Lecture Notes in Computer Science

Lecture Notes in Artificial Intelligence 16076

Founding Editor

Jörg Siekmann

Series Editors

Randy Goebel, *University of Alberta, Edmonton, Canada*
Wolfgang Wahlster, *DFKI, Berlin, Germany*
Zhi-Hua Zhou, *Nanjing University, Nanjing, China*

The series Lecture Notes in Artificial Intelligence (LNAI) was established in 1988 as a topical subseries of LNCS devoted to artificial intelligence.

The series publishes state-of-the-art research results at a high level. As with the LNCS mother series, the mission of the series is to serve the international R & D community by providing an invaluable service, mainly focused on the publication of conference and workshop proceedings and postproceedings.

Takayuki Matsuno · Honghai Liu · Lianqing Liu ·
Zhouping Yin · Xiangyang Zhu · Weihong Ren ·
Zhiyong Wang · Yixuan Sheng
Editors

Intelligent Robotics and Applications

18th International Conference, ICIRA 2025
Okayama, Japan, August 6–9, 2025
Proceedings, Part III

Editors
Takayuki Matsuno
Okayama University
Okayama, Japan

Lianqing Liu
Shenyang Institute of Automation
Shenyang, China

Xiangyang Zhu
Shanghai Jiao Tong University
Shanghai, China

Zhiyong Wang
Harbin Institute of Technology
Shenzhen, China

Honghai Liu
Harbin Institute of Technology
Shenzhen, China

Zhouping Yin
Huazhong University of Science and Technology
Wuhan, China

Weihong Ren
Harbin Institute of Technology
Shenzhen, China

Yixuan Sheng
Harbin Institute of Technology
Shenzhen, China

ISSN 0302-9743   ISSN 1611-3349 (electronic)
Lecture Notes in Artificial Intelligence
ISBN 978-981-95-2100-5   ISBN 978-981-95-2101-2 (eBook)
https://doi.org/10.1007/978-981-95-2101-2

LNCS Sublibrary: SL7 – Artificial Intelligence

© The Editor(s) (if applicable) and The Author(s), under exclusive license to Springer Nature Singapore Pte Ltd. 2026

This work is subject to copyright. All rights are solely and exclusively licensed by the Publisher, whether the whole or part of the material is concerned, specifically the rights of translation, reprinting, reuse of illustrations, recitation, broadcasting, reproduction on microfilms or in any other physical way, and transmission or information storage and retrieval, electronic adaptation, computer software, or by similar or dissimilar methodology now known or hereafter developed.
The use of general descriptive names, registered names, trademarks, service marks, etc. in this publication does not imply, even in the absence of a specific statement, that such names are exempt from the relevant protective laws and regulations and therefore free for general use.
The publisher, the authors and the editors are safe to assume that the advice and information in this book are believed to be true and accurate at the date of publication. Neither the publisher nor the authors or the editors give a warranty, expressed or implied, with respect to the material contained herein or for any errors or omissions that may have been made. The publisher remains neutral with regard to jurisdictional claims in published maps and institutional affiliations.

This Springer imprint is published by the registered company Springer Nature Singapore Pte Ltd.
The registered company address is: 152 Beach Road, #21-01/04 Gateway East, Singapore 189721, Singapore

If disposing of this product, please recycle the paper.

Preface

With the theme "AI & Robotics for Smart Society", the 18th International Conference on Intelligent Robotics and Applications (ICIRA 2025) was held in Okayama, Japan, from August 6 to 9, 2025. The conference aimed to promote high-level academic exchange and innovation in robotics and artificial intelligence, providing a global platform for researchers, engineers, and practitioners to present their latest achievements and explore emerging trends in intelligent robotics and its applications to society.

ICIRA 2025 was organized by Okayama University, and co-organized by Harbin Institute of Technology. It was technically co-sponsored by Springer. The conference received a total of 329 paper submissions from around the world. Each submitted paper underwent a rigorous peer-review process, with at least three independent reviewers per paper. Based on the reviewers' evaluations and the discussions by the Program Committee, 165 high-quality papers were accepted for publication in *Springer's Lecture Notes in Artificial Intelligence (LNAI)* series. Among these, 107 papers were presented orally and 58 papers were presented as posters.

ICIRA 2025 featured 2 plenary speeches and 8 keynote speeches, delivered by internationally renowned scholars in the field. The technical sessions covered a wide range of topics, including intelligent perception and control, human–robot interaction, robotic manipulation, biomedical and rehabilitation robotics, soft robotics, and machine learning for robotics. The conference provided a vibrant and inspiring environment for academic exchange and collaboration.

We would like to extend our heartfelt appreciation to all the authors for their valuable contributions, and to the plenary and keynote speakers for sharing their insights. We also thank the reviewers for their professional and constructive evaluations. Special thanks are due to all members of the Organizing Committee, the Technical Program Committee, and the local volunteers for their dedication and efforts that ensured the success of ICIRA 2025.

August 2025

Takayuki Matsuno
Honghai Liu
Lianqing Liu
Zhouping Yin
Xiangyang Zhu
Weihong Ren
Zhiyong Wang
Yixuan Sheng

Organization

Honorary Chair

Youlun Xiong — Huazhong University of Science and Technology, China

General Chairs

Takayuki Matsuno — Okayama University, Japan
Honghai Liu — Harbin Institute of Technology, Shenzhen, China
Lianqing Liu — Shenyang Institute of Automation, Chinese Academy of Sciences, China
Zhouping Yin — Huazhong University of Science and Technology, China
Xiangyang Zhu — Shanghai Jiao Tong University, China

Program Chairs

Guoying Gu — Shanghai Jiao Tong University, China
Duanling Li — Beijing University of Posts and Telecommunications, China
Yuichiro Toda — Okayama University, Japan
Xinyu Wu — Shenzhen Institutes of Advanced Technology, Chinese Academy of Sciences, China
Hui Zhang — Hunan University, China

Publication Chairs

Weihong Ren — Harbin Institute of Technology, Shenzhen, China
Zhiyong Wang — Harbin Institute of Technology, Shenzhen, China
Yixuan Sheng — Harbin Institute of Technology, Shenzhen, China

Award Committee Chair

Limin Zhu — Shanghai Jiao Tong University, China

International Chairs

Zhiyong Chen — University of Newcastle, Australia
Naoyuki Kubota — Tokyo Metropolitan University, Japan
Zhaojie Ju — University of Portsmouth, UK
Eric Perreault — Northwestern University, USA
Hesheng Wang — Shanghai Jiao Tong University, China
Peter Xu — University of Auckland, New Zealand
Simon Yang — University of Guelph, Canada
Xingchen Yang — Imperial College London, UK
Houxiang Zhang — Norwegian University of Science and Technology, Norway

Advisory Committee

Jorge Angeles — McGill University, Canada
Tamio Arai — University of Tokyo, Japan
Hegao Cai — Harbin Institute of Technology, China
Tianyou Chai — Northeastern University, China
Jie Chen — Tongji University, China
Jiansheng Dai — King's College London, UK
Zongquan Deng — Harbin Institute of Technology, China
Han Ding — Huazhong University of Science and Technology, China
Xilun Ding — Beihang University, China
Baoyan Duan — Xidian University, China
Xisheng Feng — Shenyang Institute of Automation, Chinese Academy of Sciences, China
Toshio Fukuda — Nagoya University, Japan
Jianda Han — Shenyang Institute of Automation, Chinese Academy of Sciences, China
Qiang Huang — Beijing Institute of Technology, China
Oussama Khatib — Stanford University, USA
Yinan Lai — National Natural Science Foundation of China, China
Jangmyung Lee — Pusan National University, South Korea

Zhongqin Lin	Shanghai Jiao Tong University, China
Hong Liu	Harbin Institute of Technology, China
Honghai Liu	University of Portsmouth, UK
Shugen Ma	Ritsumeikan University, Japan
Daokui Qu	SIASUN, China
Min Tan	Institute of Automation, Chinese Academy of Sciences, China
Kevin Warwick	Coventry University, UK
Guobiao Wang	National Natural Science Foundation of China, China
Tianmiao Wang	Beihang University, China
Tianran Wang	Shenyang Institute of Automation, Chinese Academy of Sciences, China
Yuechao Wang	Shenyang Institute of Automation, Chinese Academy of Sciences, China
Bogdan M. Wilamowski	Auburn University, USA
Ming Xie	Nanyang Technological University, Singapore
Yangsheng Xu	Chinese University of Hong Kong, China
Huayong Yang	Zhejiang University, China
Jie Zhaoc	Harbin Institute of Technology, China
Nanning Zheng	Xi'an Jiaotong University, China
Xiangyang Zhu	Shanghai Jiao Tong University, China

Contents – Part III

Magnetic Actuated Microrobots for Biomedical Engineering: Design, Control, and Application

Dynamic Parameter Identification in Haptic Robotic Systems via Artificial Bee Colony 3
   Jiachen Wang, Saeid Piri, and Huanghe Zhang

Template-Free Magnetic Programming Strategy for 3D-Transformable Soft Robots 15
   Junliang Chen, Dongdong Jin, and Xing Ma

Physics-Based Simulation of Magnetic Nanorobots Swarm 26
   Yihan Chen, Xiang Ji, Jialin Jiang, and Li Zhang

Dynamic Path Planning and Automatic Navigation for Microswarms 38
   Jialin Jiang and Li Zhang

Reinforcement Learning-Based Magnetic Levitation Control of a Capsule Endoscope for Path Tracking Using a Single Permanent Magnet 49
   Yongfeng Huang, Mingxue Cai, Guoyao Ma, Zhiqiang Chen, Chenyang Huang, Yang Yang, Hongwei Wang, and Tiantian Xu

Simulator for Identifying Contact-Prone Robot Parts to Accelerate Contact Judgment Between Needle Puncture Robot and Patient 60
   Takayuki Matsuno, Nanako Sakai, Yuichiro Toda, Tetsushi Kamegawa, Yusuke Matsui, and Takao Hirai

Innovative Design and Performance Evaluation of Robot Mechanisms

Autonomous Bolt Assembly Composite Robotic System Guided by Binocular Vision 75
   Tao Wang, Lei Zheng, Zhiran Zhang, Dailin Zhang, and Xingwei Zhao

Design and Simulation of a Bipedal Robot for Explosive Jumping Based on a Hybrid Linkage-Cam Mechanism 88
   Qiang Fu, Ke Li, Zhanchuan Qi, and Yunjiang Lou

Topological Analysis and Perception of Physical Vibration in Distributed Optical Fiber Vibration Sensing 101
   Zibin Liang, Song Wang, and Duanling Li

Design and Optimization of a Heavy-Duty Parallel Ship Motion Simulation Platform 112
  En Yang, Yan Hu, Chenbo Lang, Feng Gao, and Hao Zheng

Design and Analysis of a New Multiparameter Reconfigurable Morphing Wing 124
  Duanling Li, Ruixuan Dai, Junwei Zhang, Fengkun Xu, and Yizhu Guo

Experimental Study and Analysis of Wheel-Terrain Interaction for Crewed Lunar Vehicle Based on Single-Wheel Testbed 136
  Xinrui Wu, Huaiguang Yang, Liang Ding, Lintao Yang, Jianguo Tao, Haibo Gao, Zhehao Qiao, Ruyi Zhou, and Zongquan Deng

Research on the Dynamics Modeling and Control Method of Vector Quadrotor UAV with Variable Posture 150
  Yunfan Pang, Zhonghai Zhang, Jiahui Cai, and Duanling Li

A Probability Theory-Based Method for Calculating the Cyclical Degree of Freedom of Mechanisms 162
  Fengyi Li, Hao Chen, Weizhong Guo, and Hang Fu

Design and Analysis of Variable Geometry Truss Robot 174
  Kaijie Dong, Xiang Huai, Zhouyi Ren, Jingyao Li, and Duanling Li

AMM: An Aerial Modular Manipulator Based on Standardized Modules 185
  Yuelei Fang, Ye Li, Yijian Zhang, Ziqi Wang, Daming Liu, Shouyi Zhang, Nanlin Zhou, Sikai Zhao, Jie Zhao, and Yanhe Zhu

Structural Design and Simulation of Space Sleeve-Type Extension Arm 197
  Duanling Li, Qixiang Guo, Junwei Zhang, Junfeng huang, Shiqin Xie, and Yizhu Guo

Balloon Robot: Movement Recognition and Design of Robot 209
  Weihao Wang, Chyan Zheng Siow, Naoyuki Kubota, Azhar Aulia Saputra, Qingwei Song, and Takenori Obo

Time-Optimal Trajectory Planning for Hybrid Redundant Robotic Arm Based on Prescribed Waypoints 222
  Peng Sun, Hanqi Zhang, Zongyuan Liu, Chentao Wu, Zhe Sun, Yuan Wang, Liu Zhengqing, and Yanbiao Li

Conceptual Design and Kinematic Analysis of a Biomimetic Robot Joint (BRJ) Based on a Higher Pair Mechanism 235
  Gaohan Zhu, Shixuan Chu, Yinghui Li, and Weizhong Guo

Sensation-Perception-Actuation-Rehabilitation Oriented Technologies for Wearable Exoskeletons

Muscle Synergy-Enabled Multimodal Swimming Motion Recognition 249
   Yuchao Liu, Jiajie Guo, Yibin Chen, Weipeng Li, Kamilo Melo, and Xuan Wu

Estimation of Human Lower Limb Kinematic Parameters Based on A-Mode Ultrasound Sensing 263
   Donghan Liu, Haoran Zheng, Han Wu, Guochao Xu, and Honghai Liu

Human Lower Limb Motor Ability Estimation Based on Human-Machine Coupling Interactive Contact Model 275
   Chao Gao, Jianhua Zhang, and Hui Li

Integrated Analysis of Cortico-Muscular Coupling and Muscle Synergy for Functional Assessment in Exoskeleton-Assisted Stroke Rehabilitation 287
   Siyu Feng, Qi Kuang, Ruikai Cao, Zhuoqun Wang, and Yixuan Sheng

Multidimensional Kinematic Analysis of Walking and Turning in Older Adults Using IMUs 298
   Luobin Zhang, Yongjie Weng, Peng Chen, Wei Wei, Mingyu Du, and Shibo Cai

Development of a Functional Electrical Stimulation Device Combined with Multi-modal Muscle Status Monitoring 310
   Longjie Yu, Xiangyu Cheng, Xin Chen, Kewen Zhang, Shibo Cai, and Mingyu Du

BioKFusion-Net: Simultaneous Estimation of Ground Reaction Forces/Moments and Joint Angles from IMU Data 323
   Zhujin Chen, Yao Liu, Hui Chen, Xinyu Wu, and Chunjie Chen

Effects of Rhythmic Auditory Cues on Brain Network Characterization During Human Gait Initiation 336
   Huilin Zhou, Zefeng Shou, Tao Meng, Xuelian Wang, Tao Liu, Wenan Zhang, Guokun Zuo, and Changcheng Shi

Effects of Exoskeleton-Assisted Sit-to-Stand Training Based on Cortical-Muscular Coherence 348
   Xiaoke Peng, Shiyu Han, Guoshun Zhao, and Anqin Dong

Pattern Analysis and Machine Intelligence: Vision, Language, Multimodal Learning, and Applications

TGP: Two-Modal Occupancy Prediction with 3D Gaussian and Sparse Points for 3D Environment Awareness 361
   Mu Chen, Wenyu Chen, Mingchuan Yang, Yuan Zhang, Tao Han, Xinchi Li, Guilong Zhang, and Huaici Zhao

YOLO-HG: A Hierarchical Global Perception Method for Heavy-Duty Truck Parking Space Detection 373
   Zeyang Wang, Feng Zhao, and Dan Yang

An Accurate 3D Reconstruction Method for Large Workpieces Based on 3D Vision 386
   Shenglun Zhang, Shibo Hu, Xingwei Zhao, Dailin Zhang, and Bo Tao

Insulator and Its Defect Detection Framework Based on Feature Enhancement CenterNet 398
   Xiaoming Mai, Zehui Zhang, Shutong Yao, Shuaibing Mi, Na Dong, and Kuansheng Zou

Adaptive 3D Scene Analysis Through Multi-modal Feature Integration and Geometric Pattern Recognition 411
   Shijun Zhou, Xing Xie, and Jiandong Tian

Global to Local Mamba Low Light Image Restoration 422
   Xinhao Wu, Huijie Fan, Sen Lin, Qiang Wang, and Peng Wu

A Comparative Study of First and Second-Order Gradient Acceleration in ICP 434
   Qing Tang, Ziwei Wang, Xiaojian Zhang, Mingxu Pan, and Sijie Yan

Visual-Tactile Fusion-Driven Diffusion Policy for Robotic Excavation of Semi-buried Object in Granular Media 447
   Linan Deng, Xing Liu, Yunlong Dong, Guijun Ma, Feng Hua, Cheng Cheng, and Zuogong Yue

RCTAMP: Enhancing Rule-Constrained TAMP via Multi-agent Closed-Loop Collaboration Integrating Consensus Planning 460
   Zhongxing Wei, Xiaodong Ye, Huachen Tan, Junhong Zhao, Meiling Wang, and Yucheng Wang

Efficient Skeleton-Based Action Segmentation via Multi-granularity Perception 473
Zhihao Yang, Haoyu Ji, Wenze Huang, Bowen Chen, Zimo Jiang, Weihong Ren, Zhiyong Wang, and Honghai Liu

Tri-Axial Plantar Load Sensing for Identity Authentication with 1D-CNN Classifier 484
Zijie Liu, Yi Zhang, Hao Huang, Shabei Xu, Xiang Luo, and Jiajie Guo

Exploring the Mechanism Underlying Lower Limb Motor Dysfunction in Ischemic Stroke Based on Multimodal Signals 494
Jiaqi Shi, Hongyu Wang, Yulan Zhu, and Yanmei Zhu

FuPaD: Scalable Pose Estimation by Fusing Patch-Wise VGGT with Dense Bundle Adjustment 508
Dexin Qi, Tao Tao, Zhihong Zhang, and Xuesong Mei

ScaffoldOcc: Sparse Points Anchored Scaffold 3D Gaussian for Hierarchical Semantic Occupancy Prediction 521
Zhihong Zhang, Wenjun Wang, Dexin Qi, and Xuesong Mei

Dynamic Memory Reconciliation for Online Action Detection 534
Wenze Huang, Haoyu Ji, Zhihao Yang, Bowen Chen, Zimo Jiang, Zhiyong Wang, Weihong Ren, and Honghai Liu

Enhance Polyp Segmentation via Supervised Contrastive Learning 548
Jiejie Yan and Yizhang Ruan

Online Prediction of Surface Roughness in Robotic Grinding System for TC4 Workpieces Using PSO-XGBoost Algorithm 560
Xiangye Zhu, Yusen Li, Xiaohu Xu, Yao Chu, and Sijie Yan

Cross-Subject Respiratory State Recognition Based on Ultrasonic and IMU Signals 573
Shuo Feng, Zhiyong Wang, and Jiaole Wang

Bio-mechatronic Integration and Rehabilitation Robots

Hybrid Pole Placement and Interval Type-2 Fuzzy Control for Bio-Inspired Tendon-Driven Robotic Leg Stabilization 587
Rui Tian, Shuchen Ding, Chengyu Su, Liren Zhu, Shiyu Ma, Wensong Zhao, and Zhe Lu

Continuous Estimation Algorithm of Elbow Joint Angle Based on Mamba Model 599
   Yangfan Zhou, Jiawei Liang, Yu Lu, Liang Zhang, Bi Zhang, and Xingang Zhao

A Bone Grinding Depth Prediction Method Based on Multimodal Sensing Information 611
   Yiren Huang, Xu Liang, Guotao Li, Tingting Su, Hui Li, Kangkang Sun, Zihe Feng, Xinuo Zhang, and Yong Hai

Research on Parameter Adaptive Electrical Stimulation System Based on WBAN 622
   Jingyu Wu, Tairen Sun, and Jiantao Yang

MBGADNet: Multi-Branch Generative Adversarial Denoising Network with Semantic Preservation for EEG Artifact Removal 631
   Da Liao, Fengjun Mu, Kecheng Shi, Jun Wang, Zhe Li, Rui Huang, Zhinan Peng, and Hong Cheng

Design Optimization of Frameless Drive Motor in Robot Integrated Modular Actuator Considering Duty Cycle Suitability 650
   Zimeng Guan, Fan Yang, Songtao Cai, Wenkai Xie, Yuanbo Liu, and Tenghui Dong

Cluster-Guided State Initialization Strategy for Flexible Humanoid Locomotion 662
   Wenhao Tan, Zhiheng Li, Xing Fang, Yanyun Chen, Qian Zhang, Ran Song, and Wei Zhang

Design and Modeling of a Modular Cable-Driven Lower-Limb Exoskeleton with Compact Torque Sensors 673
   Jia Yao, Zhijun Fu, Xiao Yang, Shuowen Yi, Siyu Liu, and Zhao Guo

Author Index 687

Magnetic Actuated Microrobots for Biomedical Engineering: Design, Control, and Application

Dynamic Parameter Identification in Haptic Robotic Systems via Artificial Bee Colony

Jiachen Wang[1], Saeid Piri[2], and Huanghe Zhang[1]($\boxtimes$)

[1] School of Control Science and Engineering, Shandong University, Jinan, China
zhanghuanghe@sdu.edu.cn
[2] The Research Center for Computational Cognitive Neuroscience, System and Cybernetic Laboratory, Imam Reza International University, Mashhad, Iran

Abstract. Haptic robots are used for simulating virtual objects. Since most real objects can be modeled with a spring and damper, virtual objects are also implemented as a spring and damper (in a discrete space). Stable performance of the haptic robot results in convergent vibrations, while unstable performance leads to divergent vibrations. On one hand, the haptic robot should have negligible effective mass and friction so that its dynamics can be disregarded in comparison to the virtual object's dynamics. On the other hand, the dynamics of the user's hand affect the stability and performance of the robot. In this study, the dynamic parameters of the user's hand on the haptic robot were identified and optimized using the Artificial Bee Colony method. First, the theoretical stability boundary was presented as a function of the dynamic parameters of the user's hand on the haptic robot, the stiffness and damping coefficient of the virtual object, sampling time, and time delay. Concurrently with experiments involving the user's hand placed on the lightweight KUKA 4 robot at the PRISMA lab in Italy, the empirical stability boundary was obtained. Then, using the Artificial Bee Colony optimization method, the dynamic parameters of the user's hand on the haptic robot were determined such that the error between the theoretical and empirical stability boundaries was minimized. The evaluations indicated a high accuracy of this method in determining these parameters and consequently the stability boundary of the robot.

Keywords: Artificial Bee Colony · Haptic Robot · Stability · Numerical Optimization · Dynamic Parameter Identification of User Hand

1 Introduction

Haptic robots are utilized as interfaces to transfer virtual forces to users. These forces allow users to virtually feel the object and understand its position. So far,

---

J. Wang and S. Piri —Equal contribution.

haptic robots have been used in medicine [1] and online games [2]. Stability is a crucial condition for haptic robots because instability can harm both the robot and the user. Another factor affecting the stability of haptic robots is the user's hand. Theoretical and experimental studies have shown that the presence of the user's hand increases the stable operating range of the haptic robot [3–5]. Therefore, some researchers analyze the stability of the haptic system without considering the user's hand to achieve a simpler analysis and cautious criteria for determining the stability range (since the positive effect of the user's hand on the stability of the haptic robot means that if the haptic robot is stable without the user's hand, it will also be stable with the user's hand). Such analyses have been conducted in studies by Minsky et al. [6], Gilles et al. [3], and Moshayekhi et al. [7].

The following sections discuss the applications of haptic robots, various dynamic models of the user's hand, and types of numerical optimization methods. Section 2 provides a review of haptic robot stability and the Artificial Bee Colony optimization method. Section 3 explains the identification and optimization of the dynamic parameters of the haptic robot and the user's hand. Section 4 compares theoretical and experimental data. The discussion and conclusion are presented in Sect. 5.

1.1 Haptic Robots

Haptic robots have been studied and discussed in various tasks and applications, including medical training [1], computer games [2], enhanced sensory communication for the visually impaired [8], and surgeon training before performing surgeries [9]. For example, in online games, such as a shooting game, this robot allows the user to feel the gun when picking it up or shooting it, enhancing their experience in the game [2]. In other applications, surgeons practice with haptic robots before surgeries to improve their real surgical performance, which is a significant advancement in biomedical engineering [9].

1.2 Numerical Optimization Methods

To solve an optimization problem, the best acceptable solution is chosen based on the problem's limitations and requirements. An optimized problem may have multiple solutions. A function, called the objective function, is used to compare and select the best acceptable solution. The objective function is determined based on the overall context and physics of the problem. The purpose of optimization is to identify the problem's parameters so that the objective function is minimized or maximized [10,11]. Methods used for optimizing various problems include enumeration, computational, heuristic, and meta-heuristic methods. This article focuses on heuristic and meta-heuristic methods, also known as random search methods. These methods are inspired by nature and solve combinatorial problems, considering all possible solutions in the problem to find the global optimum. These methods can provide the best acceptable solution for complex problems in a short time [10,11]. They include the Ant Colony Algorithm, Genetic Algorithm, Natural Bee Colony, Particle Swarm Algorithm, and the Artificial Bee Colony Algorithm used in this research.

2 Literature Review

2.1 Different Models of the User Hand

The human hand has 7 degrees of freedom and is nonlinear, and various models have been proposed for its one-dimensional movement during modeling. For example, modeling has been done in two ways for fingers, hand, and arm: one with 4 degrees of freedom and the other with 5 degrees of freedom [12]. Another method of modeling the user's hand is a 5-parameter model that includes a mass representing the total hand mass and two sets of springs and dampers, one for the wrist and fingers and the other for the arm (Fig. 1) [13]. By modeling the user's hand, the transfer function between the user's hand force (F_H) and displacement (X_H) is formed according to Eq. (1) [13].

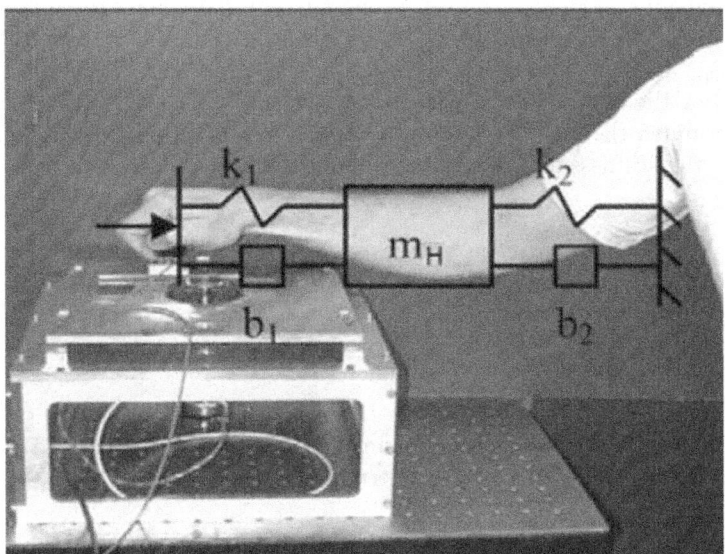

Fig. 1. Five-parameter model of the user's hand [13].

$$\frac{X_H(s)}{F_H(s)} = \frac{s}{m_H s^3 + (b_1 + b_2)s^2 + (k_1 + k_2)s} \quad (1)$$

To analyze stability, the user's hand is sometimes modeled as a single degree of freedom system comprising mass m_H, spring stiffness k_H, and damping coefficient b_H [14]. In this study, a five-parameter model is used to simulate the user's hand.

2.2 Review of Haptic Robot Stability

Haptic robots are utilized for simulating virtual objects. These robots are series robots and generally possess 6 degrees of freedom, which, given the friction in their joints, results in complex and nonlinear dynamics. Defining a stable range for these robots can be challenging. To address this issue, the multi-degree-of-freedom dynamics of the robot around the working point are simplified to a single degree of freedom system comprising an effective mass and damping coefficient. The results of this simplification indicate that the stability boundary of the robot is well defined [7,20]. The stability of haptic robots is a necessary condition for simulating virtual objects; when the robot is unstable, it can harm both itself and the user. Regarding haptic robot stability, the user's hand can contribute to the robot's stability [15,16]. In recent years, many researchers have worked on the stability of haptic robots without considering the user's hand, and specific dynamic models have been proposed. Notable among these researchers are Minsky et al. [5], Dong et al. [16], Hollin et al. [4], Gilles et al. [3], Clones et al. [17], Shakri et al. [18], and finally, in 2018, Moshayekhi et al. presented a model for the stability of haptic robots without considering the user's hand and determined the stability boundary for the haptic robot with Eq. (2), which considers the stiffness and damping of the virtual object [7].

$$K_w = T\omega^2 \times \frac{m_d \omega \cos((T+t_d)\omega) + b \sin((T+t_d)\omega)}{\sin(T\omega)} \quad (2)$$

$$B_w = T\omega \times \frac{m_d \omega \sin\left(\left(\frac{T}{2}+t_d\right)\omega\right) - b \sin\left(\left(\frac{T}{2}+t_d\right)\omega\right)}{\sin(T\omega)}$$

The above equations represent the theoretical stability boundary of the system in question. The value of ω is defined within the range from zero to ω_{max}. Additionally, the value of ω_{max} is determined by Eq. (3).

$$\omega_{max} = \frac{1}{T+t_d} \sqrt{p_2 - aq_1 + \sqrt{(p_2 - aq_1)^2 - \frac{4p_3(p_1-a)}{2(a-p_1)}}} \quad (3)$$

In Eq. (3), $a = \frac{m_d - b(T+t_d)}{m_d + b(T+t_d)}$, $q_1 = -\frac{\pi}{2}$, $p_1 = -0.4087$, $p_2 = 1.325$, $p_3 = -0.07507$ are defined, and in this way, the value of ω_{max} is determined. Additionally, Moshayekhi and colleagues further examined the stability of the robot while the user's hand was placed on the robot and proposed a dynamic model for the stability of the user's hand on the robot, presented in Fig. 2 and Eqs. (4) and (5) [5].

$$K = \frac{NUM_K}{DEN} \quad (4)$$

$$B = \frac{NUM_B}{DEN} \times \omega \quad (5)$$

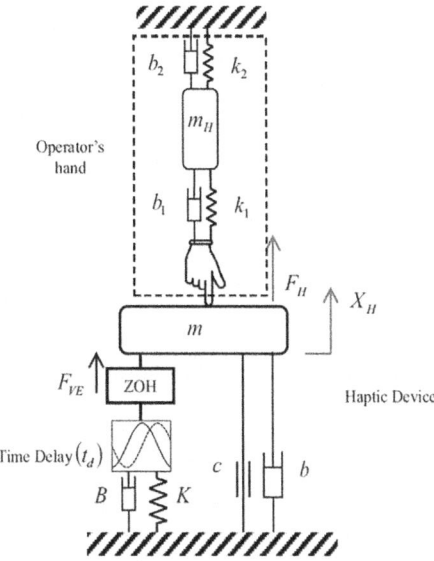

Fig. 2. Dynamic model of the haptic robot and the user's hand [5].

where:

$$NUM_K = [m\omega^6 + (m\alpha_1^2 + \beta_3\alpha_0 - \beta_0 - 2\alpha_0 m)\omega^4 + (m\alpha_0^2 + \beta_2\alpha_0 + \beta_0 - \alpha_1\beta_1)\omega^2 - \alpha_0\beta_0]$$
$$\times \cos((T + t_d)\omega)$$
$$+ [(b + \beta_3)\omega^5 + (b\alpha_1^2 + \beta_2\alpha_1 - \beta_1 - 2\alpha_0 b - \alpha_0\beta_3)\omega^3$$
$$+ (b\alpha_0^2 + \beta_1\alpha_0 - \alpha_1\beta_0)\omega]\sin((T + t_d)\omega)$$

$$NUM_B = [-(b + \beta_3)\omega^5 + (-b\alpha_1^2 - \beta_2\alpha_1 + \beta_1 + 2\alpha_0 b + \alpha_0\beta_3)\omega^3$$
$$+ (-b\alpha_0^2 - \beta_1\alpha_0 + \alpha_1\beta_0)\omega]\cos\left(\left(\frac{T}{2} + t_d\right)\omega\right)$$
$$+ [m\omega^6 + (m\alpha_1^2 + \beta_3\alpha_0 - \beta_0 - 2\alpha_0 m)\omega^4$$
$$+ (m\alpha_0^2 + \beta_2\alpha_0 + \beta_0 - \alpha_1\beta_1)\omega^2 - \alpha_0\beta_0]\sin\left(\left(\frac{T}{2} + t_d\right)\omega\right)$$

$$DEN = \cos\left(\frac{T\omega}{2}\right)(\alpha_0^2 + (-2\alpha_0 + \alpha_1^2)\omega^2 + \omega^4)$$

In the above relationships $\alpha_0 = \frac{k_1+k_2}{m_h}$, $\beta_0 = \frac{k_1 \times k_2}{m_h}$, $\alpha_1 = \frac{b_1+b_2}{m_h}$, $\beta_1 = \frac{k_1 \times b_2 + k_2 \times b_1}{m_h}$, $\beta_3 = b_1$ and $\beta_2 = \frac{m_h \times k_1 + b_1 \times b_2}{m_h}$ are defined. In this study, the parameters of the user's hand and the haptic robot were identified and optimized.

2.3 Review of the Artificial Bee Colony Algorithm

This method was introduced by Karaboga in 2005 in the article [19]. This algorithm uses the exploratory behavior of bees to solve various unconstrained optimization problems. In a bee colony, each bee has a specific role, and within the colony, bees perform their tasks through self-organization and division of labor. In the artificial bee colony, the bees that perform these tasks are divided into three groups: worker bees, scout bees, and onlooker bees. Before describing the artificial bee colony algorithm, it should be considered that in optimization, sufficient time and energy must be spent initially to generate new solutions for the given problem. Additionally, choosing the appropriate solution for the problem is essential, and trial and error are applied to refine the solution to better fit the problem [10].

In this algorithm, a number of bees randomly go to different locations (scout bees). The task of worker bees is to search and explore, finding locations with better food sources and determining the quantity of food sources. In the hive, a neighborhood is randomly selected, and the bees move towards it, bringing the honey back to the hive. Upon each return to the hive, bees share the information about the food source with the hive members using the waggle dance. If a food source is not suitable, it is discarded. Onlooker bees evaluate probabilities, compare, generate new solutions for food sources, and select the best food source location, sending more bees to that location [20]. The artificial bee colony algorithm can be summarized in three stages:

Stage 1 of the Algorithm: The initial population of food sources is randomly generated using Eq. (6).

$$X_{i,j} = X_{min,j} + rand(0,1)(X_{max,j} - X_{min,j}) \tag{6}$$

Worker bees randomly select a neighbor and move towards it according to Eq. (7).

$$V = X_{i,j} + \emptyset_{i,j}(X_{i,j} - X_{k,j}) \tag{7}$$

In this stage, if the new position (new food source) has better quality, the bee stays in the new area; otherwise, it returns to its previous area and increments the trial counter by one. The trial counter indicates the number of consecutive movements of the bee without improvement. This means that if a bee's trial counter exceeds a certain limit, it indicates that the food source is no longer suitable, and the bee should leave that area.

Stage 2 of the Algorithm: Using Eq. (8), the movement of the onlooker bees is calculated through the roulette wheel mechanism with the computed probability, and the new locations are determined using Eq. (9).

$$fit(X_i) = \begin{cases} \frac{1}{1+f(x_i)} & f(x_i) \geq 0 \\ 1 + |f(x_i)| & f(x_i) < 0 \end{cases} \tag{8}$$

$$V_i = \begin{cases} v_i & fit(v_i) > fit(x_i) \\ x_i & fit(v_i) \leq fit(x_i) \end{cases} \tag{9}$$

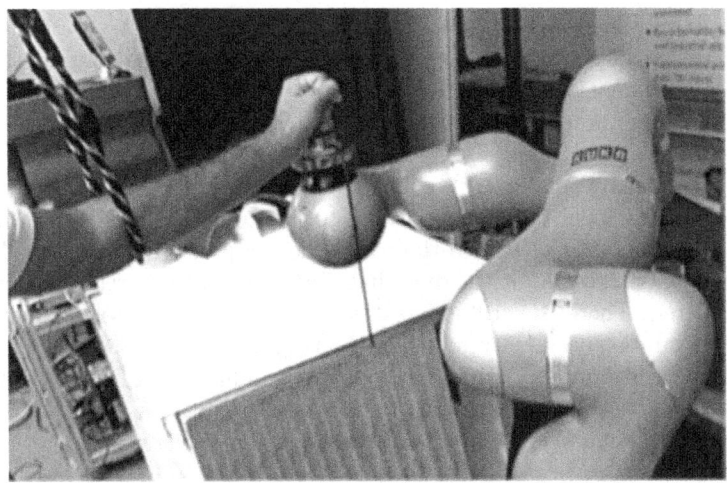

Fig. 3. The user's hand is freely placed on the KUKA robot, and the first joint of the robot is selected as the active joint [5].

Stage 3 of the Algorithm: The scout bees leave areas where the food sources are not suitable and randomly select other areas. If a better food source is not found after the trial counter reaches the set limit, a new food source is randomly initialized by the scout bees using Eq. (10) [20].

$$X_{i,j} = X_{min,j} + rand(0,1)(X_{max,j} - X_{min,j}) \quad (10)$$

The Artificial Bee Colony algorithm was selected over other meta-heuristic optimization methods for several key reasons: ABC demonstrates superior global search capabilities, effectively avoiding local optima traps [21,22]; the algorithm exhibits low sensitivity to parameter settings with stable convergence characteristics [23,24]; ABC shows excellent balance between exploration and exploitation in multi-parameter optimization problems [21]. While Genetic Algorithm and Particle Swarm Optimization have shown good performance in certain domains, ABC algorithm demonstrates better robustness and convergence properties when dealing with continuous parameter optimization problems [23,24].

3 Identification and Optimization of Dynamic Parameters of the User's Hand and the Haptic Robot

To experimentally identify and optimize the dynamic parameters of the user's hand and the haptic robot, experiments were conducted on the lightweight KUKA 4 industrial robot at the PRISMA lab in Italy, and the stability boundary was empirically determined. For this purpose, one joint of the robot was actively controlled, and a rotational virtual object with stiffness and damping was simulated. The other joints of the robot were electronically locked using the brakes embedded in the robot to minimize movement. The user's hand was then placed on the robot, and the relevant experiments were conducted (Fig. 3). In these experiments, the user attempted not to exert any voluntary force; to facilitate this, the user's hand was supported by a rope at the elbow, allowing it to move freely without applying force.

The experiments conducted on this robot with the user's hand present were performed with a fixed time delay of $t_d = 100$ ms to ensure smooth robot movement and avoid causing harm to the user. The sampling time was $T = 2$ ms. In the experiments, a value for the damping coefficient of the virtual object (B_{we}) was considered. Then, the stiffness of the virtual object was selected such that with an initial displacement applied to the robot, the robot's movement would be oscillatory with an approximately constant amplitude. In this state, the system was at the stability boundary, and the stiffness of the virtual object was considered as the empirical stability boundary (K_{we}). The experimental results are presented in Table 1.

Table 1. Empirical Stability Boundary Obtained from the Experiments.

B_{we} (Nms/rad)	0	5	10	15	20	25	30
K_{we} (Nm/rad)	46	78	96	111	93	57	32

The theoretical equations for the stiffness and damping coefficient of the virtual object are provided in Sect. 2.2 The aim of identifying and optimizing the parameters is to obtain the dynamic parameters of the user's hand (including m_h, b_1, b_2, K_1, and K_2) and the dynamic parameters of the haptic robot (including m and b), totaling 7 unknown parameters, in such a way that the error between the theoretical and empirical stability is minimized. For this purpose, given the known sampling rate and time delay, an estimate for the 7 unknown parameters is made, and then the theoretical stiffness of the virtual object is obtained from Eq. (4). The difference between the empirical and theoretical stability boundaries is then calculated using Eq. (11).

$$e_i = K_{wti} - K_{wei} \tag{11}$$

Additionally, the error between the theoretical and empirical stability boundaries has been minimized using the Artificial Bee Colony method as shown in Eq. (12).

$$\text{Minimize} \sum e_i^2 \tag{12}$$

4 Comparison of Theoretical and Experimental Data

To optimize and identify the dynamic parameters of the haptic robot using the Artificial Bee Colony method, 300 artificial bees were employed. The aim

Table 2. Identified Parameters of the User's Hand and the Haptic Robot.

Parameter	Value
m_h (kgm^2)	2.0846
b_1 (Nms/rad)	2.1956
b_2 (Nms/rad)	3.0400
k_1 (Nm/rad)	84.8094
k_2 (Nm/rad)	492.75
m (kgm^2)	1.7678
b (Nms/rad)	2.3599

was to determine the optimal numerical values for the 7 unknown parameters. The numerical range for the user's hand spring stiffness was set between 0 and 500, while the other parameters were set between 0 and 5. After optimization using the Artificial Bee Colony method, the theoretical and experimental stability boundaries showed the best match, minimizing the error according to Eq. (12), and resulting in the identification of the unknown parameters as shown in Table 2.

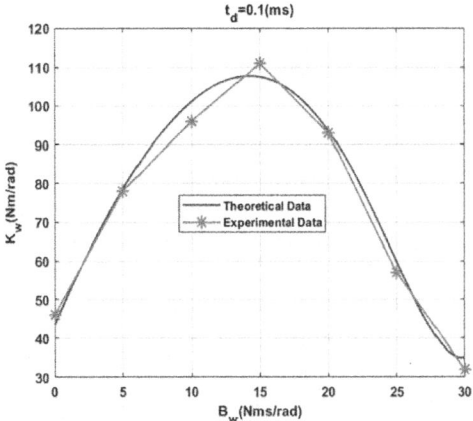

Fig. 4. Stability boundary resulting from theoretical data (obtained from identification and optimization) and experimental data obtained on the lightweight KUKA 4 robot.

With the obtained numerical values, the theoretical stability boundary is shown in Fig. 4. From Fig. 4, it can be observed that the Artificial Bee Colony optimization method has been able to identify the dynamic parameters of the user's hand and the haptic robot with good accuracy and minimize the error between the theoretical and experimental stability boundaries.

In the following section, the reason for the discrepancy between these two graphs is discussed, along with the broader implications and applications of the identified parameters.

5 Discussion and Conclusion

In this paper, the dynamic parameters of the user's hand and the haptic robot were identified and optimized using the Artificial Bee Colony method (total of 7 unknown parameters). The goal of the optimization was to minimize the error between the experimental data obtained from the tests on the user's hand on the lightweight KUKA 4 robot and the theoretical data obtained. The identified dynamic parameters present promising applications across multiple domains. In online controller design, these parameters can be utilized to real-time adjust haptic robot control strategies to accommodate different users' hand characteristics, thereby enhancing system personalization. For virtual environment modeling, accurate user hand dynamic parameters contribute to creating more realistic physical interaction models, improving immersion in virtual reality and augmented reality applications. Furthermore, in human-machine interaction prediction, these parameters can be employed to predict user operation intentions and interaction behaviors, providing essential foundations for intelligent assistance system development.

The discrepancy between the theoretical and experimental stability boundaries in Fig. 4 has valid reasons that stem from the inherent limitations of the modeling approach. Due to the voluntary force exerted by the human hand, the hand is not a completely passive system, and simulating it with passive elements (such as mass, spring, and damper) is an approximation. In the experiments, efforts were made to ensure the user did not exert voluntary force; however, potential voluntary force application can be a source of error. Moreover, even assuming no voluntary force is applied by the user, estimating the complex, non-linear, and 7-degree-of-freedom dynamics of the user's hand with a linear model (Eq. (1)) is itself an approximation. Furthermore, the behavior of the user's hand muscles in tension and compression is not the same, thus linearizing the user's hand is also an approximation.

The process of identifying and optimizing the unknown parameters using the Artificial Bee Colony method was performed on a computer with an Intel(R) Core (TM) i5-7200 processor and 6 GB of RAM. This method determines the 7 desired parameters with an accuracy better than 0.0001 (one ten-thousandth) and an average execution time of 9 min. From a computational efficiency perspective, although the ABC algorithm requires this execution time, the optimization process is typically performed offline before system deployment. For real-time application scenarios, parameter libraries can be pre-established for different user types, or simplified online learning versions can be adopted. The high precision of identified parameters ensures reliable stability boundary predictions, which is crucial for guaranteeing safe operation of haptic robots. To demonstrate the computational advantage of this approach, suppose these 7 parameters are divided into 5 segments each within their specified ranges using 7 nested codes. Given the actual range of these parameters and a minimum accuracy of 0.0001 for all parameters, finding the optimal values of these parameters would take about 10^{27} years using exhaustive search methods, which demonstrates the importance and necessity of using numerical optimization methods such as the Artificial Bee Colony algorithm. The presented methodology provides important theoretical foundations for personalized control and safe interaction of haptic robots, opening new avenues for adaptive haptic systems that can automatically adjust to individual user characteristics.

Acknowledgment. This work was supported in part by the National Key R&D Program of China under Grant 2023YFB4706102, in part by the Shandong Excellent Young Scientists Fund Program (Overseas) under Grant 2024HWYQ-019, in part by the Young Scientists Fund of the National Natural Science Foundation of China under Grant 62403281, and the Taishan Scholars Project (Young Expert Program) under Grant NO.tsqn202408040.

References

1. Li, L., et al.: Application of virtual reality technology in clinical medicine. Am. J. Trans. Res. **9**(9), 3867 (2017)
2. Xu, Z., Yu, H., Yan, S.: Motor rehabilitation training after stroke using haptic handwriting and games. In: Proceedings of the 4th International Convention on Rehabilitation Engineering and Assistive Technology (2010)
3. Gil, J.J., et al.: Stability boundary for haptic rendering: influence of damping and delay. J. Comput. Inf. Sci. Eng. **9**(1) (2009)
4. Hulin, T., Albu-Schäffer, A., Hirzinger, G.: Passivity and stability boundaries for haptic systems with time delay. IEEE Trans. Control Syst. Technol. **22**(4), 1297–1309 (2014)
5. Mashayekhi, A., Behbahani, S., Ficuciello, F., Siciliano, B.: Influence of human operator on stability of haptic rendering: a closed-form equation. Int. J. Intell. Robot. Appl. **4**(4), 403–415 (2020). https://doi.org/10.1007/s41315-020-00131-6
6. Minsky, M., et al.: Feeling and seeing: issues in force display. ACM SIGGRAPH Comput. Graphics **24**(2), 235–241 (1990)
7. Mashayekhi, A., et al.: Analytical stability criterion in haptic rendering: the role of damping. IEEE/ASME Trans. Mechatron. **23**(2), 596–603 (2018)
8. Yu, W., Ramloll, R., Brewster, S.: Haptic graphs for blind computer users. In: International Workshop on Haptic Human-Computer Interaction. Springer (2000)
9. Tse, H.Y.B.: Dental training system using haptic technology. (2008)
10. Abolghasemi, F.: Application of ant colony algorithm in network design problem. Master's thesis, Institute for Higher Research in Planning and Development (2001)
11. Tarmi, R.: Optimization of urban street network using genetic algorithm. Master's thesis, Iran University of Science and Technology (2003)
12. Dong, R.G., Dong, J.H., Wu, J.Z., Rakheja, S.: Modeling of biodynamic responses distributed at the fingers and the palm of the human hand–arm system. J. Biomech. **40**(10), 2335–2342 (2007)
13. Speich, J.E., Shao, L., Goldfarb, M.: Modeling the human hand as it interacts with a telemanipulation system. Mechatronics **15**(9), 1127–1142 (2005)

14. Marsh, R.L., Bennett, A.F.: Thermal dependence of contractile properties of skeletal muscle from the lizard Sceloporus occidentalis with comments on methods for fitting and comparing force-velocity curves. J. Exp. Biol. **126**(1), 63–77 (1986)
15. Colgate, J.E., Brown, J.M.: Factors affecting the z-width of a haptic display. In: Proceedings of the 1994 IEEE International Conference on Robotics and Automation. IEEE (1994)
16. Dang, Q.V., et al.: Analyzing the stability of the haptic interface using the linear matrix inequality approach. In: Robotics and Biomimetics (ROBIO), IEEE International Conference on. IEEE (2012)
17. Colonnese, N., Okamura, A.M.: M-Width: stability, noise characterization, and accuracy of rendering virtual mass. Int. J. Robot. Res. **34**(6), 781–798 (2015)
18. Shakari, M., Behbahani, S.: Design of fuzzy self-tuning pid for haptic robot. In: Twenty-Fifth Annual Conference on Mechanical Engineering, Tehran (2017)
19. Karaboga, D.: An idea based on honey bee swarm for numerical optimization. Technical report-tr06, Erciyes University, Engineering Faculty, Computer Engineering Department (2005)
20. Yu, Y., et al.: An enhanced artificial bee colony algorithm (EABC) for solving dispatching of hydro-thermal system (DHTS) problem. PLoS ONE **13**(1), e0189282 (2018)
21. Al-Betar, M.A., Khader, A.T., Awadallah, M.A.: New enhanced artificial bee colony (JA-ABC5) algorithm with application for reactive power optimization. Eng. Appl. Artif. Intell. **26**(8), 1758–1770 (2012)
22. Zhang, Y., Sanyang, L.: A Novel Global ABC Algorithm with Self-Perturbing. J. Intell. Syst. **25**(3), 325–339 (2016)
23. Ekinci, S.: Application and comparative performance analysis of pso and abc algorithms for optimal design of multi-machine power system stabilizers. Gazi Univ. J. Sci. **29**(2), 323–334 (2016)
24. Wang, L., et al.: Synchronous condenser excitation system parameter identification based on improved artificial bee colony algorithm. IOP Conference Series: Materials Sci. Eng. **600**(1), 012026 (2019)

Template-Free Magnetic Programming Strategy for 3D-Transformable Soft Robots

Junliang Chen, Dongdong Jin(✉), and Xing Ma(✉)

Sauvage Laboratory for Smart Materials, School of Integrated Circuits, Harbin Institute of Technology (Shenzhen), Shenzhen 518055, China
{jindongdong,maxing}@hit.edu.cn

Abstract. Soft robots have emerged as a focal point of research due to their flexible actuation mechanisms, adaptability to various environments, and safety in human-robot interactions. Among the diverse actuation strategies, magnetically actuated technologies have significantly advanced the autonomy of soft robots owing to their ability to perform remote manipulation without constraints. This necessitates the development of high-performance magneto-responsive materials and intelligent soft structures. The deformation behaviors induced by anisotropic swelling present a novel approach for constructing complex magnetic soft actuators. This study introduces a composite ink system based on shear-induced alignment of magnetic fibers, integrating the effects of anisotropic swelling with a pulsed magnetization strategy. This approach facilitates the swelling transformation of two-dimensional printed structures into predetermined three-dimensional configurations, alongside magnetic actuation. Utilizing this template-free rapid magnetic programming platform, multiple biomimetic soft actuators have been designed and fabricated, successfully demonstrating complex motion modalities, including biomimetic grasping and path navigation. This work provides a new technical paradigm for the three-dimensional deformation and design of intelligent magnetically controlled soft robots.

Keywords: Magnetic Programming · Anisotropic Swelling · Soft Robots · Magnetic Actuation

1 Introduction

Magnetically controlled soft robots (MCSRs) exhibit significant advantages in biomedical fields such as targeted drug delivery [1, 2], minimally invasive surgical intervention [3–5], and tissue engineering [6, 7], due to their unfettered manipulation capabilities and excellent biocompatibility. To broaden the medical application prospects for MCSRs, it is essential to enhance the diversity and controllability of their motion and deformation behaviors [8]. This requires precise regulation of the interaction between the magnetic components of soft robots and external magnetic fields, thus necessitating the development of rapid and accurate magnetic programming strategies. Current mainstream magnetic programming techniques include mold-assisted magnetization [9–11], assembly

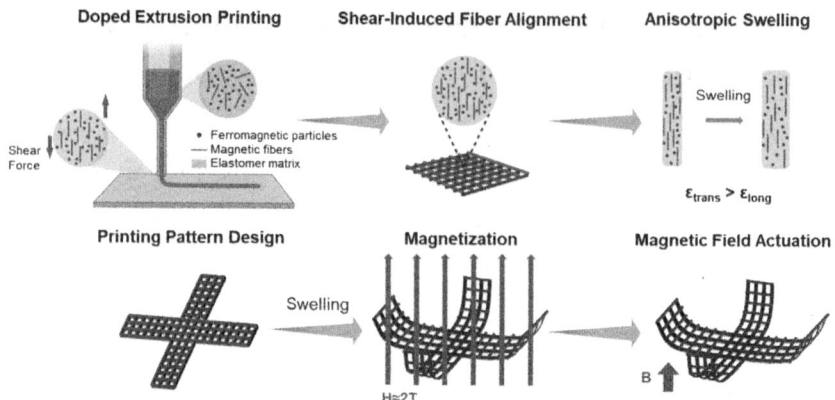

Scheme 1. Magnetic alignment-enabled doping printing and magnetic programming.

of micro-magnetic modules [12, 13], magnetic reprogramming [14, 15], and extrusion-based additive manufacturing-assisted magnetization [16, 17] for controllable deformation of soft robots. However, these technologies still face several limitations: on one hand, most magnetic programming methods are constrained by the two-dimensional design paradigm of magnetic domains, limiting their capability to edit the distribution of magnetic components only within plane structures, resulting in limited three-sdimensional morphologies through magnetic field-induced deformation [10, 18]. On the other hand, while existing 4D printing techniques can construct complex three-dimensional structures, they fail to simultaneously achieve magnetic domain orientation and programming [19, 20], posing significant challenges for the efficient fabrication of three-dimensional magnetically driven robots.

To address these challenges, this paper introduces a rapid magnetic programming strategy without the use of templates. We developed magnetic doped inks by incorporating nickel-coated carbon fibers (NiCFs) and NdFeB particles into a polydimethylsiloxane (PDMS) matrix. By leveraging the shear forces at the nozzle during the ink direct writing process, we achieved preferential alignment of fibers along the printing direction. This alignment, coupled with the induced anisotropic swelling effect, allowed the two-dimensional planar structures to spontaneously transform into preset three-dimensional shapes. Furthermore, when the structures reached a saturated state of swelling, we applied a high pulsed magnetic field, enabling the embedded NdFeB particles to "memorize" the magnetic domain distribution of the three-dimensional swollen structure. Consequently, we could trigger various complex deformations and movements under an external magnetic field (Scheme 1). The entire process eliminates the need for complex templates in magnetic programming, allowing for the definition of both the magnetization profile and the soft robot's deformation patterns in a single printing step.

This approach eliminates the need for additional template assistance; instead, it synchronously completes the design of complex three-dimensional deformation structures and editing of three-dimensional magnetic profiles solely through the coupling of structural anisotropic swelling deformation and magnetic domain memory within a single-step fabrication process. Based on this strategy, we fabricated a series of biomimetic structures with complex deformation capabilities, demonstrating the potential of these magnetically driven actuators in practical biomedical applications and providing a new paradigm for the design and development of magnetically controlled soft robots.

2 Magnetically Programmable Material System

2.1 Magnetic Composite Ink: Design and Characterization

The doped printing ink used for extrusion printing is composed of 0.5 g of nickel-coated carbon fibers (NiCFs), 1 g of NdFeB particles, 8.5 g of SE 1700, and 1.5 g of Ecoflex-30. This mixture is extruded at a pressure of 120 psi, with a printing speed of 12 mm/s, implemented in a layer-by-layer stacking approach. Following the printing process, the structure is transferred to an oven at 80 °C for a curing period of 2 h. The relevant parameters for the printing and deformation processes are detailed in Table 1. The presence of fumed silica in SE 1700 significantly enhances the rheological properties of the ink, enabling it to be printed smoothly and rapidly into complex planar or three-dimensional structures, such as helical lines, rockets, square stacked configurations, and pentagonal flowers (Fig. 1a).

Table 1. Parameters for printing and deformation processes.

Extrusion pressure	Nozzle diameter	Print speed	Soaking time	Magnetizing field	Driving field
120 psi	160 μm	12 mm/s	< 60 s	2 T	50 mT

Scanning electron microscopy (SEM) analysis reveals the distribution of NiCFs and NdFeB particles across the printed cross-grid and flat-grid structures (Fig. 1b). Further rheological testing of the printing ink indicates that the composite doping system exhibits pronounced shear-thinning behavior. Notably, the initial viscosity at low shear rates is slightly higher than that of the pure polydimethylsiloxane (PDMS) matrix, suggesting that the doped materials suppress the fluidity of the matrix (Fig. 1c). Additionally, the storage modulus of the doped system is marginally greater than its loss modulus, indicating good shape retention during the printing process, while also demonstrating excellent flow properties under high shear conditions (Fig. 1d).

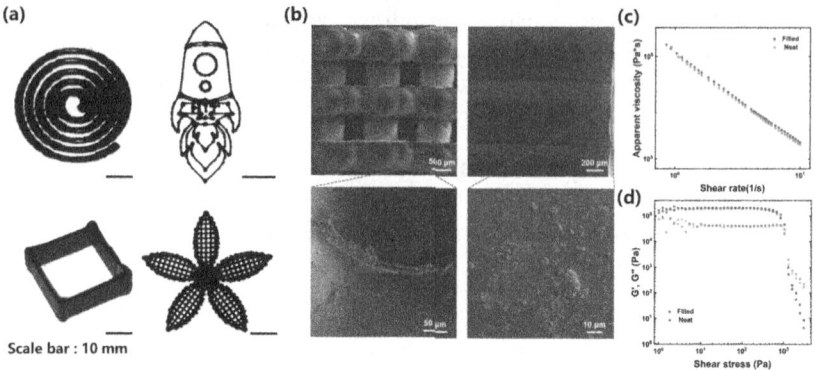

Fig. 1. Printability validation of magnetically doped inks for complex 3D architectures. a) Doped PDMS extrusion-printed structures. b) SEM images of printed grid and tiling structures. c) Relationship between apparent viscosity and shear rate. d) Variation of storage modulus G' and loss modulus G'' with shear stress; "Filled" denotes the doped system, while "Neat" refers to the undoped PDMS matrix.

2.2 Fiber Alignment and Anisotropic Behavior

During the extrusion printing process, the doped ink is subjected to shear forces at the nozzle, which alters the distribution of NiCFs within the printing matrix. A three-dimensional scan analysis of the printed filaments was conducted using micro-computed tomography (micro-CT), and Fourier analysis was employed to quantify the alignment of NiCFs in the anisotropic elastomers printed with nozzles of 160 µm, 340 µm, and 740 µm inner diameters (Fig. 2a–c). With a smaller nozzle diameter (160 µm), a pronounced peak near 0° indicates that NiCFs are more inclined to align along the direction of applied shear. Conversely, in the case of larger nozzle diameters (340 µm and 740 µm), the distribution of fibers becomes more dispersed, resulting in diminished directional alignment.

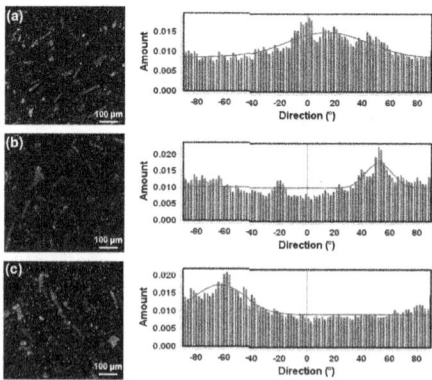

Fig. 2. Fiber distribution scans and corresponding orientation histograms after extrusion through needles of different diameters. a) 160 µm. b) 340 µm. c) 740 µm.

The distribution of NiCFs along the longitudinal direction constrains the swelling behavior of the printed filaments, thus demonstrating a more pronounced swelling strain anisotropy during extrusion with smaller nozzles (Fig. 3a). The anisotropic swelling effect observed in the flat structure printed with the smaller nozzle further corroborates this finding (Fig. 3b). This anisotropy is also reflected in the Young's modulus (E) and the strain at fracture (ε) (Fig. 3d, e). Specifically, the E and ε values along the parallel direction (approximately 534 kPa and 330%, respectively) are higher than those in the perpendicular direction (approximately 495 kPa and 218%). Thus, the printed elastomers exhibit greater rigidity in the parallel direction, which further influences the overall swelling behavior and actuation performance of the printed structures. Consequently, to achieve improved anisotropic swelling effects, all subsequent printed structures were extruded using a nozzle with a 160 μm inner diameter.

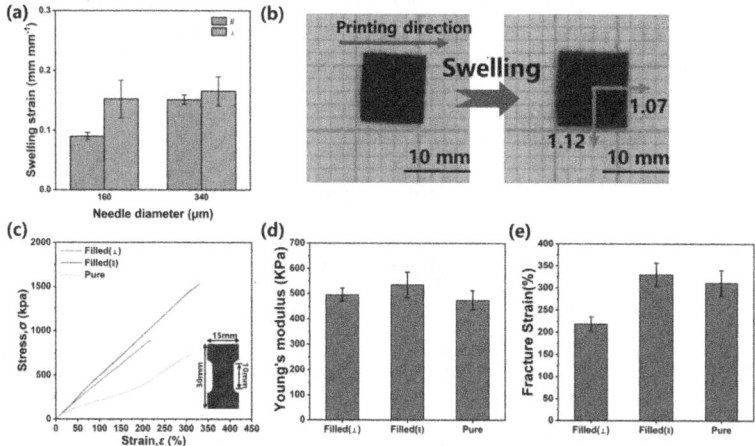

Fig. 3. Anisotropic swelling and mechanical properties of aligned composites. a) Swelling strain of extruded rod samples with different needle diameters; "∥" represents parallel to the printing direction, and "⊥" represents perpendicular to the printing direction. b) Dimensional changes of rectangular samples before and after swelling. c) stress-strain curves of Filled (⊥), Filled (∥), and pure samples. d) Young's modulus (E) and e) failure strain (ε) for the three sample types.

3 Programmable Actuation and Biomimetic Design

3.1 Geometry-Dependent 3D Transformation

Utilizing the anisotropic swelling behavior of doped elastomers in n-hexane, the actuation behavior of the composite elastomers was manipulated through the design of the printing path. For instance, in the case of the 0°/–90° dual-layer grid deformation structure (Fig. 4a, b), the printed filaments of the bottom layer are oriented perpendicularly to those of the top layer. When the printed structure swells in n-hexane, the structures on both sides gradually bend rapidly towards the central axis, ultimately reaching a saturated swelling state and forming cylindrical and cross-gripper configurations. This phenomenon arises from the disparities in the expansion directions between the upper and lower layers of the dual-layer grid structure. As both layers simultaneously expand, the requirement to maintain connectivity in the mid-plane results in internal stresses due to non-uniform expansion, which ultimately drives the structure to bend and deform.

Regarding the magnetic actuation of the printed structures, magnetization is applied via a 2 T pulsed magnetic field for 2 s while the structures are in their saturated swelling state. Subsequently, after the removal of the solvent, the printed structures can rapidly return to a state resembling their swollen deformations under the influence of an external magnetic field provided by permanent magnets with a strength of 50 mT. For the −45°/45° dual-layer grid structure, the differences in the degree of swelling between the upper and lower layers in n-hexane lead to diagonal bending along the 45° direction on both sides of the diagonal grid strips, resulting in a distinct twisting and warping of the entire strip (Fig. 4c). Further designing the diagonal grid strip into a six-petal flower structure (Fig. 4d) reveals that as swelling occurs, the six "petals" gradually lift from the plane, producing diagonal bending and twisting along the 45° direction. Ultimately, this deformation culminates in the formation of a three-dimensional flower shape within 20 s.

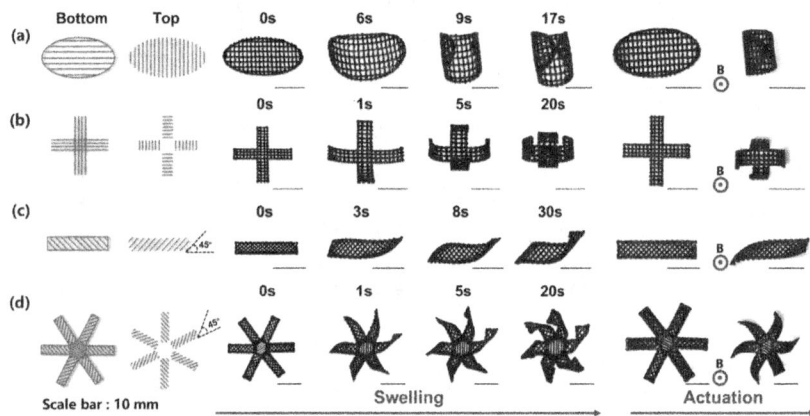

Fig. 4. Geometry-programmed 3D swelling and magnetic actuation via bilayer grids with alignment angles. a) Elliptical grids. b) Cross-grippers. c) Simple diagonal grids. d) Hexapetal flower structure; Blue lines: bottom layer printing paths; Red lines: top layer printing paths (color figure online).

Following the deformation patterns illustrated in Fig. 4, we further designed more complex biomimetic structures by planning the printing pathways, such as a biomimetic butterfly based on a dual-layer structure (Fig. 5a) and a Venus flytrap structure (Fig. 5b). The printed butterfly structure was immersed in n-hexane, and as swelling progressed, the wing structures gradually folded inward at a large angle towards the center. This bending effect reached its peak at 22 s, simultaneously exhibiting a magnetization-induced memory deformation effect, enabling the structure to mimic the repeated flapping motion of a butterfly's wings under an external magnetic field.

Similarly, the Venus flytrap structure demonstrated an inward closing behavior during swelling and exhibited a sensitive magnetic response deformation effect after magnetization. By combining single-layer printed grids with dual-layer grids, selective deformation behaviors of the printed structures could be achieved. This is exemplified by the biomimetic gesture transformations shown in Figs. 5c–e, where the structure transitions between a fist, the "6" gesture, and a peace sign. During the swelling process in n-hexane, the single-layer filling structure exhibited minimal bending, while certain finger structures adopted a dual-layer 0°/−90° grid configuration, resulting in a significant inward bending behavior directed towards the palm. The selective bending of the finger structures facilitated different gesture transformations. Upon reaching saturated swelling, magnetization completed the magnetic editing, enabling rapid deformation of the gestures under an external magnetic field.

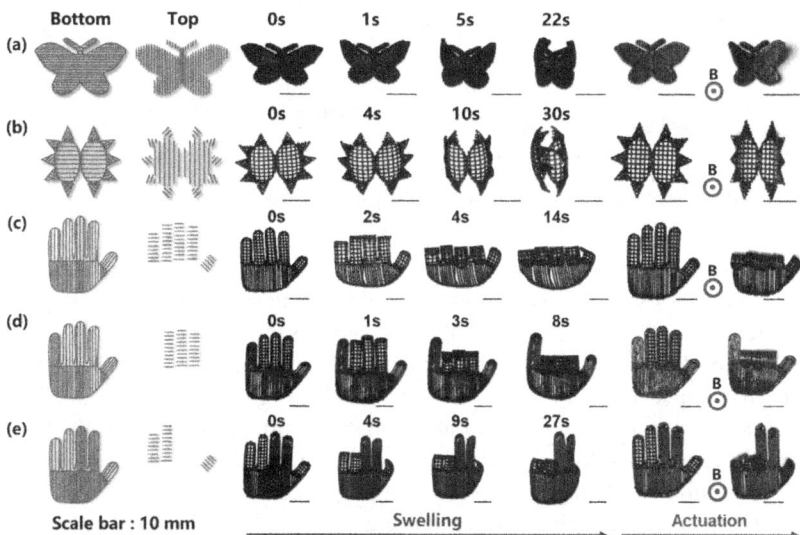

Fig. 5. Programmable shape transformation of bioinspired structures via swelling deformation and magnetic actuation. a) Bionic butterfly. b) Bionic venus flytrap. c) Clenched fist hand gesture. d) Hand gesture "6". e) Peace sign hand gesture.

3.2 Application Validation of Soft Robots

We further validated the capability of the cross-gripper structure, as illustrated in Fig. 4b, to perform cargo delivery tasks under magnetic field actuation. A red pill-shaped bead was positioned at the center of the cross gripper (Fig. 6a). Upon applying a vertical magnetic field of approximately 50 mT, generated by a permanent magnet placed perpendicular to the paper plane, the gripper structure bent to enclose the target bead (Fig. 6b). As the external magnetic field transitioned to a rotating field through manual manipulation of the permanent magnet, the cross gripper executed stable flipping and rolling motions (Figs. 6c–e). Throughout this process, the pill bead was securely contained;

upon reaching the target location, the vertical magnetic field was diminished by retracting the permanent magnet, thereby exposing the red pill bead (Fig. 6f) and completing the cargo delivery process.

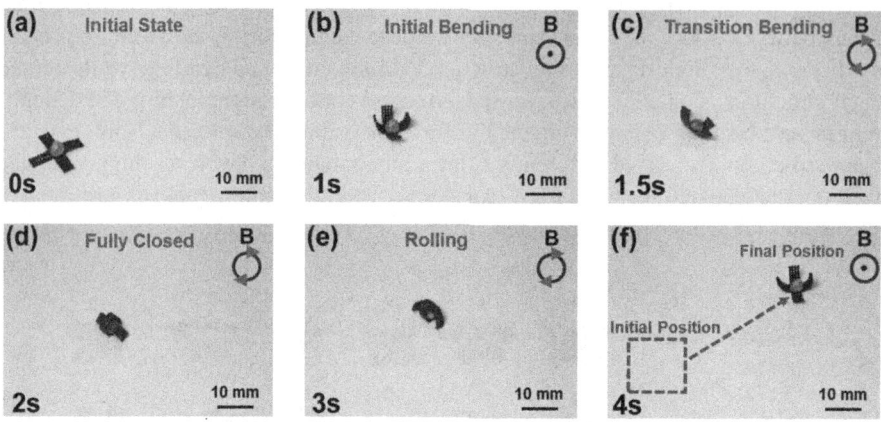

Fig. 6. Cargo delivery validation of magnetically actuated soft gripper. a) Initial state. b) Initial bending. c) Transition bending. d) Fully closed. e) Rolling. f) Final position.

Furthermore, we designed a four-legged robot by modulating the printing pathway, with the front legs exhibiting significant inward bending during the swelling process, while the rear legs, displaying minimal bending, serve as the robot's supporting structure (Fig. 7a). After deformation and magnetization, the four-legged robot was placed in a simplified U-shaped maze to assess its directional navigation capabilities (Fig. 7b). At time 0 s, the robot was positioned at the maze's starting point, with a cylindrical permanent magnet generating a gradient field of 50 mT, directed as indicated by the red arrow. This facilitated a "dragging" action that propelled the robot swiftly to the corner of the maze. At 1 s and 3 s, the robot executed a 90° turn driven by the torque from the 50 mT magnetic field generated by the moving permanent magnet. Between 4 s and 8 s, due to the smaller contact area of the front legs compared to the rear legs, the robot bent forward at the front, progressing in a manner analogous to "walking" through cyclic movements induced by the permanent magnet. Ultimately, at 10 s, the robot executed a turn at the corner of the maze under continued gradient field guidance, entering the final straight segment and reaching the endpoint of the maze at 15 s.

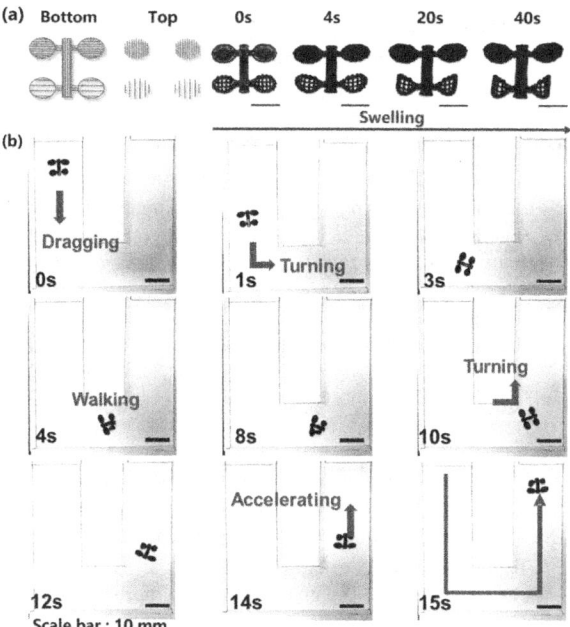

Fig. 7. Navigation of a magnetically actuated quadrupedal soft robot in a U-Shaped maze. a) Swelling-induced structural transformation. b) Motion trajectory in the confined maze.

4 Conclusion

This study presents a method for the direct writing of three-dimensional deformable magneto-responsive soft robots using magnetically doped inks featuring oriented fibers. This approach is rapid and straightforward, offering high design flexibility while achieving magnetic programming in a one-step manufacturing process. Utilizing this method, we designed biomimetic structures such as butterflies, Venus flytraps, and various hand gestures, demonstrating rapid and precise magnetic response deformations under applied magnetic fields. Additionally, we fabricated a magneto-responsive cross gripper and a four-legged robot to validate the potential applications of soft robots in cargo delivery and directional navigation.

The soft robots based on PDMS exhibit a modulus comparable to that of human tissue, ensuring that their movement does not cause mechanical damage to the surrounding tissue. The incorporated NdFeB particles and NiCFs are fully embedded within the PDMS matrix during the curing process, and no leakage of particles or fibers was observed during the swelling tests, providing significant safety assurance for their biomedical applications. Furthermore, by controlling printing parameters such as filament size, orientation, and inter-fiber spacing, it is possible to create soft robots with programmable swelling anisotropy. These structures can deform into specified target shapes when immersed in solvents, enabling precise control under external magnetic fields. Notably, our doped printing method can be further extended to various printing matrices, such as hydrogels, to meet the biocompatibility requirements of specific scenarios. This advancement opens new avenues for the design and fabrication of magneto-responsive soft robots with complex three-dimensional deformation capabilities, paving the way for future biomedical applications.

Acknowledgements. This work was supported by National Key R&D Program of China (2023YFE0208700), National Natural Science Foundation of China (92163109, 52472280, 52202348), Guangdong Basic and Applied Basic Research Foundation (2023A1515011491), Shenzhen Science and Technology Program (RCJC20231211090000001, GXWD20231129101105001, GXWD20220818224716001, KJZD20231023100302006).

Conflict of Interest. The authors declare no conflict of interest.

References

1. Sun, X., et al.: A soft capsule for magnetically driven drug delivery based on a hard-magnetic elastomer foam. ACS Biomater. Sci. Eng. **9**, 6915–6925 (2023)
2. Yim, S., Sitti, M.: Design and rolling locomotion of a magnetically actuated soft capsule endoscope. IEEE Trans. Robot. **28**, 183–194 (2012)
3. Dreyfus, R., et al.: Dexterous helical magnetic robot for improved endovascular access. Sci. Robot. **9**, eadh0298 (2024)
4. Liu, X., et al.: Magnetic soft microfiberbots for robotic embolization. Sci. Robot. **9**, eadh2479 (2024)
5. Soon, R.H., et al.: Pangolin-inspired untethered magnetic robot for on-demand biomedical heating applications. Nat. Commun. **14**, 3320 (2023)
6. Zhou, C., et al.: Ferromagnetic soft catheter robots for minimally invasive bioprinting. Nat. Commun. **12**, 5072 (2021)
7. Yang, Y., et al.: Magnetic soft robotic bladder for assisted urination. Sci. Adv. **8**, eabq1456 (2022)
8. Kim, Y., Zhao, X.: Magnetic soft materials and robots. Chem. Rev. **122**, 5317–5364 (2022)
9. Hu, W., Lum, G.Z., Mastrangeli, M., Sitti, M.: Small-scale soft-bodied robot with multimodal locomotion. Nature **554**, 81–85 (2018)
10. Gong, X., Tan, K., Deng, Q., Shen, S.: Athermal shape memory effect in magnetoactive elastomers. ACS Appl. Mater. Interfaces **12**, 16930–16936 (2020)
11. Kim, Y., Parada, G.A., Liu, S., Zhao, X.: Ferromagnetic soft continuum robots. Sci. Robot. **4**, eaax7329 (2019)
12. Zhang, J., Ren, Z., Hu, W., Soon, R.H., Yasa, I.C., Liu, Z., Sitti, M.: Voxelated three-dimensional miniature magnetic soft machines via multimaterial heterogeneous assembly. Sci. Robot. **6**, eabf0112 (2021)
13. Cui, J., et al.: Nanomagnetic encoding of shape-morphing micromachines. Nature **575**, 164–168 (2019)
14. Alapan, Y., Karacakol, A.C., Guzelhan, S.N., Isik, I., Sitti, M.: Reprogrammable shape morphing of magnetic soft machines. Sci. Adv. **6**, eabc6414 (2020)
15. Deng, H., Sattari, K., Xie, Y., Liao, P., Yan, Z., Lin, J.: Laser reprogramming magnetic anisotropy in soft composites for reconfigurable 3D shaping. Nat. Commun. **11**, 6325 (2020)
16. Kim, Y., Yuk, H., Zhao, R., Chester, S.A., Zhao, X.: Printing ferromagnetic domains for untethered fast-transforming soft materials. Nature **558**, 274–279 (2018)
17. Ma, C., et al.: Magnetic multimaterial printing for multimodal shape transformation with tunable properties and shiftable mechanical behaviors. ACS Appl. Mater. Interfaces **13**, 12639–12648 (2021)

18. Tang, D., et al.: Origami-inspired magnetic-driven soft actuators with programmable designs and multiple applications. Nano Energy **89**, 106424 (2021)
19. Boley, J.W., et al.: Shape-shifting structured lattices via multimaterial 4D printing. Proc. Natl. Acad. Sci. U.S.A. **116**, 20856–20862 (2019)
20. Sydney Gladman, A., Matsumoto, E.A., Nuzzo, R.G., Mahadevan, L., Lewis, J.A.: Biomimetic 4D printing. Nat. Mater. **15**, 413–418 (2016)

Physics-Based Simulation of Magnetic Nanorobots Swarm

Yihan Chen[1], Xiang Ji[1], Jialin Jiang[1], and Li Zhang[1,2,3,4,5](✉)

[1] Department of Mechanical and Automation Engineering, The Chinese University of Hong Kong, Hong Kong, China
lizhang@cuhk.edu.hk
[2] Chow Yuk Ho Technology Center for Innovative Medicine, The Chinese University of Hong Kong, Hong Kong, China
[3] CUHK T Stone Robotics Institute, The Chinese University of Hong Kong, Hong Kong, China
[4] Department of Surgery, The Chinese University of Hong Kong, Hong Kong, China
[5] Multi-Scale Medical Robotics Center, Hong Kong Science Park, Shatin NT, Hong Kong, China

Abstract. Micro-nanorobots swarm based on magnetic nanoparticles has many applications in the medical field such as minimally invasive surgery and drug delivery. Many studies have aimed to analyze the motion behavior of nanoparticle swarm through physical modeling. However, these physical models primarily focus on different experimental phenomena and struggle to achieve a general and real-time simulation of multiple particles. The absence of universally applicable physical modeling for nanoparticle swarm significantly increases the training cost and efficiency of using AI to control the swarm and limits its expansion in virtual reality applications. We developed a physics-based simulation of a nanoparticle swarm based on Unity, which can simulate the motion response of swarm in different magnetic fields in real-time. Initially, we analyzed the physical forces acting on particles and established functions to describe the main forces based on physical parameters. We set active region for each particle, disregarding insignificant long-range forces, greatly reducing computational complexity. By comparing simulation results with experimental outcomes under different types of magnetic field inputs, we observed good consistency between the simulation and the reality.

Keywords: Micro-nanorobots swarm · Magnetic nanoparticles · Physics-based simulation

1 Introduction

In the realm of medical applications, micro-nanorobot swarm composed of magnetic nanoparticles serves various purposes [1–3]. By flexibly altering its shape, it can perform different tasks in complex environments [4,5]. For instance, it can transform into a ribbon shape to prevent obstructions while navigating through narrow pipes, or into a vortex shape to transport or release drugs in target areas [6]. Compared to a single particle [7], a nanoparticle swarm can increase drug delivery dosages and conduct more complex tasks [8], but their physical behaviors are notably more intricate than those of individual particles [9,10]. The complex physical properties of swarm make it difficult for current methods of controlling swarm to fully automated, requiring operators with substantial experience, which greatly restricts the practical use of nanoparticle swarm in real-world scenarios [11,12].

To address this issue, some researchers used machine learning to establish swarm's control strategy [13,14]. Jiang et al. proposed a reinforcement learning-based approach that utilizes a deep Q network to plan the paths of swarm, achieving automated control [15]. However, this method only concentrates on the movement of the swarm without considering the physical properties of nanoparticles and is unable to learn the deformations of the swarm. To establish a physical model for swarm, Xie et al. analyzed the forces acting on particles in a liquid environment, separately conducting physical modeling for the responses of swarm under rotating magnetic fields and oscillating magnetic fields, and analyzing the corresponding movements [16]. However, the physical models established above primarily focus on explaining experimental phenomena and lack a comprehensive analysis of the physical properties of swarm itself, cannot fully reflect its physical characteristics and realize real-time simulation of swarm under different magnetic fields.

In this paper, we developed a physics-based swarm simulation in Unity, capable of real-time simulation and analysis of the physical behaviors of the swarm. The structure of our paper is as follows. In Sect. 2, we conduct a force analysis of magnetic nanoparticles and carry out physical modeling of the primary forces. In Sect. 3, we set active region to accelerate computations for real-time simulation. In Sect. 4, we conduct experiments to capture the real responses of swarm under different magnetic fields and compare the results with simulation. In Sect. 5, we analyzed the movement of swarm by observing the particle trajectories in the simulation. We conclude in Sect. 6.

2 Force Analysis

By modeling the physical interactions experienced by nanoparticles in fluids and magnetic fields, we can simulate corresponding physical behaviors of the swarm. The fundamental units of the swarm consist of paramagnetic particles. As shown in Fig. 1, when subjected to external magnetic fields, each particle primarily experiences various kinds of forces.

2.1 Force from External Magnetic Field

When paramagnetic particles are magnetized by an external magnetic field, the force F^B exerted on them by the external magnetic field B can be represented by the following formula [17]:

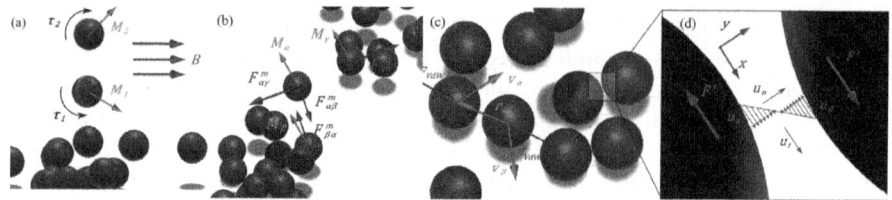

Fig. 1. Particle Force Analysis. (a) Force from external magnetic field. (b) Magnetic forces between particles. (c) Van der Waals forces between particles. (d) Tangential viscous forces between particles.

$$\boldsymbol{F}^B = (\boldsymbol{m} \cdot \nabla) \boldsymbol{B} \tag{1}$$

Here, $\boldsymbol{m}$ represents the magnetic moment of the particle, which is related to the particle's magnetization coefficient and the strength of the external magnetic field. Since in this paper, the magnetic field generation device employs Helmholtz coils, where the magnetic field in the working area can be approximated as a uniform magnetic field, the gradient of the magnetic field is nearly zero. Therefore, $\boldsymbol{F}^B$ can be neglected, and particles are only subjected to the torque of the external magnetic field. The expression of this torque $\boldsymbol{\tau}$ is as follows:

$$\boldsymbol{\tau} = \boldsymbol{B} \times \boldsymbol{m} \tag{2}$$

Due to the magnitude of the torque is significant, the particle's magnetic moment always quickly realigns with the direction of the external magnetic field. Therefore, we can consider the direction of the particle's magnetic moment to be equivalent to the direction of the external magnetic field.

2.2 Magnetic Interaction Between Particles

When particles are magnetized, they are subjected to magnetic torque and force generated by other particles. The magnetic torque, which is proportional to the product of the magnetic moments of the two particles, is much smaller than the torque from the external magnetic field and can therefore be disregarded. Thus, we only need to consider the magnetic force from other particles. The expression for the magnetic force $\boldsymbol{F}^m_{\alpha\beta}$ between particles α and β is as follows [18]:

$$\boldsymbol{F}^m_{\alpha\beta} = \frac{3\mu_0}{4\pi r^5_{\alpha\beta}} \left[(\boldsymbol{m}_\alpha \cdot \boldsymbol{r}_{\alpha\beta}) \boldsymbol{m}_\beta + (\boldsymbol{m}_\beta \cdot \boldsymbol{r}_{\alpha\beta}) \boldsymbol{m}_\alpha \right. \\ \left. + (\boldsymbol{m}_\alpha \cdot \boldsymbol{m}_\beta) \boldsymbol{r}_{\alpha\beta} - \frac{5((\boldsymbol{m}_\alpha \cdot \boldsymbol{r}_{\alpha\beta})(\boldsymbol{m}_\beta \cdot \boldsymbol{r}_{\alpha\beta}))}{r^2_{\alpha\beta}} \boldsymbol{r}_{\alpha\beta} \right] \tag{3}$$

Here, $\boldsymbol{r}_{\alpha\beta}$ represents the vector pointing from particle α to particle β.

2.3 Viscous Force in Fluid

Due to the small size of the particles, which are less than 1 micron, they move in a low Reynolds number environment where the viscous drag force $\boldsymbol{F^n}$ significantly surpasses the inertial force of the particles. The expression for this force is [19]:

$$\boldsymbol{F^n} = 6\pi\eta a \cdot (\boldsymbol{v} - \boldsymbol{v_0}) \tag{4}$$

Here, η is the viscosity coefficient of the liquid, $\boldsymbol{v}$ and $\boldsymbol{v_0}$ represent the velocity of the particle and the fluid respectively, and a denotes the particle's radius. This force arises from the resistance exerted by the surrounding fluid on the particle's motion direction. Additionally, when two particles approach each other, a tangential viscous force $\boldsymbol{F^t}$ is generated due to the difference in velocities of the two particles' boundary layers [20]. Since the normal pressure along the particle boundaries remains constant, the boundary layer equation for the two particles can be formulated as:

$$u_t \frac{\partial u_t}{\partial x} + u_n \frac{\partial u_t}{\partial y} = -\frac{1}{\rho}\frac{\partial p}{\partial x} + \frac{\eta}{\rho}\left(\frac{\partial^2 u_t}{\partial y^2}\right) \tag{5}$$

As shown in the Fig. 1, u_t is the tangential component of the fluid velocity, u_n is the normal component of the fluid velocity, ρ is the density of the fluid, and $d_{\alpha\beta}$ is the distance between the particle boundaries. Within the small-scale area of the particle boundary, we can consider that the tangential velocity u_t and the pressure p do not vary with x. At the boundary region, the fluid velocity equals the velocity of the particle boundary. By substituting the boundary conditions $u_t(0) = u_\alpha$, $u_t(r) = u_\beta$, we can derive the variation of fluid velocity in the y-direction:

$$u_t = \frac{u_\beta - u_\alpha}{d_{\alpha\beta}}y + u_\alpha \tag{6}$$

From the Eq. 7, we can calculate the tangential viscous force generated by the velocity gradient of the fluid when the tangential velocities of the two particles are u_α and u_β:

$$\boldsymbol{F^t} = C\pi a^2 \cdot \eta \frac{du_t}{dy} = C\pi a^2 \cdot \frac{\eta}{d_{\alpha\beta}}(\boldsymbol{u_\beta} - \boldsymbol{u_\alpha}) \tag{7}$$

Here, C is a constant used to modify the force area. It can be observed that the magnitude and direction of $\boldsymbol{F^t}$ depend on the distance between the two particle boundaries and the relative speed of the boundaries. When two particles approach each other, $\boldsymbol{F^t}$ acts similar to friction, causing the boundary velocities of the two particles to converge.

2.4 Van Der Waals Force

When the diameter of particles is less than 500 nanometers, the Van der Waals force between particles becomes significant. As particles come closer to each other, the Van der Waals force rapidly increases, causing adjacent particles to strongly stick together. The particles will aggregate into clusters due to the existence of the Van der Waals force. Even after removing the external magnetic field, the particles will not quickly disperse. For two spherical particles, the Van der Waals force F_{VdW} between them can be calculated using the Hamaker formula [21]:

$$F_{VdW} = \frac{\pi^2 q^2 \lambda}{6} \left\{ \frac{2(x+1)}{x^2 + 2x} - \frac{x+1}{(x^2 + 2x)^2} - \frac{2}{x+1} - \frac{1}{(x+1)^3} \right\} \qquad (8)$$

Here, q represents the atomic density, λ is the London-Van der Waals constant, x is the ratio of the distance d between the surfaces of the spherical particles to the diameter of the sphere, and y is the ratio of the diameters of the two spheres.

In the ideal scenario, when the distance d approaches zero, the value of F_{VdW} tends to infinity. However, in actual situations, the atomic density within a particle is not uniform, and there exists short-range electrostatic repulsion. Therefore, when d approaches zero, meaning when particles come into contact with each other, the Van der Waals force does not tend to infinity. Due to Brownian motion or the fluid drag force caused by the fast movement of particles, it is possible for two particles to separate.

3 Active Region of Force Calculation

In the calculation of interactions between particles, the time complexity for n particles is $O(n^2)$. Therefore, as the number of particles increases in a simulation, the required computational workload grows quadratically, posing a challenge to real-time simulation.

From Eqs. 3, 7, and 8, it is evident that the interactions between particles decrease as the distance between them increases. The significance of the interaction forces generated by particles at a greater distance is much smaller compared to those produced by adjacent particles. Therefore, setting an active region is considered, where for each particle, only forces exerted by other particles within the active region are computed, while particles outside the active region are not involved in the calculation. By employing this method, the computational complexity reduces to $O(n)$, making it acceptable for real-time simulation with a large number of particles. To validate the effectiveness of this method in reducing computational load without introducing significant errors in particle force calculations, we conducted tests within an array of 64 particles. Randomly selecting a particle, we maintained the initial conditions constant and adjusted the cell radius to define various sizes of active regions. Subsequently, we measured the forces acting on this selected particle, including magnetic forces from other particles, Van der Waals forces, and tangential viscous forces.

As the cell radius decreases, the size of the active region decreases as well. As shown in Fig. 2, the variations in magnetic and Van der Waals forces between particles are consistent in the initial stages of motion under different cell radius. This suggests that the force error induced by this method is very small, and the influence of particles outside the active region on the particle can be ignored.

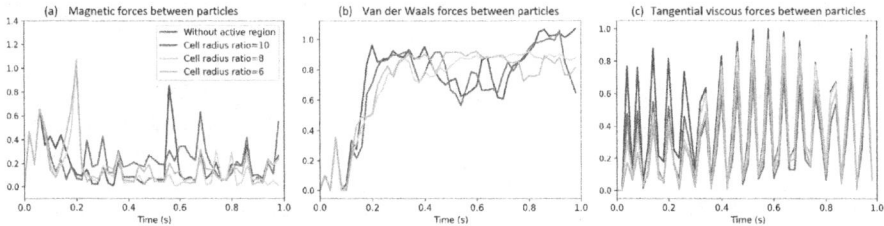

Fig. 2. Different active region sizes were set under the same initial conditions and the changes of particle forces over time were recorded. (a) Magnetic forces between particles. (b) Van der Waals forces between particles. (c) Tangential viscous forces between particles.

4 Experiment

To validate our physical simulation, we utilized Fe_3O_4@PDA nanoparticles to form a swarm, with particles radius of 200nm. The entire experiment took place in an acrylic tank, with the nanoparticles moving on a glass substrate. The liquid environment consisted of a 0.01% Tween 20 solution. An optical microscope imaging system was employed. The magnetic field generation setup utilized Helmholtz coils to produce a three-dimensional uniform magnetic field in the central working area. A computer controlled the magnetic field parameters generated and received images from the microscope. Our simulation is carried out in Unity, with the scripts written in C#. The Euler method is used for numerical integration in Unity to update the positions and velocities of particles in each frame. In this section, time step is set to be 0.02 s, the number of particles in the simulation is set to 256, and the cell radius is 10.

After numerous attempts, we experimented with three types of magnetic fields to generate the swarm, as most types of magnetic fields cannot form nanoparticles into regular shapes. As illustrated in Fig. 3, under these three types of magnetic fields, the swarm exhibited varying shapes. The first type of magnetic field was a constant field, where the field's magnitude and direction remained constant over time. Under this field, the nanoparticles formed chains with repulsion between each chain. The second type of magnetic field was an oscillating field, defined as $\boldsymbol{B} = B_x cos\left(2\pi ft\right)\hat{x} + B_y\hat{y}$, and the ratio of the oscillating component amplitude B_x to the constant component amplitude B_y is denoted as γ. In the oscillating magnetic field, the nanoparticle swarm formed ribbons, and by adjusting γ, the aspect ratio of the ribbons also changed. The third type of magnetic field was a rotating field, expressed as $\boldsymbol{B} = Bcos\left(2\pi ft\right)\hat{x} + Bsin\left(2\pi ft\right)\hat{y}$. Under the rotating field, the swarm adopted a vortex shape, and particles all revolve around the center of the vortex.

In the ribbon and vortex formations, the swarm exhibited complex dynamic behaviors. In this chapter, we will focus the performance of nanoparticles in oscillating and rotating fields in both simulation and real environments.

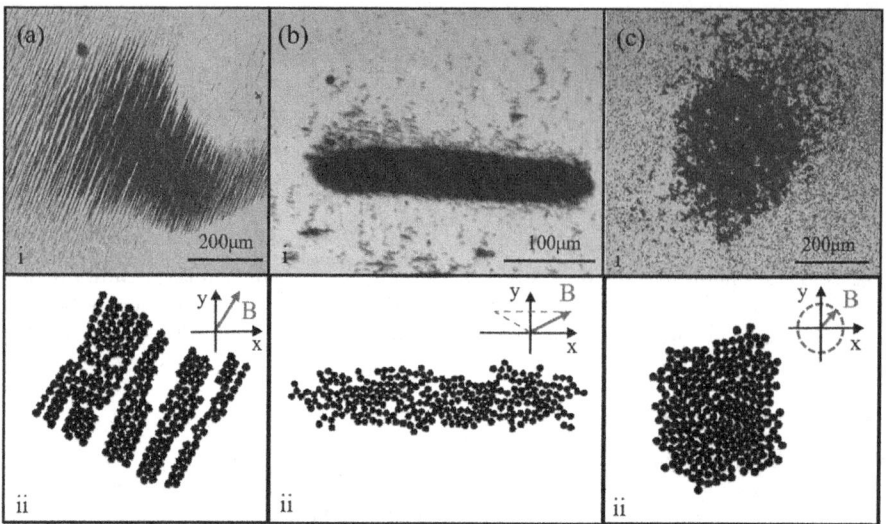

Fig. 3. Shape changes of swarm under three different types of magnetic fields, where (i) represents the reality and (ii) represents the simulated. (a) Under a constant magnetic field, the swarm forms long chains that repel each other. (b) Under an oscillating magnetic field, the swarm forms a ribbon. (c) Under a rotating magnetic field, the swarm forms a vortex.

4.1 Fusion of Ribbons

In the experiment, it was observed that when an oscillating field was applied, not all particles aggregated together to form a single ribbon. Instead, multiple ribbons of varying sizes were formed. This was due to a low initial particle density, meaning that the initial distance between particles is large. Each particle tends to form a small ribbon with surrounding particles rather than being attracted to the center to form a large ribbon. After the formation of small ribbons, the magnetic forces between ribbons rapidly decayed due to the spacing between them. Consequently, each part slowly approached each other, leading to fusion when two ribbons made contact, forming a new larger ribbon.

In the simulation, we divided the initial swarm into two parts, allowing them to form two ribbons after applying the oscillating field. The movement process in simulation was recorded to compare the fusion phenomenon of ribbons in the experiment. As shown in Fig. 4, the fusion of ribbons in reality can be divided into three stages. In the first stage (a), the two ribbons approached each other, with the speed increasing as the distance between them decreased. In the stage (b), the two ribbons made contact in the middle, forming an H shape. As the contact area expanded, in the final stage (c), they merged to form a new larger ribbon.

In the simulation, we also observed the three stages of fusion of two ribbons and can clearly observe the motion of internal particles. As the ribbons

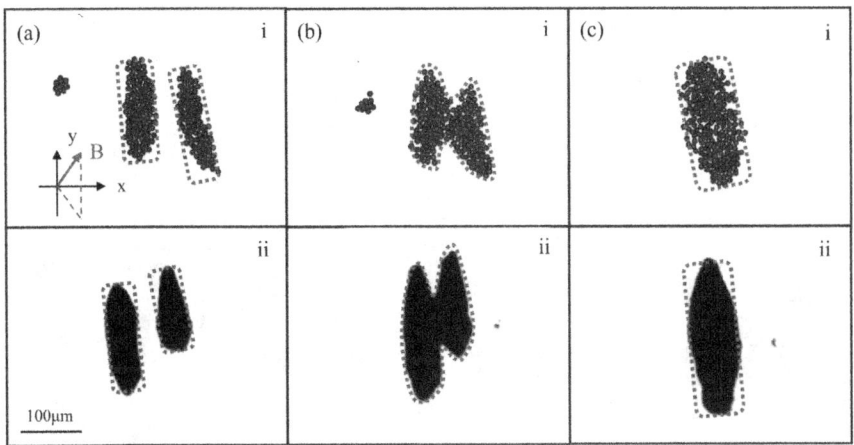

Fig. 4. Fusion process of two ribbons, where (i) represents simulation and (ii) represents reality. (a) The two ribbons approach each other at an increasing speed. (b) The two ribbons contact and begin to merge. (c) The two ribbons complete the fusion, forming a new larger ribbon.

merged, slight deformations were observed in the ribbons where both shapes bulged inward due to the presence of magnetic forces. During the fusion process, particles at the ends of the ribbons continuously filled the middle, eventually forming the ends of the new ribbon.

4.2 Fusion of Vortices

Similarly to ribbon swarm, when a rotating field is applied to unevenly dispersed nanoparticles, vortices with different sizes are formed in regions with higher particle density. Small clusters can be observed rotating around each vortex, being merged and occasionally flung out form vortices. When two vortices approach each other, fusion phenomena also occur.

In the simulation, by setting the initial conditions to form two vortices, we compared the fusion process with reality, as shown in Fig. 5. In the initial stage, the two vortices gradually approached each other until they made contact. Upon initial contact, both vortices had significant deformations, forming an S shape. As fusion progressed, the smaller vortex could not maintain its independence, transitioning from a circular shape to a silk shape. As the silk was gradually enveloped by the main vortex, the two swarms formed a new larger swarm. After the completion of fusion, the new vortex took some time to return to a circular shape. Throughout the fusion stage, the fusion behavior of the simulated swarm is similar with the reality.

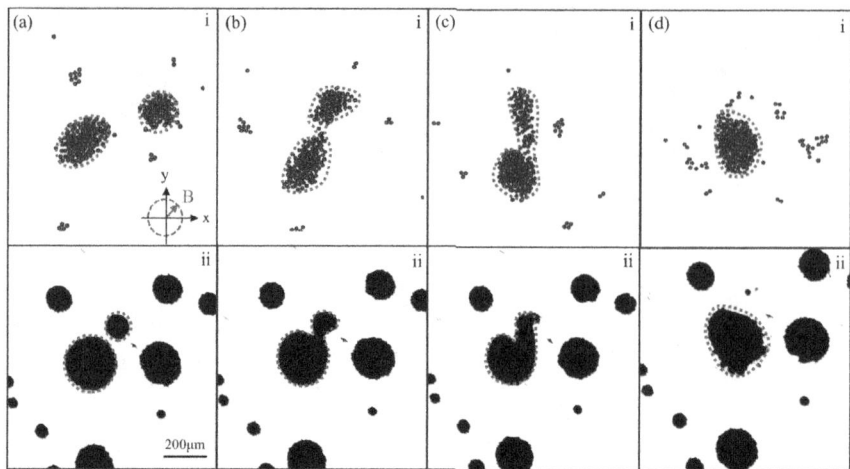

Fig. 5. Fusion process of two vortices, where (i) represents simulation and (ii) represents reality. (a) The two vortices rotate around a common center of mass while approaching each other. (b) The two vortices contact and begin to merge. (c) The smaller vortex transitions from a circular shape to a silk shape, absorbed by the larger vortex. (d) The two vortices complete the fusion, forming a new swarm.

5   Swarm Motion Analysis Based on Physical Simulation

In the Sect. 4, we observed that in physical simulations, swarms can form similar shapes to reality and produce corresponding behavior under various common magnetic fields. Additionally, individual particles can be clearly observed in physical simulations, enabling tasks that are difficult or impossible to achieve in reality. For example, due to device limitations, analyzing properties of swarms by tracking particle trajectories in real-time can be challenging, whereas this task can be easily accomplished in physical simulations. Compared to ribbon swarms, vortices exhibit more active particle exchange behavior. Therefore, in this section, we will analyze the motion of vortex swarms through particle trajectories.

Firstly, we analyze the movement of a single vortex. As shown in Fig. 6 (a), the red points represent the historical positions of particles, with lighter colors indicating earlier times. It can be observed that particles within the vortex exhibit relatively stable activity, rotating around the center. External particles rotate around the vortex, with those closer to the center rotating faster and those further away moving slowly or almost remaining stationary. Additionally, external particles tend to form clusters with scattered particles around them. By observing the movement of external particles, we can infer the approximate flow field in the environment, the internal flow field of the vortex is stable, while the external region exhibits a high-speed circular flow field, with faster speeds closer to the vortex. Particles at the edge of the vortex are in an unstable and active state, potentially detaching from or being captured by the vortex at any moment.

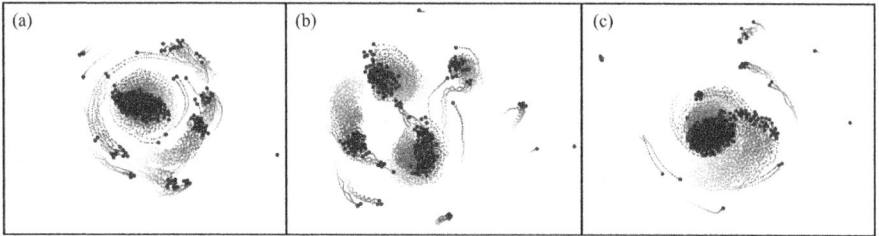

Fig. 6. Particle trajectories plot of swarm in simulation over 2 s. (a) A single vortex. (b) Multiple vortices undergoing particle exchange. (c) Two vortices undergoing fusion.

To further observe the properties of particles at the edge of the vortex, we subsequently observed multiple vortices. In Fig. 6 (b), it is evident that some edge particles of the central vortex are flung out during its rotation process. These particles undergo complex movements and are captured by the vortex on the top right, while some particles from the left vortex escape and are attracted by the central vortex, about to be captured. When multiple vortices exist, there is active particle exchange behavior between them. Particles escape from the edges of some swarms, undergo irregular movements, and are captured by other swarms. Additionally, clusters composed of 2–4 particles exhibit spiral trajectories due to the combined effect of the flow field generated by the larger vortex and their own rotation, illustrating the complexity of the flow field generated by multiple vortices.

Lastly, we observed the fusion process of vortices. In Fig. 6 (c), the image captures the moment when two vortices are on the verge of completion of fusion. During the fusion process, the two vortices rotate slowly around their center of mass. The smaller swarm transitions from a circular shape to a silk shape, with some external particles escaping during the fusion. Throughout the process, particles move towards the contact area along the silk, while the silk rotates around the center of mass until fusion is completed.

6 Conclusion

In this work, a physics-based simulation capable of modeling the response of magnetic nanoparticle swarms to magnetic fields is established. This simulation calculates the primary forces acting on particles by inputting external environmental parameters such as magnetic field strength and frequency, thereby simulating the motion response of the swarm under a given magnetic field. By setting an active region for particles, the simulation reduces the computational complexity of force calculations.

We set experiments to compare the behaviors of simulated and real swarms. The simulated swarms exhibit behaviors such as splitting and merging consistent with the swarms in real world. This physics-based simulation can accomplish tasks that are difficult to achieve in reality. By tracking particle trajectories in real-time, we analyzed the motion characteristics of vortex swarms, observing particle exchange phenomena between vortices and can infer the approximate flow fields around the vortex.

In the future, we plan to use this physics-based simulation as virtual training environment for reinforcement learning to achieve automated and robust control of swarms.

Acknowledgement. This work was supported in part by the Strategic Topics Grant (STG1/E-401/23-N, GRF14300621, GRF14301122, GRF14205823, GRF15206223 and GRF25200424), Croucher Foundation Grant with Ref. No. CAS20403, the Hong Kong Research Grants Council (RGC) with Research Impact Fund (R4015-21), the Research Fellow Scheme (project no. RFS2122-4S03), and the MultiScale Medical Robotics Center (MRC) InnoHK, at the Hong Kong Science Park, the SIAT-CUHK Joint Laboratory of Robotics and Intelligent Systems.

References

1. Kim, D.-H., Wong, P.K., Park, J., Levchenko, A., Sun, Y.: Microengineered platforms for cell mechanobiology. J. Ann. Rev. Biomed. Eng. **11**(1), 203–233 (2009)
2. Palagi, S., Fischer, P.: Bioinspired microrobots. J. Nat. Rev. Mater. **3**(6), 113–124 (2018)
3. Sitti, M., et al.: Biomedical applications of untethered mobile milli/microrobots. J. Proc. IEEE **103**(2), 205–224 (2015)
4. Yang, L., Jiang, J., Gao, X., Wang, Q., Dou, Q., Zhang, L.: Autonomous environment-adaptive microrobot swarm navigation enabled by deep learning-based real-time distribution planning. J. Nature Mach. Intell. **4**(5), 480–493 (2022)
5. Nelson, B.J., Kaliakatsos, I.K., Abbott, J.J.: Microrobots for minimally invasive medicine. J. Ann. Rev. Biomed. Eng. **12**(1), 55–85 (2010)
6. Erkoc, P., Yasa, I.C., Ceylan, H., Yasa, O., Alapan, Y., Sitti, M.: Mobile microrobots for active therapeutic delivery. J. Adv. Ther. **2**(1), 1800064 (2019)
7. Abbasi, S.A., et al.: Autonomous 3D positional control of a magnetic microrobot using reinforcement learning. J. Nature Mach. Intell. **6**(1), 92–105 (2024)
8. Rubenstein, M., Cornejo, A., Nagpal, R.: Programmable self-assembly in a thousand-robot swarm. J. Sci. **345**(6198), 795–799 (2014)
9. Floreano, D., Lipson, H.: From individual robots to robot societies. J. Sci. Robot. **6**(56), eabk2787 (2021)
10. Soria, E., Schiano, F., Floreano, D.: Predictive control of aerial swarms in cluttered environments. J. Nature Mach. Intell. **3**(6), 545–554 (2021)
11. Nauber, R., et al.: Medical microrobots in reproductive medicine from the bench to the clinic. J. Nature Commun. **14**(1), 728 (2023)
12. Liu, D., Wang, T., Lu, Y.: Untethered microrobots for active drug delivery: from rational design to clinical settings. J. Adv. Healthc. Mater. **11**(3), 2102253 (2022)
13. Tay, Z.W., et al.: Magnetic particle imaging: an emerging modality with prospects in diagnosis, targeting and therapy of cancer. J. Cancers **13**(21), 5285 (2021)

14. Ryan, P., Diller, E.: Magnetic actuation for full dexterity microrobotic control using rotating permanent magnets. J. IEEE Trans. Robot. **33**(6), 1398–1409 (2017)
15. Jiang, J., Yang, L., Zhang, L.: DQN-based on-line path planning method for automatic navigation of miniature robots. In: 2023 IEEE International Conference on Robotics and Automation (ICRA), pp. 5407–5413. IEEE (2023)
16. Xie, H., et al.: Reconfigurable magnetic microrobot swarm: multimode transformation, locomotion, and manipulation. J. Sci. Robot. **4**(28), eaav8006 (2019)
17. Kummer, M.P., Abbott, J.J., Kratochvil, B.E., Borer, R., Sengul, A., Nelson, B.J.: OctoMag: an electromagnetic system for 5-DOF wireless micromanipulation. J. IEEE Trans. Robot. **26**(6), 1006–1017 (2010)
18. Yung, K.W., Landecker, P.B., Villani, D.D.: An analytic solution for the force between two magnetic dipoles. J. Phys. Sep. Sci. Eng. **9**(1), 39–52 (1998)
19. Constantin, P., Foiaş, C.: Navier-Stokes Equations. University of Chicago Press, Chicago (1988)
20. Gersten, K.: Hermann schlichting and the boundary-layer theory. In: Hermann Schlichting–100 Years: Scientific Colloquium Celebrating the Anniversary of His Birthday, Braunschweig, Germany 2007, pp. 3–17. Springer (2009)
21. Hamaker, H.C.: The London–van der Waals attraction between spherical particles. J. Phys. **4**(10), 1058–1072 (1937)

Dynamic Path Planning and Automatic Navigation for Microswarms

Jialin Jiang[1] and Li Zhang[1,2,3,4,5](✉)

[1] Department of Mechanical and Automation Engineering, The Chinese University of Hong Kong, Hong Kong, China
lizhang@cuhk.edu.hk
[2] Department of Surgery, The Chinese University of Hong Kong, Hong Kong, China
[3] T-Stone Robotics Institute, The Chinese University of Hong Kong, Hong Kong, China
[4] Chow Yuk Ho Technology Center for Innovative Medicine, The Chinese University of Hong Kong, Hong Kong, China
[5] Multi-Scale Medical Robotics Center, Hong Kong Science Park, Hong Kong, China

Abstract. Control and autonomy of microswarms have drawn increasing attention in recent years. Especially in dynamic environments, robust navigation of swarms avoiding obstacles in real-time still remains challenging. To tackle this issue, in this work we developed an automatic navigation scheme for microswarms, including a fast path planning module and a robust motion control module. At first, we designed a discrete RRT* (d-RRT*) algorithm with enhanced searching efficiency and space availability to guarantee the real-time requirement. Then, we presented a disturbance observer (DOB) based super-twisting sliding mode controller (STSMC) to govern the trajectory following task against external disturbances and system uncertainties. Finally, we performed simulations and experiments to validate the proposed scheme. Results indicate that the d-RRT* algorithm could uniformly explore the working environments and provide a faster planning speed compared to conventional RRT* planner, and the DOB-STSMC could guarantee a tracking error within half swarm body length. Furthermore, our method successfully navigated a vortex-like microswarm to the target position while avoiding two dynamic virtual obstacles.

Keywords: Microswarms · automation at micro/nanoscale · path planning · dynamic navigation

1 Introduction

Remotely actuated micro/nanorobots have gained increasing research interest and exhibited promising application potential in biomedicine [1–3]. After decades of exploration, researchers have developed micro/nanorobots with various structures and driving mechanisms, including helical-shaped swimmers, surface rollers, soft swimmers, and bacteria [4–7]. The miniature sizes not only endow micro/nanorobots with flexibility in tortuous and narrow regions, but also raise challenges in the meantime. The motion stability, loading capacity, and imaging contrast of a single micro/nanorobot are highly limited by dimensions [8,9]. Swarm robotics could be the possible direction to tackle these issues.

A microswarm is defined as a collective consisted of numerous micro/nanoscale agents, which can maintain equilibrium under external stimuli and internal agent-agent interactions. The control and autonomy of swarms have been the research difficulties of swarm microrobotics. In comparison to conventional macroscale robot swarms, it is challenging to integrate sensors and communication modules into micro/nanorobots. All the agents of a microswarm are exposed to the same external driving field, and the control of swarm relies on tuning field parameters. The reconfiguration of microswarms could generate more diverse behaviors than single micro/nanorobots. Till now, researchers have proposed microswarms with controllable pattern distributions [8,9] and locomotion characteristics [10,11]. However, to quantatively describe these behaviors, additional variables have to be introduced and thus increase the complexity of control tasks. To realize robust identification and tracking of a magnetic microswarm, L. Yang and co-workers proposed a statistics-based algorithm [12]. Precise motion control is also demonstrated using various advanced control algorithms [12–14]. J. Yu et al. focused on the hysteresis of swarms deforming process. They designed a fuzzy logic-based controller and achieved accurate modulation of swarm distributions [15]. As for the navigation of microswarms in unstructured environments, L. Yang et al. developed a deep-learning-based scheme to plan the reference swarm patterns along the pre-designed trajectories [16]. Although impressive progress has been accomplished, the navigation of microswarms in dynamic environments still remains challenging.

Effective path planning methods are necessary for the navigation of microswarms in confined environments. Generally, path planning algorithms can be divided into off-line and on-line. Off-line (e.g., rapidly-exploring random tree (RRT) [17], A* [5], and particle swarm optimization(PSO) [18]) planners explore the working environments and provide complete reference trajectories. These methods can produce reliable planning results in both maze-like environments and obstacle-avoidance scenarios. However, the long calculation time makes them unsuitable for dynamic environments. On-line planners are mostly based on artifitial potential field [19,20], which gives reference moving directions according to the distribution of surrounding obstacles. This mechanism could generate planning results in real-time, but may not be applicable in complicated branchy environments. Although researchers have introduced deep learning algorithms for dynamic planning tasks, the relatively low success rate indicates the lack of robustness [21].

Herein, to address the path planning task of microswarms in dynamic environments, this work proposed a fast planning algorithm based on RRT method to satisfy real-time requirement. Considering the low efficiency of the random searching mechanism, we fixed the growing directions of the tree to several values to boost the planning procedure. The planner will keep updating the reference trajectory to avoid obstacles. A disturbance observer (DOB)-based super twisting sliding mode controller (STSMC) was formulated to govern the motion control and path following. Simulations are performed to compare the searching efficiency and planning speed of proposed discrete-RRT* (d-RRT*) algorithm and classic RRT* algorithm. Furthermore, experiments of steering a microswarm avoiding dynamic obstacles validated the feasibility of our navigation scheme.

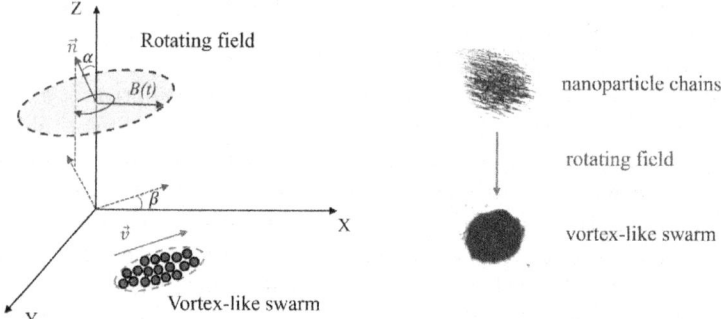

Fig. 1. The rotating magnetic field and vortex-like microswarm. The pitch angle and yaw angle control the velocity and moving direction of the swarm. The right part shows the pictures of the chain-like nanoparticle structures and the stable swarm.

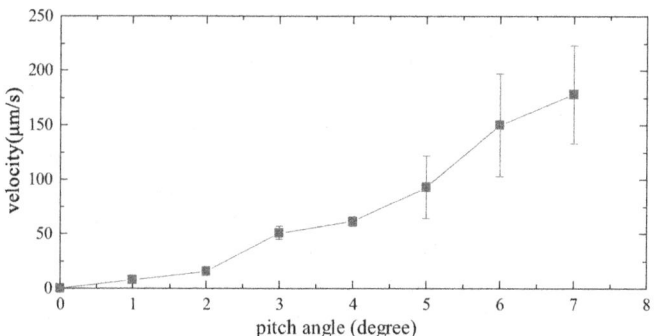

Fig. 2. The relationship between swarm velocity and pitch angle. The velocity increases linearly with the pitch angle under 7°. The error bars represent standard deviation (n = 5).

2 Model of the Microswarm

In this work, we mainly studied vortex-like microswarms. The swarms are composed of nanometer-scale magnetite particles. Rotating magnetic fields could trigger the formation of vortex-like swarms. The detailed mechanism analysis was introduced in our previous work [10]. After being magnetized by the external field, particles tend to form chain-like structures due to attraction. When the field starts to rotate, the chains will rotate accordingly, and eventually form a vortex-like swarm balancing fluidic and magnetic interactions. As depicted in Fig. 1, the locomotion of the swarm can be realized by introducing a pitch angle α to the rotating plane. The swarm velocity linearly increased with α, and the moving direction is along the yaw angle β. We tested motion characteristics of the swarm and the results are presented in Fig. 2. According to the plot, the relationship between swarm velocity and pitch angle is almost linear. It should be noticed that the standard deviations of the velocity dramatically increased when pitch angle is above 5°, indicating unstable swarm states. Thus, the maximum pitch angle in this work is limited to 5°. The system model is simplified as:

$$\begin{cases} \dot{p}_x = g_0 u_x + \xi_x \\ \dot{\xi}_x = h_x(t) \\ \dot{p}_y = g_0 u_y + \xi_y \\ \dot{\xi}_y = h_y(t), \end{cases} \quad \begin{cases} u_x = \alpha(t)\cos\beta \\ u_y = \alpha(t)\sin\beta, \end{cases} \quad (1)$$

where subscripts x and y represent the component along each axis. p is swarm coordinate, g_0 is a consent factor, u is the control effort, ξ is the lumped disturbance, and $h(t)$ is an unknow time-varying function representing the derivative of ξ.

3 Motion Control

To precisely control the swarm motion and follow the given reference trajectory, a robust controller is designed. As a classic variable structure control method, sliding mode control (SMC) has gained widespread research interest owing to its insensitivity to system uncertainties. To deal with the chattering phenomenon that is inherent for SMC, higher order SMC was proposed. Based on the system model (1), we designed a STSMC which can be formulated as:

$$u_x = \frac{\left(k_1 |S_x|^{\frac{1}{2}} sign(S_x) + k_2 \int sign(S_x)\right)}{g_0}, \quad (2)$$

since the swarm motions alon x axis and y axis are decoupled according to (1), we choose x controller for demonstration. S_x is the manually designed sliding mode manifold:

$$S_x = p_x^{ref} - p_x, \quad (3)$$

which is the tracking error along x axis. Therefore, taking 3 into 1, we can obtain the standard STSMC dynamic:

$$\begin{cases} \dot{S}_x = -k_1 |S_x|^{\frac{1}{2}} sign(S_x) + \varUpsilon - \xi_x \\ \dot{\varUpsilon} = -k_2 sign(S_x). \end{cases} \quad (4)$$

Algorithm 1. Correct the node position to fix the growing direction of the tree. Ω represents the working environment, $\mathbb{T}$ is the data tree, N_{new} is the new explored node, and N_{near} is the nearst node in $\mathbb{T}$. $NodeDiscrete(N_{near}, N_{new})$ corrects the position of N_{new} according to the direction of $\overrightarrow{N_{near}N_{new}}$. Function $LegalPath(N_{new}, N_{near})$ returns True if no blockage exists between N_{new} and N_{near}.

1: $N_{new} \leftarrow RandomNode\,(\Omega)$
2: $N_{near} \leftarrow FindNeighbour\,(N_{new}, \mathbb{T})$
3: $N_{new} \leftarrow NodeDiscrete\,(N_{near}, N_{new})$
4: $\overrightarrow{N_{near}N_{new}} \leftarrow l \cdot \frac{\overrightarrow{N_{near}N_{new}}}{\|\overrightarrow{N_{near}N_{new}}\|}$
5: **if** $LegalPath\,(N_{new}, N_{near})$ **then**
6:    **return** N_{new}
7: **else**
8:    **return** $void$
9: **end if**

In (4), k_1 and k_2 are controller factors. There is a disturbance term ξ_x, thus an observer is required for compensation. A DOB is adopted here to estimate the system states and lumped disturbance:

$$\begin{cases} \dot{\tilde{z}}_1 = g_0\beta(t)\cos\alpha + \tilde{z}_2 + L_1\,(p_x - \tilde{z}_1) \\ \dot{\tilde{z}}_2 = L_2\,(p_x - \tilde{z}_1) \\ \dot{\tilde{z}}_3 = g_0\beta(t)\sin\alpha + \tilde{z}_4 + L_3\,(p_y - \tilde{z}_3) \\ \dot{\tilde{z}}_4 = L_4\,(p_y - \tilde{z}_3), \end{cases} \quad (5)$$

where L_1-L_4 are observer factors, $\tilde{z}_1$-$\tilde{z}_4$ are observation results. Feed the estimated disturbance value to the control input, (2) can be rewritten as:

$$u_x = \frac{\left(k_1\,|S_x|^{\frac{1}{2}}\,sign\,(S_x) + k_2 \int sign\,(S_x) + \tilde{z}_x\right)}{g_0}, \quad (6)$$

4 D-RRT* Planning Method

RRT algoritm is widely applied for path planning tasks. Initialized from the start position, a tree-like data structure randomly grows to explore the working environment until it reaches the target position. The randomness of RRT guarantees an adequate search for working space and thus can return reliable planning results in various complicated scenarios. However, this mechanism also leads to a low searching efficiency. Till now, multiple modified versions of RRT (such as RRT* and B-RRT) are proposed to enhance the planning performance, yet the basic searching idea still remains unchanged. To cope with this issue, we developed d-RRT* method. In contrast to the random searching of conventional RRT, we fixed the growing direction of the tree to several discrete values (0°,

90°, 180°, and 270°). With this modification, the neighbourhood of a searched position will not be visited repeatedly during the planning process. Therefore, the searching efficiency and space availability are enhanced. The pseudo code describing of our proposed searching scheme is shown in Algorithm 1. According to the angle pointing from N_{near} to N_{new}, a $NodeDiscrete()$ function reassigns the position of the new explored node to fix the exploring direction of the tree.

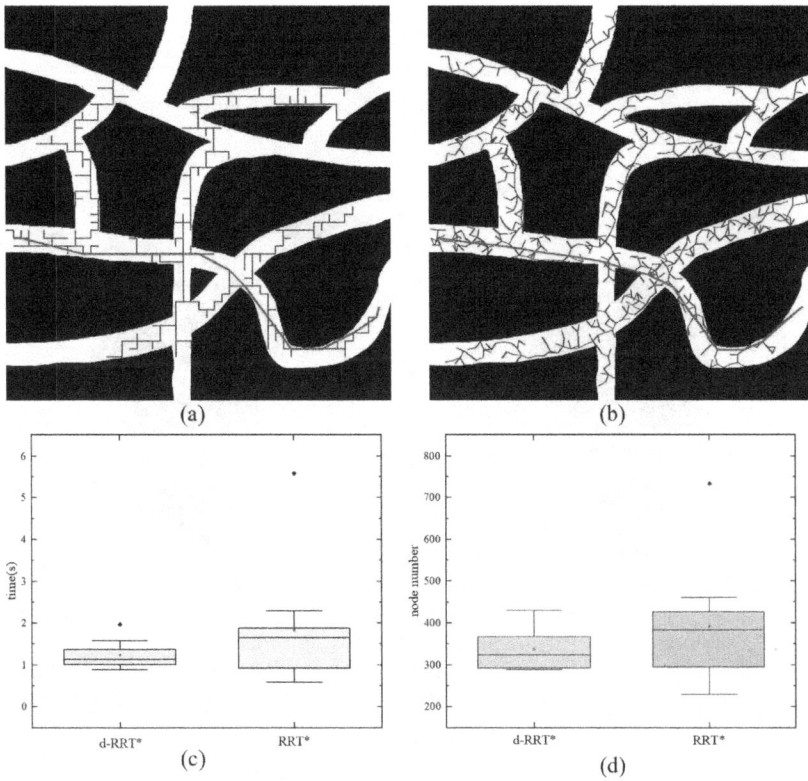

Fig. 3. The simulation results of d-RRT* algorithm and RRT* algorithm. The planning procedures are given in (a) and (b). The proposed d-RRT* method explores the working environment more randomly and possesses better space availability. (c) and (d) present the planning time and searching iterations. The d-RRT* method produces the planning result with a faster speed.

The comparison of the simulation results of the proposed d-RRT* planner and classic RRT* planner are given in Fig. 3. In a manually designed maze-like environment, with the fixed start position and target position, both algorithms plan ten times. Figures 3 (a) and (b) depict the planning procedures. The searched nodes are marked using brown branches and the final results are shown in red lines. It could be concluded that the proposed d-RRT* algorithm possess better search efficiency. The tree could uniformly explore the working environment and increase the space availability. In comparison, RRT* performed too many redundant searches in some local regions. The consumed planning time and searched nodes are recorded and plotted in Figs. 3 (c) and (d). The proposed d-RRT* possesses more stable planning performance. The average planning time and search iterations are both lower than those of RRT*. Moreover, the results of RRT* contain a dramatically abnormal value with 733 searching nodes, which takes over 5s to finish planning. This indicates that the conventional RRT* method is not suitable for real-time path update.

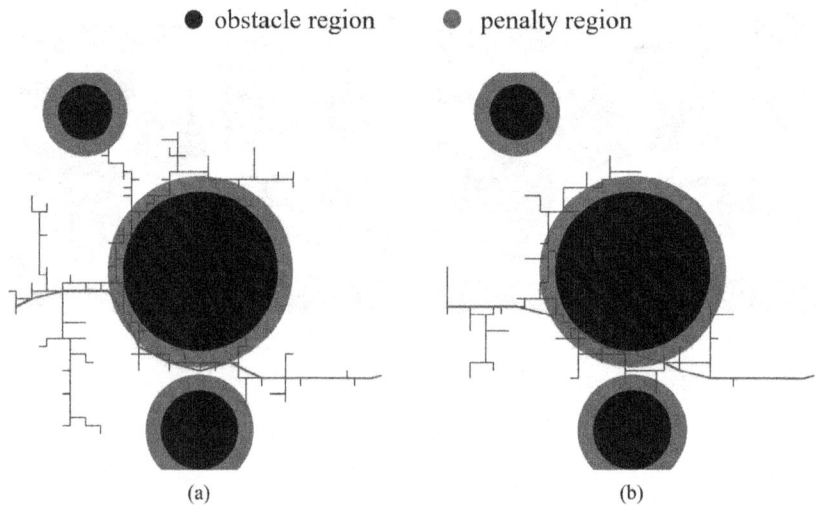

Fig. 4. The comparison between planning results (a) with penalty and (b) without penalty. The penalised trajectory could maintain a safe distance to the obstacle border, which can guarantee a robust navigation for swarms preventing collision.

Considering the physical dimension of a microswarm, a soft restraint should be introduced during planning to guarantee a safe distance between the swarm center and obstacle borders. As shown in Fig. 4, the black filled circles are obstacle regions. Without losing generality, when non-circle obstacles exist we will use fitted circumscribed circles to represent obstacles for simplification. And each obstacle is assigned a gray buffer area. The buffer areas are penalty regions. During path planning, the nodes will have a "penalty" property. The nodes insides these regions will be applied a positive penalty factor (larger than 1), which will increase the total costs of paths passing through this node. The planning resluts of d-RRT* with and without penalty factors are shown in Fig. 4. It is obvious that the trajectory with penalty could keep a safe distance to the obstacle border, yet the one without being penalised closely attached to the obstacle. In practical navigation, this path may result in the collision between swarms and obstacles.

Fig. 5. The experimental platform. The images are captured via an optical microscope, the magnetic field is generated using a Helmholtz coil system. Two host computers are employed for program processing and field calculation.

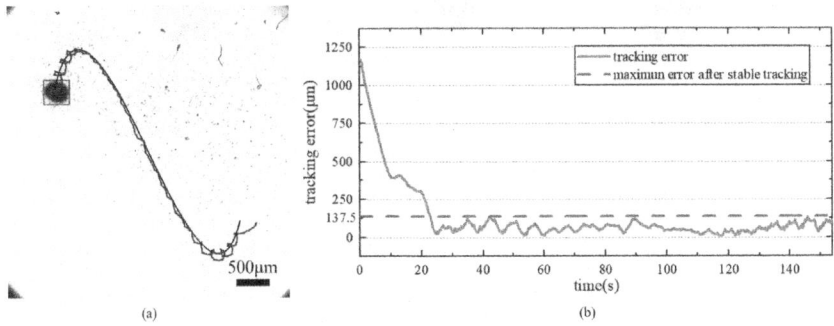

Fig. 6. The experiment result of path tracking. (a) exhibits the trajectories. The purple line is the actual trajectory and the black line is the reference trajectory. The real-time target position is represented with a blue dot. The tracking errors are plotted in (b). (Color figure online)

5 Experiments

To validate our proposed navigation scheme, we performed experiments. The hardware platform is shown in Fig. 5. The field is generated using a 3D Helmholtz coil system, a tank is placed at center of the coil system, and the swarm is inside the tank. The feedback images are captured via an optical microscope, and two host computers are utilized for program processing and field calculation. The communication between hardwares are finished using I/O cards (Model 826, Sensoray, Inc.)

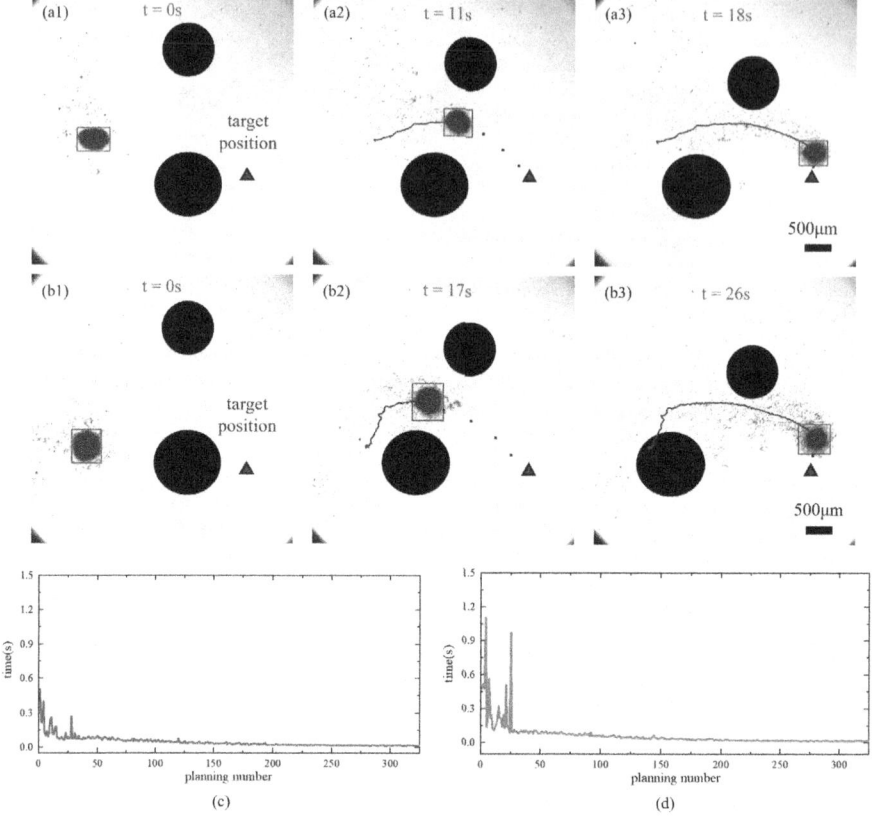

Fig. 7. The experiment result of dynamic obstacle avoidance. (a) and (b) demonstrate two navigation processes, and both swarms could be effectively steered to the target position without collision. The consumed planning times are plotted in (c) and (d), over 99% of the planning periods took less than 0.5 s, and the longest planning time is 1.017 s, which is also the only planning period longer than 1 s.

At first, the swarm was controlled by our DOB-STSMC to follow a pre-designed trajectory. The pixel coordinates of moving target can be described as:

$$\begin{cases} x = 350\cos(0.006\pi t) + 500 \\ y = 350\sin(0.012\pi t) + 500 \end{cases} \quad (7)$$

The field of vision is 1000×1000 pixels, and the obtained path is an approximate sine curve. The reference path and actual path are shown in Fig. 6 (a), the swarm could stably track the dynamic target position. The tracking errors are plotted in Fig. 6 (b). After the swarm follows the target position, the error could be limited under 137.5 μm, which is below 50% of the swarm body length.

Then we tested the navigation performance when dynamic obstacles exist in the working environments. Two virtual elliptical obstacles are assigned, the upper one moves vertically and the lower one moves horizontally. The swarm was expected to reach the target position avoiding these two obstacles. The snapshots of two navigation processes are shown in Fig. 7. The trajectories are marked using purple lines, and the swarms were able to robustly locomote the target positions without collision. The penalty mechanism can guarantee enough safe distance to obstacle borders. The consumed time periods for each planning are plotted in Figs. 7 (c) and (d). It could be concluded that only one planning took longer than 1 s (1.107 s) to update the trajectory. And over 99% of the planning periods took less than 0.5 s. This result indicates that our navigation strategy can fully satisfy the requirement of real-time planning.

6 Conclusion

This work developed a real-time navigation scheme for microswarms in dynamic environments. The path planning module is a d-RRT* with enhanced searching efficiency and planning speed compared to classic RRT*, and a penalty mechanism is introduced to provide safe distance and guarantee robust navigation. A DOB-STSMC is responsible for motion control. Simulations and experiments were performed to validate our algorithms. The swarm could be effectively steered to the target position avoiding dynamic obstacles.

Acknowledgments. This work was supported in part by the the Strategic Topics Grant (STG1/E-401/23-N, GRF14300621, GRF14301122, GRF14205823, GRF15206223 and GRF25200424), Croucher Foundation Grant with Ref. No. CAS20403, the Hong Kong Research Grants Council (RGC) with Research Impact Fund (R4015-21), the Research Fellow Scheme (project no. RFS2122-4S03), and the Multi-Scale Medical Robotics Center (MRC) InnoHK, at the Hong Kong Science Park, the SIAT-CUHK Joint Laboratory of Robotics and Intelligent Systems.

References

1. Bradly, N., Ioannis, K., Jake, A.: Microrobots for Minimally Invasive Medicine. Annu. Rev. Biomed. Eng. **12**(1), 55–85 (2010)
2. Jinxing, L., Berta, Á., Wei, G., et al: Micro/nanorobots for biomedicine: delivery, surgery, sensing, and detoxification. Sci. Robot. **2**(4), eaam6431 (2017)
3. Metin, S., Hakan, C., Wenqi, H., et al.: Biomedical applications of untethered mobile milli/microrobots. Proc. IEEE **103**(2), 205–224 (2015)
4. Li, Z., Jake, A., Lixin, D., et al.: Artificial bacterial flagella: fabrication and magnetic control. Appl. Phys. Lett. **94**(6), 064107 (2009)
5. Zhengxin, Y., Lidong, Y., Li, Z.: Autonomous navigation of magnetic microrobots in a large workspace using mobile-coil system. IEEE/ASME Trans. Mechatron. **26**(6), 3163–3174 (2021)
6. Neng, X., Bowen, J., Dong, J., et al.: Decoupling and reprogramming the wiggling motion of midge larvae using a soft robotic platform. Adv. Mater. **34**(17), 2109126 (2022)

7. Dominic, L., Ouajdi, F., Jean, T., et al.: Three-dimensional remote aggregation and steering of magnetotactic bacteria microrobots for drug delivery applications. Int. J. Robot. Res. **33**(3), 359–374 (2014)
8. Jiangfan, Y., Ben, W., Xingzhou, D., et al.: Ultra-extensible ribbon-like magnetic microswarm. Nat. Commun. **9**, 3260 (2018)
9. Hui, X., Mengmeng, S., Xinjian, F., et al: Reconfigurable magnetic microrobot swarm: multimode transformation, locomotion, and manipulation. Sci. Robot. **4**(28), eaav8006 (2019)
10. Jiangfan, Y., Lidong, Y.: Li, Z: pattern generation and motion control of a vortex-like paramagnetic nanoparticle swarm. Int. J. Robot. Res. **37**(8), 912–930 (2018)
11. Hui, X., Xinjian, F., Mengmeng, S., et al.: Programmable generation and motion control of a snakelike magnetic microrobot swarm. IEEE/ASME Trans. Mechatron. **24**(3), 902–912 (2019)
12. Lidong, Y., Jiangfan, Y., Li, Z.: Statistics-based automated control for a swarm of paramagnetic nanoparticles in 2-D space. IEEE Trans. Robot. **36**(1), 254–270 (2020)
13. Xinjian, F., Qihang, H., Lining, S., et al.: Large-scale swarm control of microrobots by a hybrid-style magnetic actuation system. IEEE Trans. Ind. Electron. **71**(9), 10998–11008 (2024)
14. Jialin, J., Lidong, Y., Bo, H., et al.: Automated microrobotic manipulation using reconfigurable magnetic microswarms. IEEE Trans. Robot. **40**, 3676–3694 (2024)
15. Jiangfan, Y., Lidong, Y., Xingzhou, D., et al.: Adaptive pattern and motion control of magnetic microrobotic swarms. IEEE Trans. Robot. **38**(3), 1552–1570 (2022)
16. Lidong, Y., Jialin, J., Xiaojie, G., et al.: Autonomous environment-adaptive microrobot swarm navigation enabled by deep learning-based real-time distribution planning. Nat. Mach. Intell. **4**(5), 480–493 (2022)
17. Liushuan, Z., Yuanjun, J., Dingran, D., et al.: 3d navigation control of untethered magnetic microrobot in centimeter-scale workspace based on field-of-view tracking scheme. IEEE Trans. Robot. **38**(3), 1583–1598 (2022)
18. Lidong, Y., Yabin, Z., Qianqian, W., et al.: Automated control of magnetic spore-based microrobot using fluorescence imaging for targeted delivery with cellular resolution. IEEE Trans. Autom. Sci. Eng. **17**(1), 490–501 (2020)
19. Jaeyeon, L., Xiao, Z., Chung, P., et al.: Real-time teleoperation of magnetic force-driven microrobots With 3D haptic force feedback for micro-navigation and micro-transportation. IEEE Robot. Autom. Lett. **6**(2), 1769–1776 (2021)
20. Hoyeon, K., U., C., Min, K.: Autonomous dynamic obstacle avoidance for bacteria-powered microrobots (BPMS) with modified vector field histogram. PLOS One **12**(10), e0185744 (2017)
21. Jialin, J., Lidong, Y., Li, Z.: DQN-based on-line path planning method for automatic navigation of miniature robots. In: 2023 IEEE International Conference on Robotics and Automation (ICRA), IEEE, London (2023)

Reinforcement Learning-Based Magnetic Levitation Control of a Capsule Endoscope for Path Tracking Using a Single Permanent Magnet

Yongfeng Huang[1,2], Mingxue Cai[2(✉)], Guoyao Ma[1,2], Zhiqiang Chen[2], Chenyang Huang[2], Yang Yang[1,2], Hongwei Wang[1,2], and Tiantian Xu[2(✉)]

[1] University of Chinese Academy of Sciences, Beijing 100049, China
[2] The Guangdong Provincial Key Laboratory of Robotics and Intelligent System, Shenzhen Institutes of Advanced Technology, Chinese Academy of Sciences, Shenzhen 518055, China
{mx.cai,tt.xu}@siat.ac.cn

Abstract. Magnetically actuated capsule endoscope enables wireless navigation for minimally invasive diagnosis and monitoring of gastrointestinal (GI) diseases. However, current studies lack reliable solutions for maintaining stable magnetic levitation at arbitrary positions within the stomach for imaging and observation during clinical procedures. This work addresses this challenge by leveraging a reinforcement learning (RL) policy to achieve magnetic levitation of capsule endoscope for path tracking under a single permanent magnet. To minimize the sim-to-real gap and enable effective policy training, we develop a simulation environment based on NVIDIA Isaac Sim. In this setup, a permanent magnet is mounted on the end-effector of a robotic arm, enabling position control of the capsule robot using magnetic gradient force. Proximal Policy Optimization (PPO) is selected as the RL algorithm due to its balance of training stability and sample efficiency. The proposed framework is implemented on a robotic platform to achieve path tracking control of a capsule endoscope in a magnetic levitation manner, demonstrating an average positional error of 0.62 mm.

Keywords: Magnetic Capsule Endoscope · Reinforcement Learning · Path Tracking

1 Introduction

Magnetically actuated capsule endoscope (MACE) has emerged as a promising technique for minimally invasive diagnostics and therapeutic procedures within the gastrointestinal (GI) tract [1–4]. By enabling wireless control of a small capsule embedded with sensors and cameras, MACE offers a more comfortable, safer, and patient-friendly alternative to traditional tethered endoscope. As the

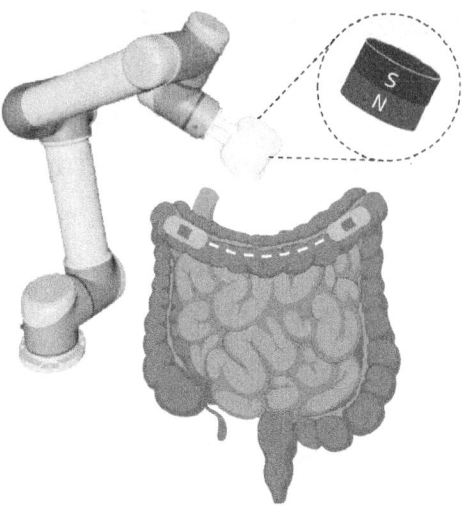

Fig. 1. The capsule endoscope is actuated using an external permanent magnet, enabling it to track a desired path within the gastrointestinal (GI) environment.

demand for non-invasive and remotely operated diagnostic technologies continues to grow–particularly in aging populations and low-resource settings—ensuring accurate and stable control of the capsule has become essential for reliable real-world deployment [5].

Currently, two primary strategies exist for magnetic actuation in capsule endoscopy: electromagnetic control and permanent magnet-based control[6,7]. Electromagnetic systems utilize externally powered coils to generate time-varying magnetic fields, enabling precise and programmable control. However, these systems often require bulky hardware, substantial power consumption, and careful electromagnetic shielding. In contrast, permanent magnet-based systems use strong neodymium magnets mounted on robotic manipulators to produce stable magnetic fields. While offering lower hardware complexity and energy demands, they typically provide less flexibility in real-time control (Fig. 1).

However, precise magnetic control in real-world conditions remains a major challenge due to the complex and nonlinear of magnetic field interactions, disturbances from the environment, and fluid dynamics within the body [8]. Traditional control methods, such as model-based and optimization-based strategies, typically rely on accurate system modeling and manual parameter tuning [9–11]. These approaches often struggle in practice due to uncertainties such as sensor noise, time delays in visual feedback, actuator inaccuracies, and network latency. Consequently, they exhibit poor generalization, limited robustness, and high sensitivity to system variations.

To address these limitations, reinforcement learning (RL) has gained attention as a promising alternative [12,13]. By learning control policies through trial-and-error interactions with the environment, RL can adapt to complex and

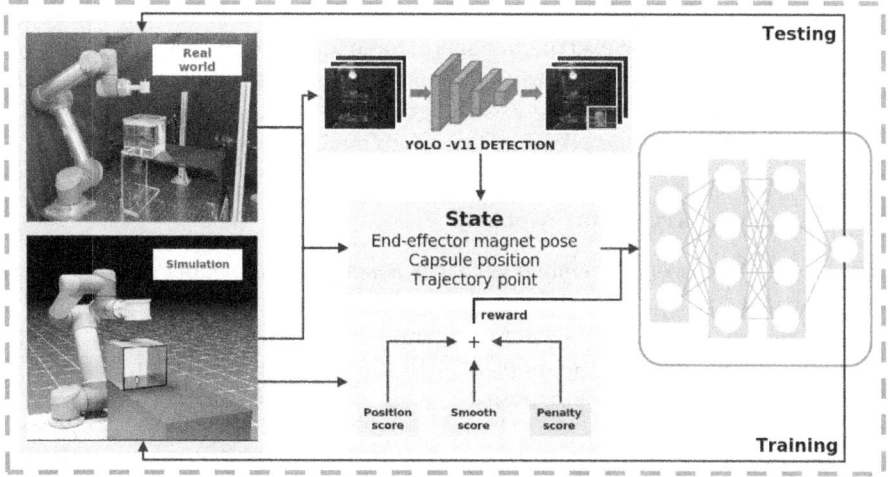

Fig. 2. The proposed reinforcement learning framework for permanent magnets consists of four components: the simulator, magnetic drive system, PPO algorithm, and YOLOv11-based visual tracking. The simulator provides the learning environment, the magnetic system models the magnetic fields, PPO optimizes the task policy, and YOLOv11 handles object detection from high-speed video frames.

uncertain dynamics without requiring explicit modeling. In particular, recent advancements in RL have shown success in robotic control tasks, demonstrating strong adaptability, robustness, and generalization capabilities [14]. In this work, we adopt Proximal Policy Optimization (PPO), a widely used on-policy RL algorithm that balances sample efficiency and stability, making it well suited for robotic applications in dynamic environments.

In this study, we propose an RL-based closed-loop control framework for magnetic capsule manipulation. The system is trained in a high-fidelity simulation environment and subsequently deployed in real-world experiments. Our framework integrates PPO with a visual tracking module based on YOLOv11 to enable accurate, real-time path tracking. Experimental results show that our method achieves improved robustness and control accuracy, offering a viable and scalable solution for practical MACE applications.

The rest of this paper is organized as follows: Section II introduces the system design and modeling; Section III presents the reinforcement learning framework and training procedure; Section IV details the experimental setup and results; and Section V concludes the paper and discusses future directions.

2 System Design and Modeling

As illustrated in Fig. 2, the system consists of a robotic manipulator equipped with a permanent magnet at its end-effector, a magnetically actuated capsule endoscope, and an external vision-based perception module. The permanent magnet generates a magnetic field that induces both translational and rotational motion of the capsule by exerting magnetic force and torque. The capsule's position is estimated in real time using a dual-camera (front-view camera and side view camera). The RL strategy was designed and evaluated through extensive parallel simulations in the NVIDIA Isaac Lab environment.

2.1 Magnetic Actuation Method

The capsule endoscope is embedded with a permanent magnet located at its center of mass, characterized by a magnetic dipole moment $\boldsymbol{m}_c \in \mathbb{R}^3$ and a position $\boldsymbol{p}_c \in \mathbb{R}^3$ expressed in the world coordinate frame. Similarly, the robotic manipulator's end-effector is equipped with a permanent magnet defined by its dipole moment $\boldsymbol{m}_e \in \mathbb{R}^3$ and position $\boldsymbol{p}_e \in \mathbb{R}^3$, also referenced in the world frame.

The magnetic field $\boldsymbol{B}(\boldsymbol{p}_c)$ at the position of the capsule endoscope, generated by the permanent magnet mounted on the robotic end-effector, is modeled using the magnetic dipole approximation [15]. Under this model, the magnetic field $\boldsymbol{B}(\boldsymbol{p}_c)$ is given by:

$$\boldsymbol{B}(\boldsymbol{p}_c) = \frac{\mu_0 \|\boldsymbol{m}_a\|}{4\pi \|\boldsymbol{p}\|^3} \left(3\hat{\boldsymbol{p}}\hat{\boldsymbol{p}}^T - I\right) \hat{\boldsymbol{m}}_a \tag{1}$$

where $\boldsymbol{p} = \boldsymbol{p}_c - \boldsymbol{p}_e$ denotes the distance from the end-effector permanent magnet to the capsule endoscope, and $I \in \mathbb{R}^{3\times 3}$ is the identity matrix.

Under the magnetic field applied by the terminal permanent magnet, the capsule endoscope experiences both magnetic force $\boldsymbol{f}_m$ and torque $\boldsymbol{\tau}_m$, expressed as follows:

$$\boldsymbol{\tau}_m = \frac{\mu_0 \|\boldsymbol{m}_a\| \|\boldsymbol{m}_c\|}{4\pi \|\boldsymbol{p}\|^3} \hat{\boldsymbol{m}}_c \times \left(3\hat{\boldsymbol{p}}\hat{\boldsymbol{p}}^T - I\right) \hat{\boldsymbol{m}}_a \tag{2}$$

$$\boldsymbol{f}_m = \frac{3\mu_0 \|\boldsymbol{m}_a\| \|\boldsymbol{m}_c\|}{4\pi \|\boldsymbol{p}\|^4} \times \left(\hat{\boldsymbol{m}}_a \hat{\boldsymbol{m}}_c^T + \hat{\boldsymbol{m}}_c \hat{\boldsymbol{m}}_a^T + \left(\hat{\boldsymbol{m}}_c^T Z \hat{\boldsymbol{m}}_a\right) I\right) \hat{\boldsymbol{p}} \tag{3}$$

We make the assumption that when the capsule endoscope operates in fluid at negligibly low velocities and infinitesimal accelerations, its dipole moment m_c can achieve near-instantaneous quasi-alignment with the magnetic field $\boldsymbol{B}(\boldsymbol{p}_c)$ produced by the terminal permanent magnet, as expressed by:

$$\hat{\boldsymbol{m}}_c \approx \hat{\boldsymbol{B}}(\boldsymbol{p}_c) \tag{4}$$

Consequently, the orientation of the capsule endoscope can be modulated by indirectly controlling its magnetic dipole moment through deliberate manipulation of the end-effector magnet's position and orientation. By substituting Eq. (4) into the theoretical model, a revised formulation for computing the magnetic force is obtained, given by:

$$\boldsymbol{f}_m \approx \frac{3\mu_0 \|\boldsymbol{m}_a\| \|\boldsymbol{m}_c\|}{4\pi \|\boldsymbol{p}\|^4 \|(3\hat{\boldsymbol{p}}\hat{\boldsymbol{p}}^T - I)\hat{\boldsymbol{m}}_a\|} \left(\hat{\boldsymbol{m}}_a \hat{\boldsymbol{m}}_a^T - \left(1 + 4\left(\hat{\boldsymbol{m}}_a^T \hat{\boldsymbol{p}}\right)^2\right) I\right) \hat{\boldsymbol{p}} \tag{5}$$

2.2 PPO Algorithm

We adopt the Proximal Policy Optimization (PPO) algorithm for training, owing to its stability and effectiveness in continuous control [16,17]. Unlike Deep Deterministic Policy Gradient (DDPG), PPO constrains policy updates via a clipping mechanism, preventing abrupt changes in control outputs. This results in smoother motion of both the robotic arm and the capsule endoscope, which is critical for reliable magnetic manipulation in mapless environments.

Environment: To overcome the inefficiency and inherent risks associated with real-world data collection, this study constructs a high-fidelity virtual simulation environment using the NVIDIA Isaac Lab platform. By integrating the platform's native physics engine with the magnetic field model presented in preceding sections, the simulation setup significantly reduces the reality gap between virtual training and physical deployment. Within this environment, Proximal Policy Optimization (PPO) is employed to train agents for magnetically actuated manipulation tasks, enabling the development of robust and generalizable control strategies. Furthermore, Isaac Lab's support for large-scale parallel simulations across multiple environments facilitates accelerated policy convergence while preserving high sample efficiency.

Observation Space: The observation space in our PPO-based framework is designed to capture key state information necessary for magnetic control of the capsule via the robotic manipulator. The state vector is defined as:

$$s_t = \{P_e, V_e, P_{ec}, V_c, T\} \tag{6}$$

where $P_e \in \mathbb{R}^7$ and $V_e \in \mathbb{R}^6$ denote the pose and velocity of the robotic arm's end-effector, respectively; $P_{ec} \in \mathbb{R}^3$ represents the relative position between the end-effector and the capsule endoscope; $V_c \in \mathbb{R}^3$ is the linear velocity of the capsule; and $T \in \mathbb{R}^6$ denotes the current path waypoint, which contains the 3D coordinates of both the current and the next target points along the desired trajectory.

Action Space: The action space is defined as a six-dimensional continuous vector representing incremental changes to the end-effector's target pose. Specifically, it comprises a 3D translational offset and a 3D rotational delta expressed in axis-angle representation, as shown below:

$$\text{Action}_t = (\Delta x, \Delta y, \Delta z, \Delta\theta_x, \Delta\theta_y, \Delta\theta_z) \tag{7}$$

where $(\Delta x, \Delta y, \Delta z)$ denote the positional offsets along the Cartesian axes, and $(\Delta\theta_x, \Delta\theta_y, \Delta\theta_z)$ represent the rotational changes around the corresponding axes in axis-angle form. The action vector is scaled appropriately and passed to a differential inverse kinematics (IK) controller, which maps it to joint-level commands for the UR5 robotic manipulator. We adopt three orientation increments primarily for the sake of consistency and generality, enabling the control policy to operate in a full 6-DoF action space. This design facilitates seamless extension to other tasks or magnetic configurations, including those where rotation about the magnet's longitudinal axis may become relevant.

Reward Function Design: The goal of this experiment is to control the magnetic field generated by the end-effector-mounted permanent magnet to guide the capsule endoscope along a predefined path, while maintaining smooth and stable motion of the robotic manipulator. Accordingly, the reward function consists of three components: waypoint achievement, robotic arm motion smoothness, and penalty terms.

1) Waypoint achievement: The desired path is defined by a sequence of time-ordered waypoints. The agent guides the capsule endoscope to follow this path by sequentially reaching each waypoint. A fixed positive reward is given when the capsule reaches a waypoint. To further ensure accurate tracking, the reward function includes a distance-based penalty term, which penalizes the squared Euclidean distance to the target waypoint, providing continuous feedback and discouraging deviations from the path.

2) Robotic arm motion smoothness: To promote smooth and stable motion of the robotic manipulator, the reward function includes an action smoothness term that penalizes abrupt variations in control inputs across successive time steps. This regularization encourages temporal continuity in the control commands, thereby reducing mechanical stress, minimizing energy consumption, and enhancing overall system stability.

3) Penalty terms: To discourage undesirable behaviors, the reward function incorporates penalty terms that assign negative rewards in response to specific adverse events. These include, but are not limited to, collisions, excessive control effort, and unstable system dynamics. By penalizing such behaviors, the agent is guided toward safer, more efficient, and physically plausible control policies.

In summary, the total reward received by the agent at time step t is formulated as the weighted sum of all individual reward components, and is expressed as:

$$r_t = \begin{cases} 100 & \text{if waypoint reached} \\ -200 & \text{if constraint violated} \\ -\lambda_1 \|a_t - a_{t-1}\|^2 & \text{motion smoothness} \\ -\lambda_2 \|p_c - p_{\text{waypoint}}\|^2 & \text{otherwise} \end{cases} \quad (8)$$

where a_t denotes the action generated by the policy network at time step t, and λ_1 and λ_2 are weighting coefficients corresponding to the associated reward components.

Loss Function Design: The total loss comprises three terms: a clipped surrogate policy loss to stabilize policy updates, a value function loss to improve

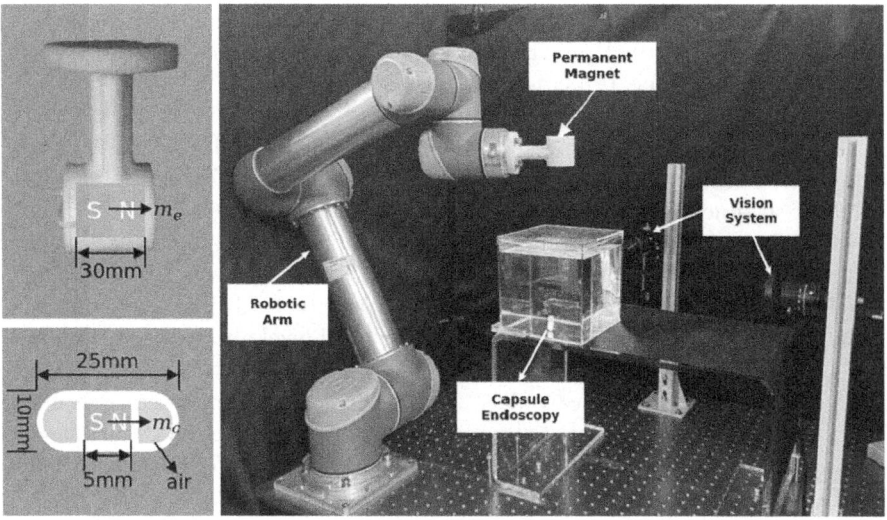

Fig. 3. Overview of the experimental setup.

return estimation accuracy, and an entropy regularization term to encourage exploration and prevent premature convergence.

$$\mathcal{L}_{\text{total}} = \mathcal{L}_{\text{policy}} + c_v \mathcal{L}_{\text{value}} + c_e \mathcal{L}_{\text{entropy}} \tag{9}$$

The policy loss is defined by the clipped surrogate objective:

$$\mathcal{L}_{\text{policy}} = \mathbb{E}_t \left[\min \left(r_t(\theta) A_t, \ \text{clip}(r_t(\theta), \ 1 - \epsilon, \ 1 + \epsilon) A_t \right) \right] \tag{10}$$

The value function loss and entropy term are given by:

$$\mathcal{L}_{\text{value}} = \mathbb{E}_t \left[(V(s_t) - R_t)^2 \right] \tag{11}$$

$$\mathcal{L}_{\text{entropy}} = -\mathbb{E}_t \left[\mathcal{H}(\pi(\cdot \mid s_t)) \right] \tag{12}$$

where c_v and c_e are weighting coefficients that balance value estimation accuracy and exploration. This loss structure ensures stable policy updates, improves value predictions, and encourages diverse behavior.

3 Experimentals

3.1 Experimental Setup

To evaluate the effectiveness of the proposed magnetic manipulation strategy, we conduct real-world experiments using a 6-degree-of-freedom UR5 robotic arm equipped with a cylindrical N52-grade NdFeB permanent magnet (30 mm diameter and height, dipole moment: 25 A m^2) mounted at the end-effector. The prototype capsule endoscope (25 mm height and 10 mm diameter) contains an internal N52-grade NdFeB magnet (5 mm × 5 mm, dipole moment: 0.137 A m^2, parallel to the capsule's principal axis), as shown in Fig. 3.

The capsule is placed in a 150 mm acrylic container filled with 100 cSt dimethyl silicone oil to provide a low-friction, controlled test environment. A stereo vision system, integrated with a YOLOv11-based detection module, enables real-time detection of the capsule from camera images.

To estimate the 3D position of the capsule endoscope, a stereo vision system comprising two orthogonally positioned cameras was employed. A YOLOv11-based object detection model was utilized to perform real-time 2D localization of the capsule in each image frame, producing pixel-level observations from both camera views. These paired detections were subsequently used to perform stereo triangulation, yielding the capsule's 3D coordinates in the camera coordinate frame. To mitigate the effects of observation noise and enhance the temporal consistency of the estimated path, an Extended Kalman Filter (EKF) was applied. The EKF fuses sequential triangulated positions and estimates both the position and velocity of the capsule over time [18,19].

3.2 Experimental Results

Two distinct 3D trajectories—a cube and an infinity-shaped path—are designed, with three trials conducted for each. In every trial, the initial positions of both the capsule and the robotic arm are randomized to test generalization. At each time step, the system receives observations comprising the robotic arm's state and vision-based recognition of the capsule. The policy's output is mapped to joint angle increments via a differential inverse kinematics controller and executed by the physical robot through ROS, enabling closed-loop control of the capsule's motion.

Figure 4 presents the real-world experimental results for two predefined 3D paths: a square path and an infinity-shaped path. Figure 4 (a1d1) and (a2d2) illustrate the manipulation process and outcome for the square path and the infinity-shaped path, respectively. In our study, we focus solely on position control of the capsule robot to achieve path tracking under magnetic levitation, while orientation control is not considered at this stage.

Figure 4 (a1)–(b1) shows an image sequence of the capsule following the square path. Subfigures (a1) and (b1) correspond to the front and side camera views, respectively. Subfigure (c1) illustrates the spatial relationship between the real-time position of the capsule and the reference path. The real-time positions are visualized using a color gradient, where the color encodes the distance from the corresponding point on the reference path, thereby providing an intuitive depiction of tracking accuracy over time. Quantitative error analysis is shown in Fig. 4 (d1), which depict the temporal evolution of the tracking error along the X, Y, and Z axes with 0.96 mm, 1.46 mm, and 1.01 mm, respectively. Furthermore, a mean perpendicular deviation of 0.55mm was observed between the capsule position and the reference path, suggesting accurate spatial alignment. The tracking and error profiles indicate the onset of mild oscillations in the motion of both the

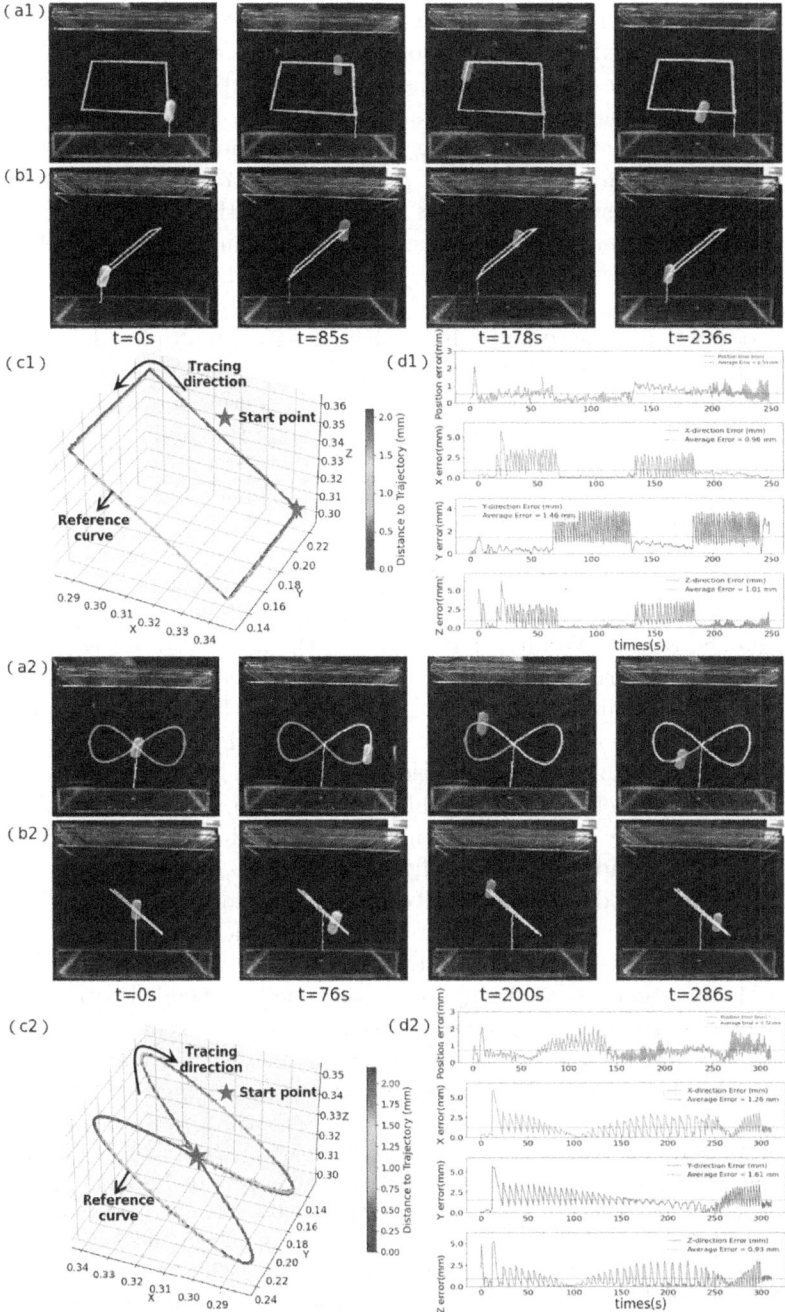

Fig. 4. Real-world demonstration of capsule endoscope path tracking. (ad) present the procedure and outcomes for a square path tracking and an infinity-shaped path tracking. (a) Frontal camera view of the capsule manipulation. (b) Side camera view providing depth observation. (c) Error distribution between the target path and real-time positions. (d) Error curve showing temporal evolution of the tracking error.

robotic arm and the capsule beginning at t = 203 s. Potential contributing factors include prolonged system operation and intermittent delays in the real-time perception module responsible for capsule position estimation.

In addition to the square path, an infinity-shaped path was employed to further evaluate the system's tracking performance under more complex spatial conditions. As shown in Fig. 4(a2)(d2), although the overall path was successfully tracked, the positional error was slightly higher than that observed in the square path experiment, with an average error of 0.72 mm. This increase in error is attributed to the greater curvature and directional changes inherent in the infinity-shaped path.

Apart from the square and infinity-shaped paths, multiple trials were also conducted for other path shapes to assess the consistency and stability of the system's tracking performance. The average tracking error across all experiments was 0.62 mm, further demonstrating the stability and reliability of the model.

4 Conclusion

In this study, we successfully demonstrated the use of a single permanent magnet controlled by a 6-DOF robotic manipulator to perform path tracking tasks with a capsule endoscope. We further investigated the application of reinforcement learning (RL) to learn the characteristics of the magnetic field and control the motion of an external magnetic field. In this framework, reinforcement learning (RL) is leveraged to optimize the control policy, allowing the robotic manipulator to interpret complex magnetic field conditions and dynamically adjust the external magnetic field, thereby enabling precise and reliable manipulation of magnetic objects. We demonstrated that the proposed strategy remains robust, even with control and localization efficiencies at 30 Hz, slight deviations in the localization system, discrepancies between the applied magnetic field and the expected field, and the presence of manipulator fatigue.

In future work, we aim to integrate onboard visual sensing by replacing the external localization system with an internal camera embedded within the capsule endoscope. By combining machine vision with reinforcement learning, this enhancement is expected to enable autonomous localization and vision-guided navigation of the capsule within complex internal environments.

Acknowledgement. This work was supported in part by National Key Research and Development Project under Grant 2023YFB4705300; in part by National Natural Science Foundation of China Under Grant U22A2064, 62403448; in part by National Natural Science Foundation of China (grant No. 62473360), in part by the Shenzhen Science and Technology Program under Grant JCYJ20240813154939050; in part by the Shenzhen Science and Technology Program under Grant JCYJ20220818101611025, Grant RCJC20231211085926038; in part by the Guangdong Basic and Applied Basic Research Foundation (2022B1515120010); in part by SIAT-CUHK Joint Laboratory of Robotics and Intelligent Systems.

References

1. Song, L., et al.: Motion control of capsule robot based on adaptive magnetic levitation using electromagnetic coil. IEEE Trans. Autom. Sci. Eng. **20**(4), 2720–2731 (2023)
2. Xu, T., Huang, C., Lai, Z., Wu, X.: Independent control strategy of multiple magnetic flexible millirobots for position control and path following. IEEE Trans. Rob. **38**(5), 2875–2887 (2022)
3. Shamsudhin, N., et al.: Magnetically guided capsule endoscopy. Med. Phys. **44**(8), e91–e111 (2017)
4. Hale, M.F., Sidhu, R., McAlindon, M.E.: Capsule endoscopy: current practice and future directions. World J Gastroenterol: WJG **20**(24), 7752 (2014)
5. Cai, M., Qi, Z., Cao, Y., Wu, X., Xu, T., Zhang, L.: Magnetic field-priority force control for automated manipulation in large workspaces with reconfigurable electromagnetic actuation system. IEEE Trans. Ind. Electron. (2024)
6. Huo, Y., Yang, L., Xu, T., Sun, D.: Design, control, and clinical applications of magnetic actuation systems: challenges and opportunities. Adv. Intell. Syst. **7**(3), 2400403 (2025)
7. Azom, M.A., Khan, M.Y.A.: Recent developments in control and simulation of permanent magnet synchronous motor systems. Control Syst. Optim. Lett. **3**(1), 84–91 (2025)
8. Huang, C., Xu, T., Yu, H., Wu, X.: A novel h-shaped soft magnetic microrobot for automatic manipulation in dynamic environments. IEEE Trans. Autom. Sci. Eng. (2024)
9. Mahoney, A.W., Abbott, J.J.: Five-degree-of-freedom manipulation of an untethered magnetic device in fluid using a single permanent magnet with application in stomach capsule endoscopy. Int. J. Robot. Res. **35**(1–3), 129–147 (2016)
10. Isitman, O., Alcan, G., Kyrki, V.: Trajectory planning and control for robotic magnetic manipulation (2024). arXiv preprint arXiv:2411.14950
11. Sun, H., Liu, J., Wang, L., Niu, C., Wang, Q.: A novel control method of magnetic navigation capsule endoscope for gastrointestinal examination. IEEE Trans. Magn. **58**(1), 1–9 (2021)
12. Wiering, M.A., Van Otterlo, M.: Reinforcement learning. Adapt. Learn. Optim. **12**(3), 729 (2012)
13. Szepesvári, C.: Algorithms for Reinforcement Learning. Springer nature (2022)
14. Tang, C., Abbatematteo, B., Hu, J., Chandra, R., Martín-Martín, R., Stone, P.: Deep reinforcement learning for robotics: a survey of real-world successes. In: Proceedings of the AAAI Conference on Artificial Intelligence. vol. 39, pp. 28694–28698 (2025)
15. Cai, M., et al.: Performance-guided rotating magnetic field control in large workspaces with reconfigurable electromagnetic actuation system. IEEE Trans. Robot. (2024)
16. Schulman, J., Wolski, F., Dhariwal, P., Radford, A., Klimov, O.: Proximal policy optimization algorithms (2017). arXiv preprint arXiv:1707.06347
17. Yu, C., et al.: The surprising effectiveness of PPO in cooperative multi-agent games. In: Advances in Neural Information Processing Systems, vol. 35, pp. 24611–24624 (2022)
18. Jiang, L., Wu, L.: Enhanced yolov8 network with extended Kalman filter for wildlife detection and tracking in complex environments. Eco. Inform. **84**, 102856 (2024)
19. Lefebvre, T., Bruyninckx, H., De Schutter, J.: Kalman filters for non-linear systems: a comparison of performance. Int. J. Control **77**(7), 639–653 (2004)

Simulator for Identifying Contact-Prone Robot Parts to Accelerate Contact Judgment Between Needle Puncture Robot and Patient

Takayuki Matsuno[1(✉)], Nanako Sakai[1], Yuichiro Toda[1], Tetsushi Kamegawa[1], Yusuke Matsui[2], and Takao Hirai[2]

[1] Okayama University, Tsushimanaka 3-1-1, Okayama, Japan
matsuno@okayama-u.ac.jp
[2] Okayama University, Shikata-cho 2-5-1, Okayama, Japan

Abstract. Interventional radiology (IR) is a minimally invasive medical procedure used for performing biopsy and needle ablation. Meanwhile, surgeons are exposed to high levels of radiation in their hands during IR procedures with current manual needle insertion under CT-guidance. In order to solve this problem, we had developed a remote-controlled IR assistance robot named Zerobot. When performing surgery using this robot, there is possibility that parts of the robot contact with surrounding devices or the patient. Therefore, there is an urgent need to build a system that predicts and warns of contact accurately and at high speed. In the previous research, triangle-based contact judgment was proposed. It was found that brute-force approach under the situation of large number of triangles requires long time to judge the contact state. Therefore, in order to shorten the calculation time, a simulator that picks up robot parts that have a possibility contact is proposed in this paper. It is confirmed that this approach is able to speed up the time to judge contact condition.

Keywords: CT-guided interventional radiology · Medical robot · Contact judgment simulation

1 Introduction

A medical procedure interventional radiology (IR) has less invasive for realizing both of the biopsy and the needle ablation. IR is a surgical procedure in which a needle or catheter is inserted into the body using imaging device, such as CT fluoroscopic imaging and X-ray fluoroscopic imaging. CT fluoroscopic systems that can display image of body inside in real time are useful as a guiding tool in IR. IR with needle puncture under CT fluoroscopic guidance has been applied to both of lung cancer treatment and biopsy [4]. IR surgery has the advantage of less invasive and performed under local anesthesia, shortening the hospital

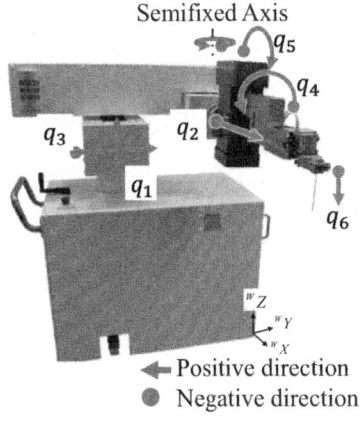
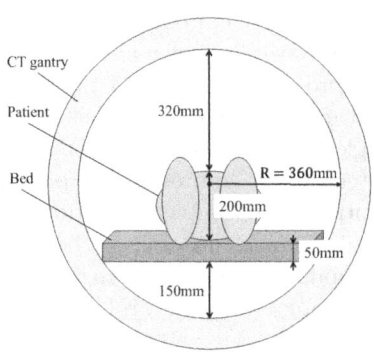

Fig. 1. Appearance of Zerobot.

Fig. 2. Workspace of Zerobot.

stay. Although there are many advantages, there is concern that the surgeon may be exposed to radiation generated during fluoroscopy. Because the surgeon has to perform the procedure close to the CT device. There is concern that the surgeon may be exposed to radiation generated during fluoroscopy. To prevent radiation exposure, surgeons wear protective clothing and use forceps, but this has not completely prevented radiation exposure. In order to reduce the radiation exposure of the surgeon, robots such as Acubot [1], CTbot [2], MAXIO [3] have been developed. Our research group developed the Zerobot in Fig. 1, which can be remotely operated by the surgeon to perform IR procedures under CT fluoroscopy without radiation exposure [4].

Through the experiments [5] and the clinical trials [6], it is found that work space is narrow for Zerobot to manipulate the gripped needle as shown in Fig. 2. When the needle inclines larger, margin of the space becomes tighter. It has possibility of contact with the patient or surrounding devices. Therefore, we have to check that planned pose of robot has no possibility to contact. In previous clinical trials, we had manually checked contact possibility. The manual checks take long time and burden the medical team. Therefore, it is need to construct a contact detection system that judges contact between robot and others in path planning procedure.

Contact judgments are used in various fields such as game programming. When detecting contact between objects, the accuracy and computation speed depend on various factors such as object geometry, the type of data used, and the computation algorithm. In general, there is a trade-off between accuracy and computation speed in object contact detection. Especially the more complex the object geometry, the more pronounced this tendency becomes. Therefore, when detailed contact detection is not required at all times, Bounding volume such as Axis-aligned bounding box (AABB) and Oriented bounding box (OBB) are used to approximate the shape to keep the computational cost low [7].

In our previous study, we focused on object data types and proposed two contact detection algorithms. One is Triangle-based Contact Detection (TCD) [8], and other is Point-cloud-based Contact Detection (PCD) [9,10]. Both algorithms have their ow n advantages and disadvantages. We have not yet to achieve accurate and fast contact prediction. In particular, TCD, which uses a method that expresses contact objects as a set of triangles and detects overlapping triangles, is computationally intensive. Furthermore, the objects subject to contact detection are limited to peripheral devices with invariable shapes, such as CT gantries, and contact detection with patients, whose physiques vary from person to person, has not yet been realized. Therefore, in this paper, we propose methods to speed up triangle-based contact detection for the purpose to judge the contact between a robot and a patient.

2 Teleoperation Surgery

2.1 Configuration of Zerobot

Zerobot has five degrees of freedoms (DOFs) in needle tip position and posture, and one DOF for puncture. As shown in Fig. 1, q_1, q_2, and q_3 are linear motion joints, q_4 and q_5 are rotational joints that change the posture of the gripped needle, and q_6 is a linear motion joint for the puncture motion. To avoid artifacts, a parallel link mechanism is used to separate the motor for puncture and angle change from the CT imaging section. To measure force and moment, the end-effector is equipped with two force sensors. The semifixed axis in Fig. 1 is a turning axis for manually rotating the direction of the end-effector.

2.2 Sequence of Preparation of Robotic Surgery

The sequence to prepare the robotic surgery is listed as below.

1. Related position of Zerobot for the IR-CT equipment is registered. That is determined by pointing the position of the needle gripped by Zerobot.
2. A patient lies down on the bed of IR-CT equipment.
3. The volume CT of the patient is scanned.
4. The surgeon determines the path plan of needle by observing scanned volume CT data. It is necessary to determine the path plan of the needle in consideration of the distance from the main organs.
5. The cross mark to insert a needle is painted on skin of patient.
6. Zerobot moves to initial pose of surgery.
7. CT fluoroscopy is scanned once so as to check the relative positions of target tumor and needle.
8. Surgeon starts the operation with Zerobot.

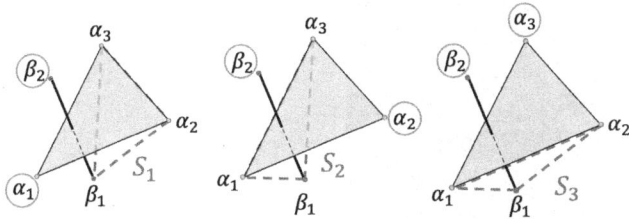

Fig. 3. Planes S_1, S_2 and S_3. Plane S_1 consists of points α_2, α_2, and β_1. Both α_1 and β_2 exist same subspace divided by S_1, if the line $\beta_2 \beta_1$ penetrates triangle α.

In the path plan of the needle, possibility to contact between the patient and Zerobot should be checked. This scheme is added due to robotic surgery. The relative positions of patient and Zerobot can be checked with three-dimensional visualization software. It is required, however, to automatically check the possibility of contact in the view of load of surgeons.

3 Contact Detection Algorithm

3.1 Overview

In this section, three methods for detecting contact condition are introduced. One is Triangle-based contact detection (TCD), and the another is Point-cloud-based contact detection (PCD). Furthermore, Triangle-line-based contact detection (TLCD), which is used to detect contact between patient surface reconstructed from CT data and Zerobot in this research, is a variant of TCD.

Those methods have obvious advantage and disadvantage respectively. Our idea is to combine those methods, so as to shorten the computational time with keeping accuracy of contact judgment.

3.2 Triangle-Based Contact Detection: TCD

The surface of contact objects is represented as gatherings of triangular polygon in TCD algorithm. Then, contact state is determined by detecting the overlap of those triangles.

Detail of sequence is described in [8]. The algorithm has the advantage of accurate contact detection, even if form of the object is concave. Because it performs a brute-force calculation on all combination of triangles. Meanwhile, it needs long time to finish due to the enormous amount of computation. Especially, computational time becomes longest in the case of no contact between objects.

3.3 Triangle-Line-Based Contact Detection: TLCD

TLCD is a method to detect contact between an object expressed with triangle and other point group. Because it takes a time to reconstruct the set of

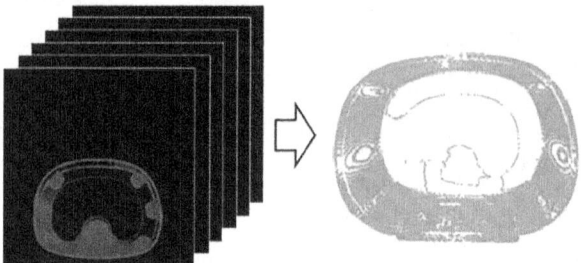

Fig. 4. Reconstruction of patient surface from volume CT data in three-dimensional space.

triangles from volume CT data, TLCD is used for detecting contact between surface of patient and Zerobot. As shown in Fig. 4, volume CT data is converted into point group with below sequence.

1. Single DICOM data is converted into a grayscale 8-bit image.
2. A grayscale 8-bit image is converted into binary image, and contour of the largest foreground object in the binary image is calculated with OpenCV library.
3. Lines are generated by connecting neighbor two points in the contour.
4. Above Lines and points are projected into real world coordinate system using the information written in DICOM data such as pixel spacing, position data.

Sequence of contact detection after projection of lines is almost same with the manner of TCD. First, it is checked that end points of the line are divided by a plane including the triangle. If so, contact is judged with the method shown in Fig. 3.

3.4 Basis of Point-Cloud-Based Contact Detection: PCD

Point-cloud-based contact detection (PCD) is explained in this subsection. There are three stage to predict the contact between a robot and a patient.

1. surface of patient body in volume CT image are converted into points in three-dimensional space.
2. Robot parts are converted into points in three dimensional space based on kinematics. The parts of robot are originally expressed with 3D CAD data. In current CAD software, CAD data can be converted into STL data. Then, edge points of STL Data are picked up.
3. Contact condition between points of the patient and points of the robot are evaluated using proposed algorithm.

First, a couple of point clouds to calculate contact condition is defined as point cloud A and B as shown in Fig. 5. Then, the center of gravity in point clouds G_A, G_B are calculated as Eq. (1).

$$G_A = \frac{1}{N_A}\sum_{k=1}^{N_A} p_a(k), \quad G_B = \frac{1}{N_B}\sum_{k=1}^{N_B} p_b(k) \qquad (1)$$

Here, N_A and N_B are number of points in point cloud A and B. p_a and p_b mean the position of each element in three dimensional space. The vector v_{AB} to connect above center of gravities is defined as Eq. (2).

$$v_{AB} = G_B - G_A. \qquad (2)$$

Next, the function to calculate the inner product between a point p and vector $v_{AB}/|v_{AB}|$ is defined as Eq. (3).

$$g(p) = \frac{(p - G_A) \cdot v_{AB}}{|v_{AB}|}. \qquad (3)$$

As shown in Fig. 5, $g(p)$ means the distance of p from G_A along the vector v_{AB}. The points p_a^{max} and p_b^{min} are defined as Eq. (4).

$$p_a^{max} = \arg\max_{k \in N_A} g(p_a(k)), \quad p_b^{min} = \arg\min_{k \in N_B} g(p_b(k)) \qquad (4)$$

It can be seen that if the point p_b^{min} is farther than point p_a^{max} with respect to point G_A, point clouds A and B are not contact. If there is possibility to contact between those point clouds as shown in Fig. 6(b), p_b^{min} and p_a^{max} have those elements respectively.

3.5 PCD Scheme Including Iteration

The total scheme including iteration is described in this subsection. Based on inner product introduced in Subsect. 3.4, the contact of point clouds is predicted using iteration method. Set of point cloud A and B are defined as S_A and S_B respectively. This means $p_a \in S_A$ and $p_b \in S_B$. For the initial condition,

$$S_A^*(1) = \{p_a | g(p_a) > g(p_b^{min})\}, \quad S_B^*(1) = \{p_b | g(p_b) < g(p_a^{max})\}$$

can be calculated. If $S_A^*(1)$ is empty, it is judged that there is no contact between point cloud A and B. Otherwise, the calculation is continued for the new sets of point cloud. After the second stage, new point data $p_a^{(i)}$ and $p_b^{(i)}$ are defined as below,

$$p_a^{(i)} \in S_A^*(i-1), \quad p_b^{(i)} \in S_B^*(i-1).$$

Here i means iteration number. Then, the calculation introduced in Subsect. 3.4 for new sets of points $p_a^{(i)}$ and $p_b^{(i)}$ is continued. Of course, the center of gravity in each is also calculated again as below,

$$G_A^{(i)} = \frac{1}{N_A^{(i)}}\sum_{k=1}^{N_A^{(i)}} p_a^{(i)}(k), \quad G_B^{(i)} = \frac{1}{N_B^{(i)}}\sum_{k=1}^{N_B^{(i)}} p_b^{(i)}(k). \qquad (5)$$

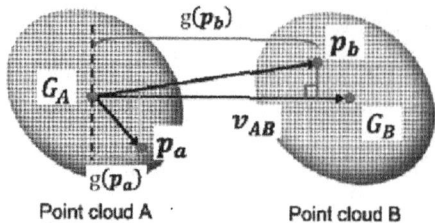

Fig. 5. Point clouds, their center of gravities and projection function $g(\cdot)$.

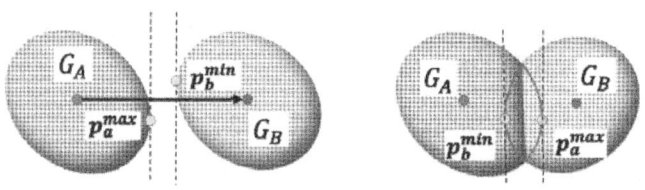

(a) Condition without contact

(b) Condition occurring contact

Fig. 6. Definition of points p_a^{max} and p_b^{min}.

Here, $N_A^{(i)}$ and $N_B^{(i)}$ are number of points $p_a^{(i)}$ and $p_b^{(i)}$ respectively. It can be explained that this algorithm picks up points, which has possibility to contact other point cloud, using projection based on inner product. There are two conditions to finish this iteration. One is that $S_A^*(i)$ becomes empty. Other is that $N_A^{(i)}$ equals $N_A^{(i-1)}$. In the later case, proposed algorithm judges that contact occurs. If $N_A^{(i)}$ does not equal $N_A^{(i-1)}$, calculation is continued.

It has the advantage of being able to judge quickly contact conditions. Meanwhile, when one object has concave shape, there is an overlap between the two points groups in one dimension. The problem with the PCD algorithm is to judge as contact condition even in the case of no contact condition. With only PCD algorithm, it will generate many false positive.

4 Strategy to Shorten Calculation Time

As described in the previous section, each of the two algorithms proposed in the previous study still has issues and has not yet achieved accurate and fast contact prediction. So as to shorten the calculation time for contact judgment, we have approaches as below.

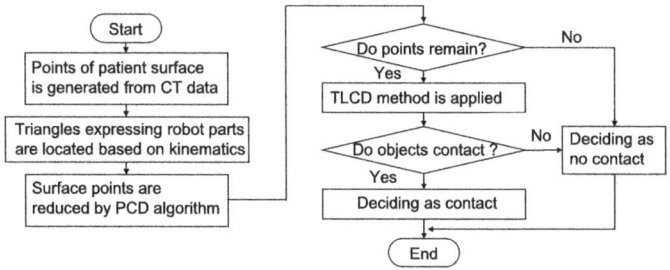

Fig. 7. Flow to judge contact condition using both of PCD and TLCD.

Table 1. Number of polygons for each part

ID No.	Part name	Number of Polygon
1	needle gripper	2,814
2	air parts	4,098
3	force sensor cover	4,088
4	upper part	16,594
5	bottom part	7,242
6	front part	200,436
7	back part	122,084
8	upper cover	3,208
9	bottom cover	3,020
10	B-axis cover	30,066
total		393,650

1. So as to reduce the number of points expressing surface of patient, PCD method is applied to those points once.
2. So as to effectively reduce the number of triangles expressing arm of robot, parts without possibility of contact with patient are deleted. A simulator using virtual patient is introduced in order to check the possibility of contact for each triangle in robot parts.

4.1 Reduction of Points by PCD

The flow to judge the contact condition using both of PCD and TLCD is shown in Fig. 7. After place both the triangles of robot parts and points expressing patient surface, once PCD algorithm is applied so as to reduce the number of points of patient surface. If there is no point expressing patients remained, algorithm finish with judgment of no contact. An example to reduce points by PCD algorithm is shown in Fig. 8. Otherwise, algorithm moves to next step. For remained points of patients and triangles of robot, TLCD algorithm is applied.

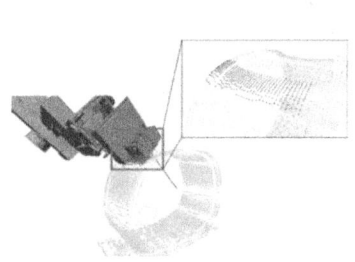
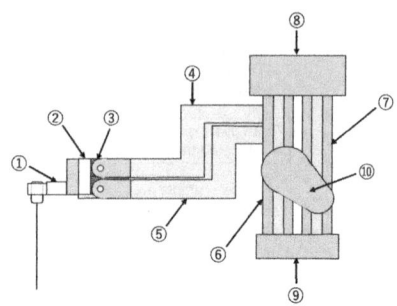

Fig. 8. Result of reducing points expressing patient surface: Pink points and Blue points indicate removed points and remained points respectively through PCD algorithm. (Color figure online)

Fig. 9. Arm parts, which moves independently, and their ID number.

4.2 Simulator for Picking up Parts with Contact Possibility

A simulator that identifies triangles with the contact possibility is proposed in order to reduce the time to judge the contact condition.

Ten parts, which move independently respond to angles of robot joints, organize the arm of robot as shown in Fig. 9. The total number of triangles in the robot arm parts reaches approximately 390,000. The number of triangles for each part is listed in Table 1. The increase in the number of triangles despite the simple structure of the robot arm is due to the rounding of the corners. It can be said that this fact is one of weakness using triangle primitives. Reducing the number of redundant triangles is essential to speed up time of the contact judgment. So as to select needful parts, simulator picks up the triangles contacting with a virtual patient under various robot poses as shown in Fig. 10. Both of the robot parts and the virtual patient in this simulator are expressed with triangles. Then, contact condition is checked by TCD algorithm. The base of virtual patient is made with software MakeHuman [11]. Then its form is modified to change the size. The virtual patient is assumed as an adult male with a height of 1,700 mm. The puncture area is set at 1,000 mm and 1,200 mm from his foot.

4.3 Result of Reducing Triangles of Robot Parts

The total number of puncture trials was 27,762, of which there is 1,883 conditions judged by TCD method to be contacts. The robot parts and triangles with the possibility of contact were identified, and the number of triangles to be calculated was successfully reduced. Seven of ten robot parts had no contact during whole contact simulation. Rest three robot parts, which have the possibility of contact, are needle gripper, force sensor cover, and bottom part. They are labeled as 1, 3, and 5 in Fig. 9. Numbers of triangles in those three parts reduced through the

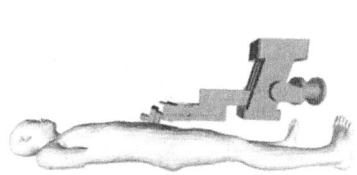
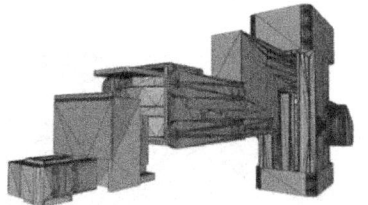

Fig. 10. Visualized appearance of simulator with virtual.

Fig. 11. Visualized result of reducing the triangles of robot arm: Triangles colored with orange have possibility of contact with a patient. Other gray triangles have no possibility and removed from the calculation target. (Color figure online)

Table 2. Number of polygons after reduction

Label No.	Part name	Number of Polygon	
		Before	After
1	needle gripper	2,814	189
3	force sensor cover	4,088	14
5	bottom part	7,242	159
–	other parts	393,288	0
total		393,650	362

simulation as shown in Table 2. It can be concluded that the simulator succeeded to significantly reduce the total number of triangles for about 390,000 triangles to about 360. Triangles with contact possibility are shown in Fig. 11. Orange triangles indicate possibility of contact with a patient. Other gray triangles have no possibility and removed from the calculation target.

5 Result of Simulation and Experiment

In this section, condition of experiment with real robot and result to compare with the contact judgment simulation are described.

The puncture postures are taken within the clinically conceivable range of rotational motion, $-45 \leq q_4 \leq 45$ for q_4 angle joint and $-15 \leq q_5 \leq 15$ for q_5 angle joint. In this range, 22 trials with various postures were conducted. With each pose, q_6 are driven to insert the needle and are stopped at the moment for a part of robot to contact. The angles of all joints are recorded and the pose of robot is reconstructed in simulation. The appearance of experiment and reconstructed situation in simulation are shown in Fig. 12. Then, the position error between actual situation and simulation along puncture direction are calculated.

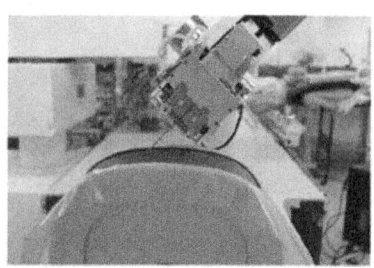
(a) Actual puncture posture

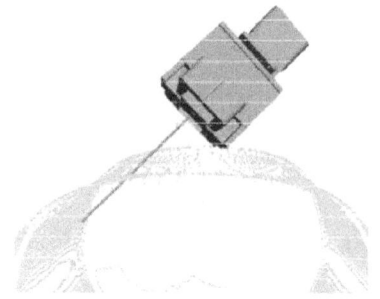
(b) Puncture posture in simulation

Fig. 12. Reproduction of robot-patient contact situations ($q_4 = -45$, $q_5 = -15$).

Table 3. Error between actual situation and contact simulation

index	Rotation angle [deg]		Error [mm]
	q_4	q_5	
1	0	0	3
2	0	15	3
3	0	−15	2
4	15	0	4
5	15	15	1
6	15	−15	2
7	30	0	7
8	30	15	2
9	30	−15	5
10	45	0	9
11	45	15	11
12	45	−15	9
13	−15	15	1
14	−15	15	0
15	−15	15	4
16	−15	−15	−3
17	−30	0	1
18	−30	15	2
19	−30	−15	1
20	−45	0	−1
21	−45	15	0
22	−45	−15	−1

Table 4. Calculation time of contact judgment

Index	Rotation angle [deg]		Calc. time [sec]	
	q_4	q_5	Contact	Non-cont.
1	0	0	0.070	0.050
2	0	15	0.091	0.076
3	0	−15	0.071	0.042
4	15	0	0.120	0.107
5	15	15	0.089	0.077
6	15	−15	0.069	0.173
7	30	0	0.416	0.420
8	30	15	0.122	0.132
9	30	−15	0.065	0.263
10	45	0	0.684	0.836
11	45	15	0.133	0.487
12	45	−15	0.065	0.337
13	−15	15	0.090	0.438
14	−15	15	0.119	0.131
15	−15	15	0.068	0.100
16	−15	−15	0.043	0.053
17	−30	0	0.057	0.086
18	−30	15	0.071	0.060
19	−30	−15	0.055	0.118
20	−45	0	0.061	0.064
21	−45	15	0.085	0.080
22	−45	−15	0.050	0.053

The error for each pose is shown in Table 3. The positive error means that the proposed algorithm judged a contact condition in real world as no contact condition. This false negative phenomenon is a problem to overcome in future. The maximum absolute error in this experiment is 11 mm. It may be due to the deflection of long arm of Zerobot. Then, the computation time required for contact judgment is measured. The results are shown in Table 4. The average computation time was 0.122 s for contact and 0.190 s for non-contact, indicating that the proposed algorithm can detect contact in short time. The computation time is less than 1.0 s for all postures, successfully shortening the time of calculation, which is a drawback of the triangle-based algorithm.

6 Conclusion

We have developed Zerobot, which enables CT-guided robotic IR to reduce radiation exposure to physicians. It has the issue of possible contact with patients due to the small workspace in CT gantry. Therefore, in order to realize accurate and fast contact judgment, we aimed to speed up the time of Triangle based method, which is capable of accurate contact detection. The approach to combine two contact detection methods is introduced. Then, a simulator for picking up the triangles with contact possibility in Zerobot is proposed. Finally, the effectiveness of proposed algorithm is confirmed through the experiment and simulation.

References

1. Stoianovici, D., et al.: AcuBot: a robot for radiological interventions. IEEE Trans. Rob. Autom. **19**(5), 927–930 (2003)
2. Maurin, B., et al.: A patient-mounted robotic platform for CT-scan guided procedures. IEEE Trans. Biomed. Eng. **55**(10), 2417–2425 (2008)
3. Koethe, Y., et al.: Accuracy and efficacy of percutaneous biopsy and ablation using robotic assistance under computed tomography guidance: a phantom study. Eur. Radiol. **24**(3), 723–730 (2013)
4. Hiraki, T., et al.: Development of a robot for CT fluoroscopy-guided intervention: free physicians from radiation. Jon J. Intervent. Radiol. **20**, 375–381 (2014)
5. Kimura, K., et al.: Needle pose adjustment based on force information with needle puncturing robot. In: Proceedings of the 2017 IEEE/SICE International Symposium on System Integration (SII2017), pp. 626–631 (2017)
6. Hiraki, T., et al.: Robotic needle insertion during computed tomography fluoroscopy-guided biopsy: prospective first-in-human feasibility trial. Eur. Radiol. **30**, 927–933 (2020)
7. Ericson, C.: Real-time collision detection. Born Digital, Inc. (2005)
8. Matsuno, T., et al.: Collision detection calculation of robot to insert needles for interventional radiology. In: The 2021 IEEE International Conference on Advanced Robotics and its Social Impacts, FrPA.13 (2013)
9. Lin, M.C.: Efficient collision detection for animation and robotics. In: Proceedings of the Third Euro-graphics Workshop on Animation Cambridge, pp. 84–85 (1992)
10. Matsuno, T., et al.: Contact prediction with patient using projection of point cloud before robotic IR surgery. In: Proceedings of The Twenty-Seventh International Symposium on Artificial Life and Robotics, pp. 1307–1310 (2022)
11. MakeHuman Community Web cite. http://www.makehumancommunity.org/. Accessed 31 Mar 2022

Innovative Design and Performance Evaluation of Robot Mechanisms

Autonomous Bolt Assembly Composite Robotic System Guided by Binocular Vision

Tao Wang, Lei Zheng, Zhiran Zhang, Dailin Zhang, and Xingwei Zhao(✉)

School of Mechanical Science and Engineering, Huazhong University of Science and Technology, Wuhan 430074, China
zhaoxingwei@hust.edu.cn

Abstract. This paper addresses the bolt assembly task for aircraft panels and proposes a vision-guided composite robotic system, which offers advantages such as a large workspace, accurate target positioning, strong assembly adaptability, and non-contact measurement. To tackle the spatial positioning problem of bolts on aircraft panels, a binocular vision-based method for bolt spatial attitude positioning is proposed. First, an autonomous bolt detection model based on the YOLOv12 neural network is developed, combined with an arc support segment fitting algorithm, to complete the feature extraction of the bolt end-face circle in the image. Then, a matching algorithm based on the SAD-BT cost is proposed to achieve bolt feature matching between the left and right camera images. Finally, using the camera calibration parameters and the triangulation positioning principle, the spatial attitude of the bolt is determined. Experiments are conducted based on assembly accuracy and process requirements, and the results demonstrate that the assembly accuracy is within 1 mm, with an assembly success rate of 100%.

Keywords: Composite Robotic System · System Calibration · Feature Matching · Visual Measurement

1 Introduction

In the entire process of aircraft manufacturing, the assembly stage accounts for 40% to 50% of the total workload and cost [1]. Meanwhile, data shows that a Boeing 747 aircraft contains 3 million assembly holes [2]. Traditional manual assembly methods face issues such as unstable product assembly quality, low efficiency, and high labor intensity. Therefore, developing an efficient, precise, and reliable automated assembly technology has become an urgent need in the aerospace manufacturing industry.

Introducing robots into aircraft assembly can improve manufacturing efficiency, relieve labor force, and also enhance product quality [3]. For large structural components like aircraft, existing robotic arm assembly systems typically use fixed robotic arm assembly systems, which are efficient and easy to operate once the process is set [4]. However, fixed robotic arm assembly systems have limitations, as the workspace of the robotic arm cannot cover multiple assembly positions of large structures. With the continuous expansion and innovation of Automated Guided Vehicle (AGV) technology, the deep integration of robotic arms and AGVs has become an advanced mobile assembly solution [5].

In the robotic assembly process, obtaining the target position is the prerequisite for robotic assembly. Therefore, the system's ability to perceive the surrounding environment becomes an integral part of its automation. With the continuous development of robotic technologies in recent years, sensors for vision, force, and other information have gradually been integrated into robotic systems. The process of information fusion can be broadly divided into single-source fusion and multi-source fusion. Single-source fusion includes vision sensors [6] and force sensors [7], while multi-source fusion involves hybrid sensors [8].

For vision-guided robotic arm operations, ensuring high-precision measurements is undoubtedly the core element of the entire process, directly affecting the accuracy and efficiency of the robot in executing tasks. However, the performance of vision sensors in achieving this high-precision goal is significantly influenced by various factors. Key parameters include imaging clarity, detail capture capability, color fidelity, and dynamic range. Additionally, the precise calibration of internal parameters [9] (such as focal length and optical center position) and external parameter calibration [10] (such as the relative position of the sensor and robotic arm) are indispensable for ensuring measurement accuracy. Automating the acquisition of targets is also a major challenge in the field of automated assembly. In complex assembly environments, target objects may appear with different postures, positions, or occlusions, which requires the vision system to have strong target recognition and positioning capabilities [11].

This paper aims to design and complete a vision-guided composite robotic system for the bolt assembly task of wall panels, focusing on the actual bolt assembly requirements. Research is carried out from the aspects of visual recognition and positioning, assembly system integration, and experimental validation. First, the YOLOv12 neural network is used to extract the bolt Region of Interest (ROI), and an arc support segment ellipse fitting algorithm is employed to obtain the feature of the bolt end-face circle in the image, achieving subpixel-level extraction of the circle center and end-face circle features. Then, a matching algorithm based on the SAD-BT cost is used to match the feature points of the same bolt obtained by the binocular camera, and, combined with binocular vision principles, a spatial set of points of the bolt end-face circle is fitted, thereby obtaining the three-dimensional spatial information of the bolt. Finally, the robotic arm is driven to complete the high-precision and high-efficiency assembly of the aerospace bolts. In summary, the contributions of this paper are as follows:

1. A composite robotic operating system for aerospace bolt assembly has been built.
2. The YOLOv12 neural network and arc support segment ellipse fitting algorithm have been introduced to achieve subpixel-level extraction of the bolt end-face circle center in the image.
3. A matching algorithm based on the SAD-BT cost and triangulation principles has been used to achieve high-efficiency and high-precision positioning of the bolt center.

2 Method

This paper presents a binocular vision-based bolt recognition and precise spatial positioning algorithm. The algorithm aims to effectively distinguish the target object from the environmental background, overcoming interference caused by lighting changes and metal reflections, and accurately extract the key feature information (end-face circle) of the target bolt, providing precise pose references for subsequent assembly operations. Additionally, the algorithm has the capability for parallel processing of multiple targets, enabling simultaneous recognition and positioning of multiple assembly targets. Based on the above analysis, the bolt positioning flowchart is shown in Fig. 1.

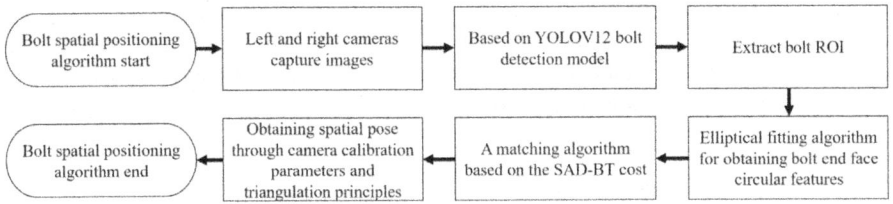

Fig. 1. Bolt Recognition and Positioning Algorithm Flowchart

2.1 YOLOv12

As deep learning-based object detection technology continues to evolve, YOLOv12, as the latest generation of the YOLO series algorithm, achieves a better balance between detection accuracy and real-time performance. This model introduces key technologies

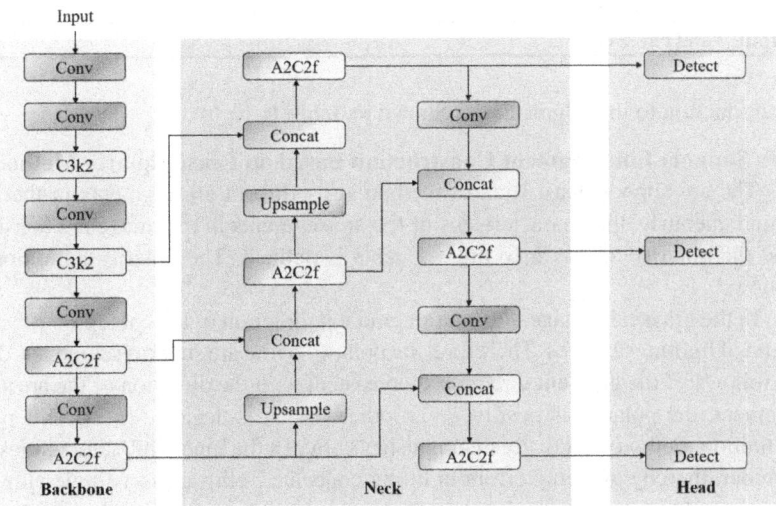

Fig. 2. YOLOv12 Network Architecture Diagram

such as multi-scale feature fusion, structural re-parameterization, and dynamic label assignment strategies, effectively improving the model's performance in small object detection scenarios. It is particularly suitable for industrial vision tasks that require precise identification of small components like bolts. The network structure of the YOLOv12 model is shown in the Fig. 2 below:

2.2 Bolt Circle Feature Extraction Based on Arc Support Segment Fitting

This paper adopts an ellipse fitting algorithm based on arc support segments [12] to extract features from the bolt's end face. This algorithm is an industrial-grade ellipse detection method, characterized by both high accuracy and high efficiency. The core idea is to simplify complex curves using arc support lines and employ a strategy that combines local and global approaches to quickly fit the ellipse. Through hierarchical clustering and saliency evaluation, the algorithm achieves high efficiency while ensuring high precision. The arc support segment algorithm is shown in Table 1.

Table 1. Arc Support Segment Fitting Algorithm

Input: Original image of the Region of Interest (ROI)
1. Utilize the least squares method (LS) to construct arc support line segments within the image, and define the polarity of the arc segments. 2. Apply constraint conditions to group the arc support segments. 3. Generate an initial set of ellipses using two complementary methods based on the grouped segments. 4. Use a mean shift-based hierarchical clustering method to optimize the generated ellipse set. 5. Define a quality rate to select high-quality ellipses from the optimized set. 6. Revalidate the selected ellipses by applying thresholds for the number of points inside the ellipses and the coverage angle.
Output: Valid circle/ellipse

Introduction to the Algorithm as Shown in Table 1:

1. **Arc Support Line Segment Construction Based on Least Squares Method.**

    The arc support least squares method is used to fit arc segments in the image. Simultaneously, the characteristics of the arc segments in the image are considered, and the polarity of the fitted arc segments is defined. The polarity definition is as follows:

    In the grayscale image, the overall gradient direction of a local region reflects the trend of lighting changes. Therefore, the polarity of the arc support segment is defined as follows: if the gradient direction is consistent with the direction of the arc support segment, the polarity is positive (+1); otherwise, it is negative (−1). This polarity definition method effectively distinguishes between the inner and outer circles in the contour, thereby avoiding errors in fitting concentric ellipses as a single ellipse and significantly improving detection accuracy.

2. Arc Support Segment Grouping

The first step is grouping the fitted arc segments by combining potential arc support line segments that belong to the same ellipse into a set. This grouping process is constrained by the continuity and convexity conditions:

Continuity Condition: The distance between the head of one arc support segment and the tail of another arc support segment should be sufficiently small.
Convexity Condition: The connected arc support segments should have the same clockwise or counterclockwise direction.

3. Generation of Initial Ellipse Set

After grouping, an initial ellipse set is constructed. Two complementary methods are used to generate this set:

Local Region: Arc support segments are individually fitted to an ellipse in the local region.
Global Region: All valid arc support segment groups are searched to reconstruct the potential ellipses in the image.

Three criteria are used during the fitting process to ensure the reliability of the line groups:

Polarity Constraint: The arc segments of the same ellipse should have the same polarity.
Region Restriction: The arc segments of the same ellipse should be located in a unified region.
Adaptive Inlier Criterion: This criterion ensures that the fitting process aligns with the reliable region.

The region restriction is illustrated in Fig. 3, and the specific formula is as follows:

$$\begin{cases} \vec{ARC}_{L_s^{gi}} \cdot \vec{P_s^{gi} P_e^{gj}} > \rho_d \\ \vec{ARC}_{L_e^{gi}} \cdot \vec{P_e^{gi} P_s^{gj}} > \rho_d \\ (Pol) \cdot Dir_\perp \left(\vec{P_s^{gi} P_e^{gj}} \right) \cdot \vec{M_i M_j} > \rho_d \end{cases} \quad (1)$$

where $\vec{ARC}_L$ is the unit vector of the arc support direction L, and $Dir_\perp \left(\vec{v} \right)$ represents the unit vector obtained by rotating v clockwise by 90°. When the polarity of $\{g_i, g_j\}$ is positive, Pol equals 1; otherwise, Pol equals -1.

Polarity Definition: If the gradient direction in the image is consistent with the arc support direction, the polarity is positive (+1); otherwise, it is negative (-1).

ρ_d is the distance threshold, and M_i is the midpoint of the line segment connecting points P_s^{gi} and P_e^{gi}, where P_s^{gi} and P_e^{gi} are the starting and ending points of the arc segment g_i, respectively.

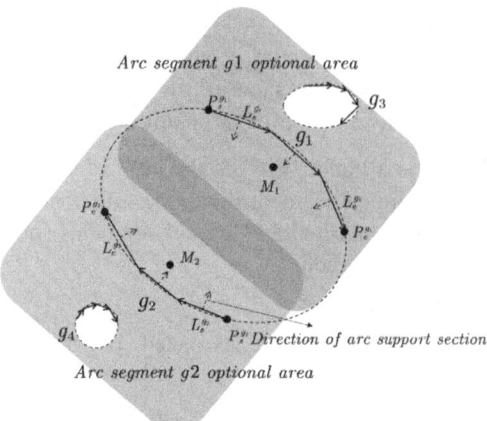

Fig. 3. Region Restriction

Adaptive Inlier Criterion: A candidate ellipse is considered valid if the number of inlier support points exceeds the length of the arc support line segment associated with that ellipse.

4. **Optimization of the Ellipse Set**

   A mean-shift-based hierarchical clustering method is used to optimize the ellipse set. Specifically, the clustering problem in the 5D ellipse parameter space is decomposed into three low-dimensional cascading space clustering problems. The clustering process utilizes the center, orientation, and semi-axes of the ellipses to cluster the initial set of ellipses.

5. **Ellipse Selection**

   The quality rate of the ellipse is defined to validate the candidate set, selecting the ellipses with higher quality rates as the final detection results. The quality rate is defined as follows:

$$G(e) = \sqrt{\frac{\#\{p_i : p_i \in SI(e)\}}{B} \cdot \frac{C}{360}} \qquad (2)$$

where, $\#\{p_i : p_i \in SI(e)\}$ is the length of the ellipse's inlier support point set, $B \approx \pi[\frac{3}{2}(a+b) - \sqrt{ab}]$ is an empirical formula, and a and b are the semi-major and semi-minor axes of the ellipse, respectively. C is the coverage angle of the inlier support points connected to the ellipse. Finally, after using the set thresholds for the number of ellipse inliers and the coverage angle, the results are re-validated, and the final output is produced.

2.3 Bolt End-Face Ellipse Point Set Matching

After accurately extracting the contours of the bolts from the stereo images, this section proposes a matching algorithm based on the SAD-BT cost to match the ellipse point sets of the captured bolts. Using the principles of triangulation, the algorithm performs calculations on the matched ellipse point sets, ultimately obtaining the spatial position information of the bolt through the matching of the bolt end-face ellipse point sets.

The matching algorithm based on the SAD-BT cost is shown in Table 2:

Table 2. Matching Algorithm Based on The SAD-BT Cost

Input: Original image and sets of ellipse points
1. Perform stereo rectification on the original image to align the epipolar lines.
2. Cluster ellipse points along the y-axis direction. Points with pixel differences within 50 are grouped into the same row.
3. For each ellipse center point, compute the Sum of Absolute Differences with Bilateral Truncation (SAD-BT) cost.
4. For ellipse centers located on the same row in the stereo image pair, compute the SAD-BT cost differences sequentially.
5. Apply the Winner-Takes-All (WTA) strategy to determine the preliminary disparity for each ellipse center based on minimum cost.
6. Cluster the obtained disparity values and select the most frequent disparity in the cluster as the standard disparity (StdDisparity).
7. In the stereo ellipse point set, identify matched points whose y-coordinate difference is within (−5, +5) pixels and x-coordinate difference is within (StdDisparity−50, StdDisparity+50) pixels.
Output: Matched ellipse point pairs

BT Cost

The Fig. 4 below shows the grayscale intensity function curves I_L and I_R along the same row in the left and right images, respectively. The grayscale intensity value at point x_i is $I_L(x_i)$, and the value at point y_i is $I_R(y_i)$.

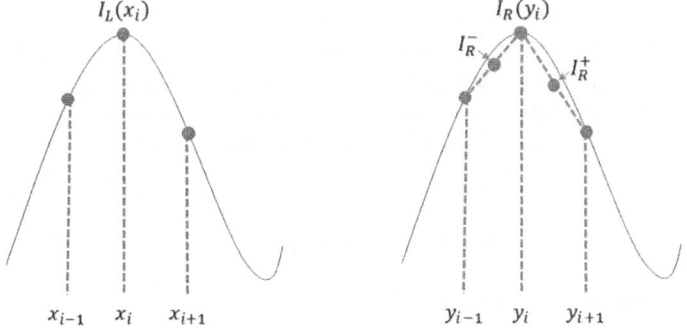

Fig. 4. Grayscale Intensity Curve

We use $d(x_i, y_i)$ to describe the similarity between points x_i and y_i.

For point y_i, we construct:

$$I_R^- = \frac{1}{2} \cdot (I_R(y_i) + I_R(y_{i-1}))$$

$$I_R^+ = \frac{1}{2} \cdot (I_R(y_i) + I_R(y_{i+1}))$$

$$I_{min} = min\{I_R^-, I_R^+, I_R(y_i)\}$$

$$I_{max} = max\{I_R^-, I_R^+, I_R(y_i)\}$$

$$\overline{d}(x_i, y_i) = \max\{0, I_L(x_i) - I_{max}, I_{min} - I_L(x_i)\} \quad (3)$$

Similarly, for point x_i, we construct:

$$I_L^- = \frac{1}{2} \cdot (I_L(x_i) + I_L(x_{i-1}))$$

$$I_R^+ = \frac{1}{2} \cdot (I_R(y_i) + I_R(y_{i+1}))$$

$$I_{min} = min\{I_R^-, I_R^+, I_R(y_i)\}$$

$$I_{max} = max\{I_R^-, I_R^+, I_R(y_i)\}$$

$$\overline{d}(x_i, y_i) = \max\{0, I_L(x_i) - I_{max}, I_{min} - I_L(x_i)\} \quad (4)$$

The BT cost is:

$$d(x_i, y_i) = \overline{d}(x_i, y_i) + \overline{d}(y_i, x_i) \quad (5)$$

X-Sobel BT and **gray BT** are fused through weighted integration.

The original BT cost is computed based on the grayscale image, resulting in BT_{gray}.

If the ellipse point set in the grayscale image is processed using Sobel-X filtering and then used as the input for BT cost computation, the resulting cost is denoted as BT_{xsobel}. The computation process of the Sobel-X filter is as follows:

$$\begin{aligned}Sobel(x, y) =\,& 2 \cdot [f(x+1, y) - f(x-1, y)] + f(x+1, y+1) \\ & - f(x-1, y+1) + f(x+1, y-1) - f(x-1, y-1)\end{aligned} \quad (6)$$

The so-called weighted fusion is defined as:

$$\text{Cost}_{combine} = BT_{xsobel} + BT_{gray} \cdot \alpha \quad (7)$$

In this paper, $\alpha = \frac{1}{4}$.

SAD-BT Cost (Neighborhood Summation Operation):

Since the BT cost is based on one-dimensional matching, it is typically combined with the Sum of Absolute Differences (SAD) approach. By performing a neighborhood summation, the SAD-BT cost is computed, resulting in a local block-based cost. In this way, the matching cost of each pixel incorporates information from its surrounding local region.

$$BT_{\text{SAD}}(p, d) = \sum_{q \in N_p} BT(q, d) \tag{8}$$

That is, the SAD-BT cost at a given point p is calculated as the sum of all BT costs within its surrounding neighborhood. This neighborhood summation operation is performed over a window N_p, which, in this paper, is defined as a 3×3 matrix.

3 Experiment

3.1 Construction of the Hardware and Software Platform for Hybrid Robotic Assembly

To meet the requirements of bolt assembly on aircraft panels, a hybrid robotic system was established. This system mainly consists of six components: a robotic arm (ROKAE-CR12), an AGV (AMB-300-D by SEER), a lifting column (LIFTKIT-0S-601), a binocular camera (Basler acA5472-gc), an end-effector, and a feeding device. The complete hybrid robotic system is shown in Fig. 5.

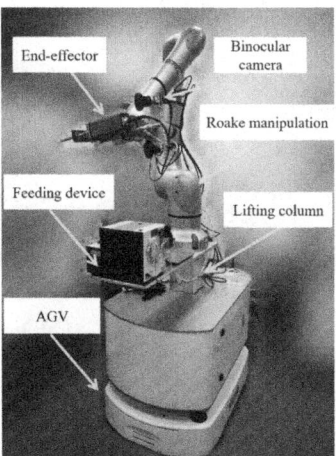

Fig. 5. Composite Robotic System

For the training of the YOLOv12 model, the hardware configuration was as follows: **CPU:** Intel(R) Core(TM) i5-12600KF @ 3.70 GHz; **GPU:** NVIDIA GeForce RTX 4070 Ti with 16 GB VRAM; **RAM:** 16 GB; **Operating System:** Windows 11.

The corresponding software environment included: **Python:** 3.9.20; **MMEngine:** 0.10.5; **CuDNN:** 8.2; **OpenCV:** 4.10.0; **PyTorch:** 1.11.0 + cu113; **TorchVision:** 0.12.0 + cu113; **CUDA:** 11.3.

The bolt dataset used for training comprised a total of 600 images with a resolution of 5472 × 3648 pixels, including 300 original images and 300 augmented samples generated through data augmentation techniques.

3.2 Feature Matching Efficiency Experiment

Due to the presence of significant noise in aircraft panel images and the small size of bolt targets within the images, traditional methods are generally limited to global or semi-global matching techniques for disparity calculation [13]. Therefore, this section employs the Semi-Global Block Matching (SGBM) algorithm [14] as a benchmark to compare with the recognition algorithm proposed in this chapter. The aim is to validate the disparity computation time for the bolt end-face centers in identical image pairs.

After image rectification, the spatial positions of the bolts were calculated using both the bolt localization algorithm proposed in this paper and the SGBM algorithm. Figure 6(a) and (b) show the fitted circular profiles of the bolt end-faces generated during the computation process of the proposed localization algorithm, while Fig. 6 (c) presents the depth map produced by the SGBM algorithm.

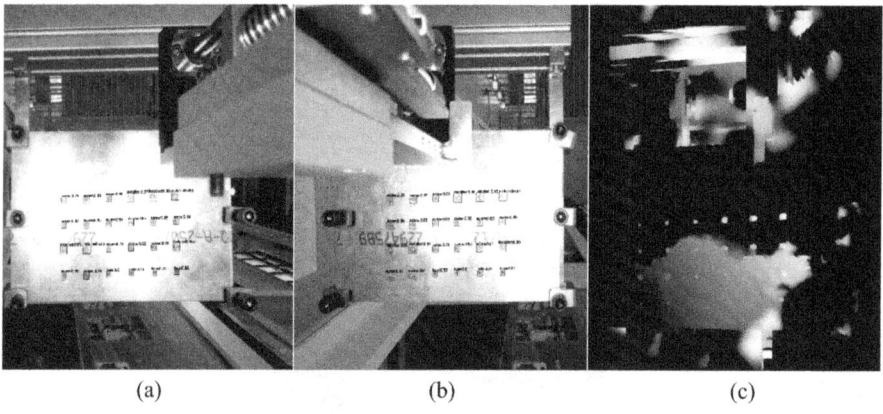

Fig. 6. ROI Extraction and Disparity Map Generation: (a) Left Image ROI; (b) Right Image ROI; (c) Disparity Map.

The average computation time over 20 runs is shown in Table 3, indicating that the Semi-Global Block Matching (SGBM) algorithm requires significantly more time than the method proposed in this paper.

Table 3. Comparison of Matching Algorithm Computation Time

Algorithm	Average Time (s)
SGBM	6.351
Proposed Recognition Algorithm	0.427

3.3 Bolt Assembly Experiment

A total of 14 assembly experiments were conducted on all identified bolt holes on the flat panel. First, the robotic arm was returned to the observation position. Then, its end-effector was moved to the computed bolt position to carry out the assembly of individual bolts. The effectiveness of each assembly was verified by observing whether the tip of the tool accurately entered the corresponding bolt hole (Fig. 7).

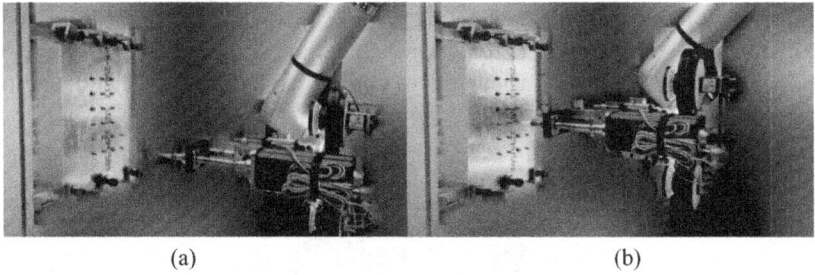

Fig. 7. Assembly Accuracy Experiment. (a) Observation Position; (b) Assembly Position

To verify positioning accuracy, a teaching step mode was used to control the end-effector's movement. The robotic arm has a repeatability error of $\pm\,0.03$ mm. As shown in Fig. 8, the deviation between the actual center of each assembled bolt and the computed position is analyzed for each assembly experiment.

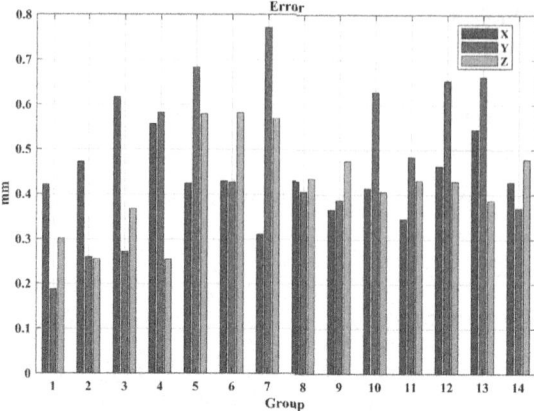

Fig. 8. Assembly Error Diagram

Given that the design tolerance of the assembly tool allows for a positional deviation of ≤ 1 mm and an angular deviation of $\leq 1°$, the assembly tasks can be successfully executed under the aforementioned accuracy conditions, achieving a 100% success rate.

Figure 9 shows the hybrid robotic system autonomously assembling aerospace bolts, including the fully automated installation of nuts. It can be observed that the designed hybrid robotic system fully meets the requirements for aerospace bolt assembly.

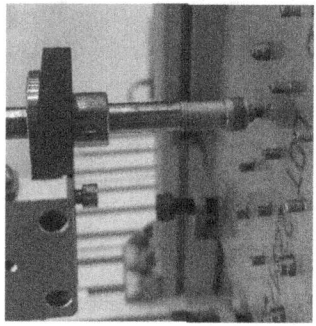

Fig. 9. Assembly Result Diagram

4 Conclusion

This paper proposes a hybrid robotic system designed to meet the task requirements of aircraft panel bolt assembly. Based on the visual characteristics of aerospace bolts, a binocular vision-guided high-precision bolt localization algorithm is developed to address the target observation challenge within the assembly system. Compared to traditional stereo matching-based localization algorithms, the proposed method reduces the average computation time for bolt feature extraction from 6.351 s to 0.427 s. Additionally, the overall assembly accuracy of the system is maintained within 1 mm. The system effectively resolves the automation challenge of panel bolt assembly and achieves fully automated operations—from localization and grasping to insertion and tightening—significantly improving both assembly efficiency and consistency.

Acknowledgment. This work was supported by the National Key Research and Development Program of China under Grant 2023YFB3408603.

References

1. Dinis, D., et al.: A supporting framework for maintenance capacity planning and scheduling: development and application in the aircraft MRO industry. Int. J. Prod. Econ. **218**, 1 (2019)
2. Pereira, B., et al.: Optimization of an autonomous robotic drilling system for the machining of aluminum aerospace alloys. Int. J. Adv. Manuf. Technol. **119**, 2429–2444 (2021)
3. Bu, Y., et al.: Corrigendum to "Stiffness analysis and optimization" in robotic drilling application. J. Precis. Eng. **49**, 388–400 (2017)
4. Zeng, F., et al.: Force/torque sensorless compliant control strategy for assembly tasks using a 6-DOF collaborative robot. IEEE Access **7**, 108795–108805 (2019)
5. Anggraeni, P., et al.: Design and development of multiple mobile manipulator robots using Gazebo-ROS. In: 2020 International Conference on Applied Science and Technology (iCAST), pp. 672–676 (2020)
6. Wu, C.-H., et al.: Target position estimation by genetic expression programming for mobile robots with vision sensors. IEEE Trans. Instrum. Meas. **62**, 3218–3230 (2013)
7. Zhao, X., et al.: Human–robot collaboration framework based on impedance control in robotic assembly. Engineering **30**, 83 (2023)
8. Roberge, E., et al.: StereoTac: a novel visuotactile sensor that combines tactile sensing with 3D vision. IEEE Robot. Automat. Lett. **8**, 6291–6298 (2023)
9. Ding, G., et al.: High precision camera calibration method based on full camera model. In: 2024 36th Chinese Control and Decision Conference (CCDC), pp. 4218–4223 (2024)
10. Yang, S., et al.: An improved hand-eye calibration method based on 3D position information. In: 2022 2nd International Conference on Algorithms, High Performance Computing and Artificial Intelligence (AHPCAI), pp. 535–541 (2022)
11. He, F., et al.: Design of remote sensing image automatic target recognition and emergency rescue assistant system based on deep learning. In: 2023 International Conference on Internet of Things, Robotics and Distributed Computing (ICIRDC), pp. 109–114 (2023)
12. Lu, C., et al.: Arc-support line segments revisited: an efficient high-quality ellipse detection. IEEE Trans. Image Process. **29**, 768–781 (2020)
13. Deng, C., et al.: Semi-global stereo matching algorithm based on multi-scale information fusion. Appl. Sci. **13**, 1027 (2023)
14. Guo, Y., et al.: Research on the improvement of semi-global matching algorithm for binocular vision based on lunar surface environment. Sensors (Basel, Switzerland) **23**, 6901 (2023)

Design and Simulation of a Bipedal Robot for Explosive Jumping Based on a Hybrid Linkage-Cam Mechanism

Qiang Fu, Ke Li, Zhanchuan Qi, and Yunjiang Lou[✉]

School of Intelligence Science and Engineering, Harbin Institute of Technology, Shenzhen, Shenzhen 518055, China
louyj@hit.edu.cn

Abstract. Humanoid robots, with their human-like structure and mobility, show great potential in rescue, exploration, industrial, and domestic applications. While significant progress has been made in basic locomotion, the achievement of highly explosive jumps remains challenging due to inefficient energy storage and delayed power release. This study proposes a bipedal jumping robot based on a hybrid linkage-cam mechanism to address these issues. A novel leg design combines an Electro-Hydrostatic Actuator (EHA), an ankle pitch motor, a spring-linkage energy storage unit, and a stroke amplification mechanism to boost instantaneous power output. A simplified seven-link leg model is developed, and both forward and inverse kinematic analyses are conducted to ensure accurate motion control. Additionally, a spring-loaded inverted pendulum (SLIP) model is constructed for jumping dynamics simulation, demonstrating the robot's strong jump performance and stability.

Keywords: humanoid robot · bipedal robot · explosive jumps · linkage-cam mechanism · SLIP

1 Introduction

With rapid advances in control, AI, sensing, and materials science, humanoid robots are evolving from theoretical research to real-world deployment. Their anthropomorphic structure and human-like mobility have made them a key focus in robotics, with applications in disaster response, space missions, industrial automation, and home assistance. Concrete application scenarios include, among others, disaster rescue operations where robots must traverse collapsed structures or wide gaps in post-earthquake environments; robotic competitions involving dynamic obstacle clearance; industrial inspections across complex terrains with vertical barriers; military reconnaissance missions requiring rapid elevation

---

Y. Lou—This work was supported by the Open Fund of Laboratory of Aerospace Servo Actuation and Transmission though Grant No. LASAT-2022-B02-01.

changes under battlefield conditions; and space missions involving humanoid robots performing tasks such as maintenance and inspection on the exterior of space stations under microgravity conditions. Compared to wheeled or tracked systems, humanoid robots utilize multi–DoF joints and flexible motions to better navigate complex environments and interact naturally in human-centered settings [1,2].

Despite significant breakthroughs in stable walking, stair climbing, and small-obstacle negotiation, achieving high-explosiveness jumping remains a formidable challenge [3–5]. Explosive leaps demand ultra–rapid energy release to overcome gravity, coupled with precise coordination of hip, knee, and ankle joints. Most existing prototypes demonstrate only preliminary jump capabilities and have yet to overcome the limitations in jump height and power output [6–8].

To address these challenges, this study introduces an innovative bipedal design based on a hybrid linkage–cam drive mechanism, targeting efficient energy storage and rapid release during jumping. We propose a novel single-leg architecture that integrates an electro-hydrostatic actuator (EHA) with an ankle-pitch servo motor, augmented by a spring–linkage energy storage unit and stroke-amplification mechanism, markedly enhancing instantaneous power output. A simplified seven-link kinematic model is then derived, with forward and inverse kinematic solutions provided to support precise jump posture control [9,10]. In addition, we establish a spring-loaded inverted pendulum (SLIP)–based model to simulate jump dynamics. The results validate the design's capability for high jumps and stable landings, paving the way for future hardware implementation.

The main contributions of this paper are threefold: (1) A hybrid linkage–cam actuation mechanism is proposed, combining an electro-hydrostatic actuator (EHA), ankle-pitch servo, and a spring–linkage energy storage with stroke amplification to enable high explosiveness jumping. (2) A simplified seven-link leg model is developed, with forward and inverse kinematics supporting accurate posture control. (3) A SLIP-based bipedal robot model is established, and dynamic simulations demonstrate improved jump height, power output, and landing stability under realistic conditions.

The rest of this paper is organized as follows. Section 2 presents the detailed design of the single-leg architecture. Section 3 describes the overall integration and hardware layout of the bipedal robot. Section 4 provides the kinematic analysis, including model derivation and solution of joint motions. Section 5 introduces the SLIP-based jumping model and reports the results of simulations. Finally, we draw the conclusions and point out the future work in the last section.

2 Leg Mechanism Design

2.1 Optimized Single-Leg Design for High-Explosiveness Jumping

To enhance the performance of bipedal robots during high-explosiveness jumping, this study proposes a single-leg design capable of efficient energy storage and controlled release, enabling rapid and powerful take-off actions.

As shown in Fig. 1, the design integrates an Electro-Hydrostatic Actuator (EHA) and an ankle pitch motor, working in coordination with an active energy storage mechanism, ankle drive linkage, and a stroke amplification system. The EHA drives the knee drive linkage between the thigh and shank, while the ankle pitch motor controls the pitch motion between the shank and footplate. To overcome the limited stroke of the EHA, a scissor-type stroke amplification mechanism is introduced, which doubles the actuator's output displacement and increases end-point velocity, meeting the demands of fast jumping.

Structurally, the robot's leg consists of a thigh, shank, and footplate, connected via hinged joints and inspired by biomimetic principles. To improve jumping performance, the overall system is lightweight, and the center of mass (CoM) is raised to the thigh region, optimizing launch posture and stability. Furthermore, to address the torque limitations of conventional motors, the proposed active energy storage mechanism uses a spring-link system and an output rod to accumulate and rapidly release energy. This approach compensates for insufficient instantaneous motor output, significantly enhancing jumping power and energy density.

By combining multiple actuation methods and structural innovations—including the ankle joint, knee drive linkage, and stroke amplification—the proposed single-leg design balances energy efficiency with explosive performance, offering a robust foundation for achieving high explosiveness jumps in complex environments.

2.2 Transmission Mechanism Design

Linkage Design. The linkage design, as illustrated on the left side of Fig. 1, positions the EHA fixedly within the robot's thigh segment. Its actuator rod is connected to a stroke amplification mechanism via a linkage component. When the EHA extends by a certain displacement, the amplification mechanism multiplies this stroke and transmits it to the knee drive linkage. The amplification ratio is determined by the configuration of the scissor-like arms. In this study, a specific arrangement enables a 1:2 stroke amplification—doubling the actuator's output displacement. This design enhances the speed and precision of knee joint rotation, providing the high explosiveness output needed for explosive jumping.

Cam Mechanism Design. As illustrated in Fig. 1 (right), the ankle pitch motor is mounted on the rear side of the thigh and transmits torque to the active energy storage mechanism, which includes a cam, compression tube, spring, and cylindrical shell. The shell is fixed to the thigh, and the cam is directly coupled to the motor shaft. A guide pin embedded in the compression tube fits into a groove on the cam, guiding the tube along a defined path. A spring between the tube and shell enables energy storage and rapid release.

The working principle of this cam mechanism is as follows: the ankle pitch motor rotates the cam, which drives the guide pin inside the compression tube to follow the cam groove, resulting in vertical movement of the compression tube.

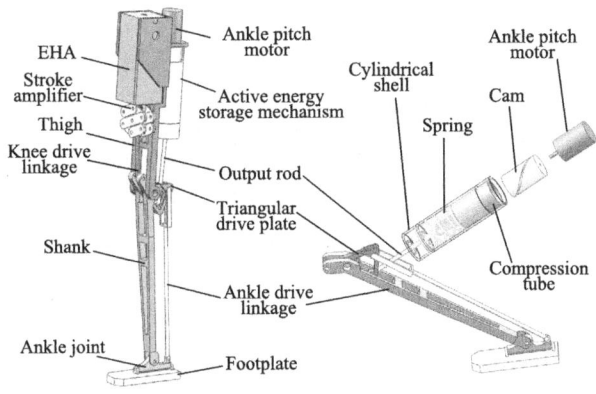

Fig. 1. Leg structure design.

One end of the compression tube is hinged to the output rod of the active energy storage mechanism, so its motion displaces the output rod, which in turn rotates the triangular transmission plate about the knee drive linkage. This triangular plate, via its hinge connection, actuates the ankle drive linkage, ultimately controlling the footplate to achieve pitch movement.

As the cam forces the tube downward, the spring compresses. Once fully compressed, further cam rotation shifts the guide pin into a straight groove, triggering rapid spring release. The tube rebounds, pushing the output rod and rotating the plate, which causes a swift upward footplate pitch and generates an explosive jump force.

This cam mechanism design enables efficient energy storage and instantaneous release, providing the high explosiveness output necessary for explosive jumping. With precise control from the ankle pitch motor, the mechanism ensures strong and rapid ankle rotation, supporting the robot in performing high-speed, high explosiveness jumping actions.

3 Bipedal Robot System Configuration

3.1 Overall Structure Design of the Bipedal Robot

In bipedal robot design, the thigh and shank must balance structural strength with minimal weight to optimize performance. This study used SolidWorks and ADAMS for iterative design and simulation, resulting in a final structure that is both lightweight and capable of withstanding jump landing impacts.

The complete structure of the bipedal robot is illustrated in Fig. 2. The robot consists of two symmetrically arranged single-leg assemblies connected by a central hip joint. This configuration enhances the robot's flexibility and adaptability in complex or harsh environments. To maximize motion capability, the hip joint is designed with three degrees of freedom (DoFs) for each leg: axial rotation

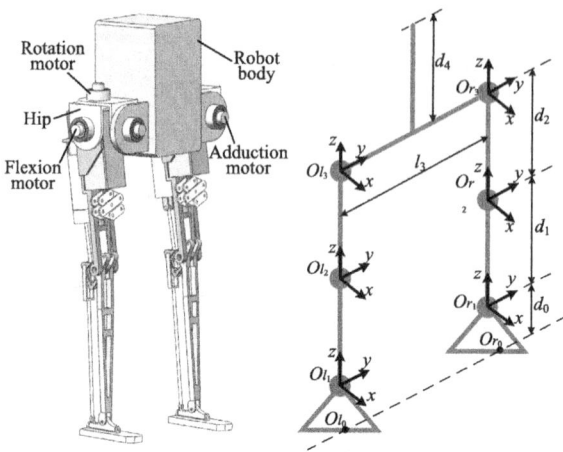

Fig. 2. Bipedal robot and link coordinate system.

around the z-axis, swing motion around the y-axis, and lateral sway around the x-axis. The knee joint provides a pitch DoF, while the ankle joint offers both pitch and roll DoFs. In total, the system possesses 12 DoFs, granting the robot high mobility and adaptability. The upper hip joint houses the robot's main body, integrating power, control systems, and sensors. These components enable precise motion and adaptability, supporting high explosiveness jumps and dynamic tasks.

3.2 Linkage Coordinate System of the Bipedal Robot

Simulating human lower-limb locomotion is a key goal in humanoid robotics. Unlike full humanoid robots, bipedal robots typically include only a torso and two legs. To simplify modeling, this study abstracts the robot as a seven-link mechanism comprising the torso, thighs, shanks, and feet. Kinematic analysis focuses on: (1) forward kinematics—computing the position and orientation of components based on joint motions; and (2) inverse kinematics—solving for joint angles given a desired pose. The analysis assumes: intersecting hip and ankle joint axes at their respective centers; the hip line remains parallel to the ground; the torso stays upright; and both feet stay level throughout the gait cycle. As shown in Fig. 2, the structure is modeled with coordinate points defined as follows: the centers of the left and right footplates are denoted as O_{l0} and O_{r0}, respectively; the centers of the ankle, knee, and hip joints of the left leg are labeled O_{l1}, O_{l2}, and O_{l3}; and those of the right leg are denoted O_{r1}, O_{r2}, and O_{r3}. The geometric parameters of the robot are defined as: d_0 for the height of the footplate, d_1 for the shank length, d_2 for the thigh length, d_3 for the distance between the two hip joints, and d_4 for the length of the torso. Local coordinate frames are established at each of these points. The frames at O_{l0} and O_{r0} remain parallel to the global inertial coordinate system O. When the robot is in a vertical posture, all local

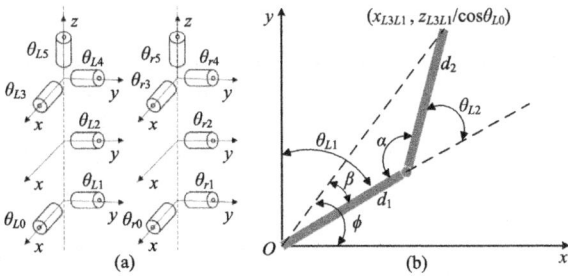

Fig. 3. DoF distribution and inverse kinematics of a planar two-link mechanism.

frames are aligned with the inertial frame, where the x-axis points outward perpendicular to the sagittal plane, the y-axis points horizontally to the right, and the z-axis points vertically upward.

4 Kinematic Analysis

The proposed single-leg structure features six DoFs: two at the ankle (pitch and roll), one at the knee (pitch), and three at the hip (roll, pitch, and yaw). To simplify kinematics and improve control accuracy, the hip's three rotational axes and the ankle's two axes are designed to intersect at a single point. This enhances coordination and reduces control complexity. The DoF distribution is shown in Fig. 3(a). Joint motions are described by the following variables: θ_{l0} and θ_{r0} (ankle roll), θ_{l1} and θ_{r1} (ankle pitch), θ_{l2} and θ_{r2} (knee pitch), and θ_{l3} to θ_{l5}, θ_{r3} to θ_{r5} (hip roll, pitch, and yaw). All rotations are defined as positive in the counterclockwise direction. To ensure stability and prevent mechanical overload, each joint's motion range is constrained based on structural limits. These ranges, balancing flexibility and strength, are summarized in Table 1.

Table 1. Joint Range of Motion for the Robot's Bipedal Legs

Joint rotation	Despription	Rotation range
θ_{l0}, θ_{r0}	Ankle roll DoF	$[-30°, 30°]$
θ_{l1}, θ_{r1}	Ankle pitch DoF	$[-60°, 60°]$
θ_{l2}, θ_{r2}	Ankle yaw DoF	$[0°, 90°]$
θ_{l3}, θ_{r3}	Knee roll DoF	$[-30°, 30°]$
θ_{l4}, θ_{r4}	Knee pitch DoF	$[-70°, 20°]$
θ_{l5}, θ_{r5}	Knee yaw DoF	$[-45°, 45°]$

4.1 Forward Kinematic

Single-Leg Forward Kinematics Model. Let the joint angles of the left leg be $\theta_{l0}, \theta_{l1}, \theta_{l2}, \theta_{l3}, \theta_{l4}, \theta_{l5}$, and those of the right leg be $\theta_{r0}, \theta_{r1}, \theta_{r2}, \theta_{r3}, \theta_{r4}, \theta_{r5}$. Let $cl \cdot i$ and $sl \cdot i$ denote $\cos(\theta l_i)$ and $\sin(\theta l_i)$, respectively, where the subscript l indicates the left leg, r indicates the right leg, and i refers to the joint index. Let d_0 represent the distance between joints. Then, the forward kinematic relationship between local coordinate frames of a single leg is as follows: The frame O_{L1} is obtained from frame O_{L0} by a rotation of θ_{l0} about the x-axis, followed by a rotation of θ_{l1} about the y-axis. Therefore, the homogeneous transformation matrix from frame O_{L0} to O_{L1} is given by:

$$H_{O_{L_0}O_{L_1}} = \begin{bmatrix} c_{11} & 0 & s_{11} & 0 \\ s_{10}s_{11} & c_{10} & -s_{10}c_{11} & 0 \\ -c_{10}s_{11} & s_{10} & c_{10}c_{11} & d_0 \\ 0 & 0 & 0 & 1 \end{bmatrix}_L \tag{1}$$

The frame O_{L2} is obtained from frame O_{L1} by a rotation of θ_{l2} about the y-axis. The corresponding homogeneous transformation matrix is given by:

$$H_{O_{L1}O_{L2}} = \begin{bmatrix} c_2 & 0 & s_2 & 0 \\ 0 & 1 & 0 & 0 \\ -s_2 & 0 & c_2 & d_1 \\ 0 & 0 & 0 & 1 \end{bmatrix}_L \tag{2}$$

$$H_{O_{L_0}O_{L_2}} = \begin{bmatrix} c_{1+2} & 0 & s_{1+2} & s_1 d_1 \\ s_0 s_{1+2} & c_0 & -s_0 c_{1+2} & -s_0 c_1 d_1 \\ -c_0 s_{1+2} & s_0 & c_0 c_{1+2} & d_0 + c_0 c_1 d_1 \\ 0 & 0 & 0 & 1 \end{bmatrix}_L \tag{3}$$

Finally, the homogeneous transformation matrix from the initial position O_{L0} to the target position O_{L5} of the robot's single leg can be obtained by sequentially multiplying the transformation matrices between each joint:

$$H_{O_{L_0}O_{L_5}} = H_{O_{L_0}O_{L_1}} \cdot H_{O_{L_1}O_{L_2}} \cdots H_{O_{L_4}O_{L_5}} \tag{4}$$

Kinematic Relationship Between Two Legs. As shown in Fig. 3(a), the coordinates of point O_{r3} with respect to the O_{l3} frame are given by $[0 \; d_3 \; 0]$, where d_3 is the distance between the left and right legs. Thus, the coordinates of point O_{r3} with respect to the O_{l0} frame can be calculated as follows:

$$\begin{bmatrix} r_{O_{10}O_{r3}} \\ 1 \end{bmatrix} = H \begin{bmatrix} 0 \\ d_3 \\ 0 \\ 1 \end{bmatrix} = \begin{bmatrix} -s_5 d_3 + s_{1+2} d_2 + s_1 d_1 \\ c_5 d_3 - s_0(c_{1+2} d_2 + c_1 d_1) \\ d_0 + c_0(c_1 d_1 + c_{1+2} d_2) \\ 1 \end{bmatrix}_l \tag{5}$$

Using the above method, we can establish the coordinate relationship between the right and left leg frames, enabling analysis of the motion relationship between the robot's two legs. Similarly, the coordinates of point O_{l3} with respect to the O_{r3} frame are $\begin{bmatrix} 0 & -d_3 & 0 \end{bmatrix}$, and the coordinates of point O_{l3} with respect to the O_{r0} frame can be calculated as follows:

$$\begin{bmatrix} r_{O_{r0}O_{13}} \\ 1 \end{bmatrix} = H \begin{bmatrix} 0 \\ -d_3 \\ 0 \\ 1 \end{bmatrix} = \begin{bmatrix} s_5 d_3 + s_{1+2} d_2 + s_1 d_1 \\ -c_5 d_3 - s_0(c_{1+2} d_2 + c_1 d_1) \\ d_0 + c_0(c_1 d_1 + c_{1+2} d_2) \\ 1 \end{bmatrix}_r \quad (6)$$

Forward kinematics allows us to determine the precise position of point O_{l3} in the right leg frame O_{r3}. This approach can also be used to compute relative positions of other joints or points, aiding spatial modeling and motion control.

4.2 Inverse Kinematic

When the robot is walking, the inverse kinematics problem can be simplified as follows: given the positions of the two ankle joints $\mathbf{r_l 1}$ and $\mathbf{r_r 1}$, the positions of the hip joints $\mathbf{r_l 3}$ and $\mathbf{r_r 3}$, as well as the yaw angle of the swing foot, the goal is to solve for the joint angles θ_{Li} (where $L = l, r$ denotes the left or right leg, and $i = 0, 1, 2, 3, 4, 5$). According to the forward kinematics relationships, we have:

$$r_{L3} - r_{L1} = \begin{bmatrix} x_{L3L1} \\ y_{L3L1} \\ z_{L3L1} \end{bmatrix} = \begin{bmatrix} s_{1+2} d_2 + s_1 d_1 \\ -s_0(c_{1+2} d_2 + c_1 d_1) \\ c_0(c_{1+2} d_2 + c_1 d_1) \end{bmatrix}_L \quad (7)$$

$$\frac{y_{\mathcal{L}_3 \mathcal{L}_1}}{z_{\mathcal{L}_3 \mathcal{L}_1}} = -\frac{s_0(c_{1+2} d_2 + c_1 d_1)}{c_0(c_{1+2} d_2 + c_1 d_1)} \bigg|_{\mathcal{L}} = -\tan \theta_{\mathcal{L}_0} \quad (8)$$

$$\theta_{\mathcal{L}_0} = \arctan - \frac{y_{\mathcal{L}_3 \mathcal{L}_1}}{z_{\mathcal{L}_3 \mathcal{L}_1}}, \theta_{\mathcal{L}_3} = -\theta_{\mathcal{L}_0} \quad (9)$$

then:
$$d_1 \sin \theta_{\mathcal{L}_1} + d_2 \sin(\theta_{\mathcal{L}_1} + \theta_{\mathcal{L}_2}) = x_{\mathcal{L}_3 \mathcal{L}_1} \quad (10)$$

$$d_1 \cos \theta_{\mathcal{L}_1} + d_2 \cos(\theta_{\mathcal{L}_1} + \theta_{\mathcal{L}_2}) = z_{\mathcal{L}_3 \mathcal{L}_1} / \cos \theta_{\mathcal{L}_0} \quad (11)$$

The inverse kinematics problem can be further simplified into a classic planar two-link problem, as shown in Fig. 3(b). By reducing the complex 3D motion into a 2D plane, joint angles can be more intuitively calculated, especially for motion transfer and inverse solving between two key points. In this simplified model, the leg is represented as two rigid links—the thigh (from hip to knee) and the shank (from knee to ankle). Ignoring ground contact, the leg motion becomes a 2D inverse kinematics problem. Given a target position (x, y) in the plane, the joint angles can be computed accordingly:

$$\begin{cases} \alpha = \arccos\left(\dfrac{d_1^2 + d_2^2 - r^2}{2d_1 d_2}\right) \\ r^2 = x_{L_3 L_1}^2 + (z_{L_3 L_1}/\cos\theta_{L_0})^2 \\ \theta_{\mathcal{L}_2} = \pi - \alpha \\ \beta = \arccos\left(\dfrac{r^2 + a_1^2 - a_2^2}{2d_1 r}\right) \\ \phi = \arctan\left(\dfrac{z_{L_3 L_1}/\cos\theta_{L_0}}{x_{L_3 L_1}}\right) \\ \theta_{\mathcal{L}_1} = \dfrac{\pi}{2} - \phi + \beta \\ \theta_{\mathcal{L}_4} = -(\theta_{\mathcal{L}_1} + \theta_{\mathcal{L}_2}) \end{cases} \qquad (12)$$

The hip yaw angle can be determined by calculating the relative position between the left and right hip joints. This angle represents the rotational relationship between the two legs and is typically used to describe the robot's orientation in the horizontal plane. Let point O_{r3} denote the reference point of the right hip joint, and O_{l3} denote the reference point of the left hip joint. Suppose the coordinates of O_{r3} relative to the left leg frame O_{l3} are given by $[x_{r3}\ y_{r3}\ z_{r3}]$, and the coordinates of O_{l3} relative to the right leg frame O_{r3} are given by $[x_{l3}\ y_{l3}\ z_{l3}]$. Then, the hip yaw angle θ_{l5} and θ_{r5} can be computed based on these relative positions.

$$\begin{cases} \mathbf{r_{r_3}} - \mathbf{r_{l_3}} = \begin{bmatrix} x_{r_3 l_3} \\ y_{r_3 l_3} \\ z_{r_3 l_3} \end{bmatrix} = \begin{bmatrix} -s_5 d_3 \\ c_5 d_3 \\ 0 \end{bmatrix}_l \\ \mathbf{r_{l_3}} - \mathbf{r_{r_3}} = \begin{bmatrix} x_{l_3 r_3} \\ y_{l_3 r_3} \\ z_{l_3 r_3} \end{bmatrix} = \begin{bmatrix} s_5 d_3 \\ -c_5 d_3 \\ 0 \end{bmatrix}_r \end{cases} \qquad (13)$$

$$\begin{cases} \dfrac{x_{r3l3}}{y_{r3l3}} = -\dfrac{\sin\theta_{l5} d_3}{\cos\theta_{l5} d_3} = -\tan\theta_{l5} \\ \dfrac{x_{l3r3}}{y_{l3r3}} = -\dfrac{\sin\theta_{r5} d_3}{\cos\theta_{r5} d_3} = -\tan\theta_{r5} \end{cases} \qquad (14)$$

$$\begin{cases} \theta_{l5} = \arctan\dfrac{x_{r3l3}}{y_{r3l3}} \\ \theta_{r5} = \arctan\dfrac{x_{l3r3}}{y_{l3r3}} \end{cases} \qquad (15)$$

Given the positions of the ankle and hip joints in the inertial frame, joint angles can be computed under level-walking constraints. The hip yaw angle, which describes the rotation between the legs, is key to maintaining stability, adjusting stride length, and adapting gait. Precise yaw control enhances performance on uneven terrain and during gait transitions.

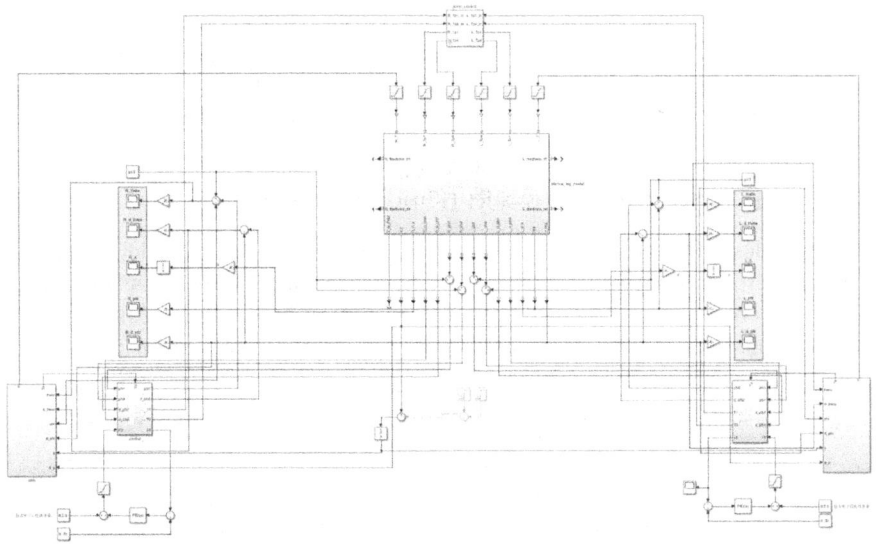

Fig. 4. Simulation Model of Bipedal Robot Jumping in Simulink.

5 Jumping Model and Simulation

This section introduces a SLIP-based jumping control framework and simulation for a bipedal robot (as shown in Fig. 4), detailing key modules and results.

5.1 Multi-DoF SLIP Model

To effectively capture the dynamic behavior of bipedal jumping, this study adopts a multi-DoF Spring-Loaded Inverted Pendulum (SLIP) model as the core abstraction for jump dynamics. Traditional SLIP models primarily focus on single-point mass dynamics with a massless spring leg, so this paper extends the framework to account for the distributed mass and jointed structure of a bipedal robot. To simplify the model, each leg is reduced to 3 DoF—hip, knee, and ankle—forming a 6-DoF system. The SLIP model treats each leg as a spring-damper, capturing mass distribution, leg length changes, and joint actuation during takeoff and landing.

In this model, the vertical and horizontal motions of the robot's CoM are governed by the elastic properties of the virtual spring elements associated with each leg. The ground contact phases are divided into stance and flight, with continuous transitions enabled by proper force control and leg retraction strategies. The leg force F is computed as a nonlinear spring-damper function:

$$F = k(l_0 - l) + d\dot{l} \tag{16}$$

where k is the stiffness coefficient, d is the damping coefficient, l_0 is the nominal leg length, l is the current leg length, and $\dot{l}$ is the leg compression rate.

These forces are projected into Cartesian coordinates to compute the resultant ground reaction forces acting on the robot's body. The enhanced SLIP framework enables realistic trajectory generation for stable, high-performance jumps and supports trajectory planning and inverse kinematics in later sections.

5.2 Jump Trajectory Generation and Inverse Kinematics

Given the desired jump height, distance, and angle, the SLIP model generates a CoM trajectory planned in both vertical and horizontal directions. Polynomial and Bézier curves are used to smooth the motion while satisfying kinematic and actuator constraints. The desired CoM trajectory $\mathbf{x}_{\text{CoM}}(t)$ is given by:

$$\mathbf{x}_{\text{CoM}}(t) = \begin{bmatrix} x(t) \\ y(t) \\ z(t) \end{bmatrix} \quad (17)$$

where $x(t)$ and $z(t)$ describe horizontal and vertical motion, respectively, and $y(t)$ ensures lateral balance. Leg trajectories follow by mapping CoM motion to foot placements via inverse kinematics.

Given each foot's desired position and orientation relative to its hip joint, inverse kinematics computes the required joint angles θ_{L_i} and θ_{R_i} for $i = 0, 1, 2$ (where $i = 0$ is the ankle, $i = 1$ is the knee, and $i = 2$ is the hip). Using the planar two-link chain geometry (thigh and shank), hip and knee angles are found by solving a standard inverse kinematics problem, then the ankle angle is set to maintain foot orientation and ground contact stability.

5.3 Joint Control and Simulation

The computed joint angles are tracked by a PD controller at each joint. The control law for joint i is:

$$\tau_i = K_p\big(\theta_i^{\text{des}} - \theta_i\big) + K_d\big(\dot{\theta}_i^{\text{des}} - \dot{\theta}_i\big) \quad (18)$$

where τ_i is the control torque, K_p and K_d are proportional and derivative gains, and θ_i^{des}, $\dot{\theta}_i^{\text{des}}$ are the desired angle and angular velocity (with θ_i, $\dot{\theta}_i$ being their measured counterparts). The bipedal robot's dynamics are simulated using a physics engine with gravity, contacts, joint constraints, and disturbances. The SLIP-based control frameworkis integrated, using state feedback for real-time joint control. Simulations show the control framework enables stable, repeatable jumps that closely follow the SLIP trajectory, with accurate foot placement and posture control. As shown in Fig. 5 (a), the robot successfully performs jumps according to the SLIP-based trajectory. Additionally, Fig. 5 (b) shows how jump length varies with jump height under different control parameters. These results validate the effectiveness of using a multi-DoF SLIP model to design dynamic jumping strategies.

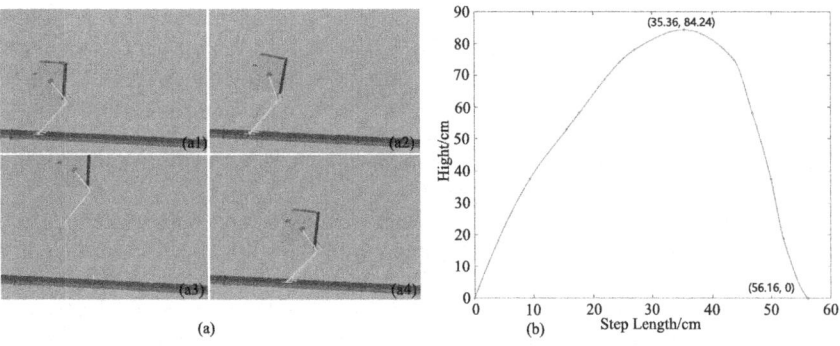

Fig. 5. Simulating bipedal robot jumping and analyzing the relationship between jump distance and vertical leap height.

6 Conclusion

This study addresses the key challenges in achieving high-explosiveness jumping for bipedal robots by proposing an innovative leg design based on a linkage-cam mechanism. A comprehensive kinematic analysis establishes the theoretical basis for motion control, demonstrating that the proposed mechanism efficiently stores and releases energy to support both explosive jumping and stable locomotion. A simulation framework based on a multi-DoF SLIP model captures the robot's dynamic behavior during jumping, with joint trajectories generated through SLIP planning and inverse kinematics. Simulation results confirm the feasibility of coordinated bipedal jumping. Future work will optimize energy transfer and control for uneven terrain and closed-loop jumping.

References

1. He, Z., Wu, J., Zhang, J., et al.: CDM-MPC: an integrated dynamic planning and control framework for bipedal robots jumping. IEEE Rob. Autom. Lett. (2024)
2. Huang, Q., Dong, C., Yu, Z., et al.: Resistant compliance control for biped robot inspired by humanlike behavior. IEEE/ASME Trans. Mechatron. **27**(5), 3463–3473 (2022)
3. Ahn, D.H., Cho, B.K.: Optimal standing jump trajectory generation for biped robots. Int. J. Precis. Eng. Manuf. **21**(8), 1459–1467 (2020)
4. Liu, X., Duan, Y., Hitzmann, A., et al.: Using the foot windlass mechanism for jumping higher: a study on bipedal robot jumping. Robot. Auton. Syst. **110**, 85–91 (2018)
5. Nishikawa, S., Tanaka, K., Shida, K., et al.: A musculoskeletal bipedal robot designed with angle-dependent moment arm for dynamic motion from multiple states. Adv. Robot. **28**(7), 487–496 (2014)
6. Bolignari, M., Mo, A., Fontana, M., et al.: Diaphragm ankle actuation for efficient series elastic legged robot hopping. In: 2022 IEEE/RSJ International Conference on Intelligent Robots and Systems (IROS), pp. 4279–4286. IEEE (2022)

7. Ding, Y., Park, H.W.: Design and experimental implementation of a quasi-direct-drive leg for optimized jumping. In: 2017 IEEE/RSJ International Conference on Intelligent Robots and Systems (IROS), pp. 300–305. IEEE (2017)
8. Sovukluk, S., Englsberger, J., Ott, C.: Whole body control formulation for humanoid robots with closed/parallel kinematic chains: Kangaroo case study. In: 2023 IEEE/RSJ International Conference on Intelligent Robots and Systems (IROS), pp. 10390–10396. IEEE (2023)
9. Romualdi, G., Dafarra, S., L'Erario, G., et al.: Online non-linear centroidal MPC for humanoid robot locomotion with step adjustment. In: 2022 International Conference on Robotics and Automation (ICRA), pp. 10412–10419. IEEE (2022)
10. Sun, H.L., Zhao, D.J., Zhao, J.S.: Screw dynamics of the upper limb of a humanoid robot. In: International Conference on Intelligent Robotics and Applications, pp. 568-577. Springer, Singapore (2023)

Topological Analysis and Perception of Physical Vibration in Distributed Optical Fiber Vibration Sensing

Zibin Liang, Song Wang[✉], and Duanling Li

School of Intelligent Engineering and Automation, Beijing University of Posts and Telecommunications, Beijing 100876, China
wongsang@bupt.edu.cn

Abstract. Distributed optical fiber vibration sensing (DOFS) monitors environmental vibrations by demodulating phase disturbances. Accurate detection of high-order vibration frequencies is essential for inferring complex physical events. To enhance the characterization of high-frequency modes in current systems, a feature extraction framework based on differential-manifold topology is proposed. First, the input signal is mapped into a high-dimensional phase-space trajectory via differential time-delay embedding, which nonlinearly reconstructs the dynamics and reveals latent high-order characteristics. Next, a simplicial structure is constructed using the Vietoris–Rips complex, and persistent homology is applied to quantify the robustness of topological features, yielding a topology-invariant persistence diagram. Finally, the Persistent Spectral Enhancement algorithm employs a convolutional network to optimize the discriminative representation of these topological features.

Keywords: DOFS · High-Order Vibration · Phase-Space Reconstruction · Persistent Homology

1 Introduction

Distributed optical fiber vibration sensing technology, because of its high sensitivity, strong immunity to electromagnetic interference, and low cost, has demonstrated significant application value in fields such as perimeter security [1], energy pipeline safety warning [2], and structural health monitoring [3]. However, in practical deployment, it faces two principal challenges: First, the high-order modes of vibration signals are difficult to accurately characterize, making it hard to capture their dynamic evolution; second, vibration signals exhibit high complexity in the time–frequency domain and strong interclass similarity, which increases the risk of misclassification by traditional pattern recognition methods.

For the identification of vibration events, Z Lyu et al. designed a data-driven, two-stage early-warning architecture that achieves precise threat detection via a cascade of primary signal filtering and secondary fine-grained classification [4]; the Sun Mingyang team proposed the Squeeze-and-Excitation WaveNet (SE-WaveNet) model, which combines the large receptivefield of a one-dimensional dilated convolutional network with a channel-wise attention mechanism to balance computational efficiency and feature-expression capacity in time-series processing [5]; Jin, Xibo et al. innovatively fused short-time Fourier transform (STFT) time–frequency analysis with a ResNet-152 deep network, obtaining high dimensional vibration-pattern representations through joint spatiotemporal feature learning; addressing signal overlap [6]; Yan et al. developed a Conv-TasNet–based vibration-signal separation framework, experimentally demonstrating that the classification-accuracy gap between separated signals and single-event measurements is only 2.4%, thus validating the effectiveness of overlapping-event decoupling; furthermore [7]. By integrating multi-scale feature fusion with deep reinforcement learning trategies, a seven-class vibration-event recognition task achieved a 96.16% cross-validation accuracy, significantly outperforming traditional unimodal methods [8]; at the theoretical level of signal processing, an improved delay-line localization algorithm—built upon a tunable fiber-delay line and a Sagnac/Mach–Zehnder hybrid structure—has extended the boundaries of zero-frequency vibration-localization theory [9]. The Huang team introduced Wigner bispectrum time–frequency energy analysis and an axial-integral bispectrum algorithm, combined with subband-partitioning techniques to balance feature-information integrity and computational complexity. Notably [10], the Zhang group incorporated unsupervised learning into φ-OTDR systems, achieving 99.4% equivalent classification accuracy for events such as wind-induced vibrations,rainfall, impacts, and noise-induced false alarms via k-means clustering [11].

These methods have advanced the intelligence of DOFS systems across multiple dimensions; however, existing research still struggles to characterize physical vibration fields in complex environments. To address the challenge of high-order mode representation, this paper proposes a robust feature- extraction mechanism based on differential-manifold topology, employing phase-space reconstruction for high-order characterization of input signals.

The remainder of this paper is organized as follows: Sect. 2 describes the problem formulation; Sect. 3 details the proposed method; Sect. 4 presents experimental results; and Sect. 5 concludes the work.

2 Problem Description

To address the inherent limitations of distributed optical fiber sensors in detecting higher-order vibration modes, this paper proposes a vibration signal feature enhancement method based on differential topological analysis. By establishing a mapping between sensing signals and topological invariants, the proposed method transforms the problem of higher-order vibration response into one of feature extraction on differential manifolds.

First, leveraging the embedding theorem of Takens, a differential time-delay embedding approach is employed to reconstruct the phase-space trajectories of the signal's dynamical system. Subsequently, the high-dimensional phase-space data are projected into a lower-dimensional space using Uniform Manifold Approximation and Projection (UMAP), which effectively preserves the local topological structure of the original manifold.

Next, a simplicial complex is constructed via the Vietoris–Rips complex, and persistent homology theory is applied to quantify the emergence and extinction of key topological features within the vibration signals. Finally, these topological features are explicitly represented through persistence diagram spectral augmentation.

This framework overcomes the limitations of conventional time–frequency analysis in capturing higher-order information in vibration signals, offering a novel analytical pathway for distributed optical fiber vibration sensing under complex operating conditions.

3 Proposed Method

3.1 Phase Space Reconstruction

Spatial events in distributed optical fiber sensing are primarily perceived through vibration energy. However, the sensed signals are typically captured as time series. Traditional delay embedding methods rely solely on signal amplitude and reconstruct the phase space in the time domain. This approach struggles to capture the higher-order vibration characteristics inherently embedded in the signal, as these are often not explicitly represented in the original time series.

To address this limitation, the differential embedding method introduces delay coordinates and higher-order derivatives as new state variables. This enables the original system to be embedded into a higher-dimensional space, thereby enhancing the dynamical perception of higher-order vibrational modes.

Leveraging Takens' embedding theorem, a differential–time delay embedding is performed on the input signal to reconstruct the corresponding phase-space trajectory. This enriched embedding strategy enhances the system's sensitivity to the dynamic features of complex vibration signals and lays the foundation for subsequent topological feature analysis.

$$\mathbf{Y}_m = \begin{bmatrix} y(t) \\ y(t+\tau) \\ y(t+2\tau) \\ \vdots \\ y(t+m\tau) \end{bmatrix} = \begin{bmatrix} x(t) & \dfrac{dx(t)}{dt} & \dfrac{d^2x(t)}{dt^2} & \cdots & \dfrac{d^n x(t)}{dt^n} \\ x(t+\tau) & \dfrac{dx(t+\tau)}{dt} & \dfrac{d^2x(t+\tau)}{dt^2} & \cdots & \dfrac{d^n x(t+\tau)}{dt^n} \\ x(t+2\tau) & \dfrac{dx(t+2\tau)}{dt} & \dfrac{d^2x(t+2\tau)}{dt^2} & \cdots & \dfrac{d^n x(t+2\tau)}{dt^n} \\ \vdots & \vdots & \vdots & \ddots & \vdots \\ x(t+m\tau) & \dfrac{dx(t+m\tau)}{dt} & \dfrac{d^2x(t+m\tau)}{dt^2} & \cdots & \dfrac{d^n x(t+m\tau)}{dt^n} \end{bmatrix} \tag{1}$$

Here, τ denotes the time delay coefficient, m is the time delay scale, and n represents the embedding order.

3.2 Dimensionality Reduction

Due to the computational burden imposed by high-dimensional data, dimensionality reduction must be applied to the obtained topological structures to meet real-time processing requirements. In this study, the Uniform Manifold Approximation and Projection algorithm is adopted for this purpose. UMAP assumes that samples are uniformly distributed on a manifold and reconstructs the manifold from finite data, projecting it into a lower-dimensional space $\mathbf{Y}_n$, where $n < m$.

Compared with other classical dimensionality reduction methods, UMAP is based on more general assumptions regarding the underlying Riemannian manifold structure of the data, making it more suitable for representing complex shapes generated by phase space reconstruction. Moreover, UMAP demonstrates superior performance in preserving global topological structures, thereby minimizing information loss during topological feature extraction.

3.3 Simple Filtering

The Vietoris–Rips complex (VR) is a method for constructing a topological space from data. Given a set of data points Y and a parameter $\varepsilon > 0$, the VR complex is defined as the collection of all subsets whose diameter is less than or equal to 2ε. That is, each data point is treated as the center of a ball with radius ε; if two such balls intersect, their centers are connected to form an edge [12]. If three balls intersect pairwise, their centers form a triangle (a 2-simplex); this process can be extended to generate higher-dimensional simplices (Fig. 1).

$$\mathrm{VR}\,(Y, \varepsilon_i) = \{\sigma \subseteq Y \mid \mathrm{diam}(\sigma) \leq 2\varepsilon_i\} \tag{2}$$

As the parameter ε_i increases monotonically, a nested sequence of simplicial complexes is obtained:

$$\mathrm{VR}\,(Y, \varepsilon_0) \subseteq \mathrm{VR}\,(Y, \varepsilon_1) \subseteq \cdots \subseteq \mathrm{VR}\,(Y, \varepsilon_m) \tag{3}$$

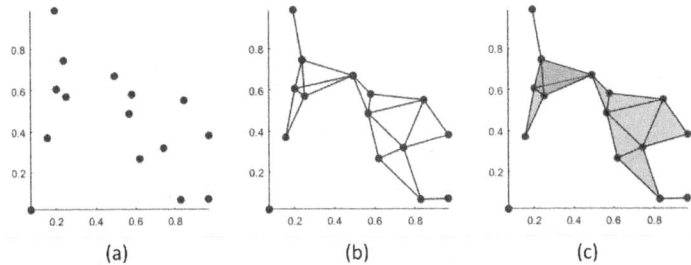

Fig. 1. The Vietoris–Rips complex of a set of randomly distributed points (a) 15 randomly distributed discrete points are shown as solid blue dots. (b) Blue edges connect pairs of points whose distance is less than or equal to ε, forming 1-simplices (edges) of the Vietoris–Rips complex. These depict local connectivity among points and result in several small connected components. (c) Triangular regions enclosed by three mutually connected points with distances $\leq \varepsilon$ are filled in to construct higher-dimensional simplices. These reflect locally dense regions in the data. (Color figure online)

When ε_j is very small, only pairs of points that are extremely close to each other will be connected by edges. Higher-dimensional simplices such as triangles and tetrahedra are either absent or very sparse, and the complex consists mainly of isolated vertices and a few edges.

As ε_i increases, more spheres begin to overlap, and corresponding edges, triangles, and higher-dimensional simplices are added to the complex. Eventually, when ε_i becomes sufficiently large, the complex tends toward a "fully connected" cluster of high-dimensional simplices.

3.4 Persistent Homology

Persistent Homology (PH), as a mathematical representation tool for the topological structure of data spaces, provides a quantitative framework for analyzing complex datasets through multiscale topological feature extraction. Built upon a sequence of parameterized nested topological spaces, this method employs homology theory from algebraic topology to systematically quantify topological features within the dataset and evaluates their geometric stability based on the principle of persistence (Fig. 2).

First, an ε-neighborhood complex sequence covering the data points is constructed. Then, the evolution of Betti numbers of homology groups at each scale is computed. Finally, the persistence diagram is used to characterize the birth b_i and death d_i of topological features in the parameter space $\varepsilon \in \mathbb{R}$.

$$D = \{(b_i, d_i)\}_{i=1}^{N} \quad (4)$$

In the framework of homology theory, given a topological space Y, its algebraic topological structure can be fully characterized by the chain complex and its homology groups $\{H_k(Y), k \geq 0\}$.

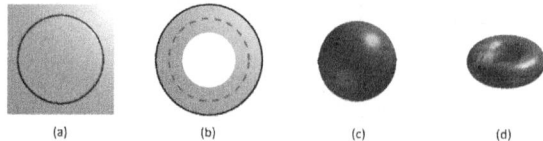

Fig. 2. Topological homology is the description of spatial holes and periodicity. (a) Single connectivity, with one connected component and one one-dimensional hole; (b) H_1 homology group, homeomorphism with the circle; (c) In a simply connected space, and all closed curves can be contracted to a point; (d) It has one one-dimensional hole and one two-dimensional hole.

The rank of $H_0(Y)$ corresponds to the number of connected components in the space Y. The generators of $H_1(Y)$ reflect one-dimensional loop structures, representing the stability of periodic oscillations. $H_2(Y)$ characterizes two-dimensional enclosed cavities defined by closed surfaces, indicating topological constraints on energy transfer paths in complex vibrational events. More generally, the k-th homology group $H_k(Y)$ describes the equivalence classes of k-cycles in Y; each generator corresponds to a k-dimensional cycle that cannot be contracted to a $(k+1)$-chain. This algebraic representation strictly corresponds to the hole hierarchy of the space. Persistent homology is applied to the filtration $\mathrm{VR}(Y, \varepsilon_i)$ of Vietoris–Rips complexes generated from low-dimensional data, where the filtration parameter is the radius ε. Rather than selecting a fixed radius ε and analyzing the homology of $\mathrm{VR}(Y, \varepsilon_i)$ at that single value, the entire range $\varepsilon \in [0, \infty)$ is considered, and the persistent homology of the filtration $\{\mathrm{VR}(Y, \varepsilon_i)\}_{\varepsilon=0}^{\infty}$ is analyzed (Fig. 3).

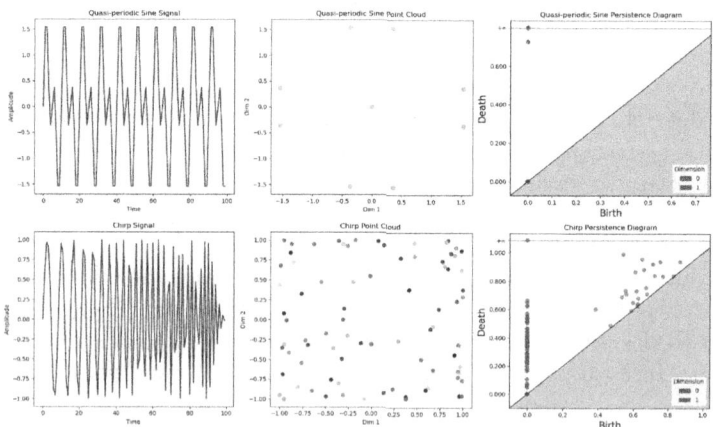

Fig. 3. Persistent homology process of Chirp signal and Quasi-periodic Sine signal.

3.5 Persistent Homology Feature Enhancement

First, a Gaussian kernel is used to perform kernel density estimation on the persistence diagram points (b_i, d_i), resulting in a two-dimensional function, which is then discretized into an image. The kernel density function is defined as:

$$\mathbf{H}(x,y) = \sum_i \exp\left(-\frac{(x-b_i)^2 + (y-d_i)^2}{2\sigma^2}\right) \tag{5}$$

For each $\mathbf{H}(x, y)$, its feature-enhanced matrix can be obtained by coupling it with a convolution kernel W. Specifically, the coupling is implemented using the convolution operation [13], which is expressed as:

$$\mathbf{G}(H, W) = \frac{\text{ReLU}(H * W)}{\max(\text{ReLU}(H * W))} \tag{6}$$

Here, the symbol "*" denotes the convolution operation; $\mathbf{G}$ represents the resulting feature enhancement matrix, with its element values constrained to the range $[0, 1]$. This normalization enhances the discriminative characteristics of sensor signal features under different types of events.

The complete procedure outlined in the above steps is as follows:

$$\begin{aligned}
x(t) &\xrightarrow{(1)} \mathbf{Y}_m \xrightarrow{(2)} \mathbf{Y}_n \\
&\xrightarrow{(3)} \{\text{VR}(Y, \varepsilon_i)\} \xrightarrow{(4)} \text{dgm}_k(\{\text{VR}(Y, \varepsilon_i)\}) \\
&\xrightarrow{(5)} \mathbf{H}(x,y) \xrightarrow{(6)} \mathbf{G}(H, W)
\end{aligned} \tag{7}$$

The procedure consists of the following steps: (1) phase space reconstruction; (2) dimensionality reduction using UMAP; (3) Vietoris–Rips (VR) complex filtration; (4) persistent homology computation; (5) persistence image generation; and (6) persistence image feature enhancement.

4 Experiment

4.1 Experimental Platform and Dataset Description

The experimental platform is equipped with an RTX 4060 GPU and an Intel Core i9-13900HX processor. MATLAB R2023b is used as the software environment.

The dataset utilized in this study is the DAS1K dataset [12], which contains distributed acoustic sensing (DAS) signals corresponding to six types of events: drilling (DL), jackhammer (JH), footsteps (FS), hand hammering (HH), shoveling, and rainfall (RA) (Fig. 4).

The signal acquisition system employs a narrow linewidth laser (NLL) with a linewidth of 5 kHz as the optical source. An erbium-doped fiber amplifier (EDFA) is used to boost the optical pulse power. The amplified spontaneous emission

(ASE) noise is suppressed using an optical bandpass filter with a passband of 0.8 nm. Subsequently, the optical pulses are launched into the fiber under test (FUT). The backscattered signals are collected by a 14-bit data acquisition card (DAC) operating at a sampling rate of 250 MS/s.

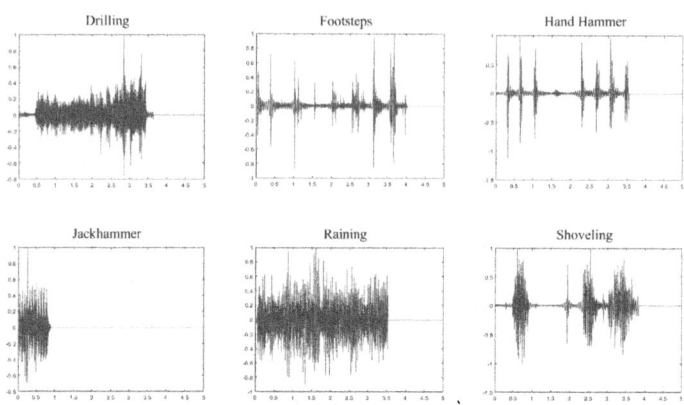

Fig. 4. Sensing signals of six types of events.

4.2 Classification Experiment

To validate the effectiveness of the proposed vibration signal feature enhancement method based on differential topological analysis in vibration event classification, this study designs a comparative evaluation scheme involving five representative algorithm categories:

a. **Unsupervised Clustering Algorithm:** K-means clustering.
b. **Time-Frequency Analysis with Machine Learning:** A combined method utilizing Short-Time Fourier Transform (STFT) and Support Vector Machine (SVM) [14].
c. **Probabilistic Graphical Models:** A joint modeling approach based on Gaussian Mixture Model (GMM) and Hidden Markov Model (HMM) [2].
d. **Deep Learning Model:** A time-series classification network based on ConvNeXt-TF, with Gramian Angular Summation Field (GASF) as the feature mapping method [1].
e. **Traditional Manifold Learning:** Phase space reconstruction using classical Time-Delay Embedding (TDE) techniques.

Table 1 presents the event classification results under different algorithms. A topological feature extraction method based on differential manifolds is proposed, demonstrating clear advantages in the classification of six types of vibration events. The method achieves an average classification accuracy of 95.03%,

Table 1. Performance comparison of different methods across scenarios

Method	DL	JH	FS	HH	SL	RA	Avg.
K-Means	72.88%	73.23%	76.67%	74.22%	70.13%	71.24%	73.06%
STFT+SVM	79.17%	80.51%	78.36%	81.02%	82.33%	79.74%	80.19%
GMM+HMM	85.10%	83.42%	84.21%	87.30%	81.27%	80.21%	83.59%
TDE	90.97%	89.16%	90.53%	92.54%	89.32%	91.43%	90.66%
GASF-ConvNeXt-TF	92.16%	94.33%	**96.09%**	92.64%	93.18%	**95.27%**	94.43%
Proposed Method	**95.27%**	**95.43%**	95.03%	**94.23%**	**96.75%**	93.52%	**95.03%**

which is 21.97% higher than that of traditional approaches such as K-means and 0.6% higher than that of deep learning methods like GASF-ConvNeXt-TF. In particular, for two representative events—high-frequency shock (HH) and periodic vibration (RA)—the classification accuracies reach 94.23% and 93.52%, respectively. These results validate the capability of topological features to capture the dynamics of high-order vibration modes and the invariance of periodic structures.

Experimental results further indicate that differential delay embedding (TDE), as the core step in phase space reconstruction, effectively maps one-dimensional signals into a high-dimensional phase space of the dynamical system. This process enables the extraction of implicit high-order derivative features, yielding performance that surpasses the 80.19% accuracy of traditional time-frequency analysis methods such as STFT+SVM, and exceeds the 90.66% accuracy of classical TDE. These findings highlight the critical role of topological features in characterizing the multi-scale geometric structures of vibration signals.

The topological framework based on differential manifolds shows a strong discriminative ability for high-order vibration patterns in signals, and these patterns are manifested as long-life H_1 features far from the diagonal in the persistence graph. This verifies its effectiveness in capturing the internal structure of the signal.

5 Summary

This study is confronted with the challenge of characterizing high-order vibration modes caused by complex multi-physical field coupling in distributed optical fiber sensing signals. A vibration-signal feature-enhancement framework based on differential-manifold topology analysis is proposed. By integrating dynamical phase-space reconstruction from differential geometry with persistent homology theory from algebraic topology, a complete analytical pipeline is established—spanning high-order signal representation to topological quantification.

Experimental results demonstrate that the proposed method achieves a classification accuracy of 95.03% across six representative event categories on a public dataset. This surpasses traditional time-frequency analysis methods and current deep learning models, effectively overcoming the limitations of conventional approaches in representing nonlinear and non-stationary signals. The method offers a novel dual-perspective paradigm, simultaneously capturing geometric structures and modeling algebraic invariants for vibration signal interpretation.

However, the explicit relationship between topological features and the underlying physical mechanisms of vibration events remains partially unresolved, limiting the model's interpretability. Future research will focus on embedding physical knowledge into the framework, aiming to establish interpretable mappings between topological descriptors and fundamental vibration dynamics. This advancement is expected to further enhance the robustness and applicability of the proposed method in industrial scenarios involving multi-physical field coupling.

References

1. Wang, Y.-J., et al.: GASF-ConvNeXt-TF algorithm for perimeter security disturbance identification based on distributed optical fiber sensing system. IEEE Internet Things J. **11**(10), 17712–17726 (2024). https://doi.org/10.1109/JIOT.2024.3360970
2. Tejedor, J., Macias-Guarasa, J., Martins, H.F., Martin-Lopez, S., Gonzalez-Herraez, M.: A contextual GMM-HMM smart fiber optic surveillance system for pipeline integrity threat detection. J. Lightwave Technol. **37**(17), 4514–4522 (2019). https://doi.org/10.1109/JLT.2019.2916687
3. Jayawickrema, U.M.N., Herath, H.M.C.M., Hettiarachchi, N.K., et al.: Fibre-optic sensor and deep learning-based structural health monitoring systems for civil structures: a review. Measurement **199**, 111514 (2022). https://doi.org/10.1016/j.measurement.2022.111514
4. Zhu, Y.-F., Xiao, Y., Dou, S.-X., Chou, S.-L.: Dynamic structural evolution and controllable redox potential for abnormal high-voltage sodium layered oxide cathodes. Cell Rep. Phys. Sci. **2**, 100631 (2021). https://doi.org/10.1016/j.xcrp.2021.100631
5. Sun, M., et al.: Man-made threat event recognition based on distributed optical fiber vibration sensing and SE-WaveNet. IEEE Trans. Instrum. Meas. **70**, 1–11 (2021). https://doi.org/10.1109/TIM.2021.3081178
6. Jin, X., et al.: Pattern recognition of distributed optical fiber vibration sensors based on ResNet 152. IEEE Sens. J. **23**, 19717–19725 (2023). https://doi.org/10.1109/JSEN.2023.3295948
7. Yan, Q., et al.: Apart and a part: overlapped vibration recognition for distributed optical fiber sensing based on deep learning separation. Opt. Laser Technol. **182**, 112083 (2025). https://doi.org/10.1016/j.optlastec.2024.112083
8. Sun, Z., et al.: Optical fiber distributed vibration sensing using grayscale image and multi-class deep learning framework for multi-event recognition. IEEE Sens. J. **21**, 19112–19120 (2021). https://doi.org/10.1109/JSEN.2021.3089004
9. Wang, Y., et al.: Optical fiber vibration sensing system using delay line method. Microw. Opt. Technol. Lett. **61**, 853–857 (2019). https://doi.org/10.1002/mop.31634

10. Huang, L., et al.: Building safety monitoring based on extreme gradient boosting in distributed optical fiber sensing. Opt. Fiber Technol. **55**, 102149 (2020). https://doi.org/10.1016/j.yofte.2020.102149
11. Zhang, J., et al.: Unsupervised learning method for events identification in φ-OTDR. Opt. Quant. Electron. **54**, 457 (2022). https://doi.org/10.1007/s11082-022-03748-y
12. Fireaizen, T., Ron, S., Bobrowski, O.: Alarm sound detection using topological signal processing. In: ICASSP 2022 - 2022 IEEE International Conference on Acoustics, Speech and Signal Processing (ICASSP), pp. 211–215 (2022). https://doi.org/10.1109/ICASSP43922.2022.9747228
13. Dan, T., Huang, Z., Cai, H., Laurienti, P.J., Wu, G.: Learning brain dynamics of evolving manifold functional MRI data using geometric-attention neural network. IEEE Trans. Med. Imaging **41**, 2752–2763 (2022). https://doi.org/10.1109/TMI.2022.3169640
14. Huayuan, M., Xinghua, L., Xingbo, X., Ying, L., Mingshou, Z., Z.F.: Research on recognition algorithm of impact vibration based on HOG feature of time–frequency spectrum. Waves Rand. Complex Media 1–18 (2022). https://doi.org/10.1080/17455030.2022.2149885

Design and Optimization of a Heavy-Duty Parallel Ship Motion Simulation Platform

En Yang, Yan Hu, Chenbo Lang, Feng Gao[(✉)], and Hao Zheng

School of Mechanical Engineering, Shanghai Jiao Tong University, Shanghai 200240, China
`gaofengsjtu@gmail.com`

Abstract. The dynamic nature of the marine environment induces six-degree-of-freedom ship motions, posing challenges to the safety of maritime operations. This paper presents a 6-PUS parallel ship motion simulation platform designed to replicate ship motion characteristics under heavy-duty conditions in a 5th sea state. The kinematic and dynamic models of the motion simulation platform were established using the closed-loop vector formulation and the Newton-Euler method. To achieve the platform's 5th sea-state simulation capability, a novel evaluation method based on the effective workspace coverage ratio was proposed to assess its motion performance. Combined with load-bearing capacity metrics, the dimensional parameters of the mechanism were optimized. The design was validated to meet the requirements for 5th sea-state simulation. To address heavy-duty driving demands, an electro-hydraulic hybrid drive system was adopted. This system counterbalances the mass of the platform assembly and payload under static conditions, significantly reducing the dynamic forces on the motor-screw modules during motion. The accuracy of the kinematic and dynamic models was verified through simulations using RecurDyn software. This research advances the application of parallel robotic mechanisms in maritime engineering, providing a robust solution for high-fidelity, heavy-duty ship motion simulation.

Keywords: Kinematic analysis · Dimensional Synthesis · Workspace · Dynamic Simulation

1 Introduction

The marine environment is characterized by variability, and ships move in six degrees of freedom (transverse, longitudinal, vertical, pendulum, transverse, longitudinal, and bow) under the action of waves. The ship's motion can cause many hazards to the offshore production operation and affect all kinds of equipment working on the ship. The six-degree-of-freedom parallel ship motion simulator can simulate ship motion on land. It can realize the characteristics of ship's motion at sea. It can shorten the test cycle, reduce the cost, and improve the reliability and safety of the test. The research of multi-degree-of-freedom parallel ship motion simulation device is of great significance to the development of parallel robot mechanism and navigation.

In 1965, D. Stewart firstly proposed a six-degree-of-freedom parallel mechanism consisting of six retractable struts connected to the upper and lower platforms by ball hinges, which was used to complete the flight simulation of an airplane [1]. Subsequently, this configuration has been widely used in motion simulation in other fields such as automobiles and ships. Various variants of this configuration of motion simulators have been derived, such as the PKM automotive motion simulator proposed by Dong W et al. and the 6-RUS and 6-PUS configurations [4, 12, 14]. Less-degree-of-freedom parallel mechanisms have also been used in motion simulation. For example, Pouliot N A, Casas S focused on the three rotational degree of freedom configuration and the lift-pitch-roll degree of freedom configuration, which were used for large transport aircraft motion simulation and earthquake simulation, respectively [2, 3, 5].Talke K et al. proposed a 3-PSR parallel mechanism for the reproduction of spectral-based wave and ship motion data, and obtained a transverse rocking-longitudinal rocking (TRL) workspace suitable for reproducing the class 4 sea state [6]. In the study of improved Steward mechanism, Nabavi S N used three performance metrics, dexterity, kinetic energy and new improved workspace metrics to optimize the 6-PUS parallel robot parameters [7]. Cao R proposed a methodology for designing the mechanism parameters based on a given workspace. The method quickly determines the mechanism parameters that satisfy the design requirements of drive stroke and joint angle by selecting the key points with the worst performance in a given workspace [8].

Due to the variability of the ship's motion at sea, the motion simulation device needs to have six degrees of freedom, and the 6-PUS has smaller running inertia and better dynamic response than the traditional Steward structure. However, there are currently few studies specifically addressing the design of mechanism dimensions tailored to the requirements of specific workspaces. Building upon an existing large-scale swing simulation platform in our laboratory (see in Fig. 1), this paper designs new dimensional parameters to address the demands of simulating sea state 5 conditions and installation space constraints. Furthermore, it proposes a drive solution suitable for heavy-duty operating conditions.

Fig. 1. Motion simulation platform prototype

2 Kinematic and Dynamic Modeling of Ship Motion Simulation Device

2.1 Mechanism Configuration and Kinematic Analysis

The 6-PUS Parallel Ship Motion Simulator consists of an end-motion platform, a fixed frame and six struts. Each link is identical in structure, with one end of the connecting rod connected to the moving sub via a Hook hinge and the other end connected to the motion platform via a ball hinge. The drive module is fixed on the frame and does not move with the motion platform, which can reduce the inertia of the mechanism. The six branch chains are divided into two groups of two, and the total is divided into three groups, which are arranged symmetrically along the vertical direction.

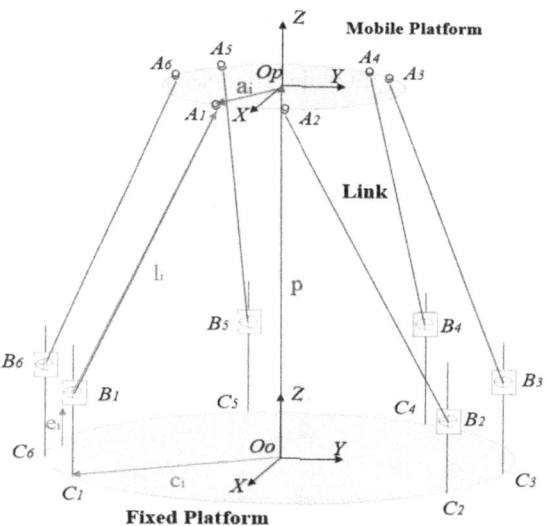

Fig. 2. Structural sketch of ship motion simulation device

For the 6-degree-of-freedom ship motion simulator, a fixed coordinate system $O_o - XYZ$ is established on the frame. A link coordinate system $O_p - XYZ$ is established at the center of the motion platform for describing the displacement and attitude of the end platform. Each branch chain has the same structure, and for any branch chain, the center point of the motion vice and the vector representation of each component are shown in Fig. 2.

Define the end generalized positional coordinates of the six-degree-of-freedom wave simulation platform as $X = [p_x\ p_y\ p_z\ \varphi\ \theta\ \phi]^T$. From this, the vector closed-loop equations for the branched chain can be written:

$$p + Ra_i = c_i + q_i e_i + l_i \qquad (1)$$

where p is the end-effector position vector, R is the end-effector rotation matrix, a_i is the position vector of point A_i on the moving platform relative to the moving coordinate system, c_i is the position vector of the driving slider relative to the polar coordinate system, $q_i e_i$ is the driving displacement, and l_i is the connecting rod position vector. Let $H_i = p + Ra_i - c_i$.

Derive and organize Eq. (1) to exclude incompatible solutions for the drive displacements of each strut at a given position:

$$q_i = H_i \cdot e_i - \sqrt{(H_i \cdot e_i)^2 - H_i^2 + L_i^2} \qquad (2)$$

where $H_i = p + Ra_i - c_i$, L_i is the length of the connecting rod. Further derivation and collation of Eq. (1) yields the mapping relationship between end velocity and drive velocity and the velocity Jacobi matrix.

$$G = \begin{bmatrix} \frac{l_1}{e_1 l_1} & \frac{l_2}{e_2 l_2} & \frac{l_3}{e_3 l_3} & \frac{l_4}{e_4 l_4} & \frac{l_5}{e_5 l_5} & \frac{l_6}{e_6 l_6} \\ \frac{Ra_1 \times l_1}{e_1 l_1} & \frac{Ra_2 \times l_2}{e_2 l_2} & \frac{Ra_3 \times l_3}{e_3 l_3} & \frac{Ra_4 \times l_4}{e_4 l_4} & \frac{Ra_5 \times l_5}{e_5 l_5} & \frac{Ra_6 \times l_6}{e_6 l_6} \end{bmatrix} \qquad (3)$$

$$\dot{X} = J\dot{q} \qquad (4)$$

where $J = (G_v^T)^{-1}$, is the velocity Jacobi matrix of this parallel mechanism. Since the positive solution analytical equation of the 6-PUS mechanism has the problems of high computational complexity and multiple solutions, which is difficult to meet the real-time control demand, this study applies the numerical iteration method to establish the positive solution model. Newton iterative method is used as the basic algorithm. Define the drive volume generalized coordinate vector q, and its function relationship with the motion platform position X can be expressed as:

$$q = F(X) \qquad (5)$$

Shifting and deforming the terms of Eq. (5) yields a system of nonlinear equations:

$$f(X) = F(X) - q = 0 \qquad (6)$$

The optimized iterative equations are finally obtained through the derivation of differential relations for the velocity Jacobi matrix:

$$X_n = X_{n-1} - J(X_{n-1})(q_{n-1} - q) \qquad (7)$$

where q_{n-1} is obtained from the inverse model, and $J(X_{n-1})$ is the Jacobi matrix at the current position. The method fully utilizes the computational advantages of the inverse model and achieves fast convergence through the real-time update of the Jacobi matrix.

2.2 Dynamic Analysis

The Newton-Euler method is used to model the dynamics of the system, which facilitates the intuitive analysis of the relationship between the binding forces of the components of the mechanism, and at the same time, the small amount of computation can be carried out quickly, which is conducive to the verification of the structural strength as well as real-time control. The ship motion simulation device can be disassembled into three main components: moving platform, connecting rod and driving slider, and the Newton-Euler equations can be constructed and solved for each group of components.

The moving platform is subjected to the binding force of six sets of connecting rods F_{Ai}, its own gravity as well as external forces F_{out} and external moments M_{out}:

$$\begin{cases} \sum_{i=1}^{6} F_{Ai} + m_p g - F_{out} = m_p \dot{v}_c \\ \sum_{i=1}^{6} ((Ra_i\prime) \times F_{Ai}) - M_{out} = I_{po}\dot{\omega} + \omega \times (I_{po}\omega) \end{cases} \quad (8)$$

where I_{po} is the moment of inertia of the moving platform with respect to the fixed coordinate system. The connecting rod is subjected to the two ends of the binding force and its own gravity, in order to facilitate the elimination of intermediate quantities on B_i to construct the moment balance equation:

$$\begin{cases} m_{li}g - F_{Ai} - F_{Bi} = m_{li}\dot{v}_{li} \\ \frac{1}{2}l_i \times m_{li}g - l_i \times F_{Ai} - \frac{1}{2}l_i \times m_{li}\dot{v}_{li} = I_{lio}\dot{\omega}_{li} + \omega_{li} \times (I_{lio}\omega_{li}) \end{cases} \quad (9)$$

where I_{lio} is the moment of inertia of the connecting rod with respect to the point B_i, v_{li} is the velocity of the connecting rod and ω_{li} is the angular velocity of the connecting rod. Further the force balance equation is established for the driving slider:

$$m_{sli}g + F_{Bi}e_i + F_{qi} = m_{sli}\ddot{q}_i \quad (10)$$

where m_{sli} is the equivalent mass of the driving slider, F_{qi} is the driving force provided to the slider by the driving system, gradually eliminating the unknown internal constraints in the Newton-Euler equations established for each independent moving part, and finally solving the mapping relationship between the driving force F_{qi} and the external force F_{out} of the moving platform as well as the external torque M_{out}, to establish the overall dynamics equations of the system.

3 Synthesis of Mechanism Dimensions for Required Workspace Under Sea State 5

The motion of a ship affected by waves is mainly influenced by the sea state and its own structural dimensions. Normally, the ship is allowed to work normally in class 5 sea state, in which the waves will produce 10° transverse rocking, 3° longitudinal rocking and 1.56 m lifting and sinking motion for the ship with the length of hull between 45.7–76.2 m [16].

It is necessary to make the six-degree-of-freedom simulation platform ensure the ability to move 1.59 m along the Z-axis when generating ± 10° transverse rocking and ± 3° longitudinal rocking attitudes, i.e., to meet the rocking ability of the class 5 sea state within the cylindrical space of H = 1.6 m, R = 0.4 m (see in Fig. 3(b)).

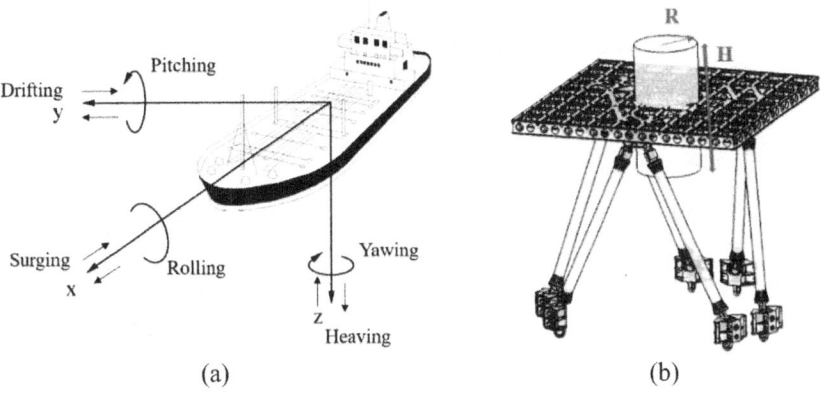

Fig. 3. Six-degree-of-freedom motion and space generated by the ship at sea (a) Schematic of the six-degree-of-freedom motion (b) Range of work required to simulate class 5 sea state

Let the radius of the bottom fixed platform P-sub mounting be r_b, the radius of the top movable platform ball-hinge mounting be r_a, the angle between the point A_1 and the point A_2 be θ_a, and the angle between the point B_1 and the point B_2 be θ_b Then the basic kinematic parameters of the device can be uniquely determined by $q_i, r_a, r_b, \theta_a, \theta_b$ and L. The kinematic parameters of the device can be uniquely determined by θ_a and L. The scale synthesis of the device is the design of the values of these five scalar parameters. The parameters r_b and θ_b are determined by the mounting dimensions of the fixed base and the selection of the drive components. r_a Under the condition of meeting the upper end of the experimental equipment carrying space, the smallest possible value is selected to reduce the end load. The above three sets of parameters are determined. The influence of the parameters θ_a and L on the workspace is investigated when the three sets of parameters are determined.

The workspace is typically separated into translational workspace and rotational workspace. The coordinate points in the space that can produce $\pm 10°$ transverse rocking and $\pm 3°$ longitudinal rocking attitude at the same time are called the effective point of the level 5 sea simulation, and a larger percentage of the effective point in the space can be considered that the device has a stronger simulation of the level 5 sea state capability. The position in 5-level sea state is input into the inverse kinematics equation to solve the driving displacement q_i, and then q_i is substituted into the positive kinematics equation to solve the position. If q_i are in the preset driving range $[-1300, 1300]$ (mm) and the difference between the positive kinematics solved position vector and the original position vector is less than 0.001. If the above conditions are met, the point is considered to be a valid point. The effective point calculation process is shown in the following diagram (see in Fig. 4).

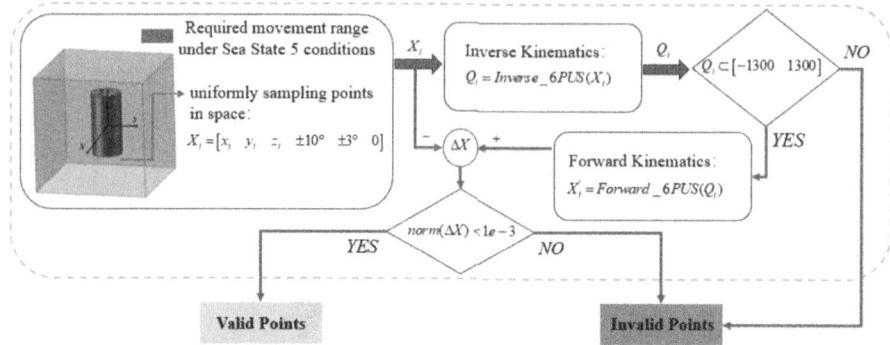

Fig. 4. Valid Points Calculation Process

The effect of these two parameters on the effective point range can be effectively investigated by searching the volume share of the effective point in space at different rod lengths L and angles θ_a, which are set between [1000.5000] (mm) for L and [0.2,1.9] (rad) for θ_a. To ensure that the moving platform is above the zero position of the drive, the constraints of $L > \sqrt{r_a^2 + r_b^2 - 2r_a r_b \cos(\theta_a/2 - \theta_b/2)}$ need to be met. At the same time, the required motion range for class 5 sea state is expanded by a margin of 10%, and the effective point is marked in red if it cannot cover the range, and the calculation results are shown below (see in Fig. 5).

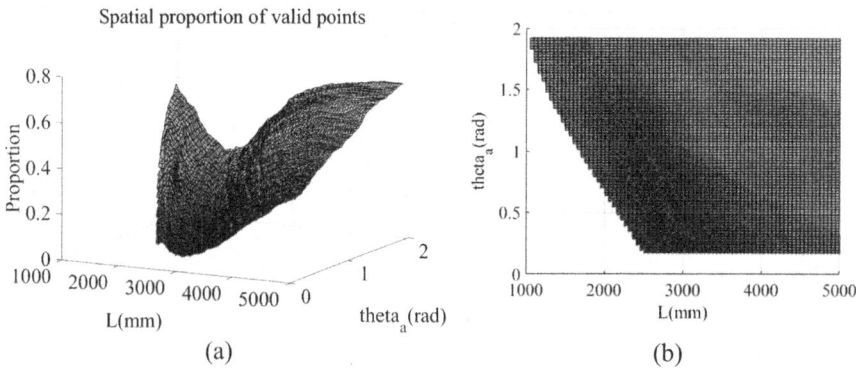

Fig. 5. Impact of Dimension Parameters on Valid Points Ratio (a) 3D view (b) Top view

From the fitted surface plots, it can be seen that increasing L and θ_a increases the percentage of effective points in space, which enhances the ability of the device to simulate class 5 sea states in the workspace. Meanwhile, L has a greater effect on the percentage of effective points than θ_a. Although increasing the length of connecting rod and the angle of ball hinge can increase the effective point ratio and increase the space motion capability, it may also increase the load of the mechanism and reduce the working load capability. The device is used for simulation of heavy load condition, which requires high load carrying capacity, and the effect of these two dimensions on the load carrying capacity needs to be further investigated.

The matrix obtained from Eq. (3) is the force Jacobi matrix and the following relationship exists between the generalized force acting on the end-effector and the end-drive force:

$$\begin{bmatrix} F \\ T \end{bmatrix} = Gf \tag{11}$$

Define the evaluation index of carrying capacity as the extreme value of the force output vector at $\|f\| = 1$ and construct the Lagrange equation to find this extreme value:

$$L = f^T G^T Gf - \lambda \left(f^T f - 1 \right) \tag{12}$$

When $\|f\| = 1$ the load-bearing extreme value is $G^T G$ maximum and minimum eigenvalue open square, using the minimum load-bearing capacity extreme value for the evaluation of the load-bearing capacity under the given positional attitude, the larger the value indicates that the overall load-bearing capacity of the organization is the stronger, take the $\alpha = \pm 10°$, $\beta = \pm 3°$ attitude of the extreme value of the integral in the workspace at the 5th level of the sea state with the ratio of the spatial volume as an evaluation index, that is:

$$\|F_{\min}\| = \sqrt{\lambda_{F\min}(G^T G)} \tag{13}$$

$$\eta_{\min} = \int_v \|F_{\min}\| dv \Big/ \int_v dv \tag{14}$$

Fitting η_{min} to a 3D surface map along with a map of the dimensional parameters of the mechanism is shown in the following Fig. 6.

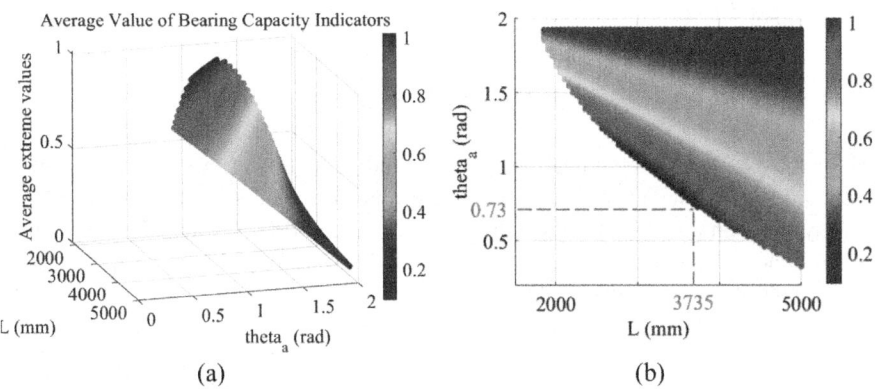

Fig. 6. Impact of Size Parameters on Bearing Capacity (a) 3D view (b) Top view

It can be seen that increasing L and θ_a will reduce the overall load carrying capacity of the organization, of which θ_a has a more significant effect on the load carrying capacity.

Under the condition of ensuring that the workspace simulation can meet level 5 sea state, we should choose the size parameter with better bearing capacity as much as possible, and the size parameter design of the ship rocking simulation platform is shown in the Table 1 (Fig. 7).

Table 1. Dimensional design of ship rocking simulation platform

r_a/mm	r_b/mm	θ_a/rad	θ_b/rad	L/mm
3000	2300	0.73	2.09	3735

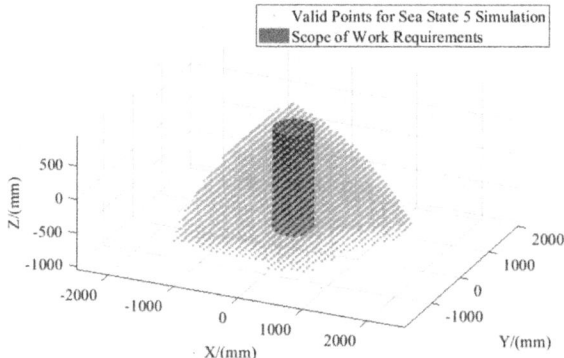

Fig. 7. Translational workspace under specific roll/pitch motion in Sea State 5

The Monte Carlo method is used to plot the translational workspace under 5 levels of sea state attitude respectively, which verifies that the mechanism can satisfy the simulation of 5 levels of sea state sway.

4 Design and Analysis of Drive Modules

The 6-PUS parallel wave simulation platform studied in this paper is driven by a motor screw module. In the face of heavy-duty conditions using electric-hydraulic composite drive system can effectively reduce the motor drive unit drive force and power, so that the equipment can complete the heavy-duty conditions of the ship motion simulation, the schematic diagram shown in Fig. 8.

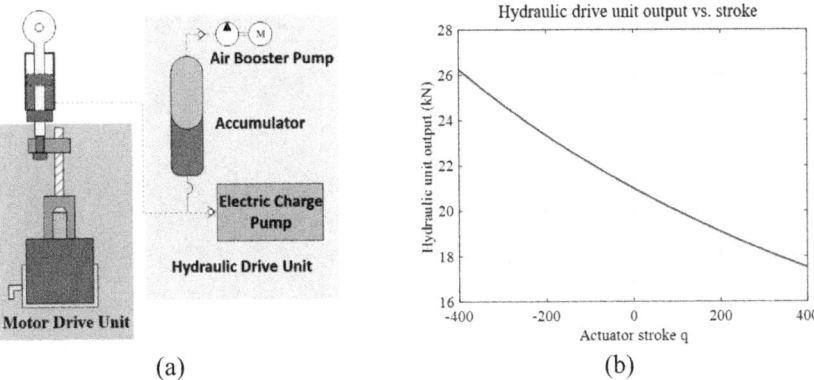

Fig. 8. Electro-hydraulic composite drive module (a) Schematic diagram (b) Curve of hydraulic drive unit force variation with stroke

The electro-hydraulic composite drive system consists of two parts: the motor drive unit and the hydraulic drive unit. Hydraulic drive unit mainly consists of pressurized gas pump, accumulator and electric charge pump. When the piston pusher moves down, the hydraulic oil is squeezed into the accumulator, the volume of gas in the accumulator is compressed so that the oil pressure increases, the role of the oil pressure on the piston pressure increases, the piston rod moves up and vice versa. Hydraulic unit output force and displacement between the non-linear relationship, the formula is as follows:

$$F = \frac{P_0 V_0 T S}{T_0 (V_0 + Sq)} \tag{15}$$

where P_0 is the initial pressure of the gas in the accumulator, T_0 is the initial temperature of the system, T is the working temperature of the system, V_0 is the initial volume of the gas in the accumulator, L_0 is the initial length of the hydraulic part in the hydraulic cylinder, S is the effective area of action of the hydraulic piston, and q is the stroke of the actuator, which is set upward for the positive direction. Assuming that the temperature of the system remains constant during operation, since the hydraulic drive unit always provides upward thrust, the control parameter $P_0 A$ makes the output force of the motor drive unit 0 when the 6-PUS mechanism carries a 5T load and is in the zero position, so as to determine the various parameters and obtain the curve of the force of the hydraulic drive unit with the change of the displacement of the actuator.

The kinematics and dynamics of the 6-PUS parallel mechanism modeled in Sect. 2 are used to calculate the driving force of the motor drive unit when the end carries a 5T load in a class 5 sea state. The motion of the end-moving platform is given as $\alpha = 10°\sin(\pi t/3)$, $\beta = 3°\sin(\pi t/3)$, $\gamma = 0$, $z = 500\sin(\pi t/3)$. The calculated driving force of the motor drive unit is shown in Fig. 9, where the left figure (a) shows the driving force case without the hydraulic drive unit and the right figure (b) shows the driving force case including the hydraulic drive unit. The hydraulic drive unit effectively reduces the maximum drive force of the motor drive at 5T load, which enables the mechanism to adapt to the simulation of ship motion under heavy load conditions (Fig. 10).

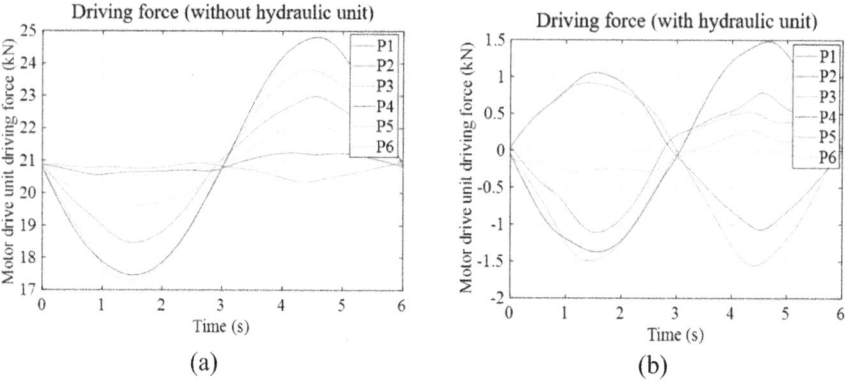

Fig. 9. Calculation curve of drive unit drive force (a) Curve of cylinder drive force without hydraulic drive module (b) Curve of cylinder drive force with hydraulic drive module

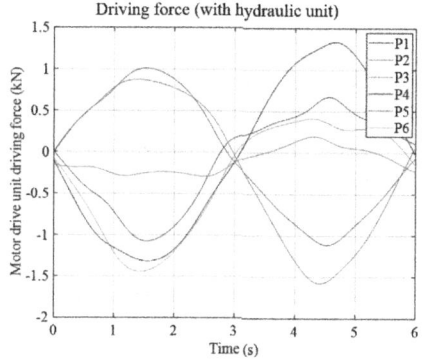

Fig. 10. RecurDyn drive simulation data curve

Using RecurDyn to perform dynamic simulation verification on a 6-PUS parallel mechanism and comparing the results with theoretical calculations, the deviation is within the permissible range, verifying the validity of the kinematic and dynamic modeling.

5 Conclusion

In this paper, by analyzing the commonly used multi-degree-of-freedom motion simulation mechanisms, a six-degree-of-freedom motion simulation platform that can satisfy the simulation of the ship's Class 5 sea state motion under heavy-duty working conditions is proposed. The kinematics and dynamics models of the mechanism are established by using the closed-loop vector method and Newtonian Eulerian method, respectively, and the positive and inverse solutions of the attitude and the driving force solution equations are obtained. Secondly, the dimensional design was completed for the attitude and workspace requirements of class 5 sea state. Finally, the electric-hydraulic composite drive is used to meet the heavy-duty working condition requirements, and its reasonableness and accuracy are verified by computation and RecurDyn dynamics simulation.

References

1. Stewart, D.: A platform with six degrees of freedom. Proc. Inst. Mech. Eng. **180**, 371–386 (1965)
2. Pouliot, N.A., Gosselin, C.M., Nahon, M.A.: Motion simulation capabilities of three-degree-of-freedom flight simulators. J. Aircr. **35**, 9–17 (1998)
3. Ottaviano, E., Ceccarelli, M., Castelli, G.: Experimental results of a 3-DOF parallel manipulator as an earthquake motion simulator. In: International Design Engineering Technical Conferences and Computers and Information in Engineering Conference, pp. 215–222. (2004)
4. Dong, W., Du, Z., Xiao, Y., Chen, X.: Development of a parallel kinematic motion simulator platform. Mechatronics **23**, 154–161 (2013)
5. Casas, S., Coma, I., Portalés, C., Fernández, M.: Optimization of 3-DOF parallel motion devices for low-cost vehicle simulators. J. Adv. Mech. Des. Syst. Manuf. **11**, JAMDSM0023-JAMDSM0023 (2017)
6. Talke, K., Drotman, D., Stroumtsos, N., de Oliveira, M., Bewley, T.: Design and parameter optimization of a 3-PSR parallel mechanism for replicating wave and boat motion. In: 2019 International Conference on Robotics and Automation (ICRA), pp. 7955–7961. IEEE (2019)
7. Nabavi, S.N., Shariatee, M., Enferadi, J., Akbarzadeh, A.: Parametric design and multi-objective optimization of a general 6-PUS parallel manipulator. Mech. Mach. Theory **152**, 103913 (2020)
8. Cao, R., Gao, F., Zhang, Y., Pan, D.: A key point dimensional design method of a 6-DOF parallel manipulator for a given workspace. Mech. Mach. Theory **85**, 1–13 (2015)
9. Zhang, J., Yu, H., Gao, F., Zhang, D., Zhao, X., Ma, C.: A 6-DOF heavy-load parallel manipulator with RFTA and its application. In: 2011 IEEE International Conference on Robotics and Automation, pp. 470–475. IEEE (2011)
10. Liu, X.-J., Wang, J., Gao, F., Wang, L.-P.: Mechanism design of a simplified 6-DOF 6-RUS parallel manipulator. Robotica **20**, 81–91 (2002)
11. Mirshekari, E., Ghanbarzadeh, A., Shirazia, K.H.: Structure comparison and optimal design of 6-RUS parallel manipulator based on kinematic and dynamic performances. Latin Am. J. Solids Struct. **13**, 2414–2438 (2016)
12. Bonev, I.A., Gosselin, C.M.: A geometric algorithm for the computation of the constant-orientation workspace of 6-RUS parallel manipulators. In: International Design Engineering Technical Conferences and Computers and Information in Engineering Conference, pp. 483–492. American Society of Mechanical Engineers (2000)
13. Halima, A.B., Bert, J., Clément, J.-F., Visvikis, D.: Development of a 6 degrees of freedom prostate brachytherapy robot with integrated gravity compensation system. In: 2021 International Symposium on Medical Robotics (ISMR), pp. 1–7. IEEE (2021)
14. Ruiz-García, J., Chaparro-Altamirano, D., Zavala-Yoe, R., Ramírez-Mendoza, R.: Direct and inverse dynamics modeling of a 6-PUS parallel robot. In: 2013 International Conference on Mechatronics, Electronics and Automotive Engineering, pp. 21–26. IEEE (2013)
15. Li, J., et al.: Parallel structure of six wheel-legged robot trajectory tracking control with heavy payload under uncertain physical interaction. Assem. Autom. **40**, 675–687 (2020)
16. Love, L.: Compensation of Wave-Induced Motion and Force Phenomena for Ship-Based High Performance Robotic and Human Amplifying Systems. Oak Ridge National Lab.(ORNL), Oak Ridge, TN (United States) (2003)

Design and Analysis of a New Multiparameter Reconfigurable Morphing Wing

Duanling Li[1], Ruixuan Dai[1], Junwei Zhang[1], Fengkun Xu[1], and Yizhu Guo[2(✉)]

[1] School of Inteligent Engineering and Automation, Beijing University of Posts and Telecommunications, Beijing 100876, China
[2] Beijing Institute of Spacecraft System Engineering, Beijing 100094, China
bamboo501@sina.com

Abstract. The challenges of expanding operational airspace/speed domains and enhancing multi-mission adaptability for future aircraft are addressed in this study through the proposal of a novel morphing-wing configuration. A reconfigurable wing integrating leading-edge mechanisms, scissor linkages, and telescopic sleeves was developed and validated through finite element simulations. The results demonstrate simultaneous adjustment of wing chord, sweep angle, and aspect ratio, enabling optimal adaptability to diverse missions ranging from low-speed cruise to high-speed penetration. Structural analysis confirms satisfactory stiffness and deformation characteristics under critical load conditions. Future research will focus on intelligent control strategies to enhance autonomous mission transition capabilities and operational reliability.

Keywords: Reconfigurable Morphing Wing · Modal Analysis · Kinematics Analysis · Statics Analysis

1 Introduction

Modern aircraft are required to adapt to expansive flight envelopes and velocity regimes while maintaining operational flexibility across diverse environmental conditions. In conventional aircraft configurations, aerodynamic and flight performance optimizations are primarily achieved through adjustments of control surfaces including elevators, rudders, flaps, and ailerons. However, such optimizations are typically effective only within specific operational parameters, with performance degradation occurring when deviating from these design conditions [1]. The limitations of fixed-geometry wings have become increasingly apparent with expanding operational domains and escalating mission adaptability requirements. Consequently, adaptive geometric adjustments of wing configurations have emerged as a critical technological focus. As an advanced technological solution, morphing wing systems have established themselves as pivotal developmental pathways in modern aerospace engineering, signifying the evolutionary trajectory of future aircraft design [2–4].

Significant research efforts have been dedicated globally to various morphing wing configurations including variable-span wings, variable-chord wings, variable-sweep wings, and variable-camber wings. A variable-span wing for unmanned aerial vehicles (UAVs) was developed by Wang Lijia [5] at Harbin Institute of Technology, incorporating scissor hinge mechanisms with comprehensive mechanical and kinematic simulations. Zhang Zuhao [6] proposed a telescopic morphing wing structure integrating rigid and flexible skin components to ensure surface continuity during deformation. J.L. Reed Jr et al. [7] investigated lead-screw driven rib-interpenetration mechanisms for chord length variation. Li Mingqi [8] from Harbin Institute of Technology designed a novel shear-type variable-sweep wing structure with topological optimization for weight reduction. Aerodynamic investigations have revealed that chordwise bending significantly influences flow separation characteristics and airfoil efficiency, while spanwise bending affects wingtip stall phenomena and lift distribution [9]. D.M. Elzey et al. [10] developed a chain-linked cellular structure enabling chordwise curvature adjustments. MANZO et al. [11] implemented segmented deformation mechanisms for spanwise camber variation. A parallel-linkage morphing wing enabling multi-modal deformations was proposed by Wang Yunfei et al. [12]. LAZOS et al. [13] achieved spanwise bending through specialized linkage systems integrated with shape memory alloy actuators. AMIN et al. [14] introduced modular-driven morphing wing architectures for multi-mode deformation control. Xiao Hong et al. [15] created a tetrahedral-unit-based morphing skeleton with linear actuators enabling torsional and bending deformations. Tian Dake et al. [16] designed an equilateral Bennett mechanism-based morphing wing structure characterized by structural simplicity and high modularity.

Current research predominantly focuses on single-degree-of-freedom morphing mechanisms, with limited exploration of multi-dimensional deformation approaches [17, 18].Consequently, the development of morphing wings capable of maintaining sufficient stability and maneuverability across diverse flight regimes and atmospheric conditions has been identified as a critical research direction in contemporary aviation technology [19]. Building upon current advancements in multi-dimensional morphing wing research, this paper proposes a novel reconfigurable morphing wing mechanism capable of simultaneous span length and sweep angle adjustments, providing theoretical references for future morphing wing designs.

2 Morphing Wing Design Scheme

2.1 System Architecture

Figure 1 illustrates the three-dimensional design of the morphing wing mechanism proposed in this study for variable-geometry aircraft. This integrated system incorporates critical components including leading-edge assemblies, scissor linkages, telescopic sleeves, wing ribs, and spars, enabling synchronous regulation of chord length, sweep angle, wing span, and surface area. The morphing mechanism is functionally divided into two operational modes.

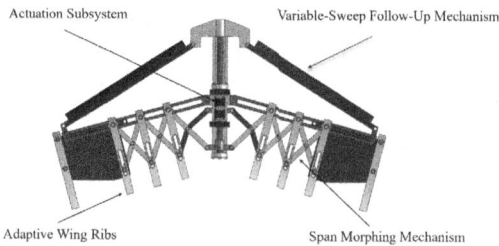

Fig. 1. Three-dimensional diagram of the morphing wing mechanism

Sweep Angle Adjustment Mode: The configuration comprises leading-edge components, rotating shafts, nut pairs, lead screws, sliding guides, drive motors, and telescopic sleeves. The sweep angle is modified through servo motor-driven rotation of lead screws, which induces coordinated translational motion of the entire wing assembly along the guide rails. Concurrent telescopic sleeve movement ensures smooth geometric transitions during angular adjustment.

Span Adjustment Mode: Centered on double-curved straight-shear units combined with multiple parallelogram mechanisms, this mode employs bidirectional lead screw-nut assemblies driven by root-mounted motors. The scissor linkage expansion/contraction is precisely controlled through this actuation system, facilitating continuous span modulation. The extended configuration enhances lift-to-drag ratio for endurance missions, while retraction optimizes aerodynamic efficiency during high-speed maneuvers.

This design methodology ensures efficient dynamic reconfiguration of wing geometry, achieving optimal flight performance across diverse operational regimes through coordinated parametric adjustments.

2.2 Sweep Angle Adjustment Mechanism

The sweep angle adjustment mechanism primarily consists of the wing leading edge, nut pair, lead screw, rotational shaft at the wing root, sliding guide rails, and drive motor, as illustrated in Fig. 2. The dynamic sweep angle adjustment is achieved through servo motor-driven rotation of the lead screw, which converts rotary motion into linear displacement via the lead screw-nut pair. This drives the entire wing assembly along the slide rails, with the telescopic sleeve functioning as a follow-up mechanism to ensure smooth and precise deformation throughout the process.

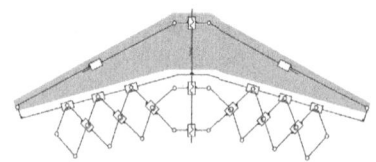

Fig. 2. Swept angle adjustment mechanism

2.3 Wingspan Adjustment Mechanism

The span adjustment system employs a combination of double-curved straight shear units and multiple parallelogram structures to form the main wing framework, shown in Fig. 3. Each modular unit is independently driven by motors located at the wing root, utilizing bidirectional lead screw-nut transmission mechanisms to control the opening/closing motion of the double-curved straight shear units and scissor linkages. This configuration not only guarantees stability and controllability during deformation but also enables continuous span adjustment through coordinated actuation of the interconnected units. The integrated design ensures synchronous operation of all components while maintaining structural integrity across varying extension.

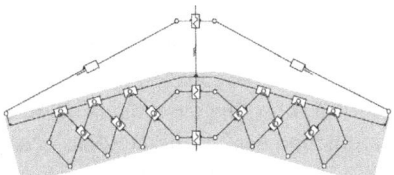

Fig. 3. Length adjustment mechanism

3 Kinematic Analysis of Morphing Mechanism

The complete kinematic diagram of the morphing wing mechanism is illustrated in Fig. 4. Each double-curved straight shear unit and its connected parallelogram unit are independently driven by motors positioned at the wing root. When maintaining constant wing span while adjusting sweep angle, a servo motor actuates the lead screw rotation. Through the lead screw-nut transmission mechanism, the entire wing assembly is propelled along sliding rails, with the telescopic sleeve functioning as a compliant follower to coordinate motion, thereby achieving dynamic sweep angle modulation. Specifically, reduced sweep angle enhances lift-to-drag ratio during low-speed flight, while increased sweep angle minimizes aerodynamic resistance in high-speed conditions.

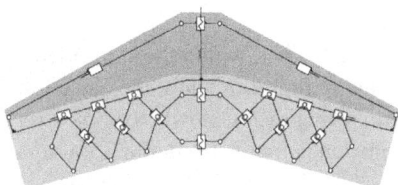

Fig. 4. Schematic diagram of the motion of the morphing wing mechanism

Conversely, when preserving sweep angle while modifying wing span, an identical servo motor drives lead screw rotation. However, the bidirectional lead screw-nut mechanism engages the double-curved straight shear units to actuate scissor linkages, enabling span adjustment. Wing extension increases span length to improve lift-to-drag ratio for extended range and endurance, whereas retraction reduces span to decrease drag and enhance maneuverability. Figure 5 demonstrates the operational effects of span and sweep angle variations.

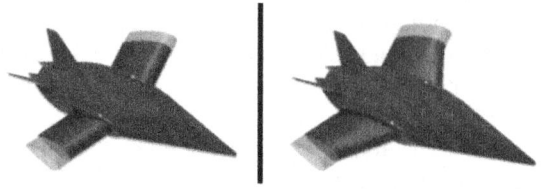

Fig. 5. Wing span and sweep angle variation effect diagram

The planar deployable reconfigurable wing mechanism comprises sequentially connected double-curved straight shear units and identical parallelogram units through revolute joints. This study focuses on analyzing individual double-curved straight shear units and parallelogram deformation modules. As all motions occur within a single plane, the mechanism is simplified to a planar linkage problem. For analytical convenience, the unit mechanism is reduced to the kinematic diagram shown in Fig. 6, consisting of fixed-length rod BD, 150° angled rod ACF, variable-length rods OA and OB. Line CH is fixed with 15° inclination relative to the x-axis, while GH remains a constant-length rod. Geometric equivalences are maintained with $l_{AC} = l_{BC} = l_{CD} = l_{CF}$ to ensure symmetric deformation characteristics.

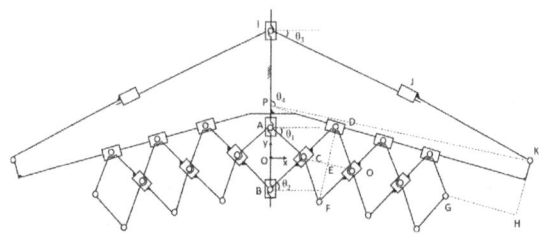

Fig. 6. Kinematic diagram of the morphing wing mechanism

A coordinate system is established within the simplified mechanism diagram of the unit structure. In this schematic representation, the closed-loop vector equation of the mechanism is systematically developed using the complex vector method. Critical links and angular parameters are mathematically defined through geometric relationships, leading to the formulation of the PBD closed-loop vector equation:

$$\vec{PB} + \vec{BD} = \vec{PD} \tag{1}$$

The closed-loop vector position equation for the morphing wing unit mechanism is expressed as Eq. (1). This equation is rewritten in complex vector form as:

$$(l_{PO} + l_{OB})e^{i\frac{\pi}{2}} + 2l_{BC}e^{i\theta_2} = l_{PD}e^{i\frac{5}{12}\pi} \tag{2}$$

Utilizing Euler's formula:

$$e^{i\theta} = \cos\theta + i\sin\theta \tag{3}$$

The real and imaginary parts are separated to obtain:

$$\begin{cases} 2l_{BC}\cos\theta_2 - l_{PD}\cos\frac{5\pi}{12} = 0 \\ l_{PO} + l_{OB} + 2l_{BC}\sin\theta_2 - l_{PD}\sin\frac{5\pi}{12} = 0 \end{cases} \tag{4}$$

Based on geometric relationships, the following are obtained:

$$\begin{cases} \overrightarrow{BC_x} = l_{AC}\cos\theta_2 \\ \overrightarrow{CE_x} = l_{CD}\cos\left[\frac{1}{2}\left(\frac{\pi}{6} + \theta_1 + \theta_2\right)\right]\cos\frac{\pi}{12} \end{cases} \tag{5}$$

This yields the expression for unilateral wingspan:

$$BH_x = \left(\frac{2l_{BC}\cos\theta_2}{\cos\frac{5\pi}{12}} + 5l_{CD}\cos\left[\frac{1}{2}\left(\frac{\pi}{6} + \theta_1 + \theta_2\right)\right] + l_{GH}\right)\cos\frac{\pi}{12} \tag{6}$$

This equation reveals the relationship between the unilateral wingspan and both θ_1 and θ_2. Through application of the cosine theorem, the following relationships are derived:

$$\begin{cases} l_{PD} = \sqrt{(l_{OP} + l_{OB})^2 + l_{BD}^2 - 2l_{BD}(l_{OP} + l_{OB})\sin\theta_2} \\ l_{BD} = \sqrt{(l_{OP} + l_{OB})^2 + l_{PD}^2 - 2l_{PD}(l_{OP} + l_{OB})\cos\frac{5\pi}{12}} \end{cases} \tag{7}$$

After rearrangement, we obtain:

$$(l_{OP} + l_{OB}) - 2l_{AC}\sin\theta_2 = \cos\frac{5\pi}{12}\sqrt{(l_{OP} + l_{OB})^2 + 4l_{AC}^2 - 2l_{BD}(l_{OP} + l_{OB})\sin\theta_2} \tag{8}$$

The variation curve of unilateral wingspan with respect to is shown in Fig. 7, as validated through simulation analysis.

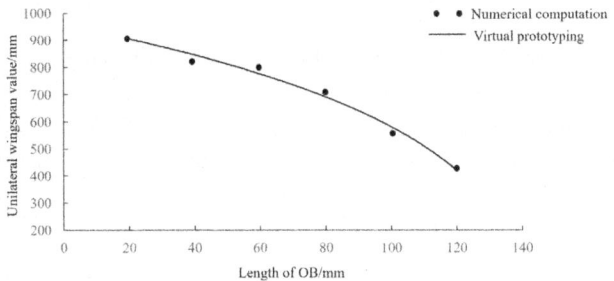

Fig. 7. Spread length varies with input drive curve

Similarly, the sweep angle variation mechanism is analyzed as follows:

Given that IP and JK are variable-length links, IJ and KP are fixed-length links, and $\theta_4 = 105°$, the vector equation is established as follows:

$$\overrightarrow{IP} + \overrightarrow{PK} = \overrightarrow{IK} \tag{9}$$

The above equation represents the closed-loop vector position equation of the variable-sweep mechanism for the morphing wing. Rewriting the equation in complex vector form:

$$l_{IP} e^{i(-\frac{\pi}{2})} + l_{PK} e^{i\theta_4} = (l_{IJ} + l_{JK}) e^{i\theta_3} \tag{10}$$

Using Euler's formula, the real and imaginary components are separated:

$$\begin{cases} l_{PK} \sin\theta_4 - l_{IP} - (l_{IJ} + l_{JK}) \sin\theta_3 = 0 \\ l_{PK} \cos\theta_4 - (l_{IJ} + l_{JK}) \cos\theta_3 = 0 \end{cases} \tag{11}$$

Further derivation yields:

$$\begin{cases} l_{JK} = \dfrac{l_{PK} \sin\theta_4 - l_{IP}}{\sin\theta_3} - l_{IP} \\ \theta_3 = \cos^{-1} \dfrac{l_{P_1 K} \cos\theta_4}{l_{IJ} + l_{JK}} \end{cases} \tag{12}$$

Simulation analysis validates that the variation of sweep angle θ_3 with the displacement of point P follows the curve shown in Fig. 8.

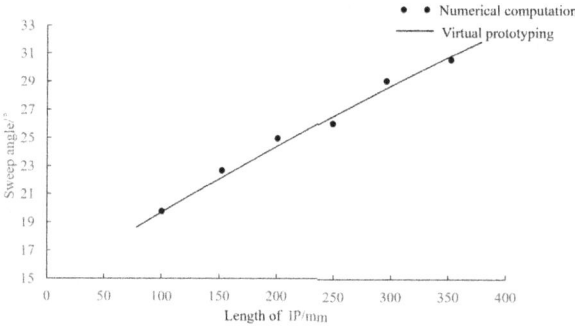

Fig. 8. Sweep Angle changes with input drive curve

Kinematic analysis of the morphing wing was conducted using ADAMS dynamics simulation software. By setting the length variation rate of l_{OB} (i.e., the velocity of point B) as shown in Fig. 9.

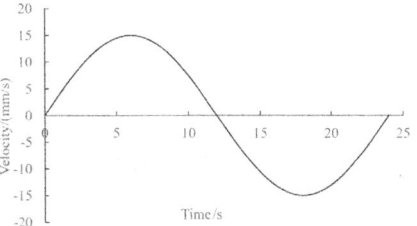

Fig. 9. The velocity of point B

The displacement, velocity, and acceleration curves of the unilateral wingspan variation were obtained (Fig. 10).

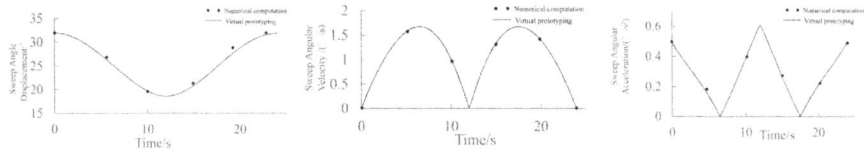

Fig. 10. Curve of displacement, velocity and acceleration with variation of unilateral span

Similarly, configuring the length variation rate of (i.e., the velocity of point P) as illustrated in Fig. 11.

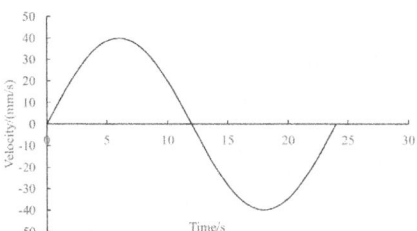

Fig. 11. The velocity of point P

Produced angular displacement, angular velocity, and angular acceleration curves for sweep angle variation (Fig. 12).

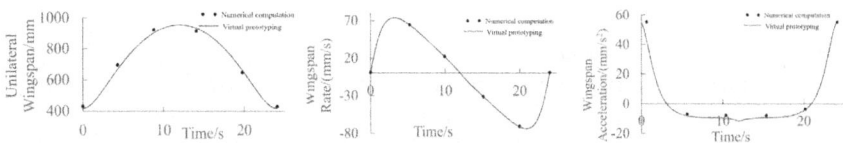

Fig. 12. The angular displacement, velocity and acceleration of sweep Angle change

The motion trajectory, velocity, and acceleration characteristics derived from the kinematic analysis confirm that the mechanism satisfies both design objectives and functional requirements during operation.

4 Static and Modal Analysis of Morphing Mechanism

Static simulation enables the analysis of stress distribution and load-bearing capacity of the morphing wing under various static loading conditions. This capability is crucial for ensuring structural integrity under anticipated operational loads while preventing failure. Additionally, static analysis evaluates the structural stability to maintain aerodynamic integrity during external force application, thereby guaranteeing normal flight performance.

A finite element simulation model of the morphing wing mechanism was developed using FEA software, with meshing results illustrated in Fig. 13.

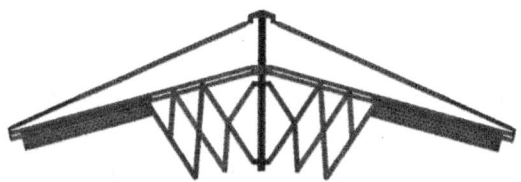

Fig. 13. Finite element meshing diagram of deformable wing mechanism

Static simulation of the morphing wing mechanism was conducted. During preprocessing, considering the alloy material used in actual wing structures, the material of the morphing wing mechanism was defined as aluminum alloy. A uniformly distributed upward load was applied to the lower surfaces of all rib plates. The lift direction and loading positions are shown in Fig. 14.

Fig. 14. Lift direction and lift loading position

Herein, to establish a standardized evaluation framework for assessing the stiffness of the morphing wing mechanism across both simulation and physical prototypes with different materials, a dimensionless parameter—load factor Lg—is proposed. This parameter is defined as the ratio of aerodynamic lift L to structural weight G, expressed mathematically as:

$$L_g = \frac{L}{G} \tag{13}$$

The simulation load parameter Lg for the morphing wing mechanism was set to 10, corresponding to an aerodynamic lift force of 362 N (10 times the structural weight). Static structural simulation under this lift condition yielded strain contour plots as shown in Fig. 15.

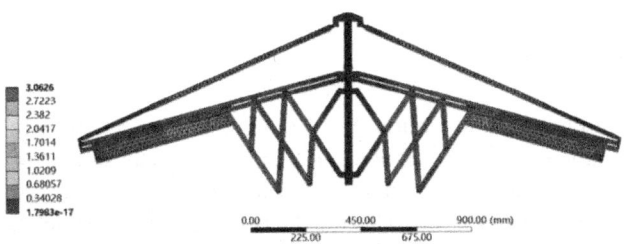

Fig. 15. Static simulation results

The results demonstrate that under loading conditions, maximum deformation occurs at the wingtip, while all structural deformations remain within acceptable safety margins.

A finite element model of the reconfigurable morphing wing mechanism was developed using FEA software, followed by dynamic characteristic simulations focusing on natural frequencies and mode shapes. Figure 16 displays the first eight natural frequencies (16.91 Hz to 53.90 Hz) and corresponding mode shapes under high-sweep, short-span configuration, all residing within the operational range of same-scale aircraft engineering applications.

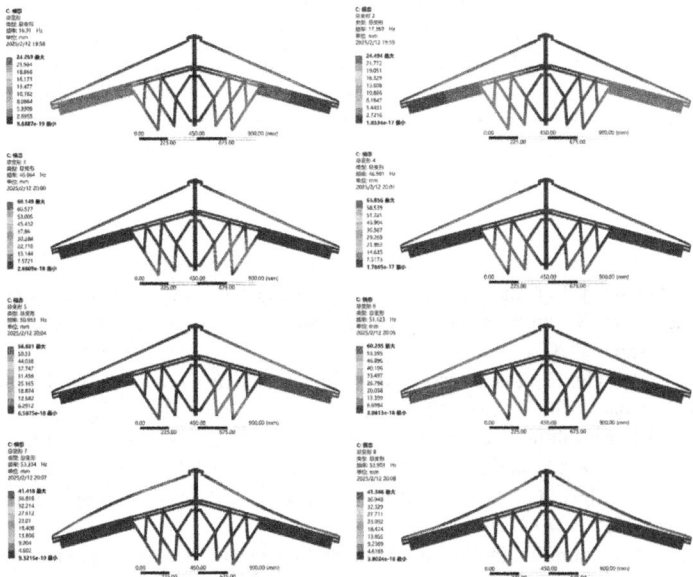

Fig. 16. Modal simulation of morphing wing mechanism

Notably, the 3rd mode demonstrates the maximum deformation magnitude of 65.856 mm at its natural frequency of 46.901 Hz. To prevent resonance-induced structural failure, operational practice must ensure avoidance of frequency matching between the mechanism's natural frequencies (especially critical modes like the 3rd) and external excitation frequencies.

5 Conclusions

This study presents a multiparameter reconfigurable morphing wing mechanism for variable-geometry aircraft, capable of simultaneous adjustment of sweep angle, wingspan, and wing area. Through highly integrated mechanism design, dynamic modulation of aerodynamic parameters during flight has been achieved. Simulation results confirm the mechanism's excellent structural stiffness and sufficient load-bearing capacity, validating its engineering feasibility.

The proposed reconfigurable morphing wing mechanism establishes a novel design paradigm for next-generation aircraft, significantly enriching the theoretical framework and methodological approaches for morphing-wing development. The innovative architecture demonstrates multi-parameter coupling control capabilities, with future research directions focusing on: Intelligent control strategies for enhanced autonomy levels and mission adaptability. Morphing efficiency optimization through lightweight design and energy consumption minimization. Multi-physics coupling analysis to address complex flight condition requirements. These advancements aim to expand operational envelopes while ensuring structural reliability across diverse flight regimes.

Acknowledgment. This work is supported by National Natural Science Foundation of China (Grant No. 52175019), Beijing Natural Science Foundations (Grant No. L222038), Beijing Nova Programme Interdisciplinary Cooperation Project (20240484699), Beijing Municipal Key Laboratory of Space-ground Interconnection and Convergence of China and Key Laboratory of IoT Monitoring and Early Warning, Ministry of Emergency Management.

References

1. Duan, F.H., Chu, Y.T., Guan, W.Q., et al.: A comprehensive review on development status of morphing wings. Mech. Electr. Eng. Technol. **50**(1), 12–18 (2021). https://doi.org/10.1234/morphwing-review-2021
2. Chu, L., Li, Q., Gu, F., et al.: Design, modeling, and control of morphing aircraft: a review. Chin. J. Aeronaut. **35**(05), 220–246 (2022)
3. Friswell, M.I.: Morphing aircraft: an improbable dream. In: Proceedings of the ASME 2014 Conference on Smart Materials, Adaptive Structures and Intelligent Systems, pp. 1–7 (2014)
4. Barbarino, S., Bilgen, O., Ajaj, R.M., et al.: A review of morphing aircraft. J. Intell. Mater. Syst. Struct. **22**, 823–877 (2011)
5. Wang, L.J.: Configuration Design and Simulation Analysis of UAV Morphing Wing. Harbin Institute of Technology, Harbin (2014)
6. Zhang, Z.H.: Research on Telescopic Morphing Wing with Continuous Aerodynamic Surface. Harbin Institute of Technology, Harbin (2019)

7. Reed Jr., J.L., Hemmelgarn, C.D., Pelley, B.M., et al.: Adaptive wing structures. In: Smart Structures and Materials 2005: Industrial and Commercial Applications of Smart Structures Technologies, vol. 5762, pp. 132–142. SPIE, San Diego (2005)
8. Li, M.: Design and Optimization of a Shear Sliding Skin Variable Sweep Wing Based on Thermal-FluidSolid Multi-Field Coupling Analysis. Harbin Institute of Technology, Harbin (2021)
9. Lu, Y.P., He, Z., Lyu, Y.: Morphing aircraft technology. Aviat. Manuf. Technol. **51**(22), 26–29 (2008). https://doi.org/10.1234/amt-morph-2008
10. Elzey, D.M., Sofla, A.Y.N., Wadley, H.N.G.: A bioinspired high-authority actuator for shape morphing structures. In: Smart Structures and Materials 2003: Active Materials: Behavior and Mechanics, vol. 5053, pp. 92–100. SPIE, San Diego (2003)
11. Manzo, J., Garcia, E.: Demonstration of an in situ morphing hyper elliptical cambered span wing mechanism. Smart Mater. Struct. **19**(2), 2–12 (2010)
12. Lazos, S.: Biologically inspired fixed-wing configuration studies. J. Aircr. **42**(5), 1089–1098 (2005)
13. Wang, Y.F., Xiao, H., Yang, G., et al.: Structural design and distributed actuation configuration of parallel-linkage morphing wing. J. Harbin Inst. Technol. **54**(01), 65–72 (2022). https://doi.org/10.1234/jhit-parallel-2022
14. Xiao, H., Guo, H.W., Zhang, D., et al.: Tetrahedral cell-based morphing wing truss structure design and analysis. Chin. J. Aeronaut. **43**(7), 425391 (2022)
15. Moosavian, A., Xi, F., Hashemi, S.: Design and motion control of fully variable morphing wings. J. Aircr. **50**(4), 11891201 (2013)
16. Tian, D.K., Zhang, J.W., Jin, L., et al.: Design and analysis of morphing wing mechanism based on equilateral Bennett linkage. J. Beijing Univ. Aeronaut. Astronaut., 1–18 (2025)
17. Joo, J.J., Sanders, B.: Optimal location of distributed actuators within an in-plane multi-cell morphing mechanism. J. Intell. Mater. Syst. Struct. **20**(4), 481 (2009)
18. Wu, B., Du, X.Z., Wang, J.X., et al.: Advances in smart structural technology for morphing aircraft. Aeronaut. Sci. Technol. **33**(12), 13–30 (2022)
19. Guo, S.J.: Research on Coordinated Flight Control for Morphing Vehicles. Nanjing University of Aeronautics and Astronautics, Nanjing (2012). https://doi.org/10.1234/nuaa-flight-coord-2012

Experimental Study and Analysis of Wheel-Terrain Interaction for Crewed Lunar Vehicle Based on Single-Wheel Testbed

Xinrui Wu, Huaiguang Yang[✉], Liang Ding, Lintao Yang, Jianguo Tao, Haibo Gao, Zhehao Qiao, Ruyi Zhou, and Zongquan Deng

State Key Laboratory of Robotics and System, Harbin Institute of Technology, Harbin 150001, China
yanghuaiguang@hit.edu.cn

Abstract. The crewed lunar vehicle (CLV) is an essential equipment for crewed lunar landing, as its mobility significantly expands the astronauts' exploration range. Studying the wheel–terrain interaction through experimental methods has become the current research trend in the design of CLVs. This study investigates the wheel–terrain mechanical properties of CLVs under high-speed and heavy-load conditions. A wheel–terrain mechanics testbed for CLVs is developed. Using this testbed, experiments are conducted by controlling a wheel under varying loads (500–3000 N), angular velocities (0.5–3 rad/s), and slip ratios (0–0.6). Data on wheel–terrain interaction parameters (drawbar pull, wheel sinkage, and driving resistance moment) are collected for analysis. The results reveal that traction performance decreases with increasing velocity, and initially increases then decreases with increasing load. Finally, based on the experimental data, the conventional semi-empirical model of wheel–terrain mechanics is revised. The prediction accuracies of the revised model for driving resistance moment, wheel sinkage, and drawbar pull are 15.9%, 12.9%, and 26.7%, respectively, showing significant improvements over conventional models.

Keywords: Crewed Lunar Vehicle · Terramechanics · Single-Wheel Testbed · Wheel-Terrain Interaction

1 Introduction

Lunar scientific exploration, as a focus of deep space exploration, has attracted significant global attention in recent years. As a critical transport equipment, the crewed lunar vehicle (CLV) plays a vital role in extending astronauts' exploration range and operational capabilities, enabling the transport of lunar samples and scientific instruments, and contributing to the construction of future lunar bases [1, 2]. Therefore, enhancing the mobility of the CLV is a key objective in its development. Moreover, the lunar surface is characterized by a rough terrain covered with soft regolith, which poses a significant challenge to the CLV's mobility [3].

To enhance the mobility performance of lunar vehicles, it is essential to conduct research in simulation, mechanical design and control, and there are many research works in these aspects [4–6]. Terramechanics is employed to analyze the effects of soil properties and driving conditions on wheel–terrain interaction through experimental and theoretical approaches. Conducting terramechanics experimental and theoretical studies on CLVs can improve simulation fidelity, support optimal wheel and suspension design, and enhance the robustness of stability control systems by incorporating force feedback mechanisms.

Currently, experimental and theoretical studies on wheel–terrain interaction have been extensively conducted for unmanned planetary rovers [7–9], whereas research on CLVs remains relatively limited. According to some design indicators [10–12], CLVs exhibit single-wheel loads ranging from several hundred to several thousand newtons, drive speeds of approximately 0.5–5 m/s, and wheel diameters typically between 600–1200 mm—all significantly larger than those of unmanned rovers. These differences necessitate the development of dedicated experimental methods for CLVs, particularly the design of single-wheel testbed. The earliest relevant research was conducted by M.G. Bekker [13], whose experiments and theoretical analyses provided foundational references for the design of the Apollo Lunar Roving Vehicle (LRV). Apostolopoulos [14] developed a circular single-wheel testbed to evaluate the drive power and endurance of the Nomad lunar rover's drive unit. In more recent studies, Jianzhong Zhu et al. [15] used a single-pass testbed to validate a proposed model describing the interaction between the flexible wheel and soil. The experimental results further informed wheel design. Zhongchao Liang conducted single-wheel experiments using a linear single-pass testbed and a mesh-patterned wheel. Based on the collected data, he revised the wheel–terrain mechanics model [16] and proposed a method for predicting acceleration from wheel torque [17].

Although previous studies have established experimental methods and conducted analyses on wheel–terrain interaction for CLVs, detailed investigations into the effects of load and travel speed remain insufficient. Therefore, this paper presents an experimental method for investigating wheel–terrain interaction in CLVs, based on an independently developed testbed. Experiments are conducted to analyze the effects of load, wheel speed, and slip ratio on wheel–terrain interaction, and the semi-empirical wheel–terrain interaction model is revised using the obtained experimental data.

2 Experimental Method for Investigating Wheel–Terrain Interaction in Crewed Lunar Vehicles

2.1 Wheel-Terrain Interaction Testbed for CLVs

Unlike conventional linear testbeds, the form of circular motion is opted in our testbed, which effectively saves field space while ensuring sufficient travel range, is suitable for experiment at high speeds, and is capable of endurance testing and fatigue testing. Although a circular motion cannot be exactly equivalent to a linear motion, the degree of freedom in the direction of the wheel axis is limited, so it can be assumed that the lateral force is provided by the testbed rather than the terrain, and that the lateral force is perpendicular to the wheel plane, there is no effect on the measurement of normal force, drawbar pull and driving resistance moment exerted by the terrain on the wheels.

Table 1 shows the design objectives of the testbed. To ensure that the circular motion can be approximated as a straight linear motion, the distance traveled of a wheel in one revolution should not be less than twice its circumference, a length of 8.8 m calculated from the maximum wheel diameter. In addition, to ensure a valid data acquisition duration of at least 3 s and to account for the wheel's acceleration phase—reaching a maximum velocity of 3 m/s under an acceleration of 0.3 g—calculations indicate that the required rotational circumference is 10.5 m, corresponding to a minimum rotation radius of 1.67 m.

Table 1. Design objectives of single-wheel testbed

Parameter	Value
Radius of circular motion (m)	1.67
Wheel loading range (N)	1000–3000
Maximum wheel angular velocity (rad/s)	7.5
Maximum linear velocity of wheel (m/s)	3
Allowable diameter range of wheel (mm)	800–1400

The testbed built from the above design requirements, as shown in Fig. 1, is arranged on a 4.8 m × 4.8 m field paved with lunar soil simulant, and consisted primarily of a rotation shaft, lifter, wheel shaft, loading cylinder, soil leveling mechanism, etc., along with sensors mounted on the mechanical structure, electrical sections, and pneumatic sections. The rotation shaft, arranged in the center of the field, extends forward with a cantilever beam driving the testbed in a circular motion. The lifter can drive the wheel shaft up and down to adjust the height of the wheel. At the same time, there is 200 mm of free movement between the wheel shaft and the lifter, ensuring the wheels can sink freely. Since the maximum load applied to the wheel is 3000 N, applying the load via counterweights is impractical. Therefore, the wheel load is controlled by adjusting the pressure of a pneumatic cylinder. The soil leveling mechanism is an adjustable-height scraper blade used to flatten the soil surface.

Some sensors are carried on testbed. The triaxial force sensor, mounted between the cylinder and the wheel shaft, measures the normal force and drawbar pull at the wheel shaft. Two rotation speed and torque sensors, mounted at the wheel shaft and at the rotation shaft, measure the wheel velocity and driving torque. Linear displacement sensor is used to measure wheel sinkage. Such that all data of the wheel-terrain interaction can be measured. Motion control of the testbed is achieved via a control software on an IPC, on which the collected experiment data is also displayed in real time.

Table 2 shows the main technical parameters of the testbed, including the performance parameters of sensors.

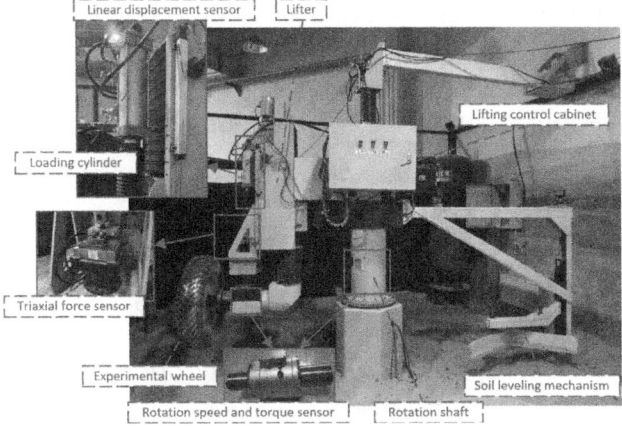

Fig. 1. Wheel-terrain interaction testbed

Table 2. Main technical parameters of the testbed

Parameter		Value
Radius of circular motion (m)		1.7
Wheel loading range (N)		0–3000
Maximum wheel angular velocity (rad/s)		7.5
Maximum linear velocity of wheel (m/s)		3
Allowable diameter range of wheel (mm)		800–1400
Data sampling frequency (Hz)		16
Range and accuracy of Sensors	Triaxial force sensor	4 kN, <0.15% FS
	Linear displacement sensor	325 mm, ±0.04 mm
	Torque sensor in wheel shaft	2000 Nm, 0.1~0.5% FS
	Rotation speed sensor in wheel shaft	2500 r/min, 0.1~0.5% FS
	Torque sensor in rotation shaft	5000 Nm, 0.1~0.5% FS
	Rotation speed sensor in rotation shaft	2500 r/min, 0.1~0.5% FS

2.2 Planetary Soil Simulant and Experimental Wheel

The planetary soil simulant HIT-MSS1 used in the experiment is the same as used in our previous work [18]. The physical property parameters are shown in Table 3.

In this paper, we study the effect of load and velocity on the wheel-terrain interaction, so to rule out the effect of wheel deformation, a rigid metal wheels with lugs is used as shown in Fig. 2, with reference to the performance indicators of a CLV. The wheel is drum shaped, with a maximum radius of 420 mm and a width of 250 mm. 24 lugs of 10 mm height and 10 mm thickness are evenly spaced on the wheel surfaces.

Table 3. Physical and mechanical parameters of planetary soil simulant [18]

Terrain	k_c (kPa/m^{n-1})	k_φ (kPa/m^n)	n	c (Pa)	φ (°)	K (m)
HIT-MSS1	13.6 ± 0.8	2259.1 ± 8.0	0.92 ± 0.08	462.3 ± 74.5	35.0 ± 1.6	0.0150

Fig. 2. Experimental wheel

2.3 Experimental Procedure

The experimental procedure is described as follows.

(1) Test preparation. First, pre-charge the pressure vessel to the required pressure level and power on the industrial PC and testbed. Then open the testbed control software to input the wheel size, rotation radius, and data file save path.
(2) Calibrate the zero point of sensors. First adjust the cylinder to lift the wheel off the ground, and keep the wheel force balanced, at this time clear the value of triaxial force sensor. Then drop the soil scraper and control the testbed rotation to level the soil, slowly lower the wheel until it is just in contact with the soil, using this height as the zero position of wheel sinkage.
(3) Applied wheel loads. Adjust the air pressure in the cylinders, making the display of the force sensor to agree with the wheel load target setting.
(4) Formal experiment. Set wheel angular and linear velocity. Start to record data before testbed motion, stop the motion after one revolution, then stop data recording.
(5) After one experiment, raise the wheels off the ground with the cylinder and drop the soil scraper to the same height as before, rotate the testbed to re level the soil, and repeat (3) (4) steps for the next experiment.

Some photos during the experiment are shown in Fig. 3. After the experiment is completed, the data are processed: selecting the data of wheel velocity and sinkage stabilization period, and the collected sinkage, drawbar pull and resistance moment are averaged as the wheel-terrain interaction data under the experiment condition.

  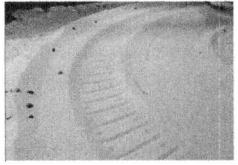

(a) Leveling the soil   (b) Testbed rotation   (c) Rut track

Fig. 3. Photos of the experimental procedure

2.4 Design of Experiments

To analyze the effect of wheel load and speed on wheel-terrain interaction, control wheel load in the range of 500–3000 N and wheel angular velocity in the range of 0.5–3 rad/s with reference to the design performance indicators of CLVs. In addition, the slip ratio is considered as an important factor affecting the wheel-terrain interaction, as defined by Eq. (1). Vary the wheel slip ratio in the 0–0.6 range by controlling the rotational speed of the testbed and the wheel. Experiments are carried out with all the combinations of experimental conditions, measuring the normal forces, drawbar pull, resistance moment (equal to driving torque) and sinkage of the wheel in the experiment. The specific design of experiments is shown in Table 4.

$$s = \begin{cases} (r\omega - v)/r\omega & (r\omega \geq v, 0 \leq s \leq 1) \\ (r\omega - v)/v & (r\omega < v, -1 \leq s < 0) \end{cases} \quad (1)$$

Table 4. Design of experiments

Experimental condition	Wheel load (N)	Slip ratio (s)	Angular velocity (rad/s)
Value	500, 1000, 1500, 2000, 2500, 3000	0, 0.1, 0.2, 0.3, 0.4, 0.5, 0.6	0.5, 1.0, 1.5, 2.0, 2.5, 3.0

3 Analysis of Experimental Results of Wheel-Terrain Interaction for CLVs

3.1 Effect of Slip Ratio on Wheel-Terrain Interaction

Figure 4 shows the effect of slip ratio on results at 1.5 rad/s. In (a) the wheel sinkage increases with the increasing slip ratio; The resistance moment increases, and its slope decreases; The drawbar pull basically increases with the increasing slip ratio, but with the increase of load, the trend of slope with slip ratio gradually changes from decreasing all the way to decreasing first and increasing later. Combined with the change rule of sinkage with slip ratio, it is shown that the large sinkage generated by the wheel cannot be converted into effective traction, but may cause the vehicle to sink at lower loads;

However, at higher levels of loading, the slope of the drawbar pull curve decreases first and then increases with increasing slip ratio, this phenomenon usually occurs at higher slip ratios ($s > 0.6$), and thus has some tolerance to the rules at low speeds with light loads, indicating that the wheel-terrain interaction is more sensitive to slip ratios under heavy load and high speed conditions as soil flowability increases.

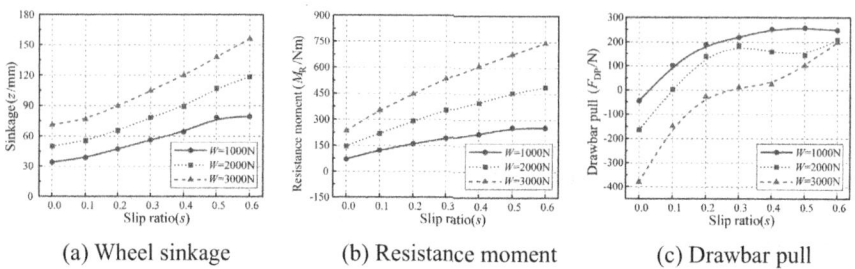

(a) Wheel sinkage (b) Resistance moment (c) Drawbar pull

Fig. 4. Influence of slip ratio on experimental results

3.2 Effect of Wheel Load on Wheel-Terrain Interaction

Figure 5 shows the effect of wheel load on the experimental results, where the wheel rotation angular velocities are all 1.0 rad/s. It can be found that with the increasing load, the wheel sinkage and resistance moment increase, and the change trend is approximately linear; While the drawbar pull decreases gradually with the increasing load or first increases and then decreases, the slope of the curve decreases gradually, and the curve shape gradually changes from decreasing to first increasing and then decreasing with the increasing slip ratio, which can be understood as increasing with slip ratio, the pole position of the curve moves towards the larger load. This may be due to an increase in wheel sinkage caused by increasing load, resulting in a significant increase in resistance of the soil on wheel, while the positive traction exerted by the soil on the wheel varies less. But on the other hand, at higher slip ratio, the soil is sheared sufficiently, and the increase in load increases the shear stress of the soil, which in turn results in an increase in drawbar pull. This phenomenon is caused by the combined effects of both roles.

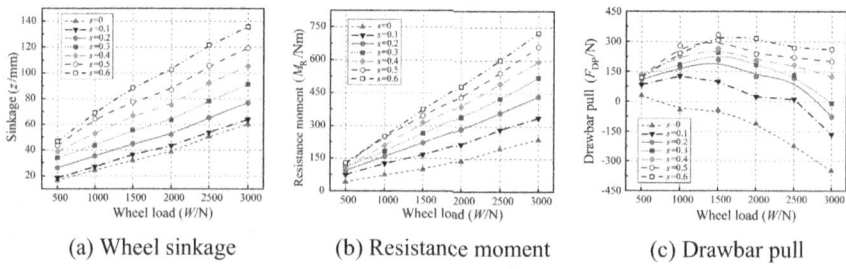

(a) Wheel sinkage (b) Resistance moment (c) Drawbar pull

Fig. 5. Influence of wheel load on experimental results

3.3 Effect of Wheel Angular Velocity on Wheel-Terrain Interaction

Figure 6 shows the effect of the wheel angular velocity on the experimental results, where the normal loads are both 2500 N. It is clear from the figure that the wheel resistance moment and sinkage change little with angular velocity, which is consistent with some experimental results of previous unmanned planetary vehicles [19]; On the other hand, the drawbar pull has an obvious decreasing trend with increasing angular velocity, and the trend is basically linear, decreasing by about 200 N from 0.5 to 3 rad/s at the same slip ratio. However, for unmanned planetary rovers, due to the very small level and range of angular velocity, the influence on the drawbar pull is usually negligible. Interestingly, this phenomenon has also been found in studies of unmanned planetary rover by David [20] et al. Therefore, it can be argued that this speed effect is a significant difference between a planetary rover in high-speed motion and a low-speed one, after which it is necessary to conduct in-depth studies to analyze the mechanism of this effect. This phenomenon illustrates that for a CLV, increasing travel speed often requires sacrificing traction performance.

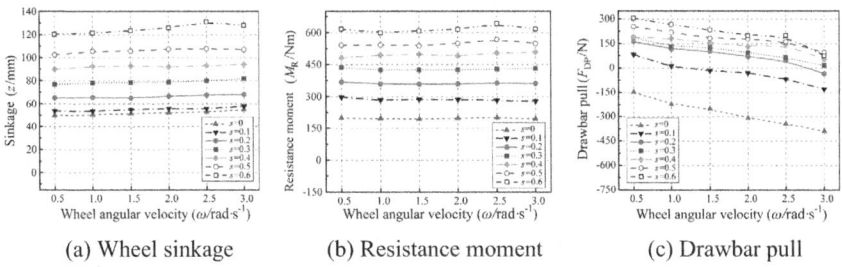

(a) Wheel sinkage   (b) Resistance moment   (c) Drawbar pull

Fig. 6. Influence of wheel angular velocity on experimental results

4 Modeling of the Wheel-Terrain Interaction for CLVs

4.1 Introduction to the Theory of Wheel-Terrain Mechanical Model

Figure 7 shows the stress distribution and concentrated force from the terrain that act on a wheel as proposed by Wong and Reece [21]. According to this theory, the wheel is subjected to normal and shear stresses exerted by the soil, distributed in the region between θ_1 and θ_2, with the maximum stress at θ_m, calculated by Eqs. (2)–(4). Where c_1, c_2 and c_3 are all empirical parameters. To facilitate later parameter identification, let c_2 be taken as 0, and this approximation is usually reasonable.

$$\theta_1 = \mathrm{acos}(1 - z/r) \qquad (2)$$

$$\theta_2 = c_3 \theta_1 \qquad (3)$$

$$\theta_m = (c_1 + c_2 s)\theta_1 \qquad (4)$$

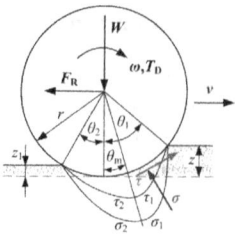

Fig. 7. Wheel-terrain mechanics model[9]

The normal stress distribution function is Eq. (5). Ding replaces the soil physical parameter n in the Wong-Reece model with N varying with the slip ratios, allowing the model to predict slip-sinkage, as shown in Eq. (6) [9]:

$$\begin{cases} \sigma_1(\theta) = (\dfrac{k_c}{b} + k_\phi) r^N (\cos\theta - \cos\theta_1)^N & (\theta_m \leq \theta \leq \theta_1) \\ \sigma_2(\theta) = (\dfrac{k_c}{b} + k_\phi) r^N \{\cos[\theta_1 - \dfrac{\theta - \theta_2}{\theta_m - \theta_2}(\theta_1 - \theta_m)] - \cos\theta_1\}^N & (\theta_2 \leq \theta < \theta_m) \end{cases} \quad (5)$$

$$N = n_0 + n_1 s \quad (6)$$

According to the Janosi formula [22], the shear stress is calculated with Eq. (7), where K is the shear modulus, and j is the shear displacement of the soil, shown in Eq. (8).

$$\tau(\theta) = [c + \sigma(\theta)\tan\varphi] \times \{1 - \exp(-j/K)\} \quad (7)$$

$$j(\theta) = r[(\theta_1 - \theta) - (1 - s)(\sin\theta_1 - \sin\theta)] \quad (8)$$

For the wheel with lugs, Ding gives the following equations for shear stress:

$$j(\theta) = r_s[(\theta'_1 - \theta) - (1 - s)(\sin\theta'_1 - \sin\theta)] \quad (9)$$

$$\theta'_1 = \operatorname{acos}[(r - z)/R_j] \quad (10)$$

$$R_j = \begin{cases} r + h & (0 \leq s \leq s_{j1}) \\ r + h(s_{j2} - s)/(s_{j2} - s_{j1}) & (s_{j1} < s < s_{j2}) \\ r & (s_{j2} \leq s \leq 1) \end{cases} \quad (11)$$

$$r_s = r + \lambda_s h \quad (12)$$

The parameter h in Eq. (11) is the height of wheel lugs. s_{j1} and s_{j2} are the transition slip ratios empirically determined, taking 0.2 and 0.5, respectively, in the calculation of Sect. 4.2. λ_s is a coefficient between 0 and 1, taken as 0.5 for later calculations.

Integrating normal and shear stresses, gives the drawbar pull F_{DP}, normal force F_N, and resistance moment M_R, exerted by the soil on the wheel, which are balanced with the resistance force F_R, the normal load W, and the driving torque T_D at the wheel shaft, respectively, as in Eq. (13).

$$\begin{cases} F_N = b\{ \int_{\theta_2}^{\theta_m} [r\sigma_2(\theta)\cos\theta + r_s\tau_2(\theta)\sin\theta]d\theta + \int_{\theta_m}^{\theta_1} [r\sigma_1(\theta)\cos\theta + r_s\tau_1(\theta)\sin\theta]d\theta \} \\ F_{DP} = b\{ \int_{\theta_2}^{\theta_m} [r_s\tau_2(\theta)\cos\theta - r\sigma_2(\theta)\sin\theta]d\theta + \int_{\theta_m}^{\theta_1} [r_s\tau_1(\theta)\cos\theta - r\sigma_1(\theta)\sin\theta]d\theta \} \\ M_R = r_s^2 b\{ \int_{\theta_2}^{\theta_m} \tau_2(\theta)d\theta + \int_{\theta_m}^{\theta_1} \tau_1(\theta)d\theta \} \end{cases} \quad (13)$$

4.2 Revision of Wheel-Terrain Mechanical Model

The wheel-terrain mechanical model contains many soil physical parameters and empirical parameters. Here, the parameters N, K, c_1 and c_3, which have a great influence on the stress distribution, are identified. Using the least squares method, the identification range includes all data at slip ratios from 0.1 to 0.6, loads from 1000 N to 3000 N, and rotation angular velocities from 0.5 to 3 rad/s.

Because the model is a system of integral equations, each parameter affects the three integration result, there is some coupling between these parameters, so after parameter identification of all data points, we mean K and c_1 in them back to the model, then identify n and c_3. The results of K and c_1 in the first identification are shown in the Table 5. It is important to note that the identified K is larger than the soil physical parameter (0.015 m), one reasonable explanation is that at higher loads and velocities, the shear displacement j is smaller due to the intensification of soil flow.

Table 5. Identification results of K and c_1

Parameter	K	c_1
Maximum	0.0059	0.9000
Minimum	0.0030	0.2438
Average value	0.0356	0.5999
Standard deviation	0.0119	0.1096
Approximate value	0.0356	0.6000

Substituting the average values of K and c_1 back to the model for a second identification, it is found that N has a linear relationship with the slip ratio, as shown in the Fig. 8(a), which basically agrees with Ding's theory, and the shape of the line remains consistent at different loads and velocities. After averaging the results corresponding to the same slip ratios, the fitted values of n_0 and n_1 are 0.873 and 0.793, respectively.

Substitute the fitted N back to identify c_3. Because c_3 doesn't vary with slip ratio according to Wong-Reece model, average the results at same slip ratios and fit c_3 according to Eq. (14). The fit results are shown in Table 6 and Fig. 8(b). To unify the units, W_0 and ω_0 are added, taking the values 500 N and 0.5 rad/s, respectively.

$$c_3 = c_{30} + c_{31}\frac{W}{W_0} + c_{32}\frac{\omega}{\omega_0} \quad (14)$$

Table 6. Fitted parameter values of c_3

Parameter	c_{30}	c_{31}	c_{32}
Fitted value	−0.192	0.0711	0.0311

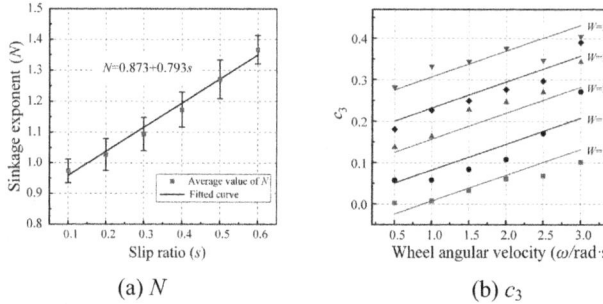

(a) N (b) c_3

Fig. 8. Identification and Fitting Results of N and $c3$

Now all parameters of model have been determined. The predicted values of model are compared with the experimental data and with the conventional models, shown in Figs. 9, 10 and 11. The overall predicted effect is listed in Table 7. The indicators of concern are the maximum relative error MRE and the coefficient of determination R^2. The revised model has a significant improvement in prediction accuracy.

Table 7. Model prediction accuracy evaluation

Parameters	Wong-Reece model		Ding's model		Revised model	
	MRE	R^2	MRE	R^2	MRE	R^2
M_R	43.0%	0.8108	46.4%	0.8059	15.9%	0.9544
z	82.2%	0.3618	26.8%	0.9879	12.9%	0.9677
F_{DP}	175.4%	0.0311	165.3%	0.1857	26.7%	0.7753

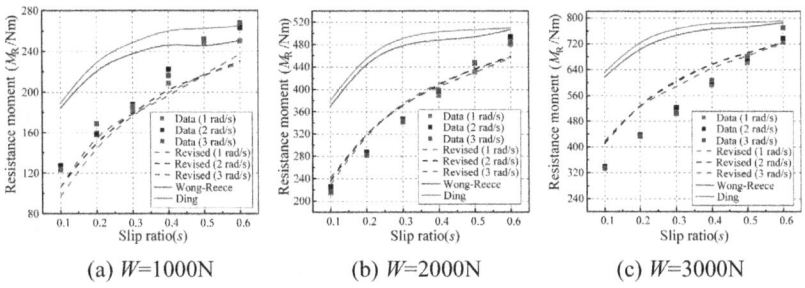

Fig. 9. Predicted results of driving resistance moment

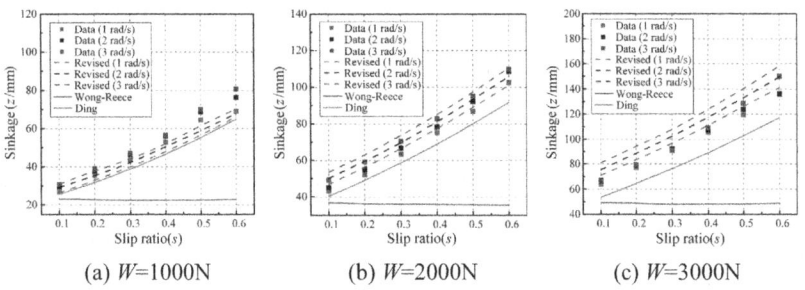

Fig. 10. Predicted results of wheel sinkage

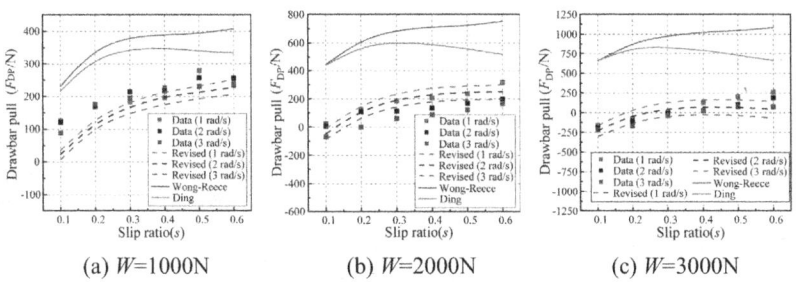

Fig. 11. Predicted results of drawbar pull

5 Conclusion and Future Work

In this paper, an experimental method for the study of wheel-terrain interaction of crewed lunar vehicles is established based on the self-developed single-wheel testbed. Based on this method, wheel-terrain interaction forces and sinkage are measured at different wheel loads (500–3000 N), angular velocities (0.5–3 rad/s) and slip ratios (0–0.6). The experimental results show that the traction performance of the wheels decreased significantly with increasing loads and speeds. Then, parameters of wheel-terrain interaction model are identified based on the experimental data, and the conventional model is revised. The revised model significantly improves the prediction accuracy of driving resistance moment, drawbar pull and sinkage.

In future work, experiments will be conducted under more diverse driving conditions, such as wheel skid and steering. Additionally, the effects of flexible wheel deformation on wheel-terrain interaction will be analyzed, and the model with higher prediction accuracy or less computational complexity will be established to better meet the requirements of wheel design, simulation and motion control of crewed lunar vehicles.

Acknowledgement. Research supported by the National Natural Science Foundation of China (Grant No. 52205011 & No. 52425502), the Self-Developed Projects of the National Key Laboratory of Aerospace Mechanism (Grant No. 2024ASM-ZY03), the National Natural Science Foundation of China, Basic Research Program for Young Students (Doctoral Students) (Grant No. 523B2039) and the Self-Planned Task of State Key Laboratory of Robotics and Systems (HIT) (Grant NO. SKLRS202503C).

References

1. Creech, S., Guidi, J., Elburn, D.: Artemis: an overview of NASA's activities to return humans to the Moon. In: 2022 IEEE aerospace conference (aero), pp. 1–7. IEEE (2022)
2. Ellery, A.: Leveraging in situ resources for lunar base construction. Can. J. Civ. Eng. **49**(5), 657–674 (2022)
3. Chan, N. T., He, X.: A review of control techniques for lunar rovers. In: Proceedings of the 2024 2nd International Conference on Frontiers of Intelligent Manufacturing and Automation, pp. 643–649 (2024)
4. Hu, W., Li, P., Unjhawala, H.M., et al.: Calibration of an expeditious terramechanics model using a higher-fidelity model, Bayesian inference, and a virtual bevameter test. J. Field Robot. **41**(3), 550–569 (2024)
5. Gao, H., Yuan, R., Liu, Z., et al.: Design and analysis of a lunar crewed vehicle with a novel versatile compliant suspension mechanism. J. Mech. Robot. **16**(12) (2024)
6. Park, B.J., Chung, H.J.: Deep reinforcement learning-based failure-safe motion planning for a 4-wheeled 2-steering lunar rover. Aerospace **10**(3), 219 (2023)
7. Shibly, H., Iagnemma, K., Dubowsky, S.: An equivalent soil mechanics formulation for rigid wheels in deformable terrain, with application to planetary exploration rovers. J. Terramech. **42**(1), 1–13 (2005)
8. Ishigami, G., Miwa, A., Nagatani, K., et al.: Terramechanics-based model for steering maneuver of planetary exploration rovers on loose soil. J. Field Robot. **24**(3), 233–250 (2007)
9. Ding, L.: Improved explicit-form equations for estimating dynamic wheel sinkage and compaction resistance on deformable terrain. Mech. Mach. Theory **86**, 235–264 (2015)
10. Harrison, D. A., Ambrose, R., Bluethmann, B., et al.: Next generation rover for lunar exploration. In: 2008 IEEE Aerospace Conference, pp. 1–14. IEEE (2008)
11. Wang, K., Sun, K., Wang, C., Ni, W., et al.: Design of integrated suspension for landing and traveling of manned lunar mobile system. In: 2022 International Conference on Advanced Robotics and Mechatronics, pp. 769–773. IEEE (2022)
12. Interbartolo, M., O'Neill, W., Chandler, A.: Forging lunar pressurized rovers for artemis. In: 2024 IEEE Aerospace Conference, pp. 1–9. IEEE (2024)
13. Apollo Lunar Roving Vehicle Documentation. https://www.nasa.gov/history/alsj/alsj-LRV docs.html/. Accessed 19 May 2025
14. Apostolopoulos, D.S.: Analytical Configuration of Wheeled Robotic Locomotion. Carnegie Mellon University (2001)

15. Zhu, J., Shen, Y., Hao, P., et al.: Modeling of flexible metal wheel for pressurized lunar rover and traction performance prediction. J. Field Robot. **40**(8), 2030–2041 (2023)
16. Liang, Z., Wang, Y., Chen, G.S., et al.: A mechanical model for deformable and mesh pattern wheel of lunar roving vehicle. Adv. Space Res. **56**(11), 2515–2526 (2015)
17. Liang, Z., Chen, J., Wang, Y.: Equivalent acceleration imitation for single wheel of manned lunar rover by varying torque on earth. IEEE-ASME Trans. Mechatron. **25**(1), 282–293 (2019)
18. Yang, H., Ding, L., Gao, H., et al.: High-fidelity dynamic modeling and simulation of planetary rovers using single-input-multi-output joints with terrain property mapping. IEEE Trans. Robot. **38**(5), 3238–3258 (2022)
19. Ding, L., Gao, H., Deng, Z., et al.: Experimental study and analysis on driving wheels' performance for planetary exploration rovers moving in deformable soil. J. Terramech. **48**(1), 27–45 (2011)
20. Rodríguez-Martínez, D., Buse, F., et al.: The effects of increasing velocity on the tractive performance of planetary rovers. arXiv preprint arXiv:2306.02167 (2023)
21. Wong, J.Y., Reece, A.R.: Prediction of rigid wheel performance based on the analysis of soil-wheel stresses part I. Performance of driven rigid wheels. J. Terramech. **4**(1), 81–98 (1967)
22. Janosi, Z.: The analytical determination of drawbar pull as a function of slip for tracked vehicles in deformable soils. In: Proceedings of the 1st International Conference of ISTVS. Turin, Italy (1961)

Research on the Dynamics Modeling and Control Method of Vector Quadrotor UAV with Variable Posture

Yunfan Pang[1], Zhonghai Zhang[1,2]($\boxtimes$), Jiahui Cai[3], and Duanling Li[3]

[1] School of Mechanical Engineering, Hebei University of Technology, Tianjin 300401, China
zhonghzhang@163.com
[2] Key Laboratory of Advanced Intelligent Protective Equipment Technology, Ministry of Education, Tianjin 300401, China
[3] School of Intelligent Engineering and Automation, Beijing University of Posts and Telecommunications, Beijing 100876, China

Abstract. With advancements in multirotor UAV technology, novel reconfigurable multirotor airframes have emerged as a prominent research focus. Conventional multirotor UAVs, as underactuated systems, face inherent limitations in attitude adjustment during hovering or flight operations due to their reliance on orientation dependent lift vector modulation. To address these constraints, this study proposes a tilt-rotor quadrotor UAV with vectored thrust capabilities. First, the structural design of this vectored rotor UAV is systematically elaborated. Subsequently, a dynamic model is derived using the wrench theorem to characterize its attitude-varying operational states. The nonlinear dynamics are then linearized via the Linear Parameter-Varying (LPV) method and incorporated into a PID control framework for system stabilization. Finally, MATLAB/Simulink simulations validate the model's performance.

Keywords: Tilting rotor · Wrench theorem · Linear Parameter-Varying method

1 Introduction

Rotor UAVs, characterized by user-friendly operation, stable flight performance, and compact portability, are particularly well-suited for mid-distance flight missions [1–3]. In recent years, multirotor UAV technology has undergone rapid development, finding extensive applications in aerial cinematography, infrastructure maintenance, search and rescue operations, crop protection, and military reconnaissance [4].

Conventional multirotor unmanned aerial vehicles, as a typical underactuated system, can only change the direction of thrust through attitude control, resulting in strong coupling between their position and attitude [5, -6]. Consequently, during the flight of UAV, a gimbal is usually required to stabilize the camera [7–9]. Furthermore, traditional UAVs cannot change their attitude during hovering or flight, and their field of view (FOV) depends entirely on the camera's installation position, resulting in significant blind spots [10].

To address the aforementioned issues, researchers have proposed an overactuated multirotor UAV design concept that increases the input of the UAV. Some scholars realize the omnidirectional thrust of the UAV by changing the number and spatial layout of rotors and using the redundancy of force driving force and direction [11, 12]. Some other scholars realize the omnidirectional thrust of UAV by controlling the thrust direction of each rotor [13–16]. For example, MA Zhenqiang [18] proposed a hexarotor UAV design with omnidirectional thrust vectoring. Through a dynamic model and PID controller, this design addresses the issues of inability to maintain horizontal attitude during low flight speeds and accelerated flight, and achieves hovering and horizontal flight. To address the challenge of decoupled position and attitude control in conventional quadrotors, LU Kaiwen [19] developed an omnidirectional thrust-vectoring tilt-rotor UAV system. By implementing an active disturbance rejection control based flight controller, this approach successfully achieves independent position and attitude regulation, effectively estimates and compensates for turbulent wind disturbances, and demonstrates strong robustness.

This study presents a tilt-rotor UAV design with servo-actuated thrust vectoring capability, where each rotor's orientation is independently controlled through precision servo mechanisms to achieve full omnidirectional thrust generation. A wrench theorem-based tilt-rotor UAV modeling and analysis method is proposed to establish the dynamics model of the UAV. Furthermore, an omnidirectional vector control model of the UAV is developed to enable decoupled control of both position and attitude of the UAV.

2 Structural Design of Vectored UAV

The structural design of the vectored rotor UAV is shown in Fig. 1, which is mainly composed of three parts: the frame, the controller and the tilt rotor.

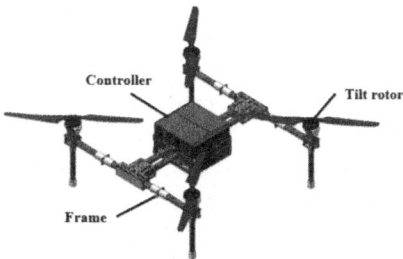

Fig. 1. Vector rotor UAV structural

The UAV adopts a H-shaped layout with four single-degree-of-freedom tilt-rotors. Each tilt-rotor has a degree of freedom for rotor thrust direction control actuated by a servo.

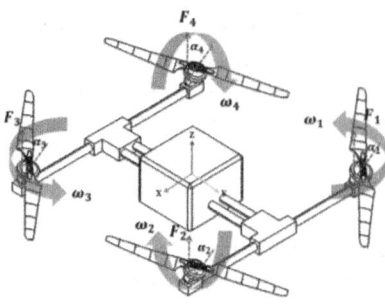

Fig. 2. Schematic and coordinates of a vector UAV

3 Dynamics Modeling of Vectored UAV

3.1 Screw Theory

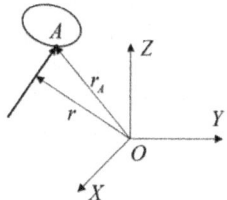

Fig. 3. Screw position and orientation vectors acting on an object

As shown in Fig. 3, the screw can be expressed as a six-dimensional vector S:

$$S = \begin{bmatrix} s \\ s_0 \end{bmatrix} = \begin{bmatrix} s \\ r \times s + hs \end{bmatrix} \quad (1)$$

where s is the axial vector of the screw S, and s_0 is the moment vector of the screw S. Both the axial vector s and the moment vector s_0 are 3×1 vectors, the moment vector s_0 is the sum of $r \times s$ and hs, where r is the position vector from the axial vector s to the origin of the coordinate system, and h is the pitch of the screw.

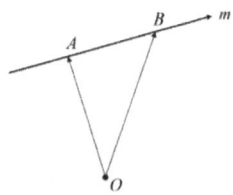

Fig. 4. Fork products of vectors

As shown in Fig. 4, points A and B are two points on the same straight line within the spatial coordinate system with origin O, and m is the direction vector of line AB. It follows that:

$$\vec{OB} \times m = (\vec{OA} + \vec{AB}) \times m = \vec{OA} \times m + \vec{AB} \times m \quad (2)$$

Since $\vec{AB}$ is collinear with m, it can be shown that $\vec{AB} \times m = 0$. It follows that:

$$\vec{OB} \times m = \vec{OA} \times m \quad (3)$$

According to Eq. (3), the screw S acts at point A in Fig. 3. Therefore, Eq. (1) can be expressed as:

$$S = \begin{bmatrix} s \\ s_0 \end{bmatrix} = \begin{bmatrix} s \\ r_A \times s + hs \end{bmatrix} \quad (4)$$

3.2 Wrench Representation of Vector UAV

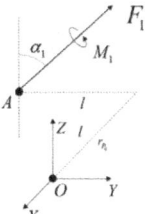

Fig. 5. Force rotation of a single rotor on a UAV

According to the wrench theorem [20–23], the rotor lift F and counter-torque M_A act at point A of the UAV coordinate system. Based on Eq. (4), the resultant force F and torque M on the UAV can be expressed as a wrench S:

$$S = \begin{bmatrix} F \\ M \end{bmatrix} = \begin{bmatrix} F \\ r_A \times F + pF \end{bmatrix} \quad (5)$$

where r_A is the vector from the origin O to the load point A, the p is the pitch of the force screw, which is a constant determined by motor parameters. Setting s as the unit vector for the force F, Eq. (5) can be expressed as follows:

$$S = |F| \begin{bmatrix} s \\ r_A \times s + ps \end{bmatrix} \quad (6)$$

where $|F|$ is the magnitude of the force vector F. As shown in Fig. 5, the force F lies parallel to XY-plane and forms an angle α with the Y-axis, given that point A has coordinates $(A_x, 0, A_z)$ in the UAV coordinate system, it follows that:

$$r_A = \begin{bmatrix} A_x \\ A_y \\ 0 \end{bmatrix}, s = \begin{bmatrix} 0 \\ \sin \alpha \\ \cos \alpha \end{bmatrix} \quad (7)$$

Substituting the vector r_A and s into Eq. (6), the wrench of a single rotor on the UAV can be obtained as:

$$S = |F| \begin{bmatrix} 0 \\ \sin \alpha \\ \cos \alpha \\ A_y \cos \alpha \\ -A_x \cos \alpha + p \sin \alpha \\ A_x \sin \alpha + p \cos \alpha \end{bmatrix} \quad (8)$$

3.3 Force Analysis of Vector UAV

Compared with the traditional rotor UAVs, the vectored rotor UAVs incorporate thrust-vectoring propulsion units. The tilt-rotor UAV analyzed in this paper features four tilt-rotor assemblies, each possessing one rotational degree of freedom. The load distribution of the UAV is shown in Fig. 6. Within the UAV coordinate system with origin O, four rotor units are positioned at points A, B, C, and D. Each rotor produces a force F along its axis and a torque M, while exhibiting one rotational degree of freedom about its own Z-axis with tilt angle α.

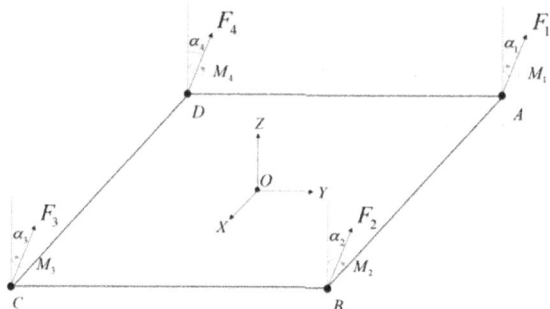

Fig. 6. Distribution of loads applied to the UAV

According to Eq. (8), the wrench of the four rotor loads on the UAV are:

$$S_1 = |F_1|\begin{bmatrix} 0 \\ \sin\alpha_1 \\ \cos\alpha_1 \\ A_y\cos\alpha_1 \\ A_x\cos\alpha_1 + p_1\sin\alpha_1 \\ A_x\sin\alpha_1 + p_1\cos\alpha_1 \end{bmatrix}, S_2 = |F_2|\begin{bmatrix} 0 \\ \sin\alpha_2 \\ \cos\alpha_2 \\ B_y\cos\alpha_2 \\ B_x\cos\alpha_2 + p_2\sin\alpha_2 \\ B_x\sin\alpha_2 + p_2\cos\alpha_2 \end{bmatrix},$$

$$S_3 = |F_3|\begin{bmatrix} 0 \\ \sin\alpha_3 \\ \cos\alpha_3 \\ C_y\cos\alpha_3 \\ C_x\cos\alpha_3 + p_3\sin\alpha_3 \\ C_x\sin\alpha_3 + p_3\cos\alpha_3 \end{bmatrix}, S_4 = |F_4|\begin{bmatrix} 0 \\ \sin\alpha_4 \\ \cos\alpha_4 \\ D_y\cos\alpha_4 \\ D_x\cos\alpha_4 + p_4\sin\alpha_4 \\ D_x\sin\alpha_4 + p_4\cos\alpha_4 \end{bmatrix} \qquad (9)$$

The wrench of the overall load acting on the UAV is:

$$S = S_1 + S_2 + S_3 + S_4 = \begin{bmatrix} F_X \\ F_Y \\ F_Z \\ M_X \\ M_Y \\ M_X \end{bmatrix} \qquad (10)$$

where:

$$\begin{aligned}
F_X &= 0 \\
F_Y &= \sum_{i=1}^{4} |F_i|\sin\alpha_i \\
F_Z &= \sum_{i=1}^{4} |F_i|\cos\alpha_i \\
M_X &= |F_1|A_y\cos\alpha_1 + |F_2|B_y\cos\alpha_2 + |F_3|C_y\cos\alpha_3 + |F_4|D_y\cos\alpha_4 \\
M_Y &= |F_1|A_x\cos\alpha_1 + |F_2|B_x\cos\alpha_2 + |F_3|C_x\cos\alpha_3 + |F_4|D_x\cos\alpha_4 + \sum_{i=1}^{4}|F_i|p_i\sin\alpha_i \\
M_Z &= |F_1|A_x\sin\alpha_1 + |F_2|B_x\sin\alpha_2 + |F_3|C_x\sin\alpha_3 + |F_4|D_x\sin\alpha_4 + \sum_{i=1}^{4}|F_i|p_i\cos\alpha_i
\end{aligned} \qquad (11)$$

3.4 Vector UAV Dynamics Modeling

Positional Dynamics Modeling

According to Newton's second law, the relationship between the linear velocity and the force of the UAV can be obtained as follows:

$$F = m\dot{v} = RT + mg \qquad (12)$$

In the formula, R is the attitude rotation matrix of the UAV in the ground coordinate system, T denotes the total rotor lift, g is the gravity acceleration, and v represents the UAV velocity vector defined as follows:

$$v = \begin{bmatrix} u & v & w \end{bmatrix}^T \tag{13}$$

According to Eqs. (11) and (12), the UAV position dynamics equations can be obtained as:

$$\begin{bmatrix} \dot{u} \\ \dot{v} \\ \dot{w} \end{bmatrix} = \begin{bmatrix} \cos\theta\cos\psi & \sin\phi\sin\theta\sin\psi - \cos\phi\sin\psi & \cos\phi\sin\theta\cos\psi + \sin\phi\sin\psi \\ \cos\theta\sin\psi & \sin\phi\sin\theta\sin\psi + \cos\phi\cos\psi & \cos\phi\sin\theta\sin\psi - \sin\phi\cos\psi \\ -\sin\theta & \sin\phi\cos\theta & \cos\phi\cos\theta \end{bmatrix} \begin{bmatrix} F_X/m \\ F_Y/m \\ F_Z/m \end{bmatrix} - \begin{bmatrix} 0 \\ 0 \\ g \end{bmatrix} \tag{14}$$

In the above equation, ϕ, θ, and ψ denote the UAV's roll, pitch, and yaw angles, respectively, with the pitch angle θ being a known control input. The roll angle ϕ, yaw angle ψ and tilt angle α of the UAV can be solved from Eq. (14).

Attitude Dynamics Modeling

According to Euler's equations, the relationship between the torque and angular velocity of the UAV can be obtained as follows:

$$M == Ga + \tau = J\dot{\omega} + \omega \times J\omega \tag{15}$$

In the above equation, J is the inertia matrix of the UAV, Ga denotes the gyroscopic moment, τ represents the propeller torque, and ω is the angular velocity of the UAV, defined as follows:

$$\omega = \begin{bmatrix} p & q & r \end{bmatrix}^T \tag{16}$$

Based on Eqs. (11) and (15) the attitude dynamic equations of the UAV can be derived as:

$$\begin{bmatrix} \dot{p} \\ \dot{q} \\ \dot{r} \end{bmatrix} = \left(\begin{bmatrix} M_X \\ M_Y \\ M_Z \end{bmatrix} - \begin{bmatrix} p \\ q \\ r \end{bmatrix} \times \begin{bmatrix} I_{xx} & 0 & 0 \\ 0 & I_{yy} & 0 \\ 0 & 0 & I_{zz} \end{bmatrix} \begin{bmatrix} p \\ q \\ r \end{bmatrix} \right) \cdot \begin{bmatrix} 1/I_{xx} & 0 & 0 \\ 0 & 1/I_{yy} & 0 \\ 0 & 0 & 1/I_{zz} \end{bmatrix} \tag{17}$$

In the above equation, I_x, I_y, and I_z are the moments of inertia of the UAV about the x, y and z axes, respectively.

According to Eq. (17), the torques of the UAV about the x, y, and z axes can be derived. Subsequently, using the total lift magnitude of the UAV, the lift forces and rotational speeds of each rotor can be determined.

System Output Calculations

Based on the forces and moments of the UAV obtained above, the magnitude of the lift for each rotor of the UAV can be solved, and the calculation formula is as follows:

$$\begin{cases} F_1 + F_2 + F_3 + F_4 = F \\ M_X = |F_1|A_z\cos\alpha_1 + |F_2|B_z\cos\alpha_2 + |F_3|C_z\cos\alpha_3 + |F_4|D_z\cos\alpha_4 + \sum_{i=1}^{4}|F_i|p_i\sin\alpha_i \\ M_Y = -|F_1|A_z\sin\alpha_1 - |F_2|B_z\sin\alpha_2 - |F_3|C_z\sin\alpha_3 - |F_4|D_z\sin\alpha_4 + \sum_{i=1}^{4}|F_i|p_i\cos\alpha_i \\ M_Z = -|F_1|A_z\cos\alpha_1 - |F_2|B_z\cos\alpha_2 - |F_3|C_z\cos\alpha_3 - |F_4|D_z\cos\alpha_4 \end{cases} \tag{18}$$

4 Control Methods and Simulation Verification for Vector UAV

4.1 UAV Vector Flight Patterns

Compared with the traditional UAVs, vectored UAVs achieve decoupled position and attitude control through tilt-rotor mechanisms, enabling adjustable attitude functionality. Traditional UAV control systems solely focus on spatial position control, with basic commands including displacement in three directions (forward/backward, left/right, up/down) and yaw angle control. In contrast, the UAV described in this paper can achieve pitch angle attitude control, adding an additional pitch angle adjustment to the four control commands of traditional UAV. The specific control modes of the UAV are illustrated in Fig. 7.

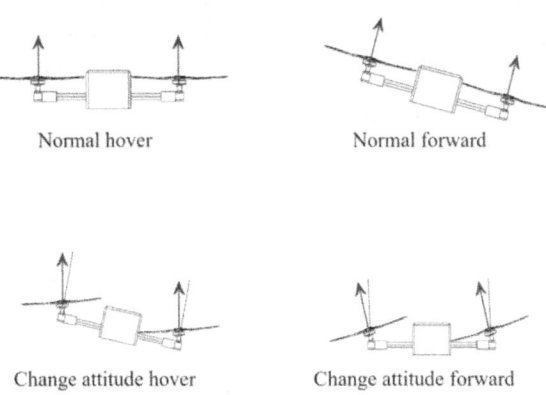

Fig. 7. UAV vector flight pattern

4.2 Vector UAV Control Method

In the current control method, we adopt the Linear Parameter-Varying method to establish a mathematical model for solving the model. The purpose of the LPV method is to achieve high-performance control of the UAV's dynamic system. The LPV controller is based on precise modeling of the system's dynamic characteristics and takes into account that system parameters may change with time or operating conditions. Then, using the LPV method, the dynamic characteristics of the system are expressed as functions of system parameters, which may vary with time or operating conditions. In this way, the LPV controller can effectively adjust the control strategy to adapt to changes in system parameters, thereby improving control performance and stability. Assume that the state equation of the system is:

$$\begin{cases} \dot{X} = AX + BU \\ Y = CX + DU \end{cases} \quad (19)$$

In the above equation, A is the coefficient matrix, $X = (\dot{x}, \dot{y}, \dot{z}, x, y, z, \dot{\phi}, \dot{\theta}, \dot{\psi}, \phi, \theta, \psi, g)^T$ is the state vector, B is the input matrix, $U = (F, M_x, M_y, M_z)^T$ is the input vector, $Y = (z, \phi, \theta, \psi)^T$ is the output quantity, C is the output vector, D is the direct transmission term. Taking the Laplace transform of the equations yields the transfer function matrix of the UAV:

$$G(s) = \frac{Y(s)}{U(s)} = C(SI - A)^{-1}B + D \qquad (20)$$

Since the UAV is equipped with four tilt-rotors, it has a total of four controllable variables. To reduce the control complexity and simplify the control model, this paper proposes that the tilt angles of the four servos on the UAV remain equal at all times, denoted as $\alpha = \alpha_1 = \alpha_2 = \alpha_3 = \alpha_4$. Additionally, during vertical takeoff and landing, low-speed flight, and hovering, the pitch and roll angles of the UAV change very little. Therefore, it can be assumed that $\theta = \phi \approx 0$, while assuming here that the $\alpha = 20°$. Substituting the data can obtain the transfer functions of each channel:

$$G(s) = \begin{bmatrix} \frac{0.4081}{0.1s^3+s^2} & 0 & 0 & 0 \\ 0 & \frac{66.1026}{0.1s^3+s^2} & 0 & 0 \\ 0 & 0 & \frac{66.1026}{0.1s^3+s^2} & 0 \\ 0 & 0 & 0 & \frac{35.3957}{0.1s^3+s^2} \end{bmatrix} \qquad (21)$$

4.3 Simulation of Vector UAV

In order to verify the correctness of the model built by the UAV, a dynamic numerical model of the UAV was built in MATLAB. The initial parameters were set as follow: UAV total mass $m = 1$kg, the acceleration of gravity is $g = 9.80$m/s², moment of inertia $I_{xx} = 3.782e^{-3}$kg·m², $I_{yy} = 3.782e^{-3}$kg·m², $I_{zz} = 7.063e^{-3}$kg·m², fuselage wheelbase $d = 0.25$m.

A control model is established based on the above transfer function and the PID control algorithm is used. The PID parameters are shown in the Table 1.

Table 1. PID parameter table

Parameter	1	2	3	4
K_p	0.1	0.04	0.04	0.05
K_i	0.01	0.001	0.001	0.001
K_d	10	0.35	0.35	0.33

In the position control of the UAV, since the designed UAV is not a fully decoupled control system, simultaneously setting the accelerations of the x, y, and z axes may lead to unsolvable situations. Therefore, it is necessary to optimize the selection of velocity constraints for each axis according to flight trajectories and actual requirements.

The system was observed and the resulting response curves for the four channels are shown in Figs. 8, 9, 10 and 11.

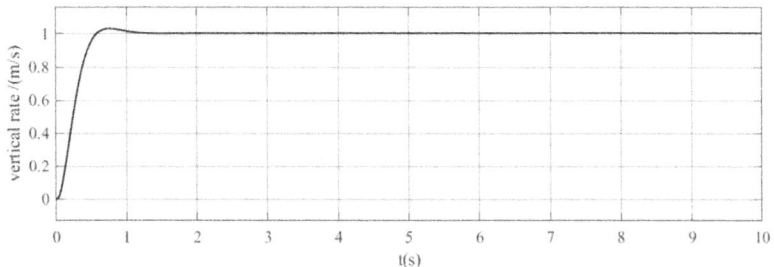

Fig. 8. Vertical rate channel response

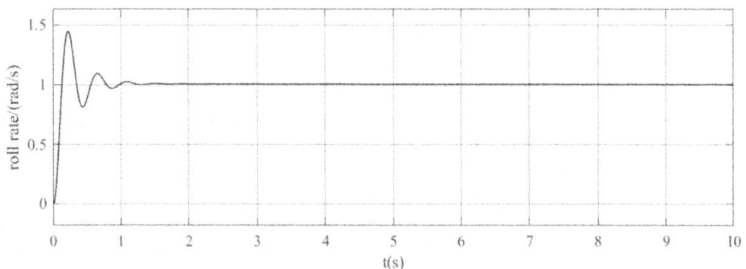

Fig. 9. Roll rate channel response

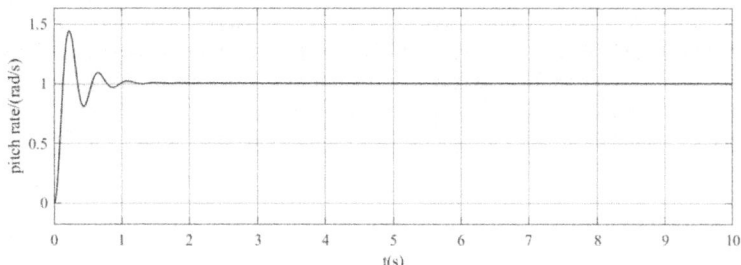

Fig. 10. Pitch rate channel response

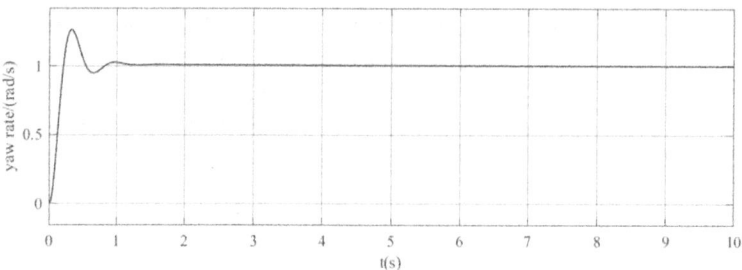

Fig. 11. Yaw rate channel response

The simulation results show that the system response is rapid, with a small overshoot, and all channels of the system quickly reach a stable state. Therefore, the design satisfies the requirements for vertical rate, roll rate, pitch rate, and yaw rate.

5 Conclusion

The traditional rotorcraft UAVs operate as underactuated systems, where thrust direction can only be altered through attitude control, and there is a strong coupling between position and attitude, making it impossible to change the attitude during hovering and flight. To address these issues, this study designs a quadrotor UAV with tilt-rotor mechanisms. The tilting rotors enable the UAV to provide thrust in any direction while maintaining a horizontal body attitude, granting it strong maneuverability. This paper first models the dynamics of the vectored-thrust UAV under variable-attitude conditions using the wrench theorem, deriving the dynamic equations under variable attitude conditions. Then, a Linear Parameter-Varying method is applied to convert the nonlinear dynamic equations into a transfer function form. Finally, the PID control law is simulated, and the simulation results show that the design satisfies the requirements for vertical rate, roll rate, pitch rate, and yaw rate. The method used in this paper can be extended to the modeling and research of various variable-form special-purpose UAVs.

Acknowledgment. This work was supported by Hebei Natural Science Foundation (Grant No. F2024202052), National Natural Science Foundation of China (Grant No. 52175019), Beijing Natural Science Foundations (Grant No. L222038), Beijing Nova Programme Interdisciplinary Cooperation Project (Grant No. 20240484699), the joint funds of Industry-university-research of Shanghai Academy of Spaceflight Technology (Grant No. SAST2022-017), Beijing Municipal Key Laboratory of Space-ground Interconnection and Convergence of China and Key Laboratory of IoT Monitoring and Early Warning, Ministry of Emergency Management.

References

1. Zhao, S., Wang, X., Chen, H., Wang, Y.: Cooperative path following control of fixed-wing unmanned aerial vehicles with collision avoidance. J. Intell. Rob. Syst. **100**(4) (2020)
2. Yu, H., Huang, J., Zou, B., Shao, W., Liu, J.: Stress-constrained shell-lattice infill structural optimisation for additive manufacturing. Virtual Phys. Prototyping 38–48 (2020)

3. Mahmood, A., Rehman, F., Okasha, M., Saeed, A.: Neural adaptive sliding mode control for camera positioner quadrotor UAV. Int. J. Aeronaut. Space Sci. **26**(2), 733–747 (2025)
4. Zhang, M., Gu, F., He, Y.: Air-water hybrid unmanned aerial/surface vehicle system design and coordinated control. Unmanned Syst. Technol. (2021)
5. Xu, J., Wang, L., Liu, Y., Xue, H.: Finite-Time Prescribed Performance Optimal Attitude Control for Quadrotor UAV. Appl. Math. Model. 752–768(2023)
6. Gao, B., Yan-Jun, L., Liu, L.: Fixed-time neural control of a quadrotor UAV with input and attitude constraints. IEEE/CAA J. Automatica Sinica **10**(1) (2023)
7. Mao, S., Li, N., Wang, C., Ling, C., Cheng, S., Li, H.: Optimized design of stabilized gimbal for multirotor UAV. Machinery **001**, 062 (2024)
8. Battistela, O.T.R.: Unit wector control of anunbalaneed three axis gimbal for application to inertiallystabilized platforms. Asian J. Control 2157–2170 (2021)
9. Altan, A.R.H.: Model predictive control of three-axis gimbal system mounted on UAV for real-time target tracking under external disturbances. Mech. Syst. Signal Process. **106548** (2020)
10. Lee, D., Kim, H.J., Sastry, S.: Feedback linearization vs. adaptive sliding mode control for a quadrotor helicopter. Int. J. Control Autom. Syst. **7**(3), 419–428 (2009)
11. Voyles, R., Jiang, G.: Hexrotor UAV platform enabling dextrous interaction with structures Preliminary work. In: IEEE International Symposium on Safety, Security, & Rescue Robotics. IEEE (2012)
12. Long, Y., Cappelleri, D.J.: Linear control design, allocation, and implementation for the Omnicopter MAV. In: 2013 IEEE International Conference on Robotics and Automation. IEEE (2013)
13. Gerber, M.J., Tsao, T.C.: Twisting and tilting rotors for high-efficiency, thrust-vectored quadrotors. J. Mech. Rob. **6** (2018)
14. Ali, R.A., Abdolreza, O., Mohammad, A.K.: A novel firefighter quadrotor UAV with tilting rotors: modeling and control. Aerospace Sci. Technol. (2024)
15. Lindokuhle, J.M., Jimoh, O.P., Jason, R.: Control-allocated sliding mode control for a single-axis tilting quadrotor UAV. IFAC-PapersOnLine **54**(21), 204–209 (2021)
16. Seongwon, Y., Changhyeon, L., Youngbin, S., Junwoo, J.S., Soohee, H.: Spinning a small-sized quadrotor efficiently to achieve a 3-D omnidirectional field of view. IEEE Trans. Aerosp. Electron. Syst. **61**(1), 266–278 (2025)
17. Hamandi, M., Sawant, K., Tognon, M.: Omni-plus-seven (O7+): an omnidirectional aerial prototype with a minimal number of unidirectional thrusters. 2020 International Conference on Unmanned Aircraft Systems (ICUAS) (2020)
18. Ma, Z., Doing, W., Xie, W., Shao, P.: Design and modeling of an omni-directional thrust vector hexarotor UAV. Flight Dyn. (2016)
19. Lu, K., Yang, Z., Zhang, Q., Xu, C., Xu, H., Xu, X.: Thrust vectoring tilt-rotor quadrotor flight control method with disturbance rejection. Control Theory Appl. **37**(6), 11 (2020)
20. Bindu, R.A., Neloy, A.A., Alam, S., Moni, N.J., Siddique, S.: Sigma-3: integration and analysis of a 6 DOF robotic arm configuration in a rescue robot (2020)
21. Wiedmeyer, W., Altoe, P., Auberle, J., Ledermannn, C., Kroeger, T.: A real-time-capable closed-form multi-objective redundancy resolution scheme for seven-DoF serial manipulators. IEEE Rob. Autom. Lett. **99**, 1 (2020)
22. Lynch, K.M., Park, F.C.: Modern robotics Cambridge University Press (2017)
23. You, W.S., Lee, Y.H., Oh, H.S., Kang, G., Choi, H.R.: Design of a 3D-printable, robust anthropomorphic robot hand including intermetacarpal joints. Intell. Serv. Rob. **12**(1), 1–16 (2018). https://doi.org/10.1007/s11370-018-0267-8

A Probability Theory-Based Method for Calculating the Cyclical Degree of Freedom of Mechanisms

Fengyi Li, Hao Chen, Weizhong Guo[✉], and Hang Fu

Shanghai Jiao Tong University, Shanghai 200240, China
wzguo@sjtu.edu.cn

Abstract. This paper presents a novel probability theory-based method for calculating the cyclical degree of freedom (DOF) of mechanisms, addressing the limitations of traditional deterministic approaches in determining cyclical DOF of complex parallel mechanisms and uncertain configurations. By integrating random sampling and significance testing, the method enables statistical evaluation of DOF across the entire motion range, ensuring reliability through binomial distribution-based hypothesis testing. The approach uses the Jacobian matrix's null space and closed-loop constraint equations to model mechanism kinematics, and iteratively optimizes samples to achieve statistically significant results. Case studies on single-loop and multi-loop mechanisms validate the accuracy, showing consistent results with modified G-K formula calculations. This framework enhances computational efficiency by reducing manual complexity and offers universality for automated DOF analysis, making it particularly suitable for complex mechanical systems with singular configurations or redundant constraints. It paves the way for integrating statistical DOF analysis into computer-aided design workflows to support data-driven mechanism design and optimization.

Keywords: Degree of freedom (DOF) · Probability theory · Significance testing

1 Introduction

With the continuous advancement of research on parallel mechanisms, the degree of freedom (DOF) calculation has become a core issue in mechanism design and analysis. DOF is a key indicator that describe the motion performance of a mechanism and determine the system's ability for independent movement in space [1]. Accurate calculation of DOF is crucial for the design, control, and optimization of mechanisms [2].

In traditional DOF calculations, the Grubler–Kutzbach (G-K) formula is one of the most commonly used formulas [3–5]. It neglects the geometric relationships between the joint axes of the mechanism, causing failure when dealing with complex spatial mechanisms. Method by calculating the null space of the Jacobian matrix is theoretically applicable to all mechanisms, yet it is highly complex and difficult, and it cannot accommodate the complexities of certain mechanisms or their DOF characteristics [6].

The screw theory demonstrates strong capabilities when dealing with complex parallel mechanisms [7–15], its application often depends on extensive manual calculations due to the mathematical complexity of screw theory. Similarly, methods based on Lie group theory and displacement subgroup theory derive the kinematic properties of mechanisms through complex algebraic operations [16–20]. Using these methods requires a deep mathematical background, and their applicability is limited when dealing with different types of mechanisms. Position and Orientation Characteristics (POC) theory can analyze the motion characteristics of parallel mechanisms and handle different constraint conditions [21–23]. However, in complex mechanism analysis it is cumbersome, requiring substantial prior knowledge and computational experience.

In recent years, research on DOF calculation has gradually shifted toward automation and efficiency. Certain research uses 3D modeling software combined with VB programming to achieve automatic DOF calculation for parallel mechanisms. Furthermore, recent studies have explored machine learning methods to enable more accurate predictions of DOF. However, most of these methods rely on specific software tools or training data, lacking universality and general applicability. Therefore, integrating probability theory into DOF calculation not only provides a new technical approach but also overcomes the limitations of existing methods when dealing with complex systems. In particular, when facing highly uncertain systems with multiple possible configurations, this approach offers a more flexible and robust analytical tool.

The innovation of this paper lies in introducing probability theory into the calculation of mechanism DOF, providing a novel statistical-based analytical framework. Through random sampling and significance testing, the proposed method can effectively address uncertainty in complex parallel mechanisms and provide a global evaluation of DOF across the entire motion range. Compared to traditional deterministic analysis methods, this approach not only improves computational efficiency and accuracy but also reduces the complexity of the calculation process through automation and optimization algorithms. By incorporating significance testing, the method ensures the statistical reliability of the results, offering a more scientific and reliable basis for the design and optimization of complex mechanisms.

The chapters of this paper are organized as follows: Sect. 2 provides a brief introduction to the theoretical background and the method for calculating DOF using probability theory. Section 3 presents application examples including single-loop mechanisms and multi-loop mechanisms. Section 4 concludes the paper.

2 The Probability Theory-Based Method for Calculating the DOF of Mechanisms

This section briefly introduces some basic theories that are essential for understanding the calculation methods.

2.1 Basic Theory

Transformation matrix. The link transformation describes the motion of each link connected by joints and relative to adjacent links. A commonly used method is Denavit-Hartenberg (DH) parameter method, which simplifies the relationship between joints with four parameters [24]: twist angle α_{i-1}, link length a_{i-1}, link offset d_i and joint angle or displacement θ_i. We can generate a transformation matrix:

$$^{i-1}_{i}T = \begin{bmatrix} cos\theta_i & -sin\theta_i & 0 & a_{i-1} \\ sin\theta_i cos\alpha_{i-1} & cos\theta_i cos\alpha_{i-1} & -sin\alpha_{i-1} & -d_i sin\alpha_{i-1} \\ sin\theta_i sin\alpha_{i-1} & cos\theta_i sin\alpha_{i-1} & cos\alpha_{i-1} & d_i cos\alpha_{i-1} \\ 0 & 0 & 0 & 1 \end{bmatrix} \quad (1)$$

The homogeneous transformation provides a convenient method to combine rotation and translation into a single matrix, allowing to describe the motion from one coordinate system to another. The general form of the homogeneous transformation matrix is:

$$T = \begin{bmatrix} R & d \\ 0 & 1 \end{bmatrix} \quad (2)$$

where R is a rotation matrix which represents orientation, and d is a translation vector. The last row represents both rotation and translation, enabling the chaining of multiple transformation matrices through matrix multiplication. For a serial manipulator with n DOF, the transformation of the end-effector relative to the initial link can be obtained by multiplying the transformation matrices of adjacent links [25]:

$$^0_n T = {}^0_1 T {}^1_2 T \cdots {}^{n-1}_n T \quad (3)$$

Closed-Loop constraint equations. The establishment of the closed-loop constraint equations originates from the geometric relationships of the mechanism. The main goal is to ensure that the closed-loop characteristics of the mechanism remain unchanged, thus maintaining the geometric consistency and constraint conditions during motion.

For a closed-loop structure, the cumulative transformation from the initial link to the end link should ultimately return to the origin or initial position. Therefore, the result of the homogeneous transformation matrix multiplication must equal the identity matrix I. Through the transformation multiplication in Eq. (3), the closed-loop constraint equations are obtained. They describe the geometric constraints between the links and ensure that the mechanism maintains its closed-loop state during motion.

$$^0_n T = I \quad (4)$$

The closed-loop constraint equations ensure the closed-loop characteristics of the mechanism and maintain the geometric consistency of the links during motion. The angle θ_i of each revolute pair must satisfy the relative spatial position and orientation of the adjacent links, thereby restricting the system's DOF. By solving the closed-loop constraint equations, we can analyze which motions in the system are independent and which are dependent on other motions.

DOF calculation via the null space of the mechanism's Jacobian matrix. Once the Jacobian matrix of the kinematic chain coupled by revolute or prismatic pairs is properly defined, the DOF of the kinematic chain can be uniquely calculated as the dimension of the null space of the above matrix. That is, the DOF of the mechanism can be determined by calculating the null space of the mechanism's Jacobian matrix, and the formula is as follows [6]:

$$M = nullity(J) \tag{5}$$

Accuracy of significance testing. Significance testing is a statistical method used to determine whether the observed results are statistically significant by evaluating the likelihood of obtaining results under random circumstances. Based on properties of specific p-value [26–28], whether the calculated DOF is comprehensive is determined.

We need to verify whether the results are significant, and therefore, we use the cumulative distribution function (CDF) of the binomial distribution:

$$X \sim Bin(n, p) \tag{6}$$

Its probability mass function is:

$$P(X \leq k) = \sum_{i=0}^{k} \binom{n}{i} p^i (1-p)^{n-i} \tag{7}$$

where $P(X \leq k)$ represents the probability of observing fewer than or equal to k successes in n independent Bernoulli trials. k is the specific success count limit used when calculating the CDF value. $\binom{n}{i}$ is the binomial coefficient which gives the number of different ways to select i successes from n trials. p is the probability of success in each trial, and n is the number of trials. The detailed steps for performing significance testing using the binomial distribution function are shown in Fig. 1.

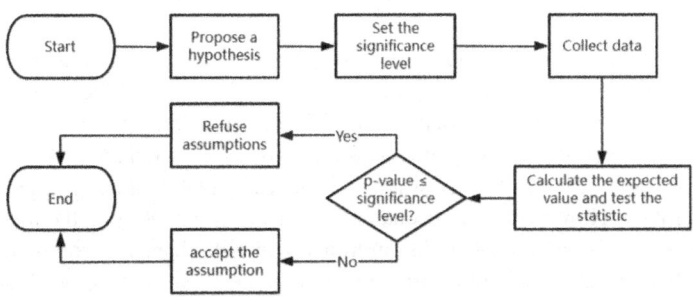

Fig. 1. Process for significance testing using binomial distribution function

2.2 Statement of the Method

For a single-loop nR DGM, its configuration space (C-space) is defined as in equation:

$$C = \{\boldsymbol{\theta} | \boldsymbol{F}(\boldsymbol{\theta}) = \boldsymbol{0}\} \tag{8}$$

where $\boldsymbol{\theta} = [\theta_1, \theta_2, \ldots, \theta_n]^T$, and θ_i represents the joint angle of the i-th revolute pair. $F(\boldsymbol{\theta})$ is a set of multivariate polynomial constraint equations about $\boldsymbol{\theta}$. $F(\boldsymbol{\theta})$ can be obtained by establishing coordinate systems on each link and performing successive homogeneous transformations, yielding up to twelve constraint equations among which six are independent. And determining which six are independent is complex because all equations are implicit. Our goal is to determine the rank of the mechanism's Jacobian matrix. These non-independent constraint equations do not affect the final result. Therefore, in numerical calculations, we directly use these equations to compute the rank of the Jacobian matrix at a given configuration. DOF of the mechanism at a given point is equal to the number of independent variables in the implicit constraint equations. In practice, it involves finding the dimension of the solution space of equations. This problem can be solved by constructing the Jacobian matrix and analyzing its rank. The Jacobian matrix provides a local linear approximation of the system, and its rank indicates the number of linearly independent constraints. The specific steps are as follows:

1. Configuration of Jacobian matrix: the implicit constraint equations given by Eq. (8) can be expressed as:

$$f_i(\theta_1, \theta_2, \ldots, \theta_n) = 0, i = 1, 2, \ldots, 12 \tag{9}$$

The mechanism's Jacobian matrix $\boldsymbol{J}$ is defined as the matrix formed by the partial derivatives of these equations with respect to all the variables:

$$\boldsymbol{J} = \begin{bmatrix} \frac{\partial f_1}{\partial \theta_1} & \frac{\partial f_1}{\partial \theta_2} & \cdots & \frac{\partial f_1}{\partial \theta_n} \\ \frac{\partial f_2}{\partial \theta_1} & \frac{\partial f_2}{\partial \theta_2} & \cdots & \frac{\partial f_2}{\partial \theta_n} \\ \vdots & \vdots & \ddots & \vdots \\ \frac{\partial f_{12}}{\partial \theta_1} & \frac{\partial f_{12}}{\partial \theta_2} & \cdots & \frac{\partial f_{12}}{\partial \theta_n} \end{bmatrix} \tag{10}$$

2. Calculating the rank of Jacobian matrix: by performing row reduction on $\boldsymbol{J}$, we obtain the number of linearly independent rows, thereby determining the rank of $\boldsymbol{J}$.
3. Determining the number of independent variables: if the rank of $\boldsymbol{J}$ is r and there are n variables, the number of independent variables is $(n - r)$, and the DOF of the mechanism is $(n - r)$. $\boldsymbol{J}$ at a single position can only reflect DOF of the mechanism at that configuration. However, for a mechanism with a cyclical DOF m, the instantaneous DOF is generally m at most configurations, and will change at singular positions. Using this property, we apply probability and statistical methods to calculate the cyclical DOF of a closed-loop mechanism. Table 1. Provides the pseudocode for the algorithm. It first defines a Boolean flag as true to control the subsequent loop process. The loop will only stop once a statistically significant DOF value is found. Each iteration of the loop executes the following steps:

   – Generate a certain number of random samples within the joint angle limits. It is difficult to find points which satisfy constraint equations, so we move to next step.
   – Set optimization options and define optimization function to correct the random sampling points obtained before. For each random sample, perform the optimization and store the results in 'optimized-samples'.

- Initialize a counter array 'DOF-Counts' to track the occurrences of each DOF. For each sample in 'optimized-samples', the algorithm computes its DOF.
- Once all samples have been processed, the algorithm identifies the most frequent DOF and calculates its statistical significance. If the p-value for the occurrence probability is less than 0.05, the algorithm confirms that this DOF is statistically significant, sets flag to false, exits the loop, and outputs this DOF value. If not, this most frequent value may not be statistically significant. In this case, the algorithm will increase the sample size and restart the loop.

Finally, when a statistically significant DOF value is found, the algorithm returns this value as the DOF of the mechanism. This process is an overall statistical validation-based DOF estimation method, which iterates until statistical significance is achieved. Since the optimized-samples are derived through optimization after the initial random sampling, they still possess some randomness, meanwhile, because the optimized-samples satisfy the constraint equations, these samples represent the characteristics of the solution space that satisfies the specific constraint conditions. Furthermore, it is meaningful to perform a significance test on the most frequent DOF value for two main reasons: the one is quantifying uncertainty. The DOF of a mechanical system is a definite physical property,

Table 1. Calculate Degree of Freedom (DOF)

Algorithm
Input: l_b, u_b, α, β, l, numSamples
Output: The most common DOF
1   Set flag to TRUE
2   Compute the constraint equations $F(\theta)$ and the Jacobian matrix $J(\theta)$ using α, β,
3   While flag is TRUE
4   Generate a set of samples within the bounds l_b and u_b
5   Define optimization options and the optimization function
6   For i from 0 to $N-1$
7   Optimize sample i using fminunc with the function fun and the options
8   Store the optimized-samples
9   End For
10   Initialize an array DOF-Counts with zeros
11   For j from 0 to $N-1$
12   Compute DOF for optimized-samples j
13   Update the count of the computed DOF in DOF-Counts
14   End For
15   Determine the most common DOF and its count from DOF-Counts
16   Compute the hypothesis test p-value for the most common DOF
17   If p-value is less than 0.05
18   Set DOF to the most common DOF
19   Set flag to FALSE
20   Else
21   Double the value of numSamples
22   End If
23   End While
24   Return the computed DOF

but sample-based calculations may be affected by sampling errors. Significance testing can help determine whether this result truly reflects the mechanism's DOF, or if it is simply due to randomness. The other is basis for decision making. Through significance testing, we can make data-driven decisions. If the test result is not significant, it also suggests that we need more data or should consider other factors.

3 Example Application

To comprehensively verify the applicability of the method, this chapter selects typical examples for analysis. For single-loop mechanisms, we have chosen planar single-DOF mechanism, planar multi-DOF mechanism, and spatial multi-DOF mechanism. For multi-loop mechanisms, we have selected planar multi-DOF mechanism, spatial single-DOF mechanism, and spatial multi-DOF mechanism to validate the method's performance in complex multi-loop structures. Through these case studies, we can more intuitively demonstrate the applicability and advantages of the method.

To facilitate the analysis of the mechanism, two coordinate systems denoted as $\{i, 1\}$ and $\{i, 2\}$ are established for each link when the mechanism is fully deployed. The coordinate system $\{i, 1\}$ is established at the center of i-th revolute pair, while $\{i, 2\}$ is established at the center of $(i + 1)$-th revolute pair. These coordinate systems allows the motion relationships between the links to be described through homogeneous transformation matrices between adjacent coordinate systems. The direction vector of the revolute pair's axis is denoted as f, where $_I^l f$ represents the direction vector of the first type of revolute pair axis, and $_{II}^l f$ represents the second type [29–32].

For mechanisms in this section, the initial conditions are provided in Tables 2 and 3. In tables, Mech. is the abbreviation of Mechanism, α_i represents the twist angle at the i-th revolute pair where $_I^l \alpha_i$ denotes the first type of revolute pair and $_{II}^l \alpha_i$ denotes the second, β_i represents the bisector angle where $_I^l \beta_i$ is of the first type and $_{II}^l \beta_i$ of the second. l is a row vector where the i-th column represents the length of the i-th link.

Table 2. Parameters of single-loop mechanisms

Type	Planar Single-dof Mech.			Planar Multi-dof Mech.			Spatial Multi-dof Mech.		
	$\alpha_i(°)$	$\beta_i(°)$	$l_i(mm)$	$\alpha_i(°)$	$\beta_i(°)$	$l_i(mm)$	$\alpha_i(°)$	$\beta_i(°)$	$l_i(mm)$
1	90	30	80	90	50	209.6	100	90	80
2	90	60	80	90	50	136.8	75	45	80
3	90	30	80	90	60	160	45	90	80
4	90	60	80	90	55	160	135	45	80
5	-	-	-	90	55	160	80	90	80
6	-	-	-	-	-	-	120	45	80
7	-	-	-	-	-	-	60	90	80
8	-	-	-	-	-	-	156.4	45	80

Table 3. Parameters of multi-loop mechanisms

Type	Planar Multi-dof Mech.						Spatial Single-dof Mech.		
	Loop 1			Loop 2			Loop 1		
	$\alpha_i(°)$	$\beta_i(°)$	$l_i(mm)$	$\alpha_i(°)$	$\beta_i(°)$	$l_i(mm)$	$\alpha_i(°)$	$\beta_i(°)$	$l_i(mm)$
1	90	45	80	90	54	80	120	90	50
2	90	45	80	90	54	80	15	45	100
3	90	45	80	90	54	80	30	45	50
4	90	45	80	90	54	80	97	90	50
5	-	-	-	90	54	80	150	45	100
6	-	-	-	-	-	-	165	45	50
Type	Spatial Single-dof Mech.			Spatial Multi-dof Mech.					
	Loop 2			Loop 1			Loop 2		
	$\alpha_i(°)$	$\beta_i(°)$	$l_i(mm)$	$\alpha_i(°)$	$\beta_i(°)$	$l_i(mm)$	$\alpha_i(°)$	$\beta_i(°)$	$l_i(mm)$
1	97	90	50	120	90	50	97	90	50
2	15	45	100	15	45	100	15	45	100
3	30	45	50	30	45	50	30	45	50
4	120	90	50	120	90	50	120	90	50
5	150	45	100	150	45	100	150	45	100
6	165	45	50	165	45	50	165	45	50

3.1 Single-Loop Mechanism

Planar single-DOF mechanism. As shown in Fig. 2(a), the planar single-loop mechanism consists of four components. Based on the method of calculating the mechanism's DOF using probability theory described in Sect. 2.2, we run the code and obtain the mechanism's DOF as:

$$M = 1, p = 0 \tag{11}$$

here, p-value being zero indicates that the DOF is cyclical. We verify the accuracy of the above result by calculating the mechanism's DOF using the modified G-K formula. The calculation gives:

$$M = d(n - g - 1) + \sum_{i=1}^{g} f_i + v - \varsigma = 3(4 - 4 - 1) + 4 = 1 \tag{12}$$

where M represents the DOF of the mechanism; d is the order of the mechanism's screw system; n is the total number of components in the mechanism; g is the number of kinematic pairs; f_i is the relative DOF of the i-th kinematic pair; v is the number of redundant constraints in a multi-loop parallel mechanism after removing the common constraint factors; and ς is the local DOF in the mechanism.

The calculation results from Eqs. (11) and (12) are consistent with each other.

Planar multi-DOF mechanism. As shown in Fig. 2(b), the planar single-loop mechanism consists of five components. Based on the method of calculating the mechanism's

DOF using probability theory described in Sect. 2.2, we have result:

$$M = 2, p = 0 \qquad (13)$$

here, p-value being zero indicates that the DOF is cyclical. We verify the result by calculating DOF using the modified G-K formula. The calculation gives:

$$M = d(n - g - 1) + \sum_{i=1}^{g} f_i + v - \varsigma = 3(5 - 5 - 1) + 5 = 2 \qquad (14)$$

The calculation results from Eqs. (13) and (14) are consistent with each other.

Spatial multi-DOF mechanism. As shown in Fig. 2(c), the spatial single-loop mechanism consists of eight components. We apply the calculating method and get:

$$M = 2, p = 0 \qquad (15)$$

here, p-value being zero indicates that the DOF is cyclical. We testify the result by applying the modified G-K formula. The calculation gives:

$$M = d(n - g - 1) + \sum_{i=1}^{g} f_i + v - \varsigma = 6(8 - 8 - 1) + 8 = 2 \qquad (16)$$

The calculation results from Eqs. (15) and (16) are consistent with each other.

3.2 Multi-loop Mechanism

Planar multi-DOF mechanism. As shown in Fig. 2(d), the planar multi-loop mechanism consists of two loops. These two loops can be viewed as a planar four-bar mechanism and a planar five-bar mechanism, respectively. Based on the method of calculating the mechanism's DOF in Sect. 2.2, we calculate the mechanism's DOF as:

$$M = 3, p = 0 \qquad (17)$$

here, p-value being zero indicates that the DOF is cyclical. We compare the result to that calculated by modified G-K formula. The calculation gives:

$$M = d(n - g - 1) + \sum_{i=1}^{g} f_i + v - \varsigma = 3(8 - 9 - 1) + 7 + 2 = 3 \qquad (18)$$

The calculation results from Eqs. (17) and (18) are consistent with each other.

Spatial single-DOF mechanism. As shown in Fig. 2(e), the spatial multi-loop mechanism consists of two loops. It is equivalent to two spatial four-bar mechanisms that are connected in parallel after removing one intermediate link. Based on the figure, the link 6 of loop 1 is rigidly connected to link 1 of loop 2, such that the output of loop 1 serves as the input for loop 2. Based on the method of calculating the mechanism's DOF using probability theory described in Sect. 2.2, we obtain the result as follow:

$$M = 1, p = 0 \qquad (19)$$

here, p-value being zero indicates that the DOF is cyclical. We verify the accuracy of the above result by using the modified G-K formula. The calculation gives:

$$M = d(n - g - 1) + \sum_{i=1}^{g} f_i + v - \varsigma = 6(9 - 10 - 1) + 10 + 3 = 1 \qquad (20)$$

The calculation results from Eqs. (19) and (20) are consistent with each other.

Spatial multi-DOF mechanism. As shown in Fig. 2(f), the spatial multi-loop mechanism consists of two loops. Similarly, when the link 6 of loop 1 is not rigidly connected to the link 1 of loop 2, as described in Sect. 3.2 - *Spatial single-DOF mechanism*, two rotational pairs are formed. In this case, the output of loop 1 is no longer the input for loop 2, and the two loops operate independently of each other. According to the method in Sect. 2.2, we calculate the mechanism's DOF as:

$$M = 2, p = 0 \tag{21}$$

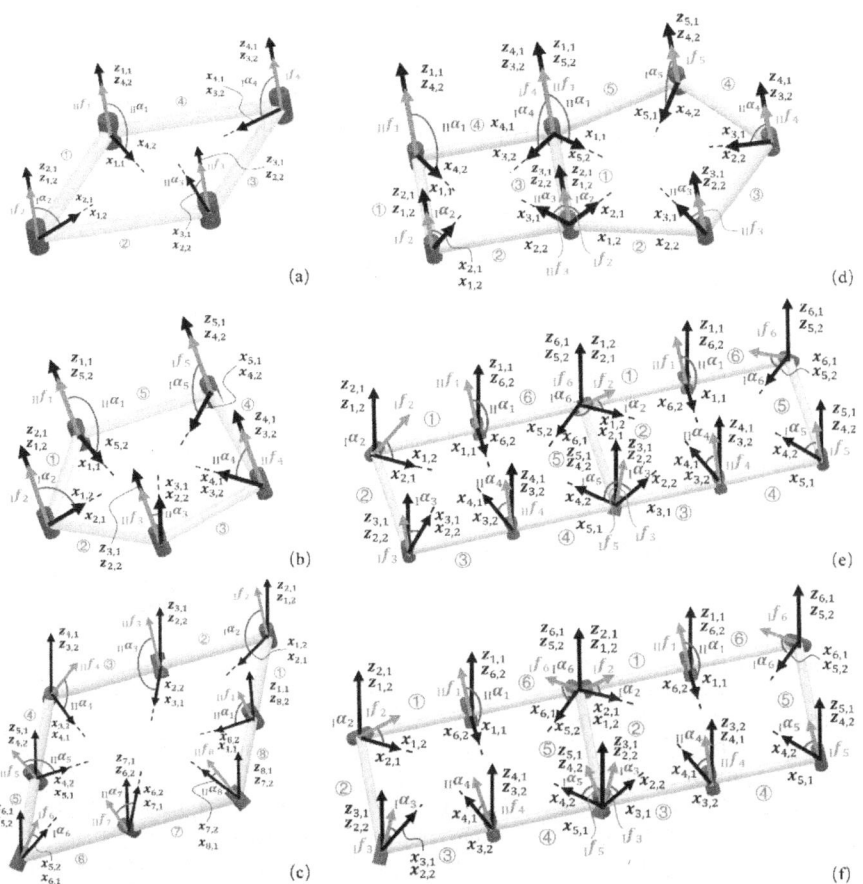

Fig. 2. Mechanisms set as example applications, (a-c) represent single-loop type mechanisms and (d-f) represent multi-loop type.

here, p-value being zero indicates that the DOF is cyclical. We check the accuracy of the above result using the modified G-K formula. The calculation gives:

$$M = d(n - g - 1) + \sum_{i=1}^{g} f_i + v - \varsigma = 6(11 - 12 - 1) + 12 + 2 = 2 \tag{22}$$

The calculation results from Eqs. (21) and (22) are consistent with each other.

4 Conclusion

This paper introduces probability theory into the calculation of the DOF of mechanisms, providing a novel method for calculating the DOF based on statistics. This method demonstrates significant advantages: first, it is highly flexible and can adapt to various types of mechanisms. Second, through random sampling and significance testing, it ensures that the calculation results are statistically reliable. Finally, the method offers a new automated calculation framework, enhancing the efficiency and accuracy of computations. It can be integrated into complex computer-aided design (CAD) software to enable the automated analysis of complex mechanisms.

The probability-based DOF calculation method offers a new research path for modern mechanism analysis. By combining statistical sampling and significance testing, this method not only overcomes the limitations of traditional DOF formulas but also makes the fully automated analysis of complex mechanisms possible.

References

1. Inoescu, G.: Terminology for mechanisms and machine science. Mech. Mach. Theory **38**(5), 819–827 (2003)
2. Zhen, H.: Spatial Mechanism, 1st edn. China Machine Press, Beijing (1991)
3. Kutzbach, K.: Mechanische leitungsverzweigung, ihre gesetze und anwendungen. Maschinenbau **8**(21), 710–716 (1929)
4. Grubler, M.: Eine Getriebelehre: Eine Theorie des Zwanglaufes und der ebenen Mechanismen, 1st edn. Springer, Berlin Heidelberg, Berlin (1917)
5. Grigore, G.: Chebyshev–Grubler–Kutzbach's criterion for mobility calculation of multi-loop mechanisms revisited via theory of linear transformations. Eur. J. Mech. A-Solids **24**(3), 427–441 (2005)
6. Angeles, J., Gosselin, C.: Determination du degre de leberte des chaines cinematique. Trans. Can. Mech. Eng. **12**(4), 219–226 (1988)
7. Voinea, R., Atanasiu, M.: Contribution a l'etude de la structure des chaines cinamatiques. Bulletinul Institutului Politehnic din Bucuresti **21**(1), 1–13 (1960)
8. Jiansheng, D., Duanling, L., Qixian, Z., et al.: Mobility analysis of a complex structured ball based on mechanism decomposition and equivalent screw system analysis. Mech. Mach. Theory **39**(4), 445–458 (2004)
9. Jiansheng, D., Zhen, H., Lipkin, H.: Mobility of overconstrained parallel mechanisms. J. Mech. Des. **128**(1), 220–229 (2006)
10. Xianwen, K., Gosselin, C.: Type synthesis of 3T1R 4-DOF parallel manipulators based on screw theory. IEEE Trans. Robot. Autom. **20**(2), 181–190 (2004)
11. Zhen, H., Jingfang, L., Daxing, Z.: A general methodology for mobility analysis of mechanisms based on constraint screw theory. Sci. China Ser. E: Technol. Sci. **52**(5), 1337–1347 (2009)
12. Zhen, H., Jingfang, L., Qinchuan, L.: A unified methodology for mobility analysis based on screw theory. In: Smart Devices and Machines for Advanced Manufacturing, pp. 49–78. Springer Publishing, London (2008)
13. Zhen, H., Jingfang, L., Yanwen, L.: On the Degree of Freedom of Mechanisms: The Universal Formula for Degree of Freedom Sought for 150 Years, 1st edn. Science Press, Beijing (2011)
14. Nazari, A.A., Hasani, A., Beedel, M.: Screw theory-based mobility analysis and projection-based kinematic modeling of a 3-CRRR parallel manipulator. J. Braz. Soc. Mech. Sci. Eng. **40**(7), 1–15 (2018). https://doi.org/10.1007/s40430-018-1277-3

15. Jingshan, Z., Fulei, C., Zhijing, F.: Mobility of Spatial Parallel Manipulators. In: Parallel Manipulators. towards New Applications, pp. 467–496. I-Tech Education Publishing, Vienna (2008)
16. Herve, M.: Analyse structurelle des mecanismes par groupe des deplacements. Mech. Mach. Theory **13**(4), 437–450 (1978)
17. Herve, M.: The LIE group of rigid body displacements, a fundamental tool for mechanism design. Mech. Mach. Theory **34**(5), 719–730 (1999)
18. Rico, M., Gallardo, J., Ravani, B.: Lie algebra and the mobility of kinematic chains. J. Robot. Syst. **20**(8), 477–499 (2003)
19. Rico, M., Ravani, B.: On mobility analysis of linkages using group theory. J. Mech. Des. **125**(1), 70–80 (2003)
20. Daniel, A., Rico, M., Gallardo, J.: Computer implementation of an improved Kutzbach–Grubler mobility criterion. In: ASME IDETC-CIE, pp. 549–557. Montreal (2002)
21. Tingli, Y., Aanxin, L., Huiping Sh., et al.: Topology design of robot mechanisms. 1st edn. Springer Singapore, Singapore (2018)
22. Tingli, Y., Dongjin, S.: A general degree of freedom formula for parallel mechanisms and multiloop spatial mechanisms. J. Mech. Robot. **4**(1), 1–17 (2012)
23. Tingli, Y., Anxin, L., Yufeng, L., et al.: Position and orientation characteristic equation for topological design of robot mechanisms. J. Mech. Des. **131**(2), 1–17 (2009)
24. John, C.: Introduction to robotics: mechanics and control, 4th edn. China Machine Press, Beijing (2018)
25. Youlun, X., Wenlong, L., Wenbin, Ch., et al.: Robotics: modeling, control, and vision. 5th edn. Huazhong University of Science and Technology Press, Wuhan (2018). (in Chinese)
26. Ming, Z., Ziyi, C., Jiagang, W.: Lectures on Mathematical Statistics. 1st edn. Fudan University Press, Shanghai (2006)
27. Alan, A., Brent, C.: Approximate is better than "exact" for interval estimation of binomial proportions. Am. Stat. **52**(2), 119–126 (1998)
28. Xiru, Ch.: Concise History of Statistics. 1st edn. Hunan Education Publishing House, Changsha (2002)
29. Hao, Ch., Weizhong, G., Zh., C., et al.: Synthesis and cross-section design of a new family of single-loop 7R deployable polygon mechanisms. Mech. Mach. Theory **198**, 105653 (2024)
30. Mingxuan, W., Hao, C., Yicheng. X., et al.: Exploring bundle folding in general line-symmetric Bricard mechanisms: dimensional synthesis and performance evaluation. Mech. Mach. Theory **210**, 106014 (2025)
31. Hao, C., Gaohan, Z., Weizhong, G., et al.: Kinematics and performance analysis for single-loop deployable polygonal mechanisms based on deployable paths. Mech. Mach. Theory **206**, 105907 (2025)
32. Hao, C., Weizhong, G., Zhenghao, W., et el.: Expanding the family of plane-symmetric 6R deployable polygon mechanisms by systematically exploring the layout of R-joint axes. Mech. Mach. Theory **202**, 105768 (2024)

Design and Analysis of Variable Geometry Truss Robot

Kaijie Dong[1,2,3(✉)], Xiang Huai[1,2,3], Zhouyi Ren[1,2,3], Jingyao Li[1,2,3], and Duanling Li[4,5]

[1] School of Mechanical Engineering, University of Science and Technology Beijing, Beijing 100083, China
dongkaijie@ustb.edu.cn
[2] National Key Laboratory of Aerospace Mechanism, Shanghai 201114, China
[3] Innovation School, University of Science and Technology Beijing, Foshan 528300, China
[4] School of Automation, Beijing University of Posts and Telecommunications, Beijing 100086, China
[5] College of Mechanical and Electrical Engineering, Shaanxi University of Science and Technology, Xi'an 710021, China

Abstract. With the development of the aerospace industry, the demand for on-orbit construction of large space platforms is increasing. However, the current on-orbit construction is in its infancy and faces the problem of error accumulation and inability to compensate, making the on-orbit construction extremely risky. To compensate for the accuracy of the on-orbit constructed truss, this project proposes a concept of a variable-geometry truss robot, which has high stiffness, large load-bearing capacity and high positioning accuracy, and can be used as a support structure and a height adjustment mechanism. In this paper, the structural design of the variable-geometry truss robot is carried out, and a modular structure composed of active nodes, passive nodes, pedestal nodes and drive rods is constructed. The forward kinematics problem of the octahedral parallel robot is deduced, and the mechanical performance analysis of the variable-geometry truss robot is carried out, including its stiffness analysis and dynamic analysis, which provides new ideas and methods for solving the problem of on-orbit construction error compensation.

Keywords: Truss robot · Structural design · Kinematic analysis · Stiffness analysis · Dynamic simulation

1 Introduction

With the aerospace industry's growth, the demand for large space platforms has surged, challenging the traditional "ground manufacturing—stowage launch—on-orbit deployment" model due to high costs and risks [1]. On-orbit construction has emerged as a key focus, but remains constrained by harsh space environments (vacuum, microgravity, extreme temperatures), modular splicing errors, and robotic precision limitations—compromising large-structure assembly accuracy [2].

To address this, a variable geometry truss robot is proposed. By integrating drive units, it adapts size/shape/pose to errors [3], offering a composite structure with high stiffness, load capacity, and positioning accuracy. Serving as both support framework and error-compensation mechanism, it resolves manufacturing constraints [4]. Its design—using statically determined truss rods for multi-DOF movement—overcomes serial robots' low stiffness and parallel robots' limited workspace [5, 6].

NASA pioneered research in the late 20th century, developing a double-octahedral deformable heavy-duty truss with a 975 kg load capacity, achieving breakthroughs in forward/inverse kinematics, trajectory planning, and static analysis. Internationally, the University of Virginia used shape memory alloys (SMA) for rigid-flexible trusses, though limited by deformation [7]. Domestic efforts, despite late start, include Harbin Institute of Technology's early VGT dynamics research [8], Sichuan University's polyhedral kinematics/control algorithms [9], and Shanghai Jiao Tong University's Lagrangian duality-based inverse kinematics optimization [10].

The variable geometry truss robot will not only endow the on-orbit construction process with higher flexibility but also break through the limitations of the traditional pure rigid construction method in technology, providing solid technical support and a new realization path for the on-orbit construction of large space platforms in China in the future [6, 11, 12].

This paper first carries out the overall scheme design of the robot based on the principle of variable geometry mechanism, then systematically analyzes the forward kinematics of the variable geometry truss robot structure and finally completes the performance analysis of the variable geometry truss robot.

2 Overall Design of Variable Geometry Truss Robot

2.1 Selection of Variable Geometry Truss Robot Cell Structure

In variable geometry truss robot design, basic unit selection significantly impacts mechanical properties, lightweight potential, and application effects. NASA's ISS/lunar-Mars base studies used hexahedral modular trusses [13], but these suffer from mechanical anisotropy—bearing capacity varies drastically under different directional loads—and have weak compression/shear resistance with low lightweight potential [14].

This paper proposes an octahedral variable geometry truss robot. Comparative analysis shows octahedrons outperform hexahedrons: their triangular truss arrangement ensures isotropy, enabling uniform multi-directional load distribution and stronger compression/shear resistance. Octahedrons also require less material for equivalent strength, offering greater lightweight potential (Figs. 1 and 3).

2.2 Structural Design of the Variable-Geometry Truss Robot

The variable-geometry truss robot unit comprises two symmetric connecting planes and a central driving plane [15]. Mirror-symmetric about the driving plane, this layout ensures mechanical balance and motion stability. The driving layer's triangular sides feature linear pairs, with revolute pairs inside; spherical pairs connect its ends to the connecting

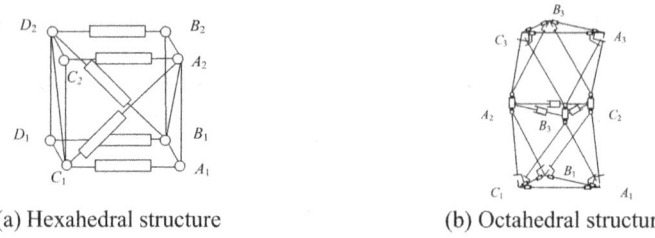

(a) Hexahedral structure   (b) Octahedral structure

Fig. 1. Cell structure configuration

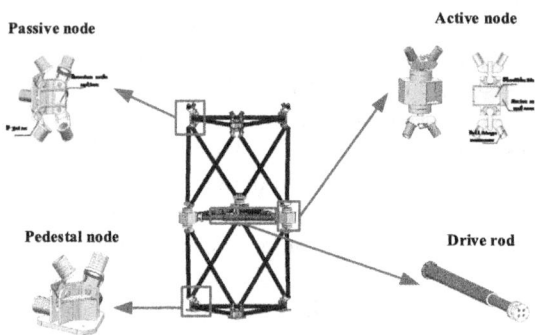 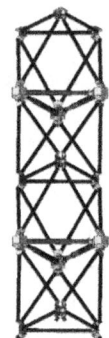

Fig. 2. Composition of Variable Geometry Truss Robot   **Fig. 3.** Modular structure design

layer, which uses a revolute-spherical pair hybrid design. The system composition is shown in Fig. 2.

The active node features a composite structure of flexible and spherical hinges. The flexible hinge enables precise elastic deformation for driving rod telescoping, while the spherical hinge allows multi-DOF rotation, together ensuring motion accuracy and force transmission. The passive node, simplified for support and guidance, uses a 150° V-type joint with optimized mechanics, ensuring central axes of rods and dowel screw intersect for stable geometric constraints. The pedestal node, similar in concept to the passive node, employs integrated processing to form a single structure of front/rear splints and base, eliminating assembly gaps for enhanced stiffness and anti-deformation. The driving rod sleeve uses lightweight high-strength carbon fiber composite pipes bonded to custom metal joints, with internal motor-screw drives for telescoping. Adjustable rods enable dynamic deformation, stiffness optimization, and multi-DOF movement between active nodes, cooperating with sensor feedback and controls for load adaptation and deployment tasks.

The structure uses modular design with symmetric double-octahedron truss units. Configurations transform by adjusting three rods in the actuator plane, ensuring high stiffness, large workspace, and good scalability.

3 Kinematic Analysis of the Variable-Geometry Truss Robot

Given that the kinematic geometric characteristics of the variable geometry truss robot are significantly different from those of traditional multi-joint robots, it is necessary to carry out kinematic analysis. For the octahedron configuration, its geometric shape is determined by the base triangle, the elbow triangle, and the top triangle. Assume that the base and top side trusses are always in the same equilateral triangle shape (i.e., $a_1 = b_1 = c_1 = a_3 = b_3 = c_3$), while the length of the side bars in the elbow plane $A_2B_2C_2$ (i.e., a_2, b_2, c_2) can vary arbitrarily. Taking the center of the base triangle as the coordinate origin, the specific definition of the basic coordinate system is shown in Fig. 4.

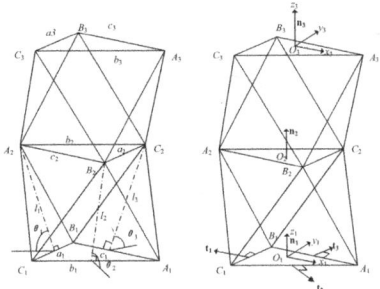

Fig. 4. Octahedron Configuration

In the case of the 4-parameter VGT robot unit, since the base triangle is an equilateral triangle, combining $l=\sqrt{1-k^2/4}$ and $r = \frac{k}{2\sqrt{3}}$ gives:

$$\overrightarrow{O_1A_2} = (r + l_1\cos\theta_1) \cdot \mathbf{t}_1 + l_1\sin\theta_1 \cdot \mathbf{n} \tag{1a}$$

$$\overrightarrow{O_1B_2} = (r + l_2\cos\theta_2) \cdot \mathbf{t}_2 + l_2\sin\theta_2 \cdot \mathbf{n} \tag{1b}$$

$$\overrightarrow{O_1C_2} = (r + l_3\cos\theta_3) \cdot \mathbf{t}_3 + l_3\sin\theta_3 \cdot \mathbf{n} \tag{1c}$$

From Eq. (1a)–(1c), the length of the elbow member can be obtained:

$$a_2^2 = 2l^2[1 - \cos(\theta_3 - \theta_2)] + 3(r + l\cos\theta_2)(r + l\cos\theta_3) \tag{2a}$$

$$b_2^2 = 2l^2[1 - \cos(\theta_1 - \theta_3)] + 3(r + l\cos\theta_3)(r + l\cos\theta_1) \tag{2b}$$

$$c_2^2 = 2l^2[1 - \cos(\theta_2 - \theta_1)] + 3(r + l\cos\theta_1)(r + l\cos\theta_2) \tag{2c}$$

By using Eq. (2a)–(2c), when a set of parameters (a_2, b_2, c_2, k) is given, a set of angles ($\theta_1, \theta_2, \theta_3$) can be calculated. From these results, the position of point A_2, B_2, C_2 can be calculated, and thus the position vector $\mathbf{g}_2$ of the center of the elbow triangle can be obtained.

The unit normal vector of the elbow triangle plane is calculated as follows:

$$\mathbf{n}_2 = \frac{\overrightarrow{O_1A_2} \times \overrightarrow{O_1B_2} + \overrightarrow{O_1B_2} \times \overrightarrow{O_1C_2} + \overrightarrow{O_1C_2} \times \overrightarrow{O_1A_2}}{||\overrightarrow{O_1A_2} \times \overrightarrow{O_1B_2} + \overrightarrow{O_1B_2} \times \overrightarrow{O_1C_2} + \overrightarrow{O_1C_2} \times \overrightarrow{O_1A_2}||} \tag{3}$$

Since the bottom equilateral triangle and the top equilateral triangle coincide with each other, the length of the diagonal is l, and the base plane $A_1B_1C_1$ and the top plane $A_2B_2C_2$ are symmetric with respect to the elbow plane $A_3B_3C_3$ respectively. The center vector $\mathbf{g}_3$ and its normal vector $\mathbf{n}_3$ of the top triangle are calculated as follows: When the following matrix is defined:

$$\mathbf{T} = 2(\mathbf{n}_2 \cdot \mathbf{n}_2^T) \tag{4}$$

The position vectors are as follows:

$$\mathbf{g}_3 = \mathbf{T}\mathbf{g}_2 \tag{5}$$

$$\mathbf{n}_3 = (\mathbf{T} - \mathbf{I})\mathbf{n}_1 \tag{6}$$

The coordinate transformation matrix $\mathbf{C}$ is given by Eqs. (5) and (6) as follows:

$$[x_3, y_3, z_3, 1]^T = \mathbf{C}[x_1, y_1, z_1, 1]^T \tag{7}$$

where:

$$\mathbf{C} = \begin{bmatrix} \frac{n_{3y}^2}{1+n_z} + n_z & -\frac{n_{3x}n_{3y}}{1+n_z} & n_{3x} & g_{3x} \\ -\frac{n_{3x}n_{3y}}{1+n_{3z}} & \frac{n_{3x}^2}{1+n_{3z}} + n_{3z} & n_{3y} & g_{3y} \\ -n_{3x} & -n_{3y} & n_{3z} & g_{3z} \\ 0 & 0 & 0 & 1 \end{bmatrix} \tag{8}$$

$$\mathbf{n}_3 = [n_{3x}, n_{3y}, n_{3z}]^T \tag{9}$$

$$\mathbf{g}_3 = [g_{3x}, g_{3y}, g_{3z}]^T \tag{10}$$

where $\mathbf{C}$ is the homogeneous transformation matrix from the base surface coordinates to the top surface coordinates. This transformation matrix represents a 2-DOF rotation and 3-DOF translation. Notably, the internal dependencies among transformation elements make the 4-parameter VGT robot have 3 effective DOFs.

4 Performance Analysis of Variable Geometry Truss Robot

4.1 Stiffness Analysis

The axial stiffness of the truss structure is an important indicator to measure its ability to resist axial deformation. Figure 5 shows the schematic diagram of the truss under the action of axial force. Since the truss has a regular octahedron structure and the three vertices have high symmetry, therefore, only the force analysis of one of the vertices needs to be carried out to obtain the axial stiffness characteristics of the entire extension arm.

Now select point A as the research object. According to the principle of force balance, we have

$$2F_b + 2F_d = F \tag{11}$$

Among them, F_b is the force on the crossbar, F_d is the force on the diagonal bar, and the two together with the external force F form a balanced force system.

The crossbar mainly undergoes bending deformation during the force application process. According to the maximum deflection formula in material mechanics, the relationship between the deformation and the force of the crossbar can be established:

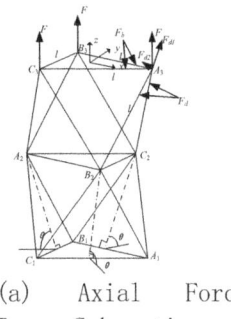 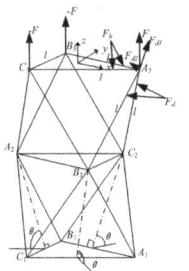 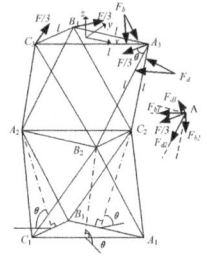

(a) Axial Force Truss Schematic   (b) Bending Force Truss Schematic   (c) Torsional Force Truss Schematic

Fig. 5. Stiffness Analysis

$$\Delta_b = \frac{F_b l^3}{3 E_b I_b} \tag{12}$$

The diagonal bar is subjected to combined tension and bending deformation, corresponding to the axial force F_{d1} and the tangential force F_{d2} in Fig. 5, and the total deformation is

$$\Delta_d = \frac{F_d \cos 30° l}{E_d A_d} + \frac{F_d \sin 30° l^3}{3 E_d I_d} \tag{13}$$

Obtained from the calculation formula of tensile stiffness

$$n\Delta_b = \frac{3FL}{EA} \tag{14}$$

Among them, n represents the total number of elements of the truss.

The expression for the deformation of the vertical crossbar and the oblique bar, obtained the axial stiffness of the truss

$$EA = \frac{9\sqrt{3} \sin\theta E_b I_b \left(\frac{9}{E_d A_d} + \frac{3\sqrt{3} l^2}{E_d I_d} + \frac{4 l^2}{E_b I_b} \right)}{l^2 \left(\frac{9}{E_d A_d} + \frac{3\sqrt{3} l^2}{E_d I_d} \right)} \tag{15}$$

Among them, l is the bar length, θ is the dihedral angle between the side of the truss and the horizontal plane, E_dA_d is the tensile stiffness of the diagonal bar, E_bI_b is the bending stiffness of the crossbar, and E_dI_d is the bending stiffness of the diagonal bar.

When studying the bending stiffness of the truss, refer to the schematic diagram of the truss under bending force shown in Fig. 5. Assume that point A is subjected to a tensile force F, while point B, C is subjected to a compressive force $-F$. The radius of the circumscribed circle of the equilateral triangle at the top of the truss is R, and the entire extension arm is subjected to a bending moment of $M = 2FR$.

Analyze the force condition of point A, and its tensile state is the same as that in the axial stiffness analysis. The total displacement of point A in tension for each layer of the truss is

$$\Delta_A = \frac{Fnl \cos 30° \sin \theta}{EA} \tag{16}$$

While the total displacement of point B in compression is

$$\Delta_B = \frac{Fnl \cos 30° \sin \theta}{EA} \tag{17}$$

The bottom of the truss is fixed, and the end is subjected to a bending moment. The schematic diagram of its bending deformation is shown in Fig. 6

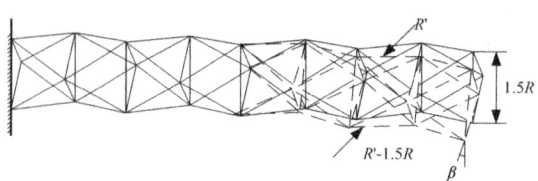

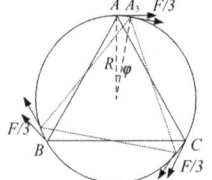

(a) Schematic diagram of the truss under bending deformation

(b) Schematic diagram of the truss under torsional deformation

Fig. 6. Schematic diagram of the truss subjected to deformation

Let the radius of curvature of the arc length after bending and stretching above the extension arm be R', the radius of curvature of the arc length after bending and compression below be $R' - \frac{3}{2}R$, and the bending angle be β.

By simultaneously solving the two equations, the deformation angle can be obtained.

$$\beta = \frac{4Fnl \cos 30° \sin \theta}{3EAR} \tag{18}$$

The bending stiffness of the truss can be obtained.

$$EI = \frac{81\sqrt{3} \sin \theta E_b I_b \left(\frac{9}{E_d A_d} + \frac{3\sqrt{3}l^2}{E_d I_d} + \frac{4l^2}{E_b I_b} \right)}{32 \left(\frac{9}{E_d A_d} + \frac{3\sqrt{3}l^2}{E_d I_d} \right)} \tag{19}$$

To study the torsional stiffness characteristics of the truss, it is assumed that the truss end is subjected to a torque of magnitude $T = FR$, that is, the three end points of the extension arm are respectively subjected to tangential forces of magnitude $F/3$, and its force diagram is shown in Fig. 5.

Taking the calculation of the deformation of point A as an example, combined with the schematic diagram of the truss under torsional deformation shown in Fig. 6, let the total torsional angle of the extension arm be φ, the torsional angle of a single unfolding unit be φ_1, $O'G$ which is the increment of the scissor rod, AA_3 is the torsional displacement of vertex B, the displacements of the diagonal rod and the cross bar are equal, the tangential force of the diagonal rod in the figure is F_{d1}, the axial force F_{d2}, the axial force of the cross bar is F_{b1}, and the tangential force F_{b2}.

$$\Delta_A = \Delta_b = F_b \left(\frac{\cos 60° l}{E_b A_b} + \frac{\sin 60° l^3}{3 E_b I_b} \right) = F_d \left(\frac{\cos \theta l}{E_d A_d} + \frac{\sin \theta l^3}{3 E_d I_d} \right) \quad (20)$$

From the geometric relationship in the figure, the calculation formula for torsional stiffness can be obtained.

$$\varphi = \frac{nTl \cos 30° \sin \theta}{GI_p} = \frac{nFRl \cos 30° \sin \theta}{GI_p}$$

$$= n\varphi_1 = n \frac{F_d \left(\frac{\cos \theta l}{E_d A_d} + \frac{\sin \theta l^3}{3 E_d I_d} \right)}{R} \quad (21)$$

By simultaneously solving the above formulas, the torsional stiffness of the truss can be obtained.

$$GI_p = \frac{3\sqrt{3} \sin \theta l^2 \left(\frac{\cos \theta}{E_d A_d} + \frac{\sin \theta l^2}{3 E_d I_d} + \frac{1}{2 E_b A_b} + \frac{\sqrt{3} l^2}{6 E_b I_b} \right)}{16 \left(\frac{1}{E_b A_b} + \frac{\sqrt{3} l^2}{3 E_b I_b} \right) \left(\frac{\cos \theta}{E_d A_d} + \frac{\sin \theta l^2}{3 E_d I_d} \right)} \quad (22)$$

Based on the theories of material mechanics and elasticity, taking the initial load of 100 N as the boundary condition, through the analytical formula and structural parameters, the theoretical value of axial stiffness can be obtained as $EA = 2.99 \times 10^8$ N/m, the theoretical value of bending stiffness as $EI = 2.10 \times 10^7$ Nm^2, and the theoretical value of torsional stiffness as $GI_p = 6.93 \times 10^7$ Nm/rad.

Figure 7 is the stiffness simulation analysis diagram. Import the three-dimensional structure model into the Ansys finite element analysis software for simulation analysis, and the simulation results of axial stiffness can be obtained as $EA = 1.49 \times 10^8$ N/m, the simulation results of bending stiffness as $EI = 1.30 \times 10^7$ Nm^2, and the simulation results of torsional stiffness as $GI_p = 4.6 \times 10^7$ Nm/rad.

According to Table 1, by comparing the values calculated theoretically with those obtained from the simulation analysis, it can be found that the orders of magnitude of the theoretical values and the simulated values are the same, which indicates that the data calculation is correct, and the simulation effect is good.

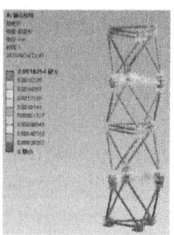 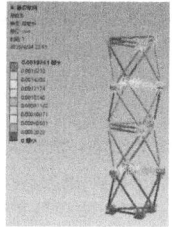 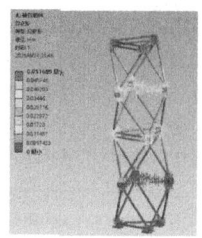 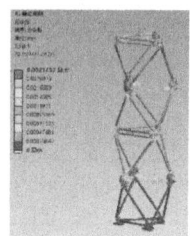

(a) Tensile Stiffness (b) Compressive Stiffness (c) Bending Stiffness (d) Torsional Stiffness

Fig. 7. Stiffness simulation analysis diagram

Table 1. Stiffness Analysis Comparison Chart

Types of Stiffness	Theoretical Calculation Value	Ansys Simulation Value
Axial Stiffness	$EA = 2.99 \times 10^8$ N/m	$EA = 1.49 \times 10^8$ N/m
Bending Stiffness	$EI = 2.10 \times 10^7$ Nm^2	$EI = 1.30 \times 10^7$ Nm^2
Torsional Stiff-ness	$GI_p = 6.93 \times 10^7$ Nm/rad	$GI_p = 4.6 \times 10^7$ Nm/rad

4.2 Simulation Analysis

A simplified simulation model of the driving surface of the variable-geometry truss robot was constructed in Adams software, and a simulation analysis was carried out on its motion process to verify the reliability of the driving rod scheme. Considering the complex structure of the driving rod, a simplified structure was used to replace the model, and it was assumed that the driving rod moved at a speed of 1 mm per second. The initial state of the angle between the driving rods was all 60°. During the simulation process, the focus was on observing the force change and angle response of the flexible hinge when the driving rod was working. Figure 8 shows the Adams simulation model. When the driving rod was stretched or compressed, the curve of the force change of the flexible hinge is shown as follows.

 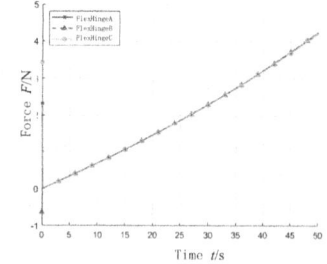

(a) Adams Simulation Model   (b) Curve of Force Change of Flexible Hinge

Fig. 8. Adams Simulation

The angle changes of the three flexible hinges are shown in Fig. 9.

Based on the analysis of the simulation data, during the motion of the driving rod, the flexible hinge structure shows significant elastic deformation characteristics, and its rotation angle change range is from 0° to 10°. It is particularly worth noting that when one driving rod is extended and the other two driving rods are compressed synchronously, the amplitude of the angle change of the flexible hinge reaches the peak value.

Verified by the prototype, when the length of the driving rod is adjusted within the range of 600–800 mm, the prototype can successfully achieve the deformation function.

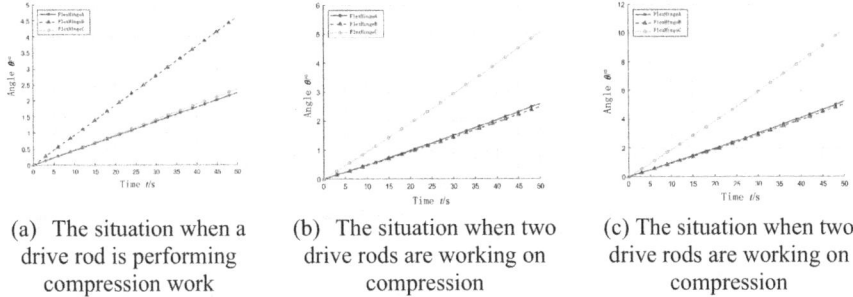

(a) The situation when a drive rod is performing compression work

(b) The situation when two drive rods are working on compression

(c) The situation when two drive rods are working on compression

Fig. 9. Diagram of Angle Change of Flexible Hinge Driven by Driving Rod

and the structural deformation amount is always controlled within the allowable tolerance range of the design (Fig. 10).

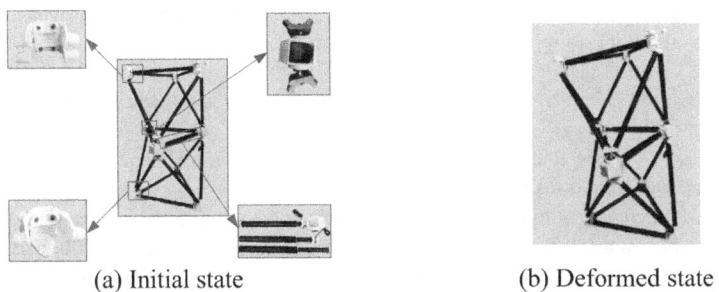

(a) Initial state

(b) Deformed state

Fig. 10. Overall structural prototype

5 Conclusions

(1) This paper proposes a variable geometry truss robot for on-orbit error compensation, designing its structure with octahedral basic units and a modular system of active/passive nodes, pedestals, and drive rods.

(2) Forward kinematics of the octahedral parallel robot is derived: assuming equilateral base and top triangles, position/normal vector expressions of the upper platform are obtained, and a homogeneous transformation matrix is built to reveal 3-DOF motion.

(3) Mechanical analysis shows Ansys-verified stiffness consistency between theory and simulation. Adams dynamics simulation compares driving rod motions to derive flexible hinge variations, validating model accuracy.

Funding. The Joint Funds of the National Natural Science Foundation of China (No. U23A20338), the National Natural Science Foundation of China (Nos. 52175019 and 52405007), the Natural Science Foundations of Beijing (Nos. 3212009 and L222038), the Guangdong Basic and Applied Basic Research Foundation (No. 2023A1515110150), the Space Drive and Manipulation Mechanism Laboratory of BICE (No. SDMM-2024-04), and the Open Project of National Key Laboratory of Aerospace Mechanism (2024ASM-KFZY02).

References

1. Xue, Z.H., Liu, J., Wu, C., et al.: Review of in-space assembly technologies. Chin. J. Aeronaut. **34**(11), 21–47 (2021)
2. Gilhooley, N.I.: In-orbit construction with a Helical Seam Pipe mill. J. Br. Interplanetary Soc. **66**, 167–170 (2013)
3. Chen, W.J.: Research on Design Principles and Deployment Dynamics Analysis Theory of Space Deployable Truss Structures. Zhejiang University, Zhejiang (1998)
4. Lee, N., Backes, P., Burdick, J., et al.: Architecture for in-space robotic assembly of a modular space telescope. J. Astron. Telescopes, Instr. Syst. **2**(4), 041207 (2016)
5. Zhao, Y., Hu, S., Yang, Y.: Inverse kinematics of asymmetric octahedral variable geometry truss manipulator with obstacle avoidance through inexact interior point optimization. Int. J. Adv. Rob. Syst. **15**(6), 1729881418817182 (2018)
6. Zhao, W., Zhang, W.: A novel redundant continuum manipulator with variable geometry trusses. International Conference on Intelligent Robotics and Applications. Cham, Springer International Publishing, pp. 199–211 (2018)
7. Zhu, S.K., Min, X., Dong, S.J.: Characteristic analysis of shape memory alloy elastic coupling system based on improved phase transformation equation. J. Mech. Eng. **60**(14), 194–205 (2024). https://doi.org/10.3901/JME.2024.14.194
8. Zhao, H.J.: Dynamic analysis and active vibration suppression of deployable truss structures. Heilongjiang, Harbin Institute of Technology (2011)
9. Lei, Y.: Kinematic solution of redundant double-octahedron variable geometry truss robot based on neural network. J. Sichuan Univ. (Eng. Sci. Ed.) **32**(2), 90–94 (2000)
10. Zhao, Y., Hu, S., Yang, Y.: Inverse kinematics for the variable geometry truss manipulator via a Lagrangian dual method. Int. J. Adv. Rob. Syst. **13**(6), 1729881416666779 (2016)
11. Zi, B., Zhao, J.H., Wang, W., et al.: Research status and development trend of key technologies for large-space rigid-flexible coupling robots. J. Mech. Eng. **60**(23), 21–42 (2024)
12. Fang, H.R., Yao, J., Hu, Z.Q., et al.: Simplified rigid body motion analysis of a novel variable geometry truss robot. Rob. Technol. Appl. **01**, 46–48 (2002)
13. Xu, H.B., Han, X.Z., Chen, Y., et al.: Discussion on on-orbit construction technology of large space load platforms. Space Electron. Technol. **15**(2), 42–48 (2018)
14. Porta, M.J., Thomas, F.: Closed-form position analysis of variable geometry trusses. Mech. Mach. Theory **109**, 14–21 (2017)
15. Qian, L.H., Hu, S.Q., Yang, Y.S.: Analytical algorithm for inverse kinematics of multi-segment double-octahedron variable geometry truss arms. J. Zhejiang Univ. (Eng. Sci. Ed.). **51**(01), 75–81+130 (2017)

AMM: An Aerial Modular Manipulator Based on Standardized Modules

Yuelei Fang[1], Ye Li[2], Yijian Zhang[1], Ziqi Wang[1], Daming Liu[1], Shouyi Zhang[1], Nanlin Zhou[1], Sikai Zhao[1], Jie Zhao[1], and Yanhe Zhu[1(✉)]

[1] State Key Laboratory of Robotics and System, Harbin Institute of Technology, Harbin 150000, China
yhzhu@hit.edu.cn

[2] The School of Astronautics, Harbin Institute of Technology, Harbin 150000, China

Abstract. In specialized missions such as rubble rescue and unstructured space exploration, aerial manipulators play a critical role. The core challenge lies in the inability of fixed-configuration aerial manipulators to adapt to dynamic environments and evolving task requirements. To address this, this study proposes an aerial modular manipulator (AMM) system based on standardized isomorphic modules. By varying module quantities and assembly configurations, this system achieves reconfigurable operational capabilities tailored to mission-specific demands. Introduce the virtual rotation axis to describe the assembly configuration relationship between modules and establish a unified kinematic model. To accommodate configuration changes arising from module reconfiguration and UAV coupling, neural network-based estimation of dynamic characteristics is implemented. An attitude extended state observer (AESO) is designed to estimate real-time attitude disturbances induced by manipulator motion and payload variations. Experimental validation demonstrates: During configuration switching, AMM exhibits a maximum attitude deviation $\leq 12°$ (recovery time: $1 \pm 0.21\,\mathrm{s}$). Success rates in grasping tasks show progressive gradients: 93.8% for lightweight deformable objects, 87.5% and 93.8% for medium-load and heavy-load irregular objects respectively, 81.3% for heterogeneous eccentric-load objects and 75.0% for heavy-load irregular objects. These results verify the system's comprehensive adaptability to geometric features, material properties, and dynamic behaviors within a $500\,\mathrm{g}$ payload range.

Keywords: Modular manipulator · Aerial manipulator · AESO

1 Introduction

With the development of low-altitude economy and robotics technology, aerial manipulators (AMs) have become a cutting-edge direction in the field of unmanned aerial vehicles (UAVs) [1–4]. Currently, the manipulators equipped

---

Y. Fang and Y. Li—Contribute equally to this work.

in AM systems can be classified into rigid and flexible types. Rigid manipulators have the advantages of strong operational capabilities and the ability to provide more degrees of freedom, but they also have the disadvantages of fixed configuration and large mass. The trade-off between mass and degrees of freedom is a research hotspot in this field. Flexible manipulators have the advantages of lightweight and flexibility, but their complex dynamic characteristics pose significant challenges in the design of controllers [1,5,6].

In the current field of robot research, the modularization concept has been widely applied in various areas, such as modularized external limbs, etc. [6–9]. However, modular manipulators capable of performing multiple predefined tasks still possess vast potential for development. Fixed-configured flying robotic arms have inherent limitations when dealing with tasks in complex environments [3,10,11]. When faced with diverse, complex, and unpredictable task demands, such AM often struggle to meet all the requirements of the tasks. For instance, when inspecting the operational status of high-voltage transmission towers, the manipulator often needs to extend over long distances; while in post-disaster ruins, it is required to reach into crevices to search for signs of life, which demands high-precision fine operations in confined spaces. Based on this issue, this study proposes an AMM system composed of a rigid robotic arm rapidly reconfigured from standard modules and a UAV. The modular manipulator (MM) in the system is formed by serially connecting multiple isomorphic basic modules, each of which has an independent rotational degree of freedom. By changing the number of modules and their configuration methods, users can configure the most suitable AMM system for the current scenario. We introduce a virtual rotation axis to represent the assembly configuration between modules and establish a regular mathematical model based on the D-H method. Since the dynamic characteristics of MM change when the number and configuration of modules change, and its combination with UAV further complicates this issue, we consider the dynamic characteristics of the base-floating manipulator in the design of the control strategy for MM to achieve better manipulation performance.

Finally, we conducted attitude control and load experiments to verify the stability of the attitude expansion observer and the overall system, demonstrating the superiority of the modular flying robotic arm in handling different load operations. The experiments verified the feasibility of the AMM system in grasping and placing tasks. Moreover, the attitude expansion state observer has strong robustness and can effectively estimate the attitude disturbance caused by the state of the manipulator and load changes, ensuring the stability of the AMM system during the operation of the manipulator.

2 Manipulator Analysis

2.1 Configuration Mode Analysis

In this study, we assembled the modular manipulator(MM) using standard modules independently developed by our team. The core of MM is based on isomorphic basic modules that can be quickly connected and separated. A basic module unit consists of two sub-modules and each module unit has one degree of rotational freedom. An MM is composed of multiple basic module units with the same structure connected in series, therefore, the overall degree of freedom of MM is determined by the number of constituent modules.

It should be noted that the operational capability of the MM is determined not only by its degrees of freedom (DOF), but also on the assembly and configuration modes between the modules. Specifically, the configuration mode between modules can be changed by rotating the module unit about the normal vector of its interface plane with the upper-level module unit. There are four configuration modes between every two standard modules (see Fig. 1). This modular design not only ensures the standardization of the structure but also achieves functional expansion through configuration diversity.

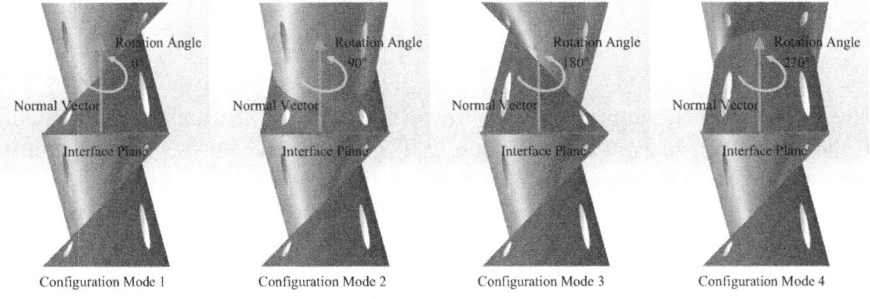

Fig. 1. Four configuration modes between two modules, achieved by rotating the interface plane about its normal vector to 0°, 90°, 180°, and 270° orientations respectively.

2.2 Kinematic Analysis

Unlike ordinary manipulators, MM have the characteristic of reconfigurability. Therefore, the D-H method needs to be modified to conduct kinematic modeling. In addition to the rotation of the module itself, we also introduce a virtual rotation axis between every two modules to describe the configuration between the modules. After introducing the virtual axis, we use the D-H method for system establishment.

The MM is constructed using isomorphic standard modules, whose homogeneous architecture endows the D-H parameters with inherent regularity. To enable unified kinematic analysis in varying module quantities and assembly configurations, we developed a normalized coordinate transformation framework through optimized mapping between the world frame and 0 frame. This methodology not only accentuates the structural periodicity of D-H parameters, but more critically establishes a generalized mathematical formulation for multi-configuration MM systems, thereby substantially enhancing the algorithmic adaptability. The D-H table is shown in Table 1.

Table 1. D-H Parameters for Modular Manipulator

i	θ_i	α_i	a_i	d_i
1	$\theta_1 \in \{0,\ \pi/2,\ 3\pi/2\}$	$\pi/4$	0	100
2	$\theta_2 \in [-\pi,\ \pi]$	$-\pi/4$	0	0
...	...	...	...	...
n	θ_n	$-1^{n+1} \times \pi/4$	0	$(n\%2) \times 100$

Where, the % operator denotes the modulo operation. When i is an odd number, θ describes the assembly configuration of the module; when i is an even number, θ represents the rotational configuration.

Through the D-H parameters, the kinematic equation of MM can be expressed as

$$_{\text{eff}}^{\text{world}}T = {}_{0}^{\text{world}}T \cdot \prod_{i=0}^{n} {}_{i+1}^{i}T \cdot {}_{\text{eff}}^{n}T \tag{1}$$

where, $_{\text{eff}}^{\text{world}}T$ is the homogeneous transformation matrix from the 0 coordinate frame to the world coordinate frame; $_{\text{eff}}^{n}T$ is the homogeneous transformation matrix from the effector coordinate frame to the n coordinate frame.

Considering the carrying capacity of the UAV, we assembled a MM composed of three basic module units onto the UAV. The UAV is responsible for moving to the target direction, and the robotic arm is responsible for achieving the target orientation. Each module has 4 assembly configurations, then the MM composed of three modules has $4^3 = 64$ assembly configurations. We selected four configuration modes: [0 0 0], [90 90 90], [180 180 180] and [270 270 270] for analysis and obtained their workspaces (see Fig. 2).

When the [0 0 0] configuration mode is adopted, the workspace of MM is a two-dimensional plane; when the [90 90 90] and [270 270 270] configuration modes are adopted, the workspaces of MM are two three-dimensional bowl-shaped spaces in opposite directions; when the [180 180 180] configuration mode is adopted, the workspace of MM is a three-dimensional torus isomorphic to a doughnut. To carry out various experiments with MM mounted on a UAV in the future, we will adopt the [180 180 180] configuration mode, which has a large workspace and a symmetric topological structure.

Since MM is only responsible for achieving the target orientation, we only solve the orientation of MM when solving the inverse kinematics. After completing the orientation solution, we bring the joint configurations into the forward kinematics of the arm, and the residual of the end position is calculated and fed back to the mobile part to achieve the target.

To adapt to the variety of MM with different number of modules and different configuration modes, we adopted the numerical method to solve the inverse kinematics of MM. The orientation residuals and regularization residuals of the robotic arm are, respectively:

$$r_q(t) = scale_q \cdot q^{-1} \cdot q_r \tag{2}$$

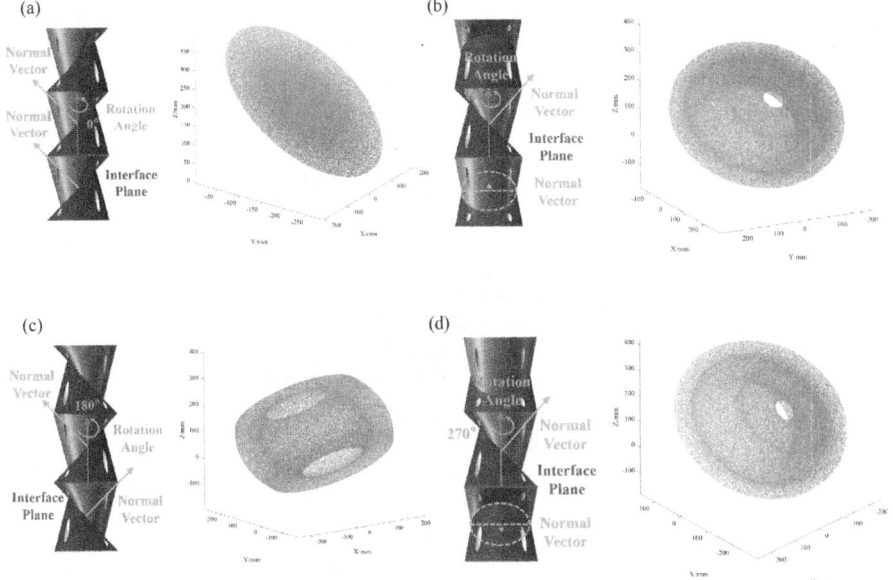

Fig. 2. Schematic diagrams of the workspace of MM. Figures (a), (b), (c), and (d) represent the workspaces of MM configured at angles of [0 0 0], [90 90 90], [180 180 180], and [270 270 270], respectively.

$$r_r(t) = scale_r \cdot (q(t) - q(t_{pre})) \quad (3)$$

where, $q(t)$ is the quaternion of the current end-effector orientation of MM, and q_r is the quaternion of the end-effector reference orientation; t_{pre} refers to the previous moment; $scale_q$ and $scale_r$ are, respectively, the proportional factors of the orientation residual and the regularization residual. Therefore, the total residual can be represented as

$$res = \begin{bmatrix} r_q(t) & r_r(t) \end{bmatrix} \quad (4)$$

Consequently, the total Jacobian matrix of inverse kinematics can be represented as follows.

$$J = \begin{bmatrix} J_o \\ J_r \end{bmatrix} \quad (5)$$

Ultimately, the iterative formula for solving inverse kinematics through numerical methods can be derived as follows:

$$\theta_{k+1} = \theta_k - \left((J^T J)^{-1} + \mu I\right)^{-1} J^T res \quad (6)$$

2.3 Floating Base Analysis

Unlike traditional mechanical systems where the base is fixed, the MM mounted on the UAV forms an aerial modular manipulator (AMM) with a floating base relative to the MM [12–14]. Due to factors such as the UAV's own system and external disturbances, the movement of the UAV will cause changes in the position and orientation of the MM's base, thereby altering the dynamics of the MM and leading to poor operation. To improve the trajectory tracking problem caused by the floating base, we establish the kinematics of the FMM (Floating Modular Manipulator) based on the kinematics of the MM (see Fig. 3).

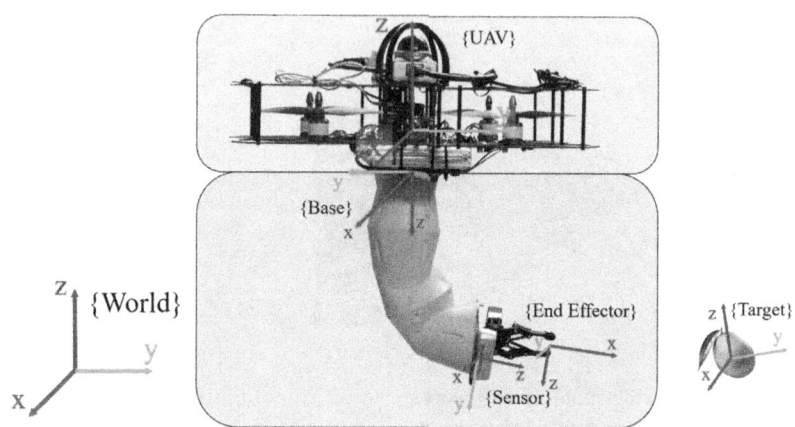

Fig. 3. Coordinate Transformation of AMM Pose with floating base.

$^W_E P$ and $^W_E R$ are, respectively the position and orientation of the end effector in the world coordinate system

$$\begin{bmatrix} ^W_E P \\ ^W_E R \end{bmatrix} = \begin{bmatrix} ^W_U P + ^W_U R \cdot ^U_E P \\ ^W_U R \cdot ^U_B R \cdot ^U_E R \end{bmatrix} \quad (7)$$

The equation of motion of a manipulator is usually expressed as

$$\tau = M\ddot{\theta} + C\dot{\theta} + g \quad (8)$$

where, M is a positive definite symmetric matrix that describes the characteristics of inertia; C is the Coriolis force and the centrifugal force term; g is the gravity term.

However, since the FMM is composed of any number of modules in any assembly configuration, the dynamic equation of the FMM will change when the number of modules and the configuration method change. In addition, due to the influence of the floating base, the position and orientation disturbances of the UAV $\delta\theta = \begin{bmatrix} \delta x & \delta y & \delta z & \delta\alpha & \delta\beta & \delta\gamma \end{bmatrix}$ and their first-order derivatives $\delta\omega = \begin{bmatrix} \delta\dot{x} & \delta\dot{y} & \delta\dot{z} & \delta\dot{\alpha} & \delta\dot{\beta} & \delta\dot{\gamma} \end{bmatrix}$ also need to be considered for their impact on the dynamic characteristics of the FMM system. Therefore, the traditional dynamic equation cannot describe well the dynamic characteristics of the FMM.

Due to the diversity of FMM and the complexity brought by the floating base, we adopt the neural network approach to approximate its dynamic characteristics, as shown in the following equation.

$$\tau_t = \text{Net}\left(\ddot{\theta}_t, \dot{\theta}_t, \theta_t, \delta\theta_t, \delta\omega_t\right) \tag{9}$$

This study adopted a MM composed of three modules in [180 180 180] configuration as the experimental platform, which was subsequently mounted on the UAV system.

3 UAV Analysis

3.1 Modeling and Control of the Attitude Loop of UAV

During the flight of the UAV, the manipulator constantly changes its orientation and load, which greatly affects the flight attitude of the UAV. The influence of this attitude cannot be directly modeled as the load changes. Therefore, an extended state observer is proposed to estimate the attitude disturbance caused by the mechanical arm and the load, in order to maintain the stability of the UAV during aerial operations.

The general interference to the unmanned aerial vehicle can be regarded as the torque disturbance caused by the operation of the manipulator, denoted as d_τ, and there exists a constant $\bar{d}_\tau$ such that $\left\|\dot{d}_\tau\right\| \leq \bar{d}_\tau$.

Based on the equations of Newton's second law and the Lagrange - Euler equations, and taking into account the aforementioned disturbances, the equation for the attitude dynamics of a quadrotor unmanned aerial vehicle is

$$M(\eta)\ddot{\eta} + C(\eta,\dot{\eta})\dot{\eta} = \tau + d_\tau \tag{10}$$

The error of the attitude loop is defined as

$$e_\eta = \eta_d - \eta \tag{11}$$

where, η_d represents the expected Euler angles and η are the current Euler angles. Therefore, the controller of the attitude loop can be expressed as

$$\tau_d = K_\eta e_\eta - K_\omega \omega - \hat{d}_\tau \tag{12}$$

where, ω represents the angular velocity in the body coordinate system, K_1 and K_2 are positive definite gain matrices, respectively, and $\hat{d}_\tau$ is the estimated attitude disturbance caused by the manipulator.

When the manipulator is working, it is desired that the UAV remains stable. Set the expected angular velocity to zero. This setting is applicable to drones operating within a small-angle range.

Defining $x_1 = \eta$, $x_2 = \Omega$ and $x_3 = d_\tau$, where Ω is the angular velocity in the world coordinate system, the attitude dynamics can be expressed as

$$\begin{cases} \dot{x}_1 = x_2 \\ \dot{x}_2 = M^{-1}(\tau - C\dot{\eta} + x_3) \\ \dot{x}_3 = \dot{d}_\tau \end{cases} \tag{13}$$

The extended state observer in the attitude loop is used to observe and estimate the angle disturbances brought about by the manipulator and the responsible party

$$\begin{cases} \dot{y}_1 = y_2 + K_1 e_1 \\ \dot{y}_2 = \hat{M}^{-1}(\tau - \hat{C} y_2 + y_3) + K_2 e_1 \\ \dot{y}_3 = K_3 e_1 \end{cases} \tag{14}$$

where, y_1, y_2 and y_3 are, respectively the estimated values of x_1, x_2 and x_3, K_1, K_2 and $K_3 \in \mathbb{R}^{3\times 3}$ are the gains of the extended state observer, $e_1 = x_1 - y_1$. $\hat{M}$ and $\hat{C}$ are the estimated values of M and C, $K = [K_1, K_2, K_3]$.

3.2 Stability Analysis of UAV

Since the flight angle of the AMM during operation is a small angle, the dynamics model of the UAV can be linearized as

$$M_0 \ddot{\eta} + C_0 \dot{\eta} = \tau + d_\tau \tag{15}$$

where, M_0 and C_0 are constant matrices, used to represent the inertia and damping matrices of the linearized approximation. Define the angle estimation error in the extended state observer as

$$e_a = x_a - z_a \tag{16}$$

where, $x_a = [x_1^T, x_2^T, x_3^T]^T$, $z_a = [z_1^T, z_2^T, z_3^T]^T$ and $e_a = [e_1^T, e_2^T, e_3^T]^T$.

Considering the state vector $\xi = [e_\eta^T, \dot{e}_\eta^T, e_a^T]^T$ that conforms to the system, construct

$$V(\xi) = \frac{1}{2} e_\eta^T P_1 e_\eta + \frac{1}{2} \dot{e}_\eta^T P_2 \dot{e}_\eta + \frac{1}{2} e_a^T P_3 e_a \tag{17}$$

where, P_1, P_2 and P_3 are positive definite matrices. Substituting the controller shown in formula (12) into formula (15) yields the dynamic of the angle tracking error

$$\ddot{e}_\eta + K_\omega \dot{e}_\eta + K_\eta e_\eta = M_0^{-1}(e_3 - \dot{d}_\tau) \tag{18}$$

The sorted result is as follows

$$\dot{\xi}_1 = A_c \xi_1 + B_c (e_3 - \dot{d}_\tau) \tag{19}$$

where, $\xi_1 = [e_\eta^T, \dot{e}_\eta^T]^T$, $A_c = \begin{bmatrix} 0 & I \\ -K_\eta & -K_\omega \end{bmatrix}$ and $B_c = \begin{bmatrix} 0 \\ M_0^{-1} \end{bmatrix}$. The dynamic of the estimation error of the angle can be expressed as

$$\dot{e}_a = We_a + D\dot{d}_\tau \tag{20}$$

where, $D = [0, 0, I]^T$, $W = \begin{bmatrix} -K_1 & I & 0 \\ -K_2 & -M_0^{-1}C_0 & M_0^{-1} \\ -K_3 & 0 & 0 \end{bmatrix}$. Differentiating formula (17) yields

$$\dot{V} = \xi_1^T \begin{bmatrix} P_1 & 0 \\ 0 & P_2 \end{bmatrix} \dot{\xi}_1 + e_a^T P_3 \dot{e}_a \tag{21}$$

Substituting formula (21) into formula (20) yields

$$\dot{V} = \xi_1^T Q_c \xi_1 + 2\xi_1^T PB_c(e_{a3} - \dot{d}_\tau) + e_a^T(W^T P_3 + P_3 W)e_a + 2e_a^T P_3 D\dot{d}_\tau \tag{22}$$

where, $Q_c = A_c^T P + PA_c$, $P = dig(P_1, P_2)$.

Since the disturbances caused by the changes in the state and load of the manipulator satisfy the condition, the Cauchy-Schwarz inequality can be applied to obtain

$$\dot{V} \leq -\lambda_c \|\xi_1\|^2 - \lambda_a \|e_a\|^2 + 2\gamma_1 \|\xi_1\| \|e_a\| + 2\gamma_2 \|e_a\| \bar{d}_\tau \tag{23}$$

where, $\lambda_c = \lambda_{\min}(Q_c)$, $W^T P_3 + P_3 W = -Q_3$, $\gamma_1 = \|PB_c\|$ and $\gamma_2 = \|P_3 D\|$. From formula (23), it can be obtained that by adjusting the gains K_η, K_ω, and K_a, the disturbance influence can be suppressed, making $\dot{V} < 0$ hold for sufficiently large $\|\xi\|$, which proves the uniform ultimate boundedness.

4 Experiment

In this section of the experimental results, to verify the mechanical robustness of the AMM and the stability of the controller, this study conducted flight tests in a real environment.

4.1 Dynamic Posture Stability Verification

The first experiment was designed to demonstrate the stability of the AMM in the air during movement of the manipulator. At the initial state ($t = 0\,\text{s}$), the manipulator was in the zero configuration. To evaluate the control system's ability to suppress random disturbances, target postures were randomly generated within the feasible region of the joint space. By changing various postures, the stability of the UAV's attitude controller was verified. The AMM completed four stepwise configuration switches within 20 s (each switch took less than 1 s), and the transient response analysis was conducted to verify the controller's ability to handle short-term discrete changes (see Fig. 4).

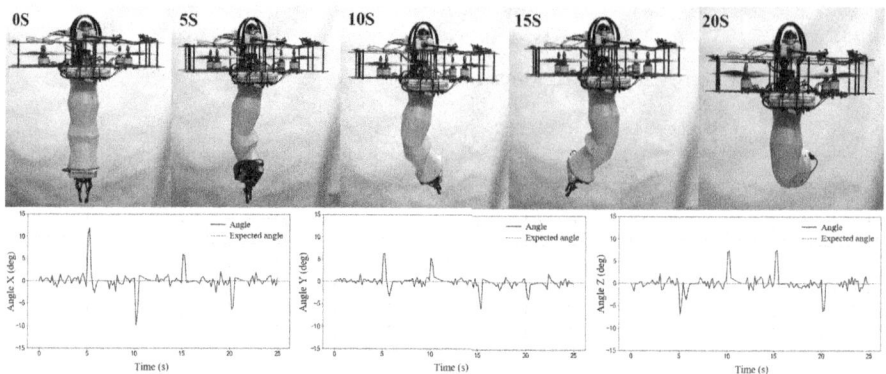

Fig. 4. AMM Airborne Morphing Experiment. The UAV completes four random motion transformations within 0 to 20 s. The three-axis angle change curves represent the angle influence brought by each transformation.

The experimental results show that when the robotic arm undergoes sudden configuration changes, the maximum deviation of the unmanned aerial vehicle's three-axis Euler angles is 12° falling within the safety tolerance threshold. The control system can converge the attitude to within the tolerance range ($\eta \leq 11.5°$) within 1 ± 0.21 s through rotor thrust redistribution, confirming the effective suppression capability of the proposed control strategy against short-term discrete disturbances.

4.2 Dynamic Posture Stability Verification

To comprehensively evaluate the load adaptability of AMM, the experiment conducted grasping experiments for five types of differentiated loads, grasping each type of item 16 times, and recorded the experimental results to obtain the grasping success rate: lightweight deformable objects (50.8 g, toothpaste), medium-load irregular objects (69.9 g, wallpaper knife), heavy-load irregular objects (290.7 g, glue gun), heterogeneous offset objects (261.3 g, headphones), and high-inertia loads (500 g, water-filled bottle) (see Fig. 5).

The experimental results show that the system's grasping success rate varies in a gradient with the complexity of the load: it reaches 93.8% for lightweight deformable objects, drops to 87.5% for medium-load irregular objects due to the torque coupling effect caused by the offset of the center of mass, maintains a 93.8% success rate for heavy-load irregular objects through the reconstruction of the rotor allocation matrix, while heterogeneous offset objects (81.3%) and heavy-load irregular objects (75.0%) are respectively constrained by material deformation and inertia coupling. The variable impedance control strategy proposed in this scheme demonstrates significant advantages: the adaptive adjustment of the grasping force based on real-time load estimation, combined with the dynamic redistribution of rotor thrust, increases the success rate in heavy-load conditions compared to the traditional fixed-gain controller, successfully overcoming 75.0% of the rotational slippage failure risks in grasping irregular objects. This result verifies AMM's comprehensive adaptability to geometric characteristics, material properties, and dynamic behaviors within a load range of 500g.

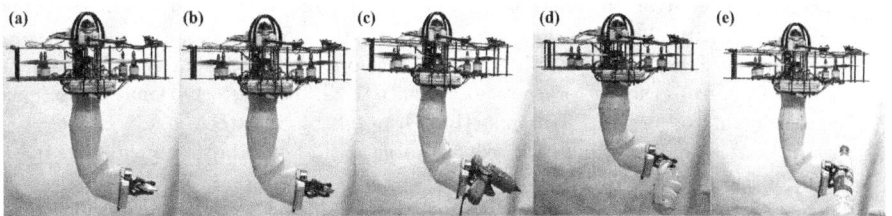

Fig. 5. AMM Airborne Deformation Load Experiment (a) toothpaste, (b) utility knife, (c) glue gun, (d) headphones, (e) water-filled bottle.

5 Conclusion

The modular manipulator MM based on standardized design of isomorphic modules demonstrates outstanding flexibility and task-driven performance. The AMM system composed of UAV carrying MM has been experimentally verified for its feasibility in grasping and placing tasks. And the attitude extended state observer has strong robustness, ensuring the stability of the AMM system during the operation of the manipulator. In the future, we will focus on improving the basic modules that make up MM to achieve lightweighting, thereby enabling more modules to be carried on UAVs to form MM to meet more complex work requirements. On the other hand, in the future, the connection methods between modules should be optimized to achieve more reliable and rapid connections, and thus realize higher self-reconfigurability with greater intelligence.

Acknowledgments. This work was supported by National Outstanding Youth Science Fund Project of National Natural Science Foundation of China [grant number 52025054].

References

1. Peng, R., Wang, Y., Lu, M., Lu, P.: A dexterous and compliant aerial continuum manipulator for cluttered and constrained environments. Nat. Commun. **16**(1), 889 (2025)
2. Ollero, A., Tognon, M., Suarez, A., Lee, D., Franchi, A.: Past, present, and future of aerial robotic manipulators. IEEE Trans. Rob. **38**(1), 626–645 (2021)

3. Peng, R., Wang, Z., Lu, P.: Aecom: an aerial continuum manipulator with imu-based kinematic modeling and tendon-slacking prevention. IEEE Trans. Syst. Man Cybern. Syst. **53**(8), 4740–4752 (2023)
4. Zhang, K., et al.: Aerial additive manufacturing with multiple autonomous robots. Nature **609**(7928), 709–717 (2022)
5. Lyu, S., Zhang, Y., Wang, J., Cheah, C.C., Yu, X.: Toward air operation aerial manipulator control with a refined anti-disturbance architecture. IEEE Trans. Autom. Sci. Eng. **22**, 4076–4091 (2024)
6. Fishman, J., Ubellacker, S., Hughes, N., Carlone, L.: Dynamic grasping with a "soft" drone: from theory to practice. In: 2021 IEEE/RSJ International Conference on Intelligent Robots and Systems (IROS), pp. 4214–4221. IEEE (2021)
7. Spröwitz, A., et al.: Roombots: reconfigurable robots for adaptive furniture. IEEE Comput. Intell. Mag. **5**(3), 20–32 (2010)
8. Sproewitz, A., et al.: Roombots—towards decentralized reconfiguration with self-reconfiguring modular robotic metamodules. In: 2010 IEEE/RSJ International Conference on Intelligent Robots and Systems, pp. 1126–1132. IEEE (2010)
9. Spröwitz, A., Moeckel, R., Vespignani, M., Bonardi, S., Ijspeert, A.J.: Roombots: a hardware perspective on 3d self-reconfiguration and locomotion with a homogeneous modular robot. Robot. Auton. Syst. **62**(7), 1016–1033 (2014)
10. Suarez, A., Heredia, G., Ollero, A.: Physical-virtual impedance control in ultra-lightweight and compliant dual-arm aerial manipulators. IEEE Rob. Autom. Lett. **3**(3), 2553–2560 (2018)
11. Lee, D., Seo, H., Kim, D., Kim, H.J.: Aerial manipulation using model predictive control for opening a hinged door. In: 2020 IEEE International Conference on Robotics and Automation (ICRA), pp. 1237–1242. IEEE (2020)
12. Zhang, Q., et al.: Motion-compensation control of supernumerary robotic arms subject to human-induced disturbances. Adv. Intell. Syst. **6**(5), 2300448 (2024)
13. Deremetz, M., et al.: Demonstrator design of a modular multi-arm robot for on-orbit large telescope assembly. In: Symposium on Advanced Space Technologies in Robotics and Automation, Noordwijk, Netherlands (2022)
14. Guggenheim, J., Hoffman, R., Song, H., Asada, H.H.: Leveraging the human operator in the design and control of supernumerary robotic limbs. IEEE Rob. Autom. Lett. **5**(2), 2177–2184 (2020)

Structural Design and Simulation of Space Sleeve-Type Extension Arm

Duanling Li[1], Qixiang Guo[1], Junwei Zhang[1], Junfeng huang[1], Shiqin Xie[1], and Yizhu Guo[2(✉)]

[1] School of Inteligent Engineering and Automation, Beijing University of Posts and Telecommunications, Beijing 100876, China
[2] Beijing Institute of Spacecraft System Engineering, Beijing 100094, China
bamboo501@sina.com

Abstract. Based on the current problem of the inability of the extension arm to balance the relationship between small mass and large-scale, this paper proposes a new type of extension arm with a grid cylinder structure, which includes four aspects: the extension arm body, the guiding system, the locking system, and the control system. The structure is simple and can effectively reduce the mass of the main structure of the extension arm. At the same time, a timing release mechanism is designed to enable the extension arm to be unfolded sequentially. Finally, a virtual prototype is established in Mechanical dynamics simulation software and the unfolding process of the extension arm in different unfolding modes is analyzed to verify the feasibility of the extension arm unfolding and the relative stability of sequential unfolding compared to synchronous unfolding.

Keywords: extension arm · Sleeve unfolding · Timing release · Kinetic analysis

1 Introduction

With growing global competition in space [1–5], space sleeve booms, crucial supports for antennas, radars, telescopes and solar panels, have become a research hotspot. Since the 21st century, advanced space exploration equipment with larger size and higher precision has imposed stricter requirements on sleeve booms' strength, stiffness and scale [6].

Extensive research has been conducted on sleeve-type extension arms on a global scale, with a particular emphasis on screw-driven and rope-driven models. The screw-driven socketed extension arm is the most widely used, with Dormier of Germany and Northrop Grumman of the United States in the leading position [7–9]. In China, Yang et al. [10] and Zhong et al. [11] have conducted research and developed the extension arm and drive locking device. However, these devices are characterized by complex structures and significant overall masses. Conversely, the rope-driven sleeve-type extension arm exhibits a reduced overall mass and a comparatively uncomplicated structure. Li et al. [12] designed the rope-driven sleeve-type extension arm utilizing the motor-driven rope sheave system, yet it was unable to be sequentially unfolded in a stable manner. Ding et al. [13] proposed a novel rope winding device and verified the feasibility. Lin et al. [14] innovated the driving mode; however, there are still drawbacks, such as the large mass.

The above-mentioned extension arm design scheme has reference significance in realizing the basic functions of the sleeve, but it can not balance the relationship between small mass and large-scale. In this paper, the rope driven extension arm is studied, and a single motor driven rope pulley system is proposed. At the same time, based on the traditional sleeve, a multi-stage sleeve timing release device with high adaptability, low complexity and low cost is designed to meet the timing release requirements of the new grid sleeve. In addition, simulation software is used to analyze the sleeve deployment process in two cases to obtain the key motion characteristics, so as to provide data support for the subsequent prototype development.

2 Design Scheme of Sleeve-Type Extension Arm

2.1 Design Scheme

The overall structure of the space sleeve-type extension arm is shown in Fig. 1. The extension arm is mainly composed of four modules, namely the three-stage sleeve-type extension arm cylinder, the guiding system, the locking system, and the control system.

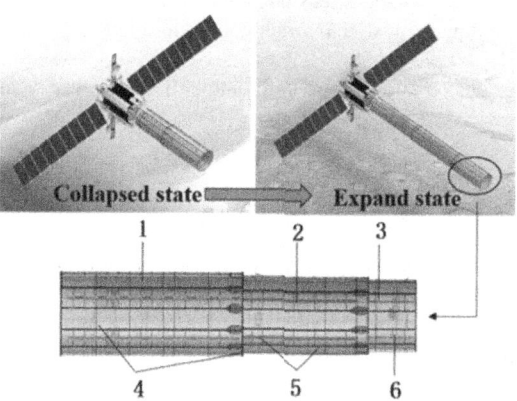

Fig. 1. Overall structure of the extension arm

1. Primary cylinder; 2. Secondary cylinder; 3. Third stage cylinder (fixed cylinder); 4. Locking system; 5. Guidance system; 6. Control system.

The specific design of the extension arm is shown in Fig. 2.

The three-stage sleeve cylinder is the main structure. Its main function is to provide support for space exploration instruments after deployment. The extension arm cylinder adopts a grid cylinder form, consisting of horizontal and vertical bars staggered at a 90° angle, thereby reducing the mass of the sleeve cylinder, reducing the transportation and launch costs of the extension arm, and facilitating the installation of larger scale space exploration instruments.

The guidance system consists of 6 pairs of inner and outer linear guides and corresponding inner and outer rollers. When deployed, the outer roller presses against the outer guide, and relative rolling is achieved through bearings. Stability is ensured by the geometric matching of the wheel and rail and material strength, and the wheel rim is used as a safety redundancy to ensure the safety of guidance. While the outer guide rail arranged at the bottom of the sleeve provides precise guidance, the inner guide rail arranged at the top of the sleeve serves as another fulcrum for deployment between the sleeves, mainly playing a supporting role to prevent the top of the sleeve from shifting and ensure the concentricity of the sleeve deployment.

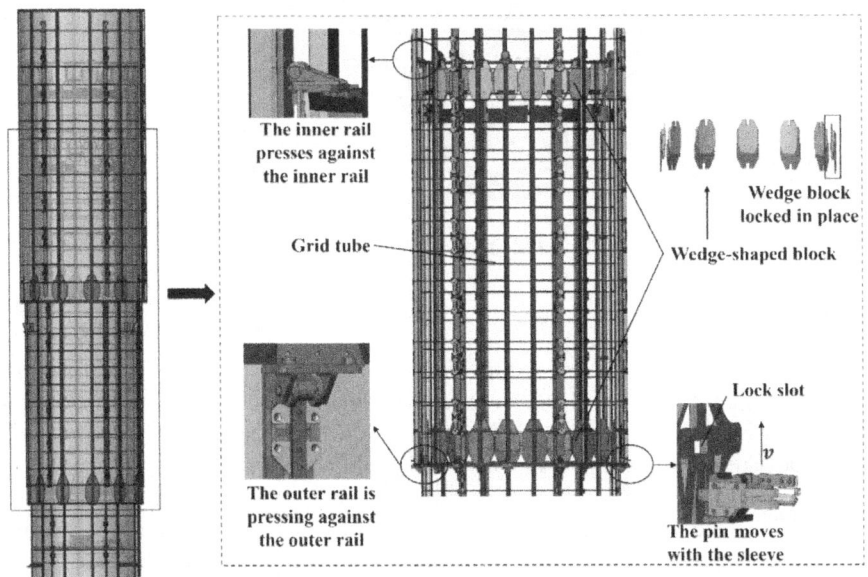

Fig. 2. Specific Design of Extension Arm

The locking system of the sleeve deployment mainly consists of wedge-shaped blocks and locking pins. When the sleeve is about to be deployed in place, the 12 corresponding wedge-shaped block groups on adjacent sleeves start to contact, reducing the instantaneous impact of the sleeve deployment in place under the action of friction and increasing the stability of deployment. When the sleeve is deployed to a certain extent, the locking pin placed at the bottom of the outer sleeve pops out under the action of the spring and bounces into the locking groove at the top of the adjacent inner sleeve, achieving limit locking and to some extent ensuring the overall stiffness of the sleeve.

The control system of the extension arm consists of a drive module and a pulley group. In order to prevent single motor failures due to current and other reasons during operation, the drive source adopts a main backup motor mode. The active motor is connected to the backup motor through a gear system and transfers torque to the winding wheel. When the active motor fails and loses power, the backup motor starts to continue providing torque. The internal structure of the active motor is concentric, and it moves with the backup motor throughout the entire process in a no current state. The rope pulley assembly includes a rope pulley, a steel wire rope, and a reversing wheel. The steel wire rope, driven by a single driving source, provides tension to three sets of rope pulleys distributed 360° in the circumferential direction through the reversing wheel, achieving the extension and contraction of the sleeve. The specific arrangement is shown in Fig. 3.

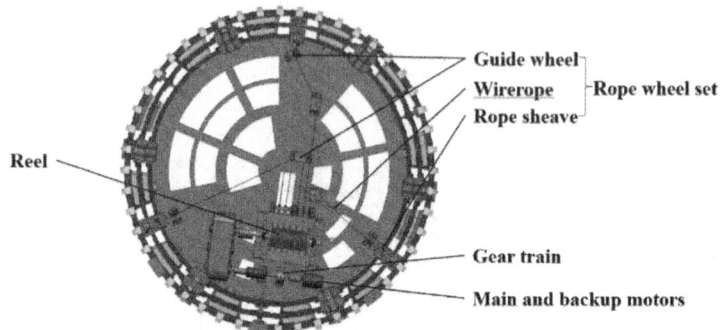

Fig. 3. Control System

2.2 Design of Rope Drive Scheme

On the premise of meeting the requirements of exhibition and collection functions, considering factors such as system simplicity and light weight, the current mainstream rope drive scheme is multi rope unfolding. Taking the three-stage sleeve as an example, three ropes are used in conjunction with pulleys to coordinate the work, connect the three-stage sleeve for force transmission, and achieve the driving of the sleeve.

The advantage of the multi rope scheme is that when one rope breaks, the other ropes can continue to run, and the multi rope scheme can also share the overall load, thereby extending the service life of the rope. Therefore, under the same conditions, the diameter of the rope can be reduced, and the design can be achieved by selecting steel wire ropes with lower mechanical properties. However, this plan has too many ropes and complex control, which puts higher demands on sensors and control systems. In addition, there may be tension imbalance between the ropes, resulting in inadequate deployment, which is particularly evident in long-distance and high load sleeve-type extension arm applications. Therefore, it can only be used as an alternative solution, and it is necessary to start from the unfolding principle to explore a solution with better performance and more suitable for large-scale sleeve-type extension arms.

Considering factors such as the number of ropes and control complexity, the multi rope system is changed to a single rope system, as shown in Fig. 4. This scheme uses a single rope to control the multi-stage sleeve deployment, which can effectively avoid the problem of insufficient sleeve deployment caused by the stretching error of the rope force. At the same time, the scheme is simplified and the control is simpler.

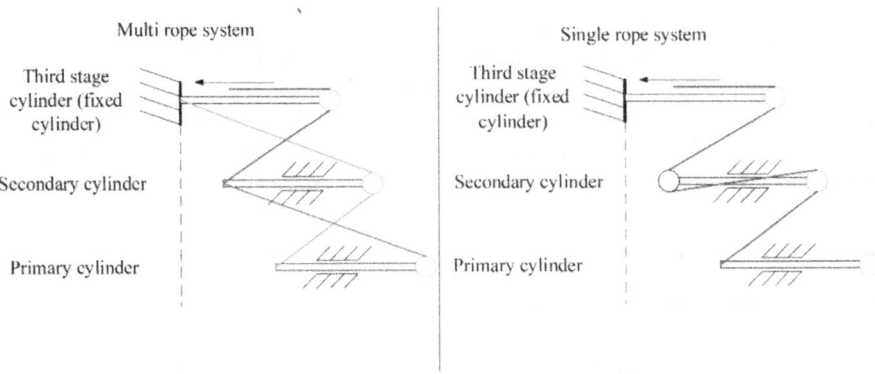

Fig. 4. Rope driven solution

Based on the above considerations, a single rope driven stretching scheme is proposed, and the specific extension and contraction process of the stretching arm is shown in Fig. 5.

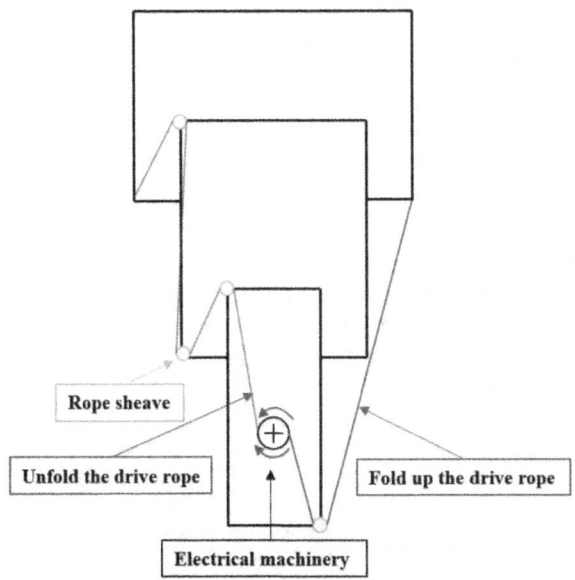

Fig. 5. The process of extension and contraction

Firstly, the motion cylinder is retracted outside the fixed cylinder, and the entire mechanism is in a retracted state. The third stage cylinder has 6 straight outer guide rails evenly distributed on the outer surface of the fixed cylinder and the outer surface of the second stage sleeve, and 6 straight inner guide rails evenly distributed on the inner surface of the second stage cylinder and the inner surface of the first stage cylinder, ensuring the linear motion accuracy of the sleeve when unfolded. The upper end of the third stage cylinder, the lower end of the first stage cylinder, and the upper and lower ends of the second stage cylinder are all equipped with pulleys. The motor drives the winding wheel in the forward direction to start winding the rope. As it is a single rope drive, the first and second sleeves synchronously unfold the extension arm as the steel wire rope between each sleeve is shortened. During the unfolding process of the sleeve, the locking system also works simultaneously to help achieve the in place locking of the sleeve.

3 Extension Arm Deployment Modeling

3.1 Euler Angle Conversion

To simulate the dynamic characteristics of the pulley system during the extension process of the deployable arm, it is necessary to import the simplified basic model from CAD package into Mechanical dynamics simulation software and remodel the pulley transmission mechanism based on the cable module. Given that modeling the cable module requires a clear spatial orientation of the pulley rotation axis, the axis direction parameters obtained in CAD package are defined based on the *xyz* Euler angle sequence, which differs from simulation software' default *zyz* rotation sequence (i.e. the Tait Bryan angle sequence around the Z-axis first, then around the Y-axis, and finally around the Z-axis). Due to the direct influence of the rotation order of Euler angles on the final orientation of space vectors, different rotation sequences will result in deviations in the parameter expression of the same axis in different coordinate systems. Therefore, it is necessary to transform the axis orientation parameters exported by CAD package through a coordinate transformation matrix to match the dynamic calculation coordinate system requirements of the simulation solver.

Assuming that the Euler angles of the rotation axis in the *xyz* rotation sequence are α, β, and γ, corresponding to the matrix $Rxyz = R_z(\gamma)R_y(\beta)R_x(\alpha)$, and the Euler angles in the *zyz* rotation sequence are φ, θ and ψ, corresponding to the matrix $Rzyz = R_z(\psi)R_y(\theta)R_x(\varphi)$. It can be inferred from this that:

$$\theta = \cos^{-1}(\cos\beta \cos\alpha) \tag{1}$$

When $\theta \neq 0$ or $\theta \neq \pi$,

$$\varphi = \tan^{-1} 2\left(\frac{\cos\beta \sin\alpha}{\sin\theta}, \frac{\sin\beta}{\sin\theta}\right) \tag{2}$$

$$\psi = \tan^{-1} 2\left(\frac{\sin\beta \cos\alpha \sin\gamma - \sin\alpha \cos\gamma}{\sin\theta}, \frac{\sin\beta \cos\alpha \cos\gamma + \sin\alpha \sin\gamma}{\sin\theta}\right) \tag{3}$$

When $\theta = 0$,

$$\varphi = 0 \tag{4}$$

$$\psi = \alpha + \gamma \tag{5}$$

When $\theta = \pi$,

$$\varphi = 0 \qquad (6)$$

$$\psi = \gamma - \alpha + \pi \qquad (7)$$

3.2 Synchronize and Extend Modeling

In the extension arm structure, a large number of components are connected in a fixed manner, which has limited impact on the dynamic simulation calculation of the model. The reach of the arm is more than ten meters, and some smaller mechanisms have little effect on the overall kinematic and dynamic parameters, but it may increase the simulation calculation of the overall virtual prototype. In order to improve the simulation calculation efficiency, the model needs to be reasonably simplified, some duplicate parts need to be removed, and replaced by setting rigid motion pairs and time scripts. Finally, the simplified model of the sleeve-type extension arm shown in Fig. 6 is obtained, which mainly consists of three parts, including the three-stage sleeve cylinder, the main limiting mechanism wedge block on the three-stage sleeve cylinder, and the force transmission structure pulley system.

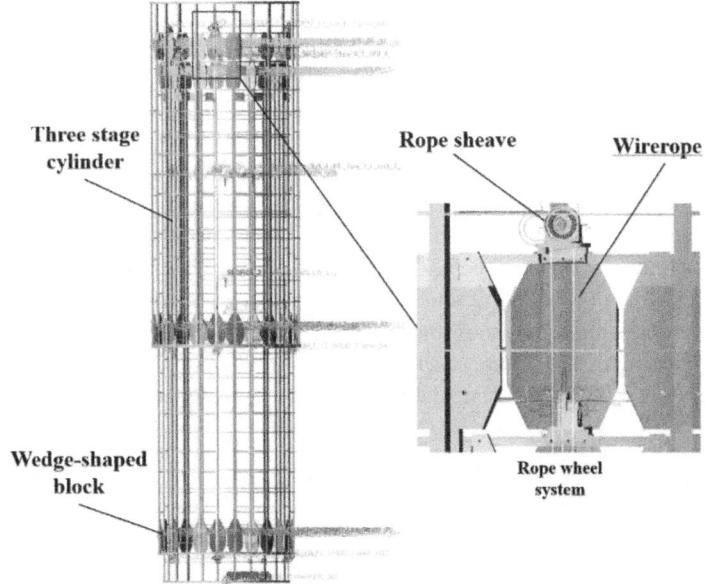

Fig. 6. Simplified model

The stretching arm model is constrained by a multi contact constraint type, with a static friction coefficient of 0.1 and a dynamic friction coefficient of 0.1 set for the internal movement of the sleeve; the static friction coefficient between wedge-shaped blocks is 1.05, and the dynamic friction coefficient is 1.4; the stretching arm material is aerospace carbon fiber T600, the wedge block material is aluminum alloy, the rope is steel wire rope, and the pulley material is titanium alloy. Table 1 shows the physical property parameters of the materials during simulation.

Table 1. Material property parameters

Material	Density (g/cm^3)	Elastic modulus (GPa)	Poisson's ratio
Carbon fiber	1.5	180	0.25
Aluminum alloy	2.6	70	0.33
Steel	7.8	210	0.27
Titanium alloy	4.4	120	0.34

The unfolding process is mainly affected by the resistance of 330 N between each sleeve. At the same time, simulate the process of the motor driving the winding wheel to drive the steel wire rope, allowing the steel wire rope to accelerate to 10 mm/s within 0-10 s, and then maintain a constant speed of 10 mm/s to stretch.

3.3 Gradual Unfolding of Mechanism Design

Due to the excessive size of the integral sleeve, previous studies on cable-driven deployable sleeve-type booms have all adopted multi-stage synchronous deployment. The drawback lies in that sleeves of different stages have different masses and moments of inertia, leading to distinct non-linear dynamic responses to cable-driven deployment. This results in overly complex dynamic responses during the overall mechanism deployment. The reach of the arm is more than ten meters. Thus, the synchronous deployment method may cause instability during the deployment process. To achieve a stable and reliable design of the sleeve-type boom, a timing release mechanism is proposed to realize the stage-by-stage deployment of the first and second-stage sleeves.

The main function of the timing release device is to restrict the movement of the secondary cylinder during the movement of the primary cylinder. After the primary cylinder is fully deployed, the timing release device is triggered to unlock, thereby releasing the restriction on the movement of the secondary cylinder and achieving sequential movement.

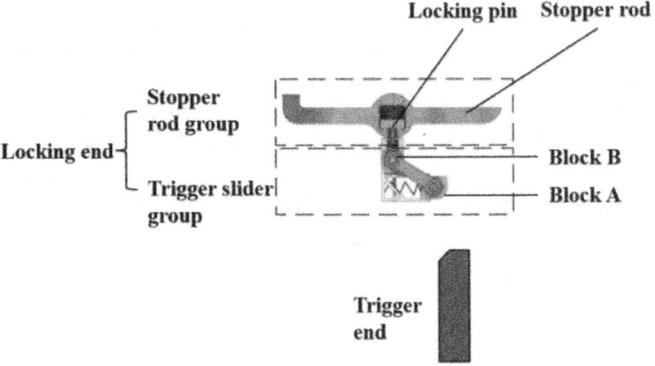

Fig. 7. Timing release device structure

As shown in Fig. 7, the proposed timing release device is divided into two parts, namely, the trigger end and the locking end. The trigger end is a wedge-shaped structure, which is installed at the bottom of the first stage cylinder. When the bottom of the first stage cylinder moves to the top of the second stage cylinder and unfolds in place, the trigger locking end is unlocked. The locking end is mainly composed of a stopper rod group and a trigger slider group, wherein the stopper rod group includes a locking pin and a stopper rod, which mainly limits the movement of the secondary barrel; the locking end is a PRRP mechanism, which is divided into two sliding blocks a and B. under the extrusion of the trigger end, block a moves to the left and pushes block B to move up, so as to press the locking pin into the gear lever to unlock the timing release device. The specific process is shown in Fig. 8.

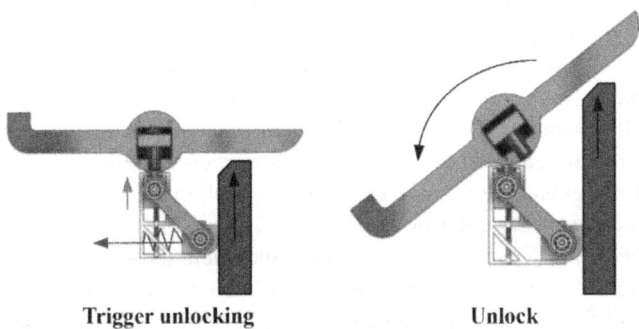

Fig. 8. Unlocking process

4 Comparative Analysis of Extension Arm Deployment

4.1 Synchronous Deployment Analysis

Under synchronous deployment, the primary and secondary cylinders of the extension arm begin to deploy under the tension of the steel wire rope, and the change of the centroid displacement is shown in Fig. 9. The deployment process of the primary drum is relatively stable. Due to the acceleration of the steel wire rope 10 s ago, the deployment of the primary drum fluctuated slightly, and then with the stability of the steel wire rope tensile speed, the deployment of the primary drum also became stable; since there is no limit on the deployment direction of the secondary barrel in the synchronous deployment mode, the secondary barrel also fluctuates up and down before the primary barrel is deployed in place. However, due to the resistance between the secondary and tertiary sleeves, the displacement is small and fluctuates up and down at 0.4 mm.

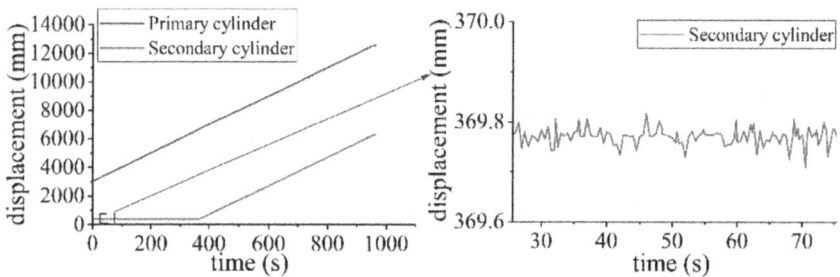

Fig. 9. Comparison of extension displacement of secondary cylinder

4.2 Comparative Analysis of Deployment Process

The sequential deployment process is similar to the synchronous deployment process, except that the constraints on the deployment direction of the secondary cylinder are added before the primary cylinder is deployed in place, so the displacement variation characteristics of the primary cylinder under the two modes are similar, as shown in Fig. 9.

By further comparing the displacement variation characteristics of the secondary barrel, as shown in Fig. 10, it can be seen that after 365 s, the displacement curves of the secondary barrel under the two extension modes tend to be consistent and enter the steady-state extension stage; while in the dynamic process 365 s ago, the displacement curve of the secondary cylinder in the sequential extension mode showed significant smooth characteristics, and the increase of sequential release mechanism effectively suppressed the displacement jitter caused by dynamic coupling in the synchronous extension mode. From the speed characteristic analysis, as shown in Fig. 10, the deployment speed of the secondary cylinder in the synchronous deployment mode presents irregular fluctuations before 365 s, with a fluctuation range of about -2 mm/s~2 mm/s, reflecting the instability of the system in the dynamic process; however, in the sequential deployment mode, the secondary cylinder remained stationary under the suppression of the sequential release mechanism, and there was no obvious speed fluctuation.

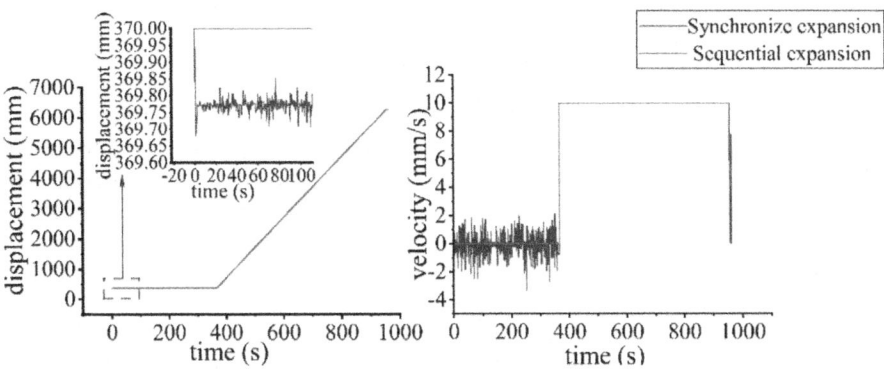

Fig. 10. Comparison of displacement and velocity of secondary cylinder under different unfolding modes

4.3 Sequential Unfolding Process Simulation

According to the above analysis, it can be concluded that the stability of the extended arm is better in the sequential unfolding state. The unfolding time in this mode is a total of 956 s, and the entire process is divided into four states: (1) initial folding state; (2) The first stage cylinder is not in place; (3) The first stage cylinder is in place and the second stage cylinder is not in place; (4) The sleeve is fully extended. The simulation process is shown in Fig. 11.

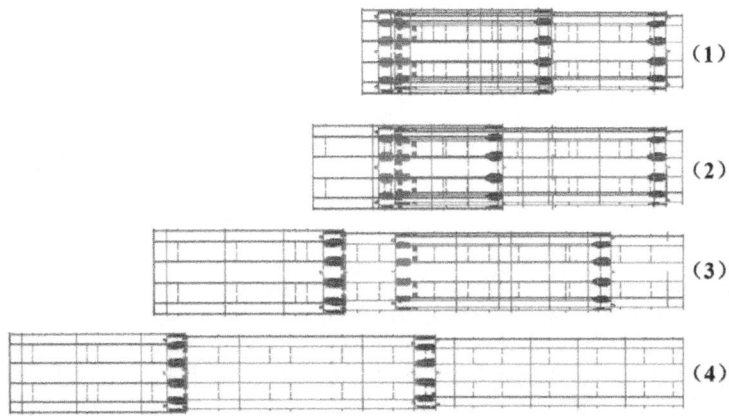

Fig. 11. The whole process of extension arm deployment

The simulation process was generally as expected, verifying the feasibility of deploying the extension arm.

5 Conclusion

This article presents a novel sleeve-type extension arm based on a grid cylinder, with a simple structure and a timing release mechanism designed to enable the extension arm to extend sequentially. Finally, a virtual prototype is established in Mechanical dynamics simulation software and the extension process of the extension arm under different extension modes is analyzed to verify the feasibility of the arm's extension and the relative stability of the sequential extension, providing reference for the development of subsequent prototypes.

Acknowledgment. Supported by National Natural Science Foundation of China (Grant No. 52175019), Beijing Natural Science Foundations (Grant Nos. L222038, 20240484699, QY25321), Project "Vice President of Science and Technology" of Changping District, Beijing.

References

1. The Space Report 2021 36th Annual Space Symposium Special Edition Just Released by Space Foundation. Satnews 23 Aug. 2021. https://news.satnews.com/2021/08/23/the-space-report-2021-36th-annual-space-symposium-special-edition-just-released-by-space-foundation/
2. Alexandra, T.E., Andrew, R., Katie, F., et al.: Space Strategy Stability, p. 9. Rand Corporation, Santa Monic (2024)
3. Shangshang, Z., Na pan, H.Z.: Analysis of the regulations and policies of military civilian commercial integration in the U.S. space field. Dual Technol. Prod. **02**, 17–23 (2025) (Chinese). https://doi.org/10.19385/j.cnki.1009-8119.2025.02.004
4. United States Space Priorities Framework. White house press releases fact sheets and briefings/FIND (2021)
5. Chinese Academy of Sciences, National Space Administration, China Manned Space Engineering Office Medium and long term development plan of National Space Science (2024–2050). Beijing, Bureau of major scientific and technological missions, National Center for Space Science (2024). (Chinese)
6. Lopatin, A.V., Morozov, E.V.: Modal analysis of the thin-walled composite spoke of an umbrella-type deployable space antenna. J. Compos. Struct. **88**(1), 46–55 (2009)
7. Zhao, Y., Yong, X., Guohui, C., et al.: Overview of space telescopic boom and design of new boom. Mech. Eng. Autom. **01**, 128–130 (2019). (Chinese)
8. Greenberg, H.S., Engler, E.E.: Development of deployable truss concept for space station. ESA Proceedings of an International Conference on Spacecraft Structures (1986)
9. Northrop Grumman Company, Inc. ISIS TELESCOPIC MAST. http://www.st.northropgrumman.com/astro-aerospace. (September 2007)
10. Yang, P., Feng, C.: Structural design and analysis of deployable telescopic telescopic boom. J. UESTC **21**(9), 9–11 (2008). (Chinese)
11. Boweng, Z.: Design and analysis of telescopic extension arm. Harbin, Harbin Institute of Technology **52**, 6–14 (2006). (Chinese)
12. Changzhou, L.: Design and analysis of the supporting mechanism of the cable driven sleeve space camera. Harbin Institute of Technology (2016). (Chinese)
13. Ding, X., Xiao, H., Yang, Q., et al.: Design and analysis of a cable-winding device driving large deployable mechanisms in astrophysics missions. Acta Astronaut. **169**, 124–137 (2020)
14. Shangmin, L.: Structural design and analysis of space extension arm. Xi'an, Xi'an University of Electronic Science and technology 19–30 (2012). (Chinese)

Balloon Robot: Movement Recognition and Design of Robot

Weihao Wang, Chyan Zheng Siow(✉), Naoyuki Kubota, Azhar Aulia Saputra, Qingwei Song, and Takenori Obo

Tokyo Metropolitan University, Tokyo, Japan
wang-weihao1@ed.tmu.ac.jp

Abstract. The feeling of being valued is essential for everyone, especially the elderly, which can motivate them to live a healthy life. Without this feeling, the elderly may feel that they are a burden to society. Therefore, we promote a concept that requires the elderly to complete the needs of the robot, thereby increasing the elderly's feeling of being valued. However, many existing robots are designed with home robots as the starting point for development. Healthcare institutions such as nursing homes need a large number of inexpensive companion/care robots. According to user needs, we first focus on development costs and robot weight. To meet this demand, we are designing an inflatable robot. We divide the robot into two parts: the upper inflatable companion/care robot and the lower smart mobile base station. The upper inflatable companion/care robot is made into an inflatable tumbler and is equipped with minimal circuits to minimize costs. In order to better accompany the elderly, we also installed IMU sensors on the upper robot to detect their movements. The lower smart mobile base station is a smart cart with McNamee wheels. The upper inflatable robot is not connected to the lower smart mobile base station one-to-one (one robot base can serve multiple balloon robots), so the development cost can be controlled. Because it is inflatable, the weight of the upper robot base can be greatly reduced. This increases the ability of the elderly to carry the robot.

Keywords: Balloon Robot · Mechanical Learning · Sense of Mattering · Pet Robot · Gesture Recognition

1 Introduction

The aging global population has led to a significant increase in the number and proportion of elderly individuals in many countries. In Japan, for instance, it's projected that by 2060, 38% of the population will be elderly [1]. As the population ages, the number of elderly people living alone is also expected to rise, which can be quite debilitating [2]. A key factor here is the loss of materiality [3]. Feeling important to others, being valued, and knowing that people care about them is significant [4]. Beyond human interaction, pets can also provide this sense of importance. Caring for a dog or cat can transform an older person's lifestyle and create a sense of being needed [5]. In a super-aged society, preventing caregiving burdens, social isolation, and loneliness among the elderly has become a pressing issue.

In response to these issues, Takanori Shibata's research team developed a pet robot called PARO [6, 7]. The object's design is reminiscent of a fluffy baby seal. The robot is charged using a "pacifier," which emulates the act of caring for an infant animal. This behavior fosters a sense of importance in the user, thereby enhancing the elderly user's sense of self-worth. However, PARO is not mobile and must be carried by the user. The device has a mass of approximately 2.5 kg, which may pose a challenge for users of advanced age. The second companion robot is an autonomous mobile pet robot called LOVOT [8], which is capable of navigating to the charging station independently. However, it is susceptible to falling during this process, necessitating assistance from the user to help it regain its footing. The device also incorporates a sleep function and a cuddling function, which are designed to enhance the user's sense of being needed. However, given its weight of approximately 4.2 kg, LOVOT may pose a challenge for elderly individuals in terms of handling and cuddling. The two robots have been designed to facilitate interaction and connection with the user. However, they do not incorporate features that would engage the user in physical movement, which could potentially enhance the user's sense of self-efficacy. Furthermore, the cost of both robots exceeds $2,000. To address these issues, a lightweight and affordable balloon robot was introduced that older users can easily pick up, move, and interact with.

In this paper, we propose the design of a detachable balloon robot that addresses the challenges posed by expensive pet robots, weight, and user motion detection. The balloon robot is composed of two components: smart mobile base station and upper balloon robot (shown as Fig. 1). The upper balloon robot and the smart mobile base station are detachable, and the upper balloon robot is lightweight enough to be easily held or hugged by older users (Figs. 2, 3, 8 and 9).

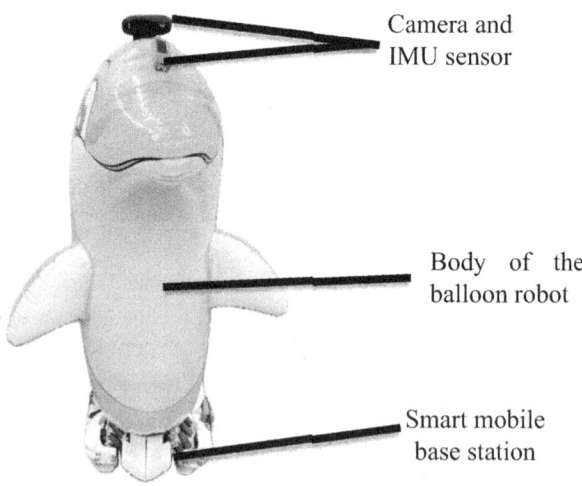

Fig. 1. Image of Balloon Robot.

The subsequent sections of this paper are as follows: Sect. 2 outlines the general design of the balloon robot, and Sect. 3 describes the research on the balloon robot so far. As delineated in Sect. 4, the 6-axis IMU sensor is utilized for the purpose of recognizing user movements. In Sect. 5, the conclusions and prospective avenues for future research are thoroughly examined.

2 Design of the Balloon Robot

Combining the two types of companion robots we mentioned earlier, the first thing we need to consider is to reduce the weight of the robot and reduce the cost of the robot. The robot should be designed to facilitate ease of handling, even by elderly individuals, and should be available in large quantities at a reasonable cost to senior service organizations. Consequently, a balloon robot was designed to reduce the weight of the robot, and a shareable smart mobile base station was developed to reduce the cost.

2.1 Design of Upper Balloon Companion Robot

The construction of the balloon robot involved the utilization of a standard inflatable tumbler as its primary structural component. Atop the robot, sensors were installed to detect the robot's posture and user movements.

A miniature wireless camera was mounted on the balloon robot, with the objective of facilitating face and gesture recognition. The installation of sensors on the upper portion of the balloon robot resulted in a shift in the center of the tumbler. To mitigate this effect, a larger mass of iron sand was introduced into the bottom of the balloon, serving as ballast to reduce the overall center of gravity of the balloon robot.

When the user holds the balloon robot in their arms, the camera mounted on the top of the robot's head experiences difficulty recognizing the user's movements due to the angle limitation. Given the potential for increased power consumption associated with the installation of multiple cameras, particularly when monitoring over an extended period, we opted for the utilization of IMU sensors for the purpose of monitoring and recognizing the user's movement. Furthermore, it can be utilized to ascertain the attitude of the balloon robot when it is positioned on the robot base.

Fig. 2. Image of Balloon Robot.

2.2 Design of Smart Mobile Base Station

In order to reduce the development cost, a smart mobile base station was designed. This base station is equipped with a McNamee wheel [9] for movement and attitude control of the balloon robot and charging it. The McNamee wheels does not require a turning mechanism and only needs to control the speed and steering of each wheel for fast steering. The McNamee wheel is a form of tireless wheel, with a series of rubberized external rollers obliquely attached to the whole circumference of its rim. These rollers typically each have an axis of rotation at 45° to the wheel plane and at 45° to the axle line. Each McNamee wheel is an independent non-steering drive wheel with its own powertrain, and when spinning generates a propelling force perpendicular to the roller axle, which can be vectored into a longitudinal and a transverse compo-nent in relation to the vehicle. The movements in any direction on flat surface can be achieved by a combination of three McNamee wheels or more than three ones. It can also steer in place, which is favorable for use in small indoor areas.

When the wheels of the Smart Mobile Base Station are elevated, the McNamee Wheel can be employed to regulate the movements (e.g., nodding, swinging, or turning) of the balloon robot positioned above it. The integration of a wireless camera within the balloon robot facilitates the implementation of face and gesture recognition capabilities. By recognizing different users, it is possible to induce the balloon robot to react in a variety of ways. For instance, the balloon robot exhibits distinct head movements in response to different individuals, and it is possible to program the balloon robot to perpetually face the user.

Fig. 3. Smart Mobile Base Station.

A high-capacity battery has been installed on the smart mobile base station for the purpose of emergency charging of the balloon robot. A charging unit was installed on the upper part of the robot base for the purpose of charging the balloon robot located on the upper part. The posterior portion of the robot base is equipped with a contact piece that can be connected to a charging station for the purpose of charging.

3 The Function of the Balloon Robot

Using the hardware described above, we have so far implemented the following functions: 1) movement of smart mobile base station; 2) control of the balloon robot's posture using the smart mobile base station; 3) long-distance gesture recognition using the camera on the balloon robot; and 4) recognition of the user's movement using the IMU sensor.

3.1 Movement of Smart Mobile Base Station

We analyzed the motion of smart mobile base station. The smart mobile base station's main directions of motion, and the direction of rotation of each wheel, as shown in Fig. 4. As the method as shown, the direction of motion of the smart mobile base station can be changed by changing the direction of rotation of the McNamee wheel.

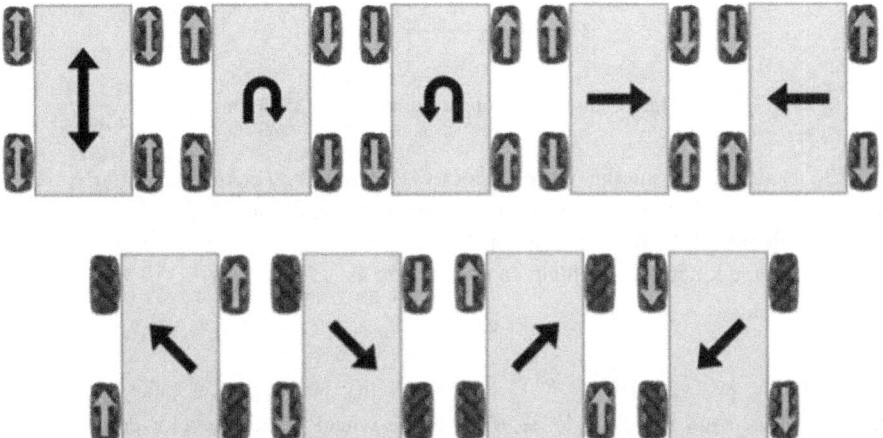

Fig. 4. The main locomotion directions of the mobile robot and the way they are achieved.

McNamee wheel that consists of free rollers with a 45° slope. Figure 5 shows the disposition of the wheel and the frames. $V_{iW}(i = 1, 2, 3, 4) \in R$ is the velocity vector corresponding to wheel revolutions, where $V_{iW} = R_w \times \omega_{iW}$, R_w is the radius of wheel, ω_{iw} is the revolution velocity of the wheel, and $V_{ir}(i = 1, 2, 3, 4) \in R$ is the tangential velocity vector of the free roller touching the floor.

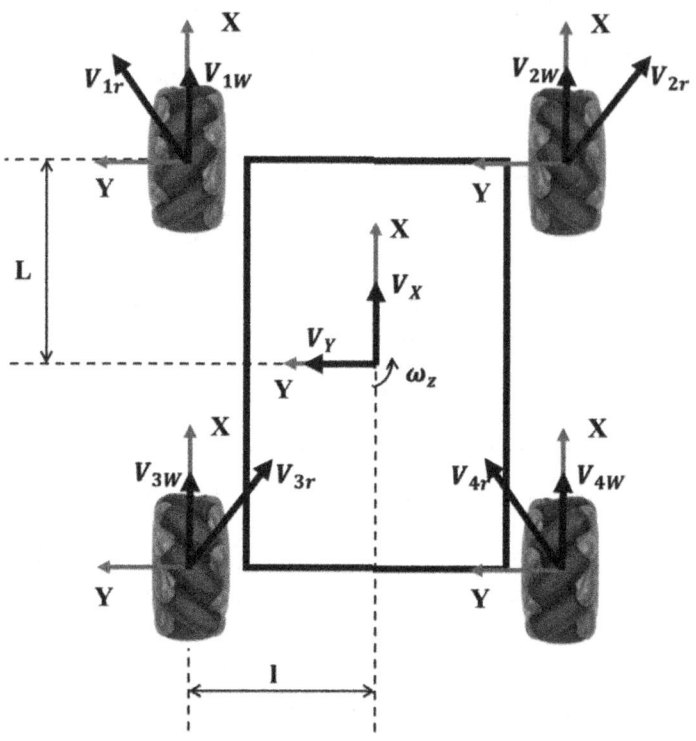

Fig. 5. Disposition of McNamee wheel and frames.

V_{iX} is derived from the wheel velocity V_{iW} and $V_{ir}/\cos 45°$. Similarly, V_{iY} is $V_{ir}/\sin 45°$ from Fig. 4. V_x, V_y are the velocity in the X and Y directions. ω_Z is the angular velocity of the robot basement.

The inverse kinematic problem can be written as:

$$V_w = J \cdot V_0 \qquad (1)$$

where $V_0 = [v_x, v_y, \omega_z]^T \in R^{3\times 1}$ is the velocity vector in Cartesian coordinates; $V_W = [V_{1W}, V_{2W}, V_{3W}, V_{4W}]^T \in R^{4\times 1}$ is the wheel velocity vector corresponding to the angular velocity.

The transformation matrix J_0 can be expressed [10]:

$$J = \begin{bmatrix} 1 & -1 & -(l+L) \\ 1 & 1 & +(l+L) \\ 1 & 1 & -(l+L) \\ 1 & -1 & +(l+L) \end{bmatrix} \in R^{4\times 3} \qquad (2)$$

According to the above equation, we can control the rotation speed of each wheel precisely, so that we can control the position, motion direction and speed of the robot basement. This enables the entire robot to move more flexibly and can be used in more confined spaces.

3.2 Behavior of Balloon Robot

As demonstrated in the foregoing analysis, the position of the balloon robot can be controlled by manipulating the wheels of the smart mobile base station. This control allows for a variety of actions, including oscillating the robot in a lateral direction and rotating it around its axis. Utilizing these rudimentary poses, the balloon robot is capable of articulating basic emotions [11]. For instance, when an individual becomes enraged, the program can respond by having the balloon robot turn its back to the user. In a positive emotional state, the balloon robot is capable of rapid oscillation.

The utilization of the camera affixed to the balloon robot entails a long-distance gesture recognition method [12], which is proposed for the purpose of guiding the robot to a charging post for the purpose of recharging. This method is expected to enhance the sense of materiality for elderly individuals. Initially, static gesture recognition is conducted, and subsequently, the results are input into a dynamic gesture recognition model to facilitate the final prediction of the gesture (as shown in Fig. 6). The subjects of this study hailed from various countries, and the findings revealed that individuals from different nations utilize distinct gestures when expressing analogous commands (e.g., Japanese students will use two hands to ask for the balloon robot to come here, while Chinese students will use one hand to ask for the robot) (as shown in Fig. 7.).

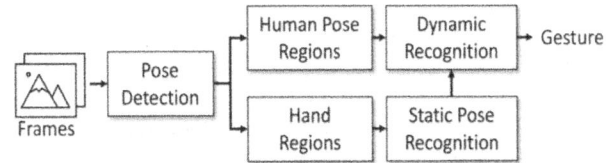

Fig. 6. Overview process of the proposed gesture recognition system.

Fig. 7. Example of video frames for "come here".

The robot is designed to encourage older adults to engage in regular physical activity and to provide positive feedback to the robot, thereby fostering a sense of connection and familiarity. This, in turn, aims to enhance the older adults' sense of self-efficacy [13]. The utilization of inertial measurement units (IMU) sensors facilitates the recognition and detection of an older adult's movements throughout the day. This capability enables the acquisition of their lifelog for the day, thereby facilitating the real-time regulation of their life. Furthermore, the robot's invitation to engage in exercises with the elderly individual has been shown to enhance their sense of purpose and contribution.

4 Movement Recognition

Since the camera mounted on the robot cannot capture the user when the robot is being held, we installed an inertial measurement unit (IMU) sensor on the head of the balloon robot to recognize the user's movements. IMU data were collected while the user held the upper part of the balloon robot, and the data were subsequently transmitted to a computer terminal for processing. Noise was removed from the raw signals, and action recognition was performed based on the cleaned data. A taxonomy of common interaction scenarios for recognition is hereby defined. These scenarios include, but are not limited to, the following: "get up and walk," "pick up the robot and walk," "walk," "walk and drop the robot down," and "exercises (a,b,c)."

To recognize the aforementioned user actions through IMU data, the IMU sensor built into the M5stick C plus microcontroller is utilized for data collection. Concurrently, the data was transmitted to a computer for processing. A group of four students was selected to perform a series of actions with the balloon robot. Prior to the initiation of data collection, the experiment did not provide any examples to the participants but rather instructed them to perform each task according to their own methods.

A selection of three light exercises was meticulously chosen to promote the maintenance of health and the recovery of older adults. The aforementioned exercises are illustrated in the figure below.

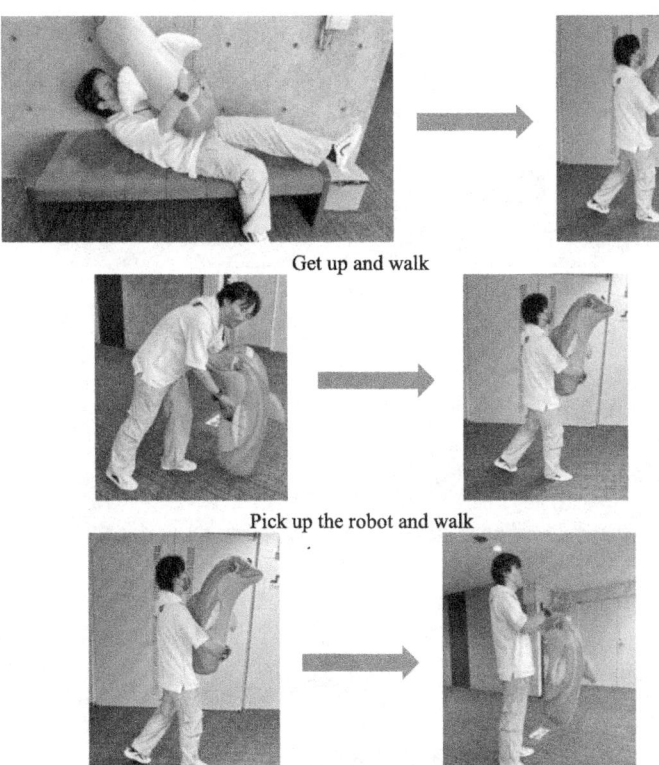

Get up and walk

Pick up the robot and walk

Walk and drop the robot down

Walk

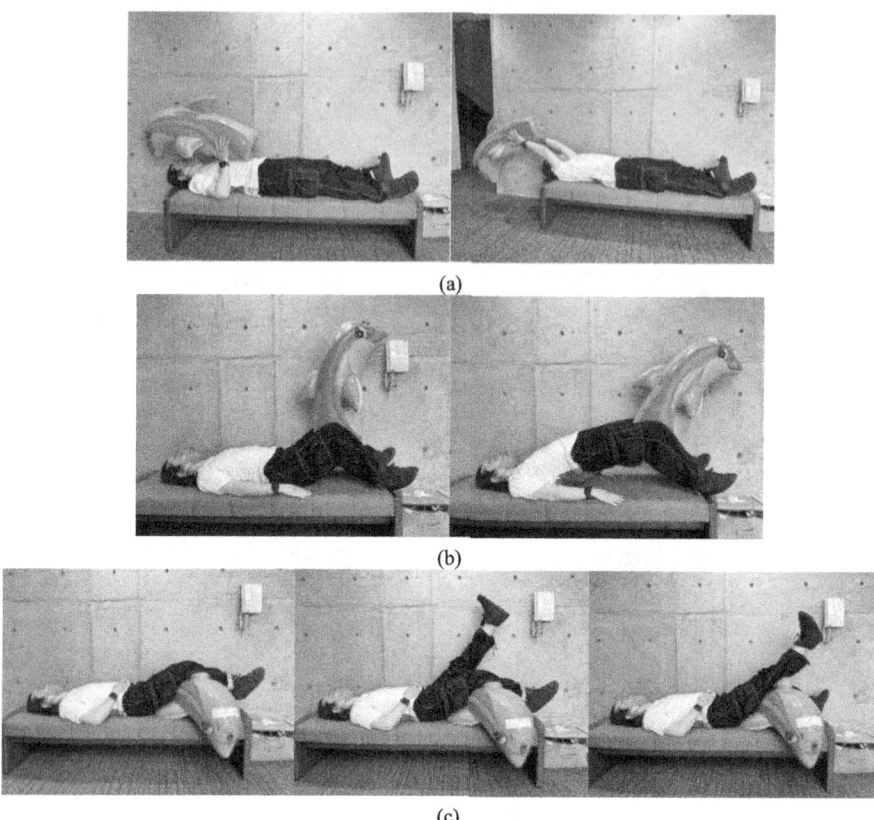

Fig. 8. Example of exercises.

It was determined that the transient actions, such as the picking up and dropping of the balloon robot, should be recognized. Therefore, the property of extracting local features was considered, and the CNN model [14] was applied. In order to detect the motion, the LSTM model [15] was implemented to detect this more complex motion. After thorough consideration, the decision was made to employ the hybrid CNN-LSTM model [16] for this experimental study.

The dataset is allocated for training, validation, and testing purposes, with 30% designated for training, 70% for validation and testing. For each subject, we windowed the data with a window size of 50 (approximately 5 s) and a window step of 10. The accuracy and F1 score results of these methods are shown in Table 1 below.

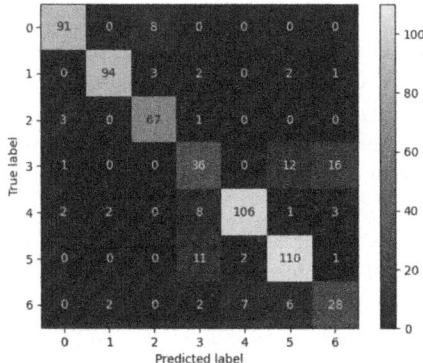

Fig. 9. Confusion matrix results.

Table 1. Experimental results of movement recognition on the collected dataset.

	precision	f1-score
Exercise 1 (0)	0.94	0.93
Exercise 2 (1)	0.96	0.94
Exercise 3 (2)	0.86	0.90
Pick up the robot and walk (3)	**0.60**	**0.58**
Wake up and walk (4)	0.92	0.89
Walk (5)	0.84	0.86
Walk and drop the robot down (6)	**0.57**	**0.60**

As illustrated in the results section, the CNN-LSTM model demonstrates suboptimal performance in recognizing actions such as picking up and dropping the balloon robot, which exhibits significant variations in instantaneous IMU data. One potential explanation for this phenomenon is that the amount of data collected may have been insufficient. Additionally, the actions exhibited certain similarities with other actions present in IMU data, which complicates the process of distinguishing them. This enhancement is regarded as a prospective undertaking.

5 Conclusion and Future Work

In this paper, we discuss the mechanical design of a companion balloon robot. In order to reduce the weight and development cost of the robot, we propose to divide the robot into an upper balloon robot and a lower robot base. The upper balloon robot relies on the lower robot base for all its motions. The motions that can be made by the upper balloon robot are clarified, and the equations of motion are established for the motion of the lower robot base.

In addition to this we used the sensors carried on the balloon robot to recognize the user's movement and to guide the robot to the charging post using hand recognition. To achieve the above tasks, we use mechanical learning to recognize and classify the IMU data. And we propose a conditional approach to solve the problem of long-distance recognition and similar patterns but different meanings. We first perform static gesture recognition and then input its results into the dynamic gesture recognition model for final gesture prediction.

After that we will focus on the study of path navigation and motion control and introduce robotic emotions to accompany the balloon robot. To make the balloon robot more like a pet and thus improve elderlies' feeling of mattering. After that we will improve the design of the robot base so that it can charge the upper balloon robot and can be connected to a charge station to charge the whole robot.

Acknowledgment. This work was partially supported by Japan Science and Technology Agency (JST), Moonshot R&D, with grant number JPMJMS2034 and TMU local 5G research support.

References

1. Matsuura, T., Ma, X.: Living arrangements and subjective well-being of the elderly in china and japan. J. Happiness Stud. **23**(3), 903–948 (2022)
2. Kojima, G., Taniguchi, Y., Kitamura, A., Fujiwara, Y.: Is living alone a risk factor of frailty? A systematic review and meta-analysis. Ageing Res. Rev. **59**, 101048 (2020)
3. Flett, G.L., Heisel, M.J.: Aging and feeling valued versus expendable during the covid-19 pandemic and beyond: a review and commentary of why mattering is fundamental to the health and well-being of older adults. International Journal of Mental Health and Addiction, pp. 1–27 (2020)
4. Rosenberg, M., McCullough, B.C.: Mattering: inferred significance and mental health among adolescents. Res. Commun. Mental Health (1981)
5. Kojima, G., Aoyama, R., Taniguchi, Y.: Associations between pet ownership and frailty: a systematic review. Geriatrics **5**(4), 89 (2020)
6. Hori, Y., et al.: Use of robotic pet in a distributed layout elderly housing with services: a case study on elderly people with cognitive impairment. J. Robot. Mechatronics **33**(4), 784–803 (2021)
7. Shibata, T., Coughlin, J.F.: Trends of robot therapy with neurological therapeutic seal robot, PARO. J. Robot. Mechatronics **26**(4), 418–425 (2014)
8. Yoshida, N., et al.: Production of character animation in a home robot: a case study of lovot. Int. J. Soc. Robot. **14**(1), 39–54 (2022)
9. Wang, Y., Chang, D.: Motion performance analysis and layout selection for motion system with four Mecanum wheels. J. Mech. Eng. **45**(5), 307–316 (2009)
10. Tătar, M.O., Popovici, C., Mândru, D., et al.: Design and development of an autonomous omni-directional mobile robot with Mecanum wheels. 2014 IEEE International Conference on Automation, Quality and Testing, Robotics. pp. 1–6, IEEE, 2014
11. Kubota, N., Nojima, Y., Baba, N., et al.: Evolving pet robot with emotional model. Proceedings of the 2000 Congress on Evolutionary Computation. CEC00 (Cat. No. 00TH8512). IEEE, **2**, 1231–1237 (2000)
12. Wang, W., Siow, C.Z., Obo, T., Kubota, N.: Long-distance gesture recognition for interactive communication. In: 2024 International Conference on Machine Learning and Cybernetics (ICMLC) (pp. 392–397). IEEE (2024)

13. Zulkosky, K.: Self-efficacy: a concept analysis. Nursing Forum. Vol. 44. No. 2. Malden, USA, Blackwell Publishing Inc (2009)
14. Huang, H., Pan, Z., Ye, L., Fangmin, S.: A lightweight attention-based CNN model for efficient gait recognition with wearable IMU sensors. Sensors **21**(8), 2866 (2021)
15. Hochreiter, S., Schmidhuber, J.: Long short-term memory. Neural Comput. **9**(8), 1735–1780 (1997)
16. Lee, C.J., Lee, J.K.: IMU-based energy expenditure estimation for various walking conditions using a hybrid CNN–LSTM model. Sensors **24**(2), 414 (2024)

Time-Optimal Trajectory Planning for Hybrid Redundant Robotic Arm Based on Prescribed Waypoints

Peng Sun, Hanqi Zhang, Zongyuan Liu, Chentao Wu, Zhe Sun, Yuan Wang, Liu Zhengqing, and Yanbiao Li[✉]

College of Mechanical Engineering, Zhejiang University of Technology, Hangzhou 310023, China
lybrory@zjut.edu.cn

Abstract. Optimizing trajectory execution time is critical for enhancing the operational efficiency of redundant robotic arms in industrial and collaborative applications. This paper proposes an improved genetic algorithm for optimizing trajectory planning in hybrid redundant robotic arms. Focusing on reducing trajectory execution time, the algorithm enhances the search strategy and fitness function to efficiently resolve complex kinematic constraints. Validated through simulations on a hybrid redundant manipulator model, the optimized trajectories achieve a significant 22.13% reduction in execution time-reducing the baseline duration to 10.31 s. The results demonstrate the effectiveness of the improved genetic algorithm in accelerating task completion while maintaining smooth joint torque profiles. This approach enables high-performance operations in time-sensitive applications, advancing the utility of redundant manipulators in dynamic environments.

Keywords: Hybrid redundant robotic arm · Trajectory planning · Improved genetic algorithm

1 Introduction

As society progresses, robotic technology has rapidly developed, demonstrating great potential in fields such as medical assistance, the aerospace industry, and intelligent manufacturing [1]. As one of the key research areas, the robotic arms need to address numerous complex practical problems, which necessitate that robotic arms possess superior motion performance, robustness, and flexibility [2]. Redundant robotic arms refer to those with more degrees of freedom than the minimum required to perform a given task. This additional freedom endows them with unique advantages in dealing with the aforementioned complex practical problems. Therefore, the research on redundant robotic arms has become a hot spot in the field of robotic engineering.

Trajectory planning for a robotic arm involves determining the time-varying motion parameters of the arm while satisfying specific constraints. Saravanan et al. [3] employed cubic B-spline curves to plan the joint trajectories of robotic arms and optimized the motion time to meet the requirements of various motion constraints. Boryga et al. [4] considered polynomial trajectories of different orders. They planned the linear acceleration curves of each coordinate of the end-effector as different polynomials and determined the displacement, velocity, acceleration, and angular jerk of each link in the kinematic chain. Pham et al. [5] extended the classical time-optimal path parameterization algorithm to redundantly actuated robotic systems. They proposed a numerical search method for approximate optimal acceleration, which transformed the human-robot arm contact into torque constraints for trajectory planning, achieved smoothness of the obtained profiles, and converted the polygon constraints back to half-plane inequalities to speed up the calculation. Pei et al. [6] divided the trajectory into several sub-trajectories and used an inverse-kinematics-based model to obtain the joint angular displacements corresponding to the final positions of the end-effector in each sub-trajectory. Zhao et al. [7] proposed an improved hybrid method combining whale optimization and particle swarm optimization. They also constructed an optimal objective function considering time and average torque to achieve the optimal time-joint path planning, reduce the vibration of the robotic arm, and improve the efficiency of the robot. Despite these advancements in trajectory planning methodologies, achieving time-optimal motion while simultaneously handling kinematic constraints and maintaining smoothness remains a critical challenge for redundant robotic arms, particularly in dynamic applications requiring real-time responsiveness.

In this work, we propose an improved genetic algorithm (GA) framework to overcome these limitations. Our approach refines the fitness evaluation and search operators to explicitly prioritize trajectory execution time minimization while preserving dynamic stability. By embedding adaptive constraint-handling mechanisms and leveraging redundant degrees of freedom for temporal optimization, the method generates kinematically feasible trajectories with a 22.13% reduction in motion duration (achieving 10.31s total execution time in validated simulations). This represents a significant leap toward high-speed, reliable operations for complex tasks in medical, aerospace, and industrial settings.

2 Related Works

2.1 Hybrid Redundant Robotic Arm

Human arm motions are completed by the shoulder, elbow, and wrist joints, which have different degrees of freedom and work together to operate complex motions. Where the shoulder joint has 3° of freedom, the elbow joint has 1° of freedom, and the wrist joint has three degrees of freedom [8]. In our study, the prototype of the hybrid redundant robotic arm, as shown in Fig. 1, is established by imitating the kinematics model of the human arm. The shoulder joint is a spherical 5R parallel mechanism, the elbow joint is a 3R serial mechanism, and the wrist joint is a 3-RRP parallel mechanism.

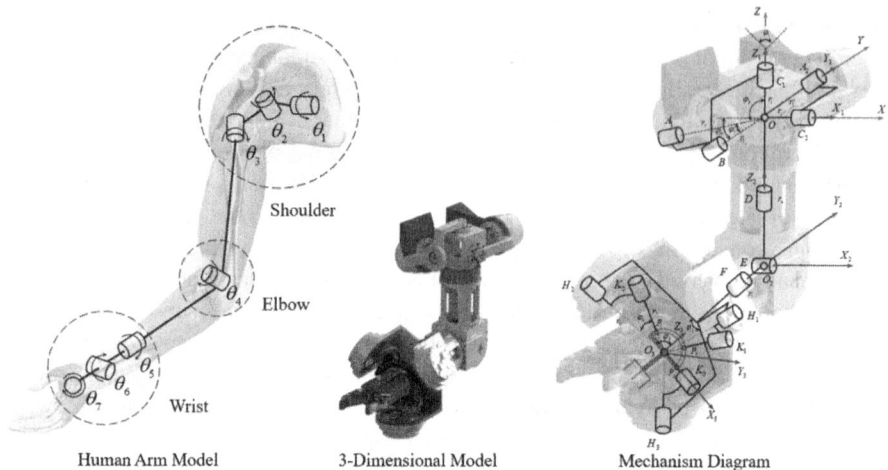

Fig. 1. Hybrid redundant robotic arm.

According to the degree-of-freedom (DOF) properties of the hybrid mechanism, we equivalent the hybrid redundant robotic arm to a serial mechanism [9]. The schematic diagram of the equivalent mechanism as shown in Fig. 2.

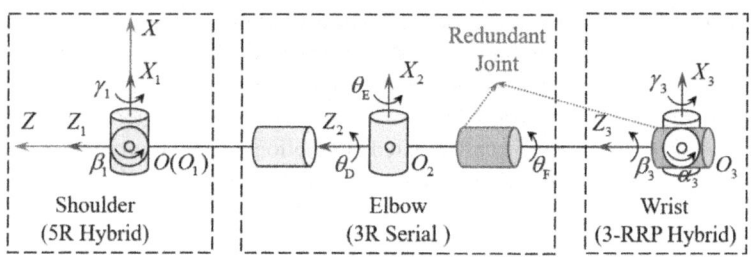

Fig. 2. The schematic diagram of the equivalent hybrid redundant robotic arm.

According to Fig. 2, $O - XYZ$ is the base reference frame of the hybrid redundant robotic arm, $O_1 - X_1Y_1Z_1$ is the moving reference frame of the shoulder joint, where point O coincides with point O_1. $O_2 - X_2Y_2Z_2$ is the moving reference frame of the elbow joint, $O_3 - X_3Y_3Z_3$ is the moving reference frame of the wrist joint. $\gamma_1, \beta_1, \theta_E, \theta_D, \theta_F, \gamma_3, \alpha_3, \beta_3$ denote the rotation input of the equivalent series robotic arm around the axes $X_1, Y_1, Z_2, X_2, Z_3, X_3, Y_3, Z_3$, respectively, where θ_F and β_3 are coaxial revolute joints rotating the Z_3 − axis, their shared rotation axis makes one joint redundant within the kinematic chain.

2.2 Inverse Kinematics Model

Based on our previous work [9], according to the screw theory and exponential product formula, the homogeneous transformation matrix g_{03} for forward motion of the equivalent series hybrid redundant robotic arm can be established as:

$$g_{03} = \exp(\hat{\xi}_{X_1}, \gamma_1) \cdot \exp(\hat{\xi}_{Y_1}, \beta_1) \cdot \exp(\hat{\xi}_{Z_2}, \theta_E) \cdot \exp(\hat{\xi}_{X_2}, \theta_D) \cdot \exp(\hat{\xi}_{Z_3}, \theta_F)$$
$$\cdot \exp(\hat{\xi}_{X_3}, \gamma_3) \cdot \exp(\hat{\xi}_{Y_3}, \alpha_3) \cdot \exp(\hat{\xi}_{Z_3}, \beta_3) \cdot g_{03}(0) \quad (1)$$

where $\hat{\xi}_{X_1}, \hat{\xi}_{Y_1}, \hat{\xi}_{Z_2}, \hat{\xi}_{X_2}, \hat{\xi}_{Z_3}, \hat{\xi}_{X_3}, \hat{\xi}_{Y_3}, \hat{\xi}_{Z_3}$ are the screw vectors of the equivalent hybrid redundant robotic arm, $g_{03}(0)$ is the initial position and orientation of the end-effector in the $O - XYZ$.

The rotation values of two joints, γ_1 and θ_F, are selected as the input variables, according to Paden–Kahan (PK [10]) problem 2, Eq. (1) can be simplified as:

$$\exp(\hat{\xi}_{Y_1}, \beta_1) \cdot \exp(\hat{\xi}_{Z_2}, \theta_E) \cdot \exp(\hat{\xi}_{X_2}, \theta_D) \cdot p_{O_3} = \exp(\hat{\xi}_{X_1}, -\gamma_1) \cdot g_{st} \cdot g_{03}^{-1}(0) \cdot p_{O_3} \quad (2)$$

where p_{O_3} is the homogeneous position vector of point O_3, g_{st} is the target position and orientation matrix of the end-effector in the $O - XYZ$, according to PK problem 3, there is:

$$\begin{cases} \exp(\hat{\xi}_{Y_1}, \beta_1) \cdot \exp(\hat{\xi}_{Z_2}, \theta_E) \cdot \left(\exp(\hat{\xi}_{X_2}, \theta_D) \cdot p_{O_3} - p_O\right) = \\ \quad \exp(\hat{\xi}_{X_1}, -\gamma_1) \cdot g_{st} \cdot g_{03}^{-1}(0) \cdot p_{O_3} - p_O \\ \left\| \exp(\hat{\xi}_{X_2}, \theta_D) \cdot p_{O_3} - p_O \right\| = \left\| \exp(\hat{\xi}_{X_1}, -\gamma_1) \cdot g_{st} \cdot g_{03}^{-1}(0) \cdot p_{O_3} - p_O \right\| \end{cases} \quad (3)$$

where p_O is the homogeneous position vector of point O, Eq. (3) obtains the value of θ_D, define $\exp(\hat{\xi}_{X_2}, \theta_D) \cdot p_{O_3} = p_{O_3}^D$, and then substitutes it into Eq. (2), the following equation is obtained:

$$\exp(\hat{\xi}_{Y_1}, \beta_1) \cdot \exp(\hat{\xi}_{Z_2}, \theta_E) \cdot p_{O_3}^D = \exp(\hat{\xi}_{X_1}, -\gamma_1) \cdot g_{st} \cdot g_{03}^{-1}(0) \cdot p_{O_3} \quad (4)$$

Apply PK problem 1 and 2 to solve (4), it can obtain β_1 and θ_D, and then substitute these two values into Eq. (1), it can be obtained:

$$\exp(\hat{\xi}_{X_3}, \gamma_3) \cdot \exp(\hat{\xi}_{Y_3}, \alpha_3) \cdot \exp(\hat{\xi}_{Z_3}, \beta_3) = \exp(\hat{\xi}_{Z_3}, -\theta_F) \cdot \exp(\hat{\xi}_{X_2}, -\theta_D) \cdot \exp(\hat{\xi}_{Z_2}, -\theta_E)$$
$$\cdot \exp(\hat{\xi}_{Y_1}, -\beta_1) \cdot \exp(\hat{\xi}_{X_1}, -\gamma_1) \cdot g_{st} \cdot g_{03}^{-1}(0) \quad (5)$$

The input variables of the wrist joint of the hybrid redundant robotic arm $\alpha_3, \beta_3, \gamma_3$ can be obtained according to Eq. (5). Then, the inverse kinematics model will be established according to Eq. (1–5).

2.3 Dynamics Model

The dynamic problem of the hybrid redundant robotic arm lies in obtaining the relationship between the external forces and joint torques during the motion process. In this paper, the principle of virtual work [11] is employed to construct the dynamic model of the hybrid redundant robotic arm:

$$\delta d_\phi^T \tau + \delta d_{\text{wrist}}^T \Gamma + \sum_i \delta d_i^T F_i = 0 \qquad (6)$$

where δd_ϕ^T is the virtual displacement of the main kinematic pair, τ is the driving torque of the main kinematic pair, $\delta d_{\text{wrist}}^T$ is the virtual displacement of the wrist joint, Γ is the terminal load, represents the displacement of each rod, represents the inertial forces and active forces of each rod.

In Sect. 2.2, the kinematics of the hybrid redundant robotic arm has been introduced, which can be utilized to relate the displacement of the active kinematic pairs to those of other links. The virtual displacement of each rod can be obtained as:

$$\begin{cases} \delta d_{\text{wrist}}^T = J_{\text{wrist}} \delta d_\phi \\ \delta d_i = J_i J_\phi^{\theta_i} \delta d_\phi \end{cases} \qquad (7)$$

Integrate and eliminate the non-zero virtual displacement according to Eq. (6) and Eq. (7), there is:

$$\tau + J_{\text{wrist}}^T \Gamma + \sum_i \left(J_i J_\phi^{\theta_i} \right)^T F_i = 0 \qquad (8)$$

Equation (8) can be combined into the standard form of the dynamic model:

$$M(\phi)\ddot{\phi} + V(\phi, \dot{\phi}) + G(\phi) = \tau \qquad (9)$$

3 Methodology

3.1 Trajectory Parameterization

During robotic motion tasks, robotic arms are often required to pass through multiple prescribed waypoints. To plan the end-effector trajectory of the robotic arm, it is necessary to fit these prescribed waypoints and then carry out parameterization analysis of the fitted trajectory.

B-spline curves are frequently utilized in robot trajectory planning because of their continuity properties [12]. The equation of the B-spline curve is expressed as:

$$C(u) = \sum_{i=0}^{k} P_i B_{i,n}(u) \qquad (10)$$

where P_i is the control points of the B-spline curve, $B_{i,n}(u)$ represent the p-order B-spline basis function, which is calculated as:

$$\begin{cases} B_{i,0}(u) = \begin{cases} 1, & u_i \leq u \leq u_{i+1} \\ 0, & \text{otherwise} \end{cases}, k = 1 \\ B_{i,n}(u) = \dfrac{(u - u_i)}{u_{i+n} - u_i} B_{i,n-1}(u) + \dfrac{(u_{i+n+1} - u)}{u_{i+n+1} - u_{i+1}} B_{i+1,n-1}(u), k \geq 2 \end{cases} \qquad (11)$$

Among Eq. (11), the interval $[u_i\ u_{i+1}]$ serves as the nodal support interval for the B-spline basis function, and its knot vector is:

$$U = \left[\underbrace{u_0, ..., u_n}_{n+1}, u_{n+1}, ..., u_{m-n-1}, \underbrace{u_{m-n}, ..., u_m}_{n+1}\right], m = i+n+1 \quad (12)$$

The time intervals between each node determine the speed of the B-spline curve. To minimize the total time T while allowing non-uniform time allocation, the free nodes in the knot vector are optimized as follows:

$$U = \left[\underbrace{0, ..., 0}_{n+1}, u_{n+1}, ..., u_{m-n-1}, \underbrace{T, ..., T}_{n+1}\right] \quad (13)$$

$u_{n+1}, ..., u_{m-n-1}$ are the free nodes that require optimization, to optimize the motion time of the end-effector trajectory of the hybrid redundant robotic arm. According to Eq. (13), the defined discrete motion time is as follows.

$$\begin{cases} \kappa_1 = u_{n+1} \\ \kappa_k = u_{k+2} - u_{k+1}, \forall k = 2, ..., n \\ \kappa_{n+1} = T - u_{m-n-1} \end{cases} \quad (14)$$

3.2 Improved Genetic Algorithm

By optimizing the motion time of each segment of the B-spline trajectory, the optimization of the entire end-effector trajectory on the time scale can be achieved. According to Eq. (14), the optimization objective can be obtained:

$$\min_\kappa T = \min_\kappa \sum_{k=1}^{n+1} \kappa_k \quad (15)$$

Owing to the physical characteristics of the hybrid redundant robotic arm, the motion of its end-effector is subject to certain velocity and acceleration constraints, and the joint motors are subject to certain torque constraints. Based on the kinematic and dynamic models derived in Sect. 2, the constraint functions for trajectory planning are as follows:

$$\begin{cases} \|v(t)\| = \left\|\dfrac{d\mathbf{C}}{dt}\right\| = \left\|\sum\limits_{i=0}^{k}\dfrac{dB_{i,n}}{dt}\mathbf{P}_i\right\| \leq v_{\max} \\ \|a(t)\| = \left\|\dfrac{d^2\mathbf{C}}{dt^2}\right\| = \left\|\sum\limits_{i=0}^{k}\dfrac{d^2 B_{i,n}}{dt^2}\mathbf{P}_i\right\| \leq a_{\max} \\ \|\tau_{1,2,...,8}\| \leq \tau_{\max} \end{cases} \quad (16)$$

The genetic algorithm [13] mimics the biological concepts of natural selection, crossover, and mutation, and possesses strong global search capabilities. In this paper, the crossover and mutation probabilities of the genetic algorithm are improved, and the penalty function is designed in combination with the kinematic and dynamic constraints of the hybrid redundant manipulator. Consequently, the operating time of the end - trajectory of the hybrid redundant manipulator is optimized. The flow chart of the improved genetic algorithm is shown in Fig. 3.

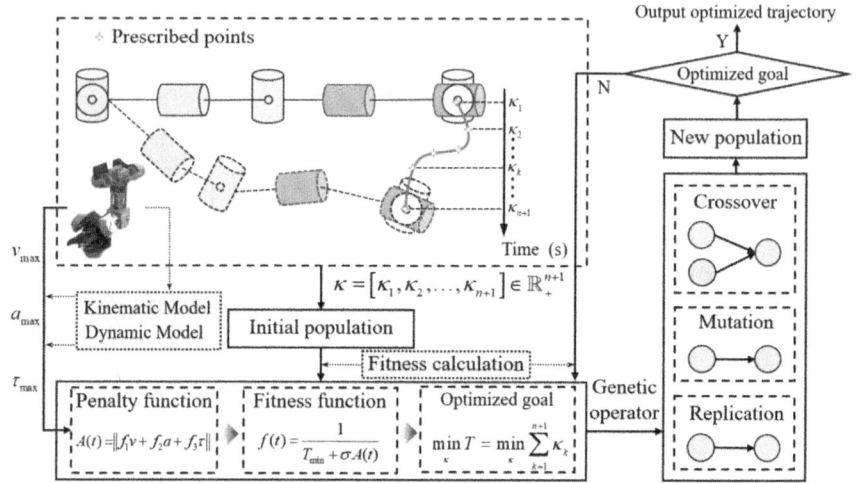

Fig. 3. Flow chart of the improved genetic algorithm

The initial population was configured according to Eq. (14), as presented below:

$$\kappa = [\kappa_1, \kappa_2, \ldots, \kappa_{n+1}] \in \mathbb{R}_+^{n+1} \quad (17)$$

Based on the kinematic and dynamic models of the hybrid redundant robotic arm, the fitness function of the improved genetic algorithm is established:

$$\begin{cases} F(t) = \frac{f(t)+f(t)_{\min}}{f(t)_{\max}+f(t)_{\min}+\delta} \\ f(t) = \frac{1}{T_{\min}+\sigma A(t)} \\ A(t) = |\max(\dot{\theta}_{\max}, \dot{\theta}(t))| + |\max(\ddot{\theta}_{\max}, \ddot{\theta}(t))| + |\max(\tau_{\max}, \tau(t))| \end{cases} \quad (18)$$

where δ is the selectivity factor, σ is the penalty factor, $f(t)$ is the individual fitness function, $A(t)$ is the penalty function, $\dot{\theta}_{\max}$ is the maximum joint speed, $\ddot{\theta}_{\max}$ is the maximum joint acceleration, $\tau_{\max}$ is the maximum joint torque.

Taking into account the complexity of the trajectory planning of hybrid redundant robotic arm, the crossover and mutation probabilities of the genetic algorithm are dynamically adjusted to enhance the algorithm's adaptability and search efficiency. The improved crossover and mutation probabilities are as follows:

$$\begin{cases} P_c = \begin{cases} \frac{P_{c\max}+P_{c\min}}{2} + \frac{P_{c\max}-P_{c\min}}{2}\sin(\frac{f_{avg}-f'}{f_{avg}-f_{\min}}\pi) & f' \leq f_{avg} \\ P_{c\max} & f' > f_{avg} \end{cases} \\ P_m = \begin{cases} \frac{P_{m\max}+P_{m\min}}{2} + \frac{P_{m\max}-P_{m\min}}{2}\sin(\frac{f_{avg}-f'}{f_{avg}-f_{\min}}\pi) & f' \leq f_{avg} \\ P_{m\max} & f' > f_{avg} \end{cases} \end{cases} \quad (19)$$

where f' is the individual fitness value of mutation, f_{min} is the minimum fitness value, f_{avg} is the average fitness value, $P_{c\,max}$ is the maximum crossover probability, $P_{c\,min}$ is the minimum crossover probability, $P_{m\,max}$ is the maximum mutation probability, $P_{m\,min}$ is the minimum mutation probability.

Based on the Eq. (19), the crossover and mutation probabilities in the algorithm change according to the fitness values of the previous generation and exhibit a non-linear trend. By introducing such a dynamic adjustment mechanism, the genetic algorithm can more flexibly adapt to different stages of the problem and the fitness of individuals, thereby improving its adaptability and search efficiency.

3.3 The Experimental System Construction

The experimental system construction is shown in Fig. 4. Based on the optimized trajectory of the end-effector of the prototype obtained by the improved genetic algorithm in Fig. 3., the real-time target system of MATLAB is utilized to regulate the joint motors of the physical prototype through the Speedgoat controller for motion execution. Specifically, EtherCAT serves as the communication protocol for the shoulder and elbow joints, whereas Ethernet is employed for the wrist joint.

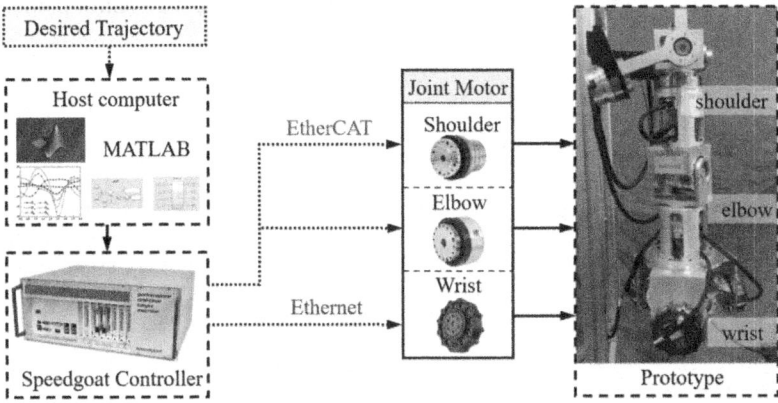

Fig. 4. Experimental system structure diagram

3.4 Terminal Trajectory Planning

Based on the improved genetic algorithm developed in Sect. 3.2, the fourth-order cubic B-spline curve was selected for optimization. First, 14 waypoints are designated, as presented in Table 1.

Table 1. Cartesian coordinates of the prescribed waypoints

Number	Waypoints (mm)			Number	Waypoints (mm)		
	X	Y	Z		X	Y	Z
1	−1	1	0	8	−5	24	24
2	0	0	0	9	−10	25	25
3	1	0	1	10	−20	35	35
4	10	5	3	11	−10	45	45
5	20	12	11	12	−1	50	50
6	10	25	24	13	0	50	50
7	5	24	25	14	1	50	50

Among these path points, points 2 and 13 represent the starting and ending positions of the fourth-order cubic B - spline trajectory. The B - spline curve generated in the three-dimensional cartesian space is depicted in Fig. 5. The red curve represents the optimized end-effector trajectory, while the blue points denote the control points of the B-spline curve.

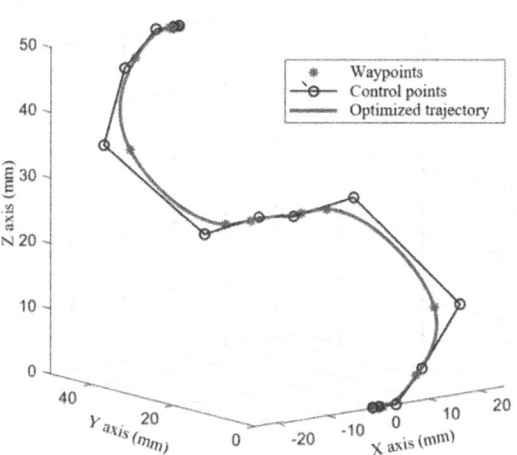

Fig. 5. Diagram of the optimized trajectory

According to Fig. 5, the optimized end-effector trajectory passes through the prescribed waypoints. To further validate the improved genetic algorithm proposed in this paper, a comparison between the standard genetic algorithm and the improved genetic algorithm was conducted based on the waypoints given in Table 1, as shown in Figs. 6 and 7.

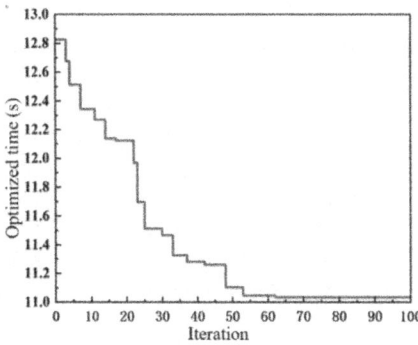

Fig. 6. Standard Genetic Algorithm

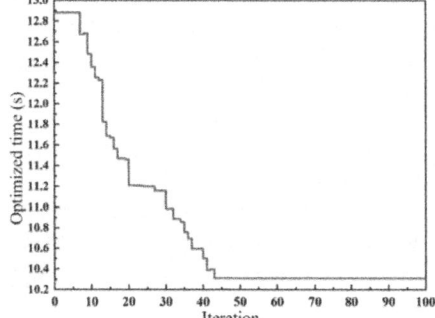

Fig. 7. Improved Genetic Algorithm

The standard genetic algorithm begins to converge after 62 iterations, while the improved genetic algorithm starts to converge after 45 iterations. This indicates that the improved genetic algorithm proposed in this paper enhances the search efficiency. In terms of optimization effect, the standard genetic algorithm shortens the trajectory running time to 11.2 s, while that of the improved genetic algorithm is 10.3 s, which verifies the optimization performance of the improved genetic algorithm.

The trajectory planned in this paper consists of 13 segments. Under the condition of meeting the given constraints. By comparing the optimization time of each trajectory segment, the effectiveness of the algorithm proposed in this paper can be further evaluated, as shown in Table 2.

Table 2. Comparison of time before and after optimization

	κ_1	κ_2	κ_3	κ_4	κ_5	κ_6	κ_7
Initial value (s)	0.111	0.108	1.093	1.693	2.422	0.549	1.099
Optimized value (s)	0.085	0.083	0.841	1.302	1.863	0.422	0.845
	κ_8	κ_9	κ_{10}	κ_{11}	κ_{12}	κ_{13}	T
Initial value (s)	0.549	1.979	2.088	1.093	0.111	0.108	13.24
Optimized value (s)	0.422	1.522	1.606	0.841	0.085	0.083	10.31

The duration of each optimized trajectory is within 2 s. The total motion time is reduced from the initial 13.24 s to 10.31 s, significantly shortening the trajectory operation time and improving the operation efficiency by 22.13%. By inputting the optimized trajectory into the controller of the experimental system built according to Fig. 4, the trajectory diagram of the hybrid redundant robotic arm shown in Fig. 8 can be obtained.

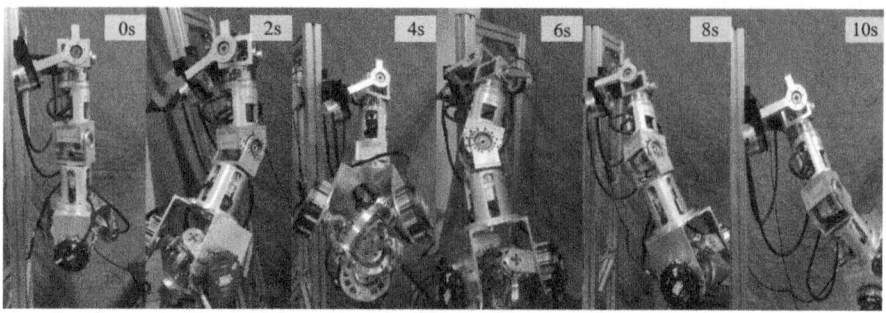

Fig. 8. Motion trajectory of the hybrid redundant robotic arm

According to the experimental results, the torques of each joint of the output robotic arm are shown in Figs. 9 and 10.

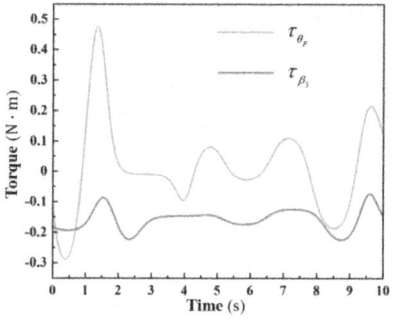

Fig. 9. Torque diagram of redundant joint θ_F and β_3

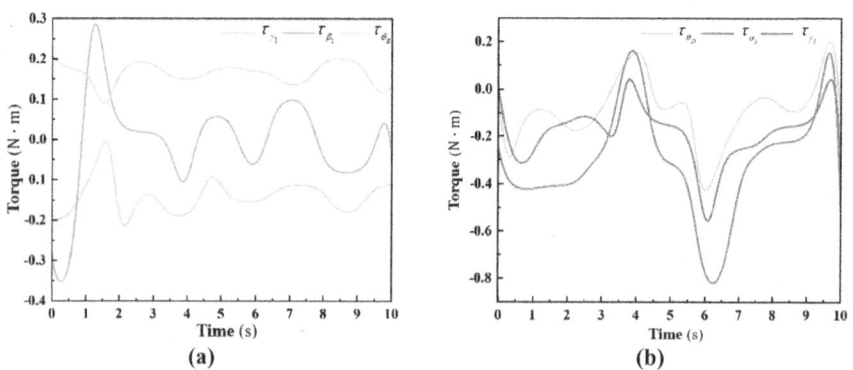

Fig. 10. Torque diagram of the rest joints: (a) joints γ_1, β_1, θ_E; (b) joints θ_D, α_3, γ_3

After inputting the optimized end-effector trajectory, the output torque curves of each joint of the hybrid redundant robotic arm are smooth without sudden changes, which further verifies the effectiveness of the proposed improved genetic algorithm.

4 Conclusion

This study presented an improved genetic algorithm for minimizing trajectory execution time in hybrid redundant robotic arm. Experiment to the prototype demonstrated a 22.13% reduction in motion duration, achieving execution in 10.31 s. The optimized trajectories retained smooth torque characteristics while drastically improving operational speed. These results confirm the capability of improved genetic algorithm to balance efficiency with dynamic performance, enabling faster task completion in industrial and collaborative settings. Future work will target real-time deployment and hardware validation.

Acknowledgement. This research was funded by the National Natural Science Foundation of China (Grant Nos. U21A20122, 52475034, 52105037), the Natural Science Foundation of Zhejiang Province (Grant No. LTGY24E050002, LD24E050003).

References

1. Licardo, J., Domjan, M., Orehovacki, T.: Intelligent robotics-A systematic review of emerging technologies and trends. Electronics **13**(3), 542–553 (2024)
2. Fareh, R., Khadraoui, S., Abdallah, M., Baziyad, M., Bettayeb, M.: Active disturbance rejection control for robotic systems: a review. Mechatronics **80**, 102671 (2021)
3. Saravan, R., Ramabalan, S., Balamurugan, C.: Multiobjective trajectory planner for industrial robots with payload constraints. Robotica **26**(6), 753–765 (2008)
4. Boryga, M., Grabos, A.: Planning of manipulator motion trajectory with higher-degree polynomials use. Mech. Mach. Theory **44**(7), 1400–1419 (2009)
5. Pham, Q., Stasse, O.: Time-optimal path parameterization for redundantly actuated robots: a numerical integration approach. IEEE/ASME Trans. Mechatron. **20**(6), 3257–3263 (2015)
6. Pei, Y., Liu, Z., Xu, J., et al.: Minimum-time trajectory planning for a 4-dof manipulator considering motion stability and obstacle avoidance. In: 5th International Conference on Mechanical, pp. 207–211 (2020)
7. Zhao, J., Zhu, X., Song, T.: Serial manipulator time-jerk optimal trajectory planning based on hybrid iwoa-pso algorithm. IEEE Access. **10**, 6592–6604 (2022)
8. Billard, A., Matarić, M.: Learning human arm movements by imitation: evaluation of a biologically inspired connectionist architecture. Robot. Auton. Syst. **37**, 145–160 (2001)
9. Sun, P., Li, Y., Wang, Z., et al.: Inverse displacement analysis of a novel hybrid humanoid robotic arm. Mech. Mach. Theory **147**, 103743 (2020)
10. Duindam, V., Xu, J., Duindam, V., Sastry, S.: Three-dimensional Motion Planning Algorithms for Steerable Needles Using Inverse Kinematics. In: 8th International Workshop on the Algorithmic Foundations of Robotics, pp. 789–800 (2010)
11. Yang, C., Geng, S., Walker, I., et al.: Geometric constraint-based modeling and analysis of a novel continuum robot with Shape Memory Alloy initiated variable stiffness. Int. J. Robot. Res. **39**(14), 1620–1634 (2020)

12. Ahmad, J., Wahab, M.: Enhancing the safety and smoothness of path planning through an integration of Dijkstra's algorithm and piecewise cubic Bezier optimization. Expert Syst. Appl. **289**, 128315 (2025)
13. Chang, W., Liu, M., Huang, Y., Lei, J., Wu, K.: Predicting the tensile strength of plant leaves based on GA-SVM. J. Natural Fibers. **22**(1), 2514081 (2025)

Conceptual Design and Kinematic Analysis of a Biomimetic Robot Joint (BRJ) Based on a Higher Pair Mechanism

Gaohan Zhu, Shixuan Chu, Yinghui Li, and Weizhong Guo[✉]

Shanghai Jiao Tong University, Shanghai 200240, China
wzguo@sjtu.edu.cn

Abstract. The human knee joint exhibits complex motion characterized by a varying instantaneous center of rotation. Mimicking this motion in mechanical systems holds significant potential for both scientific understanding and engineering design. To this end, this study investigates a design method of the biomimetic robot joint (BRJ) inspired by the human knee, aiming to accurately reproduce its motion. Firstly, the bionic concept and the design of the BRJ mechanism with one degree of freedom are introduced. The proposed mechanism incorporates a higher pair composed of three pairs of line-curve contact elements, each maintaining mutual contact and all remaining simultaneously engaged to ensure continuous and stable joint motion. Then, the profile synthesis method is presented to determine the geometry of elements forming the higher pair. Next, the kinematic model of the BRJ mechanism is developed. Finally, a case study is conducted to validate the effectiveness of the proposed design. Results indicate that the BRJ mechanism can accurately reproduce the desired complex motion with one degree of freedom, offering a novel joint solution for applications such as exoskeletons, prostheses, and rehabilitation robots.

Keywords: Bionic design · Human knee joint · One degree of freedom · Higher pair mechanisms

1 Introduction

The biomimetic design of human joints is a foundational technology in robotics, mechanism design, and biomedical engineering. Developing biomimetic robot joints that accurately reproduce human joint motion [1] while maintaining structural similarity [2] has long been a central objective of research.

The knee joint is one of the largest and most complex joints in the human body [3]. Its primary anatomical components include the bone structures formed by the femur, the tibia, and the patella; the ligament structures composed of the anterior and posterior cruciate ligaments, as well as the lateral collateral ligaments; and the muscle structures such as the quadriceps. These components collectively enable complex movement and functionality of the human knee joint (HKJ). Among these, the contact interaction between the femur and the tibia, coupled with the guiding and constraining effects of the cruciate ligaments, endows the HKJ with its unique motion pattern.

From a kinematic perspective, the primary motion of the HKJ occurs in the sagittal plane and is characterized by a varying instantaneous center of rotation (ICR) [4]. This motion pattern is analogous to that of higher pairs in mechanism theory, where relative motion is determined by point, line, or curve contact between elements with complex geometries, resulting in a continuously varying ICR. In contrast, single lower pairs, such as revolute and prismatic pairs, permit only fixed-axis rotation and linear translation, which significantly differ from the motion pattern of the HKJ.

Combining multiple kinematic pairs into a mechanism enables the reproduction of motion with a varying ICR. Most existing studies optimize the ICR path using one degree of freedom (DoF) linkage, such as four-bar [5] and six-bar linkages [6], which are widely applied in exoskeletons and prosthetics. However, 1-DoF linkages with lower pairs can only approximately reproduce the knee joint motion. Increasing the DoF of mechanisms can achieve accurate motion reproduction [7], but it also increases control complexity and reduces design compactness [8]. In contrast, higher pair mechanisms can achieve accurate motion reproduction while maintaining one DoF [9, 10], making them increasingly attractive for exoskeletons and robotic applications [1].

In previous research [10], the authors introduced the concept of biomimetic robot joints (BRJ). A BRJ is a 1-DoF higher pair mechanism in which the output and fixed links are connected by a higher pair, enabling accurate reproduction of complex motion.[1] Building upon this foundation, this study focuses on a specific type of BRJ and presents a systematic design framework that spans from the bionic concept to the profile synthesis of elements forming the higher pair, and to the kinematic modeling of the BRJ mechanism. By designing higher pairs with line-curve contact elements, the proposed schemes not only achieve accurate motion generation in a 1-DoF mechanism but also ensure that the elements maintain contact solely through their own interaction.

The remainder of this paper is structured as follows: Section 2 introduces the BRJ design concept inspired by the HKJ; Section 3 presents the profile design requirements and profile synthesis method for the elements forming the higher pair in the BRJ mechanism; Section 4 establishes the kinematic model of the BRJ mechanism; Section 5 provides case studies; and the conclusion is given in Section 6.

2 Design Concept of Biomimetic Robot Joint (BRJ)

2.1 Motion Pattern of the Human Knee Joint

The human knee joint exhibits complex motion primarily in the sagittal plane, enabling flexion and extension from 0 to 120° [11]. Its motion in the sagittal plane is characterized by two key features: 1) a complex combination of rolling and sliding motion of the femur relative to the tibia; 2) a varying ICR as the knee joint flexes or extends, resulting in a 1-DoF motion with coupled rotation and translation between the femur and tibia.

---

[1] Accurate reproduction of complex motion refers to the theoretical ability of a synthesized mechanism to accurately achieve rigid body guidance defined by a continuous position and orientation.

This motion pattern produces the moving and fixed centrodes on the femur and tibia, respectively, whose intersection point represents the ICR point, as shown in Fig. 1(a).

This research primarily reproduces the motion with a varying ICR of HKJ in the sagittal plane. Unlike traditional revolute joints with fixed-axis rotation, the varying ICR motion of the knee joint offers biomechanical advantages, such as reduced muscle force, increased joint workspace, and improved stability [12]. These features are also valuable in robotics, enhancing motion compatibility, energy efficiency, and control precision [4]. Accurately reproducing this motion is particularly important for applications in wearable devices, rehabilitation robots, and artificial joints.

To model this motion, an equivalent four-bar linkage is commonly used, as shown in Fig. 1(b), assuming constant cruciate ligament length [13]. This model simplifies analysis and serves both as a biomechanical abstraction and as a joint solution in mechanical systems [5]. However, robotic joints based on four-bar linkages can only approximately generate the desired motion [8]. To address this limitation, this research proposes a BRJ design based on higher pair mechanisms, capable of accurately reproducing knee joint motion for enhancing the humanoid movement capabilities.

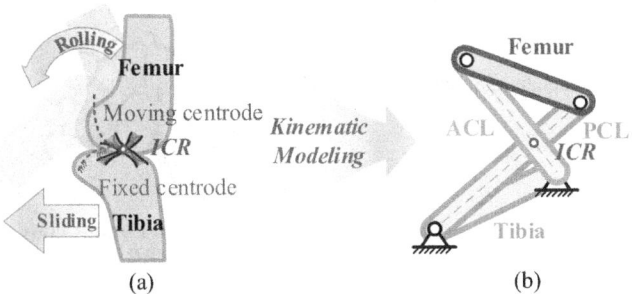

Fig. 1. Human knee joint (HKJ) and kinematic equivalent mechanism: (a) the varying instantaneous center of rotation (ICR) motion of the HKJ; (b) equivalent four-bar linkage model, including femur, tibia, anterior cruciate ligament (ACL), and posterior cruciate ligament (PCL).

2.2 Bionic Concept of BRJ Mechanism

To reproduce the varying ICR motion of the HKJ in robotic joints, it is essential to analyze the HKJ motion from a mechanism theory perspective. In our previous research [10], the key HKJ components governing the motion pattern were identified, and the concept of BRJ, inspired by the HKJ, was proposed. This research focuses on a specific structure of the BRJ mechanism, as shown in Fig. 2, where the tibiofemoral joint is represented as a higher pair, the cruciate ligaments as constraints, and the muscles as the kinematic chain.

In this mechanism, the fixed link (link 1) and the output link (link 2) represent the tibia and the femur, respectively, connected through a higher pair. The input link (link 4) and the connecting link (link 3), along with the revolute joints, form the muscle-equivalent kinematic chain. Three pairs of elements constitute the higher pair to introduce a redundant constraint, thereby ensuring contact between elements during motion. Among these, one pair mimics the conjugate surface between the femur and tibia, while the others represent ligaments (in the constraint sense, ligaments are modeled as higher pairs). The profiles of these elements are designed so that their normal vectors always intersect at the ICR point. Based on the Grübler-Kutzbach criterion [14], the DoF of a planar mechanism is calculated as

$$\text{DoF} = 3(n-1) - 2p_l - p_h + p_v \tag{1}$$

where n is the number of links; p_l and p_h. Are the number of lower and higher pairs, respectively; and p_v is the number of redundant constraints. From the equation, the DoF of the BRJ mechanism can be determined as

$$\text{DoF} = 3 \times (4-1) - 2 \times 3 - 3 + 1 = 1 \tag{2}$$

Accordingly, this joint mechanism can achieve 1-DoF motion. In addition, the connection between the output and fixed links through a higher pair enables the desired complex motion to be theoretically achieved by designing elemental profiles.

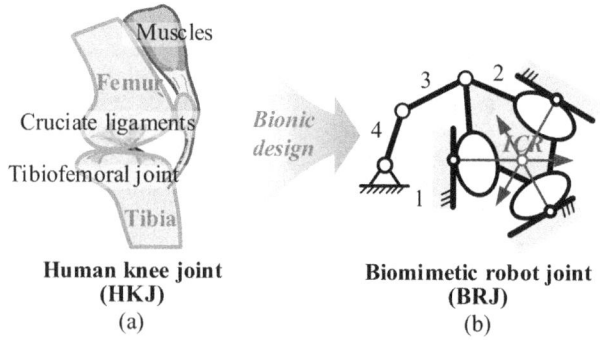

Fig. 2. Biomimetic robot joint (BRJ) mechanism inspired by HKJ: (a) HKJ; (b) BRJ.

3 Geometric Programming for Elements in the Higher Pair

3.1 Profile Design Requirements

After establishing the structure of the BRJ mechanism, the next step is to perform profile synthesis to design the elemental profiles of the higher pair for realizing the required motion [10]. However, profile synthesis alone cannot guarantee continuous contact, as directional constraints may cause element disengagement.

For planar higher pairs, the profiles of elements are typically defined by geometric forms such as curves, lines, or points. Among various combinations, point-curve, curve-curve, and line-curve types are common for reproducing the complex motion. Compared to others, the line-curve profile more easily prevents disengagement through appropriate geometric design. Accordingly, to maintain contact solely through the geometric profiles of elements, i.e., the form closure, the proposed BRJ mechanism incorporates a higher pair composed of three pairs of line-curve elements.

In the specific implementation, the elements on link 1 is designated as the line-type profiles, as shown in Fig. 3(a). The coordinate frame $O_1 - x_1 y_1$ is attached to link 1, and the local coordinate frame $P_1 - x_{p1}y_{p1}$ is used to describe the line-type profiles. The angle between the frames $O_1 - x_1y_1$ and $P_1 - x_{p1}y_{p1}$ is denoted as α_1, with the range of $[0, 2\pi/3)$. Note that the superscript on the vector denotes its representation in the corresponding coordinate frame. The position vector of point P_1 in the frame $O_1 - x_1y_1$ is denoted as $r_{p1}^{(1)}$, with its coordinates expressed as $\left[r_{p1x}^{(1)} \; r_{p1y}^{(1)} \right]^T$. The direction of the elemental profile in the frame $P_1 - x_{p1}y_{p1}$ is along the x_{p1} axis, and the angles between r_1 and r_2, r_1 and r_3 are denoted as α_{12} and α_{13}, respectively. The angles satisfy the relationship $0 < \alpha_{12} < \alpha_{13} < \pi$. The distance between the intersection point of r_1 with r_3 and point P_1 is denoted as a, and $a \geq 0$.

Based on this, the parametric representations of these linear profiles are provided. The parametric variable of the elemental profile r_i ($i = 1, 2, 3$) is denoted as θ_i. The profile r_1 can be expressed in the frame $O_1 - x_1y_1$ as

$$r_1^{(1)} = \begin{bmatrix} \theta_1 \cos(\alpha_1) + r_{p2x}^{(1)} \\ \theta_1 \sin(\alpha_1) + r_{p2y}^{(1)} \end{bmatrix} \tag{3}$$

The profile r_2 can be expressed in the frame $O_1 - x_1y_1$ as

$$r_2^{(1)} = \begin{bmatrix} \theta_2 \cos(\alpha_{12} + \alpha_1) + r_{p2x}^{(1)} \\ \theta_2 \sin(\alpha_{12} + \alpha) + r_{p2y}^{(1)} \end{bmatrix} \tag{4}$$

The profile r_3 can be expressed in the frame $O_1 - x_1y_1$ as

$$r_3^{(1)} = \begin{bmatrix} \theta_3 \cos(\alpha_{13} + \alpha_1) + a \cos(\alpha_1) + r_{p2x}^{(1)} \\ \theta_3 \sin(\alpha_{13} + \alpha) + a \sin(\alpha_1) + r_{p2y}^{(1)} \end{bmatrix} \tag{5}$$

Accordingly, the linear profiles of elements on the fixed link can be parameterized using the variables a, $r_{p1x}^{(1)}$, $r_{p1y}^{(1)}$, α_1, α_{12}, α_{13}.

3.2 Profile Synthesis Method

After determining the profiles of elements on the fixed link, the next step is to use profile synthesis to obtain the profiles of their conjugate elements on the output link. Profile synthesis refers to the process of determining a conjugate elemental profile based on the given motion and an elemental profile, using the meshing equation. The specific process of profile synthesis is detailed in Ref. [10], and here only a brief overview is provided.

As shown in Fig. 3(b), the fixed coordinate frame $O_1 - x_1y_1$ is established on the fixed link, and the moving coordinate frame $O_2 - x_2y_2$ is established on the output link. The rotation angle of frames $O_2 - x_2y_2$ relative to $O_1 - x_1y_1$ is denoted as ϕ. The position vectors of points O_2 and ICR are denoted as r_{O2} and r_{ICR}, respectively, where $r_{O2}^{(1)} = \left[r_{O2x}^{(1)} \; r_{O2y}^{(1)} \right]^T$ and $r_{ICR}^{(1)} = \left[r_{ICRx}^{(1)} \; r_{ICRy}^{(1)} \right]^T$. The conjugate profile of the elemental profile r_i is denoted as $\tilde{r}_i$, and the contact point is denoted as K_i.

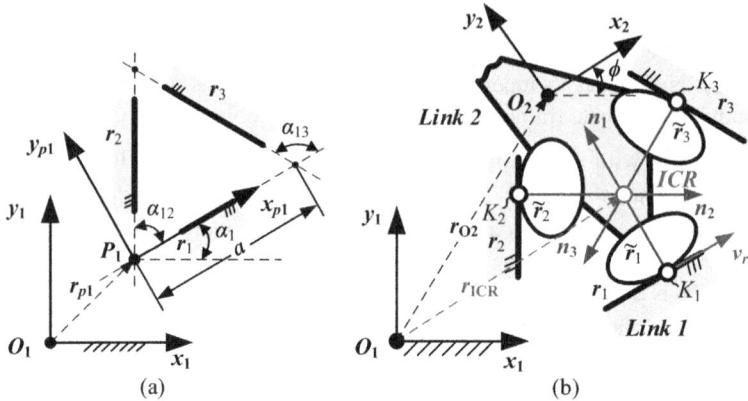

Fig. 3. Higher pair connecting the fixed and output links: (a) linear profiles of elements on the fixed link; (b) the elements with linear profiles and their conjugate elements.

Given the required motion (i.e., ϕ and r_{O2}), the path formed by the ICR on both the fixed and output links can be determined, which corresponds to fixed and moving centrodes, respectively. The fixed centrode can be expressed as

$$r_{ICR}^{(1)} = \begin{bmatrix} r_{O2x}^{(1)} - \frac{dr_{O2y}^{(1)}}{d\phi} \\ r_{O2y}^{(1)} + \frac{dr_{O2x}^{(1)}}{d\phi} \end{bmatrix} \quad (6)$$

Given the elemental profile r_i, and $r_i^{(1)} = \begin{bmatrix} r_{1x}^{(1)} & r_{1y}^{(1)} \end{bmatrix}^T$. At contact point K_i, the normal is $n_i^{(1)} = \begin{bmatrix} n_{1x}^{(1)} & n_{1y}^{(1)} \end{bmatrix}^T$, and the relative velocity is $v_{ri}^{(1)} = \dot{R}_{12}(R_{12})^{-1}\left(r_i^{(1)} - r_{ICR}^{(1)}\right)$, where R_{12} is the rotation matrix for transforming vector coordinates from frames $O_2 - x_2y_2$ to $O_1 - x_1y_1$, which can be expressed as

$$R_{12} = \begin{bmatrix} \cos(\phi) & -\sin(\phi) \\ \sin(\phi) & \cos(\phi) \end{bmatrix} \quad (7)$$

At the contact point K_i, the elemental profiles satisfy the meshing equation

$$n_i^{(1)} \cdot v_{ri}^{(1)} = 0 \quad (8)$$

The meshing equation can be rewritten as

$$\left[n_{1y}^{(1)}\left(r_{1x}^{(1)} - r_{ICRx}^{(1)}\right) - n_{1y}^{(1)}\left(r_{1y}^{(1)} - r_{ICRy}^{(1)}\right) \right]\dot{\phi} = 0 \quad (9)$$

Based on this, the profile of the conjugate element can be expressed as

$$\tilde{r}_i^{(2)} = (R_{12})^{-1}\left(r_i^{(1)} - r_{O2}^{(1)}\right) \quad (10)$$

This process outlines the general steps of profile synthesis. Due to the arbitrariness of the given profile, there are an infinite number of pairs of elemental profiles that satisfy the required motion. Therefore, profile synthesis greatly expands the design options for higher pairs. However, in practical applications, profile schemes should be selected according to specific design requirements, such as geometric continuity of elemental profiles, physical realizability, joint size limitations, and manufacturability.

4 Kinematic Modeling of the BRJ Mechanism

After obtaining the elemental profiles of the higher pair, the kinematic model of the overall mechanism is established. Given the known motion of the output link, determining the rotation angle of the input link essentially becomes an inverse kinematics problem. Accordingly, position analysis is conducted based on the vector-loop equation, followed by velocity analysis.

As shown in Fig. 4, the frames $O_k - x_k y_k$ ($k = 1, 2, 3, 4$) are attached to link k, and the frame $O_5 - x_5 y_5$ is attached to link 1. The lengths of vectors $\boldsymbol{O_1 O_2}, \boldsymbol{O_3 O_4}, \boldsymbol{O_5 O_4}, \boldsymbol{O_1 O_5}$ are L_1, L_3, L_4, L_5, respectively, and the angles between the vectors and the x_1 axis are denoted as $\phi_1, \phi_3, \phi_4, \phi_5$, respectively. The length of $\boldsymbol{O_1 O_3}$ is L_{12}, and the angle between this vector and x_1 axis is denoted as ϕ_{12}. The angle between vector $\boldsymbol{O_5 O_4}$ and x_1 axis is denoted as ϕ_I, which is also the rotation angle of the input link. Additionally, the length of vector $\boldsymbol{O_2 O_3}$ is L_2, the angle between this vector and x_2 axis is a constant, denoted as α.

The vector-loop equation can be expressed as

$$\boldsymbol{O_1 O_2} + \boldsymbol{O_2 O_3} = \boldsymbol{O_1 O_3} \tag{11}$$

Another loop vector equation can be expressed as

$$\boldsymbol{O_1 O_3} + \boldsymbol{O_3 O_4} = \boldsymbol{O_1 O_5} + \boldsymbol{O_5 O_4} \tag{12}$$

By solving the Eqs. (11) and (12), the angles of all links can be determined. The result for rotation angle of the input link is given directly as

$$\begin{cases} \phi_I = 2 \tan^{-1}\left(\frac{V - \sqrt{U^2 + V^2 - W^2}}{U + W}\right) \\ U = L_5 \cos(\phi_5) - L_{12} \cos(\phi_{12}) \\ V = L_5 \sin(\phi_5) - L_{12} \sin(\phi_{12}) \\ W = \frac{1}{2L_4}(L_3^2 - L_4^2 - L_5^2 - L_{12}^2 + 2L_{12} L_5 \cos(\phi_{12})) \end{cases} \tag{13}$$

Furthermore, by differentiating the vector-loop equation $\boldsymbol{O_1 O_5} + \boldsymbol{O_5 O_4} = \boldsymbol{O_1 O_2} + \boldsymbol{O_2 O_3} + \boldsymbol{O_3 O_4}$, the angular velocity of the input link can be obtained as

$$\begin{cases} \omega_I = \frac{E \cos(\phi_3) - F \sin(\phi_3)}{L_4 \sin(\phi_I - \phi_3)} \omega_O \\ E = L_1 \sin(\phi_1) - r_{ICRy}^{(1)} + L_2 \sin(\phi + \alpha) \\ F = L_1 \cos(\phi_1) - r_{ICRx}^{(1)} + L_2 \cos(\phi + \alpha) \end{cases} \tag{14}$$

where ω_O represents the angular velocity of the output link.

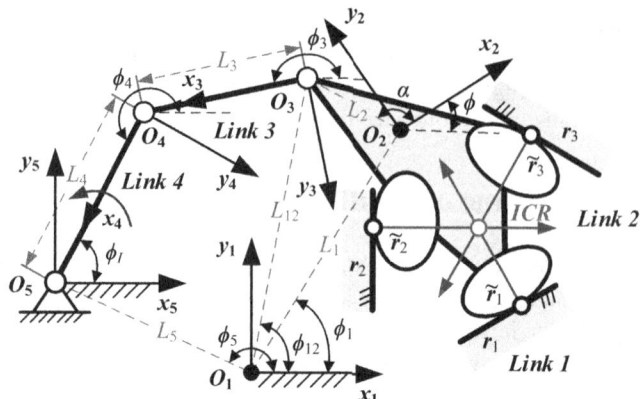

Fig. 4. Coordinate system in the scheme of the BRJ mechanism.

Through the position and velocity modeling, the kinematic parameters of the input link can be obtained. This process provides important theoretical and technical support for the design and control of the BRJ mechanism.

5 Case Study: Motion Generation of the BRJ Mechanism

This section presents case studies of the BRJ mechanism. As an extension of prior work, this research continues to use the knee joint motion described in Ref. [10] as the reproduction target. Notably, the BRJ mechanism is capable of not only accurately reproducing the motion detailed in this case but also even more complex motion. In practical applications, once the required motion is known, this method can be utilized for designing the joint mechanism.

5.1 Design of Elemental Profiles for the Higher Pair

The motion to be accurately reproduced by the BRJ mechanism is depicted in Fig. 5. Specifically, the output link exhibits motion with a varying ICR relative to the fixed link. The rotation angle of the output link ϕ changes from 0 to 120 deg in a counterclockwise direction, while the point O_2 on the output link moves. The initial position of this point in frame $O_1 - x_1 y_1$ is [20.1, 25.2] mm, and the final position is [7.1, 31.4] mm, meaning it moves approximately -13 mm and 6.2 mm along the positive directions of the x_1 and y_1 axes, respectively.

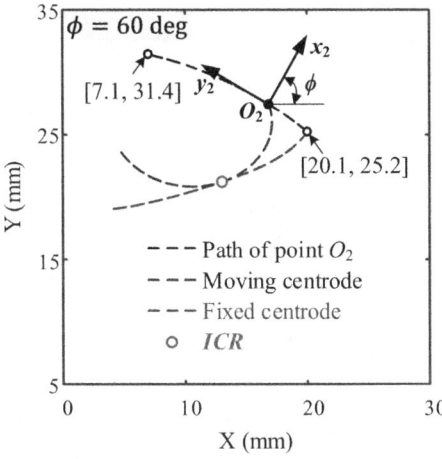

Fig. 5. Motion required to be accurately reproduced in the frame $O_1 - x_1y_1$.

As discussed earlier, the linear profiles of the elements can be parameterized using a, r_{p1x}, r_{p1y}, α_1, α_{12}, α_{13}. This section presents four sets of profile solutions for the higher pair, and the parameter values are provided as listed in Table 1. The conjugate profiles are obtained using the profile synthesis method, and the geometric shapes of the elements forming higher pairs are shown in Fig. 6.

Table 1. Parameter values for linear profiles.

Option group	Parameter Value					
	a/ mm	r_{p1x}/ mm	r_{p1y}/ mm	α_1/ deg	α_{12}/ deg	α_{13}/ deg
Option 1	60	0	10	0	80	150
Option 2	50	−6	16	0	60	140
Option 3	40	0	0	30	70	100
Option 4	40	0	0	30	60	120

As can be seen from Fig. 6, by adjusting the parameter values, different elemental profile schemes can be obtained. Additionally, reasonable changes in these parameters not only improve the geometric shape of the profiles but also reduce the overall size of the joint, resulting in a more compact design. Furthermore, the ICR remains within the triangular region formed by the linear profiles during the motion, and the contact forces between elements prevent the joint separation, maintaining the form closure of the joint as well as ensuring continuous and stable motion.

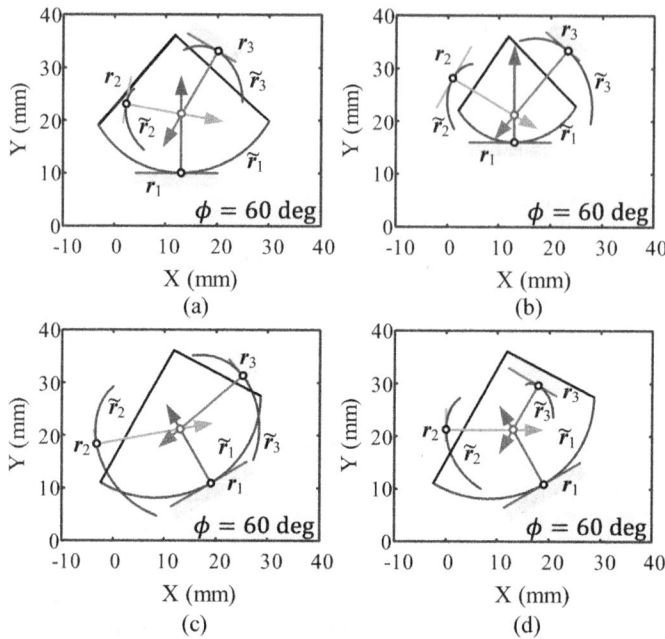

Fig. 6. Elemental profile schemes: (a) Option 1; (b) Option 2; (c) Option 3; (d) Option 4.

5.2 Kinematic Analysis of the BRJ Mechanism

As analyzed previously, the structural parameters of the joint mechanism include α, ϕ_5, L_2, L_3, L_4, L_5, which are assigned the following values in this case: $\alpha = 60$ deg, $\phi_5 = 200$ deg, $L_2 = 10$ mm, $L_3 = 38$ mm, $L_4 = 20$ mm, $L_5 = 12$ mm. Based on the given structural parameters and kinematic modeling, the relationships between ϕ_I and ϕ, as well as the ratio of ω_I to ω_O, are calculated and illustrated in Fig. 7.

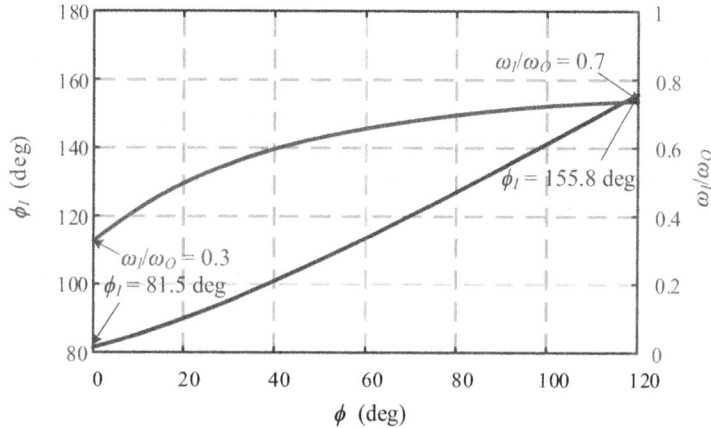

Fig. 7. Kinematic relationships between the rotation angles of the input and output links.

From Fig. 7, it can be observed that as the rotation angle of the output link ϕ increases from 0 deg to 120 deg, the input link also rotates counterclockwise, with the corresponding input angle ϕ_I increasing from 81.5 deg to 155.8 deg. During this motion, the transmission ratio ω_I/ω_O also increases from 0.3 to 0.7, indicating a variable angular velocity transmission behavior. Moreover, this transmission ratio can be adjusted in accordance with specific design requirements. These characteristics demonstrate the potential of the BRJ mechanism for applications requiring a customizable or variable transmission ratio in robotic systems.

5.3 Prototype Model of the BRJ Mechanism

Considering that Option 2 in Sect. 5.1 exhibits the smallest joint size and the shortest overall profile arc length, it is selected as the higher pair for the BRJ mechanism in this case. Based on the structural parameters provided in Sect. 5.2, a prototype of the BRJ mechanism is fabricated using 3D printing. Preliminary experiments validated the mobility of the mechanism and confirmed the form closure of the higher pair. The prototype in its initial, intermediate, and final states of motion is shown in Fig. 8.

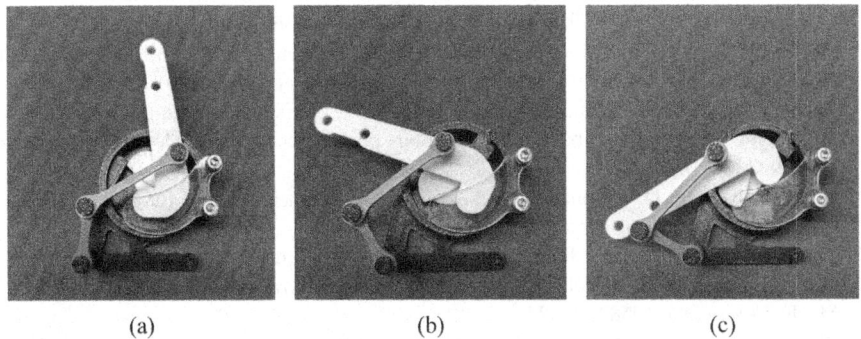

Fig. 8. Prototype model of the BRJ mechanism: (a) at the initial motion state; (b) at the intermediate motion state; (c) at the final motion state.

6 Conclusion

This paper proposes a BRJ design method based on the higher pair mechanism, enabling accurate reproduction of the varying ICR motion of the HKJ. Form closure of the higher pair is achieved through designing three pairs of line-curve contact elements, ensuring continuous and stable joint motion. Compared with biomimetic joints based on multi-bar linkages, the proposed BRJ mechanism achieves accurate reproduction of the desired complex motion while offering a simplified structure, demonstrating broad application potential in fields such as exoskeletons, prosthetics, and rehabilitation robots. However, the utilization of higher pairs in BRJ mechanisms inevitably introduces friction and wear between elements. This issue can be mitigated through the optimization of the profile geometry, the use of wear-resistant materials, and the implementation of lubrication strategies. Future research will focus on optimizing the performance of the BRJ mechanism and experimentally validating the effectiveness of the proposed design.

Acknowledgement. This work was supported by the State Key Lab of Mechanical System and Vibration Project (Grant No. MSVZD202008).

References

1. Wang, D., Lee, K.M., Guo, J., et al.: Adaptive knee joint exoskeleton based on biological geometries. IEEE/ASME Trans. Mechatron. **19**, 1268–1278 (2014)
2. Yang, H., Wei, G., Ren, L.: Enhancing the performance of a biomimetic robotic elbow-and-forearm system through bionics-inspired optimization. IEEE Trans. Rob. **40**, 2692–2711 (2024)
3. Nordin, M., Frankel, V.H.: Basic Biomechanics of the Musculoskeletal System. Lippincott Williams & Wilkins, USA (2001)
4. Tomishiro, K., Sato, R., Harada, Y., et al.: Design of robot leg with variable reduction ratio crossed four-bar linkage mechanism. In: 2019 IEEE/RSJ International Conference on Intelligent Robots and Systems (IROS), pp. 4333–4338 (2019)
5. Singh, R., Chaudhary, H., Singh, A.K.: Defect-free optimal synthesis of crank-rocker linkage using nature-inspired optimization algorithms. Mech. Mach. Theory **116**, 105–122 (2017)
6. Jin, D.W., Zhang, R.H., Dimo, H., et al.: Kinematic and dynamic performance of prosthetic knee joint using six-bar mechanism. J. Rehabil. Res. Dev. **40**, 39–48 (2003)
7. Olinski, M., Gronowicz, A., Ceccarelli, M.: Development and characterisation of a controllable adjustable knee joint mechanism. Mech. Mach. Theory **155**, 104101 (2021)
8. Zhang, Z., Zhang, Y., Zhao, J., et al.: Design method of a single degree-of-freedom planar linkage bionic mechanism based on continuous position constraints. Mech. Mach. Theory **170**, 104730 (2022)
9. Gatti, G., Mundo, D.: Optimal synthesis of six-bar cammed-linkages for exact rigid-body guidance. Mech. Mach. Theory **42**, 1069–1081 (2007)
10. Zhu, G., Guo, W., Chu, S.: Bionic concept and synthesis methods of the biomimetic robot joint mechanism for accurately reproducing the motion pattern of the human knee joint. Mech. Mach. Theory **204**, 105832 (2024)
11. Machado, M., Flores, P., Claro, J.C.P., et al.: Development of a planar multibody model of the human knee joint. Nonlinear Dyn. **60**, 459–478 (2010)
12. Etoundi, A.C., Burgess, S.C., Vaidyanathan, R.: A bio-inspired condylar hinge for robotic limbs. J. Mech. Robot. **5**, 031011 (2013)
13. Zavatsky, A.B., O'Connor, J.J.: A model of human knee ligaments in the sagittal plane: Part 1: response to passive flexion. Proc. Inst. Mech. Eng. Part H J. Eng. Med. **206**, 125–134 (1992)
14. Gogu, G.: Mobility of mechanisms: a critical review. Mech. Mach. Theory **40**, 1068–1097 (2005)

Sensation-Perception-Actuation-Rehabilitation Oriented Technologies for Wearable Exoskeletons

Muscle Synergy-Enabled Multimodal Swimming Motion Recognition

Yuchao Liu[1], Jiajie Guo[1,2(✉)], Yibin Chen[1], Weipeng Li[3], Kamilo Melo[4], and Xuan Wu[3]

[1] State Key Laboratory of Intelligent Manufacturing Equipment and Technology, School of Mechanical Science and Engineering, Huazhong University of Science and Technology, Wuhan 430074, Hubei, China
jiajie.guo@hust.edu.cn
[2] Institute of Medical Equipment Science and Engineering, Huazhong University of Science and Technology, Wuhan 430074, Hubei, China
[3] Robotics Laboratory, China Nanhu Academy of Electronics and Information Technology, Jiaxing 314000, Zhejiang, China
[4] KM-RoBoTa. Chemin de la Roche 1, 1020 Renens, Switzerland

Abstract. Accurate swimming motion recognition is crucial to underwater exoskeleton control to provide appropriate assistances to divers' motions. Because it is muscles that actuate joint motions, muscle deformation sensing is a promising alternative to traditional joint kinematics sensing in swimming monitoring. However, most previous studies directly fed the muscle deformation into "black box" machine learning models leading to opaque mechanism. Aiming to intuitively reveal the intrinsic relationship between muscle deformation and swimming motion postures, this paper characterizes the standard muscle synergy curves of four swimming modes based on the previously formulated Gaussian-based physical model, and then each muscle feature sample can be mapped into the constructed synergy curve based on their Euclidean distance, thereby enabling multimodal swimming motion recognition. Results show that average mode classification accuracy is 93.9% and phase estimation error is 6.56%. This paper validates muscle deformation sensing for swimming motion recognition with an intuitive and transparent mechanism, which is expected that can enhance swimming motion monitoring for underwater wearable robotic control.

Keywords: Muscle deformation sensing · muscle synergy · swimming motion monitoring · multimodal motion · underwater exoskeleton

1 Introduction

Swimming motion recognition is crucial to adjust the assistive torques of underwater exoskeletons to strengthen human underwater motor abilities [1]. Most existing studies usually use joint motion sensing to monitor swimming motions [2]. In the human musculoskeletal motor system, muscle activation is the "cause" and joint rotation is the "result" [3], thus the state changes of muscles precede those in joints, which is valuable to enhance the real-time performance of exoskeleton control. Compared to the electromyography (EMG) with large signal fluctuations [4], muscle mechanical deformation signals are more stable. However, most existing studies usually directly fed the muscle deformation features into "black box" machine learning models, whose opaque inner mechanism makes its reliability questionable. To intuitively reveal the relationship between human muscle deformation and swimming motion posture, previously, a Gaussian-based physical synergy model was formulated to characterize muscle-joint synergy in breaststroke. In this paper, the model is extended to construct the muscle synergy for multiple swimming modes. On this basis, the Euclidean distance method in multi-muscle space is further designed to recognize multimodal swimming motions.

The complex human musculoskeletal system can generate various signals during motions, such as the plantar force [5], joint angle [6], and EMG [7]. Herein, the foot is an important bearing structure during human walking locomotions, thus the contact force between the sole and the ground is the key information to reflect human locomotions. However, it may be ineffective for monitoring swimming motions due to horizontal body postures. The joint angles can intuitively reflect the human motion postures thus have been widely used for swimming motion monitoring [8]. Herein, the optical methods have high accuracy on land [9], and the visual obstruction caused by water splashing may result in difficulties in swimming applications [10]. Featured with the compact size and light weight, the inertial measurement unit (IMU) offers a portable method for limb joint motion monitoring [11], but its rigid properties may result in discomfort in long-term wear [12]. Because it is muscles that actuate limb joint motions, changes of muscle states can precede joint movements [13], which is beneficial to human motion intent prediction for real-time applications such as exoskeleton control. Also, compared to neural signals of EMG with low signal-to-noise ratio, mechanical signals of muscle deformations are more stable [14], which is valuable to reliable human motion recognition [15].

Previous studies directly fed the muscle deformation feature into "black box" machine learning models to monitor human motions [16], causing the relationship of muscle deformation and human movements lacks intuitive physical explanation. To reveal the relationship between muscle deformation and swimming motion posture in an intuitive perspective, our previous studies proposed a Gaussian-based physical synergy model, but it only focused on a single breaststroke mode [17]. Aiming to promote the application of muscle deformation sensing in underwater motion monitoring, based on the model, this paper constructs the lower-limb muscle synergy for four swimming modes, demonstrating the one-to-one mapping between muscle synergistic deformation and multimodal swimming motion postures. Further, based on the Euclidean distance from the input samples in multi-muscle space, the modelled synergy curve is used to achieve swimming mode classification and phase estimation.

The rest of this paper is organized below: Sect. 2 proposes the lower-limb muscle synergy-based multimodal swimming motion recognition method. Section 3 introduces the swimming experiments, and the result is given in Sect. 4, with the corresponding discussion in Sect. 5. Finally, Sect. 6 presents the conclusion.

2 Methodology

This section formulates the muscle synergy-based multimodal swimming motion monitoring method, followed by introducing the performance evaluation method.

2.1 Muscle Synergy Analysis During Swimming

As shown in Fig. 1, given that swimming is a standard cyclic motion, the evolution mechanism of muscle deformation ($\mathbf{M} = [m_1, m_2, ..., m_n]^T$, where m_n represents the deformation of the nth muscle) in different swimming cycles is theoretically exactly the same. Furthermore, because the cycle switching is continuous (human postures at the start and end points of swimming cycles are the same), the synergistic deformation $\mathbf{M}$ of n muscles within one cycle can be depicted by a smooth and closed curve $\mathbf{M}^{(T)}$ in an n-dimensional space. Due to distinct kinematic characteristics among different swimming modes (for example, the left and right leg motions in breaststroke (BrS) and butterfly (BF) are in phase, while they have a phase difference of half a cycle in front crawl (FC) and backstroke (BaS); BrS uses the frog kick, while the other three modes adopt the whip kick), their muscle synergy curves $\mathbf{M}_S^{(T)}$ are obviously different (S denotes the swimming mode: $\mathbf{M}_{BaS}^{(T)}$, $\mathbf{M}_{BrS}^{(T)}$, $\mathbf{M}_{BF}^{(T)}$, and $\mathbf{M}_{FC}^{(T)}$), and $\mathbf{M}_S = [m_{1,S}, m_{2,S}, ..., m_{n,S}]^T$.

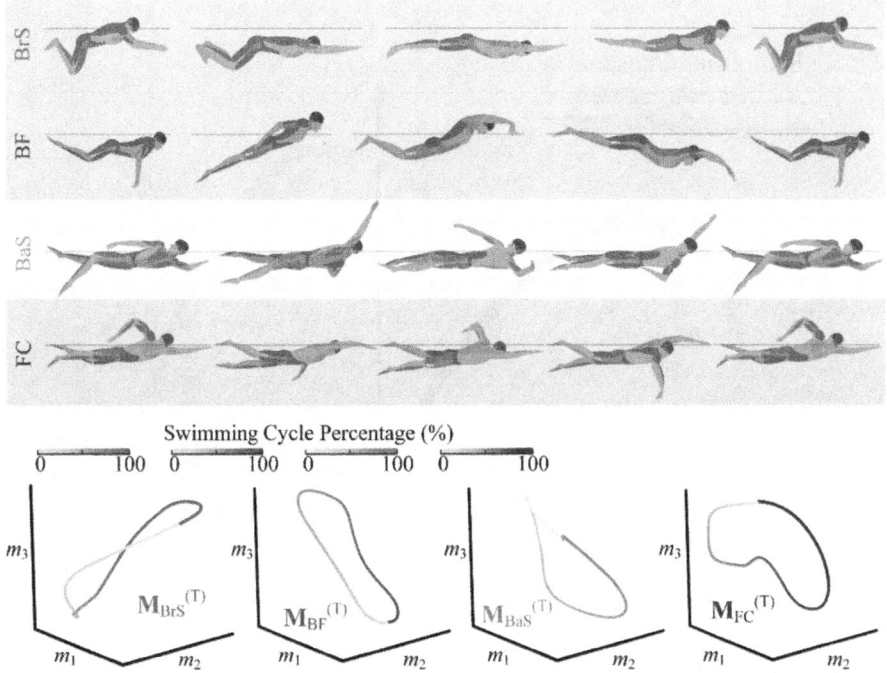

Fig. 1. Schematic diagram of muscle synergy of four swimming modes within one cycle.

2.2 Gaussian-Based Muscle Synergy Construction

Traditionally, machine learning models (such as neural networks) are used to construct the standard muscle synergy $\mathbf{M}_S^{(T)}$ by extensive training, and based on which recognize swimming motions. However, their "black box" nature makes it difficult to explain the specific meaning of the parameters. To reveal the intrinsic physical relationship between muscle deformations and swimming postures in an intuitive method, this paper extends the previously developed synergy model [17] to generate the $\mathbf{M}_S^{(T)}$ for each stroke, where the model is rigorously formulated according to swimming motion biomechanical characteristics,

$$m(\varphi) = \sum_{j=1}^{3} f_j(\varphi) + k \tag{1}$$

where three Gaussian functions $f_j = a_j \exp(-(\varphi - b_j)^2 / 2c_j^2)$ (phase $0 \leq \varphi \leq 2\pi$ and $j = 1, 2$ and 3) characterize the eccentric contraction, concentric contraction, and noise fluctuation of muscles, respectively. Within each f_j, the coefficients a_j, b_j and c_j refer to the amplitude, phase, and rate of muscle deformations, respectively, and k is the magnitude correction coefficient to compensate for initial manual installation errors. Due to continuity of cycle switching, f_1 and f_2 have the same amplitude and phase, and thus the number of coefficients in (1) can be reduced from 10 to 8 ($a_2 = a_1$ and $b_2 = b_1$). Also, each $m(\varphi)$ should be closed-looped to adapt the physical characteristics of the continuity of motion cycle transitions.

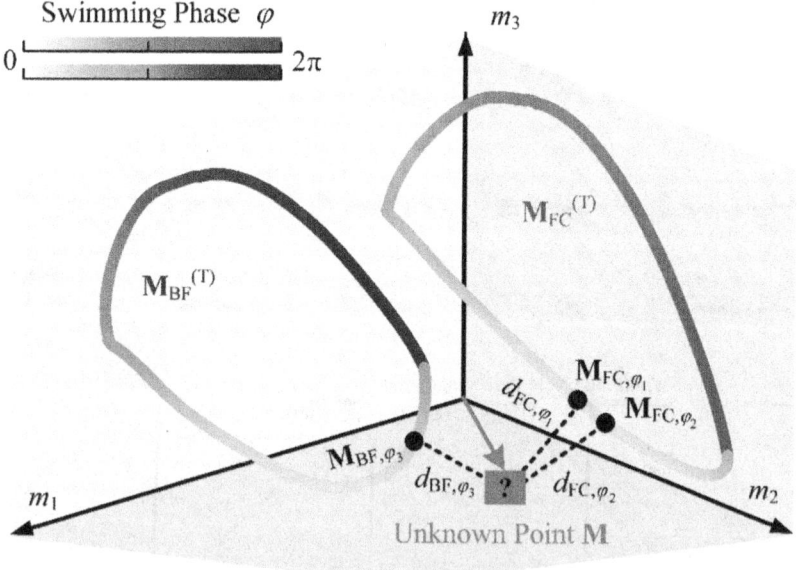

Fig. 2. Schematic diagram of the Euclidean distance-based swimming motion monitoring.

2.3 Euclidean Distance-Based Swimming Motion Monitoring

Based on the above model, the standard muscle synergy curves of various swimming modes can be constructed. In this way, for each muscle deformation **M**, the corresponding swimming mode and phase can be obtained based on the its position on the $\mathbf{M}_S^{(T)}$. However, actual experiments inevitably introduce errors, thereby causing the **M** to deviate from $\mathbf{M}_S^{(T)}$. Given that the error is unbiased, the mapping from **M** to $\mathbf{M}_S^{(T)}$ can still be conducted based on their Euclidean distance in the n-dimensional space and further achieve swimming motion monitoring.

Specifically, for an unknown sample **M**, high-frequency environmental noises and low-frequency data drift are removed through a 0.3~5 Hz bandpass filter, and then dimensional differences are eliminated by normalization. Subsequently, the Euclidean distances **D** between the **M** and all points on $\mathbf{M}_S^{(T)}$ in the n-dimensional space are calculated, where $\mathbf{D} = [d_{1,\varphi}, d_{2,\varphi}, ..., d_{S,\varphi}]^T$ ($d_{S,\varphi}$ is the distance between **M** and $\mathbf{M}_{S,\varphi}$ which denotes the point on $\mathbf{M}_S^{(T)}$ with mode S and phase φ):

$$d_{S,\varphi} = \|\mathbf{M} - \mathbf{M}_{S,\varphi}\|_2 \tag{2}$$

Based on the **D**, the k points on $\mathbf{M}_S^{(T)}$ with the minimum distance from the **M** are screened. Finally, the majority voting method is used to determine the swimming mode to which **M** belongs, and the phase is obtained based on the sample in the identified mode with the minimum distance. Figure 2 simplified the description of the proposed method in three-dimensional space ($n = 3$), two swimming modes and $k = 3$. Herein, the three points on $\mathbf{M}_S^{(T)}$ with the minimum distance from the test point **M** are $\mathbf{M}_{FC,\varphi_1}$, $\mathbf{M}_{FC,\varphi_2}$, and $\mathbf{M}_{BF,\varphi_3}$, respectively, and $\varphi_1 < \varphi_2$. Therefore, this point **M** is identified as the phase φ_2 of the BrS mode.

2.4 Performance Evaluation Method

To construct $\mathbf{M}_S^{(T)}$ and evaluate method performance, it is necessary to label the true swimming mode and phases for the **M**. In this paper, the true mode is labelled manually, and the true phase is obtained by two steps: 1) swimming cycle segmentation based on the maximum left knee flexion; 2) linearly interpolation within one cycle to obtain the true phase φ from 0 to 2π. As shown in Fig. 3, to avoid phase discontinuity during cycle switching, the φ is encoded to the two coordinates of a unit circle,

$$\mathbf{Y} = [\cos(\varphi) \quad \sin(\varphi)]^T \tag{3}$$

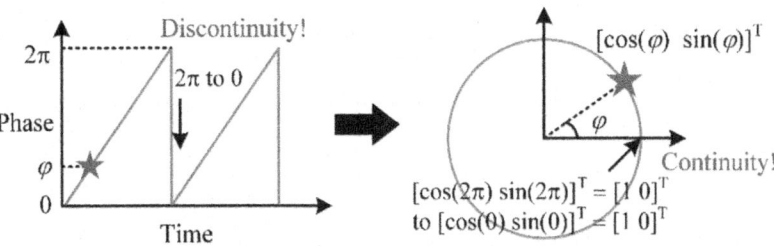

Fig. 3. Continuous mapping method of the phase.

To evaluate the accuracy of swimming mode classification, the A_S is defined as,

$$A_S = N_{correct}/N_{total} \times 100\% \quad (4)$$

where $N_{correct}$ and N_{total} are the number of correctly classified samples and total samples. Performance of swimming phase estimation is quantified by the error at each sample,

$$e_{pct} = \arccos(\mathbf{Y}_t \cdot \mathbf{Y}_p) \times 100\%/2\pi \quad (5)$$

where $\mathbf{Y}_t$ and $\mathbf{Y}_p$ are the true and predicted phase vectors, respectively. Denoting $e_{pct}(j, k)$ as the kth sample in the jth cycle of the e_{pct}, two metrics of root-mean-square and maximum errors of all measured cycles are calculated as,

$$e_{ARMS} = \sum_{j=1}^{N_c} \sqrt{\sum_{k=1}^{p_j} e_{pct}^2(j,k)/p_j} \bigg/ N_c \quad (6)$$

$$e_{MAX} = \max_{j \in 1, \ldots, N_c} \sum_{k=1}^{p_j} |e_{pct}(j,k)|/p_j \quad (7)$$

where p_j refers to the number of sampling points within the jth cycle, and N_c denotes the total number of cycles.

3 Swimming Experiment

This section introduces the swimming experiments, in which muscle deformations and joint angles were simultaneously collected to validate the proposed method.

3.1 Hardware Platform

As shown in Fig. 4, six flexible capacitive sensors were installed on muscle bellies of gluteus maximus (GMAX), rectus femoris (RF) and tibialis anterior (TA) of both legs to capture muscle deformations ($n = 6$), and two IMUs was used to detect the maximum left knee flexion for cycle segmentation. Detailed specifications of underwater wearable sensing system can be found in our previous study [17].

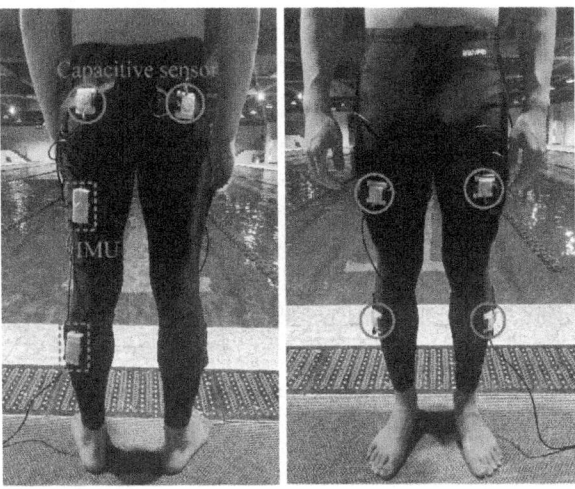

Fig. 4. Wearable sensing system for swimming experiments.

3.2 Experimental Protocol

Nine subjects (24 ± 2 years old, 177 ± 8 cm height, and 74 ± 6 kg weight) adept at all four swimming modes participated voluntarily in the experiments. Subjects were asked to swim in a constant-temperature pool. To overcome the constraint of the pool length in tests, subjects were anchored at a specific location by a cable attached at their waist to pool edge by a vacuum sucker. A 5-min break was set between two adjacent trials to prevent muscle fatigue. The average sample size for each subject is 360 cycles (90 cycles per stroke). The experiment was approved by the Institutional Review Board of Huazhong University of Science and Technology (Wuhan, Hubei, China).

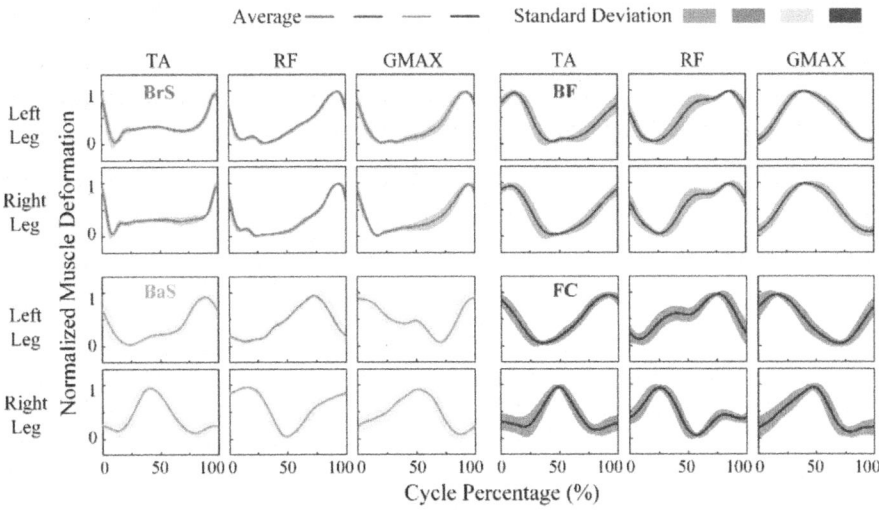

Fig. 5. Muscle deformation signals of four swimming modes within one cycle.

4 Results

In this section, the 5-fold cross validation is used to evaluate the proposed method. The total dataset **M** is randomly divided into five subsets, where four subsets $\mathbf{M}^t$ are used to generate the $\mathbf{M}_S^{(T)}$ and the remaining one $\mathbf{M}^p$ is used for prediction. The average of the five results is used for analysis.

All signals are plotted within one cycle, where the lines and shaded areas represent the averages and standard deviations of all cycles. Besides, all the numerical operations were executed employing Matlab (Mathworks R2022a) on the same computer equipped with an AMD Ryzen 5 5600G CPU with Radeon Graphics 3.90 GHz and 16 GB RAM.

4.1 Muscle Deformation Signals in Swimming

Figure 5 shows the normalized muscle deformation signals from Subject 5, which is consistent with swimming motion characteristics. Taking the BrS as an example, amplitudes of muscle deformations rapidly decrease due to the eccentric contraction during kicking and increase slowly during concentric contraction in recovery, and remain at the small value during gliding with minimum limb movements.

4.2 Muscle Synergy Construction

The $\mathbf{M}^t$ is averaged to one cycle and then construct the $\mathbf{M}_S^{(T)}$ in the six-dimensional space. Considering the motion symmetry of left and right legs, the data of the left leg was used for simplified illustration. The sum of squares error of the least square regression is used as the loss function. Figure 6 shows a representative result, where solid lines are the experimental data, and dotted lines are the constructed $\mathbf{M}_S^{(T)}$ by the (1) with the coefficients in Table 1. They exhibit the high consistency (average $R^2 = 0.99$, average e_{ARMS} within the fitted cycles are 1.685% for BrS, 0.707% for BaS, 0.737% for BF and 0.253% for FC, respectively), justifying the model can efficiently characterize muscle deformations for all four strokes. Furthermore, the $\mathbf{M}_S^{(T)}$ shows the closed-loop and no self-intersection characteristics, which indicates that there is a one-to-one mapping relationship between muscle deformations and swimming postures. In other words, for any **M**, there exists and only one swimming postures corresponding to it.

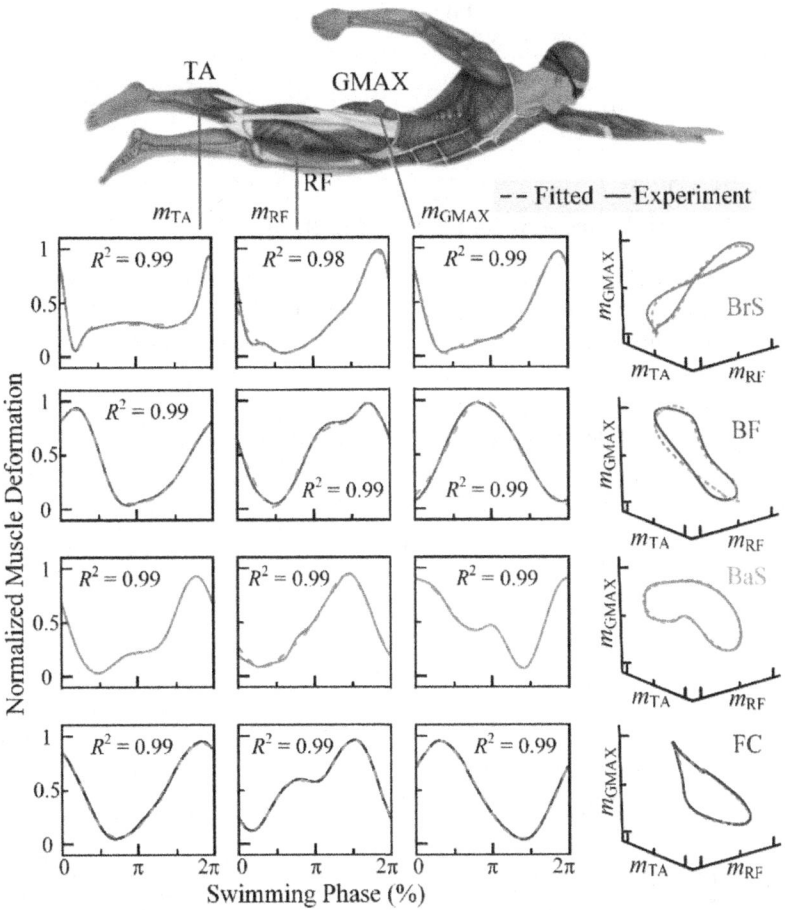

Fig. 6. Lower-limb muscle synergy modeling of four swimming modes.

Table 1. Fitting coefficients of the $M_S^{(T)}$ of four swimming modes

Coefficient		a_1	b_1	c_1	c_2	a_3	b_3	c_3	k
BrS	mTA	0.60	−0.04	0.22	0.39	−0.24	0.64	0.29	0.30
	mRF	0.41	−0.55	0.38	0.47	−0.58	1.96	1.68	0.61
	mGMAX	0.78	−0.39	0.65	0.90	−0.17	1.07	0.53	0.15
BF	mTA	0.79	0.28	0.79	1.21	0.35	1.25	0.53	0.04
	mRF	0.19	−0.94	0.02	0.34	−0.77	1.50	0.94	0.79
	mGMAX	1.01	2.80	1.41	0.31	0.68	−0.35	0.50	−0.02
BaS	mTA	1.04	−0.71	0.92	0.91	0.33	2.95	0.93	−0.12
	mRF	0.75	−1.69	4.72	0.91	−0.43	0.84	0.97	−0.13
	mGMAX	1.26	−0.05	2.03	0.98	0.47	3.30	0.63	−0.36
FC	mTA	0.96	−0.52	0.01	1.43	0.89	−0.16	0.95	−0.02
	mRF	1.16	−1.45	0.97	1.04	0.76	2.19	1.03	−0.22

(*continued*)

Table 1. (continued)

Coefficient		a_1	b_1	c_1	c_2	a_3	b_3	c_3	k
	m_{GMAX}	1.12	0.84	1.65	1.23	−0.13	−0.07	0.48	−0.16

4.3 Results of Multimodal Swimming Motion Recognition

The above constructed $M_S^{(T)}$ is used to recognize swimming modes and phases for the M^P based on $k = 15$. Table 2 and Fig. 7 present the mode classification results and corresponding confusion matrixes, where the A_S of all subjects is higher than 90%, with an average of 93.9%.

Table 2. Results of swimming mode classification

Subject	1	2	3	4	5	6	7	8	9	Mean
A_S (%)	93.2	93.8	95.1	91.7	94.1	92.4	95.8	96.2	93.1	93.9

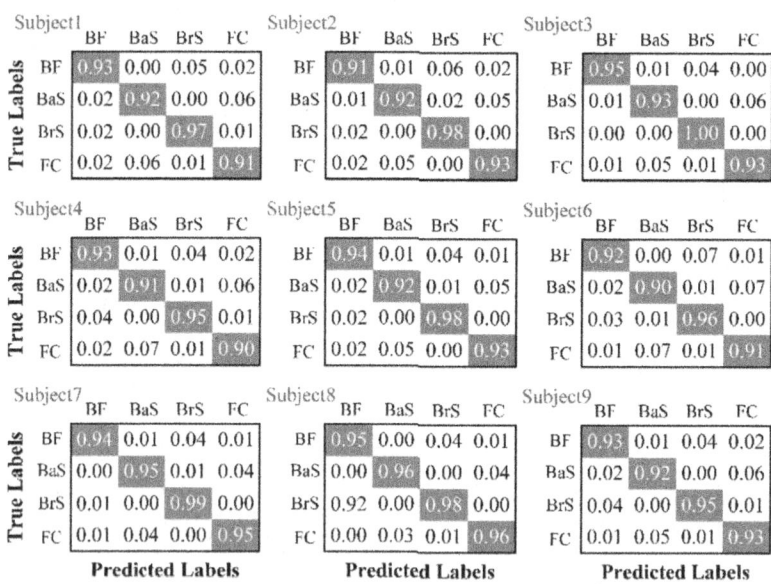

Fig. 7. Confusion matrixes of swimming mode classification.

Figure 8(a) compares the predicted and true cycle percentage ($\varphi/2\pi \times 100\%$), and Fig. 8(b) indicates that average proportion of samples within $e_{pct} < 10\%$ is more than 90%, suggesting that the method can provide an accurate prediction at the whole cycle. Errors of all nine subjects are listed in Table 3, where average e_{ARMS} are 6.36%, 6.80%,

7.09% and 6.00%, and e_{MAX} are 7.73%, 8.00%, 8.40% and 6.87% in BrS, BF, BaS, and FC.

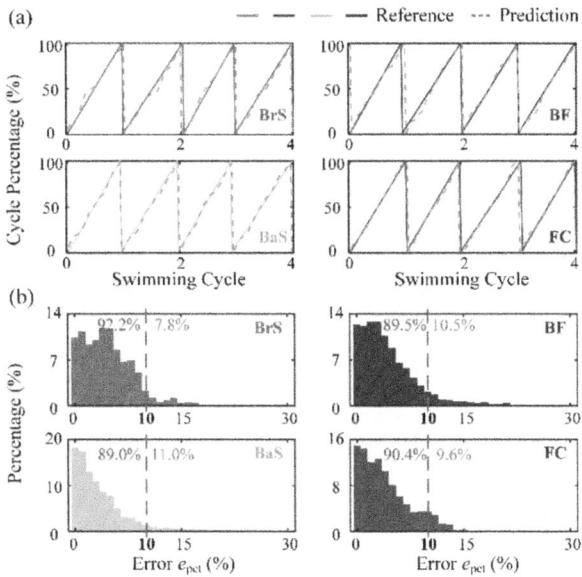

Fig. 8. Phase estimation results. (a) Time-domain analysis. (b) Error distributions of samples.

Table 3. Results of swimming phase estimation

Breaststroke					
Subject	e_{ARMS} (%)	e_{MAX} (%)	Subject	e_{ARMS} (%)	e_{MAX} (%)
1	5.88	6.61	6	7.73	8.29
2	5.33	6.92	7	4.93	7.33
3	6.96	9.17	8	5.11	7.06
4	8.08	8.86	9	7.24	8.73
5	5.94	6.59	Mean	6.36	7.73
Butterfly					
Subject	e_{ARMS} (%)	e_{MAX} (%)	Subject	e_{ARMS} (%)	e_{MAX} (%)
1	3.31	4.99	6	6.13	6.85
2	7.73	8.53	7	7.45	8.50
3	7.80	8.62	8	8.01	9.78
4	5.62	7.23	9	8.37	10.33
5	6.79	7.18	Mean	6.80	8.00
Backstroke					
Subject	e_{ARMS} (%)	e_{MAX} (%)	Subject	e_{ARMS} (%)	e_{MAX} (%)

(*continued*)

Table 3. (*continued*)

Breaststroke					
1	7.37	9.21	6	4.05	5.08
2	9.70	11.42	7	5.62	6.56
3	5.33	6.46	8	7.02	7.88
4	7.95	8.77	9	9.84	11.38
5	6.97	8.84	Mean	7.09	8.40
Front Crawl					
Subject	e_{ARMS} (%)	e_{MAX} (%)	Subject	e_{ARMS} (%)	e_{MAX} (%)
1	6.65	7.61	6	4.07	4.84
2	6.47	7.55	7	5.29	6.15
3	3.74	4.41	8	6.38	7.31
4	7.11	8.09	9	7.91	8.56
5	6.35	7.28	Mean	6.00	6.87

5 Discussion

Results are further discussed from two aspects as follows:

5.1 Analysis of the Proposed Method

Different from most related studies using the joint motion sensing (IMUs) for swimming motion monitoring, this paper proposes and validates the muscle deformation sensing, which is valuable to wearable sensing techniques. First, muscle deformation is independent from other signals such as joint kinematics, EMG and EIT, so it can promote information fusion to further improve underwater human motion recognition. Second, the robustness of muscle deformations to water makes it an alternative to other biological sensors such as EMG and EIT in humid conditions, extending working conditions of current muscle-signal-based approaches.

5.2 Improvements Over Our Previous Studies

Different from our previous studies directly inputting the muscle deformation features into the "black box" machine learning models for swimming motion monitoring [18, 19] this paper established the mapping from muscle synergistic deformations to multimodal swimming motions through a previously formulated Gaussian-based physical model [17], and then proposed the multimodal swimming motion recognition approach based on the Euclidean distance in multi-muscle synergy space. The proposed method has an intuitive and transparent working mechanism, which reveals one-to-one mapping relationship between muscle deformation and multimodal swimming motion, promoting the application of muscle deformation sensing in swimming motion monitoring.

6 Conclusion

This paper intuitively establishes the relationship of human muscle deformation and swimming motion posture through a Gaussian-based synergy model, and then validated its effectiveness by multimodal swimming motion monitoring based on Euclidean distance in multi-muscle space. In nine subjects, the model exhibits the high construction precise of muscle synergistic deformations (average $R^2 = 0.99$, average phase errors of 1.685% for BrS, 0.707% for BaS, 0.737% for BF and 0.253% for FC), and there is no intersection among them which indicates the one-to-one mapping relationship between muscle deformations and swimming postures. In multimodal swimming motion monitoring, the proposed method achieved the average swimming mode classification accuracy of 93.9% and phase estimation error of 6.56%, further demonstrating the method effectiveness. This paper promotes the application of muscle deformation sensing in swimming motion monitoring, and is anticipated that can contribute to power-assisted swimming exoskeleton control.

Acknowledgements. This work was supported by the National Key R&D Program of China (Grant No. 2023YFE0207000), National Natural Science Foundation of China (Grant No. 51875221, U22A20249, 52188102, 92248304, 52027806 and 52435005), International Science and Technology Cooperation Project from China Electronics Technology Group Corporation.

References

1. Xia, H., Khan, M.A., Li, Z., Zhou, M.: Wearable robots for human underwater movement ability enhancement: a survey. IEEE-CAA. J. Autom. Sin. **9**(6), 967–977 (2022)
2. Wang, J., Wang, Z., Gao, F., Zhao, H., Qiu, S., Li, J.: Swimming stroke phase segmentation based on wearable motion capture technique. IEEE Trans. Instrum. Meas. **69**(10), 8526–8538 (2020)
3. Winter, D.A.: Biomechanics and motor control of human movement, 4th edn. John Wiley & Sons Inc, Hoboken, New Jersey, USA (2009)
4. Rainoldi, A., Cescon, C., Bottin, A., Casale, R., Caruso, I.: Surface EMG alterations induced by underwater recording. J. Electromyogr. Kinesiol. **14**(3), 325–331 (2004)
5. Morales, I., González-Landaeta, R., Simini, F.: Force sensing resistors used as plantar impedance plethysmography electrodes. IEEE Trans. Instrum. Meas. **71**, 1–8 (2022)
6. Daemi, P., Zhou, Y., Naish, M.D., Price, A.D., Trejos, A.L.: Comprehensive kinematic model of a tendon-driven wearable tremor suppression device. IEEE Trans. Robot. **40**, 421–437 (2024)
7. Liu, R., Wang, J., Chen, Y., Liu, Y., Wang, Y., Gu, J.: Proximal policy optimization with time-varying muscle synergy for the control of an upper limb musculoskeletal system. IEEE Trans. Autom. Sci. Eng. **21**(2), 1929–1940 (2024)
8. Chen, L., Yan, X., Hu, D.: A deep learning control strategy of IMU-based joint angle estimation for hip power-assisted swimming exoskeleton. IEEE Sensors J. **23**(13), 15058–15070 (2023)
9. Wang, G., Li, H., Zhang, L., Wang, X.: Development of a low-cost and portable walker-based human motion estimation system. IEEE/ASME Trans. Mechatronics **29**(5), 3901–3911 (2024)
10. Callaway, A.J., Cobb, J.E., Jones, I.: A Comparison of video and accelerometer based approaches applied to performance monitoring in swimming. Int. J. Sports Sci. Coachiing **4**(1), 139–153 (2009)

11. Zhang, X., Tricomi, E., Missiroli, F., Lotti, N., Masia, L.: Real-Time assistive control via IMU locomotion mode detection in a soft exosuit: an effective approach to enhance walking metabolic efficiency. IEEE/ASME Trans. Mechatronics (2023)
12. Marta, G., et al.: Wearable biofeedback suit to promote and monitor aquatic exercises: a feasibility study. IEEE Trans. Instrum. Meas. **69**(4), 1219–1231 (2020)
13. Jahanandish, M.H., Rabe, K.G., Fey, N.P., Hoyt, K.: Ultrasound features of skeletal muscle can predict kinematics of upcoming lower-limb motion. Ann. Biomed. Eng. **49**(2), 822–833 (2021)
14. Kim, T., Kong, K.: Plantar flexion muscle force estimation with a soft wearable pneumatic sensor system. IEEE/ASME Trans. Mechatronics **29**(4), 2920–2928 (2024)
15. Yang, X., Chen, Z., Hettiarachchi, N., Yan, J., Liu, H.: A wearable ultrasound system for sensing muscular morphological deformations. IEEE Trans. Syst., Man, Cybern.-Syst. **51**(6), 3370–3379 (2021)
16. Sun, H., Peng, X., Wang, J., Liu, J., Fu, T., He, C.: Wearable surface deformation myography (sDMG) system for recognition of locomotion modes. IEEE J. Biomed. Health Inform. **28**, 4577–4587 (2024)
17. Guo, J., et al.: Wearable sensing for breaststroke phase monitoring with lower limb muscle-Joint synergy. IEEE Trans. Instrum. Meas. **73**, 1–12 (2023)
18. Liu, Y., et al.: Muscle deformation sensing for swimming mode identification and continuous phase estimation with two-stage network. IEEE Trans. Instrum. Meas. pp. 1–14, (2025)
19. Liu, Y., et al.: Muscle–Joint feature fusion for swimming pattern recognition with 1D–CNN classifier. IEEE Trans. Instrum. Meas. pp. 1–11 (2025)

Estimation of Human Lower Limb Kinematic Parameters Based on A-Mode Ultrasound Sensing

Donghan Liu, Haoran Zheng, Han Wu, Guochao Xu, and Honghai Liu(✉)

Harbin Institute of Technology, Shenzhen 518055, Guangdong, China
honghai.liu@hit.edu.cn

Abstract. Accurate joint angle estimation based on physiological signal-driven wearable technologies remains challenging due to their limitations, such as sensitivity to motion artifacts and signal drift, as observed in electromyography (EMG) and inertial measurement units (IMU). A-mode ultrasound signals provide real-time, non-invasive, and muscle-specific dynamic information, making them a promising alternative for kinematic parameter estimation. However, relevant research remains limited. This study focuses on extracting kinematic parameters by addressing the high-dimensional and time-dependent nature of A-mode ultrasound signals, aiming to enhance their accuracy in predicting lower limb joint angles. We propose an algorithm combining Long Short-Term Memory (LSTM) networks with a multi-path decoupled feature mapping module and a Dilated Convolutional Block Attention Module (DCBAM). The DCBAM-LSTM network captures temporal features of ultrasound signals, while the mapping module translates high-dimensional features into specific joint angles with reduced complexity. Experimental results show high prediction accuracy for hip, knee, and ankle joints, with robust performance across different prediction horizons. Prediction error increases nonlinearly with longer lead times, primarily due to posture adjustments and center-of-mass shifts. The proposed algorithm demonstrates strong accuracy, real-time capability, and generalizability, offering reliable support for motion intent recognition and human-machine interaction development based on A-mode ultrasound signals.

Keywords: A-mode ultrasound · Lower limb kinematic parameters · deep learning · DCBAM-LSTM Network · Human-Machine Interaction

1 Introduction

Wearable exoskeletons have emerged as effective tools in rehabilitation by enhancing mobility for individuals with neurological or musculoskeletal impairments. These devices assist movement by providing external mechanical support and facilitating neuroplasticity [1,2]. To synchronize seamlessly with user intent, accurate estimation of lower limb kinematics, such as joint angles and limb velocities, is essential [3,4].

Reliable human-machine interfaces (HMIs) play a vital role in real-time kinematic estimation. Wearable sensors, due to their portability and low cost, are widely adopted in HMIs [5]. Traditional modalities include surface electromyography (sEMG), inertial measurement units (IMUs), and more recently, ultrasound signals [6].

sEMG provides insights into muscle activation but suffers from noise, skin impedance, and electrode placement issues [7,8]. IMUs offer motion-related data such as acceleration and angular velocity, but long-term drift and inter-subject variability remain major limitations [9,10].

Ultrasound-based sensing, particularly A-mode ultrasound, provides a non-invasive method for visualizing internal muscle states with high wearability [11, 12]. Unlike EMG or IMU, ultrasound is less affected by external factors and offers detailed tissue-level insights [13,14].

Although previous studies have explored gesture recognition using ultrasound and classical classifiers [15], lower limb kinematic estimation using A-mode ultrasound—especially with deep learning—remains underexplored [16,17].

To address this gap, we propose a deep learning framework that leverages A-mode ultrasound signals for predicting hip, knee, and ankle joint angles with improved accuracy and generalizability.

The main contributions of this paper are:

- A deep learning model is developed for extracting joint kinematics from A-mode ultrasound signals.
- Ablation studies are conducted to assess different network configurations.
- The proposed system demonstrates superior prediction accuracy and responsiveness over IMU-based methods.

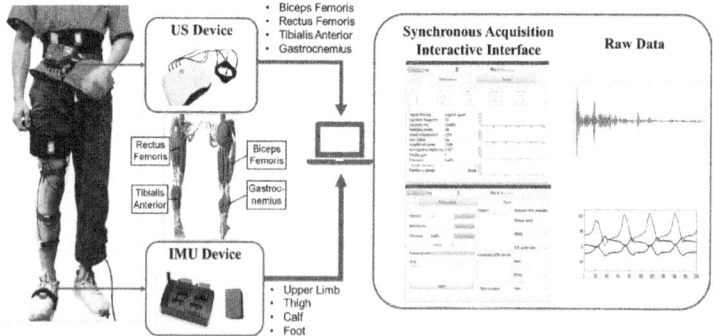

Fig. 1. IMU and A-mode Ultrasound Data Acquisition Scheme. Four A-mode ultrasound sensors are placed on the user's biceps femoris, rectus femoris, tibialis anterior, and gastrocnemius muscles. A motion capture system based on Xsens IMU is utilized. Synchronous Acquisition Interactive Interface of A-mode Ultrasound and IMU Data.

2 Dataset Collection and Experimental Design

A-mode ultrasound is investigated for its potential in estimating lower limb kinematics, with inertial measurement units (IMUs) used as a reference to provide precise ground truth values. IMUs offer reliable measurements of joint angles and body segment movements, serving as essential benchmarks for validating the accuracy of the ultrasound-based estimation models. Using IMU data as the benchmark ensures a robust and objective evaluation of A-mode ultrasound, enabling a clear comparison with established sensing technologies.

2.1 A-Mode Ultrasound and IMU System

In the execution of gait analysis and the collection of human biomechanical data, selecting wearable devices that utilize wireless connectivity is critical to minimize interference with the natural gait patterns of subjects. The prevailing IMU systems often rely on wired connections, which pose practical challenges for experimental applications. To prevent loss of IMU posture data during transmission and ensure the synchronized acquisition of data from multiple IMUs, it is imperative that the selected devices demonstrate superior real-time capabilities and synchronization. This study has opted for the MTw Awinda inertial sensing measurement unit by Xsens for its exemplary synchronization within 10 μs among gyroscopes, which guarantees the precision of measurements. Moreover, its lightweight design, at merely 16 grams, negligibly impacts the gait of subjects (Fig. 1).

In the selection of ultrasonic measuring equipment, 4-channel A-mode ultrasound was used to obtain subcutaneous muscle morphological information. Figure 1 The device system can synchronize the 4/8 channel one-dimensional ultrasonic sensor to realize multi-angle muscle information detection. With the integration of Ethernet/WIFI communication technologies, the device ensures the immediacy of signal collection and transmission, capable of collecting human muscle data at frequencies ranging from 5 to 40 Hz.

Additionally, to guarantee synchronous collection of ultrasound and IMU data during experiments, streamline the experimental protocol, and secure consistent data collection directives and storage verification across devices, a user-friendly master control interface was developed. This interface streamlines device management, command execution, and data validation storage, thereby enhancing the efficiency and reliability of the experimental setup (Fig. 1).

2.2 Experimental Setup

To evaluate the performance of ultrasound and IMU signals in human motion recognition, a total of 8 healthy participants were recruited for the experiment. The participants performed five common human gait movements: walking on flat ground, ascending stairs, descending stairs, ascending slopes, and descending slopes. Each participant performed five sets of each movement, with each set lasting 20 s. The parameters for the stair ascent and descent chosen in this study were a height of 150 mm, a length of 250 mm, and a slope angle of 15°. Figure 2 illustrates the motion paradigms of the experimental subjects.

To thoroughly validate the robustness of the fusion of ultrasound and IMU signals for motion classification, participants were instructed to gradually accelerate during the walking phases of different groups, with data being recorded at each stage. This approach was designed to explore the accuracy and stability of the fusion system in motion classification at varying speeds, thereby providing a comprehensive assessment of its effectiveness in a dynamic context.

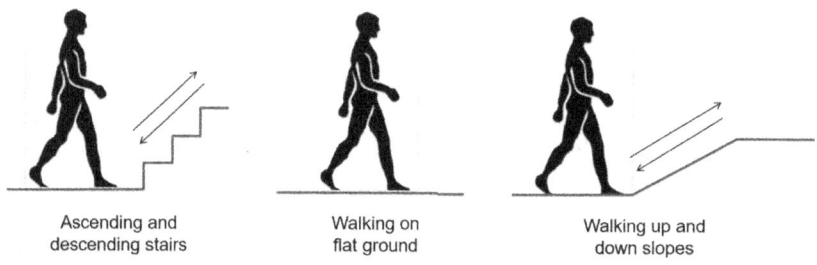

Fig. 2. Gait scene. Eight participants completed five sets of 20-second activities including ascending and descending stairs, walking on flat ground, and moving up and down slopes.

Sensor placement was determined based on the muscles activated by lower limb movements. Four muscles were selected as the subjects of study for A-mode ultrasonography: the biceps femoris, rectus femoris, tibialis anterior, and gastrocnemius. The biceps femoris and rectus femoris are primarily responsible for flexion and extension movements of the thigh at the knee joint and support at the hip joint, while the tibialis anterior and gastrocnemius are mainly responsible for dorsiflexion and extension movements at the ankle joint.

Ultrasonic data was collected at a rate of 20 frames per second, with each ultrasonic emission followed by the collection of echo data over 50 microseconds at a 20 MHz ADC sampling rate, resulting in 1000 sample points per collection. Figure 1 presents the characteristic echo signals of the ultrasonic data.

Moreover, IMU sensors were attached to the upper limbs, thighs, calves, and soles of the feet during the experiment to record motion data. The three-axis Euler angles (Roll, Pitch, Yaw), XYZ acceleration data, and three-axis angular acceleration for Roll, Pitch, and Yaw were recorded at a frequency of 40 Hz. To synchronize the IMUs with the subjects' limb movements, Velcro straps were used. Figure 1 shows the variation in limb motion data during the movements.

2.3 Data Processing

A-mode ultrasound data and IMU data were processed offline using Python. For each frame and each channel, the one-dimensional ultrasound data obtained were corrected using exponential data correction. The envelope was calculated using the Hilbert transform, and the last 40 data points were removed from the signal, resulting in a 960-dimensional raw data vector. This method enables compensation for issues such as attenuation of echo information caused by changes in muscle depth, facilitating subsequent processes including information extraction. This part of the data processing was inspired by the characteristic features of the datasets during motion and previous research on ultrasound gesture recognition [18].

For the processing of IMU data, roll axis data, which might exhibit singular values during movement, was discarded from each frame's IMU data. The remaining channel data were subjected to zero-crossing problem handling to ensure the continuity of IMU data. To calculate the actual limb angles during movement, it was necessary to subtract the measurements of the IMU data on the thigh, calf, and sole from those of the upper limb IMU, which served as the reference. This process yielded relative limb movement data during the motion, ultimately resulting in an 11-dimensional feature vector for each channel per frame. Since the sampling rate of the IMU is twice that of the ultrasound, it was necessary to downsample the IMU data by calculating the average of every two frames, ensuring that the final feature frequency of both data types was 20 Hz. By concatenating the 11-dimensional vectors from the three IMU channels after processing, a 33-dimensional total IMU feature vector was obtained.

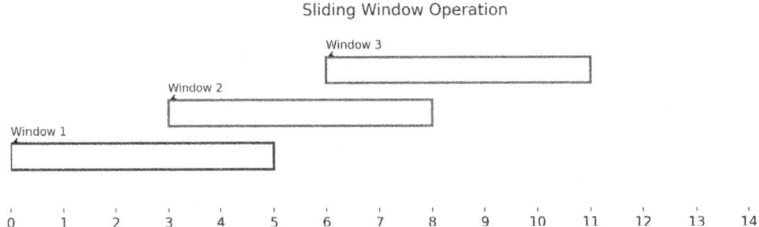

Fig. 3. Sliding Window Operation Diagram.

To construct the training and validation sets for LSTM networks, which require temporal information, a sliding window operation is applied to the data. The length and stride of the sliding window are determined based on experimental requirements, ensuring that the data within each window sufficiently captures the dynamic changes during motion. Each window contains a sequence of consecutive ultrasound feature vectors and corresponding IMU data, which serve as the input for the LSTM network to enable temporal modeling and kinematic parameter prediction. The sliding window operation is illustrated in Fig. 3.

3 Methodology

3.1 Regression Methods

Current research on ultrasound-based perception predominantly emphasizes the static feature extraction and analysis of single-frame ultrasound images, which limits the ability to effectively capture temporal dependencies during motion. The absence of robust processing methods for A-mode ultrasound signals to model dynamic and complex temporal features during continuous motion significantly constrains the accuracy of kinematic parameter estimation. To address these challenges, this study proposes a novel motion parameter estimation framework leveraging deep learning techniques which is called US-DCBAM-LSTM-(MPD-HFM)-Net. The framework integrates the Dilated Convolutional Block Attention Module (DCBAM), the Long Short-Term Memory (LSTM) module, and the Multi-Path Decoupling High-Dimensional Feature Mapping Module (MPD-HFM), enabling comprehensive modeling of both spatial and temporal features to improve estimation accuracy. The workflow of US-DCBAM-LSTM-(MPD-HFM)-Net is illustrated in Fig. 4.

Dilated Convolutional Block Attention Module. The Dilated Convolutional Block Attention Module (DCBAM) consists of two components: the Dilated Convolution and the Convolutional Block Attention Module (CBAM). Convolutional Block Attention Module (CBAM) is a lightweight attention mechanism that combines channel attention and spatial attention to enhance feature representation in convolutional neural networks [19]. It first computes channel weights using global pooling for channel refinement, followed by a spatial attention map to highlight important regions. This dual mechanism efficiently focuses on key channels and spatial information with minimal computational cost, significantly improving performance in tasks like classification, detection, and segmentation [20]. Traditional convolutional layers use fixed-size kernels to extract local features layer by layer. However, their receptive fields are typically limited, making it challenging to capture the long-range dependencies widely present in signals. To tackle the long-sequence characteristics of ultrasound data, this study introduces dilated convolution into the convolutional neural network

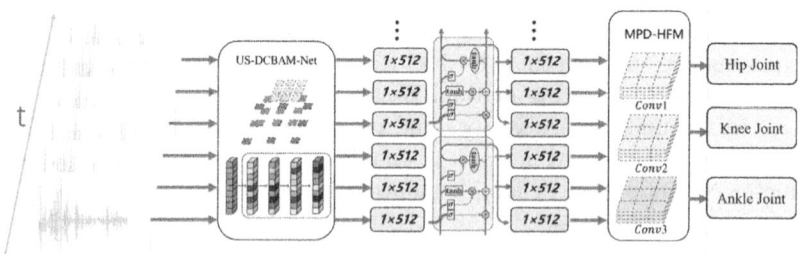

Fig. 4. The US-DCBAM-LSTM-(MPD-HFM)-Net.

(CNN). The core concept of Dilated Convolution is to expand the receptive field of the convolutional kernel by introducing a dilation rate, without significantly increasing the number of model parameters [21,22]. Specifically, dilated convolution inserts gaps between kernel elements, enabling feature extraction over a broader range. This design not only facilitates the capture of local features but also encompasses a wider range of global information, which is particularly crucial for characterizing the long-range correlations between different peaks in ultrasound signals.

In experiments involving neural network tasks, the input features are constructed by combining the 1×33 IMU feature vector with the 4×960 raw data vectors from the ultrasound channels, forming a feature tensor of 4×993 per frame. To streamline neural network propagation and parameter configuration, this feature tensor is padded to 4×1024 for each frame. The padded tensor serves as the final input representation for the neural network. Through the DCBAM module for feature extraction, each frame of the A-mode ultrasound signal is transformed into a 1×512 feature vector, serving as a fundamental representation of the muscle state. The workflow of DCBAM is illustrated in Fig. 4.

Long Short-Term Memory. Human movement is inherently a temporal process involving continuous muscle contractions and relaxations. To effectively capture such temporal dependencies in A-mode ultrasound signals, we employ Long Short-Term Memory (LSTM) networks. The gating mechanism in LSTM allows stable training and long-range sequence modeling, addressing issues like gradient vanishing. By dynamically updating memory cells over time, LSTM preserves critical sequential features, enabling robust characterization of muscle activity patterns. The resulting output vector $h_t \in \mathbb{R}^{1 \times 512}$ encapsulates temporal context and provides a compact representation of the ongoing motion state.

Multi-path Decoupling High-Dimensional Feature Mapping Module. To map the 1×512 feature vector output by the LSTM network to joint angles, this study introduces the Multi-Path Decoupling High-Dimensional Feature Mapping Module (MPD-HFM). Traditional methods either train separate networks for each joint, increasing computational cost, or use a single network for all joints, leading to feature entanglement. In contrast, MPD-HFM processes the LSTM output through three independent convolutional paths (P_1, P_2, P_3), each dedicated to one joint—hip, knee, or ankle. The joint angles are computed as:

$$y_j = \text{Conv}_{P_j}(x) \quad (j = 1, 2, 3) \tag{1}$$

$$\theta_{\text{hip}} = y_1, \quad \theta_{\text{knee}} = y_2, \quad \theta_{\text{ankle}} = y_3 \tag{2}$$

where Conv_{P_j} denotes the convolution operation in path P_j. This approach ensures complete decoupling, improving prediction accuracy and stability while reducing computational complexity.

4 Experiment Results and Discussion

4.1 Experimental Results of Angle Estimation

To validate the effectiveness of the proposed algorithm, motion data from eight experimental subjects were collected and analyzed. Based on these data, the performance of the designed motion estimation network was evaluated in terms of its ability to predict the angles of the hip, knee, and ankle joints. The predictive performance of the model was assessed using the Mean Absolute Error (MAE) metric, which quantifies the average magnitude of errors between predicted and true values. The calculation formula is as follows:

$$\text{MAE} = \frac{1}{N} \sum_{i=1}^{N} |y_i - \hat{y}_i|$$

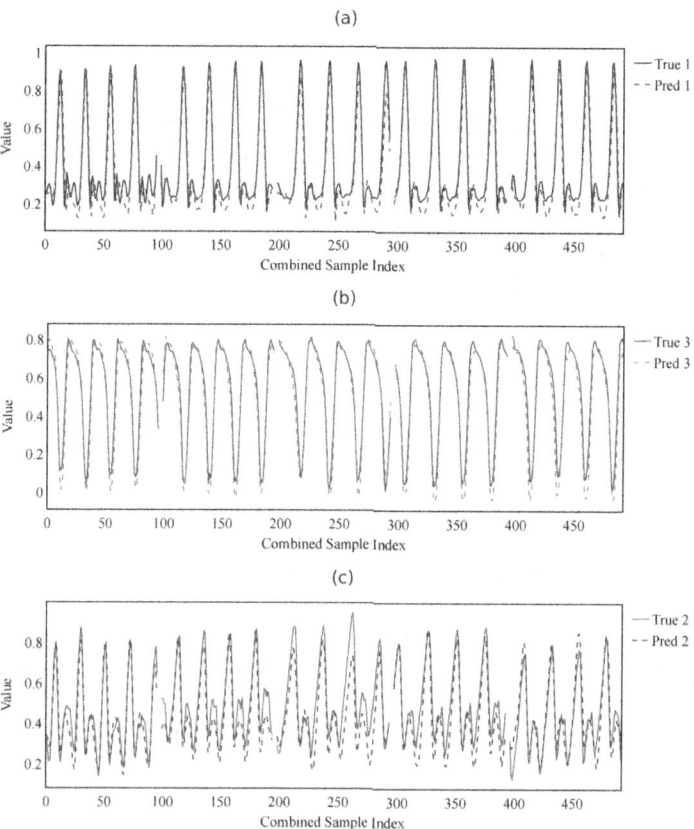

Fig. 5. Estimation curves of joint angles. (a) Hip joint. (b) Knee joint. (c) Ankle joint

Table 1. Summary of Decoding Results for Different Joints

Joint	Hip Joint	Knee Joint	Ankle Joint	Average
Error Rate	6.8%	5.4%	4.4%	5.5%

Table 1 presents the detailed results of various parameters in continuous motion decoding. The results indicate that the proposed model achieves a mean MAE of only 5.5%, demonstrating high accuracy. The experimental results are illustrated in Fig. 5.

Based on the prediction results for hip, knee, and ankle joint angles, the proposed model demonstrates high overall accuracy and stability. The specific results for each joint are as follows:

1. **Hip Joint Angle** The model achieves excellent agreement between the predicted and true hip joint angles, accurately capturing the motion trends and characteristics of the hip. The low overall error indicates the model's superior performance in predicting hip joint movement angles.
2. **Knee Joint Angle** The model also performs well in predicting knee joint angles, particularly in key regions of motion cycles such as peaks and troughs, where it closely fits the true values. However, slight deviations in some local areas suggest that the model could be further improved in capturing the dynamics of rapid knee joint motion.
3. **Ankle Joint Angle** The predicted ankle joint angles generally align well with the true values, effectively capturing periodic motion trends. However, minor discrepancies at specific points, such as near peaks and troughs, indicate room for improvement in modeling localized dynamic features of ankle motion.

Overall, the proposed model effectively captures the motion characteristics of all three joints, achieving high accuracy across the board. The consistent alignment between predicted and true values highlights the model's robustness and applicability to kinematic parameter estimation.

4.2 Ablation Experiment

In order to verify the effectiveness of each key module in the proposed algorithm, this section conducted a detailed ablation experiment Test. The algorithm framework of this article mainly includes three core modules: feature extraction module, LSTM temporal modeling Module and multi-path decoupling high-dimensional feature mapping module (MPD-HFM). By gradually removing or replacing these modules, analyze their impact on the overall performance of the system. The following four control experiments were designed for this experiment:

1. **Complete Model (Proposed)**: The full algorithm architecture, incorporating the feature extraction module, LSTM, and MPD-HFM.

2. **Without Feature Extraction Module (w/o US-DCBAM-Net)**: Directly maps the raw 4×1024 ultrasound data to a 1×512 input for the LSTM using fully connected layers, bypassing the feature extraction module.
3. **LSTM Replaced (w/o LSTM)**: Replaces the LSTM module with fully connected layers, removing the temporal modeling capability.
4. **Without Multi-path Decoupling (w/o MPD-HFM)**: Replaces the MPD-HFM module with a single fully connected layer, directly outputting the three joint angles without decoupling.

Table 2. Results of Different Model Configurations

Model Configuration	Mean Error Rate (%)
Proposed	5.5%
w/o US-DCBAM-Net	35.4%
w/o LSTM	18.5%
w/o MPD-HFM	12.33%

Based on the results of the ablation experiment shown in Table 2, the following important conclusions can be drawn from the analysis:

1. **Importance of the Feature Extraction Module** The experimental results clearly demonstrate that removing the feature extraction module increases the system's mean error rate from 5.5% to 35.4%, a significant rise of nearly 30% points. This indicates that the US-DCBAM-Net effectively extracts critical features from ultrasound data related to joint motion. The results also validate the necessity of a feature extraction architecture specifically designed for the characteristics of ultrasound signals.
2. **Significance of Temporal Modeling** Replacing the LSTM with fully connected layers raises the system's error rate to 18.5%, highlighting the substantial contribution of temporal modeling to system performance. This result demonstrates that human joint motion exhibits clear temporal continuity, and leveraging LSTM to capture these temporal dependencies significantly improves the accuracy of angle estimation.
3. **Effectiveness of the Multi-path Decoupling Strategy** Removing the MPD-HFM module increases the system's error rate to 12.33%, validating that the multi-path structure effectively decouples the modeling of different joint angles. This decoupling approach captures the unique characteristics of each joint's motion more effectively, thereby enhancing estimation accuracy.

5 Conclusion

In this paper, we proposed a deep learning framework that leverages A-mode ultrasound signals for estimating lower limb joint kinematics, aiming to enhance the accuracy and responsiveness of wearable exoskeleton systems. Compared to traditional sensing modalities such as sEMG and IMU, A-mode ultrasound offers superior wearability, stability, and deeper insights into muscle dynamics.

Our experimental results demonstrate that the proposed method can accurately predict hip, knee, and ankle joint angles, even under variations in subject-specific movement patterns. The framework shows strong potential in improving human-machine interaction for rehabilitation applications by enabling more intuitive and proactive control.

Future work will explore cross-subject generalization, real-time deployment, and multimodal sensor fusion to further enhance robustness and clinical applicability.

Acknowledgments. This work was supported by the National Key Research and Development Program of China (Grant Number: 2022YFC3601700), the Shenzhen Science and Technology Program (Grant Number: GXWD20231129102014001), and the Self-Planned Task (Grant Number: SKLRS202505C) of the State Key Laboratory of Robotics and Systems, Harbin Institute of Technology.

References

1. Chen, G., Chan, C.K., Guo, Z., Yu, H.: A review of lower extremity assistive robotic exoskeletons in rehabilitation therapy. Crit. Reviews^{TM} Biomed. Eng. **41**(4–5), (2013)
2. Dellon, B., Matsuoka, Y.: Prosthetics, exoskeletons, and rehabilitation [grand challenges of robotics]. IEEE Robot. Autom. Mag. **14**(1), 30–34 (2007)
3. Li, Y., He, K., Sun, X., Liu, H.: Human-machine interface based on multi-channel single-element ultrasound transducers: a preliminary study. In: IEEE 18th International Conference on E-health Networking, Applications and Services (Healthcom), vol. 2016, pp. 1–6, IEEE (2016)
4. Zhou, R., Luo, Q., Feng, X., Li, C.: Design of a wireless multi-channel surface EMG signal acquisition system. In: 2017 3rd IEEE International Conference on Computer and Communications (ICCC), pp. 279–283. IEEE (2017)
5. Babaei, N., Hannani, N., Dabanloo, N.J., Bahadori, S.: A systematic review of the use of commercial wearable activity trackers for monitoring recovery in individuals undergoing total hip replacement surgery. Cyborg Bionic Syst. **2022** (2022). https://spj.science.org/doi/abs/10.34133/2022/9794641
6. Scheme, E.J., Englehart, K.B.: Electromyogram pattern recognition for control of powered upper-limb prostheses: state of the art and challenges for clinical use. J. Rehabil. Res. Dev. **48**(6), 643–59 (2011). https://api.semanticscholar.org/CorpusID:14883575
7. Disselhorst-Klug, C., Schmitz-Rode, T., Rau, G.: Surface electromyography and muscle force: limits in SEMG-force relationship and new approaches for applications. Clin. Biomech. **24**(3), 225–235 (2009)
8. Duchene, J., Hogrel, J.-Y.: A model of EMG generation. IEEE Trans. Biomed. Eng. **47**(2), 192–201 (2000)
9. Zhu, L., et al.: A novel motion intention recognition approach for soft exoskeleton via IMU. Electronics **9**(12) (2020). https://www.mdpi.com/2079-9292/9/12/2176

10. Alarfaj, M., Qian, Y., Liu, H.: Detection of human body movement patterns using IMU and barometer. In: 2020 International Conference on Communications, Signal Processing, and their Applications (ICCSPA), pp. 1–6 (2021)
11. Sgambato, B.G., et al.: High performance wearable ultrasound as a human-machine interface for wrist and hand kinematic tracking. IEEE Trans. Biomed. Eng. **71**(2), 484–493 (2024)
12. Yang, X., Zhou, Y., Liu, H.: Wearable ultrasound-based decoding of simultaneous wrist/hand kinematics. IEEE Trans. Ind. Electron. **68**(9), 8667–8675 (2021)
13. Jin, Y., et al.: Estimation of joint torque in dynamic activities using wearable a-mode ultrasound. Nat. Commun. **15**(1), 5756 (2024)
14. Zeng, J., Zhou, Y., Yang, Y., Yan, J., Liu, H.: Fatigue-sensitivity comparison of SEMG and a-mode ultrasound based hand gesture recognition. IEEE J. Biomed. Health Inform. **26**(4), 1718–1725 (2021)
15. Yang, X., Sun, X., Zhou, D., Li, Y., Liu, H.; Towards wearable a-mode ultrasound sensing for real-time finger motion recognition. IEEE Trans. Neural Syst. Rehabil. Eng. **26**(6), 1199–1208 (2018)
16. Zeng, J., Zhou, Y., Yang, Y., Wang, J., Liu, H.: Feature fusion of SEMG and ultrasound signals in hand gesture recognition. In: 2020 IEEE International Conference on Systems, Man, and Cybernetics (SMC), pp. 3911–3916 (2020)
17. Hettiarachchi, N., Ju, Z., Liu, H.: A new wearable ultrasound muscle activity sensing system for dexterous prosthetic control. In: 2015 IEEE International Conference on Systems, Man, and Cybernetics, pp. 1415–1420. IEEE (2015)
18. Yang, X., Yan, J., Chen, Z., Ding, H., Liu, H.: A proportional pattern recognition control scheme for wearable a-mode ultrasound sensing. IEEE Trans. Industr. Electron. **67**(1), 800–808 (2020)
19. Woo, S., Park, J., Lee, J.Y., Kweon, I.S.: CBAM: convolutional block attention module. In: Proceedings of the European Conference on Computer Vision (ECCV), pp. 3–19 (2018)
20. Chen, L., Yao, H., Fu, J., Ng, C.T.: The classification and localization of crack using lightweight convolutional neural network with CBAM. Eng. Struct. **275**, 115291 (2023)
21. Yu, F., Koltun, V.: Multi-scale context aggregation by dilated convolutions. arXiv preprint arXiv:1511.07122 (2015)
22. Wei, Y., Xiao, H., Shi, H., Jie, Z., Feng, J., Huang, T.S: Revisiting dilated convolution: a simple approach for weakly-and semi-supervised semantic segmentation. In: Proceedings of the IEEE Conference on Computer Vision and Pattern Recognition, pp. 7268–7277 (2018)

Human Lower Limb Motor Ability Estimation Based on Human-Machine Coupling Interactive Contact Model

Chao Gao[1], Jianhua Zhang[2], and Hui Li[2(✉)]

[1] Hebei University of Technology, Tianjin 300401, China
[2] University of Science and Technology Beijing, Beijing 100083, China
15704965986@163.com

Abstract. How to meet the personalized needs of stroke patients in rehabilitation training has long been the core challenge in rehabilitation robot research. The rapid and accurate recognition of patients' motion intentions is a critical prerequisite for addressing this challenge. To address this, this paper presents a method for estimating human lower-limb motor capability based on a human-machine coupling model. Unlike the integrated equivalent model of human-machine coupling, the dynamic models of the mechanical leg and the human lower limb, along with the contact model, are established separately. Identification experiments are then designed to determine the unknown parameters. Then, the mechanical leg and human lower limb are integrated via the contact model to establish a human-machine coupling dynamic model. Based on this model and utilizing torque and interaction force sensors on the mechanical leg, the estimation of human lower-limb motor capability is indirectly realized. Finally, experiments validate the feasibility and effectiveness of the proposed approach.

Keywords: Stroke Rehabilitation · Human-Machine Coupling · Motion Intention Estimation · Dynamic Model · Human-Machine Interaction

1 Introduction

A survey published in The Lancet reveals that stroke has become one of the geriatric diseases with high disability and mortality rates in China [1]. Results from multiple small-sample clinical trials have demonstrated that robot-assisted rehabilitation outperforms traditional therapies in terms of gait independence and long-term effectiveness [2, 3]. However, owing to the heterogeneity in patient conditions, rehabilitation strategies and specific training requirements vary. Multi-posture lower-limb rehabilitation robots can address this need. This study developed a multi-posture lower-limb rehabilitation robot. As shown in Fig. 1, the robot comprises two exoskeleton mechanical legs, a suspended weight-bearing system, a retractable seat, a reclining mechanism, and a mobile support platform. The hip and knee joints of the two mechanical legs are driven by joint motors, enabling separate and combined rehabilitation training for multiple lower-limb joints in standing, sitting, and reclining positions.

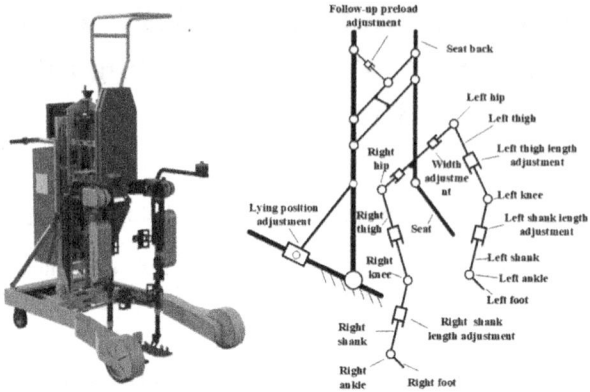

Fig. 1. Degree of freedom configuration of multi-position lower limb rehabilitation robot.

Based on clinical rehabilitation experience in stroke, the stronger the patient's awareness of active participation during rehabilitation, the more effectively rehabilitation training can stimulate the damaged brain areas, thereby promoting neural remodeling [4]. Consequently, how to quickly and accurately evaluate the motor ability of the affected limbs in patients with motor dysfunction has become a topic of widespread concern by researchers in rehabilitation robotics [5]. In [6], researchers proposed using electromyographic (EMG) information to estimate the viscoelasticity of human muscles, and based on the estimation results, proportionally adjusted the viscoelasticity of the joints of the HAL robotic exoskeleton. This study demonstrated promising results when used by normal operators. However, the user groups of power-assisted exoskeletons differ from those of rehabilitation robots. Stroke patients have damaged motor brain areas, resulting in abnormal signals being transmitted to the muscles. Additionally, due to muscle tone, it is difficult to accurately assess patients' motor ability through EMG signals and thus control the robot [7]. This paper proposes a method for estimating human lower-limb motor ability by establishing a human-machine coupling contact model. By capturing the motion and joint torque information of subjects during motor training with rehabilitation robots, the lower-limb motor ability of subjects is quickly estimated.

$$\tau = \tau_r + \tau_f + \tau_{hr} + \tau_h \tag{1}$$

As shown in Eq. (1), the output torque of the hip and knee joint motors in the lower-limb rehabilitation robot is composed of four primary components: the torque necessary for driving the exoskeleton under ideal conditions τ_r, , the torque loss caused by repetitive disturbances (primarily frictional resistance) τ_f, the torque required to drive the patient's lower limb under ideal conditions τ_h, and the loss due to human-machine interaction forces from rigid-flexible coupling τ_{hr}. The friction at the exoskeleton joint is influenced by multiple factors and is a nonlinear function of joint velocity, rendering it challenging to accurately model with linear approaches. The rehabilitation robot developed in this study is equipped with torque sensors at the joint output positions, which directly measure the joint output torque and indirectly circumvent the frictional interference component. In subsequent control research, the joint motor output torque can also be obtained from the motor current, and the torque lost to frictional interference can be derived by subtracting the measured joint output torque from this current-derived value. Since the focus of this paper is on recognizing patients' lower-limb motion intentions, this frictional interference component is temporarily set aside (Fig. 2).

2 Human-Machine Coupling Dynamic Modeling

2.1 Dynamic Modeling of Rehabilitation Robot Mechanical Leg

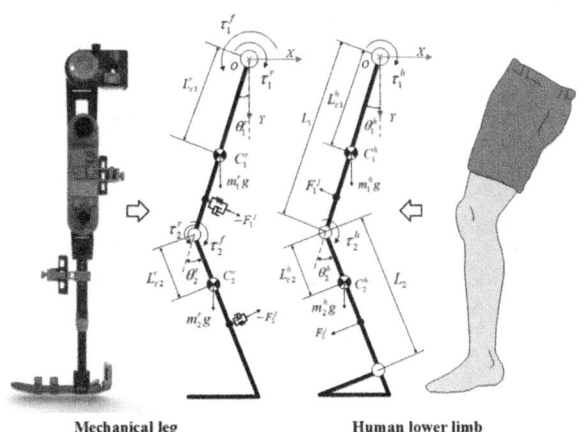

Fig. 2. Segmental Equivalent Model of Human Lower Limb-Mechanical leg.

The mechanical leg of the lower-limb rehabilitation robot is a serial rigid-link structure, whereas the human lower limb is a composite structure comprising rigid bones and flexible muscles, and skin. During rehabilitation training, the two are connected via human-machine contact units, forming a complex rigid-flexible coupling system. Accurate modeling of this coupling relationship is crucial for estimating human lower-limb motion intentions. In [8], an adaptive Kalman filter algorithm was designed for estimating human active torque, and subsequent research proposed a Gaussian process regression-based error prediction method, achieving accurate estimation results. However, when constructing the human-machine coupling dynamic model, the researchers did not account for the influence of human-machine contact. Similarly, Korean researchers [9], when estimating muscle torque during exoskeleton wear, equated the human-machine coupling system as a single entity. The above studies modeled the complex rigid-flexible coupling system equivalently as a whole, relying on the premise that the human lower limb and exoskeleton are rigidly attached—a premise that overlooks the contact issues arising from human-machine coupling. Therefore, this paper presents a segmented modeling approach for the human-machine rigid-flexible coupling relationship through segmentation.

The mechanical leg of the lower-limb rehabilitation robot is a two-degree-of-freedom (2-DOF) serial robot, directly modeled using traditional robotic dynamic modeling approaches. A coordinate system is established with the center of the hip joint rotational pair as the origin, where the joint rotation angle is defined as positive in the counterclockwise direction. The dynamic equations of the mechanical leg are:

$$\tau_r = M_r \theta_r'' + C_r \theta_r' + G_r \quad (2)$$

where, M_r, C_r, G_r are the inertia, damping, and gravity 2×2 matrix of the mechanical leg, respectively. θ_r is the joint angle 2×1 vector of the mechanical leg hip and knee, and τ_r is the output torque 2×1 vector of the mechanical leg hip and knee joints. The Lagrangian method is employed to model the mechanical leg. The total kinetic energy of the system composed of the thigh and calf segments of the mechanical leg is:

$$T_r = \frac{1}{2}m_1^r(L_{c1}^r)^2(\theta_1^{r'})^2 + \frac{1}{2}m_2^r(L_1\theta_1^{r'}\cos\theta_1^r + L_{c2}^r(\theta_1^{r'} + \theta_2^{r'})\cos(\theta_1^r + \theta_2^r))^2$$
$$+ \frac{1}{2}m_2^r(-L_1\theta_1^{r'}\sin\theta_1^r - L_{c2}^r(\theta_1^{r'} + \theta_2^{r'})\sin(\theta_1^r + \theta_2^r))^2 + \frac{1}{2}J_{c1}^r(\theta_1^{r'})^2 + \frac{1}{2}J_{c2}^r(\theta_2^{r'})^2 \quad (3)$$

The total potential energy of the mechanical leg thigh, and calf system is:

$$E_r = m_1^r g L_{c1}^r \cos\theta_1^r + m_2^r g(L_1 \cos\theta_1^r + L_{c2}^r \cos(\theta_1^r + \theta_2^r)) \quad (4)$$

The dynamic equation of the exoskeleton obtained by the Lagrangian method is:

$$L = T_r - E_r \quad (5)$$

$$\tau_i^r = \frac{d}{dt}(\frac{\partial L}{\partial \dot{\theta}_i}) - \frac{\partial L}{\partial \theta_i}, i = 1, 2 \quad (6)$$

$$\begin{bmatrix} \tau_1^r \\ \tau_2^r \end{bmatrix} = \begin{bmatrix} M_{11}^r & M_{12}^r \\ M_{21}^r & M_{22}^r \end{bmatrix} \begin{bmatrix} \theta_1^{r''} \\ \theta_2^{r''} \end{bmatrix} + \begin{bmatrix} C_{11}^r & C_{12}^r \\ C_{21}^r & C_{22}^r \end{bmatrix} \begin{bmatrix} (\theta_1^{r'})^2 \\ (\theta_2^{r'})^2 \end{bmatrix} + \begin{bmatrix} D_{11}^r & D_{12}^r \\ D_{21}^r & D_{22}^r \end{bmatrix} \begin{bmatrix} \theta_1^{r'}\theta_2^{r'} \\ \theta_2^{r'}\theta_1^{r'} \end{bmatrix} + \begin{bmatrix} G_1^r \\ G_2^r \end{bmatrix} \quad (7)$$

The variable is defined as:

$$M_{11}^r = m_1^r(L_{c1}^r)^2 + m_2^r(L_{c2}^r)^2 + m_2^r(L_1)^2 + 2m_2^r L_1 L_{c2}^r \cos(2\theta_1^r + \theta_2^r) + J_1^r;$$
$$M_{12}^r = m_2^r(L_{c2}^r)^2 + m_2^r L_1 L_{c2}^r \cos(2\theta_1^r + \theta_2^r);$$
$$M_{21}^r = m_2^r(L_{c2}^r)^2 + m_2^r L_1 L_{c2}^r \cos(2\theta_1^r + \theta_2^r);$$
$$M_{22}^r = m_2^r(L_{c2}^r)^2 + J_2^r; C_{11}^r = 0; C_{12}^r = -m_2^r L_1 L_{c2}^r \sin\theta_1^r;$$
$$C_{21}^r = m_2^r L_1 L_{c2}^r \sin\theta_2^r; C_{22}^r = 0; D_{11}^r = -2m_2^r L_1 L_{c2}^r \sin\theta_1^r; \quad (8)$$
$$D_{12}^r = D_{21}^r = D_{22}^r = 0; G_2^r = -m_2^r g L_{c2}^r \sin(\theta_1^r + \theta_2^r);$$
$$G_1^r = -m_1^r g L_{c1}^r \sin\theta_1^r - m_2^r g L_{c2}^r \sin(\theta_1^r + \theta_2^r) - m_2^r g L_1 \sin\theta_1^r;$$
$$J_{c1}^r = I_{z1}^r + I_{z2}^r + m_1^r(L_{c1}^r)^2 + m_2^r(L_{c2}^r)^2 + m_2^r(L_1^r)^2;$$
$$J_{c2}^r = I_{z2}^r + m_2^r(L_{c2}^r)^2;$$

I_{z1}^r, I_{z2}^r represent the rotational inertias of the thigh segment of the mechanical leg around the hip joint, and the rotational inertia of the lower leg segment around the knee joint.

2.2 Dynamic Modeling of Human Lower Limb

The human lower limb is typically modeled with seven degrees of freedom (7-DOF), including three DOF at the hip joint, one DOF at the knee joint, and three DOF at the ankle joint [10]. Although studies [11] have shown that high-complexity models describe lower-limb motion characteristics more accurately, their computational complexity increases exponentially. Therefore, this study balances model complexity and computational load based on practical requirements. During rehabilitation training, the coronal-plane (adduction/abduction) and horizontal-plane (internal/external rotation) DOF of the hip joint, as well as all DOF of the ankle joint (including sagittal-plane dorsiflexion/plantarflexion and coronal-plane inversion/eversion), are ignored. Only the sagittal-plane DOF of the hip and knee joints are retained, modeling the human lower limb as a 2-DOF planar linkage. Using the hip joint rotation center as the coordinate origin, the total kinetic energy of the thigh-calf system is:

$$T_h = \frac{1}{2}m_1^h(L_{c1}^h)^2(\theta_1^h)^2 + \frac{1}{2}m_2^h(L_1\theta_1^{h'}\cos\theta_1^h + L_{c2}^h(\theta_1^{h'} + \theta_2^{h'})\cos(\theta_1^h + \theta_2^h))^2 \qquad (9)$$
$$+ \frac{1}{2}m_2^h(-L_1\theta_1^{h'}\sin\theta_1^h - L_{c2}^h(\theta_1^{h'} + \theta_2^{h'})\sin(\theta_1^h + \theta_2^h))^2 + \frac{1}{2}J_{c1}^h(\theta_1^{h'})^2 + \frac{1}{2}J_{c2}^h(\theta_2^{h'})^2$$

The total potential energy of the system of the human thigh and calf is:

$$E_h = m_1^h g L_{c1}^h \cos\theta_1^h + m_2^h g (L_1 \cos\theta_1^h + L_{c2}^h \cos(\theta_1^h + \theta_2^h)) \qquad (10)$$

The dynamic equation of the human lower limb obtained by the Lagrange method is:

$$L = T_h - E_h \qquad (11)$$

$$\tau_i^h = \frac{d}{dt}\left(\frac{\partial L}{\partial \theta_i}\right) - \frac{\partial L}{\partial \theta_i}, \quad i = 1, 2 \qquad (12)$$

$$\begin{bmatrix} \tau_1^h \\ \tau_2^h \end{bmatrix} = \begin{bmatrix} M_{11}^h & M_{12}^h \\ M_{21}^h & M_{22}^h \end{bmatrix} \begin{bmatrix} \theta_1^{h''} \\ \theta_2^{h''} \end{bmatrix} + \begin{bmatrix} C_{11}^h & C_{12}^h \\ C_{21}^h & C_{22}^h \end{bmatrix} \begin{bmatrix} (\theta_1^{h'})^2 \\ (\theta_2^{h'})^2 \end{bmatrix} + \begin{bmatrix} D_{11}^h & D_{12}^h \\ D_{21}^h & D_{22}^h \end{bmatrix} \begin{bmatrix} \theta_1^{h'}\theta_2^{h'} \\ \theta_2^{h'}\theta_1^{h'} \end{bmatrix} + \begin{bmatrix} G_1^h \\ G_2^h \end{bmatrix} \qquad (13)$$

The variable is defined as:

$$M_{11}^h = m_1^h(L_{c1}^h)^2 + m_2^h(L_{c2}^h)^2 + m_2^h(L_1)^2 + 2m_2^h L_1 L_{c2}^h \cos(2\theta_1^h + \theta_2^h) + J_1^h;$$
$$M_{12}^h = m_2^h(L_{c2}^h)^2 + m_2^h L_1 L_{c2}^h \cos(2\theta_1^h + \theta_2^h);$$
$$M_{21}^h = m_2^h(L_{c2}^h)^2 + m_2^h L_1 L_{c2}^h \cos(2\theta_1^h + \theta_2^h);$$
$$M_{22}^h = m_2^h(L_{c2}^h)^2 + J_2^h;\quad C_{11}^h = 0;\quad C_{12}^h = -m_2^h L_1 L_{c2}^h \sin\theta_1^h;$$
$$C_{21}^h = m_2^h L_1 L_{c2}^h \sin\theta_2^h;\quad C_{22}^h = 0;\quad D_{11}^h = -2m_2^h L_1 L_{c2}^h \sin\theta_1^h; \qquad (14)$$
$$D_{12}^h = D_{21}^h = D_{22}^h = 0;\quad G_2^h = -m_2^h g L_{c2}^h \sin(\theta_1^h + \theta_2^h);$$
$$G_1^h = -m_1^h g L_{c1}^h \sin\theta_1^h - m_2^h g L_{c2}^h \sin(\theta_1^h + \theta_2^h) - m_2^h g L_1 \sin\theta_1^h;$$
$$J_{c1}^h = I_{z1}^h + I_{z2}^h + m_1^h(L_{c1}^h)^2 + m_2^h(L_{c2}^h)^2 + m_2^h(L_1)^2;$$
$$J_{c2}^h = I_{z2}^h + m_2^h(L_{c2}^h)^2;$$

I_{z1}^h, I_{z2}^h represent the rotational inertias of the thigh segment of the lower limbs around the hip joint, and the calf segment around the knee joint, respectively.

2.3 Human-Machine Interaction Contact Model

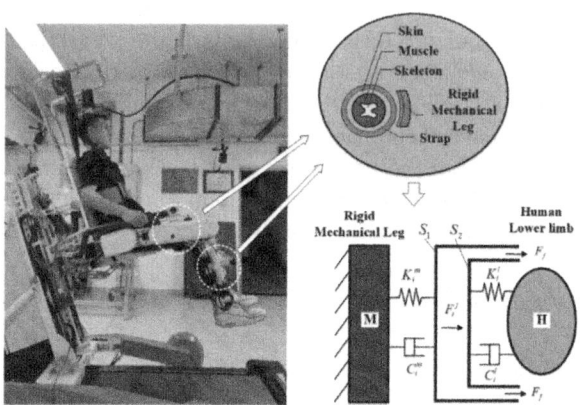

Fig. 3. Human-Machine Interaction Contact Model.

When patients use the lower-limb rehabilitation robot for training in sitting and reclining positions, their body postures are fixed, and body weight is unloaded through the multi-posture robot's seat, backrest, and weight-bearing suspension system. The lower limbs are fixed by the thigh, calf, and foot straps of the mechanical leg, and static alignment of the lower-limb joints is achieved by adjusting the mechanical leg length. Thus, this study assumes that the coordinate origin of the human hip joint coincides with that of the robot's hip joint, and the coordinate origin of the human ankle joint coincides with that of the robot's ankle joint. The relative displacement and interaction force between the human lower limb and the mechanical leg originate from the human-machine contact interface secured by straps. The relative displacement is caused by the deformation of the skin, muscles, and straps. Due to the high complexity of this coupling system, appropriate simplifications are necessary.

As shown in Fig. 3, the mechanical leg is a rigid body as a whole, coupled to the human lower limb via sponge pads (S1) and flexible straps. The interface exhibits elasticity, which can be approximated as a spring-damper system. The human lower limb, as observed in cross-section, has a rigid skeleton as the innermost layer, followed by muscle and skin layers (S2) from inner to outer. This layer undergoes the largest deformation and displacement during interaction, and is also approximated by a spring-damper system. In practical applications, S1 and S2 are in close contact. By ignoring non-sagittal plane motions, the human-machine coupling part is approximated as two spring-damper systems in series. The contact relationship at the calf follows the same logic.

The simplified contact model comprises the mechanical leg M, the human lower limb H, two equivalent springs, and two equivalent dampers. Since the contact between the human limb and the mechanical leg is established through strap binding, both normal contact force and tangential friction force act on the limb. The Coulomb friction model is suitable for modeling friction. Considering the influence of friction, the equivalent human-machine interaction contact model is finally established as:

$$F_i = \frac{K_i^m K_i^l}{K_i^m + K_i^l}(v_i^r - v_i^h) + \frac{C_i^m C_i^l}{C_i^m + C_i^l}(v_i^{r'} - v_i^{h'}) + f_{c,i} sign(v_i^{r'} - v_i^{h'}) + f_{s,i}(v_i^{r'} - v_i^{h'}) \quad (15)$$

In the formula, K_i^m and C_i^m are the elastic coefficient and damping, F_i, $i = 1, 2$ represent the human-computer interaction contact force at the thigh and calf respectively, v_i^r, v_i^h represent the displacement of exoskeleton and human lower limb segments respectively, $f_{c,i}, f_{s,i}$ represent the coulomb friction coefficient and viscous friction coefficient respectively.

2.4 Human-Machine Coupling Model

The human-machine coupling torque is characterized using the human-machine contact model. By transforming the torques of all components in the human-machine coupling system into the joint space of the rehabilitation robot exoskeleton, the human-machine coupling dynamic equation is ultimately established as:

$$\begin{aligned} & M_r \theta_r'' + C_r \theta_r' + G_r + M_{hr}(C_i^l, K_i^l, C_i^m, K_i^m, f_{c,i}, f_{s,i}) \\ & + \Phi_r^T \Phi_h^{-T}(M_h \theta_h'' + C_h \theta_h' + G_h) = \tau_r + \tau_{hr} + \tau_h \end{aligned} \quad (16)$$

In the formula, $M_{hr}()$ represents the function of the parameters of the interactive contact model, Φ_r, Φ_h are the Jacobian matrices of the mechanical leg and the human lower limbs.

3 Parameter Identification

3.1 Dynamic Parameter Identification of Mechanical Leg

Following linearization of the rehabilitation robot's mechanical leg model, the least squares method is employed for parameter identification. The identified dynamic inertia parameters of the mechanical leg are presented in Table 1:

Table 1. Identification results of mechanical leg inertial parameters.

Parameter	Value	Parameter	Value
m_1^r	3.0573 (kg)	m_2^r	2.6048 (kg)
L_1^r	458.3 (mm)	L_{c2}^r	216.5 (mm)
L_{c1}^r	293.7 (mm)	J_2^r	4132 (kg mm^2)
J_1^r	6254 (kg mm^2)	/	/

3.2 Inertial Parameter Identification of Human Lower Limb

OpenSim, a biomechanical simulation software, can perform inverse dynamics modeling of human walking using motion data and ground reaction forces, and its accuracy has been widely validated by researchers [12, 13]. Therefore, in this study, motion capture data of the subjects' lower limb (height 175 cm, weight 65 kg) movements and plantar pressure were collected. Inverse kinematics and inverse dynamics analyses were performed using OpenSim to derive the hip and knee joint torques and muscle forces of major lower limb muscles. Finally, using the joint torque and angle data, the least squares method was employed to identify the dynamic parameters of the human lower limb model. The results of the parameter identification are shown in Table 2.

Table 2. Identification results of human lower limb inertial parameters.

Parameter	Value	Parameter	Value
m_1^h	9.532 (kg)	m_2^h	3.283 (kg)
L_1^h	458.3 (mm)	L_{c2}^h	238.7 (mm)
L_{c1}^h	309.3 (mm)	J_2^h	31164 (kg mm^2)
J_1^h	128983 (kg mm^2)	/	/

3.3 Parameter Identification of Human-Machine Interaction Contact Model

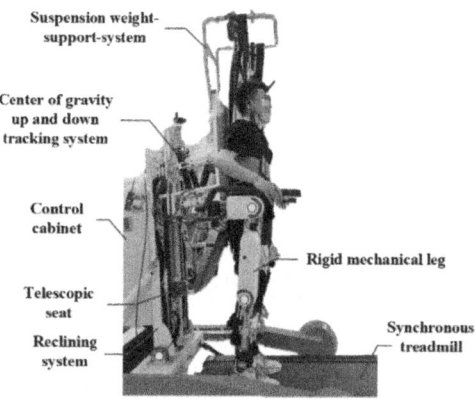

Fig. 4. Experimental Prototype Equipment.

Using the human-machine contact model presented in Eq. (15), an identification experiment for the contact model was designed. The experimental setup is shown in Fig. 4. Following the binding protocol employed in exoskeleton rehabilitation training, the subject's thigh and calf were securely attached to the mechanical leg using non-stretchable straps, ensuring optimal alignment between the subject's hip/knee joints and the robotic joints. One-dimensional force sensors were installed at the contact interfaces of the thigh and calf, with the following specifications: measurement ranges of 360 N and 200 N, resolution of 0.01 N, nonlinearity of ± 0.02% F.S., repeatability of ± 0.02% F.S., and hysteresis of ± 0.02% F.S. The rehabilitation robot was operated in passive training mode, guiding the subject's lower limb along a predefined gait trajectory without active muscular activation from the subject.

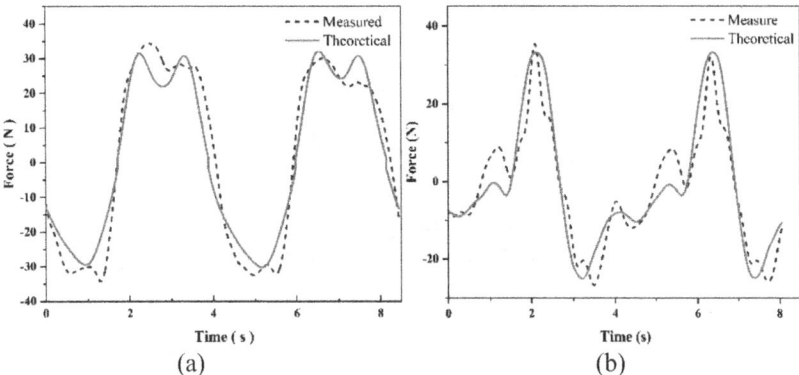

Fig. 5. Comparison between Experimental Measurements and Theoretical Calculations, (a) Thigh, (b) Calf.

Reflective markers were attached to the subject's lower limbs and the mechanical leg, and the NOKOV motion capture system was used to acquire real-time motion data of the human limbs and exoskeleton. During the experiment, motion data and interaction force data were recorded synchronously, with a total of 10 sets of data collected. After applying smoothing filtering to the collected data, the first 8 sets were selected as the experimental group for parameter identification of the human-machine contact model using a genetic algorithm, while the remaining 2 sets served as the validation group for model verification. The relevant parameter settings are as follows: the initial population size is 1000, the crossover probability is 0.8, the mutation probability is 0.01, the maximum number of iterations is 1000, and the static penalty function is used. The validation group data were input into the model to obtain theoretical torque results. Figure 5 shows the comparison between theoretical calculations and actual measurements for the validation group. The numerical fluctuations in some intervals are caused by the systematic error of the mechanical leg structure, which does not affect the overall result. An overall analysis shows that the interaction force errors for the thigh and calf were generally small, verifying the correctness of the theoretical model.

4 Experimental Verification

To validate the accuracy of the human-machine coupling model developed in this study, an experiment for estimating human lower-limb motor ability was conducted. Given the difficulty in directly measuring the active torque of human lower limbs, this paper follows the experimental protocol in related research to design a comparative experiment [14]. The first group involved the rehabilitation robot's mechanical leg driving the subject along a predefined gait trajectory, with motion and torque sensor data recorded. The second group performed the same trajectory while applying external forces to the subject's lower limb, as shown in Fig. 6.

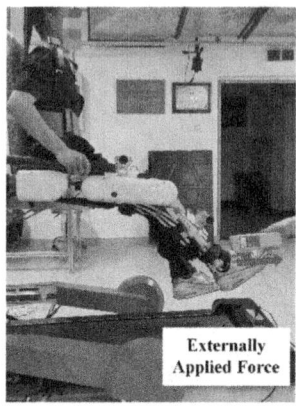

Fig. 6. Validation Experiment of Human Lower Limb Motor Ability Estimation.

The applied external forces were recorded by the dynamometer, with rehabilitation robot sensor data synchronized in real time. The human-machine coupling model proposed in this study was used to estimate the measured torque data. As shown in Fig. 7, Fig. 7(a) and (b) display the comparison between predicted and measured results for the first group, while Fig. 7(c) and (d) present the results for the second group. External forces were applied at approximately 1.5 s and 4 s, and the prediction results indicate that the applied forces were accurately estimated. The positive torque value of the hip joint indicates extension, and the positive torque value of the knee joint indicates flexion. The mean estimation torque errors for the two groups were:

$$\tau_{rmse} = \sqrt{\frac{1}{P} \sum_{i=1,2}^{p=1,\ldots,P} \left(\tau_{t,i}^{p} - \tau_{m,i}^{p}\right)^2} \tag{17}$$

In the formula, P is the number of sampling data included in the calculation; $\tau_{t,i}^{p}$, $\tau_{m,i}^{p}$, $i = 1, 2$ represent the estimated and measured torque values at the hip joint and knee joint, respectively.

The results of the human lower-limb motor ability estimation validation experiment show that although the errors are relatively large and there is a lag in the first half of the gait cycle, the predicted results are generally consistent with the actual measurements. In the validation experiment with external force application, the mean estimation error of hip joint torque was 0.5077 N·m, and that of knee joint torque was 0.2357 N·m. This indicates that the human lower-limb motor ability estimation method proposed in this paper can effectively estimate the motor ability and motion intention of the human lower limb.

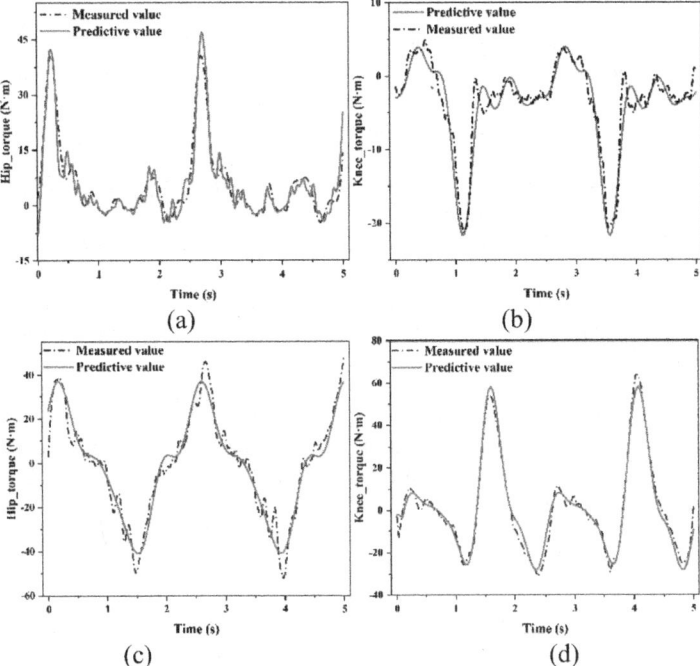

Fig. 7. Comparison between Estimated and Measured Torques. Group 1 (No external force): (a) Hip, (b) Knee; Group 2 (With external force): (c) Hip, (d) Knee.

5 Conclusion

This study presents a method for estimating human lower-limb motor ability based on a human-machine coupling dynamic model. Unlike the integrated equivalent model of the mechanical leg and human lower limb, this approach first develops dynamic models for the lower-limb rehabilitation robot's mechanical leg, human lower limb, and human-machine contact model, respectively. Subsequently, unknown parameters of each sub-model are identified through characterization experiments. Thereafter, the mechanical leg and human lower limb are coupled via the human-machine contact model to establish a human-machine coupling dynamic model. Finally, using this model and torque sensors at the hip/knee joints of the mechanical leg, along with human-machine interaction tension-compression sensors, the joint torque of the human lower limb is estimated, and the method is validated through experiments.

References

1. Zhou, M., et al.: Mortality, morbidity, and risk factors in China and its provinces, 1990–2017: a systematic analysis for the Global Burden of Disease Study 2017. (2013)
2. Rodriguez-Fernandez, A., Lobo-Prat, J., Font-Llagunes, J.M.: Systematic review on wearable lower-limb exoskeletons for gait training in neuromuscular impairments. J. Neuroeng. Rehabil. **18**(1), 22 (2021)

3. Bettella, F., Tortora, S., Menegatti, E., Petrone, N., Del Felice, A.: A scoping review on lower limb exoskeleton actuation's description and characteristics. Robotica 1–18 (2025)
4. Martin, L., Christoph, B., Niels, B., Silke, A., Cohen, L.G.J.B.: Motor learning elicited by voluntary drive. **4**, 866 (2003)
5. Dietz, V., Colombo, G., Jensen, L., Baumgartner, L.: Locomotor capacity of spinal cord in paraplegic patients. Ann. Neurol. **37**(5), 574–582 (2004)
6. Lee, S., Sankai, Y.J.I.: Power assist control for leg with HAL-3 based on virtual torque and impedance adjustment (2002)
7. Yang, M., et al.: A knowledge transfer-based personalized human-robot interaction control method for lower limb exoskeletons. IEEE Sens. J. **24**(23), 39490–39502 (2024)
8. Liang, X., et al.: Adaptive human-robot interaction torque estimation with high accuracy and strong tracking ability for a lower limb rehabilitation robot. IEEE/ASME Trans. Mechatron. **29**(6), 4814–4825 (2024)
9. Hwang, B., Jeon, D.: A method to accurately estimate the muscular torques of human wearing exoskeletons by torque sensors. Sensors **15**(4), 8337–8357 (2015)
10. Venture, G., Ayusawa, K., Nakamura, Y.: Real-time identification and visualization of human segment parameters. In: International Conference of the IEEE Engineering in Medicine & Biology Society, pp. 3983–3986
11. Maita, D., Venture, G.J.C.p.A.I.C.o.t.I.E.i.M., Medicine, B.S.I.E.i.: B.S. Conference, Influence of the model's degree of freedom on human body dynamics identification. pp. 4609–4612 (2013)
12. Sandbakk, Ø., Dembia, C.L., Silder, A., Uchida, T.K., Hicks, J.L., Delp, S.L.: Simulating ideal assistive devices to reduce the metabolic cost of walking with heavy loads. PLoS One **12**(7), (2017)
13. Rajagopal, A., Dembia, C.L., DeMers, M.S., Delp, D.D., Hicks, J.L., Delp, S.L.: Full-body musculoskeletal model for muscle-driven simulation of human gait. IEEE Trans. Biomed. Eng. **63**(10), 2068–2079 (2016)
14. Wang, W., et al.: Toward patients' motion intention recognition: dynamics modeling and identification of iLeg—An LLRR under motion constraints. IEEE Trans. Syst. Man Cyber. Syst. **46**(7), 980–992 (2016)

Integrated Analysis of Cortico-Muscular Coupling and Muscle Synergy for Functional Assessment in Exoskeleton-Assisted Stroke Rehabilitation

Siyu Feng, Qi Kuang, Ruikai Cao, Zhuoqun Wang, and Yixuan Sheng(✉)

Harbin Institute of Technology, Shenzhen 518055, Guangdong, China
shengyixuan@hit.edu.cn

Abstract. Quantitative assessment of motor function is critical for guiding rehabilitation in stroke patients. This study presents a framework that integrates cortico-muscular coupling (CMC) and muscle synergy analysis to evaluate and predict motor impairment levels during a standardized exoskeleton-assisted knee flexion-extension task. Muscle synergies were extracted from surface EMG signals and further characterized by cosine similarity and scalar descriptors. CMC was estimated using frequency domain time evolution (FDTE), distinguishing afferent and efferent cortical-muscular pathways. Group-level FDTE analysis revealed that patients exhibited elevated bidirectional CMC compared to healthy controls, suggesting higher cortical afferent demands and enhanced feedback information caused by compensatory mechanisms in stroke patients. By integrating these features, a support vector regression (SVR) model was trained to predict individual FMA scores, achieving high accuracy ($R2 = 0.9589$, $MSE = 1.91$). These results highlight the utility of combining neural coupling and synergy structure analysis during robotic-assisted movement to support objective, data-driven functional assessment in stroke rehabilitation.

Keywords: Cortico-muscular coupling · Muscle synergy · Exoskeleton-Assisted Rehabilitation · Motor function assessment

1 Introduction

Stroke is an acute cerebrovascular disorder, encompassing intracerebral hemorrhage caused by the sudden rupture of blood vessels and cerebral infarction due to vascular occlusion and insufficient cerebral blood flow. It is the second leading cause of death globally [1]. Stroke frequently results in damage to central nervous system regions such as the cerebral cortex, subcortical structures, or brainstem [2], leading to varying degrees of motor control impairment or even complete loss of voluntary movement [3]. This motor dysfunction severely compromises patients' quality of life and their ability to participate in social activities. In recent years, increasing attention has been directed toward cortico-muscular functional reorganization [4]. It aims to restore motor function by reconstructing the information transmission pathways between the brain and muscle through rehabilitation training and neuromodulation strategies. Among emerging technologies, robotic exoskeleton-assisted training has been widely applied in post-stroke lower limb rehabilitation. This method has shown great potential by enabling repetitive, controlled, and goal-directed lower-limb movements, thus facilitating precision rehabilitation for post-stroke recovery [5, 6]. Despite these advances, most exoskeleton systems primarily emphasize kinematic and mechanical parameters [7, 8], while overlooking the relationship between the brain and muscle.

Cortico-muscular coupling (CMC) analysis and other brain–muscle interaction metrics help describe the dynamic regulatory relationships between cortical regions and muscle activity. Recent studies have reported significant abnormalities in CMC among stroke survivors, such as different coupling strength [9], growing time delay [10] and disrupted directional information flow [11], which are closely associated with motor dysfunction. Besides, muscle synergy analysis enables the characterization of altered intermuscular coordination patterns [12]. After stroke, damage to the central nervous system (CNS) often leads to a reorganization of motor unit recruitment and coordination strategies, resulting in significant alterations in muscle synergy patterns. Studies have shown that stroke survivors typically exhibit a changing number of synergies and different activation patterns [13, 14].

For rehabilitation scenarios with exoskeleton assistance, Wang et al. [15] found that an ENMS-assisted training program could modulate the interaction between the cortex and muscles, and enhanced the ascending pathway to the TA muscle. And zhu et al. [16] reported that exoskeleton-assisted walking altered the synergy patterns in stroke participants, leading to a shift in activation profiles toward the normal patterns observed in healthy individuals. Despite the growing interest in neurophysiological mechanisms underlying rehabilitation, current research on lower limb motor recovery during exoskeleton-assisted therapy remains limited. In particular, studies focusing on CMC and muscle synergy in such contexts are scarce. Existing approaches often examine these two aspects in isolation, lacking an integrated framework that captures the interactions between the brain and muscle. This gap restricts the interpretability and comprehensiveness of neural rehabilitation analyses. Furthermore, few studies have explored how these neurophysiological features relate to clinically relevant motor function scores limiting their practical application in patient evaluation.

To address these issues, this study focuses on exoskeleton-assisted lower limb movements in both healthy controls and stroke patients, integrating muscle synergy analysis with bidirectional CMC derived from temporal spectral evolution (TSE) [17]. By correlating these multimodal features with clinical FMA scores, the study aims to uncover mechanisms of neural plasticity and propose a robust, interpretable assessment model for motor function evaluation.

2 Materials and Methods

2.1 Subjects

Twelve stroke patients (P1-P12; Age: 56.45 ± 17.48; 4 females and 8 males) and six healthy controls (H1-H6; habitually right-handed) participated in this experiment. The stroke patients who participated in this experiment were recruited from the Second Affiliated Hospital of Harbin Medical University (Harbin, China). The inclusion criteria was age between 40 and 79 years. All subjects signed an informed consent according to the Declaration of Helsinki, and all measurements were approved by the Medical Ethics Committee of the Second Affiliated Hospital of Harbin Medical University, with the approval number KY2022-173.

2.2 Experimental Paradigm

Prior to the experiment, participants were instructed to lie supine on a treatment bed. The affected lower limb was secured within the CHWishay Prewalk Horizontal lower limb exoskeleton sports rehabilitation training robot [18] as shown in Fig. 1. In addition to assisting patients in training and rehabilitation, the exoskeleton also limits the subject to a single degree of freedom when performing movements, allowing them to complete movements more accurately.

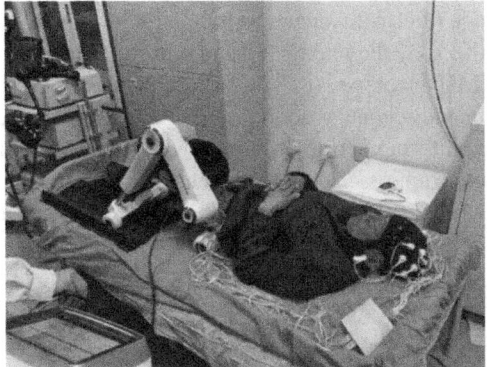

Fig. 1. Schematic diagram of experimental paradigm

Participants were fitted with a 16-channel EEG cap for cortical activity recording. Surface EMG electrodes were placed on six lower-limb muscles: rectus femoris (RF), vastus medialis (VM), biceps femoris long head (BF), semitendinosus (Semi), proximal rectus femoris (RFP), gluteus maximus (GM). And a reference electrode for EMG was placed at the Achilles tendon of the ankle. The signal acquisition equipment used was a custom-developed device designed for simultaneous EEG and EMG recording [19], with a sampling frequency set to 1000 Hz.

The experimenter simultaneously initiated the training system, EEG/EMG acquisition, and video recording. Each experimental session consisted of three trials. In each trial, participants underwent a knee flexion-extension in supine position under exoskeleton guidance for 3 min, followed by a 3-min rest period. Additionally, clinical assessments including Brunnstrom staging, FMA of the lower extremity, and ADL scores were recorded to characterize motor function and daily ability levels.

2.3 Data Preprocessing

EEG signals were first band-pass filtered between 1–45 Hz to remove slow drifts and high-frequency noise. Independent component analysis (ICA) was then applied to eliminate common artifacts such as eye blinks and muscle activity. Finally, the cleaned EEG data were normalized across channels to ensure consistency in amplitude ranges. EMG signals were processed by applying a 20–450 Hz band-pass filter to isolate physiological muscle activity while removing motion artifacts and baseline noise. The filtered signals were then full-wave rectified and smoothed to extract the envelope of muscle activation. Subsequently, the data were segmented into epochs based on each movement cycle (knee flexion and extension).

2.4 Muscle Synergy Extraction

For each muscle channel, the filtered sEMG signal was then full-wave rectified and passed through a fourth-order low-pass Butterworth filter at 5 Hz to obtain a smoothed EMG envelope. To further suppress noise and fluctuations, the envelope was smoothed using a moving average filter with a window length of 500 samples. The resulting envelope was then normalized by the maximal value during maximal voluntary contraction, yielding the scaled EMG envelope x(t). The process of muscle excitation could be modeled as a critically damped second-order linear differential system, effectively capturing the low-pass dynamic filtering nature of muscle force generation in response to neural input [20]. This modeling approach transforms the raw EMG signals into physiologically meaningful muscle activation profiles that can be used for further analysis.

Muscle synergy extraction aims to identify low-dimensional control strategies used by the central nervous system to coordinate complex muscle activities. In this study, the muscle activation was decomposed into a set of muscle synergies using Nonnegative Matrix Factorization (NMF) [21]. Besides, the number of synergies r was determined based on the variance accounted for (VAF) criterion, typically ensuring that the reconstructed signal captures more than 80% of the total variance [22].

2.5 Fourier-Domain Transfer Symbolic Entropy Analysis

Transfer entropy (TE) is an information-theoretic measure proposed by Schreiber [23] to quantify the directional information flow between two time series. Let X and Y be two discrete time series. The transfer entropy $TE_{X \to Y}$ quantifies the predictive gain of X for the future of Y, conditioned on Y's past. It is defined as:

$$TE_{X \to Y} = \sum p\left(y_t, y_{t-1}^{(l)}, x_{t-1}^{(l)}\right) \log \left(\frac{p(y_t | y_{t-1}^{(l)}, x_{t-1}^{(l)})}{p(y_t | y_{t-1}^{(l)})} \right) \quad (1)$$

where, $x_{t-1}^{(l)}$ and $y_{t-1}^{(l)}$ denote the historical embeddings of X and Y, respectively. The conventional TE method requires accurate estimation of high-dimensional joint probabilities. However, in practical applications—especially with nonstationary and noise-prone electrophysiological signals such as EEG and EMG—direct estimation of transfer entropy is often unstable and computationally expensive. In order to explore the directional coupling relationship between neural signals in the frequency domain, we adopt the method of Fourier-domain Transfer Symbolic Entropy (FDTE). This method is inspired by TSE [17].

Given two neural signals, each signal was first divided into non-overlapping time windows of length L according to the action, and each window was converted into a symbolic sequence using a quantile-based binning approach. Specifically, the amplitude of each segment $X = [x_1, x_2, ..., x_T]$ or $Y = [y_1, y_2, ..., y_T]$ was mapped to a finite symbolic alphabet based on the quantiles $\{q_1, q_2, ..., q_{k-1}\}$, where k is the symbol set size.

$$s_i^X = \begin{cases} 1, & x_i < q_1 \\ 2, & q_1 \leq x_i < q_2 \\ \vdots \\ k, & x_i \geq q_{k-1} \end{cases} \quad (2)$$

where the symbolic sequence $s^X \in A^L$ and $A = \{1, 2, ..., k\}$ is the symbol alphabet. The symbolization could be defined as a function:

$$S : R^L \to A^L, S(x) = s^X \quad (3)$$

The same process was applied to y to yield s^Y. This transformation preserves the local nonlinear dynamic structure of the signal while reducing sensitivity to amplitude variability and noise, enabling robust symbolic modeling in subsequent frequency-domain analysis.

After symbolization, Fast Fourier Transform (FFT) was performed on each symbolic sequence to extract its frequency components. Since symbolic sequences were already discrete, the resulting Fourier coefficients emphasized the oscillatory pattern of symbolic transitions rather than raw amplitudes. $s^X(t)$ and $s^Y(t)$ denoted the symbolic representations of X and Y over time, and their corresponding Fourier spectra were computed as $S^X(f)$ and $S^Y(f)$. Then this method extracted the amplitude spectrum and performed a second symbolic transformation in the frequency domain. That is, the amplitudes across all epochs at each frequency point f were binned into k_f levels to form frequency-domain symbolic sequences $\tilde{s}^X(f)$ and $\tilde{s}^Y(f)$.

Finally, the conditional probabilities of the symbolic transitions across frequencies were estimated. For each frequency bin f, this method computed the joint and conditional probability of a symbol $\tilde{s}^X(f)$ occurring in signal Y given its own previous symbol $\tilde{s}^Y(f)$ and the previous symbol of signal X, $\tilde{s}^X(f)$. Specifically, the FDTE from X to Y at frequency f is defined as:

$$FDTE_{X \to Y}(f) = \sum_{\tilde{s}_f^Y, \tilde{s}_{f-1}^Y, \tilde{s}_{f-1}^X} p(\tilde{s}_f^Y, \tilde{s}_{f-1}^Y, \tilde{s}_{f-1}^X) \log(\frac{p(\tilde{s}_f^Y | \tilde{s}_{f-1}^Y, \tilde{s}_{f-1}^X)}{p(\tilde{s}_f^Y | \tilde{s}_{f-1}^Y)}) \quad (4)$$

where $p(\cdot)$ is the empirical probability estimated from the symbolic sequences across all epochs. This formulation reflects the directional spectral coupling from X to Y, and by computing it across all frequencies, we obtain a frequency-resolved profile of directed connectivity.

2.6 Support Vector Regression Assessment Model

A support vector regression (SVR) model was developed to predict FMA scores of stroke patients based on multi-source electrophysiological features. The input features consisted of 12 subjects and were organized into a feature matrix of size 12×12, where each row represented one patient and each column represented a specific extracted feature. The feature set included twelve averaged FDTE metrics, as well as muscle synergy features comprising cosine similarity to healthy controls' synergy weights and statistical descriptors (RMS, mean, and maximum) of the synergy activation matrix H. To reduce redundancy and potential overfitting due to the high dimensionality, the feature matrix was standardized and principal component analysis (PCA) [24] was applied. The number of retained components was determined such that the cumulative explained variance exceeded 80%, resulting in a lower-dimensional representation while preserving essential information. Model performance was evaluated using mean squared error (MSE) and the coefficient of determination (R^2).

3 Results

3.1 Comparison of Muscle Synergy Between Stroke and Healthy

The paradigm of this study was the supine knee flexion and extension isokinetic exercise, which is a simple single-degree-of-freedom cyclical reciprocating motion and performed only around a single knee joint. According to method 2.4, the VAF changes of the stroke patient group and the healthy control group were calculated as shown in Fig. 2. The red dashed line in the figure indicated that the VAF is 0.80. Therefore, based on the VAF results and the nature of the movement, the number of synergies selected for subsequent research was 2.

Figure 3 illustrates the average muscle synergy for two synergies. For synergy 1, stroke patients show relatively higher weights in posterior muscles, especially Semi and GM, indicating increased reliance on the hamstring and calf muscles. In contrast, healthy controls exhibit a more balanced distribution, with BF, Semi, and GM all moderately contributing, suggesting a more coordinated posterior chain involvement. For synergy 2, stroke patients demonstrate a dominant activation of RF and VM, representing a synergy largely centered on the quadriceps group, reflecting compensatory overuse during knee extension. Healthy controls show a broader distribution with notably strong contributions from RF, BF, and RFP, indicating more diversified muscle coordination strategies during the same motor task. In addition, the activation curves in the patient group were larger and more dispersed between groups.

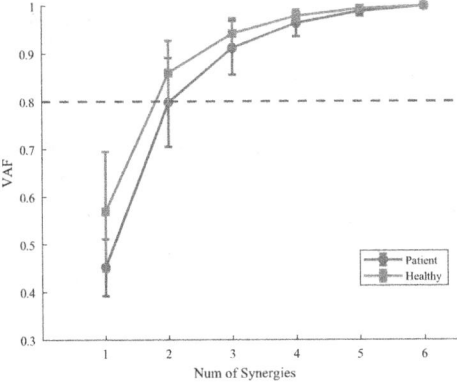

Fig. 2. VAF curves of stroke patients and healthy controls under different number of muscle synergies

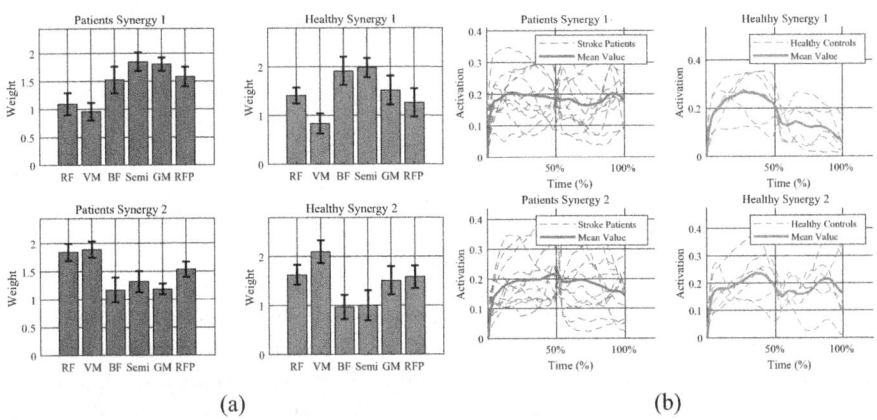

Fig. 3. Muscle synergy of stroke patients and healthy controls. (a) Muscle synergy weight matrix W. (b) Muscle synergy activation matrix H

3.2 Difference of FDTE Between Stroke Patients and Healthy Controls

To investigate cortico-muscular interaction differences between stroke patients and healthy individuals, the frequency-domain transfer entropy (FDTE) was computed between EEG signals from C3/C4 and EMG signals from two representative lower-limb muscles GM and Semi. GM and Semi were selected due to their pivotal roles in hip stabilization and knee flexion/extension during lower-limb movement. The EEG channels C3 and C4 were chosen as they correspond to the primary motor cortex responsible for contralateral leg control [25]. These regions are critically involved in voluntary motor control of the contralateral limbs, and are often affected in unilateral stroke. Besides, FDTE was computed bidirectionally to quantify the asymmetry in cortico-muscular communication. The efferent pathway refers to information flow from EEG (C3/C4) to EMG (GM/Semi), reflecting cortical command sent to peripheral effectors. The afferent pathway refers to flow from EMG to EEG, capturing peripheral feedback modulating cortical activity.

First, the differences between stroke patients and healthy subjects were compared from the perspective of frequency domain, as shown in Fig. 4. The results show that on the afferent pathway (right), stroke patients are slightly higher than healthy people. On the efferent pathway (left), the FDTE of stroke patients was significantly higher than that of healthy subjects.

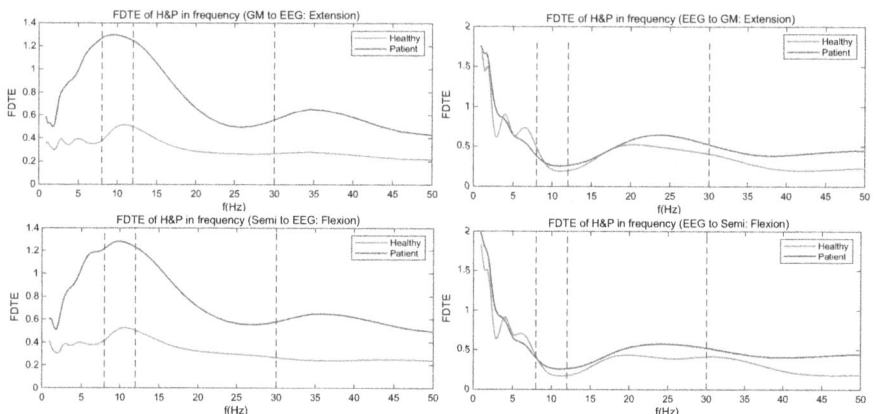

Fig. 4. Comparison of FDTE in frequency band between stroke patients and healthy controls in afferent pathway and efferent pathway

In order to obtain effective quantitative indicators, alpha, beta and gamma were calculated directional FDTE for each subject across three canonical frequency bands. As shown in Fig. 5, stroke patients exhibited significantly higher FDTE values than healthy controls in the efferent direction across alpha and beta bands ($p < 0.01$) and in the gamma band ($p < 0.05$). This suggests a greater reliance on cortical input even under assisted movement conditions, possibly due to impaired subcortical or spinal motor circuits. The presence of exoskeleton assistance may facilitate consistent kinematics, allowing clearer observation of neurophysiological deficits. And in the afferent direction, stroke patients also demonstrated elevated FDTE values in the beta and gamma bands compared to healthy controls ($p < 0.05$). This indicates altered afferent feedback or compensatory sensorimotor integration mechanisms in stroke patients. During the extension phase, a similar pattern was observed. FDTE values from efferent pathway remained significantly higher in stroke patients, particularly in the alpha and beta bands ($p < 0.01$, $p < 0.05$). For the afferent direction, stroke patients again showed significantly higher FDTE in the gamma band ($p < 0.05$).

These results reinforce the idea that stroke patients recruit additional cortical resources even when mechanical support is provided, possibly reflecting compensatory motor strategies or reduced automaticity. Interestingly, even with passive assistance, stroke patients showed exaggerated cortico-muscular information flow, highlighting persistent dysfunction in neural communication pathways. The enhanced FDTE in both top-down and bottom-up directions suggests that exoskeleton-assisted movements do not suppress pathological coupling, but may in fact make such patterns more detectable by reducing movement variability.

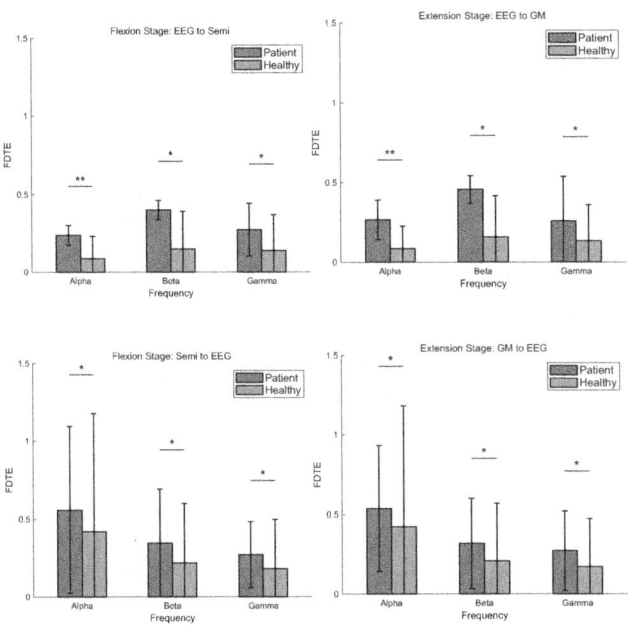

Fig. 5. Comparison of FDTE frequency band between stroke group and healthy group. The sign * denotes p < 0.05, and sign ** denotes p < 0.01.

3.3 SVR Assessment Model

Based on method 2.6, The SVR model was trained to estimate the FMA lower-limb scores as a continuous outcome. As shown in Fig. 6, The regression performance achieved a high coefficient of determination ($R^2 = 0.9589$) and a low mean squared error (MSE = 1.91), indicating excellent agreement between predicted and actual scores. In the scatter plot of predicted versus actual values, data points closely followed the diagonal line, further demonstrating the model's strong predictive capability. The results demonstrated that the inclusion of both cortical–muscular coupling features and muscle synergy information provided meaningful predictive power for functional outcome estimation, indicating the potential of combining upstream neural and downstream muscular representations for stroke rehabilitation assessment.

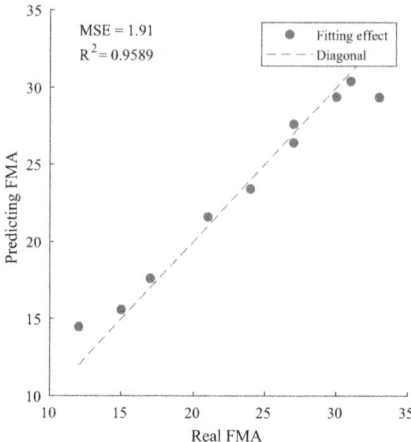

Fig. 6. The performance of motor function assessment model. The diagonal represents the location where predicted FMA is equal to the observed value.

4 Conclusion

This study presents a multimodal analytical approach that integrates cortico-muscular coherence patterns and muscle synergy structure to evaluate and predict motor function in stroke patients. By capturing both central and peripheral neuromuscular mechanisms, the extracted features provide complementary insights into motor impairment. The high predictive accuracy of the SVR model demonstrates that synergistic analysis of brain-muscle dynamics offers a robust basis for functional assessment. This study may contribute to the development of objective biomarkers for monitoring recovery progress and guiding personalized rehabilitation strategies.

Acknowledgments. This work was supported by the National Key Research and Development Program of China (Grant Number: 2022YFC3601700), the National Natural Science Foundation of China (Grant Number: 62403170), and Shenzhen Science and Technology Program (Grant Number: JCYJ20240813105129039).

References

1. Feigin, V.L., Stark, B.A., Johnson, C.O., et al.: Global, regional, and national burden of stroke and its risk factors, 1990–2019: a systematic analysis for the global burden of disease study 2019. Lancet Neurol. **20**(10), 795–820 (2021)
2. Lyu, J., Xie, D., Bhatia, T.N., et al.: Microglial/Macrophage polarization and function in brain injury and repair after stroke. CNS Neurosci. Ther. **27**(5), 515–527 (2021)
3. Tater, P., Pandey, S.: Post-stroke movement disorders: clinical spectrum, pathogenesis, and management. Neurol. India **69**(2), 272–283 (2021)
4. Liu, J., Wang, J., Tan, G., et al.: A generalized cortico-muscular-cortical network to evaluate the effects of three-week brain stimulation. IEEE Trans. Biomed. Eng. **71**(1), 195–206 (2023)

5. Louie, D.R., Mortenson, W.B., Lui, M., et al.: Patients' and therapists' experience and perception of exoskeleton-based physiotherapy during subacute stroke rehabilitation: a qualitative analysis. Disabil. Rehabil. **44**(24), 7390–7398 (2022)
6. Hsu, T.H., Tsai, C.L., Chi, J.Y., et al.: Effect of wearable exoskeleton on post-stroke gait: a systematic review and meta-analysis. Ann. Phys. Rehabil. Med. **66**(1), 101674 (2023)
7. Zou, C., Zeng, C., Huang, R., et al.: Online gait learning with assist-as-needed control strategy for post-stroke rehabilitation exoskeletons. Robotica **42**(2), 319–331 (2024)
8. Grimm, F., Kraugmann, J., Naros, G., et al.: Clinical validation of kinematic assessments of post-stroke upper limb movements with a multi-joint arm exoskeleton. J. Neuroeng. Rehabil. **18**(1), 92 (2021)
9. Chang, H., Xin, R., Sheng, Y., et al.: Post-stroke corticomuscular coupling assessment based on bilateral cerebral hemisphere difference. IEEE Trans. Neural Syst. Rehabil. Eng. (2025, in press)
10. Wang, T., Xia, M., Wang, J., et al.: Delay estimation for cortical-muscular interaction with wavelet coherence time lag. J. Neurosci. Methods **405**, 110098 (2024)
11. Wang, T., Tang, J., Xi, X., et al.: Corticomuscular coupling analysis in stroke rehabilitation based on variational mode decomposition-transfer entropy. IEEE Trans. Neural Syst. Rehabil. Eng. (2024)
12. Cheung, V.C.K., Seki, K.: Approaches to revealing the neural basis of muscle synergies: a review and a critique. J. Neurophysiol. **125**(5), 1580–1597 (2021)
13. Qing, W., Song, H., Lin, L., et al.: Reorganization of undirected and directed cortico-muscular connectivity after exoneuromusculoskeleton-assisted telerehabilitation. In: 2024 17th Int. Convention on Rehabilitation Engineering and Assistive Technology (i-CREATe), pp. 1–5. IEEE (2024)
14. Park, J.H., Shin, J.H., Lee, H., et al.: Alterations in intermuscular coordination underlying isokinetic exercise after a stroke and their implications on neurorehabilitation. J. Neuroeng. Rehabil. **18**, 1–17 (2021)
15. Wang, R., An, Q., Yang, N., et al.: Clarify sit-to-stand muscle synergy and tension changes in subacute stroke rehabilitation by musculoskeletal modeling. Front. Syst. Neurosci. **16**, 785143 (2022)
16. Zhu, F., Kern, M., Fowkes, E., et al.: Effects of an exoskeleton-assisted gait training on post-stroke lower-limb muscle coordination. J. Neural Eng. **18**(4), 046039 (2021)
17. Chen, X., Zhang, Y., Cheng, S., et al.: Transfer spectral entropy and application to functional corticomuscular coupling. IEEE Trans. Neural Syst. Rehabil. Eng. **27**(5), 1092–1102 (2019)
18. Wishay Lower Limb Exoskeleton. http://www.chwishay.com/productinfo/2350.html. Last accessed 06 Dec 2025
19. Chang, H., Cao, R., Pan, X., Sheng, Y., Wang, Z., Liu, H.: A wearable multi-channel EEG/EMG sensor system for corticomuscular coupling analysis. IEEE Sens. J. **23**(10), 11220–11230 (2023)
20. Sheng, Y., Wang, J., Tan, G., et al.: Muscle synergy plasticity in motor function recovery after stroke. IEEE Trans. Neural Syst. Rehabil. Eng. (2024)
21. Lee, D., Seung, H.S.: Algorithms for non-negative matrix factorization. Adv. Neural. Inf. Process. Syst. **13**, 556–562 (2000)
22. Turpin, N.A., Uriac, S., Dalleau, G.: How to improve the muscle synergy analysis methodology? Eur. J. Appl. Physiol. **121**(4), 1009–1025 (2021)
23. Vicente, R., Wibral, M., Lindner, M., et al.: Transfer entropy—a model-free measure of effective connectivity for the neurosciences. J. Comput. Neurosci. **30**(1), 45–67 (2011)
24. Maćkiewicz, A., Ratajczak, W.: Principal components analysis (PCA). Comput. Geosci. **19**(3), 303–342 (1993)
25. DaSilva, A.F., Volz, M.S., Bikson, M., et al.: Electrode positioning and montage in transcranial direct current stimulation. J. Vis. Exp. **51**, 2744 (2011)

Multidimensional Kinematic Analysis of Walking and Turning in Older Adults Using IMUs

Luobin Zhang[1], Yongjie Weng[1], Peng Chen[1], Wei Wei[1], Mingyu Du[1,2], and Shibo Cai[1,2(✉)]

[1] The College of Mechanical Engineering, Zhejiang University of Technology, Hangzhou 310023, China
ccc@zjut.Edu.Cn
[2] The Key Laboratory of Special Purpose Equipment and Advanced Processing Technology, Ministry of Education, Zhejiang University of Technology, Hangzhou 310023, China

Abstract. The decline in walking and postural transition functions in older adults is a critical factor contributing to increased fall risk and reduced independence. This study proposed and validated an assessment method based on a 'Multi-dimensional Kinematic Profile.' This method utilizes radar plots to intuitively present an individual's function across multiple dimensions, including motor efficiency, speed, smoothness, and symmetry, enabling a systematic and individualized quantification of functional deficits in older adults. Healthy older adults (n = 10, 70.3 ± 1.8 years) and healthy young adults (n = 10, 24.4 ± 1.4 years) were recruited for this study. Participants wore inertial measurement units (IMUs) on their lower back and feet while performing a task involving 3-m straight-line walking and a 180-degree turn. This study analyzed Kinematic data of the center of mass (CoM) and correlated with the clinical gold standard, the Timed Up and Go (TUG) test. Compared to the young group, the older group exhibited a significant decline in functional ability during the turning phase. This decline was evidenced by longer turning duration, slower means turning angular velocity, poorer movement smoothness, and lower symmetry. These parameters, which showed significant inter-group differences during turning and were highly correlated with TUG scores, were identified as core kinematic indicators for assessing postural transition ability in older adults. This assessment framework provides a crucial biomechanical basis and evaluation benchmark for designing and optimizing personalized assistive strategies for wearable exoskeletons, holding significant clinical application value.

Keywords: Gait Function · Inertial Measurement Unit · Kinematic Analysis · Postural Transition

1 Introduction

The global population is aging rapidly, and the decline in motor function among older adults has a significant impact on their quality of daily life [1]. Walking is a fundamental and crucial daily activity essential for older adults to maintain independence and effectively prevent falls [2]. With advancing age, older adults often experience issues such as reduced walking speed, decreased movement stability, increased gait variability, and a diminished ability to adapt to environmental changes [3, 4].

Compared to relatively simple, steady-state straight-line walking, postural transition tasks such as turning place higher demands on the body's dynamic balance, lower limb power output, and inter-limb coordination. Due to the natural decline in physiological functions, older adults often exhibit unstable posture [5], longer completion times, and a higher risk of falls when performing turning tasks [6, 7]. Therefore, a detailed analysis of the kinematic performance of older adults during walking tasks that include turns is particularly important for comprehensively understanding their gait function.

Currently, standard clinical methods for assessing gait function, such as the Timed Up and Go (TUG) test, are easy to administer but yield relatively macroscopic results, making it challenging to capture the nuances of movement quality [8]. In contrast, optical motion capture systems are often prohibitively expensive and complex, limiting their widespread application [9, 10]. In recent years, technology based on wearable inertial measurement units (IMUs) has provided a viable solution for motion analysis in real-world environments due to its portability, low cost, and rich data [10, 11]. However, existing research has primarily focused on comparing spatiotemporal gait parameters, and there is a lack of a comprehensive framework that integrates multidimensional information to systematically evaluate the motor function of older adults during postural transitions. A systematic assessment framework is essential for guiding rehabilitation interventions, particularly in the development of emerging assistive technologies such as wearable exoskeletons. The effectiveness of exoskeletons heavily depends on their ability to provide personalized assistance tailored to the user's specific functional deficits [12]. Relying solely on single indicators, such as walking speed, cannot provide sufficient information for exoskeleton control strategies.

Therefore, this study aimed to identify core kinematic indicators that sensitively reflect functional decline in older adults using wearable IMU technology. Building on this foundation, a systematic and multi-dimensional kinematic assessment framework is established. This framework is designed to quantify and analyze an individual's specific functional deficits during walking and turning tasks through an intuitive 'Multi-dimensional Kinematic Profile.' The goal is to provide robust biomechanical data support and establish an evaluation benchmark for clinical diagnosis, the development of personalized rehabilitation programs, and particularly for the design of intelligent, personalized assistive strategies for wearable exoskeletons.

2 Materials and Methods

2.1 Experimental Equipment

This study used three wearable IMU (HWT901C-TTL, Wit Motion, Shenzhen, China) for data acquisition. Each IMU sensor comprised a tri-axial accelerometer, a tri-axial gyroscope, and a tri-axial magnetometer. We set the measurement range of the accelerometer to ± 16 g and the gyroscope to ± 2000°/s and uniformly set the data sampling frequency for all IMUs uniformly at 100 Hz. The collected data was transmitted in real-time via a Bluetooth Low Energy module to a computer for storage and analysis. Before each experiment, this study performed static horizontal plane calibration and magnetic field calibration for all IMU sensors to minimize sensor-specific systematic errors.

2.2 Experimental Procedure

2.2.1 Participants

This study recruited a total of 20 healthy participants for this study, divided into two groups: an older group and a younger group, each consisting of 10 individuals. The older group consisted of 10 healthy older adults (5 males, 5 females; mean age, 70.3 ± 1.8 years; height, 159.4 ± 7.7 cm; weight, 61.8 ± 14.0 kg). The younger group consisted of 10 healthy young volunteers (7 males, 3 females; mean age: 24.4 ± 1.4 years; height: 169.7 ± 10.4 cm; weight: 62.9 ± 14.4 kg).

This study strictly adhered to the ethical principles of the Declaration of Helsinki. Before the experiment commenced, the researchers provided each participant with a detailed explanation of the study's purpose, procedures, potential risks, and benefits. They obtained written informed consent voluntarily signed by each participant.

2.2.2 IMU Placement and Experimental Protocol

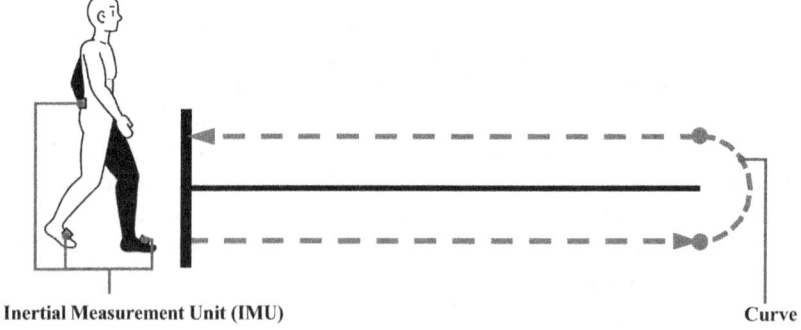

Fig. 1. Experimental setup. IMUs were fixed on the dorsum of both feet and the posterior sacrum.

Participants wore comfortable daily clothing and flat walking shoes with good anti-slip properties to simulate their natural walking state in daily life. We fixed three IMU sensors using specialized elastic straps and Velcro at the following anatomical locations: (1) Left foot instep, approximately at the distal end of the first metatarsal head, ensuring the sensor's long axis was roughly parallel to the foot's long axis. (2) Right foot instep, positioned symmetrically to the left foot. (3) Posterior sacrum, approximately at the midpoint of the line connecting the spinous processes of the fifth lumbar vertebra (L5) and the first sacral vertebra (S1).

All participants performed a standardized '3-m straight-line and turn walking test' in an indoor corridor at least 5 m long and 1.5 m wide, with a flat, dry, unobstructed surface and adequate lighting. This study marked the starting line and the 3-m turn-around point with conspicuous colors. Figure 1 illustrates the IMU sensor placement and the experimental task.

2.3 Data Processing

2.3.1 Signal Preprocessing and Gait Event Identification

This study first processed the raw tri-axial acceleration and angular velocity signals from the IMUs. It applied a fourth-order Butterworth low-pass filter with a cutoff frequency of 15 Hz to the raw signals to eliminate high-frequency noise while preserving the frequency components related to human motion. The sensor's onboard algorithm, which fuses data from the accelerometer, gyroscope, and magnetometer, provided orientation estimates to mitigate integration drift. This study automatically identified gait events, including heel strike (HS) and toe-off (TO), using a validated algorithm based on detecting peaks and zero-crossings in the foot-mounted IMUs' sagittal plane angular velocity signals [13]. A gait cycle was defined as the interval between two consecutive HS events of the same foot. The turning phase was defined as the period from the HS of the foot initiating the turn to the first HS of the contralateral foot after the body's yaw angle changed by 180 degrees.

2.3.2 Center of Mass Kinematic Parameter Calculation

This study used the motion data from the IMU placed on the posterior sacrum to characterize the movement of the human CoM. Due to the significant cumulative error associated with directly calculating displacement by double integrating acceleration signals, this study focused on dynamic characteristic parameters of CoM motion. These parameters have lower requirements for absolute positional accuracy, and drift effects can be minimized through appropriate processing methods. This study extracted and analyzed the following eight core kinematic feature indicators:

1. **Mean CoM trajectory length during swing phase (L, m):** For each swing phase within a gait cycle and for the entire turning phase (from the HS initiating the turn to the first HS after completing the turn), we calculated the CoM trajectory length by integrating the instantaneous speed of the CoM in three-dimensional space, as measured by the sacral IMU.

$$L = \int_0^T \|v(t)dt\| \tag{1}$$

where $v(t)$ is the instantaneous speed of the CoM at time t, and T is the total duration of a single swing phase.

2. **Mean CoM velocity during swing phase (v_{avg}, m/s)**: Within a single swing phase, the CoM trajectory length L divided by the total duration T of that phase.

$$v_{avg} = \frac{L_t}{T} \tag{2}$$

3. **Mean CoM displacement area during swing phase (A_{cnv}, m^2)**: Within a single swing phase, we projected the CoM trajectory onto the horizontal plane and calculated the area of the polygon enclosed by this trajectory. This parameter reflects the range of CoM activity in the horizontal plane.

$$A_{cnv} = \sum_{i=1}^{N} \frac{1}{2}|z_i| + |z_{i+1}|\sqrt{(y_i - y_{i+1})^2 + (x_i - x_{i+1})^2} \tag{3}$$

where (x_i, y_i, z_i) are the coordinates of the CoM at the current time step, and $(x_{i+1}, y_{i+1}, z_{i+1})$ are the coordinates at the next time step.

4. **Mean CoM swing amplitude (A_{avg}, m)**: Within a single swing phase, this is the mean Euclidean distance of each sampled point on the CoM trajectory to the geometric center of that trajectory.

$$A_{avg} = \frac{1}{N} \sum_{i=1}^{N} \sqrt{(r_{x,i} - C_{cen,x})^2 + (r_{y,i} - C_{cen,y})^2 + (r_{z,i} - C_{cen,z})^2} \tag{4}$$

where $(r_{x,i}, r_{y,i}, r_{z,i})$ is the CoM position of the i-th data sample, N is the number of sample points, and $C_{cen,x}$, $C_{cen,y}$, $C_{cen,z}$ represent the x, y, and z coordinates of the geometric center of the CoM swing trajectory, respectively.

5. **CoM swing symmetry (CR)**: We assessed gait symmetry by comparing the CoM trajectory lengths during swing phases supported by the left and right foot.

$$CR = \frac{|L_{lc} - L_{rc}|}{(L_{lc} + L_{rc})/2} \tag{5}$$

where L_{lc} and L_{rc} represent the CoM trajectory length during swing when walking on the left foot and right foot, respectively.

6. **CoM Jerk ($RMS\ Jerk$, m/s^3)**: We calculated the derivative of the acceleration vector from the sacral IMU in three-dimensional space with respect to time. We then computed its root mean square (RMS) value ($RMS\ Jerk$) over specific analysis periods (swing phase of straight walking, turning phase).

$$RMS\ Jerk = \sqrt{\frac{1}{T} \int_0^T \|j(t)^2 dt\|} \tag{6}$$

where $j(t)$ is the instantaneous jerk magnitude at time t, and T is the total duration of the analysis period.

7. **Turning Duration (T_{turn}, s)**: The time elapsed from the algorithmically identified gait event marking the participant's initiation of the turn (moment the body begins to show significant heading angle change) to the gait event marking the completion of the 180-degree turn and stable entry into the next straight walking segment (first HS of the outer foot after the turn).
8. **Mean Turning Angular Velocity (ω_{turn_avg}, °/s)**: Using the gyroscope data from the sacral IMU, we calculated the mean angular velocity of trunk rotation about the vertical axis during the turning duration.

2.3.3 Clinical Functional Assessment

An experienced rehabilitation therapist conducted the Timed Up and Go (TUG) test for all participants using a standardized procedure. During the test, participants rose from a standard height chair with armrests, walked straight for three meters to a marked line, turned 180 degrees, walked back to the chair, and sat down completely. This study recorded the total time required to complete the entire task. The TUG test is a comprehensive functional indicator widely used in clinical settings to assess overall mobility, dynamic balance ability, and potential fall risk in older adults [14].

3 Results

3.1 Participant Characteristics and TUG Scores

The basic demographic characteristics and TUG test scores of the older and younger group participants are shown in Table 1. As expected, there was a significant difference in age between the two groups ($p < 0.001$). This study observed no statistically significant differences in height ($p = 0.085$) or weight ($p = 0.256$) between the groups.

Table 1. Participant characteristics and TUG test scores. Data are presented as mean ± standard deviation.

Characteristic	Older Group ($n = 10$)	Younger Group ($n = 10$)	P-value
Age (years)	70.3 ± 1.8	24.4 ± 1.4	< 0.001
Height (cm)	159.4 ± 7.7	169.7 ± 10.4	0.085
Weight (kg)	61.8 ± 14.0	62.9 ± 14.4	0.256
TUG Score (s)	11.8 ± 0.8	8.2 ± 0.8	< 0.001

3.2 Kinematic Parameter Comparison: Straight Walking Phase

During the swing phase of straight-line walking, the comparison of CoM kinematic parameters between the older and younger groups is detailed in Table 2. The analysis results indicated that the older group (0.105 ± 0.028 m) had a significantly shorter mean CoM trajectory length during the straight walking swing phase compared to the younger group (0.136 ± 0.019 m). Correspondingly, the mean CoM velocity during swing phase of the older group (0.326 ± 0.082 m/s) was also significantly slower than that of the younger group (0.389 ± 0.045 m/s).

In terms of parameters reflecting the CoM's range of activity in the horizontal plane, the mean CoM displacement area during swing phase of the older group (0.009 ± 0.003 m2) was significantly smaller than that of the younger group (0.012 ± 0.003 m2). Similarly, the mean CoM swing amplitude of the older group (0.027 ± 0.007 m) was also significantly smaller than that of the younger group (0.034 ± 0.005 m). However, during the straight walking phase, the differences between the two groups in CoM swing symmetry (0.231 ± 0.123 vs 0.174 ± 0.102) and mean CoM Jerk during swing phase (0.419 ± 0.070 m/s3 vs 0.394 ± 0.111 m/s3) did not reach statistical significance. Table 2 details the comparison of these parameters, and Fig. 2 visually presents the inter-group differences for some key parameters.

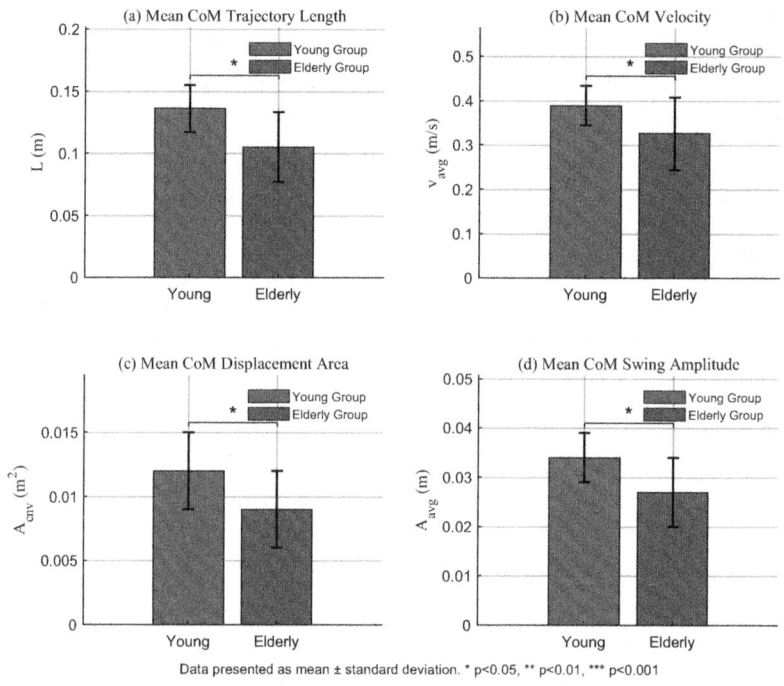

Fig. 2. Comparison of CoM kinematic parameters during swing phase of straight walking between older and younger groups. Shown are (a) mean CoM trajectory length during swing phase, (b) mean CoM velocity during swing phase, (c) mean CoM displacement area during swing phase, and (d) mean CoM swing amplitude.

3.3 Kinematic Parameter Comparison: Turning Phase

During the 180-degree turning phase, the comparison of CoM kinematic parameters between the older and younger groups is shown in Table 2. Unlike the straight walking phase, some parameters during the turning phase exhibited different patterns of inter-group differences. The differences between the older and younger groups in mean CoM trajectory length (1.040 ± 0.144 m vs 1.290 ± 0.388 m, $p = 0.073$), mean CoM velocity (0.407 ± 0.121 m/s vs 0.424 ± 0.052 m/s, $p = 0.055$), and mean CoM displacement area (0.037 ± 0.028 m2 vs 0.040 ± 0.016 m2, $p = 0.768$) during the turning phase were not significant. However, the mean CoM swing amplitude of the older group during turning was significantly larger than that of the younger group (0.249 ± 0.103 m vs 0.161 ± 0.026 m, p = 0.018).

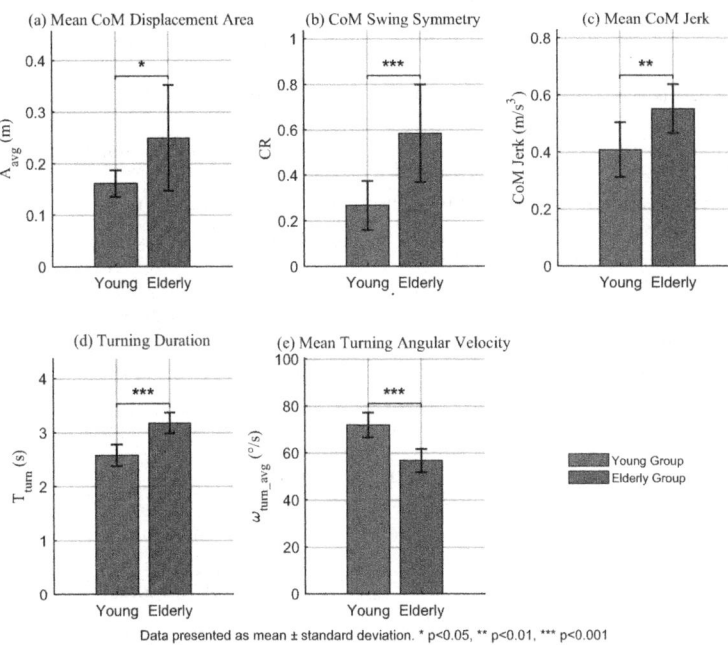

Fig. 3. Comparison of CoM kinematic parameters during turning phase between older and younger groups. Shown are (a) mean CoM swing amplitude, (b) CoM swing symmetry, (c) mean CoM Jerk, (d) turning duration, and (e) mean turning angular velocity.

In terms of motor coordination and smoothness, the CoM swing symmetry of the older group was significantly poorer than that of the younger group, indicated by a higher CR value (0.583 ± 0.215 vs 0.266 ± 0.108, $p < 0.001$), suggesting lower coordination between the two sides of the body during turning. Concurrently, the mean CoM Jerk of the older group was significantly higher than that of the younger group (0.551 ± 0.086 m/s3 vs 0.407 ± 0.097 m/s3, $p = 0.002$), indicating poorer smoothness in their turning movements. Regarding the temporal and velocity characteristics of turning, the turning duration of the older group was significantly longer than that of the younger group (3.174 ± 0.191 s vs 2.576 ± 0.204 s, $p < 0.001$). Notably, the mean turning angular velocity of the older group was significantly lower than that of the younger group (56.725 ± 4.965°/s vs 71.925 ± 5.286°/s, $p < 0.001$). Table 2 also presents the parameter comparisons for the turning phase, and Fig. 3 more clearly displays the differences in key kinematic indicators between the older and younger groups during the turning task.

Table 2. Comparison of CoM kinematic parameters during swing phase of straight walking and turning phase.

Parameter	Task Phase	Older group (n = 10)	95% CI	Younger group (n = 10)	95% CI	P-value	Cohen's d
Mean CoM Trajectory Length (L, m)	Straight phase	0.105 ± 0.028	[0.085, 0.126]	0.136 ± 0.019	[0.122,0.149]	0.012	1.245
	Turning phase	1.040 ± 0.144	[0.938,1.143]	1.290 ± 0.388	[1.012, 1.568]	0.073	-0.852
Mean CoM velocity (v_{avg}, m/s)	Straight phase	0.326 ± 0.082	[0.267, 0.385]	0.389 ± 0.045	[0.356,0.421]	0.048	0.947
	Turning phase	0.407 ± 0.121	[0.320, 0.493]	0.424 ± 0.052	[0.367,0.462]	0.055	-0.179
Mean CoM displacement area (A_{cnv}, m^2)	Straight phase	0.009 ± 0.003	[0.007, 0.012]	0.012 ± 0.003	[0.00.9,0.015]	0.016	1.194
	Turning phase	0.037 ± 0.028	[0.017,0.057]	0.040 ± 0.016	[0.028,0.052]	0.768	0.134
Mean CoM swing amplitude (A_{avg}, m)	Straight phase	0.027 ± 0.007	[0.021, 0.032]	0.034 ± 0.005	[0.031,0.037]	0.019	1.151
	Turning phase	0.249 ± 0.103	[0.175, 0.322]	0.161 ± 0.026	[0.143,0.180]	0.018	-1.166
CoM swing symmetry (CR)	Straight phase	0.231 ± 0.123	[0.143, 0.319]	0.174 ± 0.102	[0.101,0.247]	0.275	-0.504
	Turning phase	0.583 ± 0.215	[0.429, 0.737]	0.266 ± 0.108	[0.189, 0.343]	<0.001	-1.860
Mean CoM Jerk (CoM Jerk, m/s^3)	Straight phase	0.419 ± 0.070	[0.369,0.469]	0.394 ± 0.111	[0.315,0.474]	0.056	0.263
	Turning phase	0.551 ± 0.086	[0.490,0.613]	0.407 ± 0.097	[0.337, 0.477]	0.002	1.572
Turning duration (T_{turn}, s)	Turning phase	3.174 ± 0.191	[3.037, 3.311]	2.576 ± 0.204	[2.430, 2.722]	<0.001	-3.021
Mean turning angular velocity (ω_{turn_avg}, °/s)	Turning phase	56.725 ± 4.965	[52.248, 59.490]	71.925 ± 5.286	[68.143,75.706]	<0.001	-2.805

4 Discussion

This study aimed to develop and validate a quantitative assessment method using wearable IMUs to evaluate the walking and turning abilities of older adults. Our findings indicate that kinematic parameters during the turning phase are considerably more sensitive than those during the straight walking phase in differentiating age-related functional decline. Based on these findings, this study proposes a novel 'Multi-dimensional Kinematic Profile' framework, which offers a new paradigm for assessing motor function and provides a critical foundation for personalized wearable exoskeleton-assisted rehabilitation.

In the relatively simple task of straight-line walking, older adults adopted a 'conservative' gait pattern, characterized by significantly shorter CoM trajectory length, slower velocity, smaller displacement area. They reduced swing amplitude compared to the younger group. This strategy is employed to enhance stability and compensate for diminished muscle strength and balance control capabilities, which is consistent with previous literature [3, 4].

In stark contrast, the more challenging 180-degree turning task effectively 'unmasked' the underlying functional deficits in older adults. The older group exhibited significantly longer turning duration, slower mean angular velocity, higher CoM jerk, poorer symmetry, and greater CoM swing amplitude during turning. This combination of parameters depicts an inefficient, unstable, and poorly coordinated turning strategy. These deficits are directly related to the increased fall risk observed during turning maneuvers in older adults [6, 7], pinpointing specific targets for intervention. The findings highlight the inadequacy of relying on single or overly simplistic metrics for functional assessment. The proposed 'Multi-dimensional Kinematic Profile' complements traditional clinical scales like the TUG test. While the TUG provides a crucial, holistic measure of mobility, it results in a single time score. It cannot, however, specify the biomechanical reasons for poor performance.

The discrepancy in findings between straight walking and turning highlights the inadequacy of relying on single or overly simplistic metrics for functional assessment. This study selected five core kinematic indicators based on their statistical power, strong correlation with a clinical standard (TUG), and clear biomechanical interpretability.

Mean straight walking CoM velocity: Represents fundamental walking ability and efficiency. The older group was significantly slower ($p = 0.048$), which is one of the most intuitive and core manifestations of functional decline, highly correlated with macroscopic indicators such as TUG. Turning duration: Represents the efficiency of completing a postural transition task. It exhibited the most considerable inter-group difference in our study and was strongly correlated with TUG scores. Mean turning angular velocity: Reflects the dynamic capability and fluidity of the turning action itself. The older group was significantly slower ($p < 0.001$), indicating a hesitant and inefficient turning strategy. Turning CoM Jerk: Serves as a gold-standard measure of movement smoothness. The older group had significantly higher Jerk values during turning ($p = 0.002$), revealing discontinuity and instability in their motor control. Turning swing symmetry: Quantifies the bilateral coordination of the body during turning. The older group exhibited significantly poorer symmetry ($p < 0.001$), reflecting a decline in their balance control and bilateral coordination capabilities.

These five indicators—fundamental gait, turning efficiency, turning dynamics, movement smoothness, and coordination—constitute a comprehensive core set for assessing walking and postural transition abilities. As illustrated in Fig. 4, this profile provides an intuitive individual 'functional fingerprint.' It moves beyond a single score to reveal the specific dimensions of an individual's functional limitations, thereby enabling more precise diagnoses and the formulation of truly individualized rehabilitation plans [12].

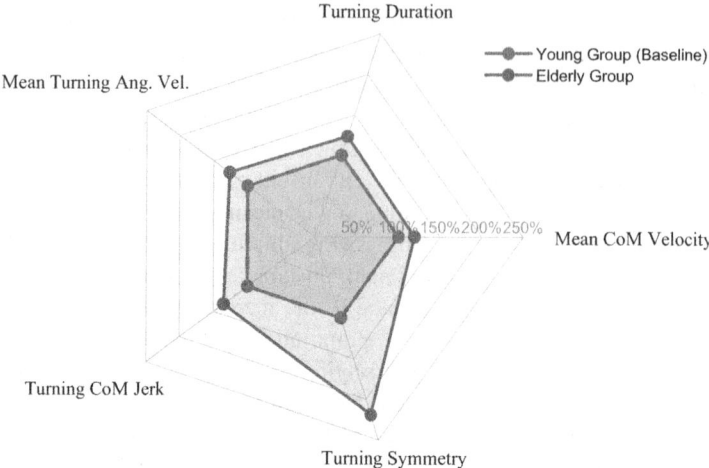

Fig. 4. The 'Multi-dimensional Kinematic Profile' radar plot. This figure illustrates the mean functional performance of the elderly group (red line) relative to the young group (blue line), which is established as the 100% functional baseline. To ensure that a value further from the center consistently represents poorer performance, all indicators were normalized. The regular pentagon of the young group at the 100% level represents the normative baseline, while the larger, irregular shape of the elderly group highlights the specific domains and magnitude of their functional decline.

This study has several limitations. First, the sample size is relatively small, which may limit the generalizability of the findings. Future research should incorporate larger and more diverse cohorts. Second, the cross-sectional design reveals age-related differences but cannot establish causality or track longitudinal changes in function. In summary, this study demonstrates that multi-dimensional kinematic analysis of walking and turning using IMUs provides a sensitive and comprehensive method for assessing age-related decline in motor function.

5 Conclusion

This study successfully developed and preliminarily validated an innovative quantitative analysis method based on wearable IMUs. By analyzing an extended set of CoM and trunk kinematic parameters, this method can comprehensively, objectively, and meticulously evaluate the walking motor function of older adults. The widespread application of this method is expected to enhance further the understanding and management of gait dysfunction in older adults, ultimately contributing positively to promoting healthy aging and improving the independence and overall quality of life of the elderly population.

Acknowledgments. This work was supported by the National Key Research and Development Program of China (Special Project on Engineering Science and Multidisciplinary Crossings, Grant No. 2024YFF0507502).

References

1. Wu, R., Ditroilo, M., Delahunt, E., De Vito, G.: Age related changes in motor function (II). Decline in motor performance outcomes. Int. J. Sports Med. **42**(03), 215–226 (2021)
2. Tiago Horta, R.d.S.: Falls prevention in older people and the role of nursing. Br. J. Commun. Nurs. **29**(7), 335–339 (2024)
3. Montero-Odasso, M., et al.: World guidelines for falls prevention and management for older adults: a global initiative. Age Ageing **51**(9), afac205 (2022)
4. Wang, J., Li, Y., Yang, G.-Y., Jin, K.: Age-related dysfunction in balance: a comprehensive review of causes, consequences, and interventions. Aging Dis. 2024.0124-1 (2024)
5. Merchant, R., Morley, J., Izquierdo, M.: Exercise, aging and frailty: guidelines for increasing function. vol. 25, pp. 405–409, Springer (2021)
6. Simpson, J.M., Worsfold, C., Reilly, E., Nye, N.: A standard procedure for using TURN180: testing dynamic postural stability among elderly people. Physiotherapy **88**(6), 342–353 (2002)
7. Baird, J.L., Van Emmerik, R.E.: Young and older adults use different strategies to perform a standing turning task. Clin. Biomech. **24**(10), 826–832 (2009)
8. Tendolkar, P., et al.: Relationship between Timed up and go performance and quantitative biomechanical measures of balance. Front. Rehabil. Sci. **5**, 1220427 (2024)
9. Suo, X., Tang, W., Li, Z.: Motion capture technology in sports scenarios: a survey. Sensors **24**(9), 2947 (2024)
10. Ghattas, J., Jarvis, D.N.: Validity of inertial measurement units for tracking human motion: a systematic review. Sports Biomech. **23**(11), 1853–1866 (2024)
11. Picerno, P., Iosa, M., D'Souza, C., Benedetti, M.G., Paolucci, S., Morone, G.: Wearable inertial sensors for human movement analysis: a five-year update. Expert Rev. Med. Devices **18**(sup1), 79–94 (2021)
12. Poggensee, K.L., Collins, S.H., How adaptation, training, and customization contribute to benefits from exoskeleton assistance. Sci. Robot. **6**(58), eabf1078 (2021)
13. Mariani, B., Rouhani, H., Crevoisier, X., Aminian, K.: Quantitative estimation of foot-flat and stance phase of gait using foot-worn inertial sensors. Gait Posture **37**(2), 229–234 (2013)
14. Podsiadlo, D., Richardson, S.: The timed "Up & Go": a test of basic functional mobility for frail elderly persons. J. Am. Geriatr. Soc. **39**(2), 142–148 (1991)

Development of a Functional Electrical Stimulation Device Combined with Multi-modal Muscle Status Monitoring

Longjie Yu[1], Xiangyu Cheng[1], Xin Chen[1], Kewen Zhang[1,2], Shibo Cai[1,2], and Mingyu Du[1,2(✉)]

[1] The College of Mechanical Engineering, Zhejiang University of Technology, Hangzhou 310023, Zhejiang, China
dumingyu@zjut.edu.cn

[2] The Key Laboratory of Special Purpose Equipment and Advanced Processing Technology, Ministry of Education, Zhejiang University of Technology, Hangzhou 310023, China

Abstract. Traditional functional electrical stimulation (FES) faces challenges in personalized parameter setting and real-time muscle status monitoring, and corresponding portable integrated hardware platforms still need to be developed. This study aimed to design and implement a novel FES device combined with multi-modal muscle status monitoring. This system seeks to establish the hardware foundation for personalized rehabilitation strategies based on multi-modal signal feedback. The system employs a modular hardware architecture. The muscle oxygenation monitoring module utilizes continuous-wave near-infrared spectroscopy (CW-NIRS) technology to monitor changes in hemoglobin concentrations. The surface electromyography (sEMG) monitoring module employs a three-electrode differential configuration to output a processed signal envelope. The FES module allows real-time adjustment of stimulation intensity, frequency, and pulse width. All modules communicate wirelessly with a host personal computer (PC) via Bluetooth Low Energy (BLE), and a PC-based Graphical User Interface (GUI) enables real-time data display and parameter control. To validate device performance, we conducted functional tests on each module. These tests included forearm vascular occlusion experiments for the muscle oxygenation monitoring module, baseline noise and signal quality assessments for the sEMG monitoring module, and output waveform verification for the FES module. Experimental results demonstrated that the muscle oxygenation monitoring module accurately captured dynamic hemo-oxygenation changes in muscle tissue. The sEMG monitoring module acquired clear signal envelopes with a high signal-to-noise ratio (SNR). Furthermore, the FES module precisely delivered user-defined stimulation parameters. This research provides a critical hardware platform that enables the future implementation of closed-loop, personalized FES rehabilitation based on multi-modal physiological signal feedback.

Keywords: Functional Electrical Stimulation · Muscle Oxygenation · Multi-modal · Rehabilitation Device · Surface Electromyography

1 Introduction

Functional electrical stimulation (FES) is a key rehabilitation technique that uses electrical currents to stimulate muscles, helping to restore motor function [1, 2] after neurological disorders like stroke [3]. However, traditional FES is limited by challenges in personalizing parameters, a lack of real-time fatigue monitoring, and open-loop control systems that cannot adapt to the muscle's changing state, which can lead to suboptimal or harmful stimulation and limits therapeutic efficacy [4].

To overcome these challenges, integrating real-time muscle status information into FES systems has become a key trend. This requires biosignals that can effectively reflect muscle status. The surface electromyography (sEMG) provides an electrophysiological window into motor intent and muscle activation timing [5]. Meanwhile, near-infrared spectroscopy (NIRS) offers a metabolic and hemodynamic window into muscle oxygen delivery and consumption, making it a valuable tool for assessing physiological load and fatigue [6, 7]. The two modalities are highly complementary: sEMG reflects the neural 'activation' command [8], while NIRS tracks the metabolic 'working' response. Their fusion provides a more comprehensive assessment of neuromuscular status than either signal alone, showing great potential for enabling closed-loop FES control and developing personalized rehabilitation protocols.

While the concept of combining FES with sEMG or NIRS exists, the practical application is hindered by the lack of a portable, highly integrated hardware platform capable of simultaneous sensing and stimulation. Therefore, this paper describes the design and implementation of a novel FES device combined with multi-modal muscle status monitoring. The development of this system validates the technical feasibility of this integrated approach and provides a critical hardware foundation to enable future research into personalized, closed-loop FES rehabilitation strategies. This work aims to facilitate more precise, safe, and effective neurorehabilitation.

2 System Hardware Design and Implementation

2.1 Overall Hardware Architecture

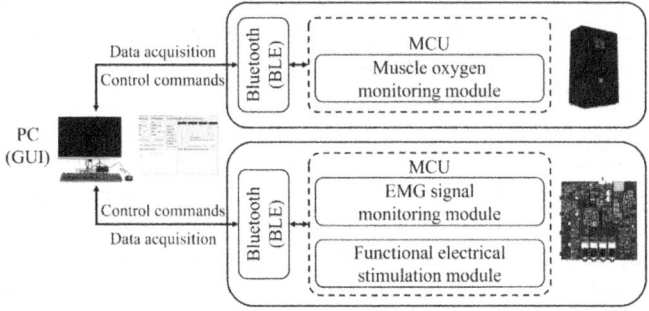

Fig. 1. Hardware architecture of the FES system combined with multi-modal muscle status monitoring.

Figure 1 illustrates the hardware architecture of the FES system combined with multi-modal muscle status monitoring. The system employed a modular design, with its core comprising a muscle oxygenation monitoring module, a sEMG monitoring module, an FES module, and a host personal computer (PC) with a Graphical User Interface (GUI).

A bidirectional Bluetooth Low Energy (BLE) link facilitated all communication between the wearable modules and a host PC. Through a central GUI, the PC transmitted downstream commands to synchronize data acquisition from the muscle oxygenation and sEMG modules and to trigger FES pulses. Concurrently, the modules streamed all acquired muscle status data upstream to the PC for real-time monitoring and logging.

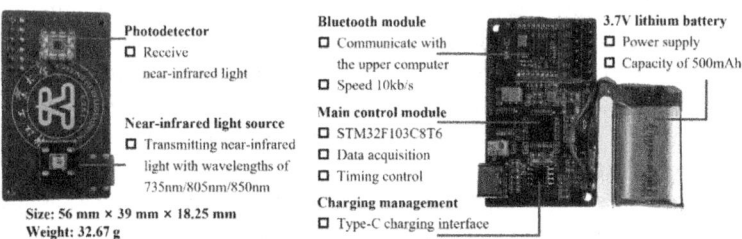

Fig. 2. Electrical function diagram of the muscle oxygen monitoring module.

2.2 Muscle Oxygen Monitoring Module

Figure 2 shows the electrical function diagram of the muscle oxygenation monitoring module. The module was composed of four primary sections: a light-emitting diode (LED) driver module, an optical acquisition module, a main control module, and a power management module.

For the LED light source driver module, we first selected a three-wavelength NIR LED (SMW735/805/850; WINWORLD, Japan). This choice was guided by the distinct absorption spectra of oxygenated (HbO_2) and deoxygenated (HHb) hemoglobin, ensuring their effective differentiation [9, 10]. We then designed a programmable constant-current driver circuit, based on a digital-to-analog converter (DAC) and an operational amplifier, to provide stable and adjustable power to this LED. This design enabled the microcontroller (MCU) to perform two key functions. First, it dynamically adjusted LED intensity via the DAC to optimize the signal-to-noise ratio (SNR) for various measurement conditions. Second, it used its GPIO ports to precisely control the LED pulsing and activation timing, a method that minimized power consumption and thermal effects and enhanced overall system flexibility.

For optical signal acquisition, we selected the OPT101 monolithic photodiode (Texas Instruments), which integrates a high-sensitivity photodiode and a transimpedance amplifier to linearly convert weak transmitted light into a voltage signal. To condition this typically weak and noisy signal, we implemented a second-order active low-pass filter with adjustable gain. This filter served a dual purpose: it removed high-frequency noise and scaled the signal amplitude to fit the optimal input range of the MCU's analog-to-digital converter (ADC). This conditioning stage was critical for maximizing the final SNR and overall measurement accuracy.

Finally, we designed the main control module, which digitized the conditioned analog optical signal for subsequent processing. This module uses an STM32F103C8T6 as its MCU, which performs data conversion via its internal 12-bit ADC. The ADC's sampling rate was adjustable to meet specific application demands. In addition to executing ADC sampling, the STM32F103C8T6 managed the LED driving timing and controlled the gain of the LED driver module. The main control module also integrated a BLE module to wirelessly transmit the acquired raw light intensity data to the PC. On the PC, custom software applies the Modified Beer-Lambert Law [11] to calculate concentration changes in oxygenated hemoglobin (ΔC_{HbO2}) and deoxygenated hemoglobin (ΔC_{HHb}), and displays these values in real-time.

2.3 sEMG Monitoring Module

The sEMG monitoring module (Fig. 3) utilized a three-electrode differential configuration to detect and process weak bioelectrical signals generated during muscle contraction. Its signal processing chain was designed to generate a final sEMG signal envelope suitable for direct acquisition by the MCU's ADC.

The signal conditioning pathway involved four sequential stages to process the weak bioelectrical signals. First, the first-stage differential amplification, which employed an AD8226 instrumentation amplifier selected for its high input impedance and common-mode rejection ratio, amplified the differential sEMG signal while suppressing common-mode noise. Next, in the full-wave rectification stage, a precision op-amp circuit converted the resulting alternating current signal into a pulsating positive direct current voltage. The signal then entered the smoothing and envelope detection stage, where an integrator circuit filtered the rectified signal to produce the sEMG envelope, a slowly varying voltage proportional to the average muscle force. Finally, the second-stage amplification, which provided adjustable gain, scaled this envelope to an optimal level for the MCU's ADC, allowing the system to adapt to signal variations between users and muscles.

The main control module's MCU and the FES module's MCU shared the same one, which will be described in Sect. 2.4.

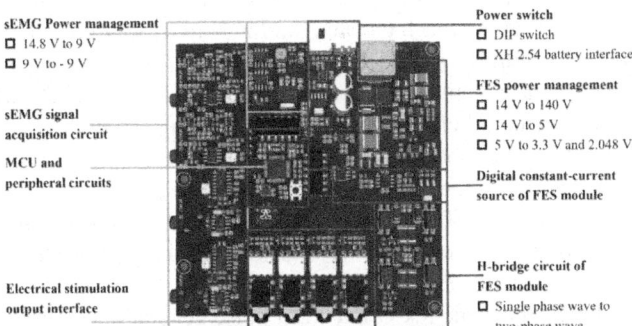

Fig. 3. Electrical function diagram of the sEMG monitoring module and FES module. The yellow box represents the sEMG monitoring module, and the red box represents the FES module.

2.4 FES Module

As shown in Fig. 3, the FES module was designed to generate precisely controllable pulsed currents to activate target muscle groups. The design of this module prioritizes five key aspects: high voltage generation, current control and pulse shaping, multi-channel design, and main control and power management module.

To overcome the high impedance of skin and tissue while maintaining a constant current output under varying loads, we designed a high-voltage generation circuit. This circuit utilized a Boost converter topology, based on an LM5022MM controller, to step-up the 14.8 V battery input to a higher, adjustable DC voltage. We implemented dynamic voltage adjustment by having the MCU control a multiplexer that switched between different feedback resistor networks. This design allowed the output voltage to be set to discrete levels (e.g., 20 V, 50 V, 100 V, and 140 V). The adjustable high-voltage output ensures the system can reliably deliver the maximum required stimulation current of 100 mA under a maximum specified load of 1.4 kΩ.

For the current control and pulse shaping, this module designed an output constant current source circuit, which used a symmetrical balanced biphasic rectangular wave. The MCU set the current amplitude by controlling a DAC via a Serial Peripheral Interface. The DAC's output voltage, V_{DAC_OUT}, served as the reference for a digitally controlled constant-current source. This source, constructed from an operational amplifier and a power transistor, utilized a negative feedback mechanism to ensure the current through the load precisely followed the DAC-set reference. The current magnitude was determined by the equation $I_{stim} = V_{DAC\_OUT}/R_{sample}$, where R_{sample} is a sampling resistor. The resulting unidirectional current pulses were then converted into biphasic current pulses by an H-bridge circuit. Through precise control of the DAC's output amplitude and the H-bridge's switching timing, the MCU achieved regulation of the final stimulation pulses.

The system utilized Time-Division Multiplexing to achieve multi-channel design, a design choice that allows for flexible stimulation of multiple muscle groups or different motor points on the same muscle. A single H-bridge circuit generated the biphasic stimulation waveform, which was then routed to the different output channels via a channel selection circuit. For this switching, we used bidirectional triac output optocouplers as solid-state relays, allowing the MCU to independently control the on/off state of each target channel. The TDM approach enabled the MCU to rapidly switch between active output channels according to a predefined program, ensuring that only one channel delivered stimulation at any given moment. By setting a very short channel-switching interval of 300 μs, we could create a pseudo-simultaneous stimulation effect that was nearly imperceptible to the user.

The sEMG monitoring and FES modules shared the same main control module, managed by the main MCU (STM32F103C8T6). In the sEMG signal pathway, the MCU acquired the processed sEMG envelope from the front-end signal conditioning circuitry and transmitted the data to the PC via a BLE module for real-time display and recording. For the FES pathway, the same MCU managed pulse generation, controlled the multi-channel outputs, triggered safety mechanisms, and handled bidirectional communication of stimulation parameters with the PC via BLE.

To address potential FES-induced electrical artifacts in the sEMG and NIRS signals, we designed the hardware to facilitate future mitigation strategies, although a dedicated removal algorithm was not implemented in this prototype. The MCU's precise timing control enables signal blanking (pausing ADC acquisition during FES pulses) at the hardware level. Additionally, software-based methods, such as adaptive filtering or template subtraction, can be applied to the data on the host PC during post-processing to address any residual artifacts.

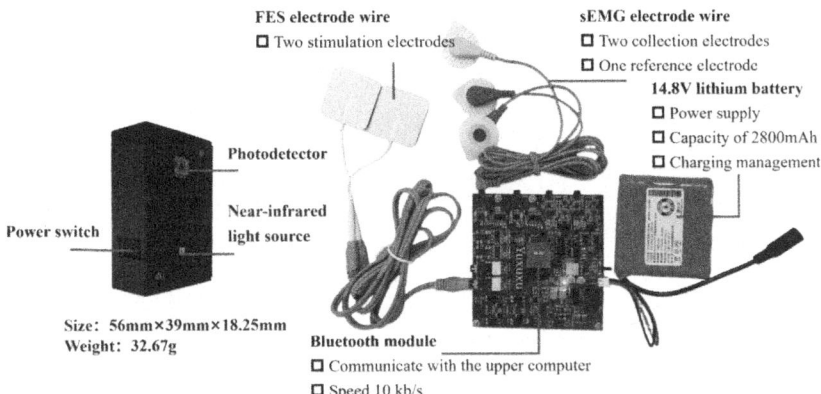

Fig. 4. The prototype of the designed device. The left side was the muscle oxygen monitoring module, and the right side was the sEMG monitoring module and FES module.

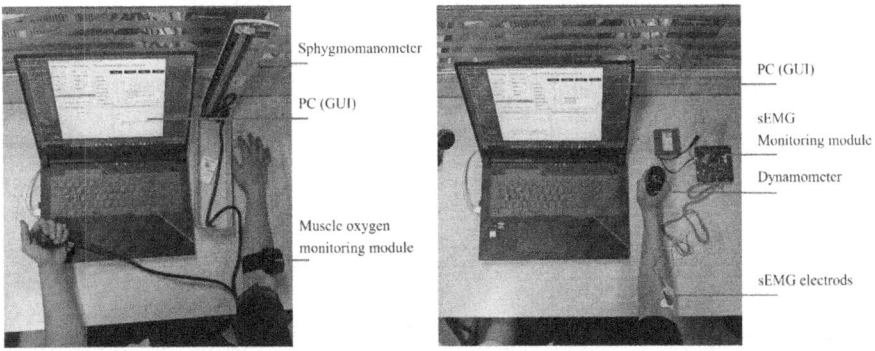

Fig. 5. Schematic diagram of experimental setup. The left side was the forearm occlusion experiment based on the muscle oxygen monitoring module, and the right side was the baseline noise and signal quality test based on the sEMG monitoring module.

3 Device Testing and Evaluation

A single healthy male participant (age 25) was recruited for the device validation experiments. The participant provided written informed consent before the study, and the experimental protocol adhered to all relevant ethical guidelines.

The experimental setup, using the prototype device developed in this study (Fig. 4), was configured as follows. The muscle oxygenation monitoring module was secured to the skin over the target muscle with an adjustable elastic band to ensure stable optical probe coupling. The main unit, containing the sEMG and FES modules, was positioned on the participant's lower back. The sEMG monitoring module was connected via lead wires to three standard Ag/AgCl hydrogel electrodes, while the FES module delivered stimulation through lead wires to specialized surface electrodes on the target muscle.

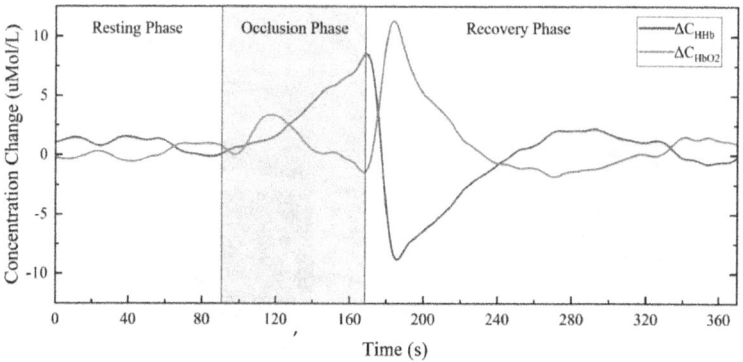

Fig. 6. The oxygenation concentration change curves during the forearm occlusion experiment.

3.1 Forearm Occlusion Experiment Based on Muscle Oxygen Monitoring Module

This study conducted a forearm occlusion experiment to validate the performance of the muscle oxygenation monitoring module in monitoring dynamic tissue oxygenation changes. The experimental setup, depicted schematically in Fig. 5, comprised the developed module, a standard sphygmomanometer, and a PC for data recording, display, and analysis.

3.1.1 Experimental Paradigm

We conducted the experiment on the participant's right arm. The optical probe of the muscle oxygenation monitoring module was secured over the brachioradialis muscle, chosen for its primary role in forearm grasping actions. A standard sphygmomanometer cuff was wrapped around the ipsilateral upper arm. Throughout the procedure, the participant sat comfortably upright with their arm resting flat on a table and was instructed to remain still to minimize motion artifacts.

The experimental protocol consisted of three sequential phases, during which we continuously acquired muscle oxygenation data at a sampling frequency of 2.5 Hz. The protocol began with a 90 s resting phase, where we recorded baseline data while the participant was relaxed and the cuff was uninflated. Next, for the 60 s occlusion phase, we rapidly inflated the cuff to 250 mmHg to induce forearm ischemia. Finally, for the recovery phase, we completely deflated the cuff and continued to record data for an additional 250 s to monitor the reperfusion process.

3.1.2 Results

The results of the forearm occlusion experiment are presented in Fig. 6. During the initial resting phase, ΔC_{HbO2} and ΔC_{HHb} remained at a stable baseline. Upon initiating the occlusion phase, the blockage of arterial blood flow caused a rapid and significant decrease in ΔC_{HbO2} with a corresponding increase in ΔC_{HHb}. At the start of the recovery phase, cuff release triggered a sharp rebound in ΔC_{HbO2} due to reactive hyperemia, which included a transient overshoot above the baseline level before gradually stabilizing. Concurrently, the influx of oxygenated blood prompted a rapid decrease in ΔC_{HHb} back toward its baseline.

These observed hemodynamic patterns are in strong agreement with established physiological principles and previously reported findings [12, 13]. The results therefore demonstrate that the developed muscle oxygenation module can accurately and reliably track dynamic changes in tissue oxygenation caused by acute events such as ischemia and reperfusion.

3.2 Baseline Noise and Signal Quality Test Based on sEMG Monitoring Module

This study conducted experiments to evaluate the signal acquisition performance of the sEMG monitoring module. The evaluation focused on two primary aspects: 1) the module's inherent noise level during periods of no muscle activity, and 2) the characteristics of sEMG signals captured during voluntary isometric contractions, specifically their response sensitivity, clarity, and SNR. The experimental setup, depicted schematically in Fig. 5, included the sEMG monitoring module, a standard handgrip dynamometer, and a PC for data recording, display, and analysis.

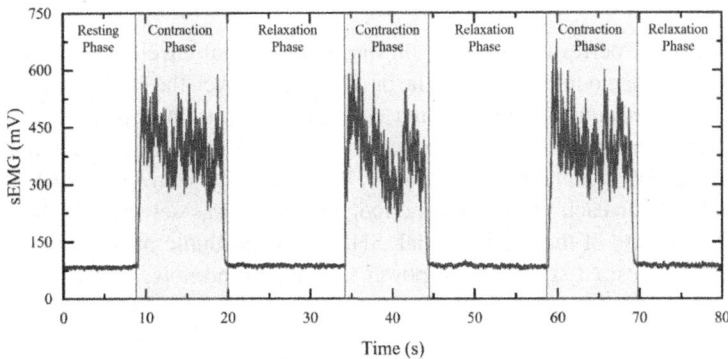

Fig. 7. sEMG signal envelope output by the module during intermittent isometric contraction.

3.2.1 Experimental Paradigm

The brachioradialis muscle was selected as the target for sEMG measurements due to its primary role in gripping actions. After preparing the skin over the target region with a medical alcohol swab to reduce impedance, three Ag/AgCl electrodes were applied in the differential configuration. Two recording electrodes were positioned over the muscle belly, parallel to the fibers with an approximate 2 cm inter-electrode distance, while the reference electrode was placed on the olecranon process.

The protocol began with determining the participant's maximum voluntary contraction (MVC), defined as the peak grip force sustained for 3–5 s using a handgrip dynamometer. The participant then performed a 95 s intermittent isometric contraction task consisting of an initial 10 s rest for baseline measurement, followed by three contraction-relaxation cycles. Each cycle involved a 10 s isometric contraction at 50% MVC, with real-time dynamometer feedback provided to help maintain the target force. The first two relaxation periods lasted 15 s each, and the final one lasted 10 s. Throughout this protocol, the sEMG module acquired signals at a 1000 Hz sampling rate and streamed the data in real-time via BLE to a host PC for display and recording.

Table 1. Baseline Noise and Signal Quality Parameters of sEMG Monitoring Module.

Parameters	Value
MVC (N)	322
RMS_{noise} (mV)	2.596
$RMS_{contraction}$ (mV)	497.243
SNR (dB)	45.647

3.2.2 Results

Our analysis was performed directly on the sEMG signal envelope generated by the sEMG monitoring module. To assess the baseline noise level, the sEMG signal envelope from the initial resting period was first corrected for baseline offset. This corrected signal's the root mean square (RMS) value RMS_{noise} was then calculated to quantify the baseline noise. For signal quality evaluation, the sEMG signal envelope's $RMS_{contraction}$ was calculated for each contraction period. The SNR was selected as the metric to evaluate the quality of the sEMG signal. SNR is a logarithmic measure that compares the power of a desired signal to the power of background noise. It was calculated as follows:

$$SNR = 20 \log_{10} \frac{RMS_{contraction}}{RMS_{noise}} \tag{1}$$

The specific parameter values are listed in Table 1. During the resting phase, the sEMG signal envelope noise's RMS_{noise} was 2.596 mV, indicating a low baseline noise level following the module's internal signal processing. During the 50% MVC isometric contraction, the amplitude of the sEMG signal envelope's $RMS_{contraction}$ increased significantly to 497.243 mV. The calculated SNR was 45.647 dB. This value, being well above 30 dB, indicates the excellent quality of the acquired myoelectric signal.

The sEMG signal envelope clearly tracked the complete muscle activity cycle of rest, contraction, and subsequent relaxation, as shown in Fig. 7. The amplitude of the envelope exhibited a strong correspondence with the muscle's activation state.

The results show that sEMG monitoring module used its built-in signal processing circuit to effectively convert weak raw sEMG signal into an sEMG envelope with a high SNR and excellent response sensitivity. This performance meets the foundational criteria for its future use in muscle status assessment and potential human-machine interface (HMI) applications.

3.3 Output Waveform Test Based on FES Module

The experimental setup for evaluating the electrical performance of the FES module is depicted in Fig. 8. The power input terminal of the FES module was connected to a 14.8 V lithium battery. A precision oscilloscope was employed to monitor the signal of the FES stimulation output channel. The stimulation channel was connected to a 2 kΩ high-power sliding rheostat, which served as a test load. For control and management, the FES module was interfaced with a PC via BLE, and the corresponding GUI control software was launched.

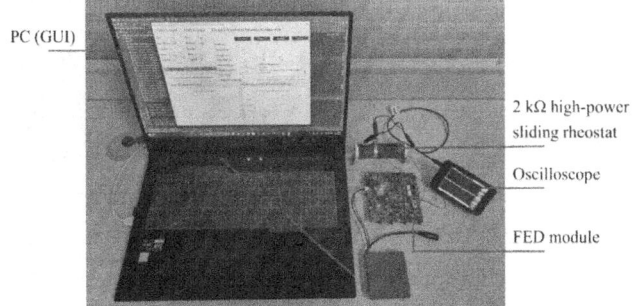

Fig. 8. The experimental setup for evaluating the electrical performance of the FES module.

3.3.1 Experimental Paradigm

This study conducted two experiments to validate the FES module's electrical performance. First, to characterize the constant-current source, we assessed the load-voltage relationship. We fixed the DAC control voltage at 0.4 V (target current: 20 mA) and varied the load resistance from 200 Ω to 2000 Ω, while recording the output voltage across the load with an oscilloscope. Second, to verify waveform accuracy, we configured the module to output a symmetric, balanced, biphasic rectangular waveform into a 421.4 Ω load. We tested the output using a representative parameter set: 30.0 mA intensity, 300 Hz frequency, 750 μs pulse width, and a 400 μs inter-phase interval. After activating the output, we used an oscilloscope to capture the stable voltage waveform and measured its actual parameters, including amplitude, frequency, pulse width, and inter-phase interval.

3.3.2 Results

The constant-current source demonstrated excellent load adaptation and control linearity. As we increased the R_L from 200 Ω to 2000 Ω, the measured output voltage increased linearly with a nearly constant slope (Fig. 9 (a)). This outcome confirmed the module's robust constant-current characteristics across the tested load range.

The verification experiment confirmed that the FES module generated the symmetric, balanced, biphasic rectangular waveform with high parameter accuracy, as shown in Fig. 9(b). We analyzed the captured oscilloscope waveform and compared the measured output values to their set points. The mean current amplitude was 30.14 mA (relative error: −0.5%), and the pulse frequency was precisely 300 Hz (no measurable error). The pulse width averaged 741.7 μs (relative error: −1.11%), and the inter-phase interval averaged 404.9 μs (relative error: +1.22%). The relative error for all key parameters remained within ±2% of their set values, confirming the high fidelity of the FES module and its ability to reliably generate precise stimulation waveforms for therapeutic or research applications.

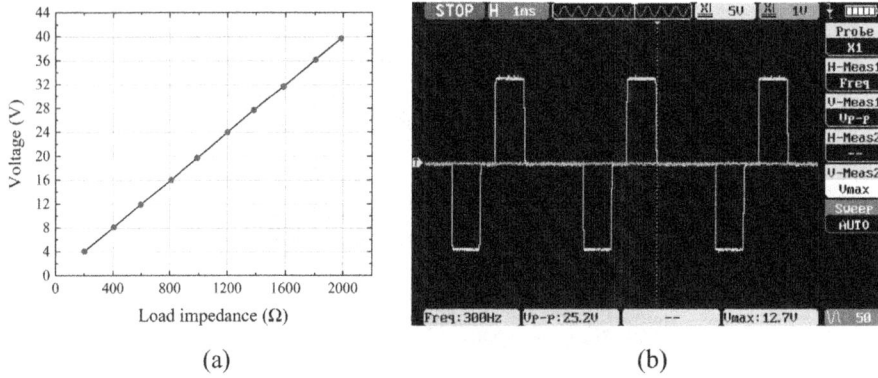

Fig. 9. (a) The voltage-load characteristic curve of the FES output. (b) The symmetric, balanced, biphasic, rectangular waveform generated by the FES module under the specific parameter set.

4 Discussion and Limitation

While validation on a single-subject established the hardware's technical feasibility as a proof-of-concept, this single-subject design inherently limits the generalizability and clinical relevance of our findings. Therefore, future research with larger, more diverse patient cohorts is required to confirm the device's clinical utility.

5 Conclusion

This study successfully designed and implemented a novel portable device that integrates multi-modal muscle status monitoring with FES capabilities. The modular system, which communicated wirelessly with a host PC via BLE, was validated through a series of hardware tests. The results confirmed that each component functioned as intended: the NIRS module accurately tracked muscle oxygenation dynamics, the sEMG module acquired high-quality signal envelopes, and the FES module delivered stimulation parameters with high fidelity. Overall, this work provides a critical, integrated hardware platform. It establishes the technical foundation necessary for future research into developing and validating closed-loop, personalized FES rehabilitation strategies guided by multi-modal physiological feedback. Future efforts will focus on system optimization and clinical efficacy studies.

Acknowledgments. This work was supported in part by the Key Research and Development Program of Zhejiang Province under Grant 2023C03159.

References

1. Qu, H., Xie, Y., Liu, X., et al.: Development of network-based multichannel neuromuscular electrical stimulation system for stroke rehabilitation. J. Rehabil. Res. Dev. **53**(2), 263–278 (2016)
2. Bélanger, M., Stein, R.B., Wheeler, G.D., et al.: Electrical stimulation: can it increase muscle strength and reverse osteopenia in spinal cord injured individuals? Arch. Phys. Med. Rehabil. **81**(8), 1090–1098 (2000)
3. Marquez-Chin, C., Popovic, M.R.: Functional electrical stimulation therapy for restoration of motor function after spinal cord injury and stroke: a review. Biomed. Eng. Online **19**(1), 34 (2020)
4. Zhang, Q., Lambeth, K., Iyer, A., et al.: Ultrasound imaging-based closed-loop control of functional electrical stimulation for drop foot correction. IEEE Trans. Control Syst. Technol. **31**(3), 989–1005 (2023)
5. Khan, M.A., Fares, H., Ghayvat, H., et al.: A systematic review on functional electrical stimulation based rehabilitation systems for upper limb post-stroke recovery. Front. Neurol. **14**, 1272992 (2023)
6. Montes, J., Goodwin, A.M., McDermott, M.P., et al.: Diminished muscle oxygen uptake and fatigue in spinal muscular atrophy. Ann. Clin. Trans. Neurol. **8**(5), 1086–1095 (2021)
7. Rennerfelt, K., Lindorsson, S., Brisby, H., et al.: Effects of exercise compression stockings on anterior muscle compartment pressure and oxygenation during running: a randomized crossover trial conducted in healthy recreational runners. Sports Med. **49**(9), 1465–1473 (2019)
8. Aranceta-Garza, A., Conway, B.A.: Differentiating variations in thumb position from recordings of the surface electromyogram in adults performing static grips, a proof of concept study. Front. Bioeng. Biotechnol. **7**, 123 (2019)
9. Ozaki, Y., Ikehata, A., Shinzawa, H.: Near-Infrared Spectroscopy in Biological Molecules and Tissues. In: Roberts, G.C.K. (ed.) Encyclopedia of Biophysics, pp. 1695–1706. Springer, Berlin, Heidelberg (2013)

10. Wang, Y., Lyu, J., Liu, H.: Development of a Multi-channel Wireless Wearable Muscle Oxygen Monitoring Device. In: Lan, X., Mei, X., Jiang, C., Zhao, F., Tian, Z. (eds.) Intelligent Robotics and Applications, ICIRA 2024, LNAI, vol. 15209, pp. 148–161. Springer, Singapore (2024)
11. Kocsis, L., Herman, P., Eke, A.: The modified Beer-Lambert law revisited. Phys. Med. Biol. **51**(5), N91 (2006)
12. Safaie, J., Grebe, R., Moghaddam, H.A., et al.: Wireless distributed acquisition system for near infrared spectroscopy – WDA-NIRS. J. Innovative Opt. Health Sci. **6**(03), 1350019 (2013)
13. Everdell, N.L., Airantzis, D., Kolvya, C., et al.: A portable wireless near-infraredspatially resolved spectroscopy system for use on brain and muscle. Medicaleng. Phys. **35**(11), 1692–1697, (2013)

BioKFusion-Net: Simultaneous Estimation of Ground Reaction Forces/Moments and Joint Angles from IMU Data

Zhujin Chen[1,2], Yao Liu[2], Hui Chen[2], Xinyu Wu[2], and Chunjie Chen[2(✉)]

[1] School of Biomedical Engineering, Shenzhen University Medical School, Shenzhen University, Shenzhen 518060, China
[2] Shenzhen Institute of Advanced Technology, Chinese Academy of Sciences, Shenzhen 518055, China
cj.chen@siat.ac.cn

Abstract. Accurate estimation of joint angles and ground reaction forces/moments (GRF/GRM) is essential for gait analysis, rehabilitation, and assistive device control, but often depends on expensive laboratory equipment. We propose **BioKFusion-Net**, a deep learning framework that simultaneously estimates GRF/GRM and joint angles from wearable inertial measurement unit (IMU) data. The architecture integrates two task-specific branches with a residual fusion module that captures biomechanical correlations between kinematics and kinetics. Experiments on six healthy subjects show high accuracy in joint angle ($R^2 = 0.966$, NRMSE = 0.027) and GRF/GRM prediction ($R^2 = 0.834$, NRMSE = 0.046), with a 3.1% improvement in force estimation due to the fusion module. This approach enables accurate, portable gait assessment without reliance on motion capture or force plates.

Keywords: IMU · gait analysis · joint angles · ground reaction force · deep learning

1 Introduction

GRF, GRM, and joint angles are key indicators of human movement quality and neuromuscular function. Their accurate estimation is critical for applications in rehabilitation training, clinical gait assessment, sports performance analysis, and assistive device control [1]. Joint angles are used to monitor the progress of stroke patients during motor recovery, while lateral GRF is commonly analyzed to assess balance and fall risk in the elderly [2,3].

Traditional methods for measuring joint angles rely on optical motion capture systems, inertial measurement units (IMUs), and electrogoniometers. A specific example is Freezing of Gait (FOG), an episodic ambulation disorder experienced by patients with Parkinson's Disease (PD), characterized by sudden inability to step forward during walking, which often leads to falls and mobility decline. Pardoel [4] used unilateral and bilateral plantar-pressure data to predict FOG events in PD, providing critical foundations for developing user-friendly FOG prediction systems. Accurate measurement of joint angles provides biomechanical basis for creating personalized training plans for athletes.

GRF/GRM are typically measured using force plates or pressure-sensitive insoles. Vertical GRF is a key biomechanical parameter for evaluating athletic performance, technical stability, and joint injury risks [5–7]. Moreover, these data serve as references for optimizing control in highly interactive human-machine devices like exoskeletons and smart prosthetics. For example, Koseki [8] proposed a decentralized controller that uses GRF to modulate joint stiffness in bipedal robots, enabling compliant locomotion.

In laboratory settings, measurement tools such as force plates and motion capture systems often require extensive preparation, impose significant restrictions on movement. For outdoor and wearable applications, insole-based foot sensors and angular sensors are commonly used as alternatives [9–11], trading off some accuracy for portability and lightness. Researchers have attempted biomechanical and forward/inverse kinematic modeling methods to compute GRF, GRM, and joint angles from limited-dimension data [11]. Refai designed a portable gait lab based on foot-worn IMUs to estimate 3D GRF [10]. However, such model-driven approaches are typically developed for specific tasks in single scenarios, struggle to adapt to changes in environmental terrain and the behavioral intent of complex individuals, and yield lower accuracy than laboratory methods. To make the models solvable, they often also require measurements from additional sensors directly contacting the skin, such as electromyography (EMG).

Recent research has increasingly focused on data-driven methods. Studies [13–16] employed various neural networks to predict lower-limb biomechanical parameters like joint torques. Lim [17] used a single lower-back IMU with machine learning to estimate gait dynamics. Zhang et al. [12] introduced GCPB-Net, a deep model leveraging IMU data to analyze skiing kinetics, offering a scalable approach for ski biomechanics.

Building on this, a multi-task deep network architecture, BioKFusion-Net, is proposed based on IMU signals to simultaneously predict joint angles and GRF/M. Two parallel Convolutional-Recurrent Neural Network (CRNN) branches are designed to learn sequence features for angles and forces. This architecture effectively captures both local temporal dependencies through convolutional layers and long-term dependencies via gated recurrent unit (GRU) layers. A learnable residual path is introduced to mitigate overfitting and gradient vanishing issues, resulting in improved optimization and stronger generalization—especially in scenarios with limited data and noisy signals.

2 Methods

2.1 Problem Formulation

For a temporal window ΔT of IMU data represented as:

$$\mathbf{I}_{\Delta T} = [\mathbf{I}_1, \mathbf{I}_2, \ldots, \mathbf{I}_{\Delta T}] \in \mathbb{R}^{\Delta T \times D_{\text{IMU}}}$$

the model predicts kinetic parameters:

$$\mathbf{G}_{\Delta T} = [\mathbf{G}_1, \mathbf{G}_2, \ldots, \mathbf{G}_{\Delta T}] \in \mathbb{R}^{\Delta T \times D_G}$$

$$\mathbf{A}_{\Delta T} = [\mathbf{A}_1, \mathbf{A}_2, \ldots, \mathbf{A}_{\Delta T}] \in \mathbb{R}^{\Delta T \times D_A}$$

Mathematically, $\mathbf{I}_{\Delta T} \to \mathbf{G}_{\Delta T}$ and $\mathbf{A}_{\Delta T}$.

Here, ΔT represents the window length of data that will be input to the model, D_{IMU} is the number of channels of IMU sensors, and D_G is the dimension of kinetics parameters of the single limb (anterior-posterior, vertical, and mediolateral components for both forces and moments), while D_A is the dimension of sagittal, frontal, and transverse plane angles for hip, knee, and ankle joints. In this problem, we use $D_{\text{IMU}} = 42$; $\Delta T = 50$; $D_G = 6$, $D_A = 9$.

2.2 Data Collection

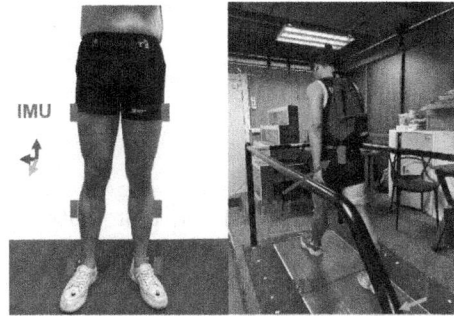

Basic Information of Subjects

Subj.	Gender	Age	Height (cm)	Weight (kg)	Leg Len. (cm)
01	F	24	164.0	50.75	85.0
02	F	29	174.0	67.60	89.0
03	M	32	175.4	77.35	84.0
04	M	25	172.2	49.55	94.0
05	M	26	181.0	91.85	98.0
06	M	26	177.2	75.00	93.0

Fig. 1. Data Collection System (L) and Subject Information (R).

Data were collected from six healthy adults (4 males, 2 females; age: 27 ± 5 years, weight: 68.68 ± 23.17 kg, height: 1.74 ± 0.10 m) with normal gait. All experimental procedures were conducted in accordance with the Declaration of Helsinki and received prior approval from the Medical Ethics Committee of Shenzhen Institute of Advanced Technology (Protocol No.SIAT-IRB-221215-H0632). Written informed consent was obtained from all participants prior to testing.

As schematically depicted in Fig. 1, seven Inertial Measurement Unit (IMU) sensors (Delsys, MA, USA) were securely affixed to each participant at the following anatomical locations: left thigh, left shank, left ankle, right thigh, right shank, right ankle, and lower back. Each IMU recorded triaxial acceleration and angular velocity at 200 Hz. All sensors were aligned to a global coordinate system with standard XYZ orientation.

During experiments, three-dimensional GRF and GRM were recorded at 200 Hz using a force plate system (AMTI, MA, USA) embedded within the treadmill, whereas three-dimensional hip, knee, and ankle joint angles were synchronously acquired at 100 Hz via a optical motion capture system (Vicon Motion Systems, Oxford, UK). All data were synchronously acquired in Vicon Nexus, ensuring strict temporal alignment throughout the experiment.

Participants performed locomotion tasks at four walking speeds (0.75, 1.25, 1.75, 2.25 and 3.25 m·s^{-1}) and one running speed (3.25 m·s^{-1}). Each speed condition lasted one minute. A stable 10–15 second window of steady-state gait was extracted from the middle portion of each trial for subsequent data analysis. Ample rest periods were provided between trials to minimize fatigue effects.

2.3 Data Processing

Firstly, raw GRF and GRM data were normalized to anthropometric parameters using:

$$\text{GRF}_{\text{norm}} = \frac{\text{GRF}}{\text{BW}} \tag{1}$$

$$\text{GRM}_{\text{norm}} = \frac{\text{GRM}}{\text{BW} \times \text{H}} \tag{2}$$

where BW denotes body weight, while H denotes body height.

IMU and kinetic data were downsampled to 100 Hz using non-overlapping mean pooling.

$$\tilde{s}[n] = \frac{1}{D} \sum_{k=nD}^{(n+1)D-1} s[k] \tag{3}$$

where $s[k]$ denotes the discrete-time sequence at f_{orig}, and $\tilde{s}[n]$ represents the downsampled output.

Finally, the resampled data were synchronized with the joint angle data collected from the motion capture system by time-stamping. All signals were filtered using a 6th-order low-pass Butterworth filter (20 Hz) to remove noise.

2.4 Training and Testing Paradigms

All experiments were executed on a computer equipped with an Intel(R) Xeon(R) W-2245 CPU (3.90 GHz) with 256 GB RAM, and an NVIDIA RTX A6000 GPU. Software dependencies included Python 3.8.0, CUDA 12.1, and PyTorch 2.3.0.

For further computational analysis, the temporal data were processed using a sliding window comprising 50 data points and a step increment of 1. The resulting segments were stacked along the channel dimension to form tensor representations, yielding a total of 46,828 data samples. The dataset was initially randomized and then partitioned into training (30,196 samples), validation (7,084 samples), and test sets (9,548 samples) following a 56:14:30 ratio. The model was trained for 300 epochs with a batch size of 32 to optimize learning efficiency. We employed the AdamW optimizer with automated hyperparameter tuning, implementing a dynamic learning rate strategy initialized between 4×10^{-6} and 1×10^{-10}. Adaptive reduction was governed by a ReduceLROnPlateau scheduler that halved the learning rate when validation loss improvement fell below a predefined threshold for consecutive epochs specified by the patience parameter, with reduction continuing until reaching the minimum learning rate.

3 BioKFusion-Net Model Architecture

BioKFusion-Net (Fig. 2) employs a dual-branch architecture comprising two parallel neural networks a joint angle prediction CRNN and a GRF/GRM prediction CRNN coupled with a residual fusion module. The twin CRNN modules extract spatiotemporal features from IMU time-series inputs to generate preliminary predictions independently. By processing the high-dimensional feature representations from both branches, the residual correction block learns latent biomechanical correlations between joint kinematics and kinetic forces to refine GRF/GRM estimates.

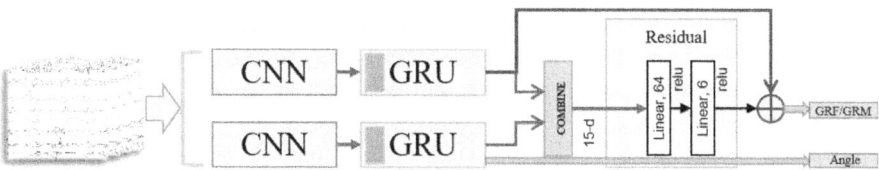

Fig. 2. BioKFusion-Net Architecture.

3.1 Convolutional Recurrent Neural Network (CRNN)

Figure 3 illustrates the structure of CRNN. Temporal signals from IMUs were structured into the tensor $\mathbf{I} \in \mathbb{R}^{B \times C \times T}$ ($B = 32$: batch size, $C = 42$: feature channels, $T = 50$: sequence length), subsequently fed into a three-layer of convolutional neural network. All convolutional layers employ symmetric padding (padding $= 1$) to preserve temporal dimensionality ($\Delta T = 50$) and ReLU activation functions, with feature channels evolving from 42 input channels to 64, 128, and 256 across successive layers respectively. The convolution operation at layer l is defined as:

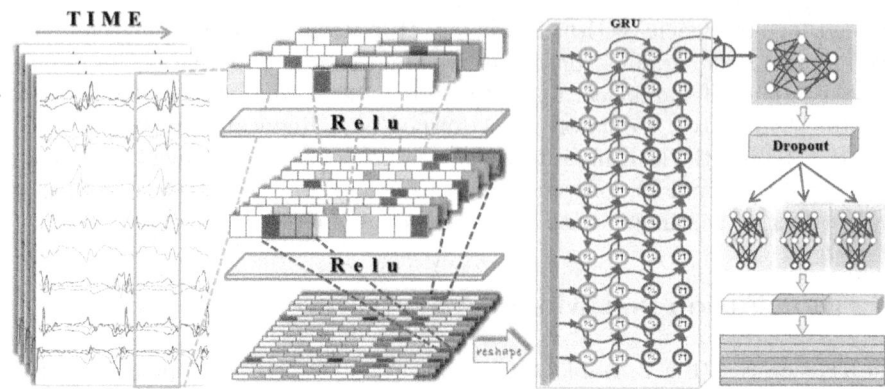

Fig. 3. Convolutional Recurrent Neural Network.

$$\mathbf{Y}^{(l)} = \text{ReLU}\left(\mathbf{W}^{(l)} * \mathbf{Y}^{(l-1)} + \mathbf{b}^{(l)}\right), \quad l = 1, 2, 3 \quad (4)$$

where the initial input $\mathbf{Y}^{(0)} = \mathbf{I}$, and $\mathbf{Y}^{(l)}$ represents the features extracted from the l_{th} layer of convolutional neural network.

The continuous state transition characteristics in the temporal dynamics modeling of human gait are highly consistent with the GRU network's update gate mechanism, which adaptively regulates the intensity of historical memory. To leverage this capability, the local short-term features $\mathbf{Y}^{(conv)}$ extracted from CNN are permuted to $\mathbf{X} \in \mathbb{R}^{B \times T \times F}$ (F = 256 features) for sequential processing. Given a hidden state $h_t \in \mathbb{R}^h$ ($h = 768$), the GRU updates its hidden state at each time step t using the following equations:

$$z_t = \sigma(W_z x_t + U_z h_{t-1} + b_z) \quad \text{(Update gate)} \quad (5)$$
$$r_t = \sigma(W_r x_t + U_r h_{t-1} + b_r) \quad \text{(Reset gate)} \quad (6)$$
$$\tilde{h}_t = \tanh(W_h x_t + U_h(r_t \odot h_{t-1}) + b_h) \quad \text{(Candidate hidden state)} \quad (7)$$
$$h_t = (1 - z_t) \odot h_{t-1} + z_t \odot \tilde{h}_t \quad \text{(Final hidden state)} \quad (8)$$

where $x_t^{(1)} \in \mathbb{R}^{B \times F}$ for layer 1 while $x_t^{(l)} \in \mathbb{R}^{B \times h}$ for $l > 1$ and $h_t^{(l)} \in \mathbb{R}^{B \times h}$, $W_*^{(l)} \in \mathbb{R}^{h \times d_{in}}$, $U_*^{(l)} \in \mathbb{R}^{h \times h}$, $b_*^{(l)} \in \mathbb{R}^h$.

Output of all time steps in each layer: $H^{(l)} \in \mathbb{R}^{B \times T \times h}$. The GRU network stacks 4 such layers. Each layer's output $H^{(l)}$ is used as input to the next layer.

3.2 Context Aggregation and Multi-task Heads

The final hidden state $\mathbf{f}_{\text{GRU}} \in \mathbb{R}^{B \times h}$ is projected via a nonlinear transformation and dropout:

$$\mathbf{h} = \text{ReLU}(\mathbf{W}_1 \mathbf{f}_{\text{GRU}} + \mathbf{b}_1), \quad \mathbf{W}_1 \in \mathbb{R}^{d \times h} \quad (9)$$

$$\mathbf{h}_{\text{drop}} = \text{Dropout}(\mathbf{h},\ 0.25) \tag{10}$$

To handle structured regression tasks involving multidimensional joint motion signals, the prediction task is decomposed into M subspaces, each processed by an independent linear layer:

$$\hat{\mathbf{y}}^{(i)} = \mathbf{W}_2^{(i)} \mathbf{h}_{\text{drop}} + \mathbf{b}_2^{(i)}, \quad i = 1, \ldots, M \tag{11}$$

For example, $M = 2$ for GRF/CRF and $M = 3$ for joint angle regression.

The final output is obtained by concatenation:

$$\hat{\mathbf{y}} = \text{Concat}(\hat{\mathbf{y}}^{(1)}, \ldots, \hat{\mathbf{y}}^{(M)}) \tag{12}$$

3.3 Residual Refinement Module

Given that the prediction of joint angles from IMU data significantly outperforms that of GRF/GRM, which aligns with our biomechanical intuition, we further leverage the richer kinematic features captured by the joint angle branch through concatenating the GRU-derived features from both CRNN branches $\mathbf{f}_{\text{joint}} \in \mathbb{R}^{B \times h_1}$ and $\mathbf{f}_{\text{force}} \in \mathbb{R}^{B \times h_2}$:

$$\mathbf{f}_{\text{concat}} = \text{Concat}(\mathbf{f}_{\text{joint}}, \mathbf{f}_{\text{force}}) \in \mathbb{R}^{B \times (h_1 + h_2)} \tag{13}$$

and then feed them into a residual refinement module:

$$\mathbf{r}_1 = \text{ReLU}(\mathbf{W}_r^{(1)} \cdot \mathbf{f}_{\text{concat}} + \mathbf{b}_r^{(1)}) \tag{14}$$

$$\hat{\mathbf{r}} = \mathbf{W}_r^{(2)} \cdot \mathbf{r}_1 + \mathbf{b}_r^{(2)} \tag{15}$$

The final prediction of GRF/GRM is obtained via residual correction:

$$\hat{\mathbf{y}}_{\text{GRF}}^{\text{final}} = \hat{\mathbf{y}}_{\text{GRF}}^{(0)} + \hat{\mathbf{r}} \tag{16}$$

Given that the joint angle prediction branch typically converges faster with higher early-stage accuracy, and to mitigate negative transfer between joint kinematics and GRF/GRM dynamics, we implement a progressive optimization strategy through selective parameter freezing. Both CRNN sub-networks are trained independently at first 150 epochs to capture their task-specific representations from IMU data. After these sub-networks converge, we freeze their parameters to preserve learned domain knowledge. Exclusive focus shifts to unfreezing and training the residual refinement module, and this targeted refinement allows the network to model latent cross-task couplings specifically to enhance GRF/GRM output predictions.

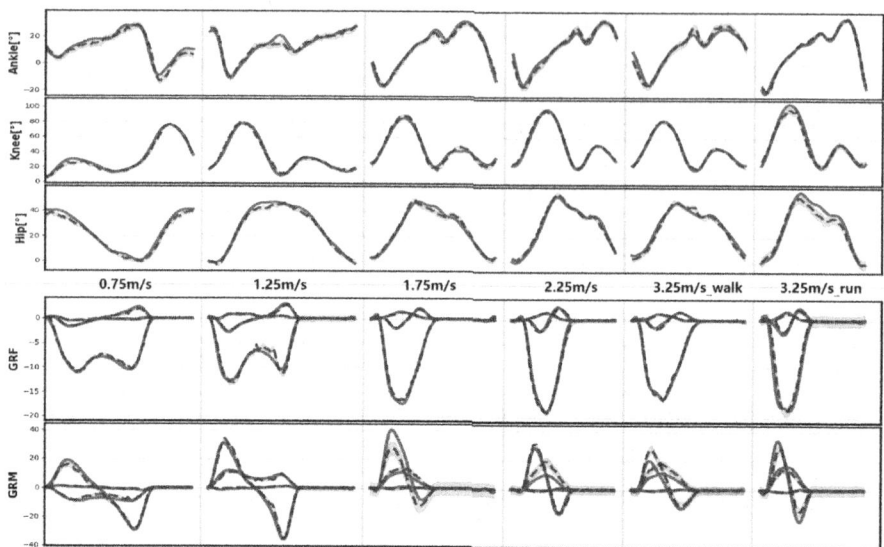

Fig. 4. Joint angles and GRF/GRM Fitting Curve. (Color figure online)

4 Result

Figure 4 depicts the fitted curve of joint angle motion (flexion and extension) in the sagittal plane, which is the most crucial indicator for human gait analysis, and three-dimensional GRF and GRM. Model predictions are shown as blue dashed lines, and their standard deviations are represented by blue shaded bands, intuitively demonstrating the excellent fitting performance of the model predictions relative to the measured ground truth values.

4.1 Module Ablation

For further measurement, we employed four metrics: the coefficient of determination (R^2), Normalized Root Mean Square Error (NRMSE), Pearson correlation coefficient (PCC), and Concordance correlation coefficient (CCC). To calculate NRMSE, the RMSE was normalized by the difference between the maximum and minimum values of the corresponding experimentally measured data. The module ablation experiments (Table 1 and Fig. 5 (R)) reveal the performance comparison of different patterns of BioKFusion-Net, demonstrating that BioKFusion-Net significantly outperforms other models across all metrics (R^2 ↑ 12.8%, NRMSE ↓ 33.3% vs No-Freeze mode, $p < 0.001$). Analysis reveals that training the network without parameter freezing constraints leads to significant performance degradation, particularly in consistency metrics (CCC decreased by 0.085 compared to BioKFusion-Net). The peak time delay also substantially increased, such as the ankle joint Y-axis delay extending from 18.7 ms to 123.0 ms.

Table 1. Performance Comparison of Different Models

Model	R^2	NRMSE	PCC	CCC
No-Freeze	0.809 ± 0.187	0.051 ± 0.025	0.912 ± 0.084	0.867 ± 0.160
CRNN-Only	0.903 ± 0.113	0.036 ± 0.016	0.950 ± 0.061	0.942 ± 0.081
BioKFusion-Net	$\mathbf{0.913 \pm 0.093}$	$\mathbf{0.034 \pm 0.015}$	$\mathbf{0.955 \pm 0.051}$	$\mathbf{0.952 \pm 0.056}$

This phenomenon may be attributed to the distinct feature requirements for different prediction tasks: joint angle prediction depends on shallow networks to capture local kinematic details (e.g., timing variations in joint rotation), while GRF/GRM prediction requires deep networks to abstract global dynamic patterns (e.g., force transmission relationships during gait cycles). Removing freezing constraints might cause excessive updates in shallow layers, where the local features crucial for joint angle prediction could be compromised by GRF learning interference. Simultaneously, the GRF task suffers from diluted gradients across all layers, hindering focused learning of high-level dynamic representations and resulting in suboptimal deep feature optimization.

For joint angle prediction, the *CRNN-Only* model (without residual blocks) achieved performance nearly identical to *BioKFusion*. Statistical analysis confirmed significant improvement from the residual module for GRF/GRM prediction ($p < 0.001$), while joint angle results showed no significant difference. This indicates that the residual structure effectively captures the underlying nonlinear relationships between joint kinematics (angles) and dynamics (GRF/GRM), thereby enhancing the model's biomechanical representation capability.

4.2 Multidimensional Error Profiling via Heatmaps

The overall RMSE heatmap (Fig. 5 (L)) illustrates the spatial distribution of prediction errors across body segments, showing that the BioKFusion-Net model achieved robust joint angle predictions overall (mean RMSE ≤ 2.8), yet with notable spatial heterogeneity. The hip joint Z-axis (4.18) and knee joint X-axis (3.45) emerged as consistent error hotspots, likely reflecting underlying biomechanical complexity. Knee flexion (X-axis) involves rapid, high-amplitude motion in the sagittal plane, making it particularly sensitive to small prediction deviations. The hip Z-axis captures vertical pelvic displacement during stance transitions, which varies across individuals due to differences in load-bearing and posture control. Notably, kinetic predictions exhibited axis-specific variation: GRF prediction was accurate along the X/Y axes (RMSE ≤ 0.28), whereas the Z-axis error increased markedly to 1.84 (a 557% rise relative to the X/Y axes), indicating a systematic bottleneck in vertical dynamic prediction—potentially due to the limitations of relying solely on body weight for GRF normalization.

Subject-specific RMSE heatmaps (Fig. 6) further highlighted pronounced variability in the same measurement channel across different individuals; for instance, Subject 2 showed an ankle joint Z-axis RMSE of 5.1 (exceeding the mean error for that joint by 163%, $p < 0.001$) and a hip joint Z-axis RMSE reaching 8.2 (equating to 196% of the group mean 4.18, $p < 0.001$), while their GRF vertical component (Fz) prediction remained stable (0.77 vs. group mean 1.84). This suggests that the subject might maintain vertical mechanical output stability through compensatory mechanisms (e.g., knee/pelvic motion adjustments), albeit at the cost of substantial inaccuracies in joint angle prediction.

Subject-specific NRMSE heatmaps (Fig. 7), normalized to eliminate unit scale effects, showed that 88% of channels had error values below 0.07, strongly validating the model's overall superior predictive performance. Furthermore, while Fig. 1 indicated a relatively high RMSE in the knee joint X-axis (3.45) and Y-axis (3.09), the corresponding NRMSE value was notably low (0.0111). This discrepancy arises because the baseline biomechanical magnitude of knee joint moments in the X-axis and Y-axis is intrinsically small, inherently amplifying any minor absolute error. However, significant aberration was observed in Subject 4's ankle joint coronal plane (Y-axis) prediction (NRMSE = 0.21), exceeding the extreme outlier threshold defined by $Q3 + 3 \times IQR$ (0.11, $p < 0.001$).

5 Discussion

This study proposes BioKFusion-Net, a biomechanics-informed deep learning framework for predicting joint angles and GRF/GRM from IMUs data. The model demonstrates high sensitivity in predicting GRF/GRM in the horizontal and coronal plane, which aligns with the findings reported by Xiao et al. [18] Compared the xiao's work, the proposed method yields a 7.3% relative improvement in R^2 for hip joint angle prediction. And is consistent with the biomechanical significance of lateral GRF in individuals with atypical gait patterns [2,3]. This observation suggests a potential interplay between biomechanical variability and modeling limitations.

In Subject 4, the detection of dual anomalies in ankle Y-axis (mediolateral) predictions (NRMSE = 0.21; RMSE = 0.75) may signify a biomechanically coherent pattern, reflecting underlying pathomechanical alterations, particularly involving subtalar joint kinematics and dynamic stabilization strategies during

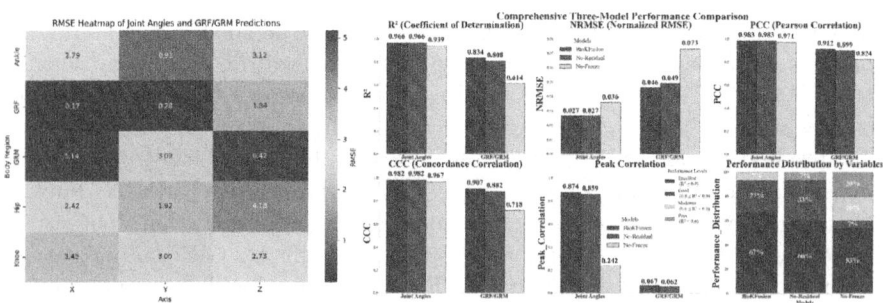

Fig. 5. Overall RMSE Heatmap(L) and Comprehensive Comparisons (R).

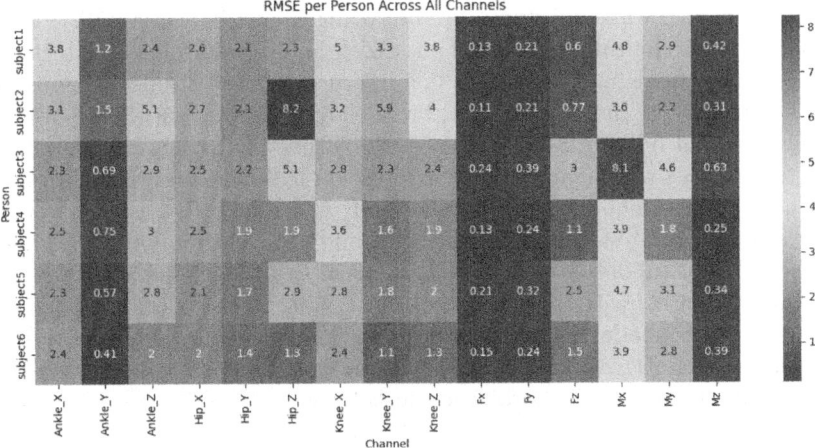

Fig. 6. RMSE Heatmap across all Channels.

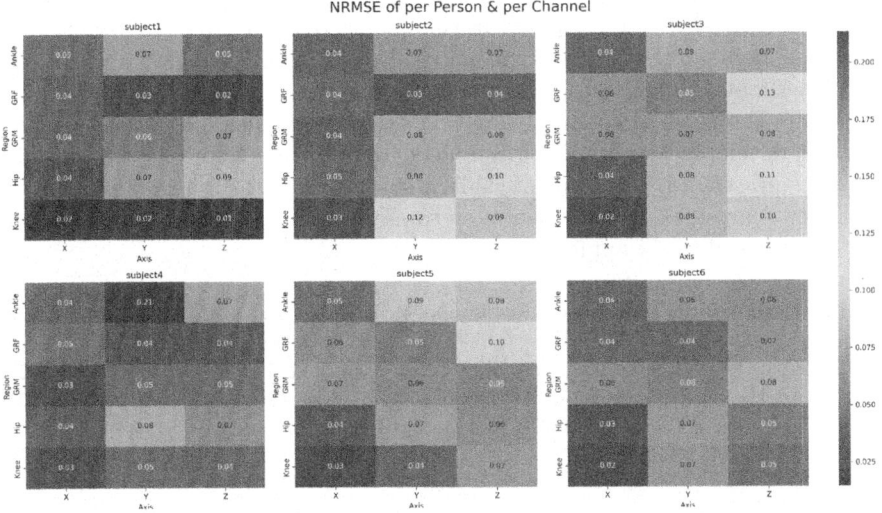

Fig. 7. NRMSE across all Channels and Subjects.

weight-bearing phases [19]. These findings provide a mechanistic entry point for refining BioKFusion-Net's biomechanical framework in future research.

Compared to purely data-driven approaches [13–16], our methods using the residual structure of the model demonstrated significant value in the prediction of dynamics, frozen training strategy effectively preserves and harmonizes multiscale gait representations spanning macroscopic movement patterns to microscopic joint kinematics. And particularly for GRF and GRM, where it outperformed non-residual architectures. This approach concurrently enhances predictive performance while substantially improving model interpretability, thereby validating the technical feasibility of implementing deep learning architectures in biomechanical modeling systems. While internal ablation studies demonstrated the effectiveness of BioKFusion-Net, broader comparisons with state-of-the-art models were not fully included in the current study due to dataset compatibility constraints. This will be an important direction in our future work.

These results highlight the potential of wearable IMU-based systems for real-world gait analysis and intelligent rehabilitation. Study limitations include laboratory-only validation and limited atypical gait samples. Future work will: 1) Expand datasets with diverse pathological gaits; 2) Incorporate electromyography (EMG) to model muscle activation mechanisms; 3) Validate in free-living environments; 4) Develop real-time computational efficiency on embedded systems for applications such as robotic exoskeletons.

6 Conclusion

The exceptional precision human walking GRM/GRF and joint angle estimation model, BioKFusion-Net, proposed in this paper, offers a promising solution for real-time monitoring of human gait, clinical pathological analysis, and assistive device control. By collecting IMU data, the model uses a data-driven approach to predict the kinematics and dynamics of the lower limbs, providing a reliable tool for developing personalized intelligent monitoring solutions. By reducing reliance on expensive equipment while maintaining measurement quality, this approach represents an important step toward portable, accessible gait analysis systems for real-world applications.

Acknowledgement. This work was supported by the National Key R&D Program of China (2022YFC3601700), the NSFC-Shenzhen Robotics Research Center Project (U2013207), the Natural Science Foundation of China (62273325, U191320, 62003327), the Natural Science Foundation of Guangdong Province (2019A1515010782), and the SIAT-CUHK Joint Laboratory of Robotics and Intelligent Systems.

References

1. Chang, W.R., Courtney, T.K., Grönqvist, R., Redfern, M.S.: Measuring Slipperiness: Human Locomotion and Surface Factors, vol. 1. CRC Press, Boca Raton (2003)
2. Slijepcevic, D., et al.: Explaining machine learning models for clinical gait analysis. ACM Trans. Comput. Healthcare **3**(2), 1–27 (2021)
3. Nüesch, C., Valderrabano, V., Huber, C., von Tscharner, V., Pagenstert, G.: Gait patterns of asymmetric ankle osteoarthritis patients. Clin. Biomech. **27**(6), 613–618 (2012)
4. Pardoel, S., Nantel, J., Kofman, J., Lemaire, E.D.: Prediction of freezing of gait in parkinson's disease using unilateral and bilateral plantar-pressure data. Front. Neurol. **13**, 831063 (2022). https://doi.org/10.3389/fneur.2022.831063. PMID: 35572938; PMCID: PMC9101469

5. Cavanagh, P.R., Lafortune, M.A.: Ground reaction forces in distance running. J. Biomech. **13**(5), 397–406 (1980)
6. Dallalana, R.J., Brooks, J.H.M., Kemp, S.P.T., Williams, A.M.: The epidemiology of knee injuries in English professional rugby union. Amer. J. Sports Med. **35**(5), 818–830 (2007)
7. Ettema, G., Braaten, S., Danielsen, J., Fjeld, B.E.: Imitation jumps in ski jumping: technical execution and relationship to performance level. J. Sports Sci. **38**(18), 2155–2160 (2020)
8. Koseki, S., Mohseni, O., Owaki, D., Hayashibe, M., Seyfarth, A., Sharbafi, M.A.: Concerted control: modulating joint stiffness using GRF for gait generation at different speeds. IEEE Rob. Autom. Lett. **10**(4), 3446–3453 (2025). https://doi.org/10.1109/LRA.2025.3542703
9. Ancillao, A., Tedesco, S., Barton, J., O'Flynn, B.: Indirect measurement of GRF and moments by means of wearable inertial sensors: a systematic review. Sensors **18**(8), 2564 (2018)
10. Refai, M.I.M., Beijnum, B.F., Buurke, J.H., Veltink, P.H.: Portable gait lab: estimating 3D GRF using a pelvis IMU in a foot IMU defined frame. IEEE Trans. Neural Syst. Rehabil. Eng. **28**(6), 1308–1316 (2020)
11. Durandau, G., Farina, D., Sartori, M.: Robust real-time musculoskeletal modeling driven by electromyograms. IEEE Trans. Biomed. Eng. **65**(3), 556–564 (2018)
12. Zhang, Y., Fei, Q., Chen, Z., Liu, X.: Estimation of normal ground reaction forces in multiple treadmill skiing movements using IMU sensors with optimized locations. IEEE Sens. J. **24**(16), 25972–25985 (2024). https://doi.org/10.1109/JSEN.2024.3418870
13. Molinaro, D.D., Kang, I., Camargo, J., Gombolay, M.C., Young, A.J.: Subject-independent, biological hip moment estimation during multimodal overground ambulation using deep learning. IEEE Trans. Med. Robot. Bionics **4**(1), 219–229 (2022)
14. Leporace, G., Batista, L.A., Metsavaht, L., Nadal, J.: Residual analysis of ground reaction forces simulation during gait using neural networks with different configurations. In: Proceedings of 37th Annual International Conference and IEEE Engineering Medical Biology Society (EMBC), pp. 2812–2815 (2015)
15. Mundt, M., et al.: Prediction of lower limb joint angles and moments during gait using artificial neural networks. Med. Biol. Eng. Comput. **58**(1), 211–225 (2020)
16. Hossain, M.S.B., Guo, Z., Choi, H.: Estimation of lower extremity joint moments and 3D ground reaction forces using IMU sensors in multiple walking conditions: a deep learning approach. IEEE J. Biomed. Health Inf. **27**(6), 2829–2840 (2023). https://doi.org/10.1109/JBHI.2023.3262164
17. Lim, H., Kim, B., Park, S.: Prediction of lower limb kinetics and kinematics during walking by a single IMU on the lower back using machine learning. Sensors **20**(1), 130 (2020)
18. Xiao, C., et al.: 3D forward dynamics modeling for gait analysis using inertial measurement units. J. Biomech. **89**, 123–131 (2019)
19. Sarrafian, S.K.: Biomechanics of the subtalar joint complex. Clin. Orthopaedics Related Res. (290) (1993). https://doi.org/10.1097/00003086-199305000-00003

Effects of Rhythmic Auditory Cues on Brain Network Characterization During Human Gait Initiation

Huilin Zhou[1,2], Zefeng Shou[1,2,3], Tao Meng[1,2,4], Xuelian Wang[1,2], Tao Liu[1,2,3], Wenan Zhang[3], Guokun Zuo[1,2(✉)], and Changcheng Shi[1,2(✉)]

[1] Ningbo Institute of Materials Engineering and Technology, Chinese Academy of Sciences, Ningbo 315201, Zhejiang, People's Republic of China
{moonstone,changchengshi}@nimte.ac.cn

[2] Ningbo Cixi Institute of Biomedical Engineering, Ningbo 315300, Zhejiang, People's Republic of China

[3] College of Information Engineering, Zhejiang University of Technology, Hangzhou 310023, Zhejiang, People's Republic of China

[4] Cixi Biomedical Research Institute, Wenzhou Medical University, Ningbo 315302, Zhejiang, People's Republic of China

Abstract. Rhythmic auditory cues (RAC) have demonstrated benefits for gait initiation (GI) in human. However, the underlying neurophysiological mechanisms remain poorly understood. This study employed electroencephalography (EEG) to characterize how RAC modulates dynamic brain network connectivity during human GI. The brain functional connectivity strengths and graph theory were analyzed during the GI tasks in 20 healthy participants under the RAC and non-rhythmic auditory cues (Non_RAC) conditions. The results showed that, compared to Non_RAC, RAC enhanced θ-band network connectivity between the prefrontal and frontal regions and suppressed α-band network connectivity in the frontal area during the GI anticipation phase. During the GI response phase, RAC elicited stronger β-band network connectivity in the frontal area but weaker network connectivity in motor area relative to Non_RAC. These findings suggest that RAC improves motor preparation efficiency and attention levels during GI anticipation, and optimizes the pattern of cognitive-motor network information interaction during the GI response to facilitate more efficient GI execution. This study provides theoretical insights supporting the application of RAC in gait modulation and other cognitive-motor tasks.

Keywords: Rhythmic Auditory Cues · Gait Initiation · Brain Networks · Functional Connectivity · Graph Theory

1 Introduction

Rhythmic auditory cues (RAC) can enhance gait and postural control during walking through externally paced rhythmic beats [1, 2]. These benefits are especially pronounced in patients with Parkinson's disease (PD), where RAC have been shown to mitigate freezing of gait (FOG) and improve key gait parameters, including speed, stride length, and symmetry [3, 4]. While gait initiation (GI) is essential for maintaining balance and locomotor coordination [5], the neural mechanisms underlying RAC-modulated GI remain poorly understood, limiting the clinical translation of RAC-based interventions for FOG. Emerging evidence suggests that RAC may effectively modulate brain network connectivity by compensating for functional deficits in the cerebellar-thalamocortical network, thereby supporting rhythmic gait control [6–8]. It has also been proposed that RAC may influence cortical network dynamics, particularly in cognitive and motor regions. However, empirical evidence delineating the spatiotemporal characteristics of RAC-induced modulation in functional brain networks during GI is lacking.

Electroencephalography (EEG), with the advantage of millisecond-level temporal resolution, is a reliable tool for investigating the functional activity of the brain during GI. Previous studies have reported RAC-induced enhancements in event-related desynchronization (ERD) and synchronization (ERS) within the α and β bands, as well as increased β power in the subthalamic nucleus and strengthened α-β coupling across frontal, parietal, and temporal cortices [9]. These changes are linked to motor performance improvements in PD and are complemented by RAC-induced θ-β coupling between prefrontal and motor regions [2]. Despite these findings, the frequency-specific and region-specific interactions in RAC-modulated brain networks during GI are yet to be clearly characterized.

Recent advances in EEG network analysis have enabled the use of functional connectivity models to probe synchronous activity across brain regions. Specifically, the weighted phase lag index (wPLI) offers a computationally efficient and volume-conduction-resistant measure of undirected functional connectivity [10]. Graph-theoretical metrics further quantify local and global network properties [11], providing insights into the efficiency and integration of neural information processing. Given that RAC may be involved in auditory, premotor, and motor networks [12], this study aims to elucidate its impact on the functional networks of these brain regions during GI.

Therefore, this study compared the brain network topological characteristic across RAC and non-rhythmic auditory cues (Non_RAC) conditions during human GI, using undirected brain network construction and graph theoretical analysis methods. The connection strength and network efficiency of the θ, α and β frequency bands of RAC modulating prefrontal, frontal, temporal, and sensorimotor areas at different phases of GI were further assessed. By investigating the influence of RAC on brain functional networks during GI process, this study will provide ideas and theoretical basis for elucidating the neural mechanism of RAC modulating GI.

2 Materials and Methods

2.1 Participants

Twenty-three healthy adults participated in this experiment, none of whom had hearing loss, visual impairments, or a history of neurological or orthopedic disorders. The experimental protocol was approved by the local research ethics committee and adhered to the Declaration of Helsinki. Informed consent was obtained from all participants. Due to significant artifacts, EEG data from three participants were excluded. The final dataset included 20 participants (12 males and 8 females; mean age 22.80 ± 2.48 years).

2.2 Procedure

The entire experiment was conducted in an electromagnetically shielded room to minimize external interference. Participants stood 1 m away from the screen displaying the paradigms with their feet approximately 5 cm apart and their arms hanging naturally by their sides. They were instructed to fixate on the prompts displayed on the screen to complete the corresponding GI tasks under two conditions: RAC (120 beats per minute (BPM) auditory cues) and Non_RAC (no auditory stimulation). The frequency of 120 bpm was chosen for auditory stimulus because it is associated with significant improvements in high-frequency EEG activity in the motor cortex of the brain [13].

Figure 1 illustrates the experimental paradigm of GI task, which consists of four phases for each condition: fixation, GI anticipation, GI response, and step back. First, a black cross appears on the screen for 1500 ms to instruct participants to maintain a standing posture. Next, a blue solid circle appears on the screen for 2500 ms to remind participants to prepare for the GI. Then, a cue to initiate movement with either the left or right foot was presented randomly on the screen for 5,000 ms, instructing the participant to step forward with the appropriate foot to complete the GI response. Finally, a return cue was presented for 4000 ms, instructing participants to return to their original position. The main differences between the RAC and Non_RAC conditions in the four phases of GI tasks mentioned above are reflected in the GI anticipation and response phases. In the Non_RAC condition, no sound stimulus is played. Participants were instructed to avoid head movements, blinking, or swallowing during the GI anticipation phase and GI response phase. We specifically analyzed the 1500 ms GI anticipation phase and 500 ms GI response phase, segmented into four periods (Time1–Time4) with 500-ms intervals.

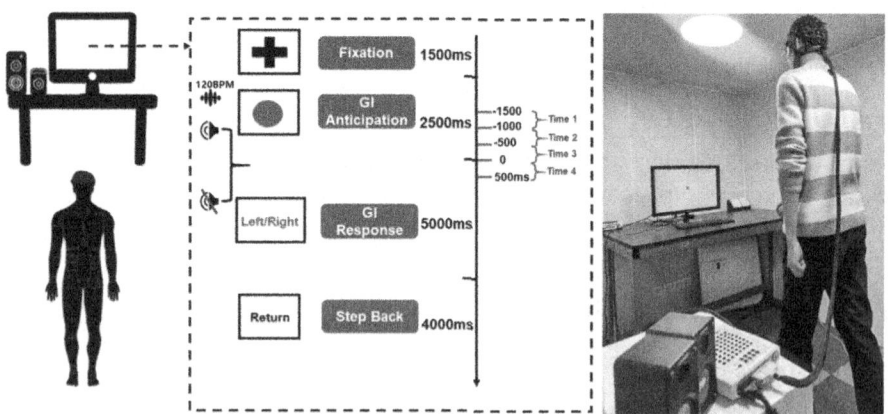

Fig. 1. Schematic diagram of RAC and Non_RAC paradigms

2.3 Data Collection

EEG data were recorded at 1000 Hz using a 64-channel SynAmps-2 system and Ag/AgCl electrodes, arranged according to the international 10–20 system. Electrode impedances were maintained below 10 kΩ. The frontal, parietal, and temporal lobes primarily mediate higher cognitive functions such as emotional processing and conflict monitoring, while the central region is mainly responsible for processing somatic sensory information and generating motor commands [14–17]. The key cortical regions include the prefrontal (FP1, FPz, FP2), frontal (F7, F5, F3, F1, Fz, F2, F4, F6, F8), central (C5, C3, C1, Cz, C2, C4, C6, CP5, CP3, CP1, CPz, CP2, CP4, CP6), and temporal (T7, TP7, T8, TP8) areas, where electrode channels are used for calculating brain functional connectivity.

2.4 Data Preprocessing

EEG data were processed using the EEGLAB toolbox (R2021b; MathWorks, USA). Continuous EEG data were re-referenced to the average of left and right mastoids, filtered with a 1 Hz high-pass, 30 Hz low-pass, and 50 Hz notch filter to remove line noise. The data were then segmented into epochs from -2500 ms to 1000 ms relative to movement onset, with baseline correction using the 500 ms pre-stimulus interval. Eye blinks and motion artifacts were removed using Independent Component Analysis (ICA) via the runica algorithm implemented in EEGLAB. Epochs with significant artifacts were manually rejected to ensure high-quality EEG signals. Artifact-free epochs of EEG signal with voltages in the range ± 100 μV were retained. Finally, band-pass filtering was applied to extract three frequency bands: θ (4−8 Hz), α (8−14 Hz), and β (14−30 Hz), yielding optimal EEG signals for functional brain network construction.

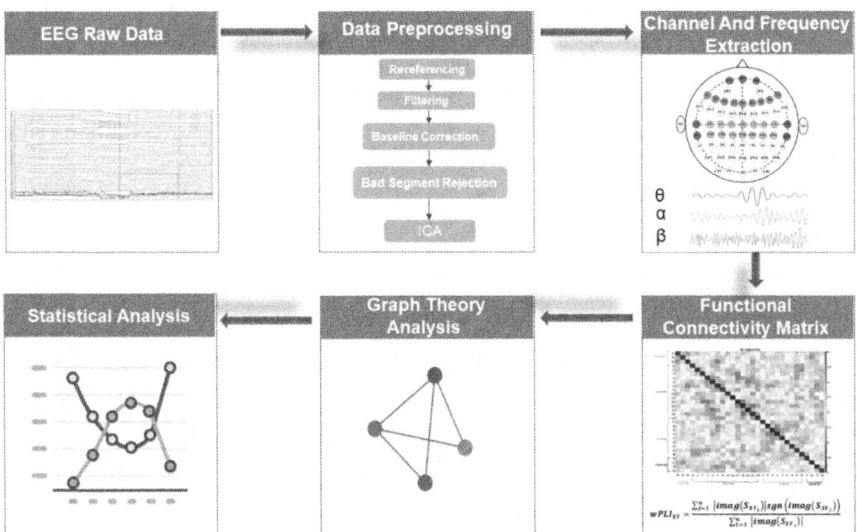

Fig. 2. Schematic diagram of brain network construction and analysis

2.5 Functional Brain Network Construction

The construction procedure of the single-layer brain network is illustrated in Fig. 2. In this study, wPLI calculations were used to construct functional brain networks, which is an optimal method for detecting phase synchronization between channels. To compute phase synchronization between two channels, we first determined the instantaneous phase of time-series signals using Hilbert transform. After extracting instantaneous phases from all channels, wPLI was calculated to obtain a functional connectivity matrix of 30 × 30. The mathematical expression of wPLI is as follows:

$$wPLI_{XY} = \frac{\sum_{t=1}^{n} |imag(S_{XY_t})| sgn(imag(S_{XY_t}))}{\sum_{t=1}^{n} |imag(S_{XY_t})|} \qquad (1)$$

where imag(·) denotes the imaginary component, sgn(·) represents the sign function, and SXYt is the cross-spectrum between variables X(t) and Y(t).

The calculation of the wPLI, implemented using the wPLI_analysis function in the FieldTrip toolbox, was performed in both RAC and Non_RAC conditions. The 30 × 30 functional connectivity matrices were computed for each participant for the three frequency bands within the four time periods (Time1-Time4).

2.6 Functional Brain Network Analysis

Prior to computing graph-theoretical metrics, the weighted functional connectivity matrices were first converted to binary adjacency matrices using density-based thresholding (11%–50% density range with 1% increments). The Brain Connectivity Toolbox (BCT) in MATLAB was employed to analyze the network properties including clustering coefficient (CC), global efficiency (GE), local efficiency (LE), and small-world (SW). For each electrode, graph metrics were calculated across all density levels and then averaged. Statistical analysis was performed in SPSS, where the area under the curve (AUC) for each metric was computed across the 11%–50% threshold range, followed by paired-sample t-tests to compare AUC values between Non_RAC and RAC conditions during the periods of Time1 to Time4.

3 Results

3.1 Functional Connectivity Strength Results

Figure 3 illustrated the comparison of θ-band functional connectivity matrices between Non_RAC and RAC conditions across Time1 to Time4. Compared to the Non_RAC, the RAC enhanced the connectivity strength of θ-band in the prefrontal-frontal areas during the GI anticipation phase (Time2 and Time3). However, during the GI response phase (Time4), the RAC generally weakened the connectivity strength of θ-band across the whole-brain compared to the Non_RAC.

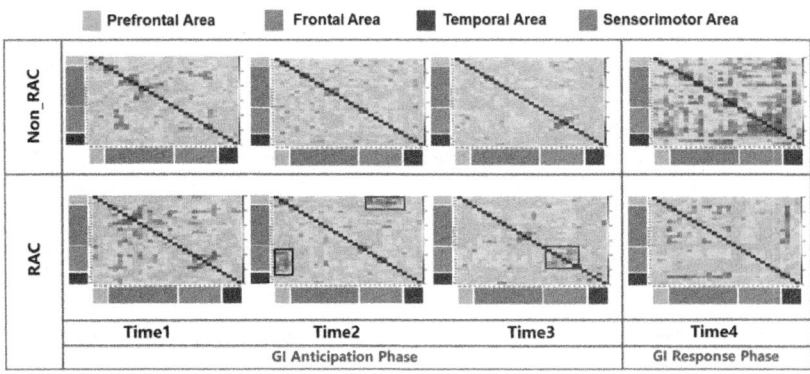

Fig. 3. Comparison of functional connectivity in the θ-band between two conditions across Time1–Time4

As shown in Fig. 4, in the α-band, RAC suppressed the frontal connectivity during the late GI anticipation phase (Time3) compared to the Non_RAC condition. During the GI response phase (Time4), both conditions exhibited strong whole-brain connectivity. Non_RAC enhanced prefrontal-frontal α-band connectivity, while RAC enhanced the intra-frontal α-band connectivity. In other words, during the GI response phase, RAC weakened the prefrontal-frontal connectivity of α-band and enhanced intra-frontal connectivity of α-band.

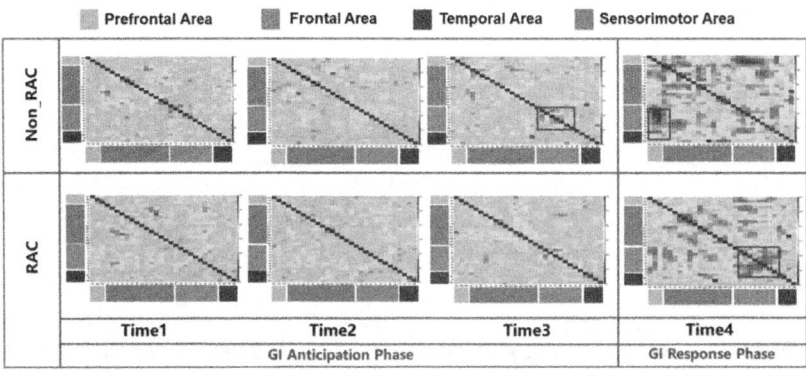

Fig. 4. Comparison of functional connectivity in the α-band between two conditions across Time1-Time4

Figure 5 illustrated the comparison of β-band functional connectivity matrices between Non_RAC and RAC conditions. The β-band connectivity results revealed that during the initial GI anticipation phase (Time1), RAC increased the intra-frontal connectivity compared to Non_RAC. During the late GI anticipation phase (Time3) and the GI response phase (Time4), RAC weakened the strength of β-band connectivity in the sensorimotor areas. Notably, during the GI response phase, the functional connectivity strength of β-band was markedly weaker than that observed in both θ and α bands.

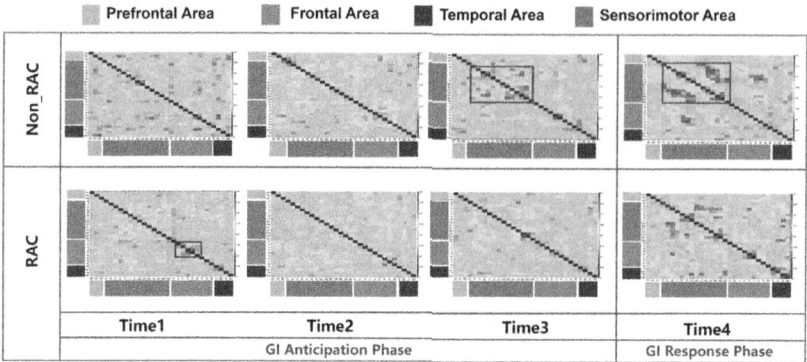

Fig. 5. Comparison of functional connectivity in the β-band between two conditions across Time1-Time4

3.2 Graph Theory Results

Figure 6 illustrated the threshold-dependent variations of graph-theoretical metrics at Time4 across all three frequency bands. And the statistical analysis was conducted on GE, LE, CC, and SW properties in three frequency bands across Time1 to Time4 under both Non_RAC and RAC conditions. Figure 7 presented the statistical results of graph-theoretical metrics across θ, α, and β bands during Time1-Time4.

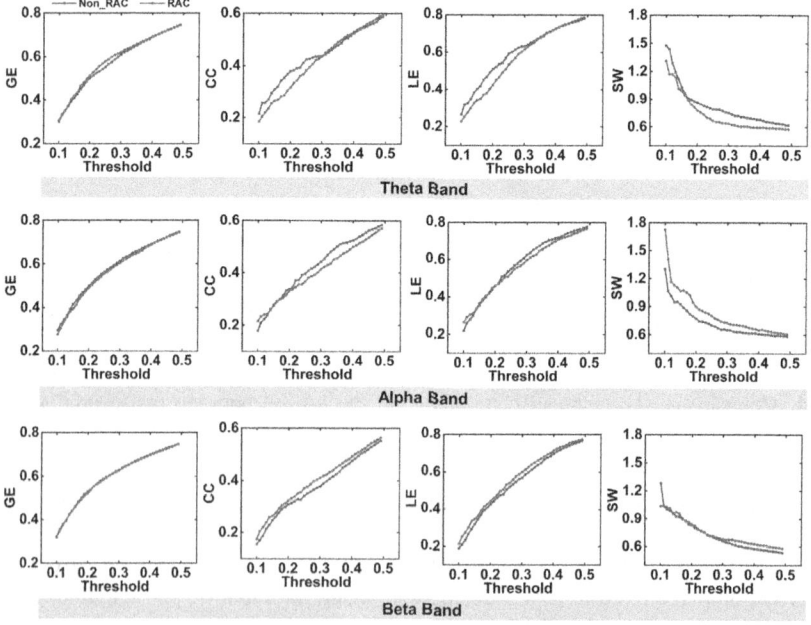

Fig. 6. Variation of graph-theoretical metrics with network sparsity at Time4 across θ, α, and β bands

In the θ-band, no significant differences were observed in the four graph-theoretical metrics between the RAC and Non_RAC conditions during Time1, indicating that RAC had not yet influenced brain network characteristics at this early stage. During Time2, RAC showed significantly higher SW values compared to Non_RAC (p = 0.048, t = −2.116), although this difference was no longer present by Time3. Visual inspection suggested marginally elevated SW properties for RAC at lower thresholds (11–25%). During GI response phase (Time4), Non_RAC exhibited significantly greater LE (p = 0.001, t = 3.965) and CC (p = 0.005, t = 3.177), alongside consistently higher SW values across thresholds (p = 0.027, t = 2.394).

In the α-band, no significant differences were observed between conditions during the GI anticipation phase (Time1-Time3). However, during the GI response phase (Time4), the CC was significantly lower in the RAC condition (p = 0.027, t = 2.391), while SW was significantly higher (p = 0.008, t = −2.969), especially across the 11%−50% threshold range.

In the β-band, no significant differences were found during the GI anticipation phase (Time1-Time3). Notably, during Time3, visual inspection revealed slightly higher SW values under RAC compared to Non_RAC within the 11%-50% threshold range. This trend suggests that RAC may have begun to exert preliminary effects on network SW properties, though not yet fully manifested. During GI response phase (Time4), the CC was significantly higher in RAC versus Non_RAC (p = 0.003, t = −3.348), with significant differences also observed in the area under the curve across the 11%−50% threshold range.

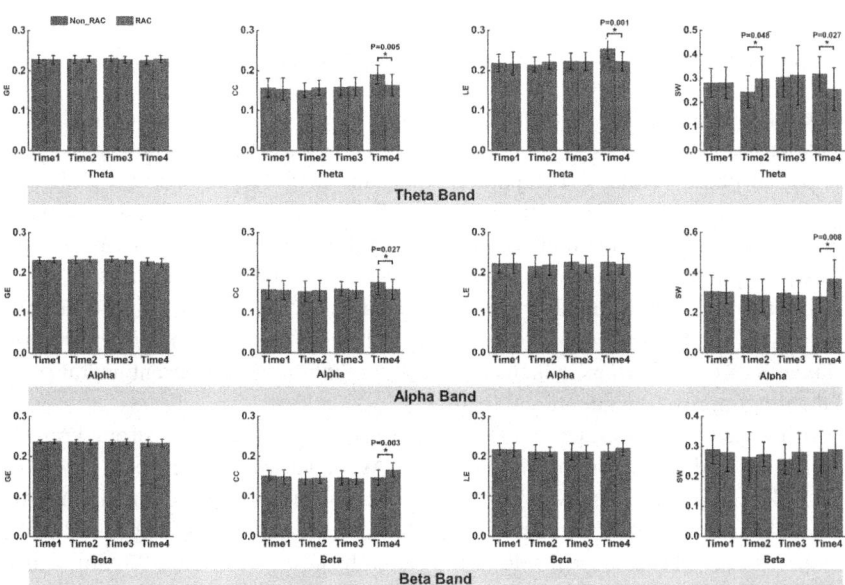

Fig. 7. Statistical analysis of graph-theoretical metrics across θ, α, and β bands during Time1−Time4

4 Discussion

This study investigated the modulatory effects of RAC on functional brain networks during GI across θ, α, and β bands. By comparing functional connectivity matrices and graph-theoretical metrics across GI anticipation to response, we elucidated the modulatory role of RAC in modulating functional connectivity and network properties of brain regions during GI, as well as their relationship with cognitive resources.

4.1 Theta-Band Functional Connectivity Linked to Motor Preparation Efficiency

In the theta band, RAC enhanced prefrontal-frontal network integration during the GI anticipation phase (Time2−Time3), as reflected in increased CC and SW metrics. Previous studies have shown that the frontal cortex is a key region for executive function [18]. RAC may enhance the efficiency of the GI anticipation phase by strengthening θ-band network connectivity between prefrontal and frontal areas [19]. The GI anticipation phase is typically associated with high cognitive load [19, 20], whereas RAC may optimize the network structure by enhancing SW and LE characteristics, thereby reducing cognitive demands [21].

During the GI response phase (Time4), global connectivity strength under the RAC condition was significantly lower than that under the Non_RAC condition. This suggests that the network optimization during the GI anticipation phase in the RAC condition reduced the subsequent requirement for extensive global brain connectivity, providing more adequate preparation for the GI response phase.

4.2 Alpha-Band Network Connectivity Modulates Attentional Levels

For the α-band, findings showed that significantly weaker frontal connectivity was exhibited under the RAC condition compared to the Non_RAC condition during the late GI anticipation phase (Time3). The pattern of α-band activity patterns was found to be strongly associated with GI anticipation [22]. The oscillations of α-band are generally considered to play a crucial inhibitory role during the sensory and GI anticipation phase [23, 24]. In particular, before GI response phase, the oscillations of α-band help the brain filter out task-irrelevant distractions to enhance the attention to motor-related neural processes. In the RAC condition, weaker frontal connectivity may be related to its modulation of α oscillations, which can effectively inhibit the irrelevant neural activity and thereby improve the attentional focus.

During the GI response phase (Time4), both conditions exhibited strong brain connectivity, but in distinct patterns. In the Non_RAC condition, the connectivity between prefrontal and frontal regions was relatively stronger, whereas the RAC condition showed enhanced connectivity within frontal regions. Previous studies have suggested that the frontal area may play a critical role in the pathophysiology of FOG [25, 26], and that auditory perception tasks also activate the frontal area [27]. Therefore, the present study suggests that RAC may promote synchronized activity within frontal regions and enhance network integration during the GI response phase.

4.3 Beta-Band Network Connectivity Shapes Cognitive-Motor Information Processing

For the β-band, the present study found that intrafrontal connections were significantly stronger in the RAC condition than in the Non-RAC condition during the early GI anticipation phase (Time1). This suggests that when receiving RAC at the initial stage of gait preparation, the brain may pre-activate certain neural circuits related to motor planning. The β-band activity is closely associated with motor coordination [28]. In the late GI anticipation phase (Time 3) and the GI response phase (Time 4), Non_RAC exhibited stronger motor area connectivity, which may reflect greater reliance on internal timing mechanisms for movement planning in the absence of external auditory cues [29], leading to increased intra-motor connectivity. In contrast, RAC optimized the information exchange between cognitive and motor networks, improving transmission efficiency and reducing the demand for high-intensity motor connectivity. This effect persisted into the GI response phase.

4.4 Neural Mechanisms of GI Modulation by RAC and Study Limitations

Overall, during the GI anticipation phase, the RAC enhanced frontal-prefrontal θ-band network connectivity to improve the efficiency of motor preparation, and attenuated frontal α-band network connectivity to inhibit extraneous neural activity and enhance the attention levels of motor preparation. During the GI response phase, β-band network connectivity under the RAC condition was enhanced in the frontal area and attenuated in motor area, optimizing the information interaction pattern between cognitive and motor networks to promote more efficient GI execution.

However, there are some limitations of the present study. First, the research was primarily conducted on healthy participants; how brain functional networks differ between healthy individuals and patients with PD under RAC remains to be explored. Second, future work should include controlled experiments with PD patients to strengthen our conclusions and provide more robust evidence. Finally, the sample size needs to be expanded to enhance statistical power.

5 Conclusions

This study investigated the effects of RAC on brain networks during GI through brain functional connectivity strength and graph theory analysis. It was found that RAC strengthened the frontal-prefrontal network connectivity during the GI anticipation phase, and improved the attention levels of motor preparation. In addition, RAC enhanced the efficiency of cognitive-motor local networks during the GI response phase and modulated these networks according to cognitive demands to facilitate more efficient GI execution. These findings not only deepen the understanding of how RAC affect brain functional network connectivity, but also provide a theoretical foundation for exploring its applications in gait control and other cognitive tasks. Further research in PD patients is needed to elucidate the neural mechanisms underlying RAC modulation of GI.

Acknowledgement. This research was supported by National Key R&D Program of China (2022YFC36017000), Natural Science Foundation of Ningbo (2022J042), Key R&D Plan Project in Zhejiang Province (2024C03101), "Scientific Innovation Yongjiang 2035" Key Technology Breakthrough Plan Projects in Ningbo City (2024Z199).

References

1. Aholt, K., et al.: A mobile solution for rhythmic auditory stimulation gait training. In: 41st Annual International Conference of the IEEE Engineering in Medicine and Biology Society (EMBC). Berlin, GERMANY, IEEE (2019)
2. Koshimori, Y., Thaut, M.H.: Rhythmic auditory stimulation as a potential neuromodulator for Parkinson's disease. Parkinsonism Relat. Disord. **113**, 105459 (2023)
3. Li, K.P., et al.: Effect of music-based movement therapy on the freezing of gait in patients with Parkinson's disease: a randomized controlled trial. Front. Aging Neurosci. **14**, 924784 (2022)
4. Cursiol, J.A., et al.: Rhythmic auditory cues improve gait asymmetry during unobstructed walking in people with Parkinson's disease but have no effect on obstacle avoidance - AsymmGait-Parkinson study. Front. Aging Neurosci. **17**, 1455432 (2025)
5. Hiraoka, K., et al.: Rhythmic movement and rhythmic auditory cues enhance anticipatory postural adjustment of gait initiation. Somatosens. Mot. Res. **37**(3), 213–221 (2020)
6. Naro, A., et al.: What about the role of the cerebellum in music-associated functional recovery? A secondary EEG analysis of a randomized clinical trial in patients with Parkinson disease. Parkinsonism Relat. Disord. **96**, 57–64 (2022)
7. Tosserams, A., Bloem, B.R., Nonnekes, J.: Compensation strategies for gait impairments in Parkinson's disease: from underlying mechanisms to daily clinical practice. Mov. Disord. Clin. Pract. **10**(Suppl 2), S56–S62 (2023)
8. Tosserams, A., et al.: Management of freezing of gait - mechanism-based practical recommendations. Nat. Rev. Neurol. **21**(6), 327–344 (2025)
9. Chen, R., et al.: Clinical neurophysiology of Parkinson's disease and parkinsonism. Clin. Neurophysiol. Pract. **7**, 201–227 (2022)
10. Vinck, M., et al.: An improved index of phase-synchronization for electrophysiological data in the presence of volume-conduction, noise and sample-size bias. Neuroimage **55**(4), 1548–1565 (2011)
11. Sancetta, B.M., et al.: Altered neural avalanche spreading in people with drug-resistant epilepsy. Neuroimage 311 (2025)
12. Pranjic, M., et al.: From sound to movement: mapping the neural mechanisms of auditory-motor entrainment and synchronization. Brain Sci. **14**(11), 1063 (2024)
13. Kucikiene, D., Praninskiene, R.: The impact of music on the bioelectrical oscillations of the brain. Acta Medica Lituanica **25**(2), 101–106 (2018)
14. Brovelli, A., et al.: Beta oscillations in a large-scale sensorimotor cortical network: directional influences revealed by granger causality. Proc. Natl. Acad. Sci. U.S.A. **101**(26), 9849–9854 (2004)
15. Miller, E.K., Cohen, J.D.: An integrative theory of prefrontal cortex function. Annu. Rev. Neurosci. **24**, 167–202 (2001)
16. Andersen, R.A., Buneo, C.A.: Intentional maps in posterior parietal cortex. Annu. Rev. Neurosci. **25**, 189–220 (2002)
17. Squire, L.R., Stark, C.E.L., Clark, R.E.: The medial temporal lobe. Annu. Rev. Neurosci. **27**, 279–306 (2004)

18. Albouy, P., et al.: Supramodality of neural entrainment: rhythmic visual stimulation causally enhances auditory working memory performance. Sci. Adv. **8**(8), eabj9782 (2022)
19. Zhou, H.L., et al.: Allocation of cognitive resources in cognitive processing of rhythmic visual stimuli before gait-related motor initiation. Front. Neurosci. **17**, 15 (2023)
20. Wu, J.J., et al.: Effects of rhythmic visual cues on cortical activation and functional connectivity features during stepping: an fNIRS study. Front. Hum. Neurosci. **18**, 11 (2024)
21. Li, J.W., et al.: Rhythmic auditory stimuli induced neural oscillation entrainment and its applications. Prog. Biochem. Biophys. **50**(6), 1371–1380 (2023)
22. Jacobsen, N.A., Ferris, D.P.: Electrocortical activity correlated with locomotor adaptation during split-belt treadmill walking. J. Physiol.-London **601**(17), 3921–3944 (2023)
23. Malcolm, B.R., et al.: Cognitive load reduces the effects of optic flow on gait and electrocortical dynamics during treadmill walking. J. Neurophysiol. **120**(5), 2246–2259 (2018)
24. Thevathasan, W., Moro, E.: What is the therapeutic mechanism of pedunculopontine nucleus stimulation in Parkinson's disease? Neurobiol. Dis. **128**, 67–74 (2019)
25. Ueno, E.: Clinical and physiological study of apraxia of gait and frozen gait. Clin. Neurol. **29**(3), 275–283 (1989)
26. Hwang, H.W., et al.: Paroxysmal freezing of gait in a patient with mesial frontal transient ischemic attacks. BMC Neurol. **17**, 4 (2017)
27. Binder, J.R., et al.: Neural correlates of sensory and decision processes in auditory object identification. Nat. Neurosci. **7**(3), 295–301 (2004)
28. Pfurtscheller, G., Stancak, A., Neuper, C.: Event-related synchronization (ERS) in the alpha band - An electrophysiological correlate of cortical idling: a review. Int. J. Psychophysiol. **24**(1–2), 39–46 (1996)
29. Fiveash, A., et al.: When visual cues do not help the beat: evidence for a detrimental effect of moving point-light figures on rhythmic priming. Front. Psychol. **13**, 7987 (2022)

Effects of Exoskeleton-Assisted Sit-to-Stand Training Based on Cortical-Muscular Coherence

Xiaoke Peng, Shiyu Han, Guoshun Zhao, and Anqin Dong[✉]

The Fifth Affiliated Hospital of Zhengzhou University, Zhengzhou 450052, Henan, China
anqindong@163.com

Abstract. This study aimed to investigate the effects of exoskeleton robot-assisted sit-to-stand training on balance, lower limb motor function, and Activities of daily living (ADL) in hemiplegic stroke patients, evaluated via cortico-muscular coherence (CMC) analysis. Forty-eight patients were randomized into an exoskeleton group and a control group. Both groups received conventional rehabilitation therapy. The exoskeleton group underwent exoskeleton-assisted sit-to-stand transfer training in addition to conventional therapy, while the control group received traditional lower limb rehabilitation training. After 3 weeks of intervention (5 days/week, 30 min/session), both groups showed significant improvements in Berg Balance Scale (BBS), Fugl-Meyer Assessment - Lower Extremity (FMA-LE), and Modified Barthel Index (MBI) scores ($P < 0.05$). The exoskeleton group demonstrated greater improvements in BBS and MBI ($P < 0.05$), with no significant difference in FMA-LE. CMC analysis revealed notable post-intervention increases in β (13–30 Hz) and γ (>30 Hz) bands for both groups, with more pronounced improvements in the exoskeleton group ($P < 0.05$). These findings indicate exoskeleton robot-assisted training outperforms conventional rehabilitation in enhancing balance and ADL, likely by improving CMC during sit-to-stand tasks.

Keywords: Exoskeleton Robot · Lower Proper Motor function · Cortical-Muscular Coherence

1 Introduction

Stroke is a leading cause of global mortality and disability, with approximately 60% of patients experiencing balance and lower limb dysfunction [1]. Post-stroke, impaired weight transfer often hinders sit-to-stand (STS) movements, compromising daily activities like walking and transfers [2]. Traditional STS training improves mobility but may inadvertently reinforce asymmetric weight-bearing toward the unaffected side due to therapist variability and patient fatigue, exacerbating abnormal movement patterns [3, 4].

Exoskeleton robotics has emerged as a promising rehabilitation tool, enabling precise joint control and repetitive task-oriented training [5, 6]. This study leverages cortico-muscular coherence (CMC)—a neurophysiological measure of brain-muscle interaction during movement—to evaluate exoskeleton-assisted STS training [7]. CMC reflects motor system functionality, with Electroencephalogram-Electromyogram (EEG-EMG) coherence in β (13–30 Hz) and γ (>30 Hz) bands linked to force control and fine movements [8–11]. Post-stroke, CMC is reduced but strengthens with motor recovery [11, 12].

While exoskeleton-assisted gait training is well-studied, STS training remains underexplored [13]. This study assesses exoskeleton-assisted STS efficacy in improving balance, lower limb function, and daily living activities in hemiplegic stroke patients, using CMC analysis to quantify neurophysiological recovery. Findings may advance exoskeleton applications in stroke rehabilitation.

2 Methods

2.1 Study Population

This single-blind randomized controlled trial enrolled 48 hemiplegic stroke inpatients from our rehabilitation department. Inclusion criteria: (1) Stroke diagnosis per Chinese guidelines 2019 with neuroimaging confirmation [14]; (2) Age 18–79 years; (3) Unilateral hemiparesis (2 weeks-6 months post-stroke); (4) Sitting balance ≥ Level 2, Brunnstrom stage II-V; (5) Cognitively intact. Exclusion criteria: (1) Unstable comorbidities; (2) Skin lesions at device contact sites; (3) Major organ failure; (4) Other neurological conditions; (5) Recent trial participation (3 months). Approved by the Medical Ethics Committee of the Fifth Affiliated Hospital of Zhengzhou University (KY2023076) and registered by China Clinical Trial Registry (CTR2400094656). This research topic is derived from the National Key Research and Development Programme of China, topic III, 'Assessment of bi-directional neural pathway remodelling and prediction of rehabilitation oriented towards postural transition' (2022YFC3601703).

2.2 Study Protocol

Randomization was performed using SPSS 27.0 by independent staff not involved in recruitment or treatment. Participants were equally allocated to control ($n = 24$) or robotic ($n = 24$) groups. Both groups received standard pharmacological and rehabilitation treatments. The control group underwent therapist-assisted sit-to-stand training using elastic bands/weights (30 min/day, 5 days/week, 3 weeks). The robotic group completed equivalent training using the ProWalk exoskeleton (Shenzhen E. Excel Vise Co., Ltd.). See Fig. 1.

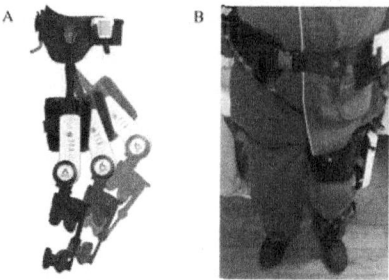

Fig. 1. A: The Prowalk unilateral wearable exoskeleton robot used in this study. B: a case of left hemiplegic stroke patient undergoing sit-stand transition training.

2.3 Outcome Indicators

This study employed the Berg Balance Scale (BBS), Fugl-Meyer Assessment for Lower Extremity (FMA-LE), and Modified Barthel Index (MBI) to evaluate both the robotic and control groups before and after the 3-week intervention. Concurrently, EEG-EMG synchronous acquisition system was used to analyze corticomuscular coupling in the robotic group: Participants wore a 16-channel Grintek EEG cap, placed according to the international 10–20 system, covering motor-related brain regions including C1, C2, C3, C4, F3, F4, FC1, FC2, FC5, FC6, CP1, CP2, CP5, CP6, P3, and P4, with EMG electrodes attached to the tibialis anterior (TA) and rectus femoris (RF) muscles on the affected lower limb and achilles tendon as reference electrode, see Fig. 2. The experiment utilized an EEG-EMG synchronous acquisition system developed by Harbin Institute of Technology (Shenzhen)) to record real-time EEG-EMG data during 3-s sit-to-stand transitions, see Fig. 3. For data analysis, EEG signals from the contralateral central motor area (C1/C2) of the affected limb and EMG signals from TA and RF muscles were selected. CMC was computed for EEG-TA and EEG-RF pairs by averaging coherence values across all time-frequency points during the 3-s movement, enabling pre-post intervention comparison.

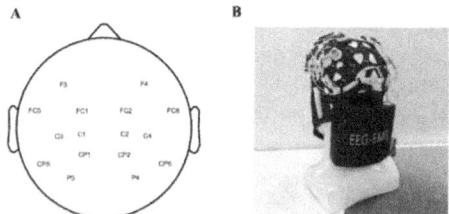

Fig. 2. A: 16-Channel EEG Electrode Placement. B: Synchronized EEG-EMG Acquisition System

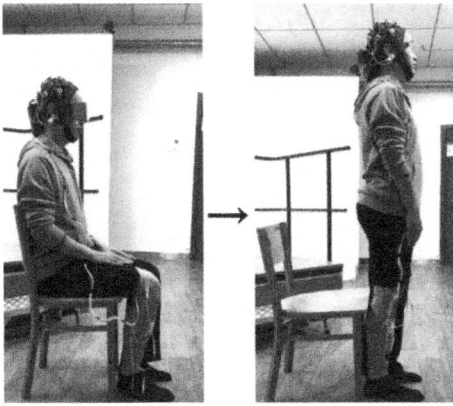

Fig. 3. Sit-to-Stand Brain-Muscle Coupling Data Collection

2.4 Data Processing

The EEG-EMG signal processing received technical support from Harbin Institute of Technology's Shenzhen campus. For EEG preprocessing, we applied bandpass filtering between 1–49 Hz and notch filtering at 50 Hz using Butterworth filters through MATLAB's EEGLAB toolbox. After filtering, artifacts were removed through visual inspection and Independent Component Analysis, which separates signal components based on their statistical independence. EMG signals underwent similar processing with 20–450 Hz bandpass filtering, rectification, and power line interference removal, see Fig. 4. The preprocessing pipeline concluded by segmenting signals into 3-s windows synchronized with movement onset through video recording alignment to ensure temporal accuracy in motion paradigm analysis. Continuous wavelets transform analyses signals using time scale functions, constructing wavelet function bases by time shifting and scale scaling. Since wavelets have time-shift and multi-scale resolution, they can be analysed simultaneously in the time-frequency domain.

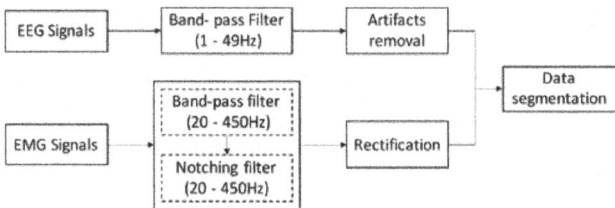

Fig. 4. Pre-processing flow of EEG data and EMG data

2.5 Statistical Analysis

Statistical analyses were performed using SPSS 27.0 and MATLAB R2023b. Data are presented as mean ± SD. Between-group differences were assessed using t-tests (Wilcoxon for non-normal data, $P < 0.05$). Within-group pre-post comparisons of clinical scales (BBS, FMA-LE, MBI) and corticomuscular coherence used paired t-tests (Wilcoxon for non-normal data). EEG-EMG coupling analysis was conducted in MATLAB (Fig. 5).

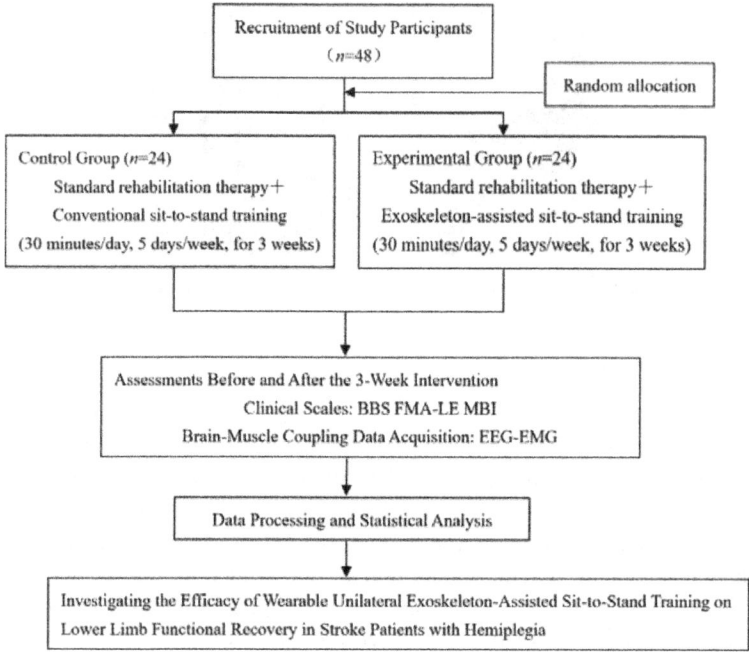

Fig. 5. Clinical Trial Flowchart

3 Results

3.1 Comparison of General Information

A total of 43 participants completed the 3-week intervention (robotic group: $n = 21$; control group: $n = 22$). Five subjects discontinued (robotic group: 2 due to early discharge, 1 due to knee discomfort; control group: 2 due to early discharge). Baseline characteristics including gender, hemiparesis side, age, disease duration, BBS, FMA-LE, and MBI scores showed no significant between-group differences ($P > 0.05$), confirming comparability. See Table 1.

Table 1. Comparison of general information in the robotic group and the control group.

		Robotic group	Control group	Statistic	P
Examples		21	22		
	Male	15	14		
Genders				$\chi^2 = 0.297$	0.586

(*continued*)

Table 1. (*continued*)

		Robotic group	Control group	Statistic	P
	Female	6	8		
Anatomy	Left	19	11	$\chi^2 = 0.220$	0.639
	Right	12	11		
Age (years)		48.52 ± 9.93	44.55 ± 10.03	t = 1.306	0.199
Duration (days)		83.14 ± 30.61	88.73 ± 30.51	t = −0.318	0.752
BBS		15.14 ± 6.75	13.50 ± 5.24	t = 0.894	0.376
FMA-LE		14.24 ± 4.15	14.50 ± 4.02	t = −0.210	0.834
MBI		39.14 ± 12.18	38.64 ± 14.65	t = 0.123	0.903

3.2 Comparison of BBS Scores

Before the intervention, there was no statistically significant difference between the BBS scores of the robot group and the control group when compared between the groups ($P > 0.05$). After 3 weeks of intervention, the BBS scores of both groups increased compared to the pre-intervention period, and the difference was statistically significant ($P < 0.001$). The difference between the BBS scores of the two groups was statistically significant ($P < 0.05$). See Table 2.

Table 2. Comparison of BBS scores between the robotic and control groups before and after intervention

	Robotic group	Control group	T	P
Examples	21	22		
Pre-intervention BBS	15.14 ± 6.75	13.50 ± 5.24	0.894	0.376
Post-intervention BBS	25.57 ± 8.01	20.32 ± 5.72	2.465	0.019*
T	−10.085	−11.070		
P	<0.001***	<0.001***		

Note: * $P<0.05$, *** $P<0.001$

3.3 Comparison of FMA-LE Scores

Before the intervention, there was no statistically significant difference between the FMA-LE scores of the robotics group and the control group when compared between the groups ($P > 0.05$). After 3 weeks of intervention, the FMA-LE scores of both groups increased compared with the pre-intervention period, and the difference was statistically significant ($P < 0.001$). The difference between the FMA-LE scores of the two groups was not statistically significant when compared between the two groups ($P > 0.05$). See Table 3.

Table 3. Comparison of FMA-LE scores between the robotic and control groups before and after intervention

	Robotic group	Control group	T	P
Examples	21	22		
Pre-intervention FMA-LE	14.24 ± 4.15	14.50 ± 4.02	−0.210	0.834
Post-intervention FMA-LE	17.48 ± 4.83	17.73 ± 3.99	−0.186	0.853
T	−7.831	−9.452		
P	<0.001***	<0.001***		

Note: * $P<0.05$, *** $P<0.001$

3.4 Comparison of MBI Scores

Before the intervention, there was no statistically significant difference between the MBI scores of the robot group and the control group when compared between the groups ($P > 0.05$). After 3 weeks of intervention, the MBI scores of both groups increased compared to the pre-intervention period, and the difference was statistically significant ($P < 0.001$). The difference between the MBI scores of the two groups was statistically significant ($P < 0.05$). For details, see Table 4.

Table 4. Comparison of MBI scores between the robotic and control groups before and after intervention

	Robotic group	Control group	T	P
Examples	21	22		
Pre-intervention MBI	39.14 ± 12.18	38.64 ± 14.65	0.123	0.903
Post-intervention MBI	53.38 ± 10.53	44.95 ± 13.40	2.285	0.028*
T	−11.224	−7.422		
P	<0.001***	<0.001***		

Note: * $P<0.05$, *** $P<0.001$

3.5 Assessment of Rehabilitation Effectiveness Based on Cortical Muscle Coherence

Time-Frequency Effects of Cortical Muscle Coherence. After the 3-week exoskeleton intervention, mean CMC values increased across α-γ frequency bands, with particularly significant EEG-EMG coherence enhancements in β and γ bands (Fig. 6).

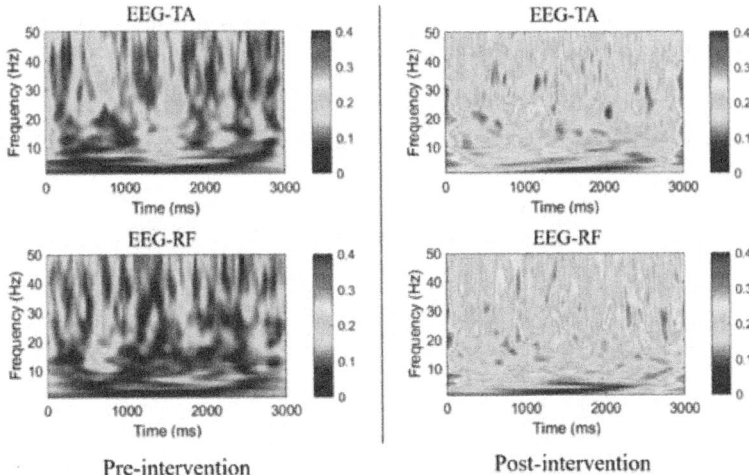

Fig. 6. Time-frequency plots of EEG-TA versus EEG-RF before intervention versus after intervention with the 3 weeks exoskeleton robot.

Comparison of Cortical Muscle Coherence in Beta and Gamma Frequency Bands. The robotic and control groups showed comparable baseline β-band CMC values in EEG-TA and EEG-RF ($P > 0.05$). Post-intervention, both groups demonstrated significant CMC increases in EEG-TA ($P < 0.001$) and EEG-RF ($P < 0.05$). Notably, the robotic group exhibited significantly greater β-band CMC improvements than controls ($P < 0.05$), indicating enhanced corticomuscular coherence with exoskeleton rehabilitation. See Table 5.

Table 5. Comparison of cortical muscle coherence in the β-band

	Robotic group	Control group	T	P
EEG-TA CMC				
Pre-intervention	0.13 ± 0.03	0.12 ± 0.03	0.596	0.559
Post-intervention	0.19 ± 0.06	0.14 ± 0.03	2.290	0.036*
T	−4.016	−2.606		
P	<0.001***	0.031*		
EEG-RF CMC				
Pre-intervention	0.12 ± 0.04	0.13 ± 0.03	−0.493	0.629
Post-intervention	0.21 ± 0.06	0.14 ± 0.03	3.201	0.006*
T	−5.047	−2.624		
P	<0.001***	0.030*		

Note: * $P<0.05$, *** $P<0.001$

Both groups showed similar baseline γ-band CMC values in EEG-TA/EEG-RF ($P > 0.05$). Post-intervention, both groups demonstrated significant CMC increases ($P <$

0.001), with the robotic group showing greater improvement than controls ($P < 0.05$), indicating enhanced γ-band corticomuscular coherence with robotic rehabilitation. See Table 6.

Table 6. Comparison of cortical muscle coherence in the gamma frequency band

	Robotic group	Control group	T	P
EEG-TA CMC				
Pre-intervention	0.13 ± 0.03	0.11 ± 0.02	1.730	0.103
Post-intervention	0.20 ± 0.06	0.15 ± 0.03	2.234	0.040*
T	−5.539	−4.299		
P	<0.001***	<0.001***		
EEG-RF CMC				
Pre-intervention	0.13 ± 0.03	0.11 ± 0.02	1.541	0.143
Post-intervention	0.21 ± 0.06	0.15 ± 0.05	2.466	0.025*
T	−5.160	−2.012		
P	<0.001***	<0.001***		

Note: * $P<0.05$, *** $P<0.001$

4 Discussion

4.1 Exoskeleton Robotics Improves Balance, Lower Limb Motor Function and Activities of Daily Living

The robotic group demonstrated significant improvements in BBS, FMA-LE, and MBI scores compared to baseline ($P < 0.001$), with greater BBS ($P = 0.019$) and MBI ($P = 0.028$) improvements versus controls, indicating enhanced balance and daily living function. These benefits likely stem from the ProWalk robot's task-specific training algorithms, which provide adjustable resistance during sitting and phase-dependent assistance during standing [15]. However, no significant between-group difference in FMA-LE scores ($P = 0.853$) suggested comparable lower limb motor recovery, consistent with mixed findings in prior exoskeleton studies [16–18]. This variability may reflect technological limitations in current exoskeleton systems.

4.2 Exoskeleton Robotic Training Improves Cortical Muscle Coherence in Patients

After the 3-week exoskeleton intervention, mean CMC values increased across α–γ frequency bands, with particularly significant EEG-EMG coherence enhancements in β and γ bands. This is consistent with previous studies [19]. Both groups showed increased EEG-TA/RF CMC post-intervention (β-band: $P < 0.05$; γ-band: $P < 0.001$), with significantly greater improvements in the robotic group ($P < 0.05$). The β-band enhancement suggests improved movement planning and postural control [20], consistent with findings that β-range coherence facilitates corticospinal interactions [21]. The γ-band improvement indicates enhanced sensorimotor integration and motor precision, supported by evidence of γ-band's role in dynamic movement control [22]. These frequency-specific CMC enhancements demonstrate exoskeleton training's superior efficacy in promoting corticomotor connectivity and functional recovery.

4.3 Limitations

There are some limitations in this study: (1) the study period is relatively short, failing to observe the long-term maintenance of the exoskeleton-assisted sitting and standing training effect; (2) the current EEG-EMG analysis only focuses on the contralateral central motor area of the affected limb (C1/C2), and in the future, we can expand the scope of data collection and increase the comparative analysis of the coherence of cortical muscles in the brain area of the healthy/affected side.

5 Conclusion

This study demonstrated that unilateral exoskeleton training significantly improved balance and daily function in stroke patients compared to conventional rehabilitation. Three-week intervention enhanced β- and γ-band corticomuscular coherence during sit-to-stand movements, revealing new neurophysiological mechanisms supporting exoskeleton-assisted rehabilitation.

References

1. Wang, W., Jiang, B., Sun, H., et al.: Prevalence, incidence, and mortality of stroke in china: results from a nationwide population-based survey of 480 687 adults. Circulation **135**(8), 759–771 (2017)
2. Liu, M., Chen, J., Fan, W., et al.: Effects of modified sit-to-stand training on balance control in hemiplegic stroke patients: a randomized controlled trial. Clin. Rehabil. **30**(7), 627–636 (2016)
3. Colón-Emeric, C.S., McDermott, C.L., Lee, D.S., et al.: Risk assessment and prevention of falls in older community-dwelling adults: a review. JAMA **331**(16), 1397–1406 (2024)
4. Pinto, E.B., Nascimento, C., Marinho, C., et al.: Risk factors associated with falls in adult patients after stroke living in the community: baseline data from a stroke cohort in Brazil. Top. Stroke Rehabil. **21**(3), 220–227 (2014)
5. Berriozabalgoitia, R., Bidaurrazaga-Letona, I., Otxoa, E., et al.: Overground robotic program preserves gait in individuals with multiple sclerosis and moderate to severe impairments: a randomized controlled trial. Arch. Phys. Med. Rehabil. **102**(5), 932–939 (2021)
6. Molteni, F., Gasperini, G., Cannaviello, G., et al.: Exoskeleton and end-effector robots for upper and lower limbs rehabilitation: narrative review. PMR **10**(9 Suppl. 2), S174–S188 (2018)
7. Keihani, A., Mohammadi, A.M., Marzbani, H., et al.: Sparse representation of brain signals offers effective computation of cortico-muscular coupling value to predict the task-related and non-task sEMG channels: a joint hdEEG-sEMG study. PLoS ONE **17**(7), e0270757 (2022)

8. Mima, T., Toma, K., Koshy, B., et al.: Coherence between cortical and muscular activities after subcortical stroke. Stroke **32**(11), 2597–2601 (2001)
9. Belardinelli, P., Laer, L., Ortiz, E., et al.: Plasticity of premotor cortico-muscular coherence in severely impaired stroke patients with hand paralysis. Neuroimage Clin. **14**, 726–733 (2017)
10. Gerloff, C., Braun, C., Staudt, M., et al.: Coherent corticomuscular oscillations originate from primary motor cortex: evidence from patients with early brain lesions. Hum. Brain Mapp. **27**(10), 789–798 (2006)
11. Mendez-Balbuena, I., Huethe, F., Schulte-Mönting, J., et al.: Corticomuscular coherence reflects interindividual differences in the state of the corticomuscular network during low-level static and dynamic forces. Cereb. Cortex **22**(3), 628–638 (2012)
12. Ritterband-Rosenbaum, A., Herskind, A., Li, X., et al.: A critical period of corticomuscular and EMG-EMG coherence detection in healthy infants aged 9–25 weeks. J. Physiol. **595**(8), 2699–2713 (2017)
13. Calafiore, D., Negrini, F., Tottoli, N., et al.: Efficacy of robotic exoskeleton for gait rehabilitation in patients with subacute stroke : a systematic review. Eur. J. Phys. Rehabil. Med. **58**(1), 1–8 (2022)
14. Chinese Medical Association Neurology Branch, Chinese Medical Association Neurology Branch, Cerebrovascular Disease Group. Diagnostic points of various major cerebrovascular diseases in China 2019. Chin. J. Neurol. **52**(9), 710-5 (2019)
15. Meyer, J.T., Weber, S., Jäger, L., et al.: A survey on the influence of CYBATHLON on the development and acceptance of advanced assistive technologies. J. Neuroeng. Rehabil. **19**(1), 38 (2022)
16. Schröder, J., Truijen, S., Van Criekinge, T., et al.: Feasibility and effectiveness of repetitive gait training early after stroke: a systematic review and meta-analysis. J Rehabil Med **51**(2), 78–88 (2019)
17. McDonald, C., Fingleton, C., Murphy, S., et al.: Stroke survivor perceptions of using an exoskeleton during acute gait rehabilitation. Sci. Rep. **12**(1), 14185 (2022)
18. Moucheboeuf, G., Griffier, R., Gasq, D., et al.: Effects of robotic gait training after stroke: a meta-analysis. Ann. Phys. Rehabil. Med. **63**(6), 518–534 (2020)
19. Liu, M., Xu, G., Yu, H., et al.: Effects of transcranial direct current stimulation on EEG power and brain functional network in stroke patients. IEEE Trans. Neural Syst. Rehabil. Eng. **31**, 335–345 (2023)
20. Muthukumaraswamy, S.D., Johnson, B.W.: Primary motor cortex activation during action observation revealed by wavelet analysis of the EEG. Clin. Neurophysiol. **115**(8), 1760–1766 (2004)
21. Kristeva, R., Patino, L., Omlor, W.: Beta-range cortical motor spectral power and corticomuscular coherence as a mechanism for effective corticospinal interaction during steady-state motor output. Neuroimage **36**(3), 785–792 (2007)
22. Omlor, W., Patino, L., Hepp-Reymond, M.C., et al.: Gamma-range corticomuscular coherence during dynamic force output. Neuroimage **34**(3), 1191–1198 (2007)

Pattern Analysis and Machine Intelligence: Vision, Language, Multimodal Learning, and Applications

TGP: Two-Modal Occupancy Prediction with 3D Gaussian and Sparse Points for 3D Environment Awareness

Mu Chen[1,4], Wenyu Chen[2,3,4], Mingchuan Yang[1], Yuan Zhang[1], Tao Han[1], Xinchi Li[1], Guilong Zhang[2,3,4], and Huaici Zhao[2,3(✉)]

[1] China Telecom Research Institute, Beijing 102200, China
[2] Key Laboratory of Opto-Electronic Information Processing, Chinese Academy of Sciences, Shenyang 110016, China
[3] Shenyang Institute of Automation, Chinese Academy of Sciences, Shenyang 110016, China
hczhao@sia.cn
[4] University of Chinese Academy of Sciences, Beijing 100049, China

Abstract. 3D semantic occupancy has rapidly emerged as a research focus in autonomous driving and robotics environment perception, owing to its capability to provide more realistic geometric perception and closer integration with downstream tasks. By performing occupancy prediction of the 3D space in the environment, it effectively enhances the ability and robustness of scene understanding. However, existing occupancy prediction tasks are predominantly modeled using voxel or point cloud-based approaches: voxel-based network structures often suffer from spatial information loss due to the voxelization process, while point cloud-based methods, though better at preserving spatial location information, face limitations in representing volumetric structural details. To address this issue, we propose a dual-modal prediction method based on 3D Gaussian sets and sparse points, which balances spatial location and volumetric structural information to achieve higher accuracy in semantic occupancy prediction. Specifically, our method adopts a Transformer-based architecture, taking 3D Gaussian sets, sparse points, and queries as inputs. Through the multi-layer structure of the Transformer, enhanced queries and 3D Gaussian sets jointly contribute to semantic occupancy prediction, and an adaptive fusion mechanism integrates the semantic outputs of both modalities to generate final prediction results. Additionally, to further improve accuracy, we dynamically refine the point cloud at each layer to enable more precise location information. Experiments conducted on the Occ3D-nuScenes dataset demonstrate superior performance of the proposed method on IoU-based metrics.

Keywords: Occupancy prediction · 3D gaussian · Environment awareness

---

M. Chen and W. Chen—These authors contributed equally to this work and should be considered co-first authors.

1 Introduction

In 3D perception for robotics and autonomous driving, cubic bounding boxes [4,9,12,26] have been widely used but have limitations in capturing the shape of irregular objects. Additionally, they require extra processing when applied to downstream tasks. On the other hand, 3D occupancy prediction [11,17,24,27] divides the space into grid cells and predicts the occupancy probability for each cell. This approach can better capture objects of any shape and offers a more unified 3D representation for tasks like 4D prediction and path planning. Due to its detailed and adaptable nature, 3D occupancy prediction has gained significant attention and rapid growth in research.

3D occupancy prediction has shifted from focusing on individual objects to enabling full-scene perception [4,9,10,27], showing great potential for broader applications. However, this progress comes with significant computational challenges, mainly due to the reliance on dense 3D representations. These dense representations are not essential for occupancy prediction tasks. Voxel-based representations, for example, have fixed resolutions and boundaries, making them inflexible, especially for targets of different sizes and shapes. In sparse scenes, many voxels remain empty, leading to inefficient resource use. To address these issues, several methods [5,8,11,24,25] have been proposed. SparseOcc [11] refines the voxel-based representation progressively, eliminating empty grids and reducing redundant computations. This is particularly efficient in sparse areas. Similarly, OPUS [24] uses a point-based strategy to replace the uniform 3D grid, offering more flexibility and precision in representing 3D space. This method also adapts better to local features, improving detection accuracy. While both approaches have made progress, voxel-based methods struggle with local information aggregation, and point-based methods face challenges in handling volumetric features.

Inspired by PV-RCNN [21] and 3D Gaussian [6,7], we innovatively proposes a sparse representation method based on the fusion of 3D Gaussians and points. In this approach, points effectively aggregate local information, while 3D Gaussians flexibly capture and represent volumetric information in high-dimensional space, thereby enhancing the ability to represent spatial details. Specifically, we design a dual-modal decoder structure based on the sparse paradigm to progressively refine 3D occupancy predictions. This dual-modal decoder structure combines a Transformer-based framework, taking queries, sparse points, and 3D Gaussian sets as inputs. Such a decoder structure is highly flexible, capable of extracting local features sufficiently at different refinement levels while effectively capturing volumetric features through Gaussian representations. Notably, the position of 3D Gaussians share the same initial values with sparse points. Each 3D Gaussian element includes attributes such as position, volume, rotation, and semantic information. In each layer of the decoder, the initial points are progressively split. These points not only enhance the query features, but also provide positional references for the refinement process in the next layer. Meanwhile, 3D Gaussians interact with the enhanced query features at a fixed number in each layer, further refining the representation of the 3D Gaussians.

Through this multi-level interaction process, the model is able to gradually optimize the 3D occupancy prediction and refine the spatial representation at each layer. Based on the semantic predictions from the enhanced queries and refined 3D Gaussian outputs in each layer, we propose an adaptive fusion method to obtain the final occupancy prediction result.

Overall, our contributions are as follows:

1) We propose an innovative dual-modal occupancy prediction decoder structure based on 3D Gaussians and points, which effectively balances position information and volumetric structure information.
2) Our method achieves good performance on the Occ3D nuScenes dataset.

2 Related Work

2.1 3D Occupancy Prediction

In recent years, image-based detection methods [4,9,12,26] have advanced significantly, improving precision and closing the gap with other sensors. However, traditional methods struggle to capture all the details of a scene in the open world. Vision-based 3D occupancy prediction methods [5,6,8,10,11,17,24,27,29] offer a promising solution by predicting the spatial occupancy and semantics of 3D voxel grids around autonomous vehicles based on image input, making them a key focus in autonomous driving. Some methods [4,9,29] use bird's-eye view (BEV) perception and multi-view representations to enhance spatial perception by improving image features. Others [7,8,11] work directly with 3D voxel representations, which minimize information loss but come with high computational costs. To address this, some methods [5,8,11,24,25] explore a coarse-to-fine feature learning approach. Voxformer [8] uses depth as a prior to predict occupancy and select valuable queries. Only the occupied queries gather information from the image, and the updated queries, along with the masked tokens, collectively reconstruct the voxel features. SparseOcc [11] reduces computational demands by prioritizing influential queries. However, these methods often require complex spatial modeling steps. In contrast, OPUS [24] adopts a point-set prediction paradigm, relying on queries to identify occupied regions, offering more flexible feature aggregation and better positional information. However, point-set-based sparse prediction does not capture the volumetric structure of the scene well. Thus, it is important to design a prediction structure that integrates both volumetric and positional representations.

2.2 3D Gaussian Splatting

3D Gaussian splatting (3D-GS) [7] has made significant progress in the field of computer graphics in recent years, particularly in 3D rendering and scene reconstruction tasks [14,16,28]. The 3D-GS technique represents scenes as multiple 3D Gaussian points or small clusters, utilizing these points for rasterization rendering, achieving high-quality rendering effects while maintaining low computational costs [2,20]. Compared to traditional mesh or voxel representations,

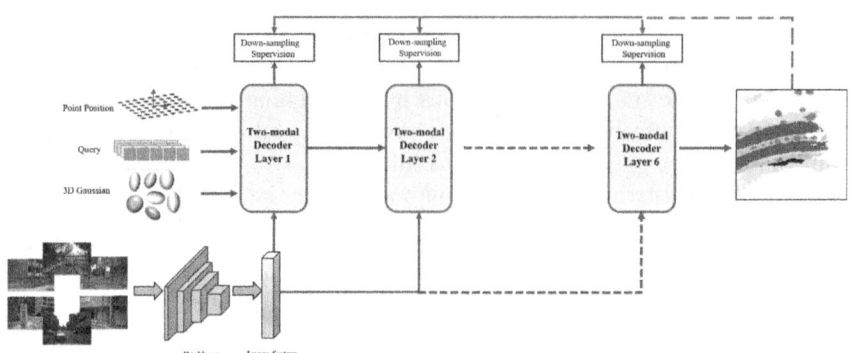

Fig. 1. Framework of the proposed occupancy prediction pipeline. The whole pipeline is designed by transformer paradigm with initial point position, 3D Gaussian representation, query, and continuous multiview image frames.

3D-GS is more flexible in representing complex geometries and offers advantages in memory usage and computational efficiency. In autonomous driving, 3D Gaussian has been widely applied in perception, mapping, path planning, and other areas [18,19,30]. GaussianFormer [6] was the first to introduce 3D Gaussian into occupancy prediction in an online manner. However, the special design mechanism using 3D convolutions to enable interaction between 3D Gaussians results in an increased computational burden.

3 Methodology

This section first outlines the network structure of our proposed method and details the key component of the two-modal decoder with Gaussian and point representations as inputs. Finally, we introduce the supervision method used.

3.1 Overview

The framework of our method is shown in Fig. 1. We use multi-view images $\mathcal{I} = \{\mathbf{I}_i \in \mathbb{R}^{3 \times H \times W} \mid i = 1, \ldots, N\}$ as input and first utilize ResNet-50 [3] as the backbone to encode image features $\mathbf{F}$. At the same time, we initialize a set of learnable queries $\mathbb{Q}$, point positions $\mathbb{P}$, and 3D Gaussians $\mathbb{G}$ to capture spatial structure and predict the occupied locations and semantic classes. In the core component, the two-modal decoder including six decoder layers shares the same form as the decoder part in Transformer [23] but with specific modifications. This decoder layer is composed of two branches. The first branch is the point decoder, which uses queries $q \in \mathbb{Q}$ and point positions $p \in \mathbb{P}$ to aggregate image features through consistent point sampling. After adaptive mixing and self-attention operation [24], the query features are generated to update the properties of the 3D Gaussians $\mathcal{G} \in \mathbb{G}$ and predict point-level semantic classification. Using the Gaussian-to-voxel splatting module from [6], local Gaussian distributions are aggregated to fuse with point-level semantics to predict 3D occupancy categories $\mathbf{O} \in \mathcal{C}^{X \times Y \times Z}$, where $\mathcal{C}$ and $\{X, Y, Z\}$ denote semantic classes and volume resolution. The predicted values at each layer of the decoder are supervised to ensure sufficient training of our end-to-end framework.

3.2 Gaussian Properties

In this paper, we use 3D Gaussians to represent regions of interest in space where potential objects may exist, unconstrained by the fixed positions of voxel grids. Compared to point-based queries, 3D Gaussians have multiple attributes, making them more suited for representing objects. The object-centered 3D Gaussian representation method allows for flexible exploration of regions of interest, progressively refining and modeling the fine-grained structure of the 3D scene in a sparse manner. Specifically, we initialize a set of Gaussian distributions $\mathcal{G}_i \in \mathbb{R}^d$, where each 3D Gaussian distribution is represented by a d-dimensional vector. The d dimension consists of $\mathbf{m} \in \mathbb{R}^3, \mathbf{s} \in \mathbb{R}^3, \mathbf{r} \in \mathbb{R}^4, \mathbf{c} \in \mathbb{R}^{|\mathcal{C}|}$. Here, $\mathbf{m}, \mathbf{s}, \mathbf{r}$, and $\mathbf{c}$ represent the mean, scale, rotation vector, and semantics, respectively. The mean and covariance characteristics allow 3D Gaussians to have various flexible shapes, providing a highly expressive capability for scene representation. The semantic attribute binds each Gaussian's position with its corresponding semantic label, thus eliminating the need for additional decoding from high-dimensional features to obtain semantic representations. In graphics, Gaussian attributes can also include glossiness, but for the purpose of controlling parameters, we exclude attributes that are more relevant to rendering but less related to occupancy prediction. Now, the Gaussian distribution $\mathcal{G}_i$ at any point $p = (x, y, z)$ in space can be computed as follows:

$$\mathcal{G}(\mathbf{p}; \mathbf{m}, \mathbf{s}, \mathbf{r}, \mathbf{c}) = \exp\left(-\frac{1}{2}(\mathbf{p} - \mathbf{m})^T \boldsymbol{\Sigma}^{-1}(\mathbf{p} - \mathbf{m})\right) \mathbf{c}$$
$$\boldsymbol{\Sigma} = \mathbf{RSS}^T \mathbf{R}^T, \quad \mathbf{S} = \mathrm{diag}(\mathbf{s}), \quad \mathbf{R} = \mathrm{q2r}(\mathbf{r}) \tag{1}$$

where $\boldsymbol{\Sigma}$, diag($\cdot$) and q2r($\cdot$) represent the covariance matrix, diagonal matrix constructor and rotation matrix constructor, respectively.

3.3 Two-Modal Decoder

The most important component is the multi-layer dual-modal decoder. Therefore, we will now describe the internal details of the decoder.

Input. In the previous section, we introduced the initial physical properties of the Gaussian distributions $\mathbb{G}_0$, which are the targets for the model to learn. However, unstructured Gaussian distributions are difficult to handle in some deformation-based attention encoding modules. Therefore, we also initialize a set of learnable 3D points $\mathbb{P}_0$, which share the same position as the 3D Gaussians, as well as high-dimensional query features $\mathbb{Q}_0$. These are used to extract image

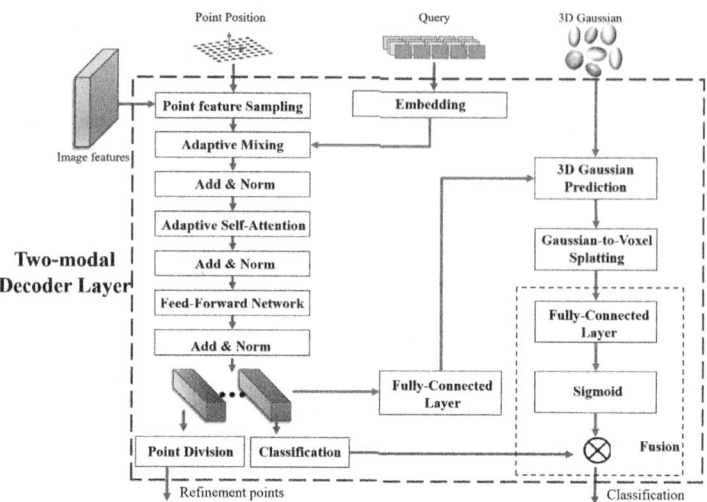

Fig. 2. The illustration of two-modal decoder layer. The decoder, as the core component of the pipeline, is designed in the transformer architecture to perform key functions, including image feature sampling, generation of query features through the attention mechanism, and updating of Gaussian attributes.

features in the consistency sampling and adaptive mixing modules, implicitly encoding 3D information, and guiding the stepwise update of the 3D Gaussians. Thus, the input to the dual-modal decoder consists of the set $\{\mathbb{G}, \mathbb{P}, \mathbb{Q}\}$. The output at each layer consists of refined point positions and intermediate results of the occupancy prediction.

Decoder Details. To improve efficiency and save computational resources, we follow OPUS and choose a fully sparse and efficient decoding method. For a given query $q \in \mathbb{R}^{Q \times 256}$ and its corresponding point position $p \in \mathbb{R}^{Q \times R \times 3}$, the decoder first performs consistent point sampling to extract image features, where Q represents the set length and R represents R points to be predicted for each query q. Given the input $\{q, p\} \in \{\mathbb{P}, \mathbb{Q}\}$, we set the number of sampled points to 4 and map their respective coordinates in the $m-th$ image feature $\mathbf{c}_m$ using the following equation:

$$\mathbf{c}_m = \mathbf{T_m r}, \text{ where } \mathbf{r} = \mathbf{m}_p + \phi(\mathbf{q}) \cdot \sigma_p \qquad (2)$$

where $\mathbf{T_m}$ represents the projection matrix from the current 3D space to the $m-th$ image coordinates. $\phi(\mathbf{q})$ uses a linear layer to generate S 3D points from the query features q. $\mathbf{m}_p$ and σ_p represent the mean and standard deviation of the R points in p, respectively. The offset $\phi(\mathbf{q})$ and the standard deviation σ_p are weighted to act as a correction mechanism, preventing the sampling process from overly focusing on more prominent points and thus causing the sampling range to become increasingly concentrated.

Subsequently, the sampled features $\mathbf{c}_m$ are adaptively mixed with the query and then passed through a self-attention layer for feature aggregation, allowing the model to focus on important information. The updated query features are then obtained through residual connections and a feed-forward network. Finally, a prediction head, composed of Linear, LayerNorm, and ReLU layers, generates the semantic class c_i and position offset Δp, which are used to update the point positions, enabling the extraction of more effective image features.

The updated query features are used to guide the correction and update of the Gaussian attributes. Specifically, we employ a multi-layer perceptron (MLP) to derive intermediate attributes $\hat{G} = (\hat{m}, \hat{s}, \hat{r}, \hat{c})$ from the query features. For the intermediate mean $\hat{m}$, it is added to the original mean m in a residual manner to obtain the updated attribute. The other intermediate attributes directly replace their original counterparts to become the updated values. As described in Equation (1), Gaussian distributions at a point p are aggregated by summation. To reduce computational complexity, we adopt the Gaussian-to-Voxel Splatting approach [6] for efficient indexing, generating point-alignment Gaussian semantic information g_i. After that, a semantic fusion mechanism is deployed to fuse c_i and g_i to generate reliable semantic classification $\mathbf{O} \in \mathcal{C}^{X \times Y \times Z}$, where subscript i denotes the $i-th$ decoder layer. As can be seen in Fig. 2, the fusion format can be formulated as:

$$\mathbf{O} = \frac{1}{2}[\text{Sigmoid}(FCN(g_i)) \cdot c_i + \text{Sigmoid}(c_i) \cdot g_i] \tag{3}$$

in which the FCN (fully-connected layer) is used to align the feature dimension of c_i and g_i. Sigmoid allows the model to softly weight each feature stream and encourages balanced interaction. This design avoids potential dominance issues seen in simple addition or multiplication and offers stable gradients. With this fusion operation, the semantic information for occupancy classification can be adaptively enhanced.

3.4 Loss Functions

Our model is efficiently trained in an end-to-end manner, using ground truth to supervise learning. Following [1,15,24], we adopt a weighted Chamfer Distance to match the predicted points set $\mathbb{P}$ with the ground truth points $\mathbb{P}_g$. This approach not only focuses on overall accuracy but also emphasizes penalizing erroneous points. The weighted Chamfer Distance is defined as:

$$\begin{array}{c} \text{CD}_R(\mathbb{P}, \mathbb{P}_g) = \frac{1}{|\mathbb{P}|} \sum_{\mathbf{p} \in \mathbb{P}} D_R(\mathbf{p}, \mathbb{P}_g) + \frac{1}{|\mathbb{P}_g|} \sum_{\mathbf{p}_g \in \mathbb{P}_g} D_R(\mathbf{p}_g, \mathbb{P}), \\ \text{where } D_R(\mathbf{x}, \mathbb{Y}) = W(d) \cdot d \text{ with } d = \min_{\mathbf{y} \in \mathbb{Y}} \|\mathbf{x} - \mathbf{y}\|_1. \end{array} \tag{4}$$

In the formula, $W(d)$ is a re-weighting function that penalizes points with large distances towards the ground truth. In the specific implementation, a step function is used to define wd. If $d \geq 0.2$, then $w(d) = 5$; otherwise, $w(d) = 1$. This weighting mechanism assigns higher penalties to points with larger errors

($d \geq 0.2$), encouraging the model to focus on correcting significant deviations during training.

For the classification task, we follow OPUS [24] to use focal loss L_{focal} to measure supervision loss. The overall loss function is defined as:

$$L = \mathrm{CD}_R\left(\mathbb{P}_0, \mathbb{P}_g\right) + \sum_{i=1}^{6}\left(\mathrm{CD}_R\left(\mathbb{P}_i, \mathbb{P}_g\right) + L^i_{focal}\right) \qquad (5)$$

4 Experiments

4.1 Experimental Setup

Dataset and Metrics. We evaluated the proposed method on the widely recognized Occ3D-nuScenes [22] dataset, a large-scale benchmark developed to support 3D occupancy prediction. The Occ3D-nuScenes dataset comprises data from six surround-view cameras, one LiDAR, and five RaDAR, encompassing a total of 600 training scenes, 150 validation scenes, and 150 test scenes, amounting to 40,000 frames. The dataset annotations include 18 categories, consisting of one free-form category and 17 semantic categories. SparseOcc [11] introduced a ray-based evaluation metric, RayIoU, to address the inconsistencies in depth penalties inherent in the traditional mIoU standard. Consequently, this study adopts the aforementioned metric and computes RayIoU at different thresholds of 1 m, 2 m, and 4 m, with the final results obtained by averaging these values.

Implementation Details. Our algorithm is implemented using PyTorch, with ResNet-50 [3] chosen as the image backbone, processing input images at a resolution of 256 × 704. We define two versions based on the number of queries, 3D Gaussians, and initial sparse points: 600 (TGP-T) and 2400 (TGP-S). The number of 3D Gaussians remains fixed at each layer, while the number of sparse points splits progressively across layers, following the same configuration used in OPUS. During training, the AdamW [13] optimizer is utilized with a learning rate of 2e-4, and a cosine annealing strategy is adopted for learning rate decay. The batch size is set to 8. All experiments are conducted with 100 epochs for validation and 24 epochs for ablation study on 4 NVIDIA A40L GPUs.

4.2 Quantitative Comparison of Results

The performance report for occupancy prediction on the Occ3D-nuScenes dataset is presented in Table 1, showcasing a comparison between our method and previous state-of-the-art approaches. As shown, our method achieves superior results across the metrics, including mIoU, RayIoU1m, RayIoU2m, RayIoU$_{4m}$, and RayIoU, with scores of 34.5, 32.8, 40.2, 45.2, and 39.4, respectively. Compared to similar point-based methods such as OPUS [24], our approach delivers significantly better performance under identical configurations, albeit with a slightly lower FPS. This trade-off suggests that combining 3D

Table 1. The performance of occupancy predcition on Occ3D-nuScenes. "8f" and "16f" means the number of input frames with 8 frames and 16 frames.

Methods	Backbone	Resolution	mIoU	$RayIoU_{1m}$	$RayIoU_{2m}$	$RayIoU_{4m}$	$RayIoU$	FPS
RenderOcc [17]	Swin-B	1408 × 512	24.5	13.4	19.6	25.5	19.5	-
BEVFormer [9]	R101	1600 × 900	39.3	26.1	32.9	38.0	32.4	3.0
BEVDet-Occ [4]	R50	704 × 256	36.1	23.6	30.0	35.1	29.6	2.6
BEVDet-Occ(8f) [4]	R50	704 × 384	39.3	26.6	33.1	38.2	32.6	0.8
FB-Occ(16f) [10]	R50	704 × 256	39.1	26.7	34.1	39.7	33.5	10.3
Sparse-Occ(8f) [11]	R50	704 × 256	-	28.0	34.7	39.4	34.0	17.3
Sparse-Occ(16f) [11]	R50	704 × 256	30.6	29.1	35.8	40.3	35.1	12.5
OPUS-T(8f) [24]	R50	704 × 256	33.2	31.7	39.2	44.3	38.4	22.4
OPUS-S(8f) [24]	R50	704 × 256	34.2	32.6	39.9	44.7	39.1	20.7
TGP-T(8f)	R50	704 × 256	33.4	31.8	39.5	44.6	38.6	18.6
TGP-S(8f)	R50	704 × 256	34.5	32.8	40.2	45.2	39.4	15.1

Gaussian representations with sparse point-based occupancy prediction enhances accuracy while incurring some loss in inference speed. In conclusion, we introduce an innovative paradigm that integrates coexisting volumes and points, providing a valuable contribution to improving occupancy prediction accuracy and offering meaningful insights for future research.

4.3 Qualitative Results

We provide detailed visualization results to further demonstrate the effectiveness of our method. As shown in Fig. 3, we illustrate various occupancy scenarios such as roads and intersections. Different colors are used to represent different object categories, enabling a clear view of their spatial occupancy through visualization. The blue boxes highlight comparative results between our method, OPUS [24] and ground truth. Upon inspection, our method clearly aligns more closely with the actual scenarios, providing more accurate estimates of the geometric structure and size of occupied regions compared to OPUS. This closer consistency enhances the advantages and effectiveness of our method in real-world applications.

4.4 Ablation Study

To validate the effectiveness of our proposed two-modal occupancy prediction framework, which combines 3D Gaussian and sparse points, we conducted ablation studies to analyze the contribution of the two-modal decoder layer (GS). The baseline is set without 3D Gaussian modality in decoder layer as same in OPUS [24]. Table 2 presents the performance improvements achieved by incorporating GS. Obviously, utilizing GS significantly enhances the performance of the occupancy prediction task when compared to the baseline, which proves

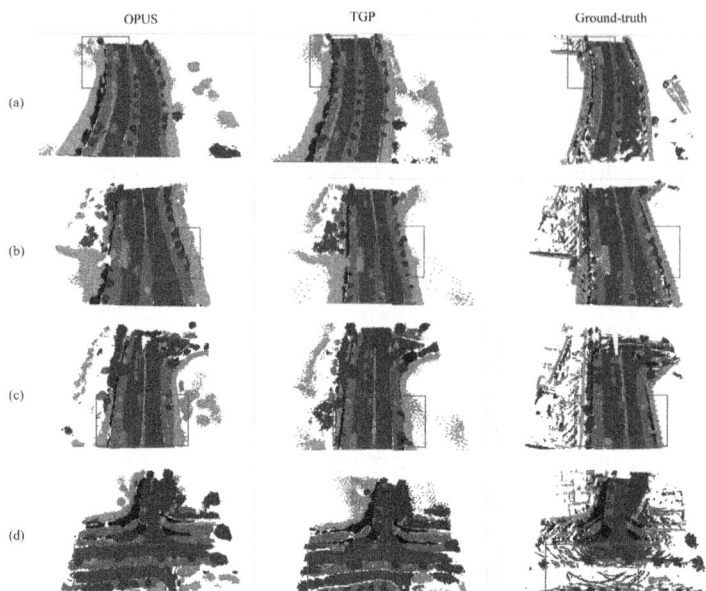

Fig. 3. Visualization comparison in four scenarios.

Table 2. Performance analysis of two-modal decoder layer (GS). The GP_s and GP_i represents initialize the 3D Gaussian with/without sharing the same value of sparse point positions.

GP_i	GP_s	mIoU	$RayIoU_{1m}$	$RayIoU_{2m}$	$RayIoU_{4m}$	$RayIoU$
-	-	32.0	30.1	37.7	43.0	36.9
✓	-	31.9	30.1	37.8	43.1	37.0
-	✓	32.3	30.2	38.1	43.4	37.2

the effectiveness of GS. Additionally, Table 2 reports a comparison of different position initialization strategies for the 3D Gaussian. It can be observed that initializing the position of the 3D Gaussian without sharing the same values as the sparse points results in only slight performance gains for the occupancy prediction task. We hypothesize that this phenomenon is due to the distribution mismatch between the 3D Gaussian and sparse points, caused by the differing position initializations. Therefore, it is crucial to ensure consistency between the 3D Gaussian and sparse points at the initialization stage.

5 Conclusion

In this work, we innovatively propose an occupancy prediction method that adopts a dual-modal representation based on 3D Gaussian and sparse points. This approach effectively integrates the volumetric occupancy information of 3D

Gaussian with the positional information of sparse points, significantly enhancing the performance of occupancy prediction. In addition, our method adopts a dynamic number of Gaussians. In future work, we will further investigate the impact of using a fixed number of Gaussians on performance, with the aim of achieving further optimization.

References

1. Fan, H., Su, H., Guibas, L.: A point set generation network for 3D object reconstruction from a single image (2016). https://arxiv.org/abs/1612.00603
2. Girish, S., Gupta, K., Shrivastava, A.: Eagles: efficient accelerated 3D gaussians with lightweight encodings. In: European Conference on Computer Vision, pp. 54–71. Springer (2024)
3. He, K., Zhang, X., Ren, S., Sun, J.: Deep residual learning for image recognition. In: Proceedings of the IEEE Conference on Computer Vision and Pattern Recognition, pp. 770–778 (2016)
4. Huang, J., Huang, G., Zhu, Z., Ye, Y., Du, D.: Bevdet: high-performance multi-camera 3D object detection in bird-eye-view (2022)
5. Huang, Y., Zheng, W., Zhang, Y., Zhou, J., Lu, J.: Tri-perspective view for vision-based 3D semantic occupancy prediction (2023). https://arxiv.org/abs/2302.07817
6. Huang, Y., Zheng, W., Zhang, Y., Zhou, J., Lu, J.: Gaussianformer: scene as gaussians for vision-based 3D semantic occupancy prediction (2024). https://arxiv.org/abs/2405.17429
7. Kerbl, B., Kopanas, G., Leimkühler, T., Drettakis, G.: 3D gaussian splatting for real-time radiance field rendering (2023). https://arxiv.org/abs/2308.04079
8. Li, Y., et al.: Voxformer: sparse voxel transformer for camera-based 3d semantic scene completion (2023). https://arxiv.org/abs/2302.12251
9. Li, Z., et al.: Bevformer: learning bird's-eye-view representation from multi-camera images via spatiotemporal transformers (2022)
10. Li, Z., et al.: FB-OCC: 3D occupancy prediction based on forward-backward view transformation (2023). https://arxiv.org/abs/2307.01492
11. Liu, H., et al.: Fully sparse 3D occupancy prediction (2024). https://arxiv.org/abs/2312.17118
12. Liu, Y., Wang, T., Zhang, X., Sun, J.: Petr: position embedding transformation for multi-view 3D object detection. In: European Conference on Computer Vision, pp. 531–548. Springer (2022)
13. Loshchilov, I., Hutter, F.: Decoupled weight decay regularization (2019). https://arxiv.org/abs/1711.05101
14. Lu, T., et al.: Scaffold-GS: structured 3D gaussians for view-adaptive rendering. In: Proceedings of the IEEE/CVF Conference on Computer Vision and Pattern Recognition (CVPR), pp. 20654–20664 (2024)
15. Mersch, B., Chen, X., Behley, J., Stachniss, C.: Self-supervised point cloud prediction using 3D spatio-temporal convolutional networks (2021). https://arxiv.org/abs/2110.04076
16. Mildenhall, B., Srinivasan, P.P., Tancik, M., Barron, J.T., Ramamoorthi, R., Ng, R.: Nerf: representing scenes as neural radiance fields for view synthesis. Commun. ACM **65**(1), 99–106 (2021). https://doi.org/10.1145/3503250
17. Pan, M., et al.: Renderocc: vision-centric 3D occupancy prediction with 2D rendering supervision (2024). https://arxiv.org/abs/2309.09502

18. Qi, Z., Ma, J., Xu, J., Zhou, Z., Cheng, L., Xiong, G.: GSPR: multimodal place recognition using 3D gaussian splatting for autonomous driving. arXiv preprint arXiv:2410.00299 (2024)
19. Qin, P., Zhang, C., Dang, M.: Gvnet: gaussian model with voxel-based 3D detection network for autonomous driving. Neural Comput. Appl. **34**(9), 6637–6645 (2022)
20. Radl, L., Steiner, M., Parger, M., Weinrauch, A., Kerbl, B., Steinberger, M.: Stopthepop: sorted gaussian splatting for view-consistent real-time rendering. ACM Trans. Graph. (TOG) **43**(4), 1–17 (2024)
21. Shi, S., et al.: PV-RCNN: point-voxel feature set abstraction for 3D object detection (2021). https://arxiv.org/abs/1912.13192
22. Tian, X., et al.: OCC3D: a large-scale 3D occupancy prediction benchmark for autonomous driving (2023). https://arxiv.org/abs/2304.14365
23. Vaswani, A., et al.: Attention is all you need. arXiv (2017)
24. Wang, J., et al.: Opus: occupancy prediction using a sparse set (2024). https://arxiv.org/abs/2409.09350
25. Wang, X., et al.: Openoccupancy: a large scale benchmark for surrounding semantic occupancy perception (2023). https://arxiv.org/abs/2303.03991
26. Wang, Y., Guizilini, V.C., Zhang, T., Wang, Y., Zhao, H., Solomon, J.: DETR3D: 3D object detection from multi-view images via 3D-to-2D queries. In: Conference on Robot Learning, pp. 180–191. PMLR (2022)
27. Wei, Y., Zhao, L., Zheng, W., Zhu, Z., Zhou, J., Lu, J.: Surroundocc: multi-camera 3D occupancy prediction for autonomous driving (2023). https://arxiv.org/abs/2303.09551
28. Yang, Z., Gao, X., Zhou, W., Jiao, S., Zhang, Y., Jin, X.: Deformable 3D gaussians for high-fidelity monocular dynamic scene reconstruction. In: Proceedings of the IEEE/CVF Conference on Computer Vision and Pattern Recognition (CVPR), pp. 20331–20341 (2024)
29. Zhang, Y., Zhu, Z., Du, D.: Occformer: dual-path transformer for vision-based 3D semantic occupancy prediction (2023). https://arxiv.org/abs/2304.05316
30. Zheng, W., et al.: Gaussianad: gaussian-centric end-to-end autonomous driving (2024). https://arxiv.org/abs/2412.10371

YOLO-HG: A Hierarchical Global Perception Method for Heavy-Duty Truck Parking Space Detection

Zeyang Wang, Feng Zhao(✉), and Dan Yang

School of Automation, Xi'an University of Posts and Telecommunications, Xi'an 710121, Shaanxi, China
hfengzhao@xupt.edu.cn

Abstract. In heavy-duty vehicle automatic parking technology, accurate parking space detection is a critical prerequisite for reliable parking. However, existing object detection methods perform poorly in complex parking lot environments. They struggle to effectively handle issues such as blurred parking space lines, occlusions, and diverse layouts. To address this, this paper proposes the YOLO-HG detection framework and designs a specialized Hierarchical Global Perception (HGP) attention mechanism. This mechanism uses non-local self-attention to model global spatial relationships. It combines geometric feature extraction and direction-sensitive filtering techniques to accurately capture the regular arrangement and boundary features of parking lots. Through a channel-spatial joint attention mechanism, it effectively fuses multi-dimensional features such as color and edges to improve feature extraction performance. Additionally, this paper integrates ODConv convolution into the C2f module to optimize the efficiency and effectiveness of feature extraction. Meanwhile, it adopts the WIoU loss function to further improve bounding box localization accuracy. The YOLO-HG built on the YOLOv8 architecture achieves excellent performance on our self-built heavy-duty vehicle parking space dataset. Experimental results show that compared to YOLOv8, this method improves mAP50 and mAP50–95 by 1.3% and 1.2% respectively. It maintains real-time inference speed, validating its effectiveness and practicality in complex parking scenarios.

Keywords: Target Detection · Parking Spot Detection · YOLO · Attention Mechanism

1 Introduction

Heavy-duty vehicles play an irreplaceable role in fields such as logistics transportation and infrastructure construction. However, parking of heavy vehicles is significantly more difficult due to their large body size and limited driving visibility. This often leads to safety accidents. Implementing automatic parking for heavy vehicles can effectively reduce traffic accident rates and operating costs. Automatic parking is a critical component of autonomous driving. It requires precise perception of the vehicle's surrounding environment. Parking space detection is the key and foundation of this process. An accurate and reliable parking space detection system not only helps vehicles identify available parking areas in real time. It also provides solid support for subsequent vehicle motion planning and control. This ensures the safety and stability of the automatic parking process.

Early traditional parking space detection methods were mainly based on image processing techniques such as geometric rules, morphological processing, color and texture analysis. For example, Tian et al. used improved Canny edge detection [1], neighborhood search clustering grouping, and random Hough transform [2] to detect parking space lines. Lee et al. proposed an available parking space identification algorithm based on parking space context analysis [3]. This algorithm compares with known parking space layout patterns to determine whether the parking space truly exists and is available. This improves detection accuracy. Suhr et al. [4] proposed a parallel line-based method. This method uses random sample consensus and template matching to fit pairs of parallel lines to represent parking space boundary lines. These methods are all based on manually designed features. They struggle to include deep semantic information of scenes. Although these methods perform well in simple backgrounds and specific conditions, they often have insufficient adaptability when facing complex backgrounds and diverse parking space types. They also suffer from low detection accuracy and high computational complexity.

With the rise of deep learning technology, deep learning-based methods have begun to be widely applied to parking space detection tasks. Leveraging advanced models such as Convolutional Neural Networks (CNN) [5–7], deep learning methods can automatically learn and extract complex features from images. Research and practice have accumulated extensively around the application of YOLO series deep learning methods in parking space detection tasks. For example, literature [8] introduced Q-block and Bi-PAN-FPN ideas based on YOLOv8. Q-block dynamically adjusts the importance between feature channels through designing lightweight attention mechanisms. Bi-PAN-FPN adopts a bidirectional feature pyramid structure to achieve bottom-up and top-down feature information flow. This improvement effectively enhances parking space detection accuracy. Literature [9] introduced a new layer to the YOLOv5 model to enhance the model's performance in tiny object detection. This new layer replaces the traditional focus layer with a multi-scale layer based on Efficient Neural Network (ENet). The multi-scale layer helps extract discriminative features from different scales. This significantly improves the model's capability in detecting objects of different sizes.

2 Methodology

2.1 YOLOv8 Network

YOLOv8 is a one-stage object detection model renowned for its balance of high accuracy and efficiency. As a newer version of the YOLO series, YOLOv8 has made several key optimizations to its network architecture: First, it replaced the C3 module in YOLOv5 with the C2f module, which has richer gradient flow, enhancing feature transfer capability. Second, it adopted an Anchor-Free detection strategy, simplifying model design and reducing computational overhead while improving adaptability to multi-scale targets

[10]. Additionally, it introduced a decoupled design for the detection head, separating classification and regression tasks into independent branches. This improves their respective representation learning capabilities, thus achieving more accurate bounding box regression and category prediction. YOLOv8 also supports diverse data augmentation strategies, including random cropping, color transformation, and other techniques, further enhancing the model's generalization ability.

This paper selects YOLOv8n as the baseline model. YOLOv8n, as a lightweight version, maintains good detection performance while having smaller model parameters and computational complexity. It can meet the requirements for real-time performance and accuracy in heavy-duty vehicle automatic parking systems. This paper introduces attention mechanisms framework for subsequent architectural improvements.

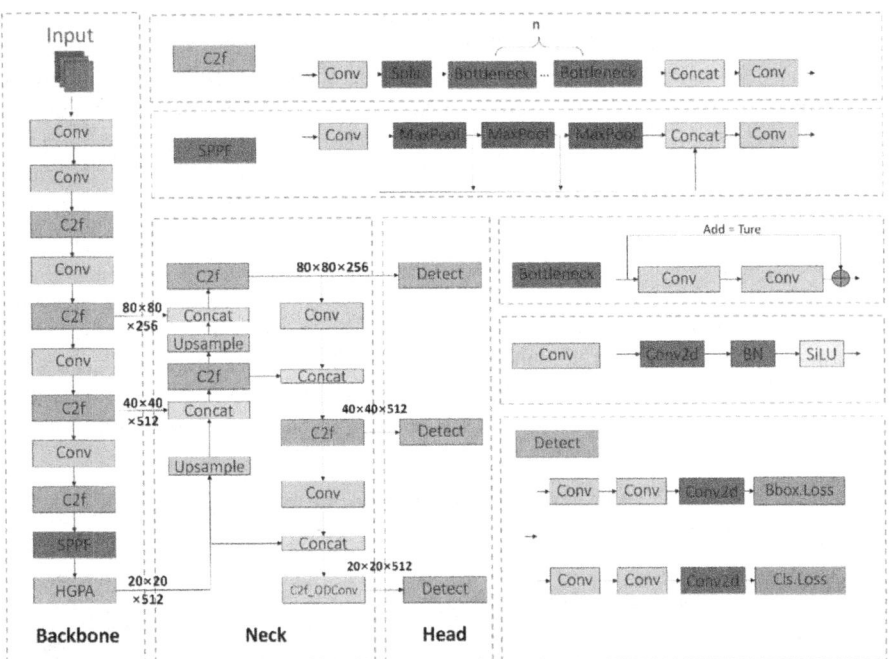

Fig. 1. The YOLO-HG architecture.

2.2 YOLO-HG

To address the multiple challenges in heavy-duty vehicle parking space detection tasks, this paper constructs the YOLO-HG detection framework. This framework uses YOLOv8n as the baseline model. Compared to the original YOLOv8, YOLO-HG's main improvement lies in embedding the HGP attention mechanism into the backbone network. This enables the model to focus on parking space-specific spatial arrangement patterns and boundary features during the feature extraction process. Then, by integrating ODConv convolution into the C2f module, it further improves the efficiency and effectiveness of feature extraction. Furthermore, YOLO-HG adopts the WIoU loss function to replace the original CIoU loss function. WIoU strengthens the influence of center distance on loss through a dynamic weighting mechanism. It can more precisely constrain the model's regression of parking space boundaries. This is particularly suitable for detection tasks like parking spaces that require high positioning accuracy. Figure 1 shows the structure diagram of YOLO-HG.

2.3 Hierarchical Global Perception Attention

This paper introduces attention mechanisms into the network. Attention mechanisms are widely applied in deep learning models, particularly in natural language processing and computer vision domains. Their significant advantage lies in their ability to effectively improve model performance. Attention mechanisms are typically categorized into four major types: channel attention mechanism, spatial attention mechanism, temporal attention mechanism, and branch attention mechanism. Heavy-duty vehicle parking space detection faces several challenges, including parking line occlusion, blurriness, and diverse layouts. To address these issues, this paper proposes a Hierarchical Global Perception (HGP) attention mechanism. HGP differs from traditional self-attention mechanisms by being specifically customized for parking space detection scenarios. It achieves hierarchical feature enhancement through three closely collaborative sub-modules. Channel attention filters important feature channels, spatial edge attention focuses on parking space boundary features, and the parking space context module models global spatial relationships while providing enhanced feature representations. The HGP module is strategically positioned only after the SPPF layer at the smallest scale feature. This design choice achieves an optimal balance between accuracy and real-time performance. By limiting HGPA to the deepest feature level, the model captures the most semantically rich representations while maintaining the efficiency required for real-time parking space detection. Figure 2 shows the HGP attention mechanism architecture.

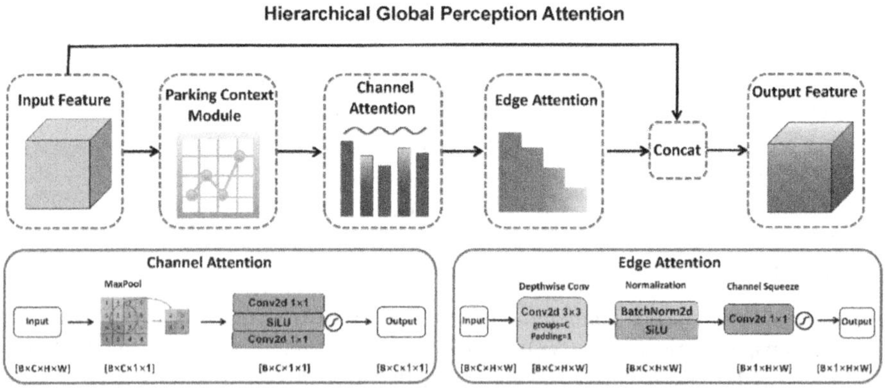

Fig. 2. The HGP attention mechanism architecture.

Channel Attention. The Channel Attention module is designed to enhance feature channels related to parking line colors. This module adopts the classic Squeeze-and-Excitation structure, compressing spatial dimensions to 1×1 through adaptive average pooling to extract global statistical information for each channel. Subsequently, a multilayer perceptron (MLP) consisting of two 1 × 1 convolutional layers learns inter-channel dependencies, where the first convolutional layer reduces the channel dimension to C/16, and the second convolutional layer restores the original channel count. Channel weights are generated through a Sigmoid activation function, enabling adaptive weighting of different feature channels. This design is particularly beneficial for strengthening channel responses related to parking lines and parking corners. The process is described as follows: Where GAP represents global average pooling, and $\odot$ denotes element-wise multiplication.

$$A_c = \sigma\left(f^{1\times 1}\left(f^{1\times 1}(\text{GAP}(F))\right)\right) \tag{1}$$

$$F_{channel} = F \odot A_c \tag{2}$$

Edge Attention. The Edge Attention module is designed to enhance parking boundary features. This module employs 3 × 3 grouped convolutions for spatial feature extraction, effectively reducing parameter count and computational complexity. After processing through batch normalization and SiLU activation functions, a 1 × 1 convolution generates a single-channel spatial attention map. The Sigmoid activation function ensures attention weights remain within the [0,1] range, achieving precise spatial position weighting. This design effectively highlights key edge features of targets, improving the model's perception capability for parking space boundaries. The process is formulated as follows: Where GroupConv3 × 3 represents the 3 × 3 grouped convolution, and BN denotes batch normalization.

$$A_e = \sigma\left(f^{1\times 1}\left(\text{ReLU}\left(\text{BN}\left(f^{3\times 3}_{groups}(F)\right)\right)\right)\right) \tag{3}$$

$$F_{edge} = F \odot A_e \tag{4}$$

Parking Contex Module. The Parking Context Module (PCM) is the core of the HGP mechanism, designed to understand the global spatial structure of parking lots. This module is based on non-local operation principles, with the key innovation lying in the construction of value vectors—unlike traditional self-attention mechanisms where value vectors undergo simple linear transformations, this module's value vectors are enhanced representations obtained by fusing geometric features and directional features. Figure 3 shows the PCM module architecture.

Specifically, the module first generates query and key vectors through three 1 × 1 convolutional layers respectively, followed by channel dimension reduction to decrease computational load. Next, the module extracts two specialized features in parallel: the geometric feature enhancement sub-module uses 3 × 3 grouped convolutions to capture structural features of parking lines, while the direction-sensitive filter employs serial connections of 1 × 5 and 5 × 1 strip convolutional kernels, a design that effectively detects L-shaped structures specifically for identifying parking corner features, which are crucial geometric characteristics. Finally, geometric and directional features are concatenated channel-wise, then fused through the parking arrangement pattern encoder (including 1 × 1 convolution, batch normalization, and SiLU activation function) to form enhanced value vectors. This fusion-enhanced value design enables the attention mechanism to rely not solely on feature similarity, but to incorporate geometric structural information specific to parking spaces, thereby extracting richer spatial feature representations.

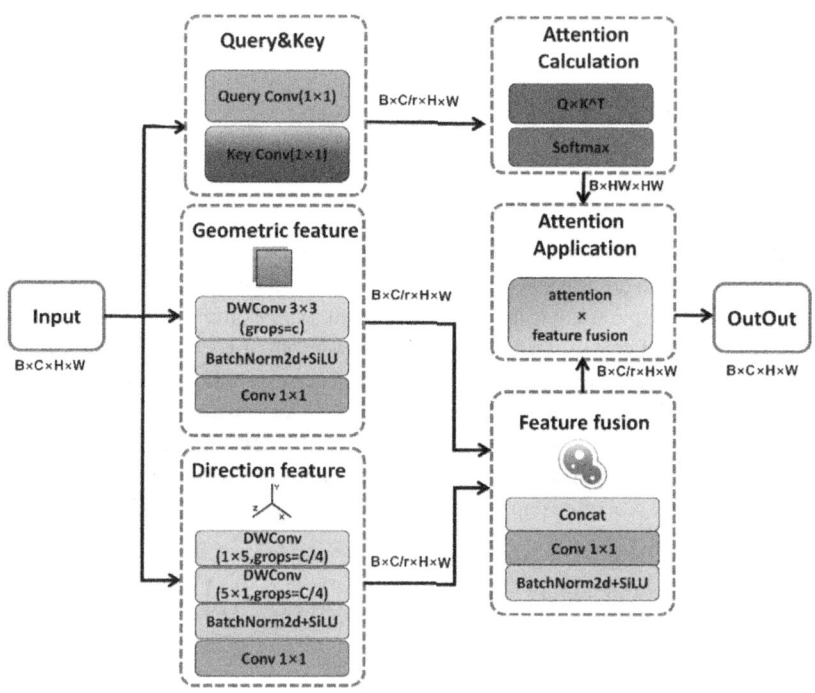

Fig. 3. The PCM module architecture.

2.4 C2f_ODConv

ODConv (Omni-dimensional Dynamic Convolution) is a dynamic convolution operation [11]. It introduces attention mechanisms across four dimensions: spatial kernel size, input channel number, output channel number, and kernel shape configuration. This achieves comprehensive adaptive regulation of the convolution process. Compared to traditional convolutions with fixed parameters, ODConv can dynamically adjust convolution weights according to input content. This significantly enhances feature representation capability and model generalization performance while maintaining computational efficiency.

This research integrates ODConv into C2f by replacing the second 3 × 3 convolution in all Bottleneck with ODConv. * MERGEFORMAT Fig. 4 shows the C2f_ODConv architecture diagram. The following equation presents the main formula for ODConv: Where, W_i is the i-th convolution kernel, α_{W_i} is the attention scalar weighted by W_i, and

∗ represents the convolution operation.

$$y = (\alpha_{W_i} W_i + \ldots + \alpha_{W_n} W_n) * x \tag{5}$$

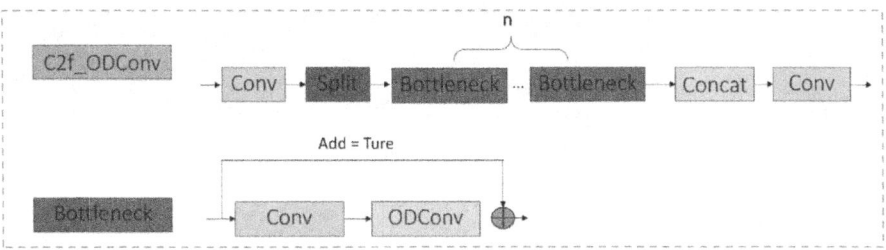

Fig. 4. The C2f_ODConv module architecture.

2.5 Loss Function

YOLOv8 employs DFL + CIoU (Complete Intersection over Union) to handle bounding boxes. It comprehensively considers the aspect ratio, center point distance, and overlapping area between predicted and ground truth boxes. This approach can, to some extent, improve network localization accuracy for targets in images. However, CIoU overly relies on target box center point distance and aspect ratio. In heavy-duty vehicle parking scenarios, targets exhibit significant aspect ratio variations, which may lead to poor detection performance. To address this issue, our research introduces WIoU (Wise IoU Loss Function) [12] as an improved loss function.

WIoU calculates IoU loss in class prediction through dynamic methods. WIoU can automatically adjust weighting according to different types of errors (such as position, size, and shape errors), better handling aspect ratio differences in target boxes. This method aims to reduce excessive penalties from geometric transformations and other factors, minimize interference with the training process, thereby enhancing model generalization capability.

3 Experiments

3.1 Dataset

Due to the scarcity of publicly available heavy-duty vehicle parking space datasets from real-world perspectives, which cannot meet practical application requirements, this research constructed a high-quality heavy-duty vehicle parking space dataset. The dataset comprises 1,420 images in total, covering various parking space types including perpendicular and angled parking spaces. The dataset exhibits rich scene diversity, including images with clear parking lines, occluded parking lines, and scenes under both sunlit and backlit conditions. The images were meticulously annotated using the LabelMe tool. Each image's annotation includes parking space bounding boxes, providing precise geometric information. The training and testing sets were split in an 8:2 ratio. Figure 5 shows typical parking spaces in the dataset.

Fig. 5. Typical parking space in the dataset

3.2 Experimental Environment

This paper designed a complete heavy-duty truck perception system solution. As shown in Fig. 6, multiple sensors were deployed at key positions on the vehicle, constructing a multi-source information fusion environmental perception system. In this experiment, only cameras on the left and right sides were used to collect environmental information (marked with black circles in the figure). This arrangement effectively expands the vehicle's perception range and provides more comprehensive environmental information. For practical system deployment, we established an industrial computer platform as the core computing unit on the heavy-duty truck. The specific hardware configuration parameters of the platform are shown in Table 1.

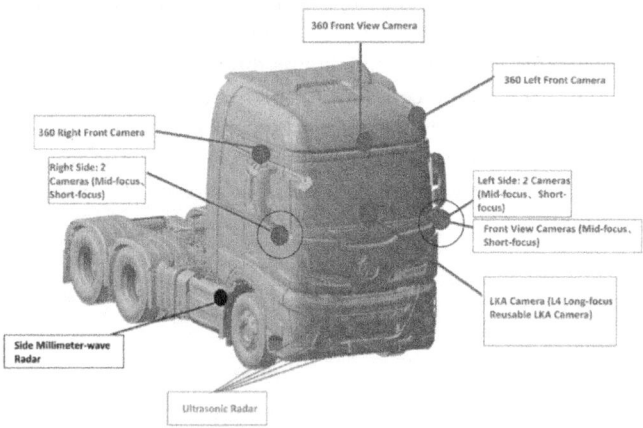

Fig. 6. Heavy-duty vehicle sensor layout

Table 1. Deployment environment information

configure	parameters
CPU	Intel(R)Xeon(R)Platinum8369BCPU@2.90 GHz
GPU	NVIDIA V100

(*continued*)

Table 1. (*continued*)

configure	parameters
Development Environment	PyTorch:2.0.1Python:3.11.0
Environment	CUDA11.8
Operating System	Ubuntu22.04.2

3.3 Evaluation Metrics

This paper uses precision, recall, and mAP as metrics to evaluate model performance. Precision measures the proportion of true positives among all samples predicted as positive. It reflects the correct prediction rate among all samples predicted as positive. Recall measures the model's ability to identify all positive samples. It is the proportion of all positive samples correctly predicted as positive. mAP is used to measure the model's overall performance across all categories. FPS indicates the number of images the model can process per second, measuring the model's real-time performance. The calculation methods for Precision, Recall, and mAP are as follows:

$$Precision = \frac{TP}{TP+FP} \tag{6}$$

$$Recall = \frac{TP}{TP+FN} \tag{7}$$

$$AP = \sum_n (R_n - R_{n-1})P_n \tag{8}$$

$$mAP = \frac{1}{N} \sum_{i=1}^{N} AP_i \tag{9}$$

3.4 Ablation Experiments

To evaluate the effectiveness of each component in the model, this paper conducted systematic ablation experiments. By sequentially adding or removing key modules, we analyzed their impact on model performance. The results are shown in Table 2.

Table 2. Ablation Experiment

Index	HGPA	C2f_ODConv	WIoU	mAP50	mAP50–95	Recall	Precision
1				0.974	0.907	0.958	0.927
2	✓			0.979	0.916	**0.964**	0.947
3		✓		0.984	0.901	0.950	0.938

(*continued*)

Table 2. (*continued*)

Index	HGPA	C2f_ODConv	WIoU	mAP50	mAP50–95	Recall	Precision
4			√	0.978	0.912	0.955	**0.957**
5	√	√		0.979	0.916	0.955	0.950
6	√		√	0.980	0.906	**0.964**	0.950
7	√	√	√	**0.987**	**0.919**	**0.964**	0.948

Using standard YOLOv8 as baseline (mAP50: 97.4%, mAP50–95: 90.7%), we tested three components individually: HGPA, C2f_ODConv, and WIoU. The results show that HGPA improves all metrics, especially increasing precision from 92.7% to 94.7%. This demonstrates its advantage in capturing global context information of parking spaces. C2f_ODConv performs well in high-threshold detection, achieving 98.4% mAP50. However, it shows a slight decrease in mAP50–95, suggesting it works best when combined with other components. The WIoU loss function significantly improves detection precision, boosting it from 92.7% to 95.7%. This validates its effectiveness in bounding box regression accuracy. Among two-component combinations, HGPA with WIoU shows the most balanced performance. It maintains high recall while significantly improving precision. Finally, combining all three components achieves the best performance. The method reaches 98.7% mAP50 and 91.9% mAP50–95, improving 1.3% and 1.2% compared to baseline. The ablation study fully validates the effectiveness of each component and their synergistic effects. This proves the superiority of our proposed method for parking space detection tasks.

3.5 Comparison Experiments

To further validate the performance of the YOLO-HG model, this paper compared it with several mainstream object detection models. We conducted comprehensive comparisons across metrics including mAP0.5, Recall, and Inference Time. The results are shown in Table 3.

Table 3. Comparative experiment

Model	mAP50	mAP50–95	Recall	Precision	FPS
YOLOv5n	0.966	0.879	0.943	0.923	138
YOLOv6n	0.970	0.901	0.917	**0.951**	175
YOLOv10n	0.961	0.890	0.878	0.896	181
YOLOv8n(Baseline)	0.974	0.907	0.958	0.927	169
YOLO-HG	**0.987**	**0.919**	**0.964**	0.948	149
YOLOv8(m)	0.984	0.939	0.966	0.950	94
YOLO-HG(m)	0.987	0.937	0.984	0.952	80

In lightweight model (n) comparisons, YOLO-HG achieved 98.7% mAP50, representing a 1.3% improvement over the baseline YOLOv8n, while reaching 91.9% mAP50–95 (+1.2%). In terms of detection recall, YOLO-HG achieved 96.4%, a 0.6% improvement over the baseline, indicating enhanced performance in reducing missed detections.

Compared to other mainstream models, YOLO-HG shows significant improvements. Compared to YOLOv5n, YOLO-HG's mAP50 improved by 2.1% and mAP50–95 improved by 4.0%, achieving significant improvements in detection accuracy. Compared to YOLOv6n, although YOLOv6n has the highest precision, its recall is only 91.7%, leaning toward conservative detection and prone to missing detections. Although YOLOv10n has faster inference speed (181 FPS), its accuracy performance is poor in parking space detection tasks, with recall only 87.8%. In terms of inference speed, due to the computational overhead introduced by the attention mechanism, YOLO-HG achieves 149 FPS, slightly lower than YOLOv8n's 169 FPS. In medium-scale model (m) comparisons, mAP50 maintained high performance at 98.7%. In terms of recall, it achieved 98.4%, surpassing YOLOv8m's 96.6%.

These comparison experiments fully validate the effectiveness of the YOLO-HG architecture design, confirming the synergistic effects of the hierarchical attention module, ODConv enhancement, and WIoU loss function, providing a superior solution for parking space detection tasks. Figure 7 shows example detection results.

Fig. 7. Example detection results. Rows 1 and 2 show improvements in false positive reduction, rows 3 and 4 show improvements in false negative reduction, and row 5 shows detection accuracy improvements.

4 Conclusion

To improve the accuracy and robustness of heavy-duty truck automatic parking space detection, this paper proposes YOLO-HG, an object detection method based on improved YOLOv8. The introduced Hierarchical Global Parking Attention (HGPA) module effectively enhances parking space recognition capability in complex scenarios by combining global contextual relationships with hierarchical modeling of local geometric features. The C2f_ODConv module enhances feature representation through omni-dimensional dynamic convolution, significantly improving object detection performance. To improve bounding box regression accuracy, this paper also employed the WIoU loss function, whose dynamic focusing mechanism better handles difficult samples. Experimental results demonstrate that YOLO-HG achieves 98.7% mAP50 and 91.9% mAP50–95 on the parking space detection dataset, representing improvements of 1.3% and 1.2% respectively compared to baseline YOLOv8n. The proposed method can accurately identify various types of parking spaces, providing effective technical support for intelligent parking systems. However, due to existing dataset limitations, this paper has not conducted sufficient testing under extreme environmental conditions such as nighttime or rainy and snowy weather. Future work can collect data from these special scenarios to further validate and optimize the model's robustness and adaptability under extreme environments.

References

1. Ding, L., Goshtasby, A.: On the Canny edge detector. Pattern Recogn. **34**(3), 721–725 (2001)
2. Illingworth, J., Kittler, J.: A survey of the Hough transform. Comput Vis. Graph. Image Process. **44**(1), 87–116 (1988)
3. Lee, S., Seo, S.-W.: Available parking slot recognition based on slot context analysis. IET Intel. Transport Syst. **10**(9), 594–604 (2016)
4. Suhr, J.K., Jung, H.G.: Automatic parking space detection and tracking for underground and indoor environments. In: IEEE Transactions on Industrial Electronics, vol. 63, pp. 5687–5698. IEEE (2016)
5. Hasan, M.D.A., Bhargav, T., Sandeep, V., et al.: Image classification using convolutional neural networks. Int. J. Mech. Eng. Res. Technol. **16**(2), 173–181 (2024)
6. Zhao, X., Wang, L., Zhang, Y., et al.: A review of convolutional neural networks in computer vision. Artif. Intell. Rev. **57**(4), 99 (2024)
7. Hung, B.T., Chakrabarti, P.: Parking lot occupancy detection using hybrid deep learning CNN-LSTM approach. In: Proceedings of 2nd International Conference on Artificial Intelligence: Advances and Applications: ICAIAA 2021, pp. 501–509. Springer Nature, Singapore (2022)
8. Wang, H., Liu, C., Cai, Y., Chen, L., Li, Y.: YOLOv8-QSD: an improved small object detection algorithm for autonomous vehicles based on YOLOv8. IEEE Trans. Instrum. Meas. **73**, 1–16 (2024)
9. Padilla Carrasco, D., Rashwan, H.A., García, M.Á., Puig, D.: T-YOLO: tiny vehicle detection based on YOLO and multi-scale convolutional neural networks. IEEE Access **11**, 22430–22440 (2023)
10. Sohan, M., Sai Ram, T., Rami Reddy, C.V.: A review on YOLOv8 and its advancements. In: International Conference on Data Intelligence and Cognitive Informatics, pp. 529–545. Springer, Singapore (2024)
11. Li, C., Zhou, A., Yao, A.: Omni-dimensional dynamic convolution (2022). arXiv preprint arXiv:2209.07947
12. Tong, Z., Chen, Y., Xu, Z., et al.: Wise-IoU: bounding box regression loss with dynamic focusing mechanism (2023). arXiv preprint arXiv:2301.10051

An Accurate 3D Reconstruction Method for Large Workpieces Based on 3D Vision

Shenglun Zhang[1], Shibo Hu[1], Xingwei Zhao[1,2](✉), Dailin Zhang[1], and Bo Tao[1]

[1] School of Mechanical Science and Engineering, Huazhong University of Science and Technology, Wuhan 430074, Hubei, China
zhaoxingwei@hust.edu.cn

[2] Huazhong University of Science and Technology-Wuxi Research Institute, Wuxi, China

Abstract. In order to achieve high-precision robot machining requirements for large workpieces, a 3D reconstruction process of the workpiece is necessary. This paper proposed an accurate 3D reconstruction method for large workpieces based on 3D vision. The method contains two steps: Considering the substantial size of large workpieces, in the first step we established a measurement-machining system that captures point cloud pieces using a point cloud camera. Using coordinate transformations, we obtained a coarse registration result. Due to factors including calibration errors and robot motion inaccuracies, etc., misalignments and displacements exist between point cloud pieces; To address this, we employed an improved Iterative Closest Point (ICP) algorithm to perform precise registration as the second step and ultimately completed the accurate 3D reconstruction process. Experimental results showed significant reductions in both point-to-tangent plane and point-to-point errors after precise registration, all within acceptable error margins. The point-to-tangent plane errors are close to point-to-point errors, which means fine alignments lies in both position and pose. These results validate the reliability and effectiveness of the measurement-machining system for large workpieces 3D reconstruction and demonstrate the high accuracy of the proposed 3D reconstruction method.

Keywords: 3D reconstruction · Point cloud registration · ICP

1 Introduction

Robots have been extensively utilized in the machining of large workpieces due to their extensive workspaces and high flexibility, effectively addressing the limitations of traditional machining methods and reducing manual labor demands [1–3]. Going through initial-forming, large workpieces often exhibit shape deviations when compared to their standard CAD models. To enhance machining precision, it is imperative to reconstruct the three-dimensional geometry of the actual workpiece and plan machining trajectories based on this reconstructed model. The reconstruction can be achieved by deploying a measurement-machining system that captures surface information of the workpiece. Among various measurement techniques, systems employing point cloud cameras have garnered significant research attention.

© The Author(s), under exclusive license to Springer Nature Singapore Pte Ltd. 2026
T. Matsuno et al. (Eds.): ICIRA 2025, LNAI 16076, pp. 386–397, 2026.
https://doi.org/10.1007/978-981-95-2101-2_32

For measuring large workpieces, a robotic measurement-machining system is typically established, wherein a point cloud camera is mounted on the robot's end-effector to perform scans. The robot's extensive workspace and flexibility facilitate comprehensive scanning of large workpieces. To accommodate the dimensions of such workpieces, these robotic measurement-machining systems are generally designed to be mobile. Zhao et al. [4] introduced a mobile robotic grinding system wherein the robot is mounted on an Automated Guided Vehicle (AGV) and equipped with a point cloud camera, laser sensors, and a force-controlled grinding tool. This configuration allows for precise calibration of the workpiece, enabling accurate 3D reconstruction and automated machining tasks. Similarly, Jiang et al. [5] proposed a mobile dual-robot machining system that achieves cooperative operations through calibration and measurement. In this system, two robots are installed on sliding rails at both sides of the workpiece, facilitating scanning and machining operations via coordinated movements.

After acquiring point cloud pieces of the large workpiece, a coarse 3D reconstruction can be performed using coordinate transformation relationships. However, due to calibration errors and robot motion inaccuracies, misalignments and displacements often exist between point cloud pieces, necessitating precise registration. The Iterative Closest Point (ICP) algorithm [6] is widely employed for point cloud registration, involving the identification of corresponding point pairs and the computation of pose transformation matrix, using point-to-point distances as the error metric. Nevertheless, when dealing with complex geometries, the ICP algorithm's reliance on point-to-point distances makes it susceptible to noise, potential convergence to local minima, and non-unique iterative directions. To address these shortcomings, various enhancements to the ICP algorithm have been proposed. Rusinkiewicz et al. [7] introduced an ICP variant based on uniform sampling in normal space, improving convergence for near-planar meshes with small features. Further, Billings et al. [8] incorporated measurement noise into the estimation of the pose transformation matrix to enhance the ICP algorithm. Beyond point-to-point distances metric, employing point-to-plane distances as the error metric can further improve ICP performance [9, 10]. Ramalingam et al. [11] proposed a minimal solution family for point-to-plane registration, addressing pose estimation and registration under various configurations. Wang et al. [12] developed an ICP variant based on point-to-plane distances, enhancing registration efficiency and robustness for surfaces with weak features. Additionally, plane-to-plane distances have been proposed as the error metric to estimate point cloud correspondences, thereby improving ICP algorithm performance [13–15].

In this paper, a 3D vision-based method for accurate 3D reconstruction of large workpieces has been proposed, comprising two main steps: coarse registration as the primary 3D reconstruction result and precise registration of point cloud pieces as the final result. A measurement-machining system has been established to scan and acquire point cloud pieces of large workpieces, facilitating the coarse registration step. Subsequently, an improved ICP algorithm is employed for the precise registration of the coarsely aligned point cloud pieces. Experimental validations confirm the effectiveness of the proposed method. The remainder of this paper is organized as follows: Sect. 2 details the composition of the measurement-machining system and the process of coarse registration. Section 3 describes the precise registration of point cloud pieces using an improved ICP algorithm. Section 4 presents the experimental results. Section 5 concludes the paper. Section 6 declares the supporting fund.

2 Coarse Registration Based on 3D Vision

In the aerospace industry, large workpieces often require surface grinding after initial-forming. Due to dimensional deviations and forming errors between the physical workpiece and its standard CAD model, it is essential to perform 3D reconstruction of the actual workpiece to facilitate accurate offline trajectory planning for robotic grinding operations. These large workpieces typically span several meters in length or diameter and possess complex surface geometries, making contact-based measurement methods impractical. Consequently, non-contact measurement techniques, such as utilizing the point cloud camera, are employed to capture surface features through scanning. However, given the limited field of view of the point cloud camera, a comprehensive measurement-machining system must be established to achieve complete scanning of the workpiece.

2.1 Establishing the Measurement-Machining System

In this paper, we established a measurement-machining system for scanning large workpieces to acquire comprehensive surface information as shown in Fig. 1. The system comprises a turntable, a vertical slider, a collaborative robot, an industrial robot, a point cloud camera, a programmable logic controller (PLC), and a host computer. The turntable serves to position the workpiece and enables multi-angle scanning through rotation, effectively eliminating measurement blind spots. The point cloud camera is mounted on the flange of the collaborative robot's end-effector. This configuration allows the camera to cover a broader scanning area, particularly beneficial for workpieces with complex surfaces. By adjusting the collaborative robot's pose, detailed surface information can be more readily captured. The collaborative robot is installed on a vertical slider to compensate for its limited workspace, thereby meeting the height requirements during the scanning process.

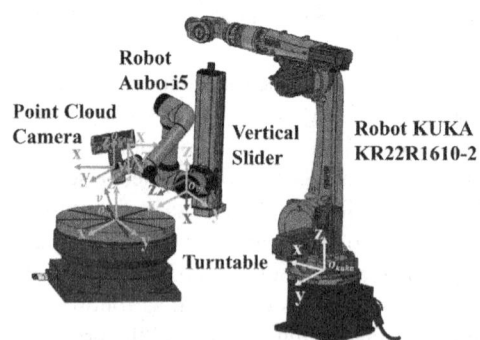

Fig. 1. The measurement-machining system and coordinate system configurations

2.2 Measurement-Machining System Coordinate Transformation Relationships and Coarse Registration

Based on the aforementioned measurement-machining system, we established the coordinate systems as depicted in Fig. 1. The turntable coordinate system is denoted as O_{rt} and the rotary axis vector is v, the collaborative robot base coordinate system is denoted as O_{base}, the industrial robot base coordinate system is denoted as O_{kuka}, the vertical slider coordinate system is denoted as O_{vs}, which is derived by rotating the robot base coordinate system 90 degrees about the y-axis. The robot end-effector flange coordinate system is represented as O_{end}, and the camera coordinate system as O_{camera}. During each scanning operation, we record the turntable rotation angle θ, the robot's height H along the vertical slider, and the robot's end-effector pose $^{base}_{end}T$. By adjusting the turntable angle, the robot's height on the vertical slider, and the robot's pose, we achieve a comprehensive scan of the entire workpiece. Utilizing the data recorded during the scanning process, we can transform the point cloud coordinates from the camera coordinate system to the industrial robot coordinate system. The specific coordinate transformation process is detailed below.

Through the hand–eye calibration relationship, we can transform the point cloud coordinates from the camera coordinate system to the collaborative robot's end-effector flange coordinate system. Let the point cloud coordinates in the camera coordinate system be denoted as ^{Cam}p, and the corresponding coordinates in the collaborative robot end-effector flange coordinate system as ^{end}p, The transformation matrix from the camera to the robot's end-effector, obtained via hand–eye calibration, is denoted as $^{end}_{Cam}T$, the transformation relationship is shown in Eq. (1):

$$^{end}p = {}^{end}_{Cam}T * {}^{Cam}p \tag{1}$$

Let the point cloud coordinates in the collaborative robot base coordinate system be denoted as ^{base}p, given the transformation matrix $^{base}_{end}T$, which represents the pose of the collaborative robot end-effector relative to the collaborative robot base, the transformation relationship is shown in Eq. (2):

$$^{base}p = {}^{base}_{end}T * {}^{end}p \tag{2}$$

Let the point cloud coordinates in the vertical slider coordinate system be denoted as ^{vs}p, given the transformation matrix $^{vs}_{base}T$, the transformation relationship is shown in Eq. (3):

$$^{vs}p = {}^{vs}_{base}T * {}^{base}p \tag{3}$$

Let the point cloud coordinates in the turntable coordinate system be denoted as ^{rt}p, given the transformation matrix $^{rt}_{vs}T$, the transformation relationship is shown in Eq. (4):

$$^{rt}p = {}^{rt}_{vs}T * {}^{vs}p \tag{4}$$

Since the point cloud coordinates under the turntable coordinate system are obtained after the turntable is rotated clockwise around the axis by an angle θ, in order to restore the actual position information of the point cloud coordinates before rotating around the axis, it is also necessary to perform a transformation that rotates counterclockwise around the turntable rotary axis, let the point cloud coordinates under the turntable coordinate system before rotation be $^{rt-static}p$ and the turntable rotary axis vector v passes through the origin of the turntable coordinate system. According to Rodriguez's equation, the rotation matrix with counterclockwise rotation angle θ around the rotary axis vector v can be obtained as $^{v\theta}R$, the transformation relationship is shown in Eq. (5):

$$^{rt-static}p = {}^{v\theta}R * {}^{rt}p \tag{5}$$

Let the transformation matrix from the collaborative robot coordinate system to the industrial robot coordinate system be $^{kuka}_{base}T$. We can get the actual point cloud coordinates ^{kuka}p before rotating in the industrial robot coordinate system as shown in Eq. (6):

$$^{kuka}p = {}^{kuka}_{base}T \, {}^{vs}_{base}T \, T^{-1}{}^{rt}_{vs} \, T^{-1 v\theta} R^{rt}_{vs} T^{vs}_{base} T^{base}_{end} T^{end}_{Cam} \, T * {}^{Cam}p \tag{6}$$

By applying coordinate transformation relationship described in Eq. (6) to the scanned point cloud pieces based on the pose data recorded during the scanning process, the coordinates of each point cloud piece can be obtained within the industrial robot coordinate system. This completes the coarse registration session in the 3D reconstruction process of the workpiece. However, due to calibration errors and robot motion inaccuracies, coarse registration errors still exist between the point cloud pieces, necessitating further precise registration process.

3 Precise Registration Based on Improved ICP Algorithm

Due to factors including calibration errors and robot motion inaccuracies, misalignments and displacements exist between point cloud pieces after coarse registration, precise registration for point cloud pieces is necessary. The registration problem between the two point cloud pieces can be summarized as follows: Given point cloud P and Q, q_i is the point coordinate in the target point cloud $Q\{q_i\}$, p_i is the point coordinate in the source point cloud to be registered $P\{p_i\}$. (q_i, p_i) is denoted as the corresponding point pair in two point clouds, totaling k pairs. The goal of registering two point cloud pieces is to minimize the distances between these corresponding point pairs. The objective optimization function for registration is described as follows:

$$minE(R, t) = \sum_{i=1}^{k} \|q_i - (Rp_i + t)\|_2 \tag{7}$$

3.1 Corresponding Point Pair Search for Partially Overlapping Point Clouds

The ICP algorithm is widely used to solve the point cloud registration problem. The ICP algorithm contains two steps, the first is the corresponding point pair search, and the second is the pose transformation matrix estimation. The corresponding point search is to find the corresponding point pairs between two point cloud pieces. The corresponding point pairs are actually the same three-dimensional coordinate points in the same coordinate system of the two point clouds. Estimating the pose transformation matrix means finding the optimal pose transformation matrix that makes the corresponding point pairs coincide, so that the target value optimization function of the registration can be minimized as much as possible.

In the ICP algorithm, the above two processes are carried out alternately. In the initial stage, the search for corresponding point pairs and the estimation of the pose transformation matrix are not accurate. Through continuous iterations, the accuracy of the corresponding relationship and the pose transformation matrix will gradually improve until convergence. However, the ICP algorithm has certain defects. Only when one point cloud is a subset of another point cloud can the accurate corresponding point pair relationship be found. When processing two point clouds with partially overlapping areas, mismatching problems will occur. In the process of coarse registration, there is only a partial overlapping area between two point clouds. Thus, a method is needed to accurately find the corresponding point pairs for point clouds with partial overlap.

In [12], a method for searching corresponding points mutually in the partial overlap area of two point clouds have been proposed. The method is shown in Fig. 2 and can be summarized as follows: p_i is the point coordinate in the source point cloud to be registered $P\{p_i\}$, by finding the point q_i that is closest to it in the target point cloud $Q\{q_i\}$, and then based on q_i, reversely find the point p_k that is closest to q_i in the source point cloud $P\{p_i\}$. Calculate the Euclidean distance l between p_i and p_k, if l is less than the given threshold, then it can be judged that (q_i, p_i) is a corresponding point pair, otherwise (q_i, p_i) is removed from the corresponding point pair set, and continue to find new corresponding point pairs.

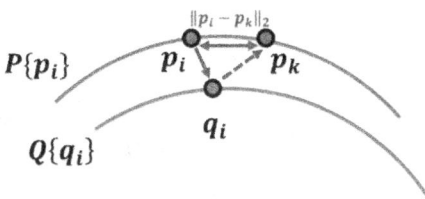

Fig. 2. Finding corresponding point pair mutually in partially overlapping point clouds, all variables were explained in the above content paragraph

3.2 Corresponding Point Pair Registration Error Criterion

In the ICP algorithm, the corresponding point search and pose transformation matrix estimation are continuously optimized through an iterative process. The Euclidean distance (point-to-point distance) is used to measure the registration error between corresponding point pairs. When the error is less than the given threshold for exiting the iteration, the ICP algorithm breaks and the pose transformation matrix at this iteration step is the optimal solution. The point-to-point distances error criterion only considers the position alignment errors of the corresponding point pairs, not including the pose alignment error. Therefore, it will lead to low registration accuracy and low efficiency.

In [12], a point-to-plane distance error metric is proposed as shown in Fig. 3, which uses the point-to-tangent plane distance error criterion instead of the point-to-point distance error criterion to improve the efficiency and robustness of the algorithm. Assuming that q_i is a point in the target point cloud $Q\{q_i\}$, the normal vector of q_i is n_{qi}, the corresponding point of q_i in the source point cloud $P\{p_i\}$ is p_i, the point-to-plane error is l_1, the point-to-point error is l_2. If there are k corresponding point pairs, the motioned error metric can be expressed as follows:

$$E_1(q_i, p_i) = \sqrt{\frac{1}{k}\sum_{i=1}^{k}\|(p_i - q_i) \cdot n_{qi}\|_2} \tag{8}$$

It was proposed in [12] that the use of the point-to-tangent plane error metric can improve the robustness and convergence speed of the ICP algorithm to noise. Based on this error metric, this paper combines the point-to-point distance as a joint error criterion to avoid the situation where the coordinates of corresponding point pairs on the same tangent plane are not aligned as shown in Fig. 3. The distance error metric between corresponding point pairs can be expressed as:

$$E_2(q_i, p_i) = \sqrt{\frac{1}{k}\sum_{i=1}^{k}\|(p_i - q_i)\|_2} \tag{9}$$

Let the threshold of the ICP interative process be $\in$, the joint error criterion J can be described as:

$$E_1(q_i, p_i) <\in \& E_2(q_i, p_i) <\in \& |E_1(q_i, p_i) - E_2(q_i, p_i)| < \in \tag{10}$$

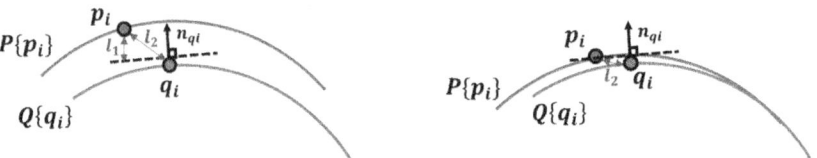

Point − to − tangent plane error criterion   misaligned situation

Fig. 3. Point-to-tangent plane error criterion and misaligned situation, all variables were explained in the above content paragraph

3.3 Improved ICP Algorithm

Considering the ICP algorithm, we replace the corresponding parts of it with the mutual corresponding point method used in [12] and the joint error criterion proposed in this paper, then we obtain the certain improved ICP algorithm pseudo code as shown in Table 1:

Table 1. Improved ICP algorithm pseudo code

Improved ICP	
Input: Point cloud P and target point cloud Q	
Output: optimal transformation matrix T	
1 Initialization: $T \leftarrow I$	
2 For i = 1,2,3,..., M	//M is the maximum steps of iterations
3 $\{(p_i, q_i)\} \leftarrow P, Q$	// Mutual finding corresponding point pairs
4 $T_i \leftarrow \min E(R, t)$	// Current optimal transformation matrix T_i
5 $P \leftarrow T_i P$	// Update Point cloud P
6 $E_1(q_i, p_i) \leftarrow \sqrt{\frac{1}{k} \sum_{i=1}^{k} \|(p_i - q_i) \cdot n_{qi}\|_2}$	// Calculate point-to-plane distance error
7 $E_2(q_i, p_i) \leftarrow \sqrt{\frac{1}{k} \sum_{i=1}^{k} \|(p_i - q_i)\|_2}$	// Calculate point-to-point Distance error
8 If $E_1 < \epsilon$ &&$E_2 < \epsilon$ &&$|E_1 - E_2| < \epsilon$	// Using the joint error criterion J
9 **Break**	
10 **End If**	
11 $T \leftarrow T_i T$	// Update optimal transformation matrix T
12 End For	

4 Experiment

In this paper, hardware devices used in the measurement-machining system mentioned in session 2 are illustrated as follows: the turntable servo motor is the Servotronix BDHDE, the vertical slider servo motor is the Servotronix BD3S, the PLC is the Inovance Easy521, the collaborative robot is the AUBO-i5, the industrial robot is the KUKA KR22R1610-2 and the point cloud camera is the Vision3D SmartScan240, the accuracy of a single frame is ±0.05 mm which meets the experiment requirements. The established experiment measurement-machining system is shown in Fig. 4.

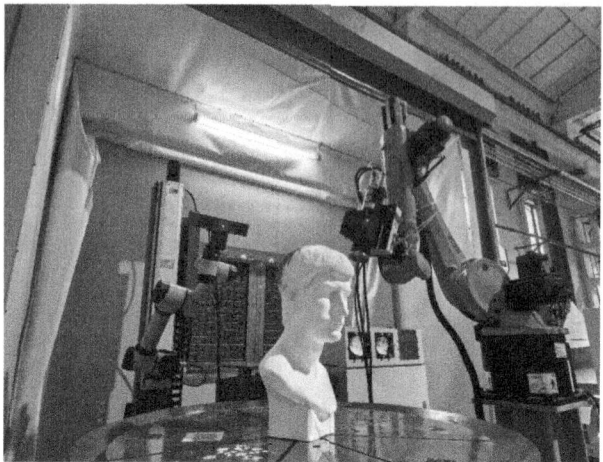

Fig. 4. Experiment measurement-machining system composition

4.1 Coarse Registration Experiment

In this paper, the workpiece is the plaster head of Roman youth which has complex surface. We placed the workpiece to be scanned on the turntable as shown in Fig. 4 and we use the measurement-machining system to perform scanning. During the scanning process, we use the host computer to record the angles of the turntable, the heights of the robot on the vertical slider, and the positions and poses of the collaborative robot. Based on Eq. (6), we can perform the coarse registration of the 3D reconstruction process, the result is shown in Fig. 5. It can be seen that there are misalignments and displacements between point cloud pieces, thus further precise registration is necessary.

4.2 Precise Registration Experiment

After we obtain the coarse registration result of the scanned workpiece, we use the improved ICP algorithm to achieve precise registration, thereby completing an accurate 3D reconstruction of the workpiece. We use the coarse registration point cloud pieces sequence as input, perform precise registration, and finally obtain the workpiece point cloud as the result as shown in Fig. 6. It can be seen that after precise registration the misalignments and displacements have been corrected. The point-to-plane errors and point-to-point errors distribution of all the point cloud pieces before and after precise registration are shown in Fig. 7. It can be seen that the mean error after precise registration is significantly lower than the mean error before, and it is within an acceptable error range. After using the joint error judgment criterion, the point-to-plane error and point-to-point error distribution of each piece are basically consistent as shown in Fig. 7, which has demonstrated that the improved ICP algorithm used in this article has a significant effect on reducing the point cloud registration errors and provides high registration accuracy.

An Accurate 3D Reconstruction Method   395

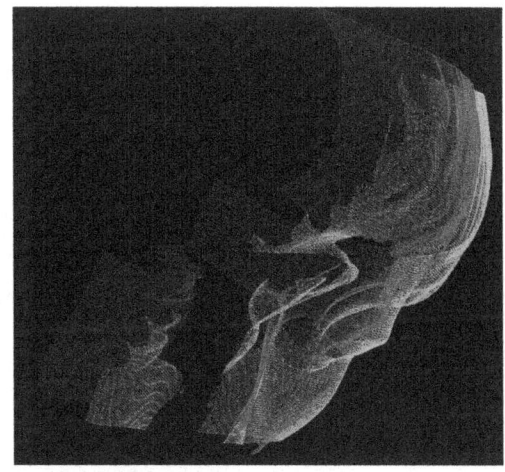

Fig. 5. Coarse registration result

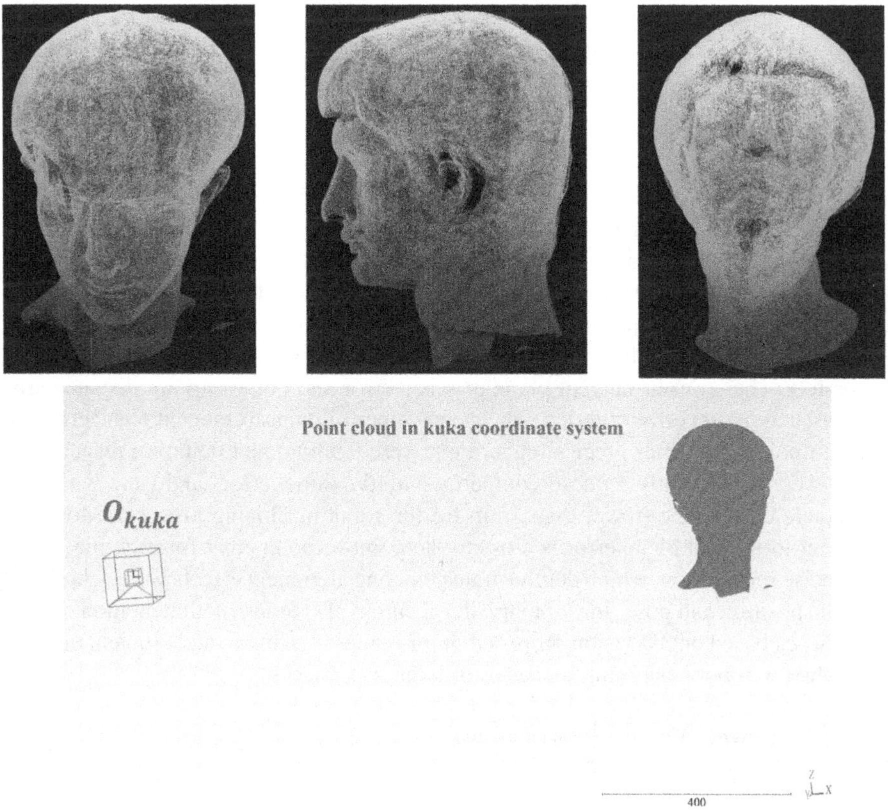

Fig. 6. Precise registration result

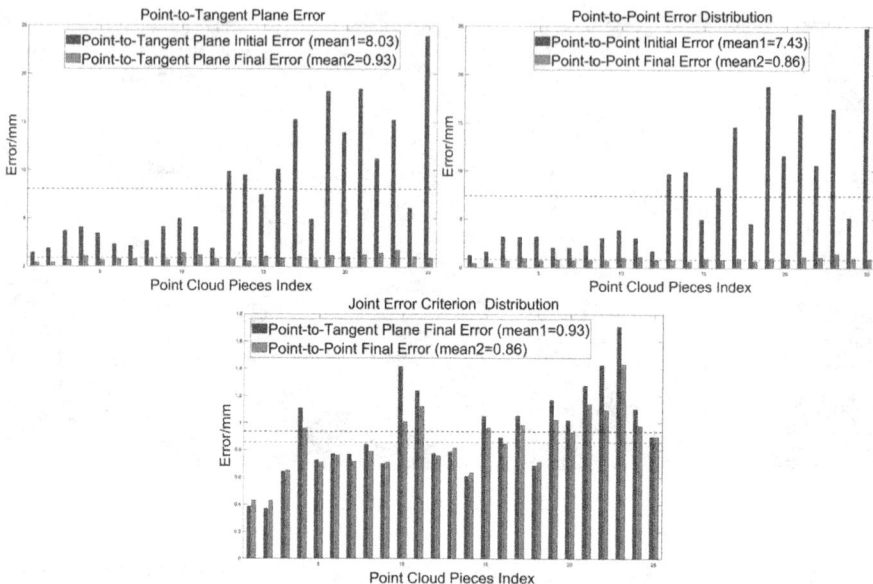

Fig. 7. Registration error analysis

5 Conclusion

In this paper, we proposed an accurate 3D reconstruction method for of large workpieces based on 3D vision. The method consists of two steps: coarse registration and precise registration. We established a measurement-machining system based on point cloud camera and performed the coarse registration through the position and pose transformation relationships. Due to the existence of calibration errors, robot motion errors, etc., we used an improved ICP algorithm to register the point cloud pieces after coarse registration accurately. The point-to-tangent plane distance error and point-to-point distance error were used as a joint error criterion. The mean values of point-to-tangent plane error and point-to-point error after precise registration were 0.93mm and 0.86mm, respectively, which were significantly reduced compared with the initial errors and were within the acceptable error range (lower than 1mm for the robot machining process). Moreover, the point-to-tangent plane error is close to the point-to-point error for each piece after the precise registration, which demonstrates that fine alignment effects were achieved in both the position and pose. In summary, the accurate 3D reconstruction method of large workpieces based on 3D vision proposed in this paper is accurate and efficient, and can be applied to robot machining scenarios of large workpieces.

Acknowledgement. This work was supported by the National Key Research and Development Program of China under Grant 2023YFB3408603.

References

1. Brogårdh, T.: Present and future robot control development—An industrial perspective. Annu. Rev. Control. **31**(1), 69–79 (2007)
2. Brogårdh, T.: Robot control overview: an industrial perspective. MIC—Model. Identif. Control **30**(3), 167 (2009)
3. Dzedzickis, A., Subačiūtė-Žemaitienė, J., Šutinys, E., Samukaitė-Bubnienė, U., Bučinskas, V.: Advanced applications of industrial robotics: new trends and possibilities. Appl. Sci. **12**(1), 135 (2022)
4. Zhao, X., Lu, H., Yu, W., Tao, B., Ding, H.: Vision-based mobile robotic grinding for large workpiece and its accuracy analysis. IEEE/ASME Trans. Mechatron. **28**(2), 895–906 (2023)
5. Jiang, C., et al.: A novel dual-robot accurate calibration method using convex optimization and lie derivative. IEEE Trans. Robot. **40**, 960–977 (2023)
6. Besl, P.J., McKay, N.D.: Method for registration of 3-D shapes. In: Sensor fusion IV: control paradigms and data structures. pp. 586–606. Spie, Boston (1992)
7. Rusinkiewicz, S., Levoy, M.: Efficient variants of the ICP algorithm. In: Proceedings third international conference on 3-D digital imaging and modeling. pp. 145–152. IEEE, Quebec (2001)
8. Billings, S.D., Boctor, E.M., Taylor, R.H.: Iterative most-likely point registration (IMLP): a robust algorithm for computing optimal shape alignment. PLoS One **10**(3), 1–45 (2015)
9. Chen, Y., Medioni, G.: Object modelling by registration of multiple range images. Image Vis. Comput. **10**(3), 145–155 (1992)
10. Khoshelham, K.: Closed-form solutions for estimating a rigid motion from plane correspondences extracted from point clouds. ISPRS J. Photogramm. Remote. Sens. **114**, 78–91 (2016)
11. Ramalingam, S., Taguchi, Y.: A theory of minimal 3D point to 3D plane registration and its generalization. Int. J. Comput. Vision **102**, 73–90 (2013)
12. Wang, J., Tao, B., Gong, Z., Yu, W., Yin, Z.: A mobile robotic 3-D measurement method based on point clouds alignment for large complex surfaces. IEEE Trans. Instrum. Meas. **70**, 1–11 (2021)
13. Brenner, C., Dold, C., Ripperda, N.: Coarse orientation of terrestrial laser scans in urban environments. ISPRS J. Photogramm. Remote. Sens. **63**, 4–18 (2008)
14. Khoshelham, K.: Automated localization of a laser scanner in indoor environments using planar objects. In: 2010 International Conference on Indoor Positioning and Indoor Navigation. pp. 1–7. IEEE (2010)
15. Forstner, W., Khoshelham, K.: Efficient and accurate registration of point clouds with plane to plane correspondences. In: Proceedings of the IEEE international conference on computer vision workshops. pp. 2165–2173. IEEE (2017)

Insulator and Its Defect Detection Framework Based on Feature Enhancement CenterNet

Xiaoming Mai[1,2], Zehui Zhang[1(✉)], Shutong Yao[1], Shuaibing Mi[1], Na Dong[1], and Kuansheng Zou[3]

[1] Tianjin Key Laboratory of Intelligent Unmanned Swarm Technology and System, School of Electrical and Information Engineering, Tianjin University, Tianjin 300072, China
zhangzh0351@tju.edu.cn
[2] The Intelligent Operation and Inspection Division of China Southern Power Grid Technology Co., Ltd., Guangzhou 510170, China
[3] School of Electrical Engineering and Automation, Jiangsu Normal University, Xuzhou 221116, China

Abstract. Power line insulator defects can lead to serious failures in transmission systems, making aerial image-based inspection a widely used technique. However, detecting insulators and their defects in aerial images remains a challenging task due to complex backgrounds and varying environmental conditions. This paper presents an automatic detection approach for insulators and their defects using aerial imagery, and proposes a novel deep learning framework based on feature-enhanced CenterNet. To improve insulator detection, we first deepen the backbone network to enhance feature extraction under complex scenes. Then, we incorporate the Res2Net module to expand the receptive field and improve multi-scale representation. Finally, a pyramid pooling module is applied to fuse multi-scale and sub-region contextual information, thereby increasing identification accuracy and reducing missed detections. To further enhance defect detection performance, we integrate an efficient channel attention mechanism during feature fusion to better capture defect-related semantic features. Additionally, we introduce a convolutional attention module in the deconvolution upsampling stage to highlight defect features while suppressing noise. Finally, we adopt CIoU Loss for bounding box regression to improve localization accuracy. Experimental results demonstrate that the proposed framework meets the accuracy and robustness requirements for insulator defect detection. Evaluated on an extended public dataset, the method achieves a mean precision of 95.06% for insulators and defects, demonstrating strong performance across diverse inspection scenarios.

Keywords: power line inspection · insulator detection · insulator defect detection · feature enhancement · CenterNet

1 Introduction

With the expansion of complex power grids globally driven by rising electricity demands [1], insulators—critical components on transmission lines play a key role in supporting conductors and preventing current leakage to ground [2,3]. Long-term outdoor exposure subjects insulators to harsh environmental stresses, leading to common defects such as fractures, detachment, and erosion. Therefore, effective insulator inspection is essential for transmission line maintenance. Traditional manual inspection methods suffer from low efficiency and limited accuracy. Recent advances in image processing and artificial intelligence have enabled deep learning-based insulator detection, allowing rapid and accurate localization of insulators and their defects, thereby reducing human workload and improving inspection efficiency. This approach also provides a reference for detecting other power equipment defects.

This paper focuses on insulator and defect detection using Convolutional Neural Networks (CNNs). To address challenges posed by complex backgrounds and small defect regions, we propose a feature-enhanced CenterNet-based detection framework. The core contributions are summarized as follows.

(1) Insulator detection: According to the characteristics of aerial insulator images, the CenterNet model is improved including: deepening the depth of the feature extraction network; improving the extraction ability of insulator features; building a pyramid pooling module and reducing the insulator leakage detection by improving the ability to obtain global context information.

(2) Insulator defect detection: To address the challenges of detecting small insulator defects in complex environments, the CenterNet model is improved by incorporating an Efficient Channel Attention (ECA) module into the pyramid pooling stage to enhance small defect feature extraction, introducing a Feature Enhancement Module (FEM) to minimize feature degradation and suppress background noise, and employing the CIoU loss function to optimize bounding box regression accuracy.

(3) Experimental demonstration: In this paper, an expended public insulator dataset is used for the experiment, and the proposed detection framework is tested and compared experimentally. Through experimental verification, the proposed framework can quickly and accurately detect insulators and its defects in various complex backgrounds.

2 Related Works

2.1 Insulator Detection

In the field of insulator detection, deep learning-based methods offer automatic and efficient feature extraction. Zhao et al. [4] improved Faster R-CNN by optimizing anchor generation to better match the aspect ratio of insulators, enhancing non-maximum suppression performance. Tan et al. [5] introduced a two-stage data augmentation strategy, first fusing real images with complex backgrounds to construct a synthetic dataset. Chen et al. [6] proposed a GAN-based insulator generation method, which generates high-resolution images through a fine-grained module. Zhuo et al. [7] developed InST-Net, which employs ResNet50 as the backbone for efficient feature extraction and introduces scale-specific detection branches embedded.

2.2 Insulator Defect Detection

Traditional insulator defect detection primarily relied on image segmentation and machine learning techniques. Cheng et al. [8] proposed a spatial feature-based method that leverages color characteristics to separate glass insulators from complex backgrounds. Chen et al. [9] transformed insulator images from RGB to LAB color space to mitigate lighting effects, followed by improved OTSU and morphological filtering for segmentation.

CNN-based object detection techniques show better performance in defect detection. Huang et al. [10] applied Fast R-CNN to learn high-level defect features and integrated low-level features such as color and texture for multi-fault recognition. Tao et al. [11] proposed a cascaded network that first locates the insulator and then detects defects within the cropped region. Gao [12] and Li [13] applied YOLOv4 and YOLOv5, respectively, without specific optimization for insulator characteristics. Yang et al. [14] improved the FPN in YOLOv3 by introducing bidirectional feature fusion to enhance small target detection, and adopted the EIoU loss function to accelerate convergence. Liu et al. [15] modified YOLOv4 by introducing a weighted balanced cross-entropy loss and a pyramid pooling structure to deepen the network and enhance detection performance.

2.3 Object Detection Based on CenterNet

Deep learning-based object detection methods are typically categorized into anchor-based and anchor-free approaches. CornerNet [16] promoted the development of anchor-free methods by providing a more flexible solution space without requiring anchor design. CenterNet [17], a representative anchor-free framework, detects objects by regressing their center points. In this work, the input image is first resized and processed through a CNN to extract initial features. These features are then upsampled via three deconvolutional layers. Subsequently, three 3×3 convolutional branches generate the heat map for category prediction, the offset map for position refinement, and the size map for bounding box regression. Final detection results are obtained by decoding these maps. The CenterNet does not set the anchor box in advance, it replaces the target with a center point, and returns the properties of the target box at the center point. A heatmap contains categorical information about the target. Each target type will produce a heat map, in each heat map there will be coordinate information.

3 Framework of Insulator and Its Defect Detection

3.1 Insulator Detection Model

The structure of the proposed insulator detection model is shown in Fig. 1. Firstly, the insulator image is sent to the Res2Net-50 network for preliminary feature extraction. Then, the extracted feature map is pooled and fused by the Pyramid Pooling Module (PPM), and the obtained feature map is upsampled to obtain a high-resolution feature map. Finally, it is fed into the detection head to complete the prediction.

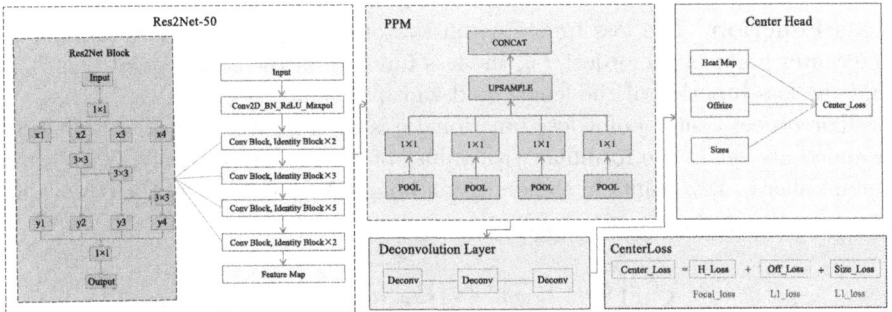

Fig. 1. The network structure of the proposed insulator detection model.

Feature Extraction Network. Insulators are usually located in the wild such as lakes, woods, urban streets etc., resulting in a complex background environment. For the feature extraction network, if the network is too shallow, and it will be difficult to effectively extract the feature information of the insulator from the complex background. If the network is too deep, too many parameters will be added, which will affect the detection speed. To better balance accuracy and efficiency, the original feature extraction network ResNet18 is deepened into a ResNet50, and the Res2Net module is added to form the Res2Net-50 architecture. As depicted in Fig. 1, the Res2Net module splits the feature map into four groups after a 1×1 convolution. The first group skips the 3×3 convolution, while the remaining three groups undergo sequential 3×3 convolutions with cross-group connections. The multi-scale features are concatenated and processed through a final 1×1 convolution, improving feature granularity and expanding the receptive field at each layer.

Pyramid Pooling Module. Strong contextual dependencies exist due to frequent co-occurrence with transmission lines and power poles. To model multi-scale context, the PPM is employed. PPM aggregates features across 1×1, 2×2, 3×3, and 6×6 pyramid scales. It first applies global pooling on the full feature map, followed by adaptive pooling on divided sub-regions. Each pooled feature is compressed via 1×1 convolution to $1/N$ of the original channel dimension, then upsampled to input size using bilinear interpolation. The compressed and upsampled features are concatenated with the original feature map, forming an enhanced global representation. This facilitates effective contextual aggregation, thus minimizing missed and false detections.

Loss Function. The loss function consists of three parts: the loss function of the center point of the object L_h, the loss function of the center point bias L_{off} and the loss function of the length and width of the object L_{size}.

The object center point loss function L_h is an improved Focal loss function. α and β are set in the formula, with values of 2 and 4 respectively; N indicates the number of key points in the detection image; Y_{xyc} represents the true value; $\hat{Y}_{xyc}$ represents the predicted value.

$$L_h = -\frac{1}{N} \sum_{x,y,c} \begin{cases} (1 - \hat{Y}_{xyc})^\alpha \log(\hat{Y}_{xyc}), & Y_{xyc} = 1 \\ (1 - Y_{xyc})^\beta (\hat{Y}_{xyc})^\alpha \times \log(1 - \hat{Y}_{xyc}), & \text{otherwise} \end{cases} \quad (1)$$

Center point bias loss function L_{off} using the $L1$ loss function. Where p indicates the coordinate position of the center point; $\hat{O}_{\tilde{p}}$ indicates the size of the preside bias value of the detection; Approximate integer coordinates $\tilde{P}$ representing the center point of the prediction.

$$L_{\text{off}} = \frac{1}{N} \sum_{p \in P} \left| \hat{O}_{\tilde{p}} - \left(\frac{p}{R} - \tilde{P} \right) \right| \quad (2)$$

L_{size} also uses the $L1$ loss function. Where s_k represents the true target frame size of the object; $\hat{S}_{pk}$ represents the predicted target box size after network regression.

$$L_{\text{size}} = \frac{1}{N} \sum_{k=1}^{N} \left| \hat{S}_{pk} - s_k \right| \quad (3)$$

3.2 Insulator Defect Detection Model

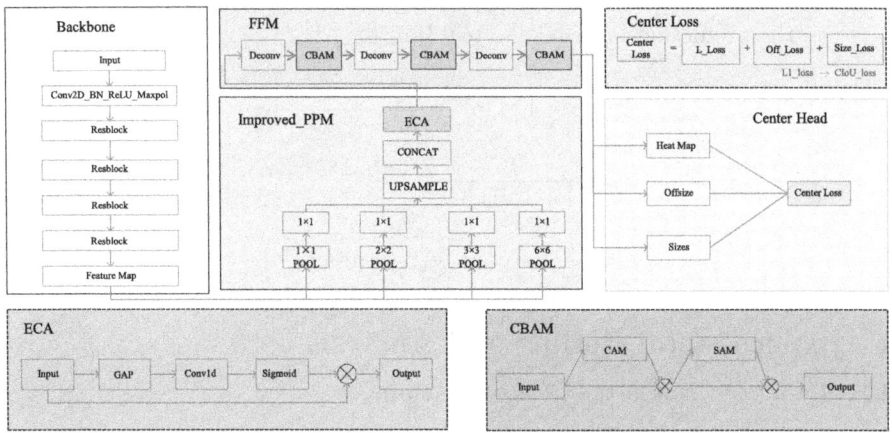

Fig. 2. Insulator defect detection framework.

The improved CenterNet detection model in the previous section achieves a good balance between accuracy and speed, but the detection effect is not very good for small targets such as insulator defects. In order to improve the detection accuracy of insulator defects, the framework is further improved, the structure of which is shown in Fig. 2.

Improved Feature Fusion Strategy. To enhance the semantic expressiveness of shallow features in insulator defect detection, the ECA module from ECA-Net is integrated into the feature fusion process. This module facilitates more effective fusion of deep and shallow features by emphasizing relevant channels and suppressing irrelevant ones. The original Concat-based fusion method ignores channel interdependencies and relative importance. To overcome this limitation, an improved fusion strategy is proposed. It combines multi-scale contextual features using PPM and refines the f used features with ECA, enabling the network to automatically learn and adaptively adjust the correlation and significance of feature channels.

Feature Enhancement Module. To mitigate the introduction of irrelevant information during direct upsampling, which adversely impacts small insulator defect detection, the Convolutional Block Attention Module (CBAM) is integrated after each deconvolutional layer to construct the Feature Enhancement Module (FEM). CBAM employs a dual-attention mechanism comprising the Channel Attention Module (CAM) and the Spatial Attention Module (SAM), which refine feature maps by recalibrating channel importance and improving spatial localization. The FEM module is therefore designed to refine feature maps during upsampling.

Loss Function. The CIoU Loss is used to optimize the length and width and center bias of the prediction box in this paper. Where α is the weighted parameter used to balance the proportion. v is used to measure the consistency of the ratio between the prediction box and the real box.

$$L_{\text{CIoU}} = 1 - \text{IoU} + \frac{\rho^2\left(b, b^{\text{gt}}\right)}{c^2} + \alpha v \tag{4}$$

$$\alpha = \frac{v}{(1 - \text{IoU}) + v}$$
$$v = \frac{4}{\pi^2}\left(\arctan\frac{w^{\text{gt}}}{h^{\text{gt}}} - \arctan\frac{w}{h}\right)^2 \tag{5}$$

4 Experimental Results and Analysis

4.1 Insulator Dataset and Expatiation

To evaluate the effectiveness of the proposed method, experiments are conducted on an expanded insulator defect dataset built upon the Chinese Power Line Insulator Dataset (CPLID) [11], which originally contains 848 aerial images, including 600 normal and 248 defective samples. To mitigate overfitting caused by the limited sample size, data augmentation techniques including geometric and color transformations are applied to increase data diversity. The expanded dataset ultimately comprises 4200 insulator images, of which 2000 contain defects.

4.2 Experimental Configuration and Evaluation Metrics

The configuration used in this paper in terms of the hardware and software platform is shown in Table 1. The experimental parameters used to train the proposed network are shown in Table 2. In order to comprehensively and objectively evaluate the detection performance, three metrics, that are, Average Precision (AP), Recall (R), and Frames Per Second (FPS) were used as the evaluation indicators of this model.

Table 1. Configuration of the experimental environment.

Platform	Configuration
Operating system	64 bit version of Windows 10
Central Processing Unit (CPU)	Intel(R) Core(TM) i9 - 10900k CPU @ 3.70GHz
Graphic Processing Unit (GPU)	NVIDIA GeForce RTX 2070 8G
Deep learning framework	PyTorch1.7
Compilers	PyCharm
Scripting language	Python 3.7
Solid State Disk (SSD)	500GB

Table 2. Experimental parameters.

Parameters	Configuration
Input Size	$512 \times 512 \times 3$
Batch size of freeze training	8
Batch size of thaw training	4
freeze training epochs	50
thaw training epochs	250
Optimizer	Adam
Learning rate of freeze training	0.001
Learning rate of thaw training	0.0001

4.3 Insulator Detection Results

The Influence of Feature Extraction Network. Based on the original CenterNet framework, ResNet18, ResNet50, and Res2Net-50 were evaluated as feature extractors in the experiments. As shown in Table 3, replacing ResNet18 with ResNet50 improved AP and R by 7.47% and 8.26%, respectively, with only a 2.46 FPS decrease. Further incorporating the Res2Net module into ResNet50 increased AP and R by 2.08% and 2.95%, respectively, while reducing FPS by just 0.05.

Table 3. The influence results of feature extraction network and PPM.

Network Model	AP(%)	R(%)	FPS(f/s)
Resnet18-CenterNet	84.30	73.12	56.02
Resnet50-CenterNet	91.77	81.38	53.56
Res2net-50-CenterNet	93.85	84.33	53.51
Res2net-50-CenterNet+PPM	96.97	89.86	53.20

The Influence of Pyramid Pooling Module. By employing Res2Net-50 as the feature extraction backbone, the model achieves an accuracy of 93.85%, yet the recall remains at 84.33%, indicating a significant number of missed detections of insulators. To address this issue and further enhance detection performance, multi-scale and subregion features are fused. As presented in Table 3, the proposed method improves AP and recall by 3.12% and 5.53%, respectively, compared to ResNet50-CenterNet, while incurring only a 0.31 f/s decrease in FPS. The incorporation of the Pyramid Pooling Module (PPM) improves detection accuracy without compromising inference speed, with recall increased to 89.86%, significantly reducing the number of missed detections. AP and recall are further improved by 12.67% and 16.74%, respectively, compared to the original CenterNet-based architecture. Experimental results demonstrate that InsulatorNet significantly reduces missed detections while achieving high detection accuracy and maintaining real-time performance.

Fig. 3. Typical insulator images used as the input.

Visualization Results and Analysis. In order to verify the detection performance in practical applications, the visualization results of the original and improved network are compared. The typical input images are shown in Fig. 3, and the compared results are shown in Fig. 4.

4.4 Insulator Defect Detection Results

The Influence of Feature Enhancement. The comparative experimental results of the feature enhancement are shown in Table 4. Experiments show that

Fig. 4. Compared detection results of the original and proposed network. (a) Original network results (b) Improved network results.

after adding the high-efficiency channel attention module ECAM, the AP values of insulators and defect parts are increased by 0.45% and 1.91%, and the mAP values are increased by 1.18%, respectively. After adding FEM, the AP values of insulators and defect parts further increased by 0.39% and 1.61%, respectively, and the mAP values increased by 1.00%. Experiments show that after adding the CIoU loss function, the AP values of insulators and defect parts further increased by 0.02% and 0.01%, respectively, and the mAP values increased by 1.00%. These improvement methods have gradually improved the performance of model.

Table 4. The influence results of improved feature extraction network

Network Model	Insulator AP(%)	Defect AP(%)	mAP(%)	FPS(f/s)
InsulatorNet	96.97	88.74	92.87	53.20
InsulatorNet +ECAM	97.44	90.65	94.05	52.34
InsulatorNet+ECAM+FEM	97.83	92.26	95.05	51.35
InsulatorNet+ ECAM+FEM+ CIoU	97.85	92.27	95.06	51.32

Comparison Results with Different Network Models. In order to further verify the detection performance, the same data set is used in the same experimental environment and compared with six network models, which are Faster-RCNN, SSD, YOLOV3, YOLOV4, YOLOV4-tiny, and YOLOX. The comparative experimental results are shown in Table 5.

Table 5. Comparison results with different network models

Network Model	AP(%)	Defect AP(%)	mAP(%)	FPS(f/s)
Faster-RCNN	92.12	83.33	87.73	8.33
SSD	83.56	74.25	78.91	35.53
YOLOV3	87.75	79.36	83.60	36.74
YOLOV4	90.46	82.54	86.50	33.58
YOLOV4-tiny	78.34	69.12	73.73	71.00
YOLOX	91.10	85.23	88.17	55.33
The Proposed Model	97.85	92.27	95.06	51.32

Compared with YOLOv4-tiny, the proposed model improves mAP by 21.33%, while reducing FPS by 17.81f/s. Compared with YOLOX, the proposed model achieves a 6.89% improvement in AP with only a 4.01f/s decrease in detection speed. Experimental results demonstrate that the proposed model achieves a better trade-off between detection accuracy and speed, making it more suitable for insulator defect detection.

Visualization Results and Analysis. To evaluate the proposed framework under real-world conditions, the model is tested on aerial insulator images with complex backgrounds. These images contain insulators of varying scales due to long shooting distances and camera shake, posing significant challenges for detecting both insulators and their defective parts. Visualization results are presented in Fig. 5.

Fig. 5. Visualization results in complex backgrounds.

The proposed model is evaluated under extreme environmental conditions, which can lead to missed or false detections due to poor visibility and image quality. Despite these challenges, the model effectively detects insulators and their defect parts, as shown in Fig. 6. This demonstrates the method's strong robustness and suitability for real-world insulator defect detection.

Fig. 6. Visualization results of insulator defect detection.

5 Conclusion

This paper proposes an insulator and defect detection framework, InsulatorNet, based on aerial images captured by UAVs. The network improves the CenterNet architecture by integrating Res2Net-50 as the backbone and constructing a feature pyramid pooling module, with transfer learning applied during training. These enhancements lead to improved detection accuracy and faster inference speed. To further enhance defect localization, a feature fusion module is designed according to the characteristics of insulator defects, incorporating a convolutional attention mechanism after the deconvolution layers and employing CIoU Loss for bounding box regression. Comparative experiments demonstrate that the proposed method achieves superior performance in detecting insulators and their defects, especially in complex and inaccessible scenes.

This paper studies insulator defect detection and achieves promising results. However, several limitations require further improvement, mainly as follows: The dataset used in this study is limited in scale and diversity. This may affect generalization under varying climatic conditions, which requires further evaluation. The current framework has not been extended to other transmission equipment or defect types. Further validation is needed to confirm its effectiveness for diverse object categories. Furthermore, to meet the demands of embedded deployment, future work should prioritize network compression and optimization for efficient integration into resource-constrained devices.

References

1. Zou, K., Jiang, Z.: Power line extraction framework based on edge structure and scene constraints. Remote Sens. **14**(18), 4575 (2022)
2. Park, K.-C., Motai, Y., Yoon, J.R.: Acoustic fault detection technique for high-power insulators. IEEE Trans. Ind. Electron. **64**(12), 9699–9708 (2017)
3. Zhai, Y., Wang, D., Zhang, M., Wang, J., Guo, F.: Fault detection of insulator based on saliency and adaptive morphology. Multimedia Tools Appl. **76**, 12051–12064 (2017)
4. Zhao, Z., Zhen, Z., Zhang, L., Qi, Y., Kong, Y., Zhang, K.: Insulator detection method in inspection image based on improved faster R-CNN. Energies **12**(7), 1204 (2019)
5. Tan, J.: Automatic insulator detection for power line using aerial images powered by convolutional neural networks. In: Journal of Physics: Conference Series, vol. 1748, p. 042012. IOP Publishing (2021)
6. Chen, W., Li, Y., Zhao, Z.: Insulatorgan: a transmission line insulator detection model using multi-granularity conditional generative adversarial nets for UAV inspection. Remote Sens. **13**(19), 3971 (2021)
7. Haoze, Z., Jiaming, H., Guoxing, Z., Zhong, Y.: Insulator string detection method based on the InST-Net network. Math. Probl. Eng. **2022**(1), 4037131 (2022)
8. Cheng, H., Zhai, Y., Chen, R., Wang, D., Dong, Z., Wang, Y.: Self-shattering defect detection of glass insulators based on spatial features. Energies **12**(3), 543 (2019)
9. Wenhao, C., Lina, Y., Fengzhe, L.: Insulator defect detection and location in UAV grid inspection. J. Comput. Appl. **39**(S1), 210–214 (2019)

10. Huang, X., Shang, E., Xue, J., Ding, H., Li, P.: A multi-feature fusion-based deep learning for insulator image identification and fault detection. In: 2020 IEEE 4th Information Technology, Networking, Electronic and Automation Control Conference (ITNEC), vol. 1, pp. 1957–1960. IEEE (2020)
11. Tao, X., Zhang, D., Wang, Z., Liu, X., Zhang, H., De, X.: Detection of power line insulator defects using aerial images analyzed with convolutional neural networks. IEEE Trans. Syst. Man Cybern. Syst. **50**(4), 1486–1498 (2018)
12. Gao, S., Qiu, G., Yang, J., Ma, Z., Pei, S., Yang, R.: Self-explosion defect detection method of glass insulator based on yolov4. In: 2021 IEEE Sustainable Power and Energy Conference (iSPEC), pp. 3686–3689. IEEE (2021)
13. Li, Q., Zhao, F., Xu, Z., Wang, J., Liu, K., Qin, L.: Insulator and damage detection and location based on yolov5. In: 2022 International Conference on Power Energy Systems and Applications (ICoPESA), pp. 17–24. IEEE (2022)
14. Yang, Z., Zheng, X., Wang, Y.: Bidirection-fusion-yolov3: an improved method for insulator defect detection using UAV image. IEEE Trans. Instrum. Meas. **71**, 1–8 (2022)
15. Liu, X., Tian, H., Yang, Y., Wang, Y., Zhao, X.: Research on image detection method of insulator defects in complex background. J. Electron. Meas. Instrum. **36**(2), 57–67 (2023)
16. Law, H., Deng, J.: Cornernet: detecting objects as paired keypoints. In: Proceedings of the European Conference on Computer Vision (ECCV), pp. 734–750 (2018)
17. Zhou, X., Wang, D., Krähenbühl, P.: Objects as points. arXiv preprint arXiv:1904.07850 (2019)

Adaptive 3D Scene Analysis Through Multi-modal Feature Integration and Geometric Pattern Recognition

Shijun Zhou[1,2], Xing Xie[1,2], and Jiandong Tian[1]

[1] State Key Laboratory of Robotics, Shenyang Institute of Automation, Chinese Academy of Sciences, Shenyang 110016, China
{zhoushijun,xiexing,tianjd}@sia.cn
[2] University of Chinese Academy of Sciences, Beijing 100049, China

Abstract. The deployment of autonomous robots in human-centric environments requires sophisticated scene understanding and adaptive visual processing capabilities. Current robotic perception systems rely predominantly on photorealistic 3D reconstruction, limiting their ability to adapt visual representations for task-specific reasoning or human-robot interaction contexts. While recent advances in 3D Gaussian Splatting have enabled real-time scene rendering for robotic applications, existing approaches for adaptive visual stylization remain computationally prohibitive for mobile robotic platforms.

We introduce a principled approach to 3D style transfer that reconceptualizes feature decoding through geometric locality rather than volumetric processing. Our Enhanced Multi-Layer Perceptron architecture leverages the intrinsic manifold structure of 3D point distributions, performing adaptive feature aggregation via K-nearest neighbor graphs coupled with learnable transformations. By reconceptualizing feature decoding through K-nearest neighbor graphs rather than volumetric convolutions, our approach achieves the computational efficiency required for autonomous operation while preserving spatial coherence essential for robotic navigation and manipulation tasks.

Experimental validation on diverse robotic scenarios demonstrates substantial efficiency improvements. Our methodology demonstrates robust generalization across diverse geometric complexities and artistic domains.

Keywords: 3D Gaussian Splatting · Neural stylization · Style Transfer

1 Introduction

The evolution of neural 3D representations has witnessed a paradigmatic shift from implicit volumetric fields to explicit geometric primitives. Neural Radiance Fields (NeRF) [10] established the foundation for neural 3D modeling through continuous implicit representations, while 3D Gaussian Splatting [1,6] has demonstrated the power of explicit primitive-based approaches for real-time applications.

This transition creates a fundamental architectural challenge: how do we design neural processing pipelines optimized for explicit 3D primitives? Traditional approaches have largely adapted techniques developed for volumetric representations, often requiring intensive volumetric convolutions that impose significant memory overhead and limit scalability. The integration of multi-modal information—geometric structures, visual features, and semantic annotations—becomes particularly computationally intensive when processing complex scenes.

Multi-modal 3D scene processing exemplifies this challenge. While feature integration techniques have matured in 2D domains, extending these concepts to explicit 3D representations requires rethinking fundamental aspects of spatial feature processing and geometric locality. The explicit nature of Gaussian primitives offers opportunities for direct geometric reasoning, yet current methodologies have not fully capitalized on these advantages.

We identify three key opportunities: (1) Geometric-aware feature aggregation that leverages the manifold structure of 3D point distributions; (2) Adaptive processing architectures that scale efficiently with scene complexity; and (3) Principled integration of deep learning techniques tailored for point-based representations.

Our approach reconceptualizes multi-modal 3D processing as a geometric learning problem, where local neighborhood structures inform adaptive feature transformations, ensuring both computational efficiency and representational fidelity.

Our contributions span multiple dimensions:

- **Theoretical Framework**: We establish a principled approach to feature processing in explicit 3D representations, grounding our method in geometric locality principles and manifold learning theory.
- **Architectural Innovation**: We introduce an Enhanced Multi-Layer Perceptron that incorporates K-nearest neighbor graph structures, residual learning pathways, and adaptive normalization schemes specifically designed for point cloud processing.
- **Efficient Spatial Processing**: Our method introduces novel chunking strategies and memory optimization techniques that enable scalable processing of large-scale 3D scenes while maintaining real-time performance guarantees.
- **Adaptive Feature Learning**: We develop a multi-scale feature aggregation mechanism that adapts to local geometric complexity, ensuring consistent style transfer quality across diverse scene regions.

2 Method

2.1 3D Scene Representation

Gaussian Splatting Primitives. We represent 3D scenes as collections of anisotropic 3D Gaussians, following the formulation introduced by Kerbl et al. [6]. Each Gaussian primitive g_i is parameterized by a set of learnable attributes:

$$g_i = (\boldsymbol{\mu}_i, \boldsymbol{s}_i, \boldsymbol{q}_i, \alpha_i, \boldsymbol{c}_i) \tag{1}$$

where $\boldsymbol{\mu}_i \in \mathbb{R}^3$ represents the 3D position, $\boldsymbol{s}_i \in \mathbb{R}^3$ denotes the scaling factors, $\boldsymbol{q}_i \in \mathbb{H}$ is a unit quaternion encoding rotation, $\alpha_i \in [0,1]$ controls opacity, and $\boldsymbol{c}_i$ encodes appearance information.

The 3D covariance matrix $\boldsymbol{\Sigma}_i$ of each Gaussian is constructed from the scaling and rotation parameters:

$$\boldsymbol{\Sigma}_i = \boldsymbol{R}_i \boldsymbol{S}_i \boldsymbol{S}_i^T \boldsymbol{R}_i^T \tag{2}$$

where $\boldsymbol{R}_i$ is the rotation matrix derived from $\boldsymbol{q}_i$ and $\boldsymbol{S}_i = \text{diag}(\boldsymbol{s}_i)$.

Differentiable Rendering. The scene is rendered through point-based α-blending, where the color $\boldsymbol{C}$ of each pixel is computed as:

$$\boldsymbol{C} = \sum_{i \in \mathcal{N}} \boldsymbol{c}_i \alpha_i \prod_{j=1}^{i-1} (1 - \alpha_j) \tag{3}$$

where $\mathcal{N}$ denotes the set of Gaussians affecting the pixel, sorted by depth. The opacity α_i is computed by evaluating the 2D Gaussian projection:

$$\alpha_i = o_i \exp\left(-\frac{1}{2}(\boldsymbol{x} - \boldsymbol{\mu}_i')^T (\boldsymbol{\Sigma}_i')^{-1} (\boldsymbol{x} - \boldsymbol{\mu}_i')\right) \tag{4}$$

where $\boldsymbol{\mu}_i'$ and $\boldsymbol{\Sigma}_i'$ are the projected mean and covariance in screen space, and o_i is the learned opacity parameter.

2.2 VGG Feature Embedding

Multi-view Feature Optimization. For style transfer, we replace the conventional RGB appearance representation $\boldsymbol{c}_i$ with high-dimensional perceptual features $\boldsymbol{f}_i \in \mathbb{R}^{256}$ extracted from a pre-trained VGG-19 network. Specifically, we utilize features from the ReLU3_1 layer, which provide a good balance between spatial resolution and semantic abstraction for style transfer tasks [3].

The feature embedding process involves optimizing per-point features $\{\boldsymbol{f}_i\}_{i=1}^N$ to match multi-view VGG feature maps through the following objective:

$$\mathcal{L}_{embed} = \sum_{v=1}^{V} \|\mathcal{R}_v(\{\boldsymbol{f}_i\}) - \Phi_{VGG}^{(3,1)}(I_v)\|_1 \tag{5}$$

where $\mathcal{R}_v$ denotes the differentiable rendering operation for camera viewpoint v, $\Phi_{VGG}^{(3,1)}$ represents VGG feature extraction from the ReLU3_1 layer, I_v is the ground truth image for view v, and V is the total number of training views.

Efficient High-Dimensional Rendering. Direct rendering of 256-dimensional features presents significant computational challenges due to memory constraints. To address this limitation, we employ a two-stage rendering strategy that factorizes the high-dimensional feature space.

First, we render compact 32-dimensional intermediate features $\boldsymbol{F}' \in \mathbb{R}^{H \times W \times 32}$:

$$\boldsymbol{F}' = \mathcal{R}(\{\boldsymbol{f}'_i\}_{i=1}^N) \tag{6}$$

where $\boldsymbol{f}'_i \in \mathbb{R}^{32}$ are learned low-dimensional features associated with each Gaussian.

Subsequently, we map these compact features to the full 256-dimensional space through a learned affine transformation:

$$\boldsymbol{F} = \boldsymbol{A}\boldsymbol{F}' + \sum_{i \in \mathcal{N}(x,y)} \boldsymbol{b}_i w_i(x,y) \tag{7}$$

where $\boldsymbol{A} \in \mathbb{R}^{256 \times 32}$ is a learnable linear transformation, $\boldsymbol{b}_i \in \mathbb{R}^{256}$ are per-Gaussian bias terms, $w_i(x,y)$ denotes the blending weight of Gaussian i at pixel (x,y), and $\mathcal{N}(x,y)$ represents the set of Gaussians contributing to that pixel.

The optimization objective for this factorized representation becomes:

$$\mathcal{L}_{factor} = \sum_{v=1}^V \|\boldsymbol{A}\mathcal{R}_v(\{\boldsymbol{f}'_i\}) + \sum_i \boldsymbol{b}_i w_{i,v} - \Phi_{VGG}^{(3,1)}(I_v)\|_1 \tag{8}$$

This factorization reduces memory consumption by approximately 8× while maintaining reconstruction fidelity.

2.3 Adaptive Style Transfer

Once the VGG features are embedded into the 3D representation, we perform style transfer using Adaptive Instance Normalization (AdaIN) [4]. For each Gaussian with embedded feature $\boldsymbol{f}_i$, the style transfer operation is defined as:

$$\boldsymbol{f}_i^{(s)} = \sigma(\boldsymbol{F}_s) \odot \frac{\boldsymbol{f}_i - \mu(\{\boldsymbol{f}_j\}_{j=1}^N)}{\sigma(\{\boldsymbol{f}_j\}_{j=1}^N) + \epsilon} + \mu(\boldsymbol{F}_s) \tag{9}$$

where $\boldsymbol{F}_s$ denotes the VGG ReLU3_1 features of the reference style image, $\mu(\cdot)$ and $\sigma(\cdot)$ represent channel-wise mean and standard deviation operations respectively, $\odot$ denotes element-wise multiplication, and $\epsilon = 10^{-5}$ is a small constant for numerical stability.

The style statistics $\mu(\boldsymbol{F}_s)$ and $\sigma(\boldsymbol{F}_s)$ are computed by spatial averaging over the style image features:

$$\mu(\boldsymbol{F}_s)_c = \frac{1}{HW}\sum_{h=1}^{H}\sum_{w=1}^{W}\boldsymbol{F}_s(h,w,c) \tag{10}$$

$$\sigma(\boldsymbol{F}_s)_c = \sqrt{\frac{1}{HW}\sum_{h=1}^{H}\sum_{w=1}^{W}(\boldsymbol{F}_s(h,w,c)-\mu(\boldsymbol{F}_s)_c)^2} \tag{11}$$

where c indexes the feature channel, and (H,W) are the spatial dimensions of the style feature map.

2.4 Enhanced Multi-layer Perceptron Decoder

Motivation and Design Philosophy. Existing approaches for decoding stylized features predominantly rely on 3D Convolutional Neural Networks (3D CNNs), which exhibit several fundamental limitations: (1) cubic computational complexity $O(N^3)$ with respect to spatial resolution, (2) substantial memory requirements for storing 3D convolution kernels, and (3) limited scalability to large point clouds due to memory constraints.

To address these challenges, we propose an Enhanced Multi-Layer Perceptron (Enhanced MLP) decoder that leverages the insight that effective local feature aggregation can be achieved through K-nearest neighbor operations followed by learned transformations. This design philosophy eliminates the need for expensive 3D convolutions while preserving the spatial coherence essential for high-quality style transfer.

K-Nearest Neighbor Feature Aggregation. The foundation of our Enhanced MLP decoder lies in local feature aggregation based on spatial proximity in 3D space. For each Gaussian g_i, we identify its K-nearest neighbors $\mathcal{N}_K(i) = \{n_1, n_2, \ldots, n_K\}$ based on Euclidean distance between their 3D positions:

$$\mathcal{N}_K(i) = \arg\min_{\{j_1,j_2,\ldots,j_K\}} \sum_{k=1}^{K}\|\boldsymbol{\mu}_i - \boldsymbol{\mu}_{j_k}\|_2 \tag{12}$$

where $\boldsymbol{\mu}_i$ and $\boldsymbol{\mu}_{j_k}$ represent the 3D positions of Gaussians i and j_k respectively. We set $K=6$ based on ablation studies that demonstrate this provides an optimal trade-off between local context preservation and computational efficiency.

The K-nearest neighbor relationships are precomputed once after scene reconstruction and remain fixed during style transfer training, ensuring computational efficiency during the decoding process.

Enhanced MLP Layer Architecture. Each Enhanced MLP layer implements a sophisticated local processing mechanism that combines neighborhood feature aggregation with modern deep learning techniques. For the ℓ-th layer processing features $\{\boldsymbol{f}_i^{(\ell-1)}\}_{i=1}^N$, the forward pass proceeds as follows:

Step 1: Neighborhood Feature Collection

$$\boldsymbol{h}_i^{(\ell)} = \text{Concat}([\boldsymbol{f}_{n_1}^{(\ell-1)}, \boldsymbol{f}_{n_2}^{(\ell-1)}, \ldots, \boldsymbol{f}_{n_K}^{(\ell-1)}]) \in \mathbb{R}^{K \times D^{(\ell-1)}} \quad (13)$$

where $\{n_k\}_{k=1}^K = \mathcal{N}_K(i)$ and $D^{(\ell-1)}$ is the feature dimension at layer $\ell - 1$.

Step 2: Primary Feature Transformation

$$\boldsymbol{z}_i^{(\ell)} = \boldsymbol{W}_1^{(\ell)} \text{Flatten}(\boldsymbol{h}_i^{(\ell)}) + \boldsymbol{b}_1^{(\ell)} \quad (14)$$

where $\boldsymbol{W}_1^{(\ell)} \in \mathbb{R}^{D^{(\ell)} \times (K \cdot D^{(\ell-1)})}$ and $\boldsymbol{b}_1^{(\ell)} \in \mathbb{R}^{D^{(\ell)}}$ are learnable parameters.

Step 3: Normalization and Activation

$$\boldsymbol{a}_i^{(\ell)} = \text{SiLU}(\text{LayerNorm}(\boldsymbol{z}_i^{(\ell)})) \quad (15)$$

We employ SiLU (Swish) activation [2] due to its superior gradient properties compared to ReLU, particularly beneficial for deep MLP architectures.

Step 4: Output Projection

$$\boldsymbol{o}_i^{(\ell)} = \boldsymbol{W}_2^{(\ell)} \boldsymbol{a}_i^{(\ell)} + \boldsymbol{b}_2^{(\ell)} \quad (16)$$

where $\boldsymbol{W}_2^{(\ell)} \in \mathbb{R}^{D^{(\ell)} \times D^{(\ell)}}$ and $\boldsymbol{b}_2^{(\ell)} \in \mathbb{R}^{D^{(\ell)}}$.

Step 5: Residual Connection. When input and output dimensions are compatible ($D^{(\ell-1)} = D^{(\ell)}$), we incorporate residual connections to facilitate gradient flow and improve training stability:

$$\boldsymbol{f}_i^{(\ell)} = \boldsymbol{o}_i^{(\ell)} + \mathcal{P}^{(\ell)}(\boldsymbol{f}_i^{(\ell-1)}) \quad (17)$$

where $\mathcal{P}^{(\ell)}$ is an identity mapping when dimensions match, or a learned linear projection when dimension adjustment is required.

Multi-layer Configuration and Progressive Refinement. Our Enhanced MLP decoder employs a three-layer architecture with channel progression [256 → 64 → 3], designed to progressively refine stylized VGG features into final RGB values:

Layer 1 (Feature Compression): Maps 256-dimensional stylized VGG features to a 64-dimensional intermediate representation. This layer performs semantic compression while preserving style-relevant information.

Layer 2 (Feature Refinement): Processes the 64-dimensional features to further refine local coherence and prepare for color generation. This layer includes residual connections to preserve important feature relationships.

Layer 3 (RGB Generation): Produces the final 3-dimensional RGB output without activation functions, allowing for unrestricted color value generation.

The mathematical formulation for the complete three-layer processing pipeline is:

$$f_i^{(1)} = \text{EnhancedMLP}_1(f_i^{(s)}, \mathcal{N}_K(i)) \in \mathbb{R}^{64} \tag{18}$$

$$f_i^{(2)} = \text{EnhancedMLP}_2(f_i^{(1)}, \mathcal{N}_K(i)) + f_i^{(1)} \in \mathbb{R}^{64} \tag{19}$$

$$c_i^{(final)} = \text{EnhancedMLP}_3(f_i^{(2)}, \mathcal{N}_K(i)) \in \mathbb{R}^3 \tag{20}$$

where $f_i^{(s)}$ denotes the stylized 256-dimensional feature from Eq. 9.

Memory Optimization and Scalability. To handle large-scale point clouds efficiently, we implement several memory optimization strategies:

Chunked Processing: Large point clouds are processed in chunks of size $C = \min(30000, \lfloor \frac{\text{GPU Memory}}{8 \times D \times K} \rfloor)$ to prevent memory overflow while maintaining processing efficiency.

2.5 Training Strategy and Loss Functions

Two-Stage Training Protocol. Our training follows a carefully designed two-stage protocol to ensure stable convergence and high-quality results:

Stage 1 - Feature Embedding: We first optimize the VGG feature embedding using Eq. 5 for 30,000 iterations with learning rate $\eta_1 = 10^{-2}$. This stage establishes a robust perceptual representation of the 3D scene.

Stage 2 - Style Transfer: Subsequently, we freeze the embedded features and train the Enhanced MLP decoder along with the style transfer module for 30,000 iterations with learning rate $\eta_2 = 5 \times 10^{-4}$.

The training objective for the style transfer stage combines multiple loss terms to ensure both style transfer fidelity and content preservation:

$$\mathcal{L}_{total} = \lambda_{content}\mathcal{L}_{content} + \lambda_{style}\mathcal{L}_{style} + \lambda_{preserve}\mathcal{L}_{preserve} \tag{21}$$

Content Loss: Ensures preservation of scene structure through VGG feature matching:

$$\mathcal{L}_{content} = \|\Phi_{VGG}^{(4,1)}(\mathcal{R}(\{c_i^{final}\})) - \Phi_{VGG}^{(4,1)}(I_{gt})\|_2^2 \tag{22}$$

Style Loss: Enforces style transfer through Gram matrix alignment across multiple VGG layers:

$$\mathcal{L}_{style} = \sum_{\ell \in \{1,2,3,4\}} \frac{1}{4N_\ell^2} \|G^{(\ell)}(\mathcal{R}(\{c_i^{final}\})) - G^{(\ell)}(I_s)\|_F^2 \tag{23}$$

Fig. 1. Multi-view style transfer results on the Train scene. Each row shows a different artistic style (0, 50, 53) applied consistently across multiple viewpoints, with the original scene and style reference shown on the right.

where $G^{(\ell)}$ computes the Gram matrix for VGG layer ℓ, N_ℓ is the number of feature channels in layer ℓ, and $\|\cdot\|_F$ denotes the Frobenius norm.

Content Preservation Loss: Provides additional regularization to maintain scene coherence:

$$\mathcal{L}_{preserve} = \|\mathcal{R}(\{c_i^{final}\}) - I_{gt}\|_1 \tag{24}$$

We empirically set the loss weights as $\lambda_{content} = 1.0$, $\lambda_{style} = 10.0$, and $\lambda_{preserve} = 0.1$ based on extensive ablation studies.

3 Experiments

3.1 Implementation Details

All experiments are conducted using PyTorch 1.12.1 with CUDA 11.6 support. Training is performed on NVIDIA RTX 3090 GPUs with 24GB memory. We use the Adam optimizer [7] with $\beta_1 = 0.9$, $\beta_2 = 0.999$, and weight decay of 10^{-4}.

For style image preprocessing, we resize all reference images to 256×256 pixels and apply standard normalization. The VGG-19 network is pre-trained on ImageNet and frozen throughout training. K-nearest neighbor computation is performed using FAISS [5] for efficiency.

We evaluate our approach on three diverse scenes from Tanks and Temples dataset [8]: **Train**, **Truck**, and **M60**, each representing different scene complexities and geometric structures. For each dataset, we test multiple style references to demonstrate the robustness and generalizability of our method across various artistic styles.

3.2 Qualitative Comparison

Figures 1, 2 and 3 demonstrate the versatility and effectiveness of our method across diverse scenes and artistic styles. We present style transfer results on various 3D scenes including indoor environments, outdoor landscapes, and object-centric scenarios. For each scene, we apply multiple reference styles ranging from

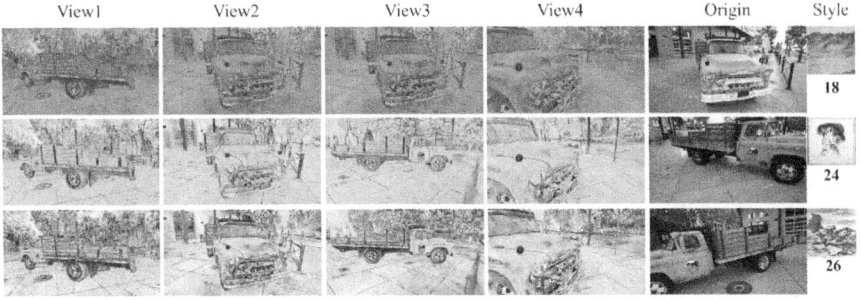

Fig. 2. Multi-view style transfer results on the Truck scene. Each row shows a different artistic style (18, 24, 26) applied consistently across multiple viewpoints, with the original scene and style reference shown on the right.

classical paintings to modern artistic interpretations. The results showcase our method's ability to faithfully transfer artistic styles while preserving the underlying 3D geometry and maintaining multi-view consistency. Each stylized scene maintains real-time rendering capabilities at 20+ fps, demonstrating the practical applicability of our approach.

Particularly noteworthy is the method's capacity to handle complex lighting conditions and intricate geometric details. The style transfer preserves important structural information such as depth relationships and surface normals while successfully incorporating the visual characteristics of the reference style images. The diverse range of scenes and styles presented validates the generalizability of our approach, showing consistent high-quality results across different content types and artistic references without requiring scene-specific parameter tuning.

3.3 Quantitative Comparison

We conduct comprehensive quantitative evaluations comparing our method with StyleGaussian [9] across multiple datasets and style references. Our evaluation focuses on the Gram Loss metric, which effectively measures the style similarity by comparing Gram matrices of VGG features between stylized and reference images.

Gram Loss Analysis Table 1 presents the Gram Loss [3] results for our method compared to StyleGaussian. The Gram Loss [3] measures the difference between Gram matrices of VGG features, where **lower values indicate better style transfer quality**.

Our method achieves lower Gram Loss values in 8 out of 9 test cases compared to StyleGaussian:

- **Train dataset:** Improvements range from 10.5% (style 50) to 20.7% (style 53), with the most significant improvement of 17.4% for style 0.

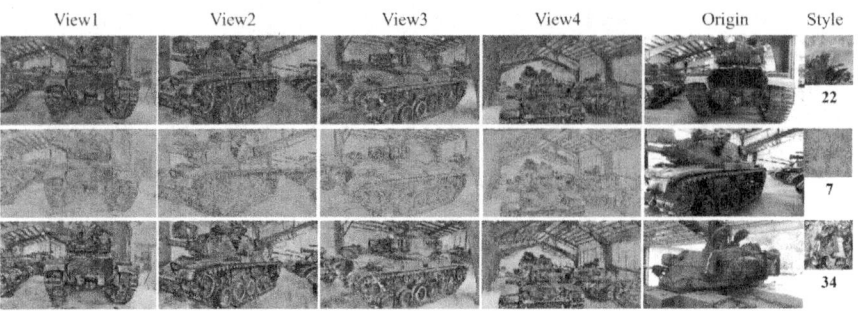

Fig. 3. Multi-view style transfer results on the M60 scene. Each row shows a different artistic style (22, 7, 34) applied consistently across multiple viewpoints, with the original scene and style reference shown on the right.

Table 1. Gram Loss comparison across different scenes and style references. Lower values indicate better style transfer quality.

Dataset	Style	StyleGaussian	Ours
Train	0	6.0338	**4.9874**
	50	0.6900	**0.6178**
	53	0.9752	**0.7736**
Truck	18	2.1167	**1.9634**
	24	0.6192	**0.5200**
	26	4.6596	**4.4687**
M60	22	0.6505	**0.3223**
	7	0.9739	1.2366
	34	4.9269	**3.7087**

- **Truck dataset:** All three styles show improvements, from 4.1% (style 26) to 16.0% (style 24).
- **M60 dataset:** Two out of three styles show substantial improvements, with style 22 achieving a remarkable 50.4% improvement. Only style 7 shows a performance decrease of 27.0%.

The consistent improvements across different scene types (Train, Truck, M60) and style references indicate that our method generalizes well to various geometric structures and content types. This robustness is particularly important for practical applications where diverse scene content is expected.

References

1. Chen, Y., Shao, G., Shum, K.C., et al.: Advances in 3D neural stylization: a survey. Int. J. Comput. Vision (2025). https://doi.org/10.1007/s11263-025-02403-9

2. Elfwing, S., Uchibe, E., Doya, K.: Sigmoid-weighted linear units for neural network function approximation in reinforcement learning. Neural Netw. **107**, 3–11 (2018). https://doi.org/10.1016/j.neunet.2017.12.012. https://www.sciencedirect.com/science/article/pii/S0893608017302976
3. Gatys, L.A., Ecker, A.S., Bethge, M.: Image style transfer using convolutional neural networks. In: Proceedings of the IEEE Conference on Computer Vision and Pattern Recognition (CVPR) (2016)
4. Huang, X., Belongie, S.: Arbitrary style transfer in real-time with adaptive instance normalization. In: Proceedings of the IEEE International Conference on Computer Vision (ICCV) (2017)
5. Johnson, J., Douze, M., Jégou, H.: Billion-scale similarity search with GPUs. IEEE Trans. Big Data **7**(3), 535–547 (2019)
6. Kerbl, B., Kopanas, G., Leimkühler, T., Drettakis, G.: 3D gaussian splatting for real-time radiance field rendering. ACM Trans. Graph. **42**(4), 139-1 (2023)
7. Kingma, D.P., Ba, J.: Adam: a method for stochastic optimization. arXiv preprint arXiv:1412.6980 (2014)
8. Knapitsch, A., Park, J., Zhou, Q.Y., Koltun, V.: Tanks and temples: benchmarking large-scale scene reconstruction. ACM Trans. Graph. **36**(4) (2017)
9. Liu, K., Zhan, F., Xu, M., Theobalt, C., Shao, L., Lu, S.: Stylegaussian: instant 3D style transfer with gaussian splatting. arXiv preprint arXiv:2403.07807 (2024)
10. Mildenhall, B., Srinivasan, P.P., Tancik, M., Barron, J.T., Ramamoorthi, R., Ng, R.: Nerf: representing scenes as neural radiance fields for view synthesis. Commun. ACM **65**(1), 99–106 (2021). https://doi.org/10.1145/3503250

Global to Local Mamba Low Light Image Restoration

Xinhao Wu[1,2], Huijie Fan[2], Sen Lin[1(✉)], Qiang Wang[2,3], and Peng Wu[2]

[1] School of Automation and Electrical Engineering, Shenyang Ligong University, Shenyang 110159, China
lin_sen6@126.com
[2] State Key Laboratory of Robotics, Shenyang Institute of Automation, Chinese Academy of Sciences, Shenyang 110016, China
[3] Key Laboratory of Manufacturing Industrial Integrated, Shenyang University, Shenyang 110044, China

Abstract. In recent years, Mamba has been playing an increasingly important role in the field of low-light image enhancement and has gradually surpassed traditional convolutional neural networks (CNNs) and Transformers. However, existing Mamba networks tend to focus exclusively on capturing global contextual semantic relations, overlooking the impact of local features on restoration under low-light conditions. Since CNNs and Transformers struggle to capture global degradation, while the state space model (SSM) within Mamba excels in long-sequence modeling, this paper introduces a novel global-to-local feature extraction approach upon integrating Mamba. We first propose the Global-to-Local Mamba Block to perform refined feature extraction in the low-frequency domain, and then complement high-frequency texture distortions via the high-frequency guided enhancement module using low-frequency features. Extensive experiments conducted on multiple datasets demonstrate that Global-to-Local Mamba achieves superior performance in low-light restoration and image enhancement.

Keywords: Mamba · low-light image enhancement · Global-to-Local Mamba Block

1 Introduction

The groundbreaking development of CNNs has propelled hierarchical feature representation-based deep learning methods to the forefront as the mainstream paradigm [1]. Through the local receptive field aggregation mechanisms enabled by multi-scale convolutional kernels, CNN architectures achieve substantial enhancements in objective metrics such as PSNR, while their intrinsic weight-sharing property effectively mitigates the risk of model overfitting. This architectural innovation not only optimizes spatial feature extraction but also establishes a robust foundation for addressing illumination-dependent degradation patterns through adaptive parameter learning. However, the inductive bias of fixed receptive fields constrains the global illumination modeling capability, while the parameter-sharing mechanism limits adaptability to diverse degradation patterns, particularly in scenarios requiring spatially variant restoration of non-uniform illumination artifacts and noise distributions. Recent advances in vision enhancement have witnessed the transformative potential of Transformer architectures, which overcome spatial constraints through self-attention mechanisms [2]. While their global attention computation establishes long-range pixel dependencies, the quadratically increasing computational demands for high-resolution images introduce a new trade-off between perceptual quality and model efficiency.

Consequently, Mamba has emerged as a promising alternative in this domain, primarily due to its selective scanning mechanism that models global information with linear complexity, drastically reducing computational overhead while maintaining a global receptive field [3]. However, Mamba's unidirectional modeling paradigm exhibits heightened sensitivity to complex noise patterns and insufficient capability in capturing localized structural features, particularly in scenarios requiring joint optimization of multi-scale texture preservation and illumination correction. This limitation underscores the necessity for architectural innovations that harmonize global contextual awareness with local discriminative power [4]. To address these limitations, researchers have proposed non-causal modeling improvements and hybrid architecture designs, alongside frequency-domain enhancement and dynamic gating mechanisms to compensate for localized biases in feature representation.

In Mamba, the Visual State Space Module (VSSM) offers linear complexity while effectively modeling long-range dependencies. Therefore, we incorporate VSSM as the global feature extraction module in our framework [4]. To address Mamba's limitations in local feature extraction, we propose a global-to-local Mamba framework that employs a CNN-based module for local feature extraction, reducing color distortion in local regions and enhancing restoration quality. A Multilayer Perceptron (MLP) is adopted as a feedforward network to capture multiscale features through sequential structures, facilitating precise recovery of textural and structural details. This framework introduces a novel approach for low-light image enhancement by integrating Mamba, wavelet transform, and the global-to-local feature extraction method within a U-Net architecture.

Our main contributions are summarized as follows: We propose a Global-to-Local Mamba-based low-light image restoration network that effectively captures complex global and local dependencies. We incorporate wavelet transform to prevent information loss during downsampling. The Global Mamba Block with VSSM for capturing long-range dependencies and the Local Feature Extraction module are integrated, adopting sequential architectures for hierarchical feature extraction. Additionally, we introduce MLP to provide multi-scale structural features. By leveraging abundant low-frequency feature information to restore high-frequency features, the network significantly enhances restoration quality. Extensive experiments conducted on multiple datasets demonstrate the model's outstanding performance.

2 Method

In this section, we present our work in three parts. The first part elaborates on the overall framework; the second part describes the processing of low-frequency blocks, specifically the LFM module; the third part focuses on the processing of the high-frequency components.

2.1 Framework Overview

The overall network decomposes images into high-frequency and low-frequency components via discrete wavelet transform(DWT), as shown in Fig. 1. We construct a Low-Frequency Mamba Block capable of extracting rich feature information, enabling the network to enhance and optimize both global and local information with linear complexity. Based on a low-frequency-guided high-frequency compensation strategy, we construct a high-frequency enhancement module. By leveraging low-frequency components with similar information, a frequency-domain attention constraint module is designed to reconstruct the spatial gradient distribution of high-frequency subbands, further establishing a cross-frequency feature coupling mechanism. This approach effectively addresses the high-frequency texture distortion issue inherent in traditional methods. Below, we outline the overall workflow of our method and provide further detailed explanations.

Fig. 1. Discrete wavelet transform decomposes the signal into low frequency subband (LL) and three high frequency subbands (LH, HL, HH) through low-pass filter and high pass filter, corresponding to the details of horizontal, vertical and diagonal directions respectively.

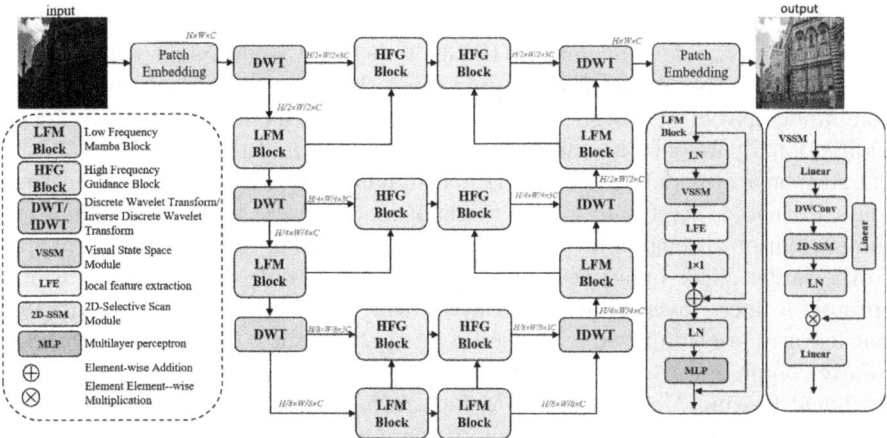

Fig. 2. The proposed global-to-local Mamba architecture establishes a hierarchical framework that incorporates wavelet transform-based upsampling and downsampling operations. Specifically, the low-frequency Mamba module (LFMBlock) conducts multi-scale feature extraction on frequency-decoupled components, while the high-frequency guided enhancement module (HFGBlock) performs detail refinement through gradient-aware attention mechanisms.

2.2 Low Frequency MambaBlock

The LFMBlock is designed to extract low-frequency features from low-light images, and by utilizing the LFMBlock, low-frequency information flow is extracted from the spatial domain of feature embeddings and modeled. As illustrated in Fig. 2 Given the low-frequency input features $\mathbf{F}_n \in \mathbb{R}^{H \times W \times C}$ we first apply Layer Normalization to stabilize feature distributions, followed by the Visual State Space Module (VSSM) to capture global contextual relationships and long-range dependencies. This hierarchical processing ensures robust representation learning while maintaining computational efficiency inherent to state-space architectures. Building upon the global semantic relationships established by the VSSM, we provide contextual guidance for subsequent local feature extraction via the Local Feature Module (LFM). To mitigate potential gradient cancellation between VSSM and LFM, a sequential architecture is adopted, forming a novel global before local feature extraction normal form. This design ensures temporal consistency in gradient update directions across modules, thereby eliminating optimization conflicts. Finally, a Multilayer perceptron (MLP) is employed to hierarchically learn and refine structural representations.

Vision State Space Module: Inspired by the advantage of linear computational complexity demonstrated by the Mamba architecture in long-range dependency modeling, this study integrates the Visual State Space Model (VSSM) into the task framework of low-light image enhancement. The VSSM architecture is illustrated in Fig. 2. Input features first undergo adjustment of channel dimensions via a linear projection layer, mapping raw data to a high-dimensional representation space to enhance feature representation capability. Subsequently, a depthwise separable convolution (DW3×3) performs lightweight extraction of local features, completing feature processing through a decomposition strategy combining spatial filtering and cross-channel fusion. Following this, the model bidirectionally unfolds the image along the main diagonal and anti-diagonal using 2D state space modeling (2D-SSM) and dynamically fuses multi-path features via a learnable directional gating mechanism. After the features are stabilized in distribution through a layer normalization operation, they are finally mapped to the target space by a linear output layer. The parallel branch, implemented through a linear layer, is activated by a SiLU activation function, and its output features are sum-fused with the target space features of the main branch to jointly complete the enhancement task.

Local Feature Module: the LFM focuses on extracting fine-grained texture details and short-range features, thereby refining low-frequency components with higher precision. The enhanced low-frequency representations subsequently guide the HFG Block to amplify high-frequency features through targeted spectral adjustments, ensuring synergistic interaction between global and local information flows. As illustrated in Fig. 3(a), the input features are first processed through Global Average Pooling (GAP), which aggregates spatial information to generate a channel-wise global descriptor capturing the overall response intensity of each channel. Subsequently, two 1×1 convolutional operations are employed to establish a cross-channel interaction pathway: the first convolution reduces the channel dimensionality while incorporating a ReLU activation function to model inter-channel dependency patterns; the second convolution restores the original dimensionality, followed by a Sigmoid function to generate normalized channel attention weights W. This sequential design enables adaptive recalibration of channel-wise feature importance through learned non-linear interactions. The resulting attention weights are then elementwise multiplied with the original features along the channel dimension, enabling adaptive feature enhancement of critical channels and dynamic suppression of redundant information.

2.3 High Frequency Guidance Block

To enhance the recovery capability of high-frequency components, this study employs a low-frequency-guided cross-frequency-domain feature transfer mechanism. By collaboratively optimizing high-frequency components using the semantic consistency features of low-frequency components, this mechanism addresses the issue of weakened high-frequency details in traditional methods. The HFG-Block adopts a dual-path collaborative architecture, which includes two key components: the Frequency Matching Attention Module (FMAM) and the Frequency-Domain Correction Feedforward Network (FCFN).

Building upon existing investigations into query effectiveness in attention mechanisms, this study proposes a low-frequency feature-guided semantic enhancement strategy to optimize the attention weight generation mechanism. As illustrated in Fig. 3(b), the Frequency matching attention module (FMAM)

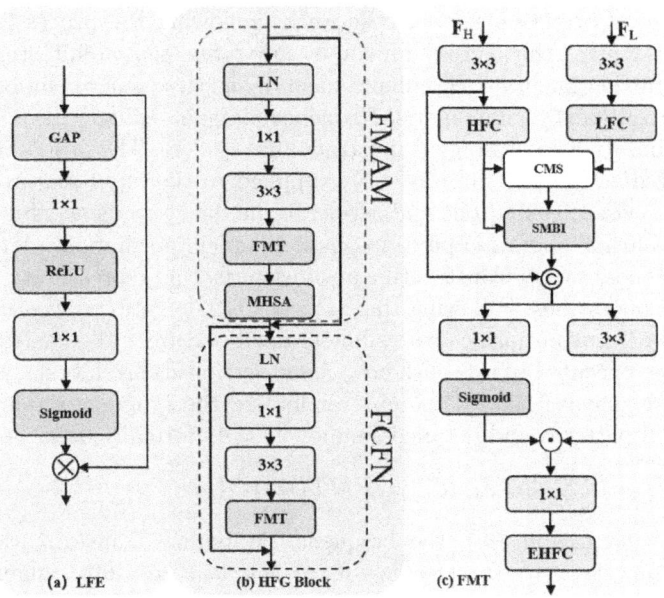

Fig. 3. (a) Local Leature Extraction. (b) High-Frequency Enhance Block. (c) Frequency Matching Transformation.

employs a dual-stage optimization design: The module first generates semantically enhanced queries (Q), keys (K), and value projections (V) through parallel 1×1 convolutional transformation W_1 and 3×3 depth-wise convolution W_3. Subsequently, the frequency matching transformation (FMT) is executed between Q and K, dynamically injecting optimized low-frequency features into the query representations while preserving high-frequency details, thereby establishing cross-band semantic correlations through adaptive frequency interaction. This design enhances the physical interpretability of attention weights and detail perception capability through a feature-level low-frequency and high-frequency cooperative mapping strategy, thereby providing a novel approach for high-frequency feature restoration in complex illumination scenarios. The workflow of the FMAM is illustrated as follows:

$$\text{FMAM}(F_H^m, F_L^e) = A(\text{FMT}(Q, F_L^e), K, V) \quad (1)$$
$$Q, K, V = \text{Split}(W_1 W_3(F_H^m)) \quad (2)$$
$$A(Q, K, V) = V \cdot \text{softmax}(\frac{K \cdot Q}{\alpha}) \quad (3)$$

The notation FMT(.), Split(.), and Softmax(.) respectively denote the Feature Modulation Transformer module, feature splitting operation, and normalized exponential function, where α serves as a learnable scaling parameter to regulate the magnitude of the dot product between keys (K) and queries (Q).

Frequency Correction Forward Network: Following the processing through the FMAM, a hierarchical cross-domain feature refinement architecture is implemented to further facilitate the enhancement of high-frequency components. This architecture achieves joint spatial-frequency domain enhancement via multistage collaborative processing, as illustrated in Fig. 3(b). The processing pipeline is formulated as follows: Initially, LN is applied to the input features to stabilize channel-wise distributions and accelerate model convergence. Subsequently, a 1×1 convolution operation performs cross-channel information interaction and dimensional adaptation, constructing an efficient feature representation space for subsequent operations. Following this, a local spatial context extraction module based on 3×3 convolutions captures fine-grained texture and edge features. The FMT is then executed to establish cross-band semantic correlations between low and high frequency features, thereby reinforcing the synergistic representation of structural patterns and detailed components. As formally described below:

$$FCFN(F'_H, F^e_L) = FMT(W_3 W_1(\text{LN}(F'_H))F^e_L) \tag{4}$$

As depicted in Fig. 3(c), the Frequency Matching Transformation (FMT) primarily functions to transfer low-frequency features into enhanced high-frequenFirst, the cross-modal similarity (CMS) between high-frequency components (HFC) and low-frequency components (LFC) is calculated to identify the optimal feature vector D. Subsequently, based on D, the most semantically aligned low-frequency components are selected as channel-specific outputs. These selected features are then concatenated with the original high-frequency features via parallel processing branches. Specifically, one branch computes attention maps using 1×1 convolutional layers coupled with Sigmoid activation to emphasize critical spatial locations, while the other branch employs 3×3 convolutions to capture contextual attention patterns. Finally, the outputs from both branches are multiplied and integrated through an additional 1×1 convolutional layer to produce the refined output enhanced high-frequency components (EHFC). The complete procedural pipeline is formally described as follows:

$$M = \text{Sim}(F_L, F_H) \tag{5}$$

$$D = \text{Top}_1(M) \tag{6}$$

$$Y_s = \text{Select}(F_L | \text{Indices}(D)) \tag{7}$$

$$Y^c_s = \text{Concat}(Y_s, F_H) \tag{8}$$

$$F^{\text{out}}_H = W_1\left(\text{Sigmoid}\left(W_1(Y^c_s)\right) \odot W_3(Y^c_s)\right) \tag{9}$$

In Equation,The notation Sim (,) denotes the similarity computation measured by Euclidean distance, $Select$ (|) represents the feature selection operation with conditional filtering, and $Indices$ (.) indicates the index retrieval operation.

3 Experimental Results and Analysis

The network architecture employs a hierarchical configuration with (1, 2, 4) LFMBlock and (1, 1, 1) HFGBlock per layer in the encoder-decoder framework.

The model utilizes 8 attention heads and maintains a channel dimension C of 32 throughout. Training is performed using the Adam W optimizer, initial-ized with a learning rate of 5×10^{-4}, which is progressively decayed to 1×10^{-7} via cosine annealing over 100k iterations. Data augmentation includes random geometric transformations (90, 180, 270) random flips, and random cropping to 512×512 patches. The Global-to-Local MambaÂăframework is optimized under and L1 loss constraint. All experiments are executed on a NVIDIA RTX 3090 GPU (24 GB) setup.

3.1 Datasets

The experimental validation employs two benchmark datasets: LOL-v1 and LOLv2-synthetic. The original Low-Light Dataset version 1, specifically designed for low-light image enhancement research, contains 500 aligned low/normal-light image pairs with a fixed resolution of 400×600 pixels. This collection comprises 485 training pairs and 15 testing pairs, predominantly featuring indoor scenarios. The enhanced LOLv2 version introduces two distinct subsets: LOLv2-real captured under authentic low-light conditions and LOLv2-synthetic generated through illumination distribution analysis of RAW images. Our experiments specifically utilize the LOL-v2-synthetic subset, which contains 1,000 synthetically generated low or normal-light image pairs divided into 900 training pairs and 100 testing pairs through systematic data partitioning.

3.2 Comparisons with State-of-the-Art Methods

In this section, we present quantitative and qualitative comparisons of our proposed Global-to-Local Mamba against state-of-the-art methods. The evaluation employs three established metrics: PSNR, SSIM, and LPIPS. PSNR measures reconstruction quality by computing pixel intensity differences between images, where higher values indicate superior reconstruction fidelity. SSIM assesses perceptual quality through luminance, contrast, and structural similarity analysis, with values closer to 1 representing better preservation of image characteristics. LPIPS quantifies perceptual similarity using deep neural networks, where lower scores correspond to enhanced human-visual alignment. These metrics collectively provide comprehensive insights into both pixel-level accuracy and perceptual authenticity across different enhancement paradigms.

The quantitative results on the LOL-v1 dataset are shown in Table 1. We evaluated the performance of Global to Local Mamba and other 12 SOTA low light image enhancement methods. The quantitative results on the LOL-v2 synthetic dataset are shown in Table 2. We evaluated the performance of Global to Local Mamba and other 11 SOTA low light image enhancement methods.

Qualitative Evaluation: Fig. 4 demonstrates a visual comparison between our method and existing approaches. Current methods exhibit insufficient illumination that fails to restore fine details, while color distortion and image degradation further compromise the enhancement outcomes of prior techniques. In contrast, our Global-to-Local Mamba framework not only effectively enhances

Table 1. Quantitative comparisons on LOL-v1 datasets.

Methods	Venue	PSNR	SSIM	LPIPS
RetinexNet [5]	BMVG 2018	16.77	0.56	0.47
KinD [6]	MM 2019	17.65	0.72	0.17
ZeroDCE [7]	CVPR 2020	14.86	0.58	0.30
RUAS [8]	CVPR 2021	16.40	0.50	0.35
EnlightenGAN [9]	TIP 2021	17.48	0.67	0.32
UFormer [10]	CVPR 2022	16.36	0.77	0.32
IAT [11]	BMVC 2022	21.30	0.82	0.11
PairLIE [12]	CVPR 2023	19.51	0.71	0.09
SCI [13]	CVPR 2022	14.78	0.50	0.36
LLFormer [14]	AAAI 2023	23.65	0.81	0.12
Wave-Mamba [15]	ACMM 2024	23.27	0.84	0.14
LTT [16]	DSP 2024	22.19	0.82	–
Ours	/	23.36	0.84	0.13

Table 2. Quantitative comparisons on LOL-v2-synthetic datasets.

Methods	VENUE	PSNR	SSIM	LPIPS
RetinexNet [5]	BMVC 2018	17.13	0.76	0.25
KinD [6]	MM 2019	18.32	0.79	0.23
DRBN [17]	CVPR 2020	23.22	0.92	–
RUAS [8]	CVPR 2021	13.76	0.63	0.20
ZeroDCE [7]	CVPR 2020	17.71	0.81	0.17
Uformer [10]	CVPR 2022	19.66	0.87	–
SNR-Net [18]	CVRR 2022	24.14	0.92	–
PairLIE [19]	CVPR 2023	19.07	0.79	0.23
LLFormer [12]	AAAI 2023	24.03	0.93	0.06
Bread [14]	IJCV 2023	17.63	0.91	0.09
QuadPrior [20]	CVPR 2024	16.10	0.79	0.26
Ours	/	24.44	0.92	0.06

brightness but also reconstructs intricate details, demonstrating superior capability in amplifying low-visibility and low-contrast regions. The proposed method reliably eliminates noise without introducing artificial artifacts and robustly preserves original chromatic information throughout the enhancement process. As the core component of the Global-to-Local Mamba framework, we perform ablation experiments to validate the functional roles of individual modules. The experimental results in Table 3 demonstrate the superiority of our proposed Mamba framework, which prioritizes global over local approaches. These findings

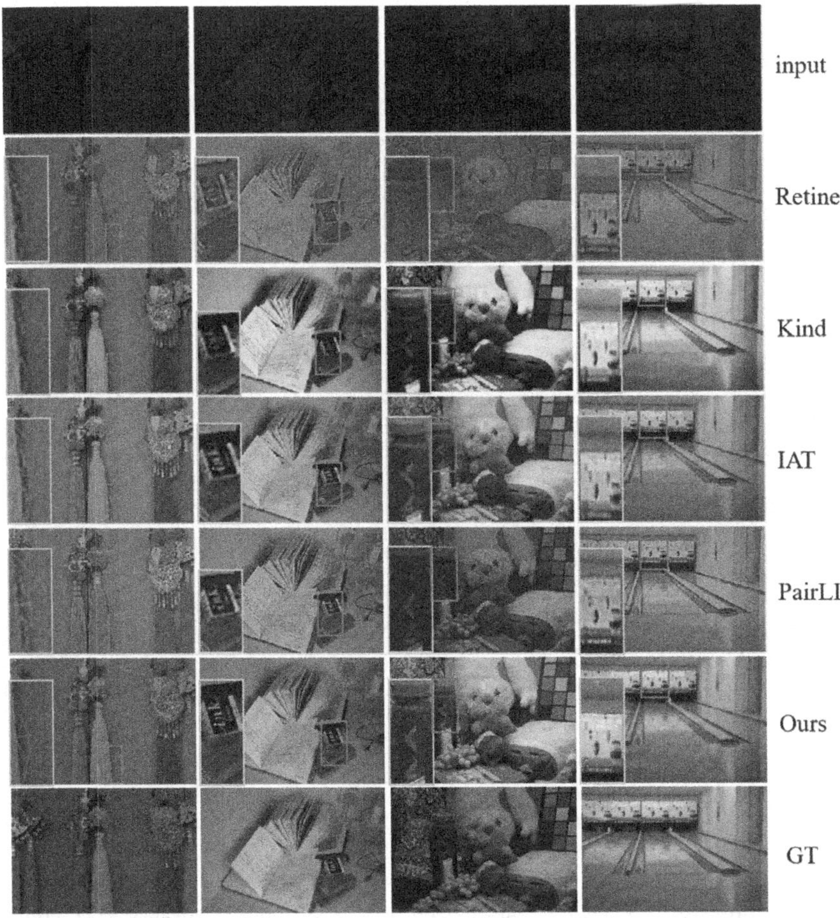

Fig. 4. Visualization of low-light enhancement model. Each column is a different image example, and each row is the prediction of models.

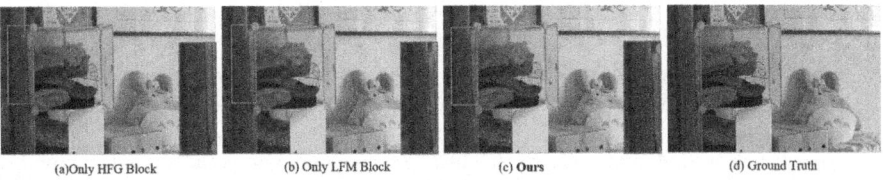

Fig. 5. We compare qualitative results on the LOL-v1 dataset using three strategies: (a) Only Retain High-Frequency Blocks, (b) Only Retain Low-Frequency Blocks, and (c) our proposed method. Zoom in for a better view.

substantiate the practical significance of low-frequency component enhancement for subsequent high-frequency refinement, while also confirming the intrinsic value of low-frequency features in low-light image restoration. Compared to the

Table 3. Ablation study on the proposed modules.

Method	PSNR	SSIM
w/o LFMBLock	22.20	0.82
w/o HFGBLock	22.34	0.83
w/o LFE	22.45	0.83
w/o MLP	23.12	0.83
w/o FMT	22.51	0.84
Full Model	23.36	0.84

LFMBlock, the HFGBlocks impose a more substantial impact on model parameters but yield a relatively minor performance gain, underscoring the efficiency superiority of our low-frequency-centric design paradigm. The visualization effect is shown in Fig. 5.

4 Conclusion

In this study, we propose an effective framework named Global to Local Mamba Low Light Image Restoration. Inspired by the wavelet transform's capability to effectively decompose high-frequency and low-frequency features, our method employs a global-to-local Mamba-based feature extraction approach to extract features from the low-frequency domain, and subsequently uses low-frequency information to correct high-frequency details. This approach has been comprehensively validated across multiple datasets, demonstrating the excellent performance of our method in the field of low-light image enhancement.

Acknowledgements. This work is supported by the National Natural Science Foundation of China (U24A201397) and the fundamental research project of SIA.

References

1. Zou, W., et al.: Cross-view hierarchy network for stereo image super-resolution. In: Proceedings of the IEEE/CVF Conference on Computer Vision and Pattern Recognition, pp. 1396–1405 (2023)
2. Albert, G., et al.: Combining recurrent, convolutional, and continuous-time models with linear state space layers. Adv. Neural. Inf. Process. Syst. **34**, 572–585 (2021)
3. Zuo, S., et al.: Efficient long sequence modeling via state space augmented transformer (2022)
4. Guo, H., Li, J., Dai, T., Ouyang, Z., Ren, X., Xia, S.-T.: Mambair: a simple baseline for image restoration with state-space model (2024)
5. Wei, C., Wang, W., Yang, W., Liu, J.: Deep retinex decomposition for low-light enhancement. In: Proceedings of the British Machine Vision Conference (2018)
6. Zhang, Y., Zhang, J., Guo, X.: Kindling the darkness: a practical low-light image enhancer. In: Proceedings of the ACM Multimedia, pp. 1632–1640. ACM (2019)

7. Guo, C., et al.: Zero-reference deep curve estimation for low-light image enhancement. In: CVPR, pp. 1777–1786 (2020)
8. Liu, R., Ma, L., Zhang, J., Fan, X., Luo, Z.: Retinex-inspired unrolling with cooperative prior architecture search for low-light image enhancement. In: Proceedings of the IEEE/CVF Conference on Computer Vision and Pattern Recognition, pp. 10561–10570 (2021)
9. Jiang, Y., et al.: EnlightenGAN: Deep light enhancement without paired supervision. IEEE Trans. Image Process. **30**, 2340–2349 (2021)
10. Wang, Z., Cun, X., Bao, J., Zhou, W., Liu, J., Li, H.: UFormer: a general U-shaped transformer for image restoration. In: Proceedings of the IEEE/CVF Conference on Computer Vision and Pattern Recognition, pp. 17683–17693 (2022)
11. Cui, Z., et al.: You only need 90k parameters to adapt light: a light weight transformer for image enhancement and exposure correction (2022)
12. Jie, H., Zuo, X., Gao, J., Liu, W., Hu, J., Cheng, S.: LLFormer: an efficient and real-time lidar lane detection method based on transformer. In: Proceedings of the 2023 5th International Conference on Pattern Recognition and Intelligent Systems, pp. 18–23 (2023)
13. Ma, L., et al.: Toward fast, flexible, and robust low-light image enhancement. In: Proceedings of the IEEE/CVF Conference on Computer Vision and Pattern Recognition (2022)
14. Guo, X., Hu, Q.: Low-light image enhancement via breaking down the darkness. Int. J. Comput. Vision **131**(1), 48–66 (2023)
15. Zou, W., Gao, H., Yang, W., Liu, T.: Wave-mamba: wavelet state space model for ultra-high-definition low-light image enhancement. In: Proceedings of the 32nd ACM International Conference on Multimedia, pp. 1534–1543 (2024)
16. Kou, K., Yin, X., Gao, X., et al.: Lightweight two-stage transformer for low-light image enhancement and object detection. Digit. Signal Process. **150**, 104521 (2024)
17. Yang, W., et al.: From fidelity to perceptual quality: a semi-supervised approach for low-light image enhancement. In: Proceedings of the IEEE/CVF Conference on Computer Vision and Pattern Recognition, pp. 3063–3072 (2020)
18. Xu, X., Wang, R., Fu, C.-W., Jia, J.: SNR-aware low-light image enhancement. In: CVPR, pp. 17693–17703. IEEE (2022)
19. Fu, Z., et al.: Learning a simple low-light image enhancer from paired low-light instances. In: Proceedings of the IEEE/CVF Conference on Computer Vision and Pattern Recognition (2023)
20. Wang, W., Yang, H., Fu, J., Liu, J.: Zero-reference low-light enhancement via physical quadruple priors. In: Proceedings of the IEEE/CVF Conference on Computer Vision and Pattern Recognition, pp. 26057–26066 (2024)

A Comparative Study of First and Second-Order Gradient Acceleration in ICP

Qing Tang[1,2], Ziwei Wang[1,2], Xiaojian Zhang[1,2], Mingxu Pan[3], and Sijie Yan[1,2(✉)]

[1] School of Mechanical Science and Engineering, Huazhong University of Science and Technology, Wuhan 430074, Hubei, China
sjyan@hust.edu.cn
[2] Huazhong University of Science and Technology-Wuxi Research Institute, Wuxi, China
[3] Shenyang Institute of Automation Chinese Academy of Sciences, Shenyang, China

Abstract. Fast point cloud registration is critical for applications in computer vision and robotics, such as 3D reconstruction, autonomous navigation, and augmented reality. While extensive research has explored ICP variants, systematic comparisons of the associated acceleration methods remain limited. This paper investigates first-order gradient methods (gradient descent, Adam, RMSprop) and second-order approaches (Newton-based methods, quasi-Newton variants) within the ICP optimization framework. Our analysis on benchmark datasets confirms the efficiency of second-order methods, reducing iteration counts by up to 50% while preserving registration precision. The Levenberg-Marquardt algorithm proved to be effective, exhibiting robust performance in all tested scenarios. Experimental results demonstrate that first-order methods require 43 to 261 s to converge. In contrast, second-order approaches achieve optimal alignment in 2 to 6 s. These findings identify which gradient-based acceleration methods perform better, supporting future real-time registration applications.

Keywords: Point cloud registration · ICP · Gradient-based acceleration methods

1 Introduction

Point cloud registration is a fundamental problem in computer vision and robotics. The task involves aligning multiple 3D point cloud datasets, acquired from different viewpoints into a common coordinate system [1]. This process is essential for constructing complete and accurate 3D models of an environment, including 3D reconstruction [2], Simultaneous Localization and Mapping (SLAM) [3], environmental perception in autonomous driving [4, 5].

The Iterative Closest Point (ICP) algorithm [9, 10] is commonly used for point cloud registration. The algorithm follows an iterative optimization process: First, corresponding points are established between source and target point clouds using nearest-neighbor search; Second, an optimal rigid transformation is computed to minimize an error metric between corresponding points, typically the sum of squared Euclidean distances; Third, the source point cloud pose is updated using the computed transformation. These steps are repeated until the convergence criteria are satisfied [11, 12].

© The Author(s), under exclusive license to Springer Nature Singapore Pte Ltd. 2026
T. Matsuno et al. (Eds.): ICIRA 2025, LNAI 16076, pp. 434–446, 2026.
https://doi.org/10.1007/978-981-95-2101-2_36

ICP implementations face convergence speed limitations as they rely on basic iterative updates without acceleration mechanisms [13–15], creating bottlenecks for real-time applications in autonomous navigation and interactive 3D modeling [16]. To address these limitations, researchers have explored different improvement strategies. Gradient-based optimization methods have received attention for their potential to enhance convergence efficiency and optimization accuracy. Maken et al. [17] employs stochastic gradient descent (SGD) within the ICP framework to minimize point-to-point distance, demonstrating acceleration effectiveness. Besides stochastic gradient descent, various first-order gradient acceleration techniques have been introduced into point cloud registration optimization. Specifically, researchers have applied methods such as Momentum [18] to smooth the update process and escape small local minima. Adaptive learning rate methods, including RMSprop [19] and Adam [20], have demonstrated effectiveness in handling non-convex optimization problems by adjusting learning rates independently for each parameter. First-order methods primarily seek faster convergence paths by refining gradient update strategies.

Second-order methods, such as Gauss-Newton [21–23] and Levenberg-Marquardt (LM) [24, 25], are applied to non-linear least squares problems. These methods approximate the Hessian matrix using first-order derivatives. Compared to first-order methods, these approaches achieve faster convergence rates and higher registration accuracy when near the optimum. Recent applications continue to employ the LM algorithm within the ICP framework for tasks such as 2D mapping [26]. Variants like Gram-Reduced LM have been developed to improve computational efficiency [27]. Quasi-Newton methods, including the Limited-memory Broyden–Fletcher–Goldfarb–Shanno (L-BFGS) algorithm [28, 29], approximate the inverse Hessian matrix using historical gradient information, providing a balance between computational cost and convergence speed [30].

Existing researches often focus on specific objective functions such as feature-based losses or rendering losses, while lacks frameworks for comparing different gradient-based accelerators on the fundamental ICP task of minimizing Euclidean distance [15, 31]. The comparison of first-order accelerated methods with second-order methods across different practical point cloud scenarios remains insufficiently explored [15, 16, 31].

We evaluate several representative first-order accelerated methods, including Steepest Descent with line search, Adam, RMSprop, and Powerball, alongside second-order and quasi-Newton methods, such as Gauss-Newton, Levenberg-Marquardt, L-BFGS, and PB-L-BFGS, on standard benchmark datasets. The study analyzes their differences in convergence speed and final registration accuracy. Moreover, we investigated the impact of varying initial parameter values on each acceleration method to identify the optimal parameter configurations.

2 Introduction of ICP

2.1 Standard ICP Algorithm

The ICP algorithm [7] is an iterative procedure designed to find the optimal rigid transformation (rotation $\mathbf{R}$ and translation $\mathbf{t}$) that aligns a source point cloud $\mathbb{P} = \{\mathbf{p}_1, \ldots, \mathbf{p}_M\}$ with a target point cloud $\mathbb{Q} = \{\mathbf{q}_1, \ldots, \mathbf{q}_N\}$, both consisting of points in $\mathbb{R}^3$. It operates by alternating between two main steps:

1. Correspondence Finding: Given the current transformation estimate $\mathbf{T}^{(k)} = \begin{bmatrix} \mathbf{R}^{(k)}_{3\times3} & \mathbf{t}^{(k)}_{3\times1} \\ 0 & 1 \end{bmatrix}$, for each point $\mathbf{p}_i$ in the source cloud $\mathbb{P}$, where i is the index of the point, find its closest point $\mathbf{q}_i$ in the target cloud $\mathbb{Q}$:

$$\mathbf{q}_i = \arg\min_{\mathbf{q}\in\mathbb{Q}} \left\| \mathbf{R}^{(k)}\mathbf{p}_i + \mathbf{t}^{(k)} - \mathbf{q} \right\|_2^2. \tag{1}$$

2. Transformation Optimization: Based on the established set of corresponding pairs $\{\mathbf{p}_i, \mathbf{q}_i\}$, update the transformation $\mathbf{T}^{(k+1)}$ by finding the rotation $\mathbf{R}^{(k+1)}$ and translation $\mathbf{t}^{(k+1)}$ that minimize the sum of squared Euclidean distances between these pairs:

$$\left(\mathbf{R}^{(k+1)}, \mathbf{t}^{(k+1)}\right) = \arg\min_{\{\mathbf{R},\mathbf{t}\}} \sum \left\| \mathbf{R}\mathbf{p}_i + \mathbf{t} - \mathbf{q}_i \right\|_2^2 + \mathbf{I}_{SO(3)}, \tag{2}$$

where $\mathbf{I}_{SO(3)}$ is an indicator function ensuring $\mathbf{R}$ is a valid rotation matrix. These two steps are repeated until a convergence criterion is met.

2.2 Lie Algebra Formulation

We use $(\cdot)^\wedge$ operator to uniformly denote the mapping from a Lie algebra vector to its matrix representation. This operator maps both a rotation vector $\omega^\wedge \in \mathfrak{so}(3)$, and a transformation vector $\boldsymbol{\xi} = \begin{pmatrix} v \\ \omega \end{pmatrix} \in \mathbb{R}^{6\times1}$ (where $v \in \mathbb{R}^3$ corresponds to translation and $\omega \in \mathbb{R}^3$ to rotation) to its 4×4 matrix representation $\boldsymbol{\xi}^\wedge \in \mathfrak{se}(3)$, with the specific forms:

$$\omega^\wedge = \begin{bmatrix} 0 & -\omega_z & \omega_y \\ \omega_z & 0 & -\omega_x \\ -\omega_y & \omega_x & 0 \end{bmatrix}, \boldsymbol{\xi}^\wedge = \begin{bmatrix} \omega^\wedge & v \\ 0^T & 0 \end{bmatrix}, \tag{3}$$

corresponding Lie algebra matrix $\boldsymbol{\xi}^\wedge$ are related via the exponential map:

$$\mathbf{T} = \exp(\boldsymbol{\xi}^\wedge), \boldsymbol{\xi}^\wedge = \log(\mathbf{T}). \tag{4}$$

Furthermore, when dealing with the relationship between points and transformations, we define $(\cdot)^\odot$ acting on the homogeneous coordinates of a point $\mathbf{p} = [\boldsymbol{\varepsilon}^T, 1]^T$ (where

$\varepsilon \in \mathbb{R}^3$ are its 3D coordinates). This operator maps the homogeneous point $\mathbf{p}$ to a 4×6 matrix $\mathbf{p}^{\odot}$:

$$\mathbf{p}^{\odot} = \begin{bmatrix} \varepsilon \\ 1 \end{bmatrix}^{\odot} = \begin{bmatrix} \mathbf{I}_{3\times 3} & -\varepsilon^{\wedge} \\ 0^T & 0^T \end{bmatrix}_{4 \times 6}. \tag{5}$$

The operator $(\cdot)^{\odot}$ converts the action of the Lie algebra matrix $\boldsymbol{\xi}^{\wedge}$ on the homogeneous point $\mathbf{p}$ into the matrix $\mathbf{p}^{\odot}$ acting on $\boldsymbol{\xi}^{\wedge}$:

$$\boldsymbol{\xi}^{\wedge}\mathbf{p} \equiv \mathbf{p}^{\odot}\boldsymbol{\xi}. \tag{6}$$

2.3 Objective Function and Parameterization

In the optimization step of ICP, we adjust the parameters $\boldsymbol{\xi}$ to minimize the objective function $f(\boldsymbol{\xi})$. This study utilizes the homogeneous coordinates $\mathbf{p}_i$, $\mathbf{q}_i$ of corresponding points, and the objective function is defined as the sum of squared 4D Euclidean distances, the corresponding 4D residual vector is $\mathbf{r}_i = \mathbf{T}(\boldsymbol{\xi}) \cdot \mathbf{p}_i - \mathbf{q}_i$:

$$f(\boldsymbol{\xi}) = \frac{1}{2} \sum \|\mathbf{T}(\boldsymbol{\xi})\mathbf{p}_i - \mathbf{q}_i\|_2^2. \tag{7}$$

The gradient $\nabla \mathbf{f}(\boldsymbol{\xi}) = \sum \nabla \mathbf{f}(\boldsymbol{\xi})_i$ with respect to $\boldsymbol{\xi}$ has contributions $\nabla \mathbf{f}(\boldsymbol{\xi})_i$ from each corresponding point pair:

$$\nabla \mathbf{f}(\boldsymbol{\xi})_i = \mathcal{J}_l(\boldsymbol{\xi})^T \left((\mathbf{T}(\boldsymbol{\xi})\mathbf{p}_i)^{\odot} \right)^T \mathbf{r}_i(\boldsymbol{\xi}). \tag{8}$$

In this gradient formula, $\mathbf{r}_i(\boldsymbol{\xi})$ is the 4D residual vector, $(\mathbf{T}(\boldsymbol{\xi})\mathbf{p}_i)^{\odot}$ is the 4×6 matrix acting on the transformed homogeneous point (as defined in Sect. 2.2), and $\mathcal{J}_l(\boldsymbol{\xi})$ represents the 6×6 left Jacobian of SE(3).

The computed gradient $\nabla \mathbf{f}(\boldsymbol{\xi})$ is then used in the optimization algorithms described in Sect. 3 to update the parameters $\boldsymbol{\xi}$.

Algorithm 1: ICP with Gradient-Based Optimization

Input: Source point cloud $\mathbb{P}$, Target point cloud $\mathbb{Q}$, Initial transformation $\boldsymbol{\xi}_0$

Output: Optimized transformation $\boldsymbol{\xi}$

1. Initialize: $\boldsymbol{\xi} = \boldsymbol{\xi}_0$, $\mathbf{P}_{source} = \mathbf{p}$, $\max_{iter} = 60$, $\text{tol}_{error} = 10^{-6}$ mm
2. For iteration = 1 to $\max_{iter}$ do
3. Find nearest neighbors $\mathbf{q}_{match}$ for $\mathbf{P}_{source}$ in $\mathbb{Q}$ using KD-tree
4. Select optimizer with parameters
5. Update $\boldsymbol{\xi}$ by minimizing $\frac{1}{2}\sum \|\mathbf{T}(\boldsymbol{\xi})\mathbf{p}_i - \mathbf{q}_i\|_2^2$ using selected optimizer

3 Gradient-Based Acceleration Methods

3.1 First-Order Methods

The choice of acceleration algorithm significantly impacts the efficiency and accuracy of the Transformation Optimization step within ICP [9–11]. We evaluate the following standard gradient-based methods applied to minimize $f(\xi)$.

Steepest Descent updates parameters along the negative gradient direction:

$$\xi_{k+1} = \xi_k - \alpha_k \nabla \mathbf{f}(\xi_k), \tag{9}$$

where ξ_k is the parameter for the k-th step and α_k is the step parameter, obtained by line search satisfying the Armijo condition [10, 21]:

$$(\xi_k - \alpha_k \nabla \mathbf{f}(\xi_k)) \leq f(\xi_k) - c\alpha_k \|\nabla \mathbf{f}(\xi_k)\|_2^2, \tag{10}$$

RMSprop [16] adapts the learning rate for each parameter individually based on a moving average of the squared gradients. We let $\mathbf{g}_k = \nabla \mathbf{f}(\xi_k)$ denote the gradient vector of the objective function f at the k-th iterate ξ_k:

$$\begin{aligned} \mathbf{E}[\mathbf{g}^2]_k &= \rho \mathbf{E}[\mathbf{g}^2]_{k-1} + (1-\rho)\mathbf{g}_k^2 \\ \xi_{k+1} &= \xi_k - \frac{\alpha_k}{\sqrt{\mathbf{E}[\mathbf{g}^2]_k + \epsilon}} \epsilon \cdot \mathbf{g}_k \end{aligned} \tag{11}$$

where ρ is the decay factor controlling the weighting of historical gradients in the moving average $\mathbf{E}[\mathbf{g}^2]_k$, and ϵ ensures stability.

Adam [17] combines RMSprop's scaling with momentum by keeping track of moving averages of both the gradient and its square:

$$\mathbf{m}_k = \beta_1 \mathbf{m}_{k-1} + (1-\beta_1)\mathbf{g}_k, \hat{\mathbf{m}}_k = \frac{\mathbf{m}_k}{1-\beta_1^k}, \mathbf{v}_k = \beta_2 \mathbf{v}_{k-1} + (1-\beta_2)\mathbf{g}_k^2, \hat{\mathbf{v}}_k = \frac{\mathbf{v}_k}{1-\beta_2^k}$$
$$\xi_{k+1} = \xi_k - \alpha_k \frac{\hat{\mathbf{m}}_k}{\sqrt{\hat{\mathbf{v}}_k} + \epsilon} \tag{12}$$

where β_1, β_2 are the decay rates, and ϵ is for stability [18, 19].

As a momentum-based approach, Powerball [29] modifies the gradient update using a non-linear transformation:

$$\mathbf{v}_{k+1} = \mu \mathbf{v}_k + \alpha_k \sigma(\mathbf{g}_k), \xi_{k+1} = \xi_k - \mathbf{v}_{k+1}, \tag{13}$$

$\sigma(\mathbf{z}) = \text{sign}(\mathbf{z})|\mathbf{z}|^\gamma$ for $\gamma \in [0, 1)$, μ is a momentum factor.

3.2 Second-Order Methods

Second-order methods utilize curvature information, which can lead to significantly faster convergence [10, 11, 21]. Let $\mathbf{J}(\xi)$ be the Jacobian matrix where the i-th row block is $\mathbf{J}_i(\xi)$. The gradient is $\nabla \mathbf{f}(\xi) = \sum \mathbf{J}_i(\xi)^T \mathbf{r}_i(\xi)$.

Gauss-Newton (GN) [11, 21, 22] is used for non-linear least squares problems, approximating the Hessian matrix $\mathbf{J}(\xi)^T \mathbf{J}(\xi)$. The update step solves the linear system:

$$\begin{aligned} \mathbf{J}(\xi)^T \mathbf{J}(\xi) \Delta \xi_k &= -\mathbf{J}(\xi)^T \mathbf{r}(\xi_k) \\ \xi_{k+1} &= \xi_k + \Delta \xi_k \end{aligned} \tag{14}$$

The Levenberg-Marquardt (LM) algorithm [23, 24] blends Steepest Descent and GN by introducing a damping factor $\lambda \geq 0$:

$$\mathbf{J}(\xi_k)^T\mathbf{J}(\xi_k) + \lambda \text{diag}(\mathbf{J}(\xi_k)^T\mathbf{J}(\xi_k))\Delta\xi_k = -\mathbf{J}(\xi_k)^T\mathbf{r}(\xi_k) = -\nabla\mathbf{f}(\xi_k)$$
$$\xi_{k+1} = \xi_k + \Delta\xi_k \quad (15)$$

λ is adjusted based on the achieved versus predicted reduction, enhancing LM's robustness over Gauss-Newton [25, 26].

L-BFGS [27] approximates the inverse Hessian $\mathbf{H}^{-1}$ using information from the last m updates. It stores m pairs of displacement vectors $\mathbf{s}_k = \xi_{k+1} - \xi_k$ and gradient differences $\mathbf{y}_k = \nabla\mathbf{f}(\xi_{k+1}) - \nabla\mathbf{f}(\xi_k)$ [21]. The update direction is computed as:

$$\mathbf{d}_k = -\mathbf{H}_k\nabla\mathbf{f}(\xi_k), \xi_{k+1} = \xi_k + \alpha_k\mathbf{d}_k. \quad (16)$$

Finally, we explore a hybrid approach, Powerball L-BFGS (PB-L-BFGS), which attempts to combine the L-BFGS framework with the non-linear gradient transformation concept from Powerball [29]:

$$\mathbf{v}_{k+1} = \mu\mathbf{v}_k + \mathbf{H}_k\sigma(\mathbf{g}_k), \xi_{k+1} = \xi_k - \alpha_k\mathbf{v}_{k+1}. \quad (17)$$

Here, the search direction incorporates momentum and the L-BFGS approximation applied to the non-linearly transformed gradient $\mathbf{g}_k$.

3.3 Algorithm Complexity Analysis

In a single iteration of ICP, the computational cost primarily stems from two stages: correspondence finding and transformation optimization. Correspondence finding, which employs a KD-tree, has a query time complexity of $O(K\log N)$ (where N is the total number of points in the target cloud), a cost common to all optimization methods. The complexity of the transformation optimization stage varies by method: the primary cost for first-order methods is gradient computation, with a time complexity of $O(K)$ and an additional space complexity of $O(1)$; second-order methods need to construct and store the Jacobian matrix, leading to a time complexity of $O(Kd)$, which simplifies to $O(K)$ as the transformation dimension $d = 6$ is a small constant. However, their additional space complexity is $O(Kd)$, which can become a memory bottleneck for large-scale point clouds. Quasi-Newton methods (L-BFGS) avoid this spatial cost by storing m sets of historical information, also having a time complexity of $O(K)$ but with an additional space complexity of only $O(md)$.

4 Experimental Results

4.1 Experimental Configuration

This section presents and discusses the comparative performance of various optimization methods across three benchmark point cloud datasets: Horse (Georgia Tech; 10,031 points), Dragon (Georgia Tech; 186,969 points), and Vertebra (Artec 3D; 10,079 points) (Figs. 1, 2, 3, 4 and 5).

Through comprehensive comparison across test range, optimal parameters were determined. These selections ensure each method operates under its optimal configuration for meaningful performance comparison (Tables 1 and 2).

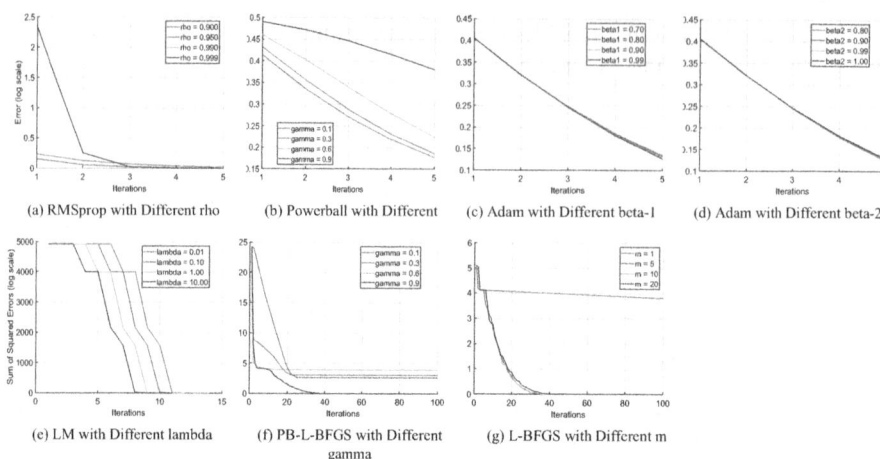

Fig. 1. Convergence Behavior Analysis of Optimization Algorithms

Table 1. Comparison of Parameter Settings for Acceleration Methods

Method	Parameter	Test Range	Optimal Value	Selection Criteria
RMSprop	ρ	[0.900,0.999][19]	0.990	Fastest convergence speed
Powerball	γ	[0.1,0.9][32]	0.1	Most stable error reduction
Adam	β_1	[0.7,0.99][17]	0.90	Best convergence performance
	β_2	[0.8,1.0][17]	0.99	Best convergence performance
LM	λ	[0.01,10.00][25]	0.01	Balance of speed and accuracy
PB-L-BFGS	γ	[0.1,0.9][23]	0.1	Fastest function value descent
L-BFGS	m	[1, 20]	5	Balance of memory usage and performance

4.2 Registration Accuracy Analysis

The alignment quality between the red (source) and blue (target) point clouds reflects the precision of each acceleration method. In this study, the final registration quality is numerically evaluated by the sum of the residual errors, denoted as r (mm), which is the value of the objective function $f(\xi)$ defined in Eq. 7. Beneath each visual alignment, the corresponding final residual error (r) is provided.

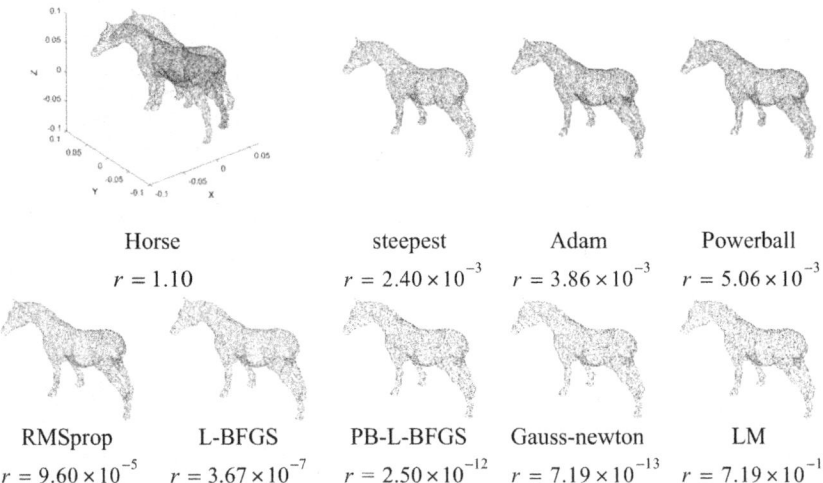

Fig. 2. Visualization comparison of registration results on the horse dataset

In the Horse point cloud alignment task, the Levenberg-Marquardt (LM) algorithm and Gauss-Newton method outperformed others. Meanwhile, the PB-L-BFGS series algorithms showed residuals close to zero.

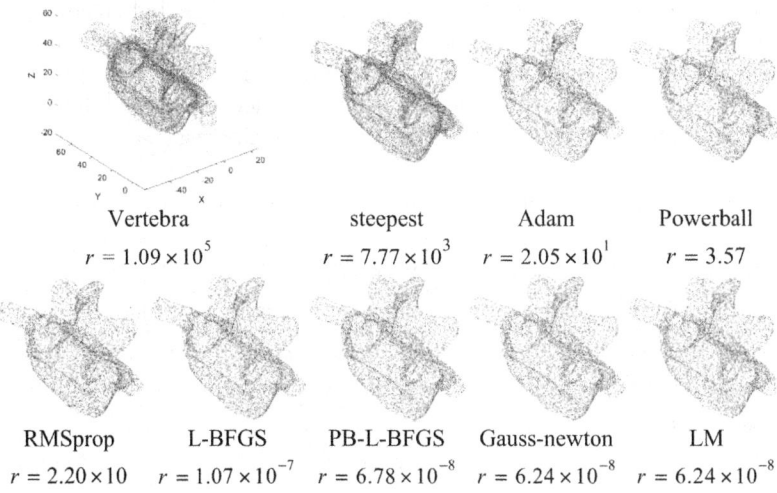

Fig. 3. Visualization comparison of registration results on the vertebra datase

Compared to the results of the vertebra model, PB-L-BFGS, Gauss-Newton, and LM algorithms demonstrate outstanding performance, reducing the error to nearly zero.

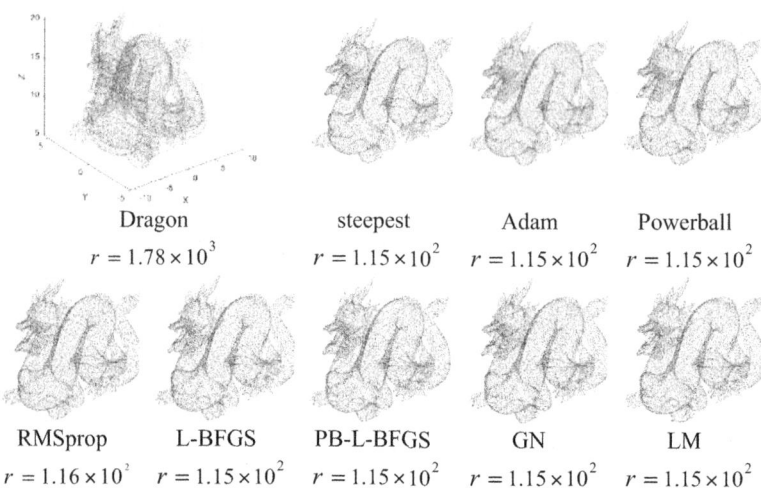

Fig. 4. Visualization comparison of registration results on the dragon dataset

On the dragon model, the performance gap between first-order and second-order methods is significantly reduced.

4.3 Convergence Speed and Stability

First-order methods exhibit variable stability characteristics. Although Adam, Powerball, and RMSprop generally maintain stable convergence trajectories, they require the full 60 iterations to reach their final results. The steepest descent method exhibits oscillatory behavior, which is particularly evident in the Horse model. This instability suggests potential convergence difficulties in complex registration scenarios.

Table 2. Runtimes across the datasets

Acceleration Methods	Horse		Vertebra		Dragon	
	Time (s)	r (mm)	Time (s)	r (mm)	Time (s)	r (mm)
steepest	86.88	2.40×10^{-3}	261.91	7.77×10^3	139.25	1.15×10^2
Adam	149.29	3.86×10^{-3}	78.09	2.05×10^1	65.38	1.15×10^2
Powerball	51.27	5.06×10^{-3}	201.72	3.57	43.23	1.15×10^2
RMSprop	43.68	9.60×10^{-5}	137.39	2.20×10	53.88	1.16×10^2
L-BFGS	12.32	3.67×10^{-7}	40.42	1.07×10^{-7}	28.81	1.15×10^2
PB-L-BFGS	14.96	2.50×10^{-12}	71.13	6.78×10^{-8}	52.90	1.15×10^2
GN	5.46	7.19×10^{-13}	5.76	6.24×10^{-8}	4.83	1.15×10^2
LM	**3.00**	7.19×10^{-13}	**2.16**	6.24×10^{-8}	**1.67**	1.15×10^2

Among second-order methods, PB-L-BFGS achieves superior convergence results compared to L-BFGS, although minor fluctuations occur in the later stages of convergence. LM demonstrates superior performance, achieving low residual errors on both the Horse and Vertebra models. GN method exhibits comparable performance, although its convergence speed is generally slightly slower than that of LM.

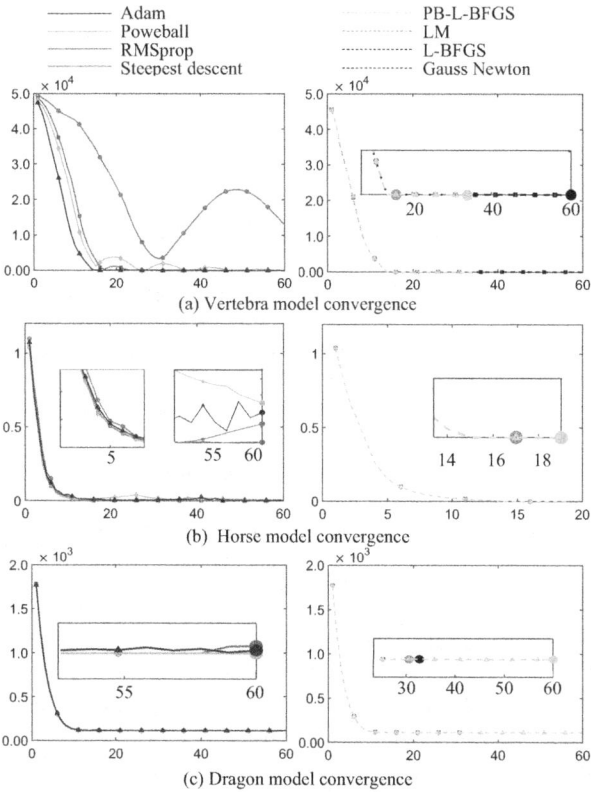

Fig. 5. Performance Evaluation of Acceleration Methods in Point Cloud Registration

5 Conclusion

This study compared first-order and second-order gradient methods for ICP point cloud registration. Second-order methods, particularly LM, outperform others in convergence speed and accuracy. GN performs similarly but is less robust. Among first-order methods, Adam and RMSprop are stable but slower. Powerball improves with L-BFGS but remains slower than second-order methods. While first-order gradient methods can achieve convergence, our experimental results suggest that second-order gradient methods generally provide faster and more accurate results under the tested conditions. In summary, LM is the most recommended algorithm, GN is a viable alternative, and Adam is suitable for use when computational resources are limited.

Future research can integrate acceleration methods with various registration techniques, including point-to-plane, plane-to-plane, and symmetric point-to-plane distance metrics, to improve registration performance. Moreover, utilizing other accelerated methods like Nesterov's Accelerated Gradient or the Heavy Ball method to improve convergence rates.

Acknowledgement. This work was supported by the National Key Research and Development Program of China (Grant Nos. 2022YFB4700500, 2024YFB4711202) and the National Natural Science Foundation of China (Grant Nos. 52375495, 52188102).

Conflict of Interests. The authors declare no conflict of interest.

References

1. Zhao, G., Li, J., Xi, J., Luo, L.: An efficient and stable registration framework for large point clouds at two different moments. Sensors (Basel) **24**(22), 7174 (2024)
2. Brightman, N., Fan, L., Zhao, Y.: Point cloud registration: a mini-review of current state, challenging issues and future directions. AIMSGEO **9**(1), 68–85 (2023)
3. Huang, S., Gojcic, Z., Usvyatsov, M., Wieser, A., Schindler, K.: Predator: registration of 3D point clouds with low overlap. Remote Sens. **15**(8), 2060 (2023)
4. Li, Y., et al.: Deep learning for lidar point clouds in autonomous driving: a review. IEEE Trans. Neural Netw. Learn. Syst. **32**(8), 3412–3432 (2021)
5. Qi, C.R., Su, H., Mo, K., Guibas, L.J.: PointNet: deep learning on point sets for 3D classification and segmentation. In: Proceedings of the IEEE Conference on Computer Vision and Pattern Recognition (CVPR), pp. 652–660. IEEE, Honolulu, HI (2017)
6. Remondino, F., Campana, S.: 3D recording and modelling in archaeology and cultural heritage: theory and best practices (BAR International Series, vol. 2598). Archaeopress, Oxford (2014)
7. Jaboyedoff, M., et al.: Use of LIDAR in landslide investigations: a review. Nat. Hazards **61**(1), 5–28 (2012)
8. Freitas, S., Catita, C., Redweik, P., Brito, M.C.: Modelling solar potential in the urban environment: state-of-the-art review. Renew. Sustain. Energy Rev. **41**, 915–931 (2015)
9. Besl, P.J., McKay, N.D.: A method for registration of 3-D shapes. IEEE Trans. Pattern Anal. Mach. Intell. **14**(2), 239–256 (1992)
10. Rusinkiewicz, S., Levoy, M.: Efficient variants of the ICP algorithm. In: Proceedings of the Third International Conference on 3-D Digital Imaging and Modeling, pp. 145–152. IEEE, Quebec City, QC (2001)
11. Koide, K., Yokozuka, M., Oishi, S., Banno, A.: LP-ICP: general localizability-aware point cloud registration for robust localization in extreme unstructured environments (2024). arXiv preprint arXiv:2401.02580
12. Koide, K., Yokozuka, M., Oishi, S., Banno, A.: GenZ-ICP: generalizable and degeneracy-robust LiDAR odometry using an adaptive weighting (2023). arXiv preprint arXiv:2311.06766

13. Pomerleau, F., Colas, F., Siegwart, R.: A review of point cloud registration algorithms for mobile robotics. Found. Trends Robot. **4**(1), 1–104 (2015)
14. Denayer, M., De Winter, J., Bernardes, E., Vanderborght, B., Verstraten, T.: Comparison of point cloud registration techniques on scanned physical objects. Sensors **24**(7), 2142 (2024)
15. Zhang, Y., Gui, J., Cong, X., Gong, X., Tao, W.: A comprehensive survey and taxonomy on point cloud registration based on deep learning. In: Proceedings of the International Joint Conference on Artificial Intelligence (IJCAI 2024), pp. 7414–7422. IJCAI, Jeju, South Korea (2024)
16. Tam, G.K., et al.: Registration of 3D point clouds and meshes: a survey from rigid to nonrigid. IEEE Trans. Visual Comput. Graphics **19**(7), 1199–1217 (2013)
17. Maken, F.A., Ramos, F., Ott, L.: Stein variational gradient descent for gaussian process inference and point cloud registration. In: Proceedings of the IEEE/CVF International Conference on Computer Vision (ICCV), pp. 13518–13527. IEEE, Paris (2021)
18. Polyak, B.T.: Some methods of speeding up the convergence of iteration methods. USSR Comput. Math. Math. Phys. **4**(5), 1–17 (1964)
19. Tieleman, T., Hinton, G.: Lecture 6.5—RMSprop: divide the gradient by a running average of its recent magnitude. COURSERA: Neural networks for machine learning **4**(2), 26–31 (2012)
20. Kingma, D.P., Ba, J.: Adam: a method for stochastic optimization. In: Proceedings of the 3rd International Conference on Learning Representations (ICLR). ICLR, San Diego, CA (2015)
21. Fletcher, R.: Practical methods of optimization, 2nd edn. John Wiley & Sons, Chichester (2000)
22. Dennis Jr, J.E., Schnabel, R.B.: Numerical methods for unconstrained optimization and nonlinear equations. SIAM Classics in Applied Mathematics, vol. 16. SIAM, Philadelphia (1996)
23. Nocedal, J., Wright, S.J.: Numerical Optimization, 2nd edn. Springer, New York (2006)
24. Levenberg, K.: A method for the solution of certain non-linear problems in least squares. Q. Appl. Math. **2**(2), 164–168 (1944)
25. Marquardt, D.W.: An algorithm for least-squares estimation of nonlinear parameters. J. Soc. Ind. Appl. Math. **11**(2), 431–441 (1963)
26. Darmawan, R., et al.: Implementation of Levenberg-Marquardt point to line iterative closest point and pose graph optimization for 2D indoor mapping. In: Proceedings of the 2023 International Conference on Computer Science, Information Technology and Engineering (ICCoSITE), vol. 1, pp. 146–151. IEEE, Medan (2023)
27. Chen, Z., Liu, Y., Luo, Z.Q.: An enhanced Levenberg–Marquardt method via gram reduction. Proc. AAAI Conf. Artif. Intell. **38**(13), 14765–14773 (2024)
28. Liu, D.C., Nocedal, J.: On the limited memory BFGS method for large scale optimization. Math. Program. **45**(1–3), 503–528 (1989)
29. Zhu, C., Byrd, R.H., Lu, P., Nocedal, J.: Algorithm 778: L-BFGS-B: fortran subroutines for large-scale bound-constrained optimization. ACM Trans. Math. Softw. **23**(4), 550–560 (1997)
30. Bottou, L., Curtis, F.E., Nocedal, J.: Optimization methods for large-scale machine learning. SIAM Rev. **60**(2), 223–311 (2018)

31. Schmidt, M., Le Roux, N., Bach, F.: Minimizing finite sums with the stochastic average gradient. Math. Program. **162**(1–2), 83–112 (2017)
32. Reddi, S.J., Kale, S., Kumar, S.: On the convergence of adam and beyond (2019). arXiv preprint arXiv:1904.09237

Visual-Tactile Fusion-Driven Diffusion Policy for Robotic Excavation of Semi-buried Object in Granular Media

Linan Deng[1], Xing Liu[1], Yunlong Dong[2], Guijun Ma[1], Feng Hua[1], Cheng Cheng[3], and Zuogong Yue[3(✉)]

[1] School of Mechanical Science and Engineering, Huazhong University of Science and Technology, Wuhan 430074, China
[2] Wuhan, China
[3] School of Artificial Intelligence and Automation, Huazhong University of Science and Technology, Wuhan 430074, China
z_yue@hust.edu.cn

Abstract. Robotic grasping of objects semi-buried in granular media (GM) is challenging due to particle resistance. Direct grasping requires excessive contact force to generate sufficient friction, easily damaging the object. In this work, we first design an adaptive gripper with multimodal sensors for excavation, integrating a binocular camera, tactile sensor array (TSA), and inertial measurement unit (IMU) to detect the object contour, the contact state, and fingertip motion. Based on the gripper, we develop a teleoperation system with visual-tactile feedback to collect high-quality human demonstration data. We then propose a visual-tactile fusion-driven diffusion policy to learn efficient excavation actions. Experiments including robotic end-pose tracking and object excavation are conducted to validate the performance of the system and the policy.

Keywords: Robotic excavation · Semi-buried object · Granular materials

1 Introduction

Robotic grasping of semi-buried objects in granular media is critical for applications such as sampling, archaeology, and search and rescue [1–3]. Most grasping methods focus on objects in air or water [4], neglecting the effects of granular media [5]. Granular media significantly alter the finger-object contact state [6], reducing the effective friction and creating unstable pressure distributions in the contact region [7]. These effects induce localized stress concentrations, risking damage to fragile objects. Therefore, an effective grasping method for semi-buried objects must overcome the interference of granular coverings.

Existing grasping methods [8] can be divided into two categories according to the generation method: analytical [9] and data-driven [10]. The analytical method refers to constructing force-closure grasping through a multi-fingered dexterous hand [11]. It is

---

Y. Dong—Individual Researcher.

assumed that the robot can obtain precise geometric models of objects, surface properties, friction coefficients, weight distribution, etc. However, this information is difficult to acquire during actual grasping, making analytical methods difficult to apply in granular environment. Data-driven methods rely on sampling infinitely possible grasping candidate postures of objects and sorting them according to specific evaluation metrics. It typically requires extensive data collection and learning in a simulation environment. Xu et al. [2] defined the grasping task of unknown buried objects as a model-free reinforcement learning problem, conducted end-to-end training in a simulation environment to learn the pushing and grasping behaviors of a two-fingered gripper. However, the particle size set in the simulation environment is much larger than actual particles such as sand, making it difficult to effectively simulate real-world scenarios. The enormous particles significantly increases the computational complexity of granular environment simulation and drastically reduces the efficiency of simulated data collection, making it difficult to learn the grasping method from the simulation environment. Deng et al. [1] proposed a coarse-fine two-stage excavation policy without simulation to remove granular coverings and grasp buried objects. The policy based only on tactile perception can overcome the lack of visual information through interaction, but it is difficult to perceive the movement of the object and inefficient at detecting the contour when the object is partially visible. Therefore, an effective excavation policy for semi-buried objects needs global visual localization and local tactile perception.

In this work, a robotic excavation system with a visual-tactile adaptive gripper is developed first. Two monocular cameras, a tactile sensor array, and an inertial measurement unit are integrated on the gripper to perceive the object contour, the fingertip contact state, and the fingertip motion. A visual-tactile fusion-driven diffusion policy is designed to detect the semi-buried object and generate effective excavation actions. Experiments on robotic end pose tracking and object excavation are conducted to validate the performance of the robotic system and the excavation policy.

The rest of this paper is organized as follows. Section 2 describes the design of the robotic excavation system. Section 3 presents the semi-buried object excavation method. Section 4 conducts experiments and discussions. Finally, this paper concludes with a discussion of future work in Sect. 5.

2 Robotic Excavation System Design

This section introduces the design of the robotic excavation system, including the visual-tactile adaptive gripper, the robotic excavation and teleoperation system, the robotic end pose control, and the action mapping of graphical user interface (GUI).

2.1 Visual-Tactile Adaptive Gripper

To excavate the semi-buried object, a visual-tactile adaptive gripper is first designed. Based on the developed robotic excavation system [1], two additional small monocular cameras (HBVCAM-1914S V44, Shenzhen Huiboshijie) are mounted in the palm of the adaptive gripper, as shown in Fig. 1. In total, the gripper integrates two cameras, a tactile sensor array (TSA) [12], and an inertial measurement unit (IMU), so as to perceive the object contour and the fingertip state.

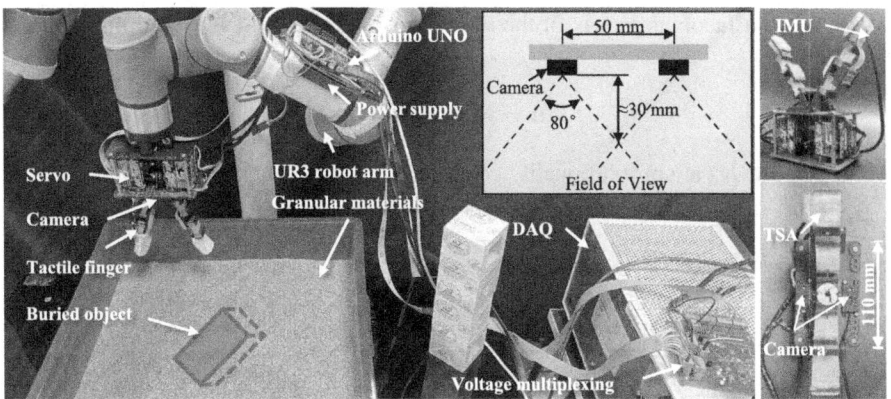

Fig. 1. Adaptive gripper with multi-modal sensors.

The field of view (FOV) of the binocular cameras is illustrated in Fig. 1. Each camera has an FOV angle of 80°, and the separation between the two cameras is 50 mm. The FOVs of the two cameras intersect at a distance of approximately 30 mm. When the vertical distance between an object and the cameras exceeds 30 mm, both cameras can capture partially overlapping images of the object, which is beneficial for recognizing and locating the contour of the object. Conversely, when the vertical distance is less than 30 mm, the two cameras will capture significantly non-overlapping images.

2.2 Robotic Excavation and Teleoperation System

Based on the designed adaptive gripper, the hardware and software of a teleoperation system are further developed to obtain high-quality demonstration data from the operator. The block diagram of the system is shown in Fig. 2. The system consists of a teleoperation platform, a robot control system, robot hardware, a sensing system, and a graphical user interface. The operator can input the desired end pose of the robot and the servo angles of the gripper through the keyboard, so as to remotely control the gripper to grasp the semi-buried object.

2.3 Robotic End Pose Control

The end pose $\mathbf{x} = [p_x, p_y, p_z, \beta_x, \beta_y, \beta_z]^T$ of the robot arm consists of the end position $[p_x, p_y, p_z]^T$ and the end orientation $[\beta_x, \beta_y, \beta_z]^T$. An proportion differentiation (PD) controller is utilized to control the end pose. First, the end pose error is denoted as:

$$\mathbf{x}_e = \mathbf{x}_{\text{ref}} - \mathbf{x}, \tag{1}$$

where $\mathbf{x}_{\text{ref}}$ is the desired end pose and $\mathbf{x}$ is the current end pose. The joint angle error of the robot arm can be calculated by differential inverse kinematics:

$$\mathbf{q}_e = \mathbf{J}^{-1}\mathbf{x}_e, \tag{2}$$

where $\mathbf{J}$ is the Jacobian matrix of the robot arm. The output of PD controller is determined by:

$$\mathbf{u} = K_p \mathbf{q}_e + K_d \dot{\mathbf{q}}_e, \qquad (3)$$

where K_p and K_d are proportionality coefficient and differential coefficient.

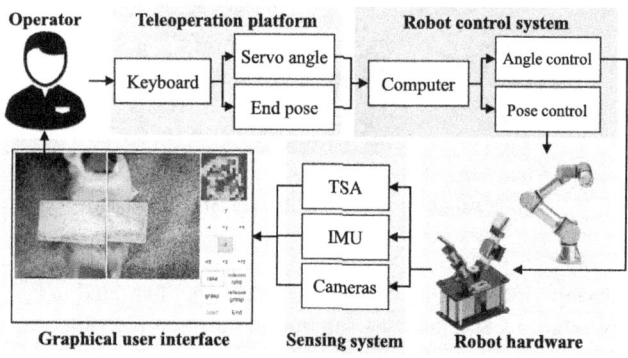

Fig. 2. Teleoperation system.

2.4 Action Mapping of GUI

First, symbols of all observations and actions are defined. For the observation at time t, data from the binocular camera is denoted as $\mathbf{o}_{t,\text{camera}} \in \mathbb{R}^{640 \times 960}$, data from TSA is denoted as $\mathbf{o}_{t,\text{tactile}} \in \mathbb{R}^{16 \times 16}$, data from IMU is denoted as $\mathbf{o}_{t,\text{imu}} \in \mathbb{R}^4$, the robotic end pose $\mathbf{o}_{t,\text{robot}} := \mathbf{x}_t \in \mathbb{R}^6$, the servo angles of the gripper are denoted as $\mathbf{o}_{t,\text{gripper}} := \boldsymbol{\alpha}_t \in \mathbb{R}^4$. The value range of all elements of $\mathbf{o}_{t,\text{gripper}}$ is $[0, 80]$. All raw observation data at time t is denoted as $\mathbf{o}_t = \{\mathbf{o}_{t,\text{camera}}, \mathbf{o}_{t,\text{tactile}}, \mathbf{o}_{t,\text{imu}}, \mathbf{o}_{t,\text{robot}}, \mathbf{o}_{t,\text{gripper}}\}$. The observation sequence with length T_o at time t is denoted as $\mathbf{O}_t = \{\mathbf{o}_{t-T_o+1}, ..., \mathbf{o}_t\}$. The action of the robot and the gripper at time t is denoted as $\mathbf{a}_t = \{\mathbf{a}_{t,\text{robot}}, \mathbf{a}_{t,\text{gripper}}\}$, where $\mathbf{a}_{t,\text{robot}} = \Delta \mathbf{o}_{t,\text{gripper}}$ and $\mathbf{a}_{t,\text{robot}} = \Delta \mathbf{o}_{t,\text{gripper}}$. The action sequence with length T_p at time t is denoted as $\mathbf{A}_t = \{\mathbf{a}_{t-T_o+1}, ..., \mathbf{a}_t, ..., \mathbf{o}_{t-T_o+T_p}\}$.

Instead of using the human motion capture [13], the keyboard is used to obtain human commands. The action mapping of GUI is illustrated in Table 1. For the key "rake" of the gripper, the fourth element of $\mathbf{o}_{t,\text{gripper}}$ is set to 80.

3 Semi-buried Object Excavation Method

In this section, a visual-tactile fusion-driven diffusion policy is proposed to generate the robotic action sequence $\mathbf{A}_t$ according to the observation sequence $\mathbf{O}_t$. The framework of the policy is shown in Fig. 3.

Table 1. Action Mapping of Graphical User Interface

Key	Action $\mathbf{a}_{t,\text{robot}}$	Key	Action $\mathbf{a}_{t,\text{gripper}}$
"±x"	$\pm[5\text{ mm}, 0, 0, 0, 0, 0]^T$	"rake"	$+[5, 5, 0, 0]^T$ (°)
"±y"	$\pm[0, 5\text{ mm}, 0, 0, 0, 0]^T$	"release rake"	$-[5, 5, 0, 0]^T$ (°)
"±z"	$\pm[0, 0, 5\text{ mm}, 0, 0, 0]^T$	"grasp"	$+[5, 5, 5, 5]^T$ (°)
"±rz"	$\pm[0, 0, 0, 0, 0, 5°]^T$	"release grasp"	$-[5, 5, 5, 5]^T$ (°)

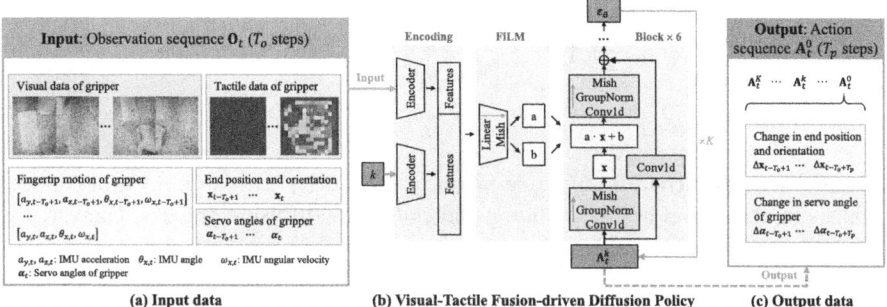

Fig. 3. Framework. (a) The input observation sequence $\mathbf{O}_t$ of the policy. (b) The visual-tactile fusion-driven diffusion policy. (c) The output action sequence $\mathbf{A}_t^0$ of the policy.

3.1 Diffusion Model for Action Learning and Generating

Denoising diffusion probabilistic model (DDPM) [14] is a latent variable model. Given a sample $\mathbf{A}^0$ from data distribution $q(\mathbf{A}^0)$, DDPM aims to learn a distribution $p_\theta(\mathbf{A}^0)$ with parameter θ that can approximate distribution $q(\mathbf{A}^0)$ and easily sampled. DDPM consists of two processes: the diffusion process and the denoising process.

Diffusion Process. The diffusion process follows a Markov chain that gradually adds Gaussian noise to the data. The parameterization of the prior distribution $q(\mathbf{A}^k|\mathbf{A}^{k-1})$ is,

$$\mathbf{A}^k = \sqrt{1-\beta^k}\mathbf{A}^{k-1} + \sqrt{\beta^k}\epsilon, \epsilon \sim \mathcal{N}(\mathbf{0}, \mathbf{I}). \tag{4}$$

where $\beta^{1:K}$, with $\beta^k \in (0, 1)$ for each k, is an incremental variance schedule. At step k, the sample $\mathbf{A}^k$ can be computed in closed form as,

$$\mathbf{A}^k = \sqrt{\bar{\alpha}^k}\mathbf{A}^0 + \sqrt{1-\bar{\alpha}^k}\epsilon, \epsilon \sim \mathcal{N}(\mathbf{0}, \mathbf{I}), \tag{5}$$

where $\alpha^k := 1-\beta^k, \bar{\alpha}^k := \prod_{s=1}^k \alpha^s$.

DDPM constructs a noise predictor ϵ_θ with parameter θ to predict the noise ϵ of $\mathbf{A}^k$, which plays an important role in the denoising process. The loss function used for the learning of ϵ_θ is,

$$\mathcal{L} = \text{MSE}\left(\epsilon, \epsilon_\theta(\sqrt{\bar{\alpha}^k}\mathbf{A}^0 + \sqrt{1-\bar{\alpha}^k}\epsilon, k)\right). \tag{6}$$

For robots, the generation process of actions is regulated by observation. Therefore, DDPM is used to approximate the conditional distribution $p_\theta(\mathbf{A}_t|\mathbf{O}_t)$ at time t. The loss in Eq. (6) can be rewritten as:

$$\mathcal{L} = \text{MSE}\left(\epsilon, \epsilon_\theta(\mathbf{O}_t, \sqrt{\bar{\alpha}^k}\mathbf{A}_t^0 + \sqrt{1-\bar{\alpha}^k}\epsilon, k)\right). \tag{7}$$

Denoising Process. The denoising process generates data $\mathbf{A}_t^0$ progressively from a random sample $\mathbf{A}_t^K \sim \mathcal{N}(\mathbf{0}, \mathbf{I})$ by,

$$\mathbf{A}_t^{k-1} = \frac{1}{\sqrt{\alpha^k}}\left(\mathbf{A}_t^k - \frac{\beta^k}{\sqrt{1-\bar{\alpha}^k}}\epsilon_\theta(\mathbf{O}_t, \mathbf{A}_t^k, k)\right) + \sigma^k \mathbf{z}, \tag{8}$$

where $\mathbf{z} \sim \mathcal{N}(\mathbf{0}, \mathbf{I})$, $(\sigma^k)^2 = \beta^k$.

Cosine Variance Schedule. Cosine variance schedule [15] is used to avoid sudden changes in noise level at the beginning and end of the diffusion process. The variance β^k is constructed according to $\bar{\alpha}^k$,

$$\bar{\alpha}^k = \frac{f(k)}{f(0)}, f(k) = \cos\left(\frac{k/K+s}{1+s}\cdot\frac{\pi}{2}\right)^2, \tag{9}$$

$$\beta^k = 1 - \frac{\bar{\alpha}^k}{\bar{\alpha}^{k-1}}, \tag{10}$$

where s is offset. $s = 0.008$ in this work.

DDIM Inference. To reduce the number of iterations of the action generation process, denoising diffusion implicit models (DDIM) [16] construct alternative non-Markovian inference processes that share the same objective function with DDPM. The new inference processes of DDIM is,

$$\mathbf{A}_t^m = \sqrt{\bar{\alpha}^m}\left(\frac{\mathbf{A}_t^k - \sqrt{1-\bar{\alpha}^k}\epsilon_\theta(\mathbf{O}_t, \mathbf{A}_t^k, k)}{\sqrt{\bar{\alpha}^k}}\right)$$
$$+ \sqrt{1-\bar{\alpha}^m - (\sigma^k)^2}\epsilon_\theta(\mathbf{O}_t, \mathbf{A}_t^k, k) + \sigma^k \mathbf{z}, \tag{11}$$

where $0 \leq m < k \leq K$, $\mathbf{z} \sim \mathcal{N}(\mathbf{0}, \mathbf{I})$, $\sigma^k = \sqrt{(1-\bar{\alpha}^m)/(1-\bar{\alpha}^k)}\sqrt{1-\bar{\alpha}^k/\bar{\alpha}^m}$.

3.2 Feature Encoder and Action Modulation

Three different encoders are constructed to extract valid information from the raw observations. The visual encoder for a single image from the monocular camera is constructed based on ResNet-18. In total, there are two visual encoders for two cameras. The detailed structures of the visual encoder, the tactile encoder, and the iteration step k encoder are shown in Fig. 4. The remaining observations are directly concatenated with these features after normalization. Finally, all features are used for action modulation via feature-wise linear modulation (FiLM). The detailed modulation process is shown in Fig. 3(b).

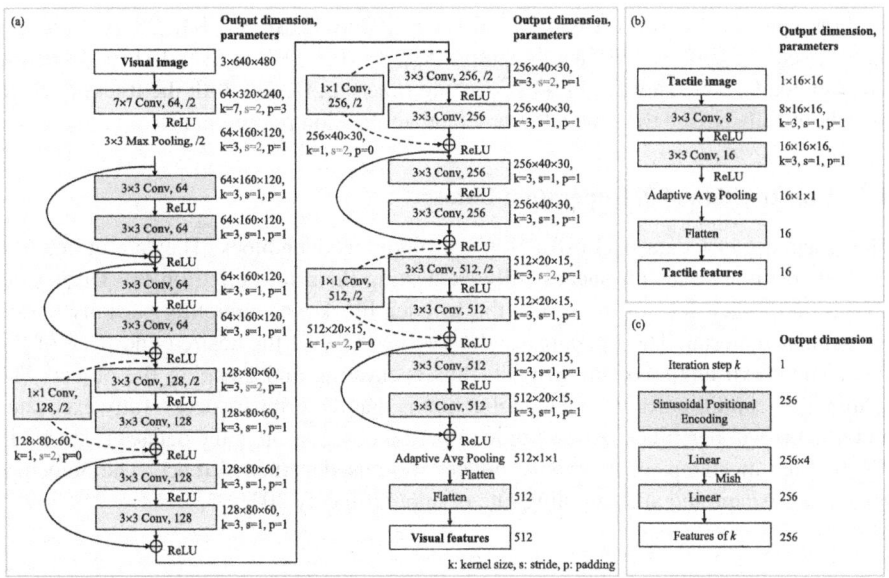

Fig. 4. Observation encoder. (a) Visual encoder. (b) Tactile encoder. (c) Iteration step k encoder.

4 Experiments and Discussions

In this section, experiments are conducted to characterize the performance of the developed system and the excavation policy, including robotic end pose tracking, Comparison of Different Sensors and Inference Method, and robotic excavation of semi-buried object.

4.1 Robotic End Pose Tracking

Tracking test of step input is conducted to evaluate the tracking performance of the teleoperation system. Tracking curves of end pose are shown in Fig. 5. Metrics including integral absolute error (IAE $= \int_0^\infty |\mathbf{x}_e(t)|\, dt$), integral square error (ISE $= \int_0^\infty \mathbf{x}_e^2(t)\, dt$), overshoot, and 2% settling time are used to evaluate the tracking performance.

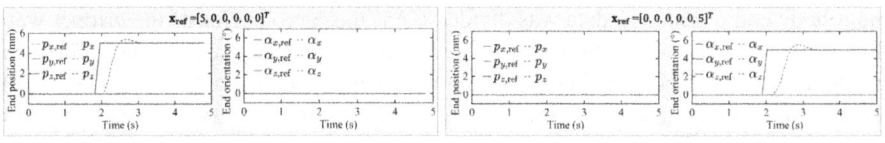

Fig. 5. Tracking curves of the step input of the robot end position and end orientation.

For input $\mathbf{x}_{\text{ref}} = (5, 0, 0, 0, 0, 0)^T$, IAE = 2.02e-03, ISE = 7.83e-06, overshoot = 6.55%, settling time = 4.7958 s. For input $\mathbf{x}_{\text{ref}} = (0, 0, 0, 0, 0, 5)^T$, IAE = 4.66e-02, ISE = 3.20e-03, overshoot = 11.44%, settling time = 5.3183 s. Both the tracking error, overshoot and settling time meet the practical application requirements.

4.2 Construction of Teleoperation Dataset

The object used for dataset construction is a cuboid wooden block. The dataset includes 100 sets of time series for successfully excavating the semi-buried object. During the collection of each set of time series, the wooden block was randomly partially buried in granular material. The operator used a keyboard to set the desired end pose of the robot and servo angles of the gripper, thus excavating and grasping the object. The termination condition for each data collection is that the gripper successfully excavates and lifts the wooden block. An example of partial observation in the dataset is shown in Fig. 6. The timestamps of two visual images were used as the reference. The binocular images were captured at a sampling rate of approximately 20 Hz.

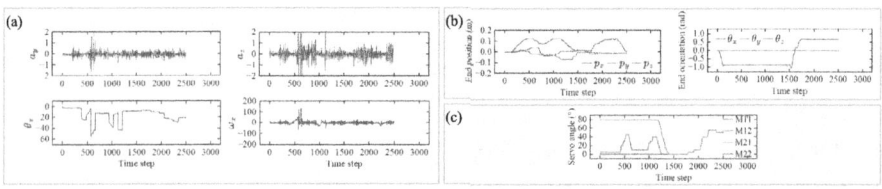

Fig. 6. An example of partial observation in the dataset. (a) Fingertip motion of gripper. (b) End position and orientation. (c) Servo angles of gripper.

After collecting 100 sets of time series and completing timestamp synchronization, each time series was segmented by randomly selecting a starting timestamp and then normalized. For time series segmentation, it should be noted that the policy model operates at a real-time frequency of approximately 2 Hz. To align the data sampling rate 20 Hz with this operational frequency, the interval between adjacent slice indices was set to 10. Using this method, each time series yields 800 observation-action slice pairs. Consequently, the complete dataset contains a total of 100×800 observation-action slice pairs.

For normalization of observation data, the image data was divided by 255, the IMU angle component was divided by 60, the robotic end position data was divided by 0.5, the robotic end orientation data was divided by π, the servo angles of the gripper were divided by 80°, and other observation data has not been processed. For normalization of action data, the robotic end position increments were divided by 0.05 (= 0.005×10), the robotic end orientation increments were divided by 0.5 (= 0.05×10), and the servo angle increments of the gripper were divided by 50 (= 5×10). After data normalization, the observation data slices fed into the policy model were of length $T_o = 2$, while the action data slices output by the policy model were of length $T_p = 8$. The executed action sequence length was 4.

4.3 Influence of Different Sensors and Inference Methods

The influence of different sensors and inference methods is investigated to evaluate the enhanced performance of sensors and determine appropriate model parameters.

Different Sensors. To study the impact of additional sensing components on model performance, this subsection gradually adds sensor data to the model input to evaluate their contributions to the overall model performance. The loss of the model trained with different sensors is shown in Fig. 7. Using visual-only data as the baseline, the final loss of the model is further reduced after progressively incorporating tactile data, IMU data, and motion data. It demonstrates that the added sensory components can provide additional useful information to the model, thereby enhancing its performance.

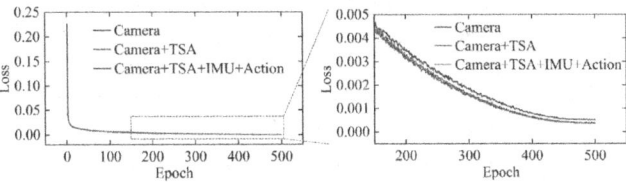

Fig. 7. Loss of model with different sensors.

Different Inference Methods. Inference time and inference error are two critical factors for practical model deployment. Comparing different inference methods aims to select appropriate parameters that balance these two metrics. MSE is used to characterize inference error,

$$\mathrm{MSE} = \frac{1}{n} \sum_{i=1}^{n} (y_i - \hat{y}_i)^2, \qquad (12)$$

where n is the number of actions. y_i and $\hat{y}_i$ are the actual value and the predicted value of the action, respectively.

DDPM inference and DDIM inference with different steps are compared. The model training was performed on a server with the following hardware specifications: GPU is NVIDIA GeForce RTX 4090, CPU is Intel(R) Xeon(R) Gold 6326 @ 2.90 GHz. Average time of 800 inferences and MSE are shown in Fig. 8, where "DDIM-100" indicates "inference method-number of iterations". As the number of iterations decreases, the average time decreases, but the MSE increases. When the number of iterations is 10, the average time is 0.1 s and MSE is 0.0015. Therefore, DDIM inference with 10 steps is used in the subsequent physical experiments.

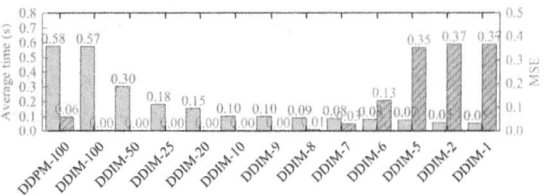

Fig. 8. Comparison between DDPM inference and DDIM inference.

4.4 Robotic Excavation of Semi-buried Object

In the semi-buried object excavation experiment, the cuboid wooden block was selected as the test object, and the experiment was repeated 10 times. The success or failure of each experiment and the time consumption were recorded. During each experiment, the cuboid wooden block was semi-buried in the sand with random orientations. The initial states of the objects in the 10 experiments are shown in Fig. 9(a), and the objects are located in different areas of the binocular field of view. The computer hardware configuration used in the experiment is as follows: the graphics card is NVIDIA GeForce GTX 1050 Ti, and the CPU is Intel(R) Core(TM) i5-8300H CPU @ 2.30 GHz.

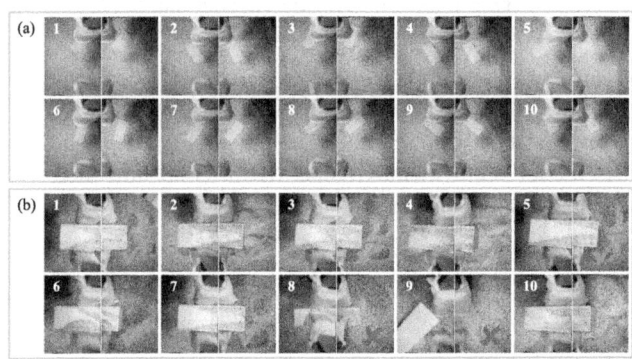

Fig. 9. States of semi-buried object in ten experiments. (a) Initial states. (b) Final states. (Color figure online)

During the object excavation, the action policy generates and executes increments of the robotic end pose and servo angles. Due to hardware limitations, the operating frequency of the policy is approximately 2 Hz. Each action generation is based on the observation data from the historical 2 steps, predicts 8 steps of actions covering both recent history and the near future, and executes the next 4 steps of actions. After executing all the action sequences generated by the policy, the final state of the object is shown in Fig. 9(b). The green checkmark in the figure indicates successful object grasping, while the red cross indicates failed object grasping.

A successful object grasping experiment demonstrates the robot excavation process in Fig. reffigspssamplespsdatasetspscamera. 0–12 s, the gripper adjusts its orientation to align with the object for excavation. 12–24 s, the gripper excavates along one side of the object. 24–36 s, the gripper is lifted and moves above the opposite side of the object. 36–48 s, the gripper excavates along the opposite side. 48–60 s, the gripper is lifted and located above the object. 60–72 s, the gripper adjusts to a perpendicular orientation for grasping. 72–84 s, the gripper attempts to grasp the object. 84–108 s, the gripper successfully grasps and lifts the object to complete the task.

During the excavation, action increments generated by the policy model are shown in Fig. 11(a). The sum of these increments and the current robot state yields the desired robotic actions, as shown in Fig. 11(b). The first two rows of the figure display the changes in the robot end position, while the third row shows the changes in the servo angles of the gripper. It is noted that compared with the original data curves of the dataset in Fig. 6, the robotic actions generated by the policy model exhibit higher smoothness, thereby reducing the jitter of the robot during task execution (Fig. 10).

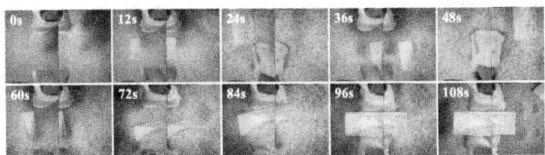

Fig. 10. Snapshots of successful excavation process.

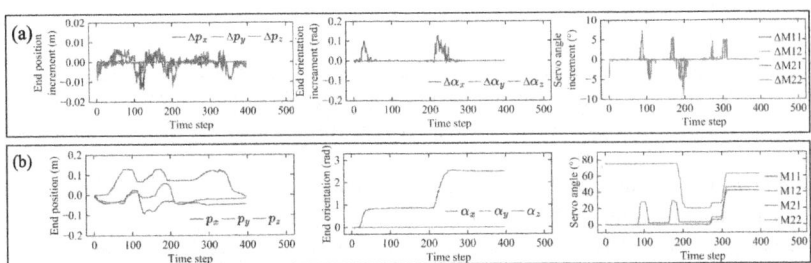

Fig. 11. Actions in actual experiment. (a) Generated action of the policy. (b) Robotic action.

Table 2 presents outcomes and time consumption of the 10 trials. The system achieves an 80% success rate in excavating the semi-buried object, with an average time consumption of 103 s. There were two failed cases in total. 1) In the 8th experiment, the gripper accidentally slipped from the gripper during grasping, causing the wooden block to overturn with its edge facing upward. Due to the smooth surface of the wooden block, the gripper failed to achieve an effective grasp, and the generated actions fell into a local stagnation state, ultimately leading to failed grasp. 2) In the 9th experiment, the policy model generated an invalid grasping configuration, resulting in failed grasp.

Table 2. Results of robotic excavation

Metrics	1	2	3	4	5	6	7	8	9	10	Average
Success	1	1	1	1	1	1	1	0	0	1	0.80
Time (s)	108	102	89	112	87	98	92	/	/	133	103

5 Conclusion and Future Work

In this work, we first develop a visual-tactile adaptive gripper and the teleoperation system. Based on the system, a visual-tactile fusion-driven diffusion policy is proposed to learn the operator demonstration and generate feasible robotic action for excavating the semi-buried object. Experiments including robotic end pose tracking and object excavation are conducted to validate the effectiveness of the robotic system and the policy. Experimental results show that 1) the system can track actions of the operator in real-time, and 2) the policy allows the gripper to perceive the dynamic change of the buried object, and generate effective actions for excavating the semi-buried object in granular media. Nevertheless, this work only considers one kind of granular media. In the future, we will also consider other granular media during the data collection process.

Acknowledgments. This work was supported by the Natural Science Foundation of China under Grant 52205520 and Grant 52188102.

References

1. Deng, L., Wang, Y., Yue, Z., Li, Z.: A robotic tactile excavation system for excavating objects buried in granular materials. IEEE/ASME Trans. Mechatron. 1–13 (2025)
2. Xu, J., et al.: Tactile-based object retrieval from granular media. arXiv preprint arXiv:2402.04536 (2024)
3. Tuomainen, N., Blanco-Mulero, D., Kyrki, V.: Manipulation of granular materials by learning particle interactions. IEEE Robot. Autom. Lett. **7**(2), 5663–5670 (2022)
4. Shen, Y., Tai, R., Zhang, J., Deng, L., Yuan, Y., Rong, S., Zhang, F., Ding, H.: Planning and motion control for underwater bimanual soft manipulator in underwater grasping task. IEEE/ASME Trans. Mechatron. **29**(4), 2487–2498 (2024)
5. Zhang, Z., et al.: GRAINS: proximity sensing of objects in granular materials. arXiv preprint arXiv:2307.05935 (2023)
6. Matl, C., Narang, Y., Bajcsy, R., Ramos, F., Fox, D.: Inferring the material properties of granular media for robotic tasks. In: 2020 IEEE International Conference on Robotics and Automation (ICRA), pp. 2770–2777 (2020)
7. Gravish, N., Umbanhowar, P.B., Goldman, D.I.: Force and flow at the onset of drag in plowed granular media. Phys. Rev. E **89**(4), 042202 (2014)
8. Bohg, J., Morales, A., Asfour, T., Kragic, D.: Data-driven grasp synthesis–a survey. IEEE Trans. Rob. **30**(2), 289–309 (2014)
9. Liu, H., Sampath, S.K., Wang, N., Yang, C.: Multifingered grasp planning based on gaussian process implicit surface and its partial differentials. IEEE/ASME Trans. Mechatron. **29**(5), 3522–3533 (2024)

10. Mahler, J., et al.: Learning ambidextrous robot grasping policies. Sci. Robot. **4**(26), eaau4984 (2019)
11. Murray, R.M., Li, Z., Sastry, S.S.: A Mathematical Introduction to Robotic Manipulation. CRC Press (2017)
12. Deng, L., Zhang, J., Yue, Z., Li, Z., Yuan, Y., Ding, H.: Active learning-aided design of a flexible tactile sensor array for recognizing properties of deformable objects. IEEE Trans. Instrum. Meas. **73**, 1–11 (2024)
13. Dong, Y., Liu, X., Wan, J., Deng, Z.: GEX: democratizing dexterity with fully-actuated dexterous hand and exoskeleton glove (2025)
14. Ho, J., Jain, A., Abbeel, P.: Denoising diffusion probabilistic models. In: Advances in Neural Information Processing Systems, vol. 33, pp. 6840–6851 (2020)
15. Nichol, A.Q., Dhariwal, P.: Improved denoising diffusion probabilistic models. In: International Conference on Machine Learning, pp. 8162–8171. PMLR (2021)
16. Song, J., Meng, C., Ermon, S.: Denoising diffusion implicit models. In: International Conference on Learning Representations (2021)

RCTAMP: Enhancing Rule-Constrained TAMP via Multi-agent Closed-Loop Collaboration Integrating Consensus Planning

Zhongxing Wei[1,2], Xiaodong Ye[1,2(✉)], Huachen Tan[3], Junhong Zhao[1,2], Meiling Wang[1], and Yucheng Wang[1]

[1] Hefei Institutes of Physical Science, Chinese Academy of Sciences, Hefei 230031, China
zxwei213@mail.ustc.edu.cn, xdye@iamt.ac.cn
[2] University of Science and Technology of China, Hefei 230026, China
[3] School of Big Data and Software Engineering, Chongqing University, Chongqing 401331, China

Abstract. Large Language Models (LLMs) have demonstrated great potential in robotic task and motion planning (TAMP). However, existing works rarely address tasks that demand both goal achievement and strict compliance with task rules, posing greater challenges for robots. Moreover, LLM-based motion failure correction methods relying solely on textual feedback struggle in complex environments. To address these issues, we propose a novel multi-agent TAMP framework that integrates consensus planning with a cross-layer motion failure correction mechanism. The framework enables hierarchical collaboration of LLM-driven multi-role agents. Specifically, at the task planning layer, multiple agents reach consensus on a semantic task plan through multi-round deliberation, ensuring its accuracy and rule compliance. At the action grounding layer, action sequences with continuous parameters are generated by the specialized agent under the guidance of the semantic plan, effectively bridging the task planning and motion planning layers. Furthermore, a cross-layer correction mechanism based on a visual reasoning agent enhances the ability to handle motion failures. Extensive experiments show that our framework significantly outperforms baselines in task success rate, rule compliance, and motion planning efficiency and robustness.

Keywords: Large language models · Task and motion planning · Multi-agent consensus

1 Introduction

With the rapid development of large language models (LLMs), they have shown great promise in robotic task planning [1–5]. LLMs enable robots to generate task plans directly from natural language, simplifying traditional manual modeling and domain-specific programming. Researchers have extended LLMs to Task and Motion Planning (TAMP), enabling them to generate action sequences with continuous parameters [6–8]. LLM-based TAMP offers superior generalization and adaptability compared to conventional methods.

However, significant challenges remain in TAMP. For task planning, most existing methods mainly focus on simple tasks and maximizing success rates, overlooking complex, context-dependent task rules such as safety constraints, action order, user preferences, and object layout. These rules are often expressed in natural language and often carry semantic ambiguity and uncertainty, imposing higher demands on language understanding and reasoning. For example, users may require robots to first group items and then arrange or stack them in a specific order. Such unstructured, context-sensitive rules pose challenges for task planning. Some studies formalize safety constraints via Linear Temporal Logic and enforce compliance through specific frameworks [9,10], which is effective for structured rules but struggles with unstructured ones like spatial semantics and preferences. As robots enter real-world environments rule compliance becomes essential for operational safety, user satisfaction, and other reasons.

For motion planning, prior work [7] shows that using LLMs as action parameter samplers improves efficiency over random sampling, but LLM-generated parameters remain stochastic, causing failures. Some methods use textual feedback to iteratively adjust parameters after failure [7,8], but this approach is inefficient in complex scenarios with stacked or occluded objects. LLMs tend to fine-tune placements repeatedly rather than adjusting action order, leading to slow convergence and motion failures. Thus, parameter-level corrections alone are insufficient for handling motion failures in complex scenes.

To address these challenges, we propose RCTAMP, a LLM-driven multi-agent TAMP framework integrating consensus planning and cross-layer motion failure correction mechanism. Our method employs multiple LLM agents to collaboratively (i) reach consensus on semantic plans that comply with task rules, (ii) ground them into action sequences with continuous parameters, and (iii) identify motion failures based on visual reasoning and correct them across both the task planning and action grounding layers. A key advantage of our approach lies in the combination of enhanced reasoning capability for task planning and improved efficiency in correcting motion failures. Together, these strengths contribute to significantly higher task success rates and better compliance with diverse rules in complex tasks.

In summary, our contributions can be summarized as follows:

(1) We propose a novel LLM-driven TAMP framework that effectively addresses complex rule-constrained tasks through hierarchical closed-loop collaboration among multi-role agents.
(2) We introduce multi-agent consensus planning to enhance task reasoning and rule compliance, along with a cross-layer correction mechanism based on visual reasoning to handle motion failures effectively.

(3) Extensive experiments demonstrate the significant advantages of our proposed method over state-of-the-art methods, highlighting its potential for further research and real-world applications.

2 Related Work

Robot Planning with LLMs. Recent studies have used LLMs for task planning [1-3,11], and TAMP [6-8]. Specifically, AutoTAMP [6] converts natural language instructions into structured representations suitable for existing TAMP algorithms via an LLM. LLM^3 [7] leverages an LLM to directly generate symbolic action sequences with continuous parameters, while iteratively reasoning and refining its planning proposals. Onto-LLM [8] further reduces semantic errors with ontology-based prompt-tuning. These studies mainly focus on enhancing task planning or improving parameters sampling efficiency with LLMs, with limited attention to joint task-motion optimization. In contrast, we aim to optimize both to significantly improve TAMP performance for rule-constrained tasks.

LLM-Based Multi-agent System. LLMs are inherently limited by issues such as hallucination, causing suboptimal outputs and reduced performance. Prior work has introduced Chain-of-Thought (CoT) [12] prompting to enhance output quality through step-by-step reasoning; other studies have adopted multi-agent systems with specialized roles to outperform single-agent systems [13-17]. While most multi-agent systems rely on a single planner, struggles with reasoning and rule compliance in complex long-horizon tasks. To address these, we combine CoT reasoning and hierarchical collaboration by explicitly decoupling high-level planning from action sequences generation. We introduce the multi-agent consensus planning method to improve both the semantic accuracy of the task plan and its compliance with task rules.

3 Method

We propose RCTAMP, an LLM-driven multi-agent TAMP framework, to handle complex rule-constrained tasks. As shown in Fig. 1, the method integrates multi-agent consensus planning (MACP) with a cross-layer motion failure correction mechanism based on visual reasoning. Five specialized agents are employed, all powered by GPT-4o, a multimodal LLM capable of processing both text and visual inputs [18]. We access GPT-4o via the OpenAI APIs.

3.1 Framework of the Proposed RCTAMP

As shown in Fig. 1, RCTAMP comprises two planners and a decision agent for task planning, a grounding agent for action grounding, a supervisor agent for failure reasoning, and uses RRT-Connect for motion planning.

At the task planning layer, two planners independently generate initial task plans. Under the guidance of a decision agent, if the plans are inconsistent or violate task rules, the system enters a consensus-seeking phase, where the planners iteratively refine their outputs to reach consensus on a rule-compliant semantic plan. The grounding agent then formalizes this semantic plan into action sequences with continuous parameters, based on the environment state. These actions are sent to the motion planner, which generates trajectories and returns motion feedback. Upon motion failure, the supervisor agent performs visual reasoning based on motion feedback and environmental context to locate the cause—whether in task planning or action parameterization—and triggers replanning or resampling accordingly. This cross-layer correction continues iteratively until a complete and executable action sequence is produced, ensuring robust task execution.

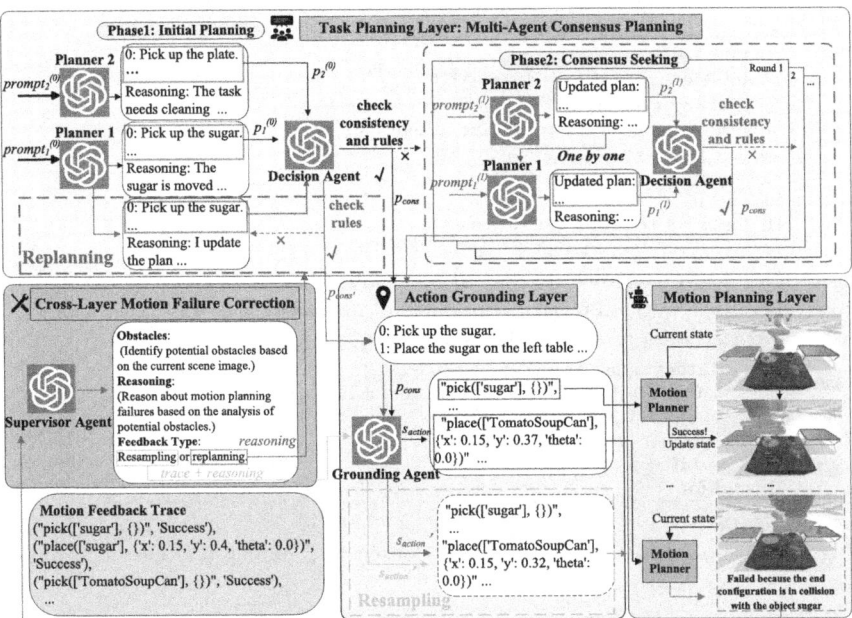

Fig. 1. Overview of our proposed framework, which consists of three layers and a cross-layer failure correction mechanism: (1) the task planning layer generates a rule-compliant semantic plan; (2) the action grounding layer formalizes the semantic plan into action sequences with continuous parameters; (3) the motion planning layer generates trajectories and feedback. A supervisor agent reasons over motion failures and adaptively triggers replanning or resampling.

3.2 Multi-agent Consensus Planning

Inspired by [17,19,20], we propose Multi-Agent Consensus Planning (MACP), a novel task planning method that enables multiple agents to reach consensus on a rule-compliant semantic plan through multi-round deliberations.

MACP includes three LLM agents: Planner 1 (P1), Planner 2 (P2), and the Decision Agent (DA). The P1 and P2 generate high-level task plans, where P1 serves as the primary planner and additionally performs replanning upon motion failures. They are differentiated by distinct contextual examples in their prompts. The DA operates in two modes: check mode evaluates plans consistency and rule compliance after each iteration to determine if further iterations are needed; selection mode chooses the optimal plan upon consensus or the final iteration.

Algorithm 1 Multi-Agent Consensus Planning

Require: Task T, Rules R, Environment State E, MaxRounds N
Ensure: Consensus Semantic Plan p_{cons}
1: Initialize empty list `history` $\leftarrow []$
2: **for** $i = 1, 2$ (for planners P_i) **do**
3: $\quad (p_i^{(0)}, r_i^{(0)}) \leftarrow \text{Prompt}_{\text{init}}(P_i, T, R, E)$
4: **end for**
5: $(decision, feedback) \leftarrow \text{DA.check}(p_1^{(0)}, p_2^{(0)}, T, R)$
6: `history.append(` $(p_1^{(0)}, r_1^{(0)}, p_2^{(0)}, r_2^{(0)}, feedback)$ `)`
7: **if** $decision \neq$ 'Need to refine' **then**
8: $\quad p_{\text{cons}} \leftarrow \text{DA.select}(p_1^{(0)}, p_2^{(0)})$
9: $\quad$ **return** p_{cons}
10: **end if**
11: **for** $n = 1$ to N **do**
12: $\quad (p_1^{(n)}, r_1^{(n)}) \leftarrow \text{Prompt}_d(P_1, \text{prompt}_1^{(n-1)}, \text{history})$
13: $\quad$ `history.append(` $(p_1^{(n)}, r_1^{(n)})$ `)`
14: $\quad (p_2^{(n)}, r_2^{(n)}) \leftarrow \text{Prompt}_d(P_2, \text{prompt}_2^{(n-1)}, \text{history})$
15: $\quad (decision, feedback) \leftarrow \text{DA.check}(p_1^{(n)}, p_2^{(n)}, T, R)$
16: $\quad$ `history.append(` $(p_2^{(n)}, r_2^{(n)}, feedback)$ `)`
17: $\quad$ **if** $decision \neq$ 'Need to refine' **or** $n = N$ **then**
18: $\quad\quad p_{\text{cons}} \leftarrow \text{DA.select}(p_1^{(n)}, p_2^{(n)})$
19: $\quad\quad$ **return** p_{cons}
20: $\quad$ **end if**
21: **end for**

Fig. 2. Pseudocode for the Multi-Agent Consensus Planning (MACP) algorithm.

As detailed in Fig. 2, initially, the two planners independently generate semantic plans and reasoning traces based on contextual information, including task descriptions, rules, and the textualized environment state. The DA then evaluates the consistency between the two plans and their compliance with task rules. If both criteria are satisfied, the DA selects one plan as the final consensus plan. It is important to note that this consistency check is based on structural alignment rather than exact textual matching, enhancing flexibility and robustness while ensuring semantic equivalence.

If inconsistencies or rule violations are detected, the system enters a consensus-seeking phase, during which the planners sequentially update their plans in each iteration. First, P1 reflects on the history of plans, reasoning traces, and feedback from the DA to decide whether to retain or optimize its plan. Subsequently, P2 incorporates the same historical information along with P1's latest update to similarly reflect and then update its plan. After each iteration, the DA evaluates consistency and rule compliance. This process continues until the two planners reach consensus on the task plan or the maximum number of iterations is exceeded, at which point the most appropriate plan is selected as the final consensus to prevent infinite iterations.

3.3 Action Grounding and Motion Planning

Action Grounding. We employ an Grounding Agent (GA) that, based on the environment state and the robot's primitive actions, converts each step in the consensus semantic plan into symbolic actions with continuous parameters, thus mapping high-level semantics to executable actions. For example, the step "Place the TomatoSoupCan to the right of the sugar on the left table" can be grounded as Place([TomatoSoupCan], 'x': 0.27,'y': 0.5,'theta': 0.0), specifying explicit target position and orientation.

Motion Planning. Each action generated by the GA is processed by a motion planning module that works with a low-level motion planner to compute feasible, collision-free trajectories for the robotic arm. We use the RRTConnect algorithm for its efficiency and reliability in constrained environments. Following [7,8], we synthesize categorized motion planning feedback using templates: (a) the end configuration is in collision with *object* (e.g., apple, cup), (b) no collision-free trajectory is found, (c) no feasible IK solution.

3.4 Cross-Layer Motion Failure Correction Mechanism

Building on the motion failure reasoning framework in [7], we enhance it by leveraging a Supervisor Agent (SA) that utilizes visual reasoning to analyze and diagnose motion failures and triggers replanning or resampling accordingly.

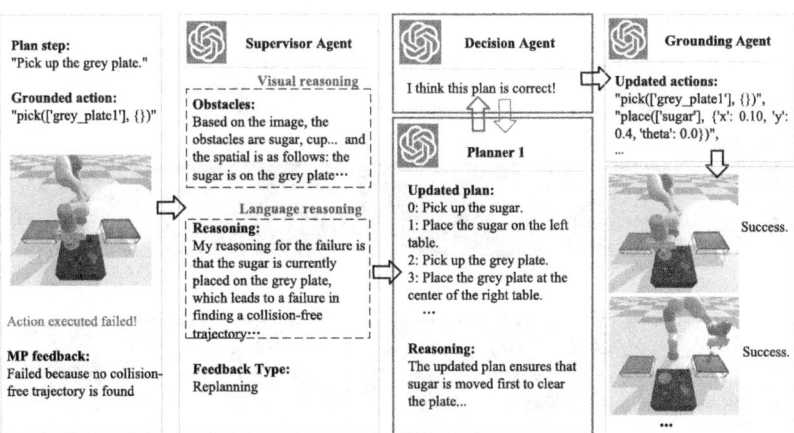

Fig. 3. Example of motion failure correction. The purple region indicates the replanning process; removing it shows the resampling process.

As illustrated in Fig. 3, when a motion failure occurs, the SA analyzes the scene image to identify potential obstacles and their spatial relationships to the target object. Based on this analysis, it reasons whether the failure stems from high-level task plan errors or suboptimal action parameters, and accordingly initiates one of the following: (1) replanning: the SA's reasoning is fed back to P1, which adjusts the task plan. The revised plan is then iteratively refined with guidance from the DA until it fully complies with task rules, followed by action grounding and motion planning; (2) resampling: the task plan remains unchanged. Instead, the SA's reasoning is incorporated into the motion trace and passed to the GA, which adjusts the action parameters before motion planning resumes. The correction process iterates until a valid executable action sequence is obtained or the iteration limit is reached.

4 Experiment

In Sect. 4.1, we separately evaluate MACP through comparative experiments in VirtualHome [21]. In Sect. 4.2, we evaluate the overall performance of RCTAMP via comparative experiments and analyze the impact of its key components through ablation studies. In Sect. 4.3, we validate the practical effectiveness of our framework in a real-world setting.

4.1 VirtualHome Simulation

To validate the effectiveness of our Multi-Agent Consensus Planning (MACP) method, we conducted comparative experiments in VirtualHome, a simulation environment rich daily scenes and objects. Agents executed multi-step plans generated by LLMs, which occasionally violated predefined task rules. Compared to Progprompt [2], our method handles such challenges more effectively.

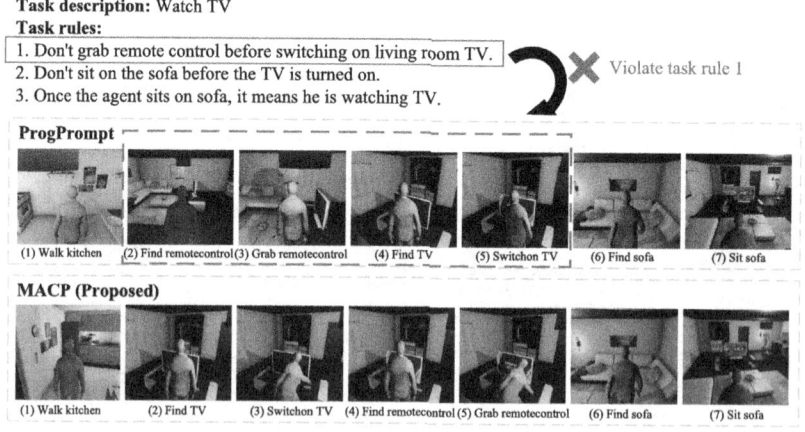

Fig. 4. Comparison of task plans generated by ProgPrompt [2] and our method for the "Watch TV" task in VirtualHome. ProgPrompt violates rule 1, while our method complies with all task rules. Rule violations are highlighted in red. (Color figure online)

As shown in Fig. 4, for the "Watch TV" task with three task rules, Prog-Prompt generated a plan that executes "Grab remote control" before "Switch on TV", violating Rule 1 and indicating limited rule awareness. In contrast, MACP employed a dual-Planner setup, where two Planners independently generate the task plan and reasoning, respectively. The Decision Agent (DA) evaluated the consistency and rule compliance of both plans and provides feedback when discrepancies or rule violations are detected, guiding the planners through iterative self-reflection and plan refinement. This process ultimately generates a semantically accurate and fully rule-compliant plan.

We conduct five iterations for each task, each with three predefined rules. $|A|$ represents the average plan length generated by the LLM. CR indicates the rule compliance rate. $Exec$ denotes the ratio of successfully executed semantic actions. SR refers to the task success rate. Unlike ProgPrompt [2], we adopt flexible success criteria based on final states of objects, allowing multiple valid outcomes. For example, the "Turn off light" task is successful if the living room light is off after execution.

Table 1. Performance comparison between MACP and ProgPrompt in VirtualHome testing tasks. Each task is associated with three predefined task rules.

Task Description	MACP				ProgPrompt [2]			
	$|A|$	CR	SR	Exec	$|A|$	CR	SR	Exec
Turn off light	3.0	1.00	1.00	1.00	4.0	1.00	1.00	0.77
Put salmon in the frige	6.0	1.00	1.00	1.00	6.4	1.00	1.00	0.98
Eat chips on the sofa	5.6	1.00	1.00	1.00	6.8	1.00	1.00	0.91
Brush teeth	6.4	1.00	1.00	1.00	7.0	1.00	1.00	0.95
Watch tv	7.2	1.00	1.00	0.98	7.4	0.73	1.00	0.98
Make toast	7.4	0.93	1.00	0.94	9.0	0.87	1.00	0.91
Throw away apple	6.4	0.93	0.80	0.95	10.6	0.87	1.00	0.90
Bring coffeepot and cupcake to the coffee table	10.4	1.00	1.00	1.00	12.6	0.73	0.20	0.85
Wash the plate	11.8	0.93	0.80	0.98	15.4	0.40	0.60	0.87
Microwave salmon	11.4	1.00	1.00	1.00	17.8	0.87	0.60	0.87

As shown in Table 1, MACP outperforms ProgPrompt across most metrics, producing more concise, efficient plans with less redundancy. Both methods show similar rule compliance and success rates on simple tasks, but ProgPrompt's performance declines significantly on complex tasks. In contrast, MACP consistently maintains high rule compliance, success rates, and executability, demonstrating strong robustness.

4.2 PyBullet Simulation

To evaluate the performance of our framework on TAMP problems, we design object sorting tasks for the Franka robotic arm in PyBullet, based on the scenario from [8], with predefined primitive actions including "Pick" and "Place".

As shown in Fig. 5, the task aims to move different categories of objects to their respective target tables. The task is described using explicit instructions ("Clean table, move plate and cup to the right table, move sugar box, tomato can, and cracker box to the left table.") and implicit instructions ("Clean dinner table, move dinnerware to the right table, and other items to the left table.") to reflect varying reasoning difficulty levels. We define five task rules: (i) avoid moving multiple objects per action; (ii) place the cup after the plate but before the cracker box; (iii) ensure the dinner table is empty in the end; (iv) place the plate at the center of the target table and arrange items on the left table in a straight line; (v) avoid placing the cup directly on the target table. These rules cover action execution, temporal order, user preferences, and spatial arrangement, significantly increasing the complexity and reasoning demands of task planning. The robot needs to comply with these diverse rules while properly organizing action sequences and spatial placements to accomplish the task accordingly.

(a) Simulation setup. (b) Task completed, rules violated. (c) Task completed, fully compliant.

Fig. 5. Examples of rule-violating and rule-compliant task completions in PyBullet.

Table 2. Performance comparison and ablation study: The table highlights the best-performing method for each task in bold. Ontology-Driven LLM is not applicable to implicit instructions and was therefore excluded from this task.

Method	Explicit Instructions				Implicit Instructions			
Baselines from [7,8]	SR	CR	#MP	#MF	SR	CR	#MP	#MF
Ontology-Driven LLM	0.10	0.12	19.9	8.6	–	–	–	–
LLM^3 backtrack	0.20	0.36	21.40	5.50	0.00	0.32	17.6	5.90
LLM^3 from scratch	0.20	0.74	27.40	4.50	0.00	0.82	20.20	4.40
Proposed Method	SR	CR	#MP	#MF	SR	CR	#MP	#MF
Overall	**0.80**	**0.94**	13.70	2.20	**0.70**	**0.92**	20.80	3.50
– w/o MACP	0.70	0.84	15.50	3.60	0.50	0.80	20.90	3.70
– w/o Grounding Agent	0.50	0.68	17.00	5.90	0.30	0.74	18.60	6.50
– w/o Failure Correction	0.10	0.20	**6.80**	–	0.10	0.10	**7.20**	–

We conducted ten iterations per task and evaluated four metrics: success rate (SR), compliance rate (CR), motion planner calls (#MP), and motion failures (#MF). SR indicates task completion regardless of rule compliance. CR measures the proportion of satisfied rules for fully executed plans. #MP and #MF together reflect the system's ability to recover from motion failures and the efficiency of motion planning. Average values are reported. As shown in Table 2, RCTAMP significantly outperforms [7,8] in SR, CR, and (#MF), with only a slightly higher (#MP) under implicit instructions. These results demonstrate RCTAMP's superior ability to handle complex task rules and implicit reasoning while maintaining high planning efficiency and robustness.

As shown in Table 2, we conducted ablation studies to assess the contribution of key modules. W/o MACP: replaces MACP with a single agent for task planning. W/o Grounding Agent: planners directly generating both semantic plans and action sequences. W/o Failure Correction: disables the cross-layer motion failure correction mechanism.

The **w/o MACP** results confirm that MACP significantly improves the rationality and rule compliance of semantic plans. This more effectively guides the grounding agent to select appropriate action parameters and generate action sequences, thereby enhancing task success rate and motion planning efficiency.

The **w/o Grounding Agent** results validate the necessity of introducing an action grounding layer to decouple semantic planning from action sequence generation. Managed by the GA, this layer reduces the burden on the high-level planner and mitigates parameter selection errors caused by overlooked environmental constraints, which often lead to task and motion failures.

The **w/o Failure Correction** results highlight its importance. In our experimental setting, tasks rarely succeed on the first attempt. Without this mechanism, the executability of action sequences decreases significantly, resulting in near-zero rule compliance and success rates.

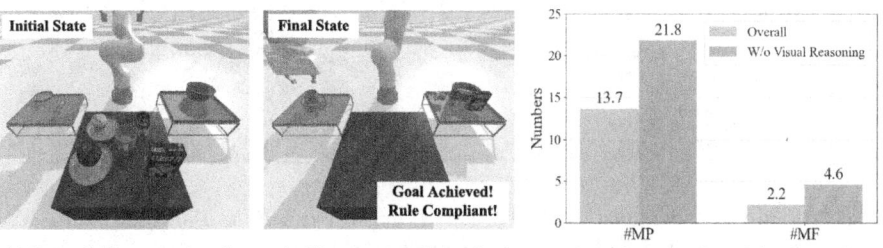

(a) Successful demonstration of our method in a more complex setting.   (b) Study on the effect of visual reasoning.

Fig. 6. Additional experiments in PyBullet.

Additionally, we conducted two supplementary experiments: one to validate RCTAMP's effectiveness in a more challenging setting, and another to assess the importance of visual reasoning in motion failure correction. As shown in Fig. 6(a), more objects and complex spatial relations increase the difficulty of action parameter selection and obstacle avoidance—ignoring stacking relations often causes motion failures. The robot must place objects correctly while following predefined rules, posing challenges to planning and execution. RCTAMP completed the tasks successfully after multiple attempts.

We ran ten iterations with explicit instructions to evaluate the effect of removing visual reasoning. As shown in Fig. 6(b), removing visual reasoning significantly increases motion failures (from 2.2 to 4.6) and planning attempts (from 12.7 to 21.8), highlighting its important contribution to the efficiency and robustness of failure correction. Compared to solely textual feedback, visual reasoning allows the SA to directly perceive spatial relationships, enabling more efficient identification of the root causes of motion failures, which results in faster recovery and fewer redundant retries.

4.3 Real Robot Demonstration

We validated our method on a real Franka Emika Panda robotic arm to demonstrate its ability to perform complex tasks while complying with task rules. We assumed a static environment where key information such as object coordinates and spatial relations was manually encoded into the LLM prompts. Figure 7 presents a qualitative evaluation where the robot placed different categories of objects on the table into designated areas without violating task rules. The successful experiment demonstrates the robustness and practical potential of our method for complex rule-constrained tasks like object sorting and household assistance.

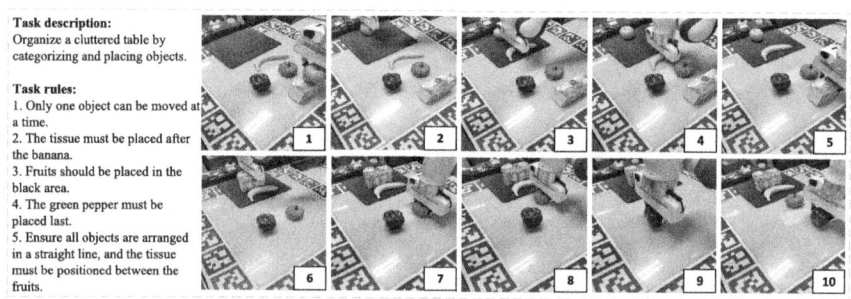

Fig. 7. Real-world demonstration: RCTAMP generated actions 1–in compliance with all task rules, and the robot executed them successfully.

5 Conclusion

This paper presents RCTAMP, an LLM-driven multi-agent TAMP framework for complex rule-constrained tasks. It integrates consensus planning and cross-layer motion failure correction mechanism within a multi-role agents hierarchical collaboration approach, significantly outperforming single-agent TAMP baselines. Extensive experiments demonstrated that RCTAMP is well-suited for complex long-horizon tasks, capable of strictly complying with task rules, and can efficiently and accurately plan and execute tasks. Future work will integrate an VLM-based perception agent with vision algorithms for object detection and scene understanding, replacing manual state encoding to improve system autonomy and scalability in real-world environments.

References

1. Brohan, A., et al.: Do as i can, not as i say: grounding language in robotic affordances. In: Conference on Robot Learning, pp. 287–318. PMLR (2023)
2. Singh, I., et al.: ProgPrompt: generating situated robot task plans using large language models. In: 2023 IEEE International Conference on Robotics and Automation (ICRA), pp. 11,523–11,530. IEEE (2023)
3. Song, C.H., Wu, J., Washington, C., Sadler, B.M., Chao, W.L., Su, Y.: LLM-planner: few-shot grounded planning for embodied agents with large language models. In: Proceedings of the IEEE/CVF International Conference on Computer Vision, pp. 2998–3009 (2023)
4. Ming, C., Lin, J., Fong, P., Wang, H., Duan, X., He, J.: HiCRISP: an LLM-based hierarchical closed-loop robotic intelligent self-correction planner. In: 2024 China Automation Congress (CAC), pp. 4310–4315. IEEE (2024)
5. Liang, J., et al.: Code as policies: language model programs for embodied control. In: 2023 IEEE International Conference on Robotics and Automation (ICRA), pp. 9493–9500. IEEE (2023)
6. Chen, Y., Arkin, J., Dawson, C., Zhang, Y., Roy, N., Fan, C.: AutoTAMP: autoregressive task and motion planning with LLMs as translators and checkers. In: 2024 IEEE International Conference on Robotics and Automation (ICRA), pp. 6695–6702. IEEE (2024)
7. Wang, S., et al.: LLM^3: large language model-based task and motion planning with motion failure reasoning. In: 2024 IEEE/RSJ International Conference on Intelligent Robots and Systems (IROS), pp. 12,086–12,092. IEEE (2024)
8. Din, M.U., et al.: Ontology-driven prompt tuning for LLM-based task and motion planning. arXiv preprint arXiv:2412.07493 (2024)
9. Wang, Z., Liu, Q., Qin, J., Li, M.: Ensuring safety in LLM-driven robotics: a cross-layer sequence supervision mechanism. In: 2024 IEEE/RSJ International Conference on Intelligent Robots and Systems (IROS), pp. 9620–9627. IEEE (2024)
10. Yang, Z., Raman, S.S., Shah, A., Tellex, S.: Plug in the safety chip: enforcing constraints for LLM-driven robot agents. In: 2024 IEEE International Conference on Robotics and Automation (ICRA), pp. 14,435–14,442. IEEE (2024)
11. Huang, W., et al.: Inner monologue: embodied reasoning through planning with language models. In: Conference on Robot Learning, pp. 1769–1782. PMLR (2023)
12. Wei, J., et al.: Chain-of-thought prompting elicits reasoning in large language models. In: Advances in Neural Information Processing Systems, pp. 24,824–24,837 (2022)
13. Argenziano, F., Brienza, M., Suriani, V., Nardi, D., Bloisi, D.D.: Empower: embodied multi-role open-vocabulary planning with online grounding and execution. In: 2024 IEEE/RSJ International Conference on Intelligent Robots and Systems (IROS), pp. 12,040–12,047. IEEE (2024)

14. Brienza, M., Argenziano, F., Suriani, V., Bloisi, D.D., Nardi, D.: Multi-agent planning using visual language models. arXiv preprint arXiv:2408.05478 (2024)
15. Devarakonda, V.N., Kaypak, A.U., Yuan, S., Krishnamurthy, P., Fang, Y., Khorrami, F.: MultiTalk: introspective and extrospective dialogue for human-environment-LLM alignment. arXiv preprint arXiv:2409.16455 (2024)
16. Singh, H., Das, R.J., Han, M., Nakov, P., Laptev, I.: MALMM: multi-agent large language models for zero-shot robotics manipulation. arXiv preprint arXiv:2411.17636 (2024)
17. Chen, H., Ji, W., Xu, L., Zhao, S.: Multi-agent consensus seeking via large language models. arXiv preprint arXiv:2310.20151 (2023)
18. Hurst, A., et al.: GPT-4o system card. arXiv preprint arXiv:2410.21276 (2024)
19. Chen, J., Saha, S., Bansal, M.: Reconcile: round-table conference improves reasoning via consensus among diverse LLMs. In: Proceedings of the 62nd Annual Meeting of the Association for Computational Linguistics (Volume 1: Long Papers), pp. 7066–7085 (2024)
20. Liang, T., et al.: Encouraging divergent thinking in large language models through multi-agent debate. In: Proceedings of the 2024 Conference on Empirical Methods in Natural Language Processing, pp. 17,889–17,904 (2024)
21. Puig, X., et al.: Virtualhome: Simulating household activities via programs. In: Proceedings of the IEEE Conference on Computer Vision and Pattern Recognition, pp. 8494–8502 (2018)

Efficient Skeleton-Based Action Segmentation via Multi-granularity Perception

Zhihao Yang, Haoyu Ji, Wenze Huang, Bowen Chen, Zimo Jiang, Weihong Ren, Zhiyong Wang, and Honghai Liu[✉]

School of Robotics and Advanced Manufacture, Harbin Institute of Technology, Shenzhen, China
honghai.liu@hit.edu.cn

Abstract. One of the major challenges in action segmentation lies in accurately partitioning action segments with varying granularities from long untrimmed videos. While existing approaches employ multi-scale strategies such as multiple sliding windows, multi-resolution attention networks, or multi-resolution loss functions, these methods inevitably incur substantial increases in model parameters and computational costs. This paper proposes a lightweight multi-granularity perception framework for action segmentation to enhance the capability of distinguishing action segments across different temporal scales. We design a progressive granularity-aware architecture consisting of four complementary modules: 1) a Channel Recalibration Attention (CReA) module for adaptive feature recalibration, 2) a Local Feature Transformer (LFT) module for fine-grained temporal modeling, 3) a Multi-scale Temporal Attention (MTA) module capturing hierarchical temporal dependencies, and 4) a Global Self-Attention (GSA) module for long-range context modeling. Through collaborative interaction of these modules, our framework achieves complementary integration of local-global feature perception and dual attention mechanisms in both channel and temporal dimensions, effectively enhancing multi-scale feature representation while maintaining low computational complexity. Experiments on two challenging benchmark datasets demonstrate competitive performance compared with existing methods.

Keywords: action segmentation · multi-granularity perception · collaborative interaction of modules · low computational complexity

1 Introduction

Human action segmentation in long untrimmed videos remains a fundamental challenge in video understanding, requiring precise identification of action boundaries across varying temporal granularities. While recent advances adopt multi-scale temporal modeling through dilated convolutions [3,6,11,12,14,24,25] or transformer architectures [4,5,16,17,23,29], they face a critical dilemma: the pursuit of multi-granularity temporal modeling inevitably leads to quadratic growth in computational complexity, particularly prohibitive for processing hour-long videos. This inefficiency stems from two inherent limitations of existing approaches: redundant feature processing where identical operations are applied across all temporal scales, and coupled gradient flows that induce optimization conflicts when learning diverse granularity patterns.

Prior attempts to address these challenges follow several categories. Some papers utilize sliding window ensembles [8,26], but suffers from fragmented temporal coherence. Some researchers utilize multi-resolution attention [22] or multi-resolution loss functions [1,13,18], yet incurs substantial memory overhead. Another direction is applying progressive pooling, but loses fine-grained temporal details. We argue that an efficient solution requires explicit decoupling of granularity-specific processing pathways while maintaining implicit interaction across temporal scales.

In this work, we present a lightweight multi-granularity collaborative network that achieves efficient action segmentation through spatially decomposed feature learning. Our key innovation lies in four complementary mechanisms: 1) A channel recalibration module (CReA) dynamically adjusts channel-wise feature responses through learnable attention weights, enhancing feature discriminability by emphasizing semantically salient channels; 2) A local feature transformer (LFT) facilitates region-specific feature transformation through position-independent processing, enabling adaptive local feature refinement; 3) A multi-scale temporal attention (MTA) integrates multi-scale downsampling and bidirectional temporal convolution, followed by attention-based feature fusion to capture hierarchical temporal dependencies; 4) A head-constrained global attention (GSA) leverages transformer-style self-attention with dimension-specific projection heads to model long-range contextual relationships. The component synergy enables decoupled multi-granularity learning through spectral channel partitioning, adaptive temporal abstraction via resolution-sensitive attention propagation, and stabilized training dynamics through hybrid residual pathways with gradient preservation.

Extensive experiments on demonstrate competitive performance with existing methods. Our main contributions are:

- A granularity-decoupled architecture that pioneers channel-wise decomposition for multi-scale temporal modeling, reducing computational complexity;
- Four lightweight modules with complementary temporal perception ranges, achieving parameter efficiency through spatial-agnostic operations and head-constrained attention;
- We conduct experiments of the proposed framework on two challenge datasets, demonstrating improvements in skeleton-based action segmentation;

2 Related Work

2.1 Temporal Action Segmentation

Temporal action segmentation aims to classify each frame into predefined action categories. Early approaches primarily employed recurrent architectures [2]

(RNNs/LSTMs/GRUs) to model temporal dependencies through sequential hidden states, albeit with inherent limitations in parallelization efficiency. Subsequent temporal convolutional networks (TCNs) [6,11,12,14] addressed this via stacked dilated 1D convolutions, effectively capturing long-range dependencies through exponentially expanding receptive fields. Recent transformer-based methods [16,17,29] further enhanced global context modeling using self-attention mechanisms. Distinct from these homogeneous architectures, our approach explicitly decouples temporal granularity processing through spectral decomposition, achieving linear computational complexity while maintaining local and global receptive fields.

2.2 Multi-scale Method

Multi-scale approaches have proven effective in video understanding by capturing hierarchical temporal patterns. Feature pyramid networks (FPN) [18] establish multi-level semantics through bidirectional feature fusion, enabling scale-aware detection. Extending this concept, DPP [13] introduces temporal pyramids to model actions across varying durations, while CBR [8] employs cascaded regression with multi-scale sliding windows for precise boundary localization. Complementary strategies include multi-scale tracking [26] that enhances spatiotemporal consistency through joint detection and tracking, and temporal aggregation networks [22] that combine max-pooling with non-local operations to fuse short/long-term dependencies. Recent architectural innovations like LWGANet [21] demonstrate efficient multi-scale modeling through group attention mechanisms. The proposed LWGA module can efficiently extract multi-scale spatial information from local to global while keeping the computational complexity unchanged by splitting the feature map into multiple sub-modules and performing attention processing separately. While existing methods rely on explicit multi-branch structures or dilated operations, our approach uniquely achieves multi-granularity perception through channel-wise feature decomposition. This intrinsic design eliminates the need for additional computational branches or dilation parameters, reducing complexity while maintaining comprehensive temporal modeling capabilities.

3 Method

Figure 1 illustrates overview of our proposed framework. Orange blocks denote our key contributions including four modules (CReA, LFT, MTA, GSA), while the other parts of the backbone are derived from DeST [16].

3.1 Preliminary

To establish the foundation of our approach, we introduce two core components as the backbone of our framework from DeST [16]: multi-scale spatial modeling, and linear transformer-based temporal modeling.

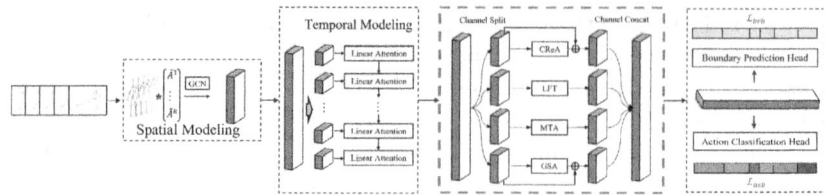

Fig. 1. Proposed framework with multi-granularity perception. Orange blocks denote our key contributions. The temporal feature are decomposed into four lightweight modules (CReA, LFT, MTA, GSA) for specialized modeling. Then features of different scales are connected to get final predictions through boundary prediction head and action classification head. Gray blocks represent the original backbone components from DeST [16]. Our design enables local-global feature complementation and dual channel-temporal attention. (Color figure online)

Multi-scale Spatial Modeling. To model anatomical and implicit correlations among joints, we employ an enhanced graph convolution paradigm [20] that integrates both physical connectivity and data-driven relationships. Let $A^{(k)} \in \mathbb{R}^{V \times V}$ denote the k-adjacency matrix that connects joints at a shortest path distance k:

$$A_{ij}^{(k)} = \begin{cases} 1, & \text{if } d(\alpha_i, \alpha_j) = k \text{ or } i = j, \\ 0, & \text{otherwise,} \end{cases} \quad (1)$$

where $d(\cdot)$ measures the shortest path between joints. To enhance flexibility, we introduce a learnable adjacency matrix $B^{(k)} \in \mathbb{R}^{V \times V}$ that adaptively captures implicit joint relationships. The multi-scale spatial features $S \in \mathbb{R}^{C^s \times T \times V}$ are aggregated through:

$$S = \text{MLP}\left(W^S X \left[(\hat{A}^{(1)} + B^{(1)}) \| \cdots \| (\hat{A}^{(K)} + B^{(K)})\right]\right), \quad (2)$$

where $\|$ denotes channel-wise concatenation, $\hat{A}^{(k)} = D^{-\frac{1}{2}} A^{(k)} D^{\frac{1}{2}}$ is the normalized adjacency matrix, and $K = 13$ controls the maximum neighborhood distance.

Temporal Modeling with Linear Transformer. To address the quadratic complexity bottleneck in conventional attention mechanisms for long sequences, we implement a linear transformer [10] with memory-efficient computation [16]:

$$\mathcal{T}(J) = \sum_{v=1}^{V} \phi(Q_v)(\phi(K_v)^T V_v) + J_v, \quad (3)$$

where Q_v, K_v, V_v are linear projections of joint-specific features, and $\phi(\cdot)$ denotes the ELU activation. These two components form the fundamental building blocks for our spatio-temporal modeling framework, enabling both localized structural awareness and efficient global temporal reasoning.

3.2 Channel Recalibration Attention (CReA)

The Channel Recalibration Attention (CReA) module adaptively recalibrates channel-wise feature responses through a lightweight gating mechanism. Given an input feature map $X \in \mathbb{R}^{C_1 \times T}$, the module first processes the features through a parameter-efficient projection layer $\mathcal{P}$ composed of two point-wise convolutional layers with intermediate batch normalization and activation:

$$\text{CReA}(X) = W_2(\sigma(\text{BN}(W_1 X))), \tag{4}$$

where $W_1 \in \mathbb{R}^{4C_1 \times C_1}$ and $W_2 \in \mathbb{R}^{C_1 \times 4C_1}$ implement channel expansion and compression respectively. This bottleneck structure captures non-linear cross-channel interactions while maintaining computational efficiency. The projected features are then transformed into channel attention weights via a sigmoid gating function $A = \text{sigmoid}(\mathcal{P}(X))$, which subsequently recalibrates the original features through element-wise multiplication $\hat{X} = X \otimes A$.

3.3 Local Feature Transformer (LFT)

The Local Feature Transformer (LFT) module enhances temporal feature representation through spatial-agnostic transformations. Given an input feature map $X \in \mathbb{R}^{C_2 \times T}$, the module implements a parameter-efficient transformation:

$$\text{LFT}(X) = \sigma(\text{BN}(WX)), \tag{5}$$

where $W \in \mathbb{R}^{C_2 \times C_2}$ denotes a point-wise convolutional layer that operates independently across temporal positions, BN represents batch normalization, and σ is the activation function. This design enables local feature enhancement without spatial context mixing, preserving the temporal structure of fine-grained action patterns.

3.4 Multi-scale Temporal Attention (MTA)

The Multi-scale Temporal Attention (MTA) module captures hierarchical temporal dependencies through bidirectional context modeling and adaptive resolution processing. Given input features $X \in \mathbb{R}^{C_3 \times T}$, the module operates through three key phases:

$$\begin{aligned} X_\downarrow &= \mathcal{P}_{\text{avg}}(\mathcal{P}_{\max}(X)), \\ \tilde{A} &= \text{BN}(\psi_\rightarrow(X_\downarrow) + \psi_\leftarrow(X_\downarrow)), \\ \text{MTA}(X) &= X \otimes \text{Interp}(\sigma(\tilde{A})), \end{aligned} \tag{6}$$

where $\mathcal{P}_{\max}$ and $\mathcal{P}_{\text{avg}}$ denote max- and average-pooling operations. $\psi_\rightarrow / \psi_\leftarrow$ represent depthwise temporal convolutions with reversed processing directions, and $\text{Interp}(\cdot)$ indicates linear interpolation for temporal resolution recovery.

The architecture achieves multi-scale perception through three-level abstraction: 1) The pooling cascade reduces temporal resolution by 3×, enabling efficient processing of long-range dependencies; 2) Bidirectional depthwise convolutions with kernel size K capture local temporal patterns from both forward and backward directions; 3) The interpolation-based attention propagation preserves temporal coherence while avoiding boundary artifacts. Compared to standard temporal attention mechanisms requiring $O(C_3 T^2)$ computations, our design reduces complexity to $O(C_3 T/3 \cdot K)$ through strategic downsampling.

3.5 Global Self-Attention (GSA)

The Global Self-Attention (GSA) module establishes long-range temporal dependencies through a multi-head self-attention mechanism. Given input features $X \in \mathbb{R}^{C_4 \times T}$, the module first projects the channel-dimension into query/key/value triplets through linear transformations:

$$Q, K, V = \text{split}(W_{qkv} X^\top) \quad \text{where} \quad W_{qkv} \in \mathbb{R}^{3H_d \times C_4}, \tag{7}$$

where H_d denotes the head dimension and $X^\top \in \mathbb{R}^{T \times C_4}$ represents the transposed temporal-channel dimensions. The attention mechanism operates in $N_h = \lfloor C_4 / H_d \rfloor$ parallel heads with scaled dot-product computation:

$$\text{GSA}(X) = \text{Softmax}\left(\frac{QK^\top}{\sqrt{H_d}}\right) V, \tag{8}$$

By dividing the features into multiple heads for independent attention calculations, the correlation in different subspaces of the features can be captured, improving the model's ability to model complex feature relationships. At the same time, each position in the feature sequence is allowed to interact with all other positions, which can capture global dependencies.

3.6 Multi-granularity Collaborative Processing

Our method integrates four complementary modules through a split-transform-merge paradigm with residual learning, as depicted in Fig. 1. Given an input feature tensor $X \in \mathbb{R}^{(C_1+C_2+C_3+C_4) \times T}$, the processing pipeline unfolds as:

$$\begin{aligned}
\{X_1, X_2, X_3, X_4\} &= \text{split}(X, [C_1, C_2, C_3, C_4]), \\
\begin{cases} X_1' = X_1 + \text{CReA}(X_1), \\ X_2' = \text{LFT}(X_2), \\ X_3' = \text{MTA}(X_3), \\ X_4' = X_4 + \text{GSA}(X_4), \end{cases} & \\
\hat{X} &= \text{concat}(X_1', X_2', X_3', X_4'), \\
Y &= X + \text{LN}(\text{DropPath}(\text{MLP}(\hat{X}))),
\end{aligned} \tag{9}$$

The channel-wise decomposition operation partitions features into four parallel streams, where CReA and GSA modules incorporate residual connections to preserve original signal fidelity, while LFT and MTA perform pure feature transformations. This architecture establishes dedicated processing pathways for distinct temporal granularities: channel-wise calibration (CReA), localized temporal enhancement (LFT), multi-scale dependency modeling (MTA), and global context integration (GSA). Through selective residual connections, the design enables decoupled gradient propagation paths to mitigate optimization conflicts, while maintaining parameter efficiency by restricting each module to operate on partitioned channel subsets rather than full-dimensional features.

3.7 Loss Function

The training objective combines two complementary loss components of action classification branch $\mathcal{L}_{asb}$ and boundary regression $\mathcal{L}_{brb}$ following DeST [16]:

$$\mathcal{L}_{asb} = \mathcal{L}_{cls} + \gamma \mathcal{L}_{smo} = -\frac{1}{T}\sum_{t=1}^{T}\log(y_{t,\hat{c}}) + \gamma\frac{1}{TC}\sum_{t=1}^{T}\sum_{c=1}^{C}(y_{t-1,c} - y_{t,c})^2,$$

$$\mathcal{L}_{brb} = -\frac{1}{T}\sum_{t=1}^{T}\left(y_t \log(\hat{y}_t) + (1-y_t)\log(1-\hat{y}_t)\right), \quad (10)$$

$$\mathcal{L} = \mathcal{L}_{asb} + \lambda \mathcal{L}_{brb},$$

where $y_{t,\hat{c}}$ denotes the predicted probability of ground truth class $\hat{c}$ at time t, with the smoothness regularization coefficient γ set to 0.15. The y_t is the ground truth label (1 for the boundary frame and 0 for others), and $\hat{y}_t$ is the predicted boundary probability. The λ controls the relative importance of boundary detection loss, defaults to 0.1.

4 Experiments

4.1 Datasets and Evaluation Metrics

Datasets. We evaluate our method on two public datasets, PKU-MMD (X-sub) [19], PKU-MMD (X-view) [19]. The PKU-MMD benchmark provides large-scale multi-modal data for skeleton-based action understanding, containing 1,009 videos across 52 action categories captured from 66 subjects under three camera views. The dataset is split into two settings: PKU-MMD(X-sub) and PKU-MMD(X-view). In the X-sub setting, the training set comprises data from 57 subjects while the testing set contains samples from the remaining 9 subjects. In the X-view setting, the training data originates from mid and right camera viewpoints, whereas testing samples are exclusively drawn from left camera views.

Evaluation Metrics. We employ the frame-wise accuracy (Acc), segmental edit score (Edit) and F1@{10, 25, 50}. Acc refers to the proportion of correctly classified frames to the total number of frames. This metric directly measures the accuracy of the model in predicting the action category on each individual frame. Edit is used to measure the difference between the segmentation result and the true annotation. It takes into account the accuracy of the segmentation boundary and the impact of redundant segmentation. Its core idea is to calculate the ratio of the minimum number of editing operations (such as insertion, deletion, and substitution) required to edit the predicted segmentation sequence into the true segmentation sequence to the length of the true segmentation sequence. F1@10, 25, 50 refers to the F1 score calculated under different overlap thresholds (10%, 25%, 50%). The F1 score is the harmonic mean of precision and recall, and is used to comprehensively evaluate the performance of the model. Different overlap thresholds correspond to different requirements for the degree of overlap between the detection results and the true annotations.

4.2 Implementation Details

The channel dimension $C_1 = C_2 = C_3 = C_4 =$ are set to 16. We build our model on a single RTX 3090 GPU. For PKU-MMD, we train the models for 300 epochs with a batch size of 1. For LARa, we train the models for 120 epochs, where the batch size is 8.

4.3 Comparisons with the State-of-the-Art

Quantitative Comparison. We compare our method with the existing methods PKU-MMD (X-sub) [19] and PKU-MMD (X-view) [19] datasets, as shown in Table 1. Our approach outperforms the DeST framework on all evaluation metrics of the PKU-MMD benchmark. Compared to DeST-Transformer (the current best variant), we achieve a 0.5% improvement in accuracy on X-sub and a 0.9% improvement in F1@50. Cross-view evaluation shows even more significant advantages: a 0.9% improvement in accuracy and a 1.0% improvement in F1@50 on X-view.

Qualitative Comparison. We further provide qualitative analysis as shown in Fig. 2. In coarse-grained action segmentation, the baseline method suffers from insufficient global context modeling, resulting in misclassification of actions as adjacent actions in the middle of long-term actions. However, this method maintains action coherence through a global attention mechanism. For fine-grained nested actions, the baseline model is prone to confusing action boundaries, while the local temporal modeling of this method accurately separates nested structures. In terms of action boundary division, the baseline method shows significant boundary blurring or deviation in the fast action switching area. In contrast, the boundary prediction of this method is more closely aligned with the true annotation. The synergistic effect of multi granularity features is significant in complex scenes, as it can capture the overall distribution of long-term actions and resolve the fine boundaries of short-term micro actions.

Table 1. Comparison with the state-of-art on PKU-MMD (X-sub, X-view) datasets. † indicates our implemented results.

Method	PKU-MMD (X-sub)					PKU-MMD (X-view)				
	Acc↑	Edit↑	F1@{10,25,50}↑			Acc↑	Edit↑	F1@{10,25,50}↑		
ST-GCN† [28]	66.2	34.6	37.3	33.4	24.7	66.5	35.4	38.6	33.9	24.9
MS-TCN [6]	65.5	–	–	–	46.3	58.2	56.6	58.6	53.6	39.4
MS-TCN++† [14]	66.0	66.7	69.6	65.1	51.5	58.4	56.7	58.7	53.2	38.7
ETSN† [15]	68.4	67.1	70.4	65.5	52.0	60.7	57.6	62.4	57.9	44.3
ASRF [9]	67.7	67.1	72.1	68.3	56.8	60.4	59.3	62.5	58.0	46.1
MS-GCN [7]	68.5	–	–	–	51.6	65.3	58.1	61.3	56.7	44.1
CTC [27]	69.2	–	69.9	66.4	53.8	–	–	–	–	–
DeST-TCN [16]	67.6	66.3	71.7	68.0	55.5	62.4	58.2	63.2	59.2	47.6
DeST-Transformer [16]	70.3	69.3	74.5	71.0	58.7	67.3	64.7	69.3	**65.6**	52.0
Ours	**70.8**	**70.5**	**74.8**	**71.0**	**59.6**	**68.2**	**65.6**	**70.8**	65.4	**53.0**

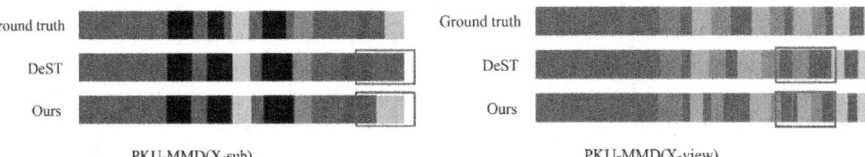

Fig. 2. Qualitative results of action segmentation on the PKU-MMD (X-sub), and PKU-MMD (X-view) datasets. Different colors represent distinct action classes. Red boxes highlight segmentation errors in other methods compared to ours. (Color figure online)

5 Conclusion

We present a lightweight multi-granularity collaborative framework for efficient action segmentation in long untrimmed videos. Through four key innovations—channel-wise feature decomposition, spatially-agnostic local transformation, bidirectional temporal attention, and head-constrained global modeling—our method achieves competitive performance while maintaining linear computational complexity. The proposed modules (CReA, LFT, MTA, GSA) demonstrate that explicit granularity decoupling with implicit feature interaction can effectively address the efficiency-accuracy trade-off that plagues conventional multi-scale approaches. Despite advancements, two limitations warrant future exploration: First, fixed 4-way channel splitting may not optimally adapt to varying video content; dynamic granularity routing could enhance flexibility. Second, while our model reduce the amount of calculation as much as possible, real-time segmentation on embedded devices requires further quantization optimization.

Acknowledgments. This work was supported in part by the National Key Research and Development Program of China under Grant 2022YFB4703200; in part by the National Natural Science Foundation of China under Grant 62261160652, Grant 52275013, Grant 62206075, and Grant 61733011; in part by Shenzhen Science and Technology Program under Grant JCYJ20240813105137049; and in part by the Science and Technology Development Fund (FDCT), Macau, SAR, under Grant 0095/2022/AFJ.

References

1. Cheng, B., et al.: Panoptic-deeplab: a simple, strong, and fast baseline for bottom-up panoptic segmentation. In: Proceedings of the IEEE/CVF Conference on Computer Vision and Pattern Recognition, pp. 12475–12485 (2020)
2. Ding, L., Xu, C.: TricorNet: A hybrid temporal convolutional and recurrent network for video action segmentation. arXiv preprint arXiv:1705.07818 (2017)
3. Ding, L., Xu, C.: Weakly-supervised action segmentation with iterative soft boundary assignment. In: Proceedings of the IEEE Conference on Computer Vision and Pattern Recognition, pp. 6508–6516 (2018)
4. Du, D., Su, B., Li, Y., Qi, Z., Si, L., Shan, Y.: Do we really need temporal convolutions in action segmentation? In: 2023 IEEE International Conference on Multimedia and Expo (ICME), pp. 1014–1019. IEEE (2023)
5. Du, Z., Wang, Q.: Dilated transformer with feature aggregation module for action segmentation. Neural Process. Lett. **55**(5), 6181–6197 (2023)
6. Farha, Y.A., Gall, J.: MS-TCN: multi-stage temporal convolutional network for action segmentation. In: Proceedings of the IEEE/CVF Conference on Computer Vision and Pattern Recognition, pp. 3575–3584 (2019)
7. Filtjens, B., Vanrumste, B., Slaets, P.: Skeleton-based action segmentation with multi-stage spatial-temporal graph convolutional neural networks. IEEE Trans. Emerg. Top. Comput. **12**(1), 202–212 (2022)
8. Gao, J., Yang, Z., Nevatia, R.: Cascaded boundary regression for temporal action detection. In: BMVC (2017)
9. Ishikawa, Y., Kasai, S., Aoki, Y., Kataoka, H.: Alleviating over-segmentation errors by detecting action boundaries. In: Proceedings of the IEEE/CVF Winter Conference on Applications of Computer Vision, pp. 2322–2331 (2021)
10. Katharopoulos, A., Vyas, A., Pappas, N., Fleuret, F.: Transformers are RNNs: fast autoregressive transformers with linear attention. In: International Conference on Machine Learning, pp. 5156–5165. PMLR (2020)
11. Lea, C., Flynn, M.D., Vidal, R., Reiter, A., Hager, G.D.: Temporal convolutional networks for action segmentation and detection. In: Proceedings of the IEEE Conference on Computer Vision and Pattern Recognition, pp. 156–165 (2017)
12. Lei, P., Todorovic, S.: Temporal deformable residual networks for action segmentation in videos. In: Proceedings of the IEEE Conference on Computer Vision and Pattern Recognition, pp. 6742–6751 (2018)
13. Li, L., Kong, T., Sun, F., Liu, H.: Deep point-wise prediction for action temporal proposal. In: Gedeon, T., Wong, K.W., Lee, M. (eds.) ICONIP 2019. LNCS, vol. 11955, pp. 475–487. Springer, Cham (2019). https://doi.org/10.1007/978-3-030-36718-3_40
14. Li, S., Farha, Y.A., Liu, Y., Cheng, M.M., Gall, J.: MS-TCN++: multi-stage temporal convolutional network for action segmentation. IEEE Trans. Pattern Anal. Mach. Intell. **45**(06), 6647–6658 (2023)

15. Li, Y., et al.: Efficient two-step networks for temporal action segmentation. Neurocomputing **454**, 373–381 (2021)
16. Li, Y., Li, Z., Gao, S., Wang, Q., Hou, Q., Cheng, M.M.: A decoupled spatio-temporal framework for skeleton-based action segmentation. arXiv preprint arXiv:2312.05830 (2023)
17. Lin, T., Chang, X., Sun, W., Zheng, W.: Prototypical transformer for weakly supervised action segmentation. In: Liu, Q., et al. (eds.) PRCV 2023. LNCS, vol. 14430, pp. 195–206. Springer, Singapore (2023). https://doi.org/10.1007/978-981-99-8537-1_16
18. Lin, T.Y., Dollár, P., Girshick, R., He, K., Hariharan, B., Belongie, S.: Feature pyramid networks for object detection. In: Proceedings of the IEEE Conference on Computer Vision and Pattern Recognition, pp. 2117–2125 (2017)
19. Liu, C., Hu, Y., Li, Y., Song, S., Liu, J.: PKU-MMD: a large scale benchmark for skeleton-based human action understanding. In: Proceedings of the Workshop on Visual Analysis in Smart and Connected Communities, pp. 1–8 (2017)
20. Liu, Z., Zhang, H., Chen, Z., Wang, Z., Ouyang, W.: Disentangling and unifying graph convolutions for skeleton-based action recognition. In: Proceedings of the IEEE/CVF Conference on Computer Vision and Pattern Recognition, pp. 143–152 (2020)
21. Lu, W., Chen, S.B., Ding, C.H., Tang, J., Luo, B.: LWGANet: a lightweight group attention backbone for remote sensing visual tasks. arXiv preprint arXiv:2501.10040 (2025)
22. Sener, F., Singhania, D., Yao, A.: Temporal aggregate representations for long-range video understanding. In: Vedaldi, A., Bischof, H., Brox, T., Frahm, J.-M. (eds.) ECCV 2020. LNCS, vol. 12361, pp. 154–171. Springer, Cham (2020). https://doi.org/10.1007/978-3-030-58517-4_10
23. Tian, X., Jin, Y., Tang, X.: Local-global transformer neural network for temporal action segmentation. Multimedia Syst. **29**(2), 615–626 (2023)
24. Wang, D., Yuan, Y., Wang, Q.: Gated forward refinement network for action segmentation. Neurocomputing **407**, 63–71 (2020)
25. Wang, Z., Gao, Z., Wang, L., Li, Z., Wu, G.: Boundary-aware cascade networks for temporal action segmentation. In: Vedaldi, A., Bischof, H., Brox, T., Frahm, J.-M. (eds.) ECCV 2020. LNCS, vol. 12370, pp. 34–51. Springer, Cham (2020). https://doi.org/10.1007/978-3-030-58595-2_3
26. Weinzaepfel, P., Harchaoui, Z., Schmid, C.: Learning to track for spatio-temporal action localization. In: Proceedings of the IEEE International Conference on Computer Vision, pp. 3164–3172 (2015)
27. Xu, L., Wang, Q., Lin, X., Yuan, L.: An efficient framework for few-shot skeleton-based temporal action segmentation. Comput. Vis. Image Underst. **232**, 103707 (2023)
28. Yan, S., Xiong, Y., Lin, D.: Spatial temporal graph convolutional networks for skeleton-based action recognition, vol. 32 (2018)
29. Yi, F., Wen, H., Jiang, T.: ASFormer: transformer for action segmentation. In: The British Machine Vision Conference (BMVC) (2021)

Tri-Axial Plantar Load Sensing for Identity Authentication with 1D-CNN Classifier

Zijie Liu[1], Yi Zhang[2], Hao Huang[2], Shabei Xu[2], Xiang Luo[2], and Jiajie Guo[1(✉)]

[1] Institute of Medical Equipment Science and Engineering, State Key Laboratory of Digital Manufacturing Equipment and Technology, School of Mechanical Science and Engineering, Huazhong University of Science and Technology, Wuhan 430074, China
jiajie.guo@hust.edu.cn

[2] Department of Neurology, Tongji Hospital, Tongji Medical College, Huazhong University of Science and Technology, Wuhan 430074, Hubei, China

Abstract. High-precision continuous identity authentication is crucial for preventing privacy breaches and safeguarding sensitive data in the digital intelligence era, garnering substantial interest from both academia and industry. However, the complexity of identity verification and the need for unperceived sensing limit the availability of suitable methods. This study proposes a novel approach using tri-axial plantar load distributions, visualized through heatmaps to highlight inter-subject feature variations and the complementary effects of multi-axial components. Identity authentication experiments, conducted on a 20-subject dataset across straight walking and turning motions using a one-dimensional convolutional neural network (1D-CNN) classifier, achieved the error rate of only 1.03%, significantly outperforming single-axis pressure sensing (3.63%). To our knowledge, this is the first study to employ tri-axial plantar load as a mechanical signature for identity authentication, which is expected to advance technologies in fields such as wearable devices and biometric security systems.

Keywords: Identity authentication · Tri-axial plantar load sensing · Wearable sensor

1 Introduction

In the era of digital intelligence, the leakage of personal data, such as location, physiological, or kinematic information, poses significant privacy risks, underscoring the critical need for identity authentication in applications like health monitoring and personalized services [1, 2]. Traditional authentication methods, such as passwords or personal identification numbers, often require a trade-off between security and usability [3]. Physiological biometric methods, including fingerprint [4], facial [5], iris [6], and voice recognition [7], offer high security and usability but are limited to static authentication, making them unsuitable for dynamic, continuous scenarios [8, 9]. Gait, as a behavioral biometric, has gained attention due to its distinct kinematic and dynamic characteristics, which are inherently difficult to replicate [10]. Gait patterns can be captured non-intrusively and analyzed in real time, enabling seamless continuous authentication.

However, existing approaches often rely on inertial measurement units [11] or electromyography sensors [12], which require additional wearable attachments. Repeated donning and doffing of these devices cause sensor misalignment, significantly degrading authentication performance [13]. Thus, developing continuous, convenient, and accurate identity authentication method remains underdeveloped and presents significant challenges.

Plantar force sensing offers a promising solution for gait-based authentication by capturing force distribution patterns during the stance phase without requiring position calibration. However, prior studies relying on plantar pressure exhibit low recognition accuracy due to the low-dimensional and single-modality data [14]. To address this, existing methods combine plantar pressure with inertial measurements [15], increasing system complexity and computational cost. Moreover, most studies require subjects to walk in straight lines to maintain reliable authentication [8], yet daily activities frequently involve non-linear motions, such as turning, which severely limits method generalizability. Notably, shear forces, which govern braking, propulsion, and steering, are particularly critical during motions [16]. Incorporating tri-axial plantar force distribution, encompassing both normal and shear forces, is expected to enhance authentication performance. However, due to the lack of suitable sensing equipment, few studies have explored tri-axial plantar force distribution for identity authentication.

Recent advances in feature fusion techniques, which integrate multi-source information, leverage the strengths of individual sensing information while mitigating their limitations [17–19]. Combined with machine learning methods [20, 21], these techniques have shown promise in gait monitoring [22], clinical diagnostics [23], and embodied navigation [24]. Multi-source fusion systems can effectively extract features from limited sensing regions, offering significant potential for unperceived identity authentication. However, some fusion methods lack reliability due to opaque physical mechanisms, underscoring the need for interpretable fusion strategies.

To address these challenges, we propose a novel identity authentication method based on tri-axial plantar load fusion, utilizing our previously developed plantar force sensing system. Unlike conventional approaches limited to straight walking, this framework integrates turning to enhance generalization for real-world gait variability. Heatmaps reveal complementary patterns in normal and shear loads across gait cycles. Based on the one-dimensional convolutional neural network (1D-CNN) classifier, this method achieves the average error rate of 1.03% across 20 subjects. This work provides the first demonstration of tri-axial plantar force distributions as unique biometric signatures, advancing identity authentication under dynamic motions.

2 Methodology of Identity Authentication

2.1 Tri-Axial Plantar Load Fusion-Based 1D-CNN

To enable effective identity authentication through tri-axial plantar load fusion, 1D-CNN classifier is developed, as illustrated in Fig. 1. At time step t, the plantar load vector along i-axis is denoted as $\mathbf{P}_{i,t} = \left[p_{i,1}^{(t)}, p_{i,2}^{(t)}, ..., p_{i,j}^{(t)} \right]^T$, where $p_{i,j}^{(t)}$ represents the i-axial load at the jth sensing node, with $i =$ x, y and z, respectively. The time-series array of i-axis load during straight walking and turning is defined as $\mathbf{L}_i = [\mathbf{P}_{i,1}, \mathbf{P}_{i,2}, ..., \mathbf{P}_{i,T}]^T$, where T is the number of time steps. The fused signal, combining tri-axial loads, is denoted as $\mathbf{L} = [\mathbf{L_x}, \mathbf{L_y}, \mathbf{L_z}]^T$.

To facilitate feature fusion, tri-axial loads are first transformed into feature spaces of identical dimensions using feature maps. The 1D-CNN model consists of two convolutional layers, each layer with the kernel size of 3×1 extracts initial features, followed by the ReLU activation and the max-pooling layer with the kernel size of 2×1 to reduce dimensionality. The pooled features are flattened and input into the fully connected layer, which maps them to a single classification score. The final authentication decision is obtained by thresholding the sigmoid output at 0.5, where values ≥ 0.5 indicate positive authentication. The 1D-CNN employs binary cross-entropy as the loss function and is optimized using the Adam optimizer with the learning rate of 0.005 and the batch size of 64, iterating for up to 500 epochs. To mitigate overfitting, early stopping is implemented if the validation loss does not decrease for ten consecutive epochs.

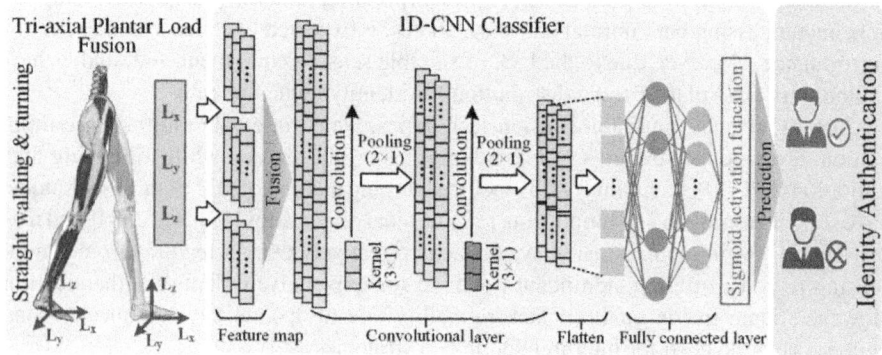

Fig. 1. Tri-axial plantar load fusion for identity authentication with the 1D-CNN classifier.

2.2 Dataset Construction and Performance Metrics

To enable robust identity authentication using tri-axial plantar load fusion, an open-set testing framework is adopted to simulate real-world scenarios, as wearable devices typically restrict access to a single authorized user while treating others as unauthorized. Collecting data from all possible unauthorized users is impractical; thus, one subject is randomly selected as the authorized user, five as unknown unauthorized users, and the remaining as known unauthorized users. The training dataset includes data from the authorized user and known unauthorized users, while the testing dataset comprises the authorized user's remaining data and all unknown unauthorized user data, evaluating the model's generalization to unseen users.

To address imbalance between authorized and unauthorized user data in the training set, which could bias the classifier toward the majority unauthorized class, a adual strategy is employed: data augmentation for authorized users and random sampling for unauthorized users. Two time-domain augmentation techniques are applied to increase the authorized user data volume while preserving original characteristics, which has been shown to be effective for temporal gait data processing. Specifically, temporal scaling via interpolation to simulate varying walking speeds and random amplitude adjustments to mimic different load conditions.

The performance of the proposed model is evaluated using the equal error rate (EER), a standard metric for biometric systems, corresponding to the point on the receiver operating characteristic (ROC) curve where the false acceptance rate (FAR) equals the false rejection rate (FRR). Specifically, EER is computed by $EER = (FAR_{\tau_{EER}} + FRR_{\tau_{EER}})/2$, where threshold $\tau_{EER} = \arg\min_{\tau \in ROC}(abs(FAR_\tau - FRR_\tau))$. Thus, a low EER signifies superior model performance.

3 Gait Experiment

3.1 Sensing System

The sensing array employed in this study is custom-designed, and implemented to support tri-axial plantar load sensing. The sensing node correlates elastomer deformation with magnetic flux density in tri-axial space, enabling force calculation through the magneto-elastomer's constitutive relations, as shown in Fig. 2(a). The sensing array employs a multilayer structure, comprising the polyimide film, circuit layer, and magneto-elastomer from bottom to top. Each insole integrates 15 sensing nodes, placed at the heel, midfoot, and forefoot load-bearing regions, with sensing ranges of 116 kPa, 113 kPa, and 433 kPa along the x-, y-, and z-axes, respectively, at the sampling rate of 144 Hz. For non-intrusive sensing, data are wirelessly transmitted via the ESP32 mounted on the shoe upper to the processing system for analysis and storage, as shown in Fig. 2(b). Real-world experimental scenarios, including straight walking and turning, are presented in Fig. 2(c, d).

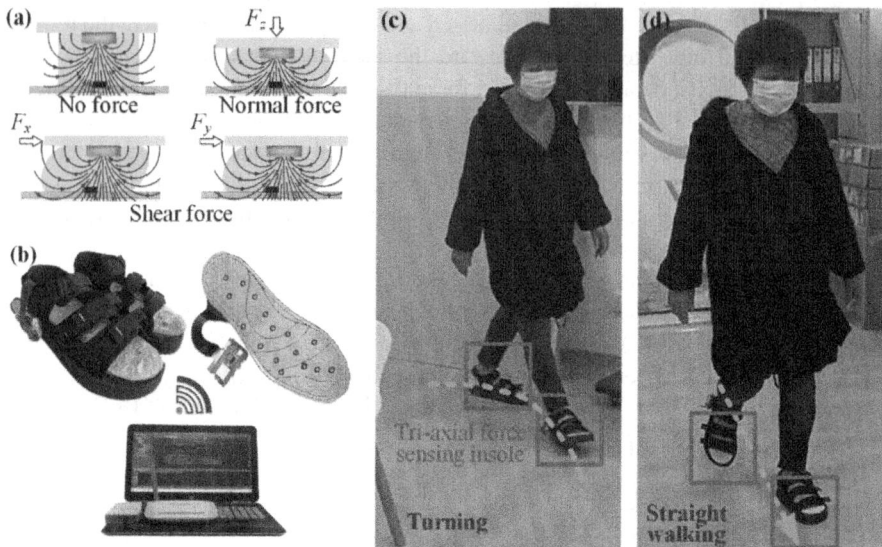

Fig. 2. Wireless tri-axial plantar force sensing system and experimental photos. (a) Tri-axial plantar force sensing mechanism (b) Prototype of the insole system (c) Experimental scenarios for turning and straight walking

3.2 Experimental Protocal

This study recruited 20 subjects (10 males, 10 females), aged 34 to 86 years (63.23 ± 8.6 years), with body weights ranging from 44 to 95 kg 63.08 ± 9.7kg) and heights from 150 to 180 cm (mean 164.96 ± 7.2 cm). All subjects were informed of and consented to the experiment's purpose and procedure. The experiment consisted of three gait patterns: straight level-ground walking (SW), left turns (LT), and right turns (RT), each spanning a 10-m distance and performed twice by subjects. The gait monitoring test was approved by the Local Ethics Committee of the Huazhong University of Science and Technology (Wuhan, China).

4 Results

4.1 Tri-Axial Plantar Load Analysis

Our prior work demonstrated distinct tri-axial plantar load distributions during SW, RT, and LT, with complementary normal and shear load patterns validated through motion recognition. This study further analyzes inter-subject variability in tri-axial load distributions, as shown in Fig. 3, which depicts spatiotemporal variations in plantar normal and shear distributions for the left feet of two subjects during SW, computed using the moving least-square method. Temporal snapshots reveal dynamic load patterns along the orthogonal x-, y-, and z-axes, where the x- and y-axis components correspond to propulsive and steering forces, respectively, and the z-axis component corresponds to normal reaction forces. During SW, normal load concentrate at the heel during heel strike, shifting to the forefoot as the center of gravity advances, which is consistent across both subjects. Variations in shear force distributions reflect individual gait differences: Subject 1 exhibits stronger x-axis shear load in the midfoot than Subject 2 at heel strike. At 10% of the gait cycle, both subjects exhibited negative y-axis shear forces at the heel, while Subject 2 simultaneously demonstrated a positive y-axis shear forces at the medial heel region. By mid-stance (45%), although negative x-axis shear forces were present in the forefoot of both subjects, Subject 2's lateral forefoot displayed the positive x-axis shear force. And at 55%, differences in x-axis shear load distributions in forefoot are evident between subjects. The observed variations in plantar load distributions capture subject-specific gait characteristics that enable accurate identity authentication.

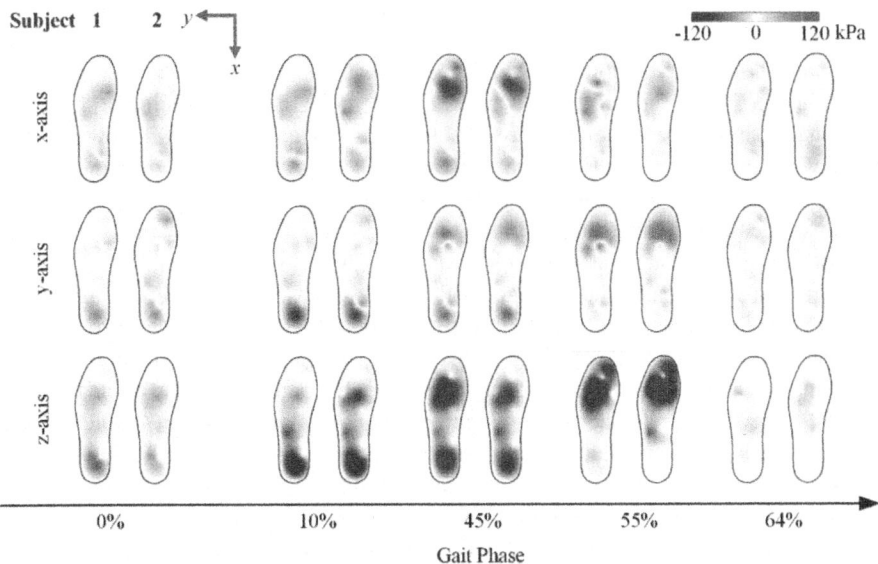

Fig. 3. Plantar tri-axial load distributions between subjects during straight walking.

4.2 1D-CNN-Based Identity Authentication

To evaluate the advantages of tri-axial plantar force distribution and the feature extraction capability of the 1D-CNN classifier, seven cases are compared, as shown in Fig. 4(a). These cases assess the contributions of sensing dimension, node counts, and motion patterns to identity authentication accuracy. Tri-axial plantar loads from both feet across three motion patterns including SW, LT, and RT, are strategically selected as model inputs. The cases are defined as follows: Case 1 employs tri-axial loads from all nodes in both feet across all patterns as inputs. Case 2 uses tri-axial loads from 5 nodes (red triangles) per foot across all patterns. Case 3 inputs only normal loads from all nodes (blue circles) on both feet across all patterns. Cases 4 and 5 utilize tri-axial loads from all nodes in left or right foot, respectively, across all patterns. Cases 6 and 7 use tri-axial loads from all nodes in both feet but only across SW or LT&RT, respectively. Figure 4(b) presents the EER of identity authentication under different cases with 10 randomly selected subjects, with the following observations:

Case 1 achieves the average EER of 1.03%, outperforming Cases 2 (1.98%) and 3 (3.68%), as shown in Fig. 4(b-i). This result indicates that more sensing dimensions and larger quantity of nodes provide richer input features of plantar load distribution, thereby enhancing authentication accuracy. Notably, the EER of Case 2 is significantly lower than that of Case 3 despite both cases utilizing the same number of inputs, as shear plantar load provides distinctive individual characteristics during motion (Fig. 3), thereby reducing ambiguity in identity authentication.

Cases 4 and 5, which rely on unilateral gait data, exhibit higher EERs of 2.24% and 3.58% respectively compared to Case 1 (Fig. 4b-ii). This degradation occurs as bilateral gait data leverages symmetry-related information across the sagittal plane, capturing additional discriminative characteristics. EER for right-foot data (Case 5) exceeds that of left-foot data (Case 4), which may be attributed to the fact that most individuals are right-handed, making the left lower limb more flexible.

Cases 1, 6, and 7 exhibit comparable EERs, indicating that turnings (LT & RT) contain discriminative gait characteristics as rich as straight walking (Fig. 4b-iii). Case 1 achieves marginally lower EERs than Cases 6 and 7, suggesting that combining features across multi patterns enhances recognition performance. Crucially, since SW, LT, and RT constitute fundamental gait patterns in daily activities, the motion diversity integrated in Case 1 ensures strong generalizability for the real-world deployment.

Figure 4(c) compares the average EER across all cases with different algorithms. The 1D-CNN achieves significantly lower EERs than LSTM and SVM, demonstrating superior feature extraction capabilities. Moreover, its lightweight architecture enables efficient deployment on edge computing platforms. In contrast, SVM exhibits the highest EER due to the reliance on handcrafted features, particularly in unilateral cases where critical symmetry-related features are inherently absent. Notably, the low EER across different algorithms demonstrates that plantar force distributions contain intrinsic biometric features, validating their reliability as an authentication biomarker.

In summary, the proposed method achieves the EER of 1.03% by fusing tri-axial loads from both feet across turning and walking via the 1D-CNN classifier. Compared to 2D-CNNs or transformer-based models, its lightweight architecture and low computational requirements enable efficient deployment on edge microprocessors. Future work will explore advanced models with attention mechanisms to support multiclassification for multi-tiered permission scenarios. Given that the model captures spatiotemporal features of plantar loads, the impact of shoe replacement on identity verification performance will be further evaluated. Furthermore, the dataset will be expanded to include complex daily activities, with subgroup analyses stratified by age, BMI, and gender to enhance generalizability.

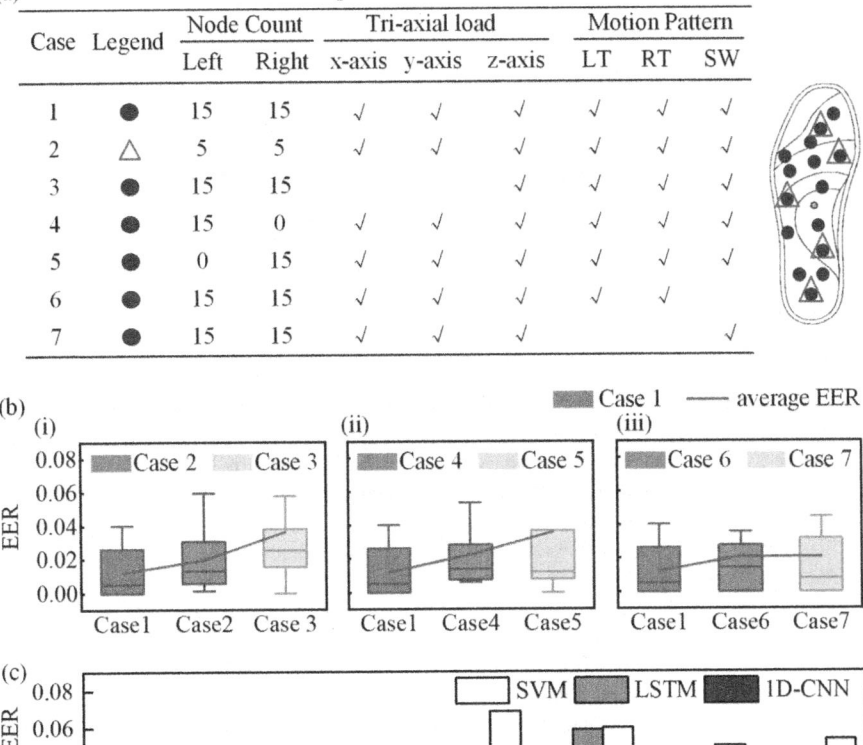

Fig. 4. Experiments for gait-based identity authentication. (a) Authentication input cases with different counts, dimensions, and patterns. (b) Comparison of EER across different cases. (c) Comparison of EER across different algorithms (color figure online).

5 Conclusion

This paper proposes a tri-axial plantar force fusion method for continuous and unperceived identity authentication during LT, RT, and SW. Tri-axial plantar force was collected from 20 subjects with plantar force insole and the 1D-CNN classifier was employed for identification. Among ten randomly selected subjects, the average EER was only 1.03%, whereas under the same conditions, relying solely on pressure resulted in the EER of 3.68%. When using a partial-node tri-axial force dataset (with the same input dimensions), the EER remained below 1.98%, suggesting that increasing sensing dimensions is more advantageous than increasing the number of sensing nodes. Experimental results also demonstrated that datasets from both feet yield lower EER than those from single-foot, and datasets incorporating multi-gait outperformed lower EER than those with single-gait pattern, providing critical insights for optimizing sensor configurations. Low EERs achieved across different algorithms highlight the intrinsic biometric patterns in tri-axial plantar force. This study is the first to introduce tri-axial plantar force into identity authentication, which is expected to advance technologies in fields such as wearable devices and biometric security systems.

Acknowledgements. This research was supported by National Natural Science Foundation of China (51875221, U22A20249, 92248304, 52188102, 52027806), Interdisciplinarity Research Support Program of Huazhong University of Science and Technology (2023JCYJ030), and Chutian Talent Program Science and Technology Innovation Team.

References

1. Boulemtafes, A., Derhab, A., Challal, Y.: Privacy-preserving deep learning for pervasive health monitoring: a study of environment requirements and existing solutions adequacy. Heal. Technol. **12**(2), 285–304 (2022)
2. Najmi, K.Y., AlZain, M.A., Masud, M., Jhanjhi, N.Z., Al-Amri, J., Baz, M.: A survey on security threats and countermeasures in IoT to achieve users confidentiality and reliability. Materials Today: Proceedings **81**, 377–382 (2023)
3. Shen, W., Tan, T.: Automated biometrics-based personal identification. Proc. Natl. Acad. Sci. **96**(20), 11065–11066 (1999)
4. Cao, K., Jain, A.K.: Automated latent fingerprint recognition. IEEE Trans. Pattern Anal. Mach. Intell. **41**(4), 788–800 (2019)
5. El Fadel, N.: Facial recognition algorithms: a systematic literature review. Journal of Imaging **11**(2). https://doi.org/10.3390/jimaging11020058
6. Kumar, A.: Insights on 'Complex-Valued Iris Recognition Network.' IEEE Trans. Pattern Anal. Mach. Intell. **47**(3), 2232–2236 (2025)
7. Peng, G., Zhou, G., Nguyen, D.T., Qi, X., Yang, Q., Wang, S.: Continuous authentication with touch behavioral biometrics and voice on wearable glasses. IEEE Trans. Human-Machine Sys. **47**(3), 404–416 (2017)
8. Ivanov, K., et al.: Identity recognition by walking outdoors using multimodal sensor insoles. IEEE Access **8**, 150797–150807 (2020)
9. Zhang, S., Liu, J.: Analysis and optimization of multiple unmanned aerial vehicle-assisted communications in post-disaster areas. IEEE Trans. Veh. Technol. **67**(12), 12049–12060 (2018)
10. Lee, S., Lee, S., Park, E., Lee, J., Kim, I.Y.: Gait-based continuous authentication using a novel sensor compensation algorithm and geometric features extracted from wearable sensors. IEEE Access **10**, 120122–120135 (2022)
11. De Marsico, M., Mecca, A., Barra, S.: Walking in a smart city: investigating the gait stabilization effect for biometric recognition via wearable sensors. Comput. Electr. Eng. **80**, 106501 (2019)
12. Raurale, S.A., McAllister, J., Rincón, J.M.D.: EMG biometric systems based on different wrist-hand movements. IEEE Access **9**, 12256–12266 (2021)
13. Maiorana, E.: A survey on biometric recognition using wearable devices. Pattern Recogn. Lett. **156**, 29–37 (2022)
14. Girão, N.S., Muller, M., Arruda, L.V.R.d.: A new biometric identification system based on plantar pressure. IEEE Sensors J. **23**(15), 16900–16906 (2023)
15. Zeng, H., Mei, Z., Lin, C., Mao, L., Yang, G., Li, Y.: Multi-modal sensing insoles for identity authentication across diverse walking activities. Measurement **242**, 116198 (2025)

16. Cong, Y., Lam, W.K., Cheung, J.T.-M., Zhang, M.: In-shoe plantar tri-axial stress profiles during maximum-effort cutting maneuvers. J. Biomech. **47**(16), 3799–3806 (2014)
17. Celik, Y., Stuart, S., Woo, W.L., Sejdic, E., Godfrey, A.: Multi-modal gait: A wearable, algorithm and data fusion approach for clinical and free-living assessment. Information Fusion **78**, 57–70 (2022)
18. Zhang, M., Liu, D., Wang, Q., Zhao, B., Bai, O., Sun, J.: Gait pattern recognition based on plantar pressure signals and acceleration signals. IEEE Trans. Instrum. Meas. **71**, 1–15 (2022)
19. Zhang, S., Zhou, H., Tchantchane, R., Alici, G.: Hand gesture recognition across various limb positions using a multimodal sensing system based on self-adaptive data-fusion and convolutional neural networks (CNNs). IEEE Sens. J. **24**(11), 18633–18645 (2024)
20. Song, B., Zhou, R., Ahmed, F.: Multi-modal machine learning in engineering design: a review and future directions. J. Comp. Info. Sci. Eng. **24**(1) (2023)
21. Hssayeni, M.D., Ghoraani, B.: Multi-modal physiological data fusion for affect estimation using deep learning. IEEE Access **9**, 21642–21652 (2021)
22. Zhang, C., Yu, Z., Wang, X., Chen, Z.-J., Deng, C., Xie, S.Q.: Exploration of deep learning-driven multimodal information fusion frameworks and their application in lower limb motion recognition. Biomed. Signal Process. Control **96**, 106551 (2024)
23. Zhao, A., et al.: Multimodal gait recognition for neurodegenerative diseases. IEEE Trans. Cybernet. **52**(9), 9439–9453 (2022)
24. Wu, Y., Zhang, P., Gu, M., Zheng, J., Bai, X.: Embodied navigation with multi-modal information: A survey from tasks to methodology. Information Fusion **112**, 102532 (2024)

Exploring the Mechanism Underlying Lower Limb Motor Dysfunction in Ischemic Stroke Based on Multimodal Signals

Jiaqi Shi, Hongyu Wang, Yulan Zhu[✉], and Yanmei Zhu[✉]

Department of Neurology, The 2nd Affiliated Hospital of Harbin Medical University,
Harbin 150086, China
zymtg1111@163.com

Abstract. Ischemic stroke (IS) is associated with high morbidity, mortality, and disability rates. The pathological mechanism of motor dysfunction in stroke need to be determined to improve the effectiveness of rehabilitation therapy.

Clinical data, electroencephalography (EEG) data, and functional magnetic resonance imaging (fMRI) data were collected from 86 patients with IS and 45 healthy controls. The EEG signals were analyzed via wavelet transform, brain network construction. The fMRI results were analyzed based on brain network construction.

Low-frequency energy activity was found in stroke patients; Neural adaptation slowed, and the number and intensity of brain network functional connectivity (FC) in patients were significantly reduced. The results of the fMRI examination revealed that the strength of the brain network correlation matrix was significantly weaker, and the brain network graph theory properties decreased considerably.

The decrease in brain network connectivity and the overall decline in the brain network graph theory attribute index may be the key mechanisms underlying the occurrence of lower limb motor dysfunction.

Keywords: Ischemic stroke · brain network · motor dysfunction

1 Introduction

Ischemic stroke (IS) is a loss of neurological function due to thrombosis or embolism blocking a certain area of the brain, resulting in a sudden decrease in blood flow [1]. Neurological dysfunction often occurs clinically and is characterized by high morbidity, disability rates, and mortality rates [2]. The dysfunction caused by stroke involves multiple aspects, the most prevalent of which is impaired motor function [3]. With the advancement of EEG, EMG, fMRI, and other technologies, the neural mechanism of stroke motor disorders has been revealed more accurately and comprehensively from multiple dimensions, such as nerve electrical activity, muscle electrical activity, and cerebral hemodynamics.

The EEG power spectrum density reflects the overall cortical electrophysiological state [4]. Using EEG, researchers can build functional brain networks in which nodes correspond to various brain regions and reflect interregional functional connectivity (FC) between edges [5]. This construction facilitates a deep understanding of the brain tissue structure and mode of information transmission. Commonly used coupling methods for the characterization of functional brain networks via EEG data include the Pearson correlation coefficient, coherence, phase lag index, and mutual information [6]. Graph theory analysis has become a key technique to assess the topological properties of brain networks, and it is widely used to quantify the global and local topological features of brain networks.

As stroke is a complex disease, the analysis of multimodal fusion and multiple physiological parameters is becoming popular. EEG can be combined with fMRI to combine the advantages of high temporal and spatial resolution to identify neural activity [7], and EEG and EMG can be combined to analyze the coupling effect of the cortical-muscle bidirectional neural pathway [8].

In recent years, neuroimaging techniques have been crucial in studying stroke mechanisms and predicting prognosis [9]. Resting-state fMRI is an effective means for mechanistic research because of its many advantages, such as its noninvasive, radiation-free, and functional imaging [10]. In the resting state, FC analysis via functional magnetic resonance imaging (fMRI) has revealed the neural connectivity mechanism during motor dysfunction and rehabilitation [11].

The pathological mechanism of motor dysfunction in stroke are not completely determined. We observed the neural network status of stroke patients during knee flexion and extension by synchronous EEG and EMG. We combined these findings with the fMRI results of patients to explore the mechanism of the occurrence of lower limb motor dysfunction during movement in stroke patients.

2 Methods

2.1 Experimental Paradigm Design

In this study, a hip/knee flexion and extension experimental paradigm was designed. The experimental steps are shown in Fig. 1. The experimental task involved knee flexion and extension movements. Each trial run consisted of four parts: "preparation, flexion, rest, and stretch".

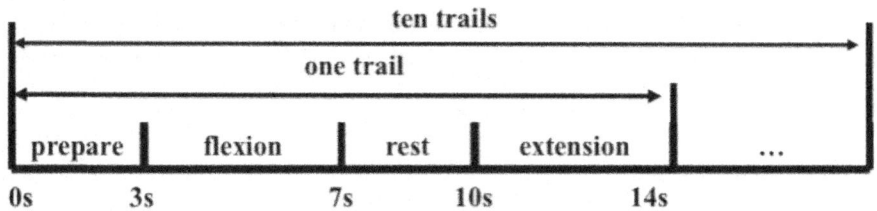

Fig. 1. Flow chart of the experiment

2.2 Subject Inclusion

Inclusion criteria

1. Those who met the diagnostic criteria for cerebral infarction in the Chinese Guidelines for the Diagnosis and Treatment of Acute Ischemic Stroke (2018);
2. Patients who were 40–79 years old;
3. Those who were first diagnosed at more than two weeks of age, with hemiplegia and a stable condition;
4. Patients whose lower limb muscle strength was Grade II or above;
5. Patients whose Simple Intelligence Status Check Scale (Mini-Mental State Examination, MMSE) score was > 17 points (total score: 30 points).
6. The patients who could understand the purpose of the study, and those patients or their family members who provided signed informed consent.

Exclusion criteria

1. Unstable vital signs;
2. Severe heart, lung, kidney, liver, and other organ diseases;
3. Lower limb motor dysfunction caused by other diseases;
4. Seizures or the use of drugs that affect cortical excitability;
5. The presence of local skin injury of the scalp and lower limbs, which can affect the detection of EEG and electromyography;
6. Patients with severe cognitive impairment, which might have prevented them from cooperating with the researchers to complete the experimental task;

Based on the above inclusion and exclusion criteria, 94 patients with stroke hemiplegia were initially included. Among them, five patients withdrew from the study due to the experimental paradigm, three were removed because of EEG and EMG interference, and 86 patients were finally enrolled. Additionally, 45 healthy controls matched by age and sex were included to complete the clinical data acquisition, synchronous EEG-EMG test, and fMRI image acquisition.

Clinical data collection

The data acquisition system independently developed by the Harbin Institute of Technology was used for clinical data collection.

2.3 Precautions for Experiments.

Before the experimental data were collected, all individuals participated in one pre-experimental trial to ensure that they fully understood the experimental paradigm.

2.4 Synchronized EEG-EMG Test

The experimental equipment used a multichannel EEG-EMG synchronous acquisition system (independently developed by the Harbin Institute of Technology) to collect the scalp EEG signals. The system supported the hardware-level synchronous acquisition of 16-channel signals, and the acquisition frequency was 1000 Hz. The major relevant muscle EMG signals during hip/knee flexion and extension were collected.

2.5 Acquisition of fMRI Data

Data acquisition for fMRI: A 3.0 T GE Architect superconducting MR scanner was used in our hospital's magnetic resonance room. In all cases, before collecting rs-fMRI data, the participants lay flat, remained silent and still, kept their eyes open, and did not perform any systematic thinking activity. The rs-fMRI scan parameters were as follows: visual field (FOV) 220 mm 220 mm, matrix 64 64 35, TR 2000 ms, TE 30 ms, dynamic scan time 240 s, number of layers 35, and layer thickness 4 mm.

2.6 Data Preprocessing

In this study, the mirror image of a right brain injury patient was regarded as the left brain injury, such that all injuries occurred in the left brain hemisphere, and all healthy participants performed right lower limb flexion and extension movements.

EEG pretreatment
Task-state data were segmented in 4s and imported into EEGLAB for preprocessing. Using the MATLAB software EEGLAB, the principal components after noise removal were determined to be the EEG components.

EMG pretreatment
The fourth-order Butterworth bandpass filtering method was applied. Based on the frequency characteristics of the EMG signal, the lower limit cutoff frequency of the filter was set to 20 Hz, and the upper limit cutoff frequency was set to 450 Hz.

fMRI pretreatment
The raw fMRI data were preprocessed via spatial smoothing, spatial filtering, normalization, and registration. The fMRI data were analyzed using structural, fine-grained, and functional macroscales. The AAL template was used to divide the brain into 116 brain regions, and the time series of all voxels in each region were averaged to obtain a time series of 116 Regions of Interest (ROIs).

2.7 EEG Analytic Procedure

Wavelet transform

The raw signal was preprocessed using the wavelet decomposition technique. A continuous wavelet transform was applied to the preprocessed signals, and the Morlet wavelet was selected as the parent wavelet. The frequency axis division of the wavelet transform used a logarithmic interval division strategy, discretizing to the specified number of frequency points within the normalized frequency range [0.005, 0.5]. The results of the transformation of the signal in the time-frequency domain were obtained by calculating the convolution of Morlet wavelets and signals at different scales. After the wavelet transformation, the signals for each category were superimposed and averaged across trials and channels to extract stable time-frequency features. Moreover, a method of sliding window segmentation was used to set the length and the overlap ratio to further enhance the temporal resolution of the time-frequency features.

Brain network construction

Electrodes distributed in different regions of the brain and corresponding to the 16 leads were used as nodes, and FC parameters between different regions were considered to be edges. In different sub-bands, the Coh and wPLI methods are used to calculate the functional connections between different brain regions and then build the brain functional network.

Analysis of brain network graph theory properties

Network efficiency is determined by calculating the average of the inverse of the shortest path length between all pairs of nodes. By comparing the clustering coefficient of the network with the clustering coefficient of a random network of the same size, the average shortest path length is calculated at the same time. If the clustering coefficient is high and the average shortest path is short, it has a small-world attribute. The nodal clustering coefficient is the ratio of the actual number of possible connections between the node neighbors to the number of possible connections. Nodal local efficiency is the efficiency of the remaining neighbor nodes in forming a subnetwork by assuming that the node and its connections are removed. The nodal shortest path is the shortest path length from this node to the others and is calculated using algorithms such as Dijkstra.

EMG analytic procedure

The integrated EMG value analysis was performed by integrating the absolute values of the EMG signals.

2.8 fMRI Analytic Procedure

(1) Construction of the brain network

    1.Node correlation measurement function
        Pearson's correlation coefficient was used to measure the dynamics between pairwise ROIs.
    2. Rarefaction strategy

(2) Brain network attribute analysis

1. Average node degree: It refers to the number of edges directly connected to the node.
2. The global efficiency is calculated based on the reciprocal average of the shortest path length in the network.
3. The methods used to calculate the small-world properties are as follows:

① Cluster coefficient (C): For a node, its C is the ratio of the actual number of connections between its neighbors to the maximum number of possible connections. ② Feature path length (L): It is the average of the shortest paths between all pairs of nodes in the network. ③ Small-world coefficient (σ): It is an indicator of whether a network has small-world characteristics. The formula used to calculate σ is as follows:

$$\sigma = \frac{C_{real}/C_{random}}{L_{real}/L_{random}}$$

2.9 Statistical Analysis

The data were analyzed using SPSS 29.0 (IBM, Armonk, NY, USA), and $P < 0.05$ was considered to indicate statistical significance. Categorical variables were expressed as counts and percentages, and differences between groups were analyzed by the Chi-square test or Fisher's exact test.

3 Results

3.1 General Data Analysis

In this study, 86 stroke patients and 45 healthy controls were included. The basic information of the study subjects was not significantly different.

3.2 Comparative Analysis of EEG WT Maps

A comparison of the superimposed average time and frequency maps of the 16 EEG channels in the patient group and the healthy control group (Fig. 2) revealed that the effective information in the patient group (right figure) was mainly concentrated at 5–10 Hz and distributed in the theta and alpha frequency bands. The highest value of the signal energy occurred after 2–3 s rather than at the beginning of the experiment. In the time-frequency chart of the healthy control group (left panel), the signal energy was mainly concentrated from 5 to 20 Hz, with the strongest signal energy ranging from 10 to 15 Hz. Additionally, the signal energy increased significantly immediately at the beginning of the experiment.

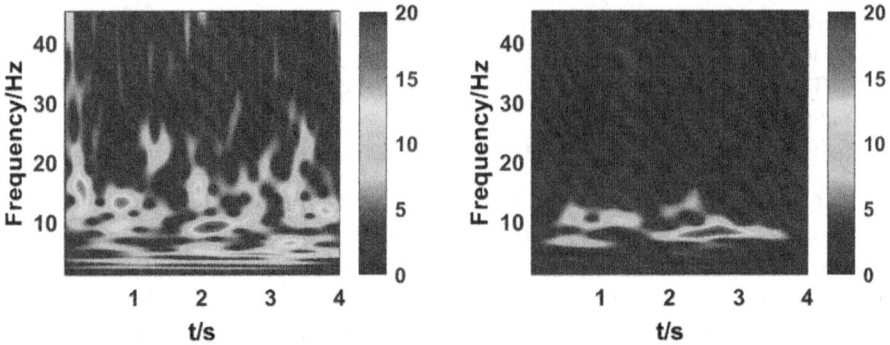

Fig. 2. Wavelet transform time-frequency graph comparison

The x-axis represents time, the y-axis represents frequency, and the color changes from blue to red indicating an increase in energy. The image on the left is the healthy control group, and the image on the right is the patient group.

3.3 Functional Connectivity of EEG Spectrum Coherence

Figure 3 illustrates the coherent functional connectivity of the patient group and the healthy controls in the alpha and beta bands. The healthy controls had rich functional connections between the alpha and beta frequency bands, with high connection strength, and the two frequency bands showed almost the same trend. Compared to that in healthy controls, the Coh FC in the alpha and beta frequency bands in IS patients was much lower in terms of connection strength and connection number. Some FC was preserved in the alpha frequency band but was weak, with greater connectivity strength between FC6-CP5, C1-C3, and CP1-P3 than between other brain regions. In the beta band, the number of connections between each brain region was small, the connection strength was weaker, and the connectivity was stronger in the left brain region than in the right brain region.

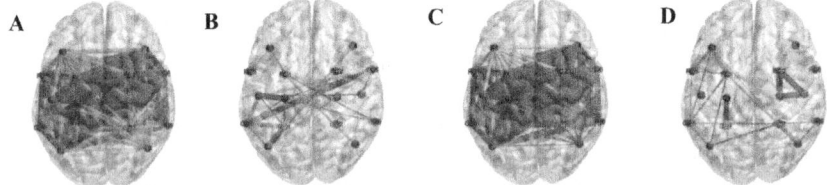

Fig. 3. Functional connectivity of Coh brain networks between patient group and healthy control group. (A)Functional connectivity of alpha band coherence in healthy individuals.(B)Functional connectivity of alpha band coherence in patients.(C)Functional connectivity of beta band coherence in healthy individuals. (D)Functional connectivity of beta band coherence in patients.

3.4 Functional Connectivity of the Brain Network According to the EEG-Weighted Phase Retardation Coefficient

Figure 4 illustrates the weighted phase lag index FC between the patient group and the healthy controls in the alpha and beta frequency bands. The healthy controls had abundant and symmetrical functional connections between brain regions in the alpha frequency band. Stroke patients had the strength and number of functional connections in the alpha frequency band. In the beta frequency band, the number of connections in stroke patients was similar to that in healthy people, but the connection strength was weaker, with significantly stronger connectivity in the left brain region than in the right brain region.

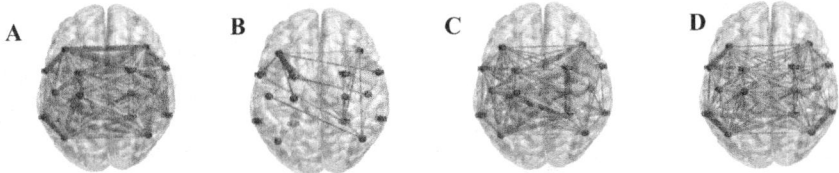

Fig. 4. Functional connectivity of wPLI brain networks between patient group and healthy control group. (A)Functional connectivity of alpha band wPLI in healthy individuals.(B)Functional connectivity of alpha band wPLI in patients.(C)Functional connectivity of beta band wPLI in healthy individuals. (D)Functional connectivity of beta band wPLI in patients.

3.5 Comparative Analysis of Brain Network Graph Theory Properties

Based on Coh and wPLI of the brain network, the differences between patients and healthy controls were analyzed for global and node attributes via graph theory (Fig. 5). The results revealed that the global attributes (network efficiency, small-world) of the Coh index in the α group were significantly lower than those in the healthy control group ($P < 0.01$), and the small-world and nodal clustering coefficients in the β group were significantly lower than those in the healthy control group ($P < 0.01$). The wPLI index in the patient group was significantly lower in the α-band small-world and nodal local efficiency than in the healthy controls ($P < 0.01$). In the β-band network efficiency, small world and nodal shortest path were significantly lower in the patient group than in the healthy controls ($P < 0.01$).

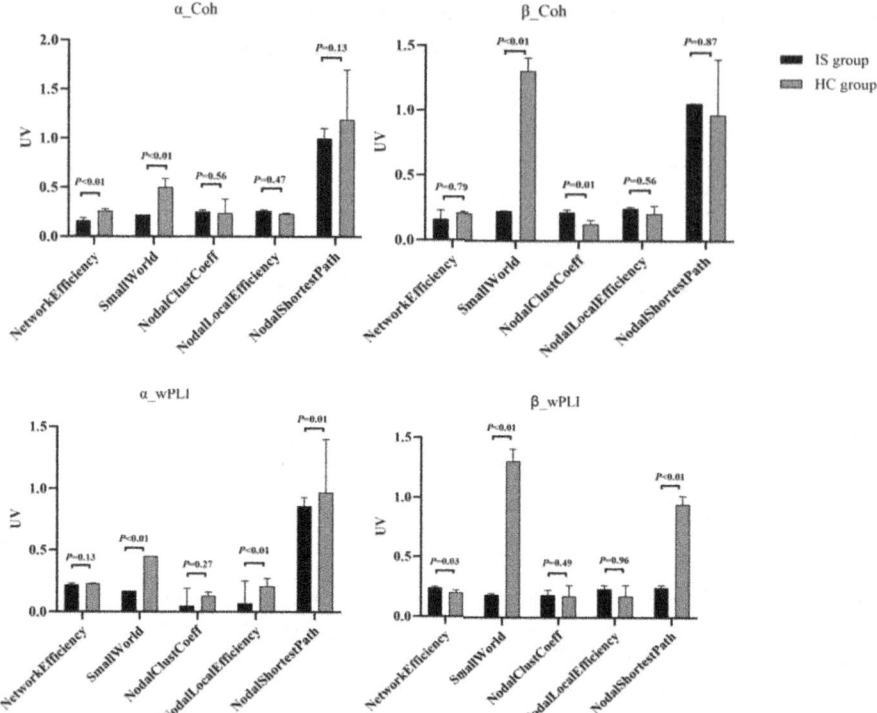

Fig. 5. Comparison of brain network graph theory properties between patient group and healthy control group. α-Coh and β-Coh represent the comparison of graph theoretic properties of Coh functional connections in alpha and beta bands, and α-wPLI and β-wPLI represent the comparison of graph theoretic properties of wPLI functional connections in alpha and beta bands, respectively. $P < 0.05$ indicates statistical significance.

3.6 Integrated EMG Values

The integrated EMG value is the integral of the absolute value of the EMG signal, reflecting the total muscle activity. When the integrated EMG values of the patient group and healthy control group were compared, the IEMG values of RF, BFLH, and Semi decreased ($P < 0.01$), and the IEMG value of the GM increased ($P < 0.01$) (Fig. 6).

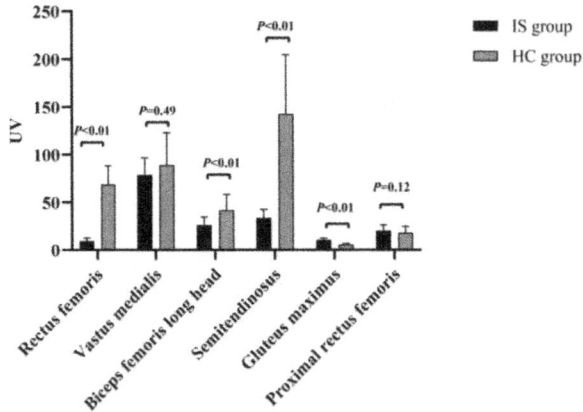

Fig. 6. IEMG comparison between patient group and healthy control group. Abbreviations: IS = Ischemic stroke. HC = Healthy control. $P < 0.05$ indicates statistical significance.

3.7 Comparative Analysis of the Correlation Matrix of 116 Brain Regions in the fMRI Brain Network AAL Template

The significance of the difference correlation coefficient matrix between the healthy control group and the patient group revealed the difference in functional connections between the two groups. By subtracting the healthy control group and patient correlation coefficient matrix, we intuitively observed the changes in pathological conditions: positive (red): the functional connections of the patient were weaker than those of healthy controls. Negative values (blue): stronger FC in the patient group than in the healthy control group. The red-blue block distribution is shown in Figure C; the pattern indicated continuous differences in functional and internetwork connectivity but modular properties (Fig. 7).

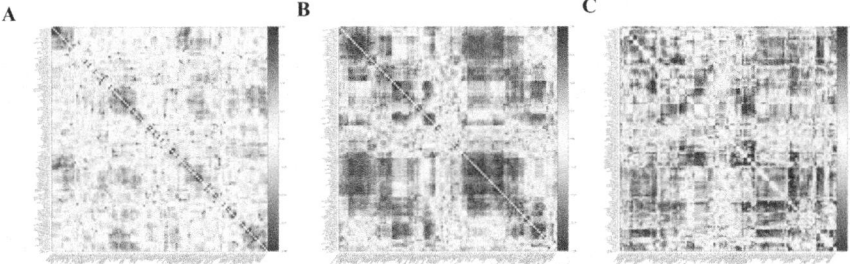

Fig. 7. Comparison of correlation matrix across 116 brain regions of fMRI brain network AAL template. (A) Patient brain region correlation matrix. (B) Healthy control group brain region correlation matrix. (C) Difference correlation matrix between healthy individuals and patients (color figure online).

3.8 Comparison Analysis of Brain Network Properties of fMRI

The average node degree, small-world attributes, and global efficiency of the brain network attributes in the stroke patient group were lower than those in the healthy control group ($P < 0.01$), reflecting that the brain functional network was significantly disrupted in the stroke patient group(Fig. 8).

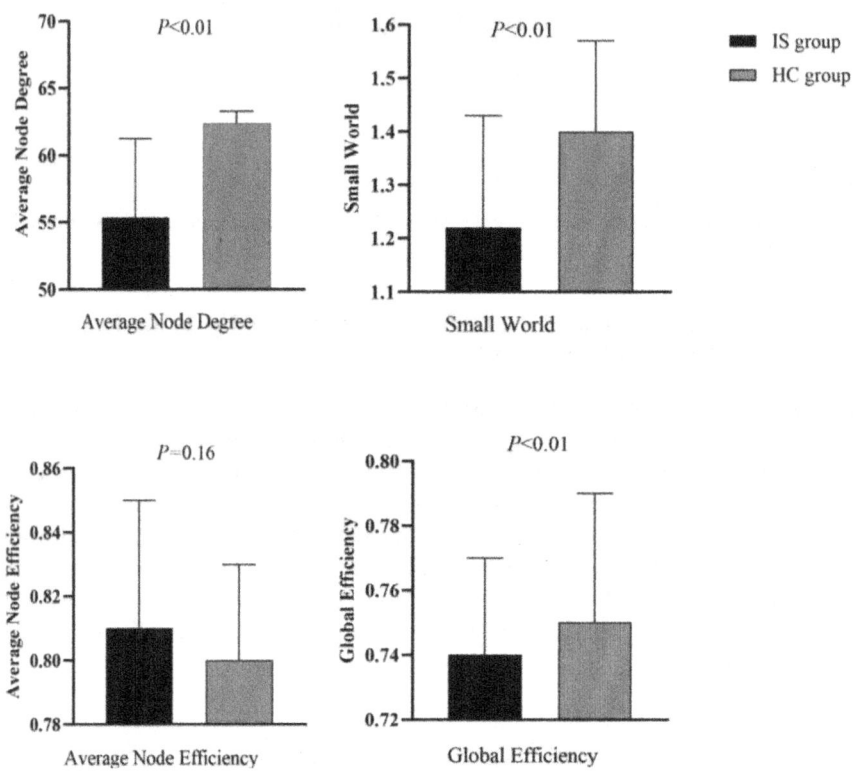

Fig. 8. Comparison map of the brain network properties between patient group and healthy control group. Abbreviations: IS = Ischemic stroke.HC = Healthy control.$P < 0.05$ indicates statistical significance.

4 Discussion

Ischemic stroke can damage the neural structure and function of the brain, leading to motor dysfunction in patients. In this study, we investigated the mechanism underlying motor dysfunction in stroke patients during lower limb motor tasks.

The results of the wavelet transform time-frequency map revealed that the EEG activity of IS patients was high in the theta and alpha frequency bands, which was consistent with the characteristics of low-frequency energy activity in stroke patients [12]. Foreman et al. Revealed that with the development of a stroke, the EEG signal shows a specific change trend; i.e., high-frequency waves become weak, and low-frequency waves become dominant [13]. Among them, the increase in the power of the δ frequency band of the electroencephalogram (EEG) signal, as a characteristic related to early ischemic stroke, has received attention [14]. The highest value of signal energy in the patient group appeared after 2–3 s, not at the beginning of the experiment, which indicates that the neural activation process in stroke patients was relatively slow; the wavelet transform time-frequency map in the healthy control group also confirmed our speculation to some extent.

A high level of brain network Coh indicates that strong synchronization between brain regions may participate in brain function activities, helping to reveal the synergistic mechanism of brain function. In this study, the alpha and beta frequency bands of healthy controls showed high connectivity, including multiple areas in the left hemisphere. These strong connections suggest that the motor and sensory functions of neural integration ability are strong in healthy controls. The Patient groups presented significantly decreased connectivity in the alpha and beta frequency bands. Most areas have reduced FC and lower strength, which indicates that the functional network of the brain is disrupted after stroke, especially the weakened synergy between the left and right hemispheres, resulting in information processing ability and motor control function, which is consistent with the findings of other studies [15].

The organization pattern of brain networks can be understood by wPLI; larger wPLI values indicate a stronger degree of phase synchronization between brain regions, i.e., stronger FC. The FC in stroke patients decreases substantially in the alpha frequency band, indicating the disruption of stroke-induced resting-state networks in the brain. In the beta frequency band, although the number of connections is large, the intensity is relatively weak, indicating that the strength of phase synchronization in the brain interval decreases in task-related motor and perceptual functions but maintains extensive FC. The FC is mainly concentrated in the left brain area, and the intensity is lower than that recorded in healthy people, reflecting the poor movement-related network function of patients and the need to restore some function through compensation.

In this study, the brain networks Coh and wPLI, combined with the global properties of graph theory and node properties, were used to analyze the differences between patients and healthy controls in the α- and β-frequency bands, which reflected the brain transmission barriers, information transmission speed, information transmission efficiency, and impaired integration and separation of brain function.

The IEMG values reflect the total amount of muscle activity in a certain period and can be used as an indicator of muscle fatigue. Stephenson et al. Reported that stroke patients have weaker lower limb muscles; inadequate knee extension; hip, knee, and ankle movement timing disorders; and poor motor coordination. These adversities further hinder the recovery of the walking ability of patients [16]. This study revealed decreased IEMG values for RF, BFLH, and SEMi ($P < 0.01$) and increased IEMG values for GM ($P < 0.01$), which was similar to the findings of another study [17].

Overall, the brain has low FC, suggesting that stroke may have damaged overall brain network function. Poorly correlated regions block information transmission between brain networks, reflecting network dysregulation after stroke. The greater correlation in some brain regions may represent the self-regulatory ability or compensatory mechanisms of the brain. Graph-theoretic attribute analysis of brain networks helps understand the processing and integration of information in the brain [18]. In this study, the brain functional network attributes of the patients decreased comprehensively, suggesting that stroke leads to local brain tissue damage and FC interruption, which decreases information transmission efficiency in the brain region.

The brain is plastic and undergoes adaptive changes after stroke, leading to reorganization and compensation of the neural network. The mechanism underlying motor function rehabilitation and brain motor network remodeling after stroke is a popular research topic. This study integrates the frontiers of medical and engineering research to further assess the neural remodeling mechanism based on the occurrence mechanism of lower limb movement disorders in stroke patients.

5 Conclusion

The results of the multimodal signal analysis led to the following conclusions: the decrease in brain network connectivity and the overall decline in brain network graph theory attribute indicators may be the key mechanisms underlying the occurrence of lower limb motor dysfunction. Additionally, the active low-frequency energy of EEG signals, the weakened synergy between the left and right hemispheres, the reduced coherence of brain-muscle coupling, and an increase in the efficiency and complexity of information transmission from muscle to the brain may jointly contribute to the occurrence of lower limb motor dysfunction.

Funding. This work was supported by the National Key R&D Program of China [grant numbers 2022YFC3601700].

Ethics Approval and Consent to Participate. The study protocol was approved by the Ethics Committee of the 2nd Affiliated Hospital of Harbin Medical University (Harbin, China), and the study was conducted according to the principles of the Helsinki Declaration II. All patients signed an informed consent form.

Competing Interests. The authors declare no competing financial interests.

References

1. Caltagirone, C., et al.: Co-Ultramicronized Palmitoylethanolamide/Luteolin in the Treatment of Cerebral Ischemia: From Rodent to Man. Transl Stroke Res **7**, 54–69 (2016)
2. Daidone, M., Cataldi, M., Pinto, A., Tuttolomondo, A.: Non-coding rnas and other determinants of neuroinflammation and endothelial dysfunction: regulation of gene expression in the acute phase of ischemic stroke and possible therapeutic applications. Neural Regen. Res. **16**, 2154–2158 (2021)
3. Sanchez-Bezanilla, S., et al.: Growth hormone promotes motor function after experimental stroke and enhances recovery-promoting mechanisms within the peri-infarct area. Int. J. Mol. Sci. **21**, 606 (2020)

4. Merica, H., Fortune, R.D.: A neuronal transition probability model for the evolution of power in the sigma and delta frequency bands of sleep eeg. Physiol. Behav. **62**, 585–589 (1997)
5. Raichle, M.E.: The restless brain. Brain Connect **1**, 3–12 (2011)
6. Yang, K., et al.: Exploration of effective electroencephalography features for the recognition of different valence emotions. Front. Neurosci. **16**, 1010951 (2022)
7. Bezmaternykh, D., et al.: Application of fmri and simultaneous fmri-eeg neurofeedback in post-stroke motor rehabilitation. Bull. Exp. Biol. Med. **171**, 379–383 (2021)
8. Averta, G., et al.: U-Limb: a multi-modal, multi-center database on arm motion control in healthy and post-stroke conditions. GigaScience **10**, giab043 (2021)
9. Wang, X., et al.: Impact of the Alberta stroke program Ct Score subregions on long-term functional outcomes in acute ischemic stroke: results from two multicenter studies in China. J. Transl. Int. Med. **12**, 197–208 (2024)
10. Tsvetanov, K.A., et al.: Extrinsic and intrinsic brain network connectivity maintains cognition across the lifespan despite accelerated decay of regional brain activation. J. Neurosci. **36**, 3115–3126 (2016)
11. White Iii, R.L., Campbell, M.C., Yang, D., Shannon, W., Snyder, A.Z., Perlmutter, J.S.: Little change in functional brain networks following acute levodopa in drug-naive parkinson's disease. Mov. Disord. **35**, 499–503 (2020)
12. 12Sun, R., Wong, W.-W., Gao, J., Wong, G.F., Tong, R.K.-Y.: Abnormal eeg complexity and alpha oscillation of resting state in chronic stroke patients. Annu. Int. Conf. IEEE Eng. Med. Biol. Soc. 6053–6057 (2021)
13. Foreman, B., Claassen, J.: Quantitative eeg for the detection of brain ischemia. Crit. Care **16**, 1–9 (2012)
14. Tolonen, U., Sulg, I.: Comparison of quantitative eeg parameters from four different analysis techniques in evaluation of relationships between eeg and Cbf in brain infarction. Electroencephalogr. Clin. Neurophysiol. **51**, 177–185 (1981)
15. Zhao, Z., et al.: Altered intra-and inter-network functional coupling of resting-state networks associated with motor dysfunction in stroke. Hum. Brain Mapp. **39**, 3388–3397 (2018)
16. Stephenson, J.L., Lamontagne, A., De Serres, S.J.: The coordination of upper and lower limb movements during gait in healthy and stroke individuals. Gait Posture **29**, 11–16 (2009)
17. Wen, H., et al.: Thigh muscle function in stroke patients revealed by velocity-encoded cine phase-contrast magnetic resonance imaging. Muscle Nerve **37**, 736–744 (2008)
18. Telesford, Q.K., Simpson, S.L., Burdette, J.H., Hayasaka, S., Laurienti, P.J.: The brain as a complex system: using network science as a tool for understanding the brain. Brain Connect **1**, 295–308 (2011)

FuPaD: Scalable Pose Estimation by Fusing Patch-Wise VGGT with Dense Bundle Adjustment

Dexin Qi[1,2,3], Tao Tao[1,2,3(✉)], Zhihong Zhang[1,2,3], and Xuesong Mei[1,2,3]

[1] School of Mechanical Engineering, Xi'an Jiaotong University, Xi'an 710049, Shaanxi, China
{dexin.qi,zhangzhihong}@stu.xjtu.edu.cn,
{taotao,xsmei}@mail.xjtu.edu.cn
[2] State Key Laboratory for Manufacturing System Engineering, Xi'an 710049, Shaanxi, China
[3] Shaanxi Key Laboratory of Intelligent Robots, Xi'an 710049, Shaanxi, China

Abstract. Pose estimation, a cornerstone of 3D computer vision, is crucial for applications such as autonomous driving and augmented reality. Global feed-forward methods, such as VGGT, demonstrate potential in direct scene reconstruction and pose inference. However, they are often constrained by prohibitive memory requirements when processing long sequences typical in large-scale environments. Furthermore, the accuracy of their single-pass predictions is often limited by the absence of explicit local geometric modeling or iterative refinement. To address these limitations, we introduce FuPaD, a novel hierarchical approach for scalable pose estimation. FuPaD integrates global pose priors derived from a tailored VGGT with the local refinement offered by dense bundle adjustment (DBA). First, a tracking-informed patch sampling strategy is introduced to select salient image patches from keyframes. These patches are subsequently processed by the tailored VGGT to yield globally consistent keyframe pose priors, meanwhile significantly reducing the memory footprint compared to frame-wise processing. These global keyframe poses are then integrated with dense local pose estimates from DBA within a pose graph optimization framework. Finally, a global DBA module further refines all poses. Such hierarchical fusion ensures the global consistency while benefiting from the fine-grained local refinement provided by DBA. Evaluation on benchmarks indicates that FuPaD achieves competitive pose accuracy, particularly in large-scale scenarios, while exhibiting computational and memory efficiency.

Keywords: Deep Learning for Visual Perception · Deep Learning Methods · Visual SLAM · 3D Reconstruction

1 Introduction

Pose estimation, the task of determining the camera's position and orientation from input images, is a fundamental and enduring research problem in computer vision. It underpins a series of applications, including autonomous navigation, augmented reality, and robotic navigation.

Traditional pose estimation methods often rely on sensor systems that directly measure depth, such as structured light, Time-of-Flight, or LiDAR. While effective, these methods can involve complex sensor systems, require substantial prior knowledge, and exhibit sensitivity to environmental conditions. Furthermore, pose estimation is inherently associated with 3D reconstruction [11,12] and Simultaneous Localization and Mapping (SLAM) systems like ORB-SLAM [2]. Despite their potential for accurate pose estimation on short sequences, these systems typically adopt an incremental estimation paradigm, often based on pair-wise image association, which can lead to the accumulation of drift over long sequences.

Deep learning has significant advancements in this domain. DROID-SLAM [15], for instance, employs a deep neural network for dense optical flow(DOF) estimation and recurrently updates poses and depth through a dense bundle adjustment(DBA) layer, demonstrating remarkable local accuracy. Concurrently, feed-forward 3D reconstruction methods also have propelled progress in pose estimation. Approaches like MASt3R [7] and DUSt3R [17] can predict per-viewpoint poses and 3D point clouds end-to-end from input images. MASt3R-SLAM [9] further leverages MASt3R's reconstruction capabilities to enhance SLAM performance. Nevertheless, such deep learning approaches, particularly those processing sequences incrementally or with limited global context, remain susceptible to the accumulation of errors, leading to well-known drifting problem. Although loop closure techniques can alleviate drifts, their effectiveness is often constrained by factors such as sparse visual overlap or perceptual aliasing.

More recently, VGGT [16] introduced an alternative approach by processing an entire image set simultaneously to infer scene geometry and camera poses globally. This method has demonstrated notable improvements in reconstruction accuracy and speed. Its feed-forward nature and ability to generate high-quality reconstructions from sparse views make it very efficient, especially for object-centric scenes where the complete set of views can be processed concurrently. However, VGGT's prerequisite of ingesting the complete image sequence poses a significant challenge for consumer-grade GPUs when dealing with large-scale environments, such as those encountered in robotics mapping, which involve extensive image sequences. Processing such long sequences directly with VGGT leads to prohibitive GPU memory consumption. Additionally, VGGT's single feed-forward prediction, without explicit modeling of local geometry or iterative refinement, makes performance sensitive to input images quality.

To overcome these challenges, we propose FuPaD (**Fu**sing **Pa**tch-wise VGGT with **D**ense Bundle Adjustment), a novel method designed to enhance long-sequence pose estimation by building upon VGGT's strengths while mitigating its limitations. First, FuPaD utilizes image patches instead of full images as input to VGGT. This patch-wise strategy reduces memory requirements, thereby enabling VGGT's application to large-scale scenes. Then, a tracking-informed patch sampling mechanism is introduced. This mechanism converts a dense input image stream into a sparse patch stream by identifying keyframes and subsequently extracting a limited set of informative, long-term tracked patches from these keyframes. Such targeted selection enhances the accuracy and robustness of the patch-wise VGGT predictions. Finally, based on the global keyframe poses obtained from patch-wise VGGT, a hierarchical pose estimation framework is employed. A pose graph integrates VGGT's global pose estimates for keyframes with precise local relative pose estimates derived from DBA. Essentially, patch-wise VGGT provides global poses for keyframes, addressing long-term drift, while DBA contributes accurate local estimations and facilitates dense refinement. This design achieves a balance between memory footprint, computational efficiency, and accuracy, enabling robust pose estimation in large-scale environments.

In summary, our main contributions are:

- We propose a novel patch-wise inference scheme for VGGT, tailored for pose estimation, which uses image patches instead of full images as input, reducing memory demands and enabling its application to long sequences.
- We introduce a tracking-informed patch sampling strategy that selects salient patches, improving the robustness and accuracy of the patch-wise VGGT.
- We develop a hierarchical pose estimation framework that fuses global keyframe poses from patch-wise VGGT with local relative poses from DBA via pose graph optimization, effectively balancing global consistency and local accuracy.
- Evaluation on benchmarks indicates that FuPaD surpasses baseline methods on pose estimation in large-scale scenes.

2 Related Work

Our work builds upon and extends recent advancements in end-to-end 3D reconstruction, and Simultaneous Localization and Mapping (SLAM). This section provides an overview of relevant literature in these interconnected fields.

2.1 Feed-Forward Pose Estimation and 3D Reconstruction

Traditional structure-from-motion (SfM) and SLAM pipelines often involve multiple stages, including feature extraction, matching, and iterative bundle adjustment. In contrast, feed-forward methods aim to directly predict camera poses and 3D scene structure from input images in a single pass through a neural network. Early works like PoseNet [5] demonstrated the feasibility of regressing camera pose from a single image in an end-to-end manner. Subsequent methods, such as DSAC [1], focused on improving the pose prediction's robustness and accuracy by the differentiable counterpart of RANSAC.

Deep learning has also facilitated end-to-end 3D reconstruction from multi-view images, often jointly with camera pose estimation. Methods have emerged that can simultaneously reconstruct 3D geometry and predict camera poses in a end-to-end manner. MASt3R [7] and DUSt3R [17] are recent introduced methods that predict both 3D pointmaps and camera poses for input view pairs in a feed-forward manner. However, these methods typically rely on pair-wise view processing, which can lead to inefficiencies and limitations in global consistency. VGGT [16] further pushed the boundaries by achieving state-of-the-art 3D reconstruction and pose estimation without explicit pair-wise view processing, instead relying on a alternative-attention module to infer global scene structure and camera poses from a set of unordered images. VGGT's ability to handle sparse views and its impressive reconstruction quality make it a strong candidate for global localization. However, as discussed, its requirement for simultaneous full-frame inputs limits its applicability to very long image sequences due to prohibitive memory consumption. Our work aims to leverage VGGT's global consistency while alleviating its memory bottleneck.

2.2 Simultaneous Localization and Mapping (SLAM)

SLAM systems aim to simultaneously track the poses of sensor observations and estimate a map for an unknown environment. SLAM methods can be broadly categorized into feature-based methods and direct methods.

Feature-Based SLAM, such as the ORB-SLAM series [2], rely on extracting salient key-points (SIFT or ORB) from images, matching them across views, and then optimizing poses and landmark positions through bundle adjustment. While generally robust, their performance can be compromised in texture-poor environments.

Direct SLAM methods, in contrast, operate on pixel intensities, optimizing poses by minimizing photometric errors between warped views. Representative examples include DSO [3] and SVO [4]. Such approaches can provide denser reconstructions and may be more effective in low-texture areas, although they can exhibit greater sensitivity to photometric variations and often require robust initialization.

Deep Learning in SLAM. The integration of deep learning has significantly impacted SLAM. DROID-SLAM [15] stands out as a leading deep learning-based direct SLAM system. It utilizes a recurrent neural network to estimate dense optical flow and confidences between frames. These correspondences are then used within a differentiable dense bundle adjustment (DBA) layer to iteratively refine camera poses and inverse depth maps. DROID-SLAM achieves remarkable accuracy, especially in local trajectory estimation. However, like other incremental methods, it can still suffer from drift over long sequences if global constraints are not sufficiently strong.

FuPaD synthesizes concepts from both feed-forward reconstruction and SLAM. A patch-wise VGGT module is leveraged for its global scene understanding, providing robust global pose priors for keyframes to mitigate long-term drift. These global pose priors are subsequently integrated with local refinement offered by DBA. This integration results in a framework tailored to be globally consistent and locally accurate, while also being scalable to extensive environments.

3 Method

The proposed FuPaD is designed to achieve accurate and scalable pose estimation for long image sequences. It operates hierarchically, first establishing globally consistent poses for a sparse set of keyframes using a memory-efficient patch-wise VGGT. Subsequently, this global information is fused with local motion estimates, and the entire trajectory is refined using dense bundle adjustment (DBA). An overview of the FuPaD pipeline is depicted in Fig. 1.

3.1 Patch-Wise VGGT for Global Keyframe Poses

The primary motivation for employing a patch-wise VGGT is to harness its capability for inferring global-consistent poses while substantially reducing its memory footprint, thereby rendering it suitable for long sequences. This module comprises two main steps: tracking-informed patch sampling and subsequent patch-based pose prediction. These steps both rely on the initial motion estimation and keyframe selection derived from a pre-processing stage as described below.

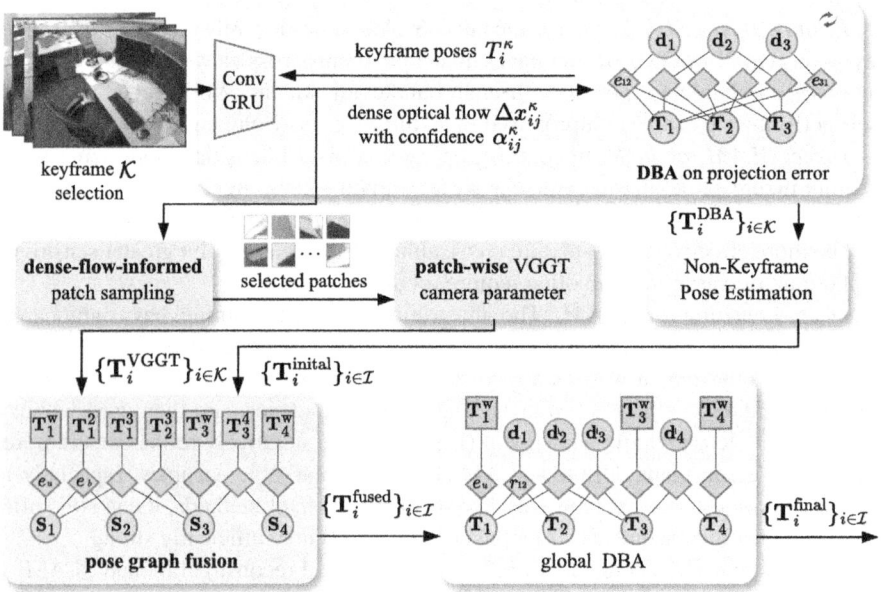

Fig. 1. Overview of the FuPaD pipeline. Patches are sampled from keyframes according to dense optical flow information and fed into the patch-wise VGGT to predict global pose priors. Then, these pose priors are fused with local relative poses by a dense bundle adjustment module to estimate the final poses.

Initial Motion Estimation and Keyframe Selection. Prior to patch sampling, the input image sequence undergoes an initial processing stage. This stage, typically performed by a system employing dense optical flow and iterative bundle adjustment (akin to DROID-SLAM), sequentially estimates relative camera poses and dense scene geometry. Specifically, a dense optical flow network provides initial estimates of optical flow fields $\Delta \mathbf{x}_{ij}$ between frame I_i and a neighboring frame I_j, along with associated confidence scores α_{ij}. These outputs are utilized to establish pixel correspondences across frames. An update operator then iteratively refines camera poses $\mathbf{T}_k \in SE(3)$ and inverse depth maps $\mathbf{d}_k$ for keyframes $I_k \in \mathcal{K}$ by minimizing a reprojection error based

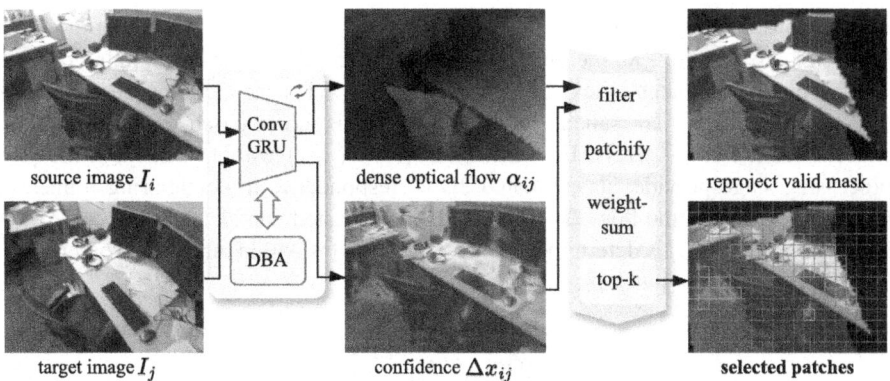

Fig. 2. Tracking-informed patch sampling. The image is divided into a grid of patches, and each patch's salience is scored based on the track-ability and confidence of its pixels. The top patches are selected for input to patch-wise VGGT.

on these flow predictions. A general form of this bundle adjustment objective, focusing on photometric or geometric consistency using flow, can be expressed as:

$$\{\mathbf{T}_k^{DBA}, \mathbf{d}_k^{DBA}\}_{k \in \mathcal{K}}^{\star} = \arg\min_{\{\mathbf{T}_k, \mathbf{d}_k\}} \sum_{k \in \mathcal{K}} \sum_{j \in \mathcal{N}_k} \sum_{\mathbf{p} \in I_k} \rho\left(\alpha_{kj} \cdot \left\|\mathbf{p}'_{kj} - \mathbf{p}^{\star}_{kj}\right\|_2^2\right) \quad (1)$$

where $\mathcal{N}_k$ are neighbors of keyframe I_k, $\mathbf{p}$ denotes a pixel in I_k, and ρ is a robust loss function. $\mathbf{p}'_{kj}$ denotes the re-projection of pixel $\mathbf{p}$ from I_k into I_j using poses $\mathbf{T}_k, \mathbf{T}_j$ and depth $\mathbf{d}_k$. $\mathbf{p}^{\star}_{kj}$ denotes the target location predicted by the dense optical flow network:

$$\mathbf{p}'_{kj} = \Pi\left(\mathbf{T}_k \mathbf{T}_j^{-1} \Pi^{-1}\left(\mathbf{p}, \mathbf{d}_k\right)\right) \quad (2a)$$

$$\mathbf{p}^{\star}_{kj} = \mathbf{p} + \Delta \mathbf{x}_{kj} \quad (2b)$$

where Π is the projection function, Π^{-1} is the back-projection.

The dense optical flow estimation and the update operator are applied alternately to mitigate convergence to local optima. To avoid processing overly dense or static segments, a subset of frames is selected as keyframes $\mathcal{K}$. A frame I_k is selected as a keyframe if the average magnitude of the initially predicted optical flow between I_k and its preceding frame I_{k-1} exceeds a predefined threshold τ_{flow}. In summary, this initial processing stage yields:

- A set of keyframes $\mathcal{K}$.
- Keyframe poses $\{\mathbf{T}_k^{DBA}\}_{k \in \mathcal{K}}$ obtained in a pair-wise manner.
- Dense optical flow fields $\Delta \mathbf{x}_{kj}$ and confidence scores α_{kj} for pixels in keyframe I_k corresponding to neighboring frames I_j (where $j \in \mathcal{N}_k$).

Those information are subsequently utilized for patch sampling.

Tracking-Informed Patch Sampling. To ensure that image patches supplied to VGGT are informative and conducive to robust global pose estimation, information derived from the aforementioned dense optical flow tracking is leveraged. As shown in Fig. 2, for each keyframe $I_k \in \mathcal{K}$, the image is divided into a grid of non-overlapping patches $p_{k,l}$ (where l is the patch index), compatible with VGGT's encoder input requirements (e.g., 14×14 pixels). The salience of each patch $p_{k,l}$ is scored based on the trackability and confidence of its pixels. For each pixel $\mathbf{p} = (u, v)$ within patch $p_{k,l}$, the pre-processing stage provides its estimated 2D correspondence in neighboring frames I_j (where $j \in \mathcal{N}_k$) via the flow $\Delta \mathbf{x}_{kj}(\mathbf{p})$, and an associated confidence score $\alpha_{kj}(\mathbf{p})$. A validity mask $m_{kj}(\mathbf{p})$ is determined (1 if $\mathbf{p} + \Delta \mathbf{x}_{kj}(\mathbf{p})$ is within image I_j, 0 otherwise). The score $S(p_{k,l})$ for patch $p_{k,l}$ is defined as:

$$S(p_{k,l}) = \sum_{\mathbf{p} \in p_{k,l}} \sum_{j \in \mathcal{N}_k} m_{kj}(\mathbf{p}) \cdot \alpha_{kj}(\mathbf{p}) \tag{3}$$

From each keyframe I_k, the top θ_{ppf} patches with the highest scores $S(p_{k,l})$ are selected. This strategy prioritizes reliably tracked and informative regions for VGGT input and ensures a consistent input structure for VGGT's frame-wise transformer.

VGGT Pose Prediction. The selected patches from all keyframes $\{I_k\}_{k \in \mathcal{K}}$, along with their original 2D coordinates, are processed by the VGGT model. The VGGT architecture, comprising a ViT image encoder followed by a view transformer, excels at establishing a global scene representation. In our application, we utilize only the camera parameter prediction head of VGGT, discarding components like the DPT depth prediction head, which require denser inputs incompatible with our patch-wise strategy. Given the set of patch features $\{\mathbf{f}_{k,l}\}$ derived from the selected patches $p_{k,l}$ of keyframes $I_k \in \mathcal{K}$, VGGT outputs a set of camera parameters $\{\mathbf{g}_k\}_{k \in \mathcal{K}}$:

$$\{\mathbf{g}_k\}_{k \in \mathcal{K}} = \mathbf{F}_{\text{camera}}(\{\mathbf{f}_{k,l} | I_k \in \mathcal{K}, l = 1..\theta_{\text{ppf}}\}) \tag{4}$$

These camera parameters $\mathbf{g}_k$ are then decoded into $SE(3)$ camera poses $\{\mathbf{T}_k^{\text{VGGT}}\}_{k \in \mathcal{K}}$. These poses are globally consistent relative to each other (sharing a common origin with $\mathbf{T}_{k=0}^{\text{DBA}} = \mathbf{T}_{k=0}^{\text{VGGT}}$) and provide a robust scaffold for mitigating long-term drift in the overall trajectory.

3.2 Hierarchical Pose Estimation with Dense Bundle Adjustment

Although our patch-wise VGGT yields globally consistent poses for sparse keyframes and significantly reduces memory requirements, it does not directly provide pose estimates for all frames in the original dense sequence. Furthermore, the overall accuracy can be enhanced by integrating these global estimates with fine-grained local motion information and performing comprehensive refinement. To this end, FuPaD employs a hierarchical pose estimation framework which involves three main stages:

1. *Initial Dense Trajectory Estimation*: Estimate poses of non-keyframes based on the dense optical flow and keyframe poses obtained from Sect. 3.1.
2. *Graph-Based Fusion with Scale Alignment*: The initial dense trajectory is fused with the global-consistent poses priors from patch-wise VGGT in a pose graph manner.
3. *Global Dense Bundle Adjustment*: A final DBA step refines all poses.

Initial Dense Trajectory Estimation. An initial dense trajectory for all input frames, denoted $\{\mathbf{T}_i^{\text{init}}\}_{i \in \mathcal{I}}$, is established based on the outputs of the initial DBA-based pre-processing stage (Sect. 3.1). Because only keyframe poses $\{\mathbf{T}_k^{\text{DBA}}\}_{k \in \mathcal{K}}$ are provided, poses for non-keyframe views I_m (where $m \in \{k_a + 1, \cdots, k_b - 1\}$) located between two consecutive keyframes I_{k_a} and I_{k_b} (with $k_a, k_b \in \mathcal{K}$) are required to solve. This is achieved by constructing a local optimization window where the poses of the bracketing keyframes, $\mathbf{T}_{k_a}^{\text{DBA}}$ and $\mathbf{T}_{k_b}^{\text{DBA}}$, are held fixed. The poses of the intermediate non-keyframes $\{\mathbf{T}_m\}$ are then refined by minimizing the reprojection error in Eq. 2, utilizing optical flow correspondences from the pre-processing stage. This stage gives every frame in the sequence an initial pose estimation $\{\mathbf{T}_i^{\text{init}}\}_{i \in \mathcal{I}}$. Note that non-keyframe poses are initialized by interpolating between $\mathbf{T}_{k_a}^{\text{DBA}}$ and $\mathbf{T}_{k_b}^{\text{DBA}}$ to accelerate convergence.

Graph-Based Fusion with Scale Alignment. A pose graph $\mathcal{G} = (\mathcal{V}, \mathcal{E})$ is constructed to fuse the global pose priors from patch-wise VGGT with local motion estimations. Given that both the initial DBA-derived poses and VGGT poses share a common coordinate origin (first keyframe pose $\mathbf{T}_{k=0}^{\text{DBA}} = \mathbf{T}_{k=0}^{\text{VGGT}}$), the primary challenge addressed is the inherent scale ambiguity of monocular systems. The nodes $\mathcal{V} = \{\mathbf{S}_i\}_{i \in \mathcal{I}}$ in this graph represent camera poses for all frames, parameterized in $Sim(3)$ to explicitly manage scale. These are initialized from $\{\mathbf{T}_i^{\text{init}}\}_{i \in \mathcal{I}}$ by augmenting them with an initial scale $s_i^{\text{init}} = 1$. The graph incorporates two types of constraints:

- *Local Relative Pose Constraints.* For temporally adjacent frames (I_i, I_j), binary edges represent the relative pose transformations $\Delta \mathbf{T}_{i,j}^{\text{DBA}}$ obtained from the pre-processing stage. The error term for these constraints, $e_b(\Delta \mathbf{T}_{i,j}^{\text{DBA}}, \mathbf{S}_i, \mathbf{S}_j)$, compares $\Delta \mathbf{T}_{i,j}^{\text{DBA}}$ with the relative motion derived from the current estimates $\mathbf{S}_i^{-1} \mathbf{S}_j$.
- *Global Keyframe Absolute Pose Priors.* For each keyframe $I_k \in \mathcal{K}$, its global pose prior $\mathbf{T}_k^{\text{VGGT}}$ from patch-wise VGGT is incorporated as a unary factor. The error term $e_u(\mathbf{T}_k^{\text{VGGT}}, \mathbf{S}_k)$ compares $\mathbf{T}_k^{\text{VGGT}}$ with the graph node $\mathbf{S}_k$. These priors guide the overall scale and global consistency of the trajectory.

The optimization problem seeks the set of $Sim(3)$ poses $\mathbf{S}^* = \{\mathbf{S}_i^*\}_{i \in \mathcal{I}}$ that minimizes:

$$\underset{\{\mathbf{S}_i\}_{i \in \mathcal{I}}}{\arg\min} \left(\sum_{k \in \mathcal{K}} \|e_u(\mathbf{T}_k^{\text{VGGT}}, \mathbf{S}_k)\|_{\boldsymbol{\Omega}_k^{\text{VGGT}}}^2 + \sum_{(i,j) \in \mathcal{E}} \|e_b(\Delta \mathbf{T}_{i,j}^{\text{DBA}}, \mathbf{S}_i, \mathbf{S}_j)\|_{\boldsymbol{\Omega}_{i,j}^{\text{DBA}}}^2 \right) \quad (5)$$

where $\boldsymbol{\Omega}_k^*$ is the information matrix. This optimization yields a global-consistent and scale-consistent trajectory, from which the fused poses $\{\mathbf{T}_i^{\text{fuse}}\}_{i \in \mathcal{I}}$ are obtained.

Global Dense Bundle Adjustment. Following pose graph optimization, a final global DBA step is performed for comprehensive refinement. This stage takes the fused poses $\{\mathbf{T}_i^{\text{fuse}}\}_{i \in \mathcal{I}}$ as initialization. It simultaneously optimizes all camera poses $\{\mathbf{T}_i\}_{i \in \mathcal{I}}$ and dense per-pixel inverse depth maps $\{\mathbf{d}_i\}$ by minimizing a reprojection error. This error is based on pixel correspondences derived from the dense optical flow estimated during the initial pre-processing stage. The objective function for this global DBA is:

$$\{\mathbf{T}_i^{\text{final}}\}^* = \underset{\{\mathbf{T}_i\}}{\arg\min} \sum_{i \in \mathcal{I}} \sum_{j \in \mathcal{N}_k'} \sum_{\mathbf{p} \in I_k} \rho \left(\alpha_{ij} \cdot \|\mathbf{p}_{ij}' - \mathbf{p}_{ij}^\star\|_2^2 \right) \quad (6)$$

$\mathcal{N}'_k$ is the new set of neighbors constructed based on the view overlap references of the fused pose. ρ is a robust loss function. $\mathbf{p}'_{ij}$ and $\mathbf{p}^\star_{ij}$ is defined in Eq. 2(b) and Eq. 2(c), respectively. This final DBA step leverages densely established pixel correspondences and globally aligned pose priors to achieve high-fidelity local detail while maintaining global consistency, resulting in the final estimated poses $\{\mathbf{T}_i^{\text{final}}\}_{i \in \mathcal{I}}$.

4 Experiments

4.1 Datasets and Metrics

We evaluate our method on a challenging real-world captured dataset, 7-Scenes [13], under monocular RGB setting, which consists of low-resolution images with severe motion blurs. Following NICER-SLAM [18], we use the 01 sequence of each scene. This dataset is suitable for evaluating pose estimation accuracy with limited scale variation and moderate camera motion. For quantitative evaluation, we primarily use the Absolute Trajectory Error (ATE) as defined in [14].

Table 1. Absolute Trajectory Error (ATE RMSE [m]) on 7-Scenes [13] (unit: m) dataset. The blue cells indicate the best and the green ones are the second best.

	Chess	Fire	Heads	Office	Pumpkin	Kitchen	Stairs	Avg.
DSO [3]	0.189	0.075	0.213	0.110	0.566	0.318	0.154	0.232
NICER-SLAM [18]	**0.033**	0.069	0.042	0.108	0.200	**0.039**	0.108	0.086
DROID-SLAM* [15]	0.047	0.038	0.034	0.136	0.166	0.080	0.044	0.078
MASt3R-SLAM [7]	0.063	0.046	0.029	0.103	**0.114**	0.074	**0.032**	0.066
SLAM3R [8]	0.063	0.053	0.045	0.124	0.117	0.095	0.093	0.084
FuPaD (Ours)	0.040	**0.037**	**0.025**	**0.097**	0.143	0.056	0.046	**0.063**

4.2 Baselines

We benchmark FuPaD against a selection of representative pose estimation methods.

- DSO [3]: A direct sparse visual odometry system that optimizes photometric errors, known for its robustness and efficiency.
- NICER-SLAM [18]: A recent method that combines neural implicit representations with SLAM, achieving state-of-the-art performance on several benchmarks.
- DROID-SLAM [15]: A leading deep learning-based SLAM system that employs a recurrent dense optical flow prediction network and a dense bundle adjustment layer for pose estimation with high local accuracy.
- MASt3R-SLAM [9]: A recent SLAM framework that integrates MASt3R's reconstruction capabilities with sequential inputs, providing a strong baseline for comparison, MASt3R-SLAM enables reconstruction with uncalibrated inputs.

– SLAM3R [8]: A recent method that combines feed-forward 3D reconstruction with SLAM, achieving competitive results on long sequences.

Publicly available implementations with their recommended configurations were utilized for all baseline methods to ensure fair comparison.

4.3 Implementation Details

Our FuPaD system is implemented in PyTorch. The patch-wise VGGT component utilizes the pre-trained DINOv2 [10] as its image encoder backbone, similar to the original VGGT. We set the number of selected patches per keyframe $\theta_{ppf} = 128$. This value is chosen to balance information content and memory efficiency. The DBA component is implementations by a CUDA function. The pose graph optimization is implemented based on the g2o [6] framework. All experiments are conducted on a workstation equipped with an NVIDIA RTX 4090 GPU with 24 GB of VRAM.

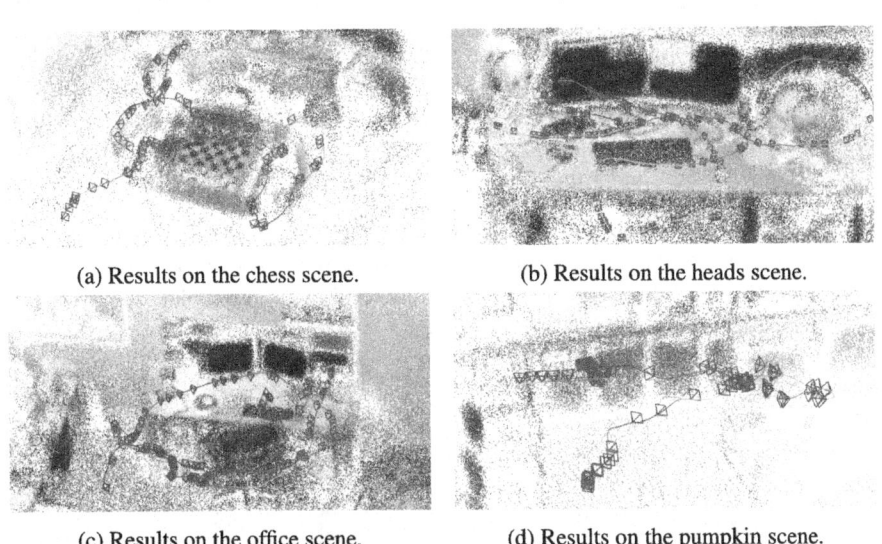

(a) Results on the chess scene.　　(b) Results on the heads scene.

(c) Results on the office scene.　　(d) Results on the pumpkin scene.

Fig. 3. Pose estimation results of FuPaD on selected sequences from the 7-Scenes dataset. The color of the segments indicates the error with respect to the ground truth trajectory. The green wireframes represent the keyframes selected by FuPaD. (Color figure online)

4.4 Comparison Experiment

Qualitative visualizations of trajectories estimated by FuPaD are provided in Fig. 3. In these visualizations, green wireframe frustums denote the keyframes selected as input to the patch-wise VGGT module for global pose prior estimation. Quantitative performance metrics on the 7-Scenes dataset are subsequently presented in Table 1. The quantitative results indicate that FuPaD surpasses baseline methods, achieving the best average ATE (0.063 m) across all seven scenes. Specifically, FuPaD achieves the top performance (indicated in blue) on three individual scenes: Fire (0.037 m), Heads (0.025 m), and Office (0.097 m). Furthermore, FuPaD secures the second-best performance (indicated in green) on the Chess (0.040 m) and Kitchen (0.056 m) scenes. Those quantitative results suggest that FuPaD benefits from its hierarchical fusion strategy, which combines the global-consistent pose priors from patch-wise VGGT with the local geometric accuracy from DBA-based refinement, is effective in challenging real-world conditions characterized by low-resolution images and motion blur.

4.5 Ablation Study on Patch Sampling Strategy

To assess the impact of the tracking-informed patch sampling strategy, an ablation study is conducted. This study focuses on the performance of the patch sampling strategy for the patch-wise VGGT module, evaluated on the 'Chess' scene from the 7-Scenes dataset. The Absolute Trajectory Error (ATE) of the poses predicted by this module is measured while varying the number of selected patches per keyframe, θ_{ppf}. The following patch sampling strategies are compared:

1. *Random Sampling*: Patches are selected randomly from each keyframe.
2. *Grid-based Sampling*: Patches are selected from a fixed, regular grid overlaid on each keyframe. If more than θ_{ppf} grid cells exist, a subset is chosen by striding.
3. *Tracking-Informed Sampling*: The proposed strategy, which selects θ_{ppf} patches based on their tracking scores as described in Eq. 3.

In each case, the selected patches are first processed by the patch-wise VGGT module to predict pose priors. Subsequently, these priors, along with interpolated poses of non-keyframes, undergo the DBA-based refinement to obtained the entire trajectory.

The results, in Fig. 4, demonstrate that the tracking-informed approach consistently achieves lower ATE compared to both random and grid sampling. Notably, even with a very limited number of patches (e.g., $\theta_{ppf} = 32$), the tracking-informed approach yields more accurate pose estimates from the patch-wise VGGT module. In contrast, both random and grid-based sampling strategies require a substantially larger number of patches to approach a comparable level of accuracy. In many cases, particularly with fewer patches, these alternative strategies result in pose estimates with errors too large to be meaningfully displayed. These findings underscore the efficiency and effectiveness of the tracking-informed patch sampling strategy.

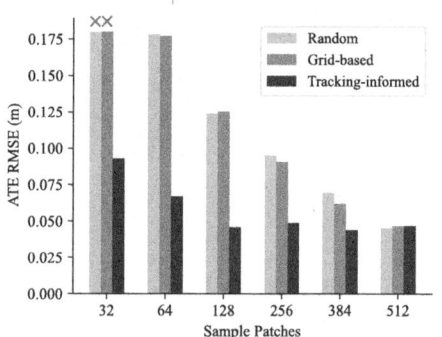

Fig. 4. Impact of different patch sampling strategies on pose estimation for the patch-wise VGGT, evaluated on the 'Chess' scene from the 7-Scenes dataset. Red crosses indicate ATE RMSE exceeding the limits. (Color figure online)

5 Conclusion

This paper presented FuPaD, a novel hierarchical framework designed for scalable pose estimation. FuPaD effectively mitigates the significant memory demands of global feed-forward models like VGGT by introducing a patch-wise inference scheme. This allows VGGT to establish globally consistent pose priors for keyframes efficiently. Subsequently, FuPaD fuses these global keyframe priors with local refinement within a pose graph optimization framework. Experimental evaluations on the 7-Scenes dataset demonstrated that FuPaD surpasses baseline methods on pose estimation. The proposed FuPaD shows promise in enhancing the efficiency of long-sequence pose estimation and reducing hardware demands, thereby contributing to the advancement of accessible and accurate 3D reconstruction and spatial understanding.

References

1. Brachmann, E., et al.: DSAC-Differentiable RANSAC for camera localization. In: IEEE Conference on Computer Vision Pattern Recognition (CVPR) (2017)
2. Campos, C., Elvira, R., Gomez, J.J., Montiel, J.M.M., Tardos, J.D.: ORB-SLAM3: an accurate open-source library for visual, visual-inertial and multi-map SLAM. IEEE Trans. Robot. Automat. 37(6), 1874–1890 (2021)
3. Engel, J., Koltun, V., Cremers, D.: Direct sparse odometry. IEEE Trans. Pattern Anal. Mach. Intell. (2018)
4. Forster, C., Zhang, Z., Gassner, M., Werlberger, M., Scaramuzza, D.: SVO: semidirect visual odometry for monocular and multicamera systems. IEEE Trans. Robot. Automat. 33(2), 249–265 (2017)
5. Kendall, A., Grimes, M., Cipolla, R.: PoseNet: a convolutional network for real-time 6-DOF camera relocalization. In: IEEE International Conference Computer Vision (ICCV) (2015). https://doi.org/10.1109/ICCV.2015.336
6. Kuemmerle, R., Grisetti, G., Strasdat, H., Konolige, K., Burgard, W.: G2o: a general framework for graph optimization. In: IEEE International Conference on Robotic Automation (ICRA). IEEE (2011)
7. Leroy, V., Cabon, Y., Revaud, J.: Grounding image matching in 3D with MASt3R. arXiv:2406.09756 (2024)
8. Liu, Y., et al.: SLAM3R: real-time dense scene reconstruction from monocular RGB videos. arXiv:2412.09401 (2024)
9. Murai, R., Dexheimer, E., Davison, A.J.: MASt3R-SLAM: real-time dense SLAM with 3D reconstruction priors. arXiv:2412.12392 (2024)
10. Oquab, M., et al.: DINOv2: learning robust visual features without supervision (2023)
11. Schneider, T., et al.: maplab: an Open Framework for Research in Visual-inertial Mapping and Localization. IEEE Robot. Automat. Lett. 3(3), 1418–1425 (2018)
12. Schönberger, J.L., Frahm, J.M.: Structure-from-motion revisited. In: IEEE Conference on Computer Vision and Pattern Recognition (CVPR) (2016)
13. Shotton, J., Glocker, B., Zach, C., Izadi, S., Criminisi, A., Fitzgibbon, A.: Scene coordinate regression forests for camera relocalization in RGB-D images. In: IEEE Conference on Computer Vision and Pattern Recognition (CVPR) (2013)
14. Sturm, J., Engelhard, N., Endres, F., Burgard, W., Cremers, D.: A benchmark for the evaluation of RGB-D SLAM systems. In: IEEE/RSJ International Conference on Intelligent Robots Systems (IROS) (2012)

15. Teed, Z., Deng, J.: DROID-SLAM: deep visual SLAM for monocular, stereo, and RGB-D cameras. Adv. Neural Inf. Process. Syst. (2021)
16. Wang, J., Chen, M., Karaev, N., Vedaldi, A., Rupprecht, C., Novotny, D.: VGGT: visual geometry grounded transformer. In: IEEE Conference on Computer Vision and Pattern Recognition (CVPR) (2025)
17. Wang, S., Leroy, V., Cabon, Y., Chidlovskii, B., Revaud, J.: Dust3R: geometric 3D vision made easy. In: IEEE Conference on Computer Vision and Pattern Recognition (CVPR) (2024)
18. Zhu, Z., et al.: Nicer-SLAM: neural implicit scene encoding for RGB slam. In: International Conference on on 3D Vision (3DV) (2024)

ScaffoldOcc: Sparse Points Anchored Scaffold 3D Gaussian for Hierarchical Semantic Occupancy Prediction

Zhihong Zhang[1,2,3], Wenjun Wang[1,2,3(✉)], Dexin Qi[1,2,3], and Xuesong Mei[1,2,3]

[1] School of Mechanical Engineering, Xi'an Jiaotong University,
Xi'an 710049, Shaanxi, China
{zhangzhihong,dexin.qi}@stu.xjtu.edu.cn,
{wenjunwang,xsmei}@mail.xjtu.edu.cn
[2] State Key Laboratory for Manufacturing System Engineering,
Xi'an Jiaotong University, Xi'an 710049, Shaanxi, China
[3] Shaanxi Key Laboratory of Intelligent Robots, Xi'an Jiaotong University,
Xi'an 710049, Shaanxi, China

Abstract. 3D semantic occupancy prediction provides fine-grained 3D scene understanding by densely predicting occupancy status and semantic labels. However, dense voxel-based methods are inefficient, as the most voxels remain empty. Recent sparse approaches such as OPUS leverage learnable queries to directly predict occupied locations, but they can struggle to capture fine volumetric structural details. Meanwhile, 3D Gaussian Splatting has emerged as a compact, detail-preserving representation. To this end, this paper proposes ScaffoldOcc, a hybrid sparse point-anchored structural 3D Gaussian representation for hierarchical semantic occupancy prediction. First, multi-scale image features are extracted and used to update a set of learnable queries to encode the global scene. Next, these queries predict a set of sparse anchor points and their associated features, each representing a local region. Around each anchor, we distribute a cluster of local 3D Gaussians to capture fine-grained volumetric details. These Gaussians form a compact structural representation from which semantic occupancy is inferred. Additionally, we introduce a hierarchical multi-layer decoding strategy that progressively learns scene representations and adaptively focuses on complex regions in a coarse-to-fine manner. Experiments on Occ3D-nuScenes demonstrate that ScaffoldOcc surpasses prior methods with less overhead.

Keywords: Machine Learning · Computer Vision · Semantic Occupancy Prediction · 3D Gaussian Splatting

1 Introduction

3D semantic occupancy prediction has emerged as a powerful scene understanding paradigm for autonomous driving and robot perception, as it seeks to recover both occupancy status and semantic labels for every voxel. Unlike bird's-eye-view (BEV), which collapse vertical structure, dense semantic occupancy captures fine-grained geometric and semantic details, naturally representing complex shapes and enabling more accurate scene understanding. MonoScene [2] first introduced the camera-only semantic occupancy prediction task. Subsequent approaches, including TPVFormer [6], VoxFormer [9], OccFormer [22], and SurroundOcc [20], have achieved remarkable results by constructing dense voxel representations to capture fine-grained scene details. However, real-world driving scenes are inherently sparse: the majority of voxels are unoccupied. Processing a full-resolution voxel grid therefore incurs substantial computational and memory overhead. Furthermore, inferring dense occupancy from limited multi-view images compounds challenges of occlusion and restricted field of view. These observations underscore the need for more efficient representations that fully exploit scene sparsity while maintaining high-fidelity geometry and semantics.

To address inefficiency, recent approaches adopt sparse representations that focus computation on informative regions. Voxel-based methods like CTF-Occ [18] use a coarse-to-fine pipeline that interacts only with voxels predicted as occupied. SparseOcc [13] further reduces overhead by progressively pruning empty regions via learned split strategies. Likewise, OccFusion [21] selects high-entropy voxels for refinement via an active coarse-to-fine scheme. While these methods effectively reduce computation by filtering empty space, they often involve complex mechanisms for voxel pruning, leading to additional implementation overhead. OPUS [19] reformulates occupancy prediction as a set prediction task: an encoder-decoder directly outputs a sparse set of occupied locations and semantic labels via learned queries. Though efficient, OPUS lacks explicit volumetric modeling, limiting its ability to capture fine geometric details such as surface curvature or thin structures. In summary, voxel-based methods suffer from inefficient local aggregation and empty-space filtering, while point-based approaches, though preserving spatial fidelity, struggle to represent continuous volumetric structural details. In contrast, 3D Gaussian splatting [8] has emerged as a compact and detail-preserving scene representation. Scaffold-GS [16] further introduces structural anchors to refine Gaussian distributions. Building on this, TGP [3] first adopts a dual-modal representation by combining 3D Gaussian with sparse points to balance global context and local detail. However, TGP lacks explicit guidance for Gaussian generation and offers limited interaction between Gaussians and sparse points, constraining its performance.

Inspired by these insights, this paper proposes ScaffoldOcc, a hybrid sparse point-anchored structural 3D Gaussian representation for hierarchical semantic occupancy prediction that combines the advantages of both structural 3D Gaussian and sparse points representations. First, multi-scale image features extracted from inputs images update a set of learnable queries that encode global scene context. These queries then predict a sparse set of 3D anchor points, each paired with a learned feature embedding. Rather than aligning anchors directly to individual voxels, we use them as anchors for local Gaussian clusters: around each anchor, we generate a small set of 3D Gaussians whose offsets and other attributes are regressed from the anchor's feature. Each Gaussian acts as a soft occupancy kernel, smoothly modeling local structure and semantics. The refined 3D Gaussians are then aggregated through Gaussian-to-Voxel [7] strategy to produce scene occupancy. This anchor-guided Gaussian construction thus provides a compact yet expressive representation, bridging sparse point predictions and dense volumetric modeling for efficient, accurate semantic occupancy.

To further improve efficiency, we introduce a hierarchical multi-layer decoding strategy that progressively learns scene representations and adaptively focuses on complex regions in a coarse-to-fine manner. Specifically, the model incrementally increases the number of anchors and Gaussians across layers to capture fine-grained occupancy details, while adaptively refining regions with high splitting probability at each stage. This joint coarse-to-fine learning and adaptive refinement paradigm enables ScaffoldOcc to achieve scalable and accurate semantic occupancy predictions, making it well-suited for autonomous driving.

Comprehensive experiments on the Occ3D-nuScenes dataset demonstrate that ScaffoldOcc surpasses prior methods. The anchor-guided Gaussians capture fine-grained details more effectively, and the hierarchical refinement strategy minimizes redundant computation without degrading performance. In summary, the main contributions of this paper are as follows:

- **Hybrid Representation**: We propose a hybrid sparse point-anchored structural Gaussian representation for semantic occupancy prediction, which marries sparse points with 3D Gaussians for high-quality scene representation.
- **Sparse Points Anchored Structural 3D Gaussian**: We innovatively introduce sparse points predicted by queries as anchors to guide the distribution of structural 3D Gaussians, forming a hybrid representation that captures fine-grained details while preserving sparsity and efficiency.
- **Hierarchical Multi-layer Decoder**: We develop a hierarchical multi-layer decoding strategy that progressively refines the representation and adaptively focus on complex regions while avoiding waste in homogeneous areas.

2 Related Works

2.1 3D Gaussian Splatting

Recent advancements in 3D Gaussian Splatting (3DGS) [8] have demonstrated remarkable potential in computer graphics, especially for high-fidelity rendering and scene reconstruction tasks [16]. Instead of relying on traditional mesh or voxel representations, 3DGS models a scene using a collection of 3D Gaussians in 3D space. These Gaussians are rendered through rasterization, enabling photorealistic outputs with significantly lower computational overhead. This representation offers greater flexibility in modeling complex geometry and exhibits superior efficiency in both memory and runtime compared to conventional volumetric methods. Given these advantages, 3D Gaussian-based representations have seen increasing adoption in autonomous driving. GaussianFormer [7] pioneers the use of 3D Gaussians for semantic occupancy prediction. GaussianFormer2 [5] extends

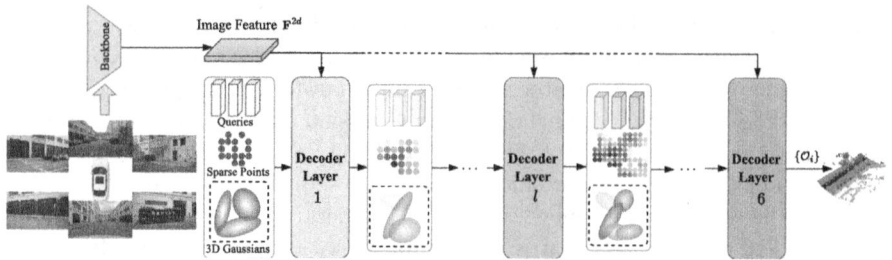

Fig. 1. Overall framework of ScaffoldOcc. The whole pipeline of ScaffoldOcc is designed as a coarse-to-fine paradigm employing hierarchical multi-layer decoder with initial queries, sparse anchor points, and 3D Gaussian representations.

this approach by introducing a probabilistic Gaussian superposition model to reduce spatial redundancy. However, thees methods still need complicated design to filter out redundant Gaussians at empty regions. This motivates the need for a more efficient and unified framework that can fully leverage the expressiveness of 3D Gaussians while minimizing computation.

2.2 Lightweight Semantic Occupancy Prediction

Due to the high memory footprint and limited inference speed of 3D occupancy prediction, recent works have explored lightweight and efficient alternatives. TPVFormer [6] introduces a tri-perspective view representation, which seeks a trade-off between the geometric completeness and representation efficiency. CTF-Occ [18] adopts a coarse-to-fine paradigm, where only the occupied voxels are selected for further interaction. SparseOcc [13] leverages a hierarchical refinement scheme which aggressively prunes empty voxels to reduce computation. OccFusion [21] further improves efficiency by actively selecting high-entropy regions for refinement. Meanwhile, OPUS [19] first reformulates occupancy prediction as a set prediction task and employs a sparse points representation for efficiency. TGP [3] further introduces a dual-modal representation that combines 3D Gaussians with sparse points, balancing global context and local detail.

3 Method

3.1 Framework Overview

The overall architecture of ScaffoldOcc is illustrated in Fig. 1. Given multi-view images $\mathbf{I} = \{\mathbf{I}_i \in \mathbb{R}^{3 \times H \times W} | i = 1, \cdots, N\}$, we first extract multi-scale image features through image backbone. The queries are first updated with image features to encode global scene context, from which sparse anchor points are subsequently predicted (Sect. 3.2). In Sect. 3.3, we generate a set of 3D Gaussians around each anchor point to model local volumetric details, enabling fine-grained encoding of geometry and semantic context. Finally, in Sect. 3.4, we propose a hierarchical multi-layer decoding strategy that progressively refines the representation and adaptively focus on complex regions in a coarse-to-fine manner. The detailed decoding process in a single layer is illustrated in Fig. 2.

3.2 Query-Based Sparse Anchor Points Prediction

In this section, we detail our query-based sparse anchor point prediction. Similar to OPUS [19], we first extract multi-scale image features from input views via image backbone, and then initialize a set of learnable queries and a sparse set of point positions to capture global spatial structure as input to the decoder.

At the beginning of the decoder, the queries are updated with the image features to encode overall scene context. From these refined queries, we then predict a set of sparse anchor points along with their associated features, each representing a local region. Each anchor point serves as a proxy for a local occupied region, with its feature encoding both geometric structure and semantic information for subsequent stages.

Query Update. Similar to SparseBEV [14], we first update the queries with the image features to encode the global scene. Specifically, at the $l-th$ layer, given the query $\mathbf{q}_i^{l-1} \in \mathbb{R}^{Q \times 256}$ and corresponding point positions $\mathbf{p}_i^{l-1} \in \mathbb{R}^{Q \times R_{l-1} \times 3}$ from the previous layer, where Q is the number of queries and the R_{l-1} is the points number that a query predicted at $l-th$ layer, we first adopt a consistent point sampling (CPS) module from OPUS [19] to extract image features. The CPS module samples a set of points from the initial query and projects them to the image space to extract image features. We then obtain the image features from the $m-th$ image at the sampled coordinates $\mathbf{c}_m$ through a bilinear interpolation operation on image feature $\mathbf{F}^{2d}$ and aggregate them across all images and sampled points for subsequent query update. At last, with the following Adaptive Mixing module [14] for feature aggregation, the sampled image features are adaptively mixed with the query, along with the self-attention among all queries, to update the queries. The overall process can be formulated as follows:

$$\mathbf{c}_m = \mathbf{T}_m \mathbf{r}, \quad \text{where} \quad \mathbf{r} = \mathbf{m}_p + \phi(\mathbf{q}) \cdot \sigma_p,$$
$$\mathbf{f}_q = \frac{1}{\sum_{m=1}^{M} |\mathbb{M}_m|} \sum_{s=1}^{S} \sum_{m=1}^{M} w_{s,m} \cdot m_{s,m} \cdot \mathcal{B}(\mathbf{F}^{2d}, \mathbf{c}_{s,m}), \qquad (1)$$
$$\mathbf{q}_i^l = \mathbf{q}_i^{l-1} + \mathcal{A}(\mathbf{f}_q, \mathbb{P}, \mathbb{Q}),$$

where $\mathbf{T}_m$ denotes the transformation matrix from the 3D point to the $m-th$ image space; $\mathbf{m}_p$ and σ_p represent the mea and standard deviation of the point locations. $\mathbb{M}_m$ is a mask set of the visible sampled points within the camera. $w_{s,m}$ denotes the weight on the $m-th$ image feature. $\mathcal{B}(\cdot)$ and $\mathcal{A}(\cdot)$ refer to the bilinear interpolation operation and the adaptive mixing module, respectively.

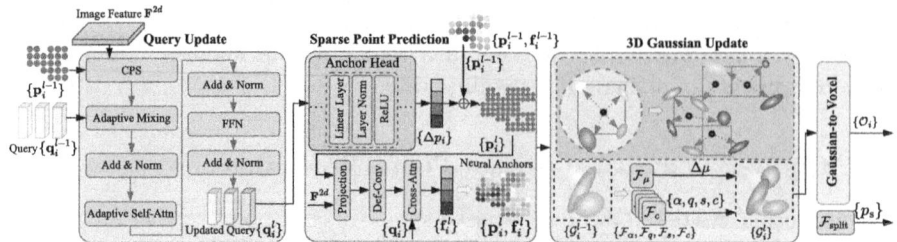

Fig. 2. Decoder layer of ScaffoldOcc. The pipeline of a decoder layer: (1) A set of learnable queries are updated with image features to encode the global scene context. (2) A sparse set of 3D anchor points are predicted from the updated queries. (3) Around each anchor point, a set of 3D Gaussians is generated, which models local volumetric details. (4) The occupancy prediction is accompanied by a split probability that guides voxel refinement in the next layer.

Sparse Anchor Points Prediction. With the updated query, we predict a set of sparse anchor points and their features, each encoding the geometry and semantic context of a local region. To this end, we employ a lightweight prediction head composed of Linear, LayerNorm, and ReLU layers. Specifically, for each updated query $\mathbf{q}_i^l$, the head outputs a position offset $\Delta \mathbf{p}_i$. Considering the points number mismatch between adjacent layers, we first compute the mean of the previous-layer anchor positions $\mathbf{p}_i^{l-1}$ across the point dimension, yielding $\bar{\mathbf{p}}^{l-1}$. We then replicate $\bar{\mathbf{p}}^{l-1}$ R_i times to match the desired count, and apply the offsets to obtain the expanded and refined anchors. The sparse anchor points prediction can be summarized as follows:

$$\Delta \mathbf{p}_i = \mathcal{F}_{\text{anchor\_head}}(\mathbf{q}_i^l),$$
$$\mathbf{p}_i^l = \bar{\mathbf{p}}^{l-1} + \Delta \mathbf{p}_i, \qquad (2)$$

Meanwhile, we also learn the corresponding feature $\mathbf{f}_i^l$ for each anchor point by integrating the updated query $\mathbf{q}_i^l$ with multi-scale image features to capture the local geometric and semantic context. To encode finer-grained information around each anchor point, we first project the updated anchor location $\mathbf{p}_i^l$ into the image space of each camera view and sample local features from the multi-scale image feature maps $\mathbf{F}^{2d}$. This is achieved via a deformable convolutional operations, which adaptively extracts local features around the projected coordinates, resulting in the sampled image features $\mathbf{f}_{i,s}^{2d}$. These features are then aggregated across multiple scales to form a unified image-aware representation $\mathbf{f}_i^{2d}$ for each anchor. Finally, we employ a cross-attention mechanism, where the updated query $\mathbf{q}_i$ attends to the aggregated image features $\mathbf{f}_i^{2d}$ to produce the final anchor feature $\mathbf{f}_i^l$. This feature serves as a comprehensive representation of the local region, encoding both geometric structure and semantic cues necessary for downstream volumetric reasoning. The whole process can be formulated as:

$$\mathbf{f}_i^{2d} = \mathcal{F}_{\text{def\_conv}}(\mathcal{F}_{\text{proj}}(\mathbf{p}_i^l), \mathbf{F}^{2d}),$$
$$\mathbf{f}_i^l = \mathcal{F}_{\text{cross\_attn}}(\mathbf{q}_i^l, \mathbf{p}_i^l, \mathbf{f}_i^{2d}), \qquad (3)$$

where $\mathcal{F}_{\text{proj}}$, $\mathcal{F}_{\text{def\_conv}}$, and $\mathcal{F}_{\text{cross\_attn}}$ denote the projection operation, deformable convolution operation, and cross-attention layer, respectively.

Instead of associating each point with a fixed voxel in OPUS [19], we treat points as a set of flexible and learnable anchors that represent local occupied regions. While OPUS encodes all scene-level information, including geometric occupancy and semantic context, within the query, our approach decouples the representation: the query encodes only the coarse-level occupancy geometry of an adaptive region, while the fine-grained local structure and semantic context are captured by sparse anchor points and their associated features. Importantly, we do not constrain each anchor point $\mathbf{p}_i^l$ to a specific voxel. Instead, each anchor represents a local occupied region, and its associated feature $\mathbf{f}_i^l$ encodes the fine-grained geometric and semantic information required for downstream Gaussian-based volumetric modeling. With these sparse anchor points and their associated features, we can learn the fine-grained local structure details and semantic context around the anchor in the next stage.

3.3 Sparse Anchor-Guided Structural Gaussian Generation

In this section, we detail the sparse anchor-guided structural Gaussian generation. Inspired by Scaffold-GS [16], we employ sparse anchor-guided structural Gaussian distribution to model local volumetric regions around each anchor, enabling effective capture of fine-grained geometric and semantic details. Unlike TGP [3], whose two-branch design limits interaction between sparse points and 3D Gaussians, we propose a unified and efficient paradigm that facilitates deep and continuous interaction between the two representations. By jointly optimizing the sparse anchors and their associated Gaussian volumes, this design allows for richer feature aggregation and more precise local volumetric details.

We distribute a cluster of local 3D Gaussians around the sparse anchors from the previous stage to model local volumetric details. Similar to Scaffold-GS, the predicted sparse points $\mathbf{p}_i^l$ can be regarded as the anchor point of local Gaussian distributions. We use a set of learnable parameters $\boldsymbol{\Theta} = \{\mu_i \in \mathbb{R}^3, \alpha_i \in \mathbb{R}, q_i \in \mathbb{R}^4, s_i \in \mathbb{R}^3, c_i \in \mathbb{R}^{|\mathcal{C}|} | i = 1, \cdots, R_l\}$ to represent the distribution of R_l Gaussians around the anchor $\mathbf{p}_i^l$. Specifically, for each visible anchor point $\mathbf{p}_i^l$ within the viewing frustum, we spawn R_l neural Gaussians at decoder layer l, and predict their attributes from corresponding anchor feature. To update the mean position $\boldsymbol{\mu}_i^l$ of each Gaussian, we predict a learnable local offset $\Delta\boldsymbol{\mu} i \in \mathbb{R}^3$ and a layer-specific scaling factor $s_l \in \mathbb{R}^3$ through an MLP $\mathcal{F}\mu$ conditioned on the anchor point $\mathbf{p}_i^l$ from the updated query. Given the increase in the number of Gaussians across layers, we first compute the centroid $\bar{\mu}^{l-1}$ of the previous layer's Gaussian. Then, the mean positions of current Gaussians are updated in a residual manner by adding the predicted offsets $\Delta\mu_i \in \mathbb{R}^3$ scaled by s_l, enabling progressively refined and spatially adaptive Gaussian placements across layers.

$$\begin{aligned}\{\Delta\mu_1, \cdots, \Delta\mu_{R_l}, s_l\} &= \mathcal{F}_\mu(\mathbf{q}_i), \\ \mu_i^l &= \bar{\mu}^{l-1} + \Delta\mu_i \cdot s_l.\end{aligned} \quad (4)$$

The remaining Gaussian attributes are directly replaced with values predicted by individual MLPs, which take as input the anchor feature $\mathbf{f}_i^l$, relative view distance $\mathbf{d}_i$, and viewing direction $\mathbf{v}_i$. Take the opacity α_i^l as examples, we generate the opacity α_i^l of the Gaussians by the opacity MLP $\mathcal{F}_\alpha$ as follows:

$$\alpha_i^l = \mathcal{F}_\alpha(\mathbf{f}_i^l, \mathbf{p}_i^l, \mathbf{d}_i, \mathbf{v}_i), \tag{5}$$

At end of current layer, we employ a Gaussian-to-Voxel (G2V) splatting approach [16] to efficiently generate semantic occupancy results.

This tightly coupled paradigm enhances the expressiveness of representation, particularly in complex regions, enabling spatially adaptive modeling of fine-grained geometric structures and semantic details.

3.4 Hierarchical Multi-layer Decoding Strategy

In this section, we introduce a hierarchical multi-layer decoding strategy that progressively refines the representation and adaptively focus on complex regions while avoiding waste in homogeneous areas in a coarse-to-fine manner.

Coarse-to-Fine Learning. To progressively learn the hybrid scene representation from the updated queries, we gradually increase the number of anchors points and associated Gaussians at each layer. As formulated in Eq. 2, anchor positions are updated in a residual manner using offsets predicted from the corresponding queries. Similarly, the number of Gaussians generated from anchors also increases layer by layer. with their mean positions updated via residual offsets predicted from the updated queries (Eq. 4). This coarse-to-fine scheme enables progressive learning of the sparse points and 3D Gaussians representation across layers, allowing the model to capture increasingly fine-grained geometric details and complex structural variations at multiple scales.

Adaptive Refinement. As pointed out in DGOcc [23], most of the voxels can be predicted at a low resolution, and only a small number of voxels need to be predicted at a high resolution. We extend this strategy and step further into sparse natural and introduce a adaptive refinement strategy.

We progressively refine the occupancy predictions across decoder layers, starting from a low-resolution occupancy map and incrementally increasing to higher resolution until reaching the full resolution as the ground truth. To improve computational efficiency and allocate resources more effectively, we predict a split probability at each layer to guide voxel refinement. Specifically, at each layer, we predict both the occupancy at the current resolution using the G2V module and a split probability via a lightweight MLP $\mathcal{F}_{\text{split}}$ from the updated query and the corresponding anchor features, as shown in Eq. 6. Then, only voxels with high split probabilities are selected for upsampling and passed to the next layer. The associated anchor points and their corresponding 3D

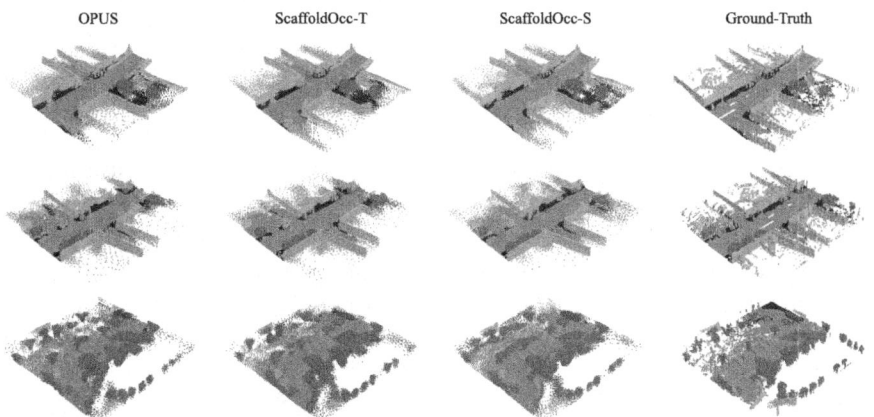

Fig. 3. Visualization comparison on the Occ3D-nuScenes dataset. The first to third column show the prediction results of OPUS, ScaffoldOcc-T, and ScaffoldOcc-S, respectively. The last columns shows the ground truth.

Gaussians are also propagated forward for further refinement at higher resolution. For these voxels, we employ multi-class version of Scene-Class Affinity Loss from DGOcc.

$$\mathbf{p}_s = \mathcal{F}_{\text{split}}(\mathbf{q}^l, \mathbf{f}^l), \tag{6}$$

The split probability indicates the likelihood that a voxel requires further refinement, effectively identifying regions with structural or semantic complexity. This mechanism focuses the model's capacity on informative regions, typically located near semantic border, while avoiding computation in homogeneous or uninformative areas. Consequently, only a small subset of voxels are selected for refinement, resulting in a marked reduction in the number of anchor points and Gaussians passed to subsequent layers. This hierarchical pruning and refine strategy allows our method to adaptively focus on complex regions, achieving high-resolution occupancy prediction with considerably reduced overhead.

The proposed hierarchical multi-layer decoding paradigm enables the model to progressively refine the scene representation, adaptively focus on complex regions, and efficiently utilize computational resources.

4 Experiments

4.1 Experimental Setup

Dataset and Metrics. We conduct comprehensive experiments on the Occ3D-nuScenes [18] dataset, a large-scale benchmark tailored for 3D semantic occupancy prediction. Built upon the nuScenes [1] dataset, Occ3D-nuScenes provides dense voxel-wise occupancy annotations across 18 categories, including one free-space class and 17 semantic classes. It contains a total of 1,000 labeled driving scenes, split into 750/150/150 scenes for training/validation/testing, respec-

Table 1. The performance of occupancy prediction on Occ3D-nuScenes [18]. "8f" and "16f" means the number of input frames with 8 frames and 16 frames, respectively. Baseline results are directly copied from their corresponding papers or the TGP [3]. FPS results are measured on an A100 GPU.

Methods	Backbone	Image Size	mIoU	RayIoU$_{1m}$	RayIoU$_{2m}$	RayIoU$_{4m}$	RayIoU	FPS
RenderOcc [17]	Swin-B	1408×512	24.5	13.4	19.6	25.5	19.5	-
BEVFormer [11]	R101	1600×900	**39.3**	26.1	32.9	38.0	32.4	3.0
BEVDet-Occ(2f) [10]	R50	704×256	36.1	23.6	30.0	35.1	29.6	2.6
BEVDet-Occ(8f) [10]	R50	704×384	**39.3**	26.6	33.1	38.2	32.6	0.8
FB-Occ(16f) [12]	R50	704×256	39.1	26.7	34.1	39.7	33.5	10.3
SparseOcc(8f) [13]	R50	704×256	30.1	28.0	34.7	39.4	34.0	17.3
SparseOcc(16f) [13]	R50	704×256	30.6	29.1	35.8	40.3	35.1	12.5
SparseOcc(16f) [13]	R50	704×256	30.9	30.2	36.8	41.2	36.1	12.5
OPUS-T(8f) [19]	R50	704×256	33.2	31.7	39.2	44.3	38.4	**22.4**
OPUS-S(8f) [19]	R50	704×256	34.2	32.6	39.9	44.7	39.1	20.7
TGP-T(8f) [3]	R50	704×256	33.4	31.8	39.5	44.6	38.6	18.6
TGP-S(8f) [3]	R50	704×256	34.5	32.8	40.2	**45.2**	39.4	15.1
ScaffoldOcc-T(8f)	R50	704×256	34.1	32.5	39.7	44.4	38.9	20.3
ScaffoldOcc-S(8f)	R50	704×256	35.1	**33.4**	**40.4**	45.0	**39.7**	18.8

tively, amounting to over 40,000 frames collected from six surround-view cameras, one LiDAR, and five radar sensors. Following previous works [3,13,19], we evaluate our method using mean Intersection over Union (mIoU) and RayIoU metrics at 1 m, 2 m, and 4 m thresholds, as well as the overall RayIoU.

Implementation Details. Following the previous works [3,13,19], we use OPUS as our codebase and employ ResNet-50 [4] to extract multi-scale features from images resized to 704 × 256. We provide two model variants, ScaffoldOcc-T and ScaffoldOcc-S. ScaffoldOcc-T uses 0.6K queries, while ScaffoldOcc-S adopts 2.4K queries. Both variants use 6 decoder layers. The number of anchors and associated 3D Gaussians progressively increases across layers. Specifically, each query predicts $\{1, 2, 4, 4, 8, 8\}$ anchors per layer, and each anchor generates $\{1, 2, 4, 4, 6, 8\}$ Gaussians, respectively, in both variants. We train it on 8 NVIDIA 4090 GPUs with batch size of 8. We use the AdamW optimizer and the learning rate is initialized to 2e-4 with a Cosine Annealing [15] weight decay scheme. The model train 100 epochs for main results and 24 epochs for ablation study.

4.2 Main Results

We compare ScaffoldOcc with recent methods, especially sparse approach including SparseOcc, OPUS and TGP, on the Occ3D-nuScenes dataset and report the results in Table 1. The results show that our method achieves better performance, while maintaining commendable efficiency. Specifically, compared to the traditional voxel-based methods, our method achieves a significant improvement in RayIoU. Moreover, in comparison to the sparse methods such as OPUS and TGP, our method achieves a higher RayIoU while maintaining a competitive FPS, demonstrating the effectiveness of our method in capturing fine-grained details and improving occupancy prediction accuracy. Thanks to our hierarchical multi-layer decoding strategy, our method can progressively refine the representation and adaptively focus on complex regions while avoiding waste in homogeneous areas, which contributes to the better efficiency compared to TGP. The predicted occupancy is shown in Fig. 3. In summary, our method demonstrates better performance in occupancy prediction on the Occ3D-nuScenes dataset, achieving a good balance between performance and efficiency.

4.3 Ablation Studies

Ablation on the Architecture. In Table 2, we conduct ablation studies using ScaffoldOcc-S to evaluate the effectiveness of different components in our method. We compare the performance of our full model with several variants that remove specific modules. The ablation study includes the following settings: (1) 3DGS: 3D Gaussians (2) C2F: coarse-to-fine learning, and (3) AdaRef: adaptive refinement. The results show that each module contributes significantly to the final performance of our method. The full model achieves the best performance.

Table 2. Model performances with different combinations of proposed strategies.

3DGS	C2F	AdaRef	mIoU	RayIoU$_{1m}$	RayIoU$_{2m}$	RayIoU$_{4m}$	RayIoU
			30.1	28.3	35.1	40.8	34.7
✓			31.9	29.7	36.6	42.2	36.2
✓	✓		32.4	30.6	37.5	43.2	37.1
✓		✓	32.9	31.0	37.9	43.7	37.5
✓	✓	✓	33.2	31.1	38.1	44.0	37.7

5 Conclusion

This paper proposed ScaffoldOcc, a hybrid sparse point-anchored structural 3D Gaussian representation for hierarchical semantic occupancy prediction that combines the advantages of both structural 3D Gaussian and sparse points representations. The proposed hierarchical multi-layer decoding strategy progressively refines the representation and adaptively focuses on complex regions. The experiments demonstrate that ScaffoldOcc surpasses recent methods and achieves competitive efficiency. ScaffoldOcc bridges sparse points and dense-volumetric paradigms, delivering both efficiency and precision for autonomous driving.

References

1. Caesar, H., et al.: nuscenes: a multimodal dataset for autonomous driving. In: IEEE Conference on Computer Vision and Pattern Recognition (CVPR) (2020)
2. Cao, A.Q., de Charette, R.: Monoscene: monocular 3D semantic scene completion. In: IEEE Conference on Computer Vision and Pattern Recognition (CVPR) (2022)
3. Chen, M., et al.: TGP: two-modal occupancy prediction with 3D gaussian and sparse points for 3D environment awareness (2025)
4. He, K., Zhang, X., Ren, S., Sun, J.: Deep residual learning for image recognition. In: IEEE Conference on Computer Vision and Pattern Recognition (CVPR) (2016)
5. Huang, Y., Thammatadatrakoon, A., Zheng, W., Zhang, Y., Du, D., Lu, J.: Gaussianformer-2: probabilistic gaussian superposition for efficient 3D occupancy prediction. In: IEEE Conference on Computer Vision and Pattern Recognition (CVPR) (2025)
6. Huang, Y., Zheng, W., Zhang, Y., Zhou, J., Lu, J.: Tri-perspective view for vision-based 3D semantic occupancy prediction. In: IEEE Conference on Computer Vision and Pattern Recognition (CVPR) (2023)
7. Huang, Y., Zheng, W., Zhang, Y., Zhou, J., Lu, J.: Gaussianformer: scene as gaussians for vision-based 3D semantic occupancy prediction. In: European Conference on Computer Vision (ECCV) (2024)
8. Kerbl, B., Kopanas, G., Leimkühler, T., Drettakis, G.: 3D gaussian splatting for real-time radiance field rendering. ACM Trans. Graph. (2023)
9. Li, Y., et al.: Voxformer: sparse voxel transformer for camera-based 3d semantic scene completion. In: IEEE Conference on Computer Vision and Pattern Recognition (CVPR) (2023)
10. Li, Y., et al.: Bevdepth: acquisition of reliable depth for multi-view 3d object detection. In: AAAI (2023)
11. Li, Z., et al.: Bevformer: learning bird's-eye-view representation from multi-camera images via spatiotemporal transformers. In: European Conference on Computer Vision (ECCV) (2022)
12. Li, Z., et al.: FB-OCC: 3D occupancy prediction based on forward-backward view transformation. arXiv preprint arXiv:2307.01492 (2023)
13. Liu, H., et al.: Fully sparse 3D occupancy prediction. In: European Conference on Computer Vision (ECCV) (2024)
14. Liu, H., Teng, Y., Lu, T., Wang, H., Wang, L.: Sparsebev: high-performance sparse 3D object detection from multi-camera videos. In: International Conference on Computer Vision (ICCV) (2023)
15. Loshchilov, I., Hutter, F.: SGDR: stochastic gradient descent with warm restarts. arXiv preprint arXiv:1608.03983 (2016)
16. Lu, T., et al.: Scaffold-GS: structured 3D gaussians for view-adaptive rendering. In: IEEE Conference on Computer Vision and Pattern Recognition (CVPR) (2024)
17. Pan, M., et al.: Renderocc: vision-centric 3D occupancy prediction with 2D rendering supervision. In: IEEE International Conference on Robotics and Automation (ICRA) (2024)
18. Tian, X., Jiang, T., Yun, L., Wang, Y., Wang, Y., Zhao, H.: OCC3D: a large-scale 3D occupancy prediction benchmark for autonomous driving. In: Advances NeurIPS (2024)
19. Wang, J., et al.: Opus: occupancy prediction using a sparse set. In: Advances NeurIPS (2024)

20. Wei, Y., Zhao, L., Zheng, W., Zhu, Z., Zhou, J., Lu, J.: Surroundocc: multi-camera 3D occupancy prediction for autonomous driving. In: International Conference on Computer Vision (ICCV) (2023)
21. Zhang, J., Ding, Y., Liu, Z.: Occfusion: depth estimation free multi-sensor fusion for 3D occupancy prediction. In: Asian Conference on Computer Vision (ACCV) (2024)
22. Zhang, Y., Zhu, Z., Du, D.: Occformer: dual-path transformer for vision-based 3D semantic occupancy prediction. In: International Conference on Computer Vision (ICCV) (2023)
23. Zhao, X., Zhang, P., Liu, B., Wu, Y.: Dgocc: depth-aware global query-based network for monocular 3d occupancy prediction. Neurocomputing (2025)

Dynamic Memory Reconciliation for Online Action Detection

Wenze Huang, Haoyu Ji, Zhihao Yang, Bowen Chen, Zimo Jiang, Zhiyong Wang, Weihong Ren(✉), and Honghai Liu

School of College of Artificial Intelligence, Harbin Institute of Technology, Shenzhen, China
renweihong@hit.edu.cn

Abstract. Online action detection (OAD) aims to recognize ongoing actions from streaming videos in real-time, which demands effective temporal modeling to capture both long-range dependencies and fine-grained local dynamics. The main challenge lies in the model's inability to utilize future data, requiring it to selectively leverage the most relevant historical and current information for predictions. To address this, we propose a novel framework integrating Shuffled Global Context (SGC) module and Adaptive Local Gating (ALG) module. The SGC module dynamically reorganizes long-term contexts through cyclic shift operations, enabling efficient cross-frame interaction. Complementarily, the ALG module adaptively regulates local feature aggregation by emphasizing spatio-temporal correlations among short-term frames, which effectively suppresses irrelevant noise and highlights discriminative cues for evolving actions. Experimental results demonstrate that our method achieves competitive performance against state-of-the-art methods.

Keywords: Online Action Detection · Global Context · Local Gating

1 Introduction

Action detection is a fundamental task in computer vision, which involves classifying action categories in untrimmed videos and precisely determining the start and end times of actions. This task is typically performed in an offline setting. However, in many real-world scenarios, real-time processing is crucial. Online action detection (OAD) [8] has thus emerged, featuring an experimental paradigm distinct from offline action detection methods. Specifically, OAD can only access historical and current data information without knowledge of future events. OAD has attracted significant research interest in fields requiring real-time feedback, such as autonomous driving [22,23], intelligent surveillance, and real-time human-computer interaction [12,13,20,21].

Existing OAD methods can be categorized into RNN-based [1,10,11,32] and Transformer -based [5,29,33,35] architectures. In early research, RNNs were widely adopted due to their ability to effectively capture temporal dependencies in action sequences and dynamically retain memory. Recently, Transformer-based architectures have demonstrated superior capability in modeling temporal action dynamics. These models typically divide video streams into long-term and short-term information components. Specifically, long-term information captures global action context over extended time spans, while short-term information focuses on local action details in neighboring frames. Finally, a query mechanism is employed to predict the action category of the latest frame. These methods highlight the importance of maintaining a comprehensive historical action context while achieving precise local action recognition. However, current approaches often perform coarse-grained compression of long-term information, causing the model to focus on irrelevant information. Additionally, existing methods lack fine-grained modeling of short-term information, limiting their ability to discern subtle temporal variations in actions.

To address the aforementioned challenges, we propose a novel framework integrating a Shuffled Global Context (SGA) module and an Adaptive Local Gating (ALG) module. The SGA module filters and refines long-term information by dynamically reorganizing historical context and employing a gating mechanism, thereby enabling the model to focus on more relevant historical cues. Meanwhile, the ALG module adaptively computes attention weights for neighboring frames based on the current frame, determining their relative importance for action recognition and achieving fine-grained temporal understanding.

Extensive experiments on two public benchmarks, THUMOS'14 and TVSeries, demonstrate that our proposed method achieves competitive performance compared to other state-of-the-art approaches. The main contributions of our work are summarized as follows:

1. We introduce the Shuffled Global Context (SGA) module, which selectively filters long-term historical information through dynamic reorganization and gating mechanisms, effectively guiding the model to focus on more relevant historical cues.
2. We propose the Adaptive Local Gating (ALG) module, which leverages the current frame to compute importance-aware attention weights for neighboring frames, enabling finer-grained action understanding.
3. Our algorithm achieves competitive results on two widely used datasets, THUMOS'14 and TVSeries, validating its effectiveness in online action detection.

The remainder of this paper is organized as follows: Sect. 2 reviews related work on OAD and temporal modeling. Subsequently, Sect. 3 provides a detailed exposition of our proposed method. Section 4 presents experimental results on two public benchmarks along with ablation studies. Finally, we conclude with final remarks in Sect. 5.

2 Related Work

2.1 Online Action Detection

The task of OAD was first introduced by Geest et al. [8], who established a fundamental framework for this research direction. Early approaches to OAD primarily focused on reinforcement learning and recurrent neural network architectures. The RED [11] method developed an encoder-decoder network incorporating a reinforcement module, achieving action prediction through sequence-level supervision. Another notable work [9] proposed a dual-stream network architecture utilizing two LSTM [14] modules to process frame features and their temporal dependencies separately. The IDU [10] approach introduced an innovative recurrent unit that selectively accumulates input information based on its relevance to current actions, enabling the learning of more discriminative action representations. TRN [32] presented a temporal recurrent network that integrated decoded future information into OAD tasks, thereby enhancing current action recognition capabilities. MiniROAD [1] implemented a minimal RNN framework that significantly improved model performance by reducing the discrepancy between training and inference phases.

In recent years, Transformer-based architectures have garnered substantial research attention in this domain. OadTR [31] pioneered the application of Transformer models to OAD tasks by proposing an encoder-decoder framework that simultaneously captures global relationships and incorporates anticipated future information as auxiliary cues. LSTR [33] introduced a Long-Short Term Transformer featuring a dual-memory mechanism, combining a coarse-scale long-term memory encoder with a fine-grained short-term memory decoder for comprehensive video stream understanding. Building upon LSTR, TeSTra [35] reformulated cross-attention using kernel methods, substantially reducing the computational complexity in streaming detection scenarios. GateHUB [5] developed a position-guided gated attention mechanism to dynamically modulate historical information, though this mechanism was primarily applied to long-term memory without achieving finer-grained understanding of short-term temporal dynamics. Most recently, MAT [29] proposed a novel memory-anticipation paradigm that models the complete temporal structure encompassing past, present, and future states for more holistic video understanding. BEDL [16] integrates Bayesian neural networks with evidential deep learning via a teacher-student architecture, effectively reducing prediction uncertainty while enabling efficient online inference. However, these methods primarily employ static or coarse-grained temporal modeling mechanisms, failing to optimize the spatiotemporal dependencies. In contrast, our proposed approach dynamically models video stream features, establishing a superior action modeling framework.

2.2 Temporal Modeling

Traditional causal time series analysis assumes the existence of a latent "state" variable that captures all historical information and updates solely with current observations [7]. We therefore directly model historical evolution to achieve current action recognition. Early methods relied on sparse frame sampling for both training and inference. While 3D CNNs [26,27] significantly expanded spatiotemporal receptive fields, they remained constrained by short-term dependency limitations. The introduction of RNNs and Transformers substantially enhanced models' capacity to capture long-range dependencies, making them dominant architectures in action detection. Other action modeling approaches further strengthened the expressiveness and efficiency of temporal feature representation. TSN [30] combined sparse temporal sampling with video-level supervision to enable efficient and effective learning of complete action videos. TallFormer [6] introduced a temporal action localization transformer that significantly reduced memory consumption and training time through long-term memory mechanisms. [24] encoded multi-scale action features, effectively modeling long-term temporal relationships at each time scale. For OAD tasks, existing methods still lack adaptive mechanisms to jointly optimize temporal dependencies under causality constraints. Our method addresses this through Shuffled Global Context and Adaptive Local Gating modules, achieving comprehensive understanding of video stream data.

3 Method

3.1 Overview

The goal of OAD is to determine the activity category in the current frame by utilizing only the historical and currently played video frames. The video stream input can be represented as $V = \{F_1, F_2, \ldots, F_T\} \in \mathbb{R}^{C_0 \times T \times H \times W}$, where F_t denotes the frame at time, with C_0, H and W denoting the number of channels, height and width of the frame. The task requires classifying the action in the latest frame F_T. Thus, the inference output of OAD is $y_T \in [0,1]^{K+1}$, where $K+1$ represents the total number of action categories plus the background class.

For the input video stream frames, we first encode them using a pre-trained feature extractor, transforming them into feature vectors $X = \{x_1, x_2, \ldots, x_T\} \in \mathbb{R}^{T \times D}$. Subsequently, we incorporate sinusoidal positional encoding [28] into each frame feature. These feature vectors are then fed into our proposed method for training and inference. Following the algorithmic setup of LSTR, which provides a strong baseline approach, we refer to the frames within a short temporal segment of the current time step as short-term memory $X_S = \{X_{T-l_S+1}, \ldots, X_T\} \in \mathbb{R}^{l_S \times D}$, while those from more distant time segments are termed long-term memory $X_L = \{X_{T-l_S-l_L+1}, \ldots, X_{T-l_S}\} \in \mathbb{R}^{l_L \times D}$, where l_L and l_S denote the sequence lengths of long-term memory and short-term memory, respectively. Specifically, the long-term memory retains broader contextual information that captures relevant background details and historical action segments associated with the current activity, thereby facilitating the interpretation of short-term behaviors. In contrast, the short-term memory focuses on processing the most immediate motion patterns, enabling the capture of fine-grained action details.

For long-term memory, we ultimately encode it into a latent representation of length M using compressed tokens η. As for short-term memory, we treat it as queries in the decoder to predict action labels for all frames in the short-term memory $y_S = \{y_{T-l_S+1}, \ldots, y_T\} \in \mathbb{R}^{l_S \times (K+1)}$, including the current timestep.

3.2 Long-Term Encoder with Shuffled Global Context Module

This section elaborates on the architecture of the Shuffled Global Context Module (SGC) and presents the compression method for long-term memory processing.

Long-term memory typically constitutes a lengthy sequence containing substantial noise. When computing attention weights, conventional cross-attention mechanisms process numerous noisy tokens, causing the model to disproportionately focus on irrelevant historical frames. Our proposed SGC module addresses this limitation by effectively capturing complex dependencies within long-term memory, thereby enabling more efficient utilization of information from different temporal intervals (Fig. 1).

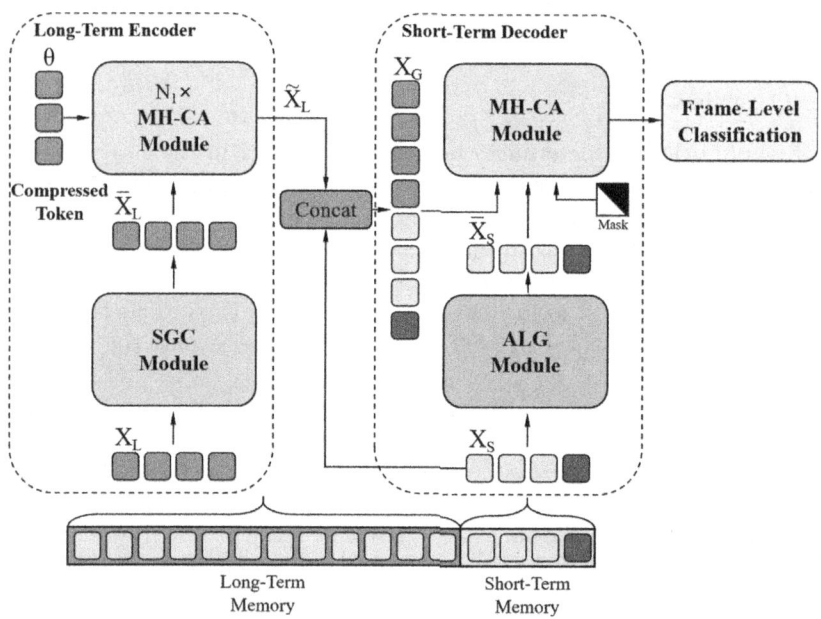

Fig. 1. The proposed network employs a long-term memory encoder and a short-term memory decoder. In the long-term memory encoder, we first process the long-term memory features using the SGC module, followed by compression through multi-head cross attention units with learnable tokens. In the short-term memory decoder, we apply the ALG module to perform spatiotemporal feature enhancement and gated filtering of short-term memories, which are subsequently decoded into frame-level prediction results.

As illustrated in Fig. 2, the input long-term memory sequence $X_L \in \mathbb{R}^{l_L \times D}$ is first partitioned into N non-overlapping segments $S = \{S_1, S_2, ..., S_N\}$, each with a fixed length of $n = \frac{l_L}{N}$. Each segment encapsulates a coherent chunk of short-term temporal information, serving as fundamental building blocks for modeling intricate long-range dependencies across the entire sequence. This segmentation strategy facilitates localized pattern extraction while maintaining the capacity to learn global temporal relationships. Subsequently, we employ spatial average pooling $\Phi AP(\cdot)$ to aggregate spatial information, followed by a context shuffle operation $\Phi CS(\cdot)$ that systematically rearranges the temporal features.

$$\widetilde{S} = \Phi AP(S) = [s_1^1, \cdots, s_n^1, s_1^2, \cdots, s_n^2, \cdots, s_1^N, \cdots, s_n^N] \quad (1)$$

$$\bar{S} = \Phi CS(\widetilde{S}) = [s_1^1, s_1^2, \cdots, s_1^N, \cdots, s_n^1, \cdots, s_n^N] \quad (2)$$

This shuffled representation is then processed through an N-tuple convolutional layer $\Phi GC(\cdot)$ to generate frame-level importance weights. Finally, these weights are restored to their original temporal order through an inverse shuffle operation, yielding the final importance-weighted representation.

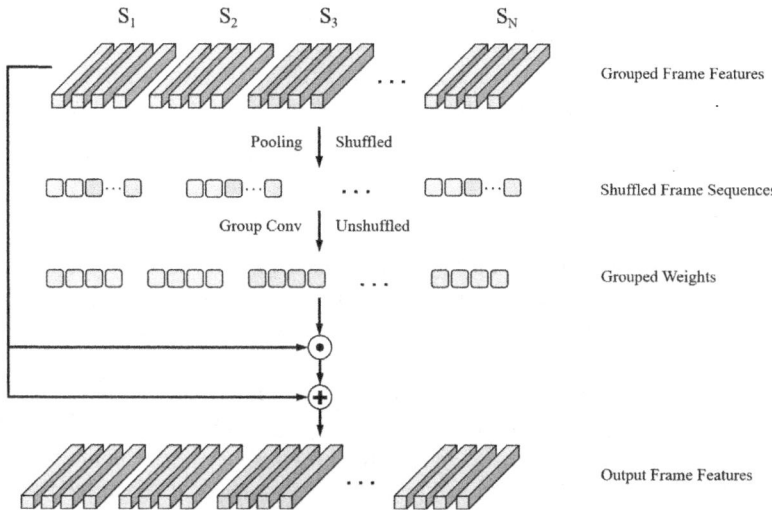

Fig. 2. The Architecture Diagram of Shuffled Global Context Module.

$$\bar{W} = \Phi CU(\Phi GC(\bar{S})) = [w_1^1, \cdots, w_n^1, w_1^2, \cdots, w_n^2, \cdots, w_1^N, \cdots, w_n^N] \quad (3)$$

where $\Phi CU(\cdot)$ is context unshuffle operation. The unshuffled weights $\bar{W}$ are partitioned into N chunks $\{W^i\}_{i=1}^N = \Phi chunk(\bar{W})$, where $\Phi chunk(\cdot)$ represents the chunk operation. Finally, we generate the output through weighted summation based on $\{W^i\}_{i=1}^N$, followed by a residual connection with the original features. This process can be formally expressed as:

$$\bar{X}_L = (\sum_{i=1}^{N} W^i * X_L^i) + X_L \qquad (4)$$

We implement long-term memory compression through M multi-head cross attention units, where each unit processes learnable compression tokens $\theta_m \in \mathbb{R}^{l_0 \times D}$ as queries and long-term memory as keys and values in the cross-attention mechanism.

$$\tilde{X}_L = MHCA(\theta_m, \bar{X}_L, \bar{X}_L) \qquad (5)$$

This usage follows LSTR. It utilizes cross-attention mechanism to trains the parameters to become effective queries that selectively weight and condense the memory. Compared to direct compression, our integration with the SGC module provides superior performance by dynamically reorganizing temporal relationships before compression, preserving critical context that would otherwise be lost in compression.

3.3 Short-Term Decoder with Adaptive Local Gating Module

In this section, we elaborate on the architecture of the Adaptive Local Gating Module (ALG), which dynamically assigns attention weights to adjacent frames based on the current frame's information and ultimately decodes frame-level prediction results.

Short-term memory contains critical action-related information, yet it is often accompanied by irrelevant or less relevant frame-level data. Direct processing of these raw temporal features typically leads to suboptimal performance. The proposed ALG module dynamically computes attention weights for adjacent frames based on their relevance to the current action, employing a learnable gating function to amplify discriminative local patterns while suppressing noise. This fine-grained processing of short-term memory dynamics complements our global context modeling, forming a comprehensive temporal understanding framework.

As illustrated in the Fig. 3, given the input short-term memory features $X_S \in \mathbb{R}^{l_S \times D}$, the ALG module enhances spatiotemporal features through a dual-branch architecture:

$$\bar{X}_S = X_S \odot \mathcal{G}(X) \odot \mathcal{B}(X) + X_S \qquad (6)$$

The gating branch $\mathcal{G}(X)$ generates a gating vector through current-frame feature extraction, which is subsequently broadcast to serve as frame-level weighting coefficients.

$$\mathcal{G}(X) = \sigma(X_{S_{[-1]}}) \qquad (7)$$

The main branch $\mathcal{B}(X)$ employs a cascaded architecture of "convolution $\rightarrow$ soft pooling $\rightarrow$ convolution" that maintains the original temporal resolution while performing feature transformation. The SoftPool layer implements adaptive feature aggregation through exponentially weighted averaging. Its core operation directly computes exponential weights from the input features, then calculates the mean of both weighted feature sums and weight sums within local receptive fields, ultimately outputting the ratio between these two values.

$$\mathcal{B}(X) = Upsample(\Phi_B(X_S)) \tag{8}$$

$$\Phi_B = \sigma \circ \mathcal{C}_2 \circ \mathcal{P} \circ \mathcal{C}_1 \tag{9}$$

We obtain frame-level prediction results through our short-term decoder. Unlike LSTR, which solely utilizes compressed long-term memory as contextual information, our approach construct enhanced global memory X_G information by concatenating the compressed long-term memory $\bar{X}_L$ and the original short-term memory X_S, which serves as the keys and values for the decoder. While utilizing the ALG-enhanced short-term memory $\bar{X}_S$ as queries for decoding through multi-head cross attention mechanisms. Furthermore, we apply a causal mask to prevent potential information leakage from future frames. The output vectors from the decoder are subsequently projected through a linear layer to generate final prediction scores y_S.

$$X_G = [\widetilde{X}_L, X_S] \tag{10}$$

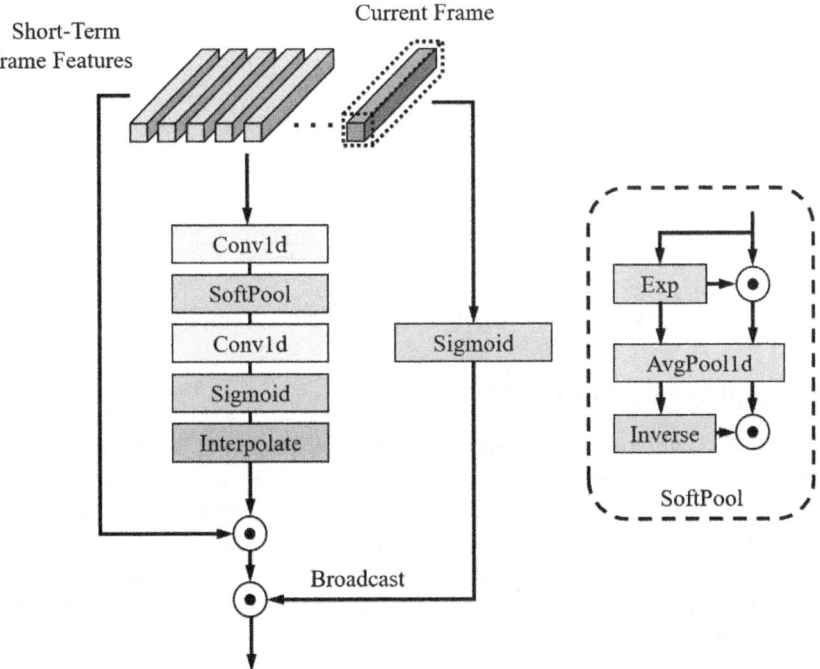

Fig. 3. The Architecture Diagram of Adaptive Local Gating Module.

$$y'_S = MHCA(\bar{X}_S, X_G, X_G) \tag{11}$$

$$y_S = FFN(y'_S) \tag{12}$$

We employ cross-entropy loss between the predicted results and ground truth annotations as the supervision for our OAD approach.

$$\mathcal{L} = -\sum_{i=0}^{K} y_S^i log(\hat{y}_S^i) \tag{13}$$

4 Experiments

4.1 Datasets and Evaluation Metric

Datasets. We assess the performance of our proposed model on two challenging datasets. THUMOS'14 [18] is a large-scale dataset consisting of over 20 h of sports videos spanning 20 action classes. Following the standard evaluation protocol in prior work [29,33], we train on the validation set (200 untrimmed videos) and evaluate on the test set (213 untrimmed videos). TVSeries [8] focuses on real-world daily actions extracted from 27 episodes of 6 popular TV shows, totaling 16 h of video. The dataset includes 30 fine-grained action classes. We train our model on 20 episodes and evaluate on the remaining 7 episodes.

Evaluation Metric. We employ perframe mean Average Precision (mAP) for evaluation on THUMOS'14 and perframe mean calibrated Average Precision (mcAP) on TVSeries.

$$cPrec = \frac{TP}{TP + \frac{FP}{\omega}} \tag{14}$$

$$cAP = \frac{\sum_k cPrec(k) \times I(k)}{\sum TP} \tag{15}$$

where ω is the ratio between negative and positive examples.

4.2 Implementation Details

Feature Extraction. Following the settings in [10,33,35], we process all videos at 24 frames per second (FPS) and divide them into non-overlapping 6-frame blocks for temporal modeling. For feature coding, we employ the Temporal Segment Network (TSN) [30] framework with a dual-stream architecture: RGB features are extracted using a ResNet-50 [17] backbone, while optical flow features are obtained using a BN-Inception [19] backbone. The backbones are pretrained on the ActivityNet [2] and Kinetics [4] separately.

Training Details. We set the training epochs to 25 and the batch size to 16. During the training process, A cosine annealing schedule with linear warm-up was applied. The learning rate schedule combines two distinct phases: a linear warm-up phase spanning the initial 10 epochs, where the learning rate linearly increases from 0 to the peak value of 7e-5, and a subsequent cosine annealing phase over the remaining 15 epochs, where the learning rate smoothly decays following a cosine function until reaching 0.

4.3 Main Result

In this subsection, we compare the performance of our proposed method with other state-of-the-art methods on THUMOS'14 and TVSeries datasets.

To ensure fair comparison, we present all results using different RGB and optical flow extraction backbones. As shown in Table 1 and Table 2, our approach demonstrates consistent improvements, achieving a 2.7% and 1.7% increase compared to the baseline method TeSTra on THUMOS'14 when using ActivityNet and Kinetics features respectively. Compared with BEDL, our method achieves performance improvements of 0.3% and 0.4% on THUMOS'14 and TVSeries datasets respectively using ActivityNet features, while demonstrating gains of 0.2% using Kinetics features.

4.4 Ablation Studies on Each Component

To rigorously validate the contribution of each component in our method, we conducted systematic ablation studies on the THUMOS'14 dataset, with detailed results presented in Table 3. The baseline model TeSTra, which employs no memory enhancement scheme and directly queries compressed long-term memory

Table 1. Comparison results on THUMOS'14 and TVSeries using ActivityNet features.

Method	Architecture	THUMOS'14 mAP	TVSeries mcAP
CDC [25]	CNN	44.4	-
RED [11]	RNN	45.3	-
TRN [32]	RNN	47.2	86.2
IDN [10]	RNN	50.0	84.7
OadTR [31]	Trans	58.3	85.4
Colar [34]	Trans	59.4	86.0
LSTR [33]	Trans	65.3	88.1
TeSTra [35]	Trans	68.2	-
GateHUB [5]	Trans	69.1	88.4
MiniROAD [1]	RNN	69.3	88.5
MAT [29]	Trans	70.4	88.6
BEDL [16]	Bayesian	70.6	88.9
Ours	Trans	**70.9**	**89.3**

Table 2. Comparison results on THUMOS'14 and TVSeries using Kinetics features.

Method	Architecture	THUMOS'14 mAP	TVSeries mcAP
TRN [32]	RNN	62.1	-
IDN [10]	RNN	60.3	86.1
OadTR [31]	Trans	65.2	87.2
Colar [34]	Trans	66.9	88.1
LSTR [33]	Trans	69.5	89.1
GateHUB [5]	Trans	70.7	89.6
TeSTra [35]	Trans	71.2	-
MiniROAD [1]	RNN	71.8	89.6
MAT [29]	Trans	71.6	89.7
E2E-LOAD [3]	Trans	72.4	**90.3**
JOADAA [15]	Trans	72.6	-
BEDL [16]	Bayesian	72.7	90.1
Ours	Trans	**72.9**	**90.3**

using short-term memory for frame-level predictions, achieves 71.2% mAP. Subsequent experiments demonstrate that when individually applying our proposed SGC and ALG modules to enhance the corresponding memory features, the mAP improves by 0.7% and 1.0% respectively, confirming the effectiveness of each module. The final results show that the combined application of both modules yields optimal performance, reaching 72.9% mAP.

Table 3. Ablation studies on the individual modules on THUMOS'14.

No.	Method	mAP(%)
1	Baseline [35]	71.2
2	w/ SGC	71.9
3	w/ ALG	72.2
4	w/ SGC and ALG	**72.9**

4.5 Efficiency Analysis

For OAD, computational efficiency is crucial. We conducted comprehensive efficiency analysis and comparisons on the THUMOS'14 dataset, with results presented in Table 4. Comparative experiments demonstrate that our proposed method achieves superior performance while maintaining competitive inference efficiency. Notably, our analysis reveals that the inference speed of current OAD methods remains constrained by optical flow computation, suggesting this as a critical bottleneck for real-time applications.

Table 4. Runtime comparison. OF. Comp., RGB Feat., and OF. Feat. represent the speed of extracting optical flows, RGB features, and optical flow features, respectively, measured in FPS.

Method	OF. Comp.	RGB Feat.	OF. Feat.	Model FPS	Overall FPS	mAP
LSTR	8.1	70.5	14.6	91.6	8.1	69.5
TeSTra				93.1	8.1	71.2
MAT				72.6	8.1	71.6
Ours				88.6	8.1	**72.9**

5 Conclution

This paper proposes a novel method for the OAD task by integrating two key components into the baseline: the Shuffled Global Context (SGA) module and the Adaptive Local Gating (ALG) module. The SGA module dynamically reorganizes long-term contextual information through a gating mechanism, effectively filtering and enhancing critical historical representations. Simultaneously, the ALG module adaptively computes fine-grained attention weights for adjacent frames based on the current frame, enabling more precise short-term action understanding. Extensive experiments conducted on THUMOS'14 and TVSeries demonstrate that our approach achieves competitive performance compared to state-of-the-art methods.

Acknowledgement. This work is supported in part by the National Key Research and Development Program of China under Grant 2022YFB4703200; in part by the National Natural Science Foundation of China under Grant 62261160652, Grant 52275013, Grant 62206075, and Grant 61733011; in part by Shenzhen Science and Technology Program under Grant JCYJ20240813105137049; and in part by the Science and Technology Development Fund (FDCT), Macau, SAR, under Grant 0095/2022/AFJ.

References

1. An, J., Kang, H., Han, S.H., Yang, M.H., Kim, S.J.: Miniroad: minimal RNN framework for online action detection. In: Proceedings of the IEEE International Conference on Computer Vision, pp. 10341–10350 (2023)
2. Caba Heilbron, F., Escorcia, V., Ghanem, B., Carlos Niebles, J.: Activitynet: a large-scale video benchmark for human activity understanding. In: Proceedings of the IEEE Conference on Computer Vision and Pattern Recognition, pp. 961–970 (2015)

3. Cao, S., Luo, W., Wang, B., Zhang, W., Ma, L.: E2e-load: end-to-end long-form online action detection. In: Proceedings of the IEEE International Conference on Computer Vision, pp. 10422–10432 (2023)
4. Carreira, J., Zisserman, A.: Quo vadis, action recognition? A new model and the kinetics dataset. In: Proceedings of the IEEE Conference on Computer Vision and Pattern Recognition, pp. 6299–6308 (2017)
5. Chen, J., Mittal, G., Yu, Y., Kong, Y., Chen, M.: Gatehub: gated history unit with background suppression for online action detection. In: Proceedings of the IEEE Conference on Computer Vision and Pattern Recognition, pp. 19925–19934 (2022)
6. Cheng, F., Bertasius, G.: Tallformer: temporal action localization with a long-memory transformer. In: Proceedings of the European Conference on Computer Vision, pp. 503–521. Springer, Cham (2022)
7. Chung, J., Gulcehre, C., Cho, K., Bengio, Y.: Empirical evaluation of gated recurrent neural networks on sequence modeling. arXiv preprint arXiv:1412.3555 (2014)
8. De Geest, R., Gavves, E., Ghodrati, A., Li, Z., Snoek, C., Tuytelaars, T.: Online action detection. In: Proceedings of the European Conference on Computer Vision, pp. 269–284 (2016)
9. De Geest, R., Tuytelaars, T.: Modeling temporal structure with LSTM for online action detection. In: 2018 IEEE Winter Conference on Applications of Computer Vision, pp. 1549–1557. IEEE (2018)
10. Eun, H., Moon, J., Park, J., Jung, C., Kim, C.: Learning to discriminate information for online action detection. In: Proceedings of the IEEE Conference on Computer Vision and Pattern Recognition, pp. 809–818 (2020)
11. Gao, J., Yang, Z., Nevatia, R.: Red: reinforced encoder-decoder networks for action anticipation. arXiv preprint arXiv:1707.04818 (2017)
12. Gao, Y., et al.: Jadfer: exploring spatial-contextual interaction with joint attention dropping for facial expression recognition. IEEE Trans. Affect. Comput. (2024)
13. Gao, Y., Ren, W., Wang, Q., Chen, X., Wang, Z., Liu, H.: Snefer: stopping the negative effect of noisy labels adaptively in facial expression recognition. IEEE Sens. J. **24**(11), 18622–18632 (2024)
14. Graves, A., Graves, A.: Long short-term memory. In: Supervised Sequence Labelling with Recurrent Neural Networks, pp. 37–45 (2012)
15. Guermal, M., Ali, A., Dai, R., Bremond, F.: Joadaa: joint online action detection and action anticipation. In: Proceedings of the IEEE/CVF Winter Conference on Applications of Computer Vision, pp. 6889–6898 (2024)
16. Guo, H., Wang, H., Ji, Q.: Bayesian evidential deep learning for online action detection. In: Proceedings of the European Conference on Computer Vision, pp. 283–301 (2024)
17. He, K., Zhang, X., Ren, S., Sun, J.: Deep residual learning for image recognition. In: Proceedings of the IEEE Conference on Computer Vision and Pattern Recognition, pp. 770–778 (2016)
18. Idrees, H., et al.: The thumos challenge on action recognition for videos "in the wild". Comput. Vis. Image Understand. **155**, 1–23 (2017)
19. Ioffe, S.: Batch normalization: accelerating deep network training by reducing internal covariate shift. In: International Conference on Machine Learning, pp. 770–778 (2015)
20. Ji, H., Chen, B., Huang, W., Ren, W., Wang, Z., Liu, H.: Snippet-aware transformer with multiple action elements for skeleton-based action segmentation. IEEE Trans. Neural Netw. Learn. Syst. (2025)

21. Ji, H., Chen, B., Xu, X., Ren, W., Wang, Z., Liu, H.: Language-assisted skeleton action understanding for skeleton-based temporal action segmentation. In: Proceedings of the European Conference on Computer Vision, pp. 400–417. Springer, Cham (2024)
22. Keller, C.G., Gavrila, D.M.: Will the pedestrian cross? A study on pedestrian path prediction. IEEE Trans. Intell. Transp. Syst. **15**(2), 494–506 (2013)
23. Kim, J., Misu, T., Chen, Y.T., Tawari, A., Canny, J.: Grounding human-to-vehicle advice for self-driving vehicles. In: Proceedings of the IEEE Conference on Computer Vision and Pattern Recognition, pp. 10591–10599 (2019)
24. Nguyen, T.T., Kawanishi, Y., Komamizu, T., Ide, I.: One-stage open-vocabulary temporal action detection leveraging temporal multi-scale and action label features. In: International Conference on Automatic Face and Gesture Recognition, pp. 1–10. IEEE (2024)
25. Shou, Z., Chan, J., Zareian, A., Miyazawa, K., Chang, S.F.: CDC: convolutional-de-convolutional networks for precise temporal action localization in untrimmed videos. In: Proceedings of the IEEE Conference on Computer Vision and Pattern Recognition, pp. 5734–5743 (2017)
26. Tran, D., Bourdev, L., Fergus, R., Torresani, L., Paluri, M.: Learning spatiotemporal features with 3d convolutional networks. In: Proceedings of the IEEE International Conference on Computer Vision, pp. 4489–4497 (2015)
27. Tran, D., Wang, H., Torresani, L., Ray, J., LeCun, Y., Paluri, M.: A closer look at spatiotemporal convolutions for action recognition. In: Proceedings of the IEEE conference on Computer Vision and Pattern Recognition, pp. 6450–6459 (2018)
28. Vaswani, A., et al.: Attention is all you need. In: Advances in Neural Information Processing Systems, vol. 30 (2017)
29. Wang, J., Chen, G., Huang, Y., Wang, L., Lu, T.: Memory-and-anticipation transformer for online action understanding. In: Proceedings of the IEEE International Conference on Computer Vision, pp. 13824–13835 (2023)
30. Wang, L., et al.: Temporal segment networks: towards good practices for deep action recognition. In: Proceedings of the European Conference on Computer Vision, pp. 20–36 (2016)
31. Wang, X., et al.: Oadtr: online action detection with transformers. In: Proceedings of the IEEE International Conference on Computer Vision, pp. 7565–7575 (2021)
32. Xu, M., Gao, M., Chen, Y.T., Davis, L.S., Crandall, D.J.: Temporal recurrent networks for online action detection. In: Proceedings of the IEEE International Conference on Computer Vision, pp. 5532–5541 (2019)
33. Xu, M., et al.: Long short-term transformer for online action detection. In: Advances in Neural Information Processing Systems, vol. 34, pp. 1086–1099 (2021)
34. Yang, L., Han, J., Zhang, D.: Colar: effective and efficient online action detection by consulting exemplars. In: Proceedings of the IEEE Conference on Computer Vision and Pattern Recognition, pp. 3160–3169 (2022)
35. Zhao, Y., Krähenbühl, P.: Real-time online video detection with temporal smoothing transformers. In: Proceedings of the European Conference on Computer Vision, pp. 485–502 (2022)

Enhance Polyp Segmentation via Supervised Contrastive Learning

Jiejie Yan[1] and Yizhang Ruan[2(✉)]

[1] Biomedical Engineering Department, Shenzhen Children's Hospital, Shenzhen 518000, China
[2] Zhejiang Open University, Hangzhou 310000, China
xmtv92@163.com

Abstract. Accurate segmentation of colorectal polyps is crucial for the early diagnosis and prevention of colorectal cancer. However, automatic polyp segmentation remains a challenging task due to the high diversity of polyps in shape, size, color, and texture, as well as their low contrast with the surrounding mucosal background. Existing deep learning-based segmentation methods, which primarily rely on pixel-wise supervised losses, may struggle to learn sufficiently discriminative features to distinguish polyps from the background. This paper proposes a novel polyp segmentation framework, namely Sup-Polyp, that enhances the model's feature representation capability by introducing supervised contrastive learning. Specifically, building upon a standard segmentation network, we first design a projection head to map the features extracted by the backbone into a dedicated embedding Space. Secondly, we construct a polyp memory bank to store and dynamically update the average feature representations of polyp regions during training. Finally, in each training iteration, we retrieve features from the memory bank and, in conjunction with the image features from the current batch, optimize them using an InfoNCE loss function. This contrastive loss pulls the features of polyp regions to move closer to the features in the memory bank within the embedding space, while simultaneously pushing them away from background features. Experimental results on public polyp segmentation datasets demonstrate that our proposed method can effectively improve segmentation performance without additional inference costs.

Keywords: Polyp Segmentation · Medical Image Analysis · Contrastive Learning

1 Introduction

Colorectal Cancer (CRC) is one of the most common malignant tumors globally, with high incidence and mortality rates [4]. Most CRCs originate from colorectal polyps; therefore, early detection and accurate resection of polyps during colonoscopy are key strategies for CRC prevention [20]. Manual detection and segmentation of polyps are not only time-consuming and labor-intensive but also highly dependent on the experience level of endoscopists, leading to potential missed diagnoses and misdiagnoses [12]. Consequently, the development of Computer-Aided Diagnosis (CAD) systems, especially automated polyp segmentation algorithms, is of great significance for improving diagnostic efficiency and accuracy.

In recent years, Convolutional Neural Networks (CNNs) based on deep learning have achieved remarkable success in the field of medical image segmentation. Various network architectures, such as U-Net [13] and DeepLabv3+ [6], have been applied to polyp segmentation tasks and have yielded promising results. However, polyp segmentation still faces numerous challenges, such as high intra-class variance, inter-class similarity, and complex imaging conditions. Polyps exhibit diverse morphologies, sizes, colors, and textures. At the same time, they may perform similar visual features to the surrounding normal intestinal mucosa, often with blurred boundaries.

Existing segmentation methods typically employ pixel-wise supervised signals (e.g., Cross-Entropy loss, Dice loss) for end-to-end training. Although these methods can learn certain semantic information, they may not fully exploit the relationships between polyp regions, leading to learned features that lack sufficient discriminative power, especially when addressing the aforementioned challenges.

To address these issues, this paper explores contrastive learning to enhance the polyp segmentation. Contrastive learning has emerged as a powerful self-supervised or supervised representation learning method, demonstrating great potential in the computer vision domain [7,11]. It learns more robust and discriminative features by pulling representations of similar samples (positive samples) closer and pushing representations of dissimilar samples (negative samples) further apart. Inspired by this, this paper aims to explore how to introduce the idea of supervised contrastive learning into the polyp segmentation task to enhance the model's ability to discern polyp features. Experimental results indicate that the proposed method can improve the accuracy and robustness of polyp segmentation.

The main contributions of this paper are as follows:

1. We propose the introduction of a projection head after the feature extraction module of a polyp segmentation model to construct a dedicated embedding space for contrastive learning, aiming to learn more refined feature representations.
2. We design a polyp region memory bank to store and iteratively update the average features extracted from polyp regions during the training process. This memory bank provides stable and representative positive prototypes for contrastive learning.
3. We utilize features extracted from the memory bank as positive anchors and, in conjunction with pixel features from the current image, optimize them using the InfoNCE loss function. This guides the model to learn a more dis-

criminative feature space, making polyp region features more compact and more clearly distinguishable from background region features.

2 Related Works

Our work is related to two main research areas: automatic polyp segmentation and contrastive learning for visual segmentation.

2.1 Polyp Segmentation

Early works on polyp segmentation relied on handcrafted features such as color, texture, and shape [2]. However, these methods often lacked robustness due to the large appearance variation of polyps. The advent of deep learning has revolutionized this field.

CNN-based Methods: Convolutional Neural Networks (CNNs), particularly encoder-decoder architectures like U-Net [13], have become the de-facto standard for polyp segmentation. Numerous variants have been proposed to enhance performance. For instance, U-Net++ [22] introduced nested and dense skip connections to reduce the semantic gap between encoder and decoder features. PraNet [10] proposed a parallel reverse attention network to mine high-level semantics and model the relationship between areas and boundaries. The strength of CNNs lies in their powerful local feature extraction capabilities and inductive biases (e.g., spatial invariance), which are well-suited for image tasks. However, their inherently limited receptive fields can make it difficult to model long-range dependencies, which is critical for distinguishing large polyps from a complex background.

Transformer-based Methods: More recently, Vision Transformers (ViTs) have been adapted for medical image segmentation to better capture global context. TransUNet [5] was a pioneering work that combined a Transformer encoder with a CNN-based decoder to leverage both global and local features. Following this, models specifically designed for polyp segmentation, such as Polyp-PVT [8], utilized a Pyramid Vision Transformer to extract multi-scale features, showing strong performance. The primary advantage of Transformers is their ability to model global context through self-attention mechanisms. However, they typically require large-scale pre-training datasets to perform well and can be computationally expensive. Furthermore, the trend in both CNN and Transformer-based models is towards increasingly complex architectures with a large number of parameters, potentially leading to overfitting and high computational costs for clinical deployment. Our work diverges from this trend by enhancing a simple backbone with a computationally efficient contrastive learning module.

2.2 Contrastive Learning for Segmentation

Contrastive learning has emerged as a dominant paradigm in self-supervised representation learning [7,11]. Its core principle is to learn an embedding space where representations of "positive" sample pairs (e.g., two augmented views of the same image) are pulled together, while representations of "negative" pairs (e.g., views from different images) are pushed apart. This principle has proven highly effective for pre-training models for various downstream tasks, including image classification and object detection.

Recently, this concept has been extended to dense prediction tasks like semantic segmentation. By treating pixels as individual instances, contrastive learning can be applied at the pixel level to learn more discriminative feature representations. For example, Wang et al. [19] proposed a dense contrastive learning framework that performs contrastive learning at both the local and global levels for self-supervised pre-training. Other works apply contrastive objectives directly during the supervised training phase to enforce feature consistency.

The application of contrastive learning to medical image segmentation is a growing but still developing area. For polyp segmentation specifically, the exploration remains limited. One related work, C-Loss [21], introduced a contrast-center loss for scribble-supervised polyp segmentation, where features from scribbled foreground pixels are pulled towards a class center. However, most existing fully-supervised polyp segmentation methods still rely solely on standard pixel-wise losses (e.g., BCE, Dice), which often neglect the crucial region-level feature consistency. These methods can be sensitive to inaccurate pixel-level annotations at the polyp boundaries and may sometimes fail to identify the entire polyp region, resulting in region-level false negatives. Our work addresses this gap by introducing a supervised contrastive learning framework with a dedicated memory bank, explicitly designed to enhance region-level feature compactness and improve the model's robustness against ambiguous boundaries and appearance variations.

3 Methodology

In this section, we will detail the proposed polyp segmentation framework based on supervised contrastive learning. The overall framework is illustrated in Fig. 1. It mainly consists of a segmentation backbone network, a projection head, a polyp region memory bank, and a joint loss function that combines segmentation loss and contrastive loss.

3.1 Overall Framework Overview

Our method is built upon a classic encoder-decoder segmentation network (e.g., U-Net or its variants). The encoder is responsible for extracting multi-level feature maps from the input image. The decoder then progressively upsamples these feature maps and fuses features from corresponding levels of the encoder to finally generate a pixel-level segmentation mask. To incorporate supervised contrastive learning, we add a projection head after the decoder's output and use the resulting embedded features for subsequent contrastive loss calculation.

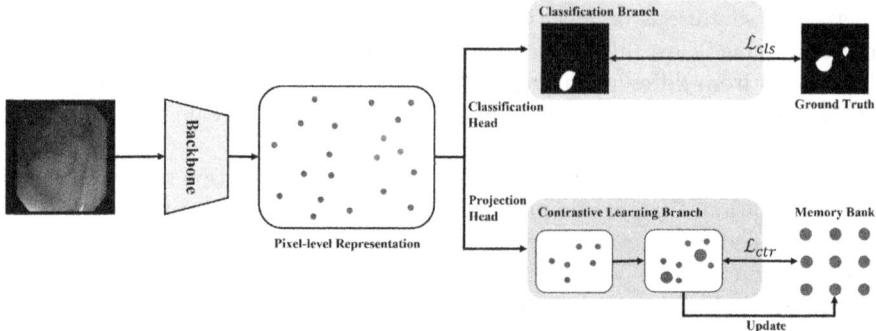

Fig. 1. The illustration of our proposed framework Sup-Polyp.

3.2 Feature Extraction and Projection Head

Given an input image $I \in \mathbb{R}^{H \times W \times 3}$, the backbone maps it to a series of feature maps. We take the feature map $F \in \mathbb{R}^{h \times w \times c}$ output by the last layer of the decoder, where h, w, c are the height, width, and number of channels of the feature map, respectively.

To construct the embedding space required for contrastive learning, we introduce a projection head $g_{\text{proj}}(\cdot)$. This projection head typically consists of one or more Multi-Layer Perceptron (MLP) layers (implemented using 1×1 convolutional layer, followed by ReLU activation and batch normalization layer). The projection head maps the features F obtained from the decoder to a embedding space, yielding embedded features $Z = g_{\text{proj}}(F) \in \mathbb{R}^{h \times w \times d'}$, where d' is the dimension of the embedding space (512 as default). This dedicated embedding space is designed to learn more discriminative representations, making features of same-class samples closer in space and features of different-class samples more distant.

3.3 Polyp Region Memory Bank

To provide stable and representative positive examples for contrastive learning, we design and maintain a Polyp Region Memory Bank M. This memory bank stores the average feature vectors extracted from polyp regions in the training data. At first, we initialize the memory bank as double empty tensor queues, for background and polyp, respectively. The size of each queue is fixed (400 as default). After each training epoch, we iterate through all images containing polyps that were trained in that epoch. For the polyp regions in each image (determined by the ground truth label $G \in \{0,1\}^{H \times W}$), we extract their corresponding pixel features in the embedding space Z. These pixel features belonging to polyp regions are averaged to obtain one or more representative polyp feature prototypes $p \in \mathbb{R}^{d'}$. For background regions, all the pixels belong to background are averaged. The computed polyp and background feature prototypes are stored in the queue of polyp and background, respectively. If the memory bank is full, a First-In, First-Out (FIFO) strategy is used for updates. In this manner, the memory bank can dynamically adapt to changes in the feature representations learned by the model during training and provide high-quality positive polyp samples for the contrastive loss.

3.4 Supervised Contrastive Loss with Hard Anchor Mining

The goal of our contrastive loss is to enforce high intra-class compactness for polyp features and high inter-class separability from background features. The effectiveness of contrastive learning is often determined by the selection of samples; focusing on "hard" samples—those that are easily confused by the model—can provide a stronger learning signal than focusing on "easy" samples [15].

To this end, we introduce a hard anchor mining strategy. In our framework, only feature vectors corresponding to polyp regions from the current training batch can serve as anchors. A polyp region is designated as a hard anchor if the model's confidence in its prediction for that region is low. Specifically, for each polyp region R in the ground truth, we calculate the average prediction confidence from the segmentation head's output mask P. If this average confidence is below a predefined threshold θ (e.g., $\theta = 0.9$), the corresponding feature prototype z_q for that region is selected as a hard anchor for contrastive loss computation. This strategy focuses the learning on polyps that the model finds most challenging.

For each selected hard anchor z_q, we construct its positive and negative sets by sampling from the memory bank. We sample a set of N_p positive prototypes $\mathcal{P}_q \subset M_p$ and a set of N_n negative prototypes $\mathcal{N}_q \subset M_b$. In our experiments, we set $N_p = N_n = 50$. When the number of samples is not enough, all the samples will be collected to generate contrastive sets. The contrastive loss for the anchor z_q is then formulated to pull it towards all sampled positive prototypes while pushing it away from all sampled negative prototypes. We adapt the InfoNCE loss for this multi-positive context as follows:

$$\mathcal{L}_{\text{ctr}}(z_q) = -\frac{1}{N_p} \sum_{p_j \in \mathcal{P}_q} \log \frac{\exp(\text{sim}(z_q, p_j)/\tau)}{\exp(\text{sim}(z_q, p_j)/\tau) + \sum_{n_k \in \mathcal{N}_q} \exp(\text{sim}(z_q, n_k)/\tau)} \quad (1)$$

where:

- $\text{sim}(u, v) = u^T v / (\|u\| \cdot \|v\|)$ is the cosine similarity.
- τ is a temperature hyperparameter.
- The loss for a single anchor z_q is the average of the InfoNCE losses calculated against each positive sample p_j from the set $\mathcal{P}_q$.

The final contrastive loss for the entire batch is the average of $\mathcal{L}_{\text{ctr}}(z_q)$ over all identified hard anchors.

3.5 Total Loss Function

The total loss function $\mathcal{L}$ of the model is a weighted combination of the standard segmentation loss $\mathcal{L}_{\text{seg}}$ (e.g., Binary Cross-Entropy loss (BCE) or Dice loss) and our proposed supervised contrastive loss $\mathcal{L}_{\text{ctr}}$:

$$\mathcal{L} = \mathcal{L}_{\text{seg}} + \lambda \cdot \mathcal{L}_{\text{ctr}} \tag{2}$$

where $\mathcal{L}_{\text{ctr}}$ is the average of the contrastive losses for all positive query features in a batch, and λ is a hyperparameter that balances the importance of the segmentation task and the contrastive learning task.

4 Experiments

In this section, we describe the experimental setup used to validate our proposed method. We detail the datasets, implementation specifics, evaluation metrics, and present a quantitative comparison against several state-of-the-art methods.

4.1 Datasets

We conducted experiments on three widely-used public datasets for polyp segmentation:

- **CVC-ClinicDB** [1]: This dataset contains 612 polyp images with a resolution of 384×288 pixels, extracted from 29 colonoscopy video sequences.
- **CVC-ColonDB** [18]: This dataset includes 380 images with a resolution of 574×500 pixels, sourced from 15 different colonoscopy videos.
- **ETIS-LARIBPOLYPDB** [3]: This dataset provides 196 images with a resolution of 1225×966 pixels, featuring polyps with significant variations in shape and size.

To ensure a fair and reproducible comparison, we adopted the same dataset preprocessing and augmentation strategy as outlined by Dumitru et al. [9]. Specifically, all images were resized to 352×352 pixels. The datasets were randomly partitioned into training, validation, and testing sets with an 80%:10%:10% ratio. We employed the same data augmentation pipeline, including random flips, color jitter, and affine transformations, to enhance model generalization.

4.2 Implementation Details

The model was implemented using the PyTorch 2.1 framework and trained on a single NVIDIA RTX 3090 GPU. We trained the network for 500 epochs with a batch size of 8. We utilized the AdamW optimizer with an initial learning rate of 1e-4, which was decayed using a cosine annealing schedule. The total loss function guiding the training is a combination of a standard segmentation loss and our proposed contrastive loss, as defined in Sect. 3.5 The segmentation loss, $\mathcal{L}_{seg}$, is a weighted sum of Binary Cross-Entropy (BCE) and Dice loss. The hyperparameter λ balancing the segmentation and contrastive losses was set to 0.1 based on validation set performance.

4.3 Evaluation Metrics

To quantitatively evaluate the performance of our method, we used five standard metrics, consistent with prior work in polyp segmentation [9]. Let TP, TN, FP, and FN represent True Positives, True Negatives, False Positives, and False Negatives, respectively. The metrics are:

1. **Dice Coefficient (DSC):** Also known as the F1-Score, it measures the overlap between the prediction and ground truth.

$$\text{DSC} = \frac{2TP}{2TP + FP + FN} \tag{3}$$

2. **Jaccard Index (Jaccard):** Measures the intersection over the union of the prediction and ground truth masks.

$$\text{Jaccard} = \frac{TP}{TP + FP + FN} \tag{4}$$

3. **Precision:** The ratio of correctly predicted positive observations to the total predicted positive observations.

$$\text{Precision} = \frac{TP}{TP + FP} \tag{5}$$

4. **Recall:** The ratio of correctly predicted positive observations to all observations in the actual class.

$$\text{Recall} = \frac{TP}{TP + FN} \tag{6}$$

5. **Accuracy:** The ratio of correctly predicted observations to the total observations.

$$\text{Accuracy} = \frac{TP + TN}{TP + TN + FP + FN} \tag{7}$$

4.4 Results

We compared our proposed method against several state-of-the-art polyp segmentation models. The quantitative results on three test sets are summarized in Table 1, Table 2, and Table 3, respectively.

As demonstrated by the results, our proposed method achieves highly competitive performance across all three datasets. The consistent improvements, especially in the Dice and Jaccard metrics which are sensitive to boundary accuracy, underscore the effectiveness of our supervised contrastive learning module. By explicitly enforcing feature compactness for polyp regions, our model learns more robust and discriminative representations, leading to more precise segmentation masks compared to methods relying solely on pixel-wise classification losses.

Figure 2 illustrates the prediction comparison among different methods. It demonstrates our proposed Sup-polyp can effectively improve the region prediction on the basement of baseline models.

Table 1. Quantitative comparison on the CVC-ClinicDB dataset. Best results are in **bold**.

Method	DSC	Jaccard	Precision	Recall	Accuracy
U-Net [13]	0.7631	0.6169	0.7989	0.7303	0.9599
HRNetV2 [17]	0.7776	0.6361	0.8260	0.7346	0.9629
PraNet [10]	0.8742	0.7766	0.9608	0.8020	0.9780
MSRF-Net [16]	0.9060	0.8282	0.9547	0.8621	0.9842
FCN-Transformer [14]	**0.9327**	**0.8740**	**0.9728**	**0.8958**	**0.9886**
Ours (U-Net)	0.8015	0.6688	0.7980	0.8051	0.9672
Ours (HRNetV2)	0.8226	0.6987	0.8245	0.8207	0.9714

Table 2. Quantitative comparison on the ETIS-LaribPolypDB dataset. Best results are in **bold**.

Method	DSC	Jaccard	Precision	Recall	Accuracy
U-Net [13]	0.7984	0.6969	0.8322	0.7724	0.9734
HRNetV2 [17]	0.4720	0.3089	0.4645	0.4797	0.9433
PraNet [10]	0.8827	0.7900	**0.9825**	0.8013	0.9877
MSRF-Net [16]	0.7791	0.6382	0.9191	0.6762	0.9797
FCN-Transformer [14]	**0.9163**	**0.8455**	0.9633	**0.8736**	**0.9915**
Ours (U-Net)	0.8164	0.6899	0.8388	0.7952	0.9780
Ours (HRNetV2)	0.5471	0.3765	0.4701	0.6655	0.9492

Table 3. Quantitative comparison on the CVC-ColonDB dataset. Best results are in **bold**.

Method	DSC	Jaccard	Precision	Recall	Accuracy
U-Net [13]	0.8032	0.7037	0.8100	0.8274	0.9807
HRNetV2 [17]	0.6383	0.4687	0.5858	0.7010	0.9565
PraNet [10]	**0.9131**	**0.8401**	**0.9657**	0.8659	**0.9901**
MSRF-Net [16]	0.8371	0.7198	0.8603	0.8151	0.9829
FCN-Transformer [14]	0.9073	0.8304	0.9107	**0.9040**	0.9899
Ours (U-Net)	0.8315	0.7116	0.8050	0.8601	0.9836
Ours (HRNetV2)	0.6852	0.5212	0.5820	0.8415	0.9611

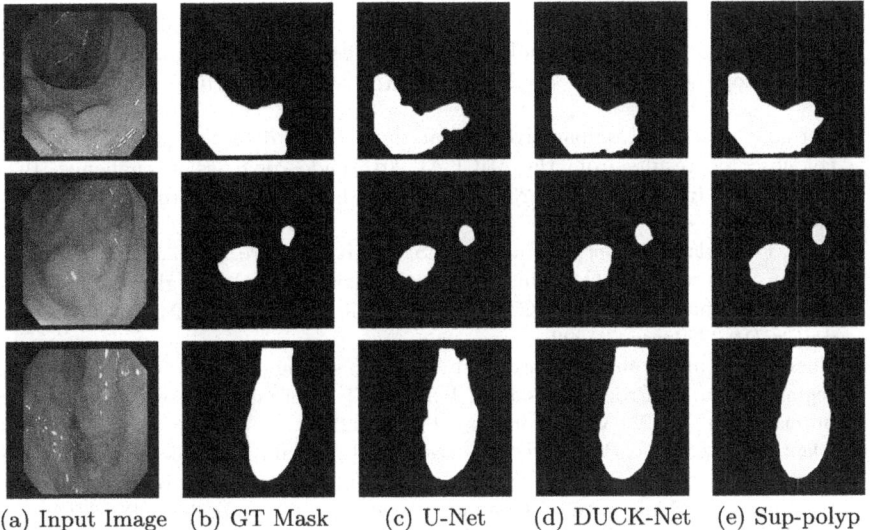

(a) Input Image (b) GT Mask (c) U-Net (d) DUCK-Net (e) Sup-polyp

Fig. 2. The visualized motion representation distribution for different parts. The *fusion* denotes the fused representations from part-level and global-level features. It can be observed that the LPL owns clearer inter-class decision boundary than DeST-Transformer and DPE.

5 Conclusion

In this paper, we presented a novel framework for polyp segmentation that leverages supervised contrastive learning to enhance feature representation. By introducing a dedicated contrastive loss, we explicitly encourage the model to learn more discriminative features, improving its ability to distinguish challenging polyps from the surrounding background tissue. Our core innovations—the use of a projection head to create a specialized embedding space, a feature memory bank to provide stable class prototypes, and a hard anchor mining strategy—are designed to directly address the common issue of low inter-class variance in polyp segmentation. We have shown that this approach can effectively regularize the feature space, leading to higher intra-class compactness and inter-class separability. This method offers a promising direction for improving polyp segmentation models by focusing on feature quality rather than solely increasing architectural complexity, providing a computationally efficient yet powerful alternative to current state-of-the-art methods.

References

1. Bernal, J., Sánchez, F.J., Fernández-Esparrach, G., Gil, D., Rodríguez, C., Vilariño, F.: WM-DOVA maps for accurate polyp highlighting in colonoscopy: validation versus saliency maps from physicians. Comput. Med. Imaging Graph. **43**, 99–111 (2015). https://doi.org/10.1016/j.compmedimag.2015.02.007

2. Bernal, J., Sánchez, F.J., Fernández-Esparrach, G., Gil, D., Rodríguez, C., Vilariño, F.: Towards automatic polyp detection with a polyp appearance model. Pattern Recogn. **45**(9), 3166–3182 (2012). https://doi.org/10.1016/j.patcog.2012.03.018
3. Bernal, J., et al.: Comparative validation of polyp detection methods in video colonoscopy: results from the MICCAI 2015 endoscopic vision challenge. IEEE Trans. Med. Imaging **36**(6), 1231–1249 (2017). https://doi.org/10.1109/TMI.2017.2664042
4. Bray, F., Ferlay, J., Soerjomataram, I., Siegel, R.L., Torre, L.A., Jemal, A.: Global cancer statistics 2018: globocan estimates of incidence and mortality worldwide for 36 cancers in 185 countries. CA: Cancer J. Clin. **68**(6), 394–424 (2018). https://doi.org/10.3322/caac.21492
5. Chen, J., et al.: Transunet: transformers make strong encoders for medical image segmentation. In: Proceedings of the IEEE/CVF International Conference on Computer Vision (ICCV) Workshops, pp. 1–11 (2021)
6. Chen, L.C., Zhu, Y., Papandreou, G., Schroff, F., Adam, H.: Encoder-decoder with atrous separable convolution for semantic image segmentation. In: Proceedings of the European Conference on Computer Vision (ECCV), pp. 801–818 (2018)
7. Chen, T., Kornblith, S., Norouzi, M., Hinton, G.: A simple framework for contrastive learning of visual representations. In: Proceedings of the 37th International Conference on Machine Learning (ICML). Proceedings of Machine Learning Research, vol. 119, pp. 1597–1607 (2020)
8. Dong, N.H., Nguyen, T.T., Do, T., Nguyen, B.M., Tjiputra, E.: Polyp-PVT: polyp segmentation with pyramid vision transformers. In: 2022 IEEE International Conference on Acoustics, Speech and Signal Processing (ICASSP), pp. 2238–2242 (2022). https://doi.org/10.1109/ICASSP43922.2022.9747209
9. Dumitru, R.G., Peteleaza, D., Craciun, C.: Using duck-net for polyp image segmentation. Sci. Rep. **13**(1), 9803 (2023). https://doi.org/10.1038/s41598-023-36940-5
10. Fan, D.P., et al.: Pranet: parallel reverse attention network for polyp segmentation. In: Medical Image Computing and Computer Assisted Intervention – MICCAI 2020. Lecture Notes in Computer Science, vol. 12264, pp. 263–273. Springer, Cham (2020). https://doi.org/10.1007/978-3-030-59752-8_26
11. He, K., Fan, H., Wu, Y., Xie, S., Girshick, R.: Momentum contrast for unsupervised visual representation learning. In: Proceedings of the IEEE/CVF Conference on Computer Vision and Pattern Recognition (CVPR), pp. 9729–9738 (2020)
12. Rex, D.K.: Quality in colonoscopy: colonoscopy miss rates and the importance of endoscopist-dependent factors. Am. J. Gastroenterol. **95**(1), 4–6 (2000). https://doi.org/10.1111/j.1572-0241.2000.01770.x
13. Ronneberger, O., Fischer, P., Brox, T.: U-net: convolutional networks for biomedical image segmentation. In: Navab, N., Hornegger, J., Wells, W.M., Frangi, A.F. (eds.) MICCAI 2015. LNCS, vol. 9351, pp. 234–241. Springer, Cham (2015). https://doi.org/10.1007/978-3-319-24574-4_28
14. Sanderson, E., Matuszewski, B.J.: FCN-transformer feature fusion for polyp segmentation. In: Medical Image Understanding and Analysis, pp. 892–907. Springer, Cham (2022)
15. Schroff, F., Kalenichenko, D., Philbin, J.: Facenet: a unified embedding for face recognition and clustering. In: Proceedings of the IEEE Conference on Computer Vision and Pattern Recognition (CVPR), pp. 815–823 (2015)
16. Srivastava, A., et al.: MSRF-net: a multi-scale residual fusion network for biomedical image segmentation. IEEE J. Biomed. Health Inform. **26**(5), 2252–2263 (2022). https://doi.org/10.1109/JBHI.2021.3138024

17. Sun, K., Xiao, B., Liu, D., Wang, J.: Deep high-resolution representation learning for human pose estimation. In: Proceedings of the IEEE/CVF Conference on Computer Vision and Pattern Recognition (CVPR), pp. 5693–5703 (2019)
18. Vázquez, D., et al.: A benchmark for endoluminal scene segmentation of colonoscopy images. J. Healthcare Eng. **2017**, 4037190 (2017). https://doi.org/10.1155/2017/4037190
19. Wang, X., Zhang, R., Shen, C., He, T., van den Hengel, A.: Dense contrastive learning for self-supervised visual pre-training. In: Proceedings of the IEEE/CVF Conference on Computer Vision and Pattern Recognition (CVPR), pp. 3024–3033 (2021)
20. Winawer, S.J., et al.: Prevention of colorectal cancer by colonoscopic polypectomy. the national polyp study workgroup. New Engl. J. Med. **329**(27), 1977–1981 (1993). https://doi.org/10.1056/NEJM199312303292701
21. Dey, R., Hong, Y.: ASC-net: adversarial-based selective network for unsupervised anomaly segmentation. In: de Bruijne, M., et al. (eds.) MICCAI 2021. LNCS, vol. 12905, pp. 236–247. Springer, Cham (2021). https://doi.org/10.1007/978-3-030-87240-3_23
22. Zhou, Z., Rahman Siddiquee, M.M., Tajbakhsh, N., Liang, J.: UNet++: a nested u-net architecture for medical image segmentation. In: Stoyanov, D., et al. (eds.) DLMIA/ML-CDS -2018. LNCS, vol. 11045, pp. 3–11. Springer, Cham (2018). https://doi.org/10.1007/978-3-030-00889-5_1

Online Prediction of Surface Roughness in Robotic Grinding System for TC4 Workpieces Using PSO-XGBoost Algorithm

Xiangye Zhu[1], Yusen Li[1], Xiaohu Xu[1,2(✉)], Yao Chu[2], and Sijie Yan[2]

[1] The Institute of Technological Sciences, Wuhan University, Wuhan 430072, China
xuxiaohu@whu.edu.cn
[2] State Key Laboratory of Intelligent Manufacturing Equipment and Technology, Huazhong University of Science and Technology, Wuhan 430074, China

Abstract. Surface roughness serves as a critical indicator of robotic machining quality for TC4 workpieces, significantly influencing functional performance and service life. However, existing approaches still struggle to achieve accurate real-time prediction of surface roughness during the robotic machining process. In order to address this gap, a novel real-time prediction model based on multisensor signal fusion using the PSO-XGBoost algorithm is developed in the paper. Initially, acoustic emission (AE) signals and triaxial vibration signals are collected and decomposed using Ensemble Empirical Mode Decomposition (EEMD) and Wavelet Packet Transform (WPT) during the robotic grinding process. Subsequently, an optimized PSO-XGBoost prediction model is proposed to enhance the generalization capability and prediction accuracy. Finally, experimental validation is performed on a robotic grinding platform for TC4 workpieces under varying machining parameters to achieve a stable and accurate real-time prediction of surface roughness compared to conventional methods.

Keywords: Roughness prediction · Features fusion · Robotic grinding

1 First Section

Due to its exceptional toughness, strength, and resistance to corrosion, TC4 titanium alloy (Ti-6Al-4V) has emerged as the preferred material for important parts such as aero-engine blades. The quality of robotic machining processes directly affects the profile accuracy and surface integrity of the blades, thereby determining the overall performance of the engine [1]. However, the increasingly precise demands of contemporary aircraft production are beyond the capabilities

---

Supported by the National Nature Science Foundation of China (Nos. 52105514, 52075204), Wuhan Natural Science Foundation (No. 20240408010202220), and State Key Laboratory of High-end Heavy-load Robots (No. HHR2025020209).

of conventional manual grinding techniques. Robotic belt grinding has become widely used in precision machining applications, such as aero-engine blades, due to its remarkable flexibility, adaptability, and machining consistency [2,3].

In the robotic belt grinding of TC4 alloy, surface quality is influenced by multiple factors. First, the discrete nature of abrasive grains on the grinding belt and their progressive wear contribute to non-uniform surface texture. Second, according to Hertz contact theory, the surface contact between the belt and the workpiece results in an elliptical non-uniform stress distribution. Additionally, belt-induced vibration generates periodic patterns on the machined surface, all of which significantly affect the final surface quality [4]. Therefore, real-time monitoring of surface roughness is crucial in robotic grinding systems to ensure machining precision. Surface roughness not only influences the mechanical properties, fatigue life, and corrosion resistance of components but also determines the assembly accuracy and functional performance [5,6].

Recent advances have been made in surface roughness prediction models during the machining process. Lipiński et al. [7] developed a feedforward multilayer neural network-based model that established a mapping relationship among machining parameters, workpiece and grinding wheel characteristics, and surface roughness using 100 training samples. Arriandiaga et al. [8] proposed a recurrent neural network model incorporating wheel wear factors, achieving a mean prediction error of less than 0.49 μm. Chandrasekaran et al. [9] developed a backpropagation (BP) neural network for predicting the surface roughness of AI-SCIP metal matrix composites in cylindrical grinding, achieving a prediction accuracy of 94.20% under the logsig transfer function. Xu et al. [10] proposed a scallop height-based model for predicting surface roughness in robotic belt grinding, accounting for elastic deformation and blade curvature. Although all the above-mentioned methods can achieve precise prediction of surface roughness, they cannot realize real-time prediction, which implies that they are unable to optimize process parameters in real time to satisfy the workpiece's surface processing quality criteria.

Real-time roughness monitoring enables dynamic assessment of the machining system's operational state. As tool or belt wear progresses, surface roughness deteriorates gradually, and real-time detection facilitates timely wear trend identification, preventing batch defects due to tool failure [11,12]. Furthermore, abnormal vibrations in the grinding machine or robotic feed system instability directly impact surface quality, and real-time roughness monitoring aids in diagnosing machine and robot health [13]. Traditional quality control relies on post-process inspection, whereas real-time monitoring lays the foundation for online feedback adjustment and closed-loop control implementation. If closed-loop control is achieved, machining accuracy and consistency can be substantially improved. Conventional roughness prediction methods operate offline, but the advancement of multi-sensor technologies now enables real-time monitoring by analyzing in-process acoustic emission (AE) and vibration signals for indirect surface quality assessment, even in harsh working conditions [14,15].

Based on the aforementioned research gaps and technological demands, a novel real-time monitoring method is presented based on multi-signal fusion. By collecting AE and vibration signals during robotic belt grinding and performing feature extraction and optimization, a PSO-XGBoost intelligent prediction model is created to realize real-time surface roughness prediction and demonstrate superior performance through multi-dimensional comparative experiments. The research findings provide critical technical support for advancing intelligent manufacturing in aerospace component production.

2 Prediction Model of Surface Roughness

In order to achieve real-time monitoring of surface roughness during the robotic abrasive belt grinding process of TC4 workpieces, a robotic grinding and monitoring system based on acoustic emission and vibration sensors is established. As illustrated in Fig. 1, the system consists of the following components: an industrial robot system, an abrasive belt grinding system, and an acoustic emission signal and vibration signal acquisition and analysis system.

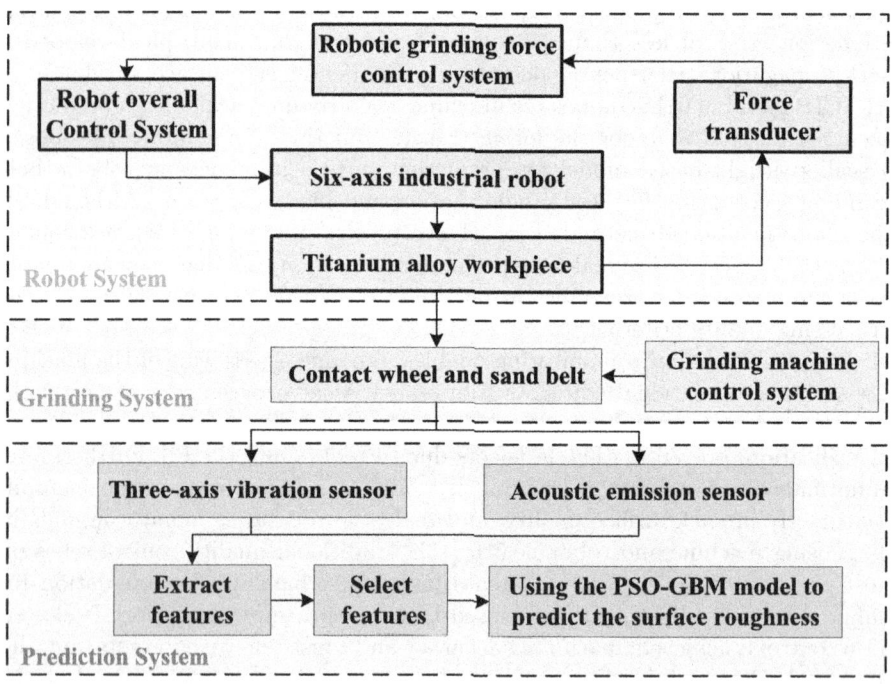

Fig. 1. The schematic of robotic grinding and monitoring system.

2.1 Signal Collection and Processing

Acoustic emission (AE) is a transient elastic wave generated by the release of energy during plastic deformation or fracture in metallic materials. It provides valuable insights into internal stress and strain conditions, which is particularly suitable for monitoring workpiece status. The application of standard Empirical Mode Decomposition (EMD) [16] of AE signal is frequently affected by mode mixing, leading to substantially impaired feature extraction. Thus, the Ensemble Empirical Mode Decomposition (EEMD) method is developed to address this issue, and it can effectively suppress mode mixing artifacts in nonlinear and non-stationary AE signals through multiple noise-assisted decompositions. The process involves:

$$x'(t) = x(t) + \eta_n(t), \quad n = 1, 2, ..., N \quad (1)$$

where $x(t)$ is the original AE signal, $\eta_i(t)$ represents the ith realization of added white noise, $x'(t)$ denotes the noise-perturbed signal, and N is the ensemble number. Subsequently, each perturbed signal $x'_n(t)$ undergoes EMD decomposition:

$$x'_n(t) = \sum_{k=1}^{K} \text{IMF}_k^{(n)}(t) + r^{(n)}(t), \quad n = 1, 2, ..., N \quad (2)$$

where $\text{IMF}_k^{(n)}(t)$ is the kth intrinsic mode function (IMF) from the nth decomposition, K is the total number of extracted IMFs, and $r^{(n)}(t)$ denotes the residual component. Resultant IMFs are obtained by ensemble averaging across all noise-realized decompositions:

$$\text{IMF}_k(t) = \frac{1}{N} \sum_{n=1}^{N} \text{IMF}_k^{(n)}(t), \quad n = 1, 2, ..., N \quad (3)$$

The acquisition of vibration signals enables real-time monitoring of mechanical equipment operational status, facilitating early fault detection [17]. Through systematic analysis of vibration signal characteristics, critical equipment conditions such as wear and imbalance can be effectively identified. Due to prolonged machine operation, the spindle of the grinding machine may generate periodic noise signals. Then the Discrete Wavelet Transform (DWT) for signal decomposition is employed to effectively isolate roughness-related information from vibration signals contaminated by noise. DWT expresses the signal as a superposition of wavelet basis functions through multiresolution analysis, decomposing the signal into components with distinct time-frequency characteristics. The vibration signal $f(t)$ is decomposed at scale j into the approximation $f_j(t)$:

$$f_j(t) = \sum_k c_{jk}\phi_{jk}(t) + \sum_k d_{jk}\psi_{jk}(t) \quad (4)$$

where $c_{jk}, \phi_{jk}(t)$ are the approximation coefficients and scaling functions at scale j and position k, which represent the low-frequency component of the signal, and $d_{jk}, \psi_{jk}(t)$ are the detail coefficients and wavelet functions at scale j and position k, which represent the high-frequency component of the signal. Thus, the approximation coefficients and detail components are denoted as A_j and D_j. The mathematical representation is given by:

$$f(t) = \sum_k A_j \phi_{jk}(t) + \sum_k D_j \psi_{jk}(t) \tag{5}$$

Table 1. Time and Frequency Domain Features

Domain	Feature	Expression
Time domain	Mean	$\frac{1}{N}\sum_{i=1}^{N} x(i)$
	Variance	$\frac{1}{N}\sum_{i=1}^{N} (x(i) - \mu)^2$
	Peak	$\max(x(i))$
	Root Mean Square	$\sqrt{\frac{1}{N}\sum_{i=1}^{N} x(i)^2}$
	Autocorrelation	$R_x(\tau) = \frac{1}{N}\sum_{i=1}^{N-|\tau|} x(i)x(i-\tau)$
Frequency domain	FC	$\frac{\sum_{k=0}^{n} \omega_k x(\omega_k)}{\sum_{k=0}^{n} x(\omega_k)}$
	RMSF	$\sqrt{\frac{\sum_{k=0}^{n} \omega_k^2 x(\omega_k)}{\sum_{k=0}^{n} x(\omega_k)}}$
	SDF	$\sqrt{\frac{\sum_{k=0}^{n} (\omega_k - X_{FC})^2 x(\omega_k)}{\sum_{k=0}^{n} x(\omega_k)}}$
	Total Energy	$\sum_f |X(f)|^2$
	Mean Magnitude	$\frac{1}{N}\sum_f |X(f)|^2$

2.2 Feature Extraction and Selection

Both the AE signal and vibration signals are decomposed to extract the features, which is performed on the obtained $IMF_k(t)$, A_j, and D_j. Five representative time-domain and frequency-domain features are selected in Table 1.

A total of $(10J + 10K)$ features were extracted from the AE signal and vibration signals. Since most of these features are redundant, the Spearman's rank correlation coefficient is used to evaluate the correlations with workpiece surface roughness, aiming to accelerate model training, decrease interference from irrelevant features, and enhance generalization performance. Subsequently, the most relevant features were selected based on their correlation strength.

Spearman's rank correlation coefficient is widely used to assess nonlinear relationships, as it does not require data normality and is robust for non-Gaussian or ordinal data. According to the previous description, the extracted K features were represented as $[X_1, X_2, ..., X_K]$ with N samples, and the workpiece roughness was represented as Y. For each feature X_k, the experimental values of X_k

and Y are first ranked as $R(X_{i,k})$ and $R(Y_i)$, respectively. The rank difference $d_i = R(X_{i,k}) - R(Y_i)$ is computed to derive Spearman's coefficient:

$$r_s = 1 - \frac{6\sum_{i=1}^{n} d_i^2}{n(n^2 - 1)} \qquad (6)$$

The value of r_s reflects the strength of correlation between the extracted features and roughness. A value closer to 1 indicates a stronger positive correlation, while a value closer to -1 indicates a stronger negative correlation.

2.3 Roughness Prediction Based on PSO-XGBoost Model

A PSO-XGBoost hybrid model is proposed to accurately predict variations in workpiece surface roughness using the selected features, which is a hybrid optimization approach that integrates the Particle Swarm Optimization (PSO) algorithm with eXtreme Gradient Boosting (XGBoost). Mostly, PSO is employed to optimize the hyperparameters of XGBoost, thereby enhancing the model's predictive efficiency and generalization capability.

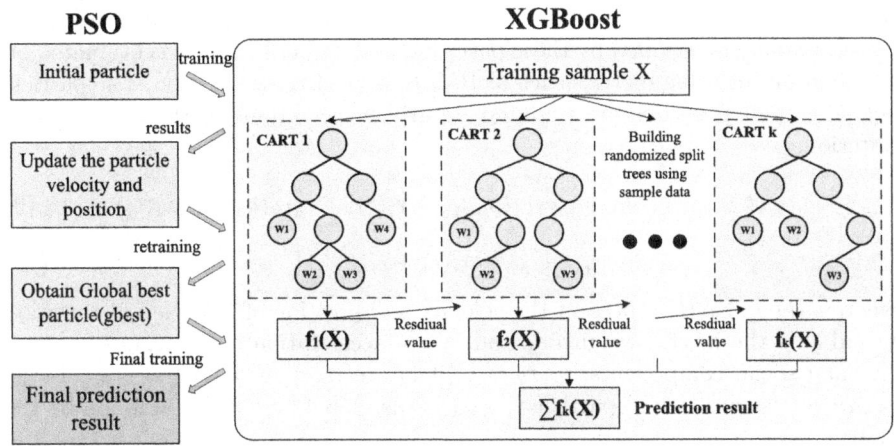

Fig. 2. The schematic of PSO-XGBoost algorithm.

XGBoost is a highly efficient, flexible, and accurate machine learning model based on Gradient Boosted Trees(GBT) [15], as illustrated in Fig. 2. Its core principle involves iteratively fitting residual errors to improve model performance. The predicted output of the model can be expressed as:

$$\hat{y}_i = \sum_{k=1}^{K} f_k(x_i), \quad f_k \in \mathcal{F} \tag{7}$$

where $\hat{y}_i$ is the predicted value for sample i, K is the number of regression trees, and f_k is a decision tree function from the functional space $\mathcal{F}$. The objective function optimized by XGBoost is expressed as:

$$\text{Obj}(\theta) = \sum_{i=1}^{n} l(y_i, \hat{y}_i) + \sum_{k=1}^{K} \Omega(f_k) \tag{8}$$

where $l(y_i, \hat{y}_i) = (y_i - \hat{y}_i)^2$ represents the training loss function and $\Omega(f_k) = \gamma T + \frac{1}{2}\lambda\|w\|^2$ denotes the regularization term that controls model complexity.

PSO is a swarm intelligence optimization algorithm inspired by bird flocking behavior, which searches for optimal solutions in multidimensional space [18]. In the process of optimizing XGBoost model training using PSO, the algorithm first randomly generates a variety of particles, where each particle represents a set of hyperparameters for XGBoost. The XGBoost model is then trained using the hyperparameters encoded by these particles, and its performance is evaluated on a validation set using metrics such as RMSE as the fitness function. The particle velocities and positions are updated iteratively according to the PSO update criterion:

$$v_i(t+1) = \omega v_i(t) + c_1 r_1(p_{\text{best}_i} - x_i(t)) + c_2 r_2(g_{\text{best}} - x_i(t)) \tag{9}$$

$$x_i(t+1) = x_i(t) + v_i(t+1) \tag{10}$$

where $v_i(t)$ and $x_i(t)$ represent the velocity and position of particle i at iteration t, and ω is the inertia weight. c_1 and c_2 are acceleration coefficients for cognitive and social components, $r_1, r_2 \sim U(0,1)$ are random numbers, p_{best_i} is the personal best position of particle i, g_{best} is the global best position found by the swarm.

The iteration continues until a termination condition is met—either a maximum number of iterations or convergence. The algorithm then outputs the optimal hyperparameters, which are used to train the final XGBoost model.

3 Experiments and Validation

3.1 Robotic Grinding Experimental Setup

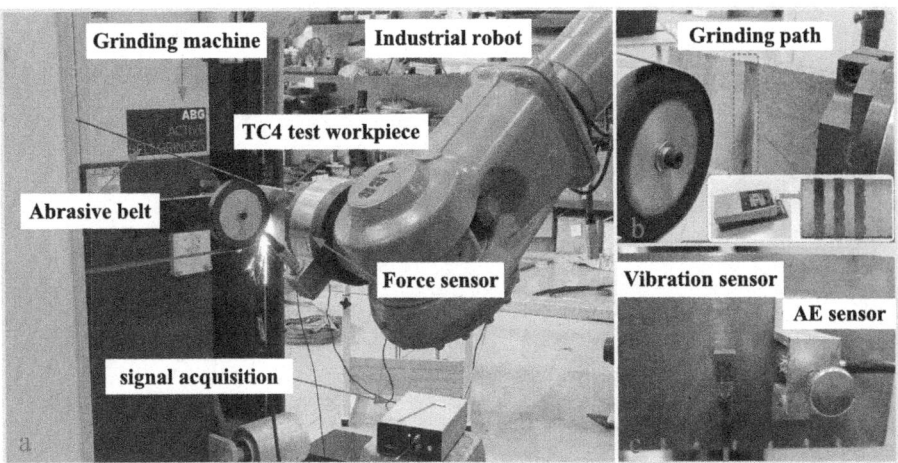

Fig. 3. Robotic grinding machining system (a); Machining details (b); AE sensor and accelerometer sensor mounting positions (c).

The robotic grinding platform consists of a six-degree-of-freedom industrial robot (ABB IRB 4400) and a self-developed belt grinding machine, as illustrated in Fig. 3. The experiment employs a constant-force grinding process, where the grinding force is controlled by a six-axis force/torque sensor (ATI Omega 160) mounted at the robot's end-effector. The data acquisition system includes an acoustic emission sensor (PX PXR15) and a triaxial accelerometer (PCB 356A44) attached to the back of the test workpiece, and all acquired signals were processed by the computer. The experiment was conducted with grinding forces set at 20 N, 30 N, and 40 N, and a robot feed rate of 5 mm/s. The abrasive belt used in this experiment was a 3M A16 pyramidal abrasive belt, and the workpiece material was a Ti-6Al-4V alloy workpiece with uniform dimensions measuring 200 mm (length) × 100 mm (width) × 20 mm (height). The surface roughness of the machined workpiece was measured using a Mitutoyo handheld surface roughness tester (SJ-210).

3.2 Signals Processing Results

The EEMD algorithm is carried out on the collected AE signals by adding noise with an amplitude of 0.2 and setting the maximum EEMD iteration count to 100, ultimately extracting eight IMF components. For the triaxial vibration signals, DWT was conducted using the db4 wavelet function with seven decomposition levels, resulting in the high-frequency components ($D_1, D_2, ..., D_7$) and the low-frequency approximation coefficient (A_7), which contains low-frequency noise. From the eight IMFs and the eight wavelet decomposition results, a total of 80 features were extracted for each signal following the criteria listed in Table 1.

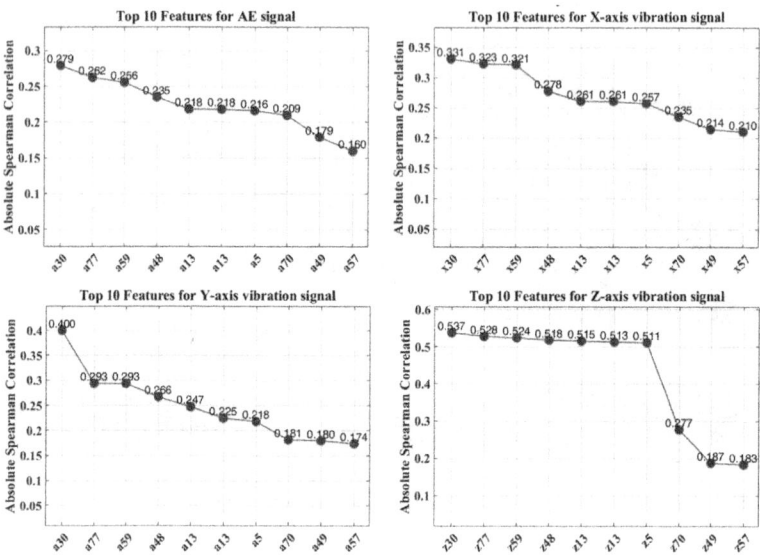

Fig. 4. Spearman correlation coefficient ranking of all signal features.

To ensure high expression capability of the selected features, the extracted features were systematically labeled: those from the AE signals were designated as $[a_1, a_2, ..., a_{80}]$, while those from the triaxial vibration signals were assigned according to their respective axes, namely $[x_1, x_2, ..., x_{80}]$, $[y_1, y_2, ..., y_{80}]$, and $[z_1, z_2, ..., z_{80}]$.

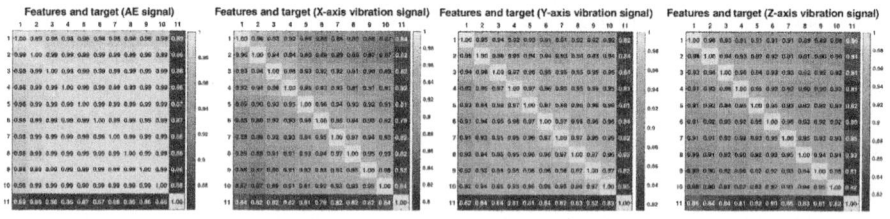

Fig. 5. Cross-correlation between selected features and surface roughness.

To ensure high relevance between the training features and workpiece surface roughness, only the top 10 features ranked by their Spearman's coefficient values were selected. The selected features for each signal are illustrated in Fig. 4. To further validate the effectiveness of these features, mitigate overfitting, and optimize model performance, cross-correlations between the selected features and surface roughness were calculated, as shown in Fig. 5. Then the deep features obtained by the proposed method exhibit high correlation, with the highest correlation coefficient reaching 0.89. Specifically, the maximum correlation coefficients derived from the four signal-based feature extractions are 0.89, 0.84, 0.84, and 0.86, respectively. Moreover, most cross-correlations between the extracted features and surface roughness exceed 0.8, further validating the effectiveness of the proposed feature extraction and screening method.

3.3 Prediction Results and Analysis

The selected features were input into the proposed PSO-XGBoost model for training. To evaluate the performance of the proposed model, the two benchmark models for comparison—SVR (Support Vector Regression) and CNN (Convolutional Neural Network)—are introduced in the paper. The SVR model, a machine learning approach, seeks an optimal balance between learning capability and accuracy under limited training samples. The CNN model, a deep learning architecture, extracts features through convolutional layers, pooling layers, and fully connected layers to perform regression predictions. These two models serve as representatives of traditional machine learning and deep learning, respectively. Comparing with them helps validate the advantages and limitations of our proposed model. As shown in Table 2 and Table 3, we tuned several hyperparameters to ensure stable model performance within an acceptable range during training.

Table 2. PSO Parameters

Parameter	Value
Number of particles	20
Max generations	100
Inertia Weight	0.5
Cognitive Learning Factor	1.5

Table 3. XGBoost Parameters

Parameter	Value
Number of estimators	[50, 500]
Max depth	[3, 500]
Learning rate	[0.01, 0.3]
L1 regularization parameter	[0.2, 0.5]

The dataset consisted of a total of 125 samples, with 80% allocated for training and 20% for testing. After training, the prediction results of the proposed model, CNN, and SVR are shown in Fig. 6, where our model demonstrates superior accuracy compared to the other models. To further evaluate the monitoring accuracy, we analyzed the models based on MAE (Mean Absolute Error) and RMSE (Root Mean Square Error) metrics, as presented in Table 4. The proposed model achieved the lowest values in both MAE and RMSE, indicating better performance than the competing models. Compared with traditional feature extraction methods, the proposed approach improved MAE by 51.55% and

62.89%, respectively. Similarly, the monitoring accuracy in terms of RMSE was enhanced by 43.24% and 56.91%, respectively.

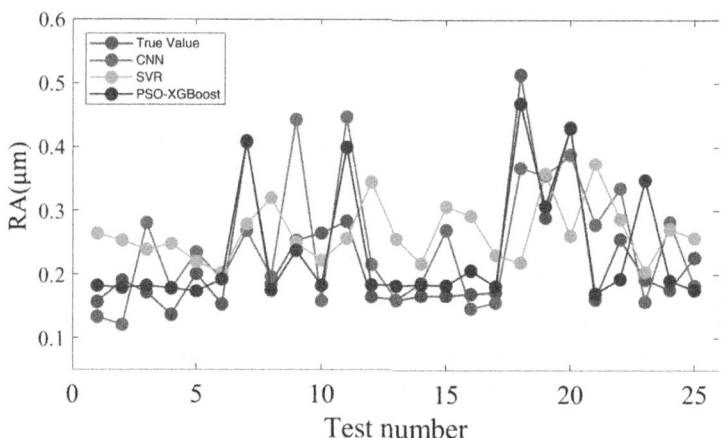

Fig. 6. Comparison of roughness prediction performance among models in multi-parameter grinding.

To verify the generalization ability of our model, experiments were conducted using 3M A45 diamond abrasive belts under grinding parameters of 20N grinding force, 8.37 m/s grinding speed and 5mm/s feed rate, where the real-time roughness predictions were performed based on the experimental data by collecting and processing 20-second acoustic emission signals and vibration signals during the machining process and feeding them into our pre-trained model, with the prediction results shown in Fig. 7.

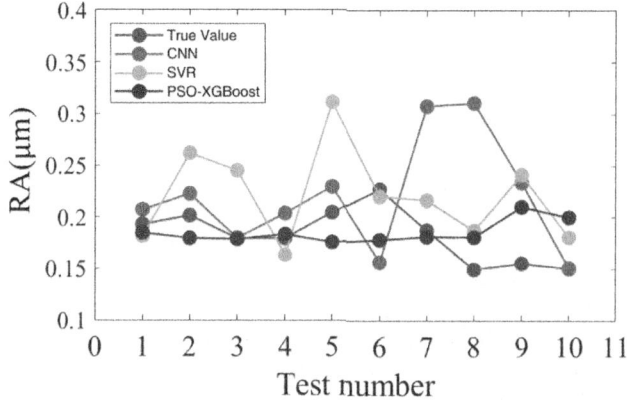

Fig. 7. Comparison of real-time roughness predictions across models.

During real-time monitoring, as evidenced by Table 4, the proposed method achieved improvements of 50.62% and 43.42% in the MAE metric compared to traditional feature extraction methods. Similarly, the model demonstrated enhanced monitoring accuracy, with reductions in RMSE by 56.18% and 41.85%, respectively. These results demonstrate that the proposed model outperforms conventional approaches, enabling highly precise and stable real-time predictions during the machining process.

Table 4. Comparison of evaluation criteria for model prediction results

Model	MAE (train)	RMSE (train)	MAE (real-time)	RMSE (real-time)
CNN	0.0710	0.0874	0.0515	0.0731
SVR	0.0927	0.1151	0.0449	0.0551
Proposed	0.0344	0.0496	0.0255	0.0320

4 Conclusion

A PSO-XGBoost-based real-time roughness prediction model is proposed for TC4 grinding in robotic processes. Key contributions include:

(1) Feature extraction from AE and triaxial vibration signals, achieving cross-correlation coefficients of 0.84–0.89 with measured roughness.
(2) PSO-optimized XGBoost improved accuracy by 51.55% (MAE) and 62.89% (RMSE) and accelerated convergence by 43.24% over conventional methods.
(3) Real-time validation demonstrates significantly lower errors under varying conditions: MAE (50.62%, 43.42%) and RMSE (56.18%, 41.85%) compared to baseline methods.

References

1. Xu, X., Chen, W., Zhu, D., Yan, S., Ding, H.: Hybrid active/passive force control strategy for grinding marks suppression and profile accuracy enhancement in robotic belt grinding of turbine blade. Robot. Cim.-Int. Manuf. **67**, 102047 (2021)
2. Zhu, D., et al.: Robotic grinding of complex components: a step towards efficient and intelligent machining - challenges, solutions, and applications. Robot. Cim.-Int. Manuf. **65**, 101908 (2020)
3. Cheng, C., Li, J., Liu, Y., Nie, M., Wang, W.: An online belt wear monitoring method for abrasive belt grinding under varying grinding parameters. J. Manuf. Process. **50**, 80–89 (2020)
4. Zhang, Y., Gong, P., Tang, L., et al.: Topography modeling of surface grinding based on random abrasives and performance evaluation. Chin. J. Mech. Eng. **37**, 93 (2024)

5. Lu, H., Zhao, X., Tao, B., Yin, Z.: Online process monitoring based on vibration-surface quality map for robotic grinding. IEEE/ASME Trans. Mechatron. **25**, 2882–2892 (2020)
6. Li, G., Bao, Y., Wang, H., Dong, Z., Guo, X., Kang, X.: An online monitoring methodology for grinding state identification based on real-time signal of CNC grinding machine. Mech. Syst. Signal Process. **200**, 110540 (2023)
7. Lipiński, D., Bałasz, B., Rypina, Ł: Modelling of surface roughness and grinding forces using artificial neural networks with assessment of the ability to data generalisation. Int. J. Adv. Manuf. Technol. **94**, 1335–1347 (2018)
8. Arriandiaga, A., Portillo, E., Sánchez, J.A., et al.: Recurrent ANN-based modelling of the dynamic evolution of the surface roughness in grinding. Neural Comput. Appl. **28**, 1293–1307 (2017)
9. Chandrasekaran, M., Devarasiddappa, D.: Artificial neural net-work modeling for surface roughness prediction in cylindrical grinding of Al-SiCp metal matrix composites and ANOVA analysis. Adv. Prod. Eng. Manag. **9**(2), 59–70 (2014)
10. Xu, X., Ye, S., Yang, Z., et al.: Analysis and prediction of surface roughness for robotic belt grinding of complex blade considering coexistence of elastic deformation and varying curvature. Sci. China Technol. Sci. **64**, 957–970 (2021)
11. Oo, H., Wang, W., Liu, Z.: Tool wear monitoring system in belt grinding based on image-processing techniques. Int. J. Adv. Manuf. Technol. **111**, 2215–2229 (2020)
12. Wang, Y., Huang, X., Ren, X., et al.: In-process belt-image-based material removal rate monitoring for abrasive belt grinding using CatBoost algorithm. Int. J. Adv. Manuf. Technol. **123**, 2575–2591 (2022)
13. Lu, H., Zhao, X., Tao, B., Yin, Z.: Online process monitoring based on vibration-surface quality map for robotic grinding. IEEE/ASME Trans. Mechatron. **5**(6), 2882–2892 (2020)
14. Xu, X., Yang, Z., Liu, Q., Yan, S., Ding, H.: Condition monitoring and mechanism analysis of belt wear in robotic grinding of TC4 workpiece using acoustic emissions. Mech. Syst. Signal Process. **188**, 109979 (2023)
15. Pan, Y., Qiao, Y., Wang, Y., et al.: Real-time prediction of grinding surface roughness based on multi-sensor signal fusion. Int. J. Adv. Manuf. Technol. **127**, 5847–5861 (2023)
16. Huang, N.E., Shen, Z., Long, S.R., et al.: The empirical mode decomposition and the Hilbert spectrum for nonlinear and non-stationary time series analysis. Proc. R. Soc. Lond. A **454**(1971), 903–995 (1998)
17. Pandiyan, V., Caesarendra, W., Tjahjowidodo, T., Tan, H.H.: In-process tool condition monitoring in compliant abrasive belt grinding process using support vector machine and genetic algorithm. J. Manuf. Process. **31**, 199–213 (2018)
18. Chen, T., Guestrin, C.: XGBoost: a scalable tree-boosting system. In: Proceedings of the 22nd ACM SIGKDD Conference on Knowledge Discovery and Data Mining, pp. 785–794 (2016)

Cross-Subject Respiratory State Recognition Based on Ultrasonic and IMU Signals

Shuo Feng, Zhiyong Wang, and Jiaole Wang(✉)

State Key Laboratory of Robotics and Systems, School of Mechanical Engineering and Automation, Harbin Institute of Technology, Shenzhen, China
23S053014@stu.hit.edu.cn, {wangzhiyong,wangjiaole}@hit.edu.cn

Abstract. Continuous and accurate respiratory monitoring is important for early disease detection and health management. This paper presents a novel multimodal data acquisition system that simultaneously collects Inertial Measurement Unit (IMU) and A-mode ultrasound signals from the chest and abdomen to monitor respiratory activity. We systematically evaluate various classification methods and fusion strategies, including feature-level vector concatenation, tensor fusion, a custom IMU-Ultrasound Convolutional Neural Network with Attention Fusion (IU-CNN-AF), decision-level max fusion, and weighted fusion, both single-subject and cross-subject respiratory state recognition across three breathing patterns (normal, deep, and high-frequency). Experiments on data from nine healthy male volunteers, using Leave-One-Group-Out cross-validation, demonstrate that multimodal fusion significantly outperforms corresponding single-modal methods, especially in more challenging cross-individual scenarios, with decision-level max fusion achieving an accuracy rate of 89.02%, outperforming other methods. Although the available dataset size limits the performance of the IU-CNN-AF network, it still demonstrates potential. These findings highlight the effectiveness and robustness of multimodal sensor fusion for wearable respiratory monitoring and provide valuable insights for future development of portable healthcare systems.

Keywords: A-mode Ultrasound · Inertial Measurement Unit · Multimodal Sensor Fusion · Sensor Fusion · Cross-Subject Recognition · Respiratory Monitoring · Wearable Healthcare

1 Introduction

Breathing is the most fundamental activity in our lives. Abnormal breathing not only affects an individual's physical health, but also may indicate the occurrence of certain diseases. Effective respiratory monitoring is crucial for the early diagnosis and treatment of diseases. The current respiratory monitoring methods mainly include spirometry, structured light plethysmography, and respiratory inductance plethysmography [4]. These methods are highly accurate, but often require large specialized equipment and operators, making it difficult to achieve portable, out-of-clinic, and real-time monitoring. In addition, some other methods have been proposed, such as video-based respiratory monitoring methods, which often require complex image processing and analysis, making it difficult to achieve real-time monitoring. Some respiratory monitoring methods are easily disturbed by external sounds, leading to inaccurate monitoring results [6]. Therefore, it is of great significance to develop a portable and real-time respiratory monitoring method. Multimodal fusion technology, by integrating data from different sensors, can offer a more comprehensive perspective and higher accuracy.

Inertial Measurement Unit (IMU) is a device that measures the three-axis attitude angles (or angular rates) and acceleration of an object. IMU can provide motion information that vision cannot provide under occlusion conditions. Current studies based on IMU mostly focus on the measurement of respiratory rate [8], while there are relatively few explorations of tidal volume and respiratory effort. However, parameters such as tidal volume and respiratory effort are crucial for the diagnosis of respiratory diseases [1]. At the same time, respiratory examinations based on IMU also face issues such as motion artifacts and noise, which can affect the accuracy of respiratory monitoring [9]. With the rapid development of sports science and rehabilitation medicine, As the basic unit of ultrasound transducer, the A-mode transducer has the advantages of small size, light mass, and low-power consumption for wearable applications [2,11]. A-mode ultrasound imaging has become an important tool for studying the dynamic changes of muscles due to its advantages such as non-invasive, real-time, portable and low power dissipation. Ultrasound can better reflect the intensity of respiratory muscle contraction and the mechanical properties of the chest and lungs, with a high spatial and temporal resolution [13].

IMU and ultrasound can complement each other, as IMU can provide dynamic motion information of the thoracic cavity, while ultrasound can provide morphological information of subcutaneous muscles. Based on this, we propose a multimodal data acquisition system based on IMU and A-mode ultrasound.

The main contributions of this work are:

1) A novel multimodal data acquisition system combining IMU and A-mode ultrasound
2) Comprehensive evaluation of fusion strategies for respiratory monitoring
3) Cross-subject validation demonstrating generalization capability

2 Dataset Collection and Experimental Design

2.1 A-Mode Ultrasound and IMU System

In the selection of inertial measurement unit, a 9-axis IMU based on JY901 was used to measure the motion information of the human thoracic cavity. The device integrates Ethernet/WIFI communication technology, which can ensure data acquisition and timely transmission at a frequency of 100 Hz. The size of the device is 45 mm * 32 mm * 13 mm, and the weight is 24 g (see Fig. 1a), which can meet the requirements of lightweight to reduce the impact on human respiratory movement.

The movement of air in and out of the lungs is accomplished by the respiratory muscles. The diaphragm and intercostal muscles are the main respiratory muscles responsible for the expansion and contraction of the thoracic cavity [7]. In order to obtain information on the morphology of subcutaneous muscles, 4-channel A-mode ultrasound technology was used. This device can synchronously collect signals from 4/8 probes, record muscle information at a frequency of 5 to 40 Hz, and transmit the information to a computer via Ethernet/Wi-Fi communication technology (see Fig. 1b).

To reduce the intervention of human factors in the experimental process, an experimental process voice prompt system was developed (see Fig. 1c). It guides volunteers to complete the experimental process through machine prompts and records the start and end stamps of each collection for convenient subsequent data processing.

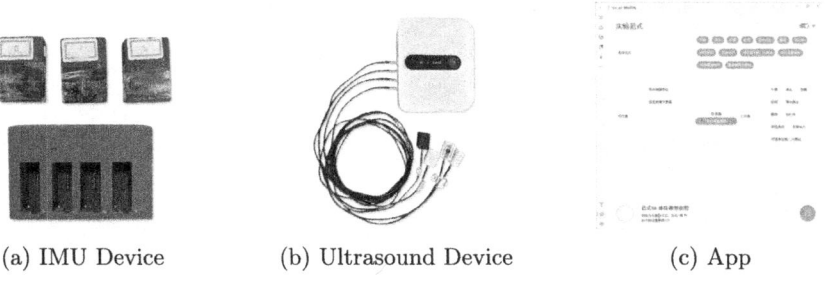

(a) IMU Device (b) Ultrasound Device (c) App

Fig. 1. Data Acquisition System.

2.2 Experimental Setup

We collected IMU and A-mode ultrasound data from 9 male healthy volunteers under different breathing exercise paradigms. The participants performed three breathing exercises in the laboratory while lying supine, including normal breathing, high-frequency breathing and deep breathing. Each participant performed three sets of each breathing type, with each set lasting 20 s.

The placement of the A-mode ultrasound probes considers the position of respiratory-related muscles, mainly placed on the anterior and lateral aspects of the thoracic cavity, including the subxiphoid region, intercostal muscles, and diaphragm (see Fig. 2). The device collects A-mode ultrasonic signals at a rate of 20 frames per second, with each frame containing 4 groups of signals, and each group consisting of 1000 sample points corresponding to the signal from one probe.

These 1000 sample points represent echo signals collected at a sampling rate of 20 MHz within 50 microseconds after each ultrasound emission, representing the intensity of ultrasound echoes at different depths. The peak positions and intensities of these echoes reflect the characteristics of tissue boundaries, thereby revealing the thickness of chest and abdominal muscles and their changes under different breathing conditions.

The IMU was placed on the abdomen at the navel to monitor breathing (see Fig. 2). During the experiment, the IMU device collected data at a frequency of 100 Hz, with each frame containing 9-dimensional signals representing acceleration, angular velocity, and angles. These signals provide dynamic information about chest movement, which is helpful for analyzing movement patterns during the breathing process.

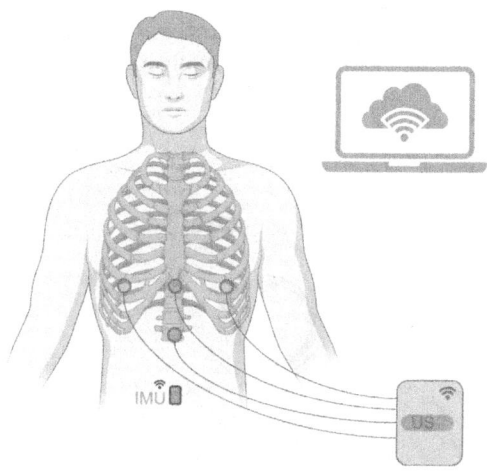

Fig. 2. IMU and A-mode Ultrasound Data Acquisition Scheme. Four A-mode ultrasound sensors and an IMU are placed on the chest and abdomen of the participant. The data is ultimately transmitted to the computer via Wi-Fi.

During the period when the participants carried out the relevant actions according to the voice instructions of the system, the computer received the signals collected by the ultrasound and IMU devices in real time. It added timestamps after each frame and stored the data locally for subsequent preprocessing and time alignment.

3 Methods

3.1 Data Processing

Data Preprocessing. To enhance the meaningful components of the original ultrasound signals, the signals were preprocessed to filter out noise and enhance meaningful components. First, 20 points were trimmed from the beginning and end of each frame's 1000 ultrasonic sample points per channel, because the first and last 20 data points of each frame of ultrasound signals contain very few meaningful components [12]. The preprocessing mainly consists of four steps: time-varying gain compensation, band-pass filtering, Hilbert transform, and logarithmic compression [5].

The ultrasonic data, which contains 1000 sample points per frame per channel after the previous processing, becomes a 960-dimensional feature vector. To accelerate subsequent computation speed, the 960-dimensional feature vector per frame per channel was downsampled to 96 dimensions through averaging. Thus, the dimension of each frame of ultrasound data becomes 4×96=384 dimensions. To facilitate subsequent sliding window processing, the data from the four channels of the same frame were concatenated end-to-end, resulting in a 384-dimensional feature vector for each frame. Now, the dimensionality of each frame feature vector for ultrasound and IMU data is 384 and 9 dimensions, respectively.

Sliding Window and Feature Extraction. A sliding window strategy was adopted to address the problem of inconsistent frequencies between the collected ultrasound and IMU data. According to actual test results, the window length and overlap were set to 10 s and 0.5 s, respectively. Features were extracted within the sliding windows mentioned above. The data was first subjected to Gaussian filtering within the time window. Then, considering the characteristics of ultrasound and IMU data, statistical features were extracted separately for each modality.

For the IMU data, the statistical characteristics within the time window were extracted: including mean absolute value, standard deviation, waveform length, zero crossings, slope sign changes, and 6th-order autoregressive coefficients [2]. In each time window, each channel of the IMU extracts 5 time-domain features and 6 AR6 coefficients of autoregressive model, totaling 11 features. For a 9-axis IMU device, 11 features are extracted per channel in each time window, resulting in a total of 9*11 = 99 features.

For the Ultrasound data, the statistical characteristics within the time window were extracted: including mean absolute value, standard deviation, waveform length and slope sign changes [3]. Within each time window, four time-domain features were extracted by ultrasound in each dimension, totaling 384*4 = 1536 features.

3.2 Classification Methods

To evaluate the classification performance of each individual modality and the fusion modality, multiple classification methods were employed.

Before classification, the data of each modality was first normalized and subjected to Principal Component Analysis (PCA) dimensionality reduction. Normalization can unify features with different scales to the same range, preventing features with larger values from dominating model training and improving algorithm convergence speed. Each modality's features were normalized to unify them within the [0, 1] interval. PCA dimensionality reduction can reduce feature dimensions, remove redundant information, and reduce computational complexity while retaining the main information of the data. In PCA dimensionality reduction, we chose to retain 95% of the variance explained ratio. Based on testing, the subsequent IU-CNN-AF network did not use PCA dimensionality reduction, while other methods all used PCA for preprocessing.

Single Sensing-Modality. The following methods were used for classification of single-modality data:

Linear Discriminant Analysis (LDA). LDA is a statistical method used to find a linear combination of features that separates two or more classes of objects or events. LDA performs well in classification and dimensionality reduction tasks by maximizing inter-class differences and minimizing intra-class differences to find the best projection direction of the data.

Support Vector Machine (SVM). SVM is a supervised learning model. It has excellent generalization ability, and it demonstrates many unique advantages in solving problems of small samples, nonlinearity and high-dimensional pattern recognition.

Multi-modal Fusion. The following methods were used for classification of multimodal data: Feature-level fusion (a.k.a., early fusion), such as vector concatenation fusion, tensor fusion, and a network based on the Multi-Head Attention Mechanism Fusion Convolutional Neural Network (CNN-AF) proposed by Wang et al. [10]. Decision-level fusion (a.k.a., late fusion), such as max fusion and weighted fusion. In this paper, decision-level fusion refers to fusion after the classifier outputs, while feature-level fusion refers to fusion before the classifier inputs. Except for the classifiers in IU-CNN-AF, SVM or LDA is used.

Feature-level Vector Concatenation Fusion. Multimodal concatenation is a simple and effective early fusion method, which is commonly used. The Ultrasound and IMU data vectors are concatenated and then input into the classifier for recognition and classification. The output of the classifier is the final recognition result. This method is simple and has less information loss, but the dimensionality increases after concatenation, which may lead to increased computational complexity.

$$\mathbf{z}^m = \begin{bmatrix} \mathbf{z}^i \\ \mathbf{z}^u \end{bmatrix} \quad (1)$$

Here $\mathbf{z}^m$ is the multimodal feature vector, $\mathbf{z}^i$ is the IMU feature vector, and $\mathbf{z}^u$ is the ultrasound feature vector.

Feature-level Tensor Fusion. The tensor generated by the Cartesian product of different modalities is used as the fusion feature. The inspiration comes from the Tensor Fusion Network (TFN) proposed by Amir Zadeh et al. in 2017 [14]. Although the computational complexity is higher than Vector Concatenation Fusion, this method can fully utilize the interaction information between different modalities, enhancing the model's expressive ability.

Specifically, suppose the dimension of the IMU data is D_{imu} and the dimension of the ultrasound data is D_{us}, then the dimension of the fused tensor is $D_{imu} \times D_{us}$.

$$\mathbf{z}^m = \begin{bmatrix} \mathbf{z}^i \\ 1 \end{bmatrix} \otimes \begin{bmatrix} \mathbf{z}^u \\ 1 \end{bmatrix} \quad (2)$$

Here $\otimes$ indicates the outer product between vectors, $\mathbf{z}^i$ and $\mathbf{z}^u$ are the unimodal embeddings of IMU and ultrasound data, respectively. In this way, we can obtain a new tensor $\mathbf{z}^m$, which contains the interaction information of IMU and ultrasound data.

Feature-level IU-CNN-AF Fusion. We propose IMU-Ultrasound Convolutional Neural Network with Attention Fusion (IU-CNN-AF), a deep learning architecture specifically designed for multimodal respiratory signal processing. The network adapts the CNN-AF framework to effectively fuse IMU motion data and A-mode ultrasound tissue information through attention mechanisms that dynamically weight the contribution of each modality (see Fig. 3).

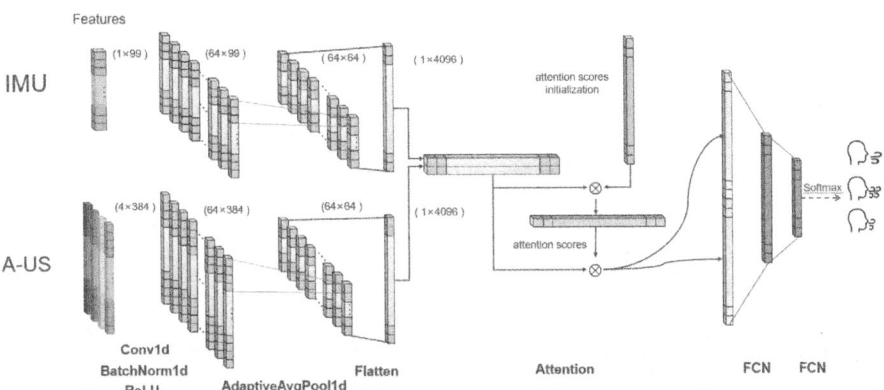

Fig. 3. IU-CNN-AF:IMU-Ultrasound Convolutional Neural Network with Attention Fusion.

Decision-Level Max Fusion. Decision-level max fusion compares the prediction probabilities of each category by the classifier, and selects the category with the highest probability value among all probabilities as the final prediction result.

$$P_{m,i} = max(P_{imu,i}, P_{us,i}) \quad (3)$$

Here, $P_{m,i}$ is the multimodal prediction rate, $P_{imu,i}$ is the IMU prediction rate, $P_{us,i}$ is the ultrasound prediction rate, and i is the index of the class.

Decision-Level Weighted Fusion. Weighted fusion of the two prediction rates of IMU and ultrasound output results, adjusting different weighting coefficients, can make the results reflect more of the data characteristics of IMU or ultrasound, thus finding a better weighted fusion scheme.

$$P_{m,i} = w_{imu} \cdot P_{imu,i} + w_{us} \cdot P_{us,i} \qquad (4)$$

Here, $P_{m,i}$ is the multimodal prediction rate, $P_{imu,i}$ is the IMU prediction rate, $P_{us,i}$ is the ultrasound prediction rate, w_{imu} and w_{us} are the weighting coefficients for IMU and ultrasound, respectively. ($w_{imu} + w_{us} = 1$), and i is the index of the class.

3.3 Data Segmentation Strategies for Fusion Technology Evaluation

Single-Subject Action Classification. In the single-subject identification experiment, the Leave-One-Group-Out (LOGO) cross-validation strategy was adopted. Specifically, in each iteration, one trial's data is left out as the test set, while the data from the remaining 2 trials is used as the training set. This is used to evaluate the performance and effect of different classification methods when processing the data of a single experimental subject.

Cross-Subject Action Classification. In the cross-subject identification experiment, the Leave-One-Group-Out (LOGO) cross-validation strategy was also adopted. Specifically, in each iteration, one volunteer's data is left out as the test set, while the data from the remaining 8 volunteers is used as the training set. This method can effectively evaluate the model's generalization ability on unseen individuals, ensuring the accuracy and reliability of the experimental results.

4 Results

The results of single-subject action classification and cross-subject action classification for each model are shown in Fig. 4 and Fig. 5, respectively. According to the two figures, it can be observed that the SVM classifier generally performs better than the LDA classifier. The reason may be that the SVM can better leverage its advantages due to the larger dimensionality compared to the data volume. The specific classification results are shown in Table 1

4.1 Single-Subject Identification Experiments

The individual recognition performance after IMU and ultrasound fusion is generally better than that of single modality approaches, with vector concatenation fusion performing the best (Accuracy: 100%) (see Fig. 4). In addition, the IU-CNN-AF network we modified for IMU and ultrasound does not perform outstandingly, possibly because deep learning networks require a large amount of data, while the experimental data is insufficient, especially for single-individual training results. This is likely the reason why the CNN-AF network is inferior to the ultrasound single modality in single-individual training.

The IMU data has fewer dimensions and sensors than the ultrasound data, resulting in ultrasound being able to extract more information, which leads to better classification performance for the ultrasound single modality. At the same time, due to the significant difference in data volume between IMU and ultrasound, the features of the ultrasound data occupy a larger proportion after concatenation, resulting in the ultrasound data features dominating the fused feature vector.

Other feature-level fusion methods, such as tensor fusion and IU-CNN-AF fusion, consider more IMU data features and require more computational resources and data volume, which may lead to a decrease in the classification performance of the fused feature vector.

Max Fusion and Weighted Fusion perform worse than feature-level fusion, possibly because feature-level fusion can make fuller use of the detailed information of the original data, especially the ultrasound data.

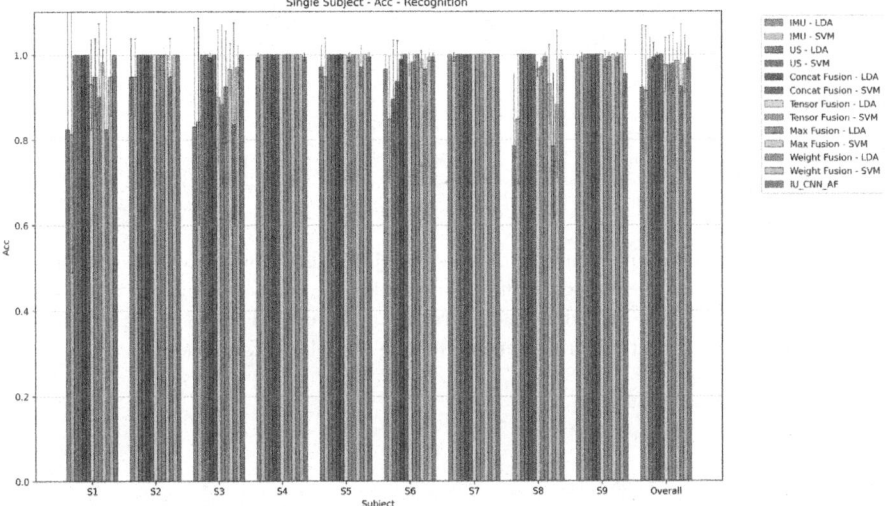

Fig. 4. The classification accuracy of single-subject tasks for each subject using 13 methods and the overall average value. The precision, recall, and F1 metrics listed in the tables are all macro precision, macro recall, and macro F1. 'S1' to 'S9' represent different individuals, and 'Overall' represents the overall average result.

4.2 Cross-Subject Action Classification Experiments

The cross-subject recognition performance after IMU and ultrasound fusion is better than that of the corresponding single-modality recognition, with decision-level max fusion using SVM achieving the best performance (Accuracy: 89.02% ± 23.81%) (see Fig. 5). This may be because decision-level max fusion has greater robustness compared to other methods and is less affected by individual differences. Weighted Fusion, Concat Fusion, and Tensor Fusion perform slightly worse than max fusion. The IU-CNN-AF network possibly requires a large amount of data, but it still performs better than the single-modality ultrasound and IMU data in cross-subject training results.

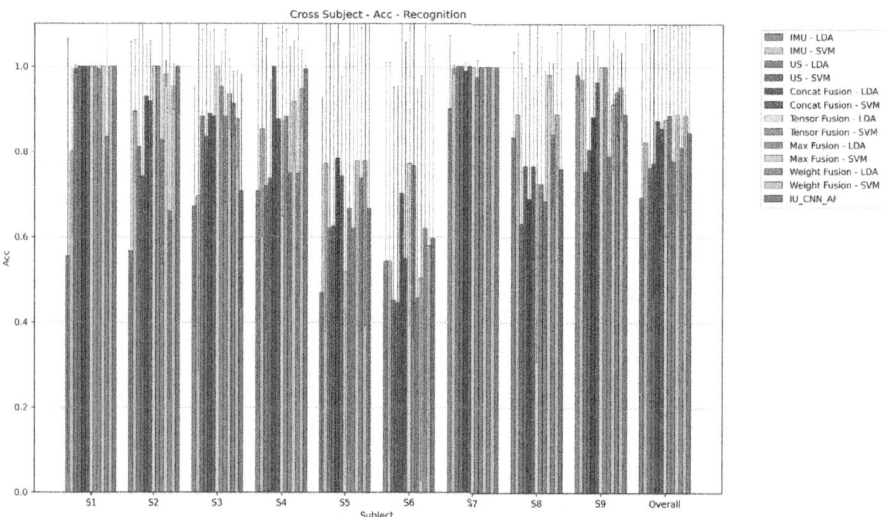

Fig. 5. The classification accuracy of cross-subject tasks for each subject using 13 methods and the overall average value. The precision, recall, and F1 metrics listed in the tables are all macro precision, macro recall, and macro F1. 'S1' to 'S9' represent different individuals, and 'Overall' represents the overall average result.

Table 1. MODEL PERFORMANCE COMPARISON

Sensor	Model		Single-Subject Scores			Cross-Subject Scores		
			Precision	Recall	F1-score	Precision	Recall	F1-score
IMU	LDA		0.9369	0.9227	0.9093	0.7724	0.6927	0.6510
	SVM		0.9536	0.9149	0.9015	0.8616	0.8239	0.8080
US	LDA		0.9929	0.9883	0.9865	0.7951	0.7628	0.7328
	SVM		0.9951	0.9929	0.9924	0.7888	0.7732	0.7475
IMU-US	IU-CNN-AF		0.9929	0.9916	0.9914	0.8639	0.8460	0.8216
	Concat Fusion	LDA	0.9981	0.9981	0.9980	0.9095	0.8739	0.8588
		SVM	1.0000	1.0000	1.0000	0.8524	0.8558	0.8407
	Tensor Fusion	LDA	0.9828	0.9747	0.9720	0.8953	0.8765	0.8587
		SVM	0.9800	0.9740	0.9723	0.8939	0.8856	0.8673
	Max Fusion	LDA	0.9879	0.9792	0.9777	0.8071	0.7784	0.7517
		SVM	0.9887	0.9851	0.9845	0.9009	0.8902	0.8779
	Weighted Fusion	LDA	0.9387	0.9246	0.9113	0.8593	0.8109	0.7897
		SVM	0.9857	0.9773	0.9735	0.9029	0.8863	0.8774

5 Conclusion

In this paper, we proposed a multimodal data acquisition system that collects IMU and A-mode ultrasound data from the chest and abdomen of participants to monitor and analyze respiratory movements. We conducted experiments to evaluate the performance of various classification methods for single-subject and cross-subject respiratory state recognition tasks. The results show that the fusion of IMU and ultrasound data generally outperforms single-modality methods, with vector concatenation fusion achieving the best performance in single-subject tasks and max fusion achieving the best performance in cross-subject tasks. Although the IU-CNN-AF network did not perform outstandingly in single-subject tasks due to the limited dataset size, it still demonstrates promising potential, especially in cross-subject experiments. These results highlight the effectiveness and robustness of multimodal sensor fusion for wearable respiratory monitoring. In future work, we will expand the dataset to include more subjects and breathing patterns, and further explore the application of deep learning methods for multimodal data fusion.

Acknowledgments. This work is supported by the National Key Research and Development Program of China under Grant 2022YFB4703200.

References

1. Fang, X., et al.: Respiration measurement technology based on inertial sensors: a review. J. Mech. Eng. **60**(20), 1–23 (2024). https://doi.org/10.3901/JME.2024.20.001
2. Huang, Y., Yang, X., Li, Y., Zhou, D., He, K., Liu, H.: Ultrasound-based sensing models for finger motion classification. IEEE J. Biomed. Health Inform. **22**(5), 1395–1405 (2018). https://doi.org/10.1109/JBHI.2017.2766249
3. Hudgins, B., Parker, P., Scott, R.: A new strategy for multifunction myoelectric control. IEEE Trans. Biomed. Eng. **40**(1), 82–94 (1993). https://doi.org/10.1109/10.204774
4. Johnson, G., Pianosi, P., Rajamani, R.: Estimation of three-dimensional thoracoabdominal displacements during respiration using inertial measurement units. IEEE/ASME Trans. Mechatron. **27**(6), 4224–4234 (2022). https://doi.org/10.1109/TMECH.2022.3151837
5. Li, Y., He, K., Sun, X., Liu, H.: Human-machine interface based on multichannel single-element ultrasound transducers: a preliminary study. In: 2016 IEEE 18th International Conference on E-Health Networking, Applications and Services (Healthcom), pp. 1–6 (2016). https://doi.org/10.1109/HealthCom.2016.7749483
6. Nabi, F.G., Sundaraj, K., Kiang, L.C., Palaniappan, R., Sundaraj, S.: Wheeze sound analysis using computer-based techniques: a systematic review. BIOMEDICAL ENGINEERING-BIOMEDIZINISCHE TECHNIK **64**(1), 1–28 (2019). https://doi.org/10.1515/bmt-2016-0219
7. Ratnovsky, A., Elad, D., Halpern, P.: Mechanics of respiratory muscles. Respir. Physiol. Neurobiol. **163**(1), 82–89 (2008). https://doi.org/10.1016/j.resp.2008.04.019
8. Romano, C., Formica, D., Schena, E., Massaroni, C.: Investigation of body locations for cardiac and respiratory monitoring with skin-interfaced inertial measurement unit sensors. IEEE Sens. J. **23**(7), 7806–7815 (2023). https://doi.org/10.1109/JSEN.2023.3245415
9. Tanweer, M., Halonen, K.A.I.: Development of wearable hardware platform to measure the ECG and EMG with IMU to detect motion artifacts. In: 2019 IEEE 22ND INTERNATIONAL SYMPOSIUM ON DESIGN AND DIAGNOSTICS OF ELECTRONIC CIRCUITS & SYSTEMS (DDECS). IEEE, New York (2019). https://doi.org/10.1109/ddecs.2019.8724639
10. Wang, H., Kang, P., Gao, Q., Jiang, S., Shull, P.B.: A novel PPG-FMG-ACC wristband for hand gesture recognition. IEEE J. Biomed. Health Inform. **26**(10), 5097–5108 (2022). https://doi.org/10.1109/JBHI.2022.3194017
11. Yang, X., Castellini, C., Farina, D., Liu, H.: Ultrasound as a neurorobotic interface: a review. IEEE Trans. Syst. Man, Cybern. Syst. **54**(6), 3534–3546 (2024). https://doi.org/10.1109/TSMC.2024.3358960
12. Yang, X., Sun, X., Zhou, D., Li, Y., Liu, H.: Towards wearable a-mode ultrasound sensing for real-time finger motion recognition
13. Yang, X., Yan, J., Liu, H.: Comparative analysis of wearable a-mode ultrasound and sEMG for muscle-computer interface. IEEE Trans. Biomed. Eng. **67**(9), 2434–2442 (2020). https://doi.org/10.1109/TBME.2019.2962499
14. Zadeh, A., Chen, M., Poria, S., Cambria, E., Morency, L.P.: Tensor fusion network for multimodal sentiment analysis (2017). https://doi.org/10.48550/arXiv.1707.07250

Bio-mechatronic Integration and Rehabilitation Robots

Hybrid Pole Placement and Interval Type-2 Fuzzy Control for Bio-Inspired Tendon-Driven Robotic Leg Stabilization

Rui Tian, Shuchen Ding(✉), Chengyu Su, Liren Zhu, Shiyu Ma, Wensong Zhao, and Zhe Lu

Suzhou University of Science and Technology, Suzhou, China
shuchendsc@sina.com

Abstract. As a novel bio-inspired robot configuration, the tendon-driven truss-type bionic mechanical leg necessitates attention to its motion stability control. The dynamic model is established based on its mechanical ontology characteristics and Lagranian Mechanics. On this basis, stability analysis is carried out for the nonlinear characteristics of the system, and the research focuses on the motion stability control problem at vertical equilibrium points. In order to achieve the control goal, this study employs the pole placement method to construct a feedback control strategy, while simultaneously developing an interval type-2 fuzzy logic controller in parallel for comparative validation. Verification through numerical simulation shows that the proposed control strategy can effectively achieve stable retention of the bionic leg at the vertical balance point. The experimental results confirm the correctness and effectiveness of the control algorithms and verify the engineering applicability of the proposed control scheme in bio-inspired robotic systems.

Keywords: Bio-inspired robotics · Stabilization Control · Pole placement · Type-2 fuzzy control

1 Introduction

With the continuous evolution of robotics technology, anthropomorphism and intelligent transformation have become its important development direction [1]. Bionics, as an interdisciplinary field that integrates biology, mechanical engineering and control theory, systematically analyzes the morphological characteristics and functional mechanisms of organisms, and then guides the innovative design of mechanical structure and control systems [2].

Currently, mainstream bionic robots generally adopt a built-in drive motor solution for axial joints [3]. This type of traditional driving architecture has significant technical limitations: the drive device needs to occupy limited joint space, which also leads to an increase in the mass of the actuator and an increase in moment of inertia, which in turn leads to a decrease in the transmission efficiency of the system and deterioration of dynamic response performance [4]. Boston Dynamics, a U.S.-based company known for its hydraulically actuated humanoid robot Petman, successfully developed the quadruped robot "BigDog" in 2011 [5]. Characterized by its high payload capacity and fast mobility, BigDog demonstrated impressive performance in rough terrain. However, the use of hydraulic actuation significantly increases the system's weight and complexity, limiting its suitability for broader applications [6]. Professor Raibert adopted the SLIP model control method proposed by Professor Blickhan [7]. This control method assumes that the legs are negligible and the mass is concentrated on the fuselage. Shigeo et al. first proposed a tendon-driven mechanism that mimics the contraction of human hand tendons, enabling the transmission of motor-generated forces to finger joints [8]. This design features a lightweight and simple structure, strong adaptability to various object shapes, and excellent conformability for grasping.

The prerequisite for the emergence of bionic robots is a deep understanding of the biological motor control mechanisms [9]. The cable-driven system simulates the efficient force transmission mechanism of biological tendons and integrates the dynamic characteristics of multi-degree of freedom coupling. However, such systems have significant technical challenges such as nonlinear dynamics and multivariable decoupling control during operation. The essence of its movement mechanism lies in solving the problem of dynamic balance under upright walking conditions [10].

This paper proposes a hybrid pole placement and IT2 fuzzy control strategy for efficient, robust control, alongside a novel bio-inspired truss-type leg robot with tendon-driven architecture. After analyzing its structure and building a dynamic model, two control methods—pole placement and interval type-2 fuzzy logic—are compared for bionic leg balance control, with simulations confirming their effectiveness. Furthermore, advanced algorithms such as MPC (Model Predictive Control) and DeepGait also demonstrate outstanding performance in complex scenarios. Due to time constraints, this paper does not conduct theoretical analysis or simulation on them at this stage.

2 Physical Structure

2.1 Physical Structure Modeling

Inspired by the coordination of multi-links of biological legs and tendon driving mechanisms, this study constructed a bionic cable-driven plane connecting rod transmission architecture based on the geometric reconfigurability of the parallelogram mechanism, aiming to achieve high-precision kinematic regulation through controllable deformation and provide hardware support for the dynamic motion simulation of bionic human legs. The system innovatively adopts two serial-connected parallelogram assemblies arranged in an upper-lower configuration, and forms a truss-shaped mechanical leg of human-like lower limbs through articulated nodes.

The system adopts a bidirectional antagonistic cable-driven strategy, which reproduces the driving mode of the biological legs "muscle-tendon": two high-strength cables run through the truss in the diagonal direction of the mechanical legs one of the cables is arranged diagonally along the front side, and a driving force for forward swing is generated by motor traction; the other one is a "backward antagonist tendon" and extends in reverse along the backside diagonal. Its tension not only balances the internal force of the system, but also realizes the function of backward swing or stable support through differential control. Each cable is precisely regulated by an independent servo motor. The structural diagram of the mechanical leg system is shown in Fig. 1.

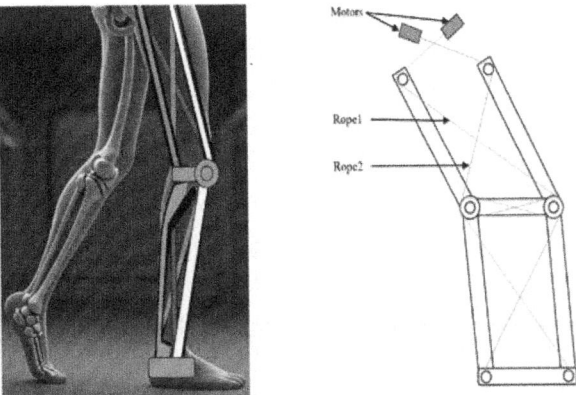

Fig. 1. Schematic diagram of bionic mechanical leg and corresponding structure

2.2 Dynamic Modeling

The dynamics of the bionic leg system describe its dynamic behavior and force-motion relationships. The system's motion can be divided into two states. The first stage is the foot remains in an unloaded state, where the sole loses contact with the supporting surface. During this phase, the system is solely subjected to inertial forces and cable tensions. The second stage is the foot contacts the supporting surface. In addition to inertial forces and cable tensions, the sole experiences external forces.

When the bionic leg system operates in the first state, the absence of ground reaction forces allows the system to be simplified as a two-link pendulum model. The horizontal and vertical directions are defined as the x-axis and y-axis respectively, with the left endpoint of the parallelogram structure positioned at the coordinate origin, as illustrated in Fig. 2(a).

All parallelogram mechanisms share identical geometric configurations, with each fundamental unit comprising two sets of parallel components of equal length. The mass parameter of the longer member is denoted as m_1, and the effective length is l; the mass parameter of the shorter member is denoted as m_2, and the effective length is b. The analysis employs the following ideal assumptions:

1. The mass of the component is evenly distributed in its geometric center
2. The density of each connecting rod is constant and the cross-sectional properties are consistent.
3. The weight and appearance dimensions of the pulley device are negligible.
4. The rope is an ideal inextensible body and has no elastic deformation.
5. There is no damping effect in the moving pair.

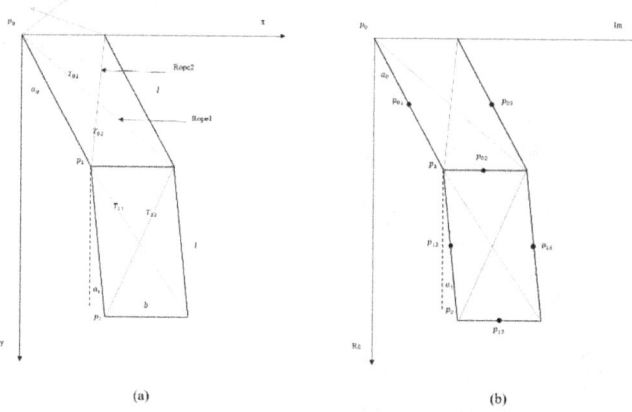

Fig. 2. Dynamic coordinate diagram in vacant state and Schematic diagram of particle selection under complex vector coordinates

The meanings of each physical quantity in the system are expressed as follows (Table 1):

Table 1. The meanings of each physical quantity

Physical symbols	Meaning
l	Long rod length
b	Short rod length
m_1	Long rod quality
m_2	Short rod quality
p_{01}	The centroid of the left strip in the upper parallelogram
p_{02}	The centroid of the short bar at the connection between the upper and lower parallelograms
p_{03}	The centroid of the right side of the strip in the upper parallelogram
p_{11}	The centroid of the left strip in the lower parallelogram
p_{12}	The centroid of the bottom short strip of the lower parallelogram
p_{13}	The centroid of the right side of the strip in the lower parallelogram
α_0	Angle between the upper parallelogram strip and the imaginary axis
α_1	The angle between the lower parallelogram strip and the imaginary axis

The energy of the mechanical leg system consists of kinetic energy and potential energy. Among them, the potential energy is:

$$V_G = -\left[2m_1 g \frac{l}{2} \cos\alpha_1 + 2m_1 g \left(\frac{l}{2}\cos\alpha_0 + l\cos\alpha_1\right) + m_2 g l \cos\alpha_1\right] \quad (1)$$

Kinetic energy includes translational kinetic energy and rotational kinetic energy:

$$T = I_0\dot{\alpha}_0^2 + I_1\dot{\alpha}_1^2 + \left(\frac{5}{4}m_1 + \frac{1}{2}m_2\right)l^2\dot{\alpha}_0^2 + \left(\frac{1}{4}m_1 + \frac{1}{2}m_2\right)l^2\dot{\alpha}_1^2 \qquad (2)$$
$$+ (m_1 + m_2)l^2\dot{\alpha}_0\dot{\alpha}_1\cos(\alpha_0 - \alpha_1)$$

where $I_i = \frac{1}{12}m_i l^2 (i = 0, 1)$ indicates the rotational moment of inertia of the long rod.

The coordinates and first-order differential forms of each mass point are represented by complex vector method, as follows:

$$\begin{cases} p_{01} = \frac{l}{2}e^{i\alpha_0} & \dot{p}_{01} = \dot{p}_{03} = i\alpha_{1,c}e^{i\alpha_0}\dot{\theta}_1 \\ p_{02} = le^{i\alpha_0} + i\frac{b}{2} & \dot{p}_{02} = ile^{i\alpha_0}\dot{\alpha}_0 \\ p_{11} = le^{i\alpha_0} + \frac{l}{2}e^{i\alpha_1} & \dot{p}_{11} = \dot{p}_{13} = ile^{i\alpha_0}\dot{\alpha}_0 + i\frac{l}{2}e^{i\alpha_1}\dot{\alpha}_1 \\ p_{12} = le^{i\alpha_0} + \frac{l}{2}e^{i\alpha_1} + i\frac{b}{2} & \dot{p}_{12} = ile^{i\alpha_0}\dot{\alpha}_0 + ile^{i\alpha_1}\dot{\alpha}_1 \end{cases} \qquad (3)$$

Bringing the above formula into the calculation can result in the Lagrangian operator:

$$L = T - V_G$$
$$= \left(\frac{4}{3}m_1 + \frac{1}{2}m_2\right)l^2\dot{\alpha}_0^2 + \left(\frac{1}{3}m_1 + \frac{1}{2}m_2\right)l^2\dot{\alpha}_1^2 + m_1gl\cos\alpha_0 \qquad (4)$$
$$+ (m_1 + m_2)\dot{\alpha}_0\dot{\alpha}_1\cos(\alpha_0 - \alpha_1) + (3m_1gl + m_2gl\cos\alpha_1)$$

Lagrangian equation:

$$\frac{d}{dt}\left(\frac{\partial L}{\partial \dot{\alpha}_i}\right) - \frac{\partial L}{\partial \alpha_i} = Q_i \ (i = 0, 1) \qquad (5)$$

Next, we need to solve the generalized force, that is, the generalized moment of each joint. The complex vector method can be used to write the complex vector of each force:

$$\begin{cases} T_{i,1} = \frac{T_1(-ib - le^{i\alpha_i})}{\sqrt{b^2 + l^2 + 2lb\sin\alpha_i}} \\ T_{i,2} = \frac{T_2(-ib - le^{i\alpha_i})}{\sqrt{b^2 + l^2 - 2lb\sin\alpha_i}} \end{cases} \qquad (6)$$

Among them, the sum represents the tension value inside the rope 1 and the rope 2. The virtual work equation of force is:

$$\delta W_T = \text{Re}\left[\sum_{i=1}^{2}(T_{i,1} + T_{i,2})\overline{\delta p_i}\right] \qquad (7)$$

where

$$\begin{cases} \delta p_0 = i\frac{l}{2}e^{i\alpha_0}\delta\alpha_0 \\ \delta p_1 = ile^{i\alpha_0}\delta\alpha_0 + i\frac{l}{2}e^{i\alpha_1}\delta\alpha_1 \end{cases} \qquad (8)$$

Comparing with the form of the virtual work Eq. (7) can obtain various generalized forces:

$$Q_i = \left(\frac{T_2}{\sqrt{b^2 + l^2 + 2lb\sin\alpha_i}} - \frac{T_1}{\sqrt{b^2 + l^2 - 2lb\sin\alpha_i}}\right)lb\cos\theta \ i = 0, 1 \qquad (9)$$

Write it into matrix form:

$$\begin{bmatrix} M_{11} & M_{12} \\ M_{21} & M_{22} \end{bmatrix} \begin{bmatrix} \ddot{\alpha}_0 \\ \ddot{\alpha}_1 \end{bmatrix} + \begin{bmatrix} C_1(\dot{\alpha}, \alpha) \\ C_2(\dot{\alpha}, \alpha) \end{bmatrix} + \begin{bmatrix} G_1(\alpha) \\ G_2(\alpha) \end{bmatrix} = \begin{bmatrix} Q_{01} & Q_{02} \\ Q_{11} & Q_{22} \end{bmatrix} \begin{bmatrix} T_1 \\ T_2 \end{bmatrix} \quad (10)$$

where

$$\begin{cases} M_{11} = \left(\frac{8}{3}m_1 + m_2\right)l^2, M_{22} = \frac{2}{3}m_1 + m_2 \\ M_{12} = M_{21} = (m_1 + m_2)l^2 \cos(\alpha_0 - \alpha_1) \\ C_1(\dot{\alpha}, \alpha) = -(m_1 + m_2)l^2(\dot{\alpha}_0 - \dot{\alpha}_1)\dot{\alpha}_1 \sin(\alpha_0 - \alpha_1) \\ \qquad + (m_1 + m_2)l^2 \dot{\alpha}_0 \dot{\alpha}_1 \sin(\alpha_0 - \alpha_1) \\ C_2(\dot{\alpha}, \alpha) = -(m_1 + m_2)l^2(\dot{\alpha}_0 - \dot{\alpha}_1)\dot{\alpha}_0 \sin(\alpha_0 - \alpha_1) \\ \qquad -(m_1 + m_2)l^2 \dot{\alpha}_0 \dot{\alpha}_1 \sin(\alpha_0 - \alpha_1) \\ G_1(\alpha) = m_1 g l \sin\alpha_0, G_2(\alpha) = (3m_1 g l + m_2 g l) \sin\alpha_1 \\ Q_{01} = \frac{-bl\cos\alpha_0}{\sqrt{b^2 + l^2 + 2lb\sin\alpha_0}}, Q_{02} = \frac{bl\cos\alpha_0}{\sqrt{b^2 + l^2 - 2lb\sin\alpha_0}} \\ Q_{11} = \frac{-bl\cos\alpha_1}{\sqrt{b^2 + l^2 + 2lb\sin\alpha_1}}, Q_{22} = \frac{bl\cos\alpha_0}{\sqrt{b^2 + l^2 - 2lb\sin\alpha_1}} \end{cases} \quad (11)$$

Write a simpler matrix equation in the following form:

$$M(\alpha)\ddot{\alpha} + C(\dot{\alpha}, \alpha) + G(\alpha) = Q(\alpha)T \quad (12)$$

When the robot foot is in contact with the ground. The interaction force between the sole of the foot and the ground mainly includes friction and normal support force, which decomposes the combined force on the sole of the foot, with the horizontal direction being F_{Im} and the vertical direction being F_{Re}.

Establishing the Jacques matrix J to represent the velocity mapping relationship between the operating space and joints, and deriving the joint angle of the sole of the foot can lead to:

$$J = \begin{bmatrix} ile^{i\alpha_0}\dot{\alpha}_0 \\ ile^{i\alpha_1}\dot{\alpha}_1 \end{bmatrix} \quad (13)$$

Definition $f = (F_{Im} \; F_{Re})^T$ is a force-bearing matrix, then the dynamic equation during contact is as follows:

$$M(\alpha)\ddot{\alpha} + C(\dot{\alpha}, \alpha) + G(\alpha) + J^T f = Q(\alpha)T \quad (14)$$

where B, C and G are the same as (11), on this basis, the transposition of the Jacobian matrix and the quantity product of the end binding force are added, fully expressing the dynamic model of the system.

3 System Properties

Consider the system balance conditions without joint damping and elastic force, and meet when the system is in equilibrium $\ddot{\alpha} = \dot{\alpha} = 0$, that is:

$$G(\alpha) = Q(\alpha)T \tag{15}$$

The equilibrium equation of n + 1th order (n = 0,1) can be expressed as:

$$m_c glsin\alpha_n = \frac{-blcos\alpha_n}{\sqrt{b^2 + l^2 + 2lbsin\alpha_n}} T_1 + \frac{blcos\alpha_n}{\sqrt{b^2 + l^2 - 2lbsin\alpha_n}} T_2 \tag{16}$$

where $m_c = \frac{G_k(\alpha)}{glsin\alpha_n}$ is the quality parameter in the formula.

Note that $\alpha_n = \frac{\pi}{2} + k\pi$ is not the solution to the equation, so the equilibrium equation can be reduced to:

$$tan\alpha_n = \frac{-1}{\sqrt{C_1 + C_2 sin\alpha_n}} \frac{T_1}{C_3} + \frac{1}{\sqrt{C_1 - C_2 sin\alpha_n}} \frac{T_2}{C_3} \tag{17}$$

where $C_1 = 1 + \frac{l^2}{b^2}, C_2 = \frac{2l}{b}, C_3 = \frac{b}{m_c g}$.

Case (1): When $T_1 = T_2 = T$, $\alpha_n = k\pi, \pi \in Z$ must be one of the equilibrium points. When T is large enough, other balance points will appear.

Case (2): When $T_1 > T_2$, for further analysis, the comparison function is constructed: $g(\alpha_n) = tan\alpha_n, f(\alpha_n) = \frac{-1}{\sqrt{C_1 + C_2 sin\alpha_n}} \frac{T_1}{C_3} + \frac{1}{\sqrt{C_1 - C_2 sin\alpha_n}} \frac{T_2}{C_3}$, at the same time, $g(\pi) = f(\pi), g(\frac{3}{2}\pi) = f(\frac{3}{2}\pi)$.

Easy to know $\dot{g}(\alpha_n) \leq 1$, so when $\dot{f}(\alpha_n) > 1$, that is $\dot{f}(\alpha_n) > \dot{g}(\alpha_n)$, according to the intravalue theorem, there must be a equilibrium point in $(\pi, \frac{3}{2}\pi)$.

From the symmetry and periodicity of the function, we can see that every $(k\pi, k\pi + \frac{1}{2}\pi)$ and $(k\pi - \frac{1}{2}\pi, k\pi)$ will periodically show a equilibrium point.

Case (3): The situation at $T_1 > T_2$ is symmetrical with $T_1 < T_2$ about the origin, and there must be a solution within $(-\frac{1}{2}\pi, 0)$.

To sum up, for any T_1 and T_2, the system has a family of equilibrium points related to the generalized force amplitude. When $T_1 = T_2 = T$, a new isolated equilibrium point will appear when the tension is sufficiently large.

4 Control Law Design and Simulation

4.1 Pole Configuration Method Control

Linearization

By performing Taylor series expansion of the nonlinear system at the equilibrium point and ignoring the higher-order perturbation terms, the original nonlinear system is approximated as a linear time-invariant system, and then applying pole configuration to achieve calm control. We can perform Taylor expansion at the equilibrium point $\alpha = 0$ and $\dot{\alpha} = 0$ $(I = 0,1)$, and keep the first item:

$$\begin{bmatrix} (\frac{8}{3}m_1 + m_2)l^2 & (m_1 + m_2)l^2 \\ (m_1 + m_2)l^2 & \frac{2}{3}m_1 + m_2 \end{bmatrix} \begin{bmatrix} \ddot{\alpha}_0 \\ \ddot{\alpha}_1 \end{bmatrix} + \begin{bmatrix} -m_1 g l \alpha_0 \\ -(3m_1 g l + m_2 g l)\alpha_1 \end{bmatrix} = \begin{bmatrix} \frac{bl}{\sqrt{b^2+l^2}} \\ \frac{bl}{\sqrt{b^2+l^2}} \end{bmatrix}(T_2 - T_1) \tag{18}$$

Substitute the parameters $m_1 = 6$, $m_2 = 5$, $l = 4$, $b = 3$, and further organize this model and write it into a more intuitive system of differential equations:

$$\begin{bmatrix} \ddot{\alpha}_0 \\ \ddot{\alpha}_1 \end{bmatrix} = \begin{bmatrix} -0.0785 & 5.6827 \\ 1.4824 & -10.848 \end{bmatrix} \begin{bmatrix} \alpha_0 \\ \alpha_1 \end{bmatrix} + \begin{bmatrix} 0.0143 \\ -0.0137 \end{bmatrix}(T_2 - T_1) \tag{19}$$

Set the status quantity and output quantity: $x_1 = \alpha_0$, $x_2 = \alpha_1$, $x_3 = \dot{\alpha}_0$, $x_4 = \dot{\alpha}_1$, $y_1 = \alpha_0$, $y_2 = \alpha_1$.

We can get the new system state - space equation:

$$\begin{cases} \dot{x} = Qx + Wu \\ y = Tx \end{cases} \tag{20}$$

Control Law Design

Based on state space model, construct a controllable discrimination matrix:

$$E = \begin{bmatrix} W & QW & Q^2W & Q^3W \end{bmatrix} \tag{21}$$

By rank determination rank(E) = 4, the controllability condition is met. The system is fully controllable.

Set the desired closed-loop pole:

$$P = [-3 + i; -3 - i; -4; -12] \tag{22}$$

Use Ackerman formula to calculate the state feedback gain matrix to obtain the feedback gain matrix:

$$K = \begin{bmatrix} 1590.10 & -4196.9 & 2886.6 & -92917 \end{bmatrix} \tag{23}$$

The feedback control method will be in this form:

$$u = -Kx \tag{24}$$

Simulation Experiment

The experimental parameters are configured as follows: the initial swing angle is set to 0.8 radians, and the simulation time is 120 s. Figure 3(a) shows the dynamic response curve of joint angle.

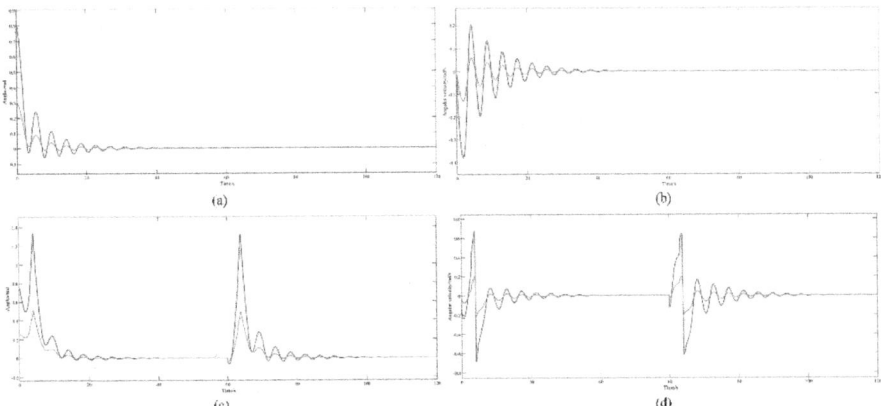

Fig. 3. Simulation of angle and angular velocity and with pulse disturbance response

The two angles of the mechanical legs can be adjusted to converge to zero, which verifies that the designed feedback control law has a control effect of asymptotic stability at the equilibrium position.

The angular velocity response presented in Fig. 3(b) further verifies the effectiveness of the control strategy.

As can be seen from the Fig. 3(c)-(d), whether it is the angle amount or the angular velocity amount, after adding external pulse interference, it can still transition smoothly to the equilibrium state at zero point, proving that the system has certain anti-interference ability.

4.2 Type 2 Fuzzy Control

This study designed one interval type-2 fuzzy controller for each of the two joints in the bionic leg system, named ITF0 and ITF1 respectively. Both controllers have identical core architectures, each equipped with two input variables—the angle error and angular velocity error of the corresponding joint—and output control commands generated through type-2 fuzzy inference. Finally, the output commands from these two controllers will be comprehensively processed to form the total control force acting on the controlled object.

Considering that IT2F0 and IT2F1 possess completely identical structural logic, the explanation process is simplified by selecting IT2F0 as a typical example to elaborate the complete design workflow of the interval type-2 fuzzy controller. Here, U_1 denotes the control command output by IT2F0.

Fuzzy Controller Design

In the specific design process, the input and output variables of the controller must be formalized through language variables: Taking the controlled joint P_0 as an example, its angle deviation is defined as the language variable e1 and the angular velocity deviation is defined as the language variable de1; the basic domain range of the input variable (e1, de1) and the output variable (U1) needs to be further determined in combination with the actual system characteristics.

The fuzzy division of the input variables adopts language subsets, and the label sets are specifically {NB, NS, O, PS, PB}. They respectively indicate negative large, negative small, zero, positive small, and positive large.

As shown in Fig. 4, the type-2 member function is designed.

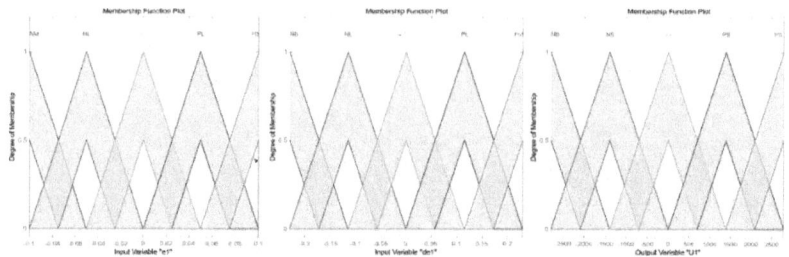

Fig. 4. Type-2 membership function of e1, de1, U1

The rules can be listed in a table as shown in Table 2.

Table 2. Fuzzy Logic Rules

e/de	NB	NL	O	PL	PM
NM	PB	PB	PB	PS	O
NL	PB	PB	PS	O	NS
O	PB	PS	O	NS	NB
PL	PS	O	NS	NB	NB
PB	O	NS	NB	NB	NB

The first rule can be written as:
IF e is NM and de is NB THEN U is PB.

That means if the input of angular deviation is the Negative Minimum (NM) and the input of angular velocity is Negative Minimum (PM), finally the Fuzzy Logic Rules system will give a Positive Big (PB) control force(U) as output. All the 25 rules of Fuzzy Logic Rules can be written and understood in the same way.

The control rules' surface could show the relationship about the two inputs and the output directly, and it is shown in Fig. 5.

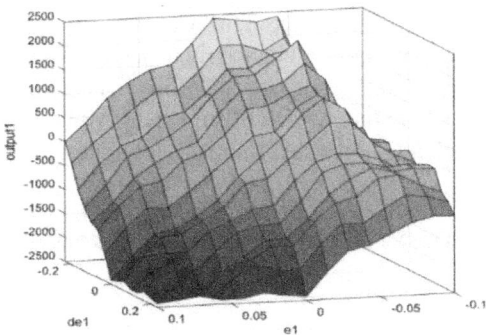

Fig. 5. Fuzzy Rules Surface of IT2F0

Simulation

The simulation result is shown in Fig. 6(a)-(b). The initial states of angles are 0.04rads and 0.01rads. Both of the angle and the angular velocity converge to zero in 3 s.

To evaluate the system's robustness, a periodic disturbance with a 4 s cycle and 0.1 rad angular offset was introduced. Simulation results as depicted in Fig. 6. (c)-(d), demonstrate that the system regains stability within 2 s, successfully achieving stabilization control and demonstrating excellent robustness.

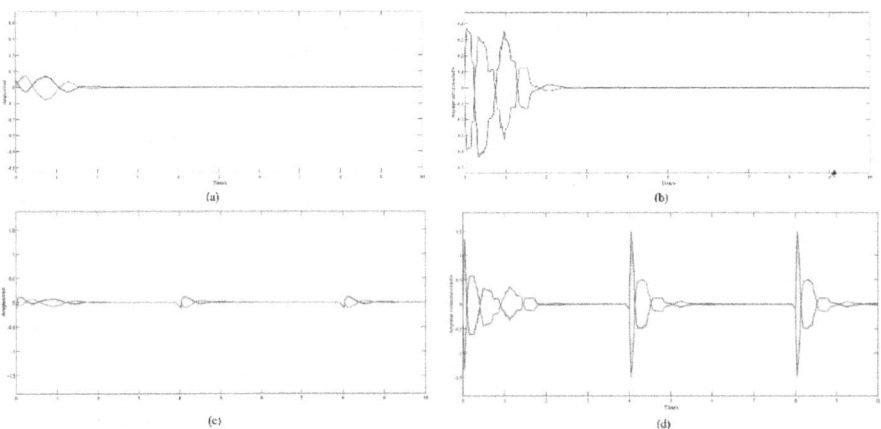

Fig. 6. IT2F0 results of angles and angular velocities and with pulse disturbance response

5 Conclusion

Inspired by the tendon-driven mechanisms of human limbs, this study innovatively designs a truss-type leg mechanism employing cable-controlled architecture to achieve multi-DOF coupled dynamic characteristics. A Lagrangian dynamic model is established to address bipedal robot balance control during upright walking. Comparative analysis between pole placement and interval type-2 fuzzy control strategies systematically evaluates their stability at vertical equilibrium and robustness. Simulations demonstrate IT2 fuzzy control's superior response speed and robustness, enabling precise dynamic stabilization of the bionic leg. Future work will implement MPC and DeepGait for further optimization while developing physical prototypes for experimental validation.

Acknowledgement. This work is supported by the National Natural Science Foundation of China (Grant No. 62303341), and the National Key Research and Development Program of China (Grant No. 2022YFB4703203).

References

1. Sara, M., Marios, K., Raquel, B.-F.: How perceptions of intelligence and anthropomorphism affect adoption of personal intelligent agents. Electronic Markets **31**, 343–364 (2021)
2. Del Vecchio, D., Dy, A.J., Qian, Y.: Control theory meets synthetic biology. The Royal Society **120**(13) (2016)
3. Ma, G.: Research evolution on biorobotics. Robot **23**(5), 463–466 (2001)
4. Ji, A., Dai, Z., Zhou, L.: Research development of bio-inspired robotics. Robot **27**(3), 284–288 (2005)
5. Woodend, Malchano, M., Blankespoor, K., et al.: Autonomous navigation for big dog. 2010 IEEE International Conference on Robotics and Automation. Anchorage: IEEE pp. 4736–4741 (2010)
6. Zhang, Y., Chai, T., Wang, D., Chen, X.: Virtual unmodeled dynamics modeling for nonlinear multivariable adaptive control with decoupling design. IEEE **48**(3), 342–353 (2018)
7. Lickhan, R.: The spring-mass model for running and hopping. J. Biomechan. **22**(11/12), 1217–1227 (1989)
8. Hirose, S., Umetani, Y.: The development of soft grip-per for the versatile robot hand. Mechan. Machi. Theory **13**(3), 351–359 (1978)
9. Xu, H., Fu, Y., Wang, S., et al.: Research on biomimetic robotics. Robot **26**(3), 283–288 (2004)
10. Ruan, X., Ren, H.: Two-wheeled self-balancing mobile robot dynamic model and balancing control. Appl. Res. Comp. **26**(1), 99–101 (2009)

Continuous Estimation Algorithm of Elbow Joint Angle Based on Mamba Model

Yangfan Zhou[1,2], Jiawei Liang[1,3], Yu Lu[4(✉)], Liang Zhang[4], Bi Zhang[1], and Xingang Zhao[1]

[1] State Key Laboratory of Robotics, Shenyang Institute of Automation, Chinese Academy of Sciences, Shenyang 110016, China
[2] University of Chinese Academy of Sciences, Beijing 100049, China
[3] School of Software, Shenyang University of Technology, Shenyang 110870, China
[4] Department of Rehabilitation Medicine, The People's Hospital of Liaoning Province, Shenyang 110016, China
dl848@lnph.com

Abstract. Continuous estimation of elbow joint angles is vital for motion intention recognition and real-time control in rehabilitation robotics. This paper proposes a novel time series prediction framework based on the Mamba model, which integrates surface electromyography (sEMG) and inertial measurement unit (IMU) signals to achieve high-precision elbow joint angle estimation. The proposed method involves synchronized feature extraction and fusion from multi-channel sEMG and IMU signals within sliding time windows, followed by advanced sequence modeling using the Mamba architecture. Experimental validation on data collected from eight healthy subjects demonstrates that the Mamba model achieves lower root mean square error (RMSE) and higher R^2 values compared to long short-term memory (LSTM) and gated recurrent unit (GRU) baselines in both single-angle and multi-angle prediction modes. The Mamba-based framework also shows robust performance under varying window lengths and advance prediction times. These results confirm the effectiveness and generalization capability of the proposed method for dynamic joint angle estimation, providing valuable support for real-time prosthetic control and multimodal human-machine interaction applications.

Keywords: Mamba Model · Elbow Joint Angle Estimation · Time Series Prediction · sEMG

1 Introduction

The human hands serve as the primary medium for interaction with the external environment and are indispensable for completing daily life and work activities. However, for stroke survivors and individuals with upper limb disabilities, the loss of control over their hands imposes significant limitations and challenges on daily activities. In China, there are currently approximately 14.9 million stroke patients, with about 3.3 million new cases diagnosed each year, and more than 1.5 million deaths annually due to stroke.

Among the survivors, nearly 80% are left with varying degrees of disability. According to the 2024 national disability survey in China, there are about 86.91 million people with disabilities, among whom approximately 24.72 million are physically disabled, accounting for 29% of the total disabled population [1]. In order to improve the quality of life for individuals with limb disabilities, the research and development of prosthetic technology has become an important direction in the field of rehabilitation engineering. With the rapid development of sensor technology, biosignal processing, and machine learning algorithms, rehabilitation robots have made significant progress in perception and motion control [2]. In particular, the use of surface electromyography (sEMG) for upper limb motion intention recognition has attracted increasing attention due to its noninvasive nature, real-time responsiveness, and high accuracy.

sEMG can be used to decode the angles of upper limb, lower limb, and even finger joints in the human body. Moreover, due to the temporal lead characteristic of sEMG, it can be utilized for predicting continuous joint angles. The estimation of joint angles first relies on effective feature extraction and dimensionality reduction of sEMG signals. Pengjie Qin et al. [3] proposed a method based on wavelet packet decomposition (WPD) and correlation dimension analysis, where multiscale features are extracted using WPD and a nonlinear autoregressive exogenous model with singular spectrum analysis (NARX-SSA) is used for joint angle prediction. Wen L et al. [4] proposed a multiple decomposition feature (MDF) representation method that combines variational mode decomposition (VMD) and wavelet packet transform (WPT) to extract richer features from multiple frequency scales, followed by joint angle regression estimation using a bidirectional long short-term memory (BiLSTM) network. Zhu M et al. [5] proposed an improved PCA algorithm based on kernel methods for dimensionality reduction to remove redundant information.

With the development of deep learning technology, an increasing number of studies have adopted deep learning methods for joint angle prediction. Li C et al. [6] utilized an attention-based long short-term memory (Attention-LSTM) model and used root mean square error (RMSE) as the evaluation metric. Lu Y et al. [7] proposed a model combining stacked convolutional neural networks and LSTM networks to predict multiple joint angles in lower limb exoskeleton movements. Song Q et al. [8] used only sEMG signals as input, performing online joint angle prediction through real-time feature extraction and normalization. Teng H et al. [9] integrated a graph convolutional neural network (GCN) with an LSTM network to predict joint angles. As research on multimodal data fusion has advanced, more studies have attempted to combine data such as IMU and vibration arthrography (VAG) to improve joint angle prediction accuracy. Delgado AL et al. [10] focused on evaluating the combination of angular velocity and EMG signals for the simultaneous and continuous prediction of 12 hand joint angles. Lin W et al. [11] proposed a gated recurrent unit (GRU) model integrating IMU and sEMG signals. However, joint angle prediction based on sEMG still faces many challenges, including insufficient modeling ability for long time series dependence, high computational overhead, limited generalization ability, limited real-time performance, and the influence of noise interference.

To address this issue, this paper extracts temporal features from sEMG signals and fuses them with angle information to construct the input features, introducing the

Mamba model based on state space modeling for continuous elbow joint angle estimation. This model has excellent global modeling capabilities, supports parallel computing and selective attention mechanisms, and can efficiently handle long-term dependent information.

2 Methodology

2.1 Experimental Setup

Data Acquisition. Eight healthy subjects were recruited for data collection in this experiment. SEMG signals were acquired using the Noraxon Ultium EMG system, with electrodes placed on the biceps brachii, medial triceps brachii, and lateral triceps brachii, which are closely related to elbow joint movement. The Noraxon myoMOTION inertial measurement unit was used to collect sagittal plane angle variations of the upper limb elbow joint. The sEMG sensors operated at a sampling frequency of 2000 Hz, while the IMU data were collected at 200 Hz.

Since muscle contraction patterns differ at various joint angles, in order to enable the prediction model to learn the mapping between angles and sEMG signals across a wide range of postures, each subject was required to perform elbow flexion and extension movements from different initial angles—specifically, with the upper arm at $90°$, $45°$, and $0°$ relative to the ground. To account for the effects of muscle fatigue, each movement at a given angle was performed for 1 min, with a 3-min rest between different movement modes and a 6-min rest between every two sets. Figure 1 shows images of the three different angle modes and sensor placements.

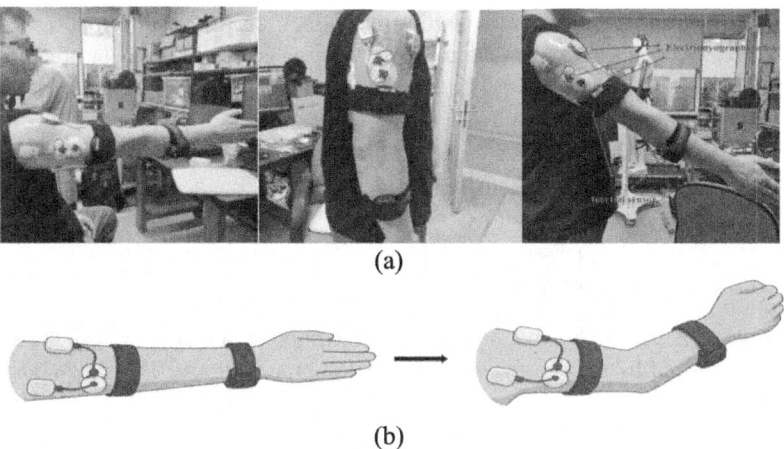

Fig. 1. (a) Experimental setup and sensor placements. (b) schematic diagram of elbow flexion.

For data preprocessing, the raw sEMG signals were first subjected to a third-order Butterworth band-pass filter with a passband range of 20 Hz to 450 Hz, retaining the valid myoelectric components of the sEMG signals. Next, full-wave rectification was performed on the band-pass filtered signals by computing their absolute values, thereby preserving the overall amplitude variation trend. Subsequently, to further obtain a smooth EMG envelope, a third-order Butterworth low-pass filter with a cutoff frequency of 4 Hz was applied to the rectified signals. The resulting low-pass filtered signal was regarded as the EMG envelope. Finally, to eliminate amplitude differences among different channels, min-max normalization was applied to each channel individually to enhance the stability of feature extraction and the convergence of model training.

Elbow Joint Angle Calculation. To accurately obtain real-time motion information of the elbow joint, this study employed two inertial measurement units, which were placed at the midpoints of the upper arm and forearm, respectively. By acquiring the pitch angles of the upper arm and forearm, the angle between them was calculated to realize real-time estimation of the elbow joint flexion-extension angle.

The upper arm IMU and the forearm IMU each record the spatial posture information of their respective locations. During upper limb flexion and extension movements, the pitch angles of the upper arm and forearm exhibit clear synchronous changes. Based on the kinematic characteristics of the upper limb, the elbow joint flexion-extension angle can be calculated using the following relationship:

$$\theta_{elbow}(t) = \theta_{forearm}(t) - \theta_{upperarm}(t) \tag{1}$$

where $\theta_{elbow}(t)$ represents the elbow flexion-extension angle at time t; $\theta_{forearm}(t)$ denotes the pitch angle recorded by the forearm IMU; and $\theta_{upperarm}(t)$ denotes the pitch angle recorded by the upper arm IMU.

The dynamic estimation process of upper limb joint angles can be described using a state space model, where the state variables include the pitch angles and angular velocities of the upper arm and forearm. By integrating muscle activity pattern information obtained from sEMG signals, time series samples are constructed for subsequent prediction by Mamba, LSTM, or GRU models. The recursive process of state update and observation update is expressed as shown in Eq. (2):

$$x_k = \begin{bmatrix} \theta_{upperarm}(k) \\ \theta_{forearm}(k) \\ \dot{\theta}_{upperarm}(k) \\ \dot{\theta}_{forearm}(k) \end{bmatrix} = Ax_{k-1} + Bu_{k-1} + w_{k-1} \tag{2}$$

where θ denotes the pitch angle; $\dot{\theta}$ represents the angular velocity; u_{k-1} is the angular velocity measured by the sensor; and w_{k-1} is the process noise. The state equation is given in Eq. (3).

$$z_k = \begin{bmatrix} \theta_{upperarm}(k) \\ \theta_{forearm}(k) \end{bmatrix} = Hx_k + v_k \tag{3}$$

where z_k is the observed value of the pitch angle calculated by the IMU, H is the observation matrix, and v_k is the observation noise.

To achieve joint analysis and feature fusion of sEMG and IMU information, the data streams from both sensors were synchronously segmented using a unified time window. Each window has a length of t_{window}, and the signal data within the window, along with the corresponding mean joint angle, are used as the feature label for that window. The window shift step is set according to the sampling frequency and movement characteristics to ensure the continuity of signals and the completeness of features across windows. The window segmentation is illustrated as follows:

$$\{X_k\} = \{x_k, x_{k+1}, \cdots, x_{k+t_{window}}\} \tag{4}$$

$$\theta_k = \frac{1}{t_{window}} \sum_{i=k}^{k+t_{window}} \theta_{elbow}(i) \tag{5}$$

where x_k denotes the sEMG feature sequence within the k-th time window, and θ_k represents the mean elbow joint angle for the corresponding time window as the label. The algorithm predicts the current joint angle based on the sEMG signals and actual joint angle values prior to (and including) time t. Since joint angle is a time-varying sequence, LSTM and GRU models are selected as baseline models for comparative experiments. The overall experimental process is shown in Fig. 2.

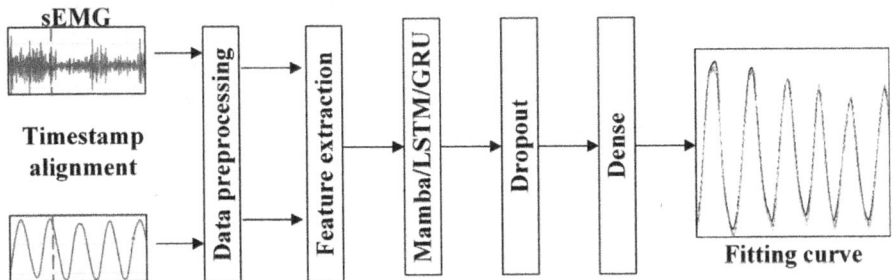

Fig. 2. The flow chart of the Angle prediction experiment

To fully utilize temporal information, the sliding window length was set to 50 data points (corresponding to 25 ms), and the step size was set to 20 data points (corresponding to 10 ms). For the sEMG signals within each window, four types of time-domain features—mean absolute value (MAV), root mean square (RMS), waveform length (WL), and zero-crossing rate (ZCR)—were extracted from each of the three channels, resulting in a 12-dimensional sEMG feature vector for each window (3 channels × 4 features). In addition, to characterize the dynamic changes of the elbow joint angle during movement, the angular velocity within each window was calculated as the difference between the end angle and the start angle of the window divided by the window length, thereby representing the joint motion speed, as shown in Eq. (6):

$$\Delta\theta = \frac{\theta_{end} - \theta_{start}}{T} \tag{6}$$

where θ_{satrt} and θ_{end} represent the elbow joint angles at the start and end of the window, respectively, and T is the window length.

$$Feature = \{f_{MAV1}, f_{RMS1}, f_{WL1}, f_{SSC1} \cdots f_{MAV3}, f_{RMS3}, f_{WL3}, f_{SSC3}, \Delta\theta\} \tag{7}$$

As a result, each window yields a feature vector consisting of 12 sEMG temporal features and 1 angular velocity, as shown in Eq. (7). For the label information, the mean joint angle within each window is used as the label value for that window.

$$Label = \frac{1}{N}\sum_{i=1}^{N}\theta(i) \qquad (8)$$

The *Label* represents the mean elbow joint angle during the corresponding time interval. All window features and their corresponding label information are stored in H5 format to facilitate subsequent reading and training by deep learning models.

2.2 Model Architecture

In general, as long as human muscles retain some contractile capability, motion intention can be recognized using sEMG signals. This is because sEMG signals can reflect muscle activity approximately 10–150 ms earlier than the actual movement occurs. In contrast, conventional sensors have the advantage of precisely calculating the current joint angle information, making the two modalities complementary. For individuals who have completely lost limb function or are unable to directly wear IMU sensors, the combined use of sEMG and IMU sensors to acquire muscle and joint angle information, along with their fusion, can enhance the stability and prediction accuracy of joint motion intention recognition. Since IMU sensors can output high-precision joint angle information in real time, their measurements can be regarded as direct references for the actual joint angle.

Among current joint angle prediction methods based on sEMG and IMU signals, recurrent neural network (RNN) such as long short-term memory (LSTM) and GRU generally outperform traditional machine learning approaches. However, these models still have certain limitations. LSTM utilizes forget, input, and output gates to control information flow, capturing long-term dependencies in sequential data and modeling complex temporal relationships. Nevertheless, the serial structure of LSTM restricts its parallel computation capability, which leads to issues such as vanishing or exploding gradients when handling long sequences, ultimately resulting in degraded performance in long-term prediction tasks. As a variant of LSTM, GRU reduces computational complexity by merging the forget and input gates, thereby improving training efficiency. However, due to its fewer parameters, GRU is less capable of modeling complex patterns compared to LSTM. Moreover, GRU cannot adaptively adjust the attention weights of different modal features when processing multimodal data, which limits its effectiveness in multimodal data fusion tasks.

To address these issues, this study adopts the Mamba model [12] for temporal modeling. Mamba is based on linear state space models (SSM) and a parallel computation mechanism, which enables it to effectively capture long-range dependencies in time series data while improving computational efficiency and enhancing the model's ability to represent complex sequential signals. Compared with LSTM and GRU, Mamba utilizes an efficient global modeling mechanism that allows for more flexible processing of joint movement data across different time steps, thereby avoiding the information forgetting problems encountered by traditional RNN models when modeling long sequences.

This, in turn, improves both the prediction accuracy and generalization capability of the model. The structure of the Mamba algorithm is illustrated in Fig. 3.

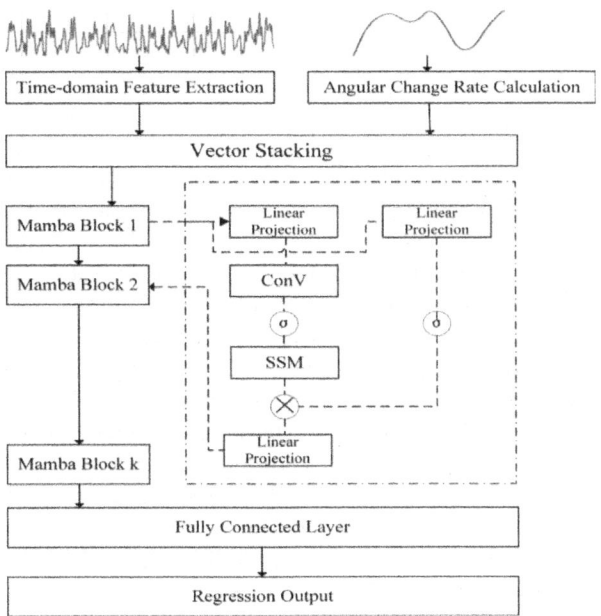

Fig. 3. Structure diagram of Mamba algorithm

2.3 Model Parameters and Evaluation Metrics

For the two baseline algorithms, both the LSTM and GRU modules were configured with 64 hidden neurons. The Mamba block was implemented using the ReLU activation function, with the Adam optimizer, 200 epochs, a batch size of 16, and an initial learning rate of 0.0006. The proposed algorithm was constructed based on Keras, with TensorFlow used as the backend engine. The model input consists of the feature vector obtained by fusing sEMG features and angle features within the current time window.

RMSE and R^2 were chosen as the evaluation metrics. RMSE is an indicator of the magnitude of the error between the predicted values and the actual values, representing the standard deviation of the prediction errors. A smaller RMSE indicates that the predicted joint angles are closer to the true values and thus reflect higher accuracy. The R^2 metric is used as a supplementary evaluation to demonstrate the correlation and goodness of fit between the model predictions and the actual data.

$$RMSE = \sqrt{\frac{1}{N} \sum_{i=1}^{N} (\theta_i - \hat{\theta}_i)^2} \qquad (9)$$

$$R^2 = 1 - \frac{\sum_{i=1}^{N} (\theta_i - \hat{\theta}_i)^2}{\sum_{i=1}^{m} (\theta_i - \overline{\theta})^2} \qquad (10)$$

where N denotes the total number of samples in the test set, θ_i represents the true joint angle value of the i-th sample, $\hat{\theta}_i$ is the predicted joint angle value, and $\overline{\theta}$ is the mean of the true joint angle values for all samples.

3 Experiment Results

3.1 Model Comparison

In this experiment, two time series prediction models, LSTM [10] and GRU [11], based on two modalities, sEMG and IMU, were selected for comparison. The latter two are both variants of the recurrent neural network RNN, while GRU is further simplified on the basis of LSTM. Each user will collect sEMG and IMU information in the multi-angle mode and divide the training set and the test set using two different data partitioning methods. The first division method divides the training set and the test set in an 8:2 ratio based on the original timing within a single Angle. The second division method uses data from different perspectives as the training set and the test set.

Tables 1 and 2 present the RMSE and R^2 results of the three models in single-angle and multi-angle modes, respectively. For each mode, models were trained and tested on the corresponding datasets to obtain RMSE and R^2 values. According to the data in Table 1, the Mamba model achieved an average RMSE of 2.783 across all eight subjects, which is significantly lower than those of LSTM and GRU, indicating that Mamba yielded the smallest prediction error for joint angles in the single-angle mode. In terms of the R^2 metric, the average R^2 for the Mamba model was 0.988 ± 0.013, which is very close to the 0.983 achieved by LSTM and superior to the 0.976 of GRU. This demonstrates that Mamba provided the best overall fit to the data trend and could accurately capture the variation of joint angles. The average RMSE for LSTM was 3.138, slightly higher than that of Mamba, indicating that the prediction error of LSTM was generally larger; however, the average R^2 for LSTM was 0.983, close to that of Mamba and much higher than that of GRU, suggesting that LSTM also has good trend fitting ability in the single-angle mode.

Table 1. Comparison of three models and RMSE and R^2 in single Angle mode

Number	Mamba/RMSE	Mamba/R2	LSTM/RMSE	LSTM/R2	GRU/RMSE	GRU/R2
1	**2.262 ± 0.61**	0.992 ± 0.013	3.023 ± 0.93	0.984 ± 0.026	3.268 ± 1.06	0.977 ± 0.044
2	2.471 ± 0.43	**0.994 ± 0.011**	4.210 ± 0.89	0.982 ± 0.022	2.466 ± 0.99	0.986 ± 0.038
3	2.613 ± 0.60	0.976 ± 0.014	3.327 ± 0.91	0.981 ± 0.023	3.689 ± 1.01	0.972 ± 0.040
4	3.298 ± 0.48	0.991 ± 0.012	4.066 ± 0.92	0.983 ± 0.024	4.296 ± 1.03	0.966 ± 0.041
5	2.386 ± 0.49	0.989 ± 0.013	3.149 ± 0.90	0.983 ± 0.023	3.392 ± 1.02	0.976 ± 0.040
6	2.637 ± 0.46	0.986 ± 0.012	3.274 ± 0.91	0.981 ± 0.022	3.636 ± 1.03	0.973 ± 0.039
7	4.194 ± 0.60	0.993 ± 0.014	2.991 ± 0.92	0.984 ± 0.026	4.236 ± 1.05	0.968 ± 0.043
8	2.318 ± 0.48	0.988 ± 0.013	3.077 ± 0.91	0.983 ± 0.024	3.321 ± 1.04	0.976 ± 0.042
Avg	2.783 ± 0.48	0.988 ± 0.013	3.138 ± 0.91	0.983 ± 0.024	3.324 ± 1.03	0.976 ± 0.041

Table 2. Comparison of three models and RMSE and R^2 in Multi Angle mode

Number	Mamba/RMSE	Mamba/R^2	LSTM/RMSE	LSTM/R^2	GRU/RMSE	GRU/R^2
1	6.12 ± 0.74	0.983 ± 0.038	6.84 ± 1.27	0.962 ± 0.048	7.39 ± 1.36	0.931 ± 0.062
2	**6.03 ± 0.82**	0.978 ± 0.041	7.91 ± 1.33	0.964 ± 0.061	8.46 ± 1.46	0.929 ± 0.066
3	6.76 ± 0.78	0.961 ± 0.039	7.62 ± 1.29	0.937 ± 0.060	8.01 ± 1.42	0.933 ± 0.064
4	7.18 ± 0.96	**0.989 ± 0.049**	8.76 ± 1.41	0.962 ± 0.069	9.12 ± 1.63	0.939 ± 0.063
5	10.37 ± 1.21	0.964 ± 0.067	11.42 ± 1.68	0.969 ± 0.073	11.86 ± 1.64	0.912 ± 0.078
6	6.46 ± 0.84	0.970 ± 0.043	7.98 ± 1.36	0.969 ± 0.063	8.24 ± 1.44	0.946 ± 0.068
7	6.91 ± 0.80	0.969 ± 0.040	7.66 ± 1.31	0.966 ± 0.061	8.02 ± 1.41	0.924 ± 0.064
8	6.32 ± 0.72	0.977 ± 0.037	6.93 ± 1.26	0.969 ± 0.049	7.36 ± 1.34	0.930 ± 0.062
Avg	6.62 ± 0.86	0.976 ± 0.044	8.13 ± 1.36	0.961 ± 0.062	8.66 ± 1.46	0.929 ± 0.068

3.2 The Influence of the Time Window

During the feature extraction stage for sEMG and angle data, it is necessary to align both types of information and extract features accordingly. The extracted feature values vary depending on different window lengths and sliding window settings. The model retains historical information, and multiple feature values from different time windows are used as inputs during actual prediction. Based on the experimental results from the previous section, the Mamba model demonstrated the best performance; therefore, it was selected for the subsequent experiments. In this section, experiments were conducted with four different window lengths. As shown in Tables 3 and 4, regardless of whether the tests were conducted in single-angle or multi-angle modes, a window length of 50 ms yielded better results than the other three window lengths. The average RMSEs were 2.383 and 6.626, respectively, both lower than those of the other window lengths.

Table 3. RMSE for different time Windows in Single Angle mode

Number	50 ms	100 ms	150 ms	200 ms
1	2.262 ± 0.614	3.104 ± 0.719	6.341 ± 1.862	18.868 ± 4.222
2	2.471 ± 0.429	3.802 ± 0.833	7.421 ± 1.926	17.609 ± 3.816
3	2.613 ± 0.602	4.110 ± 0.916	6.963 ± 1.624	16.106 ± 3.329
4	2.298 ± 0.477	3.674 ± 0.790	8.306 ± 2.004	14.892 ± 2.918
5	2.386 ± 0.488	4.208 ± 0.918	7.103 ± 1.703	16.209 ± 3.067
6	2.637 ± 0.461	3.931 ± 0.872	6.728 ± 1.642	18.603 ± 4.114
7	**2.194 ± 0.604**	3.661 ± 0.714	6.061 ± 1.423	12.804 ± 2.416
8	2.318 ± 0.479	3.943 ± 0.839	6.984 ± 1.376	19.304 ± 4.288
Avg	2.383 ± 0.481	3.916 ± 0.788	6.999 ± 1.681	16.636 ± 3.671

Table 4. RMSE for different time Windows in Multi Angle mode

Number	50 ms	100 ms	150 ms	200 ms
1	6.122 ± 0.74	10.646 ± 1.86	16.292 ± 2.68	19.689 ± 3.74
2	**6.034 ± 0.82**	11.764 ± 2.01	16.883 ± 3.11	21.242 ± 4.16
3	6.761 ± 0.78	10.667 ± 1.78	16.070 ± 2.76	19.111 ± 3.67
4	7.183 ± 0.96	12.842 ± 2.39	18.211 ± 3.49	23.474 ± 4.92
5	10.374 ± 1.21	16.213 ± 2.67	22.068 ± 4.32	28.323 ± 6.34
6	6.464 ± 0.84	11.821 ± 1.98	16.613 ± 2.83	21.682 ± 4.07
7	6.912 ± 0.80	10.784 ± 1.91	14.831 ± 2.64	18.942 ± 3.66
8	6.321 ± 0.72	9.962 ± 1.63	13.726 ± 2.41	17.631 ± 3.21
Avg	6.626 ± 0.86	11.826 ± 2.03	16.677 ± 3.03	21.494 ± 4.08

3.3 Comparison of Different Advance Prediction Times

Unlike the effect of the prediction window length, as the advance prediction time Δt increases, the prediction accuracy typically decreases and the overall prediction error gradually increases. This is because, with increasing Δt, the prediction moment becomes farther from the current time t, resulting in a weaker correlation between the current sEMG signals and the future joint angles. Theoretically, the value of Δt should be less than the lead time of the sEMG signal relative to movement; therefore, it is necessary to select Δt appropriately. However, in order to comprehensively analyze the prediction performance at different Δt values and to meet practical requirements, this section selects four advance times—50 ms, 100 ms, 150 ms, and 200 ms—for comparative experiments. The Mamba network is still used as the prediction model, with the window length set to 50 ms.

Figures 4 and 5 present the comparison curves between the predicted and actual elbow joint angles for Subject 1 under different advance times (Δt) using the Mamba model in both single-angle and multi-angle modes. It can be observed that under various Δt conditions, the prediction curves are able to track the variation trend of the true joint angles reasonably well. However, as Δt increases, the prediction curves exhibit greater lag and increased fluctuation amplitude, and the prediction error becomes more pronounced. Overall accuracy decreases, and the amplitude of prediction fluctuations increases, indicating that changes in advance time have a certain impact on prediction performance.

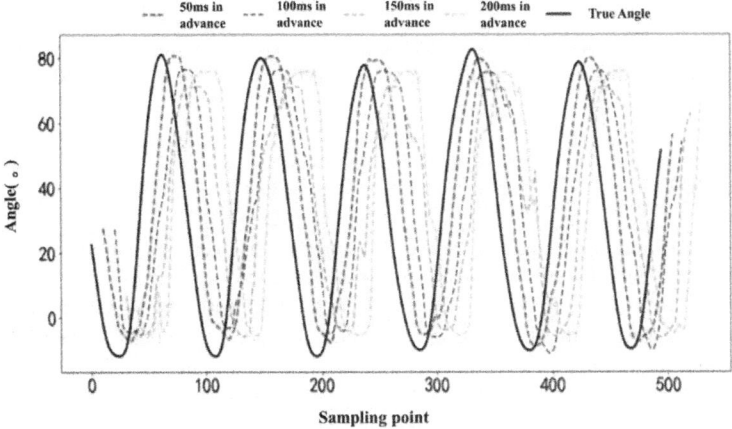

Fig. 4. Curves of true and predicted angles for different Δt in single Angle mode

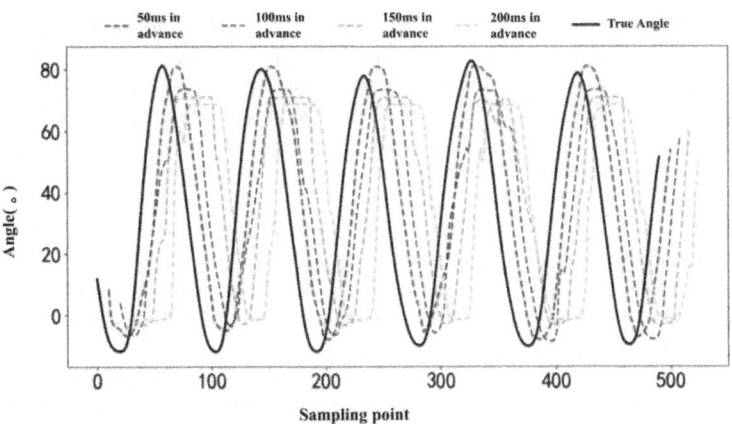

Fig. 5. Curves of true and predicted angles for different Δt of multi-angle mode

4 Conclusion

This study focused on the problem of continuous elbow joint angle estimation based on sEMG information and proposed a time series prediction framework based on the Mamba model. Experimental results demonstrated that the Mamba model achieved superior prediction accuracy and goodness of fit in both single-angle and cross-angle modes, outperforming the previously proposed LSTM and GRU models. These findings indicate that the Mamba model can more effectively capture the dynamic correlation features between sEMG and IMU signals during elbow joint movement and possesses significant advantages in multimodal motion intention recognition tasks. In addition, this study analyzed the effects of different window lengths and advance prediction times on prediction performance, providing important references for future applications in real-time prosthetic control.

Acknowledgment. This work was supported by the National Natural Science Foundation of China under Grants 62473361 and U22A2067, and is also supported by the Natural Science Foundation of Liaoning Province under Grants 2023-MSLH-117 and 2025JH6/101000028.

References

1. Chen, S., Chen, G., Zheng, X.: Survey and data of disabled population in China. J. Int. Reproduct. Health/Family Plann. **30**(3), 216–217 (2011)
2. Zheng, Y.: Research on the Design, Development and Application of High Bionic Performance Prostheses, Master's thesis. University of Chinese Academy of Sciences (Shenzhen Institute of Advanced Technology, Chinese Academy of Sciences), Shenzhen, China (2022)
3. Qin, P., Shi, X.: A novel method for lower limb joint angle estimation based on sEMG signal. IEEE Trans. Instrum. Meas. **70**, 1–9 (2021)
4. Wen, L., Xu, J., Li, D., et al.: Continuous estimation of upper limb joint angle from sEMG based on multiple decomposition feature and BiLSTM network. Biomed. Sign. Process. Contr. **80**, 104303 (2023)
5. Zhu, M., Guan, X., Li, Z., et al.: SEMG-based lower limb motion prediction using CNN-LSTM with improved PCA optimization algorithm. J. Bionic Eng. **20**(2), 612–627 (2023)
6. Li, C., He, H., Yin, S., et al.: Continuous angle prediction of lower limb knee joint based on sEMG. In: Recent Advances in Systems Science and Engineering, pp. 1–6 (2021)
7. Lu, Y., Wang, H., Zhou, B., et al.: Continuous and simultaneous estimation of lower limb multi-joint angles from sEMG signals based on stacked convolutional and LSTM models. Expert Syst. Appl. **203**, 117340 (2022)
8. Song, Q., Ma, X., Liu, Y.: Continuous online prediction of lower limb joint angles based on sEMG signals by deep learning approach. Comput. Biol. Med. **163**, 107124 (2023)
9. Teng, H., Zhang, G., Zhou, H., et al.: Estimation of elbow joint angle from EMG and IMU measurements based on graph convolution neural network. In: Mechatronics and Machine Vision in Practice, pp. 1–6 (2024)
10. Delgado, A.L., Da Rocha, A.F., León, A.S., et al.: Estimation of joint angle from sEMG and inertial measurements based on deep learning approach. In: IEEE Engineering in Medicine & Biology Society, pp. 700–703 (2021)
11. Lin, W., Su, C., An, Z., et al.: GRU-based prediction of muscle activation using IMU data: integrating VR for rehabilitation assessment. In: CYBER, pp. 599–604 (2024)
12. Gu, A., Dao, T.: Mamba: Linear-Time Sequence Modeling with Selective State Spaces. arXiv preprint arXiv:2312.00752 (2023)

A Bone Grinding Depth Prediction Method Based on Multimodal Sensing Information

Yiren Huang[1], Xu Liang[2(✉)], Guotao Li[3], Tingting Su[4], Hui Li[5], Kangkang Sun[6], Zihe Feng[7], Xinuo Zhang[7], and Yong Hai[7]

[1] Department of Mechanical and Electrical Engineering, North China University of Technology, Beijing 100144, China
[2] School of Automation and Intelligence, Beijing Jiaotong University, Beijing 100044, China
liangxu@bjtu.edu.cn
[3] State Key Laboratory of Multimodal Artificial Intelligence Systems, Institute of Automation, Chinese Academy of Sciences, Beijing 100190, China
[4] School of Information Science and Technology, Beijing University of Technology, Beijing 100124, China
[5] Beijing Lao Gan Bureau Fourth Comprehensive Service Support Center, Beijing 100083, China
[6] School of Astronautics, Harbin Institute of Technology, Harbin 150080, China
[7] Beijing Chaoyang Hospital, Capital Medical University, Beijing 100020, China

Abstract. Precision bone grinding constitutes a critical challenge for the safe operation of orthopedic surgical robots. A multi-modal sensing platform integrating force, displacement, acceleration, and laser displacement sensors was developed for comprehensive signal acquisition and depth prediction during bone grinding. A LSTM (long short-term memory) model was proposed to predict bone grinding depth. Experiments were conducted on cancellous bone samples with three densities (20, 30, and 40 pcf), and the collected experimental data were processed and mixed together for training, which showed that the mixed training strategy significantly improved the prediction accuracy and generalization ability of the LSTM model. Further testing on untrained 20 pcf cancellous bone samples showed that the model has strong robustness and high prediction accuracy. This study confirmed that the LSTM model can adapt to cancellous bone grinding scenarios with different characteristics, providing technical support for robotic applications in complex surgical scenarios.

Keywords: Multimodal sensing · Bone grinding · LSTM · Surgical robot

1 Introduction

Bone grinding is a common surgical procedure in orthopedics, and it is widely used in spinal deformity correction, joint replacement, and craniofacial surgery.

Traditional bone grinding procedures rely on manual operation of electric grinding tools, which may lead to surgeon fatigue during prolonged procedures, thereby affecting surgical precision and increasing patient risk [1]. With the development of robotics, robot-assisted bone grinding has gradually become a key research direction in orthopedic surgery due to its high precision, stability, and reduced fatigue [2]. However, current robotic systems still face challenges in terms of their sensory capabilities, particularly in maintaining stable contact force between the grinding tool and bone tissue [3].

To enhance the robot's sensory abilities and improve the recognition accuracy of grinding state, researchers have begun exploring various sensor technologies. Force sensors and accelerometers play a critical role in the surgical process by continuously monitoring grinding forces and vibration signals, optimizing feed speed and cutting depth. For example, Wang et al. [4] studied the force and torque signals during bone drilling using a spinal surgery robot system and analyzed the effects of drilling speed, feed speed, and drill diameter on force and torque. Al-Abdullah et al. [5] trained a neural network model using grinding force signals to identify bone types and adjust grinding parameters; Sun et al. [6] further expanded the recognition dimension of milling status by combining sound signals with the attention mechanism and CNN-LSTM network. Wang et al. [7] used Grey Wolf Optimizer-based BP neural networks to improve the accuracy of bone cutting forces; Chen et al. [8] proposed an accurate model for cortical bone grinding force, incorporating the stiffness characteristics of the robotic arm. Vibration signals also provide valuable information for bone grinding state monitoring. Dai et al. [9–11] and Xia et al. [12–14] successfully predicted bone tissue penetration states and enhanced robotic intelligence by analyzing vibration signals from accelerometers and laser sensors. In addition, Laser displacement sensors, as high-precision non-contact measurement tools, can accurately measure small displacements of bone tissue in real-time. Xia et al. [14] demonstrated that combining laser displacement sensors with accelerometer signals allowed for accurate recognition of key states during lamina grinding, validating its crucial role in surgical sensing. By integrating these sensor technologies, significant improvements in robotic perception and intelligence control in bone grinding procedures can be achieved.

In this paper, a bone grinding depth prediction method based on multimodal sensing information to solve the problem of limited perception ability of robots in bone grinding surgery. By collecting data from force sensors, accelerometers, displacement sensors and laser displacement sensors, a LSTM model is established to predict the target displacement in the grinding process, so as to enhance the robot's perception of the surgical environment and improve surgical accuracy and safety. The main contributions are as follows: Development of a multimodal sensing platform integrating force, displacement, acceleration, and laser displacement sensors for synchronized multidimensional data acquisition during grinding. Design of a LSTM model using force, displacement, and vibration signals to predict grinding depth. Generalization validation through experiments on bone specimens of varying densities (20, 30, and 40 pcf). The model was trained on multimodal data from these specimens and tested on an independent 20 pcf specimen, demonstrating its adaptability to bone tissue variability and supporting clinical application.

2 Experimental Setup and Signal Acquisition

2.1 Experimental Platform

The robot system used in this experiment is based on the UR5 robot arm, and a multimodal sensing platform is installed at the end to synchronously collect multi-dimensional signals during the grinding process and control the precise movement of the bone grinding tool. The main components of the platform are shown in Fig. 1.

Fig. 1. Entity diagram of the experimental device and details of the end-effector of the robotic arm.

The bone grinding drill (grinding head diameter 5mm) was used to carry out bone grinding experiments. Through the multi-modal collaborative sensing mechanism of integrated force sensor (real-time monitoring of tool-bone tissue interaction force to optimize control strategy), displacement sensor (precise detection of feed depth to ensure grinding accuracy) and accelerometer (analyzing vibration characteristics to realize bone status), it provided data support for full-parameter closed-loop control of the bone grinding process.

In addition, two springs are symmetrically installed on the sensing platform for shock absorption. To evaluate the spring stiffness, a force analysis was performed on the platform: the robotic arm pressed down 30 mm in the vertical direction, and the data of the force sensor and displacement sensor were recorded at the same time. As shown in Fig. 2, a curve was drawn with displacement as the horizontal coordinate and force as the vertical coordinate, and the least squares method was used for fitting to obtain the equation of the straight line: $y = 0.290x + 8.084$.

To further analyze the force, the total mass of the sensor, drill bit and other components was measured on an electronic scale. The weight is 783.1 g, and the gravity was about 7.674 N. During the experiment, the force F_m measured by the force sensor changes around 8 N, because the platform weighs about 7.65 N and there is elastic force F_b at this time. This shows that force sensor change can be expressed as $F_m = F_b + G$, so $F_b = F_m - 7.674N$ (Fig. 3).

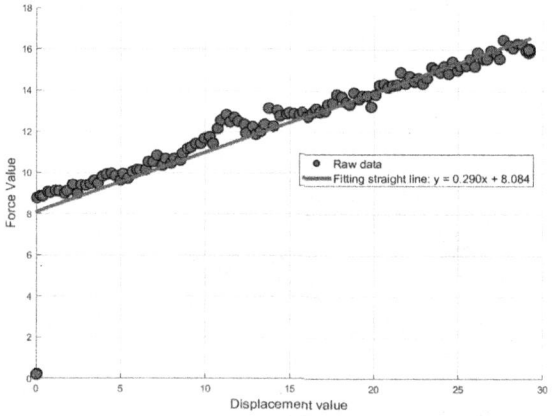

Fig. 2. Spring stiffness test.

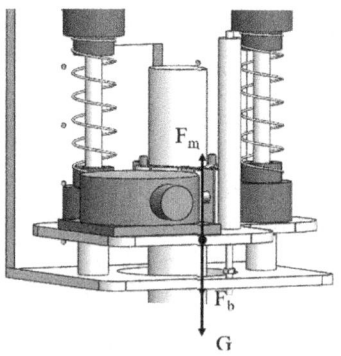

Fig. 3. Platform force analysis.

To provide high-precision ground truth data for grinding depth measurement, a laser displacement sensor was mounted on the vise platform holding the bone specimen, positioned above the robotic arm for real-time depth monitoring. These measurements served as the label column for the LSTM prediction model during network training and validation. All sensors were synchronized through a centralized data acquisition system to ensure temporal alignment of multimodal data streams. The UR-RTDE (Real-Time Data Exchange) library was employed for UR robotic arm control and data communication, with Python-based implementation enabling synchronized robotic path planning and real-time data collection.

2.2 Experimental Materials

The bone samples used in the experiment were from Sawbones, USA, including three types of bone slices with densities of 20, 30, and 40 pcf. Bone slices of different densities were used to simulate different bone conditions to evaluate the generalization ability of the proposed method. The size of the bone slices was kept consistent and fixed on the vise platform to ensure the stability of the experimental environment.

2.3 Grinding Status and Signal Acquisition System

During the experiment, the UR5 robotic arm moved 2 mm vertically downward along the Z-axis of its end effector to simulate bone grinding operations. The feed rate and acceleration were set to $0.0002\,\mathrm{m/s}$ and $0.0005\,\mathrm{m/s^2}$, respectively. The data acquisition system utilized an STM32 microcontroller-based ADC module to synchronously sample all four sensor channels at 1000 Hz. The strictly time-aligned multimodal data was transmitted to the host computer via a serial interface and ultimately stored in a database for subsequent processing and model training.

3 Experimental Process and Analysis

3.1 Experimental Process

Before the experiment begins, place the bone sample on the vise platform and secure it. Adjust the initial position of the UR5 robotic arm so that the bone-grinding drill bit installed at its end is positioned directly above the bone sample. After confirming that all sensors are functioning properly, sequentially start the bone-grinding drill bit and the data acquisition system. Then, execute the robotic arm control program to move it downward along the Z-axis at a constant speed for 2 mm. Once the reading from the laser displacement sensor stabilizes, the robotic arm stops pressing downward, and the collected data is saved as a CSV file. The experiment is conducted on bone samples with three different densities: 20 pcf, 30 pcf, and 40 pcf. One set of experiments is performed for each bone density, resulting in a total of three sets of experiments.

3.2 Data Analysis and Processing

Each group of data collects data from four sensors: force sensor, displacement sensor, accelerometer, laser displacement sensor. Since the data is transmitted to the host computer through the microcontroller at a high baud rate of 3000000, high noise values will appear during the high-speed transmission process. Therefore, before data processing, these high noise points need to be removed and corrected to improve the accuracy of subsequent analysis. First, MATLAB was used for data preprocessing. For highly noisy values, an interpolation algorithm was applied to correct the anomalies—specifically, replacing the outlier data points with values calculated from the two adjacent data points before and after the anomaly, thereby smoothing the data. To further enhance data quality, three filtering methods were employed: moving average filtering, low-pass filtering, and smooth filtering. The effects of these methods were compared. The results showed that smooth filtering not only effectively removed noise but also better preserved the overall trend of the signal, outperforming the other two methods. Therefore, after eliminating high-noise points, all experimental data were ultimately processed using smooth filtering and saved as new data files.

3.3 LSTM Network Architecture

The LSTM network constructed in this study is designed as a sequence-to-value regression model, specifically tailored to process multi-feature time series data and output a single continuous target value: grinding depth. Unlike Sun et al.'s [6] CNN-LSTM classification framework used in offline bone milling analysis, our model adopts a linear activation function in the output layer to enable continuous depth prediction. The overall architecture consists of an input layer, two stacked LSTM layers, a fully connected (dense) layer, and an output layer. The input layer receives time-series data composed of three features: force, displacement, and acceleration signals. At each time step, the input dimensionality is 3. These sequences are first processed through two LSTM layers, which extract deep temporal features. The output from the LSTM layers is then passed through a fully connected layer that maps the extracted features to an intermediate representation, followed by an output layer that produces the final prediction.

The two LSTM layers serve as the core components of the network, with each layer configured with 128 hidden units. The first LSTM layer takes in the raw input sequences and models the temporal dependencies across time steps through its internal gating mechanisms (i.e., forget gate, input gate, and output gate). The second LSTM layer further processes the output of the first LSTM layer to capture more complex and long-term dependencies within the sequence. This stacked architecture enhances the model's capacity to learn intricate temporal patterns present in the multimodal signals. Following the LSTM layers, a fully connected layer is used, with an input dimension equal to the number of hidden units in the preceding LSTM layer (128), and an output dimension of 64. This layer performs a linear transformation to further refine the learned features. Finally, the output layer maps this 64-dimensional representation to a single scalar value, representing the predicted laser displacement measurement. During the forward pass, the input sequence is processed through both LSTM layers. Each LSTM layer computes the hidden and cell states for every time step, effectively accumulating and filtering temporal information. The hidden state from the last time step of the second LSTM layer is extracted and fed into the fully connected layer. After the linear transformation, the final output is generated, representing the predicted value corresponding to the milling depth as measured by the laser displacement sensor (Table 1 and Fig. 4).

Table 1. Hyperparameter values of the training process

Parameter	Value
Learning rate	0.001
Optimizer	Adam
Batch size	32
Epochs	200
Loss function	MSE
Hidden units	128
FC neurons	64

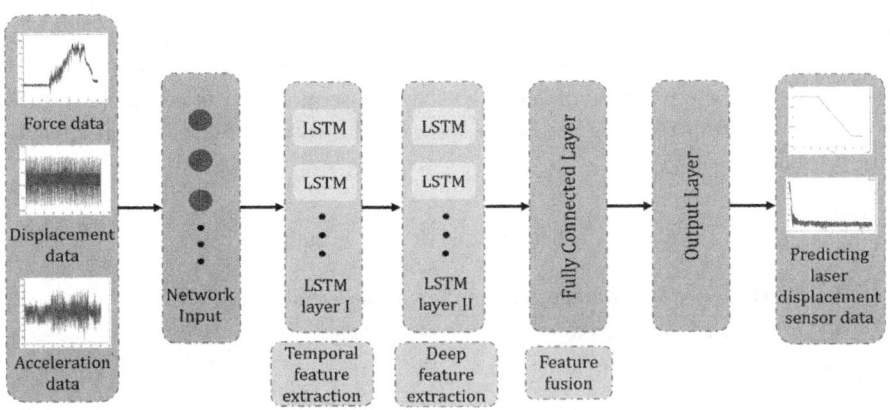

Fig. 4. Network structure diagram.

To comprehensively evaluate the prediction performance of the LSTM model, this study employs three evaluation metrics: Mean Squared Error (MSE), Root Mean Squared Error (RMSE), and the Coefficient of Determination (R^2). The formulas for these metrics are defined as follows:

$$MSE = \frac{1}{n}\sum_{i=1}^{n}(y_i - \hat{y}_i)^2 \qquad (1)$$

$$RMSE = \sqrt{\frac{1}{n}\sum_{i=1}^{n}(y_i - \hat{y}_i)^2} \qquad (2)$$

$$R^2 = 1 - \frac{\sum_{i=1}^{n}(y_i - \hat{y}_i)^2}{\sum_{i=1}^{n}(y_i - \overline{y}_i)^2} \qquad (3)$$

where n denotes the number of samples, y_i represents the ground truth, $\hat{y}_i$ denotes the predicted value, and $\overline{y}_i$ is the mean of all ground truth values.

The Adam optimizer was adopted for training, with a learning rate 1.0×10^{-3} to ensure stable convergence of the model. During training, the network parameters are iteratively updated over multiple epochs on the dataset to minimize the loss function and improve the model's prediction accuracy.

4 Experimental Results

In this experiment, bone grinding was performed on bone samples with three different densities: 20 pcf, 30 pcf, and 40 pcf. Multimodal sensor data were collected during the grinding process. The data obtained from these three bone densities were uniformly preprocessed and integrated as the training dataset, which was then input into the LSTM network. Force, displacement, and vibration signals were used as inputs to predict the grinding depth. The data measured at three different bone densities are shown in Table 2. The average grinding force increases with the increase of bone density, while the acceleration value decreases with the increase of bone density. Subsequently, the complete dataset was divided into a training set and a test set at a ratio of 8:2. The error results are presented in Fig. 5.

Table 2. Different bone density grinding values

Bone density	Average grinding force	Average acceleration value
20 pcf	3.51 N	2.08 g
30 pcf	4.13 N	2.01 g
40 pcf	4.83 N	1.96 g

To further verify the generalization capability of the trained model, a new set of grinding data was collected from a 20 pcf bone sample that was not involved in the training phase. The prediction results demonstrated small errors and high goodness of fit on the new data, indicating strong predictive performance and generalization ability of the model. The results are shown in Fig. 6 (Table 3 and Fig. 7).

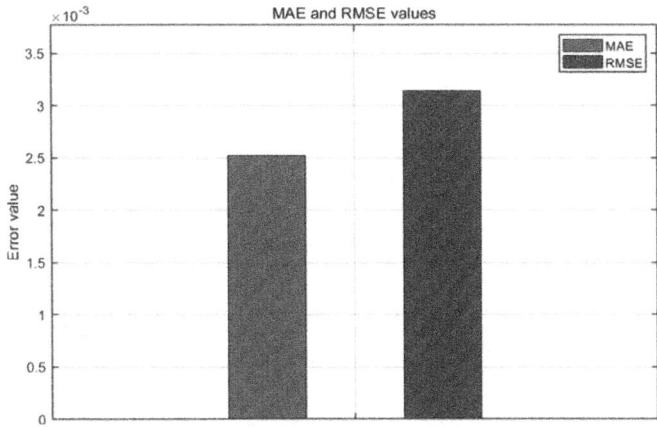

Fig. 5. Error results of the LSTM model on the test set.

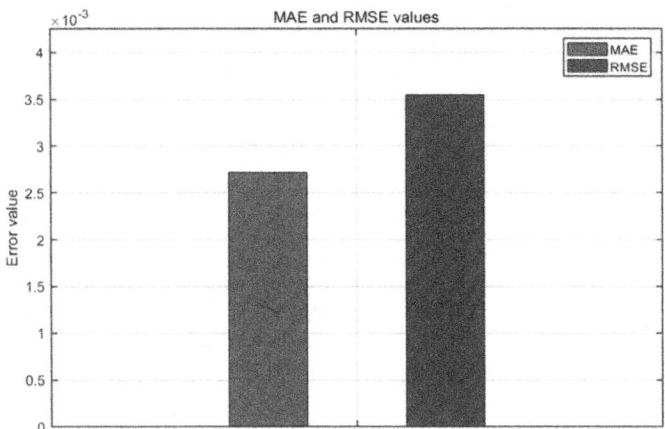

Fig. 6. Inference error results of the model on newly measured 20 pcf bone data.

Table 3. R^2 values of the model on the test set and newly measured 20 pcf samples

Data Set	R^2
Test set	0.997123
20 pcf new sample	0.985062

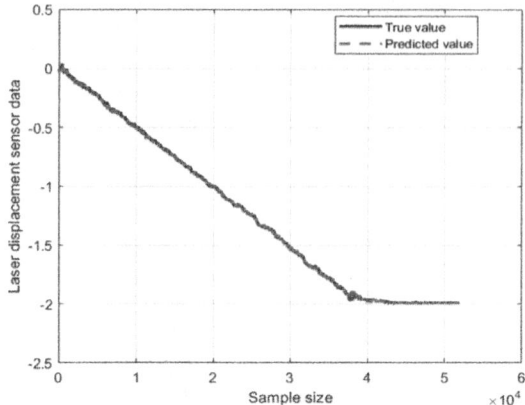

Fig. 7. Comparison between ground truth and predicted values on newly measured 20 pcf samples.

5 Conclusions

This study designed a multimodal sensing platform incorporating force sensors, displacement sensors, accelerometers, and laser displacement sensors to perform bone grinding experiments on cancellous bones with three density. The experimental data from different bone densities were combined for training the LSTM model, while the untrained bone grinding data from 20 pcf specimens was subsequently input for validation. Results indicate that this approach significantly enhances the model's prediction accuracy and generalization performance. The diversity of the dataset enhances the model's ability to learn characteristics across different bone qualities, enabling better adaptation to cancellous-bone structures. However, this study is limited to cancellous bone samples with only three density levels and does not fully validate the model's applicability across a broader range of bone densities. In particular, the model has not yet been tested on cortical bone, which has significantly different structural and mechanical properties. Future studies may expand the types and density ranges of bone samples to further explore the application potential and generalization performance of the mixed training model under complex clinical conditions. In addition, future work will involve collecting and modeling the bone grinding trajectories performed by surgeons using the UR5 robotic arm, aiming to incorporate trajectory parameters (such as velocity profile and movement direction) into the model and then combine the sensor data mentioned in this paper with the surgeon-performed trajectories to improve its predictive accuracy and adaptability.

Acknowledgments. This work is sponsored in part by the Beijing Natural Science Foundation under Grants L222053, L232021, L242101, L241058, L256048, and L222058, in part by the National Natural Science Foundation of China under Grants 62473365, U22A2056, 62373013, 62473036, and 62203144, in part by the Chinese Institutes for Medical Research, Beijing under Grant CX23YZ09, in part by the Heilongjiang Province Science Foundation for Joint Guidance under Grant LH2022F022, in part by the Beijing Nova Program under Grant 20250484860, in part by the R&D Program of Beijing Municipal Education Commission under Grant KM202210009010, and in part by the Talent Fund of Beijing Jiaotong University under Grant KAIXKRC24003532.

References

1. Huang, J., Li, Y., Huang, L.: Spine surgical robotics: review of the current application and disadvantages for future perspectives. J. Robot. Surg. **14**, 1256–1267 (2020)
2. Innocenti, B., Bori, E.: Robotics in orthopaedic surgery: why, what and how? Arch. Orthop. Trauma Surg. **141**(12), 2035–2042 (2021). https://doi.org/10.1007/s00402-021-04046-0
3. Davies, B., et al.: Active-constraint robotics for surgery. Proc. IEEE **94**(9), 1696–1704 (2006)
4. Wang, W., et al.: Experimental analysis of drilling process in cortical bone. Med. Eng. Phys. **36**(3), 261–266 (2014)
5. Al-Abdullah, K.I., et al.: A model-based bone milling state identification method via force sensing for a robotic surgical system. Int. J. Med. Robot. Comput. Assist. Surg. **15**(3), e1985 (2019)
6. Sun, J., et al.: Attention-based CNN-LSTM for enhanced perception of bone milling states in surgical robots. IEEE Trans. Instrum. Meas. **73**, 1–9 (2024)
7. Wang, L., et al.: Indirect measurement method of ultrasonic bone cutting force based on anti-node vibration displacement. J. Sound Vib. **552**, 117637 (2023)
8. Chen, Q.-S., Dai, L., Liu, Yu., Shi, Q.-X.: A cortical bone milling force model based on orthogonal cutting distribution method. Adv. Manuf. **8**(2), 204–215 (2020). https://doi.org/10.1007/s40436-020-00300-7
9. Dai, Y., Xue, Y., Zhang, J.: Human-inspired haptic perception and control in robot-assisted milling surgery. IEEE Trans. Haptics **14**(2), 359–370 (2021)
10. Dai, Y., Xue, Y., Zhang, J.: Milling state identification based on vibration sense of a robotic surgical system. IEEE Trans. Ind. Electron. **63**(10), 6184–6193 (2016)
11. Dai, Y., et al.: Motion control of milling robot based on vibration feedback. J. Tianjin Univ. (Sci. Technol.) **53**(10), 1093–1100 (2020)
12. Xia, G., et al.: Vertebral lamina state estimation in robotic bone milling process via vibration signals fusion. IEEE Trans. Instrum. Meas. **71**, 1–11 (2022)
13. Xia, G., et al.: Vibration-based cutting depth control and angle adjustment of robotic curved bone milling. IEEE Trans. Instrum. Meas. **71**, 1–10 (2022)
14. Xia, G., et al.: Tactile perception based depth and angle control during robot-assisted bent bone grinding. IEEE Trans. Ind. Inform. **20**(1), 50–61 (2024)

Research on Parameter Adaptive Electrical Stimulation System Based on WBAN

Jingyu Wu, Tairen Sun, and Jiantao Yang(✉)

University of Shanghai for Science and Technology, Shanghai 200093, China
jty@usst.edu.cn

Abstract. FES has achieved significant efficacy in the rehabilitation of patients with motor dysfunction. However, existing closed-loop electrical stimulators suffer from the drawbacks of large size and difficulty in accurately assessing fatigue level. In this study, a wearable electrical stimulator system with adaptive adjustment of parameters was proposed to address this drawback. Additionally, muscle fatigue was induced via 60% MVC, and sEMG signals were acquired during this process. MF, MPF, and SampEn were extracted to validate their relationships with muscle fatigue. A fatigue detection algorithm based on I-value was introduced to dynamically adjust the stimulation parameters in real time to avoid fatigue and injury caused by overstimulation. In addition, the system's effectiveness in real-world scenarios was validated based on different I_{at}. The WBAN heterogeneous architecture technology adopted in this paper, together with the lightweight wearable design, greatly reduces the weight of the device. The weight of the signal acquisition device is only 3g, and the electrical stimulation device is only 3.2g. All the functions of the fabricated device are basically in accordance with the expectations.

Keywords: Electrical Stimulation · sEMG · Wearable · WBAN

1 Introduction

FES has gained wide application in motor function remodeling and neuroprosthetic control [1, 2], which not only improves muscle activity but also accelerates neurological recovery [3]. However, existing systems face a dual dilemma in clinical translation: hardware-wise, traditional closed-loop devices rely on wired sensors with discrete controllers, and the weight of the whole machine generally exceeds 200g [4, 5], and heavier wearable rehabilitation devices can lead to skin pressure ulcers, which severely restricts the feasibility of long term wearability [6]; algorithmically, the choice of the stimulation parameter has a significant impact on the characteristics of muscle activation [7].

Surface electromyography (sEMG), as a commonly used means of muscle status assessment, can reflect changes in synchronization of motor unit discharges as well as reduction in muscle fiber conduction velocity by monitoring changes in Median Frequency (MF) and Root Mean Square (RMS) [8]. The flexible sEMG patch reported by Lee et al. [9] weighs only 2.1 g, but its sampling rate is limited to less than 500 Hz, which makes it difficult to capture high-frequency motor unit action potentials, and the sEMG in this study has a sampling rate of 1 kHz. The heterogeneous WBAN architecture proposed by Movassaghi et al. [10] transfers the computational load to the edge gateway through distributed signal processing. This breakthrough shows the direction for lightweight design of multimodal sensing systems.

To address the above issues, this study proposes a wearable electrical stimulation system based on sEMG adaptive regulation, which induces muscle fatigue by isometric static contraction (60% MVC), acquires sEMG (1000 Hz), extracts RMS, MF, and MPF to control the electrical stimulation parameters, and adopts the WBAN architecture to integrate the sEMG acquisition module, and the electrical stimulation terminals into a flexible substrate. The lightweight design makes long-term wear possible.

2 Hardware System Design

The hardware system's core functions include acquiring human sEMG signals and delivering electrical stimulation to target muscles. As illustrated in Fig. 1, the system based on WBAN Fig. 1(a) comprises a sEMG signal collector, electrical stimulator, wireless communication module, and data processing center. Figure 1(b) depicts the operational workflow: sEMG signals from the target muscle are sequentially processed through a signal conditioning circuit, MCU, and Bluetooth module before reaching the data processing center. Post-calculation of muscle-state-specific stimulation parameters, control commands are transmitted via Bluetooth to the ENS-001 chip, which delivers electrical stimulation to muscles through output electrodes.

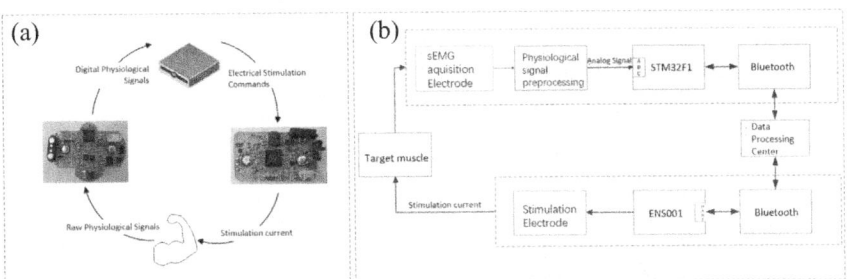

Fig. 1. System structure based on WBAN (a) Overall architecture, (b) Overall module

2.1 Design of the Electrical Stimulator

The electrical stimulation uses the ENS-001 chip as the MCU, which integrates a Boost circuit and a 32-bit ARM Cortex-M0 CPU core to control the electrical stimulation by manipulating the internal registers. This design will use Bluetooth – UART to receive control commands from the data processing center. The electrical stimulation parameters are shown in Table 1. The physical object is shown in Fig. 2.

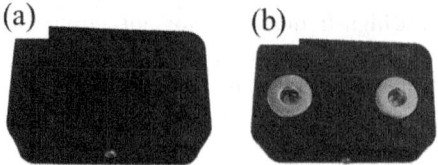

Fig. 2. Electrical stimulator, (a) Front View of the Signal Acquisition Equipment (b) Rear View.

Table 1. Electrical stimulator parameters

Parameter type	Parameter range(Unit)	
Stimulation parameters	Output current	0–55 (mA)
	Pulse width	10–1000 (uS)
	Frequency	1–1000 (Hz)
	Waveform	Square Wave
Size	Area	13.53 (cm^2)
	Weight	3.2 (g)

2.2 Design of sEMG Signal Collector

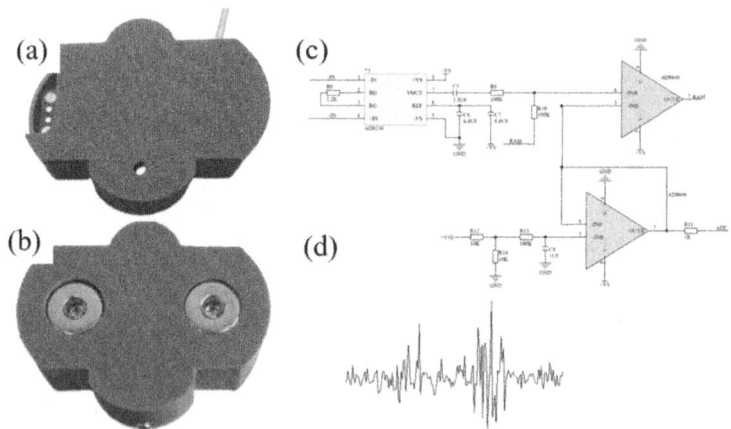

Fig. 3. (a) Front View of the Signal Acquisition Equipment (b) Rear View (c) Circuit diagram (d) surface Electromyograpy

The voltage range of sEMG signals typically falls within the range of 0–6000 uV, whereas a microcontroller ADC can only capture signals up to 3.3 V with a resolution of 12 bits. Thus, direct interfacing of the EMG signals with the microcontroller chip is insufficient for signal acquisition. To address this, an amplification circuit is employed, as shown in Fig. 3(c). The sEMG signal is introduced as a differential input along with a reference signal, where the differential signals are obtained by attaching electrodes to the muscles, while the reference signal is attached to the bone.

The differential signals first pass through the AD8636 differential amplifier for amplification, followed by a cascaded combination of pre-differential and post-amplification stages, implemented using the AD8646 chip. The pre-differential amplification stage enables differential amplification in conjunction with the reference amplifier (RAM) signal. Subsequently, a 100-fold operational amplification is applied. The physical diagram of the equipment is shown in Fig. 3(a)(b), and the acquired sEMG waveform is shown in Fig. 3(d). The sEMG signal parameters collected by the wearable device with sEMG are shown in Table 2.

Table 2. sEMG signal collector parameters

Parameter type		Parameter range(Unit)
Sample rate	sEMG	1000 (Hz)
Size	Area	13.84 (cm^2)
	Weight	3.0 (g)

2.3 Lightweight Design for Wearable

To minimize the weight, the circuit boards are manufactured using the FPC process. The electrodes of the stimulation and EMG devices are reinforced with PI material to ensure that the FPC board does not interfere with the signal and to improve bonding stability. The electrodes are soldered directly to the PCB, eliminating the need for straps when using the device. The Structure diagram is shown in Fig. 4.

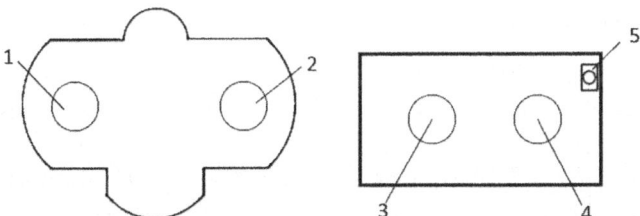

Fig. 4. Structure diagram 1, 2 – Electromyography (EMG) electrode patches; 3, 4 – Stimulation electrodes; 5 – Emergency stop switch

3 Electrical Stimulation Control Algorithm

3.1 Feature Extraction

In this paper, RMS are selected as time-domain features, and the MF and MPF are selected as frequency-domain features for the assessment of muscle functional status. RMS increased in the early stage of fatigue due to the enhanced synchronized recruitment of motor units, and decreased in the late stage with the attenuation of neural drive and muscle metabolic disorders. The formula is as follows:

$$RMS = \sqrt{\frac{1}{N}\sum_{i=1}^{N} x_i^2} \tag{1}$$

In order to visualize the distribution and variation of the sEMG in each frequency band, the sEMG is usually fast Fourier transformed to obtain the power spectrum of the sEMG. The commonly used features in the power spectrum are median frequency (MF) and mean power frequency (MPF). Compared with the time-domain features, the sEMG frequency-domain feature parameters do not change significantly with time, and thus have good noise immunity. MPF and MF are calculated as shown in (2) and (3), respectively:

$$MPF = \frac{\int_0^\infty f P(f) df}{\int_0^\infty P(f) df} \tag{2}$$

$$\int_0^{MF} P(f) df = \int_{MF}^\infty P(f) df = \frac{1}{2}\int_0^\infty P(f) df \tag{3}$$

where $P(f)$ is the power spectral density function of the signal.

3.2 Closed-Loop Control Algorithm

Introducing the nonlinear characteristic parameter I to quantify the muscle fatigue state:

$$I = \frac{u_{SampEn}}{u_{MPF}} \tag{4}$$

I is defined as the ratio of the sample entropy(u_{SampEn}) to the Mean Power Frequency (u_{MPF}). Based on I, the amplitude $A(k+1)$ and pulse width $W(k+1)$ during the stimulation cycle were dynamically adjusted using a segmented function:

$$A(k+1) = \begin{cases} A_{mit} + \frac{RMS(k)-RMS_r}{RMS_m-RMS_r} \cdot (A_{max}-A_{mit}) \cdot sign\left(\frac{I(0)}{I(k)}-b\right) & RMS(k) \in (RMS_r, RMS_m] \\ A_{min} \cdot sign\left(\frac{I(0)}{I(k)}-b\right) & RMS(k) \in (-\infty, RMS_r] \\ A_{max} \cdot sign\left(\frac{I(0)}{I(k)}-b\right) & RMS(k) \in (RMS_m, +\infty) \end{cases} \tag{5}$$

$$W(k+1) = \begin{cases} W_{mit} + \frac{RMS(k)-RMS_r}{RMS_m-RMS_r} \cdot (W_{max}-W_{mit}) \cdot sign\left(\frac{I(0)}{I(k)}-b\right) & RMS(k) \in (RMS_r, RMS_m] \\ W_{min} \cdot sign\left(\frac{I(0)}{I(k)}-b\right) & RMS(k) \in (-\infty, RMS_r] \\ W_{max} \cdot sign\left(\frac{I(0)}{I(k)}-b\right) & RMS(k) \in (RMS_m, +\infty) \end{cases} \tag{6}$$

where RMS(k) is the RMS value in the kth cycle, $I(k)$ is the real-time characteristic parameter, $I(0)$ is the initial value, b is the fatigue threshold, and sign(.) is the sign function. The algorithm integrates the baseline values with real-time feedback to achieve personalized self-activation of electrical stimulation parameters, taking into account the safety and efficacy of treatment. The sinusoidal function is corrected to optimize the neuromuscular coupling; if the RMS_m or RMS_r is exceeded or decreased, the parameters are fixed to the safety boundaries (A_{max}/A_{min}, W_{max}/W_{min}) to avoid overstimulation or ineffective contraction.

## 4 Experiment

4.1 Electrical Stimulation Performance Test

To verify the function of the system setup parameters: as this design adopts constant-current electrical stimulation, resistors with different resistance values are chosen to simulate the human load in order to observe the constancy of the output current. After actual testing and data acquisition, the results are shown in Fig. 5:

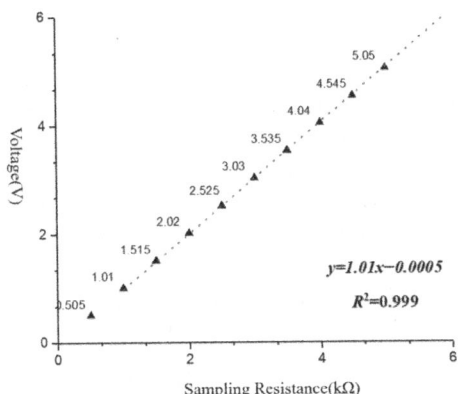

Fig. 5. Constant flow test result

The data points in the graph are closely fitted to the straight line $y = 1.01x - 0.0005$, indicating a stable correspondence between the sampling resistor voltage value and resistance value under the constant-current electrical stimulation design.

4.2 Muscle Fatigue Induction Test

In this study, constant force fatigue tests were performed with 60% MVC (Maximum Voluntary Contraction) continuous force, and sEMG were collected simultaneously. MF, MPF SampEn and I were extracted. The sliding window parameters were set to a window length of 400 points (0.4 s), a step size of 200 points (0.2 s), and an overlap rate of 50%. Subject experiments lasted 20s and corresponded to 100 windows. The correspondences between the MF, MPF, SampEn, I and the number of windows are shown in Fig. 6.

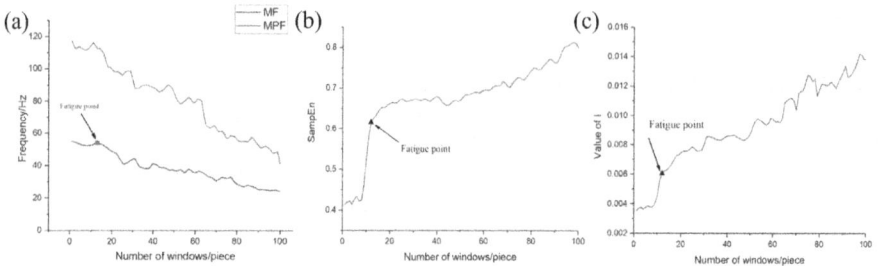

Fig. 6. Fatigue test results for MF, MPF, SampEn and I (a) Trends in MF and MPF, (b) Trend in SampEn, (c) Trend in I

As shown in Fig. 6(a), within the first 12 windows of the fatigue process, the trends of MPF and MF remain stable. As fatigue deepens, both parameters decrease to varying degrees from the 12th window onward, primarily attributed to the increase in low-frequency components following muscle fatigue. The trend of SampEn is presented in Fig. 6(b): SampEn remains within the range of 0.0035 to 0.004, indicating low and stable signal complexity. As the degree of fatigue intensifies and the muscle enters a fatigued state, SampEn gradually rises with increased fluctuations. The variation of I, as shown in Fig. 6(c), exhibits a trend similar to that of SampEn.

The synergistic verification of multi-feature effectiveness in sEMG-based fatigue monitoring provides a theoretical foundation for the design of subsequent myoelectric feedback-controlled electrical stimulation systems.

4.3 Feedback-Controlled Electrical Stimulation Test

In this study, sEMG is collected in arm muscle groups by silver chloride electrodes. Electrical stimulation parameters (pulse width and amplitude) are monitored simultaneously. Muscle exertions of different degrees cause changes in the RMS, The correspondence between electrical stimulation parameters and RMS is shown in Fig. 7.

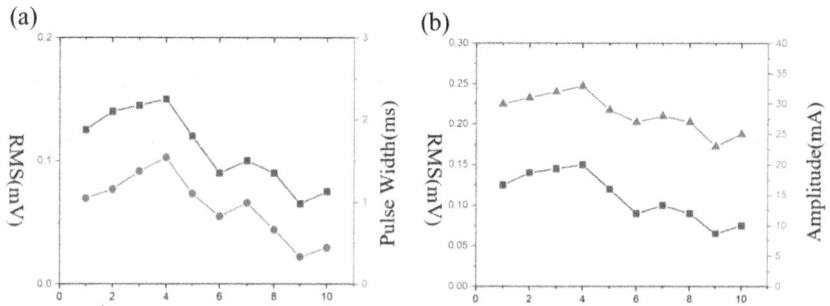

Fig. 7. Electrical Stimulation Control Test Results (a) Pulse Width, (b) Amplitude

System's electrical stimulation modulation performance during muscle fatigue experimentally verified.

4.4 Human Experiments on System Performance

To validate the performance of the I-value-based electrical stimulation fatigue monitoring system in real-world scenarios.9 subjects aged 22–35 years were selected, all of whom had no history of neuromuscular diseases and no adverse reactions to electrical stimulation. They were divided into 3 groups (3 subjects in each group) according to the fatigue threshold I_{at} set by doctors:

Group A: $I_{at} = 35\%$
Group B: $I_{at} = 40\%$
Group C: $I_{at} = 45\%$

In the experiment, the electrical stimulation fatigue monitoring system equipped with surface electrodes was applied to the forearm muscle groups, and the placement of the device and electrodes is shown in Fig. 8.

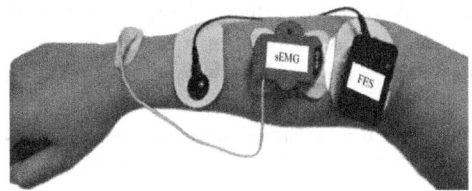

Fig. 8. The placement of the device and electrodes.

For the procedure, first, the baseline value of the resting I-value before stimulation, $I_{norm}(0)$, was collected. Then, electrical stimulation was applied, and Inorm (N) under the fatigue state was monitored in real time. The ratio $I_{norm}(N)/I_{norm}(0)$ was calculated, and the system automatically terminated the stimulation when this ratio was lower than the corresponding fatigue threshold I_{at} (35% for Group A, 40% for Group B, and 45% for Group C). The experimental data of the subjects are shown in Table 3.

Table 3. Experimental data of subjects

Volunteer	Fatigue threshold $I_{at}(\%)$	$I_{norm}(0)$	$I_{norm}(N)$	$I_{norm}(N)/I_{norm}(0)$
A1	35	1.02	0.34	0.33
A2	35	0.98	0.33	0.34
A3	35	1.05	0.35	0.33
B1	40	0.95	0.37	0.39
B2	40	1.01	0.40	0.40
B3	40	1.03	0.41	0.40
C1	45	0.97	0.43	0.44
C2	45	1.04	0.46	0.44
C3	45	0.99	0.44	0.44

The results showed that the ratios in Group A ranged from 0.33 to 0.34, those in Group B from 0.39 to 0.40, and that in Group C was 0.44, all of which were lower than the corresponding thresholds. All experimental groups triggered the automatic termination function, and the I-value at termination met the preset safety requirements. These findings indicate that the I-value-based monitoring algorithm can accurately identify the state of muscle fatigue, timely terminate electrical stimulation when the I-value drops below the threshold, and thus provide effective guarantee for the safety of treatment.

5 Conclusion

This paper presents the design of an adaptive wearable electrical stimulation system, aiming to introduce a novel and lightweight solution for electrical stimulation therapy in patients with motor dysfunction. The patient's own sEMG signal during stimulation is used to adaptively control the output parameters of the subsequent electrical stimulation cycles, making the electrical stimulation therapy more active. When fatigue is detected, the electrical stimulation can be stopped in time to avoid deep fatigue or muscle damage.

Acknowledgements. This work was supported in part by the National Natural Science Foundation of China (Grant No. 62573296). The authors would like to express their gratitude for this financial support.

References

1. Ring, H., Rosenthal, N.: Controlled study of neuroprosthetic functional electrical stimulation in subacute post-stroke rehabilitation. J. Rehabil. Med. **37**(1), 32–38 (2005)
2. Thrasher, T.A., Zivanovic, V., McIlroy, W., et al.: Rehabilitation of reaching and grasping function in severe hemiplegia using functional electrical stimulation therapy. Neurorehabil. Neural Repair **22**(6), 706–714 (2008)
3. Rikhof, C.J.H., Leerskov, K.S., Prange-Lasonder, G.B., et al.: Combining robotics and functional electrical stimulation for assist-as-needed support of leg movements in stroke patients: a feasibility study. Med. Eng. Phys. **130**, 104216 (2024)
4. Souza, D.C.D., Gaiotto, M.D.C., Nogueira Neto, G.N., et al.: Power amplifier circuits for functional electrical stimulation systems. Res. Biomed. Eng. **33**(2), 144–155 (2017)
5. Dutta, A., Ahmed, N.U.: OpenFES: development of an open-source EMG-triggered functional electrical stimulation controller for physical therapy. J. Med. Devices **4**(2), 025001 (2010)
6. Stuart, S., et al.: Critical design considerations for longer-term wear and comfort of on-body medical devices. Bioengineering **11**(11), 1058 (2024)
7. Gonnelli, F., et al.: Effects of NMES pulse width and intensity on muscle mechanical output and oxygen extraction in able-bodied and paraplegic individuals. Europ. J. Appl. Physiol. **121**(6), 1653–1664 (2021)
8. Guo-Xiang, W., He-Ping, H.: Varying characteristics of myoelectric discharge and muscle oxygen content during constant speed movement. J. Phys. Educ. (2005)
9. Lee, K.J., et al.: A wireless ECoG recording system to detect brain responses to tactile stimulation. IEEE Sens. J. **23**(12), 13692–13701 (2023)
10. Movassaghi, S., Abolhasan, M., Lipman, J., et al.: Wireless body area networks: a survey. IEEE Commun. Surv. Tutorials **16**(3), 1658–1686 (2014)

MBGADNet: Multi-Branch Generative Adversarial Denoising Network with Semantic Preservation for EEG Artifact Removal

Da Liao, Fengjun Mu, Kecheng Shi, Jun Wang, Zhe Li, Rui Huang[✉], Zhinan Peng, and Hong Cheng

School of Automation Engineering, University of Electronic Science and Technology of China, Chengdu, China
ruihuang@uestc.edu.cn

Abstract. Brain–computer interfaces (BCIs) have significant applications in neuroscience and clinical rehabilitation. However, due to the inherently low signal-to-noise ratio (SNR) of electroencephalogram (EEG) signals, they are highly susceptible to motion artifacts such as electrooculogram (EOG) and electromyogram (EMG), which severely compromises their reliability in real-world scenarios. Most existing denoising methods process the entire EEG recording directly, ignoring the coexistence of clean and contaminated segments within raw data. This often results in the unintended removal of valid neural information and degrades downstream decoding performance. Although some recent approaches attempt to segment clean and noisy regions, they still struggle with handling transition boundaries effectively. This paper proposes a Multi-Branch Generative Adversarial Denoising Network (MBGADNet) based on the WGAN-GP framework. The model comprises three core modules: (1) an improved multi-branch Inception encoder that extracts multi-scale frequency features to enhance the discrimination between EEG and artifact components; (2) a generator equipped with multihead self-attention (MHSA) to model long-range dependencies within clean EEG segments and reconstruct artifact-free signals; and (3) a dual-branch discriminator that performs both adversarial classification and artifact region segmentation, guiding the generator to achieve artifact suppression while preserving semantic integrity. Experiments were conducted on a semi-synthetic EEG dataset with varying SNR levels. Results show that MBGADNet effectively retains neural components even under low-SNR conditions and achieves superior performance over state-of-the-art methods in terms of RRMSE (0.132 vs 0.146) and SNR (11.559 dB vs 8.327 dB), demonstrating its robustness and practical potential.

Keywords: Brain–Computer Interface · Motion Artifact · EEG Denoising Method · Generative Adversarial Network

---

D. Liao and F. Mu—These authors contributed equally to this work.

1 Introduction

With the rapid development of neuroscience and artificial intelligence technologies, brain-computer interface (BCI), as an important technology connecting the brain with external devices, has shown broad application prospects in the field of medical rehabilitation [1–5]. By decoding electroencephalogram (EEG) signals, BCI systems can achieve accurate recognition of an individual's motor intention, thereby assisting stroke and spinal cord injury patients in restoring limb function. Therefore, motor intention recognition, as the core of BCI technology, directly determines the practicality and reliability of the system.

However, EEG signals themselves have an extremely low signal-to-noise ratio and are highly susceptible to interference from artifacts such as electrooculogram (EOG) and electromyogram (EMG) caused by eye and muscle movements [6]. These artifacts overlap significantly with EEG signals in frequency bands, making traditional denoising methods ineffective in separating them, which leads to a significant decrease in signal decoding accuracy. This issue severely restricts the clinical promotion of BCI technology. Therefore, how to accurately identify and remove artifacts while preserving valid neural information has become a key challenge in current EEG signal processing.

Common artifacts include EOG artifacts caused by blinking and eye movement, as well as EMG artifacts produced by facial and neck muscle activities. Current noise reduction research methods can be mainly divided into traditional approaches and deep learning-based methods. Traditional artifact removal techniques include regression (Autoregressive Model, AR) [7], blind source separation (Blind Source Separation, BSS), wavelet transform (Wavelet Transform, WT), and hybrid methods. Regression, one of the earlier applied methods, reconstructs artifact signals through a regression model and then eliminates their impact on EEG signals. Blind source separation, especially independent component analysis [8] (Independent Component Analysis, ICA), is the most commonly used method for artifact removal. It denoises by decomposing contaminated signals and removing artifact-related components. ICA manually selects components for recombination to reconstruct clean EEG signals. Wavelet transform decomposes signals into approximate and detailed wavelet coefficients and then identifies and removes relevant artifact coefficients. Each of these methods has its own advantages in artifact removal; therefore, combining different techniques has become a developmental advantage of traditional methods. Chen et al. [9] proposed a method combining ensemble empirical mode decomposition with canonical correlation analysis (Ensemble Empirical Mode Decomposition–Canonical Correlation Analysis, EEMD-CCA), focusing on several intrinsic mode functions obtained via empirical mode decomposition and effectively removing muscle artifacts from EEG signals using canonical correlation analysis. Sahoo et al. [10] proposed using principal component analysis (Principal Component Analysis, PCA) to remove ocular artifacts. Although these methods can suppress artifacts to some extent, they generally rely heavily on manual parameter tuning or strong prior assumptions, making it difficult to adapt to complex and variable real-world application scenarios.

In recent years, deep learning has emerged as a powerful end-to-end technique capable of automatic feature extraction and strong generalization, evolving from traditional shallow networks to deeper architectures in the field of EEG artifact removal. Early studies, such as those by Nguyen et al. [11] introduced improved wavelet thresholding using a wavelet neural network to handle ocular artifacts, but results were still limited. Sun et al. [12] proposed a one-dimensional residual CNN (1D-ResCNN) to remove common ocular, muscular, and cardiac artifacts from EEG signals. Later, researchers began exploring deeper and more effective denoising networks. Pu et al. [13] proposed a novel one-dimensional EEG denoising network called EEGDnet, which uses a 2D transformer module to comprehensively consider non-local and local self-similarities in EEG signals, significantly reducing the negative effects of noise and outliers. Leite et al. [14] introduced a two-dimensional deep convolutional autoencoder to filter ocular and muscle artifacts. Brophy et al. [16] employed generative adversarial networks (GANs) to remove EEG artifacts by mapping noisy EEG signals to clean ones, demonstrating the effectiveness of this method on benchmark EEG datasets and comparing it quantitatively with other deep learning-based EEG denoising techniques.

Existing networks typically process entire EEG segments directly, which can cause distortion in clean regions and lead to the loss of valuable neural information. To address this, some recent studies have introduced a "segmentation + denoising" framework by combining semantic segmentation with generative adversarial networks, enabling targeted artifact removal. For example, Li et al. [15] proposed SDNet, a segmentation-denoising joint model for single-channel EEG artifact removal.

While this paradigm improves upon traditional methods, several limitations remain:

(1) The segmentation and denoising components operate as separate modules with inconsistent feature spaces, leading to suboptimal performance, particularly at the boundaries between clean and noisy regions.
(2) The segmentation module is prone to overfitting, often misclassifying clean segments and degrading overall performance.
(3) The denoising network lacks architectural optimization specific to the spectral properties of EOG and EMG artifacts.

To overcome these challenges, we propose a novel deep learning framework that integrates semantic segmentation and adversarial denoising in a unified architecture. The key innovations are as follows:

(1) A semantics-guided multi-task discriminator that jointly performs real/fake discrimination and artifact segmentation, improving edge awareness through shared feature encoding.
(2) An adversarially trained encoder that enhances the identification and localization of structural artifacts while preserving clean EEG components.
(3) An improved MHSA-Inception module that captures both low- and high-frequency features via multi-scale convolution, offering enhanced denoising performance across varying artifact types.

2 Related Work

2.1 Multi-Head Self-Attention for EEG Modeling

Since the introduction of the Transformer architecture by Vaswani et al. [17], the self-attention mechanism has demonstrated strong capabilities in modeling long-range dependencies in sequential data. It has been widely adopted in fields such as natural language processing and time-series analysis, and is increasingly applied to biomedical signals, including EEG.

As a core component of Transformers, Multi-Head Self-Attention (MHSA) enables parallel attention computation across multiple subspaces by projecting the input sequence into multiple query, key, and value vectors. This structure enhances both expressiveness and stability, particularly in tasks requiring global temporal modeling. In image and speech domains, MHSA has shown the potential to replace certain convolutional operations by better capturing global patterns.

Despite its widespread success, the application of MHSA in EEG denoising remains limited. In this work, we incorporate MHSA into the generator to capture global temporal features in EEG signals, which complements local frequency information extracted by convolutional modules. This integration is particularly beneficial in distinguishing artifact patterns with broad temporal context, such as EOG or EMG contamination, thereby improving denoising robustness.

2.2 Adversarial Learning in EEG Artifact Removal

Conventional deep learning models are vulnerable to performance degradation in the presence of noise or adversarial perturbations. Generative Adversarial Networks (GANs) offer a promising alternative by learning robust mappings between noisy and clean domains through adversarial training.

A standard GAN framework comprises a generator and a discriminator. The generator attempts to produce artifact-free EEG signals, while the discriminator learns to distinguish between real clean signals and generated ones. However, traditional GANs often suffer from training instability, mode collapse, and vanishing gradients. To address this, Gulrajani et al. proposed WGAN-GP [18], which replaces weight clipping in WGAN [19] with a gradient penalty term, significantly stabilizing the training process.

In our work, WGAN-GP serves as the backbone of adversarial training, enabling the generator to produce realistic EEG signals. Furthermore, our discriminator extends the standard formulation with a dual-branch design: one branch for authenticity discrimination and another for artifact segmentation. This design introduces semantic feedback into adversarial learning, a novel strategy that directly supports our goal of localized denoising without over-suppressing clean segments.

2.3 Multi-scale Representation with Inception Modules

The Inception module, introduced by Szegedy et al. [21], is a multi-branch architecture that uses parallel convolutional filters of varying kernel sizes to extract multi-scale features within the same layer. This allows the network to simultaneously capture both local and global patterns, enhancing model generalizability and computational efficiency.

Originally developed for image recognition, Inception structures have been successfully applied to biomedical signals, including EEG, due to their adaptability in processing data with diverse frequency components. In EEG artifact removal tasks, where both low-frequency (EOG) and high-frequency (EMG) artifacts may coexist, multi-scale convolution is particularly advantageous.

In our approach, we propose an improved 1D Inception module tailored to EEG time-series signals. By stacking small kernels into effective large receptive fields, the module captures frequency-specific features without excessive parameter cost. This design, integrated into both the generator and the discriminator encoder, strengthens the model's capacity to distinguish between neural and non-neural components across scales.

3 Method

The single-channel EEG signal denoising network proposed in this study is illustrated in Fig. 1. It consists of two main components: a generator and a discriminator. The discriminator is responsible for performing two types of tasks: (a) semantic segmentation, and (b) scoring the quality of the generator's output, thereby providing feedback information based on semantic and adversarial learning. Furthermore, this study also proposes an improved Inception module specifically designed for EEG signals. This module effectively integrates temporal and spatial representation capabilities, not only providing a more diverse receptive field but also enhancing the network's encoding and feature expression abilities.

3.1 Improved Inception Module

The core idea of the Inception network is to use convolution kernels of multiple scales to extract features of different dimensions and then fuse them. These convolution kernels act as filters of varying sizes to capture key features from images. When it comes to time series processing, convolution kernels can be abstracted into a rectangle pulse with length T, where the main lobe width (-3dB bandwidth) is inversely proportional to $1/T$. The larger the convolution kernel, the smaller its main lobe width, resembling a low-pass narrowband filter; conversely, the smaller the convolution kernel, the larger its main lobe width, resembling a high-pass wideband filter.

As a one-dimensional time series signal, EEG signals are highly suitable for using convolution kernels of various sizes as filters with different bandwidths

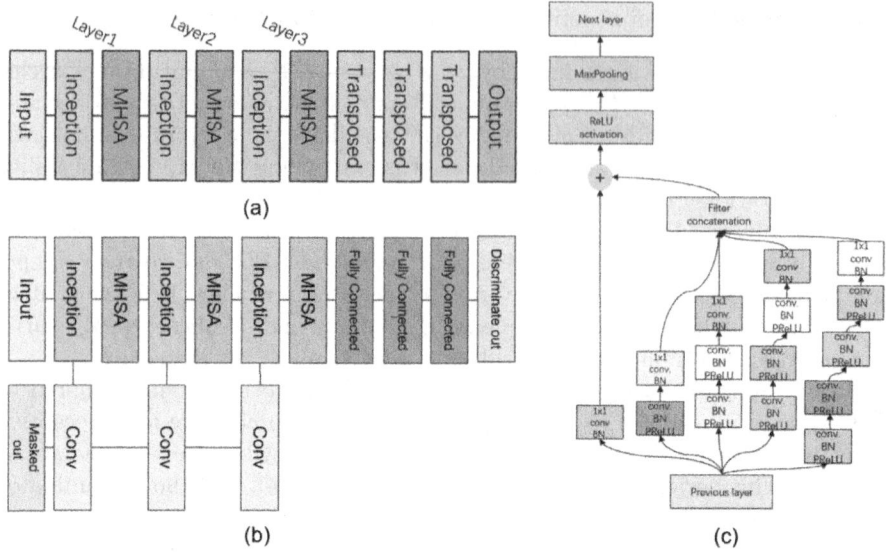

Fig. 1. MBGADNet Structures of (a) Generator, (b) Discriminator, and (c) Improved Inception Module.

to extract critical features. Moreover, EOG and EMG artifacts have distinctly different frequency characteristics. EOG has a narrower frequency band with relatively lower primary frequencies and sudden amplitude changes, often accompanied by spikes. EMG, on the other hand, has a wider frequency band with relatively higher primary frequencies and generally higher amplitudes. Therefore, using a single-sized convolution kernel makes it difficult to fully extract the key features necessary for removing both EOG and EMG artifacts.

In this study, we improved the original Inception module as shown in Fig. 1(c). Specifically, for the analysis of single-channel EEG signals, we replaced the original two-dimensional convolution blocks with one-dimensional convolutions to better suit the characteristics of EEG time-series signals. We adopted a method of stacking multiple small-sized convolution kernels to form convolution kernels of different sizes, enabling the extraction of key features from EOG and EMG artifacts. Compared to directly using large convolution kernels, stacking multiple small convolution kernels saves parameters and allows for more flexible configuration of the receptive field, forming filters with different bandwidths. This approach also enables the handling of longer EEG signals more effectively.

3.2 Multi-task Discriminator

Existing segmentation-denoising models often achieve task collaboration merely by combining loss functions. Such model architectures typically lack effective information sharing, resulting in poor generalization performance and increased parameter size. Additionally, as traditional classifiers, discriminators irregularly distinguish between real and synthetic data based on global structures or local detailed differences. This can lead to incomplete feedback for the generator, which negatively impacts the denoising performance [20].

To address the above issues, this study designs a multi-task learning discriminator that integrates semantic segmentation with authenticity discrimination. The overall architecture of the discriminator is shown in Fig. 1(b), adopting a shared encoder–dual branch decoder structure. The encoder part is composed of Inception modules, forming a stable and efficient feature extraction pathway. After the encoder, the network splits into two task-specific branches:

The authenticity discrimination task aims to determine whether the generated EEG signal is close to a real EEG signal, similar to the real/fake classification task in a traditional WGAN-GP discriminator. This process is carried out by the first task-specific path in the discriminator (see Fig. 1). The path receives high-dimensional feature representations extracted by the encoder, processes them through a series of convolutional and linear layers, and finally outputs a scalar value representing the probability that the input signal belongs to real EEG data. This task encourages the discriminator to focus on overall structural differences between real and generated EEG signals and provides global feedback to the generator to improve signal quality. The loss function adopts the Wasserstein GAN with Gradient Penalty (WGAN-GP) form, and its objective function is defined as follows:

$$\mathcal{L}_{\text{adv}} = E_{\widetilde{x} \sim P_g}\left[D\left(\widetilde{x}\right)\right] - E_{x \sim P_r}\left[D\left(x\right)\right] + \lambda \cdot E_{\hat{x} \sim P_{\hat{x}}}\left(\left|\nabla_{\hat{x}} D\left(\hat{x}\right)\right|_2 - 1\right)^2$$

Here, denotes the output of the discriminator for authenticity discrimination, and represent the distributions of real and generated EEG signals, respectively. is the gradient penalty coefficient, and is an interpolated distribution randomly sampled between real and generated samples.

The goal of the semantic segmentation task is to determine whether each time point in the EEG signal is contaminated by artifacts, enabling local structural identification and spatial localization of the signal. This task is performed by the second task-specific path in the discriminator (see Fig. 1(c)). The path employs a U-Net structure, where the encoding phase extracts multi-scale semantic features, and the decoding phase gradually restores the temporal length of the signal through skip connections and upsampling operations. Finally, a label sequence of the same length as the input is output, where each position indicates whether that time point belongs to an artifact region. The generated label map is passed to the generator as semantic feedback, assisting it in locating contaminated segments while precisely reconstructing the clean EEG signal.

The loss function for the semantic segmentation task is the Weighted Binary Cross Entropy (WBCE), formulated as follows:

$$\mathcal{L}_{\text{seg}} = -\frac{1}{T}\sum_{t=1}^{T}\left[\alpha \cdot y_t \log\left(\widehat{y}_t\right) + (1-\alpha) \cdot (1-y_t)\log\left(1-\widehat{y}_t\right)\right]$$

where is the sequence length, represents the ground truth label at the -th time step, is the network's prediction, and are the weight coefficients for positive and negative samples, respectively, which are used to address the sparsity of artifact regions.

The parameters of the network are updated according to the following formula:

$$\theta \leftarrow \theta - \alpha \left(\frac{\mathcal{L}_{\text{adv}}}{\partial \theta} + \frac{\mathcal{L}_{\text{seg}}}{\partial \theta} \right)$$

3.3 Generator

Traditional CNNs, while effective at capturing local high-frequency features in EEG signals, have limited ability to preserve global low-frequency structural information. This limitation is particularly evident when it comes to removing artifacts while maintaining the contextual semantics of the clean signal. This constraint results in a performance bottleneck for generators relying solely on local convolution operations when addressing complex temporal contamination, such as mixed EMG/EOG artifacts.

To address this, this study proposes a generator architecture that combines multi-scale Inception modules with the Multi-Head Self-Attention (MHSA) mechanism. The aim is to integrate local high-frequency details with long-range low-frequency structures in the time domain (see Fig. 1(a)). The overall structure is based on an Encoder-Decoder framework, utilizing symmetric design to preserve the signal length and employing residual connections to enhance feature reuse and information flow stability. The generator includes the following core modules:

Inception Path: Extracts frequency band features from the EEG signal by using multiple parallel convolutions with different receptive fields to capture local patterns, adapting to spectral differences between EOG (low-frequency spikes) and EMG (high-frequency oscillations) artifacts.

MHSA Path: Uses the Multi-Head Self-Attention mechanism to model long-range dependencies between different time points of the EEG, improving the ability to recognize non-local temporal structures (such as sudden artifacts or delayed interference).

Difference Channel: Directly connects the input and the feature encoding output to preserve the unpolluted original information, preventing the clean signal from being overly altered.

The final output is obtained by concatenating the three paths at the feature dimension level, followed by a convolutional layer to map it back to a single-channel EEG representation, achieving high-quality signal reconstruction. An improved Wasserstein Generative Adversarial Network (WGAN-GP) is adopted as the training strategy. Its adversarial objective function is defined as follows:

$$\mathcal{L}_G = -E_{\tilde{x} \sim P_g}\left[D\left(\tilde{x} \right) \right]$$

4 Experiments

4.1 Datasets

The experiment created two types of datasets: one with isolated EMG and EOG artifact contamination, and the other with combined EMG+EOG artifact contamination, to validate the performance and generalization ability of the model. The semi-simulated data refers to EEG data that has been contaminated by artificially added artifacts, created by overlaying clean EEG data with the added artifacts. EEGdenoiseNet [22] is a publicly available EEG dataset containing 4,514 EEG segments, 3,400 EOG segments, and 5,598 EMG segments, all sampled at 256 Hz, with each segment lasting 2 s. This study uses the full EEG-denoiseNet dataset and constructs the semi-simulated dataset according to its processing method, followed by min-max normalization for training convenience. The contaminated EEG signals are generated by linearly mixing clean EEG signals with artifacts according to the following formula:

$$X = Y + \tilde{\lambda} Z$$

In this formula, X represents the contaminated EEG signal, Y represents the clean EEG signal, and Z represents the mixed artifact. $\tilde{\lambda}$ is used to adjust the contribution of the artifacts according to the signal-to-noise ratio (SNR). The input SNR can be calculated as follows:

$$SNR(\text{dB}) = 10 \log_{10}\left(\frac{P_y}{P_z}\right) = 10 \log_{10}\left(\frac{\sum_{i=0}^{N-1} y_i^2}{\sum_{i=0}^{N-1} (\tilde{\lambda} \cdot z_i)^2}\right)$$

where P_y is the power of the clean EEG signal, P_z is the power of the mixed artifact, and N represents the length of the time series signal. By combining the above formula, $\tilde{\lambda}$ can be derived as:

$$\tilde{\lambda} = \sqrt{\frac{P_{signal}}{P_{noise}} \cdot 10^{-SNR_{\text{dB}}/10}}$$

For this study, the chosen SNR for EMG artifacts ranges from -7 dB to 4 dB [23], and the SNR for EOG artifacts ranges from -7 dB to 2 dB [24]. According to the above formula, a uniform SNR sequence is first generated based on the chosen SNR range. Then, $\tilde{\lambda}$ values are derived to obtain a sequence of linear values to be added. The resulting $\tilde{\lambda}$ values are then used to overlay the normalized EOG and EMG signals, and the final signal can be computed as follows:

$$X_{\text{noisy}} = X_{\text{clean}} + \tilde{\lambda} \cdot (N_{\text{mix}} \odot M_{\text{tag}})$$

where $\odot$ denotes element-wise multiplication, ensuring that the noise only affects the labeled regions. X_{noisy} represents the final obtained signal.

4.2 Evaluation Metrics

Three evaluation metrics—RRMSE, CC, and SNR—are used on the dataset to validate the effectiveness of the network and serve as performance comparison indicators.

The calculation process for RRMSE is as follows:

$$RRMSE = \frac{RMS(\hat{Y} - Y)}{RMS(Y)}$$

In this formula, Y and $\hat{Y}$ represent the clean EEG signal and the estimated EEG signal, respectively, while $RMS(\cdot)$ denotes the root mean square, which is defined as follows:

$$RMS(\hat{Y} - Y) = \sqrt{\frac{1}{T} \sum_{i=0}^{T-1} (\hat{y}_i - y_i)^2}$$

where T represents the number of time points. A lower RRMSE indicates better denoising performance.

The value of CC ranges from 0 to 1, with values closer to 1 indicating greater similarity between the denoised EEG and the clean EEG. The calculation process for CC is as follows:

$$CC = \frac{\mathrm{cov}(\hat{Y}, Y)}{\sigma_{\hat{Y}} \sigma_Y}$$

Here, $\mathrm{cov}(\cdot, \cdot)$ denotes the covariance, and σ denotes standard deviation.

SNR can be calculated according to the formula:

$$SNR(\mathrm{dB}) = 10 \log_{10} \left(\frac{\sum_{i=0}^{T-1} y_i^2}{\sum_{i=0}^{T-1} (\hat{y}_i - y_i)^2} \right)$$

A higher SNR indicates better quality of the generated denoised EEG signal.

4.3 Hyperparameters and Experiment Setting

Before training, the dataset was randomly divided into 90% for the training set and 10% for the validation set, ensuring uniform distribution across each SNR. All experiments were implemented in Python 3.8.2 and PyTorch 2.7.1, with hardware configured as an NVIDIA GeForce RTX 4060 Ti GPU and an Intel(R) Core(TM) i5-12400F CPU. During the experiment, the learning rate was set to 1×10^{-4}, batch size was 16, and the Adam optimizer was used with the parameters $\beta_1 = 0.5$ and $\beta_2 = 0.999$. The number of epochs was set to 200.

5 Results

5.1 Comparison with Existing Approaches

Table 1 presents the denoising results for various artifacts. From the table, it can be seen that, whether for mixed or single artifact contamination, the results of EEMD-ICA and EEMD-CCA are similar for all three metrics. The results of traditional mathematical methods are relatively poor, while deep learning-based denoising methods outperform them across all metrics. Complex-CNN, being a deeper deep learning network, achieves better denoising performance than other deep learning networks. However, methods like EEMD-CCA, EEMD-ICA, FCNN, RNN-LSTM, and Complex-CNN typically process the entire signal segment. When these methods process EEG records that include both noisy and clean segments, the artifact components decomposed from the EEG may contain useful EEG components, which could lead to distortion in some of the clean segments (Table 2).

Table 1. Average RRMSE, CC, and SNR (dB) of all methods on single type of artifact removal task

Dataset	Method	RRMSE	CC	SNR
EEG Denoisenet EMG	EEMD-CCA[27]	0.612	0.349	1.723
	EEMD-ICA[28]	0.573	0.226	1.538
	FCNN	0.375	0.722	4.248
	Simple-CNN	0.213	0.801	6.709
	RNN-LSTM	0.377	0.713	4.239
	Complex-CNN	0.184	0.863	7.341
	SDNet	0.148	0.886	7.913
	MBGADnet	0.147	0.923	8.328
EEG Denoisenet EOG	EEMD-CCA[27]	0.514	0.357	2.833
	EEMD-ICA[28]	0.433	0.245	2.454
	FCNN	0.376	0.783	4.425
	Simple-CNN	0.230	0.791	6.380
	RNN-LSTM	0.376	0.724	4.242
	Complex-CNN	0.176	0.875	7.531
	SDNet	0.146	0.877	7.967
	MBGADnet	0.156	0.891	8.546

Therefore, using segmentation networks to preserve clean segments, such as SDNet and MBGADNet, results in better denoising performance compared to other methods. Whether dealing with single or mixed artifacts, MBGADNet outperforms most deep learning networks in terms of RRMSE, CC, and SNR, and also surpasses the state-of-the-art network, SDNet. Compared to SDNet,

Table 2. Average RRMSE, CC, and SNR (dB) of all methods on mixed type of artifact removal task

Dataset	Method	RRMSE	CC	SNR
EEGDenoisenet EOG+EMG	**EEMD-CCA[27]**	0.513	0.334	3.046
	EEMD-ICA[28]	0.458	0.299	2.779
	FCNN	0.293	0.100	5.338
	Simple-CNN	0.208	0.815	6.804
	RNN-LSTM	0.273	0.547	5.630
	Complex-CNN	0.203	0.826	6.930
	SDNet	0.188	0.851	7.281
	MBGADnet	0.132	0.904	8.559

MBGADNet reduces RRMSE by 0.01 under isolated EOG artifact contamination, increases CC by 0.26, and improves SNR by 0.579 dB. Under isolated EMG artifact contamination, RRMSE is reduced by 0.001, CC increases by 0.014, and SNR improves by 0.579 dB. Under EOG and EMG mixed contamination, RRMSE is reduced by 0.056, CC increases by 0.05, and SNR improves by 1.3 dB.

5.2 Visualization Results

The visualization results are shown in Fig. 2, where the blue line represents the clean EEG, the green line represents the original noisy EEG, and the yellow line represents the denoised EEG. The denoising results from (a) to (d) are presented. The results in the figure demonstrate that MBGADNet outperforms existing state-of-the-art and popular deep learning denoising methods, with the denoised EEG closely resembling the clean EEG.

The visualization results of MBGADNet before and after denoising for different types of artifact contamination are shown in Fig. 3. The blue line represents the clean EEG, the green line represents the original noisy EEG, and the yellow line represents the denoised EEG. The denoising results from (a) to (c) correspond to EMG artifacts, EOG artifacts, and mixed artifacts, respectively. The results in the figure indicate that MBGADNet can effectively suppress various types of noise, and the denoised EEG closely resembles the clean EEG.

The denoising results of SDNet and MBGADNet are shown in Fig. 4. The blue line represents the clean EEG, the yellow line represents the denoised EEG, and the green line represents the original noisy EEG. (a) shows the denoising results of the SDNet network, while (b) shows the denoising results of the MBGADNet network. The results in the figure indicate that around 4.0 s to 4.5 s, MBGADNet provides better fitting near the edges of the noise compared to SDNet, demonstrating superior nonlinear fitting ability. This confirms that the multi-branch structure and shared encoder in MBGADNet are effective in edge perception.

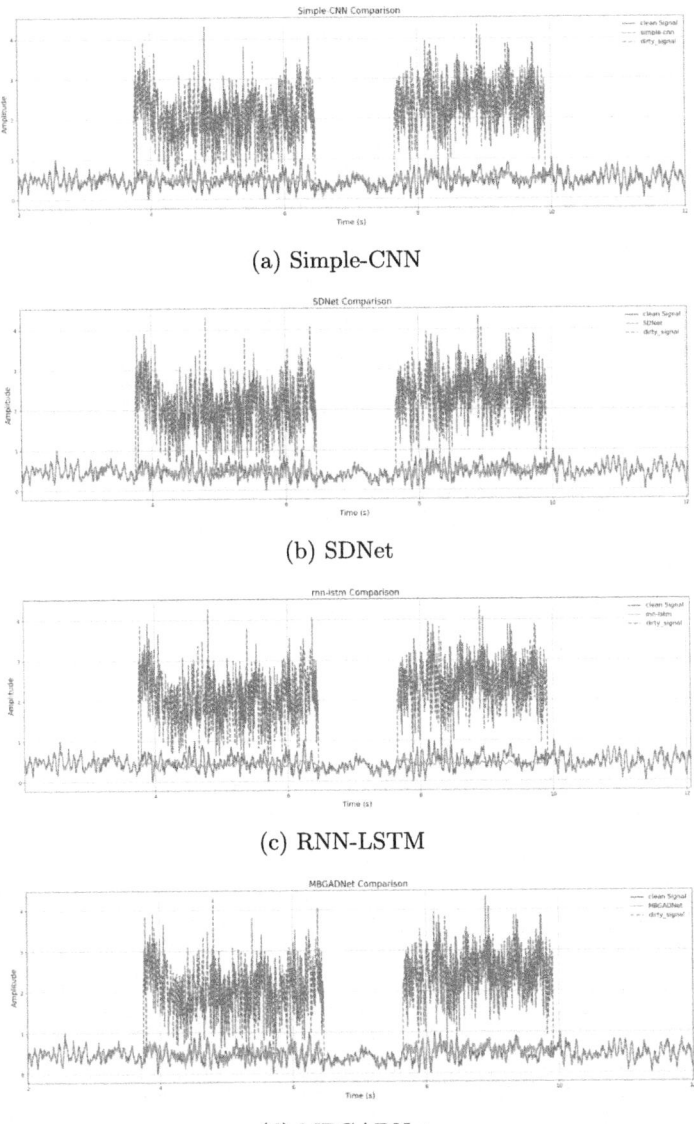

(a) Simple-CNN

(b) SDNet

(c) RNN-LSTM

(d) MBGADNet

Fig. 2. Example of artifact removal via compared approaches. Raw EEG, clean EEG, and reconstructed EEG are plotted with a green line, blue line, and orange line, respectively. (Color figure online)

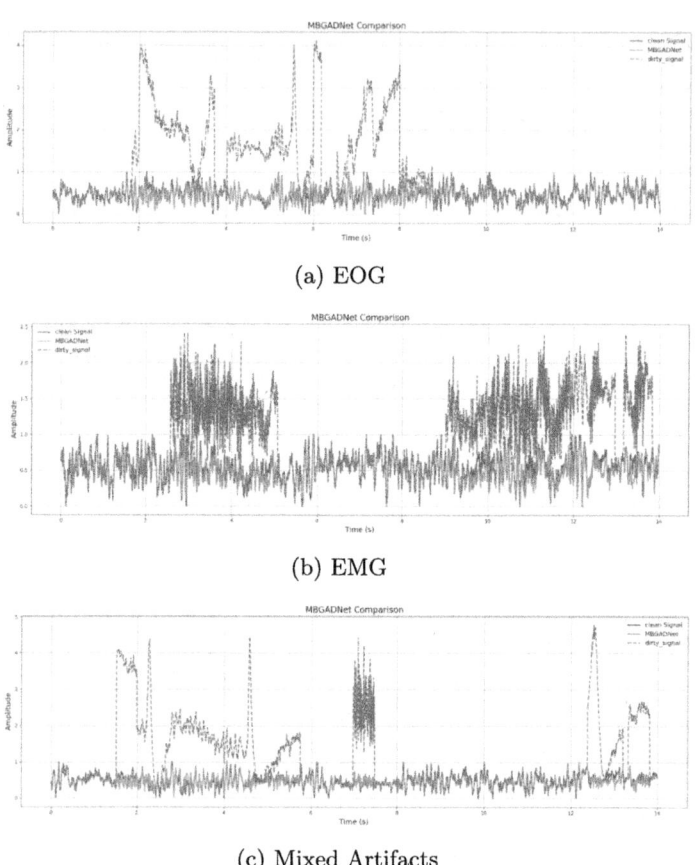

(a) EOG

(b) EMG

(c) Mixed Artifacts

Fig. 3. Typical denoising results of MBGADNet. Raw EEG, clean EEG, and reconstructed EEG are plotted with a green line, blue line, and orange line, re-spectively. (Color figure online)

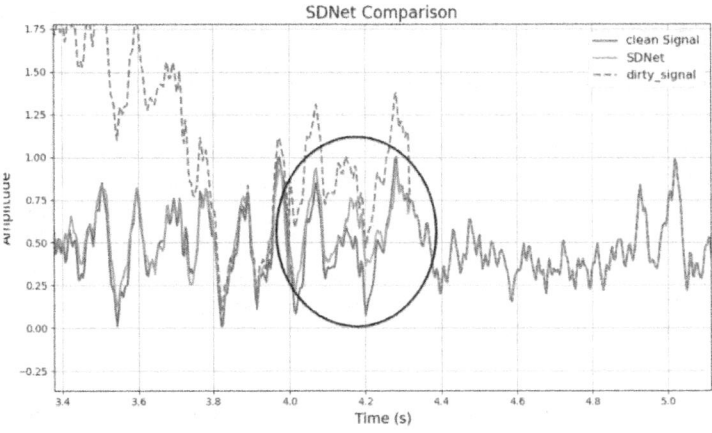

(a) Edge of SDNet's outputs

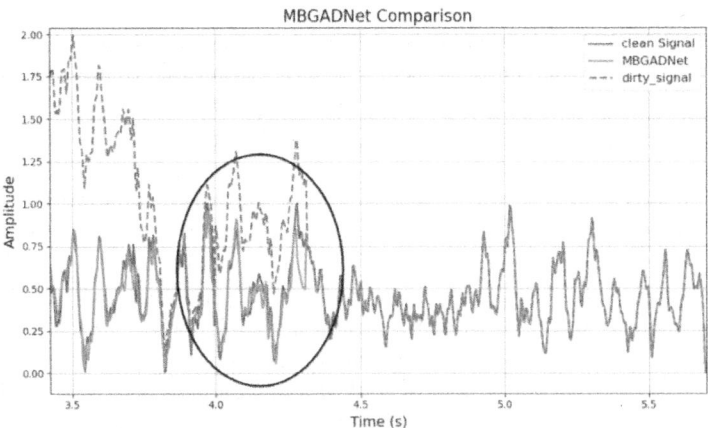

(b) Edge of MBGADNet's outputs

Fig. 4. Comparison of edge results between MBGADNet and SDNet outputs.

5.3 Ablation Experiment

The denoising network generator is the core of this study. To comprehensively assess the actual contribution of each module and design strategy to the overall performance, a series of ablation experiments were designed and conducted. By selectively removing or replacing key components in the model structure and performing performance tests under a unified dataset and evaluation metrics, a deeper understanding can be gained regarding the role and relative importance of each module in EEG signal recovery and artifact suppression.

In this section, the experiments focus on examining the following aspects: (1) Whether the segmentation structure plays a positive role in guiding the model's focus on specific regions and enhancing feature expression; (2) Whether the introduction of the improved Inception module strengthens the model's feature representation ability, capturing the key features of the signal.

Experiment setup: Under the condition that the rest of the overall structure remains unchanged, this study removed the corresponding selected modules to construct comparison models. Additionally, to maintain fairness and comparability of the results, all other hyperparameters (including learning rate, number of training epochs, loss function, etc.) were kept consistent with the original model to ensure the comparability of the experimental results. All experiments used SNR (Signal-to-Noise Ratio), relative mean squared error (MSE), and correlation coefficient (CC) for performance evaluation.

Impact of the Segmentation Structure: To evaluate the contribution of the semantic segmentation auxiliary structure in guiding the backbone network to focus on artifact regions, this experiment constructed a model variant without the semantic segmentation branch for comparison.

As shown in Fig. 5, to demonstrate the performance change in signal recovery after removing the semantic segmentation structure, this study compared three sets of waveform curves: the blue curve represents the original clean EEG signal, the green curve represents the output of the generator after removing the auxiliary semantic segmentation structure, and the yellow curve represents the denoising result after introducing the auxiliary semantic segmentation structure into the model. It can be clearly observed from the figure that after removing the auxiliary semantic segmentation structure, waveform shifts and distortions occur at multiple key details, especially around 6.4 s and 6.6 s, where the orange curve significantly deviates from the original signal, indicating that the model has difficulty handling mid-to-high frequency details.

Table 3 shows the comparison of performance metrics between the denoising net-work without Inception and the denoising network with Inception on the dataset:

In summary, the dual-branch model with multi-scale feature extraction structure performs superiorly in signal peak-trough location and amplitude restoration, indicating that the auxiliary semantic segmentation structure plays a key role in enhancing feature expression and improving complex artifact modeling.

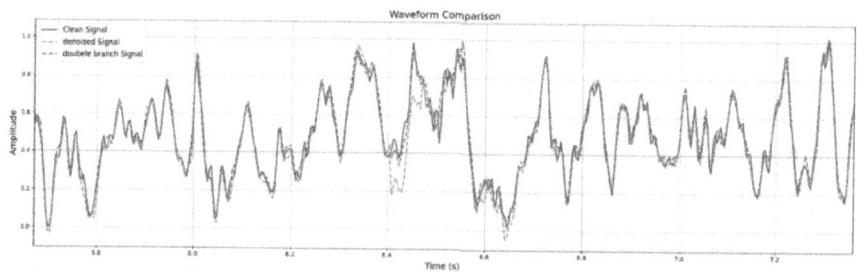

Fig. 5. Comparison of denoising details after removing the auxiliary semantic segmentation structure. (Color figure online)

Table 3. Evaluation metrics of denoising network without and with semantic segmentation.

Dataset	Method	RRMSE	CC	SNR
EEGDenoisenet EOG+EMG	MBGADNet without segmentation	0.163	0.894	7.876
	MBGADNet	0.132	0.904	8.559

Impact of Inception: To explore the importance of the Inception module in multi-scale feature extraction, this experiment replaces it with a 1×7 standard convolution layer + BN and analyzes its impact on EEG denoising performance.

As shown in Fig. 6, the blue curve represents the original clean EEG signal, the green curve represents the output after fitting with a standard single-layer convolution structure, and the yellow curve represents the denoising result after introducing the improved Inception module into the model. From the analysis of the figure, it can be seen that between 4.85 s and 5 s, the model with the Inception module more closely follows the original signal curve, showing stronger nonlinear fitting ability and better amplitude and waveform detail restoration. This indicates that the multi-scale structure has a clear advantage in extracting features of artifacts at different frequencies.

Table 4 shows the comparison of performance metrics between the denoising network without Inception and the denoising network with Inception on the dataset:

Table 4. Evaluation metrics of denoising network without and with Inception.

Dataset	Method	RRMSE	CC	SNR
EEGDenoisenet EOG+EMG	MBGADNet without Inception	0.203	0.837	6.933
	MBGADNet	0.132	0.904	8.559

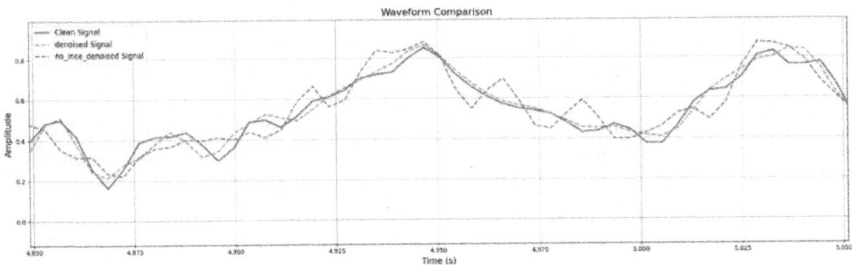

Fig. 6. Comparison of denoising details before and after removing Inception.

In summary, the Inception module, as one of the key structures for feature extraction in the model, makes a significant contribution to extracting signal features, improving denoising accuracy, and enhancing training efficiency. Its removal leads to a severe degradation in model performance.

6 Conclusion

This study proposes a multi-branch deep learning network called MBGADNet, which is based on the WGAN-GP framework and integrates the MHSA-Inception method. It jointly performs denoising and segmentation tasks. MBGADNet combines semantic segmentation and authenticity discrimination tasks into the discriminator, enhancing its edge-local perception and discrimination ability through a semantic sharing mechanism, while also improving the denoising capability of the generator. Additionally, the adversarial learning-driven shared encoder enhances MBGADNet's ability to identify and strip EEG artifacts, enabling precise localization and removal of artifact-contaminated segments. Moreover, the MHSA-improved Inception module strengthens the long-term perception capability of traditional CNN networks, effectively capturing different features of EEG signals at both high and low frequencies, and demonstrating significant performance advantages in ablation experiments. Through experiments on the semi-simulated EEGdenoiseNet dataset, we demonstrate that MBGADNet outperforms traditional methods, SDNet, and other deep learning models in removing local EEG signal artifacts. This novel deep learning approach not only provides a new method for EEG signal preprocessing but also offers new ideas for downstream tasks.

References

1. Patel, R., Janawadkar, M.P., Sengottuvel, S., Gireesan, K., Radhakrishnan, T.S.: Effective extraction of visual event-related pattern by combining template matching with ensemble empirical mode decomposition. IEEE Sensors J. **17**(7), 2146–2153 (2017)
2. Momin, R., Mir, H., Al-Nashash, H.: Cortical source localization and signal estimation without exact knowledge of the leadfield matrix. IEEE Sens. J. **17**(2), 450–458 (2017)
3. Mahmoud, R., Shanableh, T., Bodala, I.P., Thakor, N.V., Al-Nashash, H.: Novel classification system for classifying cognitive workload levels under vague visual stimulation. IEEE Sensors J. **17**(21), 7019–7028 (2017)
4. Chen, X., Wang, Z.J., McKeown, M.: Joint blind source separation for neurophysiological data analysis: multiset and multimodal methods. IEEE Signal Process. Mag. **33**(3), 86–107 (2016)
5. Zhang, Y., Zhou, G., Jin, J., Zhao, Q., Wang, X., Cichocki, A.: Sparse Bayesian classification of EEG for brain–computer interface. IEEE Trans. Neural Netw. Learn. Syst. **27**(11), 2256–2267 (2016)
6. Chen, X., et al.: Removal of muscle artifacts from the EEG: a review and recommendations. IEEE Sensors J. **19**(14), 5353–5368 (2019)

7. Klados, M.A., Papadelis, C., Braun, C., Bamidis, P.D.: REG-ICA: A hybrid methodology combining blind source separation and regression techniques for the rejection of ocular artifacts. Biomed. Signal Process. Control **6**(3), 291–300 (2011)
8. Vorobyov, S., Cichocki, A.: Blind noise reduction for multisensory signals using ICA and subspace filtering, with application to EEG analysis. Biol. Cybern. **86**(4), 293–303 (2002)
9. Zhu, H.Y., Wu, Y.L., Shen, N., et al.: The masking impact of intra-artifacts in EEG on deep learning-based sleep staging systems: a comparative study. IEEE Trans. Neural Syst. Rehabil. Eng. **30**, 1452–1463 (2022)
10. Sahoo, S.K., Mohapatra, S.K.: Recognition of ocular artifacts in EEG signal through a hybrid optimized scheme. Biomed. Res. Int. **2022**, 4875399 (2022)
11. Nguyen, H.A.T., et al.: EOG artifact removal using a wavelet neural network. Neurocomputing **97**, 374–389 (2012)
12. Sun, W., Su, Y., Wu, X., Wu, X.: A novel end-to-end 1D-ResCNN model to remove artifact from EEG signals. Neurocomputing **404**, 108–121 (2020)
13. Pu, X., et al.: EEGDnet: fusing non-local and local self-similarity for EEG signal denoising with transformer. Comput. Biol. Med. **151**, 106248 (2022)
14. Leite, N.M.N., et al.: Deep convolutional autoencoder for EEG noise filtering. In: Procedings of IEEE International Conference on Bioinformatics and Biomedicine (BIBM), pp. 1–9 (2018)
15. Li, Y., Liu, A., Yin, J., Li, C., Chen, X.: A segmentation-denoising network for artifact removal from single-channel EEG. IEEE Sensors J. **23**(13), 15115–15127 (2023)
16. Brophy, E., Redmond, P., Fleury, A., Vos, M., Boylan, G., Ward, T.: Denoising EEG signals for real-world BCI applications using GANs. Front. Neuroergonomics **2**, 805573 (2022)
17. Vaswani, A., et al.: Attention is all you need. In: Advances in Neural Information Processing System, vol. 30 (2017)
18. Gulrajani, I., et al.: Improved training of Wasserstein GANs. In: Advances in Neural Information Processing System, vol. 30 (2017)
19. Arjovsky, M., Chintala, S., Bottou, L.: Wasserstein GAN, arXiv preprint arXiv:1701.07875 (2017)
20. Tibermacine, I.E., et al.: Adversarial denoising of EEG signals: a comparative analysis of standard GAN and WGAN-GP approaches. Front. Hum. Neurosci. **19**, 1583342 (2025)
21. Szegedy, C., et al.: Going deeper with convolutions. In: Proceedings of IEEE Conference on Computer Vision and Pattern Recognition (CVPR), pp. 1–9 (2015)
22. Zhang, H., et al.: EEGdenoiseNet: a benchmark dataset for deep learning solutions of EEG denoising. J. Neural Eng. **18**(5), 056057 (2021)
23. Liu, A., et al.: A state-dependent IVA model for muscle artifacts removal from EEG recordings. IEEE Trans. Instrum. Meas. **70**, 1–13 (2021)
24. Dora, M., Holcman, D.: Adaptive single-channel EEG artifact removal with applications to clinical monitoring. IEEE Trans. Neural Syst. Rehabil. Eng. **30**, 286–295 (2022)
25. Chen, X., Liu, A., Chiang, J., Wang, Z.J., McKeown, M.J., Ward, R.K.: Removing muscle artifacts from EEG data: multichannel or single-channel techniques? IEEE Sensors J. **16**(7), 1986–1997 (2015)
26. Mijović, B., De Vos, M., Gligorijević, I., Taelman, J., Van Huffel, S.: Source separation from single-channel recordings by combining empirical-mode decomposition and independent component analysis. IEEE Trans. Biomed. Eng. **57**(9), 2188–2196 (2010)

Design Optimization of Frameless Drive Motor in Robot Integrated Modular Actuator Considering Duty Cycle Suitability

Zimeng Guan[1], Fan Yang[2], Songtao Cai[2], Wenkai Xie[1], Yuanbo Liu[1], and Tenghui Dong[1(✉)]

[1] School of Mechanical Engineering, Shanghai Jiao Tong University, Shanghai 201100, China
Tenghuidong@sjtu.edu.cn

[2] JAKA Robotics Co., Ltd., Shanghai 200240, China

Abstract. A multi-objective optimization method considering duty cycle suitability is developed for collaborative robot joint motors, addressing acceleration demands and repetitive duty cycles. The motor's operating envelope is discretized into a structured grid using trajectory-based statistics. Grid cells are statistically weighted, and representative points are selected to capture typical operating conditions; sparsely populated regions are consolidated to reduce finite-element simulation demands. This enables efficient optimization to minimize weighted loss and rotor inertia under practical constraints, solved via the Non-dominated Sorting Genetic Algorithm II. Thermal safety is then verified through transient temperature-rise simulation, and the final designs are selected based on torque-ripple performance. Compared with the original motor design, the optimized motor achieves over a 50% reduction in weighted loss, ~ 25% lower rotor inertia, and ~ 40% reduction in torque ripple, accompanied by higher efficiency and reduced temperature rise. Additionally, compared to a motor optimized solely for rated-point efficiency, the proposed method results in lower losses and heat generation over actual operating cycles, demonstrating the practical effectiveness of this optimization approach.

Keywords: Collaborative robot · Robot integrated modular actuator · Frameless drive motor · Multi-objective optimization · Duty cycle suitability

1 Introduction

Collaborative robots (cobots) are engineered to safely operate alongside humans, characterized by operational flexibility, user-friendliness, and rapid deployment [1, 2]. They enhance production efficiency through adaptive automation, addressing the increasing demand for diverse manufacturing models. As the core drive unit of robotic joint modules, drive motors fundamentally influence a robot's efficiency, reliability, and adaptability [3].

Recent advancements in sensors, control systems, and communication technologies have accelerated cobot operations, especially with the integration of intelligent management systems [4]. This evolution has significantly altered motor operational characteristics, necessitating a reevaluation of design specifications. Notably, high start-up accelerations lead to frequent overload torque conditions at low speeds, while high-speed operations often involve low torque demands. Such shifts result in a broader distribution of operating points, challenging traditional motor design assumptions and raising concerns about the thermal safety of copper windings [5].

Firstly, conventional motor optimization methodologies typically employ the rated operating condition or representative operating condition as the optimization target, or further perform generalized regional optimization, such as expanding the high-efficiency area or improving the efficiency of specific operating regions [6]. In the context of discretized operating condition distributions, this method overlooks the dynamic performance of the motor during real-world operation, resulting in difficulty in meeting the needs of complex application scenarios [7]. In recent years, operating-condition-based motor optimization methods have gained prominence, particularly in the automotive domain, with a series of optimization strategies proposed through the analysis of typical driving cycles [3, 8–13]. As a representative example, Bin Li employs the k-means clustering algorithm to segment the operating conditions into regions, identifies the energy centroid of each region as the characteristic operating points, and assigns the regional energy proportion as the weight coefficient of the representative operating conditions, thereby incorporating a more detailed consideration of energy distribution [13]. Conventional approaches typically utilize weighted averages of a few operating points (usually ≤ 8), which may not effectively capture the complexity of increasingly dispersed operating condition distributions.

Secondly, if a more lumped view of the distribution of condition data is adopted instead of selecting only a small number of representative condition points, the optimization process requires a full-domain efficiency scan. This makes the simulation computation jump by 1–2 orders of magnitude, which makes it difficult to form a large base generation for optimality seeking [14].

Considering this background, this paper proposes an optimization methodology tailored to robotic joint operating cycles, jointly considering motor losses, rotor inertia, and torque quality. Firstly, real trajectory data is analyzed to derive operating-condition statistics, integrating this information into a multi-objective optimization framework. To reduce finite element simulation demands, the operating envelope was partitioned—grids in dense areas retained their representative points, while grids in sparse areas were consolidated—significantly reducing non-critical evaluations. Building on this, the optimization is performed using NSGA-II to simultaneously minimize weighted loss and rotor inertia, subject to multidimensional constraints. Comparative simulations confirm that the optimized motor not only reduces losses and temperature rise but also aligns more closely with actual operating cycles than designs derived from conventional methods.

2 Motor Prototype and Optimized Object

The motor optimization work in this paper is carried out based on a six-degree-of-freedom cobot (S5, developed by JAKA Company). This product is made of aluminum alloy and PC material, supporting graphical drag-and-drop programming. It is equipped with embedded force sensors at the end to realize multi-dimensional force sensing, and is suitable for handling flexible assembly, welding, gluing, polishing, and sanding jobs. Figure 1 shows the composition of the integrated joint drive system. The rotor shaft of the motor is assembled in a cantilever beam design with the reducer located on the opposite side of the end plate.

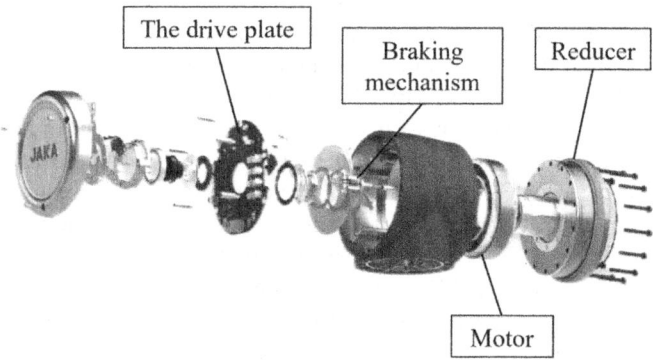

Fig. 1. The composition of the integrated joint drive system.

Figure 2 shows the permanent magnet brushless motor used in the joint, which is powered by a three-phase AC supply. The stator design uses centrally wound fractional slots and a spliced structure. The magnets are surface mounted after parallel magnetized. The specific parameters and characteristics of the motor are shown in Table 1.

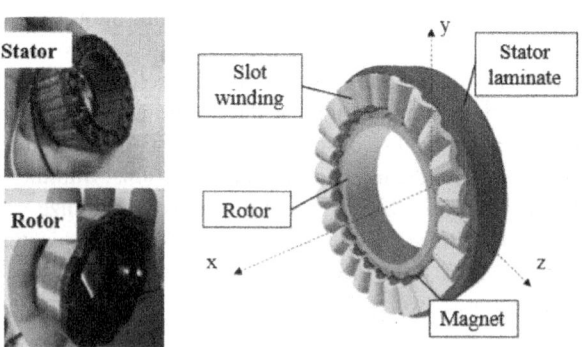

Fig. 2. Prototype of the PMSM motor.

Table 1. Basic parameters of the PMSM (original design).

Item	Value/Characteristic
Rated power/speed	1400W/3,000 rpm
Winding type	Concentrate winding
Coil arrangement in slot	Left/right
Stator lamination material	B30AHV1500
Air gap length	0.6 mm
Maximum height	26 mm
Stator diameter	118mm
Overload capability	200% (lasting at least 60 s)

3 Motor's Operation Characterization After Acceleration

In recent years, the rapid development of sensors, automation control, communication technologies, and AI-based management have led to a faster operation of the collaborative robot system. Figure 3 shows the angular position and torque output curves of the robotic joint during a representative operating cycle.

As shown, robot joint motors exhibit highly repeatable duty cycles and similar start-stop characteristics. Utilizing this feature, this study statistics a large amount of operational data of the robot's joint module in practical operation, which contains a total of 180 working cycles and more than 3,000 h of operation time, covering almost all the operating states. The sampling period of the data is 8 ms.

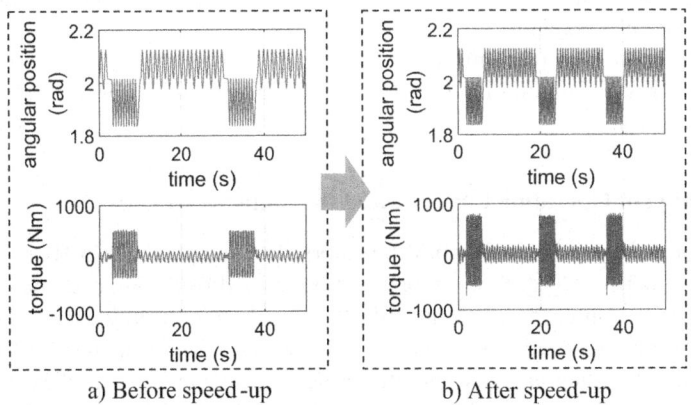

a) Before speed-up   b) After speed-up

Fig. 3. Output of the joint drive motor before and after speed-up—to perform the same motion commands at shorter time intervals, higher speed and torque are needed.

Then, to get the actual operating status of the motor, the data from the joint side is mapped to the motor side by the reduction ratio. It should be noted that the torque loss during transmission needs to be corrected by the mechanical losses of gearboxes and bearings obtained from the experimental speed-graded calibration.

Finally, the distribution of motor operating states obtained from statistics before and after operation speed-up is presented in Fig. 4. As shown in the figure, the degree of discretization of the motor's operating state in the workspace is significantly increased, with a significant increment in the number of high speed and high torque operating points.

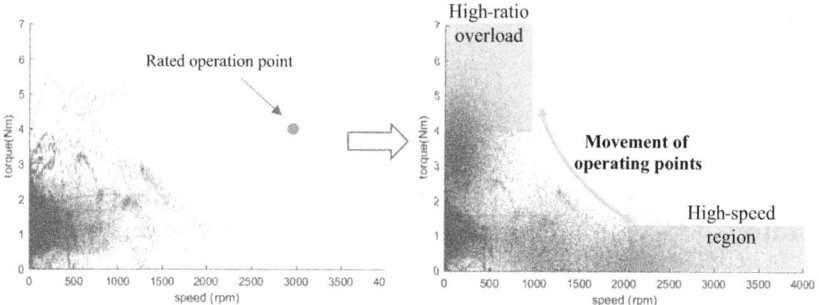

Fig. 4. Distribution of motor operating conditions before and after the acceleration of cobot operation—the degree of discretization of the motor's operating points is increased.

4 Lumped Loss Calculation

In robot-integrated modular actuators, motor efficiency is very important. In addition to the energy economy issue, more importantly, under the same volume and the same heat dissipation boundary, the smaller the heat source rate in the motor, the lower the temperature rise. This is essential to increase the power density and thermal safety of integrated modular actuators.

Therefore, the motor optimization in this study is mainly carried out on efficiency, while torque ripple and rotor inertia are adopted as references to form a multi-objective optimization seeking.

4.1 Meshing of Operating Envelope and the Statistics Matrix

For a given motor design, real-world trajectory data sampled at 125 Hz (0.008 s) are mapped into a 16 × 20 grid covering 0–4000 rpm and 0–7 Nm, and operating point counts are tallied in each cell to quantify the distribution of duty cycles. The energy centroid of each populated cell serves as its representative operating point. As illustrated in Fig. 5, this gridding and centroid clustering process yields a statistical matrix that captures the motor's operating behavior over the envelope.

The operating envelope is discretized into a structured grid, and each cell's occupancy ratio is used as a weight to perform parallel simulations. This yields a lumped loss value, representing the average heat source rate across the envelope.

To accelerate optimization over successive generations, partition the envelope into dense and sparse areas based on an occupancy threshold. Sparse area grids (occupancy <

0.5%) are consolidated into two representative points, significantly reducing the number of finite-element simulations per motor design (see Fig. 6).

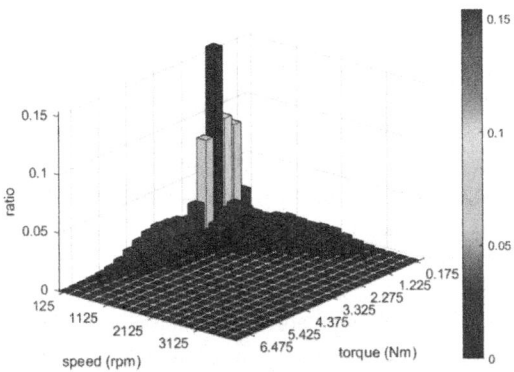

Fig. 5. The discrete distribution of the motor's operating states in the envelope.

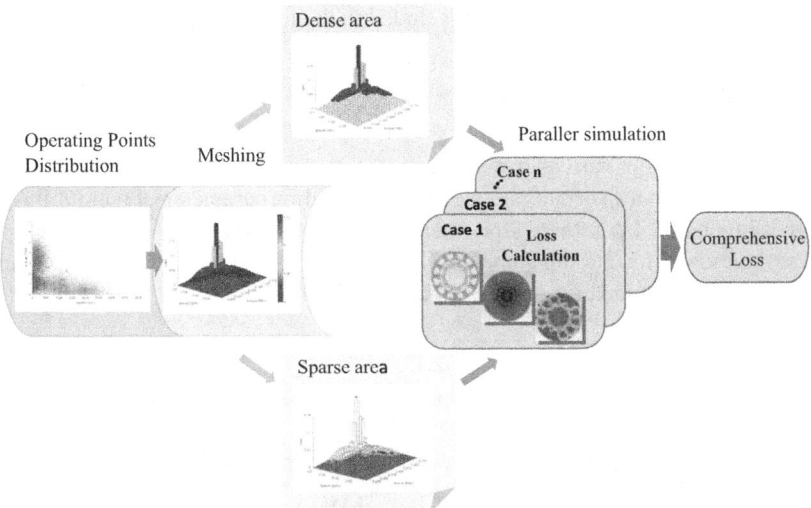

Fig. 6. Processing of the operating envelope for efficient parallel computing.

4.2 Calculation of the Lumped Losses

To accurately assess and compare the lumped efficiency of the motors under the actual operating characteristics of the robots, the loss values on the energy centers of each grid are summed up based on their probability distribution weight. Define the lumped loss value $L_{weighted}$:

$$L_{weighted} = \sum_{i=1}^{n+2} W_i \cdot L_i \tag{1}$$

In which, n denotes the number of grid cells within the motor's operating envelope where the proportion of operating points exceeds 0.5%. Each index iii corresponds to either a representative operating point from these dense grid cells or one of two representative points from the sparse region. The weight coefficient W_i represents the proportion of operating points within the region associated with the i-th representative point, while L_i denotes the loss value of the motor at this operating point.

For each representative point, the motor losses mainly consist of stator losses, rotor losses, and copper losses. The stator losses include both hysteresis and eddy current components. Hysteresis losses are calculated using the vector play model, while eddy current losses are evaluated by performing a one-dimensional transient analysis along the lamination thickness for each finite element.

Copper losses are divided into direct current (DC) and alternating current (AC) components. The DC component is computed based on Ohm's law, whereas the AC component is estimated by applying a correction factor to the DC loss [15].

Rotor losses include rotor core losses, which are calculated using the same method as for the stator core, and eddy current losses in the permanent magnets, which are computed using the Modified Winding Function Theory [16]. Additionally, the windage loss is considered negligible due to the relatively low rotational speed and compact size of the joint motor and is therefore not included in the loss calculation.

5 Optimization Algorithm

In motor optimization, various parameters are considered, encompassing not only geometric dimensions but also material selection and winding parameters. Figure 7 illustrates selected dimensional parameters pertinent to the optimization process. The variation ranges of these optimization parameters are determined based on the motor's geometric constraints and manufacturing process limitations.

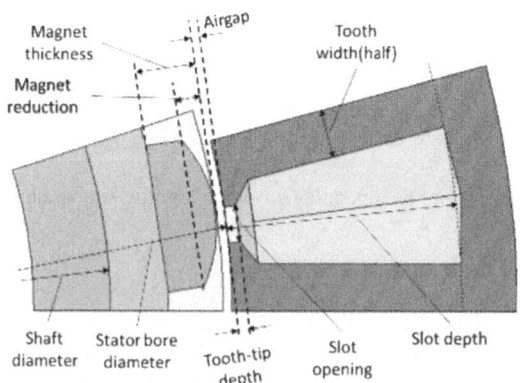

Fig. 7. Illustration of selected dimensional parameters for motor optimization

This study aims to achieve two primary optimization objectives: minimizing the weighted loss and minimizing the rotor's moment of inertia.

- Weighted Loss Minimization: The weighted loss is calculated by integrating the loss values at the center points of the efficiency map grids. Minimizing this metric enhances the motor's overall efficiency across its operational trajectory, reduces heat generation, and consequently lowers the motor's temperature rise.
- Rotor Inertia Minimization: Reducing the rotor inertia improves the motor's dynamic response, enabling faster acceleration and deceleration. This enhancement is crucial for robotic joints, requiring high responsiveness and precise control. A lower moment of inertia also contributes to improved energy efficiency and reduced mechanical stress during operation.

5.1 Multidimensional Optimization Constraints

To ensure that the optimized motor meets the required electromagnetic performance—such as delivering the rated torque, avoiding local magnetic saturation and overload, minimizing excessive torque ripple, and preventing undervoltage in high-speed regions—specific constraints are imposed during the optimization process. These constraints are applied to key performance indicators at various operating points, including torque output, voltage levels, cogging torque, and torque ripple percentage.

Additionally, manufacturing process limitations are considered to ensure the feasibility of the motor design. For instance, since winding parameters are part of the optimization, an upper limit is set on the slot fill factor to account for practical manufacturing constraints, ensuring that the proposed designs are manufacturable.

5.2 Optimization Algorithm and Implementation

This study employs the Non-dominated Sorting Genetic Algorithm II (NSGA-II) for multi-objective optimization of motor performance based on operating condition statistics. NSGA-II is chosen for its efficiency in handling complex, nonlinear, and constrained optimization problems, as well as its ability to maintain a diverse set of solutions through fast non-dominated sorting and crowding distance mechanisms.

As illustrated in Fig. 8, the optimization process begins with the generation of an initial population of motor designs, each constrained by predefined dimensional and manufacturing limits to ensure feasibility. Through iterative application of genetic operators—selection, crossover, and mutation—offspring populations are produced. Parent and offspring populations are combined and subjected to non-dominated sorting to classify solutions into different Pareto fronts. Within each front, solutions are further ranked based on crowding distance to preserve diversity. This iterative process continues until convergence criteria are met, resulting in a Pareto-optimal set of motor designs that balance multiple objectives.

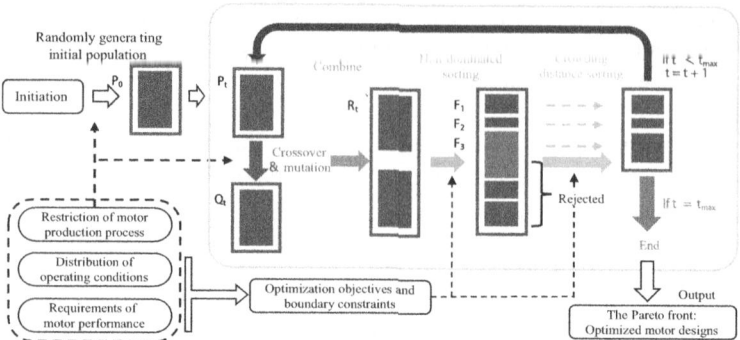

Fig. 8. NSGA-II optimization process for motor design

6 Results and Discussion

6.1 Results

There are simulation results of three motor prototypes being compared: the original design, the design optimized by minimizing rated-point efficiency, and the design optimized using weighted-loss minimization. The original motor design is a manufacturer-reduced-size version of an existing joint motor—compacted to meet the robot's lightweight requirements—without any algorithmic optimization. The only distinction between the two optimized motor designs is one of their optimization objectives, while all other design and optimization procedures remain identical.

The key performance parameters of the three motors are summarized in Table 2. It can be observed that, compared to the original motor, the optimized designs achieve higher efficiency and reduced rotor inertia while still satisfying continuous-duty requirements—demonstrating a clear improvement. Moreover, under overload conditions at rated speed and 200% rated torque for 120 s, the motor temperature remained within the safe operating range.

Table 2. Key Performance Parameters of the Three Motor Designs

Performance	Origin	Rated efficiency	Weighted loss
Rated torque (Nm)	3.77	3.81	3.79
Maximum no-load speed (rpm)	3950	4396	4421
Torque ripple percent at rated point (%)	1.74	0.99	0.90
Efficiency at rated point (%)	92.53	95.48	95.33
Weighted loss (W)	11.98	5.19	5.06
Rotor inertia (g*m2)	0.41	0.33	0.30
Temperature at extreme condition(°C)	114.7	67.4	68.1

Figure 9 presents the electromagnetic torque curves of the three motors: the optimized versions exhibit markedly lower torque ripple due to the imposed optimization constraints, while their torque magnitudes remain comparable.

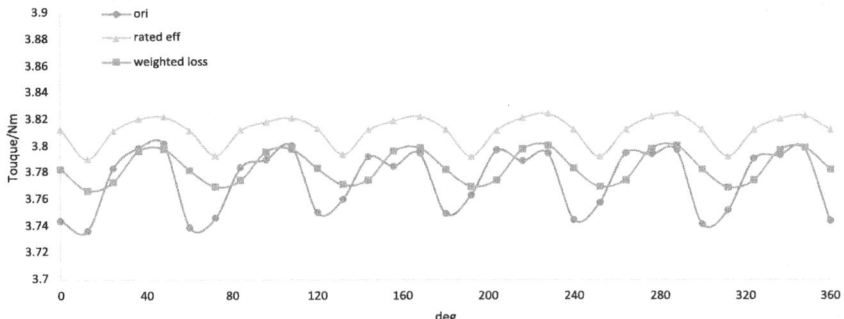

Fig. 9. Electromagnetic Torque Curves of the Three Motors —the optimized versions exhibit lower torque ripple.

To verify the thermal safety of the motor designs, transient temperature-rise simulations were conducted using a motor test bench model equipped with a 300 * 300 * 8 mm heat sink (illustrated in Fig. 10). Simulations ran until thermal steady state was reached, under both the rated operating point and the representative operating point (calculated as the weighted average across all operating cycles). The resulting temperature-rise curves are shown in Fig. 11, with the vertical axis depicting the peak winding temperature. The original motor exhibited the highest steady-state temperature. Although the optimization based on real operating conditions resulted in a slightly higher steady-state temperature at the rated point compared to the rated-efficiency-optimized motor, it achieved lower steady-state temperatures under typical operating conditions, which means less heat during practical use.

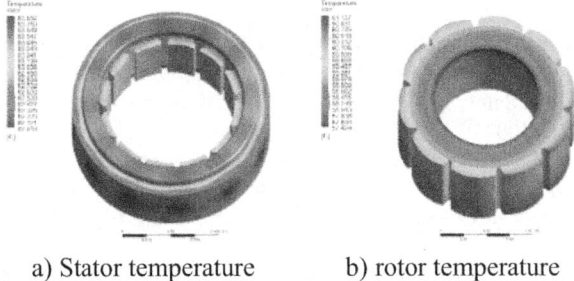

a) Stator temperature   b) rotor temperature

Fig. 10. Transient Temperature Rise Simulation

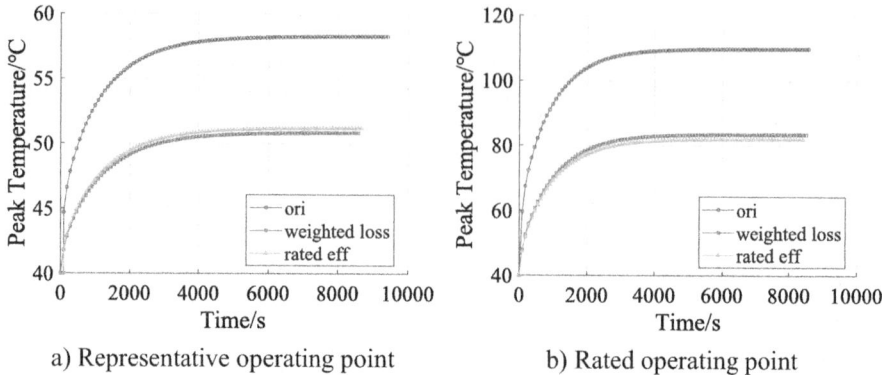

Fig. 11. Temperature Rise Curves of the Three Motors

6.2 Discussion

In this paper, an optimization method considering operating cycle suitability is proposed to address the acceleration demands and duty-cycle characteristics of robotic joint motors. Following optimization, the weighted losses are reduced by over 50%, rotor inertia is decreased by approximately 25%, and torque ripple is lowered by around 40%. These improvements translate into reduced heat generation, lower temperature rise, faster response, and decreased vibration and noise in robotic joints.

Moreover, compared to designs optimized for rated-point efficiency, those optimized for weighted loss exhibit slightly lower efficiency at the rated point but achieve significantly lower weighted losses and higher average efficiency across operational conditions. This translates to lower overall heat dissipation during actual duty cycles, thereby demonstrating the effectiveness of the proposed method.

Acknowledgments. This research work was sponsored by Shanghai Pujiang Program and JAKA Robotics Co., Ltd.

References

1. Bragança, S., Costa, E., Castellucci, I., Arezes, P.M.: A brief overview of the use of collaborative robots in industry 4.0: Human role and safety. In: Arezes, P.M., et al. (eds.) Occupational and Environmental Safety and Health. SSDC, vol. 202, pp. 641–650. Springer, Cham (2019). https://doi.org/10.1007/978-3-030-14730-3_68
2. Vicentini, F.: Collaborative robotics: a survey. J. Mech. Des. **143**(4), 040802 (2021)
3. Li, B., Zhang, Z., Gao, P., Yuan, Y., Li, G.: Optimized design of micro-joint motors using MPSO with embedded ELM indirect surrogate. IEEE Trans. Energy Convers. **39**(2), 1314–1324 (2024)
4. Sherwani, F., Asad, M.M., Ibrahim, B.S.K.K.: Collaborative robots and industrial revolution 4.0 (ir 4.0). In: 2020 International Conference on Emerging Trends in Smart Technologies (ICETST), pp. 1–5. IEEE (2020)
5. Wang, X., et al.: A critical review on thermal management technologies for motors in electric cars. Appl. Therm. Eng. **201**, 117758 (2022)

6. Chu, W., Zhu, Z., Zhang, J., Liu, X., Stone, D., Foster, M.: Investigation on operational envelops and efficiency maps of electrically excited machines for electrical vehicle applications. IEEE Trans. Magn. **51**(4), 1–10 (2015)
7. Lazari, P., Wang, J., Chen, L.: A computationally efficient design technique for electric-vehicle traction machines. IEEE Trans. Ind. Appl. **50**(5), 3203–3213 (2014)
8. Sarigiannidis, A.G., Beniakar, M.E., Kladas, A.G.: Fast adaptive evolutionary PM traction motor optimization based on electric vehicle drive cycle. IEEE Trans. Veh. Technol. **66**(7), 5762–5774 (2017)
9. Salameh, M., Brown, I.P., Krishnamurthy, M.: Fundamental evaluation of data clustering approaches for driving cycle-based machine design optimization. IEEE Trans. Transport. Electrification **5**(4), 1395–1405 (2019)
10. Fatemi, A., Demerdash, N.A.O., Nehl, T.W., Ionel, D.M.: Large-scale design optimization of PM machines over a target operating cycle. IEEE Trans. Ind. Appl. **52**(5), 3772–3782 (2016)
11. Mahmouditabar, F., Vahedi, A., Takorabet, N.: Robust design of BLDC motor considering driving cycle. IEEE Trans. Transportat. Electrification **10**(1), 1414–1424 (2024)
12. Carraro, E., Morandin, M., Bianchi, N.: Traction PMASR motor optimization according to a given driving cycle. IEEE Trans. Ind. Appl. **52**(1), 209–216 (2016)
13. Li, B., Zhang, Z., Gao, P., Li, G.: Design optimization of permanent magnet motors considering multiple operating conditions. In: 2023 26th International Conference on Electrical Machines and Systems (ICEMS), pp. 4003–4008 (2023)
14. Lei, G., Zhu, J., Guo, Y., Liu, C., Ma, B.: A review of design optimization methods for electrical machines. Energies **10**(12), 1962 (2017)
15. Wrobel, R., Salt, D.E., Griffo, A., Simpson, N., Mellor, P.H.: Derivation and scaling of AC copper loss in thermal modeling of electrical machines. IEEE Trans. Industr. Electron. **61**(8), 4412–4420 (2013)
16. Balamurali, A., Lai, C., Mollaeian, A., Loukanov, V., Kar, N.C.: Analytical investigation into magnet eddy current losses in interior permanent magnet motor using modified winding function theory accounting for pulsewidth modulation harmonics. IEEE Trans. Magn. **52**(7), 1–5 (2016)

Cluster-Guided State Initialization Strategy for Flexible Humanoid Locomotion

Wenhao Tan, Zhiheng Li, Xing Fang, Yanyun Chen, Qian Zhang, Ran Song, and Wei Zhang(✉)

Shandong University, Jinan 250014, Shandong, China
davidzhang@sdu.edu.cn

Abstract. The integration of imitation learning and reinforcement learning has demonstrated significant success in whole-body control for humanoid robots, enabling them to execute a diverse range of locomotion behaviors. However, due to the limitations of imitation targets in imitation learning and the limited exploration capacity of reinforcement learning, single-skill policies often outperform multi-skill ones on specific tasks. Furthermore, real-world tasks typically require a combination of multiple skills, which restricts the applicability of imitation learning. To address this issue, we propose a training framework based on the Fuzzy C-means clustering for imitation learning state initialization. This framework analyzes the state information of robots performing various skills within the imitation learning dataset, identifies similar motion states across different tasks, and utilizes these states to initialize training for robots learning similar skills. This framework extends the adaptability of humanoid robot motion control by leveraging the Fuzzy C-means clustering to explore the optimal training initialization for stable and flexible switching between multiple skills. It ultimately enables smooth transitions between diverse skills and control policies. In our experiments, we demonstrated the effectiveness of this approach on the H1 humanoid robot, achieving a 90.83% success rate when switching among four distinct tasks.

Keywords: Imitation learning · reinforcement learning · humanoid robots · robotic manipulation

1 Introduction

In recent years, imitation learning-based control methods [3,8,10] for legged robots have advanced significantly. Numerous studies [12–14] have shown that learning approaches that combine imitation learning and reinforcement learning can effectively enable robots to acquire a diverse set of skills. Additionally, some studies [5,22] are exploring unified frameworks that allow robots to perform multiple tasks within a single control architecture.

W. Tan and Z. Li—The two authors contribute equally to this work. This work was supported by the Key R&D Program of Shandong Province under grant 2024CXGC010212.

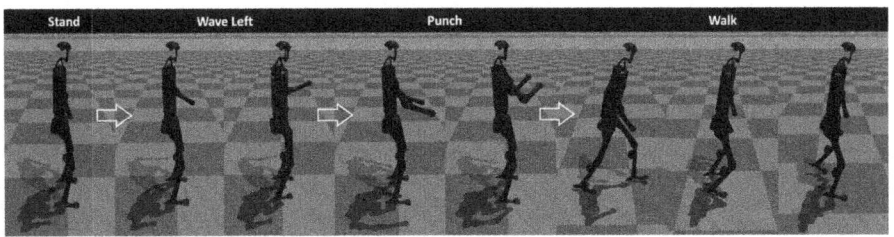

Fig. 1. Illustration of the motion switching task. Our method enables the stable and flexible motion switching via the cluster-guided state initialization strategy.

Existing imitation learning methods [1,15,17,21] have been successfully applied to tasks such as robot navigation, quadruped locomotion control, and humanoid behaviors including walking, standing, and waving. However, many of these approaches [2,19,20] are constrained by limitations related to imitation targets and the volume of demonstration data, often resulting in single-skill policies outperforming their multi-skill counterparts. Additionally, some methods [12,23] restrict a single policy to executing only one task, without support for inter-task policy switching. While a few approaches [17,21] attempt to enable multi-task switching by introducing fixed transition states—typically in the form of standing postures—such rigid mechanisms lack adaptability and are insufficient to meet the diverse and dynamic demands of real-world scenarios.

To address these issues, we propose a training framework for imitation learning and state initialization based on Fuzzy C-means clustering [16]. This framework leverages multiple specialized policies to accomplish distinct tasks, thereby maximizing the performance potential of each individual skill policy. To enable the multi-skill switching necessary for executing complex task sequences, we introduce a cluster-guided reference action analysis method that identifies appropriate states for skill switching. By integrating these similar transitional states into both the reference action dataset and the training process, our approach enhances the adaptability of each single-skill policy and enables smooth and effective transitions between multiple policies.

The proposed method clusters reference action data from multiple tasks to identify similar reference states shared across different tasks. These clusters reveal that robots often pass through analogous states while performing different tasks. Leveraging these similarities allows for policy switching at such transitional states, which minimizes the disruption caused by policy changes and enhances stability during transitions. Furthermore, this paper introduces a reference state initialization mechanism, where the robot's initial state at the beginning of each training epoch is sampled from a broader distribution of reference states. In contrast to traditional imitation learning approaches that initialize only from task-specific reference actions, this method enriches the diversity of training states, improves the robustness of the learned policies, and enables better adaptation to dynamic transitions among four tasks as shown in Fig. 1.

The main contributions of this paper are:

- We propose a clustering-based imitation learning and state initialization framework that enables robots to dynamically switch between multiple policies. This approach significantly enhances the versatility and applicability of robot motion control in multi-task scenarios.
- The framework identifies optimal switching states by searching similar reference states across different tasks. These shared states facilitate smooth transitions between policies, improving the robustness and stability of multi-skill execution.
- Using the H1 humanoid robot as a platform, we validate the effectiveness of the proposed method by demonstrating successful switching across four distinct tasks, achieving a policy transition success rate of 90.83%.

2 Related Work

2.1 Humanoid Imitation Learning

Humanoid robots are expected to proactively acquire natural and fluent motion control via imitating human reference motions. Recently, Imitation learning (IL) has emerged as an appealing technique owing to its capability to learn diverse anthropomorphic motions from human demonstrations. Predominant imitation strategies can be broadly divided into tracking-based methods and GAIL-based methods. Tracking-based methods [4,6,9] operate by providing tracking goals through high-level planning modules, and then the low-level imitation policy is optimized towards minimizing the gap between robots and the reference trajectories. For example, He et al. [7] proposed a learning-based system that leverages the human trajectories as tracking goals, enabling the versatile and dexterous whole-body control in various real-world tasks. Ji et al. [11] further integrated the robot's kinematics filter infeasible whole-body motions, ensuring stable and flexible tracking performance. On the other hand, GAIL-based methods that do not need to set tracking goals are another popular IL method for humanoid robots. Peng et al. [14] presented AMP, a generative adversarial imitation framework that extracts the human motion style from large unstructured datasets. Afterwards, Tessler et al. [18] proposed to learn the representations that capture the complexity and diversity of human motions.

2.2 Multi-skill Learning for Humanoid Robot

Inspired by the growing demand for performing complex tasks in unstructured environments, recent years have witnessed impressive progress in multi-skill learning for humanoid robots. Unlike traditional single-motion approaches, these frameworks address the dual challenges of task flexibility and behavioral diversity by enabling dynamic policy switching or integrating multiple motions into a single policy. For example, Zhang et al. [23] distilled a generalized policy from several pre-trained expert policies, allowing the humanoid robot to master various

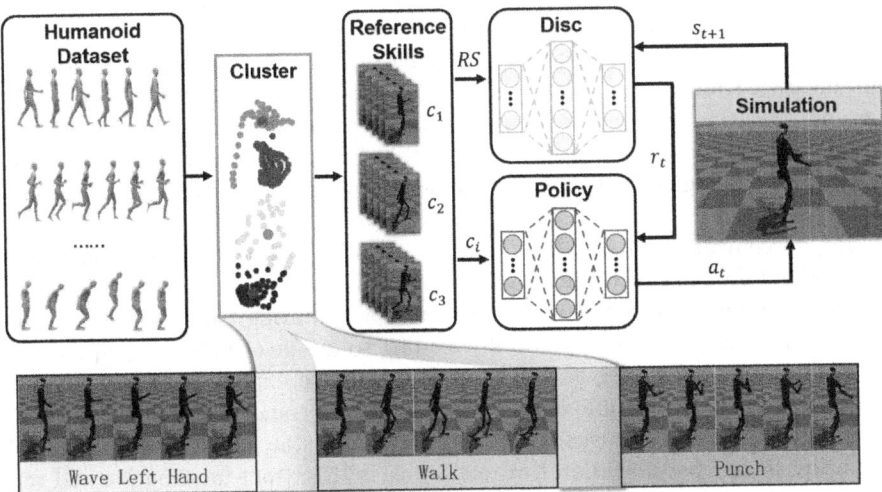

Fig. 2. Overall architecture of our method. Given a humanoid dataset, our method constructs a novel initialization sampling space based on the Fuzzy C-means cluster algorithm, enabling smooth and flexible switching between different skills.

skills. Inspired by the generative adversarial imitation learning methods, GAIL-based methods demonstrate another effective paradigm for multi-skill integration. Early methods, such as AMP [14] and ASE [13], proposed constructing a joint feature space that represents various motions, then sampling from this space to achieve the imitation of different actions. Zhang et al. [21] attempted to deploy AMP on a humanoid robot to acquire diverse anthropomorphic skills such as standing and walking. Similarly, Tang et al. [17] proposed to migrate the Wasserstein distance with the GAIL framework and successfully achieved the multi-skill integration on the humanoid robot JAXON. Although these methods have achieved promising results on multi-skill learning, they still exhibit severe flaws in multi-skill transition due to the substantial feature space disparity between various actions. The absence of smooth transitions often causes jerky motions or even system crashes during motion switching. In this paper, we emphasize the relative relationships of feature distances between different actions and propose an adaptive initialization method to ensure smooth transitions between feature clusters, thus achieving stable and flexible skill switching for humanoid robots. Compared with the state-of-the-art IL methods, our method ensures flexible and stable motion switching, while enabling each policy to unrestrictedly express smooth humanoid control signals without compromising other strategies (Fig. 2).

3 Method

Our goal is to develop a robot control framework that allows for the seamless integration and flexible switching of multiple policies, enabling robots to autonomously arrange and transition between a wide range of skills. To this end, we propose a Fuzzy C-means clustering-based imitation learning and state initialization training framework. This framework integrates reinforcement learning and imitation learning, leveraging clustering techniques to identify optimal switching states. By doing so, it enhances the robustness of individual skill strategies while enabling scalable and adaptable multi-skill execution within a unified control system.

Reinforcement learning (RL) methods optimize policies through continuous interaction between agents and their environments. However, during testing, if an agent encounters states that were not experienced during training, its behavior can become unpredictable, potentially leading to unsafe or ineffective operation. While one common policy is to encourage agents to explore as many environmental variations as possible during training, this becomes infeasible when faced with a large number of tasks or substantial changes in task dynamics. In such scenarios, leveraging imitation learning datasets to extract informative and representative states offers a practical and effective alternative for guiding robot training.

Generative Adversarial Imitation Learning. GAIL is built upon the RL paradigm that can be formulated as a Markov Decision Process (S, A, R, p_0, γ), where S represents the state space, A is the action space, p_0 denotes the initial state distribution and γ represents the discount factor. The core component of GAIL framework lies in the discriminator that accurately distinguish between the expert samples and the generated sample. During the training process, the generator endeavors to produce more realistic samples to deceive the discriminator, with the adversarial pair ideally converging to a Nash equilibrium. The objective function of the discriminator can be expressed as:

$$L_D = -E_{(s_t,s_{t+1}) \in p^M}[log(D(s_t, s_{t+1}))] - E_{(s_t,s_{t+1}) \in p^\pi}[log(1 - D(s_t, s_{t+1}))] \quad (1)$$

where p_M and p_π denote the distribution of reference motions and generated data, respectively. s_t represents the robot states at the t-th frame. $D(s_t, s_{t+1})$ is the output of the discriminator, which represents the probability that the discriminator identifies the input sample as a real one.

Traditional GAIL methods are constrained by the monotonous motion pattern of reference data, as existing imitation learning datasets are typically partitioned into sequential data by task types. Consequently, policies trained for a single task often lack the ability to coordinate effectively with policies learned for other tasks. Significant differences in robot states across tasks can make direct transitions between strategies problematic—abrupt state changes may occur during task switching, resulting in discontinuous behaviors, reduced motion smoothness, and even failure scenarios such as the robot losing balance or falling. To address this issue, we propose a novel initialization strategy to enrich the training scenarios during the training process. This strategy selects samples by measuring their membership distances via clustering, serving as transitional states to enhance the robustness and adaptability of the learned control policies.

Cluster-Guided Initialization Strategy. The heterogeneity in transition across different actions is pronounced. For example, standing-waving transitions are inherently facile, whereas switching from waving to running poses greater challenges. Therefore, we adopt the Fuzzy C-means clustering [16] to quantify the switchability between different action states. Specifically, the Fuzzy C-means computes the membership degree of each sample to predefined action categories, assigning a probabilistic value (0−1) that reflects the degree of similarity between states. Unlike hard clustering methods like K-means, this approach enables fine-grained measurement of transition feasibility, particularly valuable for dynamic scenarios where states often belong to multiple clusters. The process of updating cluster centers can be formulated as:

$$c_i = \frac{\sum_{j=1}^{n} d_{ij}^m x_j}{\sum_{j=1}^{n} d_{ij}^m} \qquad (2)$$

where c_i denotes the i-th cluster center and x_j represents the j-th motion state sample. m is the fuzzification parameter, which we set to 2 in the experiments. d_{ij} represents the membership degree of the j-th sample to the i-th cluster center, which is updated as follows:

$$d_{ij} = \frac{1}{\sum_{k=1}^{C} \left(\frac{\|x_j - c_i\|}{\|x_j - c_k\|} \right)^{\frac{2}{m-1}}} \qquad (3)$$

where C refers to the number of cluster centers. Subsequently, we leverage fuzzy membership degrees to implement a clustering-guided sample augmentation strategy, blending selected samples with original motion states to construct an enriched initialization space. This approach enables the policy to learn latent transition manifolds between distinct actions, ensuring smooth and continuous skill switching. To clearly demonstrate the clustering results, we performed dimensionality reduction with the PCA algorithm before clustering, and the results are presented in Fig. 3.

Clustering results reveal that robot states can vary significantly not only across different tasks but also within the same task at different time. Overlaps in state distributions are sometimes observed between distinct skills. These overlapping states can serve as natural transition points, enabling smooth switching between skills without the need for artificially designed intermediate states. Furthermore, even when no direct overlap exists, similar states may be identified across tasks. By leveraging such similarity, we can augment the imitation learning dataset, enrich the diversity of training samples, and alleviate the problem of low-robustness arising from overly concentrated data distributions.

Building on the expanded reference action dataset, this paper departs from approaches that rely on fixed initial states. Instead, it employs a set of randomly selected reference actions and a diverse collection of similar states—extracted from the aforementioned clustering process—as the initial state dataset. During training, these states are used both as initial state and for periodic resets throughout task execution. Furthermore, the robot's state is randomly perturbed

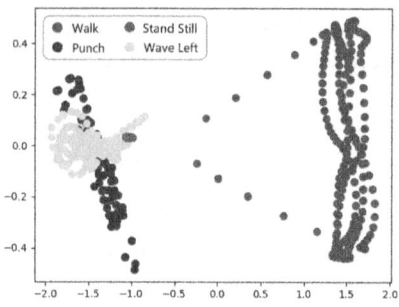
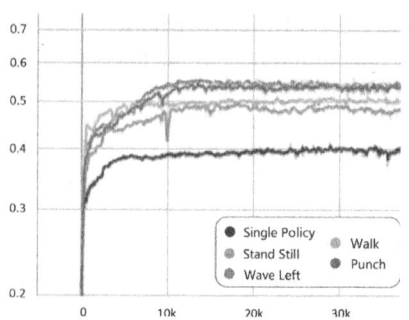

Fig. 3. Visualization of the clustering results for motion states of four different skills. The x- and y-axis represent the first two principal component vectors calculated by PCA.

Fig. 4. Qualitative comparison of training rewards between single-policy action integration and our multi-policy switching strategy.

during training to introduce additional variability. This method effectively broadens the distribution of states encountered during learning, enhances the generalization capability of the policy, and improves its robustness against environmental disturbances and task variations.

Implementation Details. The policy and critic networks are implemented as deep MLPs with a three-layer architecture, which is composed of three linear layers interleaved with two ReLU activation functions. At each timestep t, the policy takes the observation $o_t = [\omega_t, \theta_t, p_t, \dot{p}_t, a_{t-1}]$ as input and generates the action $a_{t+1} \in \mathbb{R}^{19}$. Here, p_t and $\dot{p}_t$ represent the humanoid rigidbody position and linear velocity, θ_t is the orientation, ω_t denotes the angular velocity and a_{t-1} is the previous action. We employed the PPO algorithm to optimize the policy by maximizing the expected cumulative reward: $J(\pi) = E_{\tau \in \pi}[\sum_{t=0}^{T} \gamma^t r(s_t, a_t)]$. Here, τ is the trajectory, $r(s_t, a_t)$ represents the reward for time step t. All experiments are conducted on a 24G RTX 4090 GPU.

4 Experimental Results

In this section, we evaluate both the task execution performance and the policy switching capability of the proposed framework. Using the H1 humanoid robot as the platform, we first demonstrate the effectiveness of our framework across four distinct tasks. Building on the result of clustering, we then train and evaluate policies for each task individually and assess the ability of our method to achieve seamless transitions among the four tasks, thereby validating the multi-skill integration and switching capability of the proposed framework.

In this paper, we use the humanoid rigidbody rotation as the representation of the robot state for visualization analysis. As shown in Fig. 3, by clustering the robot states across four tasks, we found that the states exhibit both significant distinctions and meaningful correlations. Specifically, the tasks of standing,

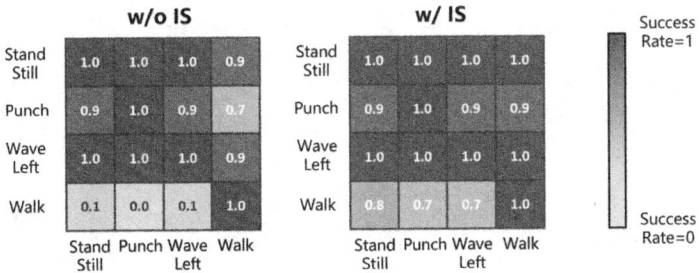

Fig. 5. Visualization of the success rates between different skills. Each element represents the success rate of switching from the vertical-axis action to the horizontal-axis action. "IS" denotes our initialization strategy.

waving, and punching share similar lower-limb movements, leading to overlapping patterns in the visualization space. In contrast, the walking task involves continuous translational motion of the entire body and substantially different lower-limb movements, resulting in distinct state distributions that are clearly separated from the other tasks. Despite these differences, overlapping or similar states are still observed between certain tasks. By assessing the relationship between state samples and cluster centers, we identify a set of representative states that can serve as effective candidates for training initialization and state reset during multi-task policy learning.

We also demonstrated the learning effectiveness of our method. As shown in Fig. 4, compared with the algorithm that learns all skills using a single policy, the proposed algorithm exhibits significantly improved learning curves when training on individual skills. This improvement is due to the limited capacity of a single policy to fit multiple skill distributions effectively. On the other hand, our method achieves higher final performance and faster convergence, demonstrating that skill-specific policies can better capture task-specific dynamics and lead to more robust and efficient learning outcomes. In addition, although a single policy is capable of learning and converging during training, it fails to perform the required tasks effectively during testing. This is primarily due to the significant differences among the tasks, which prevent the policy from appropriately balancing the learning of all four skills. As a result, the trained policy tends to overfit to tasks with similar postures—such as standing—while failing to acquire the diverse patterns needed for tasks with greater variation, such as walking.

When using multiple policies to execute tasks, it is essential to evaluate the system's ability to switch between different tasks to ensure reliable task execution. As shown in Fig. 5, we tested the success rate of switching between four distinct tasks. The results demonstrate that our method maintains a high success rate across various task transitions, indicating its effectiveness in managing policy switching without compromising performance or stability. In addition, we found a high success rate when switching between the three tasks involving lower-limb fixation. However, the success rate significantly decreases when switching between these tasks and the walking task. Interestingly, transitions

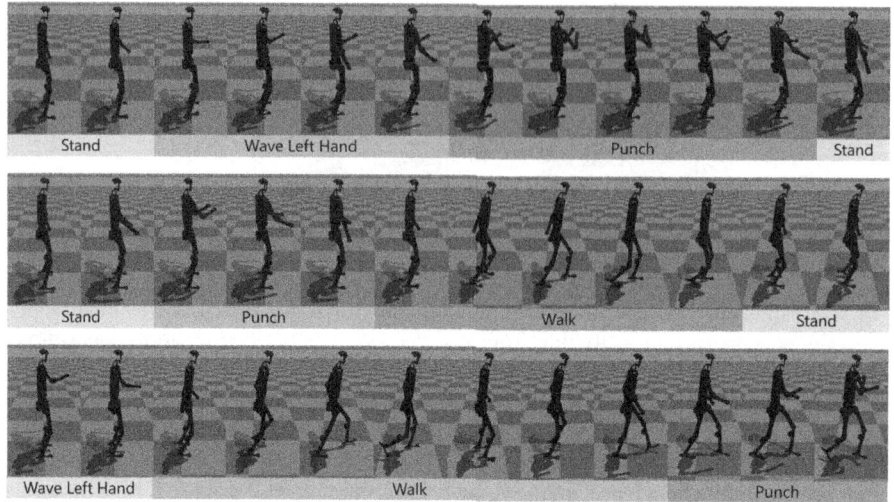

Fig. 6. Snapshots of the motion sequences generated by our method, where the skill labels are also provided. It can be seen that our method enables the stable and flexible motion transition between different skills.

from the lower-limb fixation tasks to walking yield higher success rates compared to transitions in the opposite direction. This asymmetry can be attributed to the imitation learning training process, during which the walking task is typically learned from an initial standing posture. As a result, the policy is more robust when transitioning from familiar standing-like postures into walking.

In summary, the cluster-guided state initialization strategy enables the robot to perform a wide range of tasks and achieve smooth transitions between them. To better illustrate the effectiveness of our approach, we present the robot's control performance during four tasks switching, as shown in Fig. 6. During the demonstration, our framework concurrently manages four distinct policies, each responsible for executing a specific skill. However, at any given moment, only one policy is actively engaged. The robot is capable of seamlessly switching between these policies while performing various tasks. Throughout the entire process, it consistently maintains a stable posture, demonstrating the robustness and flexibility of the proposed control framework.

5 Conclusions

In this paper, we propose a humanoid robot control framework that enables robots to learn multiple skills, specifically standing, walking, waving, and punching, and to switch smoothly between these tasks. By clustering robot states across different tasks, we identify suitable switching states to facilitate seamless transitions. Using the H1 robot as a case study, we demonstrate the effectiveness of the proposed method in performing and transitioning among the four tasks.

References

1. Al-Hafez, F., Zhao, G., Peters, J., Tateo, D.: Locomujoco: a comprehensive imitation learning benchmark for locomotion. arXiv preprint arXiv:2311.02496 (2023)
2. Celemin, C., et al.: Interactive imitation learning in robotics: a survey. Found. Trends® Robot. **10**(1-2), 1–197 (2022)
3. Cheng, X., Ji, Y., Chen, J., Yang, R., Yang, G., Wang, X.: Expressive whole-body control for humanoid robots. arXiv preprint arXiv:2402.16796 (2024)
4. Fu, Z., Zhao, Q., Wu, Q., Wetzstein, G., Finn, C.: Humanplus: humanoid shadowing and imitation from humans. arXiv preprint arXiv:2406.10454 (2024)
5. Geng, H., et al.: Roboverse: towards a unified platform, dataset and benchmark for scalable and generalizable robot learning. arXiv preprint arXiv:2504.18904 (2025)
6. He, T., et al.: Asap: aligning simulation and real-world physics for learning agile humanoid whole-body skills. arXiv preprint arXiv:2502.01143 (2025)
7. He, T., et al.: Omnih2o: universal and dexterous human-to-humanoid whole-body teleoperation and learning. arXiv preprint arXiv:2406.08858 (2024)
8. He, T., et al.: Learning human-to-humanoid real-time whole-body teleoperation. In: 2024 IEEE/RSJ International Conference on Intelligent Robots and Systems (IROS), pp. 8944–8951. IEEE (2024)
9. He, T., et al.: Hover: versatile neural whole-body controller for humanoid robots. arXiv preprint arXiv:2410.21229 (2024)
10. Ho, J., Ermon, S.: Generative adversarial imitation learning. In: Advances in Neural Information Processing Systems, vol. 29 (2016)
11. Ji, M., et al.: Exbody2: advanced expressive humanoid whole-body control. arXiv preprint arXiv:2412.13196 (2024)
12. Peng, X.B., Abbeel, P., Levine, S., Panne, M.: Deepmimic: example-guided deep reinforcement learning of physics-based character skills. ACM Trans. Graph. **37**(4), 1–14 (2018)
13. Peng, X.B., Guo, Y., Halper, L., Levine, S., Fidler, S.: Ase: Large-scale reusable adversarial skill embeddings for physically simulated characters. ACM Trans. Graph. (TOG) **41**(4), 1–17 (2022)
14. Peng, X.B., Ma, Z., Abbeel, P., Levine, S., Kanazawa, A.: Amp: Adversarial motion priors for stylized physics-based character control. ACM Trans. Graph. (ToG) **40**(4), 1–20 (2021)
15. Ratliff, N., Bagnell, J.A., Srinivasa, S.S.: Imitation learning for locomotion and manipulation. In: 2007 7th IEEE-RAS International Conference on Humanoid Robots, pp. 392–397. IEEE (2007)
16. Suganya, R., Shanthi, R.: Fuzzy c-means algorithm-a review. Int. J. Sci. Res. Publ. **2**(11), 1 (2012)
17. Tang, A., et al.: Humanmimic: learning natural locomotion and transitions for humanoid robot via wasserstein adversarial imitation. In: 2024 IEEE International Conference on Robotics and Automation (ICRA), pp. 13107–13114. IEEE (2024)
18. Tessler, C., Kasten, Y., Guo, Y., Mannor, S., Chechik, G., Peng, X.B.: Calm: conditional adversarial latent models for directable virtual characters. In: ACM SIGGRAPH 2023 Conference Proceedings, pp. 1–9 (2023)
19. Wang, Y., Dong, M., Zhao, Y., Du, B., Xu, C.: Imitation learning from purified demonstrations. arXiv preprint arXiv:2310.07143 (2023)
20. Yuan, Y., Makoviychuk, V., Guo, Y., Fidler, S., Peng, X., Fatahalian, K.: Learning physically simulated tennis skills from broadcast videos. ACM Trans. Graph **42**(4) (2023)

21. Zhang, Q., et al.: Whole-body humanoid robot locomotion with human reference. In: 2024 IEEE/RSJ International Conference on Intelligent Robots and Systems (IROS), pp. 11225–11231. IEEE (2024)
22. Zhu, Q., Zhang, H., Lan, M., Han, L.: Neural categorical priors for physics-based character control. ACM Trans. Graph. (TOG) **42**(6), 1–16 (2023)
23. Zhuang, Z., et al.: Robot parkour learning. arXiv preprint arXiv:2309.05665 (2023)

Design and Modeling of a Modular Cable-Driven Lower-Limb Exoskeleton with Compact Torque Sensors

Jia Yao, Zhijun Fu, Xiao Yang, Shuowen Yi, Siyu Liu, and Zhao Guo[✉]

Wuhan University, Wuhan 430072, China
guozhao@whu.edu.cn

Abstract. Although the application of lower limb exoskeletons has been widely studied, current designs still face challenges such as excessive weight, insufficient compliance, and limited modularity. To address these issues, this paper proposes a modular, flexibly actuated lower limb exoskeleton robot. The degrees of freedom and range of motion are determined based on an analysis of human lower limb biomechanics. A lightweight structure is achieved through the use of adjustable modular mechanisms and materials such as aluminum alloy and carbon fiber. Cable-driven actuation is employed at the knee and ankle joints, where high-strength, wear-resistant tungsten cables replace traditional steel cables, and motors are positioned on the thigh and shank to reduce inertial torque. Compact torque sensors are integrated at the hip, knee, and ankle joints, while magnetic encoders at the knee and ankle joints are used to calibrate cable-driven errors. A multidimensional hybrid sensing system is developed, incorporating torque sensors, IMUs, and encoders. For control, a PD strategy with dynamic feedforward compensation is implemented for joint angle tracking. Experimental results show that, under no-load conditions, the tracking errors are within 1.58° at the hip, 2.31° at the knee, and 1.72° at the ankle.

Keywords: Lower-limb exoskeleton · Modular design · Cable-driven actuation

1 Introduction

The global trend of population aging is accelerating, leading to a significant increase in the demand for rehabilitation services. According to the World Health Organization, the number of people aged 60 years and older worldwide is projected to grow from 1 billion in 2020 to 1.4 billion by 2030 [1]. At the same time, the incidence of cerebrovascular diseases continues to rise. In China alone, approximately 3.94 million new cases of stroke occur annually, with more than 70% of survivors experiencing long-term lower limb motor impairments [2, 3]. These pressing public health challenges have created a growing need for advancements in lower limb exoskeleton robot technologies. Traditional rehabilitation methods, which rely heavily on manual assistance and basic equipment, often suffer from low efficiency, poor standardization, and high caregiving costs [4]. Studies have shown that, compared to manual therapy, robotic-assisted gait training—enabled by precise mechanical support and gait planning—can significantly reduce gait errors [5].

In recent years, various lower limb exoskeleton robots have been developed and commercialized. For instance, the second-generation powered exoskeleton HULC developed by the University of California, Berkeley, features a lithium battery-powered hydraulic system and enables users to walk at speeds up to 16 km/h under no-load conditions [6]. The HAL exoskeleton from the University of Tsukuba in Japan allows walking speeds of up to 4 km/h, with a battery life of nearly three hours [7]. Ailegs, developed by DAI Robot in Beijing, is designed for patients with spinal cord injuries, brain injuries, cerebral palsy, or stroke. It uses electric actuators at the hip and knee joints to assist lower limb movement, and its precision control system offers personalized gait training tailored to individual rehabilitation needs [8]. However, these exoskeletons are primarily based on rigid structures, which often result in excessive weight, limited structural flexibility, and inadequate compliance [9].

Flexible Lower-Limb Exoskeletons (FLLE), as an emerging technology [10, 11], effectively address limitations of traditional rigid exoskeletons. Current FLLE structures mainly include pneumatic muscles, Bowden cables, and elastic actuators [12–14]. Among these, cable-driven method is widely adopted due to its lightweight and flexible properties. For example, Harvard's Walsh team developed the Soft Exosuit series using Bowden cables and admittance control to achieve efficient and safe joint assistance [15–17]. Nanjing University of Aeronautics and Astronautics proposed a stiffness-variable exoskeleton using cable-driven mechanisms and reconfigurable pulley systems, with only the knee joint actively actuated [18, 19]. Southern University of Science and Technology introduced an underactuated soft exoskeleton enabling timed knee extension and ankle plantarflexion using a continuum-Bowden cable system [20]. However, these systems lack force sensing and precise torque calibration, and support only fixed joint configurations, limiting flexibility and modular adaptability in assistive strategies.

The previously designed lightweight rope-driven knee exoskeleton [21] by our team has issues, including the lack of active degrees of freedom in the ankle joint and insufficient precise force sensing at each joint. To address these issues, this paper proposes a flexible rope-driven modular lower limb exoskeleton robot, with force sensors integrated at each joint. The key innovations are as follows:

1. A multi-dimensional adjustable modular structure that is personalized to fit the patient's body type, improving wearing compatibility and comfort.
2. Rope-driven knee and ankle joints, with motors placed on the thigh and calf, where the flexible rope transmission reduces joint mass and inertia torque.
3. Compact integrated torque sensors at the hip, knee, and ankle joints, enabling high-precision calibration of joint torque.
4. High-strength, high-wear-resistance tungsten wire ropes replacing traditional steel wire ropes for power transmission, enhancing the reliability of the rope-driven structure.

2 Design and Modeling of the Exoskeleton

2.1 Kinesiological Analysis and Design

The human lower limb kinematic chain is composed of the hip, knee, and ankle joints, each with distinct degrees of freedom based on their physiological structures. Human gait is essentially a periodic motion, with each gait cycle consisting of approximately 60% stance phase and 40% swing phase.

Based on the kinematic characteristics of the human body, the lower limb exoskeleton designed in this study provides five degrees of freedom (DOFs) per leg, including one active DOF at the hip joint (flexion/extension), two passive DOFs at the hip joint (abduction/adduction and internal/external rotation), one active DOF at the knee joint (flexion/extension), and one active DOF at the ankle joint (plantarflexion/dorsiflexion). The active hip joint DOF is actuated by a servo motor, while the two passive hip DOFs are realized through mechanical structures. The knee and ankle joints adopt a flexible cable-driven mechanism composed of Bowden cable housings and tungsten cables.

Compared to conventional steel cables, tungsten cables generally exhibit higher strength and hardness under the same conditions, allowing them to withstand greater tensile forces, resist higher temperatures, and offer superior wear resistance.

To accommodate users of different body types, the adjustment ranges of each exoskeleton module are designed in accordance with GB/T 10000-2023 "Anthropometric Data of Chinese Adults" [22], with the specific ranges summarized in Table 1. The exoskeleton employs an overall modular architecture, allowing rapid configuration and disassembly of individual modules, as shown in Fig. 1. The design balances structural strength with lightweight requirements: primary load-bearing components, such as the back slot and Length slider, are fabricated from metal, while other parts are made of carbon fiber panels and 3D-printed elements. The complete system weighs only 10 kg, and the mass of each joint is detailed in Table 2.

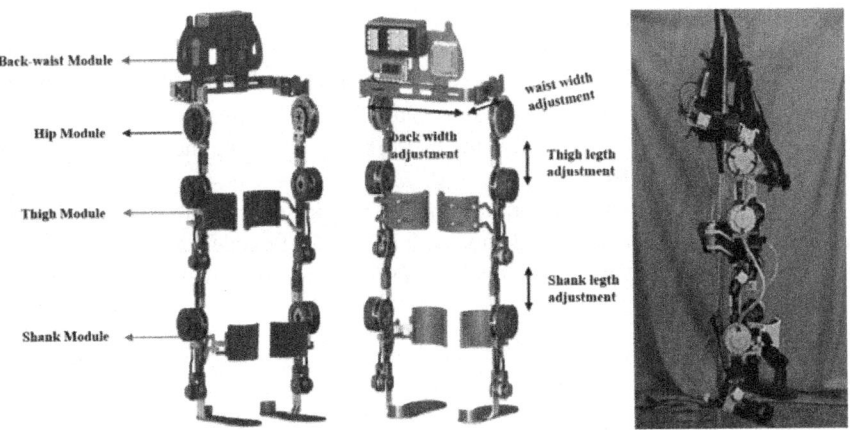

Fig. 1. Overall structure of the exoskeleton

Table 1. Structural adjustment range of the exoskeleton

Components	Adjustment Range mm
Back	330–400
Waist	155–190
Thigh	400–430
Shank-Ankle	380–420

Table 2. Measure mass of the exoskeleton components

Components	Mass per leg kg	Total mass kg	Torque density by mass N·m/kg
Back-Waist module	-	2.47	-
Hip module	0.95	1.90	24.95
Thigh module incl. Cuff	1.41	2.82	16.81
Shank-Ankle module incl. Cuff	1.62	3.24	14.63
Total mass	3.98	10.43	17.86
Total actuator mass	2.03	4.06	-

2.2 Modular Structure Implementation

Back-Waist Module

As shown in Fig. 2, the modular and adjustable design of the exoskeleton's back and waist modules is illustrated.

The back module adopts a plate-integrated structure, which accommodates the power supply and control modules of the exoskeleton. Through dual fixation using shoulder straps and a waist belt, the exoskeleton is stably secured to the user's torso. This configuration transfers part of the load to the back, thereby reducing the burden and motion inertia on the lower limbs.

The waist module employs an adjustable modular design, equipped with quick-adjustment and quick-release mechanisms. It allows for flexible adaptation of the back and waist width, effectively accommodating users of various body types and improving overall wearability.

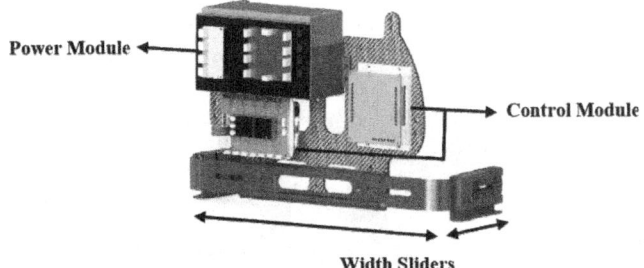

Fig. 2. Back-Waist module

Hip Module

The hip joint's flexion/extension degree of freedom is actuated by a direct-drive motor scheme, with an integrated torque sensor enabling high-precision measurement of joint torque. The passive degrees of freedom for abduction/adduction and internal/external rotation adopt coaxial rotational pair designs, employing flanged deep-groove ball bearings and thrust ball bearings to ensure smooth joint articulation, as shown in Fig. 3.

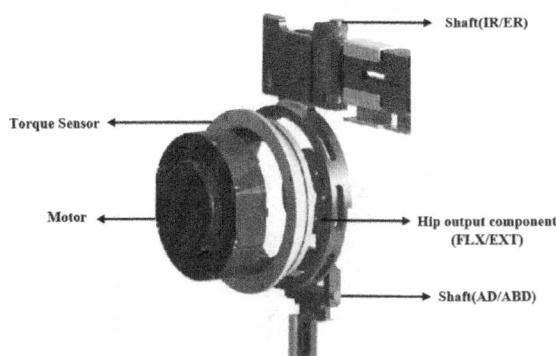

Fig. 3. Hip module

Thigh Module

The knee joint is equipped with a quick-adjustment mechanism to accommodate users with varying heights. To reduce the mass and rotational inertia at the knee joint, the drive motor is mounted on the thigh segment. A pulley–cable mechanism is employed at the joint, in which actuation force is transmitted via the cable and pulley system.

Given that friction may occur between the cable and pulley in flexible cable-driven systems, and the cable length may change over time due to wear or elongation, the motor's internal measurements can become inaccurate. To address this, a torque sensor and a magnetic encoder are installed at the knee joint to enable high-precision measurement of joint torque and angular position, as shown in Fig. 4.

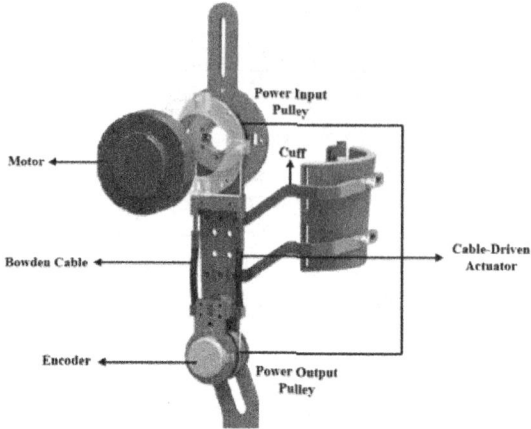

Fig. 4. Thigh module

Shank-Ankle Module

The cable-driven structure of the ankle joint in the proposed exoskeleton is similar to that of the knee joint, with only minor modifications in the dimensions of the joint axis. Therefore, a detailed structural analysis is not presented here, as shown in Fig. 5.

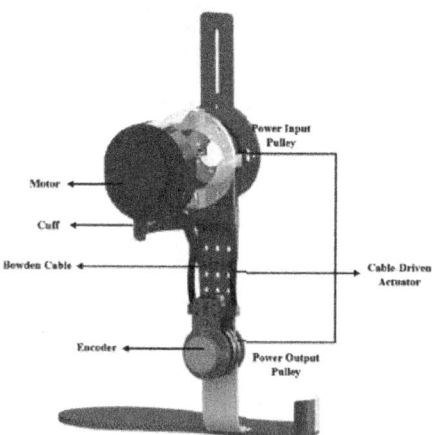

Fig. 5. Shank-Ankle module

2.3 Dynamic Modeling of a Single-Leg Exoskeleton

According to the Lagrangian equation [23], the dynamic model of the exoskeleton's single leg can be described as follows:

$$M(\theta)\ddot{\theta} + C(\theta,\dot{\theta})\dot{\theta} + G(\theta) + D = T \qquad (1)$$

In the equation, $M(\theta)$ denotes the inertia matrix, $C(\theta, \dot{\theta})$ represents the Coriolis and centrifugal matrix, $G(\theta)$ is the gravity matrix determined by the dynamic position of the center of mass, D denotes the unknown external disturbances at the joints, and T represents the output torques at the hip, knee, and ankle joints.

The dynamic modeling of a single leg of the lower limb exoskeleton robot is divided into two distinct states: swing and stance. In conducting the dynamic analysis, the degrees of freedom of the hip, knee, and ankle joints in the sagittal plane are considered, and the exoskeleton can be simplified as a linkage model. As shown in Fig. 6, the single leg of the lower limb exoskeleton robot can be equivalently represented as a four-link model.

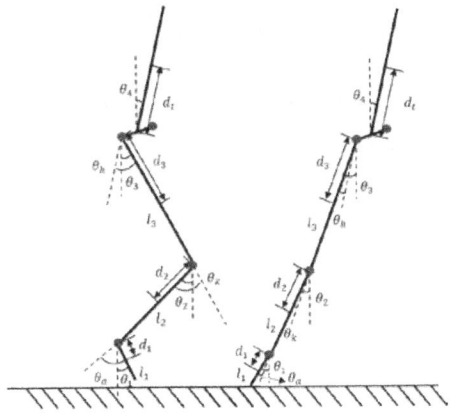

Fig. 6. Schematic diagram of dynamic model

The exoskeleton's ankle-to-foot segment is modeled as Link 1, the shank module as Link 2, the thigh module as Link 3, and the back module as Link 4. Given the approximately symmetric structure of the exoskeleton robot, it is assumed that the center of mass (COM) of each link lies along the corresponding link. Link 1 has a length l_1, a mass m_1, and its center of mass is located at a distance d_1 from the ankle joint. Link 2 has a l_2, a mass m_2, and its center of mass is located at a distance d_2 from the knee joint. Link 3 has a length l_3, a mass m_3, and its center of mass is located at a distance d_3 from the hip joint. The center of mass of Link 4 is located at a distance d_t from the midpoint of the line connecting the two hip joints.

Let θ_h denote the angles between Link 4 and Link 3, θ_k denote the angles between Link 3 and Link 2, respectively, θ_a denote the angle between Link 2 and Link 1. The angles $\theta_1, \theta_2, \theta_3, \theta_4$, represent the respective angles between Links 1 through 4 and the coronal plane.

As shown in the figure, the actual joint angles of the hip, knee, and ankle require the following coordinate transformations:

$$\theta_h = \theta_3 - \theta_4, \theta_k = \theta_2 - \theta_3, \theta_a = \theta_1 - \theta_2 \tag{2}$$

During the swing phase, the reference point is selected at the connection between the hip joint and the torso, and the dynamic model is given as follows:

$$\tau_{sw} = \begin{bmatrix} \tau_a \\ \tau_k \\ \tau_h \end{bmatrix} = \begin{bmatrix} M_{11} & M_{12} & M_{13} \\ M_{21} & M_{22} & M_{23} \\ M_{31} & M_{32} & M_{33} \end{bmatrix} \begin{bmatrix} \ddot{\theta}_a \\ \ddot{\theta}_k \\ \ddot{\theta}_h \end{bmatrix} + \begin{bmatrix} C_{11} & C_{12} & C_{13} \\ C_{21} & C_{22} & C_{23} \\ C_{31} & C_{32} & C_{33} \end{bmatrix} \begin{bmatrix} \dot{\theta}_a \\ \dot{\theta}_k \\ \dot{\theta}_h \end{bmatrix} + \begin{bmatrix} G_l \\ G_2 \\ G_3 \end{bmatrix} \quad (3)$$

During the stance phase, the reference point is defined as the intersection between Link 1 and the ground, and the dynamic model is given as follows:

$$\tau_{st} = \begin{bmatrix} \tau_a \\ \tau_k \\ \tau_h \end{bmatrix} = \begin{bmatrix} M_{11} & M_{12} & M_{13} & M_{14} \\ M_{21} & M_{22} & M_{23} & M_{24} \\ M_{31} & M_{32} & M_{33} & M_{34} \end{bmatrix} \begin{bmatrix} \ddot{\theta}_a \\ \ddot{\theta}_k \\ \ddot{\theta}_h \\ \ddot{\theta}_4 \end{bmatrix} + \begin{bmatrix} C_{11} & C_{12} & C_{13} & C_{14} \\ C_{21} & C_{22} & C_{23} & C_{24} \\ C_{31} & C_{32} & C_{33} & C_{34} \end{bmatrix} \begin{bmatrix} \dot{\theta}_a \\ \dot{\theta}_k \\ \dot{\theta}_h \\ \dot{\theta}_4 \end{bmatrix} + \begin{bmatrix} G_1 \\ G_2 \\ G_3 \end{bmatrix} \quad (4)$$

In the equation, τ_{sw} denotes the joint torques of the exoskeleton during the swing phase, τ_a represents the torque at the ankle joint, τ_k represents the torque at the knee joint, and τ_h represents the torque at the hip joint. τ_{st} denotes the joint torques of the exoskeleton during the stance phase.

Based on the dynamic model, the required joint torques of the exoskeleton robot during the swing and stance phases can be derived. These torques are used for feedforward compensation in exoskeleton control.

3 Hardware System Design

The hardware system of the lower limb exoskeleton is composed of a control module, a motor module, and a sensing module, as shown in Figs. 7 and 8.

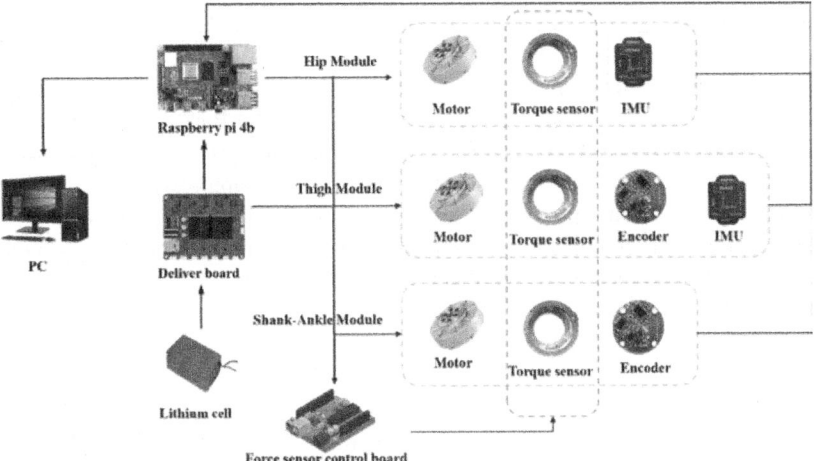

Fig. 7. Exoskeleton hardware control system

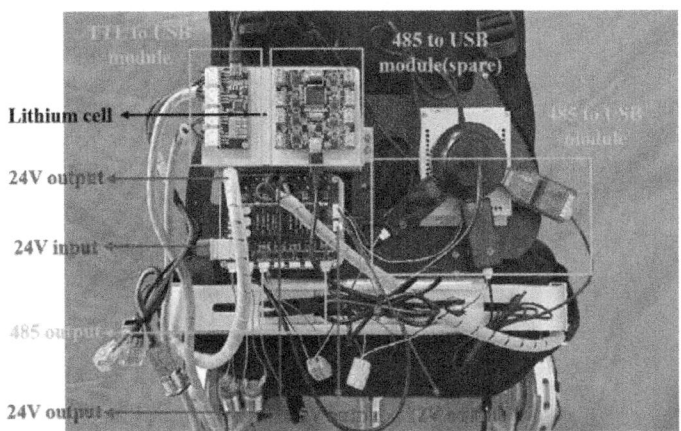

Fig. 8. Power and signal wiring diagram

3.1 Control Module

As the core of the robotic system, the control module is responsible for information exchange and motion planning. In this study, a Raspberry Pi 4B microcomputer is selected as the main controller of the lower limb exoskeleton robot. The Raspberry Pi is a microcomputer based on the ARM architecture that uses an SD/MicroSD card as memory storage and supports Bluetooth communication. However, due to the presence of four IMU sensors in the system, the Raspberry Pi may experience instability when handling multiple Bluetooth signals simultaneously, leading to sensor data distortion.

To ensure reliable data transmission, a USB-to-TTL serial module is adopted to transmit joint sensor data via wired connections.

For high-speed communication between the main controller, the motor driver, and the torque sensors, the RS485 protocol is used. Since the Raspberry Pi 4B does not natively support RS485, a USB-to-RS485 converter is employed. Additionally, a custom-designed voltage divider board is used to manage power supply and hardware control. This board supports multiple output voltages (24 V, 12 V, and 5 V) and also provides RS485 communication capability. During system operation, a computer serves as the host controller, sending control commands to the Raspberry Pi, which then reads sensor data and controls motor movement accordingly.

3.2 Motor Module

Based on the required joint torques and installation constraints of the exoskeleton, the selected joint motor provides a rated torque of 23.7 N·m and a peak rotational speed of 30 rad/s under a 24 V power supply.

3.3 Sensing Module

IMU sensors are used to directly measure sagittal-plane angle variations of the user's hip and knee joints. The IMUs support both Bluetooth and TTL serial communication and are physically attached to the user's thigh and shank. Magnetic encoders are employed to directly measure joint angles at the knee and ankle joints via the RS485 protocol. The torque sensors are custom-designed to fit the exoskeleton structure and directly measure the output torque at the knee and ankle joints. Detailed specifications are provided in Table 3.

Table 3. Specifications of the Torque Sensor

Parameter	Value
Measurement Range	±24 N·m
Accuracy	±1% FS
Resolution	0.0656 N·m(hip joint); 0.0156 N·m(knee joint & ankle joint)
Operating Voltage	5 V

4 Experiments and Results

In this study, a PD control strategy combined with feedforward torque compensation was adopted. Experiments were conducted under no-load conditions, and the control algorithm incorporated proportional-derivative (PD) control with feedforward torque compensation. The frequency of control loop is 167 Hz. The experimental results indicate that this control strategy achieved a hip joint tracking error of $\leq 1.58°$, a knee joint tracking error of $\leq 2.31°$, and an ankle joint tracking error of $\leq 1.72°$. The experiments and corresponding experimental data are shown in Fig. 9.

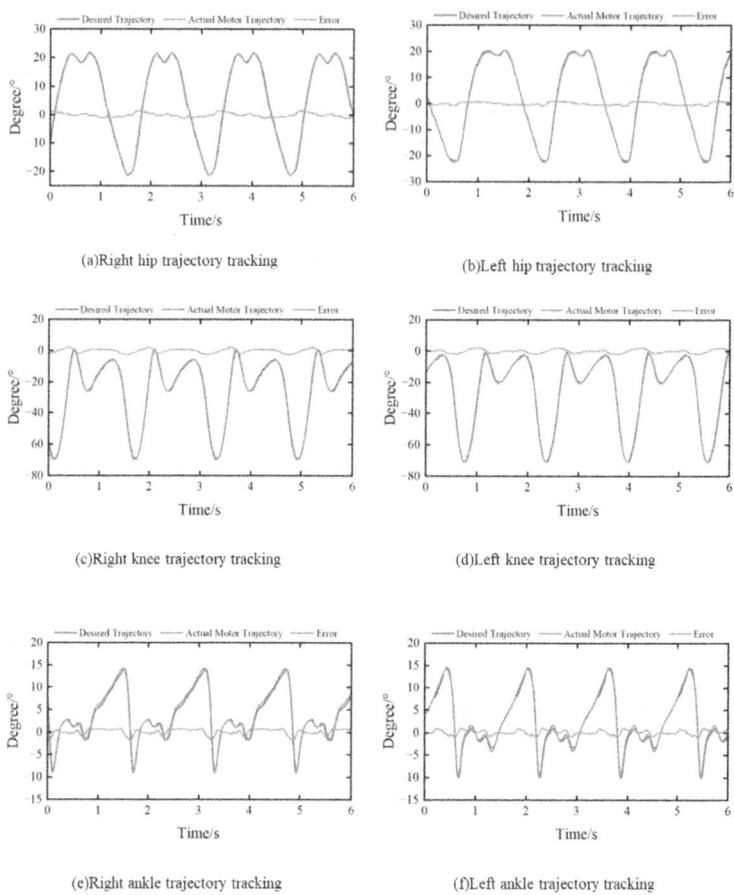

Fig. 9. Joint trajectories over multiple gait cycles

5 Conclusion

In this study, a modular lower-limb exoskeleton was developed to address the limitations of traditional rigid exoskeletons, such as excessive weight and insufficient compliance. The proposed design introduces a cable-driven mechanism for the knee and ankle joints and integrates joint torque sensors to enhance system flexibility and sensing accuracy. A multidimensional adjustable modular structure was adopted, enabling rapid configuration to accommodate users with varying body sizes.

The hip module combines direct-drive actuation for the primary degree of freedom with passive rotation enabled by a bearing assembly. Flexible transmission using Bowden cables and tungsten wires was implemented at the knee and ankle joints, with motors positioned proximally on the thigh and shank to reduce inertia and improve user comfort. The system includes torque sensors at the hip, knee, and ankle, and magnetic encoders at the knee and ankle, forming a high-precision, multi-modal sensing architecture.

A Raspberry Pi serves as the central controller, communicating with IMUs, encoders, and torque sensors via RS485 for reliable high-speed data transmission. The control system applies a PD controller enhanced by feedforward torque compensation. Experimental validation under no-load conditions demonstrated tracking accuracy within 1.58° at the hip, 2.31° at the knee, and 1.72° at the ankle.

Overall, this design achieves an effective balance between modularity, compliance, and precise torque sensing, offering a promising solution for lightweight and personalized lower-limb rehabilitation. Future work will focus on improving wearability through user feedback and enhancing control adaptability via reinforcement learning and sensor-driven real-time gait planning.

Acknowledgments. Research supported by the National Key Research and Development Program of China (No. 2023YFE0202100), and the Key Research and Development Program of Hubei Province (Grant No. 2024BCB007).

References

1. WHO: Ageing and health. https://www.who.int/news-room/fact-sheets/detail/ageing-and-health. 6 June 2025
2. National Health Commission of the People's Republic of China: Cerebrovascular Disease Prevention and Treatment Guidelines (2024 Edition). Chin. J. Magn. Reson. Imaging **16**(1), 1–8 (2025)
3. Zhao, H., et al.: Best evidence summary for rehabilitation management of stroke patients with motor dysfunction. J. Central South Univ. (Med. Sci.) **49**(4), 497–507 (2024)
4. Zhu, Y., et al.: Lower limb exoskeleton based on variable stiffness actuation. Robot **45**(3), 257–266+312 (2023)
5. Ding, Y., et al.: Research progress on wearable lower limb exoskeleton rehabilitation robots. Robot **44**(5), 522–532 (2022)
6. Yang, J, et al. A review on human intent understanding and compliance control strategies for lower limb exoskeletons. Proc. Instit. Mech. Eng., Part I: J. Syst. Control Eng. **236**(6), 1067–1086 (2022)
7. Tsukahara, A., Hasegawa, Y., Sankai, Y.: Standing-up motion support for paraplegic patient with Robot Suit HAL. IEEE Int. Conf. Rehabilit. Robot. **2009**, 211–217 (2009)
8. Wang, H., Hu, L., Wang, Z., et al.: Research progress on lower limb medical rehabilitation exoskeleton robots. Chinese Med. Equipment J. **46**(1), 88–100 (2025)
9. Bartenbach, V,. Gort, M., Riener, R.: Concept and design of a modular lower limb exoskeleton. IEEE (2016)
10. Meng, Q., Zeng, Q., Xie, Q., et al.: Flexible lower limb exoskeleton systems: a review. NeuroRehabilitation **50**(4), 367–390 (2022)
11. Khomami, A.M., Najafi, F.: A survey on soft lower limb cable-driven wearable robots without rigid links and joints. Robot. Auton. Syst. **144**, 103846 (2021)
12. Qian, W., Liao, J., Lu, L., et al.: Curer: A lightweight cable-driven compliant upper limb rehabilitation exoskeleton robot. IEEE/ASME Trans. Mechatron., (2022)
13. Yu, H., Huang, S., Chen, G., et al.: Human–robot interaction control of rehabilitation robots with series elastic actuators. IEEE Trans. Rob. **31**(5), 1089–1100 (2015)
14. Sun, J., Guo, Z., Zhang, Y., et al.: A novel design of serial variable stiffness actuator based on an archimedean spiral relocation mechanism. IEEE/ASME Trans. Mechatron. **23**(5), 2121–2131 (2018)

15. Lee. S., Karavas, N., Quinlivan, B.T., et al.: Autonomous multi-joint soft exosuit for assistance with walking overground. In: 2018 IEEE International Conference on Robotics and Automation (ICRA), pp. 2812–2819. IEEE (2018)
16. Siviy, C., et al.: Opportunities and challenges in the development of exoskeletons for locomotor assistance. Nat. Biomed. Eng. **7**(4), 456–472 (2023)
17. Baud, R., et al.: Review of control strategies for lower-limb exoskeletons to assist gait. J. Neuroeng. Rehabilit. **18**, 1–34 (2021)
18. Zhu, Y.H., Wu, Q.C., Chen, B., et al.: Design and evaluation of a novel torque-controllable variable stiffness actuator with reconfigurability. IEEE/ASME Trans. Mechatron. **27**(1), 292–303 (2021)
19. Zhu, Y.H., Wu, Q.C., Chen, B., et al.: Design and voluntary control of variable stiffness exoskeleton based on semg driven model. IEEE Robot. Autom. Lett. **7**(2), 5787–5794 (2022)
20. Ma, L., Jiang, et al.: Design an underactuated soft exoskeleton to sequentially provide knee extension and ankle plantarflexion assistance. IEEE Robot. Autom. Lett. **7**(1), 271–278 (2022)
21. Yi, S., et al.: Design and modeling of a lightweight lower limb exoskeleton with compliant knee joints. In: 2023 IEEE International Conference on Robotics and Biomimetics (ROBIO). IEEE (2023)
22. China National Institute of Standardization, Anta Co., Ltd., GAC Group Automotive Engineering Research Institute, et al.: Chinese Adult Human Dimensions. GB/T 10000–2023, p. 44 (2023)
23. Qiu, S., Pei, Z., Shi, J., et al.: Design-modeling and control of a novel wearable exoskeleton for lower-limb enhancement. IEEE Robot. Autom. Lett. **9**(7), 6640–6647 (2024)

Author Index

A
Alam, Md.Mahbub II-581
An, Peiru I-397
An, Yi II-471
Azam, Hamza II-275

B
Bai, Ruiyu I-571
Bao, Chenyu II-459
Bao, Mengyi I-363
Besari, Adnan Rachmat Anom II-129

C
Cai, Hegao II-613
Cai, Huayi II-446
Cai, Huimin I-484, I-496
Cai, Jiahui III-150
Cai, Mengchen I-459
Cai, Mingxue III-49
Cai, Shibo III-298, III-310
Cai, Songtao III-650
Cao, Ruikai III-287
Cao, Wujing II-222, II-234, II-244, II-285, II-309
Cao, Zhongzhong I-201
Chen, Bowen III-473, III-534
Chen, Chen I-373
Chen, Chunjie III-323
Chen, Genliang I-559
Chen, Hao III-162
Chen, Haochu II-155
Chen, Huangchao I-423
Chen, Hui III-323
Chen, Junliang III-15
Chen, Junru II-421
Chen, Kaixuan II-698
Chen, Mingzhi I-153
Chen, Mu III-361
Chen, Peng III-298
Chen, Wenyu III-361
Chen, Xin III-310

Chen, Xingyu I-547
Chen, Yanhu I-227
Chen, Yanyun III-662
Chen, Yibin III-249
Chen, Yihan III-26
Chen, Yinhui II-650
Chen, Yujie II-244
Chen, Yun II-483
Chen, Zhiqiang III-49
Chen, Zhujin III-323
Cheng, Cheng III-447
Cheng, Hong III-631
Cheng, Xiangyu III-310
Cheng, Yun II-446
Cheng, Zhenyu II-297
Chu, Hui II-79, II-266
Chu, Shixuan III-235
Chu, Yao III-560
Cui, Jiatong II-322

D
Dai, Ruixuan III-124
Dai, Wenjie II-373
Deng, Linan III-447
Deng, Zongquan III-136
Ding, Cheng I-91
Ding, Han I-77, I-140, II-210
Ding, Liang III-136
Ding, Ning II-483
Ding, Shuchen III-587
Ding, Tao I-446, II-497
Ding, Ye II-337, II-349
Ding, Zhe II-545
Dong, Anqin III-348
Dong, Birong I-279
Dong, Kaijie III-174
Dong, Na III-398
Dong, Tenghui III-650
Dong, Wenhui I-215
Dong, Yan II-421
Dong, Yifei II-471

Dong, Yunlong III-447
Du, Fuxin I-595
Du, Mingyu III-298, III-310
Du, Xinyang I-350, II-285, II-557

F

Fan, Huijie III-422
Fan, Shixun I-496
Fan, Xuanhe II-54
Fan, Yihui II-210
Fan, Zuxin II-567
Fang, Xing III-662
Fang, Yinfeng II-114
Fang, Yuelei III-185
Fang, Zi II-166, II-184
Fei, Xinyu I-227
Feng, Luying II-275
Feng, Shuo III-573
Feng, Siyu III-287
Feng, Zihe III-611
Fu, Chenglong II-67, II-197, II-255
Fu, Hang III-162
Fu, Qiang III-88
Fu, Zhijun III-673
Fu, Zhuang II-166, II-184

G

Gan, Yiming II-37
Gao, Ang II-361
Gao, Chao III-275
Gao, Feng III-112
Gao, Haibo III-136
Gao, Liang II-637
Gao, Naixing I-385
Gao, Qingbin II-650
Gao, Zhe II-601
Ge, Ziyun II-322
Gerževič, Mitja II-275
Gong, Kening II-175
Gou, Xuning I-547
Gu, Guoying I-65, I-547
Guan, Zimeng III-650
Guo, Hongwei I-525, I-536
Guo, Jiajie III-249, III-484
Guo, Lei I-239
Guo, Lina II-3
Guo, Liucheng II-545
Guo, Qixiang III-197
Guo, Weichao I-328

Guo, Weilun II-409
Guo, Weizhong III-162, III-235
Guo, Yikun I-77
Guo, Yizhu III-124, III-197
Guo, Ze-Sheng I-509
Guo, Zhao III-673
Guo, Zisui I-201

H

Hai, Yong III-611
Han, Bin II-421
Han, Jianda I-472
Han, Shiyu III-348
Han, Tao III-361
Han, Wei I-166
He, Jiayuan I-279
He, Shuangjiang II-54
He, Weikai I-595
Hirai, Takao III-60
Hong, Lin I-239
Hou, Haofei I-459, II-567
Hou, Licheng I-15
Hou, Siqi II-509
Hou, Zeng-Guang II-322
Hu, Hongbo I-3, I-27, I-39
Hu, Junjie II-459
Hu, Shibo III-386
Hu, Wenyu I-27
Hu, Yan III-112
Hu, Yanbo II-297
Hu, Zebin I-446
Hua, Feng III-447
Huai, Xiang III-174
Huang, Chenyang III-49
Huang, Chuwen II-234
Huang, Hao III-484
huang, Junfeng III-197
Huang, Rui III-631
Huang, Taoyuan I-65
Huang, Wenze III-473, III-534
Huang, Yedong I-583
Huang, Yiren III-611
Huang, Yongfeng III-49
Huang, Yuxiang II-545
Huo, Weiguang I-472

I

Irshad, Ahmad II-275

Author Index

J
Ji, Haoyu III-473, III-534
Ji, Xiang III-26
Ji, Yanyan II-509
Jiang, Dongjie I-103
Jiang, Gedong II-397
Jiang, Jialin III-26, III-38
Jiang, Li II-175
Jiang, Ning I-279
Jiang, Qin II-210
Jiang, Ruoyuan II-446
Jiang, Tianxiang I-115
Jiang, Xugang II-27
Jiang, Yao I-316
Jiang, Zimo III-473, III-534
Jin, Dongdong III-15
Jin, Shuxiao I-472
Jin, Taixian II-662
Jin, Wei II-567
Jin, Yaolun II-114
Jing, Fei II-166, II-184
Jing, Hongwei II-91
Ju, Haotian II-91, II-613

K
Kamegawa, Tetsushi III-60
Ke, Shuai I-77
Kuang, Qi III-287
Kubota, Naoyuki II-129, III-209

L
Lam, Tin Lun II-459
Lang, Chenbo III-112
Lei, Changjiang II-197, II-255
Leng, Yuquan II-67, II-197, II-255
Li, Bo I-571
Li, Bocong II-361
Li, Changle II-601
Li, Chuanjiang II-37
Li, Chunfeng I-536
Li, Dachuan II-433
Li, Di II-509
Li, Duanjiao II-483
Li, Duanling III-101, III-124, III-150, III-174, III-197
Li, Feng II-397
Li, Fengyi III-162
Li, Guanglin II-27
Li, Guangye I-411
Li, Guo II-397
Li, Guotao III-611
Li, Haifeng I-363
Li, Hongchen II-349
Li, Hui III-275, III-611
Li, Jianmin I-434
Li, Jiayi II-385
Li, Jinghang II-155
Li, Jingyao III-174
Li, Jinhua I-434
Li, Jinke I-350, II-143
Li, Kairu II-3
Li, Ke III-88
Li, Lele II-91
Li, Li II-54
Li, Liyi II-637
Li, Qingdu II-521
Li, Rankun II-521
Li, Shunchong I-91
Li, Tianming I-423
Li, Tiemin I-316
Li, Weimin II-409
Li, Weipeng III-249
Li, Xiangxin II-27
Li, Xinchi III-361
Li, Yanbiao III-222
Li, Yazhou II-3
Li, Ye III-185
Li, Yinghui III-235
Li, Youfu II-675, II-686
Li, Yumeng I-397
Li, Yuming I-294
Li, Yuqi I-525
Li, Yusen III-560
Li, Zhe III-631
Li, Zhiheng III-662
Li, Zhipeng II-397
Liang, Bin II-385
Liang, Cheng I-201
Liang, Dawei II-91, II-613
Liang, Guangyu II-322
Liang, Jian II-662
Liang, Jiawei III-599
Liang, Shengxiang II-222
Liang, Shuai II-37
Liang, Tian II-534
Liang, Xu III-611
Liang, Yunpeng II-624
Liang, Zhenkun I-559
Liang, Zibin III-101

Liao, Da III-631
Liao, Zhaoyang I-294
Liao, Zhao-Yang I-509
Lin, Chengyu II-67
Lin, Junkai II-509
Lin, Sen III-422
Lin, Weixian I-52
Lin, Xubin I-294
Lin, Yichen I-350, II-285, II-297, II-309, II-557
Lin, Yuchen II-497
Ling, Shaobin II-459
Liu, Bang II-166, II-184
Liu, Changquan II-197
Liu, Chongfeng I-201
Liu, Dachuan II-650
Liu, Daming III-185
Liu, Donghan III-263
Liu, Gang I-472
Liu, Gangfeng II-601
Liu, Haitao I-166
Liu, Hong II-175
Liu, Honghai III-263, III-473, III-534
Liu, Houde II-385
Liu, Jian I-140
Liu, Jianming II-483
Liu, Lianfeng I-484
Liu, Lu I-177
Liu, Rongqiang I-536
Liu, Ruiheng I-227
Liu, Runze II-409
Liu, Shengbo II-483
Liu, Siyu III-673
Liu, Tao III-336
Liu, Xing III-447
Liu, Xingyu II-686
Liu, Yao III-323
Liu, Ying II-545
Liu, Yuanbo III-650
Liu, Yuchao III-249
Liu, Yuhan II-373
Liu, Zedong II-91
Liu, Zhongtao I-595
Liu, Zijie III-484
Liu, Zongying II-129
Liu, Zongyuan III-222
Long, Xiaojing II-297
Lou, Yunjiang III-88
Lu, Chunheng II-16
Lu, Hao II-244

Lu, Honglei II-497
Lu, Wenke I-350, II-309
Lu, Xingyu I-472
Lu, Yu III-599
Lu, Yuhan I-39
Lu, Zexin I-153
Lu, Zhe III-587
Lu, Zi-Wei I-509
Luo, Mingxiang II-222
Luo, Ruijie I-411
Luo, Xiang III-484
Luo, Xin I-52, I-127
Lv, Bo I-397

M
Ma, Guijun III-447
Ma, Guoyao III-49
Ma, Shentao I-252
Ma, Shiyu III-587
Ma, Tiancheng I-127
Ma, Wei I-166
Ma, Wen II-397
Ma, Xing III-15
Ma, Yue I-350, II-234, II-285, II-309, II-557
Mai, Xiaoming III-398
Mai, Ximing I-411
Mao, Baijin I-583
Matsui, Yusuke III-60
Matsuno, Takayuki II-103, III-60
Mei, Xuesong III-508, III-521
Melo, Kamilo III-249
Meng, Jianjun I-411
Meng, Tao III-336
Mi, Shuaibing III-398
Mu, Fengjun III-631
Mu, Xinxing II-409

N
Nie, Pingyun I-115

O
Obo, Takenori III-209

P
Pan, Jie I-77
Pan, Lizhi I-434
Pan, Mingxu III-434
Pang, Wen I-153
Pang, Xufang II-483

Author Index

Pang, Yunfan   III-150
Peng, Xiaoke   III-348
Peng, Yan   II-521
Peng, Zhinan   III-631
Peng, Zhouhua   I-177
Piri, Saeid   III-3
Pradhan, Ashirbad   I-279

Q

Qi, Dexin   III-508, III-521
Qi, Jian   II-91
Qi, Zhanchuan   III-88
Qian, Huihuan   I-201
Qian, Letian   I-52
Qian, Shipang   I-227
Qiang, Junjie   I-52
Qiao, Zhehao   III-136
Qin, Pengjie   I-350, II-234, II-244
Qu, Juntian   I-583

R

Ren, Jieji   I-65
Ren, Weihong   III-473, III-534
Ren, Zengle   I-350, II-143, II-285
Ren, Zhouyi   III-174
Ruan, Lecheng   I-103, I-459, II-567
Ruan, Yizhang   III-548

S

Sakai, Nanako   III-60
Saputra, Azhar Aulia   III-209
Shan, Yihan   II-601
Shen, Xueyan   II-143, II-222
Shen, Yu   II-16
Sheng, Xinjun   I-306, I-328
Sheng, Yixuan   I-239, I-385, III-287
Shi, Changcheng   III-336
Shi, Jiaqi   III-494
Shi, Kecheng   III-631
Shi, Xiaoyu   II-581
Shi, Xin   II-244
Shi, Xulong   I-583
Shou, Zefeng   III-336
Si, Chuanyu   II-91
Siow, Chyan Zheng   II-129, III-209
Song, Ningning   II-409
Song, Qingwei   II-129, III-209
Song, Ran   III-662
Song, Rui   I-595

Song, Zhihong   II-16
Su, Chengyu   III-587
Su, Hang   II-361
Su, Tingting   III-611
Sun, Guangzhen   II-337
Sun, Jianquan   II-309, II-557
Sun, Kangkang   III-611
Sun, Peng   I-52, I-267, III-222
Sun, Shilong   II-650
Sun, Tairen   III-622
Sun, Wei   II-197
Sun, Yaowei   II-433
Sun, Zhe   I-267, III-222

T

Tan, Huachen   III-460
Tan, Wenhao   III-662
Tang, Lu   I-140
Tang, Qing   III-434
Tang, Xiaoran   II-175
Tao, Bo   I-15, I-423, II-497, III-386
Tao, Jianguo   I-536, III-136
Tao, Tao   III-508
Tian, Jiandong   III-411
Tian, Lan   II-27
Tian, Lingyan   I-373
Tian, Rui   III-587
Toda, Yuichiro   II-103, III-60
Tong, Yalong   II-3

W

Wang, Chen   II-322
Wang, Chengzhi   II-589, II-613
Wang, Chunbo   II-662
Wang, Chunfang   I-472
Wang, Chunlong   I-525
Wang, Conglin   II-37
Wang, Guofeng   I-166
Wang, Hai   I-279
Wang, Hao   I-559
Wang, Haoyu   II-275
Wang, Hongwei   III-49
Wang, Hongyu   III-494
Wang, Hui   I-91
Wang, Jiachen   II-534, III-3
Wang, Jiakang   II-534
Wang, Jiantao   I-252
Wang, Jiaole   III-573
Wang, Jingnan   II-234

Wang, Jun   III-631
Wang, Junchen   II-16
Wang, Junjie   I-239
Wang, Keyi   II-155
Wang, Lan   II-155
Wang, Liming   II-397
Wang, Lin   II-27
Wang, Lu   I-227
Wang, Meiling   III-460
Wang, Mengdi   II-497
Wang, Peixin   II-675, II-686
Wang, Peiyao   II-3
Wang, Peng   II-79, II-266
Wang, Qiang   III-422
Wang, Qining   I-103, I-459, II-567
Wang, Shengli   I-215
Wang, Shuhan   I-52
Wang, Song   III-101
Wang, Tao   III-75
Wang, Weihao   III-209
Wang, Wenjun   III-521
Wang, Xiangyang   II-557
Wang, Xiaoxin   I-385
Wang, Xu   II-79, II-266
Wang, Xuan   II-373
Wang, Xuelian   III-336
Wang, Yaling   II-234
Wang, Yanzhuo   II-155
Wang, Yi   II-3
Wang, Yuan   III-222
Wang, Yucheng   III-460
Wang, Yueming   I-340, I-363
Wang, Yunfei   II-662
Wang, Zeyang   III-373
Wang, Zhengbo   I-472
Wang, Zhiyong   II-197, III-473, III-534, III-573
Wang, Zhuoqun   III-287
Wang, Zihao   I-316
Wang, Ziqi   III-185
Wang, Ziwei   III-434
Wei, Wei   III-298
Wei, Yuxuan   I-411
Wei, Zhiao   I-77
Wei, Zhongxing   III-460
Wen, Huan   I-340, I-363
Wen, Siqi   II-37
Wen, Zhijie   I-484, I-496
Weng, Yongjie   III-298
Wu, Canhui   II-166, II-184

Wu, Chaoqun   II-446
Wu, Chenhao   II-143
Wu, Chentao   III-222
Wu, Dingze   I-189
Wu, Han   III-263
Wu, Hao   I-446
Wu, Hongmin   I-294
Wu, Hong-Min   I-509
Wu, Jianhua   I-252
Wu, Jingyu   III-622
Wu, Longyan   I-65
Wu, Peng   III-422
Wu, Tianyu   II-222
Wu, Xinhao   III-422
Wu, Xinrui   III-136
Wu, Xinyu   II-143, II-222, II-234, II-309, III-323
Wu, Xiuyuan   I-350, II-285, II-557
Wu, Xuan   III-249
Wu, Zhigang   II-210

X

Xia, Qingchao   I-189
Xia, Tian   II-497
Xia, Xin   I-279
Xia, Yan   I-536
Xia, Yu   I-472
Xia, Yulong   I-484
Xian, Haolan   II-197, II-255
Xiang, Yang   I-15
Xiang, Yuyaocen   I-583
Xiao, Han   I-267
Xiao, Hong   I-525, I-536
Xiao, Juliang   I-166
Xiao, Mubang   I-484, I-496
Xie, Bangquan   I-385
Xie, Erxuan   I-115
Xie, Shiqin   III-197
Xie, Wenkai   III-650
Xie, Xing   III-411
Xie, Yuhang   II-521
Xing, Boyang   II-698
Xing, Jianping   I-215
Xiong, Zhenhua   I-252
Xu, Enci   II-421
Xu, Fengkun   III-124
Xu, Guibin   I-446
Xu, Guochao   III-263
Xu, Jiajun   II-675, II-686
Xu, Kedi   I-340

Author Index

Xu, Qingpo   I-166
Xu, Ruoyu   I-201
Xu, Shabei   III-484
Xu, Sheng   II-471
Xu, Tiantian   II-471, III-49
Xu, Wenfu   II-650
Xu, Wenzhu   II-275
Xu, Xiaohu   III-560
Xu, Yang   I-397
Xu, Yanping   I-177
Xu, Zhantao   II-601
Xu, Zhihao   I-294
Xu, Zhi-Hao   I-509
Xu, Zhipeng   II-698

Y

Yan, Jiejie   III-548
Yan, Sijie   I-140, III-434, III-560
Yan, Weixin   II-624
Yan, Yushuai   II-67
Yang, Canjun   I-189, I-227, II-275, II-361
Yang, Chao   II-483
Yang, Chen   I-385
Yang, Dan   III-373
Yang, En   III-112
Yang, Fan   III-650
Yang, Guang   I-525, I-536
Yang, Hongkun   II-37
Yang, Huaiguang   III-136
Yang, Jiantao   III-622
Yang, Jichao   I-215
Yang, Kairui   I-103
Yang, Lintao   III-136
Yang, Mingchuan   III-361
Yang, Minghui   II-446
Yang, Siqin   II-16
Yang, Wei   II-275
Yang, Xiao   III-673
Yang, Xinyu   I-65
Yang, Yang   III-49
Yang, Zeyuan   I-140
Yang, Zhihao   III-473, III-534
Yang, Zhiyuan   II-613
Yang, Zixiang   II-244
Yao, Chong   II-601
Yao, Jia   III-673
Yao, Jianfeng   II-166, II-184
Yao, Lin   I-340, I-363
Yao, Shutong   III-398
Ye, Guoquan   II-459

Ye, Huanpeng   I-397
Ye, Linqi   II-385, II-521, II-698
Ye, Xiaodong   III-460
Yi, Shuowen   III-673
Yin, Changwei   I-595
Yin, Meng   II-234, II-285, II-309
Yin, Yanqi   I-571
Yu, Li   II-54
Yu, Longjie   III-310
Yu, Yang   I-306, I-571
Yuan, Hao   I-559
Yue, Zuogong   III-447

Z

Zang, Xizhe   II-79, II-266
Zeng, Qiming   I-385
Zha, Pengxin   I-3, I-39
Zhan, Xinrui   I-496
Zhang, Bi   III-599
Zhang, Bo   I-115
Zhang, Dailin   I-423, III-75, III-386
Zhang, Dinghuang   II-545
Zhang, Fumin   I-239
Zhang, Fuyong   I-294
Zhang, Gan   I-239
Zhang, Guilong   III-361
Zhang, Hanqi   III-222
Zhang, Haoran   I-350, II-309, II-557
Zhang, Haoshi   II-27
Zhang, Haoxiang   II-91
Zhang, Haoyan   II-662
Zhang, He   II-662
Zhang, Hongwei   I-385
Zhang, Huanghe   II-534, III-3
Zhang, Jianguo   II-483
Zhang, Jianhua   III-275
Zhang, Jiaqi   II-103, II-662
Zhang, Jiexin   I-77, I-115
Zhang, Jinnuo   I-65
Zhang, Junwei   III-124, III-197
Zhang, Kewen   III-310
Zhang, Li   III-26, III-38
Zhang, Liang   III-599
Zhang, Lunwei   I-316
Zhang, Luobin   III-298
Zhang, Ningbin   I-65
Zhang, Qian   III-662
Zhang, Shenglun   III-386
Zhang, Shisheng   II-143
Zhang, Shouyi   II-91, III-185

Zhang, Tianze I-434
Zhang, Wei III-662
Zhang, Wenan III-336
Zhang, Xiaojian III-434
Zhang, Xinuo III-611
Zhang, Xuehe II-601
Zhang, Yang I-595
Zhang, Yi III-484
Zhang, Yijian III-185
Zhang, Ying I-472, II-483
Zhang, Yuan III-361
Zhang, Yuanwen II-255
Zhang, Yuhao I-15, II-497
Zhang, Yuqi II-129
Zhang, Zehui III-398
Zhang, Zhenwei I-15, II-497
Zhang, Zhihong III-508, III-521
Zhang, Zhiran III-75
Zhang, Zhonghai III-150
Zhang, Zhongkai I-3, I-27, I-39
Zhang, Zhuowen II-662
Zhao, Chuanlin I-127
Zhao, Feng III-373
Zhao, Guoshun III-348
Zhao, Huaici III-361
Zhao, Huan I-77
Zhao, Huijuan II-54
Zhao, Jie II-589, II-601, II-613, II-637, II-662, III-185
Zhao, Junhong III-460
Zhao, Mengcheng II-675, II-686
Zhao, Ranshuo I-215
Zhao, Runchao I-536
Zhao, Shize II-589, II-613
Zhao, Shunyi I-459, II-567
Zhao, Sikai II-589, II-613, III-185
Zhao, Tianren I-166
Zhao, Wensong III-587
Zhao, Xin II-210
Zhao, Xingang III-599
Zhao, Xingwei I-15, I-423, II-497, III-75, III-386
Zhao, Xu'an II-637
Zhao, Xu'ning II-637
Zhao, Yanwei I-472
Zhao, Yanzheng II-624
Zhao, Zeming I-328

Zheng, Han II-385
Zheng, Hao III-112
Zheng, Haoran III-263
Zheng, Lei III-75
Zheng, Tianjiao II-91, II-589, II-613, II-637
Zheng, Yue II-27
Zhengqing, Liu III-222
Zhong, Lei II-662
Zhong, Yucun I-363
Zhou, Dalin II-545
Zhou, Huilin III-336
Zhou, Jiaxing I-177
Zhou, Jinglin II-197, II-255
Zhou, Juanxia II-675, II-686
Zhou, Nanlin III-185
Zhou, Puzhe I-189
Zhou, Ruyi III-136
Zhou, Shijun III-411
Zhou, Xuefei I-340
Zhou, Xuefeng I-294
Zhou, Xue-Feng I-509
Zhou, Yan I-252
Zhou, Yangfan III-599
Zhou, Zeyu I-306, I-328
Zhu, Dahu I-446
Zhu, Daqi I-153
Zhu, Gaohan III-235
Zhu, Haifei I-294
Zhu, Jintao II-567
Zhu, Linqing II-521
Zhu, Liren III-587
Zhu, Qingmiao I-15
Zhu, Wenduo I-459
Zhu, Xiangye III-560
Zhu, Xingyue I-559
Zhu, Yanhe II-91, II-589, II-613, III-185
Zhu, Yanmei III-494
Zhu, Yanzheng I-215
Zhu, Yu I-350, II-557
Zhu, Yulan III-494
Zhuang, Chungang I-3, I-27, I-39
Zou, Huaiwu I-115
Zou, Jiang I-547
Zou, Kuansheng III-398
Zou, Rui II-322
Zuo, Guokun III-336

Made in the USA
Monee, IL
03 May 2026

49438647R00391